FEDERAL COURTS, FEDERALISM AND SEPARATION OF POWERS

CASES AND MATERIALS

Fourth Edition

By

Donald L. Doernberg
Professor of Law
Pace University School of Law

C. Keith Wingate
Professor of Law
University of California,
Hastings College of Law

Donald H. Zeigler
Professor of Law
New York Law School

AMERICAN CASEBOOK SERIES®

THOMSON
—★—
WEST

Mat #40585170

American Casebook Series and West Group are trademarks registered in the U.S. Patent and Trademark Office.

COPYRIGHT © 1994 WEST PUBLISHING CO.
© West, a Thomson business, 2000, 2004
© 2008 Thomson/West
    610 Opperman Drive
    St. Paul, MN 55123
    1–800–313–9378

Printed in the United States of America

ISBN: 978–0–314–18022–3

 *TEXT IS PRINTED ON 10% POST CONSUMER RECYCLED PAPER*

The First Edition was dedicated:

To my Fathers
D.L.D

To Lilly, Clarence, Christine, and A.D.
C.K.W.

The Second Edition was dedicated:

To Cyndy
D.L.D.

To Gloria
C.K.W.

The Third Edition is dedicated:

To Chris Felts
D.L.D.

To the memories of Harriet Tubman, W.E.B. DuBois, and John Brown
C.K.W.

To my Father
D.H.Z.

The Fourth Edition is dedicated:

To Don Zeigler
D.L.D.

To Brenda, Marvin, Terry and Oliver
C.K.W.

To Brannon Heath
D.H.Z.

Preface to the Fourth Edition

The changing of the guard at the Supreme Court has resulted in the Court becoming increasingly active in some areas that had been relatively quiescent. Chief Justice Roberts' replacing Chief Justice Rehnquist and Justice Alito's taking Justice O'Connor's seat appear to have shifted the Court's alignment to some extent. To keep pace, we have had to make some difficult choices about what to retain and what to replace with newer material, always with an eye toward keeping the book teachable and of reasonable length. We retain our commitment to not letting the book become a research tool rather than a teaching tool. We also recognize, however, that teachers often have differing views about which cases are too important to reduce to notes and how they tie into the themes of the book. Accordingly, several of the full length cases that we have reduced to notes are available at full length, with their notes and questions, in the back of the Teacher's Manual for teachers to reproduce and distribute if they find it desirable to do so.

Chapter 1, dealing with justiciability, is a constant challenge. The Court has done so much with the doctrine of standing over the years that the subject could easily overwhelm the chapter and the book. Last year, the Court decided two cases, *Massachusetts v. Environmental Protection Agency* and *Hein v. Freedom from Religion Foundation*. We have made *Massachusetts v. EPA* a main case, replacing *FEC v. Akins*, which we have reduced to a note. *Hein*, on the other hand, although certainly current, seems less doctrinally important at this point, so it appears as a textual discussion following the material on *Flast v. Cohen*. We have revised the extensive notes that followed *FEC v. Akins* into what we hope is a more accessible hornbook-style section of text.

Chapter 2, Congressional Control of Jurisdiction, is fundamentally the same, but we have added some note material to take into account the Detainee Treatment Act of 2005 and the Military Commissions Act of 2006, congressional responses to the government's proceedings with regard to "enemy combatants," whether aliens or United States citizens. The Court has not decided what may turn out to be the most significant (or at least the first significant) case involving those statutes, *Boumediene v. Bush*, now awaiting argument.

Chapter 3, Federal Question Jurisdiction, has also undergone some changes because of the Court's recent decisions. The uncertainty that the majority opinion created in *Merrell Dow* finally (after almost twenty years) resulted in the Court's attempt to clarify it in *Grable*. Whether that attempt succeeded remains to be seen. In any event, *Grable* now appears as a main case following *Merrell Dow*. The Court's other federal-question-jurisdiction case, *Empire Healthchoice v. McVeigh*, appeared as a main case in the 2006 and 2007 Supplements. We have reduced *Empire* to two notes, one in Chapter 3 and one in Chapter 5. Frankly, *Empire* does not seem to add anything doctrinally to federal question jurisdiction. The major battle among the Justices concerns the choice-of-law question, and hence the case's primary significance seems to us to be a common law matter, not a jurisdictional one. The jurisdictional determination flows directly from the determination of the choice-of-law issue, much as was the case in *Lincoln Mills*. There, the Court created federal common law and so found jurisdiction; in *Empire* the majority declines to create federal common law to govern the dispute.

The Chapter 5 materials are essentially unchanged. Although *Empire Healthchoice* was predominantly a common-law battle, it does not add anything doctrinally to the Court's existing common-law jurisprudence. The Justices split over how they should strike the balance, but the balancing mechanism is unchanged.

Chapter 7 similarly did not have major changes. While we presented *Central Virginia Community College v. Katz* as a main case in the last two annual supplements, it now seems to us far more likely to end up as a special-case exception to the general rule of *Seminole Tribe*, if it survives at all given the change in membership on the Court. Accordingly, it appears as the last note following *Seminole Tribe*.

In Chapter 10, *Exxon Mobil v. SABIC* continues as a main case, replacing *Garry v. Geils*. Time will tell whether the Court's attempt to clarify the distinction between *Rooker-Feldman* and preclusion doctrine succeeds.

The habeas corpus materials, Chapter 11, remain a challenge. In no other area has the Court decided as many cases. It would not be possible to be exhaustive without being exhausting, so we have tried, in selecting cases to insert as new note materials, to distinguish between those that are doctrinally important to the functioning of the federal courts as an institution and those that are simply interpretations of the various statutes that do not directly affect the federal courts' functioning. This, too, is an area where the volume of available materials could easily overwhelm the course; we have tried to avoid that.

We continue to use editing conventions to limit length and remove matter that does not contribute to understanding. Within the cases, we omit without ellipsis citations that are not of pedagogical importance and some of the Court's footnotes. The remaining footnotes in cases retain their original numbers. Where the Court is clearly quoting itself, we omit the citation unless it is peculiarly important to understanding the substantive point. Similarly, when the Court quotes a clearly identified source (for example an IRS policy in *Allen v. Wright),* we have omitted the citation unless it is necessary for understanding. Authors' footnotes within cases are lettered rather than numbered; other authors' footnotes are consecutively numbered within each chapter. Within the material we have written, we have avoided endless repetition of citations; if we have recently cited a case, we then refer to it by its commonly-used short name. When citing state-court cases, we have included both the official reporter citation and citations to the West regional and individual-state reporters. The current version of the Bluebook may frown on it, but we think it is a service to the reader.

March, 2008

Acknowledgments

From Professor Doernberg:

Cyndy still smiles at me (despite this project).   After twenty-five years together, she still makes my universe light up. Doug and Emily were not merely supportive in a general way; they helped with some of the work the putting a book together entails (for pay, of course). I deeply appreciate their help. I predict that neither of them will ever take Federal Courts.

I have received wonderful support from the students and administration of Pace Law School. My students constantly push me to go every more deeply into the material, and I am grateful for that. They make teaching an enormous amount of fun and, whether they know it or not, they contribute to my education as I hope I do to theirs. Dean Michelle Simon has been behind this project from the very beginning. Adam Rahal has provided wonderful research assistance, and his intelligence and intellectual curiosity has helped me make many of the length and coverage decisions that inhere in this sort of endeavor.

Forty-two years ago, I met Don Zeigler in our first weekend in law school, at opposite ends of a forward pass. As the quarterback, I have always thought it fortunate that we were on the same team. We have been on the same team ever since. We went through law school together, worked in the Special Litigation Unit of the Legal Aid Society in New York together, and taught together as Pace for five years before he moved on to New York Law School. He has contributed enormously to my development as a writer, to my understanding of this subject, and to my life throughout our four-plus decades. His work on this book cannot be overstated. One of Don's real gifts is his way of imposing order and structure on confusion—as, for example, the proliferation of the Court's habeas corpus decisions.

I treasure his friendship.

From Professor Wingate:

First, I want to thank Gloria Wingate, my wife. I do not know what I would do without her, but do know it would not be nearly as much fun. Next, I would like to thank my co-authors, Don Doernberg and Don Zeigler. One could not ask for finer people to work with on any project. I again want to thank my colleague Evan Tsen Lee for his continued willingness to talk Federal Courts with me. Also, I want to thank Dean Nell Newton and Academic Dean Shuana Marshall of the University of California Hastings College of Law for all the support they have provided me to work on this new edition. It is greatly appreciated. Finally, I want to thank Stephen R. Lothrop, Beverly Taylor, Meseret Mekuria, and Divina Morgan. They make up the Office of Faculty Support, provide me with excellent secretarial assistance and administrative support, and make my life so much easier.

From Professor Zeigler:

My thanks again to Professors Doernberg and Wingate for the opportunity to contribute to the fourth edition as well as the annual supplements. Our conversations continue to enhance my understanding of the materials and help my teaching. I also thank my wife, Professor Brannon Heath, for her helpful comments and her patience as I have worked on the fourth edition and the supplements.

Preface to the Third Edition

In the four years since the second edition, the Court has focused more narrowly on some areas, leaving others entirely untouched. The third edition continues the basic organization and structure of the earlier editions. Recent years have witnessed important changes in particular areas, but the underlying themes of the course remain the same. Our editing decisions continue to be made to help elaborate those themes. There has, for example, been no significant doctrinal development in the areas of congressional control of jurisdiction (Chapter 2), federal question jurisdiction (Chapter 3), legislative courts (Chapter 4), abstention (Chapter 8) and supreme court review of state court decisions (Chapter 9). On the other hand, the Court has spoken out on standing and mootness (Chapter 1), federal common law (Chapter 5), the Eleventh Amendment (Chapter 7), and federal habeas corpus (Chapter 11). That is not to say that there has been no action in the other areas; it simply has come more as tinkering around the edges rather than major doctrinal exposition; those developments are covered in notes or text rather than as principal cases.

Chapter 1 now includes *Friends of the Earth, Inc. v. Laidlaw Environmental Services (TOC), Inc.* The case really could appear in either the standing or mootness subsections. We have chosen the latter, because the Court makes a considerable effort to compare standing and mootness, so it is desirable to have read through both subsections before undertaking *Laidlaw*.

Chapter 5 on federal common law contains *Semtek International, Inc. v. Lockheed Martin Corp.* That case surprised more than one Federal Courts scholar, because the Court appeared in *Boyle v. United Technologies Inc.* and *Atherton v. FDIC* to have interred the technique of using state law as the content of federal common law. *Semtek* demonstrates that reports of the technique's demise were indeed premature.

We have revised the Notes and Questions in Chapter 6. Some of the Notes following *Harlow v. Fitzgerald* have been reorganized in light of the recent decisions, *Saucier v. Katz* and *Hope v. Pelzer*, and we present much of the discussion as textual narrative rather than notes.

Chapter 7, on the Eleventh Amendment, has undergone significant reorganization. We have included *Giles v. Harris*, a 1903 case that, when combined with *Hans v. Louisiana*, appeared to represent the federal judiciary's complete abdication of any responsibility for enforcing the Civil War Amendments on behalf of black citizens. One may see *Ex parte Young*, a watershed case by any measure, as the Court's turning back from this course.

ix

Chapter 8 has no new main cases. The Supreme Court has not been active in the abstention area in recent years. We have substantially revised the Notes and Questions, however, and the final case of the chapter, *Wilton v. Seven Falls Company,* is reduced to a Note.

We have also made substantial revisions to the Notes and Questions in Chapter 9. The Supreme Court rulings in *Bush v. Palm Beach County Canvassing Board* and *Bush v. Gore* are discussed briefly. We clarify the Notes explaining how the Court proceeds when the respondent seeks to block Supreme Court review based on a state procedural default. Two recent cases, *Lee v. Kemna* and *Nike v. Kasky*, also are discussed.

Since the last edition came out, we have added a chapter on the *Rooker-Feldman* doctrine (at the suggestion, we might add, of Judge William Fletcher of the Ninth Circuit). The doctrine represents another arena in which the federalism battle between state and federal judiciaries plays out. This chapter now precedes the concluding chapter on federal habeas corpus.

The final chapter dealing with Federal Habeas Corpus is much changed, bearing faint resemblance to its predecessor. We have entirely reorganized the chapter, reducing some cases to text discussion or note status and highlighting others that are more doctrinally significant than we originally appreciated. The Court continues to be extremely active in this area. That is exciting, but it also challenges one to assemble a usable chapter that does not overwhelm the rest of the course. Indeed, justiciability, federal common law, the Eleventh Amendment and federal habeas corpus could each make a fine two credit seminar, the only difficulty then being that no school allocates to the Federal Courts course the twelve or thirteen credits it would then take to cover all the material in depth.

We have rewritten the introductory habeas material to clarify the doctrinal changes made by the Warren Court. Headings are revised, new cases are added, and the Notes and Questions are substantially rewritten. Several main cases in the Second Edition have been reduced to notes to make way for new material and because of space constraints. One of the trio of so-called enemy combatant cases decided June 28, 2004, *Rasul v. Bush*, is added as a main case. Another, *Padilla v. Rumsfeld*, is described in a detailed note. Although those cases do not concern the relationship of the federal government to the states, they do provide the most current indication of the Court's view of the function of the once Great Writ.

We continue to use editing conventions to limit length and remove matter that does not contribute to understanding. Within the cases, citations that are not of pedagogical importance are omitted without ellipsis, as are some of the Court's footnotes. The remaining footnotes in cases retain their original numbers. Where the Court is clearly quoting itself, the citation is omitted unless it is peculiarly important to understanding the substantive point. Similarly, when the Court quotes a clearly identified source (for example an IRS policy in *Allen v. Wright),* we have omitted the citation unless it is necessary for understanding. Authors' footnotes within cases are lettered rather than numbered; other authors' footnotes are consecutively numbered within each chapter. Within the material we have written, we have avoided endless repetition of citations; if we have recently cited a case, we then refer to it by its commonly-used short name. When citing state-court cases, we have included both the official reporter citation and citations to the West regional and individual-state reporters. The current version of the Bluebook may frown on it, but we think it is a service to the reader.

October, 2004

Acknowledgments

From Professor Doernberg:

My family still acknowledges me at the end of this project, which is remarkable testimony to their tolerance; the least I can do is to acknowledge them as well. My wife Cynthia Pope again has come to terms with the ugly reality that one does not write a casebook; one marries it, particularly so in an area in which the Court is predictably active and predictably unpredictable. She and my children Doug and Emily Pope have graciously surrendered time that should have been theirs.

As always, several students have contributed their talents. John Tenaglia, with whom I put together the *Rooker-Feldman* chapter two summers ago and Jennifer Odrobina, who did much to keep it current, were marvelous. Oren Gelber has worked with me this summer and has done a job that is simply beyond description. Her understanding, insight, willingness to offer comments and suggestions and incredible attention to detail have made this project far better than it would otherwise have been. In many ways, she has mastered this difficult subject on her own after only her first year. She has performed brilliantly, and it is my great pleasure to acknowledge my debt to her.

Chris Felts, to whom I dedicate this book, is what Isaak Walton would have called a "compleat" human being, and that is something I do not say lightly. I have known Chris since 1970, when he was four. He is in every way my son save for the small matter that we share no genes. But what does Mother Nature know anyway? In all the ways that really count, we are father and son, and the relationship has brightened my life in innumerable ways over the years, recently multiplied as Chris and his wife have made me a grandfather twice since 2000. He is an extraordinarily special fellow, and I am enriched for knowing him.

From Professor Wingate:

I seem to always be thanking the same people in my acknowledgements. My wife Gloria continues to be a great source of support and inspiration to me in everything I do, and I would be remiss not to acknowledge it. Again, I would like to thank my colleague Evan Tsen Lee for his willingness to share his vision of and ideas about Federal Courts. The Office of Faculty Support here at Hastings continues to make my life much easier with the excellent secretarial and administrative assistance it provides. Thanks to the people there, Stephen R. Lothrop, Ted Jang, Barbara Topchov, Beverly Taylor, and Cecillia Bruno. Finally, I would like to thank my students. I hope they realize that there is a method in the madness.

From Professor Zeigler:

My thanks to Professors Doernberg and Wingate for asking me to join as an author for the third edition. It is an honor to be included. In addition, our conversations about the substance of the course have deepened my understanding of the material and given me new ideas about how to teach it. My thanks also to my wife, fellow law professor Brannon Heath, for her assistance and patience.

I am also grateful for the research assistance of Annie McGuire, Class of 2005, and Julia Khalavsky and Tim Regan, Class of 2006. Ms. McGuire helped with the substantial revision of the chapter on Habeas Corpus. Understanding this complex and rapidly changing area of the law was a challenge for both of us, and her sheer analytical prowess was of real assistance. Ms. Khalavsky and Mr. Regan provided invaluable help in revising the Notes and Questions in several chapters. The Notes and Questions are sharper, clearer, and will be more valuable to students because of their efforts.

Preface to the Second Edition

The basic approach reflected in the first edition still seems to us to facilitate study of this unusually arcane subject. The intervening six years have seen some significant shifts in particular doctrines or sub-doctrines, but the basic themes of the subject as a whole remain unchanged. We have therefore tried to continue to select (and edit out) materials according to how well they elaborate those themes rather than for the particular rule of an individual case.

Chapter 1 now includes two additional cases on standing that may indicate substantial shifts in the Court's approach. At least some Members of the Court appear to be rethinking the jurisprudence of "generalized grievances," and issues of Congress's ability to create standing continue to draw judicial attention.

Chapter 2 has expanded by the addition of *Plaut v. Spendthrift Farm*, in which Congress endeavored (unsuccessfully) to undo a non-constitutional Supreme Court decision with which it disagreed. *Plaut* again brought to the fore issues of the interplay of judicial and legislative power and policymaking. There is also another conflict brewing in this area, involving the Prison Litigation Reform Act. At this writing, no case under that statute has reached the Supreme Court, but the Circuit Courts have been busy with issues reminiscent of both *Plaut* and *Klein*. It does not require much of a crystal ball to suppose that the Supreme Court will choose to address those issues in the not-too-distant future.

We have reorganized the principal cases in Chapter 5 in the wake of *Atherton v. FDIC*, which appears to mark a significant change in the Court's approach to federal common law and the vertical choice-of-law process generally.

Chapter 6 has also changed considerably. *Board of County Commissioners v. Brown* offers a new perspective on municipal liability, and Justice Breyer's explicit suggestion that the Court re-examine part of *Monell v. Department of Social Service* suggests that the law in this area is entering a period of reevaluation. In the interests of space, we have eliminated principal case coverage of the cases in the first edition from *Paul v. Davis* through *Zinermon v. Burch*, since those cases have far more to do with the contours of § 1983 *per se* than with the role of the federal courts as institutions.

The Court's decision in *Seminole Tribe of Florida v. Florida* caused us to reorganize Chapter 7. Covering the cases chronologically seems to us to make study of this complex area even more difficult. Accordingly, after presenting the basic doctrine as in the first edition, we have attempted to arrange the succeeding cases according to how they view (and affect) *Hans v. Louisiana* and *Ex parte Young*, still the foundation cases for the Court's Eleventh Amendment jurisprudence. Indeed, after *Alden v. Maine* and the *College Savings Bank* cases from the 1998 Term, *Hans* arguably takes on even greater importance than one might have thought even three years ago.

The passage of the Antiterrorism and Effective Death Penalty Act of 1996 has also caused us to take a fresh look at the Chapter 10 materials. The interaction of the statute and the Court's pre-existing doctrine is certainly not entirely clear at this point, nor is it easy to say whether or to what extent Congress has changed the underlying substantive law of the writ. The statute is less than pellucid; the inferior federal courts and ultimately the Supreme Court should be kept busy for the next few years attempting to make sense of it.

———

We have retained the editing conventions from the first edition that we used to limit length and remove matter that does not contribute to understanding. Within the cases, citations that are not of pedagogical importance are omitted without ellipsis, as are some of the Court's footnotes. The remaining footnotes in cases retain their original numbers. Where the Court is clearly quoting itself, the citation is omitted unless it is peculiarly important to understanding the substantive point. Similarly, when the Court quotes a clearly identified source (for example an IRS policy in *Allen v. Wright),* we have omitted the citation unless it is necessary for understanding. Authors' footnotes within cases are lettered rather than numbered; other authors' footnotes are consecutively numbered throughout each chapter. Within the material we have written, we have avoided endless repetition of citations; if we have recently cited a case, we then refer to it by its commonly-used short name.

January, 2000.

Acknowledgments from the Second Edition

From Professor Doernberg:

The principal burden of support for this project has fallen once again on my family: Cyndy, Emily, and of course Doug, who suggested to me on more than one occasion that my priorities were seriously out of alignment because I had to work on the book rather than to play Age of Empires™ with him on the computer. I can appreciate his viewpoint (indeed, there were times when I agreed wholeheartedly), and I am grateful all of my family for their understanding and tolerance.

I have benefited greatly over the six years since the first edition from the comments, questions, and support of Professor Eric Muller of the University of North Carolina School of Law. This product is far better for his generosity than it otherwise would have been.

I want also specifically to mention my indebtedness to all of those from schools around the country who participate in the Federal Courts faculty e-discussion group. The continuous exchange of views is enjoyable and most educational, I hope for all of us. It represents the best of what education has to offer: people exerting themselves to gain and share with others understanding of a subject truly worth thinking hard about.

Three students have borne the brunt of the research assistance for the completion of the second edition: Karen A. Anderson of the Class of 2000 worked with me for an entire calendar year, very often adding a valuable additional viewpoint of how parts of the book would work for students. When she began working with me she had not taken the course; by the time she finished she had and is now probably as well qualified to teach the course as any beginning teacher. Sally S. Benvie and Anne DeSutter of the Class of 2001 worked with me for the summer of 1999, and the project reflects their care and diligence as well. It is not possible in a short space to give enough credit to the contributions of all three as researchers, editors, welcome critics, and, most valuably, friends. Some errors have undoubtedly slipped through, but only because I still had my hands on the project after they had finished.

From Professor Wingate:

I would again like to acknowledge the support and assistance of my wife Gloria. She deserves a great deal of the credit for everything I accomplish or produce. Also, I would like to thank my colleague and Federal Courts fellow traveler Even Tsen Lee. He has always been available to offer his wisdom and valuable counsel. The Office of Faculty Support here at Hastings has provided me with excellent secretarial assistance which has made all my work much easier, including my work on this second edition. Consequently, I would like to thank the people in that office, Steven R. Lothrop, Ted Jang, Barbara Topchov, Sonja Starks, and Beverly Taylor.

As I did in the first edition, I would like to thank my Federal Courts students. They continue to teach me.

Preface to the First Edition

Federal Courts is one of the most difficult courses in the law school curriculum. The concepts are highly abstract; the doctrine is remarkably complex; the courts are open to the well-founded suspicion that their application of the doctrine is often inconsistent. Consequently, the subject presents an unusual challenge for casebook authors: to create a text that stimulates productive thought about the complexities without inundating the student with masses of impenetrable material or uncollated detail.

Federal Courts is first and foremost, a course about power. Though many of the issues concern private disputes and individual rights, two fundamental power relationships underlie them: the states versus the federal government—federalism—and the federal judiciary versus Congress—separation of powers. Moreover, many of those power struggles are played out in the context of disputes between the individual and government, a third type of power relationship. Indeed, the way federalism and separation-of-powers battles are resolved often has a major impact on the power balance between individual and government. The federal courts' primary role is to regulate these conflicts. That is what makes the federal courts special—not just another hierarchical court system.

The importance of the themes of federalism and separation of powers in the study of federal courts requires more attention to American history than in many other courses. The law of contracts, for example, was not directly affected by the Civil War; the law of federal courts was and still is. Political events stimulated many important developments in the law of federal courts. Understanding those causal relationships helps to explain federal courts doctrine.

We have elected, in choosing materials for this book, to focus on those two themes. Apparently disparate topics have in common the underlying themes of federalism and separation of powers, and it is easier to understand the forces that move the Supreme Court in a particular area if one has focused on them in other areas. Most of the chapters involve both themes, and the notes and questions following the main cases attempt to stimulate thought in those terms. Accordingly, we have elected to omit topics that do not illustrate these themes as well, such as the original jurisdiction of the Supreme Court and appellate review within the federal system.

We think there are three things a well-constructed casebook should do. First, it should present the basic themes in the subject matter in an integrated manner that demonstrates their development and interrelationships. Second, it should help students develop their analytical skills by challenging them to deal with case materials that are not too predigested and to grasp not merely the holdings of the cases but also their broader implications. Third, it should be a workable teaching and study tool that does not present the instructor with a volume. of material that cannot reasonably be covered or that is often covered in some other course, as diversity is. We hope we have charted a middle course between casebooks that contain little interpretive guidance and those that are such exhaustive scholarly exercises that they would serve as excellent research tools but are unsuited to pedagogy. The notes and questions that follow each case are designed to assist the student to understand both the individual case and its doctrinal implications. To be sure, many of the questions have no clear answers. We intend them to elicit debate on the hard issues and to explore the arguments on both sides of controversial decisions, but we have tried to avoid questions that require knowledge that students cannot reasonably have.

The chapter sequence reflects the two themes. Chapter 1, Justiciability, is a good starting point both because it is a collection of threshold doctrines and because it introduces federalism and separation of powers. Justiciability is difficult to cover as a single unit of a multi-unit course. The doctrine, particularly with respect to standing, is so convoluted that it would make a fine two-credit seminar in its own right. We have elected to cover each of the justifiability sub-doctrines with a single case supplemented by extensive notes and text commentary, resisting considerable temptation to add cases to flesh out parts of the doctrine at the expense of greatly increased length. Running throughout Chapter 1 is the primary question of whether Congress or the Supreme Court is the guardian of federalism and separation of powers.

Broadly speaking, Chapters 2, 3, and 4 concern subject matter jurisdiction, another collection of threshold doctrines. Chapter 2 discusses congressional control of federal jurisdiction. With the exception of the original jurisdiction of the Supreme Court, the federal courts derive no jurisdiction directly from the Constitution. Article III, § 2, functions primarily to enable Congress to confer jurisdiction if it wishes. That is why, almost invariably, one must find a statutory implementation of the general Article III authorization in order successfully to invoke federal jurisdiction. Chapter 2 focuses on how much latitude Congress has in conferring or withholding jurisdiction from the Supreme Court and the lower federal courts.

Chapter 3 turns to federal question jurisdiction. Most first-year Civil Procedure courses introduce the subject, but it deserves more study. A delayed return often helps cement concepts that may seem hopelessly amorphous when encountered in the first year. The doctrine is difficult, particularly with respect to declaratory judgment cases, but it illustrates the interaction between Congress and the courts and between the federal and state judicial systems.

Chapter 4, Legislative Courts, introduces a peculiar separation-of-powers problem. Most of the separation-of-powers issues raised in this volume concern whether the federal judiciary is trenching upon the powers of the other branches of the federal government, particularly Congress. In the area of legislative courts, the question is reversed, and the issue becomes whether Congress, by creating non-Article III courts, is infringing the power of the judiciary. It is an odd and interesting role reversal, casting Congress, not the courts' as the potential constitutional miscreant.

Chapter 5, Federal Common Law, further develops a subject often introduced in Civil Procedure. In our experience, few first-year students really grasp the mechanics of *Erie's* vertical choice-of-law process; fewer still understand the methods of creating federal common law when it is needed. Moreover, we suspect it is highly unusual, if not entirely unheard of, for first-year courses to focus on the separation-of-powers implications of these issues. Yet, increasingly in recent years, voices in the academy and on the bench have suggested that the *Erie* doctrine in its broadest sense properly contemplates both of the themes that animate this volume.

Chapter 6 is a place-setter; it explores the functions and limits of the Civil Rights Act of 1871, 42 U.S.C.A. § 1983. Litigation under that statute need not be in the federal courts, but most of it is. Congress intended the statute to interpose federal power between states and individuals, even though it did not make jurisdiction over § 1983 actions exclusively federal. But most of the problems that Chapters 7 and 8 discuss are played out in § 1983 litigation, so it is well to begin with a sound idea of what that section contemplates.

Chapter 7 examines the states' constitutional insulation from suits in federal court and demonstrates the importance of history in the study of federal courts. The Eleventh Amendment's roots extend back well before the Constitution, into the colonial experience with abusive central control of local affairs. The Amendment is a graphic reminder both that the battle between federal and state power is not merely historical, but continues today and that the power of the federal courts is a key part of that struggle. Moreover, it is the federal courts, primarily the Supreme Court, that determine the scope of the Amendment and thus their own power vis-à-vis the states.

Chapter 8 amplifies the federalism power struggle and begins a series of three chapters that focus on that struggle in a particular context. In these chapters we see the federal courts acting (or refusing to act) with respect to state courts particularly. Here the federalism clash is manifest in the collision of two judicial systems. Chapter 8 covers statutory and judge-made doctrines of restraint that define whether the federal courts can take a dispute away from the state courts. The Anti-Injunction Act, 28 U.S.C.A. § 2283, the doctrine of exhaustion of administrative remedies, and the abstention doctrines the Supreme Court has created all have obvious federalism implications. But they also raise important separation-of-powers questions of whether the Court is being faithful to congressional jurisdictional commands. Finally, these doctrines raise significant questions about the state courts' willingness and ability to vindicate federal rights.

Chapters 9 and 10 continue the study of federal court and state court interaction, but in a different context. Here the focus is not on the federal courts preventing state court consideration, but rather upon federal courts reviewing state adjudications. Chapter 9 discusses Supreme Court review of state court decisions. The idea of taking a case "all the way to the Supreme Court" has great colloquial currency, but not all cases can be heard there. In addition, there are a variety of doctrines that the Court invokes (apart from its discretionary certiorari policy) to weed out cases that, for one reason or another, it thinks it cannot or ought not hear. It may seem surprising that the Court lacks subject matter jurisdiction over a case with a federal constitutional issue, but that is sometimes true. Chapter 9 explores why. This Chapter also presents the only circumstance in which a federal court, as a formal matter, sits in review of a state court. The federalism implications early-on provoked a constitutional crisis in *Martin v. Hunter's Lessee,* a case well known to all students of constitutional law. The crisis has abated; the issue survives.

Finally, Chapter 10, Federal Habeas Corpus Challenges to State Custody, presents cases in which federal courts, though not as a formal matter sitting in review of state court proceedings, are in fact doing exactly that. Here, the federalism clash is intensified. In Chapter 9, the Supreme Court reviews state court judgments. In the realm of federal habeas corpus, however, the inferior federal courts may review the judgment of the highest court of a state. Moreover, the cases are far more numerous, so federal habeas corpus acts as a constant irritant to the states. Congress has provided the basic statutory framework, but the Supreme Court has played a major role in determining the degree of irritation. Consequently, federal habeas corpus is a good place to end, because we come full circle with respect to the underlying themes of this book. Even as the Supreme Court monitors federal habeas corpus on behalf of federalism, it collides with congressional authorizations of the use of the writ, thus raising separation-of-powers problems. Federal habeas corpus provides a good stage from which to present the continuing importance of these themes and an institutional question of overriding importance: As between Congress and the Court, who should be the guardian of federalism and who should be the guardian of separation of powers?

We have used some editing conventions to limit length and remove matter that does not contribute to understanding. Within the cases, citations that are not of pedagogical importance are omitted without ellipsis, as are some of the Court's footnotes. The remaining footnotes in cases retain their original numbers. Where the Court is clearly quoting itself, the citation is omitted unless it is peculiarly important to understanding the substantive point. Similarly, when the Court quotes a clearly identified source (for example an IRS policy in *Allen v. Wright)*, the citation is omitted unless needed for understanding. Authors' footnotes within cases are lettered rather than numbered; other authors' footnotes are consecutively numbered throughout each chapter. Within the material we have written, we have avoided endless repetition of citations; if a case has recently been cited, it is referred to by its commonly-used short name.

     Donald L. Doernberg

     C. Keith Wingate

January, 1994

Acknowledgements from the First Edition

     From Professor Doernberg:

Anyone who has written a book understands that the primary burden falls not upon the author, but upon those closest to him: my wife Cynthia A. Pope, fine attorney, demanding editor, welcome critic and companion of a lifetime, and my children Douglas and Emily Pope, who showed tolerance beyond their years while they wondered why Daddy was so busy. Many colleagues offered helpful comments and criticism, and sometime more. Professors Patti Alleva, Evan Tsen Lee, and Donald H. Zeigler were generous with their time and thought. Dean Steven H. Goldberg's financial support, while very much appreciated, was the least of his contribution. His insistent encouragement and faith in the project has meant more then he will ever permit himself to acknowledge. Professor Michael B. Mushlin stands in a special place. He and I have team-taught Federal Courts three times, twice from these materials. His insight, generosity, and patience is reflected throughout. If *quantum meruit* means anything, I owe him an enormous amount of tuition.

     I am indebted to many student research assistants who strove mightily to prevent me from making unpardonable blunders and did so much to help deal with the avalanche of detail that this sort of project entails: Jerome Abelman, Helen Allison, Scott Bonder, Joli Boudreaux, Richard Holahan, Cleve Lisecki, Marios Christos Sfantos, and Rona Shamoon.

     I was awarded a Charles A. Frueauff Research Professorship of Law for the 1992-93 academic year and want to express my considerable gratitude to the Charles A. Frueauff Foundation, Inc., for its generous research support for this project.

From Professor Wingate:

My, contributions to this project would not have been possible without the efforts and understanding of a number of people. My wife Gloria assisted me in so many different ways that it would not be possible to list them. My children, Brenda, Marvin, Terry, and Oliver Champion have taken on many of my duties and responsibilities to allow me to work on this book. Their support and encouragement have been appreciated. I would also like to thank my colleagues Richard Marcus and Evan Tsen lee for their willingness to listen to my strange comments and questions and, where possible, provide meaningful responses, and Danielle Ochs-Tillotson, my research assistant, whose hard work and diligence did not go unnoticed. Additionally, I must express my gratitude to Stephen Lothrop, Fran Nowve, Dwayne Eskridge, Ted Jang, and Erica Durkee, who provided excellent secretarial support, often on short notice, without complaint.

Finally, I would like to acknowledge my debt to all my Federal Courts students over the years. You have taught me a great deal.

Summary of Contents

	Page
PREFACE TO THE FOURTH EDITION	v
PREFACE TO THE THIRD EDITION	ix
PREFACE TO THE SECOND EDITION	xiii
PREFACE TO THE FIRST EDITION	xvi
TABLE OF CASES	xxxv
TABLE OF SECONDARY AUTHORITIES	li
Prologue	**1**

Chapter 1. Justiciability — **23**

Sec.

A.	Introduction	23
B.	Advisory Opinions	25
C.	Standing	34
D.	Ripeness	100
E.	Mootness	111
F.	Political Questions	144

Chapter 2. Congressional Control of Federal Jurisdiction — **163**

Sec.

A.	Introduction	163
B.	Congressional Control of the Appellate Jurisdiction of the Supreme Court	165
C.	Congressional Control of the Jurisdiction of the Lower Federal Courts	193

Chapter 3. Federal Question Jurisdiction — **223**

Sec.

A.	Introduction	223
B.	Separate Strands Intertwined	225
C.	The Special Problem of Declaratory Judgment Cases	302

Chapter 4. Legislative Courts — **321**

Sec.

| A. | Introduction | 321 |

		Page
Sec.		
B.	Limits on Legislative Courts	322
C.	The Modern Balancing Test	352
D.	Magistrate Judges As Adjuncts to the District Courts	367

Chapter 5. Federal Common Law **373**

Sec.
A.	Introduction	373
B.	The Cornerstone	375
C.	Choosing the Applicable Law and Determining Its Content: Federal Interests or Lack Thereof	387
D.	Concluding Note	506

Chapter 6. The Federal Forum, the Fourteenth Amendment, and the Civil Rights Act of 1871 .... **509**

Sec.
| A. | Introduction | 509 |
| B. | The Fourteenth Amendment and 42 U.S.C.A. § 1983 in the Remedial Scheme | 510 |

Chapter 7. The Eleventh Amendment **607**

Sec.
A.	Introduction	607
B.	The Basic Doctrine: More Than Meets the Eye	608
C.	The Basic Doctrine: Less Than Meets the Eye	629
D.	Extending and Cabining the Doctrine: The Limits of Limits	646

Chapter 8. Refusing Jurisdiction: Abstention and Related Doctrines **745**

Sec.
A.	Introduction	745
B.	Congressional Doctrines of Restraint	746
C.	Judicial Doctrines of Restraint	761

Chapter 9. Supreme Court Review of State Court Decisions **879**

Sec.
A.	Introduction	879
B.	Preliminary Jurisdictional Considerations	882
C.	Insulating State Decisions from Supreme Court Review	901

Page

Chapter 10.   The Rooker-Feldman Doctrine **993**
Sec.
A.   Introduction   993
B.   The Basic Doctrine   994
C.   Problems of Interpretation   1011

Chapter 11.   Federal Habeas Corpus...................................   **1051**
Sec.
A.   Introduction   1051
B.   The Statutory Structure   1059
C.   Habeas Corpus and the War on Terror...............................   1063
D.   Federal Court Review of State Convictions.........................   1087

Index   1201

Table of Contents

	Page
PREFACE	ix
PREFACE TO THE SECOND EDITION	xiii
PREFACE TO THE FIRST EDITION	xvi
TABLE OF CASES	xxxv
TABLE OF SECONDARY AUTHORITIES	li

Prologue ... 1
Henry J. Friendly, *Federalism: A Foreword* ... 1
Preliminary Thoughts on Separation of Powers and the
    Judiciary ... 8
Some Observations on Parity ... 13
Burt Neuborne, *The Myth of Parity* ... 14
Erwin Chemerinsky, *Ending the Parity Debate* ... 19

Chapter 1.   Justiciability ... 23
Sec.
A.   Introduction ... 23
B.   Advisory Opinions ... 25
    Muskrat v. United States ... 27
    Notes and Questions ... 33
C.   Standing ... 34
    Allen v. Wright ... 34
    Notes and Questions ... 52
    Massachusetts v. Environmental Protection Agency ... 60
    Notes and Questions ... 77
    Note on Further Problems with the Court's Stand-
        ing Jurisprudence ... 80
        1.   Constitutional Standing ... 80
            a.   Generalized Grievances ... 80
            b.   Taxpayer Standing ... 85
            c.   Citizen Standing ... 88
        2.   Prudential Standing ... 92
            a.   Statutory Substantive Rights and
                Zones of Protected Interests ... 92
            b.   Third-Party Standing ... 96
            c.   Organizational Standing ... 98
        3.   The Malleability of the Court's Standing
            Doctrine ... 98

Sec.		Page
D.	Ripeness	100
	Abbott Laboratories v. Gardner	100
	Notes and Questions	104
E.	Mootness	111
	DeFunis v. Odegaard	111
	Notes and Questions	116
	Friends of the Earth, Incorporated v. Laidlaw Environmental Services (TOC), Inc.	123
	Notes and Questions	141
F.	Political Questions	144
	Nixon v. United States	144
	Notes and Questions	158

Chapter 2.   **Congressional Control of Federal Jurisdiction** **163**

Sec.		
A.	Introduction	163
B.	Congressional Control of the Appellate Jurisdiction of the Supreme Court	165
	Ex parte McCardle	165
	Notes and Questions	167
	Ex parte Yerger	168
	Notes and Questions	172
	Leonard Ratner, *Congressional Power Over the Appellate Jurisdiction of the Supreme Court*	174
	Gerald Gunther, *Congressional Power to Curtail Federal Court Jurisdiction: An Opinionated Guide to the Ongoing Debate*	177
	Notes and Questions	180
	United States v. Klein	181
	Notes and Questions	190
	Note on External Limitations on Congressional Power to Control the Appellate Jurisdiction of the Supreme Court	191
C.	Congressional Control of the Jurisdiction of the Lower Federal Courts	193
	Sheldon v. Sill	193
	Notes and Questions	195
	Plaut v. Spendthrift Farm, Inc.	199
	Notes and Questions	217

Chapter 3.   **Federal Question Jurisdiction** **223**

Sec.		
A.	Introduction	223
B.	Separate Strands Intertwined	225
	Osborn v. Bank of the United States	225

Sec.		Page
	Notes and Questions	234
	Textile Workers Union v. Lincoln Mills	236
	Notes and Questions	245
	Donald L. Doernberg, *There's No Reason for It; It's Just Our Policy: Why the Well-Pleaded Complaint Rule Sabotages the Purposes of Federal Question Jurisdiction*	246
	Louisville and Nashville Railroad Co. v. Mottley	249
	Notes and Questions	251
	Verlinden B.V. v. Central Bank of Nigeria	255
	Notes and Questions	262
	American Well Works Co. v. Layne & Bowler Co.	262
	Notes and Questions	264
	Smith v. Kansas City Title & Trust Co.	265
	Notes and Questions	268
	Gully v. First National Bank	270
	Notes and Questions	272
	Merrell Dow Pharmaceuticals, Inc. v. Thompson	272
	Notes and Questions	283
	Grable & Sons Metal Products, Inc. v. Darue Engineering & Manufacturing	290
	Notes and Questions	296
C.	The Special Problem of Declaratory Judgment Cases	302
	Skelly Oil Co. v. Phillips Petroleum Co.	302
	Notes and Questions	305
	Franchise Tax Board v. Construction Laborers Vacation Trust	306
	Notes and Questions	316
Chapter 4.	**Legislative Courts**	**321**
Sec.		
A.	Introduction	321
B.	Limits on Legislative Courts	322
	Northern Pipeline Construction Co. v. Marathon Pipe Line Co.	322
	Notes and Questions	349
C.	The Modern Balancing Test	352
	Commodity Futures Trading Commission v. Schor	352
	Notes and Questions	364
D.	Magistrate Judges As Adjuncts to the District Courts	367
	Notes and Questions	370

		Page
Chapter 5.	**Federal Common Law**	**373**
Sec.		
A.	Introduction	373

		Page
Sec.		
B.	The Cornerstone	375
	Erie Railroad Co. v. Tompkins	375
	Notes and Questions	382
	Henry J. Friendly, *In Praise of Erie—And of the New Federal Common Law*	384
C.	Choosing the Applicable Law and Determining Its Content: Federal Interests or Lack Thereof	387
	1. Spontaneous Generation	387
	Clearfield Trust Co. v. United States	387
	Notes and Questions	389
	United States v. Kimbell Foods, Inc.	395
	Notes and Questions	405
	Boyle v. United Technologies Corporation	406
	Notes and Questions	418
	Semtek International Incorporated v. Lockheed Martin Corporation	423
	Notes and Questions	429
	Note on Discerning the Content of State Law	431
	2. Construing a Jurisdictional Command as a Command to Create Federal Common Law	433
	Textile Workers Union v. Lincoln Mills	433
	Notes and Questions	438
	3. Implying Private Rights of Action	440
	Bivens v. Six Unknown Named Agents of Federal Bureau of Narcotics	440
	Notes and Questions	453
	Introductory Note on Implying Private Rights of Action in Federal Statutes	455
	Notes and Questions	457
	Cannon v. University of Chicago	458
	Notes and Questions	469
	California v. Sierra Club	471
	Notes and Questions	476
	Schweiker v. Chilicky	480
	Notes and Questions	494
	4. Filling in Statutory Interstices	499
D.	Concluding Note	506

Page

Chapter 6. The Federal Forum, the Fourteenth Amendment, and the Civil Rights Act of 1871.. **509**

Sec.

A. Introduction 509

B. The Fourteenth Amendment and 42 U.S.C.A.
§ 1983 in the Remedial Scheme... 510

   1. Color of State Law 510
   Monroe v. Pape 510
   Notes and Questions... 526

   2. Municipalities as Defendants... 531
   Monell v. Department of Social Services........................... 531
   Notes and Questions... 550
   Board of the County Commissioners v. Brown 555
   Notes and Questions... 574

   3. Officials' Immunities 576
   Harlow v. Fitzgerald.. 580
   Notes and Questions... 585

   4. Note on Protected and Unprotected Interests 598

Chapter 7. The Eleventh Amendment............................... **607**

Sec.

A. Introduction 607

B. The Basic Doctrine: More Than Meets the Eye.................. 608
   Hans v. Louisiana 608
   Notes and Questions 615
   Giles v. Harris.. 619
   Notes and Questions 627

C. The Basic Doctrine: Less Than Meets the Eye................... 629
   Ex parte Young 629
   Notes and Questions 638

D. Extending and Cabining the Doctrine:
   The Limits of Limits... 646
   Edelman v. Jordan 646
   Notes and Questions 655
   Fitzpatrick v. Bitzer... 666
   Notes and Questions 670
   *Board of Trustees of the University of Alabama v.
   Garrett* 677
   Notes and Questions 689
   Seminole Tribe v. Florida... 697
   Notes and Questions 731
   Note on the Eleventh Amendment and
   Supplemental Jurisdiction... 736

Page

Chapter 8.   Refusing Jurisdiction: Abstention and Related Doctrines.................................... 745

Sec.
A.   Introduction 745
B.   Congressional Doctrines of Restraint 746
     Atlantic Coast Line Railroad Company v. Brother-
        hood of Locomotive Engineers.............................. 746
     Notes and Questions 757
C.   Judicial Doctrines of Restraint.................................. 761
     1.   Exhaustion 761
          Patsy v. Board of Regents of Florida............................. 762
          Notes and Questions.. 772
     2.   Abstention: The *Pullman* Doctrine........................... 774
          Railroad Commission v. Pullman Co. 774
          Notes and Questions.. 776
          Note on Post-Abstention Procedure and Tactics........... 781
     3.   Abstention: The Doctrine of *Younger v. Harris* 785
          Younger v. Harris.. 785
          Notes and Questions.. 791
          Steffel v. Thompson.. 801
          Notes and Questions.. 811
          Hicks v. Miranda 813
          Notes and Questions.. 820
          Huffman v. Pursue, Ltd.... 822
          Notes and Questions.. 829
          Note on Other Developments in *Younger* Ab-
             stention 836
          Notes and Questions.. 840
     4.   *Burford* and *Thibodaux* Abstention............................. 841
          Burford v. Sun Oil Company...................................... 841
          Notes and Questions.. 851
          Quackenbush v. Allstate Insurance Company................. 855
          Notes and Questions.. 863
     5.   *Colorado River* Abstention 865
          Colorado River Water Conservation District v.
             United States... 865
          Notes and Questions.. 874

Chapter 9.   Supreme   Court   Review   of   State Court Decisions.. 879

Sec.
A.   Introduction 879
B.   Preliminary Jurisdictional Considerations 882
     Murdock v. Memphis.. 884
     Notes and Questions 897

Sec.				Page
C.		Insulating State Decisions from Supreme Court Review		901
	1.	With Substantive Law		901
		a.	Adequacy, Independence and Certainty	901
			Fox Film Corp. v. Muller	901
			Notes and Questions	903
			Delaware v. Prouse	903
			Notes and Questions	906
			Minnesota v. National Tea Co.	906
			Questions	911
			Michigan v. Long	911
			Notes and Questions	920
		b.	Limits: Of State Incorporation of Federal and Federal Incorporation of State Law	926
			Standard Oil of California v. Johnson	926
			Notes and Questions	928
		c.	Limits: Supreme Court Review of Findings of Fact	930
			Ward v. Board of County Commissioners	930
			Notes and Questions	933
			Fiske v. Kansas	934
			Notes and Questions	938
			Norris v. Alabama	938
			Notes and Questions	946
	2.	With Procedural Law		946
			Herndon v. Georgia	946
			Notes and Questions	954
			Note on *Orr v. Orr*	956
			Henry v. Mississippi	957
			Notes and Questions	968
	3.	With the Final Judgment Rule		972
			Cox Broadcasting Corp. v. Cohn	972
			Notes and Questions	986

Chapter 10.   The Rooker-Feldman Doctrine **993**

Sec.				
A.		Introduction		993
B.		The Basic Doctrine		994
			Rooker v. Fidelity Trust Co.	994
			Notes and Questions	996
			District of Columbia Court of Appeals v. Feldman	997
			Notes and Questions	1009
C.		Problems of Interpretation		1011
	1.	The Source of the Injury: Independent Act or State Court Judgment?		1011
			Exxon Mobil Corporation v. Saudi Basic Industries Corporation	1011

Sec.		Page
	Notes and Questions	1017
2.	The Type of Relief Sought	1019
	Centifanti v. Nix	1019
	Notes and Questions	1029
3.	Appeal vs. Collateral Attack vs. Independent Action	1031
	Kamilewicz v. Bank of Boston Corporation (Panel Opinion)	1031
	Kamilewicz v. Bank of Boston Corporation (Dissent from Denial of Rehearing En banc)	1037
	Notes and Questions	1042
4.	Threading the Needle: *Rooker-Feldman* and Standing	1044
	Facio v. Jones	1044
	Notes and Questions	1048

Chapter 11. Federal Habeas Corpus Challenges to State Custody — 1051

Sec.		
A.	Introduction	1051
B.	The Statutory Structure	1059
C.	Habeas Corpus and the War on Terror	1063
	Rasul v. Bush	1065
	Notes and Questions	1080
	Note on *Rumsfeld v. Padilla*	1082
	Notes and Questions	1085
D.	Federal Court Review of State Convictions	1087
1.	State Factual Findings and Federal Evidentiary Hearings	1087
	Williams (Michael) v. Taylor	1088
	Notes and Questions	1098
2.	Constitutional Claims Cognizable on Habeas Corpus	1101
	Teague v. Lane	1101
	Notes and Questions	1112
	Williams (Terry) v. Taylor	1127
	Notes and Questions	1153
3.	Exhaustion of Remedies	1159
4.	The Effect of State Procedural Defaults	1164
	Coleman v. Thompson	1164
	Notes and Questions	1178
5.	The Problem of Successive Petitions	1183
6.	Time Limits	1193

Index — 1201

Table of Cases

Principal cases are in bold type. Cases cited or discussed in the text are in roman type. References are to pages. Cases cited within principal cases and within other quoted materials are not included.

Abrams, City of Rancho Palos Verdes v., 544 U.S. 113, 125 S.Ct. 1453, 161 L.Ed.2d 316 (2005), 530

Agency Holding Corp. v. Malley-Duff Associates, 483 U.S. 143, 107 S.Ct. 2359, 97 L.Ed.2d 121 (1987), 506

"Agent Orange" Product Liability Litigation, In re, 635 F.2d 987 (2d Cir. 1980), 419

Abbott Laboratories v. Gardner, 387 U.S. 136, 87 S.Ct. 1507, 18 L.Ed.2d 681 (1967), 100

Adickes v. S.H. Kress & Co., 398 U.S. 144 90 S.Ct. 1598, 26 L.Ed.2d 142 (1970), 529

Aetna Life Insurance Co. v. Haworth, 300 U.S. 227, 57 S.Ct. 461, 81 L.Ed. 617 (1937), 34, 106

Alabama Public Service Commission v. Southern Railway, 341 U.S. 341, 71 S.Ct. 762, 95 L.Ed. 1002 (1951), 800, 851

Aladdin's Castle, Inc., City of Mesquite v., 455 U.S. 283, 102 S.Ct. 1070, 71 L.Ed.2d 152 (1982), 118

Albright v. Oliver, 510 U.S. 266, 114 S.Ct. 807, 127 L.Ed.2d 114 (1994), 605

Albright v. Teas, 106 U.S. 613, 1 S.Ct. 550, 27 L.Ed. 295 (1882), 285

Alden v. Maine, 527 U.S. 706, 119 S.Ct. 2240, 144 L.Ed.2d 636 (1999), 607, 639, 732, 742

Alexander v. Sandoval, 532 U.S. 275, 121 S.Ct. 1511, 149 L.Ed.2d 517 (2001), 498

Allen v. Wright, 468 U.S. 737, 104 S.Ct. 3315, 82 L.Ed.2d 556 (1984), 10, 34

Amalgamated Clothing Workers v. Richman Brothers, 348 U.S. 511, 75 S.Ct. 452, 99 L.Ed.2d 600 (1955), 758

American Insurance Co. v. Canter, 26 U.S. (1 Pet.) 511, 7 L.Ed. 242 (1828), 321

American National Red Cross v. Solicitor General, 505 U.S. 247, 112 S.Ct. 2465, 120 L.Ed.2d 201 (1992), 234

American Well Works Co. v. Layne & Bowler Co., 241 U.S. 257, 36 S.Ct. 585, 60 L.Ed. 987 (1916), 262, 268, 269, 284, 306, 470

Anderson v. Creighton, 483 U.S. 635, 107 S.Ct. 3034, 97 L.Ed.2d 523 (1987), 588

Anway v. Grand Rapids Railway, 211 Mich. 592, 179 N.W. 350 (1920), 33

Arbaugh v. Y&H Corporation, 546 U.S. 500, 126 S.Ct. 1235, 163 L.Ed.2d 1097 (2006), 287

Arizonans for Official English v. Arizona, 520 U.S. 43, 117 S.Ct. 1055, 137 L.Ed.2d 170 (1997), 117, 780

Artuz v. Bennett, 531 U.S. 4, 121 S.Ct. 361, 148 L.Ed.2d 213 (2000), 1197

ASARCO Inc. v. Kadish, 409 U.S. 605, 109, S.Ct. 2037, 104 L.Ed.2d 696 (1989), 88

Ashby v. White, 92 Eng.Rep. 126 (K.B. 1703), 455

Ashwander v. TVA, 297 U.S. 288, 56 S.Ct. 466, 80 L.Ed. 688 (1936), 739, 777, 926, 989

Association of Data Processing Service Organizations v. Camp, 397 U.S. 159, 90 S.Ct. 838, 25 L.Ed.2d 192 (1970), 54, 92

Atascadero State Hospital v. Scanlon, 473 U.S. 234, 105, S.Ct. 3142, 87 L.Ed.2d 171 (1985), 645, 657, 672, 690, 731, 773

Atherton v. FDIC, 519 U.S. 213, 117 S.Ct. 666, 136 L.Ed.2d 656 (1997), 422, 503

Atlantic Coast Line Railroad Company v. Brotherhood of Locomotive Engineers, 398 U.S. 281, 90 S.Ct. 1739, 26 L.Ed.2d 234 (1970), 746, 829, 996

Avco Corp. v. Machinists, 390 U.S. 557, 88 S.Ct. 1235, 20 L.Ed.2d 126 (1968), 253, 319

Baker v. Carr, 369 U.S. 186, 82 S.Ct. 691, 7 L.Ed.2d 663 (1963), 24, 158, 159

Banco Nacional de Cuba v. Sabbatino, 376 U.S. 398, 84 S.Ct. 923, 11 L.Ed.2d 804 (1964), 373, 392

Bank of America National Trust & Savings Association v. Parnell, 352 U.S. 29, 77 S.Ct. 119, 1 L.Ed.2d 93 (1956), 390

Bank of the United States v. Deveaux, 9 U.S. (5 Cranch) 61, 3 L.Ed. 38 (1809), 235

Batson v. Kentucky, 476 U.S. 79, 106 S.Ct. 1712, 90 L.Ed.2d 69 (1986), 97

Battaglia v. General Motors Corp., 169 F.2d 254 (2d Cir. 1948), 196

Beard v. Banks, 546 U.S. 406, 124 S.Ct. 2504, 159 L.Ed.2d 494 (2004), 1113

Behrens v. Pelletier, 516 U.S. 299, 116 S.Ct. 834, 133 L.Ed.2d 773 (1996), 596

Bell v. Burson, 402 U.S. 535, 91 S.Ct. 1586, 29 L.Ed.2d 90 (1971), 599

Bell v. Cone, 535 U.S. 685, 122 S.Ct. 1842, 152 L.Ed.2d 914 (2002), 1156

Bell v. Hood, 327 U.S. 678, 66 S.Ct. 773, 90 L.Ed.2d 939 (1946), 286, 287

Bellotti v. Baird I, 428 U.S. 132, 96 S.Ct. 2857, 49 L.Ed.2d 844 (1976), 779

Bellotti v. Baird II, 443 U.S. 622, 99 S.Ct. 3035, 61 L.Ed.2d 797 (1979), 779

Beneficial National Bank v. Anderson, 539 U.S. 1, 123 S.Ct. 2058, 156 L.Ed.2d 1 (2003), 253

Benjamin v. Jacobson, 172 F.3d 144 (2d Cir. 1999), 220

Bigelow, People v., 66 N.Y.2d, 417, 488 N.E.2d 451, 497 N.Y.S.2d 630 (1985), 881

Bivens v. Six Unknown Named Agents of Fed. Bureau of Narcotics, 403 U.S. 388, 91 S.Ct. 1999, 29 L.Ed.2d 619 (1971), 286, **440**, 470, 496, 497, 578, 588, 591, 601, 602, 663

Black & White Taxicab & Transfer Company v. Brown & Yellow Taxicab & Transfer Company, 276 U.S. 518, 48 S.Ct. 404, 72 L.Ed. 681 (1928), 14

Blessing v. Freestone, 520 U.S. 329, 117 S.Ct. 1353, 137 L.Ed.2d 569 (1997), 529, 531

Board of the County Commissioners v. Brown, 520 U.S. 397, 117 S.Ct. 1382, 137 L.Ed.2d 626 (1997), 552, 555

Board of Trustees of the Univ. of Ala. v. Garrett, 531 U.S. 356, 121 S.Ct. 955, 148 L.Ed.2d 866 (2001), 677, 690

Bogan v. Scott-Harris, 523 U.S. 44, 118 S.Ct. 966, 140 L.Ed.2d 79 (1998), 577

Bolling v. Sharpe, 347 U.S. 497, 74 S.Ct. 693, 98 L.Ed. 884 (1954), 191

Boumediene v. Bush, 476 F.3d 981 (D.C. Cir.), *cert. granted,* ___ U.S.___, 127 S.Ct. 3078, 168 L.Ed.2d 755 (2007), 174, 1053, 1064, 1087

Bowsher v. Synar, 478 U.S. 714, 106 S.Ct. 3181, 92 L.Ed.2d 583 (1986), 9

Boyde v. California, 494 U.S. 370, 110 S.Ct. 1190, 108 L.Ed.2d 316 (1990), 1159

Boyle v. Landry, 401 U.S. 77, 91 S.Ct. 758, 27 L.Ed.2d 696 (1971), 800

Boyle v. United Technologies, Inc., 487 U.S. 500, 108 S.Ct. 2510, 101 L.Ed.2d 442 (1988), 406, 429, 429, 430, 503, 507

Braden v. Kentucky, 410 U.S. 484, 93 S.Ct. 1123, 35 L.Ed.2d 443 (1973), 1083

Brady v. Maryland, 373 U.S. 83, 83 S.Ct. 1194, 10 L.Ed.2d 215 (1963), 1182

Brigham City v. Stuart, 547 U.S. 398, 126 S.Ct. 1943, 164 L.Ed.2d 650 (2006), 922

Briscoe v. Lahue, 460 U.S. 325, 103 S.Ct. 1108, 75 L.Ed.2d 96 (1983), 577

Brown v. Allen, 344 U.S. 443, 73 S.Ct. 437, 97 L.Ed. 469 (1953), 17, 1052, 1057, 1058, 1101

Brown v. Board of Education, 347 U.S. 483, 74 S.Ct. 686, 98 L.Ed. 873 (1954), 87, 883

Brown v. Payton, 544 U.S. 13, 125 S.Ct. 1432, 161 L.Ed.2d 334 (2005), 1159

Buckley v. Fitzsimmons, 509 U.S. 259, 113 S.Ct. 2606, 125 L.Ed.2d 209 (1993), 577

Burford v. Sun Oil Co., 319 U.S. 315, 63 S.Ct. 1098, 87 L.Ed.2d 1424 (1943), 746, **841**

Burns v. Reed, 500 U.S. 478, 111 S.Ct. 1934, 114 L.Ed.2d 547 (1991), 577

Burton v. Stewart, ___ U.S. ___, 127 S.Ct. 793, 166 L.Ed.2d 628 (2007), 1163

Bush v. Gore, 531 U.S. 98, 121 S.Ct. 525, 148 L.Ed.2d 388 (2000), 161, 921

Bush v. Lucas, 462 U.S. 367, 103 S.Ct. 2404, 76 L.Ed.2d 648 (1983), 495

Bush v. Palm Beach County Canvassing Board, 531 U.S. 70, 121 S.Ct. 971, 148 L.Ed.2d 366 (2000), 920

Butler v. McKellar, 494 U.S. 407, 110 S.Ct. 1212, 108 L.Ed.2d 347 (1990), 1113, 1122

Butner v. United Stats, 440 U.S. 48, 99 S.Ct. 914, 59 L.Ed.2d 136 (1979), 405

Butz v. Economou, 438 U.S. 478, 98 S.Ct. 2894, 57 L.Ed.2d 895 (1978), 585

Byrd v. Blue Ridge Rural Elec. Co-op., 356 U.S. 525, 78 S.Ct. 893, 2 L.Ed.2d 953 (1958), 374

Byrne v. Karalexis, 401 U.S. 216, 91 S.Ct. 777, 27 L.Ed.2d 792 (1971), 800

Cabrera v. Martin, 973 F.2d 735 (9th Cir. 1992), 529

Caceres, United States v., 440 U.S. 741, 99 S.Ct. 1465, 59 L.Ed.2d 733 (1979), 881

Cage v. Louisiana, 498 U.S. 39, 111 S.Ct. 328, 112 L.Ed.2d 339 (199), 1122

Calderon v. Thompson, 523 U.S. 538, 118 S.Ct. 1489, 140 L.Ed.2d 728 (1998), 1186

Caldwell v. Mississippi, 472 U.S. 320, 105 S.Ct. 2633, 86 L.Ed.2d 31 (1985), 922, 1113, 1178

California v. Sierra Club, 451 U.S. 287, 101 S.Ct. 1775, 68 L.Ed.2d 101 (1981), 285, 454, **471**

Campbell v. Louisiana, 523 U.S. 392, 118 S.Ct. 1419, 140 L.Ed.2d 551 (1998), 97

Cannon v. University of Chicago, 441 U.S. 667, 99 S.Ct. 1946, 60 L.Ed.2d 560 (1979), 11, 421, **458**, 478, 495, 507, 585, 772

Cardinale v. Louisiana, 394 U.S. 437, 89 S.Ct. 1161, 22 L.Ed.2d 398 (1969), 880

Carey v. Saffold, 536 U.S. 214, 122 S.Ct. 2134, 153 L.Ed.2d 260 (2002), 1197

Carlson v. Green, 446 U.S. 14, 100 S.Ct. 1468, 64 L.Ed.2d 15 (1980), 496

Carr v. State (No. 1), 176 Ga. 55, 166 S.E. 827 (1932), 954

Carr v. State (No. 2), 176 Ga. 747, 169 S.E. 201 (1933), 955

Caterpillar, Inc. v. Williams, 482 U.S. 386, 107 S.Ct. 2425, 96 L.Ed.2d 318 (1987), 253

Centifanti v. Nix, 865 F.2d 1422 (3d Cir. 1989), 1019

Central Virginia Community College v. Katz, 546 U.S. 356, 126 S.Ct. 990, 163 L.Ed.2d 945 (2006), 734

Chappel v. Wallace, 462 U.S. 296, 103 S.Ct. 2362, 76 L.Ed.2d 586 (1983), 494

Cherry v. Warden, 1995 WL 598986 (S.D.N.Y. 1995), 220

Chisholm v. Georgia, 2 U.S. (2 Dall.) 419, 1 L.Ed. 440 (1793), 607, 642, 692, 731, 739, 740, 757

Christianson v. Colt Industries Operating Corp., 486 U.S. 800, 108 S.Ct. 2166, 100 L.Ed.2d 811 (1988), 285

City of _____ (see name of opposing party)

Clarke v. Securities Industries, 479 U.S. 388, 107 S.Ct. 750, 93 L.Ed.2d 757 (1987), 93

Clearfield Trust Co. v. United States, 318 U.S. 363, 63 S.Ct. 573, 87 L.Ed. 838 (1943), 387, 419, 506

Cohens v. Virginia, 19 U.S. (6 Wheat.) 264, 5 L.Ed.2d 257 (1821), 742, 746

Colegrove v. Green, 328 U.S. 549, 66 S.Ct. 1198, 90 L.Ed.2d 1432 (1946), 24, 159

Coleman v. Miller, 307 U.S. 433, 59 S.Ct. 972, 83 L.Ed. 1385 (1939), 161

Coleman v. Thompson, 501 U.S. 722, 111 S.Ct. 2546, 115 L.Ed.2d 640 (1991), 961, 971, 1126, **1164**, 1184

College Savings Bank v. Florida Prepaid Postsecondary Educ. Expense Bd., 527 U.S. 627, 119 S.Ct. 2199, 144 L.Ed.2d 575 (1999), 607, 676

Colorado River Water Conservation District v. United States, 424 U.S. 800, 96 S.Ct. 1236, 47 L.Ed.2d 483 (1976), 18, **865**, 878

Commissioner of Internal Revenue v. Bosch's Estate, 387 U.S. 456, 87 S.Ct. 1776, 18 L.Ed.2d 886 (1967), 432

Commodity Futures Trading Commission v. Schor, 478 U.S. 833, 106 S.Ct. 3245, 92 L.Ed.2d 675 (1986), 352

Commonwealth v. Blood, 400 Mass. 61, 507 N.E.2d 1029 (1987), 881

Construction Laborers v. Curry, 371 U.S. 542, 83 S.Ct. 531, 9 L.Ed.2d 514 (1963), 987

Correctional Services Corp. v. Malesko, 534 U.S. 61, 122 S.Ct. 515, 151 L.Ed.2d 456 (2001), 496

Cort v. Ash, 422 U.S. 66, 95 S.Ct. 2080, 45 L.Ed.2d 26 (1975), 285, 454, 455, 476, 478, 479, 498

County of Allegheny v. Frank Mashuda Co., 360 U.S. 185, 79 S.Ct. 1060, 3 L.Ed.2d 1163 (1959), 854

County of Imperial v. Munoz, 449 U.S. 54, 101 S.Ct. 289, 66 L.Ed.2d 258 (1980), 760

County of Los Angeles v. Davis, 440 U.S. 625, 99 S.Ct. 1379, 59 L.Ed.2d 642 (1979), 921

County of Oneida v. Oneida Indian Nation, 470 U.S. 226, 105 S.Ct. 1245, 84 L.Ed.2d 169 (1985), 160, 505

County of Sacramento v. Lewis, 523 U.S. 833, 118 S.Ct. 1708, 140 L.Ed.2d 626 (1998), 602

Cox Broadcasting Corp. v. Cohn, 420 U.S. 469, 95 S.Ct. 1029, 43 L.Ed.2d 328 (1975), 972, 1050

Craig v. Boren, 429 U.S. 190, 97 S.Ct. 451, 50 L.Ed.2d 397 (1976), 96, 97

Crawford v. Washington, 541 U.S. 36, 124 S.Ct. 1354, 158 L.Ed.2d 177 (2004), 1120, 1124

Crawford-El v. Britton, 523 U.S. 574, 118 S.Ct. 1584, 140 L.Ed.2d 759 (1998), 592

Crockett v. Reagan, 720 F.2d 1355 (D.C.Cir. 1983), 24

Crowell v. Benson, 285 U.S. 22, 52 S.Ct. 285, 76 L.Ed. 598 (1932), 322

DaCosta v. Laird, 471 F.2d 1146 (2d Cir. 1973), 24

DaimlerChrysler Corp. v. Cuno, 547 U.S. 332, , 126 S.Ct. 1854, 164 L.Ed.2d 589 (2006), 89

Danforth v. Minnesota, __ U.S. __, 128S.Ct. 1029, __ L.Ed.2d__ (2008), 1124

Daniels v. Allen, 345 U.S. 946, 73 S.Ct. 827, 97 L.Ed. 1370 (1953), 1055

Daniels v. United States, 254 F.3d 1180 (10th Cir. 2001), 1185

Daniels v. Williams, 474 U.S. 327, 106 S.Ct. 662, 88 L.Ed.2d 662 (1986), 601

Davidson v. Cannon, 474 U.S. 344, 106 S.Ct. 668, 88 L.Ed.2d 677 (1986), 601

Davis v. Monroe County Bd. of Educ., 526 U.S. 629, 119 S.Ct. 1661, 143 L.Ed.2d 839 (1999), 471

Davis v. Passman, 442 U.S. 228, 99 S.Ct. 2264, 60 L.Ed.2d 846 (1979), 496

Day v. McDonough, 547 U.S. 198, 126 S.Ct. 1675, 164 L.Ed.2d 376 (2006), 1194

DeFunis v. Odegaard, 416 U.S. 312, 94 S.Ct. 1704, 40 L.Ed.2d 164 (1974), 111

Delaware v. Prouse, 440 U.S. 648, 99 S.Ct. 1391, 59 L.Ed.2d 660 (1979), 903, 925

DelCostello v. International Brotherhood of Teamsters, 462 U.S. 151, 103 S.Ct. 2281, 76 L.Ed.2d 476 (1983), 505

Dellmuth v. Muth, 491 U.S. 223, 109 S.Ct. 2397, 105 L.Ed.2d 181 (1989), 673, 674

DeLovio v. Boit, 7 F.Cas. 418 (C.C.D.Mass. 1815), 440

Dennis v. Higgins, 498 U.S. 439, 111 S.Ct. 865, 112 L.Ed.2d 969 (1991), 529

Dennis v. Sparks, 449 U.S. 24, 101 S.Ct. 183, 66 L.Ed.2d 185 (1980), 529

Deposit Guaranty National Bank v. Roper, 445 U.S. 326, 100 S.Ct. 1166, 63 L.Ed.2d 427 (1980), 121

Devlin v. Scardelletti, 536 U.S. 1, 122 S.Ct. 2005, 153 L.Ed.2d 27 (2002), 1044

Dice v. Akron, Canton, and Youngstown R. Co., 342 U.S. 359, 72 S.Ct. 312, 96 L.Ed. 398 (1952), 318.

Diffenderfer v. Central Baptist Church of Miami, Inc., 404 U.S. 412, 92 S.Ct. 574, 30 L.Ed.2d 567 (1972), 119

District of Columbia Court of Appeals v. Feldman, 460 U.S. 462, 103 S.Ct. 1303, 75 L.Ed.2d 206 (1983), 997

Dodd v. United States, 545 U.S. 353, 125 S.Ct. 2478, 162 L.Ed.2d 343 (2005), 1196

Dombrowski v. Pfister, 380 U.S. 479, 85 S.Ct. 1116, 14 L.Ed.2d 22 (1965), 794

Donnelly v. DeChristoforo, 416 U.S. 637 94 S.Ct. 1868, 40 L.Ed.2d 431 (1974), 1114

Donovan v. City of Dallas, 377 U.S. 408, 84 S.Ct. 1579, 12 L.Ed.2d 409 (1964), 760, 821

Doran v. Salem Inn, Inc., 422 U.S 922, 95 S.Ct. 2561, 45 L.Ed.2d 648 (1975), 812

Douglas v. Alabama, 380 U.S. 415, 85 S.Ct. 1074, 13 L.Ed.2d 934 (1965), 970

Douglas v. City of Jeannette, 319 U.S. 157, 63 S.Ct. 877, 87 L.Ed. 1324 (1943), 791

Duke Power Co. v. Carolina Environmental Study Group, Inc. 438 U.S. 59, 98 S.Ct. 2620, 57 L.Ed.2d 595 (1978), 56

Dunn v. Blumstein, 405 U.S. 330, 92 S.Ct. 995, 31 L.Ed.2d 274 (1972), 117, 120

Dupasseur v. Rochereau, 88 U.S. (21 Wall.) 130, 22 L.Ed. 588 (1874), 429

Dyson v. Stein, 401 U.S. 200, 91 S.Ct. 769, 27 L.Ed.2d 781 (1971), 800

E. Edelmann & Co. v. Triple-A Specialty Co., 88 F.2d 852 (7th Cir. 1937), 305, 316, 318, 318

Eddings v. Oklahoma, 445 U.S. 104, 102 S.Ct. 869, 71 L.Ed.2d 1 (1982), 1118

Edelman v. Jordan, 415 U.S. 651, 94 S.Ct. 1347, 39 L.Ed.2d 662 (1974), 645, **646,** 883, 1181

Edwards v. Carpenter, 529 U.S. 446, 120 S.Ct. 1587, 146 L.Ed.2d 518 (2000), 1182

Empire Healthchoice Assurance, Inc. v. McVeigh, 547 U.S. 677, 126 S.Ct. 2121, 165 L.Ed.2d 131 (2006), 300, 429

Endo, Ex parte, 323 U.S. 283, 65 S.Ct. 209, 89 L.Ed. 243 (1944), 1083

England v. Louisiana State Board of Medical Examiners, 375 U.S. 411, 84 S.Ct. 461, 11 L.Ed.2d 440 (1964), 781

Erie Railroad v. Tompkins, 304 U.S. 64, 58 S.Ct. 817, 82 L.Ed. 1188 (1938), 11, 13, 373, **375,** 393, 405, 413, 429, 431, 440, 469, 507, 799, 922, 929

Estelle v. Gamble, 429 U.S. 97, 97 S.Ct. 285, 50 L.Ed.2d 251 (1976), 528

Evans v. Chavis, __ U.S. __, 126 S.Ct. 846, 163 L.Ed.2d 684 (2006), 1198

Ex parte _____ (see name of party)

Examining Board of Engineers v. Flores de Otero, 426 U.S. 572, 96 S.Ct. 2264, 49 L.Ed.2d 65 (1976), 778

Exxon Mobil Corp. v. Allapattah Services, Inc., 545 U.S. 546, 125 S.Ct. 2611, 162 L.Ed.2d 502 (2005), 90

Exxon Mobil Corporation v. Saudi Basic Industries Corporation, 544 U.S. 280, 125 S.Ct. 1517, 161 L.Ed.2d 454 (2005), 1011

Facio v. Jones, 929 F.2d 541 (10th Cir. 1991), 1018, **1044**

Fact Concerts, Inc., City of Newport v., 453 U.S. 247, 101 S.Ct. 2748, 69 L.Ed.2d 616 (1981), 555

Fall v. Eastin, 215 U.S. 1, 30 S.Ct. 3, 54 L.Ed. 65 (1909), 735

Farmer v. Brennan, 511 U.S. 825, 114 S.Ct. 1970, 128 L.Ed.2d 811 (1994), 601

Fay v. Noia, 372 U.S. 391, 83 S.Ct. 822, 9 L.Ed.2d 837 (1963), 971, 1055, 1184

FDIC v. Meyer, 510 U.S. 471, 114 S.Ct. 996, 127 L.Ed.2d 308 (1994), 496

Fed. Mar. Comm'n v. South Carolina State Ports Auth., 535 U.S. 743, 122 S.Ct. 1864, 152 L.Ed.2d 962 (2001), 741, 1009

Federal Election Commission v. Akins, 524 U.S. 11, 118 S.Ct. 1777, 141 L.Ed.2d 10 (1998), 83

Federated Department Stores v. Moitie, 452 U.S. 394, 101 S.Ct. 2424, 69 L.Ed.2d 103 (1981), 219

Felker v. Turpin, 518 U.S. 651, 116 S.Ct. 2333, 135 L.Ed.2d 827 (1996), 172

Fenner v. Boykin, 271 U.S. 240, 46 S.Ct. 492, 70 L.Ed. 927 (1926), 791

Finley v. United States, 490 U.S. 545, 109 S.Ct. 2003, 104 L.Ed.2d 593 (1989), 90

Fiore v. White, 531 U.S. 225, 121 S.Ct. 712, 148 L.Ed.2d 629 (2001), 1120

Firefighters Local 1784 v. Stotts, 467 U.S. 561, 104 S.Ct. 2576, 81 L.Ed.2d 483 (1984), 116

Fiske v. Kansas, 274 U.S. 380, 47 S.Ct. 655, 71 L.Ed. 1108 (1927), 934

Fitzpatrick v. Bitzer, 427 U.S. 445, 96 S.Ct. 2666, 49 L.Ed.2d 614 (1976), 666, 731, 735, 736

Flast v. Cohen, 392 U.S. 83, 88 S.Ct. 1942, 20 L.Ed.2d 947 (1968), 26, 85, 89

Flores, City of Boerne v., 521 U.S. 507, 117 S.Ct. 2157, 138 L.Ed.2d 624 (1987), 498, 628, 689

Florida Prepaid Postsecondary Educ. Expense Bd. v. College Sav. Bank, 527 U.S. 666, 119 S.Ct. 2219, 144 L.Ed.2d 605 (1999), 607, 675

Ford Motor Co. v. Dep't of the Treasury, 323 U.S. 459, 65 S.Ct. 347, 89 L.Ed. 389 (1945), 660

Ford v. Georgia, 498 U.S. 411, 111 S.Ct. 850, 112 L.Ed.2d 935 (1991), 972

Ford v. Wainwright, 477 U.S. 399, 106 S.Ct. 2595, 91 L.Ed.2d 335 (1986), 1191

Forrester v. White, 484 U.S. 219, 108 S.Ct. 538, 98 L.Ed.2d 555 (1988), 576

Fox Film Corp. v. Muller, 296 U.S. 207, 56 S.Ct. 183, 80 L.Ed. 158 (1935), 901, 970

Frady, U.S. v., 456 U.S. 152, 102 S.Ct. 1584, 71 L.Ed.2d 816 (1982), 1182

Franchise Tax Board of California v. Construction Laborers Vacation Trust, 463 U.S. 1, 103 S.Ct. 2841, 77 L.Ed.2d 420 (1983), 306

Frank v. Mangum, 237 U.S. 309, 35 S.Ct. 582, 59 L.Ed. 969 (1915), 1055

French v. Duckworth, 178 F.3d 437 (7th Cir. 1999), 220

Friends of the Earth, Inc. v. Laidlaw Envtl. Services (TOC), Inc., 528 U.S. 167, 120 S.Ct. 693, 145 L.Ed.2d 610 (2000), 123

Frothingham v. Mellon, 262 U.S. 447, 43 S.Ct. 597, 67 L.Ed. 1078 (1923), 85, 88, 89

Fuentes v. Shevin, 407 U.S. 67, 92 S.Ct. 1983, 32 L.Ed.2d 556 (1972), 796

Fusari v. Steinberg, 419 U.S. 379, 95 S.Ct. 533, 42 L.Ed.2d 521 (1975), 119

Gardner v. Florida, 430 U.S. 349, 97 S.Ct. 1197, 51 L.Ed.2d 393 (1977), 1118

Garry v. Geils, 82 F.3d 1362 (7th Cir. 1996), 1017

Gasperini v. Center for the Humanities, Inc., 518 U.S. 415, 116 S.Ct. 2211, 135 L.Ed.2d 659 (1996), 374

Gebser v. Lago Vista Independent Sch. Dist., 524 U.S. 274, 118 S.Ct. 1989, 141 L.Ed.2d 277 (1998), 471

Georgia, United States v., 546 U.S. 151, 126 S.Ct. 877, 163 L.Ed.2d 650 (2006), 694

Georgia v. McCollum, 505 U.S. 42, 112 S.Ct. 2348, 120 L.Ed.2d 33 (1992), 97

Gerstein v. Pugh, 420 U.S. 103, 95 S.Ct. 854, 43 L.Ed.2d 54 (1975), 795

Gibson v. Berryhill, 411 U.S. 564, 93 S.Ct. 1689, 36 L.Ed.2d 488 (1973), 796

Giles v. Harris, 189 U.S. 475, 23 S.Ct. 639, 47 L.Ed. 909 (1903), 619

Gitlow v. New York, 268 U.S. 652, 45 S.Ct. 625, 69 L.Ed. 1138 (1925), 954

Gladstone, Realtors v. Village of Bellwood, 441 U.S. 91, 99 S.Ct. 1601, 60 L.Ed.2d 66 (1979), 53, 59

Golden State Transit Corp. v. Los Angeles, 493 U.S. 103, 110 S.Ct. 444, 107 L.Ed.2d 420 (1989), 529

Golden v. Zwickler, 394 U.S. 103, 89 S.Ct. 956, 22 L.Ed.2d 113 (1969), 117

Goldwater v. Carter, 444 U.S. 996, 100 S.Ct. 533, 63 L.Ed.2d 428 (1979), 161

Gomez v. United States, 490 U.S. 858, 109 S.Ct. 2237, 104 L.Ed.2d 923 (1989), 369

Gonzalez v. Crosby, 545 U.S. 524, 125 S.Ct. 2641, 162 L.Ed.2d 480 (2005), 1190

Government and Civil Employees Organizing Committee v. Windsor, 353 U.S. 364, 77 S.Ct. 838, 1 L.Ed.2d 894 (1957), 781

Grable & Sons Metal Products, Inc. v. Darue Engineering & Manufacturing, 545 U.S. 308, 125 S.Ct. 2363, 162 L.Ed.2d 390 (2005), 290

Graham County Soil & Water Conservation Dist. v. United States, 545 U.S. 409, 125 S.Ct. 2444, 162 L.Ed.2d 390 (2005), 505

Graham v. Richardson, 403 U.S. 365, 91 S.Ct. 1848, 29 L.Ed.2d 534 (1971), 192

Granfinanciera, S.A. v. Nordberg, 492 U.S. 33, 109 S.Ct. 2872, 106 L.Ed.2d 493 (1989), 365

Granville-Smith v. Granville-Smith, 349 U.S. 1, 75 S.Ct. 553, 99 L.Ed. 773 (1955), 798

Gray v. Netherland, 518 U.S. 152, 116 S.Ct. 207, 135 L.Ed.2d 457 (1996), 1115

Green v. Mansour, 474 U.S. 64, 106 S.Ct. 423, 88 L.Ed.2d 371 (1985), 657

Griminger, People v., 71 N.Y.2d 635, 524 N.E.2d 409, 521 N.Y.S.2d 55 (1988), 881

Griswold v. Connecticut, 381 U.S. 479, 85 S.Ct. 1678, 14 L.Ed.2d 510 (1965), 109

Guaranty Trust Co. v. York, 326 U.S. 99, 65 S.Ct. 1464, 89 L.Ed. 2079 (1945), 374

Gully v. First National Bank, 299 U.S. 109, 57 S.Ct. 96, 81 L.Ed. 70 (1936), 262, 270, 300

Hadix v. Johnson, 144 F.3d 925 (6th Cir. 1998), 220

Hafer v. Melo, 502 U.S. 21, 112 S.Ct. 358, 116 L.Ed.2d 301 (1991), 671

Hamdan v. Rumsfeld, __ U.S. __, 126 S.Ct. 2749, 165 L.Ed.2d 723 (2006), 173, 1053, 1086

Hamdi v. Rumsfeld, 542 U.S. 507, 124 S.Ct. 2633, 159 L.Ed.2d 578 (2004), 1064

Hanna v. Plumer, 380 U.S. 460, 85 S.Ct. 1136, 14 L.Ed.2d 8 (1965), 374

Hans v. Louisiana, 134 U.S. 1, 10 S.Ct. 504, 33 L.Ed. 842 (1890), 608, 628, 638, 641, 646, 655, 670, 672, 695, 732, 733, 741

Harlow v. Fitzgerald, 457 U.S. 800, 102 S.Ct. 2727, 73 L.Ed.2d 396 (1982), 576, 580, 794, 1112

Harris County Commissioners Court v. Moore, 420 U.S. 77, 95 S.Ct. 870, 43 L.Ed.2d 32 (1975), 784

Harris v. Reed, 489 U.S. 255, 109 S.Ct. 1038, 103 L.Ed.2d 308 (1989), 1178

Harris v. Younger, 281 F.Supp. 507 (C.D. Cal. 1968), *rev'd*, 401 U.S. 37, 91 S.Ct. 746, 27 L.Ed.2d 669 (1971), 811

Harris, City of Canton v., 489 U.S. 378, 109 S.Ct. 1197, 103 L.Ed.2d 417 (1989), 553

Harrison v. NAACP, 360 U.S. 167, 79 S.Ct. 1025, 3 L.Ed.2d 1152 (1959), 778

Hastings v. United States, 802 F.Supp. 490 (D.D.C. 1992), *vacated*, 988 F.2d 1280 (D.C.Cir. 1993), 161

Hawaii Housing Authority v. Midkiff, 467 U.S. 229, 104 S.Ct. 2321, 81 L.Ed.2d 186 (1984), 820

Hayburn's Case, 2 U.S. (2 Dall.) 408, 1 L.Ed. 436 (1792), 27, 217, 220

Hays, United States v., 515 U.S. 737, 115 S.Ct. 2431, 132 L.Ed.2d 635 (1995), 84

Head v. Nixon, 342 F.Supp. 521 (E.D.La.), *aff'd*, 468 F.3d 951 (5th Cir. 1972), 24

Hein v. Freedom from Religion Foundation, Inc., __ U.S. __, 127 S.Ct. 2553, 168 L.Ed.2d 424 (2007), 86

Henry v. Mississippi, 379 U.S. 443, 85 S.Ct. 564, 13 L.Ed.2d 408 (1965), 922, 957

Herndon v. Georgia, 295 U.S. 441, 55 S.Ct. 794, 79 L.Ed. 1530 (1935), 903 946, 922, 958

Herrera v. Collins, 506 U.S. 390, 113 S.Ct. 853, 122 L.Ed.2d 203 (1993), 1189

Hess v. Port Authority Trans-Hudson Corporation, 513 U.S. 30, 115 S.Ct. 394, 130 L.Ed.2d 245 (1994), 643

Hicks v. Miranda, 422 U.S. 332, 95 S.Ct. 2281, 45 L.Ed.2d 223 (1975), 813, 831, 876

Hill v. McDonough, 547 U.S. 573, 126 S.Ct. 2096, 165 L.Ed 2d 44 (2006), 1191

Hinderlider v. LaPlata River & Cherry Creek Ditch Co., 304 U.S. 92, 58 S.Ct. 803, 82 L.Ed. 1202 (1938), 374

Holmes Group, Inc. v. Vornado Air Circulation Sys., Inc., 535 U.S. 826, 122 S.Ct. 1889, 153 L.Ed.2d 13 (2002), 252, 318

Home Telephone and Telegraph Co. v. City of Los Angeles, 227 U.S. 278, 33 S.Ct. 312, 57 L.Ed. 510 (1913), 527, 642

Honig v. Doe, 484 U.S. 305, 108 S.Ct. 592, 98 L.Ed.2d 686 (1988), 121

Hope v. Pelzer, 536 U.S. 730, 122 S.Ct. 2508, 153 L.Ed.2d 666 (2002), 587

Hopkinson v. Shillinger, 888 F.2d 1286 (10th Cir. 1989), 1114

Horn v. Banks, 536 U.S. 266, 122 S.Ct. 2147, 153 L.Ed.2d 301 (2002), 1123, 1154

Howell v. Mississippi, 543 U.S. 440, 125 S.Ct. 856, 160 L.Ed.2d 873 (2005), 880

Hudson v. Palmer, 468 U.S. 517, 104 S.Ct. 3194, 82 L.Ed.2d 393 (1984), 600

Huffman v. Pursue, Ltd. 420 U.S. 592, 95 S.Ct. 1200, 43 L.Ed.2d 492 (1975), 15, 18, 181, **822**

Hurn v. Ourlser, 289 U.S. 238, 53 S.Ct. 586, 77 L.Ed. 1148 (1933), 285

House v. Bell, 547 U.S. 518, 126 S.Ct. 2064, 165 L.Ed.2d 1 (2006), 1188

I.M. Darnell & Son Co. v. City of Memphis, 208 U.S. 113, 28 S.Ct. 247, 52 L.Ed. 413 (1908), 110

Idaho v. Coeur d'Alene Tribe, 521 U.S. 261, 117 S.Ct. 2028, 138 L.Ed.2d 438 (1997), 79, 661

Illinois v. Gates, 462 U.S. 213, 103 S.Ct. 2317, 76 L.Ed.2d 527 (1983), 881

Imbler v. Pachtman, 424 U.S. 409, 96 S.Ct. 984, 47 L.Ed.2d 128 (1976), 577

Immigration and Naturalization Service v. Chadha, 462 U.S. 919, 103 S.Ct. 2764, 77 L.Ed.2d 317 (1983), 10

Imprisoned Citizens Union v. Ridge, 169 F.3d 178 (3d Cir. 1999), 220

Industrial Communications and Electronics, Inc. v. Monroe County, 134 Fed. Appx. 314 (11th Cir. 2005), 1018

In re _____ (see name of party)

J.I. Case Company v. Borak, 377 U.S. 426, 84 S.Ct. 1555, 12 L.Ed.2d 423 (1964), 456, 456

Jackson v. Birmingham Bd. of Educ., 544 U.S. 167, 125 S.Ct. 1497, 161 L.Ed.2d 361 (2005), 471

Jackson v. Virginia, 443 U.S. 307, 99 S.Ct. 2781, 61 L.Ed.2d 560 (1979), 1101

Jaffee v.Redmond, 518 U.S. 1, 116 S.Ct. 1923, 135 L.Ed.2d 337 (1996), 439

James B. Beam Distilling Co. v. Georgia, 501 U.S. 529, 111 S.Ct. 2439, 115 L.Ed.2d 481 (1991), 504

Japan Whaling Association v. American Cetacean Society, 478 U.S. 221, 106 S.Ct. 2860, 92 L.Ed.2d 166 (1986), 161

Jett v. Dallas Independent School District, 491 U.S. 701, 109 S.Ct. 2702, 105 L.Ed.2d 598 (1989), 553

Johnson v. De Grandy, 512 U.S. 997, 114 S.Ct. 2647, 129 L.Ed.2d 775 (1994), 1044

Johnson v. Eisentrager, 339 U.S. 763, 70 S.Ct. 936, 94 L.Ed. 1255 (1950), 1080

Johnson v. Lankford, 245 U.S. 541, 38 S.Ct. 203, 62 L.Ed. 460 (1918), 736

Johnson v. Jones, 515 U.S. 304, 115 S.Ct. 2151, 132 L.Ed.2d 238 (1995), 595

Johnson v. Robison, 415 U.S. 361, 94 S.Ct. 414, 39 L.Ed.2d 389 (1974), 197

Johnson v. Zerbst, 304 U.S. 458, 58 S.Ct. 1019, 82 L.Ed. 1461 (1938), 1181

Jones v. Rath Packing Co., 430 U.S. 519, 97 S.Ct. 1305, 51 L.Ed.2d 604 (1977), 394

Juidice v. Vail, 430 U.S. 327, 97 S.Ct. 1211, 51 L.Ed.2d 376 (1977), 832, 837

Justice v. Valley National Bank, 849 F.2d 1078 (8th Cir. 1988), 395

Kalina v. Fletcher, 522 U.S. 118, 118 S.Ct. 502, 139 L.Ed.2d 471 (1997), 577

Kansas v. Marsh, 548 U.S. 163, 126 S.Ct. 2516, 165 L.Ed.2d 429 (2006), 924, 990

Kamilewicz v. Bank of Boston Corp. (dissent from denial of reh. en banc), 100 F.3d 1348 (7th Cir. 1996), 1037

Kamilewicz v. Bank of Boston Corp. (panel opinion), 92 F.3d 306 (7th Cir. 1996), 1031, 1049

Kansas v. Colorado, 533 U.S. 1, 121 S.Ct. 2033, 150 L.Ed.2d 72 (2001), 641

Karahalios v. National Federation of Federal Employees, Local 1263, 489 U.S. 527, 109 S.Ct. 1282, 103 L.Ed.2d 539 (1989), 454, 478

Keeney v. Tamayo-Reyes, 504 U.S. 1, 112 S.Ct. 1715, 118 L.Ed.2d 318 (1992), 1057, 1088, 1099

Kennedy, State v., 295 Or. 260, 666 P.2d 1316 (1983), 925

Kimbell Foods, Inc., United States v., 440 U.S. 715, 99 S.Ct. 1448, 59 L.Ed.2d 711 (1979), 394, **395,** 422, 430, 254

Kimbro, State v., 197 Conn. 219, 496 A.2d 498 (1985), 881

Kimel v. Florida Bd. of Regents, 528 U.S. 62, 120 S.Ct. 631, 145 L.Ed.2d 522 (2000), 676

Kimmelman v. Morrison, 477 U.S. 365, 106 S.Ct. 2574, 91 L.Ed.2d 305 (1986), 1101

Klein, United States v., 80 U.S. (13 Wall.) 128, 20 L.Ed. 519 (1872), 181, 217, 220, 220

Kline v. Burke Construction Co., 260 U.S. 226, 43 S.Ct. 79, 67 L.Ed. 226 (1922), 760

Kremens v. Bartley, 431 U.S. 119, 97 S.Ct. 1709, 52 L.Ed.2d 184 (1977), 118

Lake Carriers' Association v. MacMullan, 406 U.S. 498, 92 S.Ct. 1749, 32 L.Ed.2d 257 (1972), 111

Lake Country Estates, Inc. v. Tahoe Regional Planning Agency, 440 U.S. 391, 99 S.Ct. 1171, 59 L.Ed.2d 401 (1979), 643

Lampf, Pleva, Lipkind, Prupis & Petigrow v. Gilbertson, 501 U.S. 350, 111 S.Ct. 2773, 115 L.Ed.2d 321 (1991), 500

Lanier, United States v., 520 U.S. 259, 117 S.Ct. 1219, 137 L.Ed.2d 432 (1997), 532, 587

Lapides v. Board of Regents, 535 U.S. 613, 122 S.Ct. 1640, 152 L.Ed.2d 806 (2002), 660

Lauf v. E.G. Skinner & Co., Inc., 303 U.S. 323, 58 S.Ct. 578, 82 L.Ed.872 (1938), 196

Lawrence v. Florida, __ U.S. __, 127 S.Ct. 1079, 166 L.Ed.2d 924 (2007), 1060

Lawrie v. Snyder, 9 F.Supp.2d 428 (D.Del. 1998), 1099

Leatherman v. Tarrant County Narcotics Intelligence and Coordination Unit, 507 U.S. 163, 113 S.Ct. 1160, 122 L.Ed.2d 517 (1993), 595

Lee v. Kemna, 534 U.S. 362, 122 S.Ct. 877, 151 L.Ed.2d 820 (2002), 970

Lee v. Weisman, 505 U.S. 577, 112 S.Ct. 2649, 120 L.Ed.2d 467 (1992), 117

Leon, United States v., 468 U.S. 897, 104 S.Ct. 3405, 82 L.Ed.2d 677 (1984), 881

Levitt, Ex parte, 302 U.S. 633, 58 S.Ct. 1, 82 L.Ed. 493 (1937), 80

Liberty Warehouse v. Grannis, 273 U.S. 70, 47 S.Ct. 282, 71 L.Ed. 541 (1927), 105

Linda R.S. v. Richard D., 410 U.S. 614, 93 S.Ct. 1146, 35 L.Ed.2d 536 (1973), 55, 57, 142

Lobue v. Christopher, 893 F.Supp. 65 (D.D.C. 1995), rev'd on other grounds, 82 F.3d 1081 (D.C.Cir. 1996), 220

Lockyer v. Andrade, 538 U.S. 63, 123 S.Ct. 1166, 155 L.Ed.2d 144 (2003), 1157

Longest v. Langford, 274 U.S. 499, 47 S.Ct. 668, 71 L.Ed. 1170 (1927), 883

Louisiana Power & Light Co. v. City of Thibodaux, 360 U.S. 25, 79 S.Ct. 1070, 3 L.Ed.2d 1058 (1959), 854

Louisville & Nashville R.R. Co. v. Mottley, 211 U.S. 149, 29 S.Ct. 42, 53 L.Ed. 126 (1908), 249, 262, 264, 272, 627, 882, 1043

Louisville & Nashville Railroad v. Mottley, 219 U.S. 467, 31 S.Ct. 265, 55 L.Ed. 297 (1911), 251, 882

Lowe v. General Motors Corp., 624 F.2d 1373 (5th Cir. 1980), 286

Lugar v. Edmonson Oil Co., 457 U.S. 922, 102 S.Ct. 2744, 73 L.Ed.2d 482 (1982), 528

Lujan v. Defenders of Wildlife, 504 U.S. 555, 112 S.Ct. 2130, 119 L.Ed.2d 351 (1992), 53, 77, 81

Lukaszewicz v. Ortho Pharmaceutical Corp., 510 F.Supp. 961 (E.D.Wis. 1981), 286

Luther v. Borden, 48 U.S. (7 How.) 1, 12 L.Ed. 581 (1849), 24, 159

Lynch v. Donnelly, 465 U.S. 668, 104 S.Ct. 1355, 79 L.Ed.2d 604 (1984), 81

Lyons, City of Los Angeles v., 461 U.S. 95, 103 S.Ct. 1660, 75 L.Ed.2d 675 (1983), 26, 54, 105, 142, 1049

Maine v. Thiboutout, 448 U.S. 1, 100 S.Ct. 2502, 65 L.Ed.2d 555 (1980), 529

Marbury v. Madison, 5 U.S. (1 Cranch) 137, 2 L.Ed. 60 (1803), 8, 9, 34, 88

Marsala, State v., 216 Conn. 150, 579 A.2d 58 (1990), 881

Martin v. Hunter's Lessee, 14 U.S. (1 Wheat.) 304, 4 L.Ed. 97 (1816), 195, 879, 993, 1156

Martinez v. Socoma Companies, Inc., 11 Cal.3d 394, 521 P.2d 841, 113 Cal.Rptr. 585 (1974), 95

Massachusetts v. Environmental Protection Agency, __ U.S. __, 127 S.Ct. 1438, 167 L.Ed.2d 248 (2007), 60

Massachusetts v. Mellon, 262 U.S. 447, 43 S.Ct. 597, 67 L.Ed. 1078 (1923), 89

Matsushita Elec. Indus. Co. Ltd. v. Epstein, 516 U.S. 367, 116 S.Ct. 873, 134 L.Ed.2d 6 (1996), 1043

Mayle v. Felix, 545 U.S. 644, 125 S.Ct. 2562, 162 L.Ed.2d 582 (2005), 1194

McCardle, Ex parte, 74 U.S. (7 Wall.) 506, 19 L.Ed. 264 (1869), 165, 217

McCleskey v. Zant, 499 U.S. 467, 111 S.Ct. 1454, 113 L.Ed.2d 517 (1991), 1181, 1184

M'Culloch v. Maryland, 17 U.S. (4 Wheat.) 316, 4 L.Ed. 579 (1819), 234, 422

McNeese v. Board of Education, 373 U.S. 668, 83 S.Ct. 1443, 10 L.Ed.2d 622 (1963), 773, 852

Medimmune, Inc. v. Genentech, Inc., __ U.S. __, 127 S.Ct. 764, 166 L.Ed.2d 604 (2007), 106

Memorial Hospital v. Maricopa County, 415 U.S. 250, 94 S.Ct. 1076, 39 L.Ed.2d 306 (1974), 192

Mendoza-Lopez, United States v., 481 U.S. 828, 107 S.Ct. 2148, 95 L.Ed.2d 772 (1987), 198

Mercantile National Bank v. Langdeau, 371 U.S. 555, 83 S.Ct. 520, 9 L.Ed.2d 523 (1963), 987

Meredith v. City of Winter Haven, 320 U.S. 228, 64 S.Ct. 7, 88 L.Ed. 9 (1943), 777, 853

Merrell Dow Pharmaceuticals, Inc. v. Thompson, 478 U.S. 804, 106 S.Ct. 3229, 92 L.Ed.2d 650 (1986), 272, 296, 297, 298, 299, 382, 471, 874

Merrill Lynch Pierce, Fenner & Smith v. Curran, 456 U.S. 353, 102 S.Ct. 1825, 72 L.Ed.2d 182 (1982), 507

Metropolitan Life Ins. Co. v. Taylor, 481 U.S. 58, 107 S.Ct. 1542, 95 L.Ed.2d 55 (1987), 253, 254, 319

Miami Herald Publishing Co. v. Tornillo, 418 U.S. 241, 94 S.Ct. 2831, 41 L.Ed.2d 730 (1974), 987

Michel v. Louisiana, 350 U.S. 91, 76 S.Ct. 158, 100 L.Ed. 83 (1955), 969

Michigan v. Long, 463 U.S. 1032, 103 S.Ct. 3469, 77 L.Ed.2d 1201 (1983), 911, 929, 971, 1178,

Middlesex County Ethics Committee v. Garden State Bar Association, 457 U.S. 423, 102 S.Ct. 2515, 73 L.Ed.2d 46 (1982), 835

Middlesex County Sewerage Authority v. National Sea Clammers Association, 453 U.S. 1, 101 S.Ct. 2615, 69 L.Ed.2d 435 (1981), 530

Migra v. Warren City School District, 465 U.S. 75, 104 S.Ct. 892, 79 L.Ed.2d 56 (1984), 740, 781, 785

Milliken v. Bradley, 433 U.S. 267, 97 S.Ct. 2749, 53 L.Ed.2d 745 (1977), 656

Mills v. Maryland, 486 U.S. 367, 108 S.Ct. 1860, 100 L.Ed.2d 384 (1988), 1123

Minnesota v. National Tea Co., 309 U.S. 551, 60 S.Ct. 676, 84 L.Ed. 920 (1940), 906, 920

Miranda v. Arizona, 384 U.S. 436, 86 S.Ct. 1602, 16 L.Ed.2d 694 (1966), 1101

Mississippi Band of Choctaw Indians v. Holyfield, 490 U.S. 30, 109 S.Ct. 1597, 104 L.Ed.2d 29 (1989), 883

Mississippi, United States v., 380 U.S. 128, 85 S.Ct. 808, 13 L.Ed.2d 717 (1965), 733

Mitchell v. Forsyth, 472 U.S. 511, 105 S.Ct. 2806, 86 L.Ed.2d 444 (1985), 596

Mitchell v. W.T. Grant Co., 416 U.S. 600, 94 S.Ct. 1895, 40 L.Ed.2d 406 (1974), 796

Mitchum v. Foster, 407 U.S. 225, 92 S.Ct. 2151, 32 L.Ed.2d 705 (1972), 757, 761, 792, 793, 798, 830, 831

Monell v. Department of Soc. Serv., 486 U.S. 658, 98 S.Ct. 2018, 56 L.Ed.2d 611 (1978), 526, **531,** 574, 643

Monroe v. Pape, 365 U.S. 167, 81 S.Ct. 473, 5 L.Ed.2d 492 (1961), 510, 551, 552, 594, 761, 830, 1192

Mooney v. Holohan, 294 U.S. 103, 55 S.Ct. 340, 79 L.Ed. 791 (1935), 1119

Moore v. Chesapeake & Ohio Ry., 291 U.S. 205, 54 S.Ct. 402, 78 L.Ed. 755 (1934), 269, 283

Moore v. Sims, 442 U.S. 415, 99 S.Ct. 2371, 60 L.Ed.2d 994 (1979), 832

Morton v. Mancari, 417 U.S. 535, 94 S.Ct. 2474, 41 L.Ed.2d 290 (1974), 874

Moses H. Cone Memorial Hospital v. Mercury Construction Corporation, 460 U.S. 1, 103 S.Ct. 927, 74 L.Ed.2d 765 (1983), 875

Murdock v. City of Memphis, 87 S.Ct. (20 Wall.) 590, 22 L.Ed. 429 (1875), 163, **884,** 903, 929

Murdock v. The Mayor and Alderman of Memphis, 47 Tenn. 483 (1870), 900

Murray v. Carrier, 477 U.S. 478, 106 S.Ct. 2639, 91 L.Ed.2d 397 (1986), 1182, 1182

Muskrat v. United States, 219 U.S. 346, 31 S.Ct. 250, 55 L.Ed.2d 246 (1911), 27, 218

Napue v. Illinois, 360 U.S. 264, 79 S.Ct. 1173, 3 L.Ed.2d 1217 (1959), 1119

Nashville, Chattanooga & St. Louis Railway v. Wallace, 288 U.S. 249, 53 S.Ct. 345, 77 L.Ed. 730 (1933), 106

National Credit Union Administration v. First National Bank & Trust Co., 522, U.S. 479, 118 S.Ct. 927, 140 L.Ed.2d 1, (1998), 93

National Mutual Insurance Co. v. Tidewater Transfer Co., 337 U.S. 582, 69 S.Ct. 1173, 93 L.Ed. 1556 (1949), 245

Nelson v. Campbell, 541 U.S. 637, 124 S.Ct. 2117, 158 L.Ed.2d 924 (1994), 1192

Nevada Dept. of Human Res. v. Hibbs, 538 U.S. 721, 123 S.Ct. 1972, 155 L.Ed.2d 953 (2003), 691

New Orleans Public Service, Inc. v. Council of City of New Orleans, 491 U.S. 350, 109 S.Ct. 2506, 105 L.Ed.2d 298 (1989), 838, 853

New York State Association for Retarded Children, Inc. v. Rockefeller, 357 F.Supp. 752 (E.D.N.Y. 1973), 603

New York State Club Association, Inc. v. City of New York, 487 U.S. 1, 108 S.Ct. 2225, 101 L.Ed.2d 1 (1988), 26

New York State Dept. of Soc. Serv. v. Dublino, 413 U.S. 405, 93 S.Ct. 2507, 37 L.Ed.2d 688 (1973), 394

New York, In re, 256 U.S. 490, 41 S.Ct. 588, 65 L.Ed. 1057 (1921), 618

Nike, Inc. v. Kasky, 539 U.S. 654, 123 S.Ct. 2554, 156 L.Ed.2d 580 (2003), 987, 989

Nivens v. Gilchrist, 444 F.3d 237 (4th Cir. 2006), 1018

Nixon (Richard), United States v., 418 U.S. 683, 94 S.Ct. 3090, 41 L.Ed.2d 1039 (1974), 9

Nixon (Walter), United States v., 506 U.S. 224, 113 S.Ct. 732, 122 L.Ed.2d 1 (1993), 24, 144

Nixon v. Fitzgerald, 457 U.S. 731, 102 S.Ct. 2690, 73 L.Ed.2d 349 (1982), 585

Norris v. Alabama, 294 U.S. 587, 55 S.Ct. 579, 79 L.Ed. 1074 (1935), 938

North Georgia Finishing Co., Inc. v. Di-Chem, Inc., 419 U.S. 601, 95 S.Ct. 719, 42 L.Ed.2d 751 (1975), 796

North Star Steel Co. v. Thomas, 515 U.S. 29, 115 S.Ct. 1927, 132 L.Ed. 27 (1995), 506

Northeastern Florida Chapter of the Associated General Contractors of America v. City of Jacksonville, 508 U.S. 656, 113 S.Ct. 2297, 124 L.Ed.2d 586 (1993), 99, 118

Northern Pipeline Construction Co. v. Marathon Pipe Line Co., 458 U.S. 50, 102 S.Ct. 2858, 73 L.Ed.2d 598 (1982), 322, 368

Northwest Central Pipeline Corp. v. State Corp. Comm'n, 489 U.S. 493, 109 S.Ct. 1262, 103 L.Ed.2d 509 (1989), 394

Northern Insurance Co. v. Chatham County, Georgia, 547 U.S. 189, 126 S.Ct. 1689, 164 L.Ed.2d 367 (2006), 642

Occidental Life Insurance Co. v. EEOC, 432 U.S. 355, 97 S.Ct. 2447, 53 L.Ed.2d 402 (1977), 505

O'Connor v. Donaldson, 422 U.S. 563, 95 S.Ct. 2486, 45 L.Ed.2d 396 (1975), 528

O'Dell v. Netherland, 521 U.S. 151, 117 S.Ct. 1969, 138 L.Ed.2d 351 (1997), 1117

O'Shea v. Littleton, 414 U.S. 488, 94 S.Ct. 669, 38 L.Ed.2d 674 (1974), 55, 120, 795, 836, 841

O'Sullivan v. Boerckel, 526 U.S. 838, 119 S.Ct. 1728, 144 L.Ed.2d 1 (1999), 1161

Oestereich v. Selective Service System Local Board No. 11, 393 U.S. 233, 89 S.Ct. 414, 21 L.Ed.2d 402 (1968), 197

Ohio Civil Rights Commission v. Dayton Christian Schools, Inc., 477 U.S. 619, 106 S.Ct. 2718, 91 L.Ed.2d 512 (1986), 834, 836, 836

Ohio v. Roberts, 448 U.S. 56, 100 S.Ct. 2531, 65 L.Ed.2d 597 (1980), 1120

Orr v. Orr, 440 U.S. 268, 99 S.Ct. 1102, 59 L.Ed.2d 306 (1979), 901, 955

Osborn v. Bank of the United States, 22 U.S. (9 Wheat.) 738, 6 L.Ed. 204 (1824), 225, 268, 272, 438

Osborne v. Ohio, 495 U.S. 103, 110 S.Ct. 1691, 109 L.Ed.2d 98 (1990), 971

Owen Equipment & Erection Co. v. Kroger, 37 U.S. 365, 98 S.Ct. 2396, 57 L.Ed.2d 274 (1978), 89

Owen v. City of Independence, 445 U.S. 622, 100 S.Ct. 1398, 63 L.Ed.2d 673 (1980), 554

Pace v. DiGuglielmo, 544 U.S. 408, 125 S.Ct. 1807, 161 L.Ed.2d 669 (2005), 1197

Pacemaker Diagnostic Clinic v. Instromedix, Inc., 725 F.2d 537 (9th Cir. 1984), 368

Pacific Gas & Elec. Co. v. State Energy Resources Consevation & Dev. Comm'n, 461 U.S. 190, 103 S.Ct. 1713, 75 L.Ed.2d 752 (1983), 394

Panetti v. Quarterman, _ U.S. _, 127 S.Ct. 2842, 168 L.Ed.2d 662 (2007), 1191

Paramount Famous Lasky Corporation, United States v., 282 U.S. 30, 51 S.Ct. 42, 75 L.Ed. 145 (1930), 903

Parejko v. Dunn County Circuit Court, 408 F.Supp.2d 704 (W.D.Wis. 2006), 1019

Parratt v. Taylor, 451 U.S. 527, 101 S.Ct. 1908, 68 L.Ed.2d 420 (1981), 600, 603

Patsy v. Board of Regents, 457 U.S. 496, 102 S.Ct. 2557, 73 L.Ed.2d 172 (1982), 762, 1192

Paul v. Davis, 424 U.S. 693, 96 S.Ct. 1155, 47 L.Ed.2d 405 (1976), 197, 599, 676

Payne v. Tennessee, 501 U.S. 8008, 111 S.Ct. 2597, 115 L.Ed.2d 720 (1991), 734

Payner, United States v., 447 U.S. 727, 100 S.Ct. 2439, 65 L.Ed.2d 468 (1980), 96

Pembaur v. City of Cincinnati, 475 U.S. 469, 106 S.Ct. 1292, 89 L.Ed.2d 452 (1986), 552

Pennell v. City of San Jose, 485 U.S. 1, 108 S.Ct. 849, 99 L.Ed.2d 1 (1988), 108

Pennhurst State School and Hospital v. Halderman, 451 U.S. 1, 101 S.Ct. 1531, 67 L.Ed.2d 694 (1981), 529, 740, 736

Pennsylvania v. Nelson, 350 U.S. 497, 76 S.Ct. 477, 100 L.Ed. 640 (1956), 394, 394

Pennsylvania v. Union Gas Co., 491 U.S. 1, 109 S.Ct. 2273, 105 L.Ed.2d 1 (1989), 11, 645, 691, 695, 731, 732, 733, 734

Pennzoil Company v. Texaco, Inc., 481 U.S. 1, 107 S.Ct. 1519, 95 L.Ed.2d 1 (1987), 836

Penry v. Lynaugh, 492 U.S. 302, 109 S.Ct. 293, 106 L.Ed.2d 256 (1989), 1124

People v. _____ (see name of opposing party)

Peretz v. United States, 501 U.S. 923, 111 S.Ct. 2661, 115 L.Ed.2d 808 (1991), 369

Perez v. Ledesma, 401 U.S. 82, 91 S.Ct. 674, 27 L.Ed.2d 701 (1971), 800

Phillips Petroleum Co. v. Shutts, 472 U.S. 797, 105 S.Ct. 2965, 86 L.Ed.2d 628 (1985), 1042

Plaut v. Spendthrift Farm, Inc., 514 U.S. 211, 115 S.Ct. 1447, 131 L.Ed.2d 328 (1995), 27, **199,** 219, 220, 504

Plessy v. Ferguson, 163 U.S. 537, 16 S.Ct. 1138, 41 L.Ed. 256 (1896), 883

Poe v. Ullman, 367 U.S. 497, 81 S.Ct. 1752, 6 L.Ed.2d 989 (1961), 109

Polk County v. Dodson, 454 U.S. 312, 102 S.Ct. 445, 70 L.Ed.2d 509 (1981), 528

Powell v. McCormack, 395 U.S. 486, 89 S.Ct. 1944, 23 L.Ed.2d 491 (1969), 160

Powers v. Ohio, 499 U.S. 400, 111 S.Ct. 1364, 113 L.Ed.2d 411 (1991), 97

Praprotnik, City of St. Louis v., 485 U.S. 112, 108 S.Ct. 915, 99 L.Ed.2d 107 (1988), 553

Preiser v. Rodriguez, 411 U.S. 475, 93 S.Ct. 1827, 36 L.Ed.2d 439 (1973), 1192

Prentis v. Atlantic Coast Line R.R., 211 U.S. 210, 29 S.Ct. 67, 53 L.Ed. 150 (1908), 1009

Price v. Vincent, 538 U.S. 634, 123 S.Ct. 1848, 155 L.Ed.2d 877 (2003), 1158

Pulliam v. Allen, 466 U.S. 522, 104 S.Ct. 1970, 80 L.Ed.2d 565 (1984), 576, 579, 926

Quackenbush v. Allstate Insurance Company, 517 U.S. 706, 116 S.Ct. 1712, 135 L.Ed.2d 1 (1996), 855

Quern v. Jordan, 440 U.S. 332, 99 S.Ct. 1139, 59 L.Ed.2d 358 (1979), 656, 670

Raddatz, United States v., 447 U.S. 667, 100 S.Ct. 2406, 65 L.Ed.2d 424 (1980), 367

Railroad Commission v. Pullman Co., 312 U.S. 496, 61 S.Ct. 643, 85 L.Ed. 971 (1941), 774, 851, 926

Raines v. Byrd, 521 U.S. 811, 117 S.Ct. 2312, 138 L.Ed.2d 849 (1997), 55

Rakas v. Illinois, 439 U.S. 128, 99 S.Ct. 421, 58 L.Ed.2d 387 (1978), 96

Rasul v. Bush, 542 U.S. 466, 124 S.Ct. 2686, 159 L.Ed.2d 548 (2004), 1053, **1065**

Rawlings v. Kentucky, 448 U.S. 98, 100 S.Ct. 2556, 65 L.Ed.2d 633 (1980), 96

Raygor v. Regents of the Univ. of Mn., 534 U.S. 533, 122 S.Ct. 999, 152 L.Ed.2d 227 (2002), 672

Reagan v. Farmers' Loan & Trust, 154 U.S. 362, 390-91, 14 S.Ct. 1047, 1051-1052, 38 L.Ed. 1014, 1021 (1894), 736

Reconstruction Finance Corporation v. Beaver County, 328 U.S. 204, 66 S.Ct. 992, 90 L.Ed. 1172 (1946), 929

Reed v. Allen, 286 U.S. 191, 52 S.Ct. 532, 76 L.Ed.2d 1054 (1932), 219

Reed v. Ross, 468 U.S. 1, 104 S.Ct. 2901, 82 L.Ed.2d 1 (1984), 1182

Reetz v. Bozanich, 397 U.S. 82, 90 S.Ct. 788, 25 L.Ed.2d 68 (1970), 778

Regents of the State of California v. Doe, 519 U.S. 425, 117 S.Ct. 900, 137 L.Ed.2d 55 (1997), 645

Regional Rail Act Reorganization Cases, 419 U.S. 102, 95 S.Ct. 335, 42 L.Ed.2d 320 (1974), 111

Renne v. Geary, 501 U.S. 312, 111 S.Ct. 2331, 115 L.Ed.2d 288 (1991), 56, 105

Rhines v. Weber, 544 U.S. 269, 125 S.Ct. 1528, 161 L.Ed.2d 440 (2005), 1198

Rice v. Collins, 546 U.S. 333, 126 S.Ct. 969, 163 L.Ed.2d 824 (2006), 1100

Richardson, United States v., 418 U.S. 166, 94 S.Ct. 2940, 41 L.Ed.2d 678 (1974), 80

Richardson v. McKnight, 521 U.S. 399, 117 S.Ct. 2100, 138 L.Ed.2d 540 (1997), 597

Rizzo v. Goode, 423 U.S. 362, 99 S.Ct. 598, 46 L.Ed.2d 561 (1975), 15, 55, 551, 836, 841

Roe v. Wade, 410 U.S. 113, 93 S.Ct. 705, 35 L.Ed.2d 147 (1973), 23, 117, 779

Roell v. Withrow, 538 U.S. 580, 123 S.Ct. 1696, 155 L.Ed.2d 775 (2003), 370

Rooker v. Fidelity Trust Co., 263 U.S. 413, 44 S.Ct. 149, 68 L.Ed. 362 (1923), 994

Rose v. Lundy, 455 U.S. 509, 102 S.Ct. 1198, 71 L.Ed.2d 379 (1982), 1159, 1163

Rose v. Mitchell, 443 U.S. 545, 99 S.Ct. 2993, 61 L.Ed.2d 739 (1979), 1101

Rosecrans v. United States, 165 U.S. 257, 17 S.Ct. 302, 41 L.Ed. 708 (1897), 874

Ruhrgas AG v. Marathon Oil Company, 526 U.S. 574, 119 S.Ct. 1563, 143 L.Ed.2d 760 (1999), 289

Rumsfeld v. Padilla, 542 U.S. 426, 124 S.Ct. 2711, 159 L.Ed.2d 513 (2004), 1085

Saffle v. Parks, 494 U.S. 484, 110 S.Ct. 1257, 108 L.Ed.2d 415 (1990), 1113, 1120

Salve Regina College v. Russell, 499 U.S. 225, 111 S.Ct. 1217, 113 L.Ed.2d 190 (1991), 432

Samuels v. Mackell, 401 U.S. 66, 91 S.Ct. 764, 27 L.Ed.2d 688 (1971), 799, 812, 1030

Sanders v. United States, 373 U.S. 1, 83 S.Ct. 1068, 10 L.Ed.2d 148 (1963), 1055, 1183

San Remo Hotel v. City and County of San Francisco, 545 U.S. 323, 125 S.Ct. 2491, 162 L.Ed.2d 315 (2005), 784

Saucier v. Katz, 533 U.S. 194, 121 S.Ct. 2151, 150 L.Ed.2d 272 (2001), 586, 591

Sawyer v. Smith, 497 U.S. 227, 110 S.Ct. 2822, 111 L.Ed.2d 193 (1990), 1113

Sawyer v. Whitley, 505 U.S. 333, 112 S.Ct. 2514, 120 L.Ed.2d 269 (1992), 1186

Sawyer, In re, 124 U.S. 200, 8 S.Ct. 482, 31 L.Ed. 402 (1888), 791

Schenck v. United States, 249 U.S. 47, 39 S.Ct. 247, 63 L.Ed. 470 (1919), 954

Schlesinger v. Reservists Committee to Stop the War, 418 U.S. 208, 94 S.Ct. 2925, 41 L.Ed.2d 706 (1974), 80

Schlup v. Delo, 513 U.S. 298, 115 S.Ct. 851, 130 L.Ed.2d 808 (1995), 1183, 1186, 1187

Schriro v. Landrigan, __ U.S. __, 127 S.Ct. 1933, 167 L.Ed.2d 836 (2007), 1100

Schweiker v. Chilicky, 487 U.S. 412, 108 S.Ct. 2460, 101 L.Ed.2d 370 (1988), 454, 480, 600, 732, 733

Seminole Tribe v. Florida, 517 U.S. 44, 116 S.Ct. 1114, 134 L.Ed.2d 252 (1996), 662, 663, 690, 697

Semtek Int'l Inc. v. Lockheed Martin Corp., 531 U.S. 497, 121 S.Ct. 1021, 149 L.Ed.2d 32 (2001), 254, 423

Shaw v. Delta Airlines, Inc., 463 U.S. 85, 103 S.Ct. 2890, 77 L.Ed.2d 490 (1983), 317

Sheldon v. Sill, 49 U.S. (8 How.) 441, 12 L.Ed. 1147 (1850), 193

Shoshone Mining Co. v. Rutter, 177 U.S. 505, 20 S.Ct. 726, 44 L.Ed. 864 (1900), 264

Sibron v. New York, 392 U.S. 40, 88 S.Ct. 1889, 20 L.Ed.2d 917 (1968), 116

Siler v. Louisville & Nashville R. Co., 213 U.S. 175, 193, 29 S.Ct. 451, 455, 53 L.Ed. 753, 758 (1909), 736, 740

Simmons v. United States, 512 U.S. 154, 114 S.Ct. 2187, 129 L.Ed.2d 133 (1994), 1117

Simon v. Eastern Kentucky Welfare Rights Org., 426 U.S. 26, 96 S.Ct. 1917, 48 L.Ed.2d 450 (1976), 56, 57, 1030

Sims v. State Department of Public Welfare, 438 F.Supp. 1179 (S.D.Tex. 1977), rev'd sub nom. Moore v. Sims, 442 U.S. 415, 99 S.Ct. 2371, 60 L.Ed.2d 994 (1979), 834

Sioux Nation, United States v., 448 U.S. 371, 413, 100 S.Ct. 2716, 2739, 65 L.Ed.2d 844 (1980), 218

Skelly Oil Co. v. Phillips Petroleum Co., 339 U.S. 667, 70 S.Ct. 876, 94 L.Ed.1194 (1950), 302, 316, 319, 319

Skipper v. South Carolina, 476 U.S. 1, 106 S.Ct. 1669, 90 L.Ed.2d 1 (1986), 1118

Slack v. McDaniel, 529 U.S. 473, 120 S.Ct. 1595, 146 L.Ed.2d 542 (2000), 1118

Smith v. Kansas City Title & Trust Co., 255 U.S. 180, 41 S.Ct. 243, 65 L.Ed. 577 (1921), 265, 283, 470, 627, 1043

Sniadach v. Family Finance Corp., 395 U.S. 337, 89 S.Ct. 1820, 23 L.Ed.2d 349 (1969), 796

Sosna v. Iowa, 419 U.S. 393, 95 S.Ct. 553, 42 L.Ed.2d 532 (1975), 119

South Carolina v. Katzenbach, 383 U.S. 301, 86 S.Ct. 803, 15 L.Ed.2d 769 (1966), 34, 628

Southern Pacific Co. v. Jensen, 244 U.S. 205, 37 S.Ct. 524, 61 L.Ed. 1086 (1917), 440

Spallone v. United States, 493 U.S. 265, 110 S.Ct. 625, 107 L.Ed.2d 644 (1990), 56

Spencer v. Kemna, 523 U.S. 1, 118 S.Ct. 978, 140 L.Ed.2d 43 (1998), 116

Standard Oil Co., United States v., 332 U.S. 301, 67 S.Ct. 1604, 91 L.Ed. 2067 (1947), 419

Standard Oil v. Johnson, 316 U.S. 481, 62 S.Ct. 1168, 86 L.Ed. 1611 (1942), 926

Stanley, United States v., 483 U.S. 669, 107 S.Ct. 3054, 97 L.Ed.2d 550 (1987), 494

State v. _____ (see name of opposing party)

Steel Co. v. Citizens for a Better Env't, 523 U.S. 83, 118 S.Ct. 1003, 140 L.Ed.2d 210 (1998), 58, 143, 288

Steffel v. Thompson, 415 U.S. 452, 94 S.Ct. 1209, 39 L.Ed.2d 505 (1974), 110, 181, 469, 801, 821, 821, 835

Stewart Organization. Ricoh Corp., 487 U.S. 22, 108 S.Ct. 2239, 101 L.Ed.2d 22 (1988), 374

Stewart v. Martinez-Villareal, 523 U.S. 637, 118 S.Ct. 1618, 140 L.Ed.2d 849 (1998), 1162

Stone v. Powell, 428 U.S. 465, 96 S.Ct. 3037, 49 L.Ed.2d 1067 (1976), 18, 1101

Strait v. Laird, 406 U.S. 341, 92 S.Ct. 1693, 32 L.Ed.2d 141 (1972), 1083

Strickland v. Washington, 466 U.S. 668, 104 S.Ct. 2052, 80 L.Ed.2d 674 (1984), 1101, 1156, 1182, 1183

Strickler v. Greene, 527 U.S. 263, 119 S.Ct. 1936, 144 L.Ed.2d 286 (1999), 1182, 1183

Stringer v. Black, 503 U.S. 222, 112 S.Ct. 1130, 117 L.Ed.2d 367 (1992), 1113

Stump v. Sparkman, 435 U.S. 349, 98 S.Ct. 1099, 55 L.Ed.2d 331 (1978), 576

Sullivan v. Louisiana, 508 U.S. 275, 113 S.Ct. 2078, 124 L.Ed.2d 182 (1993), 1122

Summers, In re, 325 U.S. 561, 65 S.Ct. 1307, 89 L.Ed. 1795 (1945), 1010

Suter v. Artist M., 503 U.S. 347, 112 S.Ct. 1360, 118 L.Ed.2d 1 (1992), 530

Sweeney v. Abramowitz, 449 F. Supp. 213 (D.Conn. 1978), 253

Swift & Co. v. Wickham, 382 U.S. 111, 86 S.Ct. 258, 15 L.Ed.2d 194 (1965), 993, 994

Swift v. Tyson, 41 U.S. (16 Pet.) 1, 10 L.Ed. 865 (1842), 11, 383, 506

Swisher v. Brady, 438 U.S. 204, 98 S.Ct. 2699, 57 L.Ed.2d 705 (1978), 799

Syngenta Crop Protection, Inc. v. Henson, 537 U.A. 28, 123 S.Ct. 366, 154 L.Ed.2d 368 (2002), 287

Taylor, United States v., 181 F.3d 1017 (9th Cir. 1999), 220

T.B. Harms Co. v. Eliscu, 339 F.2d 823 (2d Cir. 1964), 269

Teague v. Lane, 489 U.S. 288, 109 S.Ct. 1060, 103 L.Ed.2d 334 (1989), 1061, 1101, 1153, 1162

Tennessee v. Lane, 541 U.S. 509, 124 S.Ct. 1978, 158 L.Ed.2d 820 (2004), 689, 693

Testa v. Katt, 330 U.S. 386, 67 S.Ct. 810, 91 L.Ed. 967 (1947), 195, 639

Texas & Pacific Ry. v. Rigsby, 241 U.S. 33, 36 S.Ct. 482, 60 L.Ed. 874 (1916), 285

Textile Workers Union v. Lincoln Mills, 353 U.S. 448, 77 S.Ct. 912, 1 L.Ed.2d 972 (1957), 11, 236, 433

Textron Lycoming Reciprocating Engine Division, AVCO Corp. v. United Automobile, Aerospace and Agricultural Implement Workers, 523 U.S. 653, 118 S.Ct. 1626, 140 L.Ed.2d 863 (1998), 317

Thomas v. Union Carbide Agricultural Products Co., 473 U.S. 568, 105 S.Ct. 3325, 87 L.Ed.2d 409 (1985), 350, 353, 366

Thompson v. City of Louisville, 362 U.S. 199, 80 S.Ct. 624, 4 L.Ed.2d 654 (1960), 881, 933

Thompson v. Thompson, 484 U.S. 174, 108 S.Ct. 513, 98 L.Ed.2d 52 (1988), 476

Toilet Goods Association v. Gardner, 387 U.S. 158, 87 S.Ct. 1520, 18 L.Ed.2d 697 (1967), 104

Tory v. Cochran, 544 U.S. 734, 125 S.Ct. 2108, 161 L.Ed.2d 1042 (2005), 144

Toucey v. New York Life Insurance Co., 314 U.S. 118, 62 S.Ct. 139, 86 L.Ed. 100 (1941), 760

Townsend v. Sain, 372 U.S. 293, 83 S.Ct. 745, 9 L.Ed.2d 770 (1963), 1055, 1062, 1088, 1099

Trafficante v. Metropolitan Life Insurance Co., 409 U.S. 205, 93 S.Ct. 364, 34 L.Ed.2d 416 (1972), 97

Trainor v. Hernandez, 431 U.S. 434, 97 S.Ct. 1911, 52 L.Ed.2d 486 (1977), 796, 831, 880

Trest v. Cain, 522 U.S. 87, 118 S.Ct. 478, 139 L.Ed.2d 444 (1997), 1178

Turpin v. Mailet, 579 F.2d 152 (2d Cir. 1978), 552

Tyler v. Cain, 533 U.S. 656, 121 S.Ct. 2478, 150 L.Ed.2d 632 (2001), 1121

United Food and Commercial Workers Union Local 751 v. Brown Group, Inc., 517 U.S. 544, 116 S.Ct. 1529, 134 L.Ed.2d 758 (1996), 98

United Mine Workers v. Gibbs, 383 U.S. 715, 86 S.Ct. 1130, 16 L.Ed.2d 218 (1966), 89, 285

United Public Workers v. Mitchell, 337 U.S. 75, 67 S.Ct. 556, 91 L.Ed. 754 (1947), 110

United States Civil Service Commission v. National Association of Letter Carriers, 413 U.S. 548, 93 S.Ct. 2880, 37 L.Ed.2d 796 (1973), 110

United States Department of Labor v. Triplett, 494 U.S. 715, 110 S.Ct. 1428, 108 L.Ed.2d 701 (1990), 97

United States District Court, United States v., 407 U.S. 297, 92 S.Ct. 2125, 32 L.Ed.2d 752 (1972), 9

United States Parole Commission v. Geraghty, 445 U.S. 338, 100 S.Ct. 1202, 63 L.Ed.2d 479 (1980), 120

United States v. _____ (see name of opposing party)

Utah v. Evans, 536 U.S. 452, 122 S.Ct. 2191, 153 L.Ed.2d 453 (2002), 57

Utley v. Varian Associates, Inc. 811 F.2d 1279 (9th Cir. 1987), 284

Valley Forge Christian College v. Americans United for Separation of Church and State, 454 U.S. 464, 102 S.Ct. 752, 70 L.Ed.2d 700 (1982), 80

Verlinden B.V. v. Central Bank of Nigeria, 461 U.S. 480, 103 S.Ct. 1962, 76 L.Ed.2d 81 (1983), 255, 438

Vermont Agency of Natural Resources v. United States ex rel. Stevens, 529 U.S. 765, 120 S.Ct. 1858, 146 L.Ed.2d 836 (2000), 671

W.T. Grant Co., United States v., 345 U.S. 629, 73 S.Ct. 894, 97 L.Ed.1303 (1953), 118

Wainwright v. Sykes, 433 U.S. 72, 97 S.Ct. 2497, 53 L.Ed.2d 594 (1977), 1126, 1179

Walker v. Armco Steel Corp., 446 U.S. 740, 108 S.Ct. 1978, 64 L.Ed.2d 659 (1980), 374

Ward v. Board of County Commissioners, 253 U.S. 17, 40 S.Ct. 419, 64 L.Ed. 751 (1920), 930

Warth v. Seldin, 422 U.S. 490, 95 S.Ct. 2197, 45 L.Ed.2d 343 (1975), 54, 98

Webber v. White, 422 F.Supp. 416 (N.D.Tex. 1976), 994

Webster v. Doe, 486 U.S. 592, 108 S.Ct. 2047, 100 L.Ed.2d 632 (1988), 197

West 14th Street Commercial Corp. v. 5 West 14th Street Owners Corp., 815 F.2d 188 (2d Cir. 1987), 284

West v. Atkins, 487 U.S. 42, 108 S.Ct. 2250, 101 L.Ed.2d 40 (1988), 528

White, United States v., 401 U.S. 745, 91 S.Ct. 1122, 28 L.Ed.2d 453 (1971), 881

Whorton v. Bockting, _ U.S. _, 127 S.Ct. 1173, 167 L.Ed.2d 1 (2007), 1120, 1124

Wiggins v. Smith, 539 U.S. 510, 123 S.Ct. 2527, 156 L.Ed.2d 471 (2003), 1158

Wilder v. Virginia Hospital Association, 496 U.S. 498, 110 S.Ct. 2510, 110 L.Ed.2d 2455 (1990), 529, 772

Will v. Calvert Fire Insurance Co., 437 U.S. 655, 98 S.Ct. 2552, 57 L.Ed.2d 504 (1978), 875

Will v. Michigan Department of State Police, 491 U.S. 58, 109 S.Ct. 2304, 105 L.Ed.2d 45 (1989), 554, 670

Williams (Michael) v. Taylor, 529 U.S. 420, 120 S.Ct. 1479, 146 L.Ed.2d 435 (2000), 1088

Williams (Terry) v. Taylor, 529 U.S. 362, 120 S.Ct. 1495, 146 L.Ed.2d 389 (2000), 1127

Willing v. Chicago Auditorium Association, 277 U.S. 274, 48 S.Ct. 507, 72 L.Ed. 880 (1928), 106

Willkie v. Robbins, ___ U.S. ___, 127 S.Ct. 2588, 168 L.Ed.2d 389 (2007), 499

Wilson v. Garcia, 471 U.S. 261, 105 S.Ct. 1938, 85 L.Ed.2d 254 (1985), 505

Wilson v. Layne, 526 U.S. 603, 119 S.Ct. 1692, 143 L.Ed.2d 818 (1999), 586

Wilton v. Seven Falls Company, 515 U.S. 277, 115 S.Ct. 2137, 132 L.Ed.2d 214 (1995), 876

Wingo v. Wedding, 418 U.S. 461, 94 S.Ct. 2842, 41 L.Ed.2d 879 (1974), 367

Wisconsin Department of Corrections v. Schacht, 524 U.S. 381, 118 S.Ct. 2047, 141 L.Ed.2d 364 (1998), 658

Wisconsin v. Constantineau, 400 U.S. 433, 91 S.Ct. 507, 27 L.Ed.2d 515 (1971), 598, 778, 926

Witherspoon v. Illinois, 391 U.S. 510, 88 S.Ct. 1770, 20 L.Ed.2d 776 (1968), 1181

Withrow v. Williams, 507 U.S. 680, 113 S.Ct. 1745, 123 L.Ed.2d 407 (1993), 1101

Wolff v. Selective Service Local Board No. 16, 372 F.2d 817 (2d Cir. 1967), 197

Wood v. Strickland, 420 U.S. 308, 95 S.Ct. 992, 43 L.Ed.2d 214 (1975), 579, 585, 1112

Woodford v. Ngo, 548 U.S. 81, 126 S.Ct. 2378, 165 L.Ed.2d 368 (2006), 773

Woodford v. Viscotti, 537 U.S. 19, 123 S.Ct. 357, 154 L.Ed.2d 279 (2002), 1157

Wooley v. Maynard, 430 U.S. 705, 97 S.Ct. 1428, 51 L.Ed.2d 752 (1977), 813

Worldwide Volkswagen Corp. v. Woodson, 444 U.S. 286, 100 S.Ct. 559, 62 L.Ed.2d 490 (1980), 13

Wyoming v. Oklahoma, 502 U.S. 437, 112 S.Ct. 789, 117 L.Ed.2d 1 (1992), 95

Yazell, United States v., 382 U.S. 341, 86 S.Ct. 500, 15 L.Ed.2d 404 (1966), 391, 405, 469, 507

Yee v. City of Escondido, 503 U.S. 519, 112 S.Ct. 1522, 118 L.Ed.2d 153 (1992), 108

Yerger, Ex parte, 75 U.S. (8 Wall.) 85, 19 L.Ed. 332 (1869), 168, 181

Young, Ex parte, 209 U.S. 123, 28 S.Ct. 441, 52 L.Ed. 714 (1908), 107, **629,** 661, 662, 664, 670, 732, 733, 736, 792, 993

Younger v. Harris, 401 U.S. 37 (1971), 18, 23, 552, 760, **785,** 851, 1030

Youngstown Sheet & Tube Co. v. Sawyer, 343 U.S. 579, 72 S.Ct. 863, 96 L.Ed. 1153 (1952), 9

Zablocki v. Redhail, 434 U.S. 374, 98 S.Ct. 673, 54 L.Ed.2d 618 (1978), 852

Zadvydas v. Davis, 533 U.S. 672, 121 S.Ct. 2491, 150 L.Ed.2d 653 (2001), 996

Zinermon v. Burch, 494 U.S. 113, 110 S.Ct. 975, 108 L.Ed.2d 100 (1990), 603

Zucht v. King, 260 U.S. 174, 43 S.Ct. 24, 67 L.Ed. 194 (1922), 883

Zwickler v. Koota, 389 U.S. 241, 88 S.Ct. 391, 19 L.Ed.2d 444 (1967), 509, 781, 926

Table of Secondary Authorities

Materials from which excerpts appear are in bold type. Materials cited or
discussed in the text are roman in type. References are to pages.
Materials cited in principal cases and within other quoted
materials are not included.

Alleva, Patti, *Prerogative Lost: The Trou-ble with Statutory Federal Question Doctrine After* Merrell Dow, 52 OHIO ST.L.J. 1477 (1991), 284

Althouse, Ann, *The Humble and the Trea-sonous: Judge-Made Jurisdiction Law,* 40 Case W.Res.L.Rev. 1035 (1990), 793

AMERICAN LAW INSTITUTE, FEDERAL JUDI-CIAL CODE REVISION PROJECT (2004), 298.

AMERICAN LAW INSTITUTE, STUDY OF THE DIVISION OF JURISDICTION BETWEEN STATE AND FEDERAL COURTS (1969), 320

Arkin, Marc M., *The Prisoner's Dilemma: Life in the Lower Federal Courts After* Teague v. Lane, 69 N.C.L.REV. 371 (1991), 1114, 1121, 1126

Bandes, Susan, *The* Rooker-Feldman *Doc-trine: Evaluating Its Jurisdictional Status,* 74 NOTRE DAME L.REV. 1175 (1999), 1050

Bator, Paul M., *Congressional Power over the Jurisdiction of the Federal Courts,* 27 VILL.L.REV. 1030 (1982), 192

Bator, Paul M., *Finality in Criminal Law and Federal Habeas Corpus for State Prisoners,* 76 HARV.L.REV. 441 (1963), 1054

Beermann, Jack M., *"Bad" Judicial Activ-ism and Liberal Federal–Courts Doc-trine: A Comment on Professor Doern-berg and Professor Redish,* 40 CASE W.RES.L.REV. 1053 (1989–90), 13

Beermann, Jack M., *Comments on* Rooker-Feldman *or Let State Law Be Our Guide,* 74 NOTRE DAME L.REV. 1209 (1999), 1050

Berger, Vivian, *Justice Delayed or Justice Denied—A Comment on Recent Propos-als to Reform Death Penalty Habeas Corpus,* 90 COLUM.L.REV. 1665 (1990), 1126

BLACK'S LAW DICTIONARY (8th ed. 2004), 1051

Brennan, William J., *The Bill of Rights and the States: The Revival of State Consti-tutions as Guardians of Individual Rights,* 61 N.Y.U.L.REV. 535 (1986), 881

Brown, George D., *Federal Common Law and the Role of the Federal Courts in Private Law Adjudication—A (New)* Erie *Problem,* 12 PACE L.REV. 229 (1992), 507

Brown, George D., *Letting Statutory Tails Wag Constitutional Dogs—Have the* Bivens *Dissenters Prevailed?,* 64 IND. L. J. 263 (1989), 496

Brown, George D., *Of Activism and* Erie—*The Implication Doctrine's Implication for the Nature and Role of the Federal Courts,* 69 IOWA L.REV. 617 (1984), 382

Brown, George D., *When Federalism and Separation of Powers Collide—Rethinking* Younger *Abstention,* 59 GEO.WASH.L.REV. 114 (1990), 841

Chadbourn, James H. & A. Leo Levin, *Original Jurisdiction of Federal Ques-tions,* 90 U.PA.L.REV. 639 (1942), 236

Chemerinsky, Erwin, *Ending the Parity Debate,* 71 B.U.L.REV. 593 (1991), 18

CHEMERINSKY, ERWIN, FEDERAL JURISDIC-TION (5th ed. 2007), 58, 105, 761, 785, 799, 800, 835, 875, 1048, 1051

CHOPER, JESSE H., JUDICIAL REVIEW AND THE NATIONAL POLITICAL PROCESS (1980), 865

Choper, Jesse & John Yoo, *Wartime Proc-ess: A Dialogue on Congressional Power to Remove Issues from the Fed-eral Courts,* 95 Cal. L.Rev. 1243 (2007), 199.

Cohen, William, *The Broken Compass: The Requirement that a Case Arise "Di-rectly" under Federal Law,* 115 U.PA.L.REV. 890 (1967), 320

III THE CORRESPONDENCE AND PUBLIC PAPERS OF JOHN JAY 1763-1826 (Henry P. Johnston ed. 1971), 25

Currie, David P., Ex parte Young *After* Seminole Tribe, 72 N.Y.U.L.REV. 547 (1997), 733

DePalma, Anthony, *Warming Report Warns of Increased Flooding*, N.Y. TIMES (July 11, 2007), 77.

DIRECTOR OF THE ADMINISTRATIVE OFFICE OF THE UNITED STATES COURTS, 1968 ANNUAL REPORT, 1058

DOERNBERG, DONALD L., IDENTITY CRISIS: FEDERAL COURTS IN A PSYCHOLOGICAL WILDERNESS (2001), 224.

Doernberg, Donald L., *Juridical Chameleons in the "New Erie" Canal*, 1990 UTAH L.REV. 759, 470

Doernberg, Donald L., *There's No Reason for It; It's Just Our Policy: Why the Well-Pleaded Complaint Rule Sabotages the Purposes of Federal Question Jurisdiction*, 38 HASTINGS L.J. 597 (1987), 246, 255

Doernberg, Donald L. & Michael B. Mushlin, *The Trojan Horse: How the Declaratory Judgment Act Created a Cause of Action and Expanded Federal Jurisdiction While the Supreme Court Wasn't Looking*, 36 U.C.L.A.L.REV. 529 (1989), 320

Eisenberg, Theodore, *Congressional Authority to Restrict Lower Federal Court Jurisdiction*, 83 YALE L.J. 498 (1974), 195

Ely, John Hart, *The Irrepressible Myth of Erie*, 87 HARV.L.REV. 693 (1974), 374

Eskridge, William N. Jr. & Philip P. Frickey, *Quasi-Constitutional Law: Clear Statement Rules As Constitutional Lawmaking*, 45 VAND.L.REV. 593 (1992), 674

Fallon, Richard H. Jr. & Daniel J. Meltzer, *New Law, Non-retroactivity and Constitutional Remedies*, 104 HARV.L.REV. 1731 (1991), 1126

Fallon, Richard H. Jr., *Of Legislative Courts, Administrative Agencies, and Article III*, 101 HARV.L.REV. 915 (1988), 365

Farina, Cynthia R., *Statutory Interpretation and the Balance of Power in the Administrative State*, 89 COLUM.L. REV. 452 (1989), 13

THE FEDERALIST NO. 47 (James Madison) (Jacob E. Cooke ed. 1961), 9

THE FEDERALIST NO. 48 (James Madison) (Jacob E. Cooke ed. 1961), 13

THE FEDERALIST NO. 81 (James Madison) (Jacob E. Cooke ed. 1961), 741

Feld, Alan L., *Separation of Political Powers: Boundaries or Balance?*, 21 GA.L. REV. 171 (1986), 13

Field, Martha A., *The Legitimacy of Federal Common Law*, 12 PACE L.REV. 303 (1992), 507

Fiss, Owen, Dombrowski, 86 YALE L.J. 1103 (1977), 795

Fletcher, William A., *A Historical Interpretation of the Eleventh Amendment: A Narrow Construction of an Affirmative Grant of Jurisdiction Rather Than a Prohibition Against Jurisdiction*, 35 STAN.L.REV. 1033 (1983), 616

Fletcher, William A., *The Structure of Standing*, 98 YALE L.J. 221 (1988), 54, 96

Friedman, Barry & James E. Gaylord, Rooker-Feldman from *the Ground Up*, 74 NOTRE DAME L.REV. 1129 (1999), 1050

Friedman, Barry, *Habeas and Hubris*, 45 VAND.L.REV. 797 (1992), 1126

Friendly, Henry J., *Federalism: A Foreword*, 86 YALE L.J. 1019 (1977), 1

Friendly, Henry J., *In Praise of Erie— And of the New Federal Common Law*, 39 N.Y.U.L.REV. 383 (1964), 384

Gibbons, John J., *The Eleventh Amendment and State Sovereign Immunity: A Reinterpretation*, 83 COLUM.L.REV. 1889 (1983), 616

Glennon, Robert Jerome, *The Jurisdictional Legacy of the Civil Rights Movement*, 61 TENN.L.REV. 869 (1994), 968

Goodwin, Alfred T., *International Law in the Federal Courts*, 20 CAL.W.INT'L. L.J. 157 (1990), 393

Gunther, Gerald, *Congressional Power to Curtail Federal Jurisdiction: An Opinionated Guide to the Ongoing Debate*, 36 STAN.L.REV. 895 (1984), 177, 192

Hart, Henry L., *The Power of Congress to Limit the Jurisdiction of Federal Courts: An Exercise in Dialectic*, 66 HARV.L.REV. 1362 (1953), 180

Herman, Susan N., *Why Parity Matters*, 71 B.U.L.REV. 651 (1991), 17, 18, 21

Hirschman, Linda R., *Whose Law Is It Anyway? A Reconsideration of Federal Question Jurisdiction Over Cases of Mixed State and Federal Law*, 60 IND.L.J. 17 (1984), 269

HOWARD, J. WOODFORD JR., SUPREME COURT ENFORCEMENT OF SEPARATION OF POWERS: A BALANCE SHEET, IN SEPARATION OF POWERS IN THE AMERICAN POLITICAL SYSTEM (Barbara B. Knight ed. 1989), 10

Hui, Timothy Kin Lee, *Note, The Ultimate Expansion of the* Younger *Doctrine*: Pennzoil Co. v. Texaco, Inc., 41 SW.L.J. 1055 (1987), 838

JACKSON, ROBERT, THE STRUGGLE FOR JUDICIAL SUPREMACY (1941), 471

Jackson, Vicki C., Seminole Tribe, *the Eleventh Amendment, and the Potential Evisceration of* Ex parte Young, 72 N.Y.U.L.REV. 495 (1997), 733

Jessup, Philip C., *The Doctrine of* Erie Railroad v. Tompkins *Applied to International Law*, 33 AM.J.INT.L. 740 (1939), 393

Kramer, Larry, *The Lawmaking Power of the Federal Courts*, 12 PACE L.REV. 263 (1992), 507

Lee, Evan T., *Deconstitutionalizing Justiciability: The Example of Mootness*, 105 HARV.L.REV. 603 (1992), 122

London, Ernest J., *"Federal Question" Jurisdiction—A Snare and a Delusion*, 57 MICH.L.REV. 835 (1959), 236

Massey, Calvin R., *Abstention and the Constitutional Limits of the Judicial Power of the United States*, 1991 B.Y.U.L.REV. 811, 798

Massey, Calvin R., *State Sovereignty and the Tenth and Eleventh Amendments*, 56 U.CHI.L.REV. 61 (1989), 616

MCKITRICK, ERIC L., ANDREW JOHNSON AND RECONSTRUCTION (1960), 898

Merrill, Thomas W., *The Judicial Prerogative*, 12 PACE L.REV. 327 (1992), 470, 507

Merrill, Thomas, *The Common Law Powers of Federal Courts*, 52 U.CHI.L.REV. 1 (1985), 382, 470

Monaghan, Henry P., *Third Party Standing*, 84 COLUM.L.REV. 277 (1984), 96

Neuborne, Burt, *Parity Revisited: The Uses of a Judicial Forum of Excellence*, 44 DEPAUL L.REV. 797 (1995), 19

Neuborne, Burt, *The Myth of Parity*, 90 HARV.L.REV. 1105 (1977), 14, 18, 798

Nichol, Gene R. Jr., *Ripeness and the Constitution*, 54 U.CHI.L.REV. 153 (1987), 105

Nichol, Gene, *Causation As a Standing Requirement: The Unprincipled Use of Judicial Restraint*, 69 KY.L.J. 185 (1981), 58

Nichol, Gene, *Rethinking Standing*, 72 CALIF.L.REV. 68 (1984), 58

Note, *Moore v. Sims: A Further Expansion of the* Younger *Abstention Doctrine*, 1 PACE L.REV. 149 (1980), 834

NOWAK, JOHN E. & RONALD D. ROTUNDA, CONSTITUTIONAL LAW (7th ed. 2004), 954

Peller, Gary, *In Defense of Federal Habeas Corpus Relitigation*, 16 HARV.C.R.-C.L. L. REV. 579 (1982), 1054

Pildes, Richard H., *Democracy, Anti-Democracy and the Canon*, 17 CONST. COMMENT. 295 (2000), 627

Purcell, Edward A. Jr., *The Particularly Dubious Case of* Hans v. Louisiana: *An Essay on Law, History, and "Federal Courts,"* 81 N.CAR.L.REV. 1927 (2003), 628

Ratner, Leonard, *Congressional Power over the Appellate Jurisdiction of the Supreme Court*, 109 U.PA.L.REV. 157 (1960), 174

Ratner, Leonard, *Executive Privilege, Self Incrimination, and the Separation of Powers Illusion*, 22 U.C.L.A.L.REV. 92 (1974), 8

Redish, Martin H., *Abstention, Separation of Powers, and the Limits of the Judicial Function*, 94 YALE L.J. 71 (1984), 507, 760, 793

Redish, Martin H., *Federal Common Law, Political Legitimacy, and the Interpretive Process: An "Institutionalist" Perspective*, 83 NW.L.REV. 761 (1989), 470, 507

REDISH, MARTIN H., FEDERAL JURISDICTION: TENSIONS IN THE ALLO-CATION OF JUDICIAL POWER (2d ed. 1990), 191, 269, 438

Redish, Martin H., *Judicial Parity, Litigant Choice, and Democratic Theory: A Comment on Federal Jurisdiction and Constitutional Rights*, 36 U.C.L.A.L. REV. 329, (1988), 19, 760

Redish, Martin H., *Legislative Courts, Administrative Agencies, and the* Northern Pipeline *Decision*, 1983 DUKE L.J. 197 (1983), 365

Resnik, Judith, *Tiers*, 57 S. CAL.L.REV. 840 (1984), 1058

RITZ, WILFRED, REWRITING THE HISTORY OF THE JUDICIARY ACT OF 1789 (1990), 383

Rowe, Thomas D. Jr., *Rooker-Feldman: Worth Only the Powder to Blow It Up?*, 74 NOTRE DAME L.REV. 1081 (1999), 1050

Rowe, Thomas D. Jr. & Edward L. Baskauskas, *"Inextricably Intertwined" Explicable at Last?* Rooker-Feldman *Analysis After the Supreme Court's* Exxon Mobil *Decision*, 2006 FED. CTS. L. REV. 1 (2006), 1019

SCALIA, JOHN, BUREAU OF JUSTICE STATISTICS SPECIAL REPORT: PRISONER PETITIONS FILED IN U.S. DISTRICT COURTS, 2000, WITH TRENDS 1980-2000 (2002), 1058, 1063

Sedler, Robert A., *The Assertion of Constitutional* Jus Tertii: *A Substantive Approach*, 70 CALIF.L.REV. 1308 (1982), 96

SHAKESPEARE, WILLIAM, HAMLET, 987

Shapiro, David L., *Jurisdiction and Discretion*, 60 N.Y.U.L.REV. 543, (1985), 236

Sherry, Suzanna, *Judicial Federalism in the Trenches: The* Rooker-Feldman *Doctrine in Action*, 74 NOTRE DAME L. REV. 1085 (1999), 1043, 1050

Smith, George P. II, *Title 28, Section 2255 of the United States Code—Motion to Vacate, Set Aside, or Correct Sentence: Effective or Ineffective Aid to a Federal Prisoner*, 40 NOTRE DAME L.REV. 171 (1964-65), 1058

Soifer, Aviam & H.C. Macgill, *The* Younger *Doctrine: Reconstructing Reconstruction*, 55 TEX.L.REV. 1141 (1977), 831

Stravitz, Howard B., Younger *Abstention Reaches a Civil Maturity*, 57 FORDHAM L.REV. 997 (1989), 838

Symposium, *Federalism and Parity*, 71 B.U.L.REV. 593 (1991), 798

Taylor, Telford & Everett Willis, *The Power of Federal Courts to Enjoin Proceedings in State Courts*, 42 YALE L.J. 1169 (1933), 757

TOCQUEVILLE, ALEXIS DE, DEMOCRACY IN AMERICA (Henry Steele Commager ed. 1965), 26

Tribe, Laurence H., *Jurisdictional Gerrymandering: Zoning Disfavored Rights Out of the Federal Courts*, 16 HARV.C.R.-C.L.L.REV. 129 (1981), 192

Warren, Charles, *Federal and State Court Interference*, 43 HARV.L.REV. 345 (1930), 757

Wechsler, Herbert, *The Political Safeguards of Federalism: The Role of the States in the Composition and Selection of the National Government*, 54 COLUM.L.REV. 543 (1954), 865

Wells, Michael, *Behind the Parity Debate: The Decline of the Legal Process Tradition in the Law of Federal Courts*, 71 B.U.L.REV. 609 (1991), 17

Wells, Michael, *Why Professor Redish Is Wrong About Abstention*, 19 GA.L.REV. 1097 (1985), 793

Welsh, Robert, *Reconsidering the Constitutional Relationship Between State and Federal Courts: A Critique of* Michigan v. Long, 59 NOTRE DAME L.REV. 1118 (1984), 925

Wingate, C. Keith, *The Bad Faith Harassment Exception to the* Younger *Doctrine: Exploring the Empty Universe*, 5 REV.LITIG. 123 (1986), 794

Woolhandler, Ann, *Demodeling Habeas*, 45 STAN.L.REV. 575 (1993), 1055

WRIGHT, CHARLES A. & MARY KAY KANE, LAW OF FEDERAL COURTS (6th ed. 2000), 12, 745

YACKLE, LARRY W., FEDERAL COURTS (2d ed. 2003), 1154

Yackle, Larry W., *Federal Evidentiary Hearings Under the New Habeas Corpus Statute*, 6 B.U.PUB.INT.L.J. 135 (1996), 1100

Yackle, Larry W., *A Primer on the New Habeas Corpus Statute*, 44 BUFF.L. REV. 381 (1996), 1052, 1060, 1162

Zeigler, Donald H., *An Accommodation of the* Younger *Doctrine and the Duty of the Federal Courts to Enforce Safeguards in the State Criminal Process*, 125 U.PA.L.REV. 266 (1976), 792

Zeigler, Donald H., *A Reassessment of the* Younger *Doctrine in Light of the Legislative History of Reconstruction*, 1983 DUKE L.J. 987, 1054

Zeigler, Donald H., *Rights Require Remedies: A New Approach to the Enforcement of Rights in the Federal Courts*, 38 HASTINGS L.J. 665, (1987), 454, 455, 480

Zeigler, Donald H., *Rights, Rights of Action, and Remedies: An Integrated Approach*, 76 WASH. L. REV. 67 (2001), 480

Zeigler, Donald H., *Twins Separated at Birth: A Comparative History of the Civil and Criminal Arising Under Jurisdiction of the Federal Courts and Some Proposals for Change*, 19 VT.L REV. 673 (1995), 899

Zeigler, Donald H. & Michele G. Hermann, *The Invisible Litigant: An Inside View of Pro Se Actions in the Federal Courts*, 47 N.Y.U.L.REV. 157 (1972), 1061.

FEDERAL COURTS, FEDERALISM AND SEPARATION OF POWERS

CASES AND MATERIALS

Fourth Edition

*

PROLOGUE

FEDERALISM: A FOREWORD[a]

HENRY J. FRIENDLY[*]

86 YALE L.J. 1019 (1977).

*It should never be forgotten that this slogan, "Our
Federalism," born in the early struggling days of
our Union of States, occupies a highly important
place in our Nation's history and its future.*[1]

It was fitting that in his last term Mr. Justice Black should have bequeathed to the American people the phrase "Our Federalism" and the
discussion accompanying it—the most eloquent statement on the subject
since Chief Justice Chase's reference to "an indestructible Union, composed of indestructible States." It was fitting also that he should have
emphasized Our Federalism's historic origins. The United States under
the Constitution was born federalist; it did not truly choose federalism or
have federalism thrust upon it. As Chief Justice Chase had said, "Both
the States and the United States existed before the Constitution." The
genius of the Framers lay in devising a unique form of federalism—one
in which a national government was authorized to act directly on the
people within the powers confided to it rather than solely on the states,
and was endowed with an amplitude of powers which might or might not
be used as the future would dictate. As Mr. Justice Holmes was later to
say, the Framers "called into life a being the development of which could
not have been foreseen completely by the most gifted of its begetters."

Despite the Marshall Court's resounding affirmation of the breadth
of the powers conferred on the national government, the use made of
these powers through the first century of our history under the Constitution was restrained. Congress moved speedily to exercise its powers
with respect to patents and copyrights. The national government conducted foreign affairs, raised and supported an exceedingly modest army

---

[a] Reprinted by permission of The Yale Law Journal Company and Fred B. Rothman &
Company from The Yale Law Journal, vol. 86, pp. 1019–34.

[*] Senior Judge, United States Court of Appeals for the Second Circuit; Presiding
Judge Special Court under Rail Reorganization Act of 1973.

[1] Younger v. Harris, 401 U.S. 37, 44–45 (1971) (Black, J.). The Justice regarded the
phrase as embodying "the belief that the National Government will fare best if the States
and their institutions are left free to perform their separate functions in their separate
ways." He elaborated:

> The concept does not mean blind deference to "States' Rights" any more than it
> means centralization of control over every important issue in our National Gov-
> ernment and its courts. The Framers rejected both these courses. What the
> concept does represent is a system in which there is sensitivity to the legitimate
> interests of both State and National Governments, and in which the National
> Government, anxious though it may be to vindicate and protect federal rights
> and federal interests, always endeavors to do so in ways that will not unduly in-
> terfere with the legitimate activities of the States.

1

and, over considerable protest, provided and maintained an even more modest navy, waged some foreign wars, borrowed and coined money, levied taxes (primarily import tariffs), created the first and second Banks of the United States, spent money both to purchase the Louisiana Territory and, again over much objection, to make internal improvements, and then, under the impulse of Jacksonian democracy, it withdrew from the banking field. Beyond this the national government did relatively little, and some of what it did, notably the Fugitive Slave Acts, would not be proudly regarded today. Few people remember that until 1867 we had bankruptcy acts for only seven years, 1800 to 1803 and 1841 to 1843.

The judiciary made relatively little attempt to rush in where the legislative and executive branches were unwilling to tread. Chief Justice Marshall himself authored *Barron v. Mayor of Baltimore,* which held that the guarantees of the Bill of Rights applied only to the federal government, not to the states; he thought the question to be "of great importance, but not of much difficulty." After what Professor Gunther calls "gropings," the Supreme Court arrived at the celebrated formulation of *Cooley v. Board of Wardens* that when Congress had not acted to utilize the commerce power, the states were precluded from nondiscriminatory action only when "subjects of this power are in their nature national, or admit only of one uniform system, or plan of regulation." Judged by today's standards, Congress did little indeed.

The watershed was the war between the states, the adoption of the three Reconstruction amendments, especially the Fourteenth, and enactment of the various civil rights acts with jurisdiction in the federal courts to enforce them. Although these amendments were doubtless intended primarily to safeguard the rights of the newly emancipated Negroes, Mr. Justice Miller's prophecy that this would be practically their sole effect turned out to be an exceedingly poor one. In time the due process and equal protection clauses of the Fourteenth Amendment would vest the federal judiciary, particularly the Supreme Court, with a roving authority to invalidate state statutes and, for almost all practical purposes, to reverse the decision in *Barron v. Mayor of Baltimore.* Along with these enactments Congress adopted the National Bank Act of 1864 and the Bankruptcy Act of 1867. As important as these substantive changes was the Act of March 3, 1875, which for the first time (except for the abortive Judiciary Act of 1801) vested the federal courts with general federal question jurisdiction, although subject to a jurisdictional amount.

Still another score of years elapsed, however, before enactment of the two statutes that were the real beginnings of federal regulation of interstate business—the Interstate Commerce Act of 1887, adopted in response to the Supreme Court's holding that state regulation of interstate railroad rates was not permissible under the Cooley doctrine, and the Sherman Antitrust Act of 1890. These were followed, again after the lapse of some years, by a burst of legislation in the first Wilson administration—the Clayton Act of 1914, the Federal Trade Commission Act of the same year, the Shipping Act of 1916, and, perhaps most important though least litigated, the Federal Reserve Act of 1913. The early 1920s saw four other important pieces of legislation extending federal regulatory power: the Transportation Act, 1920, which transformed the Interstate Commerce Act by placing "the railroad systems of the country more completely than ever under the fostering guardianship and control of the Commission," the Federal Water Power Act, the Packers and Stockyard Act, 1921, and the Radio Act of 1927—the forerunner of the Federal Communications Act.

Contemplating what then seemed a rather amazing array of new statutes extending national power, this writer was prompted to say in 1928:

> The steady expansion of the jurisdiction of the federal courts, especially since Reconstruction days, has been but a reflex of the general growth of federal political power. That growth will not abate, since it is responsive to deep social and economic causes.

Although this must rate as an excellent prediction, little did the author know what the next few years would bring.

If the war between the states was a watershed, the New Deal was a tidal wave. Two remarkable statutes, the Securities Act of 1933 and the Securities Exchange Act of 1934, elevated the national government from a negligible to a predominant role with respect to the issuance of and dealings in securities and the operation of the stock exchanges. An equally dramatic change in the field of labor regulation was wrought by the National Labor Relations Act of 1935 and the Fair Labor Standards Act of 1938. The Securities Exchange Act, unlike the Securities Act, provides for exclusive federal jurisdiction. Although the National Labor Relations Act does not, a good deal of preemption is furnished by the judicially fashioned rule that "[w]hen it is clear or may fairly be assumed that the activities which a State purports to regulate are protected by Section 7 of the National Labor Relations Act, or constitute an unfair labor practice under Section 8, due regard for the federal enactment requires that state jurisdiction must yield." Even when litigation under this statute can proceed in the state courts, the latter must follow not only the text of the statute but also "federal common law"—a concept representing an advance in federal power that far outweighed the abandonment in the *Erie* case of "the spurious uniformity of *Swift v. Tyson.*"

These major assertions of federal power were accompanied by a host of others—the Tennessee Valley Authority Act of 1933, the Banking Acts of 1933 and 1935, the Public Utility Holding Company Acts of 1935, the expansion of the Interstate Commerce Act to include motor carriers and water carriers, the Civil Aeronautics Act, the Federal Power Act, the Commodity Exchange Act, the Robinson–Patman Act, the 1938 amendments to the Federal Trade Commission Act and to the Securities Exchange Act, the Natural Gas Act, the Federal Food, Drug, and Cosmetic

Act, the Trust Indenture Act of 1939, and the Investment Company and
Investment Advisers Acts. Perhaps an even more important alteration
in the national-state balance was worked by a statute that could hardly
have then been thought of as creating such a change—the Social Security Act of 1935, or more accurately the portions of that Act which established assistance programs to be administered by the states in accordance with federal standards, with the national government supplying
varying percentages of funds. In this and similar enactments Congress
has found a new and powerful tool to bring the states into line with national thinking under penalty of losing the largesse from the federal fisc.

After some slowing of the congressional mill during the 1940s and
1950s, the legislative expansion of national power resumed in the next
two decades. Of prime importance was the effort, after the lapse of
nearly a century, to utilize Section 5 of the Fourteenth Amendment,
which empowers the Congress "to enforce, by appropriate legislation, the
provisions of this article." Here the basic enactments are the Civil
Rights Acts of 1957, the Voting Rights Act of 1965, the Civil Rights Act
of 1964, Title VIII of the Civil Rights Act of 1968, and the Age Discrimination in Employment Act of 1967. Along with this has come a whole
rash of statutes utilizing the commerce power for the promotion of
safety[73] and the protection of borrowers and consumers.[74] Still more important is a series of laws placing the weight of the national government
behind efforts to protect the environment.[75] Considerably more troubling to me, from the standpoint of policy and even from that of constitutionality, has been what seems a knee-jerk tendency of Congress to seek
to remedy any serious abuse by invoking the commerce power as a basis
for the expansion of the federal criminal law into areas of scant federal
concern.

The judiciary has made its own contribution to the growth of national power. I have already referred to one that seems to me wholly
salutary—the development of federal common law. More controversial

[73] The single most important is the Occupational Safety and Health Act of 1970. Oth-
ers are the National Traffic and Motor Vehicle Safety Act of 1966, the Highway Safety Act
of 1966, the Natural Gas Pipeline Safety Act of 1963, the Federal Coal Mine Health and
Safety Act of 1969, the Ports and Waterways Safety Act of 1972, the Federal Railroad
Safety Act of 1970, the Consumer Product Safety Act, the Motor Vehicle and Schoolbus
Safety Amendments of 1974, the Transportation Safety Act of 1974, the Highway Safety
Act of 1976, and the Consumer Product Safety Commission Improvements Act of 1976.

[74] These include: the Consumer Credit Protection Act, the Interstate Land Sales Full
Disclosure Act, the Fair Credit Reporting Act, the Fair Credit Billing Act, the Real Estate
Settlement Procedures Act of 1974, the Magnuson–Moss Warranty–Federal Trade Commission Improvement Act, the Equal Credit Opportunity Act, the Home Mortgage Disclosure Act of 1973, and the Consumer Leasing Act of 1976. * * *

[75] The basic statute is the National Environmental Policy Act of 1969. Other important statutes are the Water Quality Improvement Act of 1970, the Clean Air Amendments
of 1970, the Federal Water Pollution Control Act Amendments of 1972, the Federal Environmental Pesticide Control Act of 1972, the Noise Control Act of 1972, and the Deepwater
Port Act of 1974.

has been the selective incorporation doctrine whereby the due process clause of the Fourteenth Amendment has been held to make applicable to the states all the provisions of the first eight amendments except the Second, Third, and Seventh, the indictment clause of the Fifth, and the excessive bail protection of the Eighth.[78] This constitutional revolution, effectively overruling *Twining v. New Jersey* and *Adamson v. California,* became an even greater force for federalizing state criminal procedure as a result of the expansion of federal habeas corpus for state prisoners wrought initially by *Brown v. Allen* and expanded by *Fay v. Noia.* In the wake of Supreme Court decisions, notably *Monroe v. Pape,* there has been an unparalleled resort to the long-dormant civil rights acts of the Reconstruction period—not simply to prevent discrimination against blacks but to redress many other sorts of constitutional deprivations, particularly in state prisons. In carrying out this mission, federal courts have felt authorized to take on an enormous degree of supervision of the operations of state prisons and mental institutions and to impose affirmative obligations on the states. One federal court, in an effort to obtain minority representation, has ordered the complete remodeling of a city government. The risks of confrontation are serious.

Other potent weapons for increased national power recently forged by the Supreme Court are the expansion of the hearing component of due process evidenced by *Sniadach v. Family Finance Corp.* and *Goldberg v. Kelly* and their numerous progeny, the revival of substantive due process thought by some to be implicit in *Roe v. Wade,* and the holding that the Civil Rights Act of 1871 was an "expressly authorized" exception to the statute prohibiting federal court injunctions against proceedings in state courts. In addition, the Court has diluted the "reasonable ground—good faith" defense for state officials (in the particular case, members of school boards) from liability for damages under the civil rights laws by a qualification that this defense would not apply if the officer "knew or reasonably should have known that the action he took within his sphere of official responsibility" would violate a plaintiff's constitutional rights.

As if this were not enough, many believe—with much reason—that further expansion of national power is required. A former chairman of the Securities Exchange Commission, having closely and critically exam-

---

[78] The principal decisions accomplishing this include: Mapp v. Ohio (4th Amendment exclusionary rule); Robinson v. California (8th Amendment prohibition of cruel and unusual punishment); Gideon v. Wainwright (6th Amendment right to counsel); Ker v. California (4th Amendment exclusionary rule); Malloy v. Hogan (5th Amendment right to remain silent); Pointer v. Texas (6th Amendment right to confront witnesses); Klopher v. North Carolina (6th Amendment right to a speedy trial); Washington v. Texas (6th Amendment right to compulsory process); Duncan v. Louisiana (6th Amendment right to jury trial); Benton v. Maryland (5th Amendment prohibition of double jeopardy); In re Winship (proof beyond reasonable doubt). The Court has never had to say whether the Eighth Amendment's prohibition against excessive bail applies to the states, although the lower courts have held that it does, and the Court itself has hinted as much. * * *

ined what he terms "the Delaware syndrome," has called for a federal law imposing minimum standards of fiduciary responsibility and fairness on all corporations engaged in commerce with more than $1 million of assets and 300 shareholders. The proliferation of state statutes designed to aid management in retaining control of interstate enterprises that are locally based or even that simply have property within the state has led the framers of the proposed ALI Federal Securities Code to provide for preemption in the area of tender offers and takeovers. The Code proposes other preemption; some believe it should propose more to avoid the costs and delays of largely duplicative requirements in a field effectively regulated by the national government. Companies that have complied with federal environmental standards naturally object to being obliged to start all over again with the states. The adoption of many new federal statutes for the protection of consumers and borrowers may raise again the question of preemption not only in those areas but in the entire field of unfair competition and antitrust law with respect to interstate or foreign transactions. And surely we will see a federal law dealing with major aircraft accidents where there are plaintiffs from many states and defendants who can be sued in a variety of courts, state and federal, with consequences enticing to choice-of-law buffs but considerably less appealing to litigants.

Yet the movement has not been all in one direction. The cases stemming from the decision with which we began, *Younger v. Harris,* afford one illustration. The Court has advanced from its position in *Younger* that a federal court may not enjoin a pending state criminal proceeding brought in good faith even when the federal court plaintiff is suing under the Civil Rights Act, and from its simultaneous holding applying the same rule to declaratory judgments. The Court has recently held that a federal court may enjoin neither state criminal proceedings begun after the federal complaint was filed but before proceedings of substance had taken place in the federal court, nor state civil proceedings "in aid of and closely related to criminal statutes, nor state contempt proceedings." * * *

The rising tide of imposition of procedural due process on the states was checked at the 1975 Term by three decisions requiring higher thresholds for showing a legally protected interest in liberty or property. Despite the dismissal of certiorari in a case that was expected to settle the question, there may still be hope that the Court will retreat from its unexplained and, in the writer' view, ill-advised intimations that state prisoners seeking relief under the Civil Rights Act need not exhaust administrative remedies which the state has provided; if it does not, Congress may be persuaded to act. Federal habeas corpus was substantially restricted when the Court held it unavailable for Fourth Amendment claims of state prisoners to whom the state had provided an opportunity for full and fair litigation in its own courts. Any reader familiar with views I expressed some years ago will not be surprised to learn that I applaud this result, although I would have preferred to have seen it reached by a thoroughgoing judicial reconsideration of the whole subject of collateral attack on criminal convictions or, failing that, by legislation * * *.

Furthermore the Eleventh Amendment still lives, to the extent of barring federal court actions by private persons seeking funds in the state treasury even when the funds have come there through alleged violation of federal regulations concerning a federal welfare program; per contra, however, when Congress has authorized damage awards in legislation enacted pursuant to Section 5 of the Fourteenth Amendment * * *. [Consider] Professor Gunther's provocative questions:

> What are the values, historical and contemporary, of federalism? Can it still be said that federalism increases liberty, encourages diversity, promotes creative experimentation and responsive self-government? Or is it a legalistic obstruction, a harmful brake on governmental responses to pressing social issues, a shield for selfish vested interests? Is federalism a theme that constitutional law must grapple with simply because it is *there,* in the Constitution? Is the prime challenge it poses that of minimizing the obstacles that the complexities of federalism put in the way of meeting modern needs? Or does federalism embody more appealing values that deserve some of the imaginative enthusiasm with which modern constitutional law embraces the promotion of such values as equality and freedom of speech?

Clearly Mr. Justice Black, who played no small part in strengthening the role of the national government at the expense of the states, would have answered the second and the final question with a resounding "Yes." So, for what it is worth, would I. Although some state governments may be ignorant or venal, many are far-seeing and courageous; and not all wisdom reposes in Washington. There is still truth in Mr. Justice Brandeis' renowned observation:

> It is one of the happy incidents of the federal system that a single courageous State may, if its citizens choose, serve as a laboratory; and try novel social and economic experiments without risk to the rest of the country.

No-fault insurance is a sufficient example; we may end up with a uniform federal system or minimum federal standards, but we should never have had anything save for experimentation by the states. We must stand in awe and admiration of the design of the Framers and of the success of the Supreme Court in fleshing it out—preventing one state from getting in the way of others and endowing the central government with power to act on a national basis when Congress finds this to be warranted, but leaving to the states the final decision on the bulk of day-to-day matters that can best be decided by those who are closest to them. While I expect we shall be forced to pursue the centripetal path of the last century, we should not rush along it too fast or too far; the question whether action by the national government is needed should always be asked. To paraphrase T.R. Powell, how fast is too fast and far too far are matters on which the writer of a foreword need not express an opinion.

PRELIMINARY THOUGHTS ON SEPARATION OF POWERS AND THE JUDICIARY

One hesitates to play on a double bill opposite Henry Friendly, even in a prologue; it seems both presumptuous and a sure way to be on the short end of an invidious comparison. Yet, for balance it is necessary to introduce the second great theme that animates these materials. We are all poorer for Judge Friendly's not having written on separation of powers as he did on federalism. But even his silence teaches; the Supreme Court's role in elaborating this theme with respect to the functioning of the federal courts has generally been far less noticeable than its corresponding role with respect to federalism.

"Separation of powers" is a ringing phrase in American constitutional history. It brings to mind the talismanic incantation[1] of "checks and balances" and visions of bicameralism,[2] presidential veto,[3] impeachment,[4] the Senate's power to approve treaties,[5] its "advise and consent" power generally,[6] the House of Representative's special role as the originator of all revenue bills,[7] and judicial review.[8] Those who drafted the Constitution were much concerned with separation of powers, and James Madison devoted a substantial portion of the Federalist essays to it.

> One of the principal objections inculcated by the more respectable adversaries to the constitution, is its supposed violation of the political maxim, that the legislative, executive and judiciary departments ought to be separate and distinct. In the structure of the federal government, no regard, it is said, seems to have been paid to this essential precaution in favor of liberty. The several departments of power are distributed and blended in such a manner, as at once to destroy all symmetry and beauty of form; and to ex-

---

[1] Yet, as Professor Ratner warns, "[N]o matter how solemnly reiterated, the phrase provides no talismanic precept." Leonard Ratner, *Executive Privilege, Self Incrimination, and the Separation of Powers Illusion,* 22 U.C.L.A.L.REV. 92, 93 (1974).

[2] U.S. CONST. art. III, § 1.

[3] U.S. CONST. art. I, § 7.

[4] U.S. CONST. art. II, § 4.

[5] U.S. CONST. art. II, § 2, cl. 2.

[6] *Id.*

[7] U.S. CONST. art. I, § 7, cl. 1.

[8] Marbury v. Madison, 5 U.S. (1 Cranch) 137, 2 L.Ed. 60 (1803).

pose some of the essential parts of the edifice to the danger of being crushed by the disproportionate weight of other parts.

No political truth is certainly of greater intrinsic value or is stamped with the authority of more enlightened patrons of liberty than that on which the objection is founded. The accumulation of all powers legislative, executive and judiciary in the same hands, whether of one, a few or many, and whether hereditary, self-appointed, or elective, may justly be pronounced the very definition of tyranny. Were the federal constitution therefore really chargeable with this accumulation of power or with a mixture of powers having a dangerous tendency to such an accumulation, no further arguments would be necessary to inspire a universal reprobation of the system.

* * *

[I]n saying "there can be no liberty where the legislative and executive powers are united in the same person, or body of magistrates," or "if the power of judging be not separated from the legislative and executive powers," [Montesquieu] did not mean that these departments ought to have no *partial agency* in, or no *controul* over the acts of each other. His meaning, as his own words import, and still more conclusively as illustrated by the example in his eye, can amount to no more than this, that where the *whole* power of one department is exercised by the same hands which possess the *whole* power of another department, the fundamental principles of a free constitution, are subverted. * * *9

Thus did Madison endeavor to show that the checks and balances system, though it blended powers, was nonetheless consistent with and essential to separation of powers.

Constitutional law courses abound with the great decisions on separation of powers: *Marbury v. Madison*,[10] *Youngstown Sheet and Tube Co. v. Sawyer*,[11] *United States v. Nixon*,[12] *Bowsher v. Synar*,[13] *United*

---

9 THE FEDERALIST No. 47, at 323–26 (James Madison) (Jacob E. Cooke ed. 1961).

10 5 U.S. (1 Cranch) 137, 2 L.Ed. 60 (1803) (establishing judicial review of federal legislation).

11 343 U.S. 579, 72 S.Ct. 863, 96 L.Ed. 1153 (1952) (confirming judicial review of executive acts—here the government's seizure of steel mills to terminate a labor dispute during the Korean War).

12 418 U.S. 683, 94 S.Ct. 3090, 41 L.Ed.2d 1039 (1974) (confirming judicial authority to review claims of executive privilege in dispute between the President and the special prosecutor investigating the Watergate break-in).

13 478 U.S. 714, 106 S.Ct. 3181, 92 L.Ed.2d 583 (1986) (overturning congressional assignment of executive functions to Comptroller General, a legislative department official).

States v. United States District Court,[14] and *Immigration and Naturalization Service v. Chadha*,[15] to name but a few. Most of the best known decisions on separation of powers concern what the legislative and executive branches may or may not do. On occasion, however, the Supreme Court discusses separation-of-powers restraints on what the judiciary may do. One scholar notes:

> The Supreme Court, after a fragile start, has evolved into the authoritative interpreter of the U.S. Constitution, short of amendment. Judicial review of national and state action converts the tribunal into a continuous constitutional convention, which mediates between forces of continuity and change in a "living" Constitution. * * * The primary mission of the Supreme Court throughout American history has been to enforce the supremacy and uniformity of national law and of federally-created rights of individuals in the states. Enforcing separation of powers is secondary. * * * Notwithstanding its role as ultimate interpreter, the branch of the national government limited most by Supreme Court interpretation of separation of powers is the judiciary itself.[16]

Concerns about separation of powers underlie much of the Court's jurisprudence in the area of justiciability. The Article III doctrines of standing, ripeness, mootness, political questions, advisory opinions, and the overarching concept of "case or controversy" all implicate separation of powers. The Court has often declared that the case-or-controversy requirement of Article III is a specific manifestation of separation of powers because it requires the courts to limit themselves to concrete disputes, avoiding broader policy questions and more general disagreements about what the law ought to be, questions the Court reminds us are more properly left to the political branches.[17]

Separation of powers also plays a more subtle part in how the federal courts operate. The power to declare legislation unconstitutional clearly brings the judiciary into potential conflict with at least the legislature and possibly with the executive. Beyond that, every time a court interprets a statute, it gives meaning to the act of a coordinate branch. When we speak of the role of the courts in legislative interpretation, we are

---

[14] 407 U.S. 297, 92 S.Ct. 2125, 32 L.Ed.2d 752 (1972) (overturning executive's claim of authority to order searches in domestic national security cases without judicial supervision).

[15] 462 U.S. 919, 103 S.Ct. 2764, 77 L.Ed.2d 317 (1983) (disapproving legislative veto of executive branch actions unless the congressional veto goes through the normal legislative process).

[16] J. Woodford Howard, Jr., *Supreme Court Enforcement of Separation of Powers: A Balance Sheet, in* SEPARATION OF POWERS IN THE AMERICAN POLITICAL SYSTEM 81, 88 (Barbara B. Knight ed. 1989).

[17] *See, e.g.,* Allen v. Wright, 468 U.S. 737, 104 S.Ct. 3315, 82 L.Ed.2d 556 (1984), discussed in Chapter 1.

concerned with separation of powers. Should the courts, for example, search for "legislative intent," or should they confine themselves to the unadorned words of statutes no matter how clear the underlying intent of the legislature may be?[18] If the courts ignore legislative intent in favor of plain meaning, does the practice exalt separation of powers or, to the extent that a clear legislative purpose is frustrated, offend it? An example may help demonstrate the difficulty of the problem.

Suppose Congress enacts a statute creating new substantive rights for individuals, but not explicitly creating a private cause of action for enforcement of those rights. Should the courts do so? If not, congressional purpose to create effective rights may be ignored. If so, the courts may be cast into the role of "supplemental legislators," effectively amending legislation to include what the political branches omitted.[19]

The preceding example leads to the more general question of whether, in this age of statutes and administrative regulation, courts ought ever to formulate rules of law. The venerable clash of *Swift v. Tyson*[20] on one hand and *Erie Railroad v. Tompkins*[21] on the other represents a substantial federalism problem, but there are separation-of-powers undertones as well. Is it appropriate for courts to make law?

Two factors complicate that inquiry. First, the demarcation between interpretation and creation is by no means clear. Second, on occasion the legislature may invite or command the judiciary to construct rules of law.[22] In such cases, is separation of powers more offended if the courts accept or refuse the assignment?

Most of the topics covered in this volume involve separation-of-powers problems. The interplay between justiciability and separation of powers has already been noted. Congressional power to define the juris-

---

[18] Justice Scalia, at least, has suggested the latter.

> [Examination of legislative history] is appropriate * * * if one assumes that the task of a court of law is to plumb the intent of the particular Congress that enacted a particular provision. That methodology is not mine nor, I think, the one that courts have traditionally followed. It is our task, as I see it, not to enter the minds of the Members of Congress—who need have nothing in mind in order for their votes to be both lawful and effective—but rather to give fair and reasonable meaning to the text of the United States Code, adopted by various Congresses at various times.

Pennsylvania v. Union Gas Co., 491 U.S. 1, 29–30, 109 S.Ct. 2273, 2296, 105 L.Ed.2d 1, 26 (1989) (Scalia, J., concurring and dissenting).

[19] Justices Stevens and Powell debated this problem vigorously in Cannon v. University of Chicago, 441 U.S. 677, 99 S.Ct. 1946, 60 L.Ed.2d 560 (1979). *See generally* Chapter 5, Section C, Part 3.

[20] 41 U.S. (16 Pet.) 1, 10 L.Ed. 865 (1842).

[21] 304 U.S. 64, 58 S.Ct. 817, 82 L.Ed. 1188 (1938).

[22] *See, e.g.,* Textile Workers Union v. Lincoln Mills, 353 U.S. 448, 77 S.Ct. 912, 1 L.Ed.2d 972 (1957). *See generally* Chapter 5, Section C, Part 2.

diction of the federal courts within the limits of Article III represents an enormous influence by the legislature on the judiciary.[23] At the same time, the Supreme Court's efforts to construe jurisdictional statutes also affect the distribution of power among all three branches. Congress has often created "legislative" or "Article I" courts, the judges of which do not enjoy the protections available under Article III.[24] Does the existence of such courts violate separation of powers? To the extent that Congress assigns to them questions that are contemplated by Article III, § 2, is that a separate violation?

In addition to construing jurisdictional statutes, the Court occasionally recognizes that jurisdiction exists but elects not to exercise it. The abstention doctrines (Chapter 8) demonstrate this phenomenon. One might not initially characterize abstention doctrines as interbranch conflicts, but they may be. When Congress grants jurisdiction, should the Court consider the grant an invitation, or is it more like an offer that cannot be refused? Although the Court has, for the most part, developed abstention doctrines narrowly, it could theoretically create a new doctrine, deciding to abstain from exercising all diversity jurisdiction, for example.[25] If it did, would the new doctrine pose a separation-of-powers problem because of the obvious frustration of congressional intent to retain diversity jurisdiction? With respect to the more limited abstention doctrines, is the difference one in kind or merely in degree?

Complicating this entire inquiry is the fact that the Constitution never discusses separation of powers in so many words. To some extent, the document's organization exemplifies separation of powers, but the separation is far from total. In part, the elaborate system of checks and balances, by making the three branches to some extent interdependent, represents a rejection of rigid separation. James Madison thought that important. "[U]nless these departments be so far connected and blended as to give to each a constitutional control over the others, the degree of

---

[23] *See generally* Chapter 2.

[24] *See generally* Chapter 4.

[25] The Court has developed a more limited sort of abstention with respect to diversity.

> [T]here are two important areas, domestic relations cases and probate matters, where, by a judge-made exception to the [diversity] statute, the federal courts will not act though diversity is present. These two exceptions were first developed at a time when the diversity statute granted jurisdiction of "suits of a civil nature in law or in equity," and it was thought that the domestic relations and probate cases, being matters that would have been heard in the ecclesiastical courts, did not fit this description. The 1948 Judicial Code substituted the term "civil action" for the phrase used in the older statutes, but the exceptions have persisted. Today the exceptions may more rationally be defended on the ground that these are areas of the law in which the states have an especially strong interest and a well-developed competence for dealing with them.

CHARLES A. WRIGHT & MARY KAY KANE, LAW OF FEDERAL COURTS § 25, at 161 (6th ed. 2002) (footnote omitted).

separation which the maxim requires, as essential to a free government, can never in practice be duly maintained."[26] The tension between the "separate spheres" view of separation of powers and what Professor Jack Beermann has called the "overlapping" model[27] has generated much scholarly attention.[28] The Constitution's imprecision makes these problems even more difficult and subtle than they might otherwise be. Moreover, whether the federal courts act or refrain from acting because of separation of powers, they necessarily affect the relationship of the federal government to the states. As you go through this volume, keep in mind the underlying eddies and currents of interbranch relationships and their effects not merely on how each branch functions within itself, but upon federalism as well.

SOME OBSERVATIONS ON PARITY

Some cases cannot proceed in the federal courts because there is no subject matter jurisdiction. Others *must* proceed in those courts because Congress has made federal jurisdiction exclusive, as in patent and copyright cases. For the third group, however—cases for which both federal and state courts have subject matter jurisdiction—what difference does the choice of forum make? We are all familiar with cases (many encountered in the course in Civil Procedure) in which the parties do battle over the choice of forum. Often those battles turn on geography: the plaintiff wants to litigate her claim in Guam, while the defendant prefers Miami. One can readily understand issues of convenience and witness-availability that often underlie such disputes. The choice between federal and state court, however, is frequently not predominantly geographic. Recall that in *World-Wide Volkswagen Corp. v. Woodson*, 444 U.S. 286, 100 S.Ct. 559, 62 L.Ed.2d 490 (1980), the plaintiffs deliberately joined a non-diverse party in an attempt to keep the case in the state courts, and the defendants fought that assertion of personal jurisdiction (successfully) precisely so that they could remove the case to federal court. Why? The plaintiffs' counsel believed that state court juries were consistently more favorable to plaintiffs than were federal court juries (a belief apparently shared by the defense). Counsel attempted to keep the case in the state courts to enhance the chances of a favorable result.

World-Wide Volkswagen exemplifies the on-going debate about what is called "parity": the question of whether there are qualitative differences in adjudication between state and federal courts. *Erie Railroad*

---

[26] THE FEDERALIST NO. 48, at 332 (James Madison) (Jacob E. Cooke ed. 1961).

[27] Jack M. Beermann, *"Bad" Judicial Activism and Liberal Federal–Courts Doctrine: A Comment on Professor Doernberg and Professor Redish*, 40 CASE W.RES.L.REV. 1053, 1062 n. 37 (1989–90).

[28] *See, e.g.*, Alan L. Feld, *Separation of Political Powers: Boundaries or Balance?*, 21 GA.L.REV. 171 (1986); Cynthia R. Farina, *Statutory Interpretation and the Balance of Power in the Administrative State*, 89 COLUM.L.REV. 452 (1989).

Co. v. Tompkins was one attempt by the Supreme Court to deal with a demonstrated lack of parity, one stemming from choice-of-law differences between state and federal courts. Before *Erie*, suing in state court usually meant that state law would apply to key issues in a case and suing in federal court meant that federal common law would apply, choice of forum was often equivalent to choice of result.[29] Although *Erie* sought to eliminate one particular kind of forum/result linkage, many remain. Battles between litigants over personal jurisdiction often deal less with convenience than with the parties' recognition that forum choice-of-law rules can determine the outcome of disputes touching more than one state. It is still true, to some extent, that choosing among available state forums may directly and predictably determine the outcome in some cases.

The choice between federal and state courts often involves considerations far less tangible than choice of law. Many academics, practitioners, and litigants believe that the federal courts are qualitatively better.[30] One observes the manifestations of these beliefs primarily in two phenomena. Plaintiffs vote with their feet, by electing to file in one forum or the other. Defendants vote with motion (or removal) papers, seeking dismissal, removal, transfer, or abstention. The parity debate outside of academia plays itself out in those terms, with the underlying motivations rarely being discussed. Others have approached the subject more directly. As Professor Neuborne indicates in the following excerpt, the debate is quite important, not least because the Supreme Court quite explicitly bases some of its jurisdictional and other decisional rules on the assumption that there is no qualitative difference between the two court systems, or at least none of which the courts ought to take notice.

THE MYTH OF PARITY[b]
BURT NEUBORNE
90 HARV.L.REV. 1105 (1977).

In *Stone v. Powell*, Justice Powell responded to the assertion that federal habeas corpus review of state exclusionary rule determinations was essential to the vigorous enforcement of the fourth amendment by rejecting any notion that federal judges are institutionally more receptive to federal constitutional norms than are their state counterparts. Rather, Justice Powell appeared to assume that state and federal courts are functionally interchangeable forums likely to provide equivalent pro-

---

[29] Perhaps the most famous example is Black & White Taxicab & Transfer Company v. Brown & Yellow Taxicab & Transfer Company, 276 U.S. 518, 48 S.Ct. 404, 72 L.Ed. 681 (1928), where the plaintiff changed the state of its incorporation so that it could bring a diversity action to enforce a contract that was lawful under federal common law but that the state courts would have declared invalid.

[30] Some or many judges in both systems may agree, but they are far less likely to make their feelings known for obvious institutional reasons.

[b] Copyright © 1977 The Harvard Law Review Association. Reprinted by permission.

tection for federal constitutional rights. If it existed, this assumed parity between state and federal courts, which characterizes much of the current Court's approach to problems of federal jurisdiction, would render the process of allocating judicial business between state and federal forums an outcome-neutral exercise unrelated to the merits.

Unfortunately, I fear that the parity which Justice Powell celebrated in *Stone* exists only in his understandable wish that it were so. I suggest that the assumption of parity is, at best, a dangerous myth, fostering forum allocation decisions which channel constitutional adjudication under the illusion that state courts will vindicate federally secured constitutional rights as forcefully as would the lower federal courts. At worst, it provides a pretext for funneling federal constitutional decisionmaking into state courts precisely because they are less likely to be receptive to vigorous enforcement of federal constitutional doctrine. As a result, I view forum allocation decisions like *Stone* not as outcome-neutral allocations of judicial business but as indirect decisions on the merits, which weaken disfavored federal constitutional rights by remitting their enforcement to less receptive state forums.

The attempt by lawyers to utilize an ostensibly outcome-neutral federalism analysis to influence indirectly the merits of constitutional litigation is hardly new. During the past century, litigators have consistently advanced ostensibly outcome-neutral federalism arguments, assertedly unrelated to the merits, to channel constitutional adjudication into forums calculated to advance the substantive interests of their clients. Although the political persuasion and economic status of the constitutional litigants have varied with the changing nature of the rights invoked, one factor has remained constant: interests and groups seeking expansive definition and vigorous application of federal constitutional rights have sought a federal judicial forum while their opponents, attempting to narrow federal rights and weaken their implementation, have emphasized the facially neutral federalism concerns which argue in favor of state judicial enforcement of federal constitutional rights.

One of the current Court's most vigorous proponents for channelling constitutional challenges against state officials into the state courts has been Justice Rehnquist.[89] Professor David Shapiro, recently assessing Justice Rehnquist's performance on the Court, has suggested that his opinions have been guided by three basic principles:

> (1) Conflicts between an individual and the government should, whenever possible, be resolved against the individual;

> (2) Conflicts between state and federal authority, * * * should, whenever possible, be resolved in favor of the states; and

---

[89] *See, e.g.*, Paul v. Davis, 424 U.S. 693 (1976); Rizzo v. Goode, 423 U.S. 362 (1976); Doran v. Salem Inn, Inc., 422 U.S. 922 (1975); Huffman v. Pursue, Ltd., 420 U.S. 592 (1975).

(3) Questions of the exercise of federal jurisdiction, * * * should, whenever possible, be resolved against such exercise.[90]

As Professor Shapiro noted, these principles "often overlap and reinforce each other." I suggest that not only do they "often overlap"; they are, in fact, integrally related by the perception that state judicial forums are less likely to operate as strong countermajoritarian power centers than are federal district courts. Were one to reformulate Professor Shapiro's first proposition more charitably, it might read:

> In a democracy, actions bearing the imprimatur of democratic decisionmaking should be overturned by courts only when absolutely necessary; all doubts should be resolved in favor of upholding a collective societal judgment.

If the views of Justice Rehnquist and those of a current majority of his brethren reflect not merely a preference for government at the expense of the individual, but rather a principled theory of deference to majoritarian decisionmaking,[92] the Court's increasing preference for state court adjudication and its distrust of federal jurisdiction are explicable as the logical forum allocation corollaries to its major substantive premise. As subsidiary propositions they rest, I suggest, on an understanding that the only judicial forums in our system capable of enforcing countermajoritarian checks in a sustained, effective manner are the federal courts and that, to the extent that constitutional cases can be shifted from federal to state trial courts, the capacity of individuals to mount successful challenges to collective decisions will be substantially diminished. It is the recognition of that fact and its troubling ramifications for the viability of constitutional rights—and not an uncritical assumption of parity—which should be the critical factor in current federal-state forum allocation decisions.

Professor Neuborne addresses the issue of parity head-on, but even defining the terms of debate is not easy. Professor Susan Herman notes that

> Parties to the parity debate have framed the issue in a variety of ways: whether federal and state court judges are "equally talented and equally sympathetic" to federal constitutional claims; whether state court judges show "widespread disregard" for federal constitutional claims; or whether the federal and state courts can be con-

---

[90] David Shapiro, *Mr. Justice Rehnquist: A Preliminary View*, 90 HARV.L.REV. 293, 294 (1976).

[92] Justice Rehnquist has articulated such a view in William H. Rehnquist, *The Notion of a Living Constitution*, 54 TEX.L.REV. 693 (1976). *But see* National League of Cities v. Usery, 426 U.S. 833 (1976).

sidered "functionally interchangeable."[31]

Professor Michael Wells observes that parity is an ambiguous term that can be interpreted in two ways:

> The assertion of parity between state and federal courts may refer to a claim that a litigant will receive a constitutionally adequate hearing on a federal claim in state court. In contrast with this "weak" sense of parity, the "strong" sense of the term signifies the fungible nature of state and federal courts and the absence of a systematic difference in outcomes whether cases are allotted to state or federal courts.[32]

He finds that "most participants in the parity debate believe in the weak sense of parity," but that there is a consensus that "strong" parity does not exist.[33]

In the 1950s and 1960s, Supreme Court decisions mandating desegregation met considerable resistance from some state courts. Many state judges, particularly (though not exclusively) in the South, were hostile to plaintiffs who sought to take advantage of the Court's (and other federal courts') decisions. Simultaneously, the Warren Court expanded federal constitutional rights in criminal cases through the process of incorporation, applying Bill of Rights provisions to the states through the Due Process Clause of the Fourteenth Amendment, both on direct review and collateral attack on state criminal convictions through federal habeas corpus. The Court was obviously concerned that individuals asserting constitutional rights against state governments did not receive fair adjudication on the state level, and it therefore saw federal courts as necessary to enforce federal constitutional rights against state encroachment.[34] This concern assumed, though it did not articulate, a lack of parity between state and federal courts.

In the late 1960s and early 1970s, appointments of conservative Justices resulted in a resurgence of deference to state power. While the Warren Court saw federal courts as essential to enforcing expanded federal constitutional rights, the more conservative Burger Court restricted the availability of federal remedies. The Court had an increasing tendency to channel constitutional challenges to state action into the state courts, basing its forum allocation choices on concerns about federalism,

---

[31] Susan N. Herman, *Why Parity Matters*, 71 B.U.L.REV. 651, 651-52 (1991) (footnotes omitted).

[32] Michael Wells, *Behind the Parity Debate: The Decline of the Legal Process Tradition in the Law of Federal Courts*, 71 B.U.L.REV. 609, 610 (1991).

[33] *Id.* at 610-11.

[34] *See, e.g.,* Brown v. Allen, 344 U.S. 443, 511, 73 S.Ct. 437, 448, 97 L.Ed. 469, 517 (1953) (Frankfurter, J., concurring) (noting that "even the highest state courts" had failed to uphold federal constitutional rights).

judicial economy, and the federal courts' caseload. Apart from the
Court's explicit bows to parity, as Professor Neuborne mentioned, one
sees its judicial philosophy in the expansion of door-closing doctrines,
such as *Younger* abstention and *Pullman* abstention, and the Court's
creation of new barriers to federal adjudication, such as *Colorado River*
abstention.[35]

The modern parity debate ensued when the Court began to express
its view that state courts were as competent as federal courts to adjudicate federal constitutional challenges and restricted federal court power
based on an assumption of parity.[36] As Professor Neuborne noted, "The
Supreme Court * * * presently seems bent on resolving forum allocation
decisions by assuming that no factors exist which render federal district
courts more effective than state trial or appellate courts for the enforcement of federal constitutional rights."[37] Professor Erwin Chemerinsky
suggested that the Court "profess[ed] parity to justify diverting cases to
state courts, which, the Court believed, would rule quite differently from
their federal counterparts."[38] Professor Herman posited the Court's willingness to tolerate some disparity at the expense of federal constitutional rights, "because this cost offsets what the Court perceives as the
enormous countervailing cost of not adequately respecting the values of
federalism."[39]

Professor Neuborne, an experienced constitutional litigator, generated academic debate when he urged that the importance of having constitutional claims heard by a "more sympathetic and competent forum"
be considered along with the traditional factors of judicial economy and
caseload when allocating business between state and federal courts. He
argued that federal courts, rather than state courts, were the appropriate forum to adjudicate federal constitutional rights and identified three
institutional characteristics of the federal judiciary responsible for federal superiority in adjudicating federal claims: 1) the greater prestige
and higher pay of federal judgeships, which helps to attract superior tal-
ent, 2) the long-standing federal tradition of upholding federal constitutional rights, and 3) the fact that federal judges enjoy lifetime tenure
and are thus shielded from public pressures when enforcing countermajoritarian rights (unlike state trial judges who must undergo periodic

---

[35] Chapter 8 discusses the abstention doctrines.

[36] *See, e.g.,* Stone v. Powell, 428 U.S. 465, 494 n.35, 96 S.Ct. 3037, 3052 n.35, 49
L.Ed.2d 1067, 1087 n.35 (1976) (noting that the Court was "unwilling to assume that there
now exists a general lack of appropriate sensitivity to constitutional rights in the trial and
appellate courts of the several States"); Huffman v. Pursue, Ltd., 420 U.S. 592, 611, 95
S.Ct. 1200, 1211, 43 L.Ed.2d 482, 496 (1975) (refusing to "base a rule on the assumption
that state judges will not be faithful to constitutional responsibilities).

[37] Burt Neuborne, *The Myth of Parity*, 90 HARV.L.REV. 1105, 1118 (1977).

[38] Erwin Chemerinsky, *Ending the Parity Debate*, 71 B.U.L.REV. 593, 598 (1991).

[39] Susan N. Herman, *Why Parity Matters*, 71 B.U.L.REV. 651, 655 (1991).

elections, thereby making them vulnerable to majoritarian pressure when deciding constitutional cases). These factors permitted Professor Neuborne to argue that institutional differences, not "bad faith," account for state judges being less likely than federal judges to resolve arguable issues in favor of protecting federal constitutional rights.[40]

Much has changed since the debate over parity emerged. Openly ideological appointments to the federal judiciary have altered the federal courts and, perhaps equally important, perceptions of the federal courts. Some state courts have emerged as champions of state constitutional jurisprudence, protecting individual rights at the state level as the Supreme Court has withdrawn federal constitutional protection. Eighteen years after *The Myth of Parity*, Professor Neuborne observed that ever since its publication, academicians have disputed "the existence of qualitative differences between state and federal courts and it has been impossible to resolve the dispute empirically, principally because no agreement exists about what we mean as better."[41]

ENDING THE PARITY DEBATE[c]
ERWIN CHEMERINSKY
71 B.U.L.REV. 593 (1991).

In the 1990s, parity seems a relic of an earlier time and a previous set of issues. First, there now is great uncertainty about how to compare the quality of federal and state courts. In the 1950s and 1960s, the desirability of courts enforcing desegregation orders and complying with Bill of Rights provisions was largely accepted in academic circles. But the standard for evaluating courts is now unsettled. More protection of individual liberties is hardly accepted as an unquestioned good: there is a deep division among scholars and on the bench as to the appropriate role for the judiciary. Even the desirability of rights as a concept has come under attack. Furthermore, if federal courts are more likely than state courts to protect individual liberties aggressively, there is no agreement that this is desirable. It is impossible to discuss parity without having some agreed upon baseline for comparison. Unfortunately, no baseline appears to exist.

Second, the domination of federal courts by judges appointed by Re-

---

[40] Professor Redish thinks the point beyond debate. "So many obvious, undisputed institutional differences between state and federal courts exist that one must truly close one's eyes to avoid seeing them." Martin H. Redish, *Judicial Parity, Litigant Choice, and Democratic Theory: A Comment on Federal Jurisdiction and Constitutional Rights*, 36 U.C.L.A.L.REV. 329, 332 (1988).

[41] Burt Neuborne, *Parity Revisited: The Uses of a Judicial Forum of Excellence*, 44 DEPAUL L.REV. 797, 798 (1995).

[c] Volume 71:4, Boston University Law Review (1991) 598-600. Reprinted with permission. Copyright © 1991 The Trustees of Boston University. Forum of original publication. Boston University bears no responsibility for any errors that have occurred in reproducing the article.

publican presidents undermines any basis for confidence in the federal bench as a source of systematic protection of individual liberties. More than half of the current federal judges were appointed by President Ronald Reagan. From 1968 until at least 1992, for twenty of twenty-four years, Republicans will have occupied the White House and selected federal judges. If the assumption of federal courts superiority stemmed, in part, from years of Democratic appointees, then this sustained period of Republican domination diminishes any basis for greater trust in federal courts.

Third, the differences between federal and state courts do not necessarily translate into decisions that are more protective of individual liberties. Most commentators appear to believe that the general quality of the federal bench is greater than the average quality of state judges. But there is no reason to believe that "better" judges will produce decisions that systematically favor individual rights. Jurists such as Justice Antonin Scalia and Ninth Circuit Judge Alex Kozinski are respected for their brilliance, but they hardly instill confidence that federal courts will protect individual rights more often than their state counterparts.

Nor does the greater independence of federal courts necessarily mean that state judges are more likely to compromise constitutional rights. Although all federal judges have life tenure, state court judges generally have some degree of insulation by virtue of features such as long terms, a tradition of non-partisanship and strong support for incumbent judges, and non-contested retention elections. A survey of twenty years of election data from 1964 to 1984 found that in 1,864 judicial elections, only twenty-two judges (1.2%) were defeated. Electoral accountability only undermines state judicial independence if state court judges fear that voters will use their decisions as the basis for casting their votes. But how many cases are of sufficient visibility to influence voters? Realistically, it is unlikely that many cases are decided differently because of fear of voter rejection at the next election. In fact, it appears that few voters are able to distinguish between judges in retention elections.

Fourth and finally, the analytical problems in demonstrating parity or the lack thereof seem insurmountable. * * * [P]arity is an empirical question—which court system will perform better at a particular task—for which no empirical answer is likely to exist. Additionally, the usefulness of any empirical answer is questionable. At best, data could provide an aggregate comparison of all state courts with all federal courts. State courts differ greatly from one another, however, and federal courts lack homogeneity as well. The parity question demands an overall comparison of the federal courts with the state courts. This comparison appears largely useless given the likelihood that on some issues, in some places, at some times, the federal courts will seem preferable for vindicating rights, while at other times and places the state courts will appear to be better. Absent marked overall differences between the systems, there is no reason to engage in a comparison.

All of the above suggests that the parity debate is futile and danger-ous. If the defense of federal court jurisdiction in constitutional rights cases rests on the assumption of federal court superiority, then there is little reason to preserve such jurisdiction if parity is assumed. This is not to suggest that Congress is likely to eliminate section 1331 or that the Court will gut it in the foreseeable future. Rather, emphasizing the parity issue poses a risk for those who believe in the availability of fed-eral courts for constitutional cases. The more the question is phrased in terms of parity, the more it seems that federal court jurisdiction should be based exclusively on this judgment. A meaningful approach to federal jurisdiction must transcend the focus on parity.

Perhaps so, but it is difficult to ignore the elephant in the room, and one might even posit that the appropriately zealous advocate cannot ethically ignore the real-world concerns upon which the parity debate focuses. As Professor Herman observed, "parity will continue to be an issue * * * because the issue arises every time a litigant chooses whether to raise a constitutional claim in federal or state court."[42] Professor Chemerinsky may be correct on a theoretical level that it would be better that the debate end, but there seems to be little doubt that it will con-tinue without resolution.

---

[42] Susan N. Herman, *Why Parity Matters*, 71 B.U.L.REV. 651, 662 (1991).

Chapter 1

JUSTICIABILITY

A. INTRODUCTION

"Justiciability" subsumes several doctrines that, like subject matter jurisdiction, are threshold doctrines. At the federal level, justiciability concerns in large part, though not exclusively, limitations on jurisdiction that flow from Article III's Case-or-Controversy Clause, which all but one of the doctrines implicate. Whether a particular piece of litigation constitutes a case or controversy depends on whether the parties are those appropriate to seek judicial intervention (standing), whether the dispute is sufficiently well-developed (ripeness) and not too far along (mootness) to justify resort to the courts, and whether there is a true practical dispute between the parties as opposed to a question of merely academic interest (advisory opinions). Only the political question doctrine cannot easily fit into the case-or-controversy mold.

Standing concerns whether the plaintiff is the appropriate person to present the dispute to the courts. For example, a bystander to an accident lacks standing to sue for the injuries suffered by one of the participants, even if he should undertake to pay all of the medical bills and lost wages of the injured party. Simply stating the focus of the doctrine of standing, however, masks a plethora of sub-issues that the Supreme Court has identified as contributing to the standing inquiry.

Ripeness involves whether a dispute has progressed far enough to make judicial review appropriate. For example, a married couple's challenge to an abortion-restricting statute is not ripe for adjudication unless the woman is pregnant, even if the woman should avoid pregnancy for medical reasons and even if the couple alleges the detrimental effect of having to choose between refraining from normal sexual relations or endangering the woman's health through a possible pregnancy.[1] The courts consider such a controversy too hypothetical and speculative to permit judicial review.

There are also two ways in which disputes can be "too ripe." The better-known manifestation of overripeness is the doctrine of mootness.[2]

---

[1] *See* Roe v. Wade, 410 U.S. 113, 127, 93 S.Ct. 705, 714, 35 L.Ed.2d 147, 163 (1973).

[2] The second example of "overripeness" does not involve justiciability, but inheres in the abstention doctrine of Younger v. Harris, 401 U.S. 37, 91 S.Ct. 746, 27 L.Ed.2d 669

There the dispute between the parties is stale; judicial intervention would no longer be useful. For example, an individual who wishes to raise an equal protection challenge seeking a declaration that the manner in which grand jury pools are selected in his county is unconstitutional might be unable to do so if the county voluntarily changes the practice of which he complains. However, the courts must be sensitive to two problems regarding mootness. First, a defendant may in bad faith seek to manipulate the doctrine, discontinuing a challenged practice when an action is filed but reinstituting it after the litigation is dismissed. Second, some problems are of such limited duration that judicial resolution cannot be obtained quickly enough. For example, if a pregnant woman wants to take an experimental drug during her pregnancy because she and her physician believe it promotes fetal health, and the government opposes its use, nine months may well elapse before the courts can resolve the controversy. If the woman and her physician seek to sue on behalf of the class of all women in that circumstance, should the court dismiss the case after she gives birth? If it does, no one is likely ever to be able to challenge the policy.

Finally, the political question doctrine causes the courts occasionally to refuse to adjudicate disputes because the Constitution commits their resolution to other branches of government or because the Court determines that the other branches are better suited to resolve them. Historically, such cases have included questions of whether a particular state government complies with the requirements of the Guaranty Clause,[3] whether questions of legislative apportionment are justiciable,[4] whether the United States may fund and participate in an undeclared war,[5] and whether the Senate has constitutionally conducted an impeachment trial.[6]

(1971), discussed in Chapter 8. A dispute between an individual and a state government about the constitutionality of a criminal statute may be insufficiently ripe to permit adjudication if the individual has no reason to suspect imminent enforcement of the statute against him, but too ripe if he has already been arrested under the statute. In such a circumstance, the federal courts must abstain from adjudicating the dispute regarding the statute's unconstitutionality in favor of resolution of that issue in the state courts, with possible ultimate review in the Supreme Court. In this sense, ripeness acts as a forum selector rather than as a determinant of the propriety of judicial review.

[3] U.S. CONST. art. IV, § 4. *See* Luther v. Borden, 48 U.S. (7 How.) 1, 12 L.Ed. 581 (1849).

[4] *See, e.g.,* Baker v. Carr, 369 U.S. 186, 82 S.Ct. 691, 7 L.Ed.2d 663 (1962); Colegrove v. Green, 328 U.S. 549, 66 S.Ct. 1198, 90 L.Ed. 1432 (1946). *Baker,* discussed more fully at page 159, is particularly interesting because while it reaffirmed *Colegrove*'s holding that apportionment questions are nonjusticiable under the Guaranty Clause, it held that they are justiciable as equal protection matters.

[5] *See* Crockett v. Reagan, 720 F.2d 1355 (D.C.Cir.1983) (constitutionality of United States' assistance to El Salvador); DaCosta v. Laird, 471 F.2d 1146 (2d Cir.1973) (constitutionality of aerial operations in Cambodia); Head v. Nixon, 342 F.Supp. 521 (E.D.La.), *affirmed* 468 F.2d 951 (5th Cir.1972) (constitutionality of Vietnam war generally).

[6] Nixon v. United States, 506 U.S. 224, 113 S.Ct. 732, 122 L.Ed.2d 1 (1993). *Nixon* appears as the principal case in Section F of this Chapter, at page 144.

B.   ADVISORY OPINIONS

The first specific mentions of advisory opinions appear in a famous letter from then-Secretary of State Thomas Jefferson to the Supreme Court and the Court's subsequent reply to President Washington, on whose behalf Jefferson had written.[7] Washington and Jefferson clearly entertained doubts about the propriety of the Court acting in such a manner.

> Gentlemen:
>
> The war which has taken place among the powers of Europe produces frequent transactions within our ports and limits, on which questions arise of considerable difficulty, and of greater importance to the peace of the United States. These questions depend for their solution on the construction of our treaties, on the laws of nature and nations, and on the laws of the land, and are often presented under circumstances *which do not give a cognisance of them to the tribunals of the country.* Yet their decision is so little analogous to the ordinary functions of the executive, as to occasion much embarrassment and difficulty to them. The President therefore would be much relieved if he found himself free to refer questions of this description to the opinions of the judges of the Supreme Court of the United States, whose knowledge of the subject would secure as against errors dangerous to the peace of the United States, and their authority to insure the respect of all parties. He has therefore asked the attendance of such of the judges as could be collected in time for the occasion, to know, in the first place, their opinion, whether the public may, with propriety, be availed of their *advice on these questions?* And if they may, to present, for their advice, the abstract questions which have already occurred, or may soon occur, from which they will themselves strike out such as any circumstance might, in their opinion, forbid them to pronounce on. I have the honour to be with sentiments of the most perfect respect, gentlemen, Your most obedient and humble servant * * * .

Chief Justice Jay's response to President Washington confirmed Washington's and Jefferson's suspicions about the Court's limited role.

> Sir:
>
> We have considered the previous question stated in a letter written by your direction to us by the Secretary of State on the 18th of last month, [regarding] the lines of separation drawn by the Constitution between the three departments of the government. These being in certain respects checks upon each other, and our being judges of a court in the last resort, are considerations which afford

---

[7] III THE CORRESPONDENCE AND PUBLIC PAPERS OF JOHN JAY 1763–1826 486-87 (Henry P. Johnston ed. 1971).

strong arguments against the propriety of our extra-judicially deciding the questions alluded to, especially as the power given by the Constitution to the President, of calling on the heads of departments for opinions, seems to have been *purposely* as well as expressly united to the *executive* departments.

We exceedingly regret every event that may cause embarrassment to your administration, but we derive consolation from the reflection that your judgment will discern what is right, and that your usual prudence, decision, and firmness will surmount every obstacle to the preservation of the rights, peace, and dignity of the United States.

We have the honour to be, with perfect respect, sir, your most obedient and humble servants.

The Court thus refused, as a matter of separation of powers, to permit itself to be drawn by request into the decision of questions that apparently could not assume ordinary judicial form.[8]

One might disapprove of advisory opinions either as a matter of constitutional imperative or in the view that they are bad policy. The Supreme Court has repeatedly linked advisory opinions with the Case-or-Controversy Clause, leaving little doubt that the prohibition is constitutionally based.[9] Moreover, the Court has made clear that the Case-or-Controversy Clause helps to implement the more general principle of separation of powers by keeping the courts from addressing problems in the absence of a specific, limited conflict, much as the legislative and executive branches do. *See Flast v. Cohen,* 392 U.S. 83, 88 S.Ct. 1942, 20 L.Ed.2d 947 (1968). The federal courts thus avoid general, prescriptive pronouncements thought to be more appropriate for the other branches, simultaneously avoiding entanglement in the workings of the other branches and preserving their own independence and legitimacy.

The Jefferson-Jay correspondence involved "pure advice seeking" by the executive from the judiciary. Congress, from time to time, endeavors to authorize particular forms of cases in traditional judicial form, but the Court has not always been willing to permit adjudication in such circum-

---

[8] Some have suggested that that is a small set of questions indeed. *See, e.g.,* ALEXIS DE TOCQUEVILLE, DEMOCRACY IN AMERICA 207 (Henry Steele Commager ed. 1965) ("Scarcely any question arises in the United States which does not become, sooner or later, a subject of judicial debate.").

[9] *See, e.g.,* City of Los Angeles v. Lyons, 461 U.S. 95, 129 n. 20, 103 S.Ct. 1660, 1680 n. 20, 75 L.Ed.2d 675, 710 n. 20 (1983) ("[A] court must have the power to fashion some appropriate remedy. This concern, an aspect of the more general case or controversy requirement, reflects the view that the adjudication of rights which a court is powerless to enforce is tantamount to an advisory opinion.") *See also* New York State Club Association, Inc. v. City of New York, 487 U.S. 1, 8 n. 2, 108 S.Ct. 2225, 2231 n. 2, 101 L.Ed.2d 1, 13 n. 2 (1988); Flast v. Cohen, 392 U.S. 83, 96 n. 14, 88 S.Ct. 1942, 1950 n. 14, 20 L.Ed.2d 947, 959 n. 14 (1968).

stances. In 1792, a congressional scheme called for the federal courts to make preliminary findings and recommendations to the Secretary of War about disability benefits to be paid to Revolutionary War veterans. The Secretary was authorized to disregard the courts' findings. Although the Supreme Court itself did not expressly hold the statute unconstitutional, five of the Court's six Justices, serving as Circuit Court judges, found that the scheme violated separation of powers because it subjected individual judicial actions to review and revision by executive officials. *Hayburn's Case*, 2 U.S. (2 Dall.) 408, 1 L.Ed. 436 (1792). The decisions in *Hayburn's Case* and in more recent cases have been taken to signify that a case is not justiciable unless the judiciary's decision will have final, not merely preliminary, effect. Moreover, when a case is justiciable, the finality principle means that Congress cannot reverse the final decision by the judicial branch by mandating a new judicial proceeding with a different result. *See Plaut v. Spendthrift Farm, Inc.*, 514 U.S. 211, 115 S.Ct. 1447, 131 L.Ed.2d 328 (1995), at page 199. The Judiciary has the power not only to consider cases, but also to decide them dispositively. The next logical step was for Congress to attempt to create and authorize a case in traditional judicial form in which the judicial decision *would* be final. Such an attempt resulted in the following case.

MUSKRAT v. UNITED STATES
Supreme Court of the United States, 1911.
219 U.S. 346, 31 S.Ct. 250, 55 L.Ed. 246.

MR. JUSTICE DAY delivered the opinion of the Court:

These cases arise under an act of Congress undertaking to confer jurisdiction upon the court of claims, and upon this Court, on appeal, to determine the validity of certain acts of Congress hereinafter referred to.

Case No. 330 was brought by David Muskrat and J. Henry Dick, in their own behalf, and in behalf of others in a like situation, to determine the constitutional validity of the act of Congress of April 26, 1906 and to have the same declared invalid in so far as the same undertook to increase the number of persons entitled to share in the final distribution of lands and funds of the Cherokees beyond those enrolled on September 1, 1902, in accordance with the act of Congress passed July 1, 1902. The acts subsequent to that of July 1, 1902, have the effect to increase the number of persons entitled to participate in the division of the Cherokee lands and funds, by permitting the enrolment of children who were minors, living on March 4, 1906, whose parents had theretofore been enrolled as members of the Cherokee tribe, or had applications pending for that purpose.

Case No. 331 was brought by Brown and Gritts on their own behalf and on behalf of other Cherokee citizens having a like interest in the property allotted under the act of July 1, 1902. Under this act, Brown and Gritts received allotments. The subsequent act of March 11, 1904 empowered the Secretary of the Interior to grant rights of way for pipe lines over lands allotted to Indians under certain regulations. Another act purported to extend to a period of twenty-five years the time within which full-blooded Indians of the Cherokee, Choctaw, Chickasaw, Creek, and Seminole tribes were forbidden to alienate, sell, dispose of, or encumber certain of their lands.

The object of the petition of Brown and Gritts was to have the subsequent legislation of 1904 and 1906 declared to be unconstitutional and void, and to have the lands allotted to them under the original act of July 1, 1902, adjudged to be theirs free from restraints upon the rights to sell and convey the same. From this statement it is apparent that the purpose of the proceedings instituted in the court of claims, and now appealed to this Court, is to restrain the enforcement of such legislation subsequent to the act of July 1, 1902, upon the ground that the same is unconstitutional and void. The court of claims sustained the validity of the acts and dismissed the petitions.

These proceedings were begun under the supposed authority of an act of Congress passed March 1, 1907 (a part of the Indian appropriation bill). As that legislation is important in this connection, so much of the act as authorized the beginning of these suits is here inserted in full:

> That William Brown and Levi B. Gritts, on their own behalf and on behalf of all other Cherokee citizens, having like interests in the property allotted under the act of July first, nineteen hundred and two, entitled, "An Act to Provide for the Allotment of Lands of the Cherokee Nation, for the Disposition of Town Sites Therein, and for Other Purposes," and David Muskrat and J. Henry Dick, on their own behalf, and on behalf of all Cherokee citizens enrolled as such for allotment as of September first, nineteen hundred and two, be, and they are hereby, authorized and empowered to institute their suits in the court of claims to determine the validity of any acts of Congress passed since the said act of July first, nineteen hundred and two, in so far as said acts, or any of them, attempt to increase or extend the restrictions upon alienation, encumbrance, or the right to lease the allotments of lands of Cherokee citizens, or to increase the number of persons entitled to share in the final distribution of lands and funds of the Cherokees beyond those enrolled for allotment as of September first, nineteen hundred and two, and provided for in the said act of July first, nineteen hundred and two.

> And jurisdiction is hereby conferred upon the court of claims, with the right of appeal, by either party, to the Supreme Court of the United States, to hear, determine, and adjudicate each of said suits.

> The suits brought hereunder shall be brought on or before September first, nineteen hundred and seven, against the United States as a party defendant, and, for the speedy disposition of the

questions involved, preference shall be given to the same by said courts, and by the Attorney General, who is hereby charged with the defense of said suits.

Upon the rendition of final judgment by the court of claims or the Supreme Court of the United States, denying the validity of any portion of the said acts authorized to be brought into question, in either or both of said cases, the court of claims shall determine the amount to be paid the attorneys employed by the above-named parties in the prosecution thereof for services and expenses, and shall render judgment therefor, which shall be paid out of the funds in the United States Treasury belonging to the beneficiaries, under the said act of July first, nineteen hundred and two.

This act is the authority for the maintenance of these two suits.

The first question in these cases, as in others, involves the jurisdiction of the Court to entertain the proceeding, and that depends upon whether the jurisdiction conferred is within the power of Congress, having in view the limitations of the judicial power, as established by the Constitution of the United States.

* * *

The subject underwent a complete examination [when] * * * an act of Congress was held invalid which undertook to confer jurisdiction upon the court of claims, and thence by appeal to this Court, the judgment, however, not to be paid until an appropriation had been estimated therefor by the Secretary of the Treasury; and * * * the result was that neither court could enforce its judgment by any process, and whether it was to be paid or not depended on the future action of the Secretary of the Treasury and of Congress. "The Supreme Court," says the Chief Justice,

does not owe its existence or its powers to the legislative department of the government. It is created by the Constitution, and represents one of the three great divisions of power in the government of the United States, to each of which the Constitution has assigned its appropriate duties and powers, and made each independent of the other in performing its appropriate functions. The power conferred on this Court is exclusively judicial, and it cannot be required or authorized to exercise any other.

* * *

It therefore becomes necessary to inquire what is meant by the judicial power thus conferred by the Constitution upon this Court, and, with the aid of appropriate legislation, upon the inferior courts of the United States. "Judicial power," says Mr. Justice Miller, in his work on the Constitution, "is the power of a court to decide and pronounce a judgment and carry it into effect between persons and parties who bring a case before it for decision."

As we have already seen, by the express terms of the Constitution, the exercise of the judicial power is limited to "cases" and "controversies." Beyond this it does not extend, and unless it is asserted in a case or controversy within the meaning of the Constitution, the power to exercise it is nowhere conferred.

What, then, does the Constitution mean in conferring this judicial power with the right to determine "cases" and "controversies." A "case" was defined by Mr. Chief Justice Marshall as early as the leading case of *Marbury v. Madison* to be a suit instituted according to the regular course of judicial procedure. And what more, if anything, is meant in the use of the term "controversy?" That question was dealt with by Mr. Justice Field, at the circuit. Of these terms that learned justice said:

> The judicial article of the Constitution mentions cases and controversies. The term "controversies," if distinguishable at all from "cases," is so in that it is less comprehensive than the latter, and includes only suits of a civil nature. By cases and controversies are intended the claims of litigants brought before the courts for determination by such regular proceedings as are established by law or custom for the protection or enforcement of rights, or the prevention, redress, or punishment of wrongs. Whenever the claim of a party under the Constitution, laws, or treaties of the United States takes such a form that the judicial power is capable of acting upon it, then it has become a case. The term implies the existence of present or possible adverse parties, whose contentions are submitted to the court for adjudication.

The power being thus limited to require an application of the judicial power to cases and controversies, Is the act which undertook to authorize the present suits to determine the constitutional validity of certain legislation within the constitutional authority of the court? This inquiry in the case before us includes the broader question, When may this Court, in the exercise of the judicial power, pass upon the constitutional validity of an act of Congress? That question has been settled from the early history of the Court, the leading case on the subject being *Marbury v. Madison.*

In that case Chief Justice Marshall, who spoke for the Court, was careful to point out that the right to declare an act of Congress unconstitutional could only be exercised when a proper case between opposing parties was submitted for judicial determination; that there was no general veto power in the Court upon the legislation of Congress; and that the authority to declare an act unconstitutional sprang from the requirement that the Court, in administering the law and pronouncing judgment between the parties to a case, and choosing between the requirements of the fundamental law established by the people and embodied in the Constitution and an act of the agents of the people, acting under authority of the Constitution, should enforce the Constitution as the supreme law of the land. The Chief Justice demonstrated, in a manner which has been regarded as settling the question, that with the choice thus given between a constitutional requirement and a conflicting statutory enactment, the plain duty of the Court was to follow and enforce the Constitution as the supreme law established by the people. And the Court recognized, in *Marbury v. Madison* and subsequent cases, that the exercise of this great power could only be invoked in cases which came regularly before the courts for determination * * * .

Again, in the case of *Cohen v. Virginia,* Chief Justice Marshall, amplifying and reasserting the doctrine of *Marbury v. Madison,* recognized the limitations upon the right of this Court to declare an act of Congress unconstitutional, and granting that there might be instances of its violation which could not be brought within the jurisdiction of the courts, and referring to a grant by a state of a patent of nobility as a case of that class, and conceding that the Court would have no power to annul such a grant, said:

> This may be very true; but by no means justifies the inference drawn from it. The article does not extend the judicial power to every violation of the Constitution which may possibly take place, but to "a case in law or equity" in which a right under such law is asserted in a court of justice. If the question cannot be brought into a court, then there is no case in law or equity, and no jurisdiction is given by the words of the article. But if, in any controversy depending in a court, the cause should depend on the validity of such a law, that would be a case arising under the Constitution, to which the judicial power of the United States would extend.

* * *

Applying the principles thus long settled by the decisions of this Court to the act of Congress undertaking to confer jurisdiction in this case, we find that William Brown and Levi B. Gritts * * * are authorized and empowered to institute suits in the court of claims to determine the validity of acts of Congress passed since the act of July 1, 1902 * * * .

The jurisdiction was given for that purpose first to the Court of Claims, and then upon appeal to this Court. That is, the object and purpose of the suit is wholly comprised in the determination of the constitutional validity of certain acts of Congress; and furthermore, in the last paragraph of the section, should a judgment be rendered in the Court of Claims or this Court, denying the constitutional validity of such acts, then the amount of compensation to be paid to attorneys employed for the purpose of testing the constitutionality of the law is to be paid out of funds in the Treasury of the United States belonging to the beneficiaries, the act having previously provided that the United States should be made a party, and the Attorney General be charged with the defense of the suits.

It is therefore evident that there is neither more nor less in this procedure than an attempt to provide for a judicial determination, final in this Court, of the constitutional validity of an act of Congress. Is such a determination within the judicial power conferred by the Constitution, as the same has been interpreted and defined in the authoritative decisions to which we have referred? We think it is not. That judicial power, as we have seen, is the right to determine actual controversies arising between adverse litigants, duly instituted in courts of proper jurisdiction. The right to declare a law unconstitutional arises because an act of Congress relied upon by one or the other of such parties in determining their rights is in conflict with the fundamental law. The exercise of this, the most important and delicate duty of this Court, is not given to it as a body with revisory power over the action of Congress, but because the rights of the litigants in justiciable controversies require the court to choose between the fundamental law and a law purporting to be enacted within constitutional authority, but in fact beyond the power delegated to the legislative branch of the government. This attempt to obtain a judicial declaration of the validity of the act of Congress is not presented in a "case" or "controversy," to which, under the Constitution of the United States, the judicial power alone extends. It is true the United States is made a defendant to this action, but it has no interest adverse to the claimants. The object is not to assert a property right as against the government, or to demand compensation for alleged wrongs because of action upon its part. The whole purpose of the law is to determine the constitutional validity of this class of legislation, in a suit not arising between parties concerning a property right necessarily involved in the decision in question, but in a proceeding against the government in its sovereign capacity, and concerning which the only judgment required is to settle the doubtful character of the legislation in question. Such judgment will not conclude private parties, when actual litigation brings to the court the question of the constitutionality of such legislation. In a legal sense the judgment could not be executed, and amounts in fact to no more than an expression of opinion upon the validity of the acts in question. Confining the jurisdiction of this Court within the limitations conferred by the Constitution, which the Court has hitherto been careful to observe, and whose boundaries it has refused to transcend, we think the Congress, in the act of March 1, 1907, exceeded the limitations of legislative authority, so far as it required of this Court action not judicial in its nature within the meaning of the Constitution.

Nor can it make any difference that the petitioners had brought suits in the supreme court of the District of Columbia to enjoin the Secretary of the Interior from carrying into effect the legislation subsequent to the act of July 1, 1902, which suits were pending when the jurisdictional act here involved was passed. The latter act must depend upon its own terms and be judged by the authority which it undertakes to confer. If such actions as are here attempted, to determine the validity of legislation, are sustained, the result will be that this Court, instead of keeping within the limits of judicial power, and deciding cases or controversies arising between opposing parties, as the Constitution intended it should, will be required to give opinions in the nature of advice concerning legislative action,—a function never conferred upon it by the Constitution, and against the exercise of which this Court has steadily set its face from the beginning.

The questions involved in this proceeding as to the validity of the legislation may arise in suits between individuals, and when they do and are properly brought before this Court for consideration they, of course, must be determined in the exercise of its judicial functions. For the reasons we have stated, we are constrained to hold that these actions present no justiciable controversy within the authority of the Court, acting within the limitations of the Constitution under which it was created. As Congress, in passing this act, as a part of the plan involved, evidently intended to provide a review of the judgment of the court of claims in this Court, as the constitutionality of important legislation is concerned, we think the act cannot be held to intend to confer jurisdiction on that court separately considered.

The judgments will be reversed and the cases remanded to the Court of Claims, with directions to dismiss the petitions for want of jurisdiction.

Notes and Questions

1. Does the Court suggest that the constitutional questions the plaintiffs sought to litigate would be justiciable in a suit with the proper parties? Does that mean that if only Congress had designated the correct defendants the case could have gone forward? Could Congress have done that?

2. Does Congress's goal here differ in any substantial way from what a declaratory judgment seeks to accomplish? If the federal Declaratory Judgment Act (not enacted until 1934) had been in effect in 1911, could the Court have entertained an action to determine the constitutionality of the post-1902 legislation? If so, then did the Court here create a distinction without a difference? If not, then is the Declaratory Judgment Act unconstitutional?

3. Early opinion thought declaratory judgments presented insurmountable constitutional problems because they "looked" advisory.[10] In one of the first cases involving a declaratory judgment, the Michigan Supreme Court reacted harshly not just to the friendly nature of the suit (in which the defendant admitted all of the allegations of the plaintiff's complaint), but to the declaratory judgment device itself, declaring the Michigan Declaratory Judgment Act unconstitutional. *See Anway v. Grand Rapids Railway,* 211 Mich. 592, 179 N.W. 350 (1920). A trio of United States Supreme Court cases in the late 1920's also viewed declaratory judgments as inherently violating federal constitutional limitations. The Court reversed itself five years

---

[10] There was also concern that such disputes were not ripe. Note 3 at page 105 discusses this aspect of declaratory judgments.

later, repudiating what it referred to as the "denunciatory dicta" of the earlier cases, and eventually ruled that the Declaratory Judgment Act of 1934 was constitutional. *See Aetna Life Ins. Co. v. Haworth,* 300 U.S. 227, 57 S.Ct. 461, 81 L.Ed. 617 (1937).

4. It would be a mistake to conclude that any congressional attempt to authorize judicial review of particular matters is necessarily void as seeking an advisory opinion. In *South Carolina v. Katzenbach,* 383 U.S. 301, 86 S.Ct. 803, 15 L.Ed.2d 769 (1966), the state challenged several provisions of the Voting Rights Act of 1964, particularly one that automatically suspended state voting regulations enacted after November 1, 1964, until approval by the United States Attorney General or a declaratory judgment by the United States District Court for the District of Columbia that the new regulations did not violate the Fifteenth Amendment. Section 5 of the Act authorized such declaratory judgments actions. Georgia, appearing *amicus curiae,* argued that the provision sought to authorize advisory opinions and therefore violated Article III. The Court disagreed.

> Nor has Congress authorized the District Court to issue advisory opinions, in violation of the principles of Article III * * * . The Act automatically suspends the operation of voting regulations enacted after November 1, 1964, and furnishes mechanisms for enforcing the suspension. A State or political subdivision wishing to make use of a recent amendment to its voting laws therefore has a concrete and immediate "controversy" with the Federal Government.

Does the Court's approach in *South Carolina v. Katzenbach* suggest alternative strategies for Congress in a situation like that in *Muskrat?*

5. One of the difficulties presented by the prohibition against advisory opinions is that such opinions can arise very subtly. For example, it may not be immediately obvious that a case from a state's highest court being reviewed by the United States Supreme Court raises the possibility of an advisory opinion if it contains both federal and state grounds that might support the judgment. Yet the Supreme Court routinely has held that to be the case. Chapter 9 covers this aspect of the advisory opinion doctrine more fully.

C. STANDING

ALLEN v. WRIGHT
Supreme Court of the United States, 1984.
468 U.S. 737, 104 S.Ct. 3315, 82 L.Ed.2d 556.

JUSTICE O'CONNOR delivered the opinion of the Court.

Parents of black public school children allege in this nationwide class action that the Internal Revenue Service (IRS) has not adopted sufficient standards and procedures to fulfill its obligation to deny tax-exempt status to racially discriminatory private schools. They assert that the IRS thereby harms them directly and interferes with the ability of their children to receive an education in desegregated public schools. The issue before us is whether plaintiffs have standing to bring this suit. We hold that they do not.

I

The Internal Revenue Service denies tax-exempt status * * * and hence eligibility to receive charitable contributions deductible from income taxes to racially discriminatory private schools. The IRS policy requires that a school applying for tax-exempt status show that it "admits the students of any race to all the rights, privileges, programs, and activities generally accorded or made available to students at that school and that the school does not discriminate on the basis of race in administration of its educational policies, admissions policies, scholarship and loan programs, and athletic and other school-administered programs." To carry out this policy, the IRS has established guidelines and procedures for determining whether a particular school is in fact racially nondiscriminatory. Failure to comply with the guidelines "will ordinarily result in the proposed revocation of" tax-exempt status.

* * *

The IRS rules require a school applying for tax-exempt status to give a breakdown along racial lines of its student body and its faculty and administrative staff, as well as of scholarships and loans awarded. They also require the applicant school to state the year of its organization, and to list "incorporators, founders, board members, and donors of land or buildings," and state whether any of the organizations among these have an objective of maintaining segregated public or private school education. The rules further provide that, once given an exemption, a school must keep specified records to document the extent of compliance with the IRS guidelines. Finally, the rules announce that any information concerning discrimination at a tax-exempt school is officially welcomed.

In 1976 respondents challenged these guidelines and procedures in a suit filed in Federal District Court against the Secretary of the Treasury and the Commissioner of Internal Revenue. The plaintiffs named in the complaint are parents of black children who, at the time the complaint was filed, were attending public schools in seven States in school districts undergoing desegregation. They brought this nationwide class action "on behalf of themselves and their children, and * * * on behalf of all other parents of black children attending public school systems undergoing, or which may in the future undergo, desegregation pursuant to court order [or] HEW regulations and guidelines, under state law, or voluntarily." They estimated that the class they seek to represent includes several million persons.

Respondents allege in their complaint that many racially segregated private schools were created or expanded in their communities at the time the public schools were undergoing desegregation. According to the complaint, many such private schools, including 17 schools or school systems identified by name in the complaint (perhaps some 30 schools in all), receive tax exemptions either directly or through the tax-exempt status of "umbrella" organizations that operate or support the schools. Respondents allege that, despite the IRS policy of denying tax-exempt status to racially discriminatory private schools and despite the IRS guidelines and procedures for implementing that policy, some of the tax-exempt racially segregated private schools created or expanded in desegregating districts in fact have racially discriminatory policies. Respondents allege that the IRS grant of tax exemptions to such racially discriminatory schools is unlawful.

Respondents allege that the challenged Government conduct harms them in two ways. The challenged conduct

> (a) constitutes tangible federal financial aid and other support for racially segregated educational institutions, and

> (b) fosters and encourages the organization, operation and expansion of institutions providing racially segregated educational opportunities for white children avoiding attendance in desegregating public school districts and thereby interferes with the efforts of federal courts, HEW and local school authorities to desegregate public school districts which have been operating racially dual school systems.

Thus, respondents do not allege that their children have been the victims of discriminatory exclusion from the schools whose tax exemptions they challenge as unlawful. Indeed, they have not alleged at any stage of this litigation that their children have ever applied or would ever apply to any private school. Rather, respondents claim a direct injury from the mere fact of the challenged Government conduct and, as indicated by the restriction of the plaintiff class to parents of children in desegregating school districts, injury to their children's opportunity to receive a desegregated education. The latter injury is traceable to the IRS grant of tax exemptions to racially discriminatory schools, respondents allege, chiefly because contributions to such schools are deductible from income taxes and the "deductions facilitate the raising of funds to organize new schools and expand existing schools in order to accommodate white students avoiding attendance in desegregating public school districts."

Respondents request only prospective relief. They ask for a declaratory judgment that the challenged IRS tax-exemption practices are unlawful. They also ask for an injunction requiring the IRS to deny tax exemptions to a considerably broader class of private schools than the class of racially discriminatory private schools. Under the requested injunction, the IRS would have to deny tax-exempt status to all private schools

> which have insubstantial or nonexistent minority enrollments, which are located in or serve desegregating public school districts,

and which either—

(1) were established or expanded at or about the time the public school districts in which they are located or which they serve were desegregating;

(2) have been determined in adversary judicial or administrative proceedings to be racially segregated; or

(3) cannot demonstrate that they do not provide racially segregated educational opportunities for white children avoiding attendance in desegregating public school systems.

Finally, respondents ask for an order directing the IRS to replace its 1975 guidelines with standards consistent with the requested injunction.

* * * The District Court * * * granted the defendants' motion to dismiss the complaint, concluding that respondents lack standing, that the judicial task proposed by respondents is inappropriately intrusive for a federal court, and that awarding the requested relief would be contrary to the will of Congress expressed in the 1979 ban on strengthening IRS guidelines.

The United States Court of Appeals for the District of Columbia reversed, concluding that respondents have standing to maintain this lawsuit. The court acknowledged that *Simon v. Eastern Kentucky Welfare Rights Org.* "suggests that litigation concerning tax liability is a matter between taxpayer and IRS, with the door barely ajar for third party challenges." The court concluded, however, that the *Simon* case is inapposite because respondents claim no injury dependent on taxpayers' actions: "[t]hey claim indifference as to the course private schools would take." Instead, the court observed, "[t]he sole injury [respondents] claim is the denigration they suffer as black parents and schoolchildren when their government graces with tax-exempt status educational institutions in their communities that treat members of their race as persons of lesser worth." The court held this denigration injury enough to give respondents standing * * *. The court accordingly remanded the case to the District Court for further proceedings, enjoining the defendants meanwhile from granting tax-exempt status to any racially discriminatory school.

* * * We granted certiorari, and now reverse.

II

A

Article III of the Constitution confines the federal courts to adjudicating actual "cases" and "controversies." As the Court [has] explained, the "case or controversy" requirement defines with respect to the Judicial Branch the idea of separation of powers on which the Federal Government is founded. The several doctrines that have grown up to elaborate that requirement are "founded in concern about the proper—and properly limited—role of the courts in a democratic society."

> All of the doctrines that cluster about Article III—not only standing but mootness, ripeness, political question, and the like—relate in part, and in different though overlapping ways, to an idea, which is more than an intuition but less than a rigorous and explicit theory, about the constitutional and prudential limits to the powers of an unelected, unrepresentative judiciary in our kind of government.

Vander Jagt v. O'Neill, 699 F.2d 1166, 1178-79 (1983) (Bork, J., concurring). The case-or-controversy doctrines state fundamental limits on federal judicial power in our system of government.

The Art. III doctrine that requires a litigant to have "standing" to invoke the power of a federal court is perhaps the most important of these doctrines. "In essence the question of standing is whether the litigant is entitled to have the court decide the merits of the dispute or of particular issues." Standing doctrine embraces several judicially self-imposed limits on the exercise of federal jurisdiction, such as the general prohibition on a litigant's raising another person's legal rights, the rule barring adjudication of generalized grievances more appropriately addressed in the representative branches, and the requirement that a plaintiff's complaint fall within the zone of interests protected by the law invoked. The requirement of standing, however, has a core component derived directly from the Constitution. A plaintiff must allege personal injury fairly traceable to the defendant's allegedly unlawful conduct and likely to be redressed by the requested relief.

Like the prudential component, the constitutional component of standing doctrine incorporates concepts concededly not susceptible of precise definition. The injury alleged must be, for example, " 'distinct and palpable,' " and not "abstract" or "conjectural" or "hypothetical." The injury must be "fairly" traceable to the challenged action, and relief from the injury must be "likely" to follow from a favorable decision. These terms cannot be defined so as to make application of the constitutional standing requirement a mechanical exercise.

* * * [T]he law of Art. III standing is built on a single basic idea—the idea of separation of powers. It is this fact which makes possible the gradual clarification of the law through judicial application. * * *

* * * Typically, * * * the standing inquiry requires careful judicial examination of a complaint's allegations to ascertain whether the particular plaintiff is entitled to an adjudication of the particular claims asserted. Is the injury too abstract, or otherwise not appropriate, to be considered judicially cognizable? Is the line of causation between the illegal conduct and injury too attenuated? Is the prospect of obtaining relief from the injury as a result of a favorable ruling too speculative? These questions and any others relevant to the standing inquiry must be

answered by reference to the Art. III notion that federal courts may exercise power only "in the last resort, and as a necessity," and only when adjudication is "consistent with a system of separated powers and [the dispute is one] traditionally thought to be capable of resolution through the judicial process."

B

Respondents allege two injuries in their complaint to support their standing to bring this lawsuit. First, they say that they are harmed directly by the mere fact of Government financial aid to discriminatory private schools. Second, they say that the federal tax exemptions to racially discriminatory private schools in their communities impair their ability to have their public schools desegregated.

In the Court of Appeals, respondents apparently relied on the first injury. Thus, the court below asserted that "[t]he sole injury [respondents] claim is the denigration they suffer" as a result of the tax exemptions. In this Court, respondents have not focused on this claim of injury. Here they stress the effect of the tax exemptions on their "equal educational opportunities," renewing reliance on the second injury described in their complaint.

Because respondents have not clearly disclaimed reliance on either of the injuries described in their complaint, we address both allegations of injury. We conclude that neither suffices to support respondents' standing. The first fails under clear precedents of this Court because it does not constitute judicially cognizable injury. The second fails because the alleged injury is not fairly traceable to the assertedly unlawful conduct of the IRS.[19]

1

Respondents' first claim of injury can be interpreted in two ways. It might be a claim simply to have the Government avoid the violation of law alleged in respondents' complaint. Alternatively, it might be a claim of stigmatic injury, or denigration, suffered by all members of a racial group when the Government discriminates on the basis of race. Under neither interpretation is this claim of injury judicially cognizable.

---

[19] The "fairly traceable" and "redressability" components of the constitutional standing inquiry were initially articulated by this Court as "two facets of a single causation requirement." C. WRIGHT, LAW OF FEDERAL COURTS § 13, at 68 n.43 (4th ed. 1983). To the extent there is a difference, it is that the former examines the causal connection between the assertedly unlawful conduct and the alleged injury, whereas the latter examines the causal connection between the alleged injury and the judicial relief requested. Cases such as this, in which the relief requested goes well beyond the violation of law alleged, illustrate why it is important to keep the inquiries separate if the "redressability" component is to focus on the requested relief. Even if the relief respondents request might have a substantial effect on the desegregation of public schools, whatever deficiencies exist in the opportunities for desegregated education for respondents' children might not be traceable to IRS violations of law—grants of tax exemptions to racially discriminatory schools in respondents' communities.

This Court has repeatedly held that an asserted right to have the Government act in accordance with law is not sufficient, standing alone, to confer jurisdiction on a federal court. [T]he Court rejected a claim of citizen standing to challenge Armed Forces Reserve commissions held by Members of Congress as violating the Incompatibility Clause of Art. I, § 6, cl. 2, of the Constitution. As citizens, the Court held, plaintiffs alleged nothing but "the abstract injury in nonobservance of the Constitution * * *." More recently, we rejected a claim of standing to challenge a Government conveyance of property to a religious institution. Insofar as the plaintiffs relied simply on " 'their shared individuated right' " to a Government that made no law respecting an establishment of religion, we held that plaintiffs had not alleged a judicially cognizable injury. "[A]ssertion of a right to a particular kind of Government conduct, which the Government has violated by acting differently, cannot alone satisfy the requirements of Art. III without draining those requirements of meaning." Respondents here have no standing to complain simply that their Government is violating the law.

Neither do they have standing to litigate their claims based on the stigmatizing injury often caused by racial discrimination. There can be no doubt that this sort of noneconomic injury is one of the most serious consequences of discriminatory government action and is sufficient in some circumstances to support standing. Our cases make clear, however, that such injury accords a basis for standing only to "those persons who are personally denied equal treatment" by the challenged discriminatory conduct.

[T]he Court [has] held that the plaintiff had no standing to challenge a club's racially discriminatory membership policies because he had never applied for membership. [T]he Court [has also] held that the plaintiffs had no standing to challenge racial discrimination in the administration of their city's criminal justice system because they had not alleged that they had been or would likely be subject to the challenged practices. * * * In each of those cases, the plaintiffs alleged official racial discrimination comparable to that alleged by respondents here. Yet standing was denied in each case because the plaintiffs were not personally subject to the challenged discrimination. Insofar as their first claim of injury is concerned, respondents are in exactly the same position: * * * they do not allege a stigmatic injury suffered as a direct result of having personally been denied equal treatment.

The consequences of recognizing respondents' standing on the basis of their first claim of injury illustrate why our cases plainly hold that such injury is not judicially cognizable. If the abstract stigmatic injury were cognizable, standing would extend nationwide to all members of the particular racial groups against which the Government was alleged to be discriminating by its grant of a tax exemption to a racially discriminatory school, regardless of the location of that school. All such persons could claim the same sort of abstract stigmatic injury respondents assert in their first claim of injury. A black person in Hawaii could challenge the grant of a tax exemption to a racially discriminatory school in Maine. Recognition of standing in such circumstances would transform the federal courts into "no more than a vehicle for the vindication of the value interests of concerned bystanders." Constitutional limits on the role of the federal courts preclude such a transformation.

2

It is in their complaint's second claim of injury that respondents allege harm to a concrete, personal interest that can support standing in some circumstances. The injury they identify—their children's diminished ability to receive an education in a racially integrated school—is, beyond any doubt, not only judicially cognizable but, * * * one of the most serious injuries recognized in our legal system. Despite the constitutional importance of curing the injury alleged by respondents, however, the federal judiciary may not redress it unless standing requirements are met. In this case, respondents' second claim of injury cannot support standing because the injury alleged is not fairly traceable to the Government conduct respondents challenge as unlawful.[22]

The illegal conduct challenged by respondents is the IRS' grant of tax exemptions to some racially discriminatory schools. The line of causation between that conduct and desegregation of respondents' schools is attenuated at best. From the perspective of the IRS, the injury to respondents is highly indirect and "results from the independent action of some third party not before the court." As the Court pointed out in *Warth v. Seldin,* "the indirectness of the injury * * * may make it substantially more difficult to meet the minimum requirement of Article III * * * ."

The diminished ability of respondents' children to receive a desegregated education would be fairly traceable to unlawful IRS grants of tax exemptions only if there were enough racially discriminatory private schools receiving tax exemptions in respondents' communities for withdrawal of those exemptions to make an appreciable difference in public-school integration. Respondents have made no such allegation. It is, first, uncertain how many racially discriminatory private schools are in fact receiving tax exemptions. Moreover, it is entirely speculative, as

---

[22] Respondents' stigmatic injury, though not sufficient for standing in the abstract form in which their complaint asserts it, is judicially cognizable to the extent that respondents are personally subject to discriminatory treatment. The stigmatic injury thus requires identification of some concrete interest with respect to which respondents are personally subject to discriminatory treatment. That interest must independently satisfy the causation requirement of standing doctrine. * * *

In this litigation, respondents identify only one interest that they allege is being discriminatorily impaired—their interest in desegregated public-school education. Respondents' asserted stigmatic injury, therefore, is sufficient to support their standing in this litigation only if their school-desegregation injury independently meets the causation requirement of standing doctrine.

respondents themselves conceded in the Court of Appeals, whether with-drawal of a tax exemption from any particular school would lead the school to change its policies. It is just as speculative whether any given parent of a child attending such a private school would decide to transfer the child to public school as a result of any changes in educational or fi-nancial policy made by the private school once it was threatened with loss of tax-exempt status. It is also pure speculation whether, in a par-ticular community, a large enough number of the numerous relevant school officials and parents would reach decisions that collectively would have a significant impact on the racial composition of the public schools.

The links in the chain of causation between the challenged Govern-ment conduct and the asserted injury are far too weak for the chain as a whole to sustain respondents' standing. [T]he Court [has] held that standing to challenge a Government grant of a tax exemption to hospi-tals could not be founded on the asserted connection between the grant of tax-exempt status and the hospitals' policy concerning the provision of medical services to indigents. The causal connection depended on the decisions hospitals would make in response to withdrawal of tax-exempt status, and those decisions were sufficiently uncertain to break the chain of causation between the plaintiffs' injury and the challenged Govern-ment action. The chain of causation is even weaker in this case. It in-volves numerous third parties (officials of racially discriminatory schools receiving tax exemptions and the parents of children attending such schools) who may not even exist in respondents' communities and whose independent decisions may not collectively have a significant effect on the ability of public-school students to receive a desegregated education.

The idea of separation of powers that underlies standing doctrine explains why our cases preclude the conclusion that respondents' alleged injury "fairly can be traced to the challenged action" of the IRS. That conclusion would pave the way generally for suits challenging, not spe-cifically identifiable Government violations of law, but the particular programs agencies establish to carry out their legal obligations. Such suits, even when premised on allegations of several instances of viola-tions of law, are rarely if ever appropriate for federal-court adjudication.

> Carried to its logical end, [respondents'] approach would have the
> federal courts as virtually continuing monitors of the wisdom and
> soundness of Executive action; such a role is appropriate for the
> Congress acting through its committees and the "power of the
> purse"; it is not the role of the judiciary, absent actual present or
> immediately threatened injury resulting from unlawful govern-
> mental action.

The same concern for the proper role of the federal courts is reflected in cases like *O'Shea v. Littleton, Rizzo v. Goode,* and *City of Los Angeles v. Lyons.* In all three cases plaintiffs sought injunctive relief directed at certain systemwide law enforcement practices. The Court held in each case that, absent an allegation of a specific threat of being subject to the challenged practices, plaintiffs had no standing to ask for an injunction. Animating this Court's holdings was the principle that "[a] federal court * * * is not the proper forum to press" general complaints about the way in which government goes about its business.

* * * Most relevant to this case is the principle [that]:

> When a plaintiff seeks to enjoin the activity of a government agency, even within a unitary court system, his case must contend with "the well-established rule that the Government has traditionally been granted the widest latitude in the 'dispatch of its own internal affairs.'"

When transported into the Art. III context, that principle, grounded as it is in the idea of separation of powers, counsels against recognizing standing in a case brought, not to enforce specific legal obligations whose violation works a direct harm, but to seek a restructuring of the apparatus established by the Executive Branch to fulfill its legal duties. The Constitution, after all, assigns to the Executive Branch, and not to the Judicial Branch, the duty to "take Care that the Laws be faithfully executed." U.S. Const., Art. II, § 3. We could not recognize respondents' standing in this case without running afoul of that structural principle.[26]

* * *

III

"The necessity that the plaintiff who seeks to invoke judicial power stand to profit in some personal interest remains an Art. III requirement." Respondents have not met this fundamental requirement. The judgment of the Court of Appeals is accordingly reversed, and the injunction issued by that court is vacated.

It is so ordered.

JUSTICE BRENNAN, dissenting.

Once again, the Court "uses 'standing to slam the courthouse door against plaintiffs who are entitled to full consideration of their claims on the merits.'" And once again, the Court does so by "wax[ing] eloquent" on considerations that provide little justification for the decision at hand. This time, however, the Court focuses on "the idea of separation of powers," as if the mere incantation of that phrase provides an obvious solu-

---

[26] We disagree with Justice Stevens' suggestions that separation of powers principles merely underlie standing requirements, have no role to play in giving meaning to those requirements, and should be considered only under a distinct justiciability analysis. Moreover, our analysis of this case does not rest on the more general proposition that no consequence of the allocation of administrative enforcement resources is judicially cognizable. Rather, we rely on separation of powers principles to interpret the "fairly traceable" component of the standing requirement.

tion to the difficult questions presented by these cases.

One could hardly dispute the proposition that Article III of the Constitution, by limiting the judicial power to "cases" or "controversies," embodies the notion that each branch of our National Government must confine its actions to those that are consistent with our scheme of separated powers. But simply stating that unremarkable truism provides little, if any, illumination of the standing inquiry that must be undertaken by a federal court faced with a particular action filed by particular plaintiffs. "The question whether a particular person is a proper party to maintain the action does not, by its own force, raise separation of powers problems related to improper judicial interference in areas committed to other branches of the Federal Government."

The Court's attempt to obscure the standing question must be seen, therefore, as no more than a cover for its failure to recognize the nature of the specific claims raised by the respondents in these cases. By relying on generalities concerning our tripartite system of government, the Court is able to conclude that the respondents lack standing to maintain this action without acknowledging the precise nature of the injuries they have alleged. In so doing, the Court displays a startling insensitivity to the historical role played by the federal courts in eradicating race discrimination from our nation's schools—a role that has played a prominent part in this Court's decisions. Because I cannot join in such misguided decisionmaking, I dissent.

* * *

II

Persons seeking judicial relief from an Article III court must have standing to maintain their cause of action. At a minimum, the standing requirement is not met unless the plaintiff has "such a personal stake in the outcome of the controversy as to assure that concrete adverseness which sharpens the presentation of issues upon which the court so largely depends." Under the Court's cases, this "personal stake" requirement is satisfied if the person seeking redress has suffered, or is threatened with, some "distinct and palpable injury," and if there is some causal connection between the asserted injury and the conduct being challenged.

A

In these cases, the respondents have alleged at least one type of injury that satisfies the constitutional requirement of "distinct and palpable injury."[3] In particular, they claim that the IRS' grant of tax-exempt

---

[3] Because I conclude that the second injury alleged by the respondents is sufficient to satisfy constitutional requirements, I do not need to reach what the Court labels the "stigmatic injury." I note, however, that the Court has mischaracterized this claim of injury by

status to racially discriminatory private schools directly injures their children's opportunity and ability to receive a desegregated education. As the complaint specifically alleges, the IRS action being challenged

> fosters and encourages the organization, operation and expansion of institutions providing racially segregated educational opportunities for white children avoiding attendance in desegregating public school districts and thereby interferes with the efforts of federal courts, HEW and local school authorities to desegregate public school districts which have been operating racially dual school systems.

The Court acknowledges that this alleged injury is sufficient to satisfy constitutional standards. It does so only grudgingly, however, without emphasizing the significance of the harm alleged. Nonetheless, we have consistently recognized throughout the last 30 years that the deprivation of a child's right to receive an education in a desegregated school is a harm of special significance; surely, it satisfies any constitutional requirement of injury in fact. Just last Term, for example, we acknowledged that "[a]n unbroken line of cases following *Brown v. Board of Education* establishes beyond doubt this Court's view that racial discrimination in education violates a most fundamental national public policy, *as well as the rights of individuals.*" ([E]mphasis added). "The right of a student not to be segregated on racial grounds in schools * * * is indeed so fundamental and pervasive that it is embraced in the concept of due process of law."

In the analogous context of housing discrimination, the Court has similarly recognized that the denial of an opportunity to live in an integrated community is injury sufficient to satisfy the constitutional requirements of standing. In particular, we have recognized that injury is properly alleged when plaintiffs claim a deprivation "of the social and professional benefits of living in an integrated society." Noting "the importance of the 'benefits [obtained] from interracial associations,' " as well as the oft-stated principle "that noneconomic injuries may suffice to provide standing," we have consistently concluded that such an injury is "sufficient to satisfy the constitutional standing requirement of actual or threatened harm."

---

misreading the complaint filed by the respondents. In particular, the respondents have not simply alleged that, as blacks, they have suffered the denigration injury "suffered by all members of a racial group when the Government discriminates on the basis of race." Rather, the complaint, fairly read, limits the claim of stigmatic injury from illegal governmental action to black children attending public schools in districts that are currently desegregating yet contain discriminatory private schools benefitting [*sic*] from illegal tax exemptions. Thus, the Court's "parade of horribles" concerning black plaintiffs from Hawaii challenging tax exemptions granted to schools in Maine is completely irrelevant for purposes of Article III standing in this action. Indeed, even if relevant, that criticism would go to the scope of the class certified or the relief granted in the lawsuit, issues that were not reached by the District Court or the Court of Appeals and are not now before this Court.

* * *

B

Fully explicating the injury alleged helps to explain why it is fairly traceable to the governmental conduct challenged by the respondents. As the respondents specifically allege in their complaint:

Defendants have fostered and encouraged the development, operation and expansion of many of these racially segregated private schools by recognizing them as "charitable" organizations described in Section 501(c)(3) of the Internal Revenue Code, and exempt from federal income taxation under Section 501(a) of the Code. Once the schools are classified as tax-exempt * * *, contributions made to them are deductible from gross income on individual and corporate income tax returns * * *. Moreover, [the] organizations * * * are also exempt from federal social security taxes * * * and from federal unemployment taxes * * *. The resulting exemptions and deductions provide tangible financial aid and other benefits which support the operation of racially segregated private schools. In particular, the resulting deductions facilitate the raising of funds to organize new schools and expand existing schools in order to accommodate white students avoiding attendance in desegregating public school districts. Additionally, the existence of a federal tax exemption amounts to a federal stamp of approval which facilitates fund raising on behalf of racially segregated private schools. Finally, by supporting the development, operation and expansion of institutions providing racially segregated educational opportunities for white children avoiding attendance in desegregating public schools, defendants are thereby interfering with the efforts of courts, HEW and local school authorities to desegregate public school districts which have been operating racially dual school systems.

Viewed in light of the injuries they claim, the respondents have alleged a direct causal relationship between the government action they challenge and the injury they suffer: their inability to receive an education in a racially integrated school is directly and adversely affected by the tax-exempt status granted by the IRS to racially discriminatory schools in their respective school districts. Common sense alone would recognize that the elimination of tax-exempt status for racially discriminatory private schools would serve to lessen the impact that those institutions have in defeating efforts to desegregate the public schools.

The Court admits that "[t]he diminished ability of respondents' children to receive a desegregated education would be fairly traceable to unlawful IRS grants of tax exemptions * * * if there were enough racially discriminatory private schools receiving tax exemptions in respondents' communities for withdrawal of those exemptions to make an appreciable difference in public-school integration," but concludes that "[r]espondents have made no such allegation." With all due respect, the Court has either misread the complaint or is improperly requiring the respondents to prove their case on the merits in order to defeat a motion to dismiss. For example, the respondents specifically refer by name to at least 32 private schools that discriminate on the basis of race and yet continue to benefit illegally from tax-exempt status. Eighteen of those schools—including at least 14 elementary schools, two junior high schools, and one high school—are located in the city of Memphis, Tennessee, which has been the subject of several court orders to desegregate. Similarly, the respondents cite two private schools in Orangeburg, South Carolina that continue to benefit from federal tax exemptions even though they practice race discrimination in school districts that are desegregating pursuant to judicial and administrative orders. At least with respect to these school districts, as well as the others specifically mentioned in the complaint, there can be little doubt that the respondents have identified communities containing "enough racially discriminatory private schools receiving tax exemptions * * * to make an appreciable difference in public-school integration."

Moreover, the Court has previously recognized the existence, and constitutional significance, of such direct relationships between unlawfully segregated school districts and government support for racially discriminatory private schools in those districts. In *Norwood v. Harrison,* for example, we considered a Mississippi program that provided textbooks to students attending both public and private schools, without regard to whether any participating school had racially discriminatory policies. In declaring that program constitutionally invalid, we noted that "a state may not induce, encourage or promote private persons to accomplish what it is constitutionally forbidden to accomplish." We then spoke directly to the causal relationship between the financial aid provided by the state textbook program and the constitutional rights asserted by the students and their parents:

> The District Court laid great stress on the absence of a showing by appellants that "any child enrolled in private school, if deprived of free textbooks, would withdraw from private school and subsequently enroll in the public schools." * * * *We do not agree with the District Court in its analysis of the legal consequences of this uncertainty, for the Constitution does not permit the State to aid discrimination even when there is no precise causal relationship between state financial aid to a private school and the continued well-being of that school. A State may not grant the type of tangible financial aid here involved if that aid has a significant tendency to facilitate, reinforce, and support private discrimination.*

([E]mphasis added). Thus, *Norwood* explicitly stands for the proposition that governmental aid to racially discriminatory schools is a direct impediment to school desegregation.

The Court purports to distinguish *Norwood* from the present litigation because " '[t]he plaintiffs in *Norwood* were parties to a school desegregation order' " and therefore "had acquired a right to have the State 'steer clear' of any perpetuation of the racially dual school system that it had once sponsored," whereas the "[r]espondents in this lawsuit * * * have no injunctive rights against the IRS that are allegedly being harmed." There is nothing to suggest, however, that the relevant injunction in *Norwood* was anything more than an order to desegregate the schools in Tunica County, Mississippi. Given that many of the school districts identified in the respondents' complaint have also been the subject of court-ordered integration, the standing inquiry in these cases should not differ. And, although the respondents do not specifically allege that they are named parties to any outstanding desegregation orders, that is undoubtedly due to the passage of time since the orders were issued, and not to any difference in the harm they suffer.

Even accepting the relevance of the Court's distinction, moreover, that distinction goes to the injury suffered by the respective plaintiffs, and not to the causal connection between the harm alleged and the governmental action challenged.

* * *

[T]he Court is forced to place primary reliance on our decision in *Simon v. Eastern Kentucky Welfare Rights Org.* In that case, the Court denied standing to plaintiffs who challenged an IRS revenue ruling that granted charitable status to hospitals even though they failed to operate to the extent of their financial ability when refusing medical services for indigent patients. The Court found that the injury alleged was not one "that fairly can be traced to the challenged action of the defendant." In particular, it was "purely speculative" whether the denial of access to hospital services alleged by the plaintiffs fairly could be traced to the government's grant of tax-exempt status to the relevant hospitals, primarily because hospitals were likely making their service decisions without regard to the tax implications.

Even accepting the correctness of the causation analysis included in that decision, however, it is plainly distinguishable from the case at hand. The respondents in this case do not challenge the denial of any service by a tax-exempt institution; admittedly, they do not seek access to racially discriminatory private schools. Rather, the injury they allege, and the injury that clearly satisfies constitutional requirements, is the deprivation of their children's opportunity and ability to receive an education in a racially integrated school district. This injury, as the Court admits, and as we have previously held, is of a kind that is directly traceable to the governmental action being challenged. The relationship between the harm alleged and the governmental action cannot simply be deemed "purely speculative" * * * .

III

More than one commentator has noted that the causation component of the Court's standing inquiry is no more than a poor disguise for the Court's view of the merits of the underlying claims. The Court today does nothing to avoid that criticism. What is most disturbing about today's decision, therefore, is not the standing analysis applied, but the indifference evidenced by the Court to the detrimental effects that racially segregated schools, supported by tax-exempt status from the federal government, have on the respondents' attempt to obtain an education in a racially integrated school system. I cannot join such indifference, and would give the respondents a chance to prove their case on the merits.

JUSTICE STEVENS, with whom JUSTICE BLACKMUN joins, dissenting.

Three propositions are clear to me: (1) respondents have adequately alleged "injury in fact"; (2) their injury is fairly traceable to the conduct that they claim to be unlawful; and (3) the "separation of powers" principle does not create a jurisdictional obstacle to the consideration of the merits of their claim.

* * *

II

In final analysis, the wrong the respondents allege that the Government has committed is to subsidize the exodus of white children from schools that would otherwise be racially integrated. The critical question in this case, therefore, is whether respondents have alleged that the Government has created that kind of subsidy.

* * *

An organization that qualifies for preferential treatment under § 501(c)(3) of the Internal Revenue Code, because it is "operated exclusively for * * * charitable * * * purposes," 26 U.S.C. § 501(c)(3), is exempt from paying federal income taxes, and under § 170 of the Code, persons who contribute to such organizations may deduct the amount of their contributions when calculating their taxable income. Only last Term we explained the effect of this preferential treatment:

> Both tax exemptions and tax-deductibility are a form of subsidy that is administered through the tax system. A tax exemption has much the same effect as a cash grant to the organization of the amount of tax it would have to pay on its income. Deductible contributions are similar to cash grants of the amount of a portion of the individual's contributions.

The purpose of this scheme, like the purpose of any subsidy, is to promote the activity subsidized; the statutes "seek to achieve the same basic goal of encouraging the development of certain organizations through the grant of tax benefits." If the granting of preferential tax treatment would "encourage" private segregated school to conduct their "charitable" activities, it must follow that the withdrawal of the treatment would "discourage" them, and hence promote the process of desegregation.[2]

* * *

We have held that when a subsidy makes a given activity more or less expensive, injury can be fairly traced to the subsidy for purposes of standing analysis because of the resulting increase or decrease in the ability to engage in the activity.

* * *

This causation analysis is nothing more than a restatement of elementary economics: when something becomes more expensive, less of it will be purchased. Sections 170 and 501(c)(3) are premised on that recognition. If racially discriminatory private schools lose the "cash grants" that flow from the operation of the statutes, the education they provide will become more expensive and hence less of their services will be purchased. Conversely, maintenance of these tax benefits makes an education in segregated private schools relatively more attractive, by decreasing its cost. Accordingly, without tax exempt status, private schools will

---

[2] Respondents' complaint is premised on precisely this theory. The complaint * * * describes a number of private schools which receive preferential tax treatment and which allegedly discriminate on the basis of race, providing white children with "a racially segregated alternative to attendance" in the public schools which respondents' children attend. The complaint then states:

> There are thousands of other racially segregated private schools which operate or serve desegregating public school districts and which function under the umbrella of organizations which have received, applied for, or will apply for, federal tax exemptions. Moreover, many additional public school districts will in the future begin desegregating pursuant to court order or [government] regulations and guidelines, under state law or voluntarily. Additional racially segregated private schools may be organized or expanded, many of which will be operated by organizations which have received, applied for, or will apply for federal tax exemptions. As in the case of those representative organizations and private schools described in paragraphs 39-48, supra, such organizations and schools provide, or will provide, white children with a racially segregated alternative to desegregating public schools. *By recognizing these organizations as exempt from federal taxation, defendants facilitate their development, operation and expansion and the provision of racially segregated educational opportunities for white children avoiding attendance in desegregating public school systems. Defendants thereby also interfere with the efforts of federal courts, [the Federal Government] and local school authorities to eliminate racially dual school systems.*

([E]mphasis supplied). Thus, like Justice Brennan, I do not understand why the Court states that the complaint contains no allegation that the tax benefits received by private segregated schools "make an appreciable difference to public-school integration," unless the Court requires "intricacies of pleading that would have gladdened the heart of Baron Parke." Chayes, *The Role of the Judge in Public Law Litigation,* 89 HARV.L.REV. 1281, 1305 (1976).

either not be competitive in terms of cost, or have to change their admissions policies, hence reducing their competitiveness for parents seeking "a racially segregated alternative" to public schools, which is what respondents have alleged many white parents in desegregating school districts seek.[5] In either event the process of desegregation will be advanced in the same way that it was advanced in *Gilmore* and *Norwood*—the withdrawal of the subsidy for segregated schools means the incentive structure facing white parents who seek such schools for their children will be altered. Thus, the laws of economics, not to mention the laws of Congress embodied in §§ 170 and 501(c)(3), compel the conclusion that the injury respondents have alleged—the increased segregation of their children's schools because of the ready availability of private schools that admit whites only—will be redressed if these schools' operations are inhibited through the denial of preferential tax treatment.

III

Considerations of tax policy, economics, and pure logic all confirm the conclusion that respondents' injury in fact is fairly traceable to the Government's allegedly wrongful conduct. The Court therefore is forced to introduce the concept of "separation of powers" into its analysis. The Court writes that the separation of powers "explains why our cases preclude the conclusion" that respondents' injury is fairly traceable to the conduct they challenge.

The Court could mean one of three things by its invocation of the separation of powers. First, it could simply be expressing the idea that if the plaintiff lacks Article III standing to bring a lawsuit, then there is no "case or controversy" within the meaning of Article III and hence the matter is not within the area of responsibility assigned to the Judiciary by the Constitution. As we have written in the past, through the standing requirement "Art. III limit[s] the federal judicial power 'to those disputes which confine federal courts to a role consistent with a system of separated powers and which are traditionally thought to be capable of resolution through the judicial process.' " While there can be no quarrel with this proposition, in itself it provides no guidance for determining if the injury respondents have alleged is fairly traceable to the conduct they have challenged.

Second, the Court could be saying that it will require a more direct causal connection when it is troubled by the separation of powers implications of the case before it. That approach confuses the standing doctrine with the justiciability of the issues that respondents seek to raise.

---

[5] It is this "racially segregated alternative" to public schools—the availability of schools that "receive tax exemptions on the basis of adopting and certifying—but not implementing—a policy of nondiscrimination," which respondents allege white parents have found attractive, and which would either lose their cost advantage or their character as a segregated alternative if denied tax exempt status because of their discriminatory admissions policies.

The purpose of the standing inquiry is to measure the plaintiff's stake in the outcome, not whether a court has the authority to provide it with the outcome it seeks: "[T]he standing question is whether the plaintiff 'has alleged such a personal stake in the outcome of the controversy' as to warrant *his* invocation of federal-court jurisdiction and to justify the exercise of the court's remedial powers on his behalf."

Thus, the " 'fundamental aspect of standing' is that it focuses primarily on the *party* seeking to get his complaint before the federal court rather than 'on the issues he wishes to have adjudicated.' " The strength of the plaintiff's interest in the outcome has nothing to do with whether the relief it seeks would intrude upon the prerogatives of other branches of government; the possibility that the relief might be inappropriate does not lessen the plaintiff's stake in obtaining that relief. If a plaintiff presents a nonjusticiable issue, or seeks relief that a court may not award, then its complaint should be dismissed for those reasons, and not because the plaintiff lacks a stake in obtaining that relief and hence has no standing. * * *

Third, the Court could be saying that it will not treat as legally cognizable injuries that stem from an administrative decision concerning how enforcement resources will be allocated. This surely is an important point. Respondents do seek to restructure the IRS' mechanisms for enforcing the legal requirement that discriminatory institutions not receive tax-exempt status. Such restructuring would dramatically affect the way in which the IRS exercises its prosecutorial discretion. The Executive requires latitude to decide how best to enforce the law, and in general the Court may well be correct that the exercise of that discretion, especially in the tax context, is unchallengeable.

However, as the Court also recognizes, this principle does not apply when suit is brought "to enforce specific legal obligations whose violation works a direct harm." Here, respondents contend that the IRS is violating a specific constitutional limitation on its enforcement discretion.

* * *

In short, I would deal with the question of the legal limitations on the IRS' enforcement discretion on its merits, rather than by making the untenable assumption that the granting of preferential tax treatment to segregated schools does not make those schools more attractive to white students and hence does not inhibit the process of desegregation. I respectfully dissent.

Notes and Questions

1. *Allen* presents the basic framework of the Court's modern standing jurisprudence. Particular aspects of standing doctrine deserve greater scrutiny and are discussed in the notes that follow, but some overarching questions should be considered at the outset because they bear upon all aspects of the doctrine.

a) Separation-of-powers questions abound. Given that Article III sets out the basic requirement for standing, is it appropriate for the Court to embellish the constitutional requirements as opposed to interpreting them? What is the authority for the Court's creation of the various "prudential" parts of the standing doctrine?

b) To the extent that Article III is the constitutional component of the standing inquiry, standing is clearly jurisdictional and the courts should raise it *sua sponte* if the parties do not. Do the prudential aspects of the doctrine call for the same treatment? Are they jurisdictional and thus appropriate for the courts to raise *sua sponte,* or are they less structural and therefore only for the parties to raise?

2. Both the constitutional and prudential components of the standing inquiry have developed over time, and each deserves individualized attention. Although one might infer from *Allen* that the enumerated considerations are completely distinct, they often blend into each other. For example, one may view "generalized grievances" (of which the Court clearly is chary) as a separate prudential category, as Justice O'Connor seems to do in *Allen* and as the Court clearly did in *Gladstone, Realtors v. Village of Bellwood,* 441 U.S. 91, 120, 99 S.Ct. 1601, 1618, 60 L.Ed.2d 66, 89 (1979), or as incapable of giving rise to a cognizable injury in fact, part of the Article III aspect of standing jurisprudence. *Lujan v. Defenders of Wildlife,* 504 U.S. 555, 112 S.Ct. 2130, 119 L.Ed.2d 351 (1992), *infra* at 81, for example, seemed to characterize the generalized-grievance component as constitutionally compelled.

a) *Constitutional Components—Injury in Fact.* Where in Article III is the injury-in-fact requirement? Is it inherent in the constitutionally-undefined concept of case or controversy? Why should the Case-or-Controversy Clause be interpreted to concern standing at all?

Given that the injury-in-fact requirement is part of Article III, by what process does the Court determine whether an alleged injury is constitutionally sufficient? What criteria does, or should, it use? In the general case, how does it give meaning to its view of injury in fact?

Is it possible to access the constitutional sufficiency of an injury without consideration of the nature of the legal rights which have allegedly been violated? Is a plaintiff's loss of sleep too abstract an injury to support the standing requirements of Article III? Or does it depend on the nature of the substantive claim he is asserting? If one of the plaintiffs in *Allen* alleged that he was unable to sleep because racially discriminatory schools obtained tax-exempt status under the challenged guidelines, would such a claimed injury be too abstract to support standing? Suppose a plaintiff in a nuisance case alleged that the barking of a neighbor's dog interfered with his ability to sleep. Would such an injury be too abstract to support standing? Is the first plaintiff's loss of sleep different from that of the second plaintiff? An excellent article argues that the Court's entire standing jurisprudence is really a mischaracterized examination of the merits of the cases. " '[I]njury in fact' is a meaningless concept when applied to a plaintiff who is telling the truth about the injury she feels she has suffered, for injury can only be assessed against some normative structure. In the legal system, injury is assessed against the normative structure provided by particular rights." William A. Fletcher, *The Structure of Standing*, 98 YALE L.J. 221, 248-49 (1988). Judge Fletcher argues that when the Court asks if someone has been injured in fact, it is really asking whether the hurt that the plaintiff perceives is one that society is prepared to remedy through the legal system. He views that inquiry as indistinguishable from whether the plaintiff can state, in federal terms, "a claim upon which relief may be granted." FED.R.CIV.P. 12(b)(6). Is Judge Fletcher correct? On occasion, dissenting Justices have asserted that denial of standing reflected only the majority's view on the merits. *See, e.g., Warth v. Seldin* (1975) (Brennan, J., dissenting) ("[T]he opinion * * * can be explained only by an indefensible hostility to the claim on the merits."). Does the choice of analytical framework—standing or merits—constitutionalize or deconstitutionalize the underlying disputes? Is it possible that in some cases it may do one and in some the other? If the majority in *Allen* addressed the merits of the plaintiffs' claim, would only the vocabulary of the decision change or might the result change as well?

Must the injury that satisfies Article III be one against which the law offers specific affirmative protection? Suppose one suffers pecuniary loss by reason of an action taken by a third party that violates the law, but not a law designed to protect or directly to benefit the injured party. Has the injured party met the requirements of Article III? *See Association of Data Processing Service Organizations v. Camp,* 397 U.S. 159, 90 S.Ct. 838, 25 L.Ed.2d 192 (1970).

If someone has been injured by a continuing governmental practice or policy that is alleged to be unconstitutional, does that person have standing to seek an injunction? Although the intuitive response might be "yes," the Court has refused standing because of the plaintiff's inability to show that he would again be subject to the complained-of conduct. For example, in *City of Los Angeles v. Lyons,* 461 U.S. 95, 103 S.Ct. 1660, 75 L.Ed.2d 675 (1981), the plaintiff complained that he had been choked into unconsciousness by police who stopped him for a minor traffic violation. Los Angeles police policy permitted officers to use either of two chokeholds in circumstances that did not justify deadly force; sixteen people had died as a result of police chokeholds. The Court found Lyons lacked standing because he could not demonstrate that he was a) likely to be arrested again and b) likely to be choked even if he was arrested. Justice Marshall, joined by three colleagues, dissented:

> By fragmenting the standing inquiry and imposing a separate standing hurdle with respect to each form of relief sought, the decision today departs significantly from this Court's traditional conception of the standing requirement and of the remedial powers of the federal courts. We have never required more than that a plaintiff have standing to litigate a claim. Whether he will be entitled to obtain particular forms of relief should he prevail has never been understood to be an issue of standing. * * *
>
> Our cases uniformly state that the touchstone of the Article III standing requirement is the plaintiff's personal stake in the underlying dis-

pute, not in the particular types of relief sought. Once a plaintiff establishes a personal stake in the dispute, he has done all that is necessary * * * .

See also Rizzo v. Goode, 423 U.S. 362, 96 S.Ct. 598, 46 L.Ed.2d 561 (1975); *O'Shea v. Littleton,* 414 U.S. 488, 94 S.Ct. 669, 38 L.Ed.2d 674 (1974). Should the Court continue to evaluate standing according to the type of relief sought? If it does, what are the implications for plaintiffs' ability to seek systemic relief?

In *Raines v. Byrd,* 521 U.S. 811, 117 S.Ct. 2312, 138 L.Ed.2d 849 (1997), the Court declined to reach the issue of the constitutionality of the Line Item Veto Act, 2 U.S.C.A. §§ 681 *et seq.* (1997), because the Justices found that Members of Congress who had voted against the Act lacked standing, despite Congress's attempt to create it by statute in 2 U.S.C.A. § 692(a) (1997). The Court ruled that no Member who had voted against the Act had any personal stake likely to be redressed by invalidation of the Act. Chief Justice Rehnquist, sounding as if he was modifying the Court's "generalized grievance" rubric, also noted that the harm to any Member of Congress because of the Act was equally shared by all Members. Finally, having suggested no injury-in-fact and generalized grievance, the Court also suggested that the controversy was not ripe because the plaintiffs "have not alleged that they voted for a specific bill, that there were sufficient votes to pass the bill, and that the bill was nonetheless deemed defeated." Perhaps this implies that a Member of Congress would have standing in such a situation, though it is not immediately apparent why that creates any more of a personal stake for the Member than the original passage of the Act.

b) *Constitutional Components—Traceability & Redressability.* Traceability and redressability are linked causation requirements that look in different directions. "Traceability" refers to whether the plaintiff's injury arises from the defendant's action. It is, in other words, backward-looking. "Redressability," on the other hand, is forward-looking, asking whether the relief requested is likely to improve the situation for the plaintiff.

If the plaintiff is an intended beneficiary of a criminal statute enacted to protect a class of people, does non-enforcement of the statute give rise to a cognizable injury sufficient to create standing, or must the plaintiff demonstrate that but for the non-enforcement of the statute she would not have suffered injury, and that if the statute is enforced the injury will cease? How close a causal connection should the plaintiff have to demonstrate? *See Linda R.S. v. Richard D.,* 410 U.S. 614, 93 S.Ct. 1146, 35 L.Ed.2d 536 (1973).

In *Linda R.S.,* a Texas statutory scheme allowed prosecution of parents who did not pay child support for legitimate children, but did not permit prosecution of defaulting parents of illegitimate children. The plaintiff argued that the scheme violated the Equal Protection Clause. The Court's denial of standing rested upon its perception that granting relief would have made it no more probable (or insufficiently probable) that support payments to the individual plaintiff would commence. On the Court's rationale, would the defaulting parent of a legitimate child have had standing to challenge the statutory scheme, at least if threatened with prosecution? Manifestly, such an individual would benefit directly from a judicial victory; no prosecution could ensue. If the Court had allowed standing in that case, what anomalies would that have created?

For a plaintiff seeking equitable relief, should standing doctrine require the plaintiff to demonstrate that the relief requested will "cure" the plaintiff's problem? If so, to what degree of certainty must the plaintiff prove redressability? If not, then is the court's subsequent grant of relief, at least potentially, an advisory opinion in contravention of Article III? *See Simon v. Eastern Kentucky Welfare Rights Organization,* 426 U.S. 26, 96 S.Ct. 1917, 48 L.Ed.2d 450 (1976). In *Simon,* the Court found no standing to challenge IRS's continuing allowance of charitable-organization status to hospitals that allegedly did not offer service to those unable to pay. The Court reasoned that there was not a sufficient showing that removal of the hospitals' tax exempt status would cause them to change the behavior of which the plaintiffs complained. Is the Court's refusal to find standing consistent with its recognition of progressive fines for contempt of court, the underlying assumption of which is that continued and increasing financial pressure is effective to alter behavior? *See, e.g., Spallone v. United States,* 493 U.S. 265, 110 S.Ct. 625, 107 L.Ed.2d 644 (1990).

Suppose a plaintiff sues for an injunction against the defendant's continuing excavation on defendant's adjacent parcel of land. If, at trial, the plaintiff is unable to demonstrate either that the subsidence of his land will be stopped by preventing defendant's activity or that it will continue if defendant continues, is the proper disposition of the case dismissal for lack of standing? Is it not more likely that plaintiff would be defeated for failure of his cause of action? Should the same type of analysis inform standing inquiries in cases concerning challenges to governmental action?

Suppose that the same conduct may tend to be both promoted or prohibited by more than one statute or state constitutional provision. Must a prospective plaintiff who wants to assert the unconstitutionality of one provision actually challenge both in order to avoid redressability problems? *See Renne v. Geary,* 501 U.S. 312, 111 S.Ct. 2331, 115 L.Ed.2d 288 (1991).

On occasion, plaintiffs have survived the Court's inquiry into traceability and redressability only to lose on the merits. In *Duke Power Co. v. Carolina Environmental Study Group, Inc.,* 438 U.S. 59, 98 S.Ct. 2620, 57 L.Ed.2d 595 (1978), the plaintiffs challenged the Price-Anderson Act's limitation of civil liability of companies building and operating nuclear reactors. The Court found that only because of the Price-Anderson Act did the defendant build the nuclear facility, and further found that plaintiffs were injured. The plaintiffs alleged that they were injured because of the plant's emission of small amounts of non-natural radiation and its use of the water of two recreational lakes for steam generation and cooling of the reactor, resulting in a "sharp increase" in water temperature accompanied by adverse environmental and aesthetic consequences. The Court found these allegations to be sufficient to establish standing because the defendant would not have built the facility but for the Price-Anderson Act. The Court then upheld the Act. Did the Court apply the traceability and redressability requirements with the same rigor in this case as in *Allen*?

Does it make any difference whether a case is dismissed for lack of standing, for failure of the plaintiff to state a claim upon which relief may be granted, or for failure of proof?

Why should traceability and redressability be viewed as components of Article III standing? How much certainty of redress should be required before a federal court can act? To the extent that the plaintiff's burden as to traceability and redressability is substantial, does the plaintiff have a Herculean task establishing standing in all cases where conduct is alleged to cause injury indirectly?

In *Utah v. Evans*, 536 U.S. 452, 122 S.Ct. 2191, 153 L.Ed.2d 453 (2002), the state challenged the 2000 census's use of a method called "hot-deck imputation." Utah claimed that violated a statutory provision forbidding "sampling," *see* 13 U.S.C.A. § 195 (2002), and the constitutional requirement of an "actual Enumeration." *See* U.S. CONST. art. I, § 2, cl. 3. North Carolina intervened, since Utah would gain a seat in the House of Representatives at North Carolina's expense if House seats were reapportioned based on an adjusted count. North Carolina argued that Utah lacked standing because even if the Secretary of Commerce were to certify new figures, that would not automatically change the congressional representation because other officials from the legislative and executive branches would have to act before seats could be redistributed. Therefore, North Carolina argued, even a change in the official census figures would not guarantee Utah the relief it needed. An 8-to-1 Court found that Utah had standing (a prelude to deciding against Utah on the merits). The majority noted that although there was no guarantee that the President and the Clerk of the House of Representatives would act on new census data, "we believe it likely that Utah's victory would bring about the ultimate relief that Utah seeks. * * * Under these circumstances, it would seem, as in *Franklin* [*Department of Commerce v. Montana*, 503 U.S. 442 (1992)], 'substantially likely that the President and other executive and congressional officials would abide by an authoritative interpretation of the census statute and constitutional provision * * * .' "

Is the Court's reasoning in *Evans* compatible with *Simon v. Eastern Kentucky Welfare Rights Organization*? There the Court refused to assume that loss of a tax exemption would change hospitals' decisions to refuse care to those unable to pay. Similarly, in *Linda R.S. v. Richard D.*, the Court refused to find that allowing criminal prosecution of parents failing to support illegitimate children would cause such parents to begin paying child support. Note that in *Evans*, the Court concluded that a judgment that would have no direct effect at all on the officials whose action Utah needed for redress would nonetheless be likely to achieve Utah's desired results. By contrast, in *Simon* and *Linda R.S.* the Court refused to conclude that judgments that would have had a direct impact on the finances or liberty of the persons opposing the plaintiffs would likely redress plaintiffs' injuries.

Commentators have assailed the Court's jurisprudence in this area as too protean. *See, e.g.,*

> Alan Bakke, a white male, was denied admission to the University of
> California at Davis Medical School and filed suit challenging the
> school's practice of setting aside sixteen spots for minority students out
> of an entering class of 100. The state argued that Bakke lacked stand-
> ing based on the redressability requirement. Even if the affirmative
> action program were declared unconstitutional, Bakke still might not
> be admitted to the medical school. In other words, if the Court charac-
> terized Bakke's injury as a denial of admission, there was no assurance
> that a favorable court decision would redress the injury. But the Court
> chose a different characterization of the harm. The Court stated that
> Bakke's injury was an inability to compete for all 100 spots and, there-
> fore, a judicial decision declaring the set-aside of sixteen spots uncon-
> stitutional would remedy the injury and give him a chance to compete
> for all the slots.

ERWIN CHEMERINSKY, FEDERAL JURISDICTION, § 2.3, at 81 (5th. ed. 2007)
(footnotes omitted). *See also* Gene Nichol, *Causation As a Standing Requirement: The Unprincipled Use of Judicial Restraint,* 69 KY.L.J. 185
(1981); Gene Nichol, *Rethinking Standing,* 72 CALIF.L.REV. 68, 79 (1984).
Consider the phenomenon Professor Chemerinsky addresses in the context
of *Linda R.S.* and *Simon.* Is there the same ability to manipulate in those
cases? Is it possible to articulate the traceability and redressability requirements in a way that is not conducive to manipulation?

The Court took a narrow view of redressability in *Steel Company v. Citizens for a Better Environment,* 523 U.S. 83, 118 S.Ct. 1003, 140 L.Ed.2d 210
(1998). Plaintiff CBE sued under the Emergency Planning and Community
Right-to-Know Act of 1986 (EPCRA), alleging that the defendant had failed
timely to file reports required by the Act with respect to the presence of toxic
or other hazardous chemicals at its site. After the plaintiff had notified defendant and relevant federal and state officials of the non-filing, defendant
filed all of the overdue reports. Plaintiff nonetheless exercised its statutory
right to sue. Defendant moved to dismiss for lack of subject matter jurisdiction and for failure to state a claim upon which relief could be granted, arguing that by the time the action was filed, there was no violation and that
EPCRA does not authorize an action for past violations. All nine Justices
concurred in the judgment directing dismissal of the action, but reached that
conclusion via different routes. The Court's majority declined to reach the
question of whether deprivation of information is an injury-in-fact that satisfies Article III, holding instead that the complaint could not satisfy the redressability requirement that the majority identified as one of the "irreducible constitutional minim[a] of standing * * * ."

> The complaint asks for (1) a declaratory judgment that petitioner vio-
> lated EPCRA; (2) authorization to inspect periodically petitioner's facil-
> ity and records (with costs borne by petitioner); (3) an order requiring
> petitioner to provide respondent copies of all compliance reports sub-
> mitted to the EPA; (4) an order requiring petitioner to pay civil penal-
> ties of $25,000 per day for each violation of §§ 11022 and 11023; (5) an

award of all respondent's "costs, in connection with the investigation and prosecution of this matter, including reasonable attorney and expert witness fees, as authorized by Section 326(f) of [EPCRA]"; and (6) any such further relief as the court deems appropriate. None of the specific items of relief sought, and none that we can envision as "appropriate" under the general request, would serve to reimburse respondent for losses caused by the late reporting, or to eliminate any effects of that late reporting upon respondent.

Since it was undisputed that the defendant had failed timely to file the reports, thus violating the Act, the request for declaratory relief did not support standing. Civil penalties, the only damages authorized by the Act, were payable to the United States, not to the plaintiff. Thus, the request for civil penalties did not meet the redressability requirement. Moreover, the majority noted that "[t]he litigation must give the plaintiff some other benefit besides reimbursement of costs that are a byproduct of the litigation itself." Consequently, the request for investigation and prosecution costs did not establish standing. The majority recognized that deterrence of future injury could be remedial for Article III purposes, but demurred at recognizing it in this case. "If respondent had alleged a continuing violation or the imminence of a future violation, the injunctive relief requested would remedy that alleged harm. But there is no allegation here—and on the facts of the case, there seems no basis for it." The Court also rejected the notion that voluntary cessation of illegal activity gives rise to a presumption that the activity will be resumed, distinguishing this situation from a case where the defendant argues mootness after voluntary cessation. If the defendant here had characterized the ground for dismissal as mootness because it had filed the required forms, do you think the majority would have had to come out the other way? Was the result determined simply by defendant's artfulness in selecting the basis for objecting to the action, combined with plaintiff's inartfulness in failing to allege the likelihood of continuing violations?

Justice Breyer, concurring in the result, suggested that in some cases, it might be proper for the Court to bypass a thorny standing (constitutional) question and to rule on the merits where the merits decision would come out in favor of the party seeking dismissal on standing grounds. Were the Court to adopt his suggestion, what difficulties might it encounter?

Justice Stevens, joined in part by Justices Souter and Ginsburg, also concurred, but argued that the Court should have bypassed the standing question in favor of resolving what he characterized as a different jurisdictional question: whether EPCRA conferred jurisdiction on the district court to decide cases involving only past (rather than on-going) violations of the Act. He also argued that even if the statutory construction question were regarded as a 12(b)(6) (failure to state a claim) issue rather than a 12(b)(1) (subject matter jurisdiction) issue, it would be proper for the Court to decide that issue first. This aspect of Justice Stevens's opinion is discussed at page 288.

3. When should a court determine standing? In *Gladstone, Realtors v. Village of Bellwood*, 441 U.S. 91, 115 n. 31, 99 S.Ct. 1601, 1616 n. 31, 60

L.Ed.2d 66, 86 n. 31 (1979), the Court said: "Although standing generally is a matter dealt with at the earliest stages of litigation, usually on the pleadings, it sometimes remains to be seen whether the factual allegations of the complaint necessary for standing will be supported adequately by the evidence adduced at trial." Does this mean that after all the evidence is in the court may dismiss the case for lack of standing? The Court at least suggested so in *Gladstone:* "The presence of a genuine injury should be ascertainable on the basis of discrete facts presented at trial." Standing is thus being treated, for some purposes at least, as akin to subject matter jurisdiction. If the defendant raises no question about the plaintiff's standing, should the court? If so, should the court limit its *sua sponte* inquiry to the constitutional components of standing?

MASSACHUSETTS v. ENVIRONMENTAL PROTECTION AGENCY
Supreme Court of the United States, 2007.
__ U.S. __, 127 S.Ct. 1438, 167 L.Ed.2d 248.

JUSTICE STEVENS delivered the opinion of the Court.

A well-documented rise in global temperatures has coincided with a significant increase in the concentration of carbon dioxide in the atmosphere. Respected scientists believe the two trends are related. For when carbon dioxide is released into the atmosphere, it acts like the ceiling of a greenhouse, trapping solar energy and retarding the escape of reflected heat. It is therefore a species—the most important species—of a "greenhouse gas."

Calling global warming "the most pressing environmental challenge of our time," a group of States, local governments, and private organizations, alleged in a petition for certiorari that the Environmental Protection Agency (EPA) has abdicated its responsibility under the Clean Air Act to regulate the emissions of four greenhouse gases, including carbon dioxide. Specifically, petitioners asked us to answer two questions concerning the meaning of § 202(a)(1) of the Act: whether EPA has the statutory authority to regulate greenhouse gas emissions from new motor vehicles; and if so, whether its stated reasons for refusing to do so are consistent with the statute.

In response, EPA, supported by 10 intervening States and six trade associations, correctly argued that we may not address those two questions unless at least one petitioner has standing to invoke our jurisdiction under Article III of the Constitution. Notwithstanding the serious character of that jurisdictional argument and the absence of any conflicting decisions construing § 202(a)(1), the unusual importance of the underlying issue persuaded us to grant the writ.

I

Section 202(a)(1) * * * provides:

The [EPA] Administrator shall by regulation prescribe (and from time to time revise) in accordance with the provisions of this section, standards applicable to the emission of any air pollutant from any class or classes of new motor vehicles or new motor vehicle engines, which in his judgment cause, or contribute to, air pollution which may reasonably be anticipated to endanger public health or welfare * * * ."

The Act defines "air pollutant" to include "any air pollution agent or combination of such agents, including any physical, chemical, biological, radioactive * * * substance or matter which is emitted into or otherwise enters the ambient air." "Welfare" is also defined broadly: among other things, it includes "effects on * * * weather * * * and climate."

When Congress enacted these provisions, the study of climate change was in its infancy. In 1959, shortly after the U.S. Weather Bureau began monitoring atmospheric carbon dioxide levels, an observatory in Mauna Loa, Hawaii, recorded a mean level of 316 parts per million. This was well above the highest carbon dioxide concentration—no more than 300 parts per million—revealed in the 420,000-year-old ice-core record. By the time Congress drafted § 202(a)(1) in 1970, carbon dioxide levels had reached 325 parts per million.[10]

In the late 1970's, the Federal Government began devoting serious attention to the possibility that carbon dioxide emissions associated with human activity could provoke climate change. In 1978, Congress enacted the National Climate Program Act, which required the President to establish a program to "assist the Nation and the world to understand and respond to natural and man-induced climate processes and their implications." President Carter, in turn, asked the National Research Council, the working arm of the National Academy of Sciences, to investigate the subject. The Council's response was unequivocal: "If carbon dioxide continues to increase, the study group finds no reason to doubt that climate changes will result and no reason to believe that these changes will be negligible * * * . A wait-and-see policy may mean waiting until it is too late."

Congress next addressed the issue in 1987 * * * . Finding that "manmade pollution-the release of carbon dioxide, chlorofluorocarbons, methane, and other trace gases into the atmosphere-may be producing a long-term and substantial increase in the average temperature on Earth," Congress directed EPA to propose to Congress a "coordinated national policy on global climate change," § and ordered the Secretary of State to work "through the channels of multilateral diplomacy" and coordinate diplomatic efforts to combat global warming. Congress emphasized that "ongoing pollution and deforestation may be contributing now

---

[10] A more dramatic rise was yet to come: In 2006, carbon dioxide levels reached 382 parts per million, a level thought to exceed the concentration of carbon dioxide in the atmosphere at any point over the past 20-million years.

to an irreversible process" and that "[n]ecessary actions must be identified and implemented in time to protect the climate."

Meanwhile, the scientific understanding of climate change progressed. In 1990, the Intergovernmental Panel on Climate Change (IPCC), a multinational scientific body organized under the auspices of the United Nations, published its first comprehensive report on the topic. Drawing on expert opinions from across the globe, the IPCC concluded that "emissions resulting from human activities are substantially increasing the atmospheric concentrations of * * * greenhouse gases [which] will enhance the greenhouse effect, resulting on average in an additional warming of the Earth's surface."

Responding to the IPCC report, the United Nations convened the "Earth Summit" in 1992 in Rio de Janeiro. The first President Bush attended and signed the United Nations Framework Convention on Climate Change (UNFCCC), a nonbinding agreement among 154 nations to reduce atmospheric concentrations of carbon dioxide and other greenhouse gases for the purpose of "prevent[ing] dangerous anthropogenic [*i.e.,* human-induced] interference with the [Earth's] climate system." The Senate unanimously ratified the treaty.

Some five years later—after the IPCC issued a second comprehensive report in 1995 concluding that "[t]he balance of evidence suggests there is a discernible human influence on global climate"—the UNFCCC signatories met in Kyoto, Japan, and adopted a protocol that assigned mandatory targets for industrialized nations to reduce greenhouse gas emissions. Because those targets did not apply to developing and heavily polluting nations such as China and India, the Senate unanimously passed a resolution expressing its sense that the United States should not enter into the Kyoto Protocol. President Clinton did not submit the protocol to the Senate for ratification.

II

On October 20, 1999, a group of 19 private organizations filed a rulemaking petition asking EPA to regulate "greenhouse gas emissions from new motor vehicles under § 202 of the Clean Air Act." Petitioners maintained that 1998 was the "warmest year on record"; that carbon dioxide, methane, nitrous oxide, and hydrofluorocarbons are "heat trapping greenhouse gases"; that greenhouse gas emissions have significantly accelerated climate change; and that the IPCC's 1995 report warned that "carbon dioxide remains the most important contributor to [man-made] forcing of climate change." The petition further alleged that climate change will have serious adverse effects on human health and the environment. As to EPA's statutory authority, the petition observed that the agency itself had already confirmed that it had the power to regulate carbon dioxide. In 1998, Jonathan Z. Cannon, then EPA's General Counsel, prepared a legal opinion concluding that "CO_2 emissions are within the scope of EPA's authority to regulate," even as he recognized that EPA had so far declined to exercise that authority. Cannon's successor, Gary S. Guzy, reiterated that opinion before a congressional committee just two weeks before the rulemaking petition was filed.

Fifteen months after the petition's submission, EPA requested public comment on "all the issues raised in [the] petition," adding a "particular" request for comments on "any scientific, technical, legal, economic or other aspect of these issues that may be relevant to EPA's consideration of this petition." EPA received more than 50,000 comments over the next five months.

Before the close of the comment period, the White House sought "assistance in identifying the areas in the science of climate change where there are the greatest certainties and uncertainties" from the National Research Council, asking for a response "as soon as possible." The result was a 2001 report titled Climate Change: An Analysis of Some Key Questions (NRC Report), which, drawing heavily on the 1995 IPCC report, concluded that "[g]reenhouse gases are accumulating in Earth's atmosphere as a result of human activities, causing surface air temperatures and subsurface ocean temperatures to rise. Temperatures are, in fact, rising."

On September 8, 2003, EPA entered an order denying the rulemaking petition.

* * *

III

Petitioners, now joined by intervenor States and local governments, sought review of EPA's order in the United States Court of Appeals for the District of Columbia Circuit. Although each of the three judges on the panel wrote a separate opinion, two judges agreed "that the EPA Administrator properly exercised his discretion under § 202(a)(1) in denying the petition for rule making." The court therefore denied the petition for review.

In his opinion announcing the court's judgment, Judge Randolph avoided a definitive ruling as to petitioners' standing, reasoning that it was permissible to proceed to the merits because the standing and the merits inquiries "overlap[ped]." Assuming without deciding that the statute authorized the EPA Administrator to regulate greenhouse gas emissions that "in his judgment" may "reasonably be anticipated to endanger public health or welfare," Judge Randolph concluded that the exercise of that judgment need not be based solely on scientific evidence, but may also be informed by the sort of policy judgments that motivate congressional action. Given that framework, it was reasonable for EPA to base its decision on scientific uncertainty as well as on other factors, including the concern that unilateral regulation of U.S. motor-vehicle emissions could weaken efforts to reduce greenhouse gas emissions from other countries.

Judge Sentelle wrote separately because he believed petitioners failed to "demonstrat[e] the element of injury necessary to establish standing under Article III." In his view, they had alleged that global warming is "harmful to humanity at large," but could not allege "particularized injuries" to themselves. While he dissented on standing, however, he accepted the contrary view as the law of the case and joined Judge Randolph's judgment on the merits as the closest to that which he preferred.

Judge Tatel dissented. Emphasizing that EPA nowhere challenged the factual basis of petitioners' affidavits, he concluded that at least Massachusetts had "satisfied each element of Article III standing-injury, causation, and redressability." In Judge Tatel's view, the " 'substantial probability' " that projected rises in sea level would lead to serious loss of coastal property was a "far cry" from the kind of generalized harm insufficient to ground Article III jurisdiction. He found that petitioners' affidavits more than adequately supported the conclusion that EPA's failure to curb greenhouse gas emissions contributed to the sea level changes that threatened Massachusetts' coastal property. As to redressability, he observed that one of petitioners' experts, a former EPA climatologist, stated that " '[a]chievable reductions in emissions of CO_2 and other [greenhouse gases] from U.S. motor vehicles would * * * delay and moderate many of the adverse impacts of global warming.' " He further noted that the one-time director of EPA's motor-vehicle pollution control efforts stated in an affidavit that enforceable emission standards would lead to the development of new technologies that " 'would gradually be mandated by other countries around the world.' " On the merits, Judge Tatel explained at length why he believed the text of the statute provided EPA with authority to regulate greenhouse gas emissions, and why its policy concerns did not justify its refusal to exercise that authority.

IV

Article III of the Constitution limits federal-court jurisdiction to "Cases" and "Controversies." Those two words confine "the business of federal courts to questions presented in an adversary context and in a form historically viewed as capable of resolution through the judicial process." It is therefore familiar learning that no justiciable "controversy" exists when parties seek adjudication of a political question, when they ask for an advisory opinion, or when the question sought to be adjudicated has been mooted by subsequent developments,. This case suffers from none of these defects.

The parties' dispute turns on the proper construction of a congressional statute, a question eminently suitable to resolution in federal court. Congress has moreover authorized this type of challenge to EPA action. That authorization is of critical importance to the standing inquiry: "Congress has the power to define injuries and articulate chains of causation that will give rise to a case or controversy where none existed before." *Lujan* [1992] (Kennedy, J., concurring in part and concurring in judgment). "In exercising this power, however, Congress must at the very least identify the injury it seeks to vindicate and relate the injury to the class of persons entitled to bring suit." We will not, therefore, "entertain citizen suits to vindicate the public's nonconcrete interest in the proper administration of the laws."

EPA maintains that because greenhouse gas emissions inflict widespread harm, the doctrine of standing presents an insuperable jurisdictional obstacle. We do not agree. At bottom, "the gist of the question of standing" is whether petitioners have "such a personal stake in the outcome of the controversy as to assure that concrete adverseness which sharpens the presentation of issues upon which the court so largely depends for illumination." As Justice Kennedy explained in his *Lujan* concurrence:

> While it does not matter how many persons have been injured by the challenged action, the party bringing suit must show that the action injures him in a concrete and personal way. This requirement is not just an empty formality. It preserves the vitality of the adversarial process by assuring both that the parties before the court have an actual, as opposed to professed, stake in the outcome, and that the legal questions presented * * * will be resolved, not in the rarified [*sic*] atmosphere of a debating society, but in a concrete factual context conducive to a realistic appreciation of the consequences of judicial action.

To ensure the proper adversarial presentation, *Lujan* holds that a litigant must demonstrate that it has suffered a concrete and particularized injury that is either actual or imminent, that the injury is fairly traceable to the defendant, and that it is likely that a favorable decision will redress that injury. However, a litigant to whom Congress has "accorded a procedural right to protect his concrete interests,"—here, the right to challenge agency action unlawfully withheld—"can assert that right without meeting all the normal standards for redressability and immediacy." When a litigant is vested with a procedural right, that litigant has standing if there is some possibility that the requested relief will prompt the injury-causing party to reconsider the decision that allegedly harmed the litigant.

Only one of the petitioners needs to have standing to permit us to consider the petition for review. We stress here, as did Judge Tatel below, the special position and interest of Massachusetts. It is of considerable relevance that the party seeking review here is a sovereign State and not, as it was in *Lujan,* a private individual.

Well before the creation of the modern administrative state, we recognized that States are not normal litigants for the purposes of invoking federal jurisdiction. As Justice Holmes explained in *Georgia v. Tennes-*

see Copper Co. (1907), a case in which Georgia sought to protect its citizens from air pollution originating outside its borders:

> The case has been argued largely as if it were one between two private parties; but it is not. The very elements that would be relied upon in a suit between fellow-citizens as a ground for equitable relief are wanting here. The State owns very little of the territory alleged to be affected, and the damage to it capable of estimate in money, possibly, at least, is small. This is a suit by a State for an injury to it in its capacity of *quasi*-sovereign. In that capacity the State has an interest independent of and behind the titles of its citizens, in all the earth and air within its domain. It has the last word as to whether its mountains shall be stripped of their forests and its inhabitants shall breathe pure air.

Just as Georgia's "independent interest * * * in all the earth and air within its domain" supported federal jurisdiction a century ago, so too does Massachusetts' well-founded desire to preserve its sovereign territory today. That Massachusetts does in fact own a great deal of the "territory alleged to be affected" only reinforces the conclusion that its stake in the outcome of this case is sufficiently concrete to warrant the exercise of federal judicial power.

When a State enters the Union, it surrenders certain sovereign prerogatives. Massachusetts cannot invade Rhode Island to force reductions in greenhouse gas emissions, it cannot negotiate an emissions treaty with China or India, and in some circumstances the exercise of its police powers to reduce in-state motor-vehicle emissions might well be pre-empted.

These sovereign prerogatives are now lodged in the Federal Government, and Congress has ordered EPA to protect Massachusetts (among others) by prescribing standards applicable to the "emission of any air pollutant from any class or classes of new motor vehicle engines, which in [the Administrator's] judgment cause, or contribute to, air pollution which may reasonably be anticipated to endanger public health or welfare." Congress has moreover recognized a concomitant procedural right to challenge the rejection of its rulemaking petition as arbitrary and capricious. Given that procedural right and Massachusetts' stake in protecting its quasi-sovereign interests, the Commonwealth is entitled to special solicitude in our standing analysis.[17]

---

[17] The Chief Justice accuses the Court of misreading *Tennessee Copper* and "devis[ing] a new doctrine of state standing." But no less an authority than HART & WECHSLER'S THE FEDERAL COURTS AND THE FEDERAL SYSTEM understands *Tennessee Copper* as a standing decision. Indeed, it devotes an entire section to chronicling the long development of cases permitting States "to litigate as *parens patriae* to protect quasi-sovereign interests—*i.e.,* public or governmental interests that concern the state as a whole."

Drawing on *Massachusetts v. Mellon* (1923) and *Alfred L. Snapp & Son, Inc. v. Puerto Rico ex rel. Barez,* 458 U.S. 592 (1982), the Chief Justice claims that we "overloo[k] the fact

With that in mind, it is clear that petitioners' submissions as they pertain to Massachusetts have satisfied the most demanding standards of the adversarial process. EPA's steadfast refusal to regulate greenhouse gas emissions presents a risk of harm to Massachusetts that is both "actual" and "imminent." There is, moreover, a "substantial likelihood that the judicial relief requested" will prompt EPA to take steps to reduce that risk.

The Injury

The harms associated with climate change are serious and well recognized. Indeed, the NRC Report itself—which EPA regards as an "objective and independent assessment of the relevant science,"—identifies a number of environmental changes that have already inflicted significant harms, including "the global retreat of mountain glaciers, reduction in snow-cover extent, the earlier spring melting of rivers and lakes, [and] the accelerated rate of rise of sea levels during the 20th century relative to the past few thousand years * * * ."

Petitioners allege that this only hints at the environmental damage yet to come. According to the climate scientist Michael MacCracken, "qualified scientific experts involved in climate change research" have reached a "strong consensus" that global warming threatens (among other things) a precipitate rise in sea levels by the end of the century, "severe and irreversible changes to natural ecosystems," a "significant reduction in water storage in winter snowpack in mountainous regions with direct and important economic consequences," and an increase in the spread of disease. He also observes that rising ocean temperatures may contribute to the ferocity of hurricanes.[18]

That these climate-change risks are "widely shared" does not minimize Massachusetts' interest in the outcome of this litigation. According to petitioners' unchallenged affidavits, global sea levels rose somewhere between 10 and 20 centimeters over the 20th century as a result of

---

that our cases cast significant doubt on a State's standing to assert a quasi-sovereign interest * * * against the Federal Government." Not so. *Mellon* itself disavowed any such broad reading when it noted that the Court had been "called upon to adjudicate, not rights of person or property, not rights of dominion over physical domain, [and] *not quasi sovereign rights actually invaded or threatened*." ([E]mphasis added). In any event, we held in *Georgia v. Pennsylvania R. Co.* (1945) that there is a critical difference between allowing a State "to protect her citizens from the operation of federal statutes" (which is what *Mellon* prohibits) and allowing a State to assert its rights under federal law (which it has standing to do). Massachusetts does not here dispute that the Clean Air Act *applies* to its citizens; it rather seeks to assert its rights under the Act.

[18] In this regard, MacCracken's 2004 affidavit—drafted more than a year in advance of Hurricane Katrina—was eerily prescient. Immediately after discussing the "particular concern" that climate change might cause an "increase in the wind speed and peak rate of precipitation of major tropical cyclones (i.e., hurricanes and typhoons)," MacCracken noted that "[s]oil compaction, sea level rise and recurrent storms are destroying approximately 20-30 square miles of Louisiana wetlands each year. These wetlands serve as a 'shock absorber' for storm surges that could inundate New Orleans, significantly enhancing the risk to a major urban population."

global warming. These rising seas have already begun to swallow Massachusetts' coastal land. Because the Commonwealth "owns a substantial portion of the state's coastal property," it has alleged a particularized injury in its capacity as a landowner. The severity of that injury will only increase over the course of the next century: If sea levels continue to rise as predicted, one Massachusetts official believes that a significant fraction of coastal property will be "either permanently lost through inundation or temporarily lost through periodic storm surge and flooding events." Remediation costs alone, petitioners allege, could run well into the hundreds of millions of dollars.[21]

Causation

EPA does not dispute the existence of a causal connection between man-made greenhouse gas emissions and global warming. At a minimum, therefore, EPA's refusal to regulate such emissions "contributes" to Massachusetts' injuries.

EPA nevertheless maintains that its decision not to regulate greenhouse gas emissions from new motor vehicles contributes so insignificantly to petitioners' injuries that the agency cannot be haled into federal court to answer for them. For the same reason, EPA does not believe that any realistic possibility exists that the relief petitioners seek would mitigate global climate change and remedy their injuries. That is especially so because predicted increases in greenhouse gas emissions from developing nations, particularly China and India, are likely to offset any marginal domestic decrease.

But EPA overstates its case. Its argument rests on the erroneous assumption that a small incremental step, because it is incremental, can never be attacked in a federal judicial forum. Yet accepting that premise would doom most challenges to regulatory action. Agencies, like legislatures, do not generally resolve massive problems in one fell regulatory swoop. They instead whittle away at them over time, refining their preferred approach as circumstances change and as they develop a more-nuanced understanding of how best to proceed. That a first step might be tentative does not by itself support the notion that federal courts lack jurisdiction to determine whether that step conforms to law.

And reducing domestic automobile emissions is hardly a tentative step. Even leaving aside the other greenhouse gases, the United States transportation sector emits an enormous quantity of carbon dioxide into

---

[21] In dissent, the Chief Justice dismisses petitioners' submissions as "conclusory," presumably because they do not quantify Massachusetts' land loss with the exactitude he would prefer. He therefore asserts that the Commonwealth's injury is "conjectur[al]." Yet the likelihood that Massachusetts' coastline will recede has nothing to do with whether petitioners have determined the precise metes and bounds of their soon-to-be-flooded land. Petitioners maintain that the seas are rising and will continue to rise, and have alleged that such a rise will lead to the loss of Massachusetts' sovereign territory. No one, save perhaps the dissenters, disputes those allegations. Our cases require nothing more.

the atmosphere—according to the MacCracken affidavit, more than 1.7 billion metric tons in 1999 alone. That accounts for more than 6% of worldwide carbon dioxide emissions. To put this in perspective: Considering just emissions from the transportation sector, which represent less than one-third of this country's total carbon dioxide emissions, the United States would still rank as the third-largest emitter of carbon dioxide in the world, outpaced only by the European Union and China. Judged by any standard, U.S. motor-vehicle emissions make a meaningful contribution to greenhouse gas concentrations and hence, according to petitioners, to global warming.

The Remedy

While it may be true that regulating motor-vehicle emissions will not by itself *reverse* global warming, it by no means follows that we lack jurisdiction to decide whether EPA has a duty to take steps to *slow* or *reduce* it. Because of the enormity of the potential consequences associated with man-made climate change, the fact that the effectiveness of a remedy might be delayed during the (relatively short) time it takes for a new motor-vehicle fleet to replace an older one is essentially irrelevant. Nor is it dispositive that developing countries such as China and India are poised to increase greenhouse gas emissions substantially over the next century: A reduction in domestic emissions would slow the pace of global emissions increases, no matter what happens elsewhere.

We moreover attach considerable significance to EPA's "agree[ment] with the President that 'we must address the issue of global climate change,' " and to EPA's ardent support for various voluntary emission-reduction programs. As Judge Tatel observed in dissent below, "EPA would presumably not bother with such efforts if it thought emissions reductions would have no discernable impact on future global warming."

In sum—at least according to petitioners' uncontested affidavits—the rise in sea levels associated with global warming has already harmed and will continue to harm Massachusetts. The risk of catastrophic harm, though remote, is nevertheless real. That risk would be reduced to some extent if petitioners received the relief they seek. We therefore hold that petitioners have standing to challenge the EPA's denial of their rulemaking petition.[24]

---

[24] In his dissent, the Chief Justice expresses disagreement with the Court's holding in *United States v. Students Challenging Regulatory Agency Procedures (SCRAP)* (1973). He does not, however, disavow this portion of Justice Stewart's opinion for the Court:

> Unlike the specific and geographically limited federal action of which the petitioner complained in *Sierra Club* (1972), the challenged agency action in this case is applicable to substantially all of the Nation's railroads, and thus allegedly has an adverse environmental impact on all the natural resources of the country. Rather than a limited group of persons who used a picturesque valley in California, all persons who utilize the scenic resources of the country, and indeed all who breathe its air, could claim harm similar to that alleged by the environmental groups here. But we have already made it clear that standing is

* * *

[The Court's discussion of the merits is omitted.]

VIII

The judgment of the Court of Appeals is reversed, and the case is remanded for further proceedings consistent with this opinion.

It is so ordered.

CHIEF JUSTICE ROBERTS, with whom JUSTICE SCALIA, JUSTICE THOMAS, and JUSTICE ALITO join, dissenting.

Global warming may be a "crisis," even "the most pressing environmental problem of our time." Indeed, it may ultimately affect nearly everyone on the planet in some potentially adverse way, and it may be that governments have done too little to address it. It is not a problem, however, that has escaped the attention of policymakers in the Executive and Legislative Branches of our Government, who continue to consider regulatory, legislative, and treaty-based means of addressing global climate change.

Apparently dissatisfied with the pace of progress on this issue in the elected branches, petitioners have come to the courts claiming broad-ranging injury, and attempting to tie that injury to the Government's alleged failure to comply with a rather narrow statutory provision. I would reject these challenges as nonjusticiable. Such a conclusion involves no judgment on whether global warming exists, what causes it, or the extent of the problem. Nor does it render petitioners without recourse. This Court's standing jurisprudence simply recognizes that redress of grievances of the sort at issue here "is the function of Congress and the Chief Executive," not the federal courts. I would vacate the judgment below and remand for dismissal of the petitions for review.

I

* * *

Our modern framework for addressing standing is familiar: "A plaintiff must allege personal injury fairly traceable to the defendant's allegedly unlawful conduct and likely to be redressed by the requested relief." Applying that standard here, petitioners bear the burden of al-

---

not to be denied simply because many people suffer the same injury. Indeed some of the cases on which we relied in *Sierra Club* demonstrated the patent fact that persons across the Nation could be adversely affected by major governmental actions. *To deny standing to persons who are in fact injured simply because many others are also injured, would mean that the most injurious and widespread Government actions could be questioned by nobody.* We cannot accept that conclusion." ([C]itations omitted and emphasis added).

It is moreover quite wrong to analogize the legal claim advanced by Massachusetts and the other public and private entities who challenge EPA's parsimonious construction of the Clean Air Act to a mere "lawyer's game."

leging an injury that is fairly traceable to the Environmental Protection Agency's failure to promulgate new motor vehicle greenhouse gas emission standards, and that is likely to be redressed by the prospective issuance of such standards.

Before determining whether petitioners can meet this familiar test, however, the Court changes the rules. It asserts that "States are not normal litigants for the purposes of invoking federal jurisdiction," and that given "Massachusetts' stake in protecting its quasi-sovereign interests, the Commonwealth is entitled to *special solicitude* in our standing analysis." ([E]mphasis added).

Relaxing Article III standing requirements because asserted injuries are pressed by a State, however, has no basis in our jurisprudence, and support for any such "special solicitude" is conspicuously absent from the Court's opinion. The general judicial review provision cited by the Court affords States no special rights or status. The Court states that "Congress has ordered EPA to protect Massachusetts (among others)" through the statutory provision at issue and that "Congress has * * * recognized a concomitant procedural right to challenge the rejection of its rulemaking petition as arbitrary and capricious." The reader might think from this unfortunate phrasing that Congress said something about the rights of States in this particular provision of the statute. Congress knows how to do that when it wants to, but it has done nothing of the sort here. Under the law on which petitioners rely, Congress treated public and private litigants exactly the same.

Nor does the case law cited by the Court provide any support for the notion that Article III somehow implicitly treats public and private litigants differently. The Court has to go back a full century in an attempt to justify its novel standing rule, but even there it comes up short. The Court's analysis hinges on *Georgia v. Tennessee Copper Co.* (1907)—a case that did indeed draw a distinction between a State and private litigants, but solely with respect to available remedies. The case had nothing to do with Article III standing.

In *Tennessee Copper,* the State of Georgia sought to enjoin copper companies in neighboring Tennessee from discharging pollutants that were inflicting "a wholesale destruction of forests, orchards and crops" in bordering Georgia counties. Although the State owned very little of the territory allegedly affected, the Court reasoned that Georgia—in its capacity as a "*quasi*-sovereign"—"has an interest independent of and behind the titles of its citizens, in all the earth and air within its domain." The Court explained that while "[t]he very elements that would be relied upon in a suit between fellow-citizens as a ground for equitable relief [were] wanting," a State "is not lightly to be required to give up *quasi*-sovereign rights for pay." Thus while a complaining private litigant would have to make do with a *legal* remedy—one "for pay"—the State was entitled to *equitable* relief.

In contrast to the present case, there was no question in *Tennessee Copper* about Article III injury. There was certainly no suggestion that the State could show standing where the private parties could not; there was no dispute, after all, that the private landowners had "an action at law." *Tennessee Copper* has since stood for nothing more than a State's right, in an original jurisdiction action, to sue in a representative capacity as *parens patriae*. Nothing about a State's ability to sue in that capacity dilutes the bedrock requirement of showing injury, causation, and redressability to satisfy Article III.

A claim of *parens patriae* standing is distinct from an allegation of direct injury. Far from being a substitute for Article III injury, *parens patriae* actions raise an additional hurdle for a state litigant: the articulation of a "quasi-sovereign interest" "*apart* from the interests of particular private parties." ([E]mphasis added). Just as an association suing on behalf of its members must show not only that it represents the members but that at least one satisfies Article III requirements, so too a State asserting quasi-sovereign interests as *parens patriae* must still show that its citizens satisfy Article III. Focusing on Massachusetts's interests as quasi-sovereign makes the required showing here harder, not easier. The Court, in effect, takes what has always been regarded as a *necessary* condition for *parens patriae* standing-a quasi-sovereign interest-and converts it into a *sufficient* showing for purposes of Article III.

What is more, the Court's reasoning falters on its own terms. The Court asserts that Massachusetts is entitled to "special solicitude" due to its "quasi-sovereign interests," but then applies our Article III standing test to the asserted injury of the State's loss of coastal property. In the context of *parens patriae* standing, however, we have characterized state ownership of land as a "nonsovereign interes[t]" because a State "is likely to have the same interests as other similarly situated proprietors."

On top of everything else, the Court overlooks the fact that our cases cast significant doubt on a State's standing to assert a quasi-sovereign interest—as opposed to a direct injury—against the Federal Government. As a general rule, we have held that while a State might assert a quasi-sovereign right as *parens patriae* "for the protection of its citizens, it is no part of its duty or power to enforce their rights in respect of their relations with the Federal Government. In that field it is the United States, and not the State, which represents them."

All of this presumably explains why petitioners never cited *Tennessee Copper* in their briefs before this Court or the D.C. Circuit. It presumably explains why not one of the legion of *amici* supporting petitioners ever cited the case. And it presumably explains why not one of the three judges writing below ever cited the case either. Given that one purpose of the standing requirement is " 'to assure that concrete adverseness which sharpens the presentation of issues upon which the court so largely depends for illumination,' " it is ironic that the Court today adopts a new theory of Article III standing for States without the benefit of briefing or argument on the point.[1]

II

It is not at all clear how the Court's "special solicitude" for Massachusetts plays out in the standing analysis, except as an implicit concession that petitioners cannot establish standing on traditional terms. But the status of Massachusetts as a State cannot compensate for petitioners' failure to demonstrate injury in fact, causation, and redressability.

When the Court actually applies the three-part test, it focuses, as did the dissent below, on the State's asserted loss of coastal land as the injury in fact. If petitioners rely on loss of land as the Article III injury, however, they must ground the rest of the standing analysis in that specific injury. That alleged injury must be "concrete and particularized," and "distinct and palpable." Central to this concept of "particularized" injury is the requirement that a plaintiff be affected in a "personal and individual way," and seek relief that "directly and tangibly benefits him" in a manner distinct from its impact on "the public at large." Without "particularized injury, there can be no confidence of 'a real need to exercise the power of judicial review' or that relief can be framed 'no broader than required by the precise facts to which the court's ruling would be applied.' "

The very concept of global warming seems inconsistent with this particularization requirement. Global warming is a phenomenon "harmful to humanity at large," and the redress petitioners seek is focused no more on them than on the public generally—it is literally to change the atmosphere around the world.

If petitioners' particularized injury is loss of coastal land, it is also that injury that must be "actual or imminent, not conjectural or hypothetical," "real and immediate," and "certainly impending."

As to "actual" injury, the Court observes that "global sea levels rose somewhere between 10 and 20 centimeters over the 20th century as a result of global warming" and that "[t]hese rising seas have already begun to swallow Massachusetts' coastal land." But none of petitioners' declarations supports that connection. One declaration states that "a rise in sea level due to climate change is occurring on the coast of Massachusetts, in the metropolitan Boston area," but there is no elaboration. And the declarant goes on to identify a "significan[t]" *non*-global-warming cause of Boston's rising sea level: land subsidence. Thus, aside

---

[1] The Court seems to think we do not recognize that *Tennessee Copper* is a case about *parens patriae* standing, but we have no doubt about that. The point is that nothing in our cases (or HART & WECHSLER) suggests that the prudential requirements for *parens patriae* standing, can somehow substitute for, or alter the content of, the "irreducible constitutional minimum" requirements of injury in fact, causation, and redressability under Article III. * * *

from a single conclusory statement, there is nothing in petitioners' 43 standing declarations and accompanying exhibits to support an inference of actual loss of Massachusetts coastal land from 20th century global sea level increases. It is pure conjecture.

The Court's attempts to identify "imminent" or "certainly impending" loss of Massachusetts coastal land fares no better. One of petitioners' declarants predicts global warming will cause sea level to rise by 20 to 70 centimeters *by the year 2100*. Another uses a computer modeling program to map the Commonwealth's coastal land and its current elevation, and calculates that the high-end estimate of sea level rise would result in the loss of significant state-owned coastal land. But the computer modeling program has a conceded average error of about 30 centimeters and a maximum observed error of 70 centimeters. As an initial matter, if it is possible that the model underrepresents the elevation of coastal land to an extent equal to or in excess of the projected sea level rise, it is difficult to put much stock in the predicted loss of land. But even placing that problem to the side, accepting a century-long time horizon and a series of compounded estimates renders requirements of imminence and immediacy utterly toothless. "Allegations of possible future injury do not satisfy the requirements of Art. III. A threatened injury must be *certainly impending* to constitute injury in fact."

III

Petitioners' reliance on Massachusetts's loss of coastal land as their injury in fact for standing purposes creates insurmountable problems for them with respect to causation and redressability. To establish standing, petitioners must show a causal connection between that specific injury and the lack of new motor vehicle greenhouse gas emission standards, and that the promulgation of such standards would likely redress that injury. As is often the case, the questions of causation and redressability overlap. And importantly, when a party is challenging the Government's allegedly unlawful regulation, or lack of regulation, of a third party, satisfying the causation and redressability requirements becomes "substantially more difficult."

Petitioners view the relationship between their injuries and EPA's failure to promulgate new motor vehicle greenhouse gas emission standards as simple and direct: Domestic motor vehicles emit carbon dioxide and other greenhouse gases. Worldwide emissions of greenhouse gases contribute to global warming and therefore also to petitioners' alleged injuries. Without the new vehicle standards, greenhouse gas emissions-and therefore global warming and its attendant harms-have been higher than they otherwise would have been; once EPA changes course, the trend will be reversed.

The Court ignores the complexities of global warming, and does so by now disregarding the "particularized" injury it relied on in step one, and using the dire nature of global warming itself as a bootstrap for finding causation and redressability. First, it is important to recognize the extent of the emissions at issue here. Because local greenhouse gas emissions disperse throughout the atmosphere and remain there for anywhere from 50 to 200 years, it is global emissions data that are relevant. According to one of petitioners' declarations, domestic motor vehicles contribute about 6 percent of global carbon dioxide emissions and 4 percent of global greenhouse gas emissions. The amount of global emissions at issue here is smaller still; § 202(a)(1) of the Clean Air Act covers only *new* motor vehicles and *new* motor vehicle engines, so petitioners' desired emission standards might reduce only a fraction of 4 percent of global emissions.

* * *

Petitioners are never able to trace their alleged injuries back through this complex web to the fractional amount of global emissions that might have been limited with EPA standards. In light of the bit-part domestic new motor vehicle greenhouse gas emissions have played in what petitioners describe as a 150-year global phenomenon, and the myriad additional factors bearing on petitioners' alleged injury—the loss of Massachusetts coastal land—the connection is far too speculative to establish causation.

IV

Redressability is even more problematic. To the tenuous link between petitioners' alleged injury and the indeterminate fractional domestic emissions at issue here, add the fact that petitioners cannot meaningfully predict what will come of the 80 percent of global greenhouse gas emissions that originate outside the United States. As the Court acknowledges, "developing countries such as China and India are poised to increase greenhouse gas emissions substantially over the next century," so the domestic emissions at issue here may become an increasingly marginal portion of global emissions, and any decreases produced by petitioners' desired standards are likely to be overwhelmed many times over by emissions increases elsewhere in the world.

Petitioners offer declarations attempting to address this uncertainty, contending that "[i]f the U.S. takes steps to reduce motor vehicle emissions, other countries are very likely to take similar actions regarding their own motor vehicles using technology developed in response to the U.S. program." In other words, do not worry that other countries will contribute far more to global warming than will U.S. automobile emissions; someone is bound to invent something, and places like the People's Republic of China or India will surely require use of the new technology, regardless of cost. The Court previously has explained that when the existence of an element of standing "depends on the unfettered choices made by independent actors not before the courts and whose exercise of broad and legitimate discretion the courts cannot presume either to control or to predict," a party must present facts supporting an assertion that the actor will proceed in such a manner. The declarations' conclusory (not to say fanciful) statements do not even come close.

No matter, the Court reasons, because *any* decrease in domestic emissions will "slow the pace of global emissions increases, no matter what happens elsewhere." Every little bit helps, so Massachusetts can sue over any little bit.

The Court's sleight-of-hand is in failing to link up the different elements of the three-part standing test. What must be *likely* to be redressed is the particular injury in fact. The injury the Court looks to is the asserted loss of land. The Court contends that regulating domestic motor vehicle emissions will reduce carbon dioxide in the atmosphere, *and therefore* redress Massachusetts's injury. But even if regulation *does* reduce emissions—to some indeterminate degree, given events elsewhere in the world—the Court never explains why that makes it *likely* that the injury in fact—the loss of land—will be redressed. Schoolchildren know that a kingdom might be lost "all for the want of a horseshoe nail," but "likely" redressability is a different matter. The realities make it pure conjecture to suppose that EPA regulation of new automobile emissions will *likely* prevent the loss of Massachusetts coastal land.

V

Petitioners' difficulty in demonstrating causation and redressability is not surprising given the evident mismatch between the source of their alleged injury—catastrophic global warming—and the narrow subject matter of the Clean Air Act provision at issue in this suit. The mismatch suggests that petitioners' true goal for this litigation may be more symbolic than anything else. The constitutional role of the courts, however, is to decide concrete cases—not to serve as a convenient forum for policy debates.

When dealing with legal doctrine phrased in terms of what is "fairly" traceable or "likely" to be redressed, it is perhaps not surprising that the matter is subject to some debate. But in considering how loosely or rigorously to define those adverbs, it is vital to keep in mind the purpose of the inquiry. The limitation of the judicial power to cases and controversies "is crucial in maintaining the tripartite allocation of power set forth in the Constitution." In my view, the Court today—addressing Article III's "core component of standing"—fails to take this limitation seriously.

To be fair, it is not the first time the Court has done so. Today's decision recalls the previous high-water mark of diluted standing requirements, *United States v. Students Challenging Regulatory Agency Procedures (SCRAP)* (1973). *SCRAP* involved "[p]robably the most attenuated injury conferring Art. III standing" and "surely went to the very outer limit of the law"—until today. In *SCRAP,* the Court based an environmental group's standing to challenge a railroad freight rate surcharge on the group's allegation that increases in railroad rates would cause an increase in the use of nonrecyclable goods, resulting in the increased need for natural resources to produce such goods. According to the group, some of these resources might be taken from the Washington area, resulting in increased refuse that might find its way into area parks, harming the group's members.

Over time, *SCRAP* became emblematic not of the looseness of Article III standing requirements, but of how utterly manipulable they are if not taken seriously as a matter of judicial self-restraint. *SCRAP* made standing seem a lawyer's game, rather than a fundamental limitation ensuring that courts function as courts and not intrude on the politically accountable branches. Today's decision is *SCRAP* for a new generation.[2]

Perhaps the Court recognizes as much. How else to explain its need to devise a new doctrine of state standing to support its result? The good news is that the Court's "special solicitude" for Massachusetts limits the future applicability of the diluted standing requirements applied in this case. The bad news is that the Court's self-professed relaxation of those Article III requirements has caused us to transgress "the proper—and properly limited—role of the courts in a democratic society."

I respectfully dissent.

Notes and Questions

1. The majority, quoting *Lujan v. Defenders of Wildlife* (*see* pages 81-83), asserts the if Congress creates a procedural right, then the person seeking to assert that right is to some unspecified extent excused from meeting the ordinary requirements of redressability and immediacy of the harm threatened. If those requirements are functions of Article III standing, how is it possible for Congress to create exceptions to them?

2. What is the constitutional basis for declaring states to be "special" litigants for purposes of standing? Does the *Tennessee Copper* case that Justice Stevens cites stand for that proposition, or does it merely recognize that states *qua* states have certain substantive rights, violation of which may give rise to injuries-in-fact of a type that individuals cannot suffer?

3. a) What precisely is the injury-in-fact that Massachusetts claims? If it is the loss of coastal land, is the Chief Justice correct in his dissent that it is neither impending nor redressable? *See* Anthony DePalma, *Warming Report Warns of Increased Flooding*, N.Y. TIMES (July 11, 2007) ("One-

---

[2] The difficulty with *SCRAP*, and the reason it has not been followed, is not the portion cited by the Court. Rather, it is the *attenuated* nature of the injury there, and here, that is so troubling. Even in *SCRAP*, the Court noted that what was required was "something more than an ingenious academic exercise in the conceivable," and we have since understood the allegation there to have been "that the string of occurrences alleged would happen *immediately*." That is hardly the case here.

The Court says it is "quite wrong" to compare petitioners' challenging "EPA's parsimonious construction of the Clean Air Act to a mere 'lawyer's game.'" Of course it is not the legal challenge that is merely "an ingenious academic exercise in the conceivable," but the assertions made in support of standing.

hundred-year floods could come as often as once every 10 years by the end of this century, Long Island lobsters could disappear and New York apples could be just a memory if nothing is done to reduce greenhouse gas emissions, according to a new report on the impact of global warming by the Union of Concerned Scientists.") If it is harm to the climate, is he correct that it is not individualized?

b) If Massachusetts' injury is the loss of coastal land, which, as Justice Stevens notes, gives rise to "a particularized injury in its capacity as a landowner," then is it proper simultaneously to treat Massachusetts as a state? In other words, is the majority trying to have it both ways, characterizing Massachusetts as a state entitled to special rules for purposes of satisfying the imminence and redressability inquiries but as an individual for purposes of the injury-in-fact inquiry?

4. Near the beginning of the dissent, the Chief Justice argues that the Court's standing jurisprudence merely remits Massachusetts to the political process for addressing this difficulty. Massachusetts, of course, may have the view that the political process has already spoken and that it is simply trying to get the courts to enforce the very statute that Congress passed. Is the Chief Justice saying that the law is unconstitutional, or is he instead saying that a law may confer specific rights without those rights being judicially enforceable? If it is the latter, does that raise separation-of-powers problems?

5. Does the Chief Justice argue that Massachusetts has no standing because a) it has not demonstrated that it has any injury-in-fact, or b) that even if it does suffer injury-in-fact, noticeable injury will not occur for so long a time that the injury is not "impending," or c) because he thinks that the remedy that Massachusetts seeks can have no measurable impact on the problem of which the state complains? There are potential problems with each alternative.

a) If the difficulty is lack of injury-in-fact *simpliciter*, how long must Massachusetts wait until it acquires a justiciable injury? Presumably, if the EPA acted in a way that caused the rapid and perceptible loss of several square miles of Massachusetts coast land, the state would have standing to protest. How long is too long for an injury to accrue for purposes of standing? Should it make any difference that the injury process may be irreversible by the time it is perceptible? Should the answer to that question depend in any part on whether the plaintiff seeks legal or equitable relief?

b) If the difficulty is that the injury is not sufficiently imminent, is the Chief Justice implicitly adapting the common law year-and-a-day rule for causation in homicide cases to the standing context? Inhalation of asbestos fibers causes mesothelioma, an almost-always-fatal form of cancer. The symptoms, however, may not appear for decades following the exposure and inhalation. If a tenant can prove that his landlord's improper handling of asbestos removal caused the tenant to inhale a large quantity of asbestos fibers, would the tenant lack standing to bring a diversity case against the landlord? In the Chief Justice's view, if the tenant would not have standing at the outset, at what point might he acquire standing? Should the answer to this question depend at all on whether ameliorative treatments are available before that point? Suppose such treatments exist, but the tenant cannot afford them.

One is tempted to say that it would and should preclude an action because so many things might happen to cause the victim's death sooner, so that the harm is conjectural. Consider, though, that in ordinary torts cases, juries may award damages for both future pain and suffering, medical expenses and future earnings over the victim's expected lifetime, despite the fact that something may happen to end the victim's life long before the time the actuaries predict.

c) If the difficulty is that the remedy through the EPA will not have a measurable impact on the problem, has the Chief Justice drawn an unusually blurry line? One assumes he would not take the position that qualifying under the redressability prong of standing doctrine is not an all-or-nothing matter. Does he offer any guidance for when available relief is *de minimis* for standing purposes?

That aside, has not Congress already made the policy judgment that this approach to the problem is worth pursuing through the mechanism that it enacted? If so, does the Chief Justice propose that the Court use standing doctrine to override that legislative policy judgment? Alternatively, must the Chief Justice then be prepared to say that Congress's policy judgment as represented in the statute is unconstitutional under Article III standing doctrine?

6. The Chief Justice also argues that states are not entitled to any special consideration in their capacity as landowners. His position makes an interesting contrast with the position taken by the Court's majority in *Idaho v. Coeur d'Alene Tribe* (1997) (*see* page 661), where it relied precisely on Idaho's special status as a state in a dispute over ownership of land in order to bar relief under the Eleventh Amendment. Ironically, in the very next paragraph, the Chief Justice alludes to the federal government's special status when he acknowledges the curious concept of *quasi*-sovereignty but notes that the Court has not permitted states to invoke that concept in disputes with the federal government.

7. On page 73, the dissent appears to conflate two concepts in discussing the nature of the remedy. The opinion argues that the relief Massachusetts seeks would not benefit the state in any way different from the benefit that the whole world would presumably reap from a reduction in greenhouse gases. Is the dissent suggesting that not only the injury-in-fact but also the remedy must be particularized to the plaintiff? In other words, assuming that the requested remedy would benefit the plaintiff, is it somehow suspect for standing purposes if it would also benefit many others?

8. At bottom, is the Chief Justice's real concern with standing, or is it that he thinks that Massachusetts either cannot or should not prevail on the merits? Note his comments on page 75 on the speculative nature of Massachusetts's injury. Is the dissent subtly equating the only-partial-effectiveness of relief with the causation inquiry?

NOTE ON FURTHER PROBLEMS WITH THE COURT'S STANDING JURISPRUDENCE

1. CONSTITUTIONAL STANDING

a. *Generalized Grievances*

Massachusetts v. EPA is only the latest case to consider widely-shared harms as injuries-in-fact. The Court's generalized-grievance jurisprudence has always caused difficulties. The variety of the cases demonstrates the scope of the problem.

In 1937, a brave attorney challenged Hugo Black's appointment to the Supreme Court on the ground that Black had been a member of the Senate when it passed a bill increasing the retirement pay of associate justices. The plaintiff argued that the appointment violated the Ineligibility Clause (art. I, § 6, cl. 2): "No Senator or Representative shall, during the Time for which he was elected, be appointed to any civil Office under the Authority of the United States, * * * the Emoluments whereof shall have been encreased during such time * * * ." The Court, in a *per curiam* opinion, found the plaintiff lacked standing and never reached the merits. *Ex parte Levitt,* 302 U.S. 633, 58 S.Ct. 1, 82 L.Ed. 493 (1937). Suppose that Levitt was correct on the merits. What remedy would he or anyone else have?

The Vietnam War sparked many judicial challenges to various governmental practices. *United States v. Richardson,* 418 U.S. 166 (1974), refused to find standing for a taxpayer challenging the CIA's accounting methods as inconsistent with the Accounts Clause, U.S. CONST. art. I, § 9, cl. 7. In *Schlesinger v. Reservists Committee to Stop the War,* 418 U.S. 208, 94 S.Ct. 2925, 41 L.Ed.2d 706 (1974), present and former members of military reserve units challenged the constitutionality of members of Congress also holding reserve commissions in violation of the Incompatibility Clause, U.S. CONST. art. I, § 6, cl. 2. There, too, the Court refused to find standing and made it clear that what it called "generalized grievances" were insufficient to satisfy the Case-or-Controversy Clause. In *Schlesinger,* as in *Richardson,* the Court asserted that the plaintiffs' remedy was political, not judicial.

What are the advantages and disadvantages of remitting citizens to the political process to raise issues about the constitutionality of governmental conduct? What are the disadvantages of permitting cases like *Levitt, Richardson* and *Schlesinger* to be resolved by the judiciary?

Suppose the federal government proposed to convey as a gift a valuable parcel of land to a sectarian institution of higher education engaged primarily in training ministers. Who would have standing to seek to enjoin the transfer as violative of the Establishment Clause? Suppose, instead of donating land, the government decided to make a gift of $500,000 to such an institution. *See Valley Forge Christian College v. Americans United for Separation of Church and State,* 454 U.S. 464, 102

S.Ct. 752, 70 L.Ed.2d 700 (1982). Consider whether, in the typical Establishment Clause case, any individual or group is likely to be able to show a personalized injury sufficient to satisfy the Court's evolving standard under Article III. The *Valley Forge* Court dismissed this potential problem.

> Respondents' claim of standing implicitly rests on the presumption that violations of the Establishment Clause typically will not cause injury sufficient to confer standing under the "traditional" view of Art. III. But "[t]he assumption that if respondents have no standing to sue, no one would have standing, is not a reason to find standing."

Sometimes the Court considers Establishment Clause challenges on their merits without mentioning standing. *See, e.g., Lynch v. Donnelly*, 465 U.S. 668, 104 S.Ct. 1355, 79 L.Ed.2d 604 (1984) (city residents and ACLU challenge to city's inclusion of nativity scene in holiday display).

Note that whether the category of "generalized grievances" is a constitutional or prudential impediment is a matter of some importance. Congress may attempt to create standing to overcome a prudential requirement but cannot so treat an Article III requirement. Which position makes more sense?

Even if "generalized grievances" is a constitutional component, Congress may be able to create standing. Congress can create new substantive rights and thereby define new "injuries in fact." For example, the patent laws define a substantive right—the right not to have others copy and sell one's invention—and thereby create a new type of injury-in-fact. The common law of torts, property, or contracts would not have recognized the inventor's loss of business because someone copied his invention as a cognizable legal injury. When Congress does so, it can authorize private rights of action by those injured in the enjoyment of the newly-created rights. Must the injury be individualized? *Lujan v. Defenders of Wildlife*, 504 U.S. 555, 112 S.Ct. 2130, 119 L.Ed.2d 351 (1992), seems to say so. Part of the Endangered Species Act, 16 U.S.C.A. § 1531 *et seq.* (1982), requires each federal agency to insure that its actions not threaten any protected species. Another provision permits a civil suit by "any person" to enjoin violations. When a dispute arose over whether the Act applies to federal involvement outside the United States, Defenders of Wildlife and several of its individual members sued to establish that it does. The plaintiffs alleged that defendants' actions threatened species in Egypt and Sri Lanka, but did not allege that the individual plaintiffs had concrete plans to visit those areas again. The Court refused to find standing and elaborated upon the requirement of concrete injury.

> It is clear that the person who observes or works with a particular animal threatened by a federal decision is facing perceptible harm, since the very subject of his interest will no longer exist. It is even

plausible—though it goes to the outermost limits of plausibility—to think that a person who observes or works with animals of a particular species in the very area of the world where that species is threatened by a federal decision is facing such harm, since some animals that might have been the subject of his interest will no longer exist. It goes beyond the limit, however, and into pure speculation and fantasy, to say that anyone who observes or works with an endangered species, anywhere in the world, is appreciably harmed by a single project affecting some portion of that species with which he has no more specific connection.

With respect to the "citizen-suit" provision, the Court noted:

> We have consistently held that a plaintiff raising only a generally available grievance about government—claiming only harm to his and every citizen's interest in proper application of the Constitution and laws, and seeking relief that no more directly and tangibly benefits him than it does the public at large—does not state an Article III case or controversy.

> * * *

> To be sure, our generalized grievance cases have typically involved Government violation of procedures assertedly ordained by the Constitution rather than the Congress. But there is absolutely no basis for making the Article III inquiry turn on the source of the asserted right. Whether the courts were to act on their own, or at the invitation of Congress, in ignoring the concrete injury requirement described in our cases, they would be discarding a principle fundamental to the separate and distinct constitutional role of the Third Branch—one of the essential elements that identifies those "Cases" and "Controversies" that are the business of the courts rather than of the political branches. * * * Vindicating the *public* interest (including the public interest in government observance of the Constitution and laws) is the function of Congress and the Chief Executive. The question presented here is whether the public interest in proper administration of the laws * * * can be converted into an individual right by a statute that denominates it as such, and that permits all citizens * * * to sue. If the concrete injury requirement has the separation-of-powers significance we have always said, the answer must be obvious: To permit Congress to convert the undifferentiated public interest in executive officers' compliance with the law into an "individual right" vindicable in the courts is to permit Congress to transfer from the President to the courts the Chief Executive's most important constitutional duty, to "take Care that the Laws be faithfully executed * * * ."

Does *Lujan* suggest that Congress may be able to create standing, but it must find a way to convert what would otherwise be a mere "generalized grievance" into a violation that can visit a specific and distinctive harm on an individual? Does this possibility operate the same way with respect to constitutional and statutory rights?

In *Federal Election Commission v. Akins*, 524 U.S. 11, 118 S.Ct. 1777, 141 L.Ed.2d 10 (1998), the Court again considered Congress's ability to create standing. The Federal Election Campaign Act (FECA) mandates limits on the amounts that individuals, corporations, political committees and political parties can directly contribute to candidates for federal office. Part of FECA imposes both recordkeeping and disclosure requirements on political committees, which the Act defines as "any committee, club, association or other group of persons which receives" or makes certain defined contributions or expenditures.[11] The *Akins* plaintiffs challenged the FEC's refusal to treat the American Israel Public Affairs Committee (AIPAC) as a political committee. They asserted that AIPAC was violating certain provisions of FECA and demanded that FEC order AIPAC to make the disclosures required of a political committee under FECA. There was a lively dispute between the plaintiffs and AIPAC about the nature of some of the latter's revenue (contributions) and disbursements (expenditures). FEC sought and received summary judgment in the district court, which upheld FEC's interpretation of FECA's requirements. A panel of the District of Columbia Circuit affirmed on the substantive point after finding that the plaintiffs had standing. The en banc Circuit vacated the panel decision, agreeing on the standing point but finding that the plaintiff's interpretation of FECA was correct. Accordingly, it reversed the district court's grant of summary judgment and remanded.

When the case reached the Supreme Court, a six-Member majority agreed with the District of Columbia Circuit that there was standing, but vacated the Circuit decision and remanded so that the FEC could reconsider whether, under proposed new FEC rules concerning who qualified as a member of organizations like AIPAC, APIAC was a political committee within the meaning of FECA.

With respect to standing, the majority rejected FEC arguments that the plaintiffs satisfied neither the constitutional nor the prudential requirements of the Court's doctrine. Regarding the prudential standing challenge, the Court found that Congress explicitly authorized people like the *Akins* plaintiffs—a group of voters—to challenge FEC dismissal of an administrative complaint demanding that the FEC proceed against an entity under FECA, thus bringing voters with the "zone of interests" that the statute protected.

The FEC's constitutional standing argument fared no better. FEC

---

[11] The definition is somewhat more complex because it goes into what constitutes contributions to such committees and qualifying expenditures by them, but the precise contours are not important here.

argued that the plaintiffs had suffered no injury-in-fact, and that their case was analogous to *United States v. Richardson, supra* at 80, because they expressed only a generalized grievance. The *Akins* majority noted that *Richardson* refused to find standing because the Court found "no 'logical nexus' between the [plaintiffs'] asserted status of taxpayer and the claimed failure of the Congress to require the Executive to supply a more detailed report of the [CIA's] expenditures." By contrast, the court noted that the *Akins* plaintiffs wanted the information they said FECA required to "help them (and others to whom they would communicate it) to evaluate candidates for public office, especially candidates who received assistance from AIPAC, and to evaluate the role that AIPAC's financial assistance might play in a specific election." Thus, having the FECA information might directly affect the plaintiffs' exercise of their franchise, validating congressional creation of voter standing. The Court also noted that *Richardson* was a taxpayer-standing, not a voter-standing, case.

Ultimately, the Court characterized the generalized-grievance attack as the FEC's strongest argument, but rejected it (explicitly without placing the generalized-grievance doctrine squarely in either the constitutional or prudential standing requirements), finding that the plaintiffs' interest in obtaining the information was neither abstract nor undifferentiated from the entitlement of the populace generally. "[T]he informational injury here, directly related to voting, the most basic of political rights, is sufficiently concrete and specific such that the fact that it is widely shared does not deprive Congress of constitutional power to authorize its vindication in the federal courts."

The three dissenting Justices disagreed with the majority that any voter could be aggrieved within the meaning of FECA's authorization to sue. The dissent distinguished between the FEC's refusal to make public information in its possession, which the dissent appeared to concede was actionable, and the FEC's refusal to undertake enforcement action to collect information. Those Justices also thought *Akins* precisely in the mold of *Richardson*, partly on the ground that *Richardson* had treated voter standing as indistinguishable from taxpayer standing. For the dissenters, the plaintiffs could not show that their asserted injury from not having the information they claimed FECA mandated be available was any different from the injury that any other member of the voting public might assert. Justice Scalia found plaintiffs' injury to be undifferentiated in the same way that the *Richardson* majority had found Richardson's complaint wanting. *See also United States v. Hays*, 515 U.S. 737, 115 S.Ct. 2431, 132 L.Ed.2d 635 (1995) (holding voters outside of an allegedly racially gerrymandered district without standing to raise an equal protection challenge). *Hays* also appeared to locate the generalized-grievance doctrine within the constitutional, not prudential, criteria for standing. Query whether *Akins* casts doubt on that conclusion.

b. *Taxpayer Standing*

When government embarks upon a course of conduct alleged to be unconstitutional and the conduct requires expenditure of public funds, should a federal taxpayer have standing to challenge the perceived misuse of tax revenues? For many years, the Court's answer has been a uniform "no." *See Frothingham v. Mellon,* 262 U.S. 447, 43 S.Ct. 597, 67 L.Ed. 1078 (1923), in which the Court, although noting that municipal taxpayer standing had been upheld, refused to find standing for a taxpayer challenging the constitutionality of a federal expenditure:

> [T]he relation of a taxpayer of the United States to the federal government is very different. His interest in the moneys of the treasury—partly realized from taxation and partly from other sources—is shared with millions of others, is comparatively minute and indeterminable, and the effect upon future taxation, of any payment out of the funds, so remote, fluctuating and uncertain, that no basis is afforded for an appeal to the preventive powers of a court of equity * * * . If one taxpayer may champion and litigate such a cause, then every other taxpayer may do the same, not only in respect of the statute here under review, but also in respect of every other public appropriation act and statute whose administration requires the outlay of public money, and whose validity may be questioned. The bare suggestion of such a result, with its attendant inconveniences, goes far to sustain the conclusion which we have reached, that a suit of this character cannot be maintained.

Would or should the answer be different if the challenged expenditure were a substantial part of the federal budget, or if the individual taxpayer pays enough in taxes to make an identifiable contribution? What if the tax is not general, but is a specialized "use" tax?

In the only exception to denial of taxpayer standing, a sharply divided Court ruled in *Flast v. Cohen,* 392 U.S. 83, 88 S.Ct. 1942, 20 L.Ed.2d 947 (1968), that a taxpayer had standing to challenge action that specifically violated the taxing power itself. The plaintiffs presented an Establishment Clause challenge to federal expenditures of funds to support education in religious schools. A five-to-four majority found standing for the plaintiffs as taxpayers because they satisfied a two-part nexus test:

> *First* the taxpayer must establish a logical link between that status and the type of legislative enactment attacked. Thus, a taxpayer will be a proper party to allege the unconstitutionality only of exercises of congressional power under the taxing and spending clause of Art. I, § 8, of the Constitution. It will not be sufficient to allege an incidental expenditure of tax funds in the administration of an essentially regulatory statute * * * . *Secondly,* the taxpayer must establish a nexus between that status and the precise nature of the constitutional infringement alleged. Under this requirement, the

taxpayer must show that the challenged enactment exceeds specific constitutional limitations imposed upon the exercise of the congressional taxing and spending power and not simply that the enactment is generally beyond the powers delegated to Congress by Art. I, § 8. When both nexuses are established, the litigant will have shown a taxpayer's stake in the outcome of the controversy and will be a proper and appropriate party to invoke a federal court's jurisdiction.

The best measure of the difficulty of satisfying the two-pronged test that *Flast* sets out may be that since *Flast* no one has been found to have federal taxpayer standing. The *Flast* Court viewed the Establishment Clause as a specific restriction on governmental expenditures; that allowed the plaintiffs to satisfy the second branch of the nexus test. Are there any other constitutional provisions that fit that description?

Hein v. Freedom from Religion Foundation, Inc., ___ U.S. ___, 127 S.Ct. 2553, 168 L.Ed.2d 424 (2007), reaffirmed the shakiness of the ground on which *Flast* stands. The plaintiff organization challenged the allocation of executive branch funds to the White House Office of Faith-Based and Community Initiatives and to the corresponding Executive Department Centers for Faith-Based and Community Initiatives established in several federal agencies and departments. President Bush instituted the programs by executive orders in 2001 to ensure that "private and charitable community groups, including religious ones * * * have the fullest opportunity permitted by law to compete [for federal financial support] on a level playing field, so long as they achieve valid public purposes * * * ." The plaintiff argued that the funding violated the Establishment Clause. A five-to-four Court held that the plaintiff lacked standing. There was, however, no majority opinion. Justice Alito, writing for himself, Chief Justice Roberts and Justice Kennedy, distinguished *Flast* on the ground that it rested on a challenge to a congressional Taxing-and-Spending-Clause appropriation that specifically endorsed spending federal money to support parochial schools. In *Hein*, the money came from Congress's general allocation of funds to the executive branch. Consider, however, that the expenditures in *Flast* were made pursuant to a federal statute appropriating $100 million to local educational agencies to help educate low-income students. Although the Act contemplated that resources would be spent on private elementary and secondary schools, it apparently did not explicitly authorize funds for religious schools. In *Hein*, by contrast, Congress apparently informally "earmarked" portions of its general Executive Branch appropriations to fund the very offices and centers the suit challenged. Arguably, then, the legislative mandate was more "express" and the appropriation more "specific" in *Hein* than in *Flast*. Justice Alito responded to this dilemma by assuming that Congress "surely understood that much of the aid mandated by the statute would find its way to religious schools" since the majority of American private schools were associated with a church in the 1960s, and by saying that informal earmarks don't matter because they do not "impose legally binding restrictions." Does this distinction persuade you?

In a separate concurrence, Justice Kennedy worried that allowing standing in *Hein* would expand *Flast*'s "narrow exception" to *Frothingham*'s taxpayer-standing rule without limits. Justice Scalia, joined by Justice Thomas, concurred in the judgment only. He wanted the Court simply to overrule *Flast*, in part because he could see no logical distinction between permitting standing in *Flast* and denying it in *Hein*. He challenged the Court either to extend *Flast* to what he saw as the limits of his logic or to jettison it entirely. In the process, he distinguished between what he labeled as "wallet injury" and "psychic injury," arguing that only the former could create a justiciable case or controversy within the meaning of Article III. In his view, permitting standing in a case where the plaintiffs allege only psychic injury allows plaintiffs to evade the traceability and redressability parts of the Court's standing jurisprudence, because they will always be able to allege that their psychic injury is traceable to the expenditure and will cease if the courts prevent the expenditure.

Establishment-Clause challenges of the type that *Hein* represents are not, of course, the only cases in which plaintiffs allege psychic rather than wallet injury. The Court's decision in *Brown v. Board of Education*, 347 U.S. 483, 74 S.Ct. 686, 98 L.Ed. 873 (1954), rested heavily on the psychic impact that separate-but-equal educational philosophy and practice had on African-American children. There was no allegation of wallet injury. Justice Scalia's opinion made no mention of such cases. For that matter, tort actions seeking compensation for intentionally inflicted extreme emotional distress are now commonplace. Would Justice Scalia argue that the federal courts cannot adjudicate such cases under their diversity jurisdiction?

The four dissenting Justices agreed with Justice Scalia that *Flast*'s logic compelled a finding of standing in *Hein*. They argued that the mere fact that the designation of expenditures to aid religion came from the executive rather than the legislative branch did not turn the matter from a case presenting a justiciable case to one that did not. For them, it was sufficient that the money funding the executive branch offices came directly from a congressional exercise of power under the Taxing and Spending Clause.

Hein suggests that Congress and the President may act together to expend federal funds in support of religion if only Congress is careful not to specify the purpose of the expenditures. In theory, given Justice Alito's and Justice Scalia's opinions, even if the President were to specify that unallocated executive branch funds should go to a designated religion, no individual or group would have standing to mount a judicial challenge. Justice Alito's opinion indicated that in the face of egregious executive branch endorsement or support of religion, "Congress could quickly step in." Does the Court's approach relegate what may be constitutional violations to the political process, undermining the Court's assertion, dating from *Marbury*, that it is the supreme expositor of the meaning of the Constitution?

c. *Citizen Standing*

Can Congress create citizen standing? The answer seems to be a qualified "yes." This requires renewed consideration of whether the generalized grievance sub-doctrine is constitutional or prudential. Clearly, if it is merely prudential, then there is no impediment to a contrary legislative rule; one of our legal system's working assumptions is legislative primacy within the bounds of the Constitution. As the Court has said on many occasions, Congress is free to do foolish things; it just may not do unconstitutional things.

May state law allow citizen-standing actions in the state courts that would not qualify as Article III cases or controversies? If so, may the Supreme Court review the ensuing state court decisions without running afoul of Article III? The Court has suggested an affirmative answer to both questions, with some significant qualifications, but a recent dismissal of a grant of certiorari suggests that the answers are far from clear.

In *ASARCO Inc. v. Kadish*, 409 U.S. 605, 109 S.Ct. 2037, 104 L.Ed.2d 696 (1989), taxpayers sought a declaration that a state law concerning mineral leases on state lands was invalid. They prevailed in the state court, after which the defendant class of mineral lessees sought Supreme Court review. The Court held that Article III standing existed, although it recognized that had the action been commenced in the federal courts, long-established law would have required its dismissal because the taxpayer plaintiffs would have been unable to demonstrate injury-in-fact and thus would have lacked standing under *Frothingham v. Mellon*, 262 U.S. 447, 43 S.Ct. 597, 67 L.Ed. 1078 (1923). Nonetheless, the Court found that the defendant class, having suffered an adverse judgment in the state courts that would have invalidated their mineral leases, did have standing.

Although the Court stated clearly that the plaintiffs would have lacked standing in an original federal action, it did not address the question, not presented by the case in its posture on review, of whether there would have been Supreme Court jurisdiction to review if the state courts had ruled adversely to the plaintiffs. To be sure, the plaintiffs would have lacked standing to commence their action in the federal district court, but after an adverse state court ruling, would they have been in position to claim that the state court's erroneous judgment then caused them injury and, in effect, conferred standing?

The latest case to present the state-versus-federal standing problem is *DaimlerChrysler Corp. v. Cuno,* 547 U.S. 332, , 126 S.Ct. 1854, 164 L.Ed.2d 589 (2006). Taxpayers in Ohio, including some in Toledo, sued DaimlerChrysler and municipal and state tax officials objecting to local (a municipal tax exemption) and state tax benefits (in the form of a property tax credit) offered to the company in exchange for its agreement to expand its Jeep plant in Toledo. The plaintiffs argued that the benefits would have the effect of increasing their own tax burdens and violated the Commerce Clause. They commenced the action in the Ohio state courts, but DaimlerChrysler removed the case to the federal courts. Plaintiffs moved to remand, expressing doubts that they could satisfy the federal requirements for standing. The district court denied the remand, finding that the plaintiffs had standing under the municipal taxpayer rule that *Massachusetts v. Mellon* (1923), a companion case to *Frothingham v. Mellon* (1923) had recognized. That court denied relief under the Commerce Clause. The Sixth Circuit agreed with the district court as to the municipal tax exemption but disagreed as to the state franchise tax credit. Both sides sought certiorari.

The Court's discussion of taxpayer standing is unremarkable. Chief Justice Roberts's opinion rehearsed the history of the Court's approach to taxpayer standing from *Frothingham* forward. The Court made clear that the taxpayer standing rule rests on the Article III requirement of case or controversy and is, therefore, jurisdictional. In the course of the discussion, the Chief Justice tied the Court's taxpayer standing rules to the Constitution's concern with separation of powers, quoting, among other sources, a speech that Chief Justice Marshall made to the House of Representatives. The Court also reiterated its opposition to recognizing standing for what it has called "generalized grievances." The plaintiffs also attempted to use *Flast v. Cohen* (1968) to their advantage, but the Court firmly rejected the invitation to extend its spending-power doctrine, noting the special place of that Establishment Clause case in the structure of standing. With *Flast* essentially limited to its facts (but certainly not repudiated), the Court refused to recognize standing for the plaintiffs as state taxpayers.

The plaintiffs were not quite through, however. As noted above, the district court upheld plaintiffs' standing as municipal taxpayers to challenge the municipal tax exemption, and there was no issue as to that ruling in either the Sixth Circuit or the Supreme Court. In what one certainly must view as creative lawyering, the plaintiffs argued that since jurisdiction over the municipal tax exemption claim was secure, the federal courts could hear the *state*-taxpayers claims under their supplemental jurisdiction. The Court declined this invitation as well, noting that it had read *United Mine Workers v. Gibbs* (1966) narrowly, and relying for that assertion in part on *Owen Equipment & Erection Co. v.*

Kroger (1978) and *Finley v. United States* (1989).[12] In the course of the discussion of *Gibbs*, the Court limited *Gibbs*'s one-constitutional-case approach to Article III considerations other than standing.[13] The Chief Justice noted the gate-opening effects that the plaintiffs' suggested "ancillary-standing" reading of *Gibbs* would have and turned away from the parade of horribles that the Court envisioned.[14]

So saying, the Court reversed the Sixth Circuit's grant of relief and remanded the case with directions that the plaintiffs' challenge to the state franchise tax credit be dismissed, leaving in place the judgment of the lower courts upholding the municipal property tax exemption. It is at this point that interesting questions begin to arise. Why, for example, did the Court not remand with directions that the district court remand the case to the state court from which it came, pursuant to 28 U.S.C. § 1447(c)?[15] It is true, of course, that the statute refers to remand "before final judgment," but that term has varying meanings, depending on the context. For purposes of the preclusion doctrines, for example, a judgment is final even while it is on appeal and may serve as the predicate for either claim or issue preclusion. In this sense, the Supreme Court's action in the case certainly did not come before final judgment. On the other hand, in the law of federal habeas corpus, a judgment is not final for purposes of beginning the statute of limitations period until "the

---

[12] The latter reliance was perhaps a bit odd, given that the Court recognized in *Exxon Mobil Corp. v. Allapattah Services, Inc.* (2005) that the supplemental jurisdiction statute, 28 U.S.C. § 1367, had overruled *Finley*, a fact that Chief Justice Roberts noted in the sentence following his *Finley* citation.

[13]   What we have never done is apply the rationale of *Gibbs* to permit a federal court to exercise supplemental jurisdiction over a claim that does not by itself satisfy those elements of the Article III inquiry, such as constitutional standing, that "serv[e] to identify those disputes which are appropriately resolved through the judicial process * * * ." We see no reason to read the language of *Gibbs* so broadly, particularly since our standing cases confirm that a plaintiff must demonstrate standing for each claim he seeks to press. * * * We have insisted, for instance, that "a plaintiff must demonstrate standing separately for each form of relief sought."

[14]   Yet if *Gibbs*' "common nucleus" formulation announced a new definition of "case" or "controversy" for all Article III purposes, a federal court would be free to entertain moot or unripe claims, or claims presenting a political question, if they "derived from" the same "operative fact[s]" as another federal claim suffering from non of these defects. Plaintiffs' reading of *Gibbs*, therefore, would amount to a significant revision of our precedent interpreting Article III. With federal courts thus deciding issues they would not otherwise be authorized to decide, the " 'tripartite allocation of power' " that Article III is designed to maintain would quickly erode; our emphasis on the standing requirement's role in maintaining this separation would be rendered hollow rhetoric. As we have explained, "[t]he actual-injury requirement would hardly serve the purpose * * * of preventing courts from undertaking tasks assigned to the political branches[,] if once a plaintiff demonstrated harm from one particular inadequacy in government administration, the court were authorized to remedy *all* inadequacies in that administration."

[15] In pertinent part, the statute reads: "If at any time before final judgment it appears that the district court lacks subject matter jurisdiction, the case shall be remanded."

date on which the judgment became final by the conclusion of direct review or the expiration of the time for seeking such review."[16] Using that standard, perhaps the Court should have directed the district court to remand. As a practical matter, it may make little difference, since the plaintiffs retain the option of refiling in the state court under the Ohio law discussed in the next paragraph.

The Court has said that the Article III standing requirements are jurisdictional, preventing the federal courts from considering the plaintiffs' claims on the merits. Those requirements do not, of course, apply to the state courts. If plaintiffs refile their state court claim[17] that the state tax credit is unlawful, what should happen? Although the case as originally filed was removable (because the Supreme Court had not spoken definitively on the issue), the Court's decision in *DaimlerChrysler* now makes clear that the case is not removable because there is no jurisdiction.[18]

Assume the plaintiffs do litigate their challenge to the state tax credit in the state courts. Under *ASARCO, Inc. v. Kadish*, if the plaintiffs win the defendants presumably would have standing to seek review of the Ohio Supreme Court's decision in the United States Supreme Court. Thus, under *DaimlerChrysler*, defendants lack Article III standing to invoke the removal jurisdiction of the federal courts but have standing under *ASARCO* to invoke the Supreme Court's appellate jurisdiction. Can these cases be harmonized, or are the results simply inconsistent?

Suppose instead that the defendants were to prevail in the Ohio Supreme Court. Do the plaintiffs then acquire Article III standing under *ASARCO*, which found that an adverse state judgment can itself create injury-in-fact that permits Supreme Court review? If nothing else, would such a situation require the Supreme Court to decide the merits of the plaintiffs' constitutional claims with respect to the state-tax-credit claim? If that is not the case, has *DaimlerChrysler* (in combination with *ASARCO*) bequeathed a situation in which the decision of the Ohio Supreme Court may or may not create Article III standing, depending which way it goes? Some might think that anomalous. Either plaintiffs or defendants might seek review of the same Fourteenth Amendment issues: whether the state tax credit violates the Due Process or Equal Protection Clauses. Does resolution of the Article III standing issue de-

---

[16] 28 U.S.C. § 2244(d)(1)(A) (2000).

[17] Ohio law allows refiling in this situation either until the end of the normal limitation period or within one year from the Supreme Court's decision, whichever is later. *See* OHIO REV. CODE ANN. § 2305.19(a) (2005).

[18] Indeed, counsel now seeking to remove the case would run a considerable risk of Rule 11 sanctions, since there is no longer a good-faith argument that there is federal jurisdiction.

pend on who asks the question?[19]

2. PRUDENTIAL STANDING

a. *Statutory Substantive Rights and Zones of Protected Interests.*

A clearly prudential standing requirement exists with respect to statutory rights. The interest that the plaintiff seeks to vindicate must be arguably within the zone of interests that the statute upon which she relies protects or regulates. *Association of Data Processing Service Organizations v. Camp,* 397 U.S. 150, 90 S.Ct. 827, 25 L.Ed.2d 184 (1970), originally articulated that test. The Comptroller of the Currency had ruled that national banks could provide data processing services to other banks and to bank customers "as an incident to their banking services." Petitioners, a data processors' association and a data processing firm, challenged the ruling, alleging that it was inconsistent with a federal statute that allowed banks to engage in incidental activities only when such activities were "necessary to carry on the business of banking." Additionally, the petitioners argued that the Comptroller's ruling violated another federal statute that restricted banks to performing "bank services" for banks. The Supreme Court asserted that it was easy to identify those whose interests were directly affected by the statutes and concluded that competitors of the banks providing data processing services were within the statutorily protected zone of interests. The Court introduced the zone-of-interests test as a rejection of the previously-used protected-legal-interest test. "The 'legal interest' test goes to the merits. The question of standing is different."[20]

In 1987, the Court elaborated further.

> The "zone of interest" test is a guide for deciding whether, in view of Congress' evident intent to make agency action presumptively reviewable, a particular plaintiff should be heard to complain of a particular agency decision. In cases where the plaintiff is not itself the subject of the contested regulatory action, the test denies a right of review if the plaintiff's interests are so marginally related

---

[19] The Court has created this sort of anomaly before. In *Franchise Tax Board v. Construction Laborer' Vacation Trust,* text at 264, the question to which both parties wanted an answer in the form of a declaratory judgment was, "Does ERISA pre-empt?" The Court made clear that there was federal question jurisdiction if the Trust commenced an action asking the question but not if the Franchise Tax Board commenced an action asking the same question.

[20] At least for Justice Brennan, the change in vocabulary was not sufficient.

> I had thought we discarded the notion of any additional requirement when we discussed standing solely in terms of its constitutional content in *Flast v. Cohen.* By requiring a second, nonconstitutional step, the Court comes very close to perpetuating the discredited requirement that conditioned standing on a showing by the plaintiff that the challenged governmental action invaded one of his legally protected interests.

to or inconsistent with the purposes implicit in the statute that it cannot reasonably be assumed that Congress intended to permit the suit. The test is not meant to be especially demanding; in particular, there need be no indication of congressional purpose to benefit the would-be plaintiff.

Clarke v. Securities Industry Association, 479 U.S. 388, 399-400, 107 S.Ct. 750, 757, 93 L.Ed.2d 757, 769 (1987). Does the quotation distinguish the zone-of-interests test from the legally-protected-interest-test that *Data Processing* purported to reject, or is Justice Brennan correct that the new test is merely the old traveling *incognito*?

National Credit Union Administration v. *First National Bank & Trust Co.,* 522 U.S. 479, 118 S.Ct. 927, 140 L.Ed.2d 1 (1998), is a more recent example of the Court's application of the zone-of-interests test. Respondents, five banks and the American Bankers Association, challenged the National Credit Union Administration's (NCUA) interpretation of a federal statute it administered. The statute limited membership of federal credit unions to "groups having a common bond of occupation or association, or to groups within a well-defined neighborhood, community, or rural district." Before 1982, NCUA had interpreted the common bond provision to require that all members of the credit union be united by occupation, but it changed its interpretation in 1982 to apply only to each employer group within multi-group credit unions. Thus, as long as each employer group was united by a common bond, federal credit unions could be composed of entirely unrelated groups and still meet the requirements of the statute. When the NCUA allowed a particular credit union to add several unrelated employer groups, respondents sued. The Supreme Court again declared that in applying the zone-of-interests test there is no need to determine whether Congress intended the statutory provision to benefit those in the plaintiff's position. Rather, a court must first ascertain the interests the statute arguably protects and then ask if the plaintiff's interests are among them. The Court found that one of the protected interests was an interest in limiting the markets that federal credits can serve by limiting their membership and restricting the availability of their services to members only. As competitors, respondents also had an interest in limiting the markets the credit unions could serve, and the NCUA's interpretation of the statute affected that interest by allowing the credit unions to increase their base of customers. Consequently, respondents were arguably within the statute's zone of protected interests and had standing.

Four Justices joined in a vigorous dissent, arguing that the majority's application of the zone-of-interests test was inconsistent with precedent and all but eliminated the requirement. The majority's view of the relevant protected interest amounted to an examination of the interest in *enforcing* the statute. The common-bond requirement limited the customers a credit union can serve, and because respondents were competitors, they also had an interest in the same limitation. Thus, according to the majority, respondents had an interest in enforcing the statute. Instead, the dissent argued that the critical inquiry should be whether the injury of which the plaintiff complains is within the zone of interests the statute seeks to protect. The dissenters concluded that neither the statutory language, its operation, nor the circumstances surrounding its enactment demonstrated congressional intent to restrict competition. Thus, the injury plaintiffs asserted was not within the statute's zone of protected interests. The dissent argued that Congress required a common bond among members of federal credit unions to ensure that, as lenders, credit unions would be more knowledgeable about their borrowers and that the borrowers would be more reluctant to default.

Does *National Credit Union Administration* say that Congress may protect an interest (for purposes of standing) without having intended to do so? The majority opinion quoted *Clarke*'s assertion that "there need be no indication of congressional purpose to benefit the would-be plaintiff." Was it suggesting that Congress may not actually have intended to benefit the plaintiff but might have if it had thought about it, thus making this test a watered-down version of congressional intent? Alternatively, did it mean that reasonable people could conclude that a legislature intended the benefit claimed by the plaintiff, even if the particular legislature that passed the statute did not? In short, just what did the juxtaposition of these themes in the majority opinion mean? The only limitation the majority seemed to express on a plaintiff's coming within the zone-of-interests test was " 'if the plaintiff's interests * * * are [only] marginally related to or inconsistent with the purposes implicit in the statute.' "

The dissent, on the other hand, seemed to read the test as one of congressional intent. Is the dissent correct that the majority made the zone-of-interest test simply a mutated form of the constitutionally-required injury-in-fact? If injury-in-fact is all that the majority is talking about, what of its exclusion from standing of plaintiffs whose interests are only "marginally related to or inconsistent with the purposes implicit in the statute"? To the extent that the majority's test is not simply injury-in-fact, does it become a form of sophisticated causation requirement, with the Court asserting that it is unwilling to find that challenged agency action proximately caused plaintiffs' the injury-in-fact?

Suppose the Federal Communications Commission, acting pursuant to a congressional grant of authority, denies television broadcast stations permission to offer electronically-based services (such as shopping, banking, or other informational services) other than entertainment, simply because the FCC thinks it too difficult to regulate such a broad spectrum of operations. Such a decision would permit (perhaps implicitly encourage) development of cable services. If the FCC were then to overcome its concerns and reverse its ruling, would cable companies have standing to object?

Is the zone-of-interests test analogous to the contracts rule that only intended third-party beneficiaries may sue to enforce a contract? *See, e.g., Martinez v. Socoma Companies, Inc.,* 11 Cal.3d 394, 113 Cal.Rptr. 585, 521 P.2d 841 (1974) (class of disadvantaged unemployed persons cannot recover for defendant's failure to honor contractual provision with United States government requiring defendant to hire certain numbers of such persons, since they were not intended beneficiaries):

> American law generally classifies persons having enforceable rights under contracts to which they are not parties as either creditor beneficiaries or donee beneficiaries.
>
> A person cannot be a creditor beneficiary unless the promisor's performance of the contract will discharge some form of legal duty owed to the beneficiary by the promisee.
>
> A person is a donee beneficiary only if the promisee's contractual intent is either to make a gift to him or to confer on him a right against the promisor.

When the Court says that a plaintiff falls outside a statute's zone of interests, is it really saying that the plaintiff is, at best, an incidental third-party beneficiary rather than a creditor or donee beneficiary? Justice Scalia has suggested that analogy. *Wyoming v. Oklahoma,* 502 U.S. 437, 473, 112 S.Ct. 789, 810, 117 L.Ed.2d 1, 34 (1992) (Scalia, J., dissenting) ("The 'zone of interests' test performs the same role as * * * the limitation on suits by third-party beneficiaries of contracts * * * .").

Should the zone-of-interests test apply in litigation seeking relief under constitutional provisions? Is it possible in a principled way to speak of the zone of interests addressed by a constitutional provision?

Suppose a state passes a law requiring a locally-regulated industry to purchase a certain percentage of its raw materials from in-state sources, a change from the commercial practice formerly followed by the industry. It is clear that former suppliers in other states might challenge the law under the Commerce Clause. May the states in which the former suppliers are located file their own judicial challenges on the ground that the new statute has deprived them of tax revenues that they otherwise would have gotten from raw material sales? Is such a state within the zone of interests protected by the Commerce Clause? In *Wyoming v. Oklahoma* the majority found standing but did not mention the zone-of-interests test. Justice Scalia, joined by Chief Justice Rehnquist and Justice Thomas, dissented on the ground that Wyoming's interests were at best only marginally related to those protected by the Commerce Clause, since Wyoming was not itself seeking to engage in interstate commerce.

In at least one area, the Court has used zone-of-interest analysis as part of its inquiry in constitutional cases, though it has assiduously avoided labeling it as such. In a line of cases restricting defendants' standing to challenge searches and seizures on Fourth Amendment grounds, the Court articulated its findings in terms of the defendants' "reasonable expectation of privacy." *See, e.g., Rakas v. Illinois,* 439 U.S. 128, 99 S.Ct. 421, 58 L.Ed.2d 387 (1978); *Rawlings v. Kentucky,* 448 U.S. 98, 100 S.Ct. 2556, 65 L.Ed.2d 633 (1980); *United States v. Payner,* 447 U.S. 727, 100 S.Ct. 2439, 65 L.Ed.2d 468 (1980). In each of those cases, the Court held that defendants convicted on the basis of evidence seized in violation of the Fourth Amendment had no standing because they had no reasonable expectation of privacy in the area searched. Clearly each search caused a defendant injury in fact; the seized evidence was crucial to conviction. Was the Court saying, in effect, that the defendants were outside the zone of interests of the Fourth Amendment? Explicit application of the zone-of-interest test, a prudential rather than constitutional requirement, would allow Congress prospectively to overrule the Court's standing analysis. In the Fourth Amendment cases, the Court eliminated that possibility by declaring, in *Rakas:*

> the question necessarily arises whether it serves any useful analytical purpose to consider this principle as a matter of standing, distinct from the merits of a defendant's Fourth Amendment claim * * *. [T]he type of standing requirement * * * reaffirmed today is more properly subsumed under substantive Fourth Amendment doctrine * * *. The inquiry under either approach is the same. But we think the better analysis forthrightly focuses on the extent of a particular defendant's rights under the Fourth Amendment, rather than on any theoretically separate, but invariably intertwined concept of standing.

Does the Court's recognition of the interrelationship of standing and the merits support the argument that all standing inquiries ought instead to be treated as questions about the merits?

b. *Third-Party Standing*

May an individual assert the rights of third persons? That apparently simple question, to which one might intuitively (but not always correctly) answer "no," has provoked substantial scholarly comment, *see, e.g.,* William A. Fletcher, *The Structure of Standing,* 98 YALE L.J. 221 (1988); Henry P. Monaghan, *Third Party Standing,* 84 COLUM.L.REV. 277 (1984); Robert A. Sedler, *The Assertion of Constitutional* Jus Tertii: *A Substantive Approach,* 70 CALIF.L.REV. 1308 (1982), and not inconsiderable judicial attention. For example, if a state statute prohibits the purchase of alcoholic beverages by males under the age of twenty-one and by females under the age of eighteen, may a vendor of alcoholic beverages sue arguing that the statute violates the Equal Protection Clause? *See Craig v. Boren,* 429 U.S. 190, 97 S.Ct. 451, 50 L.Ed.2d 397 (1976). The vendor almost certainly suffers injury, since males between the ages of eighteen and twenty-one are excluded from his customer base, but the substantive entitlement upon which he relies is an equal protection right that extends to someone else.

Alternatively, consider a situation that arose from the Civil Rights Act of 1968, 42 U.S.C.A. § 3610(a) (1988), which prohibited housing discrimination. White residents of an apartment complex charged the landlord with violating the Act by excluding blacks. Should the white residents have had standing? A unanimous Court found that they did. *Trafficante v. Metropolitan Life Insurance Co.,* 409 U.S. 205, 93 S.Ct. 364, 34 L.Ed.2d 415 (1972). Was *Trafficante* a true third-party standing case, or were the plaintiffs asserting merely their own rights?

Perhaps surprisingly, similar standing questions can also arise in criminal cases. For example, in *Batson v. Kentucky,* 476 U.S. 79, 106 S.Ct. 1712, 90 L.Ed.2d 69 (1986), the black defendant successfully challenged the prosecution's use of peremptory challenges systematically to exclude blacks from the jury. Does a defendant not of the same race as the excluded jurors have standing to protest the prosecution's use of peremptory challenges? Similarly, if the defense uses its peremptory challenges in a racially discriminatory manner, does the state have standing to raise the equal protection claim? *See Powers v. Ohio,* 499 U.S. 400, 111 S.Ct. 1364, 113 L.Ed.2d 411 (1991) (criminal defendant had standing to object to race-based exclusions of jurors through the use of peremptory challenges even though the defendant and the excluded jurors were not of the same race); *Georgia v. McCollum,* 505 U.S. 42, 112 S.Ct. 2348, 120 L.Ed.2d 33 (1992) (state may raise equal protection rights of jurors excluded by criminal defendant on the basis of race). *See also Campbell v. Louisiana,* 523 U.S. 392, 118 S.Ct. 1419, 140 L.Ed.2d 551 (1998) (criminal defendant had third-party standing to challenge race-based selection of grand jury forepersons even though not of the same race as the excluded individuals).

It would be a mistake to conclude that *Craig v. Boren,* which allowed third-party standing, was an aberration. For example, in *United States Department of Labor v. Triplett,* 494 U.S. 715, 110 S.Ct. 1428, 108 L.Ed.2d 701 (1990), the Court permitted an attorney to challenge fee-limiting provisions of the federal Black Lung Benefits Act of 1972 on the ground that they violated the Fifth Amendment rights of miners who, because of the provisions, might not be able to obtain qualified counsel to assist them. Justice Scalia's opinion noted an exception to the rule against third-party standing: "When * * * enforcement of a restriction against the litigant prevents a third party from entering into a relationship with the litigant (typically a contractual relationship), to which relationship the third party has a legal entitlement (typically a constitutional entitlement), third-party standing has been held to exist." As a policy matter, why should that exception exist? Would it be better to characterize the litigant's interest as cognizable for standing purposes?

How should the Court determine what is, in its words, "the meaning of constitutionally cognizable injury"? Particularly for those Justices who adhere more or less closely to the idea of original intent, is the described exercise appropriate for the judiciary? Even if the Court undertakes the exercise, are there any objective principles it can use to determine whether allowing standing would be "prudent," or will decisions necessarily be generated only by the Justices own predilections about what sorts of cases the judiciary ought to hear?

c. *Organizational Standing*

May an organization ever bring suit on behalf of one or more of its members? May it do so even if the members upon whose behalf the suit is brought themselves have to participate in the action? The Supreme Court faced these issues in *United Food and Commercial Workers Union Local 751* v. *Brown Group, Inc.*, 517 U.S. 544, 116 S.Ct. 1529, 134 L.Ed.2d 758 (1996). A federal statute, the Worker Adjustment and Retraining Notification Act (the WARN Act), requires certain employers to provide workers or their union at least 60 days' notice before a mass layoff or plant closing. The Act authorizes employees to bring suit to obtain back pay for each day of the violation and specifically authorizes the union to bring suit on their behalf in the alternative. In a previous case the Court had set forth a three part test for situations where an organization would have standing to bring suit on behalf of a member: 1) the members would otherwise have standing to sue on their own behalf; 2) the interests the group seeks to protect are germane to its purpose; and 3) neither the claim asserted nor the remedy sought requires the participation of individual group members in the action. The participation of the individual union members was required so that their right to damages and the amount thereof could be determined based upon particularized proof. Thus, the Court had to determine whether Congress could constitutionally authorize the union to bring suit upon the employees' behalf, despite the fact that their individual presence was required.

The Court held that Congress had that power, characterizing the requirement that the presence of individual group members not be required as prudential. In its view the first and second requirements assured vigorous advocacy on the part of the organization in pursing a claim for which its member had Article III standing, and there was no constitutional necessity for anything else.

In an organizational standing case, is it essential that the organization itself have suffered some injury? A footnote in *United Food and Commercial Workers Union* asserted that the Court's holding made it unnecessary for it to address the issue. If the organization need not suffer any injury, how is the constitutional requirement of injury-in-fact met? Can Congress authorize any third-party to bring suit on behalf of an injured plaintiff?

3.   THE MALLEABILITY OF THE COURT'S STANDING DOCTRINE

In *Warth v. Seldin*, 422 U.S. 490, 95 S.Ct. 2197, 45 L.Ed.2d 343

(1975), the Court combined many of the preceding grounds to drive away an apparently comprehensive assortment of plaintiffs. Plaintiffs sued the Rochester, New York, suburb of Penfield and the members of its zoning, planning and town boards, claiming that town ordinances deliberately prevented persons of low and moderate income from living in the town, in violation of the First, Ninth, and Fourteenth Amendments and various civil rights statutes. The plaintiffs included: 1) potential residents of Penfield, each of low or moderate income and a member of a minority racial or ethnic group, 2) a builders' association whose members built residential housing, 3) Rochester taxpayers, who alleged that their taxes were higher as a direct result of Penfield's exclusionary policies because Rochester then had a disproportionate share of low and moderate income housing that required support from tax abatements, increasing the tax burden, and 4) an association of Penfield residents, which asserted, with echoes of *Trafficante,* that its members were deprived of the benefits of a diverse community. The Court found that the first group of plaintiffs had not alleged that they personally had been excluded and, although they each alleged attempts to find affordable housing in Penfield, the Court declared that they could not trace their inability to find such housing to the constitutional and statutory violations attributed to the defendants. "Petitioners must allege facts from which it reasonably could be inferred that, absent the respondents' restrictive zoning practices, there is a substantial probability that they would have been able to purchase or lease in Penfield and that, if the court affords the relief requested, the asserted inability of petitioners will be removed." The Court denied standing to the builders' group because it failed to allege that the zoning ordinances frustrated any specific building project. The Court said the taxpayers' claim was too conjectural and characterized it as an attempt to assert the rights of others. The Court viewed the Penfield residents' group as similarly attempting to assert third-party standing. *But see Northeastern Florida Chapter of the Associated General Contractors of America v. City of Jacksonville,* 508 U.S. 656, 113 S.Ct. 2297, 124 L.Ed.2d 586 (1993) (contractors' association challenging affirmative action plan based on percentage "goals" for minority participation need not show that any member would have been awarded a contract but for the challenged ordinance; alleged loss of opportunity to compete on equal terms establishes standing).

Assume for the moment that the defendants in *Warth* were violating the constitutional and statutory provisions upon which the plaintiffs relied. Given the Court's approach, how would you structure litigation to challenge the Penfield ordinances? Does the Court's approach signal that such conduct is unchallengeable in the federal courts?

D.   RIPENESS

ABBOTT LABORATORIES v. GARDNER
Supreme Court of the United States, 1967.
387 U.S. 136, 87 S.Ct. 1507, 18 L.Ed.2d 681.

MR. JUSTICE HARLAN delivered the opinion of the Court.

In 1962 Congress amended the Federal Food, Drug, and Cosmetic Act to require manufacturers of prescription drugs to print the "established name" of the drug "prominently and in type at least half as large as that used thereon for any proprietary name or designation for such drug," on labels and other printed material. The "established name" is one designated by the Secretary of Health, Education, and Welfare; the "proprietary name" is usually a trade name under which a particular drug is marketed. The underlying purpose of the 1962 amendment was to bring to the attention of doctors and patients the fact that many of the drugs sold under familiar trade names are actually identical to drugs sold under their "established" or less familiar trade names at significantly lower prices. The Commissioner of Food and Drugs, exercising authority delegated to him by the Secretary, published proposed regulations designed to implement the statute. After inviting and considering comments submitted by interested parties the Commissioner promulgated the following regulation for the "efficient enforcement" of the Act: "If the label or labeling of a prescription drug bears a proprietary name or designation for the drug or any ingredient thereof, the established name, if such there be, corresponding to such proprietary name or designation, shall accompany each appearance of such proprietary name or designation." A similar rule was made applicable to advertisements for prescription drugs.

The present action was brought by a group of 37 individual drug manufacturers and by the Pharmaceutical Manufacturers Association, of which all the petitioner companies are members, and which includes manufacturers of more than 90% of the Nation's supply of prescription drugs. They challenged the regulations on the ground that the Commissioner exceeded his authority under the statute by promulgating an order requiring labels, advertisements, and other printed matter relating to prescription drugs to designate the established name of the particular drug involved every time its trade name is used anywhere in such material.

The District Court, on cross motions for summary judgment, granted the declaratory and injunctive relief sought, finding that the statute did not sweep so broadly as to permit the Commissioner's "every time" interpretation. The Court of Appeals for the Third Circuit reversed without reaching the merits of the case. It held first that under the statutory scheme provided by the Federal Food, Drug, and Cosmetic Act pre-enforcement review of these regulations was unauthorized and therefore beyond the jurisdiction of the District Court. Second, the Court of Appeals held that no "actual case or controversy" existed and, for that reason, that no relief under the Administrative Procedure Act or under the Declaratory Judgment Act was in any event available. Because of the general importance of the question, and the apparent conflict with the decision of the Court of Appeals for the Second Circuit, we granted certiorari.

I

[The Court concluded that there is no indication that Congress intended to preclude pre-enforcement review of this agency action under the Administrative Procedure Act, "which embodies the basic presumption of judicial review to one 'suffering legal wrong because of the agency action, or adversely affected or aggrieved by agency action within the meaning of a relevant statute,' 5 U.S.C. § 702, so long as no statute precludes such relief or the action is not one committed by law to agency discretion."]

II

A further inquiry must, however, be made. The injunctive and declaratory judgment remedies are discretionary, and courts traditionally have been reluctant to apply them to administrative determinations unless these arise in the context of a controversy "ripe" for judicial resolution. Without undertaking to survey the intricacies of the ripeness doctrine it is fair to say that its basic rationale is to prevent the courts, through avoidance of premature adjudication, from entangling themselves in abstract disagreements over administrative policies, and also to protect the agencies from judicial interference until an administrative decision has been formalized and its effects felt in a concrete way by the challenging parties. The problem is best seen in a twofold aspect, requiring us to evaluate both the fitness of the issues for judicial decision and the hardship to the parties of withholding court consideration.

As to the former factor, we believe the issues presented are appropriate for judicial resolution at this time. First, all parties agree that the issue tendered is a purely legal one: whether the statute was properly construed by the Commissioner to require the established name of the drug to be used every time the proprietary name is employed. Both sides moved for summary judgment in the District Court, and no claim is made here that further administrative proceedings are contemplated. It is suggested that the justification for this rule might vary with different circumstances, and that the expertise of the Commissioner is relevant to passing upon the validity of the regulation. This of course is true, but the suggestion overlooks the fact that both sides have approached this case as one purely of congressional intent, and that the Government made no effort to justify the regulation in factual terms.

Second, the regulations in issue we find to be "final agency action" within the meaning of § 10 of the Administrative Procedure Act as construed in judicial decisions. An "agency action" includes any "rule," defined by the Act as "an agency statement of general or particular applicability and future effect designed to implement, interpret, or prescribe law or policy." The cases dealing with judicial review of administrative actions have interpreted the "finality" element in a pragmatic way.

* * *

We find decision in the present case following *a fortiori* from * * * precedents. The regulation challenged here, promulgated in a formal manner after announcement in the Federal Register and consideration of comments by interested parties is quite clearly definitive. There is no hint that this regulation is informal or only the ruling of a subordinate official or tentative. It was made effective upon publication, and the Assistant General Counsel for Food and Drugs stated in the District Court that compliance was expected.

The Government argues, however, that the present case can be distinguished from cases like *Frozen Food Express* on the ground that in those instances the agency involved could implement its policy directly, while here the Attorney General must authorize criminal and seizure actions for violations of the statute. In the context of this case, we do not find this argument persuasive. These regulations are not meant to advise the Attorney General, but purport to be directly authorized by the statute. Thus, if within the Commissioner's authority, they have the status of law and violations of them carry heavy criminal and civil sanctions. Also, there is no representation that the Attorney General and the Commissioner disagree in this area; the Justice Department is defending this very suit. It would be adherence to a mere technicality to give any credence to this contention. Moreover, the agency does have direct authority to enforce this regulation in the context of passing upon applications for clearance of new drugs, or certification of certain antibiotics.

This is also a case in which the impact of the regulations upon the petitioners is sufficiently direct and immediate as to render the issue appropriate for judicial review at this stage. These regulations purport to give an authoritative interpretation of a statutory provision that has a direct effect on the day-to-day business of all prescription drug companies; its promulgation puts petitioners in a dilemma that it was the very purpose of the Declaratory Judgment Act to ameliorate. As the District Court found on the basis of uncontested allegations, "Either they must comply with the every time requirement and incur the costs of changing over their promotional material and labeling or they must follow their present course and risk prosecution." The regulations are clear-cut, and were made effective immediately upon publication; as noted earlier the agency's counsel represented to the District Court that immediate compliance with their terms was expected. If petitioners wish to comply they must change all their labels, advertisements, and promotional materials; they must destroy stocks of printed matter; and they must invest heavily in new printing type and new supplies. The alternative to compliance—continued use of material which they believe in good faith meets the statutory requirements, but which clearly does not meet the regulation of the Commissioner—may be even more costly. That course would risk serious criminal and civil penalties for the unlawful distribution of "misbranded" drugs.

It is relevant at this juncture to recognize that petitioners deal in a sensitive industry, in which public confidence in their drug products is especially important. To require them to challenge these regulations only as a defense to an action brought by the Government might harm them severely and unnecessarily. Where the legal issue presented is fit for judicial resolution, and where a regulation requires an immediate and significant change in the plaintiffs' conduct of their affairs with serious penalties attached to noncompliance, access to the courts under the Administrative Procedure Act and the Declaratory Judgment Act must be permitted, absent a statutory bar or some other unusual circumstance, neither of which appears here.

The Government does not dispute the very real dilemma in which petitioners are placed by the regulation, but contends that "mere financial expense" is not a justification for pre-enforcement judicial review. It is of course true that cases in this Court dealing with the standing of particular parties to bring an action have held that a possible financial loss is not by itself a sufficient interest to sustain a judicial challenge to governmental action. But there is no question in the present case that petitioners have sufficient standing as plaintiffs: the regulation is directed at them in particular; it requires them to make significant changes in their everyday business practices; if they fail to observe the Commissioner's rule they are quite clearly exposed to the imposition of strong sanctions. * * *

The Government further contends that the threat of criminal sanctions for noncompliance with a judicially untested regulation is unrealistic; the Solicitor General has represented that if court enforcement becomes necessary, "the Department of Justice will proceed only civilly for an injunction * * * or by condemnation." We cannot accept this argument as a sufficient answer to petitioners' petition. This action at its inception was properly brought and this subsequent representation of the Department of Justice should not suffice to defeat it.

Finally, the Government urges that to permit resort to the courts in this type of case may delay or impede effective enforcement of the Act. We fully recognize the important public interest served by assuring prompt and unimpeded administration of the Pure Food, Drug, and Cosmetic Act, but we do not find the Government's argument convincing. First, in this particular case, a pre-enforcement challenge by nearly all prescription drug manufacturers is calculated to speed enforcement. If the Government prevails, a large part of the industry is bound by the decree; if the Government loses, it can more quickly revise its regulation.

* * *

Reversed and remanded.

Notes and Questions

1. The Commissioner of the Food and Drug Administration issued a regulation that provided that he could immediately suspend certification service to any company that refused to permit authorized FDA employees unrestricted access to any company facilities involved in manufacturing color additives. Cosmetics containing additives that have not been certified cannot be sold in interstate commerce. Companies could challenge suspension of certification services through an administrative procedure and were entitled to judicial review of adverse determinations. Although it was unclear whether the Commissioner would actually order inspections and, if so, under what circumstances, several cosmetics companies sued, alleging that the Commissioner had exceeded his authority when he issued the regulation. Among other things, the companies were concerned that safeguards the Commissioner might devise would not adequately protect their trade secrets. Was the dispute ripe for adjudication? *See Toilet Goods Association v. Gardner*, 387 U.S. 158, 87 S.Ct. 1520, 18 L.Ed.2d 697 (1967).

2. There are potential difficulties distinguishing ripeness from standing. One might ask three questions: 1) whether the type of injury alleged by the plaintiff is justiciable, 2) whether the plaintiff personally has suffered or will suffer the injury, and 3) whether the plaintiff is sufficiently close to suffering the injury to make judicial intervention appropriate. Consider the following:

> In measuring whether the litigant has asserted an injury that is real and concrete rather than speculative and hypothetical, the ripeness inquiry merges almost completely with standing analysis. The standing requirement, the cornerstone of the Burger Court's article III jurisprudence, demands that a litigant show that he personally "has suffered some threatened or actual injury" as the result of the conduct of the defendant. This requirement of particularized actual injury repeatedly has been treated by the Court not only as constitutionally mandated, but as the very core of the standing determination.

> What then is the distinction between the standing doctrine's demand for "threatened or actual injury" and the ripeness cases' focus on "direct and immediate" harm? Analytically, the two concepts could be segregated, despite the similar phraseology of their standards. The standing doctrine might be used to analyze the nature and magnitude of *present* injuries. Only if such harms could be considered concrete, objective, and judicially cognizable would the standing barrier be overcome. The ripeness requirement, on the other hand, would focus on the substantiality of threatened or actually pending *future* injuries. Applying injury analysis on a forward-looking time frame, the ripeness demand would measure the present effects and hardships imposed by the threat of future government action. In theory, therefore, each doc-

trine could serve distinct but related functions.

It is clear, however, that no such line of demarcation can be located in the cases. The "natural" overlap between standing and ripeness analysis occurs in the measurement of the cognizability of contingent or threatened harms. In such cases, the Burger Court appears to have used the two lines of inquiry interchangeably.

Gene R. Nichol, Jr., *Ripeness and the Constitution,* 54 U.CHI.L.REV. 153, 172-73 (1987) (footnotes omitted). Dean Nichol is not alone in his view. *See, e.g.,* ERWIN CHEMERINSKY, FEDERAL JURISDICTION § 2.4.1, at 117-18 (5th ed. 2007).

Dean Nichol's reservations about the limitations of the present/future dichotomy seem well-founded in at least some cases. For example, in *City of Los Angeles v. Lyons,* 461 U.S. 95, 103 S.Ct. 1660, 75 L.Ed.2d 675 (1983), the plaintiff challenged a city police practice of using chokeholds when deadly force was not justified. Although the plaintiff had been choked, the Court found him without *standing* to seek injunctive relief against the practice because he could not show with any certainty that he would ever be choked again. The Court clearly viewed *Lyons* as a standing case, but under Dean Nichol's hypothesis it appears that it should be a ripeness case.

On the other hand, in *Renne v. Geary,* 501 U.S. 312, 111 S.Ct. 2331, 115 L.Ed.2d 288 (1991), the Court considered challenges to a California constitutional provision that prohibited party endorsements of candidates for judicial, school, county or city offices. The Court found the challenges non-justiciable, noting in part:

> [W]e have no reason to believe that § 6(b) had any impact on the conduct of those involved. The committee made these endorsements "despite objections from some that such endorsements are prohibited" by the provision at issue. Nothing in the record suggests that any action was taken to enforce § 6(b) as a result of those endorsements. We know of no adverse consequences suffered by the Republican Committee or its members due to the apparent violation of § 6(b).

Although the Court sounds like it is discussing injury in fact, it concluded that no "ripe controversy" existed. Under Dean Nichol's model, the Court would have focused on the "nature and magnitude of *present* injuries" and therefore would have discussed standing.

Does the standing inquiry turn upon the certainty that the plaintiff will suffer injury or be a member of the affected class, while ripeness asks when an injury clearly threatening the plaintiff is likely to occur? Does this formulation do any better at describing the results reached by the Court? At bottom, does it make any difference whether a case is dismissed as unripe or for plaintiff's lack of standing?

3. Cases seeking declaratory relief can obviously present ripeness problems. The Court disparaged early declaratory judgment statutes as attempts to permit adjudication of cases that presented no Article III case or controversy. *See, e.g., Liberty Warehouse v. Grannis,* 273 U.S. 70, 47 S.Ct.

282, 71 L.Ed. 541 (1927); *Willing v. Chicago Auditorium Association,* 277 U.S. 274, 48 S.Ct. 507, 72 L.Ed. 880 (1928). But the Court's hostility seemed to erode five years later in *Nashville, Chattanooga & St. Louis Railway v. Wallace,* 288 U.S. 249, 53 S.Ct. 345, 77 L.Ed. 730 (1933), and in 1937, the Court had no trouble affirming the federal Declaratory Judgment Act's constitutionality. *Aetna Life Ins. Co. v. Haworth,* 300 U.S. 227, 57 S.Ct. 461, 81 L.Ed. 617 (1937). It is important to remember, however, that while one of the purposes of declaratory judgment statutes is to accelerate the commencement of litigation, the Supreme Court's approval does not mean that all ripeness problems have disappeared. One still must analyze each case under the Court's ripeness standards.

The Court continues to struggle with the distinction between standing and ripeness and with declaratory judgment actions. *Medimmune, Inc. v. Genentech, Inc.,* ___ U.S. ___, 127 S.Ct. 764, 166 L.Ed.2d 604 (2007), involved a dispute between a patentee (Genentech) and a patent licensee (Medimmune). The license covered an existing patent and a pending application for a second patent, and it required royalty payments to continue until the relevant patent expired or was authoritatively declared not to bar any particular product. Medimmune had been manufacturing Synagis for some years and did not pay royalties on it, apparently because neither party thought the existing patent covered the product. When the Patent Office issued the second patent, the patentee advised the licensee to begin paying royalties on Synagis. The licensee wanted to challenge the patent as invalid and unenforceable and further wanted to establish that Synagis did not infringe the second patent. The licensee faced the classic dilemma of an alleged patent infringer: pay royalties, discontinue the challenged activity or persist in its conduct, with the risk, as Justice Scalia noted, of incurring treble damages, liability for attorney's fees and an injunction preventing further manufacture and sale of the product, which accounted for more than 80% of Medimmune's revenues in recent years. Medimmune paid the demanded royalties "under protest and with reservation of all of [its] rights." It commenced an action seeking declaratory relief. The Court had to decide:

> whether Article III"s limitation of federal courts" jurisdiction to "Cases" and "Controversies," reflected in the "actual controversy" requirement of the Declaratory Judgment Act * * * requires a patent licensee to terminate or be in breach of its license agreement before it can seek a declaratory judgment that the underlying patent is invalid, unenforceable, or not infringed.

> Finding that the matter satisfied the case-or-controversy requirement, the Court reversed the lower courts' dismissal of the declaratory judgment claim and remanded.

Justice Scalia's opinion for an eight-Member majority observed that "*Aetna* [*Life Ins. Co. v. Haworth* (1937)] and the cases following it do not draw the brightest of lines between those declaratory-judgment actions that satisfy the case-or-controversy requirement and those that do not." The potential justiciability difficulty arose because the licensee's under-protest royalty payments prevented hostile action by the patentee, so the issue was whether the threat to the licensee was sufficient. The Court noted the difficulty in characterizing the problem:

> The justiciability problem that arises, when the party seeking declaratory relief is himself preventing the complained-of injury from occurring, can be described in terms of standing (whether plaintiff is threatened with "imminent" injury in fact " 'fairly * * * trace[able] to the challenged action of the defendant,' " or in terms of ripeness (whether there is sufficient "hardship to the parties [in] withholding court consideration" until there is enforcement action. As respondents acknowledge, standing and ripeness boil down to the same question in this case.

That may be so, given the Court's convoluted standing jurisprudence. Consider, however, whether the Justices might find the characterization of the problem simpler if they confined the standing inquiry to the question of identity (whether the party suing is the proper plaintiff) and remitted questions of timing (*imminent* injury in fact) to the ripeness inquiry.

The Court noted that where threatened government action is concerned, the Court has not required plaintiffs to risk liability or prosecution before suing, and Justice Scalia found no reason to use a different approach when the threatened action comes from a private source. Citing established precedents (including *Ex parte Young* (1908) (*infra* at 629) and *Steffel v. Thompson* (1974) (*infra* at 801)), the Court noted that "[i]n each of these cases, the plaintiff had eliminated the imminent threat of harm by simply not doing what he claimed the right to do. . . . That did not preclude subject-matter jurisdiction because the threat-eliminating behavior was effectively coerced."

In one way, both *Young* and *Steffel* support the idea that Medimmune need not have risked liability to Genentech by continuing the disputed activity, but *Young* seems better authority. *Steffel* is a bit of a problem because of its unique facts. Steffel and a companion had been handing out antiwar handbills at a shopping center. Employees asked them to desist and then called the police. When threatened with arrest by the police on that occasion, both left. On a second occasion, there was a repeat performance except that Steffel left while his companion stayed and continued to distribute handbills until the police arrested him—the perfect control case. Justice Brennan's majority opinion relied in part on that arrest as demonstrating the reality (and hence the justiciability) of the threat to Steffel. In *Ex parte Young*, however, there was no control case and no articulated threat of prosecution other than the challenged statute itself. *Young*, therefore, is a better parallel to *Medimmune*, where there is also no control case.

4. Justice Harlan mentions several factors that affect whether issues are fit for judicial determination. Does the Court suggest that the more fact-specific a dispute, the less appropriate is early judicial intervention? Why might that be a desirable rule?

In San Jose, California, a city rent control ordinance provided that hearing officers could consider hardship to tenants when evaluating a landlord's application for a rent increase. A landlords' association and individual land-lords challenged the ordinance, arguing that it violated the Due Process and Equal Protection Clauses and, separately, that it was a constitutionally im-permissible taking. The Court ruled on the merits of the first two chal-lenges, but declined to adjudicate the takings challenge.

> We think it would be premature to consider this contention on the pre-sent record. As things stand, there simply is no evidence that the "tenant hardship clause" has in fact ever been relied upon by a Hear-ing Officer to reduce a rent below the figure it would have been set at on the basis of the other factors set forth in the Ordinance. In addi-tion, there is nothing in the Ordinance requiring that a Hearing Offi-cer in fact reduce a proposed rent increase on grounds of tenant hard-ship. Section 5703.29 does make it mandatory that hardship be con-sidered—it states that "the Hearing Officer *shall* consider the economic hardship imposed on the present tenant"—but it then goes on to state that if "the proposed increase constitutes an unreasonably severe fi-nancial or economic hardship * * * he *may* order that the excess of the increase" be disallowed. ([E]mphasis added). Given the "essentially ad hoc, factual inquir[y]" involved in the takings analysis, we have found it particularly important in takings cases to adhere to our admonition that "the constitutionality of statutes ought not be decided except in an actual factual setting that makes such a decision necessary." [F]or ex-ample, we found that a challenge to the Surface Mining Control and Reclamation Act of 1977 was "premature" and "not ripe for judicial resolution," because the property owners had not identified any prop-erty that had allegedly been taken by the Act, nor had they sought administrative relief from the Act's restrictions on surface mining. Similarly, in this case we find that the mere fact that a Hearing Officer is enjoined to consider hardship * * * does not present a sufficiently concrete factual setting for the adjudication of the takings claim appel-lants raise here.

Pennell v. City of San Jose, 485 U.S. 1, 9-10, 108 S.Ct. 849, 856, 99 L.Ed.2d 1, 13 (1988).

Contrast *Yee v. City of Escondido,* 503 U.S. 519, 112 S.Ct. 1522, 118 L.Ed.2d 153 (1992), with *Pennell.* Owners of mobile home parks challenged a local rent control ordinance as a constitutionally impermissible taking, arguing it effectively gave mobile home owners a transferable right of per-petual occupation of the park owner's land and simultaneously regulated the rents a park owner could charge. Said the Court:

> As a preliminary matter, we must address respondent's assertion that a regulatory taking claim is unripe because petitioners have not sought rent increases. While respondent is correct that a claim that the ordi-nance effects a regulatory taking as applied to petitioners' property would be unripe for this reason * * * petitioners mount a facial chal-lenge to the ordinance. They allege in this Court that the ordinance does not " 'substantially advance' " a " 'legitimate state interest' " no matter how it is applied. * * * As this allegation does not depend on

the extent to which petitioners are deprived of the economic use of their particular pieces of property or the extent to which these particular petitioners are compensated, petitioners' facial challenge is ripe.

Are *Pennell* and *Yee* reconcilable? Are they consistent with *Abbott Laboratories*?

How much development of the fact pattern underlying a dispute of law should the Court demand? In *Poe v. Ullman*, 367 U.S. 497, 81 S.Ct. 1752, 6 L.Ed.2d 989 (1961), physicians and their patients challenged Connecticut statutes that prohibited use of contraceptives or giving medical advice as to their use.

> In proceedings seeking declarations of law [the state] court has ruled that these statutes would be applicable in the case of married couples and even under claim that conception would constitute a serious threat to the health or life of the female spouse.
>
> Appellants' complaints * * * do not * * * allege that appellee Ullman threatens to prosecute [them]. The allegations are merely that, in the course of his public duty, he intends to prosecute any offenses against Connecticut law, and that he claims that use of and advice concerning contraceptives would constitute offenses.

The majority ruled that despite Ullman's statements of intention to prosecute violations, the controversy was not ripe. The Court relied in part upon the fact that the statutes had been on the books for nearly a century without enforcement.[13] Justice Harlan, later to author *Gardner*, dissented.

> I do not think these appeals may be dismissed for want of "ripeness" as that concept has been understood in its "varied applications." There is no lack of "ripeness" in the sense that is exemplified by [many prior] cases. In all of those cases the lack of ripeness inhered in the fact that the need for some further procedure, some further contingency of application or interpretation, whether judicial, administrative or executive, or some further clarification of the intentions of the claimant, served to make remote the issue which was sought to be presented to the Court. Certainly the appellants have stated in their pleadings fully and unequivocally what it is that they intend to do; no clarifying or resolving contingency stands in their way before they may embark on that conduct. Thus there is no circumstance besides that of detection or prosecution to make remote the particular controversy. And it is clear beyond cavil that the mere fact that a controversy such as this is rendered still more unavoidable by an actual prosecution, is not alone sufficient to make the case too remote, not ideally enough "ripe" for adjudication, at the prior stage of anticipatory relief.
>
> Moreover, it follows from what has already been said that there is no

---

[13] Griswold v. Connecticut, 381 U.S. 479, 85 S.Ct. 1678, 14 L.Ed.2d 510 (1965), held those statutes unconstitutional, vacating the convictions of several persons prosecuted under the century-old statute.

such want of ripeness as was presented in * * * [cases] where the records presented for adjudication a controversy so artificially truncated as to make the cases not susceptible to intelligent decision. I cannot see what further elaboration is required to enable us to decide the appellants' claims, and indeed neither the plurality opinion nor the concurring opinion—notwithstanding the latter's characterization of this record as "skimpy"—suggests what mere grist is needed before the judicial mill could turn.

Is the majority's position in *Poe* inconsistent with the Court's apparent approval of adjudication on the merits of the dispute underlying *I.M. Darnell & Son Co. v. City of Memphis,* 208 U.S. 113, 28 S.Ct. 247, 52 L.Ed. 413 (1908)? A Minnesota statute set rate ceilings for railroads and imposed severe penalties for violations. Railroad shareholders sought to prohibit the railroad from complying and to enjoin enforcement. They sued and won in the Circuit Court for the District of Minnesota. Young was the Attorney General of Minnesota, and when he commenced a prosecution in defiance of the Circuit Court's order, the court held him in contempt and jailed him. The Supreme Court heard his petition for a writ of habeas corpus. Should the Court have ruled that the original controversy was not ripe, given that there had been no prosecutions and the statute was not even in effect?

For a more modern setting, consider *Steffel v. Thompson,* 415 U.S. 452, 94 S.Ct. 1209, 39 L.Ed.2d 505 (1974), (*infra* at 801) where plaintiff challenged the constitutionality of a statute that would have prohibited him from distributing leaflets at a local shopping center. He had twice been warned to stop distributing leaflets or face arrest, and his companion, who continued to distribute, was arrested. The Court ruled on the merits. Would the plaintiffs in *Poe* have been better off if only they had been able to get Ullman to threaten them specifically? What if they could have arranged for someone else to be prosecuted?

5. The second component of the ripeness inquiry revolves around the hardship to the parties of withholding judicial resolution. Justice Harlan makes clear that this factor is critical, yet the Court has not been particularly rigorous or consistent in applying it. Consider the following cases.

a) The Hatch Act prohibits federal employees from participating in political campaigns. The penalty for engaging in the prohibited activity is dismissal from federal employment. If federal employees who wish to campaign sue to have the Hatch Act declared unconstitutional, is the matter ripe? *United Public Workers v. Mitchell,* 330 U.S. 75, 67 S.Ct. 556, 91 L.Ed. 754 (1947), held that it was not.

b) Although the Hatch Act still exists, members of a federal employees union allege that they desire to participate in a wide variety of political activities, including running for local office, being a delegate to a party convention, and campaigning for various candidates, but have refrained because of the statute. Democratic and Republican political organizations allege that they cannot get people to run for certain local offices or even to be members of Democratic or Republican committees because of the Act. Is an action brought by those groups under the Declaratory Judgment Act ripe? *United*

States Civil Service Commission v. National Association of Letter Carriers, 413 U.S. 548, 93 S.Ct. 2880, 37 L.Ed.2d 796 (1973), held that it was, but did not overrule *Mitchell.*

c) A state statute forbids discharge of sewage from boats, though officials have stated that they will not seek to enforce the statute until on-shore pumping facilities are available. A group of ship owners wishes to challenge the statute's constitutionality. They have already begun modifying their vessels to comply with the law when it is finally implemented. Is an action to declare the statute unconstitutional ripe? *Lake Carriers' Association v. MacMullan,* 406 U.S. 498, 92 S.Ct. 1749, 32 L.Ed.2d 257 (1972), says it is.

d) Can one harmonize *Mitchell,* never overruled, with the latter two cases? In 1974, the Court said, "Where the inevitability of the operation of a statute against certain individuals is patent, it is irrelevant to the existence of a justiciable controversy that there will be a time delay before the disputed provisions will come into effect." *Regional Rail Act Reorganization Cases,* 419 U.S. 102, 143, 95 S.Ct. 335, 358, 42 L.Ed.2d 320, 353 (1974). Does that language suggest that the Court would view *Mitchell* differently today? In any event, how much harm must a plaintiff allege from the withholding of judicial relief in order to make a case ripe?

6. Is ripeness a constitutional or prudential concern? To be sure, at some point a plaintiff's request for pre-enforcement review of a proposed statute or regulation will raise substantial case-or-controversy problems. Should those be dealt with under the rubric of ripeness or standing? If a prospective plaintiff seeking pre-enforcement review has suffered an injury in fact for standing purposes, is there any legitimate constitutional or prudential policy reason to superimpose a ripeness requirement also?

E.   MOOTNESS

DEFUNIS v. ODEGAARD

Supreme Court of the United States, 1974.
416 U.S. 312, 94 S.Ct. 1704, 40 L.Ed.2d 164.

PER CURIAM.

In 1971 the petitioner Marco DeFunis, Jr., applied for admission as a first-year student at the University of Washington Law School, a state-operated institution. The size of the incoming first-year class was to be limited to 150 persons, and the Law School received some 1,600 applications for these 150 places. DeFunis was eventually notified that he had been denied admission. He thereupon commenced this suit in a Washington trial court, contending that the procedures and criteria employed by the Law School Admissions Committee invidiously discriminated against him on account of his race in violation of the Equal Protection Clause of the Fourteenth Amendment to the United States Constitution.

DeFunis brought the suit on behalf of himself alone, and not as the representative of any class, against the various respondents, who are officers, faculty members, and members of the Board of Regents of the

University of Washington. He asked the trial court to issue a mandatory injunction commanding the respondents to admit him as a member of the first-year class entering in September 1971, on the ground that the Law School admissions policy had resulted in the unconstitutional denial of his application for admission. The trial court agreed with his claim and granted the requested relief. DeFunis was, accordingly, admitted to the Law School and began his legal studies there in the fall of 1971. On appeal, the Washington Supreme Court reversed the judgment of the trial court and held that the Law School admissions policy did not violate the Constitution. By this time DeFunis was in his second year at the Law School.

He then petitioned this Court for a writ of certiorari, and Mr. Justice Douglas, as Circuit Justice, stayed the judgment of the Washington Supreme Court pending the "final disposition of the case by this Court." By virtue of this stay, DeFunis has remained in law school, and was in the first term of his third and final year when this Court first considered his certiorari petition in the fall of 1973. Because of our concern that DeFunis' third-year standing in the Law School might have rendered this case moot, we requested the parties to brief the question of mootness before we acted on the petition. In response, both sides contended that the case was not moot. The respondents indicated that, if the decision of the Washington Supreme Court were permitted to stand, the petitioner could complete the term for which he was then enrolled but would have to apply to the faculty for permission to continue in the school before he could register for another term.[2]

We granted the petition for certiorari on November 19, 1973. The case was in due course orally argued on February 26, 1974.

In response to questions raised from the bench during the oral argument, counsel for the petitioner has informed the Court that DeFunis has now registered "for his final quarter in law school." Counsel for the respondents have made clear that the Law School will not in any way seek to abrogate this registration. In light of DeFunis' recent registration for the last quarter of his final law school year, and the Law School's assurance that his registration is fully effective, the insistent question again arises whether this case is not moot, and to that question we now turn.

The starting point for analysis is the familiar proposition that "federal courts are without power to decide questions that cannot affect the rights of litigants in the case before them." The inability of the federal judiciary "to review moot cases derives from the requirement of Art. III of the Constitution under which the exercise of judicial power depends

---

[2] By contrast, in their response to the petition for certiorari, the respondents had stated that DeFunis "will complete his third year (of law school) and be awarded his J.D. degree at the end of the 1973-74 academic year regardless of the outcome of this appeal."

upon the existence of a case or controversy." Although as a matter of
Washington state law it appears that this case would be saved from
mootness by "the great public interest in the continuing issues raised by
this appeal," the fact remains that under Art. III "[e]ven in cases arising
in the state courts, the question of mootness is a federal one which a federal court must resolve before it assumes jurisdiction."

The respondents have represented that, without regard to the ultimate resolution of the issues in this case, DeFunis will remain a student
in the Law School for the duration of any term in which he has already
enrolled. Since he has now registered for his final term, it is evident
that he will be given an opportunity to complete all academic and other
requirements for graduation, and, if he does so, will receive his diploma
regardless of any decision this Court might reach on the merits of this
case. In short, all parties agree that DeFunis is now entitled to complete
his legal studies at the University of Washington and to receive his degree from that institution. A determination by this Court of the legal
issues tendered by the parties is no longer necessary to compel that result, and could not serve to prevent it. DeFunis did not cast his suit as a
class action, and the only remedy he requested was an injunction commanding his admission to the Law School. He was not only accorded
that remedy, but he now has also been irrevocably admitted to the final
term of the final year of the Law School course. The controversy between the parties has thus clearly ceased to be "definite and concrete"
and no longer "touch[es] the legal relations of parties having adverse legal interests."

It matters not that these circumstances partially stem from a policy
decision on the part of the respondent Law School authorities. The respondents, through their counsel, the Attorney General of the State,
have professionally represented that in no event will the status of DeFunis now be affected by any view this Court might express on the merits
of this controversy. And it has been the settled practice of the Court, in
contexts no less significant, fully to accept representations such as these
as parameters for decision.

There is a line of decisions in this Court standing for the proposition
that the "voluntary cessation of allegedly illegal conduct does not deprive
the tribunal of power to hear and determine the case, *i.e.*, does not make
the case moot." These decisions and the doctrine they reflect would be
quite relevant if the question of mootness here had arisen by reason of a
unilateral change in the admissions procedures of the Law School. For it
was the admissions procedures that were the target of this litigation,
and a voluntary cessation of the admissions practices complained of
could make this case moot only if it could be said with assurance "that
'there is no reasonable expectation that the wrong will be repeated.'"
Otherwise, "[t]he defendant is free to return to his old ways," and this
fact would be enough to prevent mootness because of the "public interest
in having the legality of the practices settled." But mootness in the pre-

sent case depends not at all upon a "voluntary cessation" of the admissions practices that were the subject of this litigation. It depends, instead, upon the simple fact that DeFunis is now in the final quarter of the final year of his course of study, and the settled and unchallenged policy of the Law School to permit him to complete the term for which he is now enrolled.

It might also be suggested that this case presents a question that is "capable of repetition, yet evading review," and is thus amenable to federal adjudication even though it might otherwise be considered moot. But DeFunis will never again be required to run the gantlet of the Law School's admission process, and so the question is certainly not "capable of repetition" so far as he is concerned. Moreover, just because this particular case did not reach the Court until the eve of the petitioner's graduation from Law School, it hardly follows that the issue he raises will in the future evade review. If the admissions procedures of the Law School remain unchanged, there is no reason to suppose that a subsequent case attacking those procedures will not come with relative speed to this Court, now that the Supreme Court of Washington has spoken. This case, therefore, in no way presents the exceptional situation in which the *Southern Pacific Terminal* doctrine might permit a departure from "[t]he usual rule in federal cases * * * that an actual controversy must exist at stages of appellate or certiorari review, and not simply at the date the action is initiated."

Because the petitioner will complete his law school studies at the end of the term for which he has now registered regardless of any decision this Court might reach on the merits of this litigation, we conclude that the Court cannot, consistently with the limitations of Art. III of the Constitution, consider the substantive constitutional issues tendered by the parties.[5] Accordingly, the judgment of the Supreme Court of Washington is vacated, and the cause is remanded for such proceedings as by that court may be deemed appropriate.

It is so ordered.

MR. JUSTICE BRENNAN, with whom MR. JUSTICE DOUGLAS, MR. JUSTICE WHITE, and MR. JUSTICE MARSHALL concur, dissenting.

I respectfully dissent. Many weeks of the school term remain, and petitioner may not receive his degree despite respondents' assurances that petitioner will be allowed to complete this term's schooling regardless of our decision. Any number of unexpected events—illness, economic necessity, even academic failure—might prevent his graduation at

---

[5] It is suggested in dissent that "[a]ny number of unexpected events—illness, economic necessity, even academic failure—might prevent his graduation at the end of the term." "But such speculative contingencies afford no basis for our passing on the substantive issues [the petitioner] would have us decide," in the absence of "evidence that this is a prospect of 'immediacy and reality.'"

the end of the term. Were that misfortune to befall, and were petitioner required to register for yet another term, the prospect that he would again face the hurdle of the admissions policy is real, not fanciful; for respondents warn that "Mr. DeFunis would have to take some appropriate action to request continued admission for the remainder of his law school education, and *some discretionary action by the University on such request would have to be taken.*" ([E]mphasis supplied). Thus, respondents' assurances have not dissipated the possibility that petitioner might once again have to run the gantlet of the University's allegedly unlawful admissions policy. The Court therefore proceeds on an erroneous premise in resting its mootness holding on a supposed inability to render any judgment that may affect one way or the other petitioner's completion of his law studies. For surely if we were to reverse the Washington Supreme Court, we could insure that, if for some reason petitioner did not graduate this spring, he would be entitled to re-enrollment at a later time on the same basis as others who have not faced the hurdle of the University's allegedly unlawful admissions policy.

In these circumstances, and because the University's position implies no concession that its admissions policy is unlawful, this controversy falls squarely within the Court's long line of decisions holding that the "[m]ere voluntary cessation of allegedly illegal conduct does not moot a case." Since respondents' voluntary representation to this Court is only that they will permit petitioner to complete this term's studies, respondents have not borne the "heavy burden," of demonstrating that there was not even a "mere possibility" that petitioner would once again be subject to the challenged admissions policy. On the contrary, respondents have positioned themselves so as to be "free to return to [their] old ways."

* * *

[I]n endeavoring to dispose of this case as moot, the Court clearly disserves the public interest. The constitutional issues which are avoided today concern vast numbers of people, organizations, and colleges and universities, as evidenced by the filing of twenty-six *amicus curiae* briefs. Few constitutional questions in recent history have stirred as much debate, and they will not disappear. They must inevitably return to the federal courts and ultimately again to this Court. Because avoidance of repetitious litigation serves the public interest, that inevitability counsels against mootness determinations, as here, not compelled by the record. Although the Court should, of course, avoid unnecessary decisions of constitutional questions, we should not transform principles of avoidance of constitutional decisions into devices for sidestepping resolution of difficult cases.

* * *

Notes and Questions

1. a) Is the majority accurate that "all parties agree that DeFunis is now entitled to receive his degree"? Does not Justice Brennan's dissent argue persuasively that the parties only agreed that DeFunis could finish the current term? It is far from unheard-of for circumstances to arise that cause a student unexpectedly to have to take a leave of absence or otherwise to interrupt his legal education. Should that possibility, which the majority calls a "speculative contingency," be sufficient to avoid a finding of mootness? If not, should the Court consider the effect on scarce judicial resources if DeFunis were forced to reapply and, presumably, to relitigate constitutional claims that have already been through three levels of courts?

b) Perhaps the majority is correct that the case is moot, but for a different reason. Even if DeFunis did not finish his degree program without interruption, upon seeking re-entry he would be competing for a seat with potential transfer and visiting students, not with the incoming first-year class. Is the school's affirmative action policy relevant at all? Even if it is, does its application in the new context present issues sufficiently similar to the original issues to warrant hearing the case?

2. Four primary categories of cases present special mootness problems. Whether they are actually moot cases that the courts hear or are not moot at all, it is important to understand each category. Consider the following.

a) A defendant is convicted, the conviction secured in part through the use of evidence the defendant claims was obtained in violation of his Fourth and Fourteenth Amendment rights. The state courts refuse bail pending appeal. After pursuing his appeals through the state court system, the defendant successfully petitions for a writ of certiorari. One month before oral argument, the defendant is released. Is the case moot? *See Sibron v. New York*, 392 U.S. 40, 88 S.Ct. 1889, 20 L.Ed.2d 917 (1968).

In contrast with *Sibron*, consider the following. An inmate serving a sentence is released on parole. Subsequently, his parole is revoked in a proceeding that the inmate claims is constitutionally tainted. He seeks federal habeas corpus relief from his reincarceration. Does his release from custody upon the expiration of his complete sentence moot the habeas proceeding? *See Spencer v. Kemna*, 523 U.S. 1, 118 S.Ct. 978, 140 L.Ed.2d 43 (1998).

An individual discharged from employment sues claiming discrimination. The company reinstates the individual in circumstances that make it clear that the reinstatement is not simply a ruse to dispose of the pending litigation. Is the case moot? *See Firefighters Local 1784 v. Stotts*, 467 U.S. 561, 104 S.Ct. 2576, 81 L.Ed.2d 483 (1984).

Sibron, *Kemna*, and *Stotts* address mootness in the context of what has been called "collateral consequences." Clearly the complaining parties are primarily interested in the sentence of imprisonment and the loss of employment. But are there other matters at stake than merely whether Sibron or Kemna is in jail or the fire fighter is on the job? If so, are they sufficient to avoid mootness?

In *Arizonans for Official English v. Arizona*, 520 U.S. 43, 117 S.Ct. 1055, 137 L.Ed.2d 170 (1997), the original plaintiff, a state employee, sought to challenge the state's constitutional amendment that required the conduct of state business only in English. The District Court found the statute unconstitutional, which generated cross-appeals, with the bill's sponsor seeking reversal and the employee seeking nominal damages. The original plaintiff, however, resigned her position before the Ninth Circuit decided the appeal. The Court of Appeals affirmed the finding of unconstitutionality and rejected a suggestion of mootness because of the possibility of nominal damages running directly against Arizona, which had waived its Eleventh Amendment immunity from federal proceedings. The Supreme Court found several problems with the case. The Justices noted that although Arizona had eliminated any Eleventh Amendment problem, § 1983 does not contemplate state defendants—an unwaivable problem. The Court also disapproved the obvious close cooperation between the employee and Arizona's Attorney General in attempting to save the case from premature demise. The bottom line was that the Court found the case mooted.

b) *Roe v. Wade,* 410 U.S. 113, 93 S.Ct. 705, 35 L.Ed.2d 147 (1973), deals with one of the most important social issues of the past few decades. Yet should the Court have decided it at all? By the time the case reached the Supreme Court, the plaintiff was no longer pregnant. The majority observed, "the normal 266-day human gestation period is so short that the pregnancy will come to term before the usual appellate process is complete. If that termination makes a case moot, pregnancy litigation seldom will survive much beyond the trial stage, and appellate review will effectively be denied." Without disputing the Court's factual conclusion, one may nonetheless ask whether the Court could have done anything to affect the plaintiff's legal situation. If not, was the case moot?

Suppose a newly-arrived domiciliary of a state seeks to register to vote only to be told that there is a one-year residency requirement. He brings a federal action challenging the requirement on First and Fourteenth Amendment grounds, and secures a preliminary injunction requiring the state to permit him to vote in the upcoming election. If the next election will not occur until after he has been a state resident for one year, does his case become moot as soon as he casts his ballot? Suppose instead that he obtains a final judgment from the federal district court declaring the state statute unconstitutional. If, pending the state's appeal, the election occurs or the plaintiff completes his year of residence, does the case then become moot? If not, why not? If so, should the appellate court remand with directions to dismiss the case as moot? *See Dunn v. Blumstein,* 405 U.S. 330, 92 S.Ct. 995, 31 L.Ed.2d 274 (1972). *Cf. Golden v. Zwickler,* 394 U.S. 103, 89 S.Ct. 956, 22 L.Ed.2d 113 (1969).

There are many situations that may be characterized as "capable of repetition, yet evading review." For example, in *Lee v. Weisman,* 505 U.S. 577, 112 S.Ct. 2649, 120 L.Ed.2d 467 (1992), a public middle school student and her parent challenged the school district's practice of having a local clergyman deliver a nonsectarian invocation at the beginning of each commencement ceremony. The suit began only four days before the ceremony, and the district court declined to consider it. The student attended commencement, which included a prayer. Subsequently, the student's parent sought a permanent injunction, arguing that the practice violated the Establishment Clause. The Court ruled on the merits, without mentioning mootness. But should it have? Was the controversy moot at the end of the commencement ceremony? Is it significant that the student would be enrolled in the public high school and might, four years later, be a participant in another commencement? Would the case have been moot if at the time of the initial challenge she had been a high school student? Suppose on the facts of the original case that her parents decided to send her to a private high school because of the distant threat of a prayer at her high school commencement. Would that moot the case or intensify the need to adjudicate it?

Is the "capable of repetition, yet evading review" case truly not moot, or is it a circumstance in which the ordinary strictures of the mootness doctrine ought to be loosened? If the circumstances that caused the individual plaintiff to sue have changed, and the particular problem has disappeared, how can the court know that there is a continuing controversy in any but the most academic sense? If the plaintiff's interest in the litigation is sufficient to keep the case alive for mootness purposes, should it be for standing and ripeness purposes as well?

c) If a plaintiff seeks to enjoin a policy or practice and the defendant announces that it has discontinued the conduct, does that moot the case? The Court has generally held that it does not, on the theory that the defendant remains free to resume the challenged practice. The leading case is *United States v. W.T. Grant Co.,* 345 U.S. 629, 73 S.Ct. 894, 97 L.Ed. 1303 (1953), in which the federal government's challenge to corporate interlocking directorships on antitrust grounds was met by the corporations' announcement that they had abandoned and would not resume the practice. The Court refused to dismiss on mootness grounds. The Justices did say that "[t]he case may nevertheless be moot if the defendant can demonstrate that there is no reasonable expectation the wrong will be repeated. The burden is a heavy one."

Suppose that instead of merely announcing the cessation of a practice, a governmental entity repeals the statute or ordinance that aggrieved the plaintiff. Should that sort of formalized voluntary cessation moot the action? Nothing, obviously, then prevents reenactment of the challenged provision. *See generally Kremens v. Bartley,* 431 U.S. 119, 97 S.Ct. 1709, 52 L.Ed.2d 184 (1977). *But see City of Mesquite v. Aladdin's Castle, Inc.,* 455 U.S. 283, 102 S.Ct. 1070, 71 L.Ed.2d 152 (1982).

Alteration of a challenged statute presents an even more difficult mootness question. How much of a change is sufficient to moot the original question? The Court split on this issue in *Northeastern Florida Chapter of the Associated General Contractors of America v. City of Jacksonville,* 508 U.S. 656, 113 S.Ct. 2297, 124 L.Ed.2d 586 (1993), where the petitioner originally challenged a municipal set-aside ordinance that required 10% of city contract expenditures to go to minority businesses. The petitioner challenged the ordinance on equal protection grounds, winning preliminary relief in the district court but suffering reversal in the Eleventh Circuit for lack of standing. Three weeks after the Supreme Court granted certiorari, Jacksonville replaced the ordinance with one that (a) applied only to women and blacks, rather than all minorities, (b) established participation "goals" of 5 to 16%, and (c) provided five alternative methods for reaching the goals. Jacksonville moved to dismiss the case as moot; the Court refused, arguing that the new ordinance worked no essential change in petitioner's complaint. Justices O'Connor and Blackmun dissented, arguing that

> precedents establish that, where a challenged statute is replaced with more narrowly drawn legislation pending our review, and the plaintiff seeks only prospective relief, we generally should decline to decide the case. The controversy with respect to the old statute is moot, because a declaration of its invalidity or an injunction against the law's future enforcement would not benefit the plaintiff. Where we cannot be sure how the statutory changes will affect the plaintiff's claims, dismissal avoids the possibility that our decision will prove advisory.

See also Diffenderfer v. Central Baptist Church of Miami, Inc., 404 U.S. 412, 92 S.Ct. 574, 30 L.Ed.2d 567 (1972) (*per curiam*); *Fusari v. Steinberg*, 419 U.S. 379, 95 S.Ct. 533, 42 L.Ed.2d 521 (1975).

The Court's hesitation about letting defendants too easily escape with insincere and temporary changes of behavior is understandable. But consider a circumstance in which a plaintiff fears that the defendant is about to undertake an unlawful activity. Is such a case ripe? Ordinarily, the plaintiff bears a heavy burden to show that the complained-of activity is imminent. Why should that burden be shifted to the defendant in circumstances of voluntary cessation?

Why doesn't *DeFunis* survive the mootness challenge as a "voluntary cessation" case? The University had no intention of abandoning its policy and candidly conceded that if anything interrupted DeFunis's march to his diploma, the policy might again apply to him. Does that meet the "heavy burden" upon which the Court insisted in *W.T. Grant*?

d) Does mooting the claim of a class representative require dismissal of the action? That pattern can arise in many contexts. In *Sosna v. Iowa*, 419 U.S. 393, 95 S.Ct. 553, 42 L.Ed.2d 532 (1975), the class representative challenged Iowa's one-year residency prerequisite for divorce actions. The plaintiff lost on the merits in the district court. Before the Supreme Court could review the case, Ms. Sosna satisfied the residency requirement. The Court refused to find the case moot, although the majority noted that "[i]f appellant had sued only on her own behalf, both the fact that she now satisfies the one-year residency requirement and the fact that she has obtained a divorce elsewhere would make this case moot and require dismissal." In addition, the Court declined to categorize the case as one "capable of repetition, yet evading review," recognizing the extreme unlikelihood that the plaintiff would again face the durational residency requirement. "The controversy may exist, however, between a named defendant and a member of the class represented by the named plaintiff, even though the claim of the named plaintiff has become moot." The majority was similarly untroubled by the named plaintiff's unrepresentativeness of the class when the case was reviewed. "In the present suit, where it is unlikely that segments of the class appellant represents would have interests conflicting with those she has sought to advance, and where the interests of that class have been competently urged at each level of the proceeding, we believe that the test of Rule 23(a) is met."

Justice White dissented vigorously, arguing that Sosna lacked standing to represent the class, since she no longer had any personal stake in the outcome. He chided the majority with language from the Court's then-recent decision in *O'Shea v. Littleton*, 414 U.S. 488, 94 S.Ct. 669, 38 L.Ed.2d 674 (1974):

> "[I]f none of the named plaintiffs purporting to represent a class establishes the requisite of a case or controversy with the defendants, none may seek relief on behalf of himself or any other member of the class." * * * In reality, there is no longer a named plaintiff in the case, no member of the class before the Court. The unresolved issue, the attorney, and a class of unnamed litigants remain. None of the anonymous members of the class is present to direct counsel and ensure that class interests are being properly served. For all practical purposes, this case has become one-sided and has lost the adversary quality necessary to satisfy the constitutional "case or controversy" requirement. A real issue unquestionably remains, but the necessary adverse party to press it has disappeared.
>
> The Court thus dilutes the jurisdictional command of Art. III to a mere prudential guideline.

Is *Sosna* not consistent with *Dunn v. Blumstein*, where the Court (including Justice White) ruled upon Professor Blumstein's challenge to Tennessee's durational residency voting requirement even though by the time the case reached the Court he had satisfied the requirement? Does *Sosna* call *Dunn*'s legitimacy into question? Justice White notes in his *Sosna* dissent that he joined the majority in *Dunn*, but argues that the mootness question was never contested by the parties or addressed by the Court. Yet if he is correct that mootness goes to the constitutional jurisdictional requirements of Article III, should not the Court have raised it *sua sponte*? Does the Court's failure to do so cast light on the mootness requirement's place in the constitutional hierarchy?

Whether one agrees with the rationale or not, the Court has been quite consistent in allowing certified class actions to proceed despite the disappearance of the claims of the named parties. But what if the class has not been certified when the representative's claims become moot? In *United States Parole Commission v. Geraghty*, 445 U.S. 388, 100 S.Ct. 1202, 63 L.Ed.2d 479 (1980), a prisoner challenged the Parole Commission's guidelines. The district court refused to certify the plaintiff class, and before Geraghty's appeal from the denial of certification could be decided, he was released from custody. Does that not moot the case? The Court ruled that it did not. Yet, despite the Court's confident assertion that the plaintiff retained sufficient personal stake in the controversy to satisfy Article III, what, exactly, was the plaintiff's personal stake, and how did it differ from that of anyone else with an interest in prison problems and parole guidelines? *See also Deposit Guaranty National Bank v. Roper*, 445 U.S. 326, 100 S.Ct. 1166, 63 L.Ed.2d 427 (1980), decided the same day as *Geraghty*.

Is the Court's approach to class actions and the mootness doctrine sound? If the Court were to reverse its position, what would be the practical effects?

3. a) *DeFunis* clearly states the basis for the mootness doctrine, which seems not to embrace the same two-levels of consideration—constitutional and prudential—as does standing. On the contrary, the Court characterizes mootness as derived exclusively from constitutional limitations. That view raises some substantial problems for the Court's mootness jurisprudence. If the doctrine is of constitutional stature, how is it possible to have exceptions to it? Would it be permissible for the Court to hear a case where there was admittedly no injury in fact?

Chief Justice Rehnquist raised the question of whether the case-or-controversy view of the mootness doctrine is accurate.

> The Court implies in its opinion, and the dissent [by Justice Scalia] expressly states, that the mootness doctrine is based upon Art. III of the Constitution. There is no doubt that our recent cases have taken that position * * *. But it seems very doubtful that the earliest case I have found discussing mootness, was premised on constitutional constraints; Justice Gray's opinion in that case nowhere mentions Art. III.
>
> If it were indeed Art. III which—by reason of its requirement of a case or controversy for the exercise of federal judicial power—underlies the mootness doctrine, the "capable of repetition yet evading review" exception relied upon by the Court in this case would be incomprehensible. If our mootness doctrine were forced upon us by the case or controversy requirement of Art. III itself, we would have no more power to decide lawsuits which are "moot" but which also raise questions which are capable of repetition but evading review than we would to decide cases which are "moot" but raise no such questions.

> * * *

> The logical conclusion to be drawn from [earlier "capable of repetition"] cases, and from the historical development of the principle of mootness, is that while an unwillingness to decide moot cases may be connected to the case or controversy requirement of Art. III, it is an attenuated connection that may be overridden where there are strong reasons to override it.

Honig v. Doe, 484 U.S. 305, 330-31, 108 S.Ct. 592, 607-08, 98 L.Ed.2d 686, 711-12 (1988) (Rehnquist, Ch. J., concurring). Chief Justice Rehnquist further suggested that the Court ought to be especially reluctant to dismiss a case as moot where the supervening events occurred after the decision to review.

To me the unique and valuable ability of this Court to decide a case—

we are, at present, the only Art. III court which can decide a federal question in such a way as to bind all other courts—is sufficient reason either to abandon the doctrine of mootness altogether in cases which this Court has decided to review, or at least to relax the doctrine of mootness in such a manner as the dissent accuses the majority of doing here. I would leave the mootness doctrine as established by our cases in full force and effect when applied to the earlier stages of a lawsuit, but I believe that once this Court has undertaken a consideration of a case, an exception to that principle is just as much warranted as where a case is "capable of repetition, yet evading review."

Justice Scalia dissented sharply, arguing that mootness is an inescapable component of Article III. "There is no more reason to intuit that mootness is merely a prudential doctrine than to intuit that initial standing is. Both doctrines have equivalently deep roots in the common-law understanding, and hence the constitutional understanding, of what makes a matter appropriate for judicial disposition." At the same time, he seemed to approve, with limitations, the capable-of-repetition exception.

> Jurisdiction on the basis that a dispute is "capable of repetition, yet evading review" is limited to the "exceptional situatio[n]" * * * where the following two circumstances simultaneously occur " '(1) the challenged action [is] in its duration too short to be fully litigated prior to its cessation or expiration, and (2) there [is] a reasonable expectation that the same complaining party would be subjected to the same action again.' "

Is Chief Justice Rehnquist's advocacy of mootness as a prudential doctrine weakened by his admission that it may have at least an attenuated connection with Article III? What, exactly, does he mean by that phrase? If Article III compels the mootness doctrine, how can even the strongest policy reason override it? For an article arguing that justiciability generally and mootness particularly ought to be regarded as non-constitutional doctrines, see Evan T. Lee, *Deconstitutionalizing Justiciability: The Example of Mootness*, 105 HARV.L.REV. 603 (1992).

Does not Justice Scalia's argument have some problems also? He strongly urges the constitutional underpinning of the mootness doctrine. How, then, as Chief Justice Rehnquist points out, can he approve any exception based on nonconstitutional criteria, even the two restrictive criteria that Justice Scalia recites?

b) Can one solve the hierarchical problem outlined above by approaching the problem as definitional and characterizing marginal cases as simply not being moot at all? What changes, if any, would such an approach make in the categories outlined in Note 2?

FRIENDS OF THE EARTH, INCORPORATED
v. LAIDLAW ENVIRONMENTAL SERVICES (TOC), INC.

Supreme Court of the United States, 2000.
528 U.S. 167, 120 S.Ct. 693, 145 L.Ed.2d 610.

JUSTICE GINSBURG delivered the opinion of the Court.

This case presents an important question concerning the operation of the citizen-suit provisions of the Clean Water Act. Congress authorized the federal district courts to entertain Clean Water Act suits initiated by "a person or persons having an interest which is or may be adversely affected." To impel future compliance with the Act, a district court may prescribe injunctive relief in such a suit; additionally or alternatively, the court may impose civil penalties payable to the United States Treasury. In the Clean Water Act citizen suit now before us, the District Court determined that injunctive relief was inappropriate because the defendant, after the institution of the litigation, achieved substantial compliance with the terms of its discharge permit. The court did, however, assess a civil penalty of $405,800. The "total deterrent effect" of the penalty would be adequate to forestall future violations, the court reasoned, taking into account that the defendant "will be required to reimburse plaintiffs for a significant amount of legal fees and has, itself, incurred significant legal expenses."

The Court of Appeals vacated the District Court's order. The case became moot, the appellate court declared, once the defendant fully complied with the terms of its permit and the plaintiff failed to appeal the denial of equitable relief. "[C]ivil penalties payable to the government," the Court of Appeals stated, "would not redress any injury Plaintiffs have suffered." Nor were attorneys' fees in order, the Court of Appeals noted, because absent relief on the merits, plaintiffs could not qualify as prevailing parties.

We reverse the judgment of the Court of Appeals. The appellate court erred in concluding that a citizen suitor's claim for civil penalties must be dismissed as moot when the defendant, albeit after commencement of the litigation, has come into compliance. In directing dismissal of the suit on grounds of mootness, the Court of Appeals incorrectly conflated our case law on initial standing to bring suit with our case law on post-commencement mootness. A defendant's voluntary cessation of allegedly unlawful conduct ordinarily does not suffice to moot a case. The Court of Appeals also misperceived the remedial potential of civil penalties. Such penalties may serve, as an alternative to an injunction, to deter future violations and thereby redress the injuries that prompted a citizen suitor to commence litigation.

I

A

In 1972, Congress enacted the Clean Water Act (Act) * * * .   33
U.S.C. § 1342 provides for the issuance, by the Administrator of the Environmental Protection Agency (EPA) or by authorized States, of National Pollutant Discharge Elimination System (NPDES) permits.
NPDES permits impose limitations on the discharge of pollutants, and
establish related monitoring and reporting requirements, in order to improve the cleanliness and safety of the Nation's waters. Noncompliance
with a permit constitutes a violation of the Act. § 1342(h).

* * * [A] suit to enforce any limitation in an NPDES permit may be
brought by any "citizen," defined as "a person or persons having an interest which is or may be adversely affected." Sixty days before initiating a citizen suit, however, the would-be plaintiff must give notice of the
alleged violation to the EPA, the State in which the alleged violation occurred, and the alleged violator. "[T]he purpose of notice to the alleged
violator is to give it an opportunity to bring itself into complete compliance with the Act and thus * * * render unnecessary a citizen suit." Accordingly, we have held that citizens lack statutory standing under
§ 505(a) to sue for violations that have ceased by the time the complaint
is filed. The Act also bars a citizen from suing if the EPA or the State
has already commenced, and is "diligently prosecuting," an enforcement
action.

The Act authorizes district courts in citizen-suit proceedings to enter
injunctions and to assess civil penalties, which are payable to the United
States Treasury. In determining the amount of any civil penalty, the
district court must take into account "the seriousness of the violation or
violations, the economic benefit (if any) resulting from the violation, any
history of such violations, any good-faith efforts to comply with the applicable requirements, the economic impact of the penalty on the violator, and such other matters as justice may require." In addition, the
court "may award costs of litigation (including reasonable attorney and
expert witness fees) to any prevailing or substantially prevailing party,
whenever the court determines such award is appropriate."

B

In 1986, defendant-respondent Laidlaw Environmental Services
(TOC), Inc., bought a hazardous waste incinerator facility in Roebuck,
South Carolina, that included a wastewater treatment plant.   * * *
Shortly after Laidlaw acquired the facility, the South Carolina Department of Health and Environmental Control (DHEC) * * * granted Laidlaw an NPDES permit authorizing the company to discharge treated water into the North Tyger River. The permit, which became effective on
January 1, 1987, placed limits on Laidlaw's discharge of several pollutants into the river, including—of particular relevance to this case—

mercury, an extremely toxic pollutant. The permit also regulated the flow, temperature, toxicity, and pH of the effluent from the facility, and imposed monitoring and reporting obligations.

Once it received its permit, Laidlaw began to discharge various pollutants into the waterway; repeatedly, Laidlaw's discharges exceeded the limits set by the permit. In particular, despite experimenting with several technological fixes, Laidlaw consistently failed to meet the permit's stringent 1.3 ppb (parts per billion) daily average limit on mercury discharges. The District Court later found that Laidlaw had violated the mercury limits on 489 occasions between 1987 and 1995.

On April 10, 1992, plaintiff-petitioners Friends of the Earth (FOE) and Citizens Local Environmental Action Network, Inc. (CLEAN) (referred to collectively in this opinion, together with later joined plaintiff-petitioner Sierra Club, as "FOE") took the preliminary step necessary to the institution of litigation. They sent a letter to Laidlaw notifying the company of their intention to file a citizen suit against it * * * after the expiration of the requisite 60-day notice period, *i.e.*, on or after June 10, 1992. Laidlaw's lawyer then contacted DHEC to ask whether DHEC would consider filing a lawsuit against Laidlaw. The District Court later found that Laidlaw's reason for requesting that DHEC file a lawsuit against it was to bar FOE's proposed citizen suit through the operation of 33 U.S.C. § 1365(b)(1)(B). DHEC agreed to file a lawsuit against Laidlaw; the company's lawyer then drafted the complaint for DHEC and paid the filing fee. On June 9, 1992, the last day before FOE's 60-day notice period expired, DHEC and Laidlaw reached a settlement requiring Laidlaw to pay $100,000 in civil penalties and to make " 'every effort' " to comply with its permit obligations.

On June 12, 1992, FOE filed this citizen suit against Laidlaw under § 505(a) of the Act, alleging noncompliance with the NPDES permit and seeking declaratory and injunctive relief and an award of civil penalties. Laidlaw moved for summary judgment on the ground that FOE had failed to present evidence demonstrating injury in fact, and therefore lacked Article III standing to bring the lawsuit. In opposition to this motion, FOE submitted affidavits and deposition testimony from members of the plaintiff organizations. The record before the District Court also included affidavits from the organizations' members submitted by FOE in support of an earlier motion for preliminary injunctive relief. After examining this evidence, the District Court denied Laidlaw's summary judgment motion, finding—albeit "by the very slimmest of margins"—that FOE had standing to bring the suit.

Laidlaw also moved to dismiss the action on the ground that the citizen suit was barred * * * by DHEC's prior action against the company. The United States, appearing as *amicus curiae*, joined FOE in opposing the motion. After an extensive analysis of the Laidlaw-DHEC settlement and the circumstances under which it was reached, the District

Court held that DHEC's action against Laidlaw had not been "diligently prosecuted"; consequently, the court allowed FOE's citizen suit to proceed.[1] The record indicates that after FOE initiated the suit, but before the District Court rendered judgment, Laidlaw violated the mercury discharge limitation in its permit 13 times. The District Court also found that Laidlaw had committed 13 monitoring and 10 reporting violations during this period. The last recorded mercury discharge violation occurred in January 1995, long after the complaint was filed but about two years before judgment was rendered.

On January 22, 1997, the District Court * * * found that Laidlaw had gained a total economic benefit of $1,092,581 as a result of its extended period of noncompliance with the mercury discharge limit in its permit. The court concluded, however, that a civil penalty of $405,800 was adequate in light of the guiding factors listed in 33 U.S.C. § 1319(d). In particular, the District Court stated that the lesser penalty was appropriate taking into account the judgment's "total deterrent effect." In reaching this determination, the court "considered that Laidlaw will be required to reimburse plaintiffs for a significant amount of legal fees." The court declined to grant FOE's request for injunctive relief, stating that an injunction was inappropriate because "Laidlaw has been in substantial compliance with all parameters in its NPDES permit since at least August 1992."

FOE appealed the District Court's civil penalty judgment, arguing that the penalty was inadequate, but did not appeal the denial of declaratory or injunctive relief. Laidlaw cross-appealed, arguing, among other things, that FOE lacked standing to bring the suit and that DHEC's action qualified as a diligent prosecution precluding FOE's litigation. The United States continued to participate as *amicus curiae* in support of FOE.

* * * The Court of Appeals assumed without deciding that FOE initially had standing to bring the action, but went on to hold that the case had become moot. The appellate court stated, first, that the elements of Article III standing—injury, causation, and redressability—must persist at every stage of review, or else the action becomes moot. Citing our decision in *Steel Co.*, the Court of Appeals reasoned that the case had become moot because "the only remedy currently available to [FOE]—civil penalties payable to the government—would not redress any injury [FOE has] suffered." The court therefore vacated the District Court's order and remanded with instructions to dismiss the action. In a foot-

[1] The District Court noted that "Laidlaw drafted the state-court complaint and settlement agreement, filed the lawsuit against itself, and paid the filing fee." Further, "the settlement agreement between DHEC and Laidlaw was entered into with unusual haste, without giving the Plaintiffs the opportunity to intervene." The court found "most persuasive" the fact that "in imposing the civil penalty of $100,000 against Laidlaw, DHEC failed to recover, or even to calculate, the economic benefit that Laidlaw received by not complying with its permit."

note, the Court of Appeals added that FOE's "failure to obtain relief on the merits of [its] claims precludes any recovery of attorneys' fees or other litigation costs because such an award is available only to a 'prevailing or substantially prevailing party.'"

According to Laidlaw, after the Court of Appeals issued its decision but before this Court granted certiorari, the entire incinerator facility in Roebuck was permanently closed, dismantled, and put up for sale, and all discharges from the facility permanently ceased.

We granted certiorari to resolve the inconsistency between the Fourth Circuit's decision in this case and the decisions of several other Courts of Appeals, which have held that a defendant's compliance with its permit after the commencement of litigation does not moot claims for civil penalties under the Act.

II

A

The Constitution's case-or-controversy limitation on federal judicial authority underpins both our standing and our mootness jurisprudence, but the two inquiries differ in respects critical to the proper resolution of this case, so we address them separately. Because the Court of Appeals was persuaded that the case had become moot and so held, it simply assumed without deciding that FOE had initial standing. But because we hold that the Court of Appeals erred in declaring the case moot, we have an obligation to assure ourselves that FOE had Article III standing at the outset of the litigation. We therefore address the question of standing before turning to mootness.

In *Lujan v. Defenders of Wildlife* we held that, to satisfy Article III's standing requirements, a plaintiff must show (1) it has suffered an "injury in fact" that is (a) concrete and particularized and (b) actual or imminent, not conjectural or hypothetical; (2) the injury is fairly traceable to the challenged action of the defendant; and (3) it is likely, as opposed to merely speculative, that the injury will be redressed by a favorable decision. An association has standing to bring suit on behalf of its members when its members would otherwise have standing to sue in their own right, the interests at stake are germane to the organization's purpose, and neither the claim asserted nor the relief requested requires the participation of individual members in the lawsuit.

Laidlaw contends first that FOE lacked standing from the outset even to seek injunctive relief, because the plaintiff organizations failed to show that any of their members had sustained or faced the threat of any "injury in fact" from Laidlaw's activities. In support of this contention Laidlaw points to the District Court's finding, made in the course of setting the penalty amount, that there had been "no demonstrated proof of harm to the environment" from Laidlaw's mercury discharge violations.

The relevant showing for purposes of Article III standing, however, is not injury to the environment but injury to the plaintiff. To insist upon the former rather than the latter as part of the standing inquiry (as the dissent in essence does) is to raise the standing hurdle higher than the necessary showing for success on the merits in an action alleging noncompliance with an NPDES permit. Focusing properly on injury to the plaintiff, the District Court found that FOE had demonstrated sufficient injury to establish standing. For example, FOE member Kenneth Lee Curtis averred in affidavits that he lived a half-mile from Laidlaw's facility; that he occasionally drove over the North Tyger River, and that it looked and smelled polluted; and that he would like to fish, camp, swim, and picnic in and near the river between 3 and 15 miles downstream from the facility, as he did when he was a teenager, but would not do so because he was concerned that the water was polluted by Laidlaw's discharges. Curtis reaffirmed these statements in extensive deposition testimony. For example, he testified that he would like to fish in the river at a specific spot he used as a boy, but that he would not do so now because of his concerns about Laidlaw's discharges.

Other members presented evidence to similar effect. CLEAN member Angela Patterson attested that she lived two miles from the facility; that before Laidlaw operated the facility, she picnicked, walked, birdwatched, and waded in and along the North Tyger River because of the natural beauty of the area; that she no longer engaged in these activities in or near the river because she was concerned about harmful effects from discharged pollutants; and that she and her husband would like to purchase a home near the river but did not intend to do so, in part because of Laidlaw's discharges. CLEAN member Judy Pruitt averred that she lived one-quarter mile from Laidlaw's facility and would like to fish, hike, and picnic along the North Tyger River, but has refrained from those activities because of the discharges. FOE member Linda Moore attested that she lived 20 miles from Roebuck, and would use the North Tyger River south of Roebuck and the land surrounding it for recreational purposes were she not concerned that the water contained harmful pollutants. In her deposition, Moore testified at length that she would hike, picnic, camp, swim, boat, and drive near or in the river were it not for her concerns about illegal discharges. CLEAN member Gail Lee attested that her home, which is near Laidlaw's facility, had a lower value than similar homes located further from the facility, and that she believed the pollutant discharges accounted for some of the discrepancy. Sierra Club member Norman Sharp averred that he had canoed approximately 40 miles downstream of the Laidlaw facility and would like to canoe in the North Tyger River closer to Laidlaw's discharge point, but did not do so because he was concerned that the water contained harmful pollutants.

These sworn statements, as the District Court determined, adequately documented injury in fact. We have held that environmental plaintiffs adequately allege injury in fact when they aver that they use the affected area and are persons "for whom the aesthetic and recreational values of the area will be lessened" by the challenged activity.

* * * *Lujan* is not to the contrary. In that case an environmental organization assailed the Bureau of Land Management's "land withdrawal review program," a program covering millions of acres, alleging that the program illegally opened up public lands to mining activities. The defendants moved for summary judgment, challenging the plaintiff organization's standing to initiate the action under the Administrative Procedure Act. We held that the plaintiff could not survive the summary judgment motion merely by offering "averments which state only that one of [the organization's] members uses unspecified portions of an immense tract of territory, on some portions of which mining activity has occurred or probably will occur by virtue of the governmental action."

In contrast, the affidavits and testimony presented by FOE in this case assert that Laidlaw's discharges, and the affiant members' reasonable concerns about the effects of those discharges, directly affected those affiants' recreational, aesthetic, and economic interests. These submissions present dispositively more than the mere "general averments" and "conclusory allegations" found inadequate in [*Lujan*]. Nor can the affiants' conditional statements—that they would use the nearby North Tyger River for recreation if Laidlaw were not discharging pollutants into it—be equated with the speculative " 'some day' intentions" to visit endangered species halfway around the world that we held insufficient to show injury in fact in [*Lujan*].

Los Angeles v. Lyons, relied on by the dissent, does not weigh against standing in this case. In *Lyons*, we held that a plaintiff lacked standing to seek an injunction against the enforcement of a police chokehold policy because he could not credibly allege that he faced a realistic threat from the policy. In the footnote from *Lyons* cited by the dissent, we noted that "[t]he reasonableness of Lyons' fear is dependent upon the likelihood of a recurrence of the allegedly unlawful conduct," and that his "subjective apprehensions" that such a recurrence would even take place were not enough to support standing. Here, in contrast, it is undisputed that Laidlaw's unlawful conduct—discharging pollutants in excess of permit limits—was occurring at the time the complaint was filed. Under *Lyons*, then, the only "subjective" issue here is "[t]he reasonableness of [the] fear" that led the affiants to respond to that concededly ongoing conduct by refraining from use of the North Tyger River and surrounding areas. Unlike the dissent, we see nothing "improbable" about the proposition that a company's continuous and pervasive illegal discharges of pollutants into a river would cause nearby residents to curtail their recreational use of that waterway and would subject them to other economic and aesthetic harms. * * * [T]he District Court found it was true in this case, and that is enough for injury in fact.

Laidlaw argues next that even if FOE had standing to seek injunctive relief, it lacked standing to seek civil penalties. Here the asserted defect is not injury but redressability. Civil penalties offer no redress to private plaintiffs, Laidlaw argues, because they are paid to the government, and therefore a citizen plaintiff can never have standing to seek them.

Laidlaw is right to insist that a plaintiff must demonstrate standing separately for each form of relief sought. But it is wrong to maintain that citizen plaintiffs facing ongoing violations never have standing to seek civil penalties.

We have recognized on numerous occasions that "all civil penalties have some deterrent effect." More specifically, Congress has found that civil penalties in Clean Water Act cases do more than promote immediate compliance by limiting the defendant's economic incentive to delay its attainment of permit limits; they also deter future violations. This congressional determination warrants judicial attention and respect. "The legislative history of the Act reveals that Congress wanted the district court to consider the need for retribution and deterrence, in addition to restitution, when it imposed civil penalties. * * * [The district court may] seek to deter future violations by basing the penalty on its economic impact."

It can scarcely be doubted that, for a plaintiff who is injured or faces the threat of future injury due to illegal conduct ongoing at the time of suit, a sanction that effectively abates that conduct and prevents its recurrence provides a form of redress. Civil penalties can fit that description. To the extent that they encourage defendants to discontinue current violations and deter them from committing future ones, they afford redress to citizen plaintiffs who are injured or threatened with injury as a consequence of ongoing unlawful conduct.

The dissent argues that it is the availability rather than the imposition of civil penalties that deters any particular polluter from continuing to pollute. This argument misses the mark in two ways. First, it overlooks the interdependence of the availability and the imposition; a threat has no deterrent value unless it is credible that it will be carried out. Second, it is reasonable for Congress to conclude that an actual award of civil penalties does in fact bring with it a significant quantum of deterrence over and above what is achieved by the mere prospect of such penalties. A would-be polluter may or may not be dissuaded by the existence of a remedy on the books, but a defendant once hit in its pocketbook will surely think twice before polluting again.[2]

---

[2] The dissent suggests that there was little deterrent work for civil penalties to do in this case because the lawsuit brought against Laidlaw by DHEC had already pushed the level of deterrence to "near the top of the graph." This suggestion ignores the District Court's specific finding that the penalty agreed to by Laidlaw and DHEC was far too low to remove Laidlaw's economic benefit from noncompliance, and thus was inadequate to deter

We recognize that there may be a point at which the deterrent effect of a claim for civil penalties becomes so insubstantial or so remote that it cannot support citizen standing. The fact that this vanishing point is not easy to ascertain does not detract from the deterrent power of such penalties in the ordinary case. Justice Frankfurter's observations for the Court, made in a different context nearly 60 years ago, hold true here as well:

> How to effectuate policy—the adaptation of means to legitimately sought ends—is one of the most intractable of legislative problems. Whether proscribed conduct is to be deterred by qui tam action or triple damages or injunction, or by criminal prosecution, or merely by defense to actions in contract, or by some, or all, of these remedies in combination, is a matter within the legislature's range of choice. Judgment on the deterrent effect of the various weapons in the armory of the law can lay little claim to scientific basis.

In this case we need not explore the outer limits of the principle that civil penalties provide sufficient deterrence to support redressability. Here, the civil penalties sought by FOE carried with them a deterrent effect that made it likely, as opposed to merely speculative, that the penalties would redress FOE's injuries by abating current violations and preventing future ones—as the District Court reasonably found when it assessed a penalty of $405,800.

Laidlaw contends that the reasoning of our decision in *Steel Co.* directs the conclusion that citizen plaintiffs have no standing to seek civil penalties under the Act. We disagree. *Steel Co.* established that citizen suitors lack standing to seek civil penalties for violations that have abated by the time of suit. We specifically noted in that case that there was no allegation in the complaint of any continuing or imminent violation, and that no basis for such an allegation appeared to exist. In short, *Steel Co.* held that private plaintiffs, unlike the Federal Government, may not sue to assess penalties for wholly past violations, but our decision in that case did not reach the issue of standing to seek penalties for violations that are ongoing at the time of the complaint and that could continue into the future if undeterred.[4]

---

future violations. And it begins to look especially farfetched when one recalls that Laidlaw itself prompted the DHEC lawsuit, paid the filing fee, and drafted the complaint.

[4] In insisting that the redressability requirement is not met, the dissent relies heavily on *Linda R.S. v. Richard D.* That reliance is sorely misplaced. In *Linda R. S.*, the mother of an out-of-wedlock child filed suit to force a district attorney to bring a criminal prosecution against the absentee father for failure to pay child support. In finding that the mother lacked standing to seek this extraordinary remedy, the Court drew attention to "the special status of criminal prosecutions in our system" and carefully limited its holding to the "unique context of a challenge to [the non-enforcement of] a criminal statute." Furthermore, as to redressability, the relief sought in *Linda R. S.*—a prosecution which, if successful, would automatically land the delinquent father in jail for a fixed term, with predictably negative effects on his earning power—would scarcely remedy the plaintiff's lack of child support payments. In this regard, the Court contrasted "the civil contempt model whereby

B

Satisfied that FOE had standing under Article III to bring this action, we turn to the question of mootness.

The only conceivable basis for a finding of mootness in this case is Laidlaw's voluntary conduct—either its achievement by August 1992 of substantial compliance with its NPDES permit or its more recent shutdown of the Roebuck facility. It is well settled that "a defendant's voluntary cessation of a challenged practice does not deprive a federal court of its power to determine the legality of the practice." "[I]f it did, the courts would be compelled to leave '[t]he defendant * * * free to return to his old ways.'" In accordance with this principle, the standard we have announced for determining whether a case has been mooted by the defendant's voluntary conduct is stringent: "A case might become moot if subsequent events made it absolutely clear that the allegedly wrongful behavior could not reasonably be expected to recur." The "heavy burden of persua[ding]" the court that the challenged conduct cannot reasonably be expected to start up again lies with the party asserting mootness.

The Court of Appeals justified its mootness disposition by reference to *Steel Co.*, which held that citizen plaintiffs lack standing to seek civil penalties for wholly past violations. In relying on *Steel Co.*, the Court of Appeals confused mootness with standing. The confusion is understandable, given this Court's repeated statements that the doctrine of mootness can be described as "the doctrine of standing set in a time frame: The requisite personal interest that must exist at the commencement of the litigation (standing) must continue throughout its existence (mootness)."

Careful reflection on the long-recognized exceptions to mootness, however, reveals that the description of mootness as "standing set in a time frame" is not comprehensive. As just noted, a defendant claiming that its voluntary compliance moots a case bears the formidable burden of showing that it is absolutely clear the allegedly wrongful behavior could not reasonably be expected to recur. By contrast, in a lawsuit brought to force compliance, it is the plaintiff's burden to establish standing by demonstrating that, if unchecked by the litigation, the de-

---

the defendant 'keeps the keys to the jail in his own pocket' and may be released whenever he complies with his legal obligations." The dissent's contention, that "precisely the same situation exists here" as in *Linda R. S.* is, to say the least, extravagant.

Putting aside its mistaken reliance on *Linda R. S.*, the dissent's broader charge that citizen suits for civil penalties under the Act carry "grave implications for democratic governance" seems to us overdrawn. Certainly the federal Executive Branch does not share the dissent's view that such suits dissipate its authority to enforce the law. In fact, the Department of Justice has endorsed this citizen suit from the outset, submitting *amicus* briefs in support of FOE in the District Court, the Court of Appeals, and this Court. As we have already noted, the Federal Government retains the power to foreclose a citizen suit by undertaking its own action. And if the Executive Branch opposes a particular citizen suit, the statute allows the Administrator of the EPA to "intervene as a matter of right" and bring the Government's views to the attention of the court.

fendant's allegedly wrongful behavior will likely occur or continue, and that the "threatened injury [is] certainly impending." Thus, in *Lyons*, as already noted, we held that a plaintiff lacked initial standing to seek an injunction against the enforcement of a police chokehold policy because he could not credibly allege that he faced a realistic threat arising from the policy. Elsewhere in the opinion, however, we noted that a citywide moratorium on police chokeholds—an action that surely diminished the already slim likelihood that any particular individual would be choked by police—would not have mooted an otherwise valid claim for injunctive relief, because the moratorium by its terms was not permanent. The plain lesson of these cases is that there are circumstances in which the prospect that a defendant will engage in (or resume) harmful conduct may be too speculative to support standing, but not too speculative to overcome mootness.

Furthermore, if mootness were simply "standing set in a time frame," the exception to mootness that arises when the defendant's allegedly unlawful activity is "capable of repetition, yet evading review" could not exist. * * * Standing admits of no similar exception; if a plaintiff lacks standing at the time the action commences, the fact that the dispute is capable of repetition yet evading review will not entitle the complainant to a federal judicial forum.

We acknowledged the distinction between mootness and standing most recently in *Steel Co.*:

> The United States * * * argues that the injunctive relief does constitute remediation because "there is a presumption of [future] injury when the defendant has voluntarily ceased its illegal activity in response to litigation," even if that occurs before a complaint is filed * * *. This makes a sword out of a shield. The "presumption" the Government refers to has been applied to refute the assertion of mootness by a defendant who, when sued in a complaint that alleges present or threatened injury, ceases the complained-of activity* * *. It is an immense and unacceptable stretch to call the presumption into service as a substitute for the allegation of present or threatened injury upon which initial standing must be based.

Standing doctrine functions to ensure, among other things, that the scarce resources of the federal courts are devoted to those disputes in which the parties have a concrete stake. In contrast, by the time mootness is an issue, the case has been brought and litigated, often (as here) for years. To abandon the case at an advanced stage may prove more wasteful than frugal. This argument from sunk costs does not license courts to retain jurisdiction over cases in which one or both of the parties plainly lacks a continuing interest, as when the parties have settled or a plaintiff pursuing a nonsurviving claim has died. But the argument surely highlights an important difference between the two doctrines.

In its brief, Laidlaw appears to argue that, regardless of the effect of

Laidlaw's compliance, FOE doomed its own civil penalty claim to mootness by failing to appeal the District Court's denial of injunctive relief. This argument misconceives the statutory scheme. * * * [T]he district court has discretion to determine which form of relief is best suited, in the particular case, to abate current violations and deter future ones. "[A] federal judge sitting as chancellor is not mechanically obligated to grant an injunction for every violation of law." Denial of injunctive relief does not necessarily mean that the district court has concluded there is no prospect of future violations for civil penalties to deter. Indeed, it meant no such thing in this case. The District Court denied injunctive relief, but expressly based its award of civil penalties on the need for deterrence. As the dissent notes, federal courts should aim to ensure " 'the framing of relief no broader than required by the precise facts.' " In accordance with this aim, a district court in a Clean Water Act citizen suit properly may conclude that an injunction would be an excessively intrusive remedy, because it could entail continuing superintendence of the permit holder's activities by a federal court—a process burdensome to court and permit holder alike.

Laidlaw also asserts, in a supplemental suggestion of mootness, that the closure of its Roebuck facility, which took place after the Court of Appeals issued its decision, mooted the case. The facility closure, like Laidlaw's earlier achievement of substantial compliance with its permit requirements, might moot the case, but—we once more reiterate—only if one or the other of these events made it absolutely clear that Laidlaw's permit violations could not reasonably be expected to recur. The effect of both Laidlaw's compliance and the facility closure on the prospect of future violations is a disputed factual matter. FOE points out, for example—and Laidlaw does not appear to contest—that Laidlaw retains its NPDES permit. These issues have not been aired in the lower courts; they remain open for consideration on remand.

C

[The Court declined to discuss whether plaintiffs were entitled to attorney's fees, since the district court, though indicating that it might award fees, had delayed its final decision until final appellate disposition of the case.]

* * *

For the reasons stated, the judgment of the United States Court of Appeals for the Fourth Circuit is reversed, and the case is remanded for further proceedings consistent with this opinion.

It is so ordered.

JUSTICE STEVENS, concurring.

Although the Court has identified a sufficient reason for rejecting the Court of Appeals' mootness determination, it is important also to note that the case would not be moot even if it were absolutely clear that respondent had gone out of business and posed no threat of future permit violations. The District Court entered a valid judgment requiring respondent to pay a civil penalty of $405,800 to the United States. No post-judgment conduct of respondent could retroactively invalidate that judgment. A record of voluntary post-judgment compliance that would justify a decision that injunctive relief is unnecessary, or even a decision that any claim for injunctive relief is now moot, would not warrant vacation of the valid money judgment.

Furthermore, petitioners' claim for civil penalties would not be moot even if it were absolutely clear that respondent's violations could not reasonably be expected to recur because respondent achieved substantial compliance with its permit requirements after petitioners filed their complaint but before the District Court entered judgment. As the Courts of Appeals (other than the court below) have uniformly concluded, a polluter's voluntary post-complaint cessation of an alleged violation will not moot a citizen-suit claim for civil penalties even if it is sufficient to moot a related claim for injunctive or declaratory relief. This conclusion is consistent with the structure of the Clean Water Act, which attaches liability for civil penalties at the time a permit violation occurs. It is also consistent with the character of civil penalties, which, for purposes of mootness analysis, should be equated with punitive damages rather than with injunctive or declaratory relief. No one contends that a defendant's post-complaint conduct could moot a claim for punitive damages; civil penalties should be treated the same way.

The cases cited by the Court in its discussion of the mootness issue all involved requests for injunctive or declaratory relief. In only * * * *Los Angeles v. Lyons* did the plaintiff seek damages, and in that case the opinion makes it clear that the inability to obtain injunctive relief would have no impact on the damages claim. There is no precedent, either in our jurisprudence, or in any other of which I am aware, that provides any support for the suggestion that post-complaint factual developments that might moot a claim for injunctive or declaratory relief could either moot a claim for monetary relief or retroactively invalidate a valid money judgment.

JUSTICE SCALIA, with whom JUSTICE THOMAS joins, dissenting.

The Court begins its analysis by finding injury in fact on the basis of vague affidavits that are undermined by the District Court's express finding that Laidlaw's discharges caused no demonstrable harm to the environment. It then proceeds to marry private wrong with public remedy in a union that violates traditional principles of federal standing—thereby permitting law enforcement to be placed in the hands of private individuals. Finally, the Court suggests that to avoid mootness one needs even less of a stake in the outcome than the Court's watered-down requirements for initial standing. I dissent from all of this.

I

Plaintiffs, as the parties invoking federal jurisdiction, have the burden of proof and persuasion as to the existence of standing. The plaintiffs in this case fell far short of carrying their burden of demonstrating injury in fact. The Court cites affiants' testimony asserting that their enjoyment of the North Tyger River has been diminished due to "concern" that the water was polluted, and that they "believed" that Laidlaw's mercury exceedances had reduced the value of their homes. These averments alone cannot carry the plaintiffs' burden of demonstrating that they have suffered a "concrete and particularized" injury. General allegations of injury may suffice at the pleading stage, but at summary judgment plaintiffs must set forth "specific facts" to support their claims. And where, as here, the case has proceeded to judgment, those specific facts must be " 'supported adequately by the evidence adduced at trial.' " In this case, the affidavits themselves are woefully short on "specific facts," and the vague allegations of injury they do make are undermined by the evidence adduced at trial.

Typically, an environmental plaintiff claiming injury due to discharges in violation of the Clean Water Act argues that the discharges harm the environment, and that the harm to the environment injures him. This route to injury is barred in the present case, however, since the District Court concluded after considering all the evidence that there had been "no demonstrated proof of harm to the environment," , that the "permit violations at issue in this citizen suit did not result in any health risk or environmental harm," that "[a]ll available data * * * fail to show that Laidlaw's actual discharges have resulted in harm to the North Tyger River," and that "the overall quality of the river exceeds levels necessary to support * * * recreation in and on the water."

The Court finds these conclusions unproblematic for standing, because "[t]he relevant showing for purposes of Article III standing * * * is not injury to the environment but injury to the plaintiff." This statement is correct, as far as it goes. We have certainly held that a demonstration of harm to the environment is not enough to satisfy the injury-in-fact requirement unless the plaintiff can demonstrate how he personally was harmed. In the normal course, however, a lack of demonstrable harm to the environment will translate, as it plainly does here, into a lack of demonstrable harm to citizen plaintiffs. While it is perhaps possible that a plaintiff could be harmed even though the environment was not, such a plaintiff would have the burden of articulating and demonstrating the nature of that injury. Ongoing "concerns" about the environment are not enough, for "[i]t is the reality of the threat of repeated injury that is relevant to the standing inquiry, not the plaintiff's subjective apprehensions." *Los Angeles v. Lyons.* At the very least, in the present case, one would expect to see evidence supporting the affidavits' bald assertions regarding decreasing recreational usage and declining home values, as well as evidence for the improbable proposition that Laidlaw's violations, even though harmless to the environment, are somehow responsible for these effects. Plaintiffs here have made no attempt at such a showing, but rely entirely upon unsupported and unexplained affidavit allegations of "concern."

Indeed, every one of the affiants deposed by Laidlaw cast into doubt the (in any event inadequate) proposition that subjective "concerns" actually affected their conduct. Linda Moore, for example, said in her affidavit that she would use the affected waterways for recreation if it were not for her concern about pollution. Yet she testified in her deposition that she had been to the river only twice, once in 1980 (when she visited someone who lived by the river) and once after this suit was filed. Similarly, Kenneth Lee Curtis, who claimed he was injured by being deprived of recreational activity at the river, admitted that he had not been to the river since he was "a kid," and when asked whether the reason he stopped visiting the river was because of pollution, answered "no." As to Curtis's claim that the river "looke[d] and smell[ed] polluted," this condition, if present, was surely not caused by Laidlaw's discharges, which according to the District Court "did not result in any health risk or environmental harm." The other affiants cited by the Court were not deposed, but their affidavits state either that they would use the river if it were not polluted or harmful (as the court subsequently found it is not), or said that the river looks polluted (which is also incompatible with the court's findings). These affiants have established nothing but "subjective apprehensions."

The Court is correct that the District Court explicitly found standing—albeit "by the very slimmest of margins," and as "an awfully close call." That cautious finding, however, was made in 1993, long before the court's 1997 conclusion that Laidlaw's discharges did not harm the environment. As we have previously recognized, an initial conclusion that plaintiffs have standing is subject to reexamination, particularly if later evidence proves inconsistent with that conclusion. Laidlaw challenged the existence of injury in fact on appeal to the Fourth Circuit, but that court did not reach the question. Thus no lower court has reviewed the injury-in-fact issue in light of the extensive studies that led the District Court to conclude that the environment was not harmed by Laidlaw's discharges.

Inexplicably, the Court is untroubled by this, but proceeds to find injury in fact in the most casual fashion, as though it is merely confirming a careful analysis made below. Although we have previously refused to find standing based on the "conclusory allegations of an affidavit," the Court is content to do just that today. By accepting plaintiffs' vague, contradictory, and unsubstantiated allegations of "concern" about the environment as adequate to prove injury in fact, and accepting them even in the face of a finding that the environment was not demonstrably harmed, the Court makes the injury-in-fact requirement a sham. If there are permit violations, and a member of a plaintiff environmental organization lives near the offending plant, it would be difficult not to satisfy today's lenient standard.

II

The Court's treatment of the redressability requirement—which would have been unnecessary if it resolved the injury-in-fact question correctly—is equally cavalier. As discussed above, petitioners allege ongoing injury consisting of diminished enjoyment of the affected waterways and decreased property values. They allege that these injuries are caused by Laidlaw's continuing permit violations. But the remedy petitioners seek is neither recompense for their injuries nor an injunction against future violations. Instead, the remedy is a statutorily specified "penalty" for past violations, payable entirely to the United States Treasury. Only last Term, we held that such penalties do not redress any injury a citizen plaintiff has suffered from past violations. The Court nonetheless finds the redressability requirement satisfied here, distinguishing *Steel Co.* on the ground that in this case the petitioners allege ongoing violations; payment of the penalties, it says, will remedy petitioners' injury by deterring future violations by Laidlaw. It holds that a penalty payable to the public "remedies" a threatened private harm, and suffices to sustain a private suit.

That holding has no precedent in our jurisprudence, and takes this Court beyond the "cases and controversies" that Article III of the Constitution has entrusted to its resolution. Even if it were appropriate, moreover, to allow Article III's remediation requirement to be satisfied by the indirect private consequences of a public penalty, those consequences are entirely too speculative in the present case. The new standing law that the Court makes—like all expansions of standing beyond the traditional constitutional limits—has grave implications for democratic governance. I shall discuss these three points in turn.

A

* * *

* * * The principle that "in American jurisprudence * * * a private citizen lacks a judicially cognizable interest in the prosecution or non-prosecution of another" applies no less to prosecution for civil penalties payable to the State than to prosecution for criminal penalties owing to the State.

The Court's opinion reads as though the only purpose and effect of the redressability requirement is to assure that the plaintiff receive some of the benefit of the relief that a court orders. That is not so. If it were, a federal tort plaintiff fearing repetition of the injury could ask for tort damages to be paid, not only to himself but to other victims as well, on the theory that those damages would have at least some deterrent effect beneficial to him. Such a suit is preposterous because the "remediation" that is the traditional business of Anglo-American courts is relief specifically tailored to the plaintiff's injury, and not any sort of relief that has some incidental benefit to the plaintiff. Just as a "generalized grievance" that affects the entire citizenry cannot satisfy the injury-in-fact requirement even though it aggrieves the plaintiff along with everyone else, so also a generalized remedy that deters all future unlawful activity against all persons cannot satisfy the remediation requirement, even though it deters (among other things) repetition of this particular unlawful activity against these particular plaintiffs.

Thus, relief against prospective harm is traditionally afforded by way of an injunction, the scope of which is limited by the scope of the threatened injury. In seeking to overturn that tradition by giving an individual plaintiff the power to invoke a public remedy, Congress has done precisely what we have said it cannot do: convert an "undifferentiated public interest" into an "individual right" vindicable in the courts. The sort of scattershot redress approved today makes nonsense of our statement that the requirement of injury in fact "insures the framing of relief no broader than required by the precise facts." A claim of particularized future injury has today been made the vehicle for pursuing generalized penalties for past violations, and a threshold showing of injury in fact has become a lever that will move the world.

B

* * *

If the Court had undertaken the necessary inquiry into whether significant deterrence of the plaintiffs' feared injury was "likely," it would have had to reason something like this: Strictly speaking, no polluter is deterred by a penalty for past pollution; he is deterred by the fear of a penalty for future pollution. That fear will be virtually nonexistent if the prospective polluter knows that all emissions violators are given a free pass; it will be substantial under an emissions program such as the federal scheme here, which is regularly and notoriously enforced; it will be even higher when a prospective polluter subject to such a regularly enforced program has, as here, been the object of public charges of pollution and a suit for injunction; and it will surely be near the top of the graph when, as here, the prospective polluter has already been subjected to state penalties for the past pollution. The deterrence on which the plaintiffs must rely for standing in the present case is the marginal increase in Laidlaw's fear of future penalties that will be achieved by adding federal penalties for Laidlaw's past conduct.

I cannot say for certain that this marginal increase is zero; but I can say for certain that it is entirely speculative whether it will make the difference between these plaintiffs' suffering injury in the future and these plaintiffs' going unharmed. In fact, the assertion that it will "likely" do so is entirely farfetched. The speculativeness of that result is much greater than the speculativeness we found excessive in *Simon v. Eastern Ky. Welfare Rights Organization,* where we held that denying § 501(c)(3) charitable-deduction tax status to hospitals that refused to treat indigents was not sufficiently likely to assure future treatment of the indigent plaintiffs to support standing. And it is much greater than the speculativeness we found excessive in *Linda R.S. v. Richard D.,* where we said that "the prospect that prosecution [for nonsupport] will * * * result in payment of support can, at best, be termed only speculative."

In sum, if this case is, as the Court suggests, within the central core of "deterrence" standing, it is impossible to imagine what the "outer limits" could possibly be. The Court's expressed reluctance to define those "outer limits" serves only to disguise the fact that it has promulgated a revolutionary new doctrine of standing that will permit the entire body of public civil penalties to be handed over to enforcement by private interests.

* * *

III

Finally, I offer a few comments regarding the Court's discussion of whether FOE's claims became moot by reason of Laidlaw's substantial compliance with the permit limits. I do not disagree with the conclusion that the Court reaches. Assuming that the plaintiffs had standing to pursue civil penalties in the first instance (which they did not), their claim might well not have been mooted by Laidlaw's voluntary compliance with the permit, and leaving this fact-intensive question open for consideration on remand, as the Court does, seems sensible.[4] In reaching this disposition, however, the Court engages in a troubling discussion of the purported distinctions between the doctrines of standing and mootness. I am frankly puzzled as to why this discussion appears at all.

---

[4] In addition to the compliance and plant-closure issues, there also remains open on remand the question whether the current suit was foreclosed because the earlier suit by the State was "diligently prosecuted." Nothing in the Court's opinion disposes of the issue. The opinion notes the District Court's finding that Laidlaw itself played a significant role in facilitating the State's action. But there is no incompatibility whatever between a defendant's facilitation of suit and the State's diligent prosecution—as prosecutions of felons who confess their crimes and turn themselves in regularly demonstrate. Laidlaw was entirely within its rights to prefer state suit to this private enforcement action; and if it had such a preference it would have been prudent—given that a State must act within 60 days of receiving notice of a citizen suit, and given the number of cases State agencies handle—for Laidlaw to make sure its case did not fall through the cracks. South Carolina's interest in the action was not a feigned last minute contrivance. It had worked with Laidlaw in resolving the problem for many years, and had previously undertaken an administrative enforcement action resulting in a consent order. South Carolina has filed an *amicus* brief arguing that allowing citizen suits to proceed despite ongoing state enforcement efforts "will provide citizens and federal judges the opportunity to relitigate and second-guess the enforcement and permitting actions of South Carolina and other States."

Laidlaw's claimed compliance is squarely within the bounds of our "voluntary cessation" doctrine, which is the basis for the remand.[5] There is no reason to engage in an interesting academic excursus upon the differences between mootness and standing in order to invoke this obviously applicable rule.

* * *

By uncritically accepting vague claims of injury, the Court has turned the Article III requirement of injury in fact into a "mere pleading requirement," and by approving the novel theory that public penalties can redress anticipated private wrongs, it has come close to "mak[ing] the redressability requirement vanish." The undesirable and unconstitutional consequence of today's decision is to place the immense power of suing to enforce the public laws in private hands. I respectfully dissent.

Notes and Questions

1. a) Justice Ginsburg notes that while the DHEC action was pending, Laidlaw continued to violate its NPDES permit. Why is that relevant to the district court's inquiry? Shouldn't that be a matter of concern for the South Carolina executive branch in deciding what sort of settlement is acceptable? Has Congress made all such settlements subject to court supervision much in the manner of FED.R.CIV.P 23(e)?

b) Is it appropriate for Congress effectively to have directed the courts to determine whether the government has "diligently prosecuted" an action? Should the federal courts be in the position of determining how well or poorly a litigant has prosecuted or defended an action, apart from their role in rendering a judgment? To the extent that that there may be a problem with this role for the federal courts, is the problem more acute if the federal government (rather than a state government, as here) prosecutes the action?

c) Justice Scalia suggested that the idea of private attorneys general might violate Article II. Does the statute here, with its emphasis on "diligently prosecuted," inject the courts into a consideration of whether the executive has "faithfully executed" the laws, thus creating another potential constitutional problem?

2. a) What, precisely, is the injury-in-fact that plaintiffs claim to have suffered? Was Justice Scalia correct in his implication that lack of harm to

---

[5] Unlike Justice Stevens' concurrence, the opinion for the Court appears to recognize that a claim for civil penalties is moot when it is clear that no future injury to the plaintiff at the hands of the defendant can occur. The concurrence suggests that civil penalties, like traditional damages remedies, cannot be mooted by absence of threatened injury. The analogy is inapt. Traditional money damages are payable to compensate for the harm of past conduct, which subsists whether future harm is threatened or not; civil penalties are privately assessable (according to the Court) to deter threatened future harm to the plaintiff. Where there is no threat to the plaintiff, he has no claim to deterrence. The proposition that impossibility of future violation does not moot the case holds true, of course, for civil-penalty suits by the government, which do not rest upon the theory that some particular future harm is being prevented.

the environment virtually compels the conclusion that none of the plaintiffs suffered harm even though they may have wholly subjective fears about environmental safety? The plaintiffs, of course, argued at least implicitly that Laidlaw's unlawful discharges damaged their aesthetic interest in the environment and their ability to enjoy the recreational opportunities of the North Tyger River. For many years the Court has found that cognizable as injury-in-fact. Should it, or does that give weight to Justice Scalia's charge that the Court's approach makes standing a mockery?

b) As Justice Scalia pointed out, much of the plaintiffs' injury-in-fact argument rested not on what Laidlaw's activities forced them to discontinue but rather upon what they alleged they "would" do. Should the Court have distinguished between two types of conditional statements for standing purposes, the first where the plaintiffs have been engaged in activities and "would" continue but for the defendant's conduct, and the second where the plaintiffs have never (or not for decades) engaged in such activities but allege that they "would" begin but for the defendant's conduct?

c) Is Justice Scalia's reliance on *City of Los Angeles v. Lyons* well-placed? What does the possibility of aesthetic injury-in-fact suggest?

d) Justice Scalia argues that "an initial conclusion that plaintiffs have standing is subject to reexamination, particularly if later evidence proves inconsistent with that conclusion." Does he thereby suggest that the standing inquiry remains open throughout the trial and appellate process? How far would he take that idea? Suppose a plaintiff filed a diversity action seeking to recover damages caused by the defendant's negligent driving. At the conclusion of the trial, if the jury's special verdict indicates that although the defendant drove negligently, his driving was not the proximate cause of plaintiff's injuries, should the court dismiss the action for lack of standing?

3. The Court's treatment of redressability demands consideration, not least the Court finds itself in a bind from having to defend its past decisions.

a) Justice Ginsburg notes that the Court has acknowledged the deterrent effect of civil penalties. Is that important, or is it only important that Congress intended the civil penalties to act as deterrents of future unlawful conduct? Who should evaluate the effectiveness of penalties—the legislature or the courts? If the former, then do the courts have any role at all, or could Congress effectively circumvent the injury-in-fact requirement of Article III by providing clearly nominal penalties and declaring them effective? If the latter, what standards should the courts use to determine efficacy?

b) *Linda R.S. v. Richard D.* (page 55), poses a problem for the Court. The majority in that case held that it was "only speculative" that the threat of criminal penalties against a parent refusing child support might cause him to commence payments. The statute in question prescribed a fixed jail term for violators. If it is too speculative to conclude that the threat of jail might be an incentive for compliance, how can the majority conclude that the threat (or imposition) of civil penalties is not too speculative as a deterrent?

The *Linda R.S.* Court argued that if the plaintiff were granted relief, the non-supporting father would be incapacitated from paying support. Might not imposition of that penalty deter future noncompliance in much the way that Justice Ginsburg's majority hypothesized that civil penalties would? Justice White dissented in *Linda R.S.*, finding the majority's reasoning "very odd." "I had always thought our civilization has assumed that the threat of penal sanctions had something more than a 'speculative effect' on a person's conduct." In other words, should Justice Ginsburg have tried so hard to live with *Linda R.S.* and its reasoning?

c) Justice Scalia argued that mere availability of civil penalties, rather than actual imposition, creates the deterrent effect. Do you think he would take the same position with respect to criminal statutes? He also argued that the sanction in the DHEC action was as great a deterrent as possible. The structure of the statute suggests that Congress felt differently. How can a court, rather than a legislature, make such a judgment?

4. Does the Court's treatment of *Steel Co.* (also discussed *infra* at 288) persuade you? There the Court held that the plaintiffs lacked standing because the defendant had ceased its violations, but specifically noted that payment of fines to the government could not remedy the injury (failure timely to report environmental data) that the plaintiffs alleged.

> [T]he civil penalties authorized by the statute might be viewed as a sort of compensation or redress to respondent if they were payable to the respondent. But they are not. These penalties—the only damages authorized * * * —are payable to the United States Treasury. In requesting them, therefore, respondent seeks not remediation of its own injury—reimbursement for the costs it incurred as a result of the late filing—but vindication of the rule of law—the "undifferentiated public interest in the faithful execution of [the law].

Note that the *Steel Co.* Court's discussion in this respect does not turn on the timing of the action; it turns on who gets the money. Why does the deterrent value of the civil penalties suffice for redressability in *Laidlaw* but not in *Steel Co.*? In both cases, the plaintiffs surely relied upon the idea that civil penalties encourage future compliance, whether it be with respect to reporting requirements or environmentally damaging discharges. Has the majority in *Laidlaw* created a distinction without a difference?

5. a) For mootness, how much voluntary cessation is enough? As the Court notes, if the defendant can show that events have eliminated any reasonable expectation of recurrence of the offending conduct, then the case is moot. "According to Laidlaw, after the Court of Appeals issued its decision but before this Court granted certiorari, the entire incinerator facility in Roebuck was permanently closed, dismantled, and put up for sale, and all discharges from the facility permanently ceased." Does that satisfy the Court's heightened cessation standard? The majority accepted FOE's argument that Laidlaw's retention of the NPDES permit might prevent a finding that there was no reasonable possibility of recurrence. How might such recurrence happen?

b) Does FOE have standing simply based on Laidlaw's permit to seek an injunction against further violations? If Laidlaw announced its intention to build another facility on the North Tyger River, would FOE be able immediately to seek an injunction against additional violations of the NPDES permit? Would it have standing? Would the case be ripe?

6. The Court suggests that mootness and standing call for different evaluations, not merely influenced by the passage of time. "[T]he prospect that a defendant will engage in (or resume) harmful conduct may be too speculative to support standing, but not too speculative to support mootness." To the extent that mootness, like standing, finds its constitutional footing in Article III, is there anything in that Article to justify the different treatment to which Justice Ginsburg adverts? If the bottom-line question is whether the plaintiff has suffered injury-in-fact and has a live controversy with the defendant, how can the Court justify what it characterizes as the "exception" to mootness of cases "capable of repetition, yet evading review"?

It may be that mootness, like standing, has both constitutional and prudential components; certainly that division seems implicit in the Court's cost-benefit analysis: "To abandon the case at an advanced stage may prove more wasteful than frugal." Does the Case-or-Controversy Clause rest on concepts of frugality?

7. *Tory v. Cochran*, 544 U.S. 734, 125 S.Ct. 2108, 161 L.Ed.2d 1042 (2005), held that a case resulting in an injunction restraining Mr. Tory from picketing and making any oral or written public statements about the well-known attorney Johnnie Cochran was not mooted by Mr. Cochran's death. California law did not automatically render the injunction invalid upon Mr. Cochran's death; apparently, a court order was necessary to determine its continued force. Moreover, the widow had an interest in enforcing the injunction. The Court also concluded, however, that the injunction as written amounted to an overly broad prior restraint on speech because the basic reason for the injunction, which was to keep Tory from trying to coerce Mr. Cochran to pay " 'amounts of money to which Tory was not entitled' as a 'tribute' or a 'premium' for desisting * * * ," had lost much of its force. The Court remanded to the state courts to consider whether a more narrowly tailored injunction was appropriate.

F. POLITICAL QUESTIONS

NIXON v. UNITED STATES
Supreme Court of the United States, 1993.
506 U.S. 224, 113 S.Ct. 732, 122 L.Ed.2d 1.

CHIEF JUSTICE REHNQUIST delivered the opinion of the Court.

Petitioner Walter L. Nixon, Jr., asks this court to decide whether Senate Rule XI, which allows a committee of Senators to hear evidence against an individual who has been impeached and to report that evidence to the full Senate, violates the Impeachment Trial Clause, Art. I, § 3, cl. 6. * * * But before we reach the merits of such a claim, we must decide whether it is "justiciable," that is, whether it is a claim that may be resolved by the courts. We conclude that it is not.

Nixon, a former Chief Judge of the United States District Court for the Southern District of Mississippi, was convicted by a jury of two counts of making false statements before a federal grand jury and sentenced to prison. * * * Because Nixon refused to resign from his office as a United States District Judge, he continued to collect his judicial salary while serving out his prison sentence.

On May 10, 1989, the House of Representatives adopted three articles of impeachment for high crimes and misdemeanors. The first two articles charged Nixon with giving false testimony before the grand jury and the third article charged him with bringing disrepute on the Federal Judiciary.

After the House presented the articles to the Senate, the Senate voted to invoke its own Impeachment Rule XI, under which the presiding officer appoints a committee of Senators to "receive evidence and take testimony."[1] The Senate committee held four days of hearings, during which 10 witnesses, including Nixon, testified. Pursuant to Rule XI, the committee presented the full Senate with a complete transcript of the proceeding and a report stating the uncontested facts and summarizing the evidence on the contested facts. Nixon and the House impeachment managers submitted extensive final briefs to the full Senate and delivered arguments from the Senate floor during the three hours set aside for oral argument in front of that body. Nixon himself gave a personal appeal, and several Senators posed questions directly to both parties. The Senate voted by more than the constitutionally required two-thirds majority to convict Nixon on the first two articles. The presiding officer then entered judgment removing Nixon from his office as United States District Judge.

Nixon thereafter commenced the present suit, arguing that Senate Rule XI violates the constitutional grant of authority to the Senate to

---

[1] Specifically, Rule XI provides:

> [I]n the trial of any impeachment the Presiding Officer of the Senate, if the Senate so orders, shall appoint a committee of Senators to receive evidence and take testimony at such times and places as the committee may determine, and for such purpose the committee so appointed and the chairman thereof, to be elected by the committee, shall (unless otherwise ordered by the Senate) exercise all the powers and functions conferred upon the Senate and the Presiding Officer of the Senate, respectively, under the rules of procedure and practice in the Senate when sitting on impeachment trials.

Unless otherwise ordered by the Senate, the rules of procedure and practice in the Senate when sitting on impeachment trials shall govern the procedure and practice of the committee so appointed. The committee so appointed shall report to the Senate in writing a certified copy of the transcript of the proceedings and testimony had and given before such committee, and such report shall be received by the Senate and the evidence so received and the testimony so taken shall be considered to all intents and purposes, subject to the right of the Senate to determine competency, relevancy, and materiality, as having been received and taken before the Senate, but nothing herein shall prevent the Senate from sending for any witness and hearing his testimony in open Senate, or by order of the Senate having the entire trial in open Senate.

"try" all impeachments because it prohibits the whole Senate from taking part in the evidentiary hearings. Nixon sought a declaratory judgment that his impeachment conviction was void and that his judicial salary and privileges should be reinstated. The District Court held that his claim was nonjusticiable, and the Court of Appeals for the District of Columbia Circuit agreed.

A controversy is nonjusticiable—*i.e.,* involves a political question—where there is "a textually demonstrable constitutional commitment of the issue to a coordinate political department; or a lack of judicially discoverable and manageable standards for resolving it * * *." But the courts must, in the first instance, interpret the text in question and determine whether and to what extent the issue is textually committed. As the discussion that follows makes clear, the concept of a textual commitment to a coordinate political department is not completely separate from the concept of a lack of judicially discoverable and manageable standards for resolving it; the lack of judicially manageable standards may strengthen the conclusion that there is a textually demonstrable commitment to a coordinate branch.

In this case, we must examine Art. I, § 3, cl. 6, to determine the scope of authority conferred upon the Senate by the Framers regarding impeachment. It provides:

> The Senate shall have the sole Power to try all Impeachments. When sitting for that Purpose, they shall be on Oath or Affirmation. When the President of the United States is tried, the Chief Justice shall preside: And no Person shall be convicted without the Concurrence of two thirds of the Members present.

The language and structure of this Clause are revealing. The first sentence is a grant of authority to the Senate, and the word "sole" indicates that this authority is reposed in the Senate and nowhere else. The next two sentences specify requirements to which the Senate proceedings shall conform: the Senate shall be on oath or affirmation, a two-thirds vote is required to convict, and when the President is tried the Chief Justice shall preside.

Petitioner argues that the word "try" in the first sentence imposes by implication an additional requirement on the Senate in that the proceedings must be in the nature of a judicial trial. From there petitioner goes on to argue that this limitation precludes the Senate from delegating to a select committee the task of hearing the testimony of witnesses, as was done pursuant to Senate Rule XI. " '[T]ry' means more than simply 'vote on' or 'review' or 'judge.' In 1787 and today, trying a case means hearing the evidence, not scanning a cold record." Petitioner concludes from this that courts may review whether or not the Senate "tried" him before convicting him.

There are several difficulties with this position which lead us ultimately to reject it. The word "try," both in 1787 and later, has considerably broader meanings than those to which petitioner would limit it. Older dictionaries define try as "[t]o examine" or "[t]o examine as a judge." In more modern usage the term has various meanings. For example, try can mean "to examine or investigate judicially," "to conduct the trial of," or "to put to the test by experiment, investigation, or trial." * * * [W]e cannot say that the Framers used the word "try" as an implied limitation on the method by which the Senate might proceed in trying impeachments. * * *

The conclusion that the use of the word "try" in the first sentence of the Impeachment Trial Clause lacks sufficient precision to afford any judicially manageable standard of review of the Senate's actions is fortified by the existence of the three very specific requirements that the Constitution does impose on the Senate when trying impeachments * * *. These limitations are quite precise, and their nature suggests that the Framers did not intend to impose additional limitations on the form of the Senate proceedings by the use of the word "try" in the first sentence.

Petitioner devotes only two pages in his brief to negating the significance of the word "sole" in the first sentence of Clause 6. As noted above, that sentence provides that "[t]he Senate shall have the sole Power to try all Impeachments." We think that the word "sole" is of considerable significance. Indeed, the word "sole" appears only one other time in the Constitution—with respect to the House of Representatives' *sole* Power of Impeachment." ([E]mphasis added). The common sense meaning of the word "sole" is that the Senate alone shall have authority to determine whether an individual should be acquitted or convicted. The dictionary definition bears this out. "Sole" is defined as "having no companion," "solitary," "being the only one," and "functioning * * * independently and without assistance or interference." If the courts may review the actions of the Senate in order to determine whether that body "tried" an impeached official, it is difficult to see how the Senate would be "functioning * * * independently and without assistance or interference."

* * *

Petitioner also contends that the word "sole" should not bear on the question of justiciability because Art. II, § 2, cl. 1, of the Constitution grants the President pardon authority "except in Cases of Impeachment." He argues that such a limitation on the President's pardon power would not have been necessary if the Framers thought that the Senate alone had authority to deal with such questions. But the granting of a pardon is in no sense an overturning of a judgment of conviction by some other tribunal; it is "[a]n executive action that mitigates or sets aside *punishment* for a crime." ([E]mphasis added). Authority in the Senate to determine procedures for trying an impeached official, unreviewable by the courts, is therefore not at all inconsistent with authority in the President to grant a pardon to the convicted official. The exception from the President's pardon authority of cases of impeachment was a separate determination by the Framers that executive clemency should not be available in such cases.

Petitioner finally argues that even if significance be attributed to the word "sole" in the first sentence of the clause, the authority granted is to the Senate, and this means that "the Senate—not the courts, not a lay jury, not a Senate Committee—shall try impeachments." It would be possible to read the first sentence of the Clause this way, but it is not a natural reading. Petitioner's interpretation would bring into judicial purview not merely the sort of claim made by petitioner, but other similar claims based on the conclusion that the word "Senate" has imposed by implication limitations on procedures which the Senate might adopt. Such limitations would be inconsistent with the construction of the Clause as a whole, which, as we have noted, sets out three express limitations in separate sentences.

The history and contemporary understanding of the impeachment provisions support our reading of the constitutional language. The parties do not offer evidence of a single word in the history of the Constitutional Convention or in contemporary commentary that even alludes to the possibility of judicial review in the context of the impeachment powers. This silence is quite meaningful in light of the several explicit references to the availability of judicial review as a check on the Legislature's power with respect to bills of attainder, *ex post facto* laws, and statutes.

The Framers labored over the question of where the impeachment power should lie. Significantly, in at least two considered scenarios the power was placed with the Federal Judiciary. Indeed, Madison and the Committee of Detail proposed that the Supreme Court should have the power to determine impeachments. Despite these proposals, the Convention ultimately decided that the Senate would have "the sole Power to Try all Impeachments." According to Alexander Hamilton, the Senate was the "most fit depositary of this important trust" because its members are representatives of the people. The Supreme Court was not the proper body because the Framers "doubted whether the members of that tribunal would, at all times, be endowed with so eminent a portion of fortitude as would be called for in the execution of so difficult a task" or whether the Court "would possess the degree of credit and authority" to carry out its judgment if it conflicted with the accusation brought by the Legislature—the people's representative. In addition, the Framers believed the Court was too small in number * * * .

There are two additional reasons why the Judiciary, and the Supreme Court in particular, were not chosen to have any role in impeachments. First, the Framers recognized that most likely there would be two sets of proceedings for individuals who commit impeachable offenses—the impeachment trial and a separate criminal trial. In fact, the

Constitution explicitly provides for two separate proceedings. The Framers deliberately separated the two forums to avoid raising the specter of bias and to ensure independent judgments * * *. Certainly judicial review of the Senate's "trial" would introduce the same risk of bias as would participation in the trial itself.

Second, judicial review would be inconsistent with the Framers' insistence that our system be one of checks and balances. In our constitutional system, impeachment was designed to be the *only* check on the Judicial Branch by the Legislature. On the topic of judicial accountability, Hamilton wrote: "The precautions for their responsibility are comprised in the article respecting impeachments. They are liable to be impeached for mal-conduct by the house of representatives, and tried by the senate, and if convicted, may be dismissed from office and disqualified for holding any other. *This is the only provision on the point, which is consistent with the necessary independence of the judicial character, and is the only one which we find in our own constitution in respect to our own judges.*" ([E]mphasis added). Judicial involvement in impeachment proceedings, even if only for purposes of judicial review, is counterintuitive because it would eviscerate the "important constitutional check" placed on the Judiciary by the Framers. Nixon's argument would place final reviewing authority with respect to impeachments in the hands of the same body that the impeachment process is meant to regulate.

Nevertheless, Nixon argues that judicial review is necessary in order to place a check on the Legislature. Nixon fears that if the Senate is given unreviewable authority to interpret the Impeachment Trial Clause, there is a grave risk that the Senate will usurp judicial power. The Framers anticipated this objection and created two constitutional safeguards to keep the Senate in check. The first safeguard is that the whole of the impeachment power is divided between the two legislative bodies, with the House given the right to accuse and the Senate given the right to judge. This split of authority "avoids the inconvenience of making the same persons both accusers and judges; and guards against the danger of persecution from the prevalency of a factious spirit in either of those branches." The second safeguard is the two-thirds supermajority vote requirement. * * *

In addition to the textual commitment argument, we are persuaded that the lack of finality and the difficulty of fashioning relief counsel against justiciability. We agree with the Court of Appeals that opening the door of judicial review to the procedures used by the Senate in trying impeachments would "expose the political life of the country to months, or perhaps years, of chaos." This lack of finality would manifest itself most dramatically if the President were impeached. The legitimacy of any successor, and hence his effectiveness, would be impaired severely, not merely while the judicial process was running its course, but during any retrial that a differently constituted Senate might conduct if its first judgment of conviction were invalidated. Equally uncertain is the question of what relief a court may give other than simply setting aside the judgment of conviction. Could it order the reinstatement of a convicted federal judge, or order Congress to create an additional judgeship if the seat had been filled in the interim?

Petitioner finally contends that a holding of nonjusticiability cannot be reconciled with our opinion in *Powell v. McCormack.* The relevant issue in *Powell* was whether courts could review the House of Representatives' conclusion that Powell was "unqualified" to sit as a Member because he had been accused of misappropriating public funds and abusing the process of the New York courts. We stated that the question of justiciability turned on whether the Constitution committed authority to the House to judge its members' qualifications, and if so, the extent of that commitment. Article I, § 5 provides that "Each House shall be the Judge of the Elections, Returns and Qualifications of its own Members." In turn, Art. I, § 2 specifies three requirements for membership in the House: The candidate must be at least 25 years of age, a citizen of the United States for no less than seven years, and an inhabitant of the State he is chosen to represent. We held that, in light of the three requirements specified in the Constitution, the word "qualifications"—of which the House was to be the Judge—was of a precise, limited nature.

Our conclusion in *Powell* was based on the fixed meaning of "[q]ualifications" set forth in Art. I, § 2. The claim by the House that its power to "be the Judge of the Elections, Returns and Qualifications of its own Members" was a textual commitment of unreviewable authority was defeated by the existence of this separate provision specifying the only qualifications which might be imposed for House membership. The decision as to whether a member satisfied these qualifications was placed with the House, but the decision as to what these qualifications consisted of was not.

In the case before us, there is no separate provision of the Constitution which could be defeated by allowing the Senate final authority to determine the meaning of the word "try" in the Impeachment Trial Clause. We agree with Nixon that courts possess power to review either legislative or executive action that transgresses identifiable textual limits. As we have made clear, "whether the action of [either the Legislative or Executive Branch] exceeds whatever authority has been committed, is itself a delicate exercise in constitutional interpretation, and is a responsibility of this Court as ultimate interpreter of the Constitution." But we conclude, after exercising that delicate responsibility, that the word "try" in the Impeachment Clause does not provide an identifiable textual limit on the authority which is committed to the Senate.

For the foregoing reasons, the judgment of the Court of Appeals is

Affirmed.

JUSTICE WHITE, with whom JUSTICE BLACKMUN joins, concurring in the judgment.

Petitioner contends that the method by which the Senate convicted him on two articles of impeachment violates Art. I, § 3, cl. 6 of the Constitution, which mandates that the Senate "try" impeachments. The Court is of the view that the Constitution forbids us even to consider his contention. I find no such prohibition and would therefore reach the merits of the claim. I concur in the judgment because the Senate fulfilled its constitutional obligation to "try" petitioner.

I

It should be said at the outset that, as a practical matter, it will likely make little difference whether the Court's or my view controls this case. This is so because the Senate has very wide discretion in specifying impeachment trial procedures and because it is extremely unlikely that the Senate would abuse its discretion and insist on a procedure that could not be deemed a trial by reasonable judges. Even taking a wholly practical approach, I would prefer not to announce an unreviewable discretion in the Senate to ignore completely the constitutional direction to "try" impeachment cases. When asked at oral argument whether that direction would be satisfied if, after a House vote to impeach, the Senate, without any procedure whatsoever, unanimously found the accused guilty of being "a bad guy," counsel for the United States answered that the Government's theory "leads me to answer that question yes." Especially in light of this advice from the Solicitor General, I would not issue an invitation to the Senate to find an excuse, in the name of other pressing business, to be dismissive of its critical role in the impeachment process.

Practicalities aside, however, since the meaning of a constitutional provision is at issue, my disagreement with the Court should be stated.

II

* * *

A

The majority finds a clear textual commitment in the Constitution's use of the word "sole" in the phrase "the Senate shall have the sole Power to try all impeachments." It attributes "considerable significance" to the fact that this term appears in only one other passage in the Constitution. The Framers' sparing use of "sole" is thought to indicate that its employment in the Impeachment Trial Clause demonstrates a concern to give the Senate exclusive interpretive authority over the Clause.

* * * The significance of the Constitution's use of the term "sole" lies not in the infrequency with which the term appears, but in the fact that it appears exactly twice, in parallel provisions concerning impeachment. That the word "sole" is found only in the House and Senate Impeach-

ment Clauses demonstrates that its purpose is to emphasize the distinct role of each in the impeachment process. As the majority notes, the Framers, following English practice, were very much concerned to separate the prosecutorial from the adjudicative aspects of impeachment. Giving each House "sole" power with respect to its role in impeachments effected this division of labor. While the majority is thus right to interpret the term "sole" to indicate that the Senate ought to " 'functio[n] independently and without assistance or interference,' " it wrongly identifies the judiciary, rather than the House, as the source of potential interference with which the Framers were concerned when they employed the term "sole."

Even if the Impeachment Trial Clause is read without regard to its companion clause, the Court's willingness to abandon its obligation to review the constitutionality of legislative acts merely on the strength of the word "sole" is perplexing. Consider, by comparison, the treatment of Art. I, § 1, which grants "All legislative powers" to the House and Senate. As used in that context "all" is nearly synonymous with "sole"—both connote entire and exclusive authority. Yet the Court has never thought it would unduly interfere with the operation of the Legislative Branch to entertain difficult and important questions as to the extent of the legislative power. Quite the opposite, we have stated that the proper interpretation of the Clause falls within the province of the judiciary. Addressing the constitutionality of the legislative veto, for example, the Court found it necessary and proper to interpret Art. I, § 1 as one of the "[e]xplicit and unambiguous provisions of the Constitution [that] prescribe and define the respective functions of the Congress and of the Executive in the legislative process."

* * *

The majority's review of the historical record * * * explains why the power to try impeachments properly resides with the Senate. It does not explain, however, the sweeping statement that the judiciary was "not chosen to have any role in impeachments." Not a single word in the historical materials cited by the majority addresses judicial review of the Impeachment Trial Clause. And a glance at the arguments surrounding the Impeachment Clauses negates the majority's attempt to infer nonjusticiability from the Framers' arguments in support of the Senate's power to try impeachments.

What the relevant history mainly reveals is deep ambivalence among many of the Framers over the very institution of impeachment, which, by its nature, is not easily reconciled with our system of checks and balances. As they clearly recognized, the branch of the Federal Government which is possessed of the authority to try impeachments, by having final say over the membership of each branch, holds a potentially unanswerable power over the others. In addition, that branch, insofar as it is called upon to try not only members of other branches, but also its own, will have the advantage of being the judge of its own members' causes.

It is no surprise, then, that the question of impeachment greatly vexed the Framers. The pages of the Convention debates reveal diverse plans for resolving this exceedingly difficult issue. * * *

The historical evidence reveals above all else that the Framers were deeply concerned about placing in any branch the "awful discretion, which a court of impeachments must necessarily have." Viewed against this history, the discord between the majority's position and the basic principles of checks and balances underlying the Constitution's separation of powers is clear. In essence, the majority suggests that the Framers' [sic] conferred upon Congress a potential tool of legislative dominance yet at the same time rendered Congress' exercise of that power one of the very few areas of legislative authority immune from any judicial review. While the majority rejects petitioner's justiciability argument as espousing a view "inconsistent with the Framers' insistence that our system be one of checks and balances," it is the Court's finding of nonjusticiability that truly upsets the Framers' careful design. In a truly balanced system, impeachments tried by the Senate would serve as a means of controlling the largely unaccountable judiciary, even as judicial review would ensure that the Senate adhered to a minimal set of procedural standards in conducting impeachment trials.

B

The majority also contends that the term "try" does not present a judicially manageable standard. It notes that in 1787, as today, the word "try" may refer to an inquiry in the nature of a judicial proceeding, or, more generally, to experimentation or investigation. In light of the term's multiple senses, the Court finds itself unable to conclude that the Framers used the word "try" as "an implied limitation on the method by which the Senate might proceed in trying impeachments." Also according to the majority, comparison to the other more specific requirements listed in the Impeachment Trial Clause * * * indicates that the word "try" was not meant by the Framers to constitute a limitation on the Senate's conduct and further reveals the term's unmanageability.

It is apparently on this basis that the majority distinguishes *Powell v. McCormack.* * * * The majority finds this case different from *Powell* only on the grounds that, whereas the qualifications of Art. I, § 2 are readily susceptible to judicial interpretation, the term "try" does not provide an "identifiable textual limit on the authority which is committed to the Senate."

This argument comes in two variants. The first, which asserts that one simply cannot ascertain the sense of "try" which the Framers employed and hence cannot undertake judicial review, is clearly untenable. To begin with, one would intuitively expect that, in defining the power of a political body to conduct an inquiry into official wrongdoing, the Framers used "try" in its legal sense. That intuition is borne out by reflection on the alternatives. The third clause of Art. I, § 3 cannot seriously be read to mean that the Senate shall "attempt" or "experiment with" impeachments. It is equally implausible to say that the Senate is charged with "investigating" impeachments given that this description would substantially overlap with the House of Representatives' "sole" power to draw up articles of impeachment. That these alternatives are not realistic possibilities is finally evidenced by the use of "tried" in the third sentence of the Impeachment Trial Clause ("[w]hen the President of the United States is tried * * *"), and by Art. III, § 2, cl. 3 ("[t]he Trial of all Crimes, except in Cases of Impeachment * * *").

The other variant of the majority position focuses not on which sense of "try" is employed in the Impeachment Trial Clause, but on whether the legal sense of that term creates a judicially manageable standard. The majority concludes that the term provides no "identifiable textual limit." Yet, as the Government itself conceded at oral argument, the term "try" is hardly so elusive as the majority would have it. Were the Senate, for example, to adopt the practice of automatically entering a judgment of conviction whenever articles of impeachment were delivered from the House, it is quite clear that the Senate will have failed to "try" impeachments. Indeed in this respect, "try" presents no greater, and perhaps fewer, interpretive difficulties than some other constitutional standards that have been found amenable to familiar techniques of judicial construction, including, for example, "Commerce * * * among the several States," and "due process of law."[3]

* * *

III

The majority's conclusion that "try" is incapable of meaningful judicial construction is not without irony. One might think that if any class of concepts would fall within the definitional abilities of the judiciary, it would be that class having to do with procedural justice. Examination of the remaining question—whether proceedings in accordance with Senate Rule XI are compatible with the Impeachment Trial Clause—confirms

---

[3] The majority's *in terrorem* argument against justiciability—that judicial review of impeachments might cause national disruption and that the courts would be unable to fashion effective relief—merits only brief attention. In the typical instance, court review of impeachments would no more render the political system dysfunctional than has this litigation. Moreover, the same capacity for disruption was noted and rejected as a basis for not hearing *Powell*. The relief granted for unconstitutional impeachment trials would presumably be similar to the relief granted to other unfairly tried public employee-litigants. Finally, as applied to the special case of the President, the majority's argument merely points out that, were the Senate to convict the President without any kind of a trial, a constitutional crisis might well result. It hardly follows that the Court ought to refrain from upholding the Constitution in all impeachment cases. Nor does it follow that, in cases of Presidential impeachment, the Justices ought to abandon their Constitutional responsibilities because the Senate has precipitated a crisis.

this intuition.

Petitioner bears the rather substantial burden of demonstrating that, simply by employing the word "try," the Constitution prohibits the Senate from relying on a fact-finding committee. It is clear that the Framers were familiar with English impeachment practice and with that of the States employing a variant of the English model at the time of the Constitutional Convention. Hence there is little doubt that the term "try" as used in Art. I, § 3, cl. 6 meant that the Senate should conduct its proceedings in a manner somewhat resembling a judicial proceeding. Indeed, it is safe to assume that Senate trials were to follow the practice in England and the States, which contemplated a formal hearing on the charges, at which the accused would be represented by counsel, evidence would be presented, and the accused would have the opportunity to be heard.

Petitioner argues, however, that because committees were not used in state impeachment trials prior to the Convention, the word "try" cannot be interpreted to permit their use. It is, however, a substantial leap to infer from the absence of a particular device of parliamentary procedure that its use has been forever barred by the Constitution. And there is textual and historical evidence that undermines the inference sought to be drawn in this case.

The fact that Art. III, § 2, cl. 3 specifically exempts impeachment trials from the jury requirement provides some evidence that the Framers were anxious not to have additional specific procedural requirements read into the term "try." Contemporaneous commentary further supports this view. Hamilton, for example, stressed that a trial by so large a body as the Senate (which at the time promised to boast 26 members) necessitated that the proceedings not "be tied down to * * * strict rules, either in the delineation of the offence by the prosecutors, or in the construction of it by the Judges * * * ." In his extensive analysis of the Impeachment Trial Clause, Justice Story offered a nearly identical analysis, which is worth quoting at length.

[I]t is obvious, that the strictness of the forms of proceeding in cases of offences at common law is ill adapted to impeachments. The very habits growing out of judicial employments; the rigid manner, in which the discretion of judges is limited, and fenced in on all sides, in order to protect persons accused of crimes by rules and precedents; and the adherence to technical principles, which, perhaps, distinguishes this branch of the law, more than any other, are all ill adapted to the trial of political offences, in the broad course of impeachments. And it has been observed with great propriety, that a tribunal of a liberal and comprehensive character, confined, as little as possible, to strict forms, enabled to continue its session as long as the nature of the law may require, qualified to view the charge in all its bearings and dependencies, and to appropriate on sound principles of public policy the defence of the accused, seems indispensable to the value of the trial. The history of impeachments, both in England and America, justifies the remark. There is little technical in the mode of proceeding; the charges are sufficiently clear, and yet in a general form; there are few exceptions, which arise in the application of the evidence, which grow out of mere technical rules and quibbles. And it has repeatedly been seen, that the functions have been better understood, and more liberally and justly expounded by statesmen, than by mere lawyers.

It is also noteworthy that the delegation of fact-finding by judicial and quasi-judicial bodies was hardly unknown to the Framers. Jefferson, at least, was aware that the House of Lords sometimes delegated fact-finding in impeachment trials to committees and recommended use of the same to the Senate. The States also had on occasion employed legislative committees to investigate whether to draw up articles of impeachment. More generally, in colonial governments and state legislatures, contemnors appeared before committees to answer the charges against them. Federal courts likewise had appointed special masters and other fact finders "[f]rom the commencement of our Government." Particularly in light of the Constitution's grant to each House of the power to "determine the Rules of its Proceedings," the existence of legislative and judicial delegation strongly suggests that the Impeachment Trial Clause was not designed to prevent employment of a factfinding committee.

In short, textual and historical evidence reveals that the Impeachment Trial Clause was not meant to bind the hands of the Senate beyond establishing a set of minimal procedures. Without identifying the exact contours of these procedures, it is sufficient to say that the Senate's use of a factfinding committee under Rule XI is entirely compatible with the Constitution's command that the Senate "try all impeachments." Petitioner's challenge to his conviction must therefore fail.

IV

Petitioner has not asked the Court to conduct his impeachment trial; he has asked instead that it determine whether his impeachment was tried by the Senate. The majority refuses to reach this determination out of a laudable desire to respect the authority of the legislature. Regrettably, this concern is manifested in a manner that does needless violence to the Constitution.[4] The deference that is owed can be found in

---

[4] Although our views might well produce identical results in most cases, the same objection may be raised against the prudential version of political question doctrine presented by Justice Souter. According to the prudential view, judicial determination of whether the Senate has conducted an impeachment trial would interfere unacceptably with the Senate's work and should be avoided except where necessitated by the threat of grave harm to the constitutional order. As articulated, this position is missing its premise: no explana-

the Constitution itself, which provides the Senate ample discretion to determine how best to try impeachments.

JUSTICE SOUTER, concurring in the judgment.

I agree with the Court that this case presents a nonjusticiable political question. Because my analysis differs somewhat from the Court's, however, I concur in its judgment by this separate opinion.

* * *

Whatever considerations feature most prominently in a particular case, the political question doctrine is "essentially a function of the separation of powers," existing to restrain courts "from inappropriate interference in the business of the other branches of Government," and deriving in large part from prudential concerns about the respect we owe the political departments. Not all interference is inappropriate or disrespectful, however, and application of the doctrine ultimately turns, as Learned Hand put it, on "how importunately the occasion demands an answer."

This occasion does not demand an answer. The Impeachment Trial Clause commits to the Senate "the sole Power to try all Impeachments," subject to three procedural requirements: the Senate shall be on oath or affirmation; the Chief Justice shall preside when the President is tried; and conviction shall be upon the concurrence of two-thirds of the Members present. It seems fair to conclude that the Clause contemplates that the Senate may determine, within broad boundaries, such subsidiary issues as the procedures for receipt and consideration of evidence necessary to satisfy its duty to "try" impeachments. Other significant considerations confirm a conclusion that this case presents a nonjusticiable political question: the "unusual need for unquestioning adherence to a political decision already made," as well as "the potentiality of embarrassment from multifarious pronouncements by various departments

---

tion is offered as to why it would show disrespect or cause disruption or embarrassment to review the action of the Senate in this case as opposed to, say, the enactment of legislation under the Commerce Clause. The Constitution requires the courts to determine the validity of statutes passed by Congress when they are challenged, even though such laws are passed with the firm belief that they are constitutional. The exercise of judicial review of this kind, with all of its attendant risk of interference and disrespect, is not conditioned upon a showing in each case that without it the Republic would be at risk. Some account is therefore needed as to why prudence does not counsel against judicial review in the typical case, yet does so in this case.

In any event, the prudential view cannot achieve its stated purpose. The judgment it wishes to avoid—and the attendant disrespect and embarrassment—will inevitably be cast because the courts still will be required to distinguish cases on their merits. Justice Souter states that the Court ought not to entertain petitioner's constitutional claim because "[i]t seems fair to conclude," that the Senate tried him. In other words, on the basis of a preliminary determination that the Senate has acted within the "broad boundaries" of the Impeachment Trial Clause, it is concluded that we must refrain from making that determination. At best, this approach offers only the illusion of deference and respect by substituting impressionistic assessment for constitutional analysis.

on one question." As the Court observes, judicial review of an impeachment trial would under the best of circumstances entail significant disruption of government.

One can, nevertheless, envision different and unusual circumstances that might justify a more searching review of impeachment proceedings. If the Senate were to act in a manner seriously threatening the integrity of its results, convicting, say, upon a coin-toss, or upon a summary determination that an officer of the United States was simply " 'a bad guy,' " judicial interference might well be appropriate. In such circumstances, the Senate's action might be so far beyond the scope of its constitutional authority, and the consequent impact on the Republic so great, as to merit a judicial response despite the prudential concerns that would ordinarily counsel silence. "The political question doctrine, a tool for maintenance of governmental order, will not be so applied as to promote only disorder."

Notes and Questions

1. Is the political question doctrine constitutional or prudential? If it is constitutional, from what part of the Constitution does it spring? If it is prudential, what should the courts do when a matter arguably involving the doctrine is nonetheless explicitly within their Article III jurisdiction and an appropriate statutory jurisdictional grant? In *Nixon*, for example, there is no question that there is an actual case or controversy (as the Court's opinion notes) that presents a federal question. On what basis can the Court refuse to exercise jurisdiction?

2. a) The Court seems concerned with identifiable standards. Is its own standard of whether a particular type of question is textually committed elsewhere sufficiently precise to permit principled decision making, or is Justice White correct that it is illusory? As he points out, many functions are initially committed to the non-judicial branches; that does not ipso facto make them non-justiciable.

b) The Court, quoting *Baker v. Carr*, 369 U.S. 186, 82 S.Ct. 691, 7 L.Ed.2d 663 (1962), characterizes the political question doctrine as having two branches: " 'a textually demonstrable constitutional commitment of the issue to a coordinate political department; or a lack of judicially discoverable and manageable standards for resolving it * * * .' " In light of Justice White's objection, should the two parts be conjunctive rather than disjunctive?

3. a) Justice Rehnquist spends some time discussing the meaning of the verb "try." Given the conclusion that the case is nonjusticiable, should that analysis even appear in the opinion? Does not that discussion drag the Court into considering the merits, at least in some preliminary sense?

b) Consider also Justice Souter's concurrence. He says he agrees with the Court that the issue presented is a nonjusticiable political question, but that if the Senate's procedure were sufficiently *outré*, judicial intervention might be appropriate. Is he saying that whether an issue is a political question ultimately depends on the resolution of that issue on the merits? How is that possible? Justice Souter says that Senate action "so far beyond the scope of its constitutional authority" might be reviewed. How far is far enough? Can something be a little unconstitutional for Justice Souter?

4. *Baker v. Carr* considered whether questions of legislative apportionment were justiciable. It found that they are, but carefully distinguished the Guaranty Clause, Art. IV, § 4, from the Equal Protection Clause as possible bases for decision. As to the former, the Court reaffirmed its position in *Colegrove v. Green*, 329 U.S. 828, 67 S.Ct. 199, 91 L.Ed. 703 (1946), that issues arising under the Guaranty Clause are nonjusticiable. The *Baker* Court, on the other hand, ruled on the basis of equal protection.

Baker articulated more factors to be considered for political question purposes than *Nixon*.

> Prominent on the surface of any case held to involve a political question is found a textually demonstrable constitutional commitment of the issue to a coordinate political department; or a lack of judicially discoverable and manageable standards for resolving it; or the impossibility of deciding without an initial policy determination of a kind clearly for nonjudicial discretion; or the impossibility of a court's undertaking independent resolution without expressing lack of the respect due coordinate branches of government; or an unusual need for unquestioning adherence to a political decision already made; or the potentiality of embarrassment from multifarious pronouncements by various departments on one question.

The Court counseled against confusing political "questions" with political "cases," and noted the "impossibility of resolution by any semantic cataloguing." Do the additional factors in *Baker* assist in determining whether a case presents a nonjusticiable political question?

5. If the political question doctrine is a servant of separation of powers within the federal government, why are Guaranty Clause cases necessarily nonjusticiable political questions? Why is not any Guaranty Clause case involving state government, as *Luther v. Borden*, 48 U.S. (7 How.) 1, 12 L.Ed. 581 (1849), did, justiciable? *Luther* involved disputes between supporters of conflicting governments in the state of Rhode Island. After 1783, Rhode Island did not adopt a new state constitution, but continued to operate the form of government established by charter in the seventeenth century. In 1841, some of the people of Rhode Island purported to hold a constitutional convention and to adopt a state constitution, under which elections were held and a new government declared. The "charter government" did not yield to those proceedings, but convened its own constitutional convention, which resulted in certification of a new government. In *Luther*, the plaintiff called upon the Supreme Court to adjudicate a trespass claim that depended upon a determination of which of the two "governments" of Rhode Island should be recognized as the lawful government. The plaintiff relied upon the Guaranty Clause, U.S. CONST. art. IV, § 4: "The United States shall guarantee to every State in this Union, a Republican Form of Government, and shall protect each of them against Invasion; and on Application of

the Legislature, or of the Executive (when the Legislature cannot be convened), against domestic Violence." The Supreme Court found the dispute a nonjusticiable political question, declining to place any federal *imprimatur* on either of the two state governments. It observed that the courts of the state had determined the legitimacy of one of the governments as a matter of state law in which the federal courts could not intervene. Additionally, the Court concluded that the Guaranty Clause gave Congress the power to decide what government was the established one in a state. Congress had to decide what government was established before it could decide whether it was "republican" or not. By admitting the senators and representatives from a state, Congress recognized the authority by which they were designated to represent the state and, hence, the state government's republican character.

Does the text of the Guaranty Clause indicate that disputes concerning it are not subject to judicial review?

6. Suppose Congress passed a statute specially conferring on the federal courts subject matter jurisdiction with respect to a class of cases (involving the legislature) that the Court had determined were political questions. Which way would the separation of powers argument then cut? Alternatively, to the extent that the doctrine is a function of separation of powers, should the burden be on Congress affirmatively to exclude from federal jurisdiction classes of cases that it does not want the federal courts to adjudicate because they are "political"?

7. What does it mean for an issue to be committed to a coordinate branch? Consider the following cases.

a) The House of Representatives refuses to seat one of its members who has been re-elected, excluding him on the ground that in a previous term he had filed false travel vouchers seeking reimbursement to which he was not entitled and had otherwise misused government funds. Article I, § 5 declares that each house of Congress is the judge of the qualifications of its own members and that it may "determine the Rules of its Proceedings, punish its Members for disorderly Behaviour, and, with the Concurrence of two thirds, expel a Member." On the other hand, Article I, § 2, cl. 2 lists the qualifications for membership in the House and limits them to age, citizenship, and residence. The excluded member and his constituents sue to compel the House to seat him on the grounds that he meets all of the qualification requirements. Should the case be dismissed as non-justiciable? *See Powell v. McCormack*, 395 U.S. 486, 89 S.Ct. 1944, 23 L.Ed.2d 491 (1969).

b) Certain Tribes sue several counties of a state for damages representing the fair rental value of land allegedly conveyed from the Tribes to the state in violation of a treaty providing that "no sale of lands made by any Indians, or any nation or tribe of Indians within the United States, shall be valid to any person * * * unless * * * held under the authority of the United States." The state's purchase of the land (nearly 200 years before the lawsuit) was not supervised by the federal government. Article I, § 3 explicitly gives Congress responsibility for Indian affairs. Is the case justiciable? *See County of Oneida v. Oneida Indian Nation*, 470 U.S. 226, 105 S.Ct. 1245, 84

L.Ed.2d 169 (1985).

c) Federal statutes require the Secretary of Commerce to certify nations violating whale harvesting quotas set by the International Whaling Commission, an organization established by a fifteen-nation treaty to which the United States is a party. The statutes require economic sanctions against such nations. The United States and Japan enter into a bilateral agreement concerning whale harvests that the Secretary of Commerce thinks do not undermine the treaty. Plaintiffs sue to compel the Secretary to certify Japan as being in violation of the treaty. Is the case justiciable? *See Japan Whaling Association v. American Cetacean Society*, 478 U.S. 221, 106 S.Ct. 2860, 92 L.Ed.2d 166 (1986).

When the United States announced in late 1978 that it would recognize the People's Republic of China on January 1, 1979, President Carter also gave notice to the Republic of China that he would abrogate the Mutual Defense Treaty of 1954 between that nation and the United States, pursuant to an article of that Treaty that permitted cancellation on one year's notice. Members and one former member of Congress challenged the President's power to cancel a treaty without senatorial or congressional consultation and approval. Was the case justiciable? *See Goldwater v. Carter*, 444 U.S. 996, 100 S.Ct. 533, 62 L.Ed.2d 428 (1979).

d) In 1924, Congress proposed a child labor amendment to the Constitution. In 1937, the Kansas Senate divided evenly on whether to ratify the amendment, and the state's lieutenant governor then cast his vote for ratification. After the Kansas House had also ratified the amendment, some members of both houses sued the Kansas Secretary of State, seeking to compel him to erase an endorsement of the Senate resolution approving the amendment. The Secretary of State of Kansas argued that the federal courts should not hear cases concerning state legislatures' ratification procedures. The plaintiffs argued that the proposed amendment had lost its vitality by lapse of time and that the Kansas legislature therefore could not ratify it. Was the case justiciable? *See Coleman v. Miller*, 307 U.S. 433, 59 S.Ct. 972, 83 L.Ed. 1385 (1939).

e) In *Nixon*, would it make any difference if the judge had been acquitted of the criminal charges but impeached on the basis of the same evidence nonetheless, and if the judge had voiced his objections to the procedure before the Senate acted? *See Hastings v. United States*, 802 F.Supp. 490 (D.D.C.1992), *vacated* 988 F.2d 1280 (D.C.Cir.1993).

8. Should the Court abandon the political question doctrine? The answer depends in part on whether the doctrine is constitutionally compelled or is merely prudential. Whether it is constitutionally compelled or not, is it sound policy?

9. In *Bush v. Gore*, 531 U.S. 98, 121 S.Ct. 525, 148 L.Ed. 2d 388 (2000), the United States Supreme Court essentially resolved the disputed presidential election of that year. The election depended upon which candidate received Florida's electoral votes, and the Florida popular vote was extremely close. In a suit filed by then Vice-President Al Gore, one of the candidates,

the Florida Supreme Court had ordered manual recounts in all Florida counties where "undervotes," ballots that the vote scanning machines had reported as not indicating a preference for president, had not been subject to manual tabulation. After Governor George W. Bush of Texas, the other major candidate sought review, the Supreme Court reversed the Florida Supreme Court's order and remanded the case for further proceedings in a five-to-four decision. In a *per curiam* opinion the Court concluded that the Florida court's manual recount order did not meet the minimum standards required by the Equal Protection Clause. There were no uniform guidelines as to how the voters' intent was to be discerned when ballots had not been marked properly, and different counties had followed, and presumably would follow, different standards in tabulating the votes.

Justice Breyer dissented, in an opinion joined in part by Justices Stevens, Ginsburg, and Souter. He contended that the state court could have resolved the equal protection problem by imposing a uniform standard upon remand. Therefore, he did not think the Supreme Court had to act to vindicate a fundamental constitutional right. Justice Breyer went on to discuss why the majority action was not only legally wrong, but unfortunate. He noted that in characterizing political disputes that the federal courts should refrain from deciding, the Court should consider the strangeness of the issue, its intractability to judicial judgment, its momentousness, and the vulnerability of the courts as important factors, and he found that there are all present in the case. Breyer asserted that by acting in such a politicized dispute in such a divided manner, the majority risked undermining public confidence in the Court as an institution. Do you agree? If so, does that mean the Court should in no circumstances have decided the equal protection issue or that it would have been all right to decide it if it appeared that all Justices agreed?

Chapter 2

CONGRESSIONAL CONTROL
OF FEDERAL JURISDICTION

A. INTRODUCTION

Members of Congress have often introduced bills that would have prohibited the Supreme Court, the lower federal courts, or both from exercising jurisdiction over cases dealing with controversial issues. Over the last two decades, these have included abortion, busing, and school prayer. The members who introduce these bills generally disagree with Supreme Court interpretations of some provision of the Constitution. By restricting the jurisdiction of the federal courts, they hope to circumvent (or at least limit) the effect of the Court's decisions. They believe that state courts will hand down more palatable decisions. The constitutionality of jurisdiction-stripping proposals is a serious question that goes to the heart of separation of powers. In addition, important federalism issues arise because such bills would limit the federal courts' ability to enforce federal rights (often against the states themselves), transferring that role to the state courts.

The Constitution clearly gives Congress some power over the appellate jurisdiction of the Supreme Court. Article III, § 2, allows the Court appellate jurisdiction "with such exceptions, and under such regulations as the Congress shall make." The first Congress exercised that power by limiting the circumstances in which the Supreme Court could review state court interpretations of federal law. The first Judiciary Act[1] authorized Supreme Court review of such determinations only if the state court rejected the contention of the party relying upon federal law. Thus, from the beginning of our history, Congress has determined which state court cases are eligible for Supreme Court review. But how broad is that power? Could Congress completely eliminate appellate review by the Supreme Court? Could it prohibit the Court from exercising appellate jurisdiction over a category of constitutional cases because of disagreement with the Court's decisions, as many jurisdiction-limiting bills have attempted to do?

Similar questions regarding the jurisdiction of the lower federal courts also arise. One of the great controversies at the Constitutional

---

[1] Act of Sept. 29, 1789, § 25, 1 Stat. 73, 85. This section of the statute is reproduced in *Murdock v. City of Memphis* in Chapter 9 at pages 884-885.

Convention was the existence of federal courts other than the Supreme Court. Many delegates thought lower federal courts were essential to the new national government's survival. Others, however, argued that a large federal judiciary would permit too much federal encroachment on state courts and state power. The solution was a compromise. Article III, § 1, does not mandate the existence of the lower federal courts, but rather provides for "such inferior courts as the Congress may from time to time ordain and establish." Consequently, many scholars contend that because Congress has the power to create or eliminate inferior federal courts, it has plenary power over their jurisdiction and has exercised it since the Judiciary Act of 1789. For example, the Act provided trial court jurisdiction in diversity cases only when the amount in controversy exceeded $500 and did not grant any jurisdiction over civil cases that arose under federal law. Indeed, with minor exceptions, Congress did not grant the lower federal courts jurisdiction over federal question cases until 1875.[2] Some argue that this history demonstrates that although proposals to strip the lower federal courts of jurisdiction over specific categories of cases may be unwise, they are not unconstitutional.

Others have questioned this conclusion by pointing to other language in the text of Article III or to other constitutional provisions. Article III does say that "[t]he judicial Power * * * *shall* be vested * * *," [emphasis added] not that it may be vested. Additionally, some have argued that any jurisdiction-stripping statute would violate another constitutional provision by excluding classes of litigants or cases entitled to constitutional protection. As with congressional control of the appellate jurisdiction of the Supreme Court, the issue continues to be the subject of heated debate.

Questions also arise as to whether Congress can totally preclude federal court review of specific issues by both cutting off the appellate jurisdiction of the Supreme Court and stripping the lower federal courts of jurisdiction as well. Even if one accepts congressional power to engage in either course of conduct, would it be unconstitutional for Congress to do both? Some scholars contend that the federal judicial power has to be available in either its appellate or original form over all federal question cases. As with the other issues discussed above, there is still debate among scholars on this matter. However, the so-called "War on Terror" has made the debate more than academic. Congress has severely limited the rights of aliens either suspected of being or determined to be enemy combatants to assert federal constitutional challenges to their confinement. It has further limited the fed-

---

[2] Congress did briefly grant general federal question jurisdiction in the famous Midnight Judges Act that spawned Marbury v. Madison, 5 U.S. (1 Cranch) 137, 2 L.Ed. 60 (1803), but the incoming Jeffersonian Congress repealed the grant a year later. Act of Feb. 13, 1801, ch. 4, § 11, 2 Stat. 89, 92, *repealed by* Act of Mar. 8, 1802, ch. 8, § 1, 2 Stat. 132. There were also, from time to time, specialized grants of federal question jurisdiction, discussed in Chapter 3 at page 224 n.4.

eral forums that can hear those challenges that are allowed. Thus, the federal courts themselves may soon have to answer the questions which thus far have primarily been discussed by scholars.

B.   CONGRESSIONAL CONTROL OF THE APPELLATE JURISDICTION OF THE SUPREME COURT

EX PARTE MCCARDLE
Supreme Court of the United States, 1869.
74 U.S. (7 Wall.) 506, 19 L.Ed. 264.

[Following the Civil War, newspaperman William H. McCardle wrote several editorials that contained bitter attacks on Reconstruction and the military leaders responsible for implementing it. Military authorities arrested and held him pursuant to the Military Reconstruction Act of 1867, which was the legislative foundation of Congress' reconstruction program. The Act established military jurisdiction in 10 Southern states and authorized military commissions to try civilians accused of violating its provisions. McCardle was charged with libel, impeding Reconstruction, inciting to insurrection and disorder, and disturbing the peace. He petitioned a federal circuit court for a writ of habeas corpus, alleging that he was being held in military custody in violation of his constitutional rights. The court held that his imprisonment was lawful, but ordered his release on bond pending appeal to the Supreme Court.

McCardle appealed pursuant to the Habeas Corpus Act of 1867. Prior to that statute, the Supreme Court had exercised appellate jurisdiction over cases in which persons held under federal authority sought habeas relief, pursuant to section 14 of the Judiciary Act of 1789. The Habeas Corpus Act of 1867 authorized the federal courts for the first time to issue writs of habeas corpus whenever persons held in *state* custody challenged it on federal grounds. In addition, the Act provided an alternate basis for federal habeas relief for those held in federal custody and an alternate authorization of Supreme Court review.

When McCardle's appeal reached the Court, the government moved to dismiss on the ground that the Court lacked jurisdiction. The Court unanimously found jurisdiction based upon the Habeas Corpus Act of 1867. *Ex Parte McCardle,* 73 U.S. (6 Wall.) 318, 18 L.Ed. 816 (1868). The Court then heard argument on the merits. Before the Court announced a decision, Congress passed the Repealer Act (over President Johnson's veto), which provided that so much of the Habeas Corpus Act of 1867 "as authorizes an appeal from the judgment of the circuit court to the Supreme Court of the United States, or the exercise of any such jurisdiction by said Supreme Court on appeals which have been made or may hereafter be taken, be, and the same is, hereby repealed." Congress evidently wanted to prevent the Court from hearing McCardle's appeal and ruling on the constitutionality of the Military Reconstruction Act and Reconstruction itself. The government again moved to dismiss for lack of jurisdiction.]

THE CHIEF JUSTICE delivered the opinion of the court.

The first question necessarily is that of jurisdiction; for, if the act of March, 1868, takes away the jurisdiction defined by the act of February, 1867, it is useless, if not improper, to enter into any discussion of other questions.

It is quite true, as was argued by the counsel for the petitioner, that the appellate jurisdiction of this court is not derived from acts of Congress. It is, strictly speaking, conferred by the Constitution. But it is conferred "with such exceptions and under such regulations as Congress shall make."

It is unnecessary to consider whether, if Congress had made no exceptions and no regulations, this court might not have exercised general appellate jurisdiction under rules prescribed by itself. For among the earliest acts of the first Congress, at its first session, was the act of September 24th, 1789, to establish the judicial courts of the United States. That act provided for the organization of this court, and prescribed regulations for the exercise of its jurisdiction.

The source of that jurisdiction, and the limitations of it by the Constitution and by statute, have been on several occasions subjects of consideration here. In the case of *Durousseau v. The United States* particularly, the whole matter was carefully examined, and the court held, that while "the appellate powers of this court are not given by the judicial act, but are given by the Constitution," they are, nevertheless, "limited and regulated by that act, and by such other acts as have been passed on the subject." The court said, further, that the judicial act was an exercise of the power given by the Constitution to Congress "of making exceptions to the appellate jurisdiction of the Supreme Court." "They have described affirmatively," said the court, "its jurisdiction, and this affirmative description has been understood to imply a negation of the exercise of such appellate power as is not comprehended within it."

The principle that the affirmation of appellate jurisdiction implies the negation of all such jurisdiction not affirmed having been thus established, it was an almost necessary consequence that acts of Congress, providing for the exercise of jurisdiction, should come to be spoken of as acts granting jurisdiction, and not as acts making exceptions to the constitutional grant of it.

The exception to appellate jurisdiction in the case before us, however, is not an inference from the affirmation of other appellate jurisdiction. It is made in terms. The provision of the act of 1867, affirming the appellate jurisdiction of this court in cases of habeas corpus is expressly repealed. It is hardly possible to imagine a plainer instance of positive exception.

We are not at liberty to inquire into the motives of the legislature. We can only examine into its power under the Constitution; and the power to make exceptions to the appellate jurisdiction of this court is given by express words.

What, then, is the effect of the repealing act upon the case before us? We cannot doubt as to this. Without jurisdiction the court cannot proceed at all in any cause. Jurisdiction is power to declare the law, and when it ceases to exist, the only function remaining to the court is that of announcing the fact and dismissing the cause. And this is not less clear upon authority than upon principle.

Several cases were cited by the counsel for the petitioner in support of the position that jurisdiction of this case is not affected by the repealing act. But none of them, in our judgment, afford any support to it. They are all cases of the exercise of judicial power by the legislature, or of legislative interference with courts in the exercising of continuing jurisdiction.

On the other hand, the general rule, supported by the best elementary writers, is, that "when an act of the legislature is repealed, it must be considered, except as to transactions past and closed, as if it never existed."

* * *

It is quite clear, therefore, that this court cannot proceed to pronounce judgment in this case, for it has no longer jurisdiction of the appeal; and judicial duty is not less fitly performed by declining ungranted jurisdiction than in exercising firmly that which the Constitution and the laws confer.

Counsel seem to have supposed, if effect be given to the repealing act in question, that the whole appellate power of the court, in cases of habeas corpus, is denied. But this is an error. The act of 1868 does not except from that jurisdiction any cases but appeals from Circuit Courts under the act of 1867. It does not affect the jurisdiction which was previously exercised.

The appeal of the petitioner in this case must be dismissed for want of jurisdiction.

Notes and Questions

1. Should the Court have found the Repealer Act ineffective because it had already heard arguments on the merits? Would it matter if the Court had not only heard arguments on the merits, but had discussed the case in conference? If the Court had already reached a decision but had simply not published its opinion, should that alter the result?

2. Could the Court have decided McCardle's appeal on the merits without ignoring the Repealer Act? If so, should it have?

3. Did the Repealer Act make an "exception" to the appellate jurisdiction of the Supreme Court? If so, describe the cases excluded. If not, what was the constitutional authority for it?

EX PARTE YERGER
Supreme Court of the United States, 1869.
75 U.S. (8 Wall.) 85, 19 L.Ed. 332.

[Military authorities acting pursuant to the Military Reconstruction Act of 1867 arrested Yerger, also a newspaper editor, and charged him with murder. The Act provided for trial by military commission without a jury. Yerger was not and had never been connected with the United States' armed forces. He filed a petition for a writ of habeas corpus in the Circuit Court of the United States for the Southern District of Mississippi. That court found his imprisonment lawful and dismissed the habeas petition. Yerger appealed to the Supreme Court pursuant to section 14 of the Judiciary Act of 1789. "On the suggestion of the Attorney-General," the Court directed argument on the issue of jurisdiction.]

THE CHIEF JUSTICE delivered the opinion of the court.

* * *

The general question of jurisdiction in this case resolves itself necessarily into two other questions:

1. Has the court jurisdiction, in a case like the present, to inquire into the cause of detention, alleged to be unlawful, and to give relief, if the detention be found to be in fact unlawful, by the writ of habeas corpus, under the Judiciary Act of 1789?

2. If, under that act, the court possessed this jurisdiction, has it been taken away by the second section of the act of March, 27, 1868, repealing so much of the act of February 5, 1867, as authorizes appeals from Circuit Courts to the Supreme Court?

Neither of these questions is new here. The first has, on several occasions, received very full consideration, and very deliberate judgment.

A cause, so important as that which now invokes the action of this court, seems however to justify a reconsideration of the grounds upon which its jurisdiction has been heretofore maintained.

The great writ of habeas corpus has been for centuries esteemed the best and only sufficient defence of personal freedom.

In England, after a long struggle, it was firmly guaranteed by the famous Habeas Corpus Act of May 27, 1679, "for the better securing of the liberty of the subject," which, as Blackstone says, "is frequently considered as another Magna Charta."

It was brought to America by the colonists, and claimed as among the immemorial rights descended to them from their ancestors.

Naturally, therefore, when the confederated colonies became United States, and the formation of a common government engaged their deliberations in convention, this great writ found prominent sanction in the Constitution. That sanction is in these words: "The privilege of the writ of habeas corpus shall not be suspended unless when in cases of rebellion or invasion the public safety may require it."

The terms of this provision necessarily imply judicial action. In England, all the higher courts where open to applicants for the writ, and it is hardly supposable that, under the new government, founded on more liberal ideas and principles, any court would be, intentionally, closed to them.

We find, accordingly, that the first Congress under the Constitution, after defining, by various sections of the act of September 24, 1789, the jurisdiction of the District Courts, the Circuit Courts, and the Supreme Court in other cases, proceeded, in the 14th section, to enact, "that all the beforementioned courts of the United States shall have power to issue writs of *scire facias,* habeas corpus, and all other writs, not specially provided by statute, which may be necessary for the exercise of their respective jurisdictions, and agreeable to the principles and usages of law." In the same section, it was further provided "that either of the Justices of the Supreme Court, as well as Judges of the District Courts, shall have power to grant writs of habeas corpus for the purpose of an inquiry into the cause of commitment; provided that writs of habeas corpus shall in no case extend to prisoners in jail, unless they are in custody, under, or by color of the authority of the United States, or are committed for trial before some court of the same, or are necessary to be brought into court to testify."

* * *

The judicial power of the United States extends to all cases in law and equity arising under the Constitution, the laws of the United States, and treaties made under their authority, and to large classes of cases determined by the character of the parties, or the nature of the controversy.

That part of this judicial power vested in this court is defined by the Constitution in these words:

> In all cases affecting ambassadors, other public ministers, and consuls, and those in which a State shall be a party, the Supreme Court shall have original jurisdiction. In all the other cases before mentioned, the Supreme Court shall have appellate jurisdiction, both as to law and fact, with such exceptions, and under such regulations as the Congress shall make.

If the question were new one, it would, perhaps, deserve inquiry whether Congress might not, under the power to make exceptions from this appellate jurisdiction, extend the original jurisdiction to other cases than those expressly enumerated in the Constitution; and especially, in view of the constitutional guaranty of the writ of habeas corpus, to cases arising upon petition for that writ.

But, in the case of *Marbury v. Madison,* it was determined, upon full consideration, that the power to issue writs of mandamus, given to this court by the 13th section of the Judiciary Act, is, under the Constitution, an appellate jurisdiction, to be exercised only in the revision of judicial decisions. And this judgment has ever since been accepted as fixing the construction of this part of the Constitution.

It was pronounced in 1803. In 1807 the same construction was given to the provision of the 14th section relating to the writ of habeas corpus.

* * *

The doctrine of the Constitution and of the cases thus far may be summed up in these propositions:

(1) The original jurisdiction of this court cannot be extended by Congress to any other cases than those expressly defined by the Constitution.

(2) The appellate jurisdiction of this court, conferred by the Constitution, extends to all other cases within the judicial power of the United States.

(3) This appellate jurisdiction is subject to such exceptions, and must be exercised under such regulations as Congress, in the exercise of its discretion, has made or may see fit to make.

(4) Congress not only has not excepted writs of habeas corpus and mandamus from this appellate jurisdiction, but has expressly provided for the exercise of this jurisdiction by means of these writs.

* * *

The great and leading intent of the Constitution and the law must be kept constantly in view upon the examination of every question of construction.

That intent, in respect to the writ of habeas corpus, is manifest. It is that every citizen may be protected by judicial action from unlawful imprisonment. To this end the act of 1789 provided that every court of the United States should have power to issue the writ. The jurisdiction thus given in law to the Circuit and District Courts is original; that given by the Constitution and the law to this court is appellate. Given in general terms, it must necessarily extend to all cases to which the judicial power of the United States extends, other than those expressly excepted from it.

* * *

We are obligated to hold, therefore, that in all cases where a Circuit Court of the United States has, in the exercise of its original jurisdiction, caused a prisoner to be brought before it, and has, after inquiring into the cause of detention, remanded him to the custody from which he was taken, this court, in the exercise of its appellate jurisdiction, may, by the writ of habeas corpus, aided by the writ of certiorari, revise the decision of the Circuit Court, and if it be found unwarranted by law, relieve the prisoner from the unlawful restraint to which he has been remanded.

This conclusion brings us to the inquiry whether the 2d section of the act of March 27th, 1868, takes away or affects the appellate jurisdiction of this court under the Constitution and the acts of Congress prior to 1867.

In *McCardle*'s case * * * we expressed the opinion that it does not, and we have now re-examined the grounds of that opinion.

The circumstances under which the act of 1868 was passed were peculiar.

On the 5th of February, 1867, Congress passed the act to which reference has already been made, extending the original jurisdiction by habeas corpus of the District and Circuit Courts, and of the several judges of these courts, to all cases of restraint of liberty in violation of the Constitution, treaties, or laws of the United States. This act authorized appeals to this court from judgments of the Circuit Court, but did not repeal any previous act conferring jurisdiction by habeas corpus, unless by implication.

* * *

The effect of the act was to oust the court of its jurisdiction of the particular case then before it on appeal, and it is not to be doubted that such was the effect intended. Nor will it be questioned that legislation of this character is unusual and hardly to be justified except upon some imperious public exigency.

It was, doubtless, within the constitutional discretion of Congress to determine whether such an exigency existed; but it is not to be presumed that an act, passed under such circumstances, was intended to have any further effect than that plainly apparent from its terms.

It is quite clear that the words of the act reach, not only all appeals pending, but all future appeals to this court under the act of 1867; but they appear to be limited to appeals taken under that act.

The words of the repealing section are, "that so much of the act approved February 5th, 1867, as authorizes an appeal from the judgment of the Circuit Court to the Supreme Court of the United States, or the exercise of any such jurisdiction by said Supreme Court on appeals which have been, or may be hereafter taken, be, and the same is hereby repealed."

These words are not of doubtful interpretation. They repeal only so much of the act of 1867 as authorized appeals, or the exercise of appellate jurisdiction by this court. They affected only appeals and appellate jurisdiction authorized by that act. They do not purport to touch the appellate jurisdiction conferred by the Constitution, or to except from it any cases not excepted by the act of 1789. They reach no act except the act of 1867.

* * *

We could come to no other conclusion without holding that the whole appellate jurisdiction of this court, in cases of habeas corpus, conferred by the Constitution, recognized by law, and exercised from the foundation of the government hitherto, has been taken away, without the expression of such intent, and by mere implication, through the operation of the acts of 1867 and 1868.

* * *

The argument having been confined, by direction of the court, to the question of jurisdiction, this opinion is limited to that question. The jurisdiction of the court to issue the writ prayed for is affirmed.

Notes and Questions

1. Despite finding jurisdiction, the Court never did decide Yerger's constitutional claims on the merits. Following the jurisdictional decision, the military dismissed the charges, again avoiding Supreme Court review of the constitutionality of Reconstruction.

2. Do *McCardle* and *Yerger* establish congressional power completely to eliminate the appellate jurisdiction of the Supreme Court? Do they at least establish congressional power to eliminate Supreme Court review in a specific category of constitutional cases?

3. In *Felker v. Turpin*, 518 U.S. 651, 116 S.Ct. 2333, 135 L.Ed.2d 827 (1996), the issue of congressional power to control the appellate jurisdiction of the Supreme Court again arose in the context of statutory restrictions on the review of habeas petitions. The Antiterrorism and Effective Death Penalty Act of 1996 places severe restrictions on a state prisoner's second or successive federal habeas application. The prospective applicant must move the court of appeals for leave to file such an application in the district court. A three-judge appellate panel plays a "gatekeeping" role by determining whether the prisoner has made a showing sufficient to meet the statutory requirements. Title 28 U.S.C. § 106(b)(3)(E) of the Act provides that "[t]he grant or denial of an authorization by a court of appeals to file a second or successive application shall not be appealable and shall not be the subject of a petition for rehearing or for a writ of certiorari." When the Eleventh Circuit denied Felker's motion for leave to file a second habeas petition, he sought certiorari from the Supreme Court, arguing that the

statute unconstitutionally restricts the Court's jurisdiction. The Court granted certiorari but unanimously rejected his claim. After an extended discussion of *Yerger*, the Court "for reasons similar to those stated in" that case concluded that the Act had not repealed its power to entertain original habeas petitions pursuant to 28 U.S.C. § 2241, pointing out that the provision does not mention that jurisdiction. Consequently, the Court held that there was no substantial argument that the Act deprives it of appellate jurisdiction in violation of Article III. The Court then denied Felker's petition for an original writ of habeas corpus.

Justice Stevens concurred, joined by Justices Souter and Breyer, asserting that the Court's original habeas jurisdiction extends to review of "gatekeeping" orders by the court of appeals and provides the parties with the substantial equivalent of direct review. Additionally, Justice Stevens noted that the Act does not expressly limit the Court's power to review "gatekeeping" orders pursuant to the All Writs Act, 28 U.S.C. § 1651 or when it is reviewing an interlocutory order under 28 U.S.C. § 1254(2). Thus, he found at least three reasons to reject Felker's constitutional claim. Does Justice Stevens's interpretation of the statute deny it its intended effect?

Justice Souter, joined by Justices Stevens and Breyer, also concurred to note that if all statutory avenues for the Court to review "gatekeeping" determinations were subsequently closed, the question of whether Congress had exceeded its power under the Exceptions Clause would be open.

4. The Detainee Treatment Act of 2005, Pub. L. 109-148, 119 Stat. 2739 (10 U.S.C.A. § 801 Note (Supp. 2006)), addresses a broad range of issues related to persons detained in U.S. custody. Section 1005 of the Act places significant restrictions on the jurisdiction of the federal courts to hear actions brought by aliens detained at Guantanamo Bay, Cuba. Prior to enactment of the statute, Salim Ahmed Hamdan, a Guantanamo detainee, filed a federal habeas corpus petition challenging the President's decision to try him by military commission. The case worked its way through the lower courts and was pending in the Supreme Court when the Act became effective. The Government moved to dismiss the case, claiming the Act deprived the federal courts, including the Supreme Court, of subject matter jurisdiction over habeas petitions, future or pending, by Guantanamo detainees. The Court denied the motion, and in an opinion of enormous significance for separation of powers as between Congress and the President, held that the military commission convened to try Hamdan could not proceed because its structure and procedures violated the Uniform Code of Military Justice and the Geneva Conventions. *Hamdan v. Rumsfeld*, ___ U.S. ___, 126 S.Ct. 2749, 165 L.Ed.2d 723 (2006).

The jurisdiction question turned on whether the Act applied to pending applications. Hamdan argued that the Government's argument raised serious questions about Congress' power to restrict the Supreme Court's appellate jurisdiction, particularly in habeas cases, and that the Government's interpretation of the Act would unconstitutionally suspend the writ of habeas corpus. The Court, however, declined to reach these issues by interpreting the statute not to require dismissal of pending cases.

Congress responded to *Hamdan* by passing the Military Commissions Act of 2006, Pub. L. No. 109-366, 120 Stat. 2600 (2006), which became law on October 17, 2006. Section 7 of the Act declared that "[n]o court, justice, or judge shall have jurisdiction" to entertain a habeas corpus petition or any other action against the federal government or its agents concerning "any aspect of the detention, transfer, treatment, trial or conditions of confinement" of an alien who has either been determined to be an enemy combatant or is awaiting such a determination. Section 7(b) of the Act declared that this prohibition "shall apply to all cases, without exception, pending on or after the date of enactment of this Act." On its face, the Act plainly appears to require the dismissal of pending habeas petitions filed by Guantanamo detainees.

On February 20, 2007, the United States Court of Appeals for the District of Columbia Circuit decided *Boumediene v. Bush*, which involved consolidated appeals from decisions of various district judges in the District of Columbia in cases brought by Guantanamo detainees. The majority and dissent agreed that the Act withdrew jurisdiction over pending cases, thus raising the issue of whether the Act violates the Suspension Clause of the Constitution, which states that "The Privilege of the Writ of Habeas Corpus shall not be suspended, unless when in Cases of Rebellion or Invasion the public Safety may require it." U.S. CONST. art. 1, § 9, cl. 2. The majority held that the Act did not violate the Suspension Clause because the writ simply did not extend to aliens without presence or property within the United States. The dissenting judge reached a contrary conclusion, stating:

> The Suspension Clause limits the removal of habeas corpus, at least as the writ was understood at common law, to times of rebellion or invasion unless Congress provides as adequate alternative remedy. The writ would have reached the detainees at common law, and Congress has neither provided an adequate alternative remedy * * * nor invoked the exception to the Clause by making the required findings to suspend the writ.

Initially the Supreme court denied certiorari, but on June 29, 2007, reversed itself, granted certiorari and will hear the case in the 2007 Term.

CONGRESSIONAL POWER OVER THE APPELLATE JURISDICTION OF THE SUPREME COURT
LEONARD RATNER
109 U.PA.L.REV. 157 (1960)[a]

The Constitution gives the Supreme Court appellate jurisdiction "with such Exceptions, and under such Regulations as the Congress shall make" over all cases within the judicial power of the United States originating in state or lower federal courts. From time to time since 1796 the Supreme Court has used language in its opinions suggesting that by virtue of the exceptions and regulations clause its appellate ju-

[a] Copyright © 1960 by the University of Pennsylvania Law Review. Reprinted by permission.

risdiction is subject to unlimited congressional control, and this language has generally been regarded as establishing that Congress has such power.

Constitutional authority to create and abolish inferior federal courts gives Congress plenary control over their jurisdiction. If Congress also has plenary control over the appellate jurisdiction of the Supreme Court, then Congress may constitutionally do any of the following:

(1) Deprive the Supreme Court of all appellate jurisdiction and abolish the lower federal courts, thereby confining the judiciary of the United States to a single court exercising original jurisdiction over cases affecting ambassadors, public ministers, and consuls, or in which a state is a party.

(2) Deprive the Supreme Court of appellate jurisdiction and other federal courts of all jurisdiction over cases involving the validity, under the Constitution, of state statutes or the conduct of state officials, thereby leaving to the highest court of each state the final determination of such questions.

(3) Deprive the Supreme Court of appellate jurisdiction over any case arising under the Constitution, laws, or treaties of the United States, thereby allowing the federal courts of appeals and the highest state courts to become, in their respective jurisdictions, the final interpreters of federal law.

If such legislation is permissible, Congress can by statute profoundly alter the structure of American government. It can all but destroy the coordinate judicial branch and thus upset the delicately poised constitutional system of checks and balances. It can distort the nature of the federal union by permitting each state to decide for itself the scope of its authority under the Constitution. It can reduce the supreme law of the land as defined in article VI to a hodgepodge of inconsistent decisions by making fifty state courts and eleven federal courts of appeals the final judges of the meaning and application of the Constitution, laws, and treaties of the United States.

* * *

Does the exceptions and regulations clause confer power of such magnitude upon Congress? The answer requires an analysis of the function of the Supreme Court as a part of the governmental structure created by the Constitution.

* * *

One of the most significant aspects of the federal union is disclosed by the declaration in article VI of the Constitution that "this Constitution, and the Laws of the United States which shall be made in Pursuance thereof; and all Treaties made, or which shall be made, under the

Authority of the United States, shall be the supreme Law of the Land; and the Judges in every State shall be bound thereby, any Thing in the Constitution or Laws of any State to the Contrary notwithstanding." This constitutional mandate requires (a) that there shall be one supreme federal law throughout the land and (b) that in the event of conflict between that law and the law or authority of any state, the federal law shall prevail.

The supremacy clause standing alone, however, is no more than an exhortation. A tribunal with nationwide authority is needed to interpret and apply the supreme law. Such a tribunal is created by article III, which vests the judicial power of the United States in one Supreme Court and such inferior courts as Congress may establish and extends that power to every case involving the supreme law of the land. The only court created by the article is designated as supreme in contrast to the inferior courts which Congress in its discretion may establish. That court alone is expressly given appellate jurisdiction over cases involving the supreme law of the land whether those cases are initiated in state or federal courts. It is thus the constitutional instrument for implementing the supremacy clause. As such, its essential appellate functions under the Constitution are: (1) to provide a tribunal for the ultimate resolution of inconsistent or conflicting interpretations of federal law by state and federal courts, and (2) to provide a tribunal for maintaining the supremacy of federal law when it conflicts with state law or is challenged by state authority.

The process of carrying out these functions is necessarily a flexible one. A Supreme Court decision is not required in every case that involves a state challenge to federal law or an interpretation of federal law in conflict with other cases. A measure of inconsistency in the interpretation and application of federal law is inevitable, and immediate correction is not always imperative. But some avenue must remain open to permit ultimate resolution by the Supreme Court of persistent conflicts between state and federal law or in the interpretation of federal law by lower courts. For this purpose discretionary review through certiorari can be as effective as mandatory review by writ of error or appeal. Although these essential functions would not ordinarily be disrupted by a procedural limitation restricting the availability of Supreme Court review in some but not all cases involving a particular subject, legislation denying the Court jurisdiction to review any case involving that subject would effectively obstruct those functions in the proscribed area.

CONGRESSIONAL POWER TO CURTAIL FEDERAL COURT JURISDICTION: AN OPINIONATED GUIDE TO THE ONGOING DEBATE
GERALD GUNTHER
36 STAN.L.REV. 895, 901-08 (1984)[b]

* * *

On its face, the exceptions clause of article III, section 2, seems to grant a quite unconfined power to Congress to withhold from the Court a large number of classes of cases potentially within its appellate jurisdiction. Moreover, those who would find substantial constitutional restraints on congressional power over Supreme Court appellate jurisdiction within article III itself face formidable obstacles in the historical congressional practice and in numerous statements by the Supreme Court. Nevertheless, there have been extensive academic efforts to articulate substantial internal limits on congressional authority.

* * *

Far and away the most widely voiced modern argument for internal limitations is that the "exceptions" power of Congress cannot be exercised in a way that would interfere with the "essential" or "core" functions of the Supreme Court. The origin of the argument is traceable to a remark in the deservedly famous Socratic dialogue written by the late Henry Hart in 1953. Hart suggested (with somewhat ambiguous import) that the "exceptions" power cannot be used in a manner that "will destroy the essential role of the Supreme Court in the constitutional plan." The most insistent modern advocate of this type of limit is Leonard Ratner. In Ratner's view, the "essential constitutional functions of the Court" are "to maintain the supremacy and uniformity of federal law." A plenary congressional "exceptions" power, he insists, is "not consistent with the constitutional plan."

Although much of the modern academic literature goes on at considerable length to explain why Ratner's thesis is unpersuasive, he does not stand alone in advocating this "essential functions" limit. Recently, his position has been adopted in substance by a powerful ally outside of academia—William French Smith, the Reagan Administration's Attorney General. In May 1982, Attorney General Smith sent a lengthy letter to Senator Strom Thurmond, the Chairman of the Senate Judiciary Committee, in response to inquiries about the constitutionality of the portion of the Helms bill that would withdraw the Court's appellate jurisdiction over cases relating to "voluntary" prayers. The Attorney General, while recognizing that "the question of the limits of Congress' authority under the Exceptions Clause is an extraordinarily difficult one," argued that Congress may not constitutionally "make 'exceptions' to Supreme Court jurisdiction which would intrude upon the core functions of the Supreme Court as an independent and equal branch in our system of separation of powers." Rather, "Congress can limit the Supreme Court's appellate jurisdiction only up to the point where it impairs the Court's core functions in the constitutional scheme."

What are the pros and cons of the widely debated "essential" or "core" functions position? Proponents of the thesis cannot readily (and do not) rely on the constitutional language: there is simply no "essential functions" limit on the face of the exceptions clause. They claim to find helpful language in some Supreme Court opinions, but they discount the far more numerous statements from the Court suggesting a very broad congressional authority by arguing that the Court has really never had to face a situation in which Congress sought to bar all access to the Court in an "essential" area. Proponents rely above all on historical expectations and structural considerations allegedly demonstrating that appellate review must be available to assure that the Court will be able to provide the "essential" uniformity and supremacy of important (especially constitutional) issues of federal law. Critics of the thesis question the legitimacy of importing the "essential functions" limit into the Constitution, emphasize the vague, slippery, open-ended nature of the limit, and challenge its various underpinnings at length.

The most concrete source of the arguments lies in statements made by the Supreme Court itself. The advocates of an "essential functions" limit can indeed point to various dicta endorsing the desirability of Court review to ensure the supremacy and uniformity of federal law. An early, extensive, and eloquent example is in Joseph Story's opinion for the Court in *Martin v. Hunter's Lessee,* which sustained the constitutionality of section 25 of the 1789 Judiciary Act against an attack from the highest court of Virginia. But, as I have argued elsewhere, Justice Story's statements are more plausibly read as exhortations regarding desirable policy than as expressions of constitutional commands, particularly in view of his own later decisions and his contemporaneous legislative lobbying activities advocating congressional extension of the Judiciary Act. In any event, as critics such as William Van Alstyne have pointed out, the Court's sporadic paeans of praise to uniformity and supremacy seem far outweighed by its considerably more frequent expressions of deference to congressional delineations of appellate jurisdiction.

* * *

But the main support invoked by those who assert a broad "essential functions" limit on the "exceptions" power does not rest on such slender reeds. Instead the arguments rely most heavily on general expectations, historical and contemporary, about the Supreme Court's role—on the "constitutional plan" and its evolution. The main question raised by this kind of argument is whether it confuses the familiar with the necessary, the desirable with the constitutionally mandated. In recent decades, the Court certainly has enjoyed very broad statutory jurisdiction to review constitutional rulings by state and lower federal courts. The central and expanding role of the Court in our modern polity helps explain the recurrent outrage expressed in the media and in academia in response to proposed congressional assertions of power over jurisdiction. But is there sufficient basis, in history and in principle, for insistence upon substantial internal, article III restraints on congressional power?

The strongest basis for such restraints lies in expectations reflected in the debates at the Constitutional Convention. The major point of controversy during the evolution of article III was whether the Constitution should mandate the establishment of lower federal courts. Nationalists insisted that lower federal courts were necessary to assure adequate enforcement of federal law; localists countered that state judges, compelled to apply federal law under the supremacy clause, were adequate for the initial interpretation and enforcement of federal requirements, and that ultimate review by the Supreme Court would assure sufficient supremacy and uniformity. In one of the Convention's great compromises, article III emerged: the article mandated the creation of the Supreme Court, but left to the discretion of Congress the establishment of any "inferior" courts.

Advocates of the "essential functions" limit on congressional power can draw some legitimate comfort from these debates, for an expectation of Supreme Court review of state court judgments was indeed widespread. But is that expectation tantamount to a constitutional limitation on congressional authority over appellate jurisdiction? After all, the same Convention did insert the exceptions clause, the textual nub of the controversy. Even more damaging to the case for an unreachable, "essential" Court role of assuring supremacy and uniformity is congressional practice, beginning in the earliest period, when there was a considerable overlap among delegates to the Constitutional Convention and members of the First Congress. The Judiciary Act of 1789 did not grant to the Court all of the potential article III appellate jurisdiction, even in constitutional cases, necessary to assure that the Supreme Court would be the ultimate provider of both supremacy and uniformity. Rather, section 25 of the Act, dealing with review of state court decisions, was essentially a supremacy-assuring device; it was not primarily concerned with uniformity. Supreme Court review was available only when a state court denied a federal claim; when the state court sustained a federal claim, even when its reading of federal law differed from that of federal tribunals, review was unavailable. Such was the scheme of the jurisdictional statutes for more than a century, until 1914. Proponents of the "essential functions" thesis have difficulty explaining the long life of the section 25 scheme. They counter that section 25 did, after all, assure supremacy. But their thesis is that assurance of uniformity as well as supremacy is the "essential function" of the Court, and uniformity was conspicuously lacking from the congressionally devised and judicially implemented jurisdictional scheme until Congress chose to modify it early in this century.

The advocates of a narrow reading of the "exceptions" power then fall back to a broader ground: the alleged implications of the role of an independent judiciary in a system of separation of powers. A large part of Attorney General Smith's narrow reading of the "exceptions" power, for example, is based on just such premises. "Essential to the principle of separation of powers," he argues, "was the proposition that no one Branch of Government should have the power to eliminate the fundamental constitutional role of either of the other Branches." But of course the constitutional scheme is one of checks and balances as well as separation. Article III does provide for an independent judiciary, but independence does not mean total insulation of the judicial branch any more than it does for the other branches. No one denies, for example, that the political branches govern the selection of personnel for the Bench, a selection process that often has a profound impact on the course of decisions. And article III does not specify the size of the Supreme Court, leaving open the technique of "packing" the Court that Franklin D. Roosevelt advocated—a technique widely recognized as constitutionally authorized albeit criticizable in the strongest terms as a matter of policy. Ultimately, arguments stemming from the lack of power of one branch to interfere with the "fundamental constitutional role" of another tend to be question-begging. Even the proponents of the "essential" or "core" functions limitation recognize that Congress may legitimately react to constitutional rulings through the constitutional amendment route; they simply insist that that is the only legitimate route. But the question remains whether the "fundamental constitutional role" of the Court leaves any significant role for Congress under its "exceptions" power. In a sense, then, much of the debate turns on whether arguments about sensible and desirable judicial structures can be converted into constitutionally mandated ones. Much of the "essential functions" theory of Professor Ratner and Attorney General Smith strikes me as failing to heed the warning I voiced earlier about confusing wisdom and constitutionality, confusing what Congress ought not to do with what it cannot do.

Notes and Questions

1. As Professor Gunther points out, Professor Henry Hart originated the "essential functions" theory in an article written over forty years ago and still frequently cited in debates on this topic. *See* Henry L. Hart, *The Power of Congress to Limit the Jurisdiction of Federal Courts: An Exercise in Dialectic,* 66 HARV.L.REV. 1362 (1953).

2. Is there any language in Article III that supports the "essential functions" theory? If not, does the Exceptions Clause connote that while it may be desirable for the Court to perform the core functions set forth by the theory, it is not constitutionally mandated? If the Exceptions Clause embraces

the essential functions theory, does Congress have a substantial role in determining the Supreme Court's appellate jurisdiction?

3. Do *McCardle* and *Yerger* support or contradict the "essential functions" theory?

4. Is Professor Gunther correct that the Judiciary Act of 1789 was inconsistent with the "essential functions" theory?

5. Is recognition of broad congressional power over the appellate jurisdiction of the Supreme Court a greater threat to the Court's independence than the checks on it that are universally recognized, such as selection of justices by the political branches or congressional power to determine the number of justices and thereby "pack" the Court?

6. Eliminating Supreme Court review over a particular category of constitutional cases would not eliminate the "undesirable" decisions that may motivate efforts to restrict the Court's appellate jurisdiction. State court judges have an obligation under the Supremacy Clause to follow Supreme Court precedents notwithstanding congressional opposition to them. The Court has often (particularly in recent years) asserted that state and federal courts are equally willing and able to apply federal constitutional principles. *See, e.g., Huffman v. Pursue, Ltd.,* 420 U.S. 592, 604, 95 S.Ct. 1200, 1208, 43 L.Ed.2d 482, 492 (1975); *Steffel v. Thompson,* 415 U.S. 452, 461, 94 S.Ct. 1209, 1216, 39 L.Ed.2d 505, 515-16 (1974) (both supporting federal abstention on the ground that intervention "reflect['s] negatively upon the state courts' ability to enforce constitutional principles."). *See generally* Chapter 8, Section D. If that assertion is correct, what would Congress accomplish by eliminating Supreme Court review? If it is not, are there implications for the legitimacy of the jurisdiction-stripping legislation?

UNITED STATES v. KLEIN
Supreme Court of the United States, 1872.
80 U.S. (13 Wall.) 128, 20 L.Ed. 519.

[In 1863, United States Treasury agents seized 664 bales of cotton belonging to V.F. Wilson, sold it, and paid the proceeds, $125,300, into the Treasury. Wilson had aided the Confederacy by signing, as surety, two official bonds of Confederate Army officers. After his death, the estate's administrators sued in the Court of Claims to recover the proceeds pursuant to the Abandoned and Captured Property Act, which conditioned recovery upon a showing that the property owner had never given any aid or comfort to the rebellion. *United States v. Padelford,* 76 U.S. (9 Wall.) 531, 19 L.Ed. 788 (1869), had held that even though Padelford had participated in the rebellion, his presidential pardon made him as innocent under the law as if he had never participated. Based on *Padelford,* the Court of Claims concluded that Wilson was relieved of any charge of disloyalty; he, too, had received a presidential pardon. Consequently, the court held that Klein, the surviving administrator, was entitled to the proceeds of the cotton sale. The government appealed to the Supreme Court.

While the appeal was pending, Congress attached the following *proviso* to an appropriations bill that was enacted:

Provided, That no pardon or amnesty granted by the President, whether general or special, by proclamation or otherwise, nor any acceptance of such pardon or amnesty, nor oath taken, or other act performed in pursuance or as a condition thereof, shall be admissible in evidence on the part of any claimant in the Court of Claims as evidence in support of any claim against the United States, or to establish the standing of any claimant in said court, or his right to bring or maintain suit therein; nor shall any such pardon, amnesty, acceptance, oath, or other act as aforesaid, heretofore offered or put in evidence on behalf of any claimant in said court, be used or considered by said court, or by the appellate court on appeal from said court, in deciding upon the claim of said claimant, or any appeal therefrom, as any part of the proof to sustain the claim of the claimant, or to entitle him to maintain his action in said Court of Claims, or on appeal therefrom; but the proof of loyalty required by the Abandoned and Captured Property Act, and by the sections of several acts quoted, shall be made by proof of the matters required, irrespective of the effect of any executive proclamation, pardon, amnesty, or other act of condonation or oblivion. And in all cases where judgment shall have been heretofore rendered in the Court of Claims in favor of any claimant, on any other proof of loyalty than such as is above required and provided, and which is hereby declared to have been and to be the true intent and meaning of said respective acts, the Supreme Court shall, on appeal, have no further jurisdiction of the cause, and shall dismiss the same for want of jurisdiction.

And provided further, That whenever any pardon shall have heretofore been granted by the President of the United States to any person bringing suit in the Court of Claims for the proceeds of abandoned or captured property under the said act, approved 12th March, 1863, and the acts amendatory of the same, and such pardon shall recite in substance that such person took part in the late rebellion against the government of the United States, or was guilty of any act of rebellion against, or disloyalty to, the United States; and such pardon shall have been accepted in writing by the person to whom the same issued without an express disclaimer of, and protestation against, such fact of guilt contained in such acceptance, such pardon and acceptance shall be taken and deemed in such suit in the said Court of Claims, and on appeal therefrom, conclusive evidence that such person did take part in, and give aid and comfort to, the late rebellion, and did not maintain true allegiance or consistently adhere to the United States; and on proof of such pardon and acceptance, which proof may be heard summarily on motion or otherwise, the jurisdiction of the court in the case shall cease, and the court shall forthwith dismiss the suit of such claimant.

The government then asked the Supreme Court to remand the case with the mandate that it be dismissed for want of jurisdiction.]

THE CHIEF JUSTICE delivered the opinion of the Court.

The general question in this case is whether or not the *proviso* relating to suits for the proceeds of abandoned and captured property in the Court of Claims, contained in the appropriation act of July 12th, 1870, debars the defendant in error from recovering, as administrator of V.F. Wilson, deceased, the proceeds of certain cotton belonging to the decedent, which came into the possession of the agents of the Treasury Department as captured or abandoned property, and the proceeds of which were paid by them according to law into the Treasury of the United States.

The answer to this question requires a consideration of the rights of property, as affected by the late civil war, in the hands of citizens engaged in hostilities against the United States.

It may be said in general terms that property in the insurgent States may be distributed into four classes:

1st. That which belonged to the hostile organizations or was employed in actual hostilities on land.

2d. That which at sea became lawful subject of capture and prize.

3d. That which became the subject of confiscation.

4th. A peculiar description, known only in the recent war, called captured and abandoned property.

The first of these descriptions of property, like property of other like kind in ordinary international wars, became, wherever taken, ipso facto, the property of the United States.

The second of these descriptions comprehends ships and vessels with their cargoes belonging to the insurgents or employed in aid of them; but property in these was not changed by capture alone but by regular judicial proceeding and sentence.

Accordingly it was provided in the Abandoned and Captured Property Act of March 12th, 1863, that the property to be collected under it "shall not include any kind or description used or intended to be used for carrying on war against the United States, such as arms, ordnance, ships, steamboats and their furniture, forage, military supplies, or munitions of war."

Almost all the property of the people in the insurgent States was included in the third description, for after sixty days from the date of the President's proclamation of July 25th, 1862, all the estates and property of those who did not cease to aid, countenance, and abet the rebellion became liable to seizure and confiscation, and it was made the duty of the President to cause the same to be seized and applied, either specifically or in the proceeds thereof, to the support of the army. But it is to be observed that tribunals and proceedings were provided, by which alone such property could be condemned, and without which it remained unaffected in the possession of the proprietors.

It is thus seen that, except to property used in actual hostilities, as mentioned in the first section of the act of March 12th, 1863, no titles were divested in the insurgent States unless in pursuance of a judgment rendered after due legal proceedings. The government recognized to the fullest extent the humane maxims of the modern law of nations, which exempt private property of non-combatant enemies from capture as booty of war. Even the law of confiscation was sparingly applied. The cases were few indeed in which the property of any not engaged in actual hostilities was subjected to seizure and sale.

The spirit which animated the government received special illustration from the act under which the present case arose. We have called the property taken into the custody of public officers under that act a peculiar species, and it was so. There is, so far as we are aware, no similar legislation mentioned in history.

The act directs the officers of the Treasury Department to take into their possession and make sale of all property abandoned by its owners or captured by the national forces, and to pay the proceeds into the national treasury.

That it was not the intention of Congress that the title to these proceeds should be divested absolutely out of the original owners of the property seems clear upon a comparison of different parts of the act.

We have already seen that those articles which became by the simple fact of capture the property of the captor, as ordnance, munitions of war, and the like, or in which third parties acquired rights which might be made absolute by decree, as ships and other vessels captured as prize, were expressly excepted from the operation of the act; and it is reasonable to infer that it was the purpose of Congress that the proceeds of the property for which the special provision of the act was made should go into the treasury without change of ownership. Certainly such was the intention in respect to the property of loyal men. That the same intention prevailed in regard to the property of owners who, though then hostile, might subsequently become loyal, appears probable from the circumstance that no provision is anywhere made for confiscation of it; while there is no trace in the statute book of intention to divest ownership of private property not excepted from the effect of this act, otherwise than by proceedings for confiscation.

In the case of *Padelford,* we held that the right to the possession of private property was not changed until actual seizure by proper military authority, and that actual seizure by such authority did not divest the title under the provisions of the Abandoned and Captured Property Act. The reasons assigned seem fully to warrant the conclusion. The government constituted itself the trustee for those who were by that act declared entitled to the proceeds of captured and abandoned property, and for those whom it should thereafter recognize as entitled. By the act itself it was provided that any person claiming to have been the owner of such property might prefer his claim to the proceeds thereof, and, on proof that he had never given aid or comfort to the rebellion, receive the amount after deducting expenses.

This language makes the right to the remedy dependent upon proof of loyalty, but implies that there may be proof of ownership without proof of loyalty. The property of the original owner is, in no case, absolutely divested. There is, as we have already observed, no confiscation, but the proceeds of the property have passed into the possession of the government, and restoration of the property is pledged to none except to those who have continually adhered to the government. Whether restoration will be made to others, or confiscation will be enforced, is left to be determined by considerations of public policy subsequently to be developed.

* * *

We conclude, therefore, that the title to the proceeds of the property which came to the possession of the government by capture or abandonment, with the exceptions already noticed, was in no case divested out of the original owner. It was for the government itself to determine whether these proceeds should be restored to the owner or not. The promise of the restoration of all rights of property decides that question affirmatively as to all persons who availed themselves of the proffered pardon. It was competent for the President to annex to his offer of pardon any conditions or qualifications he should see fit; but after those conditions and qualifications had been satisfied, the pardon and its connected promises took full effect. The restoration of the proceeds became the absolute right of the persons pardoned, on application within two years from the close of the war. It was, in fact, promised for an equivalent. "Pardon and restoration of political rights" were "in return" for the oath and its fulfilment. To refuse it would be a breach of faith not less "cruel and astounding" than to abandon the freed people whom the Executive had promised to maintain in their freedom.

What, then, was the effect of the provision of the act of 1870 upon the right of the owner of the cotton in this case? He had done certain acts which this court has adjudged to be acts in aid of the rebellion; but he abandoned the cotton to the agent of the Treasury Department, by whom it has been sold and the proceeds paid into the Treasury of the United States; and he took, and has not violated, the amnesty oath under the President's proclamation. Upon this case the Court of Claims pronounced him entitled to a judgment for the net proceeds in the treasury. This decree was rendered on the 26th of May, 1869; the appeal to this court made on the 3d of June, and was filed here on the 11th of December, 1869.

The judgment of the court in the case of *Padelford,* which, in its essential features, was the same with this case, was rendered on the 30th of April, 1870. It affirmed the judgment of the Court of Claims in his favor.

Soon afterwards the provision in question was introduced as a *proviso* to the clause in the general appropriation bill, appropriating a sum of money for the payment of judgments of the Court of Claims, and became a part of the act, with perhaps little consideration in either House of Congress.

This *proviso* declares in substance that no pardon, acceptance, oath, or other act performed in pursuance, or as a condition of pardon, shall be admissible in evidence in support of any claim against the United States in the Court of Claims, or to establish the right of any claimant to bring suit in that court; nor, if already put in evidence, shall be used or considered on behalf of the claimant, by said court, or by the appellate court on appeal. Proof of loyalty is required to be made according to the provisions of certain statutes, irrespective of the effect of any executive proclamation, pardon, or amnesty, or act of oblivion; and when judgment has been already rendered on other proof of loyalty, the Supreme Court, on appeal, shall have no further jurisdiction of the cause, and shall dismiss the same for want of jurisdiction. It is further provided that whenever any pardon, granted to any suitor in the Court of Claims, for the proceeds of captured and abandoned property, shall recite in substance that the person pardoned took part in the late rebellion, or was guilty of any act of rebellion or disloyalty, and shall have been accepted in writing without express disclaimer and protestation against the fact so recited, such pardon or acceptance shall be taken as conclusive evidence in the Court of Claims, and on appeal, that the claimant did give aid to the rebellion; and on proof of such pardon, or acceptance, which proof may be made summarily on motion or otherwise, the jurisdiction of the court shall cease, and the suit shall be forthwith dismissed.

The substance of this enactment is that an acceptance of a pardon, without disclaimer, shall be conclusive evidence of the acts pardoned, but shall be null and void as evidence of the rights conferred by it, both in the Court of Claims and in this court on appeal.

* * *

The Court of Claims is * * * constituted one of those inferior courts which Congress authorizes, and has jurisdiction of contracts between the government and the citizen, from which appeal regularly lies to this court.

Undoubtedly the legislature has complete control over the organization and existence of that court and may confer or withhold the right of appeal from its decisions. And if this act did nothing more, it would be our duty to give it effect. If it simply denied the right of appeal in a particular class of cases, there could be no doubt that it must be regarded as an exercise of the power of Congress to make "such exceptions from the appellate jurisdiction" as should seem to it expedient.

But the language of the *proviso* shows plainly that it does not intend to withhold appellate jurisdiction except as a means to an end. Its great and controlling purpose is to deny to pardons granted by the President the effect which this court had adjudged them to have. The *proviso* declares that pardons shall not be considered by this court on appeal. We had already decided that it was our duty to consider them and give them effect, in cases like the present, as equivalent to proof of loyalty. It provides that whenever it shall appear that any judgment of the Court of Claims shall have been founded on such pardons, without other proof of loyalty, the Supreme Court shall have no further jurisdiction of the case and shall dismiss the same for want of jurisdiction. The *proviso* further declares that every pardon granted to any suitor in the Court of Claims and reciting that the person pardoned has been guilty of any act of rebellion or disloyalty, shall, if accepted in writing without disclaimer of the fact recited, be taken as conclusive evidence in that court and on appeal, of the act recited; and on proof of pardon or acceptance, summarily made on motion or otherwise, the jurisdiction of the court shall cease and the suit shall be forthwith dismissed.

It is evident from this statement that the denial of jurisdiction to this court, as well as to the Court of Claims, is founded solely on the application of a rule of decision, in causes pending, prescribed by Congress. The court has jurisdiction of the cause to a given point; but when it ascertains that a certain state of things exists, its jurisdiction is to cease and it is required to dismiss the cause for want of jurisdiction.

It seems to us that this is not an exercise of the acknowledged power of Congress to make exceptions and prescribe regulations to the appellate power.

The court is required to ascertain the existence of certain facts and thereupon to declare that its jurisdiction on appeal has ceased, by dismissing the bill. What is this but to prescribe a rule for the decision of a cause in a particular way? In the case before us, the Court of Claims has rendered judgment for the claimant and an appeal has been taken to this court. We are directed to dismiss the appeal, if we find that the judgment must be affirmed, because of a pardon granted to the intestate of the claimants. Can we do so without allowing one party to the controversy to decide it in its own favor? Can we do so without allowing that the legislature may prescribe rules of decision to the Judicial Department of the government in cases pending before it?

We think not; and thus thinking, we do not at all question what was decided in the case of *Pennsylvania v. Wheeling Bridge Company.* In that case, after a decree in this court that the bridge, in the then state of the law, was a nuisance and must be abated as such, Congress passed an act legalizing the structure and making it a postroad; and the court, on a motion for process to enforce the decree, held that the bridge had ceased to be a nuisance by the exercise of the constitutional powers of Congress, and denied the motion. No arbitrary rule of decision was prescribed in that case, but the court was left to apply its ordinary rules to the new circumstances created by the act. In the case before us no new circumstances have been created by legislation. But the court is forbidden to give the effect to evidence which, in its own judgment, such evidence should have, and is directed to give it an effect precisely contrary.

We must think that Congress has inadvertently passed the limit which separates the legislative from the judicial power.

It is of vital importance that these powers be kept distinct. The Constitution provides that the judicial power of the United States shall be vested in one Supreme Court and such inferior courts as the Congress shall from time to time ordain and establish. The same instrument, in the last clause of the same article, provides that in all cases other than those of original jurisdiction, "the Supreme Court shall have appellate jurisdiction both as to law and fact, with such exceptions and under such regulations as the Congress shall make."

Congress has already provided that the Supreme Court shall have jurisdiction of the judgments of the Court of Claims on appeal. Can it prescribe a rule in conformity with which the court must deny to itself the jurisdiction thus conferred, because and only because its decision, in accordance with settled law, must be adverse to the government and favorable to the suitor? This question seems to us to answer itself.

The rule prescribed is also liable to just exception as impairing the effect of a pardon, and thus infringing the constitutional power of the Executive.

It is the intention of the Constitution that each of the great coordinate departments of the government—the Legislative, the Executive, and the Judicial—shall be, in its sphere, independent of the others. To the executive alone is intrusted the power of pardon; and it is granted without limit. Pardon includes amnesty. It blots out the offence pardoned and removes all its penal consequences. It may be granted on conditions. In these particular pardons, that no doubt might exist as to their character, restoration of property was expressly pledged, and the pardon was granted on condition that the person who availed himself of it should take and keep a prescribed oath.

Now it is clear that the legislature cannot change the effect of such a pardon any more than the executive can change a law. Yet this is attempted by the provision under consideration. The court is required to receive special pardons as evidence of guilt and to treat them as null and void. It is required to disregard pardons granted by proclamation on condition, though the condition has been fulfilled, and to deny them their legal effect. This certainly impairs the executive authority and directs the court to be instrumental to that end.

We think it unnecessary to enlarge. The simplest statement is the best.

We repeat that it is impossible to believe that this provision was not inserted in the appropriation bill through inadvertence; and that we shall not best fulfill the deliberate will of the legislature by Denying the motion to dismiss and Affirming the judgment of the Court of Claims; which is accordingly done.

MR. JUSTICE MILLER (with whom concurred MR. JUSTICE BRADLEY), dissenting.

I cannot agree to the opinion of the court just delivered in an important matter; and I regret this the more because I do agree to the proposition that the *proviso* to the act of July 12th, 1870, is unconstitutional, so far as it attempts to prescribe to the judiciary the effect to be given to an act of pardon or amnesty by the President. This power of pardon is confided to the President by the Constitution, and whatever may be its extent or its limits, the legislative branch of the government cannot impair its force or effect in a judicial proceeding in a constitutional court. But I have not been able to bring my mind to concur in the proposition that, under the act concerning captured and abandoned property, there remains in the former owner, who had given aid and comfort to the rebellion, any interest whatever in the property or its proceeds when it had been sold and paid into the treasury or had been converted to the use of the public under that act. I must construe this act, as all others should be construed, by seeking the intention of its framers, and the intention to restore the proceeds of such property to the loyal citizen, and to transfer it absolutely to the government in the case of those who had given active support to the rebellion, is to me too apparent to be disregarded. In the one case the government is converted into a trustee for the former owner; in the other it appropriates it to its own use as the property of a public enemy captured in war. Can it be inferred from anything found in the statute that Congress intended that this property should ever be restored to the disloyal? I am unable to discern any such intent. But if it did, why was not some provision made by which the title of the government could at some time be made perfect, or that of the owner established? Some judicial proceeding for confiscation would seem to be necessary if there remains in the disloyal owner any right or interest whatever. But there is no such provision, and unless the act intended to forfeit absolutely the right of the disloyal owner, the proceeds remain in a condition where the owner cannot maintain a suit for its recovery, and the United States can obtain no perfect title to it.

This statute has recently received the attentive consideration of the court in two reported cases.

In the case of the *United States v. Anderson,* in reference to the relation of the government to the money paid into the treasury under this act, and the difference between the property of the loyal and disloyal owner, the court uses language hardly consistent with the opinion just read. It says that Congress, in a spirit of liberality, constituted the government a trustee for so much of this property as belonged to the faithful Southern people, and while it directed that all of it should be sold and its proceeds paid into the treasury, gave to this class of persons an opportunity to establish their right to the proceeds. Again, it is said, that "the measure, in itself of great beneficence, was practically important only in its application to the loyal Southern people, and sympathy for their situation doubtless prompted Congress to pass it." These views had the unanimous concurrence of the court. If I understand the present opinion, however, it maintains that the government, in taking possession of this property and selling it, became the trustee of all the former owners, whether loyal or disloyal, and holds it for the latter until pardoned by the President, or until Congress orders it to be restored to him.

The other case which I refer to is that of *United States v. Padelford.* In that case the opinion makes a labored and successful effort to show that Padelford, the owner of the property, had secured the benefit of the amnesty proclamation before the property was seized under the same statute we are now considering. And it bases the right of Padelford to recover its proceeds in the treasury on the fact that before the capture his status as a loyal citizen had been restored, and with it all his rights of property, although he had previously given aid and comfort to the rebellion. In this view I concurred with all my brethren. And I hold now that as long as the possession or title of property remains in the party, the pardon or the amnesty remits all right in the government to forfeit or confiscate it. But where the property has already been seized and sold, and the proceeds paid into the treasury, and it is clear that the statute contemplates no further proceeding as necessary to divest the right of the former owner, the pardon does not and cannot restore that which has thus completely passed away. And if such was not the view of the court when Padelford's case was under consideration I am at a loss to discover a reason for the extended argument in that case, in the opinion of the court, to show that he had availed himself of the amnesty before the seizure of the property. If the views now advanced are sound, it was wholly immaterial whether Padelford was pardoned before or after the seizure.

Notes and Questions

1. Is *Klein* consistent with *McCardle*?

2. Did Congress have the power to disqualify classes of former property

owners from receiving compensation? If so, why is the use of that power in *Klein* unconstitutional? How does it differ from other situations where Congress has amended statutes to achieve certain results?

Does *Klein* indicate that Congress cannot make such changes applicable to pending cases? Generally appellate courts apply the law as it exists at the time of their decisions, even if it was not the law at the time the suit was filed. *See* MARTIN REDISH, FEDERAL JURISDICTION: TENSIONS IN THE ALLOCA-TION OF JUDICIAL POWER 49 (2d ed. 1990). Does *Klein* establish an exception to this rule for cases where the federal government is a party? If so, why? If not, is *Klein* based upon some other exception to the general rule, or is the general rule mentioned above irrelevant to the decision? If the latter, what makes it irrelevant?

3. Can one characterize the statute in *Klein* as not making an exception to the Court's appellate jurisdiction? If so, what does it do? Does that raise constitutional concerns?

4. Does the discussion of separation of powers refer to possible congressional intrusion on the power of the judiciary, the pardon power of the President, or both? Should the answer affect the Court's analysis of the constitutionality of the statute?

5. Some scholars have distinguished between "internal" limitations on congressional power to make exceptions—those found within Article III itself—and "external" limitations—those found in other constitutional provisions. Is the limitation recognized by the Court in *Klein* internal or external? What difference does it make?

6. Does *Klein* answer the question of congressional power to restrict the Supreme Court's appellate jurisdiction over a category of cases because Congress disagrees with the Court's decisions?

NOTE ON EXTERNAL LIMITATIONS ON CONGRESSIONAL POWER TO CONTROL THE APPELLATE JURISDICTION OF THE SUPREME COURT

It is generally recognized that there are some external limitations on congressional power to make exceptions to the appellate jurisdiction of the Supreme Court. For example, Congress probably cannot limit the appellate jurisdiction of the Supreme Court to appeals filed by whites. The Due Process Clause of the Fifth Amendment includes an "equal protection" component. *See, e.g., Bolling v. Sharpe*, 347 U.S. 497, 74 S.Ct. 693, 98 L.Ed. 884 (1954). The hypothesized limitation would therefore likely be unconstitutional because it would violate the Fifth Amendment rights of excluded litigants. Congressional action under the Exceptions Clause is as subject to the limitations imposed by the Bill of Rights or other constitutional provisions as it is when Congress is exercising any of its other powers.

However, there is controversy about how far such limitations extend. Suppose Congress passed a statute prohibiting the Supreme Court from exercising appellate jurisdiction over cases dealing with abortion rights, perhaps anticipating that state courts would issue more congenial decisions than would the Supreme Court. Would such a statute violate any external constitutional provision? Some scholars contend that it would violate the equal protection component of the Fifth Amendment Due Process Clause, just as the hypothetical statute limiting Supreme Court access to whites. *See, e.g.,* Laurence H. Tribe, *Jurisdictional Gerrymandering: Zoning Disfavored Rights Out of the Federal Courts,* 16 HARV.C.R.-C.L.L.REV. 129 (1981). They contend that a congressional decision to withdraw Supreme Court protection from some rights and not others would invite hostile state action against those who exercise the disfavored rights. Consequently, the statute would burden the exercise of those rights and would have to survive "strict scrutiny." In other words, it would have to be necessary to accomplish a compelling state interest. *See, e.g., Graham v. Richardson,* 403 U.S. 365, 91 S.Ct. 1848, 29 L.Ed.2d 534 (1971).

The argument is analogous to *Memorial Hospital v. Maricopa County,* 415 U.S. 250, 94 S.Ct. 1076, 39 L.Ed.2d 306 (1974), which held that a statute requiring a year's residence as a condition precedent to an indigent's receiving non-emergency hospital or medical care at state expense created an invidious classification that burdened the constitutional right to interstate travel and therefore was subject to strict scrutiny. Arguably, a statute denying Supreme Court review in abortion cases creates an invidious classification, impinges on constitutionally-recognized privacy rights, and thus requires strict scrutiny. Since making it more difficult for litigants to protect constitutional rights is not likely to qualify as a compelling state interest, such statutes will almost inevitably be unconstitutional.

On the other hand, many scholars reject the generality of such an analysis. *See, e.g.,* Gerald Gunther, *Congressional Power to Curtail Federal Jurisdiction: An Opinionated Guide to the Ongoing Debate,* 36 STAN.L.REV. 895, 916-22 (1984); Paul M. Bator, *Congressional Power over the Jurisdiction of the Federal Courts,* 27 VILL.L.REV. 1030 (1982). They argue that although the Constitution prohibits racial discrimination, nothing in it requires that the Supreme Court have appellate jurisdiction in all categories of constitutional cases. Instead, Article III itself provides that the appellate jurisdiction of the Supreme Court is subject to the "exceptions" created by Congress. Thus, the Constitution specifically authorizes Congress to remove categories of cases from Supreme Court review when it deems that course prudent. The Framers intended Congress to regulate the flow of federal question cases among the federal and state courts. That intent is evidenced not only by the Exceptions Clause, but also by the discretion granted Congress regarding the creation of inferior federal courts. Thus, if Congress decides that a particular class of cases, such as those dealing with abortion rights, should be adjudicated in the state courts, it is not "burdening" those rights; it is merely exercising its power to determine the forum in which they will be adjudicated. Additionally, these scholars question the assumption that state courts will be less protective of constitutional rights than federal courts, though none disputes that Congress might believe that.

The controversy rages on. It is not likely to be resolved until Congress passes such a statute. Indeed, many contend that the controversy itself has played a major role in preventing such legislation. Moreover, many of the scholars who believe the congressional power exists nonetheless oppose such statutes on policy grounds. Thus, the debate continues.

C.   CONGRESSIONAL CONTROL OF THE JURISDICTION OF THE LOWER FEDERAL COURTS

SHELDON v. SILL
Supreme Court of the United States, 1850.
49 U.S. (8 How.) 441, 12 L.Ed. 1147.

MR. JUSTICE GRIER delivered the opinion of the court.

The only question which it will be necessary to notice in this case is, whether the Circuit Court had jurisdiction.

Sill, the complainant below, a citizen of New York, filed his bill in the Circuit Court of the United States for Michigan, against Sheldon, claiming to recover the amount of a bond and mortgage, which had been assigned to him by Hastings, the President of the Bank of Michigan.

Sheldon, in his answer, among other things, pleaded that "the bond and mortgage in controversy, having been originally given by a citizen of Michigan to another citizen of the same state, and the complainant being assignee of them, the Circuit Court had no jurisdiction."

The eleventh section of the Judiciary Act, which defines the jurisdiction of the Circuit Courts, restrains them from taking "cognizance of any suit to recover the contents of any promissory note or other chose in action, in favor of an assignee, unless a suit might have been prosecuted in such court to recover the contents, if no assignment had been made, except in cases of foreign bills of exchange."

The third article of the Constitution declares that "the judicial power of the United States shall be vested in one Supreme Court, and such inferior courts as the Congress may, from time to time, ordain and establish." The second section of the same article enumerates the cases and controversies of which the judicial power shall have cognizance, and, among others, it specifies "controversies between citizens of different states."

It has been alleged, that this restriction of the Judiciary Act, with regard to assignees of choses in action, is in conflict with this provision of the Constitution, and therefore void.

It must be admitted, that if the Constitution had ordained and established the inferior courts, and distributed to them their respective powers, they could not be restricted or divested by Congress. But as it has made no such distribution, one of two consequences must result,—either that each inferior court created by Congress must exercise all the judicial powers not given to the Supreme Court, or that Congress, having the power to establish the courts, must define their respective jurisdictions. The first of these inferences has never been asserted, and could not be defended with any show of reason, and if not, the latter would seem to follow as a necessary consequence. And it would seem to follow, also, that, having a right to prescribe, Congress may withhold from any court of its creation jurisdiction of any of the enumerated controversies. Courts created by statute can have no jurisdiction but such as the statute confers. No one of them can assert a just claim to jurisdiction exclusively conferred on another, or withheld from all.

The Constitution has defined the limits of the judicial power of the United States, but has not prescribed how much of it shall be exercised by the Circuit Court; consequently, the statute which does prescribe the limits of their jurisdiction, cannot be in conflict with the Constitution, unless it confers powers not enumerated therein.

Such has been the doctrine held by this court since its first establishment. To enumerate all the cases in which it has been either directly advanced or tacitly assumed would be tedious and unnecessary.

In the case of *Turner v. Bank of North America,* 4 Dall. [4 U.S.], 10, it was contended, as in this case, that, as it was a controversy between citizens of different states, the Constitution gave the plaintiff a right to sue in the Circuit Court, notwithstanding he was an assignee within the restriction of the eleventh section of the Judiciary Act. But the court said,—"The political truth is, that the disposal of the judicial power (except in a few specified instances) belongs to Congress; and Congress is not bound to enlarge the jurisdiction of the Federal courts to every subject, in every form which the Constitution might warrant." This decision was made in 1799; since that time, the same doctrine has been frequently asserted by this court.

The only remaining inquiry is, whether the complainant in this case is the assignee of a "chose in action," within the meaning of the statute.

* * *

The complainant in this case is the purchaser and assignee of a sum of money, a debt, a chose in action, not of a tract of land. He seeks to recover by this action a debt assigned to him. He is therefore the "assignee of a chose in action," within the letter and spirit of the act of Congress under consideration, and cannot support this action in the Circuit Court of the United States, where his assignor could not.

The judgment of the Circuit Court must therefore be reversed, for want of jurisdiction.

Notes and Questions

1. Why did Congress limit the lower federal courts' jurisdiction in assignment cases? Does *Sheldon* mean that Congress has the power to remove original jurisdiction over a category of constitutional cases because it is unhappy with federal decisions? Do the due process arguments made against congressional power to limit the appellate jurisdiction of the Supreme Court apply with the same force in this context?

2. Could Congress simply have never created any lower federal courts? In *Martin v. Hunter's Lessee,* 14 U.S. (1 Wheat.) 304, 331, 4 L.Ed. 97, 104 (1816), Justice Story, in dicta, expressed the view that Congress had a duty to vest the whole judicial power of the United States either in original or appellate form in some federal court. He based this conclusion on the language of Article III, § 1: "the judicial power of the United States *shall* be vested."[3] [Emphasis added.] He reasoned that state courts might lack jurisdiction to adjudicate some cases within the federal judicial power but not within the original jurisdiction of the Supreme Court.[4] Thus, without inferior federal courts, the whole Article III judicial power could not be vested, from which Justice Story inferred that the Constitution required Congress to create some inferior federal courts. Is Justice Story's view consistent with language or holding of *Sill,* the leading decision on this topic? Is it consistent with the rest of the language of Article III, § 1? Even if Justice Story is correct that the entire federal judicial power must be vested, does that necessarily require the creation of lower federal courts?

3. One scholar has concluded that even though Congress need not have initially created the lower federal courts, it cannot abolish them now without violating the Constitution. Theodore Eisenberg, *Congressional Authority to Restrict Lower Federal Court Jurisdiction,* 83 YALE L.J. 498 (1974). This theory relies upon the circumstances of Supreme Court review that the Framers expected. They probably believed that appellate review by the Supreme Court would provide litigants with Article III cases the federal hearing to which they were entitled, not anticipating that the Supreme Court would only be able to review a very small percentage of the cases in which litigants seek that review. Indeed, for the first 100 years of our history,

---

[3] Justice Story placed such heavy reliance upon the word "shall" after comparing the beginning language of the first three articles of the Constitution. He argued that no one, upon reading that the legislative power shall be vested in Congress or the executive power in the President, understood that language to mean that any further act of the legislature was required to make the vesting of power effective in those branches and urged that there was no reason to construe the parallel language of Article III differently.

[4] Although Justice Story did not elaborate, his theory may have been that the jurisdiction of the state courts depended upon state constitutional and legislative grants, which might not include certain classes of federal cases. Thus, in his view, a federal case might be excluded from both state and federal courts. He apparently did not consider the possibility that the Constitution might compel states to entertain federal actions. *See* Testa v. Katt, 330 U.S. 386, 67 S.Ct. 810, 91 L.Ed. 967 (1947).

there was no discretionary device for the Court to use to control its docket, as certiorari functions today. The existence today of discretionary review and the Court's inability to handle the volume of cases qualifying for federal adjudication means that to meet the Framers' original expectation that cases within the federal judicial power would be heard by a federal court, Article III must now be interpreted to prohibit the abolition of the inferior federal courts. This theory also recognizes, however, that the lower federal courts need not have jurisdiction over all cases within the judicial power if granting such jurisdiction would undermine the federal judicial system, because the Framers would not have demanded such a self-defeating exercise. Thus, in his view, current restrictions on federal jurisdiction, such as the amount-in-controversy limitation, are consistent with Article III.

Is Professor Eisenberg's interpretation of Article III compelled by, or at least consistent with, the constitutional text? If not, is the justification he offers for departing from the text persuasive?

4. In *Lauf v. E.G. Shinner & Co., Inc.,* 303 U.S. 323, 58 S.Ct. 578, 82 L.Ed. 872 (1938), the Court confronted a provision of the Norris-LaGuardia Act, 29 U.S.C.A. §§ 101 *et seq.,* that prohibited federal courts from exercising jurisdiction to issue injunctions in labor disputes in the absence of specific findings. Congress had passed the statute in response to the widely-held view that federal courts had been hostile to the labor movement in the early decades of this century. The district court in *Lauf* enjoined the defendant union on the theory that the case was not a labor dispute within the meaning of the statute, and the court of appeals affirmed. The Supreme Court disagreed and noted:

> There can be no question of the power of Congress thus to define and limit the jurisdiction of the inferior courts of the United States. The District Court made none of the required findings save as to irreparable injury and lack of remedy at law. It follows that in issuing the injunction it exceeded its jurisdiction.

Is there a conceptual difference between congressional power to limit the remedies federal courts can provide in certain classes of cases and its power to exclude those cases from the courts' jurisdiction entirely? Is there any practical difference when the remedy denied is the only effective one?

Is congressional power over the remedies broader in statutory or constitutional cases? Does *Lauf* establish congressional power to prohibit federal courts from ordering busing in school desegregation cases? Does it mean that Congress has the power to oust the lower federal courts of jurisdiction over a category of constitutional cases, like school desegregation cases, altogether?

5. Assuming that Congress can prohibit the Supreme Court from exercising appellate jurisdiction in categories of constitutional cases and also has the power to prohibit the exercise of original jurisdiction over such cases in the lower federal courts, can it do both?

6. Can Congress eliminate state jurisdiction as well as federal jurisdiction over such categories of cases? In *Battaglia v. General Motors Corp.,* 169

F.2d 254 (2d Cir.1948), the Second Circuit considered a constitutional challenge to a federal statute that prohibited the exercise of jurisdiction by any court, state or federal. The court indicated that although Congress had the power to restrict the jurisdiction of the lower federal courts, "it must not so exercise that power as to deprive any person of life, liberty, or property without due process of law or to take private property without just compensation." Having said that, the court avoided declaring the statute unconstitutional by finding that the plaintiffs had no established property right that could serve as the predicate for a due process analysis.[5]

7. For its part, in order to avoid the "serious constitutional question" that would otherwise arise, the Supreme Court has gone to great lengths in a series of cases to construe federal statutes not to eliminate judicial review completely. *See, e.g., Webster v. Doe,* 486 U.S. 592, 108 S.Ct. 2047, 100 L.Ed.2d 632 (1988); *Johnson v. Robison,* 415 U.S. 361, 94 S.Ct. 1160, 39 L.Ed.2d 389 (1974).

In *Oestereich v. Selective Service System Local Board No. 11,* 393 U.S. 233, 89 S.Ct. 414, 21 L.Ed.2d 402 (1968), however, the majority interpreted a statute to allow judicial review without relying on the need to avoid the constitutional issue. Oestereich was a divinity student and thus entitled to exemption from service under § 6(g) of the Military Selective Service Act of 1967. He had received the exemption, but when he returned his registration certificate to express his opposition to the involvement of the United States in the War in Vietnam, his Local Board responded by declaring him delinquent for failure to have the certificate in his possession and for failure to provide the Board with notice of his local status. It then reclassified him I-A: ready for induction. Oestereich filed an administrative appeal but lost and was ordered to report for induction. He sued, alleging that he was illegally deprived of his exemption and that his induction order was therefore void.

Generally, the courts had held that the Selective Service Act did not permit pre-induction judicial review of draft classifications. Registrants could challenge classifications in the courts in only two ways: by raising improper classification as a defense to criminal prosecution for refusing to be inducted or, if the registrant accepted induction, by seeking discharge from the military through a writ of habeas corpus. Then, in *Wolff v. Selective Service Local Board No. 16,* 372 F.2d 817 (2d Cir.1967), the court permitted pre-induction review of the punitive reclassification of two young men who had demonstrated against the war. Congress disliked the decision and amended the Selective Service Act. Thus, when Oestereich filed his complaint, the pertinent language of § 10(b)(3) provided:

No judicial review shall be made of the classification or processing of

---

[5] The court's analysis is similar to the analysis the Supreme Court would later use in *Paul v. Davis,* 424 U.S. 693, 96 S.Ct. 1155, 47 L.Ed.2d 405 (1976), to find that a state official's labeling an individual a convicted criminal without an adjudication was not actionable under the Due Process Clause of the Fourteenth Amendment because the individual had no constitutionally cognizable liberty or property interest in his reputation. *See generally* Chapter 6, Section B, Part 4.

any registrant by local boards, appeal boards, or the President, except as a defense to a criminal prosecution instituted under section 12 of this title, after the registrant has responded either affirmatively or negatively to an order to report for induction * * * .

Legislative history confirmed that Congress meant to restrict judicial review to the two situations generally recognized before *Wolff.* Nonetheless, the Supreme Court held that pre-induction judicial review was available to Oestereich.

The Court concluded that Congress had never authorized the use of delinquency regulations to deprive a registrant of an exemption to which he was entitled. Once a person had qualified for an exemption, he could not be deprived of it because of conduct unrelated to the basis for the exemption. If Oestereich's allegations were true, his local board had acted completely outside its authority. The Court distinguished cases where the Board evaluated evidence and exercised its discretion in determining whether a registrant qualified for a claimed exemption. In regard to the language of § 10(b)(3), the Court asserted:

> To hold that a person deprived of his statutory exemption in such a blatantly lawless manner must either be inducted and raise his protest through habeas corpus or defy induction and defend his refusal in a criminal prosecution is to construe the Act with unnecessary harshness. As the Solicitor General suggests, such literalness does violence to the clear mandate of § 6(g) governing the exemption. Our construction leaves § 10(b)(3) unimpaired in the normal operations of the Act.

Justice Harlan concurred in a separate opinion. He read Oestereich's claim as one that the procedure by which he was reclassified was unlawful. Such a challenge was beyond the competence of the Board to hear and determine. Consequently, if Oestereich was not allowed pre-induction judicial review in this case, he would be deprived of his liberty without the prior opportunity to challenge the legality of the procedure by which he was inducted. Justice Harlan thought such a construction "would raise serious constitutional problems."

Thus, most of the Supreme Court's confrontations with statutes purporting to preclude all judicial review have resulted in the Court, perhaps straining a bit, construing the statutes to permit judicial review after all.[6] That approach avoids the serious constitutional question to which Justice Harlan adverted; one can only speculate what the Court might do if forced to confront the issue.

8. Re-read Note 4 following *Yerger*, on pages 172-173. Thus, Congress has prohibited any court from hearing a habeas petition or other suit by an alien who either has been determined to be an enemy combat-

---

[6] In United States v. Mendoza-Lopez, 481 U.S. 828, 107 S.Ct. 2148, 95 L.Ed.2d 772 (1987), however, a majority held that a statutory scheme that made prior deportation a conclusive predicate for felonious unlawful entry violated due process because Congress had permitted too limited judicial review of administrative deportation orders.

ant or is awaiting such a determination if the suit seeks to challenge his confinement or the conditions thereof. Instead, the Detainee Treatment Act of 2005 and the Military Commissions Act of 2006 authorize the United States Court of Appeals for the District of Columbia to exercise exclusive jurisdiction to review final decisions of Combatant Status Review Tribunals. The Defense Department were established these tribunals to review the basis for the decisions to detain alien enemy combatants at Guantanamo Bay. Such review, however, is limited to whether the determination of the petitioner's status was "consistent with the procedures specified by Secretary of Defense for Combatant Status Review Tribunals" and "whether the use of such standards and procedures to make the determination is consistent with the Constitution and laws of the United States." Pub. L. No. 109-63, Div. A Title XIV, section 1405(e)(2)(C)(i)-(ii), 119 Stat. 3476, 3478 (2006) (see 10 U.S.C.A. § 801 Note at 6 (Supp. 2007)). Thus, the court may not itself determine whether the petitioner is wrongfully detained, for example because of insufficient evidence. *See* Jesse Choper & John Yoo, *Wartime Process: A Dialogue on Congressional Power to Remove Issues from the Federal Courts,* 95 CAL.L.REV. 1243, 1245 (2007). Thus, to a great extent Congress has removed such cases from the jurisdiction of the courts. Did it violate the Constitution in doing so?

PLAUT v. SPENDTHRIFT FARM, INC.
Supreme Court of the United States, 1995.
514 U.S. 211, 115 S.Ct. 1447, 131 L.Ed.2d 328.

JUSTICE SCALIA delivered the opinion of the Court.

The question presented in this case is whether § 27A(b) of the Securities Exchange Act of 1934, to the extent that it requires federal courts to reopen final judgments in private civil actions under § 10(b) of the Act, contravenes the Constitution's separation of powers or the Due Process Clause of the Fifth Amendment.

I

In 1987, petitioners brought a civil action against respondents in the United States District Court for the Eastern District of Kentucky. The complaint alleged that in 1983 and 1984 respondents had committed fraud and deceit in the sale of stock in violation of § 10(b) of the Securities Exchange Act of 1934 and Rule 10b-5 of the Securities and Exchange Commission. The case was mired in pretrial proceedings in the District Court until June 20, 1991, when we decided *Lampf, Pleva, Lipkind, Prupis & Petigrow v. Gilbertson,* 501 U.S. 350, 111 S.Ct. 2773, 115 L.Ed.2d 321 (1991). *Lampf* held that "[l]itigation instituted pursuant to § 10(b) and Rule 10b-5 must be commenced within one year after the discovery of the facts constituting the violation and within three years after such violation." We applied that holding to the plaintiff-respondents in *Lampf* itself, found their suit untimely, and reinstated a summary judgment previously entered in favor of the defendant-petitioners. On the same day we decided *James B. Beam Distilling Co. v. Georgia*, 501 U.S. 529, 111 S.Ct. 2439, 115 L.Ed.2d 481 (1991), in which a majority of the Court held, albeit in different opinions, that a new rule of federal law that is applied to the parties in the case announcing the rule must be applied as well to all cases pending on direct review. The joint effect of *Lampf* and *Beam* was to mandate application of the 1-year/3-year limitations period to petitioners' suit. The District Court, finding that petitioners' claims were untimely under the *Lampf* rule, dismissed their action with prejudice on August 13, 1991. Petitioners filed no appeal; the judgment accordingly became final 30 days later.

On December 19, 1991, the President signed the Federal Deposit Insurance Corporation Improvement Act of 1991. Section 476 of the Act—a section that had nothing to do with FDIC improvements—became § 27A of the Securities Exchange Act of 1934. It provides:

> (a) Effect on pending causes of action "The limitation period for any private civil action implied under section 78j(b) of this title [§ 10(b) of the Securities Exchange Act of 1934] that was commenced on or before June 19, 1991, shall be the limitation period provided by the laws applicable in the jurisdiction, including principles of retroactivity, as such laws existed on June 19, 1991.

> (b) Effect on dismissed causes of action "Any private civil action implied under section 78j(b) of this title that was commenced on or before June 19, 1991—

> > (1) which was dismissed as time barred subsequent to June 19, 1991, and

> > (2) which would have been timely filed under the limitation period provided by the laws applicable in the jurisdiction, including principles of retroactivity, as such laws existed on June 19, 1991, shall be reinstated on motion by the plaintiff not later than 60 days after December 19, 1991.

On February 11, 1992, petitioners returned to the District Court and filed a motion to reinstate the action previously dismissed with prejudice. The District Court found that the conditions set out in §§ 27A(b)(1) and (2) were met, so that petitioners' motion was required to be granted by the terms of the statute. It nonetheless denied the motion, agreeing with respondents that § 27A(b) is unconstitutional. The United States Court of Appeals for the Sixth Circuit affirmed. We granted certiorari.[1]

II

Respondents bravely contend that § 27A(b) does not require federal

---

[1] Last Term this Court affirmed, by an equally divided vote, a judgment of the United States Court of Appeals for the Fifth Circuit that held § 27A(b) constitutional. That ruling of course lacks precedential weight.

courts to reopen final judgments, arguing first that the reference to "the laws applicable in the jurisdiction * * * as such laws existed on June 19, 1991" (the day before *Lampf* was decided) may reasonably be construed to refer precisely to the limitations period provided in *Lampf* itself, in which case petitioners' action was time barred even under § 27A. It is true that "[a] judicial construction of a statute is an authoritative statement of what the statute meant before as well as after the decision of the case giving rise to that construction." But respondents' argument confuses the question of what the law *in fact* was on June 19, 1991, with the distinct question of what § 27A *means* by its *reference* to what the law was. We think it entirely clear that it does not mean the law enunciated in *Lampf*, for two independent reasons. First, *Lampf* provides a uniform, national statute of limitations (instead of using the applicable state limitations period, as lower federal courts had previously done.) If the statute referred to *that* law, its reference to the "laws applicable *in the jurisdiction*" (emphasis added) would be quite inexplicable. Second, if the statute refers to the law enunciated in *Lampf* it is utterly without effect, a result to be avoided if possible. It would say, in subsection (a), that the limitation period is what the Supreme Court has held to be the limitation period; and in subsection (b), that suits dismissed as untimely under *Lampf* which were timely under *Lampf* (a null set) shall be reinstated. To avoid a constitutional question by holding that Congress enacted and the President approved a blank sheet of paper would indeed constitute "disingenuous evasion."

As an alternative reason why § 27A(b) does not require the reopening of final judgments, respondents suggest that the subsection applies only to cases still pending in the federal courts when § 27A was enacted. This has only half the defect of the first argument, for it makes only half of § 27A purposeless—§ 27A(b). There is no need to "reinstate" actions that are still pending; § 27A(a) (the new statute of limitations) could and would be applied by the courts of appeals. On respondents' reading, the only consequence of § 27A(b) would be the negligible one of permitting the plaintiff in the pending appeal from a statute-of-limitations dismissal to return *immediately* to the district court, instead of waiting for the court of appeals' reversal. To enable § 27A(b) to achieve such an insignificant consequence, one must disregard the language of the provision, which refers generally to suits "dismissed as time barred." It is perhaps arguable that this does *not* include suits that are not yet *finally* dismissed, *i.e.*, suits still pending on appeal; but there is *no* basis for the contention that it includes *only* those. In short, there is no reasonable construction on which § 27A(b) does not require federal courts to reopen final judgments in suits dismissed with prejudice by virtue of *Lampf*.

III

Respondents submit that § 27A(b) violates both the separation of powers and the Due Process Clause of the Fifth Amendment. Because the latter submission, if correct, might dictate a similar result in a challenge to state legislation under the Fourteenth Amendment, the former is the narrower ground for adjudication of the constitutional questions in the case, and we therefore consider it first. We conclude that in § 27A(b) Congress has exceeded its authority by requiring the federal courts to exercise "the judicial Power of the United States," U.S. CONST., Art. III, § 1, in a manner repugnant to the text, structure and traditions of Article III.

Our decisions to date have identified two types of legislation that require federal courts to exercise the judicial power in a manner that Article III forbids. The first appears in *United States v. Klein*, where we refused to give effect to a statute that was said "[t]o prescribe rules of decision to the Judicial Department of the government in cases pending before it." Whatever the precise scope of *Klein*, however, later decisions have made clear that its prohibition does not take hold when Congress "amend[s] applicable law." Section 27A(b) indisputably does set out substantive legal standards for the Judiciary to apply, and in that sense changes the law (even if solely retroactively). The second type of unconstitutional restriction upon the exercise of judicial power identified by past cases is exemplified by *Hayburn's Case*, which stands for the principle that Congress cannot vest review of the decisions of Article III courts in officials of the Executive Branch. Yet under any application of § 27A(b) only courts are involved; no officials of other departments sit in direct review of their decisions. Section 27A(b) therefore offends neither of these previously established prohibitions.

We think, however, that § 27A(b) offends a postulate of Article III just as deeply rooted in our law as those we have mentioned. Article III establishes a "judicial department" with the "province and duty * * * to say what the law is" in particular cases and controversies. *Marbury v. Madison*. The record of history shows that the Framers crafted this charter of the judicial department with an expressed understanding that it gives the Federal Judiciary the power, not merely to rule on cases, but to *decide* them, subject to review only by superior courts in the Article III hierarchy—with an understanding, in short, that "a judgment conclusively resolves the case" because "a 'judicial Power' is one to render dispositive judgments." Easterbrook, *Presidential Review*, 40 CASE W. RES. L. REV. 905, 926 (1990). By retroactively commanding the federal courts to reopen final judgments, Congress has violated this fundamental principle.

A

The Framers of our Constitution lived among the ruins of a system of intermingled legislative and judicial powers, which had been prevalent in the colonies long before the Revolution, and which after the Revolution had produced factional strife and partisan oppression. In the 17th and 18th centuries colonial assemblies and legislatures functioned as courts of equity of last resort, hearing original actions or providing appellate review of judicial judgments. Often, however, they chose to correct the judicial process through special bills or other enacted legislation. It was common for such legislation not to prescribe a resolution of the dispute, but rather simply to set aside the judgment and order a new trial or appeal. Thus, as described in our discussion of *Hayburn's Case*, such legislation bears not on the problem of interbranch review but on the problem of finality of judicial judgments.

* * *

* * * [A] sense of a sharp necessity to separate the legislative from the judicial power, prompted by the crescendo of legislative interference with private judgments of the courts, triumphed among the Framers of the new Federal Constitution. The Convention made the critical decision to establish a judicial department independent of the Legislative Branch by providing that "the judicial Power of the United States shall be vested in one supreme Court, and in such inferior Courts as the Congress may from time to time ordain and establish." Before and during the debates on ratification, Madison, Jefferson, and Hamilton each wrote of the factional disorders and disarray that the system of legislative equity had produced in the years before the framing; and each thought that the separation of the legislative from the judicial power in the new Constitution would cure them. Madison's Federalist No. 48, the famous description of the process by which "[t]he legislative department is every where extending the sphere of its activity, and drawing all power into its impetuous vortex," referred to the report of the Pennsylvania Council of Censors to show that in that State "cases belonging to the judiciary department [had been] frequently drawn within legislative cognizance and determination." Madison relied as well on Jefferson's Notes on the State of Virginia, which mentioned, as one example of the dangerous concentration of governmental powers into the hands of the legislature, that "the Legislature * * * in many instances decided rights which should have been left to judiciary controversy." ([E]mphasis deleted).[4]

If the need for separation of legislative from judicial power was plain, the principal effect to be accomplished by that separation was even plainer. As Hamilton wrote in his exegesis of Article III, § 1, in Federalist No. 81:

> It is not true * * * that the parliament of Great Britain, or the legislatures of the particular states, can rectify the exceptionable decisions of their respective courts, in any other sense than might be

---

[4] Read in the abstract these public pronouncements might be taken, as the Solicitor General does take them, to disapprove only the practice of having the legislature itself sit as a court of original or appellate jurisdiction. But against the backdrop of history, that reading is untenable. Many, perhaps a plurality, of the instances of legislative equity in the period before the framing simply involved duly enacted laws that nullified judgments so that new trials or judicial rulings on the merits could take place.

done by a future legislature of the United States. The theory neither of the British, nor the state constitutions, authorises the revisal of a judicial sentence, by a legislative act * * *. A legislature without exceeding its province cannot reverse a determination once made, in a particular case; though it may prescribe a new rule for future cases.

The essential balance created by this allocation of authority was a simple one. The Legislature would be possessed of power to "prescrib[e] the rules by which the duties and rights of every citizen are to be regulated," but the power of "[t]he interpretation of the laws" would be "the proper and peculiar province of the courts." The Judiciary would be, "from the nature of its functions, * * * the [department] least dangerous to the political rights of the constitution," not because its acts were subject to legislative correction, but because the binding effect of its acts was limited to particular cases and controversies. Thus, "though individual oppression may now and then proceed from the courts of justice, the general liberty of the people can never be endangered from that quarter: * * * so long as the judiciary remains truly distinct from both the legislative and executive."

Judicial decisions in the period immediately after ratification of the Constitution confirm the understanding that it forbade interference with the final judgments of courts. * * *

The state courts of the era showed a similar understanding of the separation of powers, in decisions that drew little distinction between the federal and state constitutions. * * *

By the middle of the 19th century, the constitutional equilibrium created by the separation of the legislative power to make general law from the judicial power to apply that law in particular cases was so well understood and accepted that it could survive even *Dred Scott v. Sandford.* * * * And the great constitutional scholar Thomas Cooley addressed precisely the question before us in his 1868 treatise: "If the legislature cannot thus indirectly control the action of the courts, by requiring of them a construction of the law according to its own views, it is very plain it cannot do so directly, by setting aside their judgments, compelling them to grant new trials, ordering the discharge of offenders, or directing what particular steps shall be taken in the progress of a judicial inquiry."

B

Section 27A(b) effects a clear violation of the separation-of-powers principle we have just discussed. It is, of course, retroactive legislation, that is, legislation that prescribes what the law was at an earlier time, when the act whose effect is controlled by the legislation occurred—in this case, the filing of the initial Rule 10b-5 action in the District Court. When retroactive legislation requires its own application in a case already finally adjudicated, it does no more and no less than "reverse a determination once made, in a particular case." The Federalist No. 81. Our decisions stemming from *Hayburn's Case*—although their precise holdings are not strictly applicable here—have uniformly provided fair warning that such an act exceeds the powers of Congress. * * * Today those clear statements must either be honored, or else proved false.

It is true, as petitioners contend, that Congress can always revise the judgments of Article III courts in one sense: When a new law makes clear that it is retroactive, an appellate court must apply that law in reviewing judgments still on appeal that were rendered before the law was enacted, and must alter the outcome accordingly. Since that is so, petitioners argue, federal courts must apply the "new" law created by § 27A(b) in finally adjudicated cases as well; for the line that separates lower court judgments that are pending on appeal (or may still be appealed), from lower-court judgments that are final, is determined by statute and so cannot possibly be a *constitutional* line. But a distinction between judgments from which all appeals have been forgone or completed, and judgments that remain on appeal (or subject to being appealed), is implicit in what Article III creates: not a batch of unconnected courts, but a judicial *department* composed of "inferior Courts" and "one supreme Court." Within that hierarchy, the decision of an inferior court is not (unless the time for appeal has expired) the final word of the department as a whole. It is the obligation of the last court in the hierarchy that rules on the case to give effect to Congress's latest enactment, even when that has the effect of overturning the judgment of an inferior court, since each court, at every level, must "decide according to existing laws." Having achieved finality, however, a judicial decision becomes the last word of the judicial department with regard to a particular case or controversy, and Congress may not declare by retroactive legislation that the law applicable *to that very case* was something other than what the courts said it was. Finality of a legal judgment is determined by statute, just as entitlement to a government benefit is a statutory creation; but that no more deprives the former of its constitutional significance for separation-of-powers analysis than it deprives the latter of its significance for due process purposes.

To be sure, § 27A(b) reopens (or directs the reopening of) final judgments in a whole class of cases rather than in a particular suit. We do not see how that makes any difference. The separation-of-powers violation here, if there is any, consists of depriving judicial judgments of the conclusive effect that they had when they were announced, not of acting in a manner—*viz.*, with particular rather than general effect—that is unusual (though, we must note, not impossible) for a legislature. To be sure, a general statute such as this one may reduce the perception that legislative interference with judicial judgments was prompted by individual favoritism; but it is legislative interference with judicial judgments nonetheless. Not favoritism, nor even corruption, but *power* is the object of the separation-of-powers prohibition. The prohibition is violated when an individual final judgment is legislatively rescinded for even the *very best* of reasons, such as the legislature's genuine conviction (supported by all the law professors in the land) that the judgment was wrong; and it is violated 40 times over when 40 final judgments are legislatively dissolved.

It is irrelevant as well that the final judgments reopened by § 27A(b) rested on the bar of a statute of limitations. The rules of finality, both statutory and judge-made, treat a dismissal on statute-of-limitations grounds the same way they treat a dismissal for failure to state a claim, for failure to prove substantive liability, or for failure to prosecute: as a judgment on the merits. Petitioners suggest, directly or by implication, two reasons why a merits judgment based on this particular ground may be uniquely subject to congressional nullification. First, there is the fact that the length and indeed even the very existence of a statute of limitations upon a federal cause of action is entirely subject to congressional control. But virtually *all* of the reasons why a final judgment on the merits is rendered on a federal claim are subject to congressional control. Congress can eliminate, for example, a particular element of a cause of action that plaintiffs have found it difficult to establish; or an evidentiary rule that has often excluded essential testimony; or a rule of offsetting wrong (such as contributory negligence) that has often prevented recovery. To distinguish statutes of limitations on the ground that they are mere creatures of Congress is to distinguish them not at all. The second supposedly distinguishing characteristic of a statute of limitations is that it can be extended, without violating the Due Process Clause, after the cause of the action arose and even after the statute itself has expired. But that also does not set statutes of limitations apart. To mention only one other broad category of judgment-producing legal rule: rules of pleading and proof can similarly be altered after the cause of action arises, and even, if the statute clearly so requires, after they have been applied in a case but before final judgment has been entered. Petitioners' principle would therefore lead to the conclusion that final judgments rendered on the basis of a stringent (or, alternatively, liberal) rule of pleading or proof may be set aside for retrial under a new liberal (or, alternatively, stringent) rule of pleading or proof. This alone provides massive scope for undoing final judgments and would substantially subvert the doctrine of separation of powers.

The central theme of the dissent is a variant on these arguments. The dissent maintains that *Lampf* "announced" a new statute of limitations, in an act of "judicial * * * lawmaking" that "changed the law." That statement, even if relevant, would be wrong. The point decided in *Lampf* had never before been addressed by this Court, and was therefore an open question, no matter what the lower courts had held at the time. But the more important point is that *Lampf* as such is irrelevant to this case. The dissent itself perceives that "[w]e would have the same issue to decide had Congress enacted the *Lampf* rule," and that the *Lampf* rule's genesis in judicial lawmaking rather than, shall we say, legislative lawmaking, "should not affect the separation-of-powers analysis." Just so. The issue here is not the validity or even the source of the legal rule that produced the Article III judgments, but rather the immunity from legislative abrogation of those judgments themselves. The separation-of-powers question before us has nothing to do with *Lampf*, and the dissent's attack on *Lampf* has nothing to do with the question before us.

C

Apart from the statute we review today, we know of no instance in which Congress has attempted to set aside the final judgment of an Article III court by retroactive legislation. That prolonged reticence would be amazing if such interference were not understood to be constitutionally proscribed. The closest analogue that the Government has been able to put forward is the statute at issue in *United States v. Sioux Nation*, 448 U.S. 371, 100 S.Ct. 2716, 65 L.Ed.2d 844 (1980). That law required the Court of Claims " '[n]otwithstanding any other provision of law * * * to review on the merits, without regard to the defense of res judicata or collateral estoppel,' " a Sioux claim for just compensation from the United States—even though the Court of Claims had previously heard and rejected that very claim. We considered and rejected separation-of-powers objections to the statute based upon *Hayburn's Case* and *United States v. Klein*. The basis for our rejection was a line of precedent that stood, we said, for the proposition that "Congress has the power to waive the res judicata effect of a prior judgment entered in the Government's favor on a claim against the United States." And our holding was as narrow as the precedent on which we had relied: "In sum, * * * Congress' mere waiver of the res judicata effect of a prior judicial decision rejecting the validity of a legal claim against the United States does not violate the doctrine of separation of powers."[5]

The Solicitor General suggests that even if *Sioux Nation* is read in accord with its holding, it nonetheless establishes that Congress may require Article III courts to reopen their final judgments, since "if res judicata were compelled by Article III to safeguard the structural independence of the courts, the doctrine would not be subject to waiver by any party litigant." But the proposition that legal defenses based upon doctrines central to the courts' structural independence can never be waived simply does not accord with our cases. Certainly one such doctrine consists of the "judicial Power" to disregard an unconstitutional statute; yet none would suggest that a litigant may never waive the defense that a statute is unconstitutional. What may follow from our holding that the judicial power unalterably includes the power to render final

---

[5] The dissent quotes a passage from the opinion saying that Congress " 'only was providing a forum so that a new judicial review of the Black Hills claim could take place.' " That is quite consistent with the res judicata holding. Any party who waives the defense of res judicata provides a forum for a new judicial review.

judgments, is not that waivers of res judicata are always impermissible, but rather that, as many federal Courts of Appeals have held, waivers of res judicata need not always be accepted—that trial courts may in appropriate cases raise the res judicata bar on their own motion. Waiver subject to the control of the courts themselves would obviously raise no issue of separation of powers, and would be precisely in accord with the language of the decision that the Solicitor General relies upon. We [have] held * * * that, although a litigant had consented to bring a state-law counterclaim before an Article I tribunal, we would nonetheless choose to consider his Article III challenge, because "where these Article III limitations are at issue, notions of consent and waiver cannot be *dispositive*."

Petitioners also rely on a miscellany of decisions upholding legislation that altered rights fixed by the final judgments of non-Article III courts, or administrative agencies, or that altered the prospective effect of injunctions entered by Article III courts. These cases distinguish themselves; nothing in our holding today calls them into question. Petitioners rely on general statements from some of these cases that legislative annulment of final judgments is not an exercise of judicial power. But even if it were our practice to decide cases by weight of prior dicta, we would find the many dicta that reject congressional power to revise the judgments of *Article III* courts to be the more instructive authority.

Finally, petitioners liken § 27A(b) to Federal Rule of Civil Procedure 60(b), which authorizes courts to relieve parties from a final judgment for grounds such as excusable neglect, newly discovered evidence, fraud, or "any other reason justifying relief * * * ." We see little resemblance. Rule 60(b), which authorizes discretionary judicial revision of judgments in the listed situations and in other "extraordinary circumstances," does not impose any legislative mandate-to-reopen upon the courts, but merely reflects and confirms the courts' own inherent and discretionary power, "firmly established in English practice long before the foundation of our Republic," to set aside a judgment whose enforcement would work inequity. Thus, Rule 60(b), and the tradition that it embodies, would be relevant refutation of a claim that reopening a final judgment is always a denial of property without due process; but they are irrelevant to the claim that legislative instruction to reopen impinges upon the independent constitutional authority of the courts.

The dissent promises to provide "[a] few contemporary examples" of statutes retroactively requiring final judgments to be reopened, "to demonstrate that [such statutes] are ordinary products of the exercise of legislative power." That promise is not kept. The relevant retroactivity, of course, consists not of the requirement that there be set aside a judgment that has been rendered *prior to its being setting aside*—for example, a statute passed today which says that all default judgments rendered in the future may be reopened within 90 days after their entry. In that sense, *all* requirements to reopen are "retroactive," and the designa-

tion is superfluous. Nothing we say today precludes a law such as that.
The finality that a court can pronounce is no more than what the law in
existence at the time of judgment will permit it to pronounce. If the law
then applicable says that the judgment may be reopened for certain reasons, that limitation is built into the judgment itself, and its finality is so
conditioned. The present case, however, involves a judgment that Congress subjected to a reopening requirement which did not exist when the
judgment was pronounced. The dissent provides not a single clear prior
instance of such congressional action.

The dissent cites, first, Rule 60(b), which it describes as a "familiar
remedial measure." As we have just discussed, Rule 60(b) does not provide a new remedy at all, but is simply the recitation of pre-existing judicial power. The same is true of another of the dissent's examples, 28
U.S.C. § 2255, which provides federal prisoners a statutory motion to
vacate a federal sentence. This procedure " 'restates, clarifies and sim-
plifies the procedure in the nature of the ancient writ of error *coram no-
bis.*' " It is meaningless to speak of these statutes as applying "retroactively," since they simply codified judicial practice that pre-existed.
Next, the dissent cites the provision of the Soldiers' and Sailors' Civil
Relief Act of 1940, which authorizes courts, upon application, to reopen
judgments against members of the Armed Forces entered while they
were on active duty. It could not be clearer, however, that this provision
was not retroactive. It says: "If any judgment *shall be rendered* in any
action or proceeding governed by this section against any person in military service during the period of such service * * * *such judgment* may
* * * be opened * * * ." (Emphasis added).

The dissent also cites a provision of the Handicapped Children's Protection Act of 1986, which provided for the award of attorney's fees under
the Education for All Handicapped Children Act of 1975. This changed
the law regarding attorney's fees under the Education for All Handicapped Children Act, after our decision in *Smith v. Robinson* found such
fees to be unavailable. The provision of the Statutes at Large adopting
this amendment to the United States Code specified, in effect, that it
would apply not only to proceedings brought after its enactment, but also
to proceedings pending at the time of, or brought after, the decision in
Smith. The amendment says nothing about reopening final judgments,
and the retroactivity provision may well mean nothing more than that it
applies not merely to new suits commenced after the date of its enactment, but also to *previously* filed (but not yet terminated) suits of the
specified sort. This interpretation would be consistent with the only case
the dissent cites, which involved a court-entered consent decree not yet
fully executed. Alternatively, the statute can perhaps be understood to
create a new cause of action for attorney's fees attributable to already
concluded litigation. That would create no separation-of-powers problem, and would be consistent with this Court's view that "[a]ttorney's fee
determinations * * * are 'collateral to the main cause of action' and

'uniquely separable from the cause of action to be proved at trial.' "

The dissent's perception that retroactive reopening provisions are to be found all about us is perhaps attributable to its inversion of the statutory presumption regarding retroactivity. Thus, it asserts that Rule 60(b) must be retroactive, since "[n]ot a single word in its text suggests that it does not apply to judgments entered prior to its effective date." This reverses the traditional rule, confirmed only last Term, that statutes do *not* apply retroactively *unless* Congress expressly states that they do. The dissent adds that "the traditional construction of remedial measures * * * support[s] construing [Rule 60(b)] to apply to past as well as future judgments." But [we have rejected] reliance on the vaguely remedial purpose of a statute to defeat the presumption against retroactivity * * * .

The dissent sets forth a number of hypothetical horribles flowing from our assertedly "rigid holding"—for example, the inability to set aside a civil judgment that has become final during a period when a natural disaster prevented the timely filing of a certiorari petition. That is horrible not because of our holding, but because the underlying statute *itself* enacts a "rigid" jurisdictional bar to entertaining untimely civil petitions. Congress could undoubtedly enact *prospective* legislation permitting, or indeed requiring, this Court to make equitable exceptions to an otherwise applicable rule of finality, just as district courts do pursuant to Rule 60(b). It is no indication whatever of the invalidity of the constitutional rule which we announce, that it produces unhappy consequences when a legislature lacks foresight, and acts belatedly to remedy a deficiency in the law. That is a routine result of constitutional rules.

* * *

Ultimately, the concurrence agrees with our judgment only "[b]ecause the law before us embodies risks of the very sort that our Constitution's 'separation of powers' prohibition seeks to avoid." But the doctrine of separation of powers is a *structural safeguard* rather than a remedy to be applied only when specific harm, or risk of specific harm, can be identified. In its major features (of which the conclusiveness of judicial judgments is assuredly one) it is a prophylactic device, establishing high walls and clear distinctions because low walls and vague distinctions will not be judicially defensible in the heat of interbranch conflict. * * * We think legislated invalidation of judicial judgments deserves the same categorical treatment accorded by *Chadha* to congressional invalidation of executive action. The delphic alternative suggested by the concurrence (the setting aside of judgments is all right so long as Congress does not "impermissibly tr[y] to *apply*, as well as *make*, the law,") simply prolongs doubt and multiplies confrontation. Separation of powers, a distinctively American political doctrine, profits from the advice authored by a distinctively American poet: Good fences make good neighbors.

* * *

We know of no previous instance in which Congress has enacted retroactive legislation requiring an Article III court to set aside a final judgment, and for good reason. The Constitution's separation of legislative and judicial powers denies it the authority to do so. Section 27A(b) is unconstitutional to the extent that it requires federal courts to reopen final judgments entered before its enactment. The judgment of the Court of Appeals is affirmed.

It is so ordered.

JUSTICE STEVENS, with whom JUSTICE GINSBURG joins, dissenting.

* * *

Throughout our history, Congress has passed laws that allow courts to reopen final judgments. Such laws characteristically apply to judgments entered before as well as after their enactment. When they apply retroactively, they may raise serious due process questions,[2] but the Court has never invalidated such a law on separation-of-powers grounds until today. Indeed, only last Term we recognized Congress' ample *power* to enact a law that "in effect 'restored' rights that [a party] reasonably and in good faith thought he possessed before the surprising announcement" of a Supreme Court decision. We conditioned our unambiguous restatement of the proposition that "Congress had the power to enact legislation that had the practical effect of restoring the status quo retroactively" only on Congress' clear expression of its intent to do so.

* * *

I

Respondents conducted a public offering of common stock in 1983. Petitioners, suing on behalf of themselves and other purchasers of the stock, filed a 10b-5 action in 1987 in the United States District Court for the Eastern District of Kentucky, alleging violations of substantive federal rules that had been in place since 1934. Respondents moved to dis-

---

[2] Because the Court finds a separation-of-powers violation, it does not reach respondents' alternative theory that § 27A(b) denied them due process under the Fifth Amendment, a theory the Court of Appeals did not identify as an alternative ground for its holding. In my judgment, the statute easily survives a due process challenge. Section 27A(b) is rationally related to a legitimate public purpose. Given the existence of statutes and rules, such as Rule 60(b), that allow courts to reopen apparently "final" judgments in various circumstances, respondents cannot assert an inviolable "vested right" in the District Court's post-*Lampf* dismissal of petitioners' claims. In addition, § 27A(b) did not upset any "settled expectations" of respondents. * * * Before 1991 no one could have relied either on the yet-to-be-announced rule in *Lampf* or on the Court's unpredictable decision to apply that rule retroactively. All of the reliance interests that ordinarily support a presumption against retroactivity militate in favor of allowing retroactive application of § 27A.

miss the complaint as untimely because petitioners had filed it more than three years after the events in dispute. At that time, settled law in Kentucky and elsewhere in the United States directed federal courts to determine statutes of limitations applicable to 10b-5 actions by reference to state law. The relevant Kentucky statute provided a 3-year limitations period, which petitioners contended ran from the time the alleged fraud was or should have been discovered. A Magistrate agreed with petitioners and recommended denial of respondents' motion to dismiss, but by 1991 the District Court had not yet ruled on that issue. The factual question whether petitioners should have discovered respondents' alleged 10b-5 violations more than three years before they filed suit remained open for decision by an Article III judge on June 20, 1991.

On that day, this Court's decision in *Lampf* changed the law. The Court concluded that every 10b-5 action is time barred unless brought within three years of the alleged violation and one year of its discovery. Moreover, it applied that novel rule to pending cases. As Justice O'Connor pointed out in her dissent, the Court held the plaintiffs' suit "time barred under a limitations period that did not exist before," a holding that "depart[ed] drastically from our established practice and inflict[ed] an injustice on the [plaintiffs]." The inequitable consequences of *Lampf* reached beyond the parties to that case, injuring a large class of litigants that includes petitioners. Without resolving the factual issue that would have determined the timeliness of petitioners' complaint before *Lampf*, the District Court dismissed the instant action as untimely under the new limitations period dictated by this Court. Because *Lampf* had deprived them of any non-frivolous basis for an appeal, petitioners acquiesced in the dismissal, which therefore became final on September 12, 1991.

Congress responded to *Lampf* by passing § 27A, which became effective on December 19, 1991. The statute changed the substantive limitations law, restoring the pre-*Lampf* limitations rule for two categories of 10b-5 actions that had been pending on June 19, 1991. Subsection (a) of § 27A applies to cases that were still pending on December 19, 1991. The courts of appeals have uniformly upheld the constitutionality of that subsection, and its validity is not challenged in this case. Subsection (b) applies to actions, like the instant case, that (1) were dismissed after June 19, 1991, and (2) would have been timely under the pre-*Lampf* regime. This subsection authorized the district courts to reinstate dismissed cases if the plaintiff so moved within 60 days after the effective date of § 27A. The amendment was not self-executing: Unless the plaintiff both filed a timely motion for reinstatement and then satisfied the court that the complaint had been timely filed under applicable pre-*Lampf* law, the dismissal would remain in effect.

In this case petitioners made the required showing, but the District Court refused to reinstate their case. Instead, it held § 27A(b) unconstitutional. The Court of Appeals for the Sixth Circuit, contrary to an earlier decision of the Fifth Circuit, affirmed.

* * *

III

The lack of precedent for the Court's holding is not, of course, a sufficient reason to reject it. Correct application of separation-of-powers principles, however, confirms that the Court has reached the wrong result. As our most recent major pronouncement on the separation of powers noted, "we have never held that the Constitution requires that the three branches of Government 'operate with absolute independence.' " Rather, our jurisprudence reflects "Madison's flexible approach to separation of powers." In accepting Madison's conception rather than any "hermetic division among the Branches," "we have upheld statutory provisions that to some degree commingle the functions of the Branches, but that pose no danger of either aggrandizement or encroachment." Today's holding does not comport with these ideals.

Section 27A shares several important characteristics with the remedial statutes discussed above. It does not decide the merits of any issue in any litigation but merely removes an impediment to judicial decision on the merits. The impediment it removes would have produced inequity because the statute's beneficiaries did not cause the impediment. It requires a party invoking its benefits to file a motion within a specified time and to convince a court that the statute entitles the party to relief. Most important, § 27A(b) specifies both a substantive rule to govern the reopening of a class of judgments—the pre-*Lampf* limitations rule—and a procedure for the courts to apply in determining whether a particular motion to reopen should be granted. These characteristics are quintessentially legislative. They reflect Congress' fealty to the separation of powers and its intention to avoid the sort of *ad hoc* excesses the Court rightly criticizes in colonial legislative practice. In my judgment, all of these elements distinguish § 27A from "judicial" action and confirm its constitutionality. A sensible analysis would at least consider them in the balance.

Instead, the Court myopically disposes of § 27A(b) by holding that Congress has no power to "requir[e] an Article III court to set aside a final judgment." That holding must mean one of two things. It could mean that Congress may not impose a mandatory duty on a court to set aside a judgment even if the court makes a particular finding, such as a finding of fraud or mistake, that Congress has not made. Such a rule, however, could not be correct. Although Rule 60(b), for example, merely authorizes federal courts to set aside judgments after making appropriate findings, Acts of Congress characteristically set standards that judges are obligated to enforce. Accordingly, Congress surely could add to Rule 60(b) certain instances in which courts *must* grant relief from final judgments if they make particular findings—for example, a finding that a member of the jury accepted a bribe from the prevailing party. The Court, therefore, must mean to hold that Congress may not *unconditionally* require an Article III court to set aside a final judgment. That rule is both unwise and beside the point of this case.

A simple hypothetical example will illustrate the practical failings of the Court's new rule. Suppose Congress, instead of endorsing the new limitations rule fashioned by the Court in *Lampf*, had decided to return to the pre-*Lampf* regime (or perhaps to enact a longer uniform statute). Subsection (a) of § 27 would simply have provided that the law in effect prior to June 19, 1991, would govern the timeliness of all 10b-5 actions. In that event, subsection (b) would still have been necessary to remedy the injustice caused by this Court's failure to exempt pending cases from its new rule. In my judgment, the statutory correction of the inequitable flaw in *Lampf* would be appropriate remedial legislation whether or not Congress had endorsed that decision's substantive limitations rule. The Court, unfortunately, appears equally consistent: Even though the class of dismissed 10b-5 plaintiffs in my hypothetical would have been subject to the same substantive rule as all other 10b-5 plaintiffs, the Court's reasoning would still reject subsection (b) as an impermissible exercise of "judicial" power.

The majority's rigid holding unnecessarily hinders the Government from addressing difficult issues that inevitably arise in a complex society. This Court, for example, lacks power to enlarge the time for filing petitions for certiorari in a civil case after 90 days from the entry of final judgment, no matter how strong the equities. If an Act of God, such as a flood or an earthquake, sufficiently disrupted communications in a particular area to preclude filing for several days, the majority's reasoning would appear to bar Congress from addressing the resulting inequity. If Congress passed remedial legislation that retroactively granted movants from the disaster area extra time to file petitions or motions for extensions of time to file, today's holding presumably would compel us to strike down the legislation as an attack on the finality of judgments. Such a ruling, like today's holding, would gravely undermine federal courts' traditional power "to set aside a judgment whose enforcement would work inequity."[16]

Even if the rule the Court announces today were sound, it would not control the case before us. In order to obtain the benefit of § 27A, petitioners had to file a timely motion and persuade the District Court they had timely filed their complaint under pre-*Lampf* law. In the judgment of the District Court, petitioners satisfied those conditions. Congress reasonably could have assumed, indeed must have expected, that some

---

[16] The Court also appears to bar retroactive application of changes in the criminal law. Its reasoning suggests that, for example, should Congress one day choose to abolish the federal death penalty, the new statute could not constitutionally save a death row inmate from execution if his conviction had become final before the statute was passed.

movants under § 27A(b) would fail to do so. The presence of an important condition that the District Court must find a movant to have satisfied before it may reopen a judgment distinguishes § 27A from the unconditional congressional directives the Court appears to forbid.

Moreover, unlike the colonial legislative commands on which the Court bases its holding, § 27A directed action not in "a civil case," but in a large category of civil cases.[17] The Court declares that a legislative direction to reopen a class of 40 cases is 40 times as bad as a direction to reopen a single final judgment because "power is the object of the separation-of-powers prohibition." This self-evident observation might be salient if § 27A(b) unconditionally commanded courts to reopen judgments even absent findings that the complaints were timely under pre-*Lampf* law. But Congress did not decide—and could not know how any court would decide—the timeliness issue in any particular case in the affected category. Congress, therefore, had no way to identify which particular plaintiffs would benefit from § 27A. It merely enacted a law that applied a substantive rule to a class of litigants, specified a procedure for invoking the rule, and left particular outcomes to individualized judicial determinations—a classic exercise of legislative power.

"All we seek," affirmed a sponsor of § 27A, "is to give the victims [of securities fraud] a fair day in court." A statute, such as § 27A, that removes an unanticipated and unjust impediment to adjudication of a large class of claims on their merits poses no danger of "aggrandizement or encroachment."[19] This is particularly true for § 27A in light of Congress' historic primacy over statutes of limitations. The statute contains several checks against the danger of congressional overreaching. The Court in *Lampf* undertook a legislative function. Essentially, it supplied a statute of limitations for 10b-5 actions. The Court, however, failed to adopt the transition rules that ordinarily attend alterations shortening the time to sue. Congress, in § 27A, has supplied those rules. The statute reflects the ability of two coequal branches to cooperate in providing for the impartial application of legal rules to particular disputes. The

---

[17] At the time Congress was considering the bill that became § 27A, a House Subcommittee reported that *Lampf* had resulted in the dismissal of 15 cases, involving thousands of plaintiffs in every State (of whom over 32,000 had been identified) and claims totaling over $692.25 million. In addition, motions to dismiss based on *Lampf* were then pending in 17 cases involving thousands of plaintiffs in every State and claims totaling over $4.578 billion.

[19] Today's decision creates a new irony of judicial legislation. A challenge to the constitutionality of § 27A(a) could not turn on the sanctity of final judgments. Section 27A(a) benefits litigants who had filed appeals that *Lampf* rendered frivolous; petitioners and other law-abiding litigants whose claims *Lampf* rendered untimely had acquiesced in the dismissal of their actions. By striking down § 27A(b) on a ground that would leave § 27A(a) intact, the Court indulges litigants who protracted proceedings but shuts the courthouse door to litigants who proceeded with diligence and respect for the *Lampf* judgment.

Court's mistrust of such cooperation ill serves the separation of powers.[21]

IV

The Court has drawn the wrong lesson from the Framers' disapproval of colonial legislatures' appellate review of judicial decisions. The Framers rejected that practice, not out of a mechanistic solicitude for "final judgments," but because they believed the impartial application of rules of law, rather than the will of the majority, must govern the disposition of individual cases and controversies. Any legislative interference in the adjudication of the merits of a particular case carries the risk that political power will supplant evenhanded justice, whether the interference occurs before or after the entry of final judgment. Section 27A(b) neither commands the reinstatement of any particular case nor directs any result on the merits. Congress recently granted a special benefit to a single litigant in a pending civil rights case, but the Court saw no need even to grant certiorari to review that disturbing legislative favor. In an ironic counterpoint, the Court today places a higher priority on protecting the Republic from the restoration to a large class of litigants of the opportunity to have Article III courts resolve the merits of their claims.

"We must remember that the machinery of government would not work if it were not allowed a little play in its joints." The three Branches must cooperate in order to govern. We should regard favorably, rather than with suspicious hostility, legislation that enables the judiciary to overcome impediments to the performance of its mission of administering justice impartially, even when, as here, this Court has created the impediment.[23] Rigid rules often make good law, but judgments in areas such as the review of potential conflicts among the three coequal

---

[21] Although I agree with Justice Breyer's general approach to the separation-of-powers issue, I believe he gives insufficient weight to two important features of § 27A. First, he fails to recognize that the statute restored a preexisting rule of law in order to remedy the manifest injustice produced by the Court's retroactive application of *Lampf.* The only " 'substantial deprivation' " Congress imposed on defendants was that properly filed lawsuits proceed to decisions on the merits. Second, he understates the class of defendants burdened by § 27A: He finds the statute underinclusive because it provided no remedy for potential plaintiffs who may have failed to file timely actions in reliance on pre-*Lampf* limitations law, but he denies the importance of § 27A(a), which provided a remedy for plaintiffs who appealed dismissals after *Lampf.* The coverage of § 27A is coextensive with the retroactive application of the general rule announced in *Lampf.* If Congress had enacted a statute providing that the *Lampf* rule should apply to all cases filed after the statute's effective date and that the pre-*Lampf* rule should apply to all cases filed before that date, Justice Breyer could not reasonably condemn the statute as special legislation. The only difference between such a statute and § 27A is that § 27A covered all cases pending on the date of *Lampf*—June 20, 1991—rather than on the effective date of the statute—December 19, 1991. In my opinion, § 27A has sufficient generality to avoid the characteristics of a bill of attainder.

[23] Of course, neither the majority nor I would alter its analysis had Congress, rather than the Court, enacted the *Lampf* rule without any exemption for pending cases, then later tried to remedy such unfairness by enacting § 27A. Thus, the Court's attribution of § 27A to "the legislature's genuine conviction (supported by all the law professors in the land) that [*Lampf*] was wrong" is quite beside the point.

Branches of the Federal Government partake of art as well as science. That is why we have so often reiterated the insight of Justice Jackson:

> The actual art of governing under our Constitution does not and cannot conform to judicial definitions of the power of any of its branches based on isolated clauses or even single Articles torn from context. While the Constitution diffuses power the better to secure liberty, it also contemplates that practice will integrate the dispersed powers into a workable government. It enjoins upon its branches separateness but interdependence, autonomy but reciprocity.

We have the authority to hold that Congress has usurped a judicial prerogative, but even if this case were doubtful I would heed Justice Iredell's admonition that "the Court will never resort to that authority, but in a clear and urgent case." An appropriate regard for the interdependence of Congress and the judiciary amply supports the conclusion that § 27A(b) reflects constructive legislative cooperation rather than a usurpation of judicial prerogatives.

Accordingly, I respectfully dissent.

Notes and Questions

1. *Plaut* is different from the other cases discussed in this chapter because it clearly does not involve any attempt by Congress to limit the subject-matter jurisdiction of the federal courts as such. It does, however, concern limits on Congress's ability to control judicial authority. Congress attempted to mandate the results in several federal court actions, and the Supreme Court found the attempt unconstitutional on separation-of-powers grounds. Is the decision analogous to *Klein*? Why or why not? Does *Plaut* support the notion that the separation of powers restricts Congress's ability to limit the jurisdiction of the federal courts? If so, describe the restriction.

2. *Plaut* shows the impact of the Case-or-Controversy Clause (discussed in Chapter 1) in a new light. In *Hayburn's Case*, the Clause prevented the Supreme Court from giving advice to the other branches. Here, rather than circumscribing the judiciary, the Clause protects an area from incursion by the political branches. Read together, these cases demonstrate that the Case-or-Controversy Clause defines a boundary between mutually exclusive areas of federal power.

3. The boundary may, however, be movable. Congress certainly can define cases or controversies through its control over substantive law. When Congress creates new substantive rights that include private rights of action, for example, it expands the reach of the Case-or-Controversy Clause. It remains to decide when the boundary becomes fixed.

Justice Scalia's opinion seems to acknowledge that Congress can affect pending cases, changing the substantive law in a manner that controls pending cases, including those on appeal. *Ex parte McCardle* is an example of this power. Why is a congressional attempt to affect the result in a case like *McCardle* less of an intrusion on the judiciary's exclusive power over cases or controversies than the congressional attempt here? Are you satisfied with the Court's explanation?

Perhaps the Case-or-Controversy Clause really describes three areas: 1) an area outside of the Clause, closed to the courts because there is no case or controversy, as exemplified by *Hayburn's Case* and *Muskrat v. United States*, 2) an area within the Clause in which the political branches and the judiciary can both act (and in which the former can affect the latter's ability to act), exemplified by *Ex parte McCardle*, and 3) an area within the Clause from which the political branches are excluded, as exemplified by *Plaut*, though the judiciary may still act (for example, under Rule 60 or what Justice Scalia calls the judiciary's "inherent" power).

4. Part of the majority's job is to distinguish *Sioux Nation*, in which Congress allowed the plaintiff to bring an already adjudicated action a second time, notwithstanding res judicata. If Congress had parroted the *Sioux Nation* statute here, purporting to permit "review on the merits, without regard to any defense based upon either res judicata or limitation of the time in which to commence an action," would the Court have come out the other way? If so, does *Plaut* merely represent a legislative drafting blunder? If not, what distinguishes *Plaut* from *Sioux Nation*?

5. The majority notes that "waivers of res judicata need not always be accepted." When will or should the courts decline to permit waiver of the defense? What standards do or should govern the decision? To the extent res judicata is a doctrine "central to the courts' structural independence," therefore permitting the courts to refuse to allow waiver, does that suggest that res judicata is part and parcel of defining a case or controversy within the meaning of Article III? If that is so, when is res judicata part of Article III and thereby not waivable? What can take it out of Article III so that it becomes waivable?

6. Justice Scalia and the majority decline to recognize Rule 60 as a legislative authorization to reopen final judgments, arguing that the Rule merely reflects the courts' inherent discretionary power over their own judgments. Does that argument read Rule 60 to be "utterly without effect, a result to be avoided if possible," as Justice Scalia said with respect to petitioners' reading of § 27A? Isn't Justice Scalia trying to have it both ways? If Rule 60 does nothing at all, then it seems to be subject to the vice he condemns (perhaps more so, given that the Court itself promulgates the Federal Rules of Civil Procedure). If Rule 60 does in some respect affect the judiciary's power with respect to final judgments, then it provides more support for petitioners than the Court acknowledges.

7. The majority seems to draw a sharp line between cases that are pending (including on appeal) and those in which no further action is possible. In effect, Justice Scalia takes the position that the judicial department has not spoken until a case is no longer subject to judicial action.

a) Given that Rule 60 permits (or, in Justice Scalia's terms, confirms the inherent power of) the judiciary to reopen judgments, when can one say with certainty that the judicial department has spoken? After all, the Rule itself contemplates judicial revision in some cases more than one year after the entry of judgment.

b) Is it so obvious that a judgment is not a judicial department decision until there are no further possibilities of judicial action? Certainly that is not universally true. In *Federated Department Stores v. Moitie*, 452 U.S. 394, 101 S.Ct. 2424, 69 L.Ed.2d 103 (1981), the Court's opinion by then-Justice Rehnquist made clear that a judgment on appeal is entitled to full res judicata recognition, reaffirming *Reed v. Allen*, 286 U.S. 191, 52 S.Ct. 532, 76 L.Ed. 1054 (1932):

> [A]n "erroneous conclusion" reached by the court in the first suit does not deprive the defendants in the second action "of their right to rely upon the plea of res judicata * * * . A judgment merely voidable because based upon an erroneous view of the law is not open to collateral attack, but can be corrected only by a direct review and not by bringing another action upon the same cause [of action]."

In the majority's view, an erroneous judgment is open to collateral *legislative* attack as long as it is on appeal or is appealable. Can that position be reconciled with the Court's twice-expressed disinclination to permit collateral *judicial* attack on such a judgment?

8. The dissent also has its problems. Are there any limits to Congress's ability to affect judgments that without legislative action would be regarded as final? The dissent attempts to distinguish statutes like that in *Plaut* from illegitimate legislative interference on the ground that the *Plaut* statute does not seek to determine the merits of the litigation, but simply to ensure that the judiciary reaches the merits. Are you persuaded?

9. Title 18 U.S.C. § 3184 sets out the procedures to be followed when a foreign country seeks to have the United States extradite an individual charged with committing a crime in that country. A federal judge conducts a hearing to determine whether the statutory prerequisites to extradition have been established. Those requirements are: (1) the offense charged is extraditable under the applicable treaty; (2) the criminal conduct alleged is unlawful not only in the requesting country, but the United States as well; and (3) there is probable cause to believe that the individual did commit the crime. If the judge concludes that all of these criteria have been met, she certifies the accused as extraditable. The Secretary of State then has sole discretion as to whether actually to extradite. The statute permits the Secretary to decide not to extradite for no reason or for any reason, including a determination that the judge erroneously concluded that the statutory prerequisites were met. If the judge concludes that all of the criteria have not been met, the individual is released. However, the judge's finding of non-extraditability has no res judicata effect, and there is no limit on the number of times the government can seek extradition of the same individual on the same charges. There are no provisions for judicial appeals of extraditability determinations. Essentially the same procedures have been in effect for over 150 years.

Is this statutory scheme vulnerable to constitutional attack under *Plaut* and *Hayburn's Case*? Or is this scheme distinguishable because extradition involves political and foreign policy judgments, which are uniquely within the purview of the Executive Branch? If not, can the scheme be amended to allow the Executive Branch to exercise its judgment without violating separation of powers concerns? Or is the decision of whether the individual is extraditable analogous to a magistrate's decision on an application for a search warrant? Such decisions are not given res judicata effect, and it is not generally thought that a decision by a law enforcement official not to execute a warrant violates separation of powers. *Compare Lobue v. Christopher*, 893 F.Supp. 65 (D.D.C. 1995), *rev'd on other grounds*, 82 F.3d 1081 (D.C.Cir. 1996) *with Cherry v. Warden*, 1995 WL 598986 (S.D.N.Y. 1995).

10. The Prison Litigation Reform Act of 1995, codified as scattered sections of Titles 18, 28 and 42 U.S.C. is one of the newest statutes to raise separation-of-powers problems similar to those in *Plaut* and *Klein*.

a) On its face, the statute mandates vacating judgments that are "final" in the sense that the parties could have, and indeed may have, appealed (under 28 U.S.C. § 1291) the relief that the district court ordered. In response to the Act's passage, prison authorities in several states moved to terminate relief granted in previous litigation. Prisoners' representatives opposed the motions on the ground that the PLRA's authorization of such termination unconstitutionally intrudes upon Article III courts and their final judgments.

Consider first the potential *Plaut* problems. A court may properly modify an equitable decree when there has been a significant change in the factual or legal circumstances that make it inequitable to give the original order continued prospective application. Do you think 28 U.S.C. § 3626(b) violates the rule of *Plaut*? For *Plaut* purposes, should the courts distinguish between "final" judgments and "executory" judgments? *See Benjamin v. Jacobson*, 172 F.3d 144 (2d Cir. 1999) (en banc); *Taylor v. United States*, 181 F.3d 1017 (9th Cir. 1999) (en banc). Does it matter whether the underlying claims rest upon the Constitution rather than upon federal statutes?

b) Section 3626(e)(2) appears to direct a court to stay existing injunctive relief when the state has made a motion to terminate that relief pursuant to § 3626(b). Does the statute permit a court to exercise any discretion as to whether to enter the stay? *See Hadix v. Johnson*, 144 F.3d 925 (6th Cir. 1998). If it does not, does it then constitute a legislative incursion into the judicial process in violation of *Klein* or *Plaut*? *See French v. Duckworth*, 178 F.3d 437 (7th Cir. 1999).

c) With respect to *Klein*, do the provisions of § 3626(a) violate its rule? Has Congress permissibly prescribed a substantive standard that applies to pending cases, or has it endeavored to tell the federal courts how to weigh evidence and determine facts? *See Imprisoned Citizens Union v. Ridge*, 169 F.3d 178 (3d Cir. 1999). With respect to the Act as a whole, do you think Congress wanted to influence the outcome this particular kind of dispute? Assuming that it did, is there anything improper about that?

How should one draw the line between permissible—even desirable—

congressional involvement in formulation of substantive social policies and impermissible congressional involvement in the courts' function as adjudicators of particular disputes under the law? To what extent should *Plaut* and *Klein* limit Congress's undoubted entitlement to change substantive and jurisdictional law?

Chapter 3

FEDERAL QUESTION JURISDICTION

A. INTRODUCTION

The United States' legal system is federal; state and national governments exist side by side. The Constitution allocates power in some cases exclusively to the states or the federal government, but often to both concurrently. The scope of federal jurisdiction greatly affects the relationship between the federal and state governments. If federal jurisdiction is broad, cases that would otherwise be in the state courts can be brought in the federal courts, thus diminishing the role of the state courts. On the other hand, if federal jurisdiction is narrowly circumscribed, state power increases proportionally to the number of cases forced into the state courts.

Moreover, it is not just a question of numbers. The power to adjudicate a case often necessarily includes the power to adjudicate issues from the "other" level of government. Many cases present issues of federal and state law. The broader federal jurisdiction, the more hybrid cases and therefore the more state law issues the federal courts will adjudicate. This increases federal influence on state law. Conversely, if federal jurisdiction were narrower, state courts would adjudicate more hybrid cases and have a correspondingly greater influence on federal law.

Finally, the court hearing a case necessarily makes choice-of-law decisions about whether federal or state law applies to each issue. As a practical matter, of course, for many issues the choice is so obvious that one never consciously considers the question. For example, in a negligence action between citizens of the same state, that state rather than federal law governs the standard of care is so plain that no discussion of choice of law ensues. Nonetheless, the choices are being made, even if *sub silentio*. Although this process is primarily important with respect to the existence and scope of federal common law, it is also significant for subject matter jurisdiction, since the jurisdictional decision will determine whether a federal or state court will make the choice-of-law decisions. Thus, a federal or state court to some extent determines for itself the questions to which it will apply the law of the "other" system.

Article III, § 2 of the Constitution establishes the scope of possible jurisdiction over cases involving questions of federal law.[1] Note, however, that the judicial power described in Article III, § 2, cl. 1 is not self-executing. Compare that clause with the next,[2] which, rather than describing the reach of the judicial power generally, vests jurisdiction in a named court. Under Article III, the inferior federal courts need not even have existed, and Art. III, § 2, cl. 1 has always been understood to describe the power that Congress may, if it wishes, vest in the federal courts.[3]

Except for a brief period in 1801–02, Congress did not confer general federal question jurisdiction on the lower federal courts until 1875.[4] It is not clear whether Congress intended to grant the full scope of Article III jurisdiction to the federal trial courts, but note the similarity of language in the two provisions.[5] The only contemporaneous comment was made

---

[1] "The judicial Power shall extend to all Cases, in Law and Equity, arising under this Constitution, the Laws of the United States, and Treaties made, or which shall be made, under their Authority * * *."

[2] "In all Cases affecting Ambassadors, other public Ministers and Consuls, and those in which a State shall be a Party, the Supreme Court shall have original Jurisdiction." U.S. Const. art. III, § 2, cl. 2.

[3] This is why it is necessary, in order to find subject matter jurisdiction in the inferior federal courts, to find a statute conferring the jurisdiction in addition to finding that the case falls within those described in Article III, § 2. A case merely within Article III does not by that fact alone gain entry to the district court. Were that not so, for example, Congress' attempt to limit diversity jurisdiction to cases exceeding $75,000 would be unavailing.

[4] The common view is that Congress did enact a few specialized grants of jurisdiction for the federal trial courts from time to time before 1875. *E.g.* Act of Sept. 24, 1789, ch. 20, § 26, 1 Stat. 73, 87 (jurisdiction over cases involving federal penalties and forfeitures); *id.* at 77 (jurisdiction over tort suits brought by aliens under international law or federal treaty); Act of April 10, 1790, ch. 7, § 5, 1 Stat. 109, 111 (jurisdiction over wrongfully secured patents); Act of Feb. 21, 1793, § 6, 1 Stat. 318, 322 (patent infringement actions). From time to time, Congress permitted removal of cases of particular federal interest, especially those involving direct state challenges to federal power. *E.g.* Act of Feb. 4, 1815, ch. 31, § 3, 3 Stat. 195, 196 (actions against federal officials collecting war revenue); Act of Mar. 2, 1833, ch. 57, § 3, 4 Stat. 632, 633 (actions against federal officials for acts done pursuant to federal revenue laws). In the aftermath of the Civil War, some of the shift of power away from the states to the federal government was effected in jurisdictional statutes. *E.g.* Act of Apr. 9, 1866, ch. 31, 14 Stat. 27 (Civil Rights Act of 1866); Act of July 27, 1866, ch. 288, 14 Stat. 306 (general civil cause removal statute for state actions seeking more than $500 from non-citizens); Act of Mar. 2, 1867, ch. 196, 14 Stat. 558 (removal by non-citizens (plaintiff or defendant) upon showing of local prejudice); Act of Feb. 28, 1871, ch. 94, §§ 15–16, 16 Stat. 433, 439–40 (cases involving voting registration irregularities). Professor Doernberg contests that view. "[W]hen Congress was creating substantive federal law involving rights or obligations of individuals with respect to the federal government, it ordinarily did create inferior federal court jurisdiction for resolving disputes." DONALD L. DOERNBERG, IDENTITY CRISIS: FEDERAL COURTS IN A PSYCHOLOGICAL WILDERNESS 32–33 (2001). *See generally id.* at 30–37.

[5] The constitutional language is reproduced in note 1, *supra.* The 1875 Act provided:

> That the circuit courts of the United States shall have original cognizance, concurrent with the courts of the several States, of all suits of a civil nature at common law or in equity, where the matter in dispute exceeds, exclusive of costs, the sum or value of five hundred dollars, and arising under the Constitu-

by Senator Carpenter, who, after noting that prior enactments had not vested all constitutionally-allowed jurisdiction, said, "This bill gives precisely the power which the Constitution confers—nothing more, nothing less." Nonetheless, the Supreme Court has interpreted the constitutional provision more broadly than the statutory provision. As you begin to understand the differences between the constitutional and statutory standards for federal question jurisdiction, consider whether the Court has drawn wise and workable distinctions. Initially, why might it be a good idea to interpret the constitutional provision more broadly?

As a final preliminary matter, one must keep in mind two distinct concepts regarding federal question jurisdiction. The first involves the placement of the federal issue—whether it comes up in the complaint, the answer, or elsewhere. The second concerns the substantiality of the federal issue. Regrettably, cases do not always fall neatly into one category or the other, and the Court has not always been clear either about which issue it is addressing or about precisely what the concept of substantiality, in this context, entails. Nonetheless, it is important to remember both issues and to be aware of the distinctions between them.

In this area, as in others, it is wise to be aware of the broader themes. Apart from whether a court should exercise jurisdiction in a particular case, consider the purpose of having any federal question jurisdiction. Why was it mentioned in the Constitution? Why not leave preliminary adjudication of federal questions to the state courts, with review in the United States Supreme Court when necessary? After all, that system prevailed until 1875. What might have provoked Congress to make so broad a change?

B.   CONSTITUTIONAL AND STATUTORY "ARISING UNDER"—SEPARATE STRANDS INTERTWINED

OSBORN v. BANK OF THE UNITED STATES
Supreme Court of the United States, 1824.
22 U.S. (9 Wheat.) 738, 6 L.Ed. 204.

The bill filed in this cause, was exhibited in the Court below, at September term, 1819, in the name of the respondents, and signed by solicitors of the Court, praying an injunction to restrain Ralph Osborn, Auditor of the State of Ohio, from proceeding against the complainants, under an act of the Legislature of that State, passed February the 8th, 1819, entitled, "An act to levy and collect a tax from all banks, and individuals, and companies, and associations of individuals, that may transact banking business in this State, without being allowed to do so by the laws thereof." This act, after reciting that the Bank of the United States pur-

---

tion or laws of the United States, or treaties made, or which shall be made, under their authority * * *.

Act of Mar. 3, 1875, ch. 137, § 1, 18 Stat. 470.

sued its operations contrary to a law of the State, enacted, that if, after the 1st day of the following September, the said Bank, or any other, should continue to transact business in the State, it should be liable to an annual tax of 50,000 dollars on each office of discount and deposit. And that on the 15th day of September, the Auditor should charge such tax to the Bank, and should make out his warrant, under his seal of office, directed to any person, commanding him to collect the said tax, who should enter the banking house, and demand the same, and if payment should not be made, should levy the amount on the money or other goods of the Bank, the money to be retained, and the goods to be sold * * * . If no effects should be found in the banking room, the person having the warrant was authorized to go into every room, vault, &c. and to open every chest, &c. in search of what might satisfy his warrant.

[Pursuant to the statute, and despite the grant of an injunction by the circuit court forbidding such a seizure, an agent of Osborn's broke into the bank and seized approximately $100,000. The Bank returned to the federal courts seeking relief.]

MR. CHIEF JUSTICE MARSHALL delivered the opinion of the Court, and, after stating the case, proceeded as follows:

At the close of the argument, a point was suggested, of such vital importance, as to induce the Court to request that it might be particularly spoken to. That point is, the right of the Bank to sue in the Courts of the United States. It has been argued, and ought to be disposed of, before we proceed to the actual exercise of jurisdiction, by deciding on the rights of the parties.

The appellants contest the jurisdiction of the Court on two grounds:

1st. That the act of Congress has not given it.

2d. That, under the constitution, Congress cannot give it.

1. The first part of the objection depends entirely on the language of the act. The words are, that the Bank shall be "made able and capable in law," "to sue and be sued, plead and be impleaded, answer and be answered, defend and be defended, in all State Courts having competent jurisdiction, and in any Circuit Court of the United States."

These words seem to the Court to admit of but one interpretation. They cannot be made plainer by explanation. They give, expressly, the right "to sue and be sued," "in every Circuit Court of the United States," and it would be difficult to substitute other terms which would be more direct and appropriate for the purpose. The argument of the appellants is founded on the opinion of this Court, in *The Bank of the United States v. Deveaux*. In that case it was decided, that the former Bank of the United States was not enabled, by the act which incorporated it, to sue in the federal Courts. The words of the 3d section of that act are, that the Bank may "sue and be sued," & c. "in Courts of record, or any other place whatsoever." The Court was of opinion, that these general words, which are usual in all acts of incorporation, gave only a general capacity to sue, not a particular privilege to sue in the Courts of the United States; and this opinion was strengthened by the circumstance that the 9th rule of the 7th section of the same act, subjects the directors, in case of excess in contracting debt, to be sued in their private capacity, "in any Court of record of the United States, or either of them." The express grant of jurisdiction to the federal Courts, in this case, was considered as having some influence on the construction of the general words of the 3d section, which does not mention those Courts. Whether this decision be right or wrong, it amounts only to a declaration, that a general capacity in the Bank to sue, without mentioning the Courts of the Union, may not give a right to sue in those Courts. To infer from this, that words expressly conferring a right to sue in those Courts, do not give the right, is surely a conclusion which the premises do not warrant.

The act of incorporation, then, confers jurisdiction on the Circuit Courts of the United States, if Congress can confer it.

2. We will now consider the constitutionality of the clause in the act of incorporation, which authorizes the Bank to sue in the federal Courts.

In support of this clause, it is said, that the legislative, executive, and judicial powers, of every well constructed government, are co-extensive with each other; that is, they are potentially co-extensive. The executive department may constitutionally execute every law which the Legislature may constitutionally make, and the judicial department may receive from the Legislature the power of construing every such law. All governments which are not extremely defective in their organization, must possess, within themselves, the means of expounding, as well as enforcing, their own laws. If we examine the constitution of the United States, we find that its framers kept this great political principle in view. The 2d article vests the whole executive power in the President; and the 3d article declares, "that the judicial power shall extend to all cases in law and equity arising under this constitution, the laws of the United States, and treaties made, or which shall be made, under their authority."

This clause enables the judicial department to receive jurisdiction to the full extent of the constitution, laws, and treaties of the United States, when any question respecting them shall assume such a form that the judicial power is capable of acting on it. That power is capable of acting only when the subject is submitted to it by a party who asserts his rights in the form prescribed by law. It then becomes a case, and the constitution declares, that the judicial power shall extend to all cases arising under the constitution, laws, and treaties of the United States.

The suit of *The Bank of the United States v. Osborn* and others, is a case, and the question is, whether it arises under a law of the United States?

The appellants contend, that it does not, because several questions may arise in it, which depend on the general principles of the law, not on any act of Congress.

If this were sufficient to withdraw a case from the jurisdiction of the federal Courts, almost every case, although involving the construction of a law, would be withdrawn; and a clause in the constitution, relating to a subject of vital importance to the government, and expressed in the most comprehensive terms, would be construed to mean almost nothing. There is scarcely any case, every part of which depends on the constitution, laws, or treaties of the United States. The questions, whether the fact alleged as the foundation of the action, be real or fictitious; whether the conduct of the plaintiff has been such as to entitle him to maintain his action; whether his right is barred; whether he has received satisfaction, or has in any manner released his claims, are questions, some or all of which may occur in almost every case; and if their existence be sufficient to arrest the jurisdiction of the Court, words which seem intended to be as extensive as the constitution, laws, and treaties of the Union, which seem designed to give the Courts of the government the construction of all its acts, so far as they affect the rights of individuals, would be reduced to almost nothing.

In those cases in which original jurisdiction is given to the Supreme Court, the judicial power of the United States cannot be exercised in its appellate form. In every other case, the power is to be exercised in its original or appellate form, or both, as the wisdom of Congress may direct. With the exception of these cases, in which original jurisdiction is given to this Court, there is none to which the judicial power extends, from which the original jurisdiction of the inferior Courts is excluded by the constitution. Original jurisdiction, so far as the constitution gives a rule, is co-extensive with the judicial power. We find, in the constitution, no prohibition to its exercise, in every case in which the judicial power can be exercised. It would be a very bold construction to say, that this power could be applied in its appellate form only, to the most important class of cases to which it is applicable.

The constitution establishes the Supreme Court, and defines its jurisdiction. It enumerates cases in which its jurisdiction is original and exclusive; and then defines that which is appellate, but does not insinuate, that in any such case, the power cannot be exercised in its original form by Courts of original jurisdiction. It is not insinuated, that the judicial power, in cases depending on the character of the cause, cannot be exercised in the first instance, in the Courts of the Union, but must first be exercised in the tribunals of the State; tribunals over which the government of the Union has no adequate control, and which may be closed to any claim asserted under a law of the United States.

We perceive, then, no ground on which the proposition can be maintained, that Congress is incapable of giving the Circuit Courts original jurisdiction, in any case to which the appellate jurisdiction extends.

We ask, then, if it can be sufficient to exclude this jurisdiction, that the case involves questions depending on general principles? A cause may depend on several questions of fact and law. Some of these may depend on the construction of a law of the United States; others on principles unconnected with that law. If it be a sufficient foundation for jurisdiction, that the title or right set up by the party, may be defeated by one construction of the constitution or law of the United States, and sustained by the opposite construction, provided the facts necessary to support the action be made out, then all the other questions must be decided as incidental to this, which gives that jurisdiction. Those other questions cannot arrest the proceedings. Under this construction, the judicial power of the Union extends effectively and beneficially to that most important class of cases, which depend on the character of the cause. On the opposite construction, the judicial power never can be extended to a whole case, as expressed by the constitution, but to those parts of cases only which present the particular question involving the construction of the constitution or the law. We say it never can be extended to the whole case, because, if the circumstance that other points are involved in it, shall disable Congress from authorizing the Courts of the Union to take jurisdiction of the original cause, it equally disables Congress from authorizing those Courts to take jurisdiction of the whole cause, on an appeal, and thus will be restricted to a single question in that cause; and words obviously intended to secure to those who claim rights under the constitution, laws, or treaties of the United States, a trial in the federal Courts, will be restricted to the insecure remedy of an appeal upon an insulated point, after it has received that shape which may be given to it by another tribunal, into which he is forced against his will.

We think, then, that when a question to which the judicial power of the Union is extended by the constitution, forms an ingredient of the original cause, it is in the power of Congress to give the Circuit Courts jurisdiction of that cause, although other questions of fact or of law may be involved in it.

The case of the Bank is, we think, a very strong case of this description. The charter of incorporation not only creates it, but gives it every faculty which it possesses. The power to acquire rights of any description, to transact business of any description, to make contracts of any description, to sue on those contracts, is given and measured by its charter, and that charter is a law of the United States. This being can acquire no right, make no contract, bring no suit, which is not authorized by a law of the United States. It is not only itself the mere creature of a law, but all its actions and all its rights are dependent on the same law. Can a being, thus constituted, have a case which does not arise literally, as well as substantially, under the law?

Take the case of a contract, which is put as the strongest against the

Bank.

When a Bank sues, the first question which presents itself, and which lies at the foundation of the cause, is, has this legal entity a right to sue? Has it a right to come, not into this Court particularly, but into any Court? This depends on a law of the United States. The next question is, has this being a right to make this particular contract? If this question be decided in the negative, the cause is determined against the plaintiff; and this question, too, depends entirely on a law of the United States. These are important questions, and they exist in every possible case. The right to sue, if decided once, is decided for ever; but the power of Congress was exercised antecedently to the first decision on that right, and if it was constitutional then, it cannot cease to be so, because the particular question is decided. It may be revived at the will of the party, and most probably would be renewed, were the tribunal to be changed. But the question respecting the right to make a particular contract, or to acquire a particular property, or to sue on account of a particular injury, belongs to every particular case, and may be renewed in every case. The question forms an original ingredient in every cause. Whether it be in fact relied on or not, in the defence, it is still a part of the cause, and may be relied on. The right of the plaintiff to sue, cannot depend on the defence which the defendant may choose to set up. His right to sue is anterior to that defence, and must depend on the state of things when the action is brought. The questions which the case involves, then, must determine its character, whether those questions be made in the cause or not.

The appellants say, that the case arises on the contract; but the validity of the contract depends on a law of the United States, and the plaintiff is compelled, in every case, to show its validity. The case arises emphatically under the law. The act of Congress is its foundation. The contract could never have been made, but under the authority of that act. The act itself is the first ingredient in the case, is its origin, is that from which every other part arises. That other questions may also arise, as the execution of the contract, or its performance, cannot change the case, or give it any other origin than the charter of incorporation. The action still originates in, and is sustained by, that charter.

The clause giving the Bank a right to sue in the Circuit Courts of the United States, stands on the same principle with the acts authorizing officers of the United States who sue in their own names, to sue in the Courts of the United States. The Postmaster General, for example, cannot sue under that part of the constitution which gives jurisdiction to the federal Courts, in consequence of the character of the party, nor is he authorized to sue by the Judiciary Act. He comes into the Courts of the Union under the authority of an act of Congress, the constitutionality of which can only be sustained by the admission that his suit is a case arising under a law of the United States. If it be said, that it is such a case, because a law of the United States authorizes the contract, and authorizes the suit, the same reasons exist with respect to a suit brought by the Bank. That, too, is such a case; because that suit, too, is itself authorized, and is brought on a contract authorized by a law of the United States. It depends absolutely on [t]hat law, and cannot exist a moment without its authority.

If it be said, that a suit brought by the Bank may depend in fact altogether on questions unconnected with any law of the United States, it is equally true, with respect to suits brought by the Postmaster General. The plea in bar may be payment, if the suit be brought on a bond, or nonassumpsit, if it be brought on an open account, and no other question may arise than what respects the complete discharge of the demand. Yet the constitutionality of the act authorizing the Postmaster General to sue in the Courts of the United States, has never been drawn into question. It is sustained singly by an act of Congress, standing on that construction of the constitution which asserts the right of the Legislature to give original jurisdiction to the Circuit Courts, in cases arising under a law of the United States.

The clause in the patent law, authorizing suits in the Circuit Courts, stands, we think, on the same principle. Such a suit is a case arising under a law of the United States. Yet the defendant may not, at the trial, question the validity of the patent, or make any point which requires the construction of an act of Congress. He may rest his defence exclusively on the fact, that he has not violated the right of the plaintiff. That this fact becomes the sole question made in the cause, cannot oust the jurisdiction of the Court, or establish the position, that the case does not arise under a law of the United States.

* * *

Upon the best consideration we have been able to bestow on this subject, we are of opinion, that the clause in the act of incorporation, enabling the Bank to sue in the Courts of the United States, is consistent with the constitution, and to be obeyed in all Courts.

* * *

MR. JUSTICE JOHNSON, dissenting.

The argument in this cause presents three questions: 1. Has Congress granted to the Bank of the United States, an unlimited right of suing in the Courts of the United States? 2. Could Congress constitutionally grant such a right? and 3. Has the power of the Court been legally and constitutionally exercised in this suit?

I have very little doubt that the public mind will be easily reconciled to the decision of the Court here rendered; for, whether necessary or unnecessary originally, a state of things has now grown up, in some of the States, which renders all the protection necessary, that the general government can give to this Bank. The policy of the decision is obvious, that is, if the Bank is to be sustained; and few will bestow upon its legal correctness, the reflection, that it is necessary to test it by the constitution and laws, under which it is rendered.

* * *

[In this section of the opinion, Justice Johnson took issue with the majority on Congress's intent. He argued that Marshall's view would ultimately make everything a federal question case. He thought, to the contrary, that Congress had intended not to create jurisdiction, but only to authorize the Bank to use its corporate name in bringing suit.]

* * *

I will dwell no longer on a point, which is in fact secondary and subordinate; for if Congress can vest this jurisdiction, and the people will it, the act may be amended, and the jurisdiction vested. I next proceed to consider, more distinctly, the constitutional question, on the right to vest the jurisdiction to the extent here contended for.

And here I must observe, that I altogether misunderstood the counsel, who argued the cause for the plaintiff in error, if any of them contended against the jurisdiction, on the ground that the cause involved questions depending on general principles. No one can question, that the Court which has jurisdiction of the principal question, must exercise jurisdiction over every question. Neither did I understand them as denying, that if Congress could confer on the Circuit Courts appellate, they could confer original jurisdiction. The argument went to deny the right to assume jurisdiction on a mere hypothesis. It was one of description, identity, definition; they contended, that until a question involving the construction or administration of the laws of the United States did actually arise, the *casus fœderis* was not presented, on which the constitution authorized the government to take to itself the jurisdiction of the cause. That until such a question actually arose, until such a case was actually presented, *non constat,* but the cause depended upon general principles, exclusively cognizable in the State Courts; that neither the letter nor the spirit of the constitution sanctioned the assumption of jurisdiction on the part of the United States at any previous stage.

And this doctrine has my hearty concurrence in its general application. A very simple case may be stated, to illustrate its bearing on the question of jurisdiction between the two governments. By virtue of treaties with Great Britain, aliens holding lands were exempted from alien disabilities, and made capable of holding, aliening, and transmitting their estates, in common with natives. But why should the claimants of such lands, to all eternity, be vested with the privilege of bringing an original suit in the Courts of the United States? It is true, a question might be made, upon the effect of the treaty, on the rights claimed by or through the alien; but until that question does arise, nay, until a decision against the right takes place, what end has the United States to subserve in claiming jurisdiction of the cause?

* * *

Efforts have been made to fix the precise sense of the constitution, when it vests jurisdiction in the general government, in "cases arising under the laws of the United States." To me, the question appears susceptible of a very simple solution; that all depends upon the identity of the case supposed; according to which idea, a case may be such in its very existence, or it may become such in its progress. An action may "live, move, and have its being," in a law of the United States; such is that given for the violation of a patent-right, and four or five different actions given by this act of incorporation; particularly that against the President and Directors for over-issuing; in all of which cases the plaintiff must count upon the law itself as the ground of his action. And of the other description, would have been an action of trespass, in this case, had remedy been sought for an actual levy of the tax imposed. Such was the case of the former Bank against Deveaux, and many others that have occurred in this Court, in which the suit, in its form, was such as occur in ordinary cases, but in which the pleadings or evidence raised the question on the law or constitution of the United States. In this class of cases, the occurrence of a question makes the case, and transfers it, as provided for under the twenty-fifth section of the Judiciary Act, to the jurisdiction of the United States. And this appears to me to present the only sound and practical construction of the constitution on this subject; for no other cases does it regard as necessary to place under the control of the general government. It is only when the case exhibits one or the other of these characteristics, that it is acted upon by the constitution. Where no question is raised, there can be no contrariety of construction; and what else had the constitution to guard against? As to cases of the first description, *ex necessitate rei,* the Courts of the United States must be susceptible of original jurisdiction; and as to all other cases, I should hold them, also, susceptible of original jurisdiction, if it were practicable, in the nature of things, to make out the definition of the case, so as to bring it under the constitution judicially, upon an original suit. But until the plaintiff can control the defendant in his pleadings, I see no practical mode of determining when the case does occur, otherwise than by permitting the cause to advance until the case for which the constitution provides shall actually arise. If it never occurs, there can be nothing to complain of; and such are the provisions of the twenty-fifth section. The cause might be transferred to the Circuit Court before an adjudication takes place; but I can perceive no earlier stage at which it can possibly be predicated of such a case, that it is one within the constitution; nor any possible necessity for transferring it then, or until the Court has acted upon it to the prejudice of the claims of the United States. It is not, therefore, because Congress may not vest an original jurisdiction, where they can constitutionally vest in the Circuit Courts *appellate* jurisdiction, that I object to this general grant of the right to sue; but, because that the peculiar nature of this jurisdiction is such, as to render it impossible to exercise it in a strictly original form, and because the principle of a possible occurrence of a question as a ground of jurisdiction, and placing the bounds of the constitution, and placing it on a ground which will admit of an *enormous accession,* if not an *unlimited assumption,* of jurisdiction.

* * *

Notes and Questions

1. a) How many tests did Chief Justice Marshall articulate in *Osborn*? Are they different formulations of the same test, or are they alternative standards by which to adjudicate jurisdictional questions?

b) What tests would Justice Johnson use? Are his tests like any of those suggested by the majority opinion? Does he differ on the proper standard for subject matter jurisdiction or on its application to the facts?

Justice Johnson's dissent is worth careful attention. He divides cases in which there might be an argument for inferior federal court jurisdiction into two categories. What are they, and how would he treat them differently for purposes of establishing jurisdiction?

2. In *Osborn,* the Bank asserted that the Supremacy Clause forbade the Ohio tax, citing *M'Culloch v. Maryland,* 17 U.S. (4 Wheat.) 316, 4 L.Ed. 579 (1819). The case thus presented a clear federal constitutional issue. Obviously, an authorization to the federal courts to hear cases in which the federal issue was so central would have been well within the bounds of Article III. But Marshall thought Congress had gone further by authorizing jurisdiction whenever the Bank of the United States was a party, even if the substantive issues involved were not federal. Thus, the jurisdictional statute, while constitutional as applied in *Osborn,* seemed to authorize a far broader scope of jurisdiction. Chief Justice Marshall therefore decided to evaluate the outer limits of the statute under constitutional standards.

a) Note that the Court hypothesized suits by or against the Bank that did not involve so central a federal issue, as in Marshall's contract example. What federal issue did Marshall think would arise in that kind of case? Why would such a suit present a more difficult case for federal jurisdiction?

b) Should the federal courts be permitted to hear cases containing potential federal issues that neither party intends to raise? What policies might be served by allowing jurisdiction in such cases? What policies might be harmed?

3. Statutes similar to the one in *Osborn* continue to torment the Court. In *American National Red Cross v. Solicitor General,* 505 U.S. 247, 112 S.Ct. 2465, 120 L.Ed.2d 201 (1992), the federal charter authorized the Red Cross "to sue and be sued in courts of law and equity, State or Federal, within the jurisdiction of the United States." The issue, as in *Osborn,* was whether that language conferred subject matter jurisdiction on the federal courts for every

action to which the Red Cross is a party. A five-to-four Court held that it did. The majority argued that cases from *Deveaux* (discussed in *Osborn*) onward "support the rule that a congressional charter's 'sue and be sued' provision may be read to confer federal court jurisdiction if, but only if, it specifically mentions the federal courts." Thus, the majority distinguished *Deveaux* but embraced *Osborn* and cases with similar statutes that followed it.

Justice Scalia, writing for the minority, argued strongly that the "capacity" language of the statute did not grant jurisdiction. He pointed out that the *Deveaux* Court had distinguished two statutory provisions. The first, quoted in *Osborn*, gave the bank capacity to be a litigant in courts of record. The second, not mentioned in *Osborn*, "provided that certain actions against the directors of the Bank 'may * * * be brought * * * in any court of record of the United States * * * .' " Justice Scalia argued that *Deveaux* turned upon the distinction between the language in the two statutory sections, not upon the happenstance of the mention of federal courts in an otherwise capacity-granting statute. He distinguished *Osborn* from *Deveaux* and *Red Cross:*

> By granting the Bank power to sue, not in all courts generally (as in *Deveaux*), but in *particular* federal courts, this suggested a grant of jurisdiction rather than merely of capacity to sue. And that suggestion was strongly confirmed by the fact that the Bank was empowered to sue in state courts "having competent jurisdiction," but in federal circuit courts *simpliciter*. If the statute had jurisdiction in mind as to the one, it must as to the other as well.

Justice Scalia also took issue with *Osborn*'s reading of *Deveaux:*

> In distinguishing *Deveaux, Osborn* noted, *and apparently misunderstood* as the Court today does, that case's contrast between the "express grant of jurisdiction to the federal Courts" over suits against directors and the "general words" of the "sue and be sued" clause, "which [did] not mention those Courts." All it concluded from that, however, was that *Deveaux* established that "a general capacity in the Bank to sue, without mentioning the Courts of the Union, may not give a right to sue in those Courts." There does not logically follow from that the rule which the Court announces today: that *any* grant of a general capacity to sue *with* mention of federal courts will suffice to confer jurisdiction.

(Emphasis added). Justice Souter replied. "The dissent accuses us of repeating what it announces as Chief Justice Marshall's misunderstanding, in *Osborn*, of his own previous opinion in *Deveaux*. We are honored."

Is the majority's or the dissent's reasoning more persuasive? One's reaction, of course, may turn ultimately upon how persuasively *Osborn* made the case for broad interpretation of the statute. Does it make any difference that Congress has continued to enact similarly-worded statutes and apparently acquiesced in the Court's reading? The majority thought so.

> [W]e do not face a clean slate. Beginning with Chief Justice Marshall's opinion [in *Deveaux*] in 1809, we have had several occasions to consider

whether the "sue and be sued" provision of a particular federal corporate charter conferred original federal jurisdiction over cases to which that corporation was a party, and our readings of those provisions not only represented our best efforts at divining congressional intent retrospectively, but have also placed Congress on prospective notice of the language necessary and sufficient to confer jurisdiction * * * .

4. At what point in a case should the court determine the existence of federal jurisdiction? At what point should it be determinable? The Supreme Court and some commentators have suggested that federal jurisdiction must appear at the outset of the litigation—that is, when the complaint is filed. *See, e.g.,* James H. Chadbourn & A. Leo Levin, *Original Jurisdiction of Federal Questions,* 90 U.Pa.L.Rev. 639, 648 (1942); David L. Shapiro, *Jurisdiction and Discretion,* 60 N.Y.U.L.Rev. 543, 567 (1985). How will it ever be possible, at the complaint stage, to know whether a federal issue identified by the plaintiff will be contested? *See* Ernest J. London, *"Federal Question" Jurisdiction—A Snare and a Delusion,* 57 Mich.L.Rev. 835, 846–47 (1959). On the other hand, if jurisdiction is to be judged at some later stage in the proceeding, what stage is appropriate?

5. Note that *Osborn* contains the earliest clearly identifiable reference to what later became known as pendent and ancillary (now supplemental) jurisdiction, as Chief Justice Marshall espoused the principle that a court properly exercising jurisdiction may decide all questions presented, whether or not each has a federal component. The polar position is that federal courts should entertain only cases presenting federal questions exclusively. Is there a possible middle position?

TEXTILE WORKERS UNION v. LINCOLN MILLS, 353 U.S. 448, 77 S.Ct. 912, 1 L.Ed.2d 972 (1957).

The Court considered the relationship between Congress' powers under Article I of the Constitution and its power to provide federal question jurisdiction under Article III, particularly whether Congress may allow federal question jurisdiction in areas in which it *could* legislate under Article I, or whether, by contrast, it is restricted to areas in which it *has* legislated. The Labor Management Relations Act of 1947 (the Taft-Hartley Act) granted jurisdiction over actions concerning violations of labor-employer contracts. Congress had not, however, enacted substantive law concerning such contracts, which continued to be governed by state law. Clearly, however, Congress could have enacted such substantive law, exercising its power under the Commerce Clause.

The majority construed the jurisdictional grant to be a command to the federal courts to fashion a body of federal common law dealing with labor-management contractual relations.[6] Then, finding that the con-

---

[6] Such a command raises other significant questions concerning the existence and

tractual cause of action was based upon federal law, the majority had no trouble concluding that federal question jurisdiction existed. Justice Frankfurter dissented, arguing that Congress did not intend the federal courts to create federal common law in this area. That conclusion led him to explore the jurisdictional question at some length.

The second ground of my dissent from the Court's action is more fundamental. Since I do not agree with the Court's conclusion that federal substantive law is to govern in actions under § 301, I am forced to consider * * * the constitutionality of a grant of jurisdiction to federal courts over contracts that came into being entirely by virtue of state substantive law, a jurisdiction not based on diversity of citizenship, yet one in which a federal court would, as in diversity cases, act in effect merely as another court of the State in which it sits. The scope of allowable federal judicial power that this grant must satisfy is constitutionally described as "Cases, in Law and Equity, arising under this Constitution, the Laws of the United States, and Treaties made, or which shall be made, under their Authority." While interpretive decisions are legion under general statutory grants of jurisdiction strikingly similar to this constitutional wording, it is generally recognized that the full constitutional power has not been exhausted by these statutes.

Almost without exception, decisions under the general statutory grants have tested jurisdiction in terms of the presence, as an integral part of plaintiff's cause of action, of an issue calling for interpretation or application of federal law. Although it has sometimes been suggested that the "cause of action" must derive from federal law, it has been found sufficient that some aspect of federal law is essential to plaintiff's success. The litigation-provoking problem has been the degree to which federal law must be in the forefront of the case and not collateral, peripheral or remote.

In a few exceptional cases, arising under special jurisdictional grants, the criteria by which the prominence of the federal question is measured against constitutional requirements have been found satisfied under circumstances suggesting a variant theory of the nature of these requirements. The first, and the leading case in the field, is *Osborn v. Bank of United States.* There, Chief Justice Marshall sustained federal jurisdiction in a situation—hypothetical in the case before him but presented by the companion case of *Bank of United States v. Planters' Bank*—involving suit by a federally incorporated bank upon a contract. Despite the assumption that the cause of action and the interpretation of the contract would be gov-

scope of federal common law. *See* Chapter 5. For example, assuming that Congress did intend such a command, do not substantial separation-of-powers questions arise from delegation of comprehensive legislative authority? Is it appropriate for courts to act as legislatures merely because Congress has instructed them to do so?

erned by state law, the case was found to "arise under the laws of the United States" because the propriety and scope of a federally granted authority to enter into contracts and to litigate might well be challenged. This reasoning was subsequently applied to sustain jurisdiction in actions against federally chartered railroad corporations. The traditional interpretation of this series of cases is that federal jurisdiction under the "arising" clause of the Constitution, though limited to cases involving potential federal questions, has such flexibility that Congress may confer it whenever there exists in the background some federal proposition that might be challenged, despite the remoteness of the likelihood of actual presentation of such a federal question.[4]

The views expressed in *Osborn* and the *Pacific Railroad Removal Cases* were severely restricted in construing general grants of jurisdiction. But the Court later sustained this jurisdictional section of the Bankruptcy Act of 1898:

The United States district courts shall have jurisdiction of all controversies at law and in equity, as distinguished from proceedings in bankruptcy, between trustees as such and adverse claimants concerning the property acquired or claimed by the trustees, in the same manner and to the same extent only as though bankruptcy proceedings had not been instituted and such controversies had been between the bankrupts and such adverse claimants.

Under this provision the trustee could pursue in a federal court a private cause of action arising under and wholly governed by state law. To be sure, the cases did not discuss the basis of jurisdiction. It has been suggested that they merely represent an extension of the approach of the *Osborn* case; the trustee's right to sue might be challenged on obviously federal grounds—absence of bankruptcy or irregularity of the trustee's appointment or of the bankruptcy proceedings. So viewed, this type of litigation implicates a potential federal question.

Apparently relying on the extent to which the bankruptcy cases involve only remotely a federal question, Mr. Justice Jackson concluded in *Tidewater Transfer Co.,* that Congress may confer jurisdiction on the District Courts as incidental to its powers under Article I. No attempt was made to reconcile this view with the restrictions of Article III; a majority of the Court recognized that Article III defined the bounds of valid jurisdictional legislation and rejected the notion that jurisdictional grants can go outside these limits.

---

[4] *Osborn* might possibly be limited on the ground that a federal instrumentality, the Bank of the United States, was involved, but such an explanation could not suffice to narrow the holding in the *Pacific Railroad Removal Cases.*

With this background, many theories have been proposed to sustain the constitutional validity of § 301. Judge Wyzanski suggested, among other possibilities, that § 301 might be read as containing a direction that controversies affecting interstate commerce should be governed by federal law incorporating state law by reference, and that such controversies would then arise under a valid federal law as required by Article III. Whatever may be said of the assumption regarding the validity of federal jurisdiction under an affirmative declaration by Congress that state law should be applied as federal law by federal courts to contract disputes affecting commerce, we cannot argumentatively legislate for Congress when Congress has failed to legislate. To do so disrespects legislative responsibility and disregards judicial limitations.

Another theory, relying on *Osborn* and the bankruptcy cases, has been proposed which would achieve results similar to those attainable under Mr. Justice Jackson's view, but which purports to respect the "arising" clause of Article III. Called "protective jurisdiction," the suggestion is that in any case for which Congress has the constitutional power to prescribe federal rules of decision and thus confer "true" federal question jurisdiction, it may, without so doing, enact a jurisdictional statute, which will provide a federal forum for the application of state statute and decisional law. Analysis of the "protective jurisdiction" theory might also be attempted in terms of the language of Article III—construing "laws" to include jurisdictional statutes where Congress could have legislated substantively in a field. This is but another way of saying that because Congress could have legislated substantively and thereby could give rise to litigation under a statute of the United States, it can provide a federal forum for state-created rights although it chose not to adopt state law as federal law or to originate federal rights.

Surely the truly technical restrictions of Article III are not met or respected by a beguiling phrase that the greater power here must necessarily include the lesser. In the compromise of federal and state interests leading to distribution of jealously guarded judicial power in a federal system, it is obvious that very different considerations apply to cases involving questions of federal law and those turning solely on state law. It may be that the ambiguity of the phrase "arising under the laws of the United States" leaves room for more than traditional theory could accommodate. But, under the theory of "protective jurisdiction," the "arising under" jurisdiction of the federal courts would be vastly extended. For example, every contract or tort arising out of a contract affecting commerce might be a potential cause of action in the federal courts, even though only state law was involved in the decision of the case. At least in *Osborn* and the bankruptcy cases, a substantive federal law was present somewhere in the background. But this theory rests on the supposition that Congress could enact substantive federal law to govern the particular case. It was not held in those cases, nor is it clear, that federal law could be held to govern the transactions of all persons who subsequently become bankrupt, or of all suits of a Bank of the United States.

"Protective jurisdiction," once the label is discarded, cannot be justified under any view of the allowable scope to be given to Article III. "Protective jurisdiction" is a misused label for the statute we are here considering. That rubric is properly descriptive of safeguarding some of the indisputable, staple business of the federal courts. It is a radiation of an existing jurisdiction. "Protective jurisdiction" cannot generate an independent source for adjudication outside of the Article III sanctions and what Congress has defined. The theory must have as its sole justification a belief in the inadequacy of state tribunals in determining state law. The Constitution reflects such a belief in the specific situation within which the Diversity Clause was confined. The intention to remedy such supposed defects was exhausted in this provision of Article III.[5] That this "protective" theory was not adopted by Chief Justice Marshall at a time when conditions might have presented more substantial justification strongly suggests its lack of constitutional merit. Moreover, Congress in its consideration of § 301 nowhere suggested dissatisfaction with the ability of state courts to administer state law properly. Its concern was to provide access to the federal courts for easier enforcement of state-created rights.

Another theory also relies on *Osborn* and the bankruptcy cases as an implicit recognition of the propriety of the exercise of some sort of "protective jurisdiction" by the federal courts. Professor Mishkin tends to view the assertion of such a jurisdiction, in the absence of any exercise of substantive powers, as irreconcilable with the "arising" clause since the case would then arise only under the jurisdictional statute itself, and he is reluctant to find a constitutional basis for the grant of power outside Article III. Professor Mishkin also notes that the only purpose of such a statute would be to insure impartiality to some litigant, an objection inconsistent with Article III's recognition of "protective jurisdiction" only in the specified situation of diverse citizenship. But where Congress has

---

[5] To be sure, the Court upheld the removal statute for suits or prosecutions commenced in a state court against federal revenue officers on account of any act committed under color of office. The Court, however, construed the action of Congress in defining the powers of revenue agents as giving them a substantive defense against prosecution under state law for commission of acts "warranted by the Federal authority they possess." That put federal law in the forefront as a defense. In any event, the fact that officers of the Federal Government were parties may be considered sufficient to afford access to the federal forum.

"an articulated and active federal policy regulating a field, the 'arising under' clause of Article III apparently permits the conferring of jurisdiction on the national courts of all cases in the area—including those substantively governed by state law." In such cases, the protection being offered is not to the suitor, as in diversity cases, but to the "congressional legislative program." Thus he supports § 301: "even though the rules governing collective bargaining agreements continue to be state-fashioned, nonetheless the mode of their application and enforcement may play a very substantial part in the labor-management relations of interstate industry and commerce—an area in which the national government has labored long and hard."

Insofar as state law governs the case, Professor Mishkin's theory is quite similar to that advanced by Professors Hart and Wechsler and followed by the Court of Appeals for the First Circuit: The substantive power of Congress, although not exercised to govern the particular "case," gives "arising under" jurisdiction to the federal courts despite governing state law. The second "protective jurisdiction" theory has the dubious advantage of limiting incursions on state judicial power to situations in which the State's feelings may have been tempered by early substantive federal invasions.

Professor Mishkin's theory of "protective jurisdiction" may find more constitutional justification if there is not merely an "articulated and active" congressional policy regulating the labor field but also federal rights existing in the interstices of actions under § 301. Therefore, before resting on an interpretation of § 301 that would compel a declaration of unconstitutionality, we must * * * defer to the strong presumption—even as to such technical matters as federal jurisdiction—that Congress legislated in accordance with the Constitution.

* * *

* * * " 'But avoidance of a difficulty will not be pressed to the point of disingenuous evasion.' * * * 'Here the intention of the Congress is revealed too distinctly to permit us to ignore it because of mere misgivings as to power.' "

* * *

There is a point, however, at which the search may be ended with less misgiving regarding the propriety of judicial infusion of substantive provisions into § 301. The contribution of federal law might consist in postulating the right of a union, despite its amorphous status as an unincorporated association, to enter into binding collective-bargaining contracts with an employer. The federal courts might also give sanction to this right by refusing to comply with any state law that does not admit that collective bargaining may result in an enforceable contract. It is hard to see what serious federal-state conflicts could arise under this view. At most, a state court might dismiss the action, while a federal court would entertain it. Moreover, such a function of federal law is closely related to the removal of the procedural barriers to suit. Section 301 would be futile if the union's status as a contracting party were not recognized. The statement in § 301(b) that the acts of the agents of the union are to be regarded as binding upon the union may be used in support of this conclusion. This provision, not confined in its application to suits in the District Court under § 301(a), was primarily directed to responsibility of the union for its agents' actions in authorizing strikes or committing torts. It can be construed, however, as applicable to the formation of a contract. So applied, it would imply that a union must be regarded as contractually bound by the acts of its agents, which in turn presupposes that the union is capable of contract relations.

Of course, the possibility of a State's law being counter to such a limited federal proposition is hypothetical, and to base an assertion of federal law on such a possibility, one never considered by Congress, is an artifice. And were a State ever to adopt a contrary attitude, its reasons for so doing might be such that Congress would not be willing to disregard them. But these difficulties are inherent in any attempt to expand § 301 substantively to meet constitutional requirements.

Even if this limited federal "right" were read into § 301, a serious constitutional question would still be present. It does elevate the situation to one closely analogous to that presented in *Osborn*.[6] Section 301 would, under this view, imply that a union is to be viewed as a juristic entity for purposes of acquiring contract rights under a collective-bargaining agreement, and that it has the right to enter into such a contract and to sue upon it. This was all that was immediately and expressly involved in the *Osborn* case, although the historical setting was vastly different and the juristic entity in that case was completely the creature of federal law, one engaged in carrying out essential governmental functions. Most of these special considerations had disappeared, however, at the time and in the circumstances of the decision of the *Pacific Railroad Removal Cases*. There is force in the view that regards the latter

---

[6] Enunciation of such a requirement could in fact bring federal law somewhat further to the forefront than was true of *Osborn,* the *Pacific Railroad Removal Cases,* or the bankruptcy cases in the few cases where an assertion could be made that state law did not sufficiently recognize collective agreements as contracts. But there appears to be no State that today possesses such a rule. Most and probably all cases arising under § 301—certainly the present ones—would never present such a problem.

as a "sport" and finds that the Court has so viewed it. * * * The question is whether we should now so consider it and refuse to apply its holding to the present situation.

I believe that we should not extend the precedents of *Osborn* and the *Pacific Railroad Removal Cases* to this case even though there be some elements of analytical similarity. *Osborn,* the foundation for the *Removal Cases,* appears to have been based on premises that today * * * are subject to criticism. The basic premise was that every case in which a federal question might arise must be capable of being commenced in the federal courts, and when so commenced it might, because jurisdiction must be judged at the outset, be concluded there despite the fact that the federal question was never raised. Marshall's holding was undoubtedly influenced by his fear that the bank might suffer hostile treatment in the state courts that could not be remedied by an appeal on an isolated federal question. There is nothing in Article III that affirmatively supports the view that original jurisdiction over cases involving federal questions must extend to every case in which there is the potentiality of appellate jurisdiction. We also have become familiar with removal procedures that could be adapted to alleviate any remaining fears by providing for removal to a federal court whenever a federal question was raised. In view of these developments, we would not be justified in perpetuating a principle that permits assertion of original federal jurisdiction on the remote possibility of presentation of a federal question. Indeed, Congress, by largely withdrawing the jurisdiction that the *Pacific Railroad Removal Cases* recognized, and this Court, by refusing to perpetuate it under general grants of jurisdiction, have already done much to recognize the changed atmosphere.

Analysis of the bankruptcy power also reveals a superficial analogy to § 301. The trustee enforces a cause of action acquired under state law by the bankrupt. Federal law merely provides for the appointment of the trustee, vests the cause of action in him, and confers jurisdiction on the federal courts. Section 301 similarly takes the rights and liabilities which under state law are vested distributively in the individual members of a union and vests them in the union for purposes of actions in federal courts, wherein the unions are authorized to sue and be sued as an entity. While the authority of the trustee depends on the existence of a bankrupt and on the propriety of the proceedings leading to the trustee's appointment, both of which depend on federal law, there are similar federal propositions that may be essential to an action under § 301. Thus, the validity of the contract may in any case be challenged on the ground that the labor organization negotiating it was not the representative of the employees concerned, a question that has been held to be federal, or on the ground that subsequent change in the representative status of the union has affected the continued validity of the agreement. Perhaps also the qualifications imposed on a union's right to utilize the facilities of the National Labor Relations Board * * * might be read as restrictions on the right of the union to sue under § 301, again providing a federal basis for challenge to the union's authority. Consequently, were the bankruptcy cases to be viewed as dependent solely on the background existence of federal questions, there would be little analytical basis for distinguishing actions under § 301. But the bankruptcy decisions may be justified by the scope of the bankruptcy power, which may be deemed to sweep within its scope interests analytically outside the "federal question" category, but sufficiently related to the main purpose of bankruptcy to call for comprehensive treatment. Also, although a particular suit may be brought by a trustee in a district other than the one in which the principal proceedings are pending, if all the suits by the trustee, even though in many federal courts, are regarded as one litigation for the collection and apportionment of the bankrupt's property, a particular suit by the trustee, under state law, to recover a specific piece of property might be analogized to the ancillary or pendent jurisdiction cases in which, in the disposition of a cause of action, federal courts may pass on state grounds for recovery that are joined to federal grounds.

If there is in the phrase "arising under the laws of the United States" leeway for expansion of our concepts of jurisdiction, the history of Article III suggests that the area is not great and that it will require the presence of some substantial federal interest, one of greater weight and dignity than questionable doubt concerning the effectiveness of state procedure. The bankruptcy cases might possibly be viewed as such an expansion. But even so, not merely convenient judicial administration but the whole purpose of the congressional legislative program—conservation and equitable distribution of the bankrupt's estate in carrying out the constitutional power over bankruptcy—required the availability of federal jurisdiction to avoid expense and delay. Nothing pertaining to § 301 suggests vesting the federal courts with sweeping power under the Commerce Clause comparable to that vested in the federal courts under the bankruptcy power.

In the wise distribution of governmental powers, this Court cannot do what a President sometimes does in returning a bill to Congress. We cannot return this provision to Congress and respectfully request that body to face the responsibility placed upon it by the Constitution to define the jurisdiction of the lower courts with some particularity and not to leave these courts at large. Confronted as I am, I regretfully have no choice. For all the reasons elaborated in this dissent, even reading into § 301 the limited federal rights consistent with the purposes of that section, I am impelled to the view that it is unconstitutional in cases such as the present ones where it provides the sole basis for exercise of jurisdiction by the federal courts.

Notes and Questions

1. Can Congress grant federal jurisdiction in cases involving no existing federal substantive law but touching upon areas in which Congress could legislate? What interests would be served if that were allowed? What interests might be compromised?

2. A related issue surfaced in a slightly different way in *National Mutual Insurance Co. v. Tidewater Transfer Co.,* 337 U.S. 582, 69 S.Ct. 1173, 93 L.Ed. 1556 (1949). Congress conferred jurisdiction on the district courts for non-federal suits between citizens of the District of Columbia and citizens of a state. Well-established precedent held that the District of Columbia was not a state for purposes of Article III diversity jurisdiction, and the Court showed no disposition to overturn those cases. Nonetheless, a splintered Court upheld the grant. Justice Jackson, joined by two other Justices, took an expansive view of Congress's ability to create jurisdiction notwithstanding the apparent limits of Article III. Noting that Congress has plenary authority under Article I to govern the District of Columbia, he continued:

> However, it is contended that Congress may not combine this function, under Art. I, with those under Art. III, in district courts of the United States. One is that no jurisdiction other than that specified in Art. III can be imposed on courts that exercise the judicial power of the United States thereunder. The other is that Art. I powers over the District of Columbia must be exercised solely within that geographic area.

> * * * [A]lthough District of Columbia courts are Art. III courts, they can also exercise judicial power conferred by Congress pursuant to Art. I. The fact that District of Columbia courts, as local courts, can also be given administrative or legislative functions which other Art. III courts cannot exercise, does but emphasize the fact that, although the latter are limited to the exercise of judicial power, it may constitutionally be received from either Art. III or Art. I, and that congressional power over the District, flowing from Art. I, is plenary in every respect.

* * *

We concluded that where Congress in the exercise of its powers under Art. I finds it necessary to provide those on whom its power is exerted with access to some kind of court or tribunal for determination of controversies that are within the traditional concept of the justiciable, it may open the regular federal courts to them regardless of lack of diversity of citizenship. The basis of the holdings we have discussed is that, when Congress deems that for such purposes it owes a forum to claimants and trustees, it may execute its power in this manner. The Congress, with equal justification, apparently considers that it also owes such a forum to the residents of the District of Columbia in execution of its power and duty under the same Article. We do not see how the one could be sustained and the other denied.

Does Justice Jackson's position suggest that the jurisdiction of Article III courts is actually limited not by that Article but by Article I? Under this theory, could Congress open the Article III courts to private disputes between parties regulated by statutes under the Commerce Clause, even if their dispute involved neither interpretation, application nor constitutionality of those statutes? If so, is the potential jurisdictional reach of Article III courts effectively illimitable? If not, how can such a case be distinguished from *Tidewater Transfer*?

THERE'S NO REASON FOR IT; IT'S JUST OUR POLICY: WHY THE WELL-PLEADED COMPLAINT RULE SABOTAGES THE PURPOSES OF FEDERAL QUESTION JURISDICTION
DONALD L. DOERNBERG
38 HASTINGS L.J. 597, 601-07 (1987)[a]

The constitutional language creating federal question jurisdiction has not changed since 1787. Congress first permitted the exercise of this jurisdiction in the famous "Midnight Judges Act" of 1801, which substantially tracked the constitutional language: "[T]he said circuit courts respectively shall have cognizance of * * * all cases in law or equity, arising under the constitution and laws of the United States, and treaties made, or which shall be made, under their authority." The Act did not, however, survive the Federalists' departure from power for long; it was repealed barely one year later by the Jeffersonian Congress.

It was not until 1875 that Congress again granted federal question jurisdiction to the inferior federal courts. The 1875 Act, still the foundation for such jurisdiction, provided:

> That the circuit courts of the United States shall have original cognizance, concurrent with the courts of the several States, of all suits of a civil nature at common law or in equity, where the matter in dispute exceeds, exclusive of costs, the sum or value of five hundred dollars, and arising under the Constitution or laws of the United States, or treaties made, or which shall be made, under their authority * * * .

This statute, too, substantially tracked the constitutional language, except that the 1875 statute specified that federal question jurisdiction shall be concurrent with the states and used "or" rather than "and" as a conjunction between "Constitution," "laws," and "treaties."

The 1875 Act also provided for removal jurisdiction in federal question cases for the first time:

> [A]ny suit of a civil nature, at law or in equity, now pending or

---

hereafter brought in any State court where the matter in dispute exceeds, exclusive of costs, the sum or value of five hundred dollars, and arising under the Constitution or laws of the United States, or treaties made, or which shall be made, under their authority, * * * either party may remove said suit into the circuit court of the United States for the proper district.

The meaning of the provision is reasonably clear apart from what one may think of its grammar and syntax: arising-under cases were made removable at the instance of either party. One may wonder why a plaintiff might wish to remove a federal question case, since he might well have brought it in federal court initially. The only logical explanation is that plaintiffs were given removal power in the event that the answer or reply raised a federal question. No other explanation is plausible. The significance of this provision for the development of the *Mottley* rule should not be underestimated.

The 1875 statute contained one other paragraph destined to become central to the century-long debate about the meaning of "arising under." Section 5 provided:

> That if, in any suit commenced in a circuit court or removed from a State court to a circuit court of the United States, it shall appear to the satisfaction of said circuit court, at any time after such suit has been brought or removed thereto, that such suit does not really and substantially involve a dispute or controversy properly within the jurisdiction of said circuit court, * * * the said circuit court shall proceed no further therein, but shall dismiss the suit or remand it to the court from which it was removed as justice may require.

This language might suggest several meanings, and it has been the subject of some scholarly debate. It might suggest that a case arising under federal law within the meaning of the Constitution and the first section of the 1875 Act could nonetheless be considered too insubstantial to warrant the expenditure of federal judicial energy.[22] On the other hand, as Professor Forrester has contended, it might have been intended only to permit the court to review its subject matter jurisdiction *sua sponte*, eliminating the need for a party to enter a plea in abatement. Finally, it may represent Congress' rejection, for statutory purposes, of Chief Justice Marshall's argument in *Osborn v. Bank of the United States* that an underlying federal issue, even if not disputed by the parties, was sufficient to confer jurisdiction under the constitutional provision. In any case, the 1875 Act used language that later became central to the morass surrounding the *Mottley* rule.

---

[22] * * * In Merrell Dow Pharmaceuticals v. Thompson, 106 S.Ct. 3229 (1986), the Court seems also to have adopted this view of statutory arising-under jurisdiction. * * *

There is almost no legislative history concerning the intended scope of "arising under" in the 1875 Act, but what little exists is unambiguous. Senator Carpenter, recalling Justice Story's argument that Congress was constitutionally required to vest the full scope of federal judicial power in the inferior federal courts, declared, "This bill does [vest such power] * * * . This bill gives precisely the power which the Constitution confers—nothing more, nothing less."[26]   The only contemporaneous commentator adopted Senator Carpenter's view, explaining Congress' action in light of the Civil War and the continuing reconstruction effort. Many later commentators have expressed a similar understanding.

Shortly after 1875, in cases construing the Act, the Court appeared to adopt this broad view. Its repeated citations of cases construing constitutional "arising under" jurisdiction suggests that the Court believed that Congress intended the constitutional language to define the scope of the statute. In 1893, referring to the statute as amended in 1887 and 1888, a unanimous Court declared:

> The intention of Congress is manifest, at least as to cases of which the courts of the several States have concurrent jurisdiction, and which involve a certain amount or value, to vest in the Circuit Courts of the United States full and effectual jurisdiction, as contemplated by the Constitution, over each of the classes of controversies above mentioned * * * .

Notwithstanding this history, however, it is clear that the statutory provision has not generally been accorded the same breadth as the constitutional grant.

In 1887, Congress amended the 1875 Act in several respects. It made no change in the original jurisdiction of the trial courts except to increase the jurisdictional amount from $500 to $2000. The statutory language governing removal, however, was radically altered:

> [A]ny suit of a civil nature, at law or equity, arising under the Constitution or laws of the United States, or treaties made, or which shall be made, under their authority, of which the circuit courts of the United States are given original jurisdiction by the preceding section, which may now be pending, or which may hereafter be brought, in any State court, may be removed by the defendant or defendants therein to the circuit court of the United States for the proper district * * * .

This language reflects two significant changes. First, Congress deleted the language that had closely paraphrased the "arising under" clause of

---

[26] 2 CONG.REC. 4986-87 (1874) (statement of Sen. Carpenter). Senator Carpenter (R.Wis.) was president *pro tempore* of the Senate and apparently the only legislator to comment on the 1875 Act on the Senate floor. The fact that Justice Story's interpretation of Congress' obligation was never widely adopted does nothing to undercut the scope or clarity of Senator Carpenter's remarks.

the Constitution and replaced it with a reference to the section of the statute conferring original jurisdiction, a section that had remained substantially unchanged from the 1875 version. Second, the plaintiff's power to remove was eliminated.

* * *

In 1888, Congress tried to clarify the poorly drafted language of the 1887 Act. But, the 1888 statute left the language conferring original jurisdiction unchanged, while amending the section dealing with removal jurisdiction to eliminate the run-on sentence. The amended section continued to restrict removal to defendants and to refer to the original jurisdiction language of the preceding section of the statute.

Beginning in 1911, Congress recodified the statutory provisions concerning original and removal jurisdiction on several occasions, making only minor changes in the language. Thus, for practical purposes, by 1888 Congress had settled on the final statutory contours of federal question jurisdiction, whether invoked originally or by removal.

LOUISVILLE AND NASHVILLE RAILROAD COMPANY v. MOTTLEY

Supreme Court of the United States, 1908.
211 U.S. 149, 29 S.Ct. 42, 53 L.Ed. 126.

The bill alleged that in September, 1871, plaintiffs, while passengers upon the defendant railroad, were injured by the defendant's negligence, and released their respective claims for damages in consideration of the agreement for transportation during their lives, expressed in the contract. It is alleged that the contract was performed by the defendant up to January 1, 1907, when the defendant declined to renew the passes. The bill then alleges that the refusal to comply with the contract was based solely upon that part of the act of Congress of June 29, 1906, 34 Stat. 584, which forbids the giving of free passes or free transportation. The bill further alleges: First, that the act of Congress referred to does not prohibit the giving of passes under the circumstances of this case; and, second, that if the law is to be construed as prohibiting such passes, it is in conflict with the Fifth Amendment of the Constitution, because it deprives the plaintiffs of their property without due process of law. The defendant demurred to the bill. The judge of the Circuit Court overruled the demurrer, entered a decree for the relief prayed for, and the defendant appealed directly to this court.

Mr. Justice Moody, after making the foregoing statement, delivered the opinion of the court.

Two questions of law were raised by the demurrer to the bill, were brought here by appeal, and have been argued before us. They are, first, whether that part of the act of Congress of June 29, 1906 (34 Stat. 584), which forbids the giving of free passes or the collection of any different compensation for transportation of passengers than that specified in the tariff filed, makes it unlawful to perform a contract for transportation of persons, who in good faith, before the passage of the act, had accepted such contract in satisfaction of a valid cause of action against the railroad; and, second, whether the statute, if it should be construed to render such a contract unlawful, is in violation of the Fifth Amendment of the Constitution of the United States. We do not deem it necessary, however, to consider either of these questions, because, in our opinion, the court below was without jurisdiction of the cause. Neither party has questioned that jurisdiction, but it is the duty of this court to see to it that the jurisdiction of the Circuit Court, which is defined and limited by statute, is not exceeded. This duty we have frequently performed of our own motion.

There was no diversity of citizenship and it is not and cannot be suggested that there was any ground of jurisdiction, except that the case was a "suit * * * arising under the Constitution and laws of the United States." It is the settled interpretation of these words, as used in this statute, conferring jurisdiction, that a suit arises under the Constitution and laws of the United States only when the plaintiff's statement of his own cause of action shows that it is based upon those laws or that Constitution. It is not enough that the plaintiff alleges some anticipated defense to his cause of action and asserts that the defense is invalidated by some provision of the Constitution of the United States. Although such allegations show that very likely, in the course of the litigation, a question under the Constitution would arise, they do not show that the suit, that is, the plaintiff's original cause of action, arises under the Constitution. In *Tennessee v. Union & Planters' Bank,* the plaintiff, the State of Tennessee, brought suit in the Circuit Court of the United States to recover from the defendant certain taxes alleged to be due under the laws of the State. The plaintiff alleged that the defendant claimed an immunity from the taxation by virtue of its charter, and that therefore the tax was void, because in violation of the provision of the Constitution of the United States, which forbids any State from passing a law impairing the obligation of contracts. The cause was held to be beyond the jurisdiction of the Circuit Court, the court saying, by Mr. Justice Gray, "a suggestion of one party, that the other will or may set up a claim under the Constitution or laws of the United States, does not make the suit one arising under that Constitution or those laws." Again, in *Boston & Montana Consolidated Copper & Silver Mining Company v. Montana Ore Purchasing Company,* the plaintiff brought suit in the Circuit Court of the United States for the conversion of copper ore and for an injunction against its continuance. The plaintiff then alleged, for the purpose of showing jurisdiction, in substance, that the defendant would set up in defense certain laws of the United States. The cause was held to be beyond the jurisdiction of the Circuit Court, the court saying, by Mr. Justice Peckham:

It would be wholly unnecessary and improper in order to prove complainant's cause of action to go into any matters of defence which the defendants might possibly set up and then attempt to reply to such defence, and thus, if possible, to show that a Federal question might or probably would arise in the course of the trial of the case. To allege such defence and then make an answer to it before the defendant has the opportunity to itself plead or prove its own defence is inconsistent with any known rule of pleading so far as we are aware, and is improper.

The rule is a reasonable and just one that the complainant in the first instance shall be confined to a statement of its cause of action, leaving to the defendant to set up in his answer what his defence is and, if anything more than a denial of complainant's cause of action, imposing upon the defendant the burden of proving such defence.

Conforming itself to that rule the complainant would not, in the assertion or proof of its cause of action, bring up a single Federal question. The presentation of its cause of action would not show that it was one arising under the Constitution or laws of the United States.

The only way in which it might be claimed that a Federal question was presented would be in the complainant's statement of what the defence of defendants would be and complainant's answer to such defence. Under these circumstances the case is brought within the rule laid down in *Tennessee v. Union & Planters' Bank.* That case has been cited and approved many times since * * * .

The interpretation of the act which we have stated was first announced in *Metcalf v. Watertown,* and has since been repeated and applied [in seventeen other cases decided by the Supreme Court following *Metcalf*].

* * *

The application of this rule to the case at bar is decisive against the jurisdiction of the Circuit Court. * * *

Notes and Questions

1. The Mottleys were not to be denied their day in court, or even their day in federal court. They returned to the state courts and brought an action identical to the dismissed federal action. They succeeded in the Kentucky courts, but the railroad appealed to the United States Supreme Court, which finally ruled on the federal issues it had declined to adjudicate three years earlier. The Mottleys lost. *Louisville & Nashville Railroad v. Mottley,* 219 U.S. 467, 31 S.Ct. 265, 55 L.Ed. 297 (1911)

2. a) The rule from *Mottley,* commonly known as the well-pleaded complaint rule, substantially antedates *Mottley* itself. Nonetheless, *Mottley* is

the case most often associated with the rule and cited for it.

b) In evaluating cases like *Mottley* to see if they qualify for statutory federal question jurisdiction, one should get into the habit of drafting the complaint. Only in that manner can one reliably determine the jurisdictional issue. What pleading standards should be used to determine whether a particular document satisfies the *Mottley* test? A good test should distinguish between cases of artful pleading and those presenting substantial federal issues for adjudication.

3. What is achieved by limiting federal question jurisdiction in the manner mandated by *Mottley*? The only apparent issues between the parties were the applicability of the no-free-pass law to the Mottleys and its constitutionality. Does the Court's decision to refuse the case make sense?

4. Could Congress overrule *Mottley*? Should it? Is it significant that Congress has recodified federal question jurisdiction several times since *Mottley* without commenting on it?

5. The Court continues to insist on the *Mottley* rule even when one might suspect that the rule frustrates congressional intent. In *Holmes Group, Inc. v. Vornado Air Circulation Systems Inc.*, 535 U.S. 826, 122 S.Ct. 1889, 153 L.Ed.2d 13 (2002), the plaintiff sought a declaratory judgment that it was not infringing the defendant's trade dress, and the defendant responded with a patent law counterclaim. The district court entered judgment for the plaintiff, but stayed all proceedings on the defendant's counterclaim. The defendant appealed to the Federal Circuit, which has exclusive jurisdiction over "an appeal from a final decision of a district court of the United States * * * if the jurisdiction of that court was based, in whole or in part," on 28 U.S.C. § 1338. *See* 28 U.S.C. § 1295. The Court held that because the well-pleaded-complaint rule applies to actions under § 1338 just as it does to actions under § 1331, the district court's jurisdiction could not rest on § 1338 because the *plaintiff* stated no patent claim. Justice Scalia's opinion reaffirmed that counterclaims cannot serve as the basis for arising-under jurisdiction. The defendant argued that Congress created the Federal Circuit and gave it exclusive jurisdiction in order to achieve uniformity in patent law. Justice Scalia rebuffed the suggestion that the exclusive appellate jurisdiction should come into play whenever a case contains a patent law counterclaim. "Our task here is not to determine what would further Congress's goal of ensuring patent-law uniformity, but to determine what the words of the statute must fairly be understood to mean. * * * It would be an unprecedented feat of interpretive necromancy to say that § 1338's 'arising under' language means one thing (the well-pleaded-complaint rule) in its own right, but something quite different (respondent's complaint-or-counterclaim rule) when referred to by § 1295(a)(1)." Justices Ginsburg and O'Connor argued that "when the claim stated in a compulsory counterclaim 'aris[es]' under federal patent law and is adjudicated on the merits by a federal district court, the Federal Circuit has exclusive appellate jurisdiction over that adjudication and other determinations made in the same case * * * ," although they concurred in the judgment because the district court had not actually adjudicated the patent counterclaim.

6. How does the scope of statutory federal question jurisdiction as interpreted in *Mottley* differ from the scope of constitutional federal question jurisdiction as delineated in *Osborn*? What practical difference do the distinctions between Article III and statutory federal question jurisdiction make?

7. Some justify the *Mottley* rule by arguing that adjudication of federal issues in state courts can be followed by Supreme Court review, as in *Mottley* itself. Consider, however, whether that is realistic. As a practical matter, cases brought in the state courts have a slim chance of Supreme Court review. One result, then, of the *Mottley* rule is that important federal issues may be finally adjudicated in the state courts. Presumably the federal courts have greater expertise in federal law than the state courts and will make fewer errors dealing with it. If state courts make more errors, the Supreme Court may feel compelled to review cases it would otherwise not hear were they originally handled by the lower federal courts. Thus, lessening the case load of the district courts may be at the expense of the load of the Supreme Court, a body substantially less elastic in its work capacity than the District Court with its 680 authorized judges.

8. Suppose that a plaintiff could plead federal law as an ingredient of a claim within the meaning of *Mottley* but elects not to do so and sues in the state courts. May the defendant remove the action on the ground that the plaintiff is avoiding federal law that properly should be part of the complaint? In *Metropolitan Life Ins. Co. v. Taylor*, 481 U.S. 58, 107 S.Ct. 1542, 95 L.Ed.2d 55 (1987), the Court held that the Employee Retirement Income Security Act (ERISA) had so completely preempted state law that the plaintiff's attempt to plead a state claim was unavailing; ERISA had, in effect, federalized the state claim. *Metropolitan*'s theory followed *Avco Corp. v. Machinists*, 390 U.S. 557, 88 S.Ct. 1235, 20 L.Ed.2d 126 (1968), *affirming* 376 F.2d 337, 340 (6th Cir.1967): "[s]tate law does not exist as an independent source of private rights to enforce collective bargaining contracts" governed by the Labor Management Relations Act. And, in *Sweeney v. Abramovitz*, 449 F.Supp. 213 (D.Conn.1978), the court held that artificial omission of a federal allegation did not prevent the defendant from removing to federal court.

On the other hand, in *Caterpillar, Inc. v. Williams*, 482 U.S. 386, 107 S.Ct. 2425, 96 L.Ed.2d 318 (1987), the Supreme Court limited *Avco* by ruling that the Labor Management Relations Act preempted state law only with respect to contracts between employers and unions, not with respect to individual employment contracts between employers and employees. Although the employees could have proceeded under the collective bargaining agreement, they elected not to do so. The Court held that "[t]he [*Mottley*] rule makes the plaintiff the master of the claim; he or she may avoid federal jurisdiction by exclusive reliance on state law." Thus, *Caterpillar* seemed sharply to limit the reach of *Metropolitan, AVCO*, and *Sweeney*.

Beneficial National Bank v. Anderson, 539 U.S. 1, 123 S.Ct. 2058, 156 L.Ed.2d 1 (2003), returned to *Avco* preemption theory. Anderson sued Beneficial to recover damages, alleging that Beneficial charged interest in excess of that permitted by Alabama common law and an Alabama usury statute.

However, the National Bank Act, 12 U.S.C. §§ 85, 86, in addition to specifying the maximum lawful rate of interest chargeable by national banks, includes a private right of action for debtors subjected to usurious interest charges. Plaintiff commenced his action in an Alabama state court, and defendant removed. The district court denied plaintiff's motion to remand, but the Eleventh Circuit reversed on the ground that the complaint did not allege a federal claim and that Congress had given no indication in the National Bank Act that it intended to permit removal of actions brought under § 86. A 6-to-3 majority of the Justices found that the National Bank Act so completely preempts the area that the plaintiff could not state a claim under Alabama law at all. Regarding removal, the majority effectively found that the Eleventh Circuit had improperly conceived the issue; the question was not whether Congress had indicated in § 86 that such actions were removable, but rather whether § 86 contained any indication that the ordinary removal rules of 28 U.S.C. § 1441 did not apply. With respect to the preemption issue, the Court stated that congressional intent to preempt state remedies was paramount: "Only if Congress intended § 86 to provide the exclusive cause of action for usury claims against national banks would the statute be comparable to the provisions that we construed in the *Avco* and *Metropolitan Life* cases." The majority wasted no time in finding that Congress did so intend, and therefore found that although the plaintiff may have thought that he was pleading two state claims, he was actually pleading a single federal claim.

Justice Scalia, joined by Justice Thomas, dissented. In his view, the long-established rule that the plaintiff is the master of the claim prevented the Court's majority from recharacterizing the plaintiff's state claims as a federal claim. Preemption, he argued, is simply one species of defense to a state claim. He therefore felt that the well-pleaded-complaint rule should have kept the case out of the federal court, on the authority of *Caterpillar*'s statement that "a case may *not* be removed to federal court on the basis of the defense of pre-emption." Justice Scalia also mounted a frontal attack on *Avco*'s legitimacy, arguing that *Avco* rested unjustifiably on *dictum* from *Lincoln Mills* that Justice Scalia thought the *Avco* Court had taken out of context. He saw *Metropolitan Life Ins. Co. v. Taylor* as an empty echo of *Avco*: "*Taylor*, in other words, rests upon a sort of statutory incorporation of *Avco*. *Avco* itself, on the other hand, continues to rest upon nothing."

Justice Scalia also questioned the entire notion of federalizing state claims. He distinguished the federal courts' occasional adoption of the content of a state rule as federal common law[7] from conversion of a state claim into a federal claim. In his view, complete federal preemption (which he did not dispute) compelled the conclusion that the state claims had met their demise, requiring dismissal of the action.

> [T]he mere fact that a state-law claim is invalid no more deprives it of its character as a state-law claim which [sic] does not raise a federal

---

[7] *United States v. Kimbell Foods, Inc.* (page 395 of the text) and *Semtek International Incorporated v. Lockheed Martin Corporation* (*infra* at 423) discuss and exemplify this phenomenon.

question, than does the fact that a federal claim is invalid deprives it of its character as a federal claim which [*sic*] does raise a federal question. The proper response to the presentation of a nonexistent claim to a state court is *dismissal*, not the "federalize-and-remove" dance authorized by today's opinion.

Is Justice Scalia's argument persuasive? If so, what drove the majority to expand *Avco* to cover this situation?

9. One of the authors has suggested abandoning the well-pleaded complaint rule and allowing any action presenting an outcome-determinative federal issue to be heard in the federal courts, either originally, by permitting the plaintiff to anticipate federal defenses or replies, or by removal at the instance of either party after a federal issue has been injected into the case by pleadings after the complaint. *See* Donald L. Doernberg, *There's No Reason for It; It's Just Our Policy: Why the Well-Pleaded Complaint Rule Sabotages the Purposes of Federal Question Jurisdiction*, 38 HASTINGS L.J. 597 (1987). What new difficulties might adoption of that suggestion create? What old problems might it solve?

VERLINDEN B.V. v. CENTRAL BANK OF NIGERIA
Supreme Court of the United States, 1983.
461 U.S. 480, 103 S.Ct. 1962, 76 L.Ed.2d 81.

CHIEF JUSTICE BURGER delivered the opinion of the Court.

We granted certiorari to consider whether the Foreign Sovereign Immunities Act of 1976, by authorizing a foreign plaintiff to sue a foreign state in a United States District Court on a non-federal cause of action, violates Article III of the Constitution.

I

On April 21, 1975, the Federal Republic of Nigeria and petitioner Verlinden B.V., a Dutch corporation with its principal offices in Amsterdam, The Netherlands, entered into a contract providing for the purchase of 240,000 metric tons of cement by Nigeria. The parties agreed that the contract would be governed by the laws of the Netherlands and that disputes would be resolved by arbitration before the International Chamber of Commerce, Paris, France.

The contract provided that the Nigerian government was to establish an irrevocable, confirmed letter of credit for the total purchase price through Slavenburg's Bank in Amsterdam. According to petitioner's amended complaint, however, respondent Central Bank of Nigeria, an instrumentality of Nigeria, improperly established an unconfirmed letter of credit payable through Morgan Guaranty Trust Company in New York.

In August 1975, Verlinden subcontracted with a Liechtenstein corporation, Interbuco, to purchase the cement needed to fulfill the contract. Meanwhile, the ports of Nigeria had become clogged with hundreds of ships carrying cement, sent by numerous other cement suppliers with whom Nigeria also had entered contracts. In mid-September, Central Bank unilaterally directed its correspondent banks, including Morgan Guaranty, to adopt a series of amendments to all letters of credit issued in connection with the cement contracts. Central Bank also directly notified the suppliers that payment would be made only for those shipments approved by Central Bank two months before their arrival in Nigerian waters.

Verlinden then sued Central Bank in United States District Court for the Southern District of New York, alleging that Central Bank's actions constituted an anticipatory breach of the letter of credit. Verlinden alleged jurisdiction under § 2 of the Foreign Sovereign Immunities Act, 28 U.S.C. § 1330.[4] Respondent moved to dismiss for, among other reasons, lack of subject matter and personal jurisdiction.

The District Court first held that a federal court may exercise subject matter jurisdiction over a suit brought by a foreign corporation against a foreign sovereign. Although the legislative history of the Foreign Sovereign Immunities Act does not clearly reveal whether Congress intended the Act to extend to actions brought by foreign plaintiffs, Judge Weinfeld reasoned that the language of the Act is "broad and embracing. It confers jurisdiction over 'any nonjury civil action' against a foreign state." Moreover, in the District Court's view, allowing *all* actions against foreign sovereigns, including those initiated by foreign plaintiffs, to be brought in federal court was necessary to effectuate "the Congressional purpose of concentrating litigation against sovereign states in the federal courts in order to aid the development of a uniform body of federal law governing assertions of sovereign immunity." The District Court also held that Article III subject matter jurisdiction extends to suits by foreign corporations against foreign sovereigns, stating:

> [The Act] imposes a single, federal standard to be applied uniformly by both state and federal courts hearing claims brought against foreign states. In consequence, even though the plaintiff's claim is one grounded upon common law, the case is one that "arises under" a federal law because the complaint compels the application of the uniform federal standard governing assertions of sovereign immunity. In short, the Immunities Act injects an essential federal element into all suits brought against foreign states.

---

[4] Section 2, 28 U.S.C. § 1330, provides:

> (a) The district courts shall have original jurisdiction without regard to amount in controversy of any nonjury civil action against a foreign state as defined in section 1603(a) of this title as to any claim for relief in personam with respect to which the foreign state is not entitled to immunity either under sections 1605–1607 of this title or under any applicable international agreement.

> (b) Personal jurisdiction over a foreign state shall exist as to every claim for relief over which the district courts have jurisdiction under subsection (a) where service has been made under section 1608 of this title.

The District Court nevertheless dismissed the complaint, holding that a foreign instrumentality is entitled to sovereign immunity unless one of the exceptions specified in the Act applies. After carefully considering each of the exceptions upon which petitioner relied, the District Court concluded that none applied, and accordingly dismissed the action.[5]

The Court of Appeals for the Second Circuit affirmed, but on different grounds. The court agreed with the District Court that the Act was properly construed to permit actions brought by foreign plaintiffs. The court held, however, that the Act exceeded the scope of Article III of the Constitution. In the view of the Court of Appeals, neither the diversity clause nor the "arising under" clause of Article III is broad enough to support jurisdiction over actions by foreign plaintiffs against foreign sovereigns; accordingly it concluded that Congress was without power to grant federal courts jurisdiction in this case, and affirmed the District Court's dismissal of the action.

We granted certiorari, and we reverse and remand.

II

* * *

In 1976, Congress passed the Foreign Sovereign Immunities Act in order to free the Government from the case-by-case diplomatic pressures, to clarify the governing standards, and to "assur[e] litigants that * * * decisions are made on purely legal grounds and under procedures that insure due process." To accomplish these objectives, the Act contains a comprehensive set of legal standards governing claims of immunity in every civil action against a foreign state or its political subdivisions, agencies or instrumentalities.

For the most part, the Act codifies, as a matter of federal law, the restrictive theory of sovereign immunity. A foreign state is normally immune from the jurisdiction of federal and state courts, 28 U.S.C. § 1604, subject to a set of exceptions specified in §§ 1605 and 1607. Those exceptions include actions in which the foreign state has explicitly or impliedly waived its immunity, and actions based upon commercial activities of the foreign sovereign carried on in the United States or causing a di-

---

[5] The District Court dismissed "for lack of personal jurisdiction." Under the Act, however, both statutory subject matter jurisdiction (otherwise known as "competence") and personal jurisdiction turn on application of the substantive provisions of the Act. Under § 1330(a), federal district courts are provided subject matter jurisdiction if a foreign state is "not entitled to immunity either under sections 1605-1607 * * * or under any applicable international agreement;" § 1330(b) provides personal jurisdiction wherever subject matter jurisdiction exists under subsection (a) and service of process has been made under § 1608 of the Act. Thus, if none of the exceptions to sovereign immunity set forth in the Act applies, the District Court lacks both statutory subject matter jurisdiction and personal jurisdiction. The District Court's conclusion that none of the exceptions to the Act applied therefore signified an absence of both competence and personal jurisdiction.

rect effect in the United States. When one of these or the other specified exceptions applies, "the foreign state shall be liable in the same manner and to the same extent as a private individual under like circumstances."

The Act expressly provides that its standards control in "the courts of the United States and of the States," and thus clearly contemplates that such suits may be brought in either federal or state courts. However, "[i]n view of the potential sensitivity of actions against foreign states and the importance of developing a uniform body of law in this area," the Act guarantees foreign states the right to remove any civil action from a state court to a federal court. The Act also provides that any claim permitted under the Act may be brought from the outset in federal court. If one of the specified exceptions to sovereign immunity applies, a federal district court may exercise subject matter jurisdiction under § 1330(a); but if the claim does not fall within one of the exceptions, federal courts lack subject matter jurisdiction. In such a case, the foreign state is also ensured immunity from the jurisdiction of state courts by § 1604.

* * *

IV

We now turn to the core question presented by this case: whether Congress exceeded the scope of Article III of the Constitution by granting federal courts subject matter jurisdiction over certain civil actions by foreign plaintiffs against foreign sovereigns where the rule of decision may be provided by state law.

This Court's cases firmly establish that Congress may not expand the jurisdiction of the federal courts beyond the bounds established by the Constitution. Within Article III of the Constitution, we find two sources authorizing the grant of jurisdiction in the Foreign Sovereign Immunities Act: the diversity clause and the "arising under" clause. The diversity clause, which provides that the judicial power extends to controversies between "a State, or the Citizens thereof, and foreign States," covers actions by citizens of states. Yet diversity jurisdiction is not sufficiently broad to support a grant of jurisdiction over actions by foreign plaintiffs, since a foreign plaintiff is not "a State, or [a] Citize[n] thereof." We conclude, however, that the "arising under" clause of Article III provides an appropriate basis for the statutory grant of subject matter jurisdiction to actions by foreign plaintiffs under the Act.

The controlling decision on the scope of Article III "arising under" jurisdiction is Chief Justice Marshall's opinion for the Court in *Osborn v. Bank of the United States*. In *Osborn*, the Court upheld the constitutionality of a statute that granted the Bank of the United States the right to sue in federal court on causes of action based upon state law. There, the Court concluded that the "judicial department may receive * * * the power of construing every * * * law" that "the Legislature may constitutionally make." The rule was laid down that:

> [I]t [is] a sufficient foundation for jurisdiction, that the title or right set up by the party, may be defeated by one construction of the constitution or law[s] of the United States, and sustained by the opposite construction.

Osborn thus reflects a broad conception of "arising under" jurisdiction, according to which Congress may confer on the federal courts jurisdiction over any case or controversy that might call for the application of federal law. The breadth of that conclusion has been questioned. It has been observed that, taken at its broadest, *Osborn* might be read as permitting "assertion of original federal jurisdiction on the remote possibility of presentation of a federal question." We need not now resolve that issue or decide the precise boundaries of Article III jurisdiction, however, since the present case does not involve a mere speculative possibility that a federal question may arise at some point in the proceeding. Rather, a suit against a foreign state under this Act necessarily raises questions of substantive federal law at the very outset, and hence clearly "arises under" federal law, as that term is used in Article III.

By reason of its authority over foreign commerce and foreign relations, Congress has the undisputed power to decide, as a matter of federal law, whether and under what circumstances foreign nations should be amenable to suit in the United States. Actions against foreign sovereigns in our courts raise sensitive issues concerning the foreign relations of the United States, and the primacy of federal concerns is evident.

To promote these federal interests, Congress exercised its Article I powers by enacting a statute comprehensively regulating the amenability of foreign nations to suit in the United States. The statute must be applied by the District Courts in every action against a foreign sovereign, since subject matter jurisdiction in any such action depends on the existence of one of the specified exceptions to foreign sovereign immunity, 28 U.S.C. § 1330(a). At the threshold of every action in a District Court against a foreign state, therefore, the court must satisfy itself that one of the exceptions applies—and in doing so it must apply the detailed federal law standards set forth in the Act. Accordingly, an action against a foreign sovereign arises under federal law, for purposes of Article III jurisdiction.

In reaching a contrary conclusion, the Court of Appeals relied heavily upon decisions construing 28 U.S.C. § 1331, the statute which grants district courts general federal question jurisdiction over any case that "arises under" the laws of the United States. The court placed particular emphasis on the so-called "well-pleaded complaint" rule, which provides, for purposes of statutory "arising under" jurisdiction, that the federal question must appear on the face of a well-pleaded complaint and may not enter in anticipation of a defense. In the view of the Court of Appeals, the question of foreign sovereign immunity in this case arose solely as a defense, and not on the face of Verlinden's well-pleaded complaint.

Although the language of § 1331 parallels that of the "arising under" clause of Article III, this Court never has held that statutory "arising under" jurisdiction is identical to Article III "arising under" jurisdiction. Quite the contrary is true. Section 1331, the general federal question statute, although broadly phrased,

> has been continuously construed and limited in the light of the history that produced it, the demands of reason and coherence, and the dictates of sound judicial policy which have emerged from the [statute's] function as a provision in the mosaic of federal judiciary legislation. *It is a statute, not a Constitution, we are expounding.*

([E]mphasis added). In an accompanying footnote, the Court further observed, "Of course the many limitations which have been placed on jurisdiction under § 1331 are not limitations on the constitutional power of Congress to confer jurisdiction on the federal courts." As these decisions make clear, Article III "arising under" jurisdiction is broader than federal question jurisdiction under § 1331, and the Court of Appeals' heavy reliance on decisions construing that statute was misplaced.

In rejecting "arising under" jurisdiction, the Court of Appeals also noted that § 2 of the Foreign Sovereign Immunities Act, 28 U.S.C. § 1330, is a jurisdictional provision.[22] Because of this, the court felt its conclusion compelled by prior cases in which this Court has rejected Congressional attempts to confer jurisdiction on federal courts simply by enacting jurisdictional statutes. * * *

From these cases, the Court of Appeals apparently concluded that a jurisdictional statute can never constitute the federal law under which the action arises, for Article III purposes. Yet the statutes at issue in these prior cases sought to do nothing more than grant jurisdiction over a particular class of cases. As the Court stated in *The Propeller Genesee Chief,* "The law * * * contains no regulations of commerce * * * . *It merely confers a new jurisdiction on the district courts; and this is its only object and purpose* * * * . It is evident * * * that Congress, in passing [the law], did not intend to exercise their power to regulate commerce * * * ." (Emphasis added).

---

[22] Although a major function of the Act as a whole is to regulate jurisdiction of federal courts over cases involving foreign states, the Act's purpose is to set forth "comprehensive rules governing sovereign immunity." H.R.REP. NO. 94-1487, at 12. The Act also prescribes procedures for commencing lawsuits against foreign states in federal and state courts and specifies the circumstances under which attachment and execution may be obtained against the property of foreign states. In addition, the Act defines "Extent of Liability," setting out a general rule that the foreign sovereign is "liable in the same manner and to the same extent as a private individual," subject to certain specified exceptions, 28 U.S.C. § 1606. In view of our resolution of this case, we need not consider petitioner's claim that § 1606 itself renders every claim against a foreign sovereign a federal cause of action.

In contrast, in enacting the Foreign Sovereign Immunities Act, Congress expressly exercised its power to regulate foreign commerce, along with other specified Article I powers. As the House Report clearly indicates, the primary purpose of the Act was to "se[t] forth comprehensive rules governing sovereign immunity"; the jurisdictional provisions of the Act are simply one part of this comprehensive scheme. The Act thus does not merely concern access to the federal courts. Rather, it governs the types of actions for which foreign sovereigns may be held liable in a court in the United States, federal or state. The Act codifies the standards governing foreign sovereign immunity as an aspect of substantive federal law, and applying those standards will generally require interpretation of numerous points of federal law. Finally, if a court determines that none of the exceptions to sovereign immunity applies, the plaintiff will be barred from raising his claim in any court in the United States—manifestly, "the title or right set up by the party, may be defeated by one construction of the * * * laws of the United States, and sustained by the opposite construction." *Osborn v. Bank of the United States.* That the inquiry into foreign sovereign immunity is labeled under the Act as a matter of jurisdiction does not affect the constitutionality of Congress' action in granting federal courts jurisdiction over cases calling for application of this comprehensive regulatory statute.

Congress, pursuant to its unquestioned Article I powers, has enacted a broad statutory framework governing assertions of foreign sovereign immunity. In so doing, Congress deliberately sought to channel cases against foreign sovereigns away from the state courts and into federal courts, thereby reducing the potential for a multiplicity of conflicting results among the courts of the 50 states. The resulting jurisdictional grant is within the bounds of Article III, since every action against a foreign sovereign necessarily involves application of a body of substantive federal law, and accordingly "arises under" federal law, within the meaning of Article III.

V

A conclusion that the grant of jurisdiction in the Foreign Sovereign Immunities Act is consistent with the Constitution does not end the case. An action must not only satisfy Article III but must also be supported by a statutory grant of subject matter jurisdiction. As we have made clear, deciding whether statutory subject matter jurisdiction exists under the Foreign Sovereign Immunities Act entails an application of the substantive terms of the Act to determine whether one of the specified exceptions to immunity applies.

In the present case, the District Court, after satisfying itself as to the constitutionality of the Act, held that the present action does not fall within any specified exception. The Court of Appeals, reaching a contrary conclusion as to jurisdiction under the Constitution, did not find it necessary to address this statutory question. Accordingly, on remand the Court of Appeals must consider whether jurisdiction exists under the Act itself. If the Court of Appeals agrees with the District Court on that issue, the case will be at an end. If, on the other hand, the Court of Appeals concludes that jurisdiction does exist under the statute, the action may then be remanded to the District Court for further proceedings.

It is so ordered.

Notes and Questions

1. What does *Verlinden* mean for the constitutional tests of federal question jurisdiction that *Osborn* articulated? Does it endorse *Osborn*? Which case involves a more expansive exercise of federal question jurisdiction?

2. What does *Verlinden* suggest about the well-pleaded complaint rule?

3. Since the federal question in *Verlinden* is the existence of sovereign immunity, and since sovereign immunity is tied to subject matter jurisdiction by 28 U.S.C.A. § 1330(a), did not the plaintiff satisfy *Mottley* because pursuant to FED.R.CIV.P. 8(a)(1) a complaint must plead subject matter jurisdiction? If that is so, then is the Court's discussion of the well-pleaded complaint rule merely *dictum*?

4. As a policy matter, why is it desirable for cases like *Verlinden* to be handled in the federal courts at all? This country's only apparent connection with the case is through the correspondent bank, which is not even individually exposed to liability. In *Gully v. Meridian National Bank* (*supra* at 270), Justice Cardozo observed that a "case does not arise under a law renouncing a defense." The Foreign Sovereign Immunities Act, in these circumstances, does just that. Given that all of the parties are aliens, is not *Verlinden* the paradigmatic example of why the federal courts should not get involved in cases like this?

AMERICAN WELL WORKS CO.
v. LAYNE & BOWLER CO.
Supreme Court of the United States, 1916.
241 U.S. 257, 36 S.Ct. 585, 60 L.Ed. 987.

MR. JUSTICE HOLMES delivered the opinion of the court.

This is a suit begun in a state court, removed to the United States Court, and then, on motion to remand by the plaintiff, dismissed by the latter court, on the ground that the cause of action arose under the patent laws of the United States, that the state court had no jurisdiction, and that therefore the one to which it was removed had none.[b] There is

---

[b] [AUTHORS' NOTE] Until 1986, removal jurisdiction was considered wholly derivative, so that the federal district court could not acquire subject matter jurisdiction if the state court had lacked it. This led to the anomalous result exemplified by the federal trial court here. The plaintiff's case, viewed by the court as exclusively federal, was dismissed by the federal court so that the plaintiff could refile the case in federal court. The addition of 28 U.S.C.A. § 1441(e) eliminated this bizarre dance.

a proper certificate and the case comes here direct from the District Court.

Of course the question depends upon the plaintiff's declaration. That may be summed up in a few words. The plaintiff alleges that it owns, manufactures and sells a certain pump, has or has applied for a patent for it, and that the pump is known as the best in the market. It then alleges that the defendants have falsely and maliciously libeled and slandered the plaintiff's title to the pump by stating that the pump and certain parts thereof are infringements upon the defendant's pump and certain parts thereof and that without probable cause they have brought suits against some parties who are using the plaintiff's pump and that they are threatening suits against all who use it. The allegation of the defendants' libel or slander is repeated in slightly varying form but it all comes to statements to various people that the plaintiff was infringing the defendants' patent and that the defendant would sue both seller and buyer if the plaintiff's pump was used. Actual damage to the plaintiff in its business is alleged to the extent of $50,000 and punitive damages to the same amount are asked.

It is evident that the claim for damages is based upon conduct, or, more specifically, language, tending to persuade the public to withdraw its custom from the plaintiff and having that effect to its damage. Such conduct having such effect is equally actionable whether it produces the result by persuasion, by threats or by falsehood, and it is enough to allege and prove the conduct and effect, leaving the defendant to justify if he can. If the conduct complained of is persuasion, it may be justified by the fact that the defendant is a competitor, or by good faith and reasonable grounds. If it is a statement of fact, it may be justified, absolutely or with qualifications, by proof that the statement is true. But all such justifications are defences and raise issues that are no part of the plaintiff's case. In the present instance it is part of the plaintiff's case that it had a business to be damaged; whether built up by patents or without them does not matter. It is no part of it to prove anything concerning the defendants' patent or that the plaintiff did not infringe the same—still less to prove anything concerning any patent of its own. The material statement complained of is that the plaintiff infringes—which may be true notwithstanding the plaintiff's patent. That is merely a piece of evidence. Furthermore, the damage alleged presumably is rather the consequence of the threat to sue than of the statement that the plaintiff's pump infringed the defendants' rights.

A suit for damages to business caused by a threat to sue under the patent law is not itself a suit under the patent law. And the same is true when the damage is caused by a statement of fact—that the defendant has a patent which is infringed. What makes the defendants' act a wrong is its manifest tendency to injure the plaintiff's business and the wrong is the same whatever the means by which it is accomplished. But whether it is a wrong or not depends upon the law of the State where the act is done, not upon the patent law, and therefore the suit arises under the law of the State. A suit arises under the law that creates the cause of action. The fact that the justification may involve the validity and infringement of a patent is no more material to the question under what law the suit is brought than it would be in an action of contract. If the State adopted for civil proceedings the saying of the old criminal law: the greater the truth the greater the libel, the validity of the patent would not come in question at all. In Massachusetts the truth would not be a defence if the statement was made from disinterested malevolence. The State is master of the whole matter, and if it saw fit to do away with actions of this type altogether, no one, we imagine, would suppose that they still could be maintained under the patent laws of the United States.

Judgment reversed.

Notes and Questions

1. Is the test *American Well Works* announced consistent with the approach to federal question jurisdiction *Mottley* exemplified? Was it appropriate for Justice Holmes to write the opinion without even citing *Mottley*, either to follow, modify, or overrule it? The decision was only eight years old, and he had been a member of the unanimous Court that announced it. Does *Mottley* shed any light on the proper disposition of *American Well Works*? Although today a plaintiff in a trade libel action must plead and prove the falsity of the defendant's statements, that apparently was not the case when the Court decided *American Well Works*, as Justice Holmes's language on the preceding page makes clear. Would today's pleading requirements for a trade libel action make a difference for *Mottley* purposes? If so, how?

2. Does *American Well Works* hold that federal question jurisdiction exists whenever federal law creates the cause of action?

In *Shoshone Mining Co. v. Rutter,* 177 U.S. 505, 20 S.Ct. 726, 44 L.Ed. 864 (1900), the Supreme Court refused jurisdiction in a case involving conflicting miners' claims to tracts of western land. Despite a federal cause of action in a comprehensive congressional scheme for resolving such disputes, the Court found no jurisdiction. Although Congress had authorized the cause of action for adverse claims, it had also provided that local law should govern most claims involving land. The Court pointed out that Congress had not even incorporated such law as a body of federal law; it had merely made its use permissible. The statute authorizing the adverse-claim action provided only that such claims could be brought in a "court of competent jurisdiction." The Court observed that in most cases, the controversy between the parties would be resolved on issues of fact or of local law, with no provision of federal law being disputed either as to its meaning or its application. The Justices expressed their concern about the federal courts being inundated with essentially local suits and found that although federal law created the underlying cause of action, Congress did not intend, merely by doing so, to expand federal jurisdiction. Does *American Well Works* overrule

Shoshone?

3. Justice Holmes's test for federal question jurisdiction clearly has the advantage of simplicity. If this bright-line test were rigorously applied, new categories of cases would be included in and excluded from federal jurisdiction. For example, a dispute involving title to western lands originally granted under a federal land patent might arise under federal law, contrary to the result in *Shoshone*. On the other hand, disputes like that in *American Well Works* itself, where apparently the only contested issues revolve around the patents, would be consigned to the state courts. Are those boundaries desirable? If not, is the remedy to reinterpret the statute or to redraft it? If the latter, how?

SMITH v. KANSAS CITY TITLE & TRUST CO.
Supreme Court of the United States, 1921.
255 U.S. 180, 41 S.Ct. 243, 65 L.Ed. 577.

MR. JUSTICE DAY delivered the opinion of the court.

A bill was filed in the United States District Court for the Western Division of the Western District of Missouri by a shareholder in the Kansas City Title & Trust Company to enjoin the Company, its officers, agents and employees from investing the funds of the Company in farm loan bonds issued by Federal Land Banks or Joint Stock Land Banks under authority of the Federal Farm Loan Act of July 17, 1916.

The relief was sought on the ground that these acts were beyond the constitutional power of Congress. The bill avers that the Board of Directors of the Company are about to invest its funds in the bonds to the amount of $10,000 in each of the classes described, and will do so unless enjoined by the court in this action. The bill avers the formation of twelve Federal Land Banks, and twenty-one Joint Stock Land Banks under the provisions of the act.

* * *

Section 27 of the act provides that Farm Loan Bonds issued under the provisions of the act by Federal Land Banks or Joint Stock Land Banks shall be a lawful investment for all fiduciary and trust funds, and may be accepted as security for all public deposits. The bill avers that the defendant Trust Company is authorized to buy, invest in and sell government, state and municipal and other bonds, but it cannot buy, invest in or sell any such bonds, papers, stocks or securities which are not authorized to be issued by a valid law or which are not investment securities, but that nevertheless it is about to invest in Farm Loan Bonds; that the Trust Company has been induced to direct its officers to make the investment by reason of its reliance upon the provisions of the Farm Loan Acts, especially §§ 21, 26 and 27, by which the Farm Loan Bonds are declared to be instrumentalities of the Government of the United States, and as such with the income derived therefrom, are declared to be exempt from federal, state, municipal and local taxation, and are further declared to be lawful investments for all fiduciary and trust funds. The bill further avers that the acts by which it is attempted to authorize the bonds are wholly illegal, void and unconstitutional and of no effect because unauthorized by the Constitution of the United States.

The bill prays that the acts of Congress authorizing the creation of the banks, especially §§ 21, 26 and 27 thereof, shall be adjudged and decreed to be unconstitutional, void and of no effect, and that the issuance of the Farm Loan Bonds, and the taxation exemption feature thereof, shall be adjudged and decreed to be invalid.

* * * The Kansas City Title & Trust Company filed a motion to dismiss in the nature of a general demurrer, and upon hearing the District Court entered a decree dismissing the bill. From this decree appeal was taken to this court.

No objection is made to the federal jurisdiction, either original or appellate, by the parties to this suit, but that question will be first examined. The Company is authorized to invest its funds in legal securities only. The attack upon the proposed investment in the bonds described is because of the alleged unconstitutionality of the acts of Congress undertaking to organize the banks and authorize the issue of the bonds. No other reason is set forth in the bill as a ground of objection to the proposed investment by the Board of Directors acting in the Company's behalf. As diversity of citizenship is lacking, the jurisdiction of the District Court depends upon whether the cause of action set forth arises under the Constitution or laws of the United States.

The general rule is that where it appears from the bill or statement of the plaintiff that the right to relief depends upon the construction or application of the Constitution or laws of the United States, and that such federal claim is not merely colorable, and rests upon a reasonable foundation, the District Court has jurisdiction under this provision.

At an early date, considering the grant of constitutional power to confer jurisdiction upon the federal courts, Chief Justice Marshall said: "A case in law or equity consists of the right of the one party, as well as of the other, and may truly be said to arise under the Constitution or a law of the United States, whenever its correct decision depends on the construction of either," and again, when "the title or right set up by the party may be defeated by one construction of the Constitution or law of the United States, and sustained by the opposite construction." *Osborn v. Bank of the United States.*

This characterization of a suit arising under the Constitution or laws of the United States has been followed in many decisions of this and other federal courts.

* * *

The jurisdiction of this court is to be determined upon the principles laid down in the cases referred to. In the instant case the averments of the bill show that the directors were proceeding to make the investments in view of the act authorizing the bonds about to be purchased, maintaining that the act authorizing them was constitutional and the bonds valid and desirable investments. The objecting shareholder avers in the bill that the securities were issued under an unconstitutional law, and hence of no validity. It is, therefore, apparent that the controversy concerns the constitutional validity of an act of Congress which is directly drawn in question. The decision depends upon the determination of this issue.

The general allegations as to the interest of the shareholder, and his right to have an injunction to prevent the purchase of the alleged unconstitutional securities by misapplication of the funds of the corporation, give jurisdiction * * * . We are, therefore, of the opinion that the District Court had jurisdiction under the averments of the bill, and that a direct appeal to this court upon constitutional grounds is authorized.

* * *

[The Court examined the constitutional grounds that Smith urged and concluded that his claims were without merit.]

It follows that the decree of the District Court is

Affirmed.

MR. JUSTICE HOLMES, dissenting.

No doubt it is desirable that the question raised in this case should be set at rest, but that can be done by the Courts of the United States only within the limits of the jurisdiction conferred upon them by the Constitution and the laws of the United States. As this suit was brought by a citizen of Missouri against a Missouri corporation the single ground upon which the jurisdiction of the District Court can be maintained is that the suit "arises under the Constitution or laws of the United States" within the meaning of § 24 of the Judicial Code. I am of opinion that this case does not arise in that way and therefore that the bill should have been dismissed.

It is evident that the cause of action arises not under any law of the United States but wholly under Missouri law. The defendant is a Missouri corporation and the right claimed is that of a stockholder to prevent the directors from doing an act, that is, making an investment, alleged to be contrary to their duty. But the scope of their duty depends upon the charter of their corporation and other laws of Missouri. If those laws had authorized the investment in terms the plaintiff would have had no case, and this seems to me to make manifest what I am unable to deem even debatable, that, as I have said, the cause of action arises wholly under Missouri law. If the Missouri law authorizes or forbids the investment according to the determination of this Court upon a point under the Constitution or acts of Congress, still that point is material only because the Missouri law saw fit to make it so. The whole foundation of the duty is Missouri law, which at its sole will incorporated the other law as it might incorporate a document. The other law or document depends for its relevance and effect not on its own force but upon the law that took it up, so I repeat once more the cause of action arises wholly from the law of the State.

But it seems to me that a suit cannot be said to arise under any other law than that which creates the cause of action. It may be enough that the law relied upon creates a part of the cause of action although not the whole, as held in *Osborn v. Bank of the United States,* which perhaps is all that is meant by the less guarded expressions in *Cohens v. Virginia.* I am content to assume this to be so, although the *Osborn Case* has been criticized and regretted. But the law must create at least a part of the cause of action by its own force, for it is the suit, not a question in the suit, that must arise under the law of the United States. The mere adoption by a state law of a United States law as a criterion or test, when the law of the United States has no force *proprio vigore,* does not cause a case under the state law to be also a case under the law of the United States, and so it has been decided by this Court again and again.

I find nothing contrary to my views in *Brushaber v. Union Pacific R.R. Co.* It seems to me plain that the objection that I am considering was not before the mind of the Court or the subject of any of its observations, if open. I am confirmed in my view of that case by the fact that in the next volume of reports is a decision, reached not without discussion and with but a single dissent, that "a suit arises under the law that creates the cause of action." That was the *ratio decidendi* of *American Well Works Co. v. Layne & Bowler Co.* I know of no decisions to the contrary and see no reason for overruling it now.

Notes and Questions

1. Note the similarity between the test articulated in *Smith* and one test from *Osborn v. Bank of the United States.* Did the Court thus intend to signal that statutory federal question jurisdiction was co-extensive with the bounds described in Article III, § 2?

2. What did the complaint in *Smith* look like? Was Justice Holmes correct in asserting that the cause of action arose "not under any law of the United States, but *wholly* under Missouri law"? (Emphasis added).

3. In 1916, only five years before *Smith,* the Court had voted six to one[8] for Justice Holmes's law-that-creates-the-cause-of-action test. Chief Justice White and Justices Hughes, McReynolds, Pitney and Van Devanter joined Justice Holmes in refusing jurisdiction; Justice McKenna dissented. In

---

[8] Justice Lamar had died; his seat was vacant when the Court decided *American Well Works.* Justice Day did not participate in the decision.

1921, a six-to-two Court found jurisdiction in *Smith* in a situation clearly inconsistent with Holmes's test. Justice McKenna, now in the majority, was joined by Chief Justice White and Justices Clarke, Day, Pitney and Van Devanter. Justice McReynolds was still with Justice Holmes, now in dissent. Justice Brandeis did not participate. Thus, Chief Justice White and Justices Van Devanter and Pitney, who had opposed jurisdiction in *American Well Works,* supported it in *Smith.* Why? Had three members of the Court changed their views on so fundamental a matter as subject matter jurisdiction within the space of five years? If so, why did none of them offer an explanation? Is it possible that they did not see their positions as inconsistent? Can you construct a view of *American Well Works* and *Smith* that permits simultaneous support of the results in each case?

4. Scholars have been hard pressed to reconcile *American Well Works* and *Smith.* Professor Hirschman noted that "[t]he almost simultaneous decisions in *Smith* and *American Well Works* set up a situation where two incompatible approaches to the problem enjoyed equal precedential status." Linda R. Hirschman, *Whose Law Is It Anyway? A Reconsideration of Federal Question Jurisdiction Over Cases of Mixed State and Federal Law,* 60 IND.L.J. 17, 31 (1984). She suggests that *American Well Works* is the more closely followed, *Smith* being aberrant. Professor Redish, however, comparing *Smith* and *American Well Works* (before the 1986 decision in *Merrell Dow Pharmaceuticals, Inc. v. Thompson*) suggested that "*Smith* continues to provide the most cogent basis for a modern construction of section 1331 * * *. *Smith*'s expansion of the *American Well Works* principle has been widely followed in the federal courts * * *." MARTIN H. REDISH, FEDERAL JURISDICTION: TENSIONS IN THE ALLOCATION OF JUDICIAL POWER 69 (1980). Which rule seems better to fulfill the purposes of federal question jurisdiction?

5. Judge Friendly, partly because of clash between the theories of *Smith* and *American Well Works,* suggested that Holmes's test is "more useful for inclusion than for the exclusion for which it was intended." *T.B. Harms Co. v. Eliscu,* 339 F.2d 823, 827 (2d Cir.1964), *cert. denied* 381 U.S. 915, 85 S.Ct. 1534, 14 L.Ed.2d 435 (1965). But, as Professor Redish points out:

> It is not even entirely accurate, however, to say that federal question jurisdiction exists whenever the cause of action is created by federal law, for on occasion federal question jurisdiction has been rejected even where the cause of action derived solely from federal law. *Shoshone Mining Co. v. Rutter* is an example.

MARTIN H. REDISH, FEDERAL JURISDICTION: TENSIONS IN THE ALLOCATION OF JUDICIAL POWER 103 (2d ed. 1990) (footnote omitted).

6. While it is a struggle to reconcile *American Well Works* and *Smith,* it is even more difficult to harmonize *Smith* with *Moore v. Chesapeake & Ohio Ry.,* 291 U.S. 205, 54 S.Ct. 402, 78 L.Ed. 755 (1934). Moore sought damages for injuries suffered during his employment by the railroad. He stated two counts, one under the Federal Employers Liability Act, the other under a parallel Kentucky provision, certain regulations of the Interstate Commerce Act, and the Federal Safety Appliance Act. Kentucky law incorporated fed-

eral law, stating that an employer's negligence could not be negated by the employee's contributory negligence or assumption of risk if the employer had violated any state or federal employee-safety statute.

The case is unusual because, although the plaintiff sued in federal court, he also argued that there was no federal question jurisdiction because the federal regulations and statute involved in his claim under Kentucky law required actions to be prosecuted in the employer's home state. Moore had sued in Indiana, his home; the defendant was a Virginia citizen. Moore thus invoked diversity jurisdiction and did not need federal question jurisdiction. The railroad sought dismissal for improper venue under the federal regulations. Moore countered that the action was not federal, and therefore was not governed by the ICC's special venue provisions. The Court agreed with Moore and held that the second cause of action arose under Kentucky law despite that law's wholesale adoption of federal safety standards.

Are *Smith* and *Moore* reconcilable? In light of the purposes of federal question jurisdiction, which case reaches a sounder result, or can they both be justified? Draft the complaint in *Moore*. What did the plaintiff have to allege to state his claim for relief? How should the federal issue arise?

GULLY v. FIRST NATIONAL BANK, 299 U.S. 109, 57 S.Ct. 96, 81 L.Ed. 70 (1936).

During the Depression, First National Bank purchased the assets and assumed the liabilities of a predecessor national bank. One of the liabilities was a state tax obligation, assessed pursuant to a federal statute permitting such taxation, thus avoiding the constitutional problem addressed in *M'Culloch v. Maryland* (1819). The statute also prescribed that tax assessments be made either against the shareholders of such banks, to be collected from the banks themselves as agents, or against the banks directly based upon their income only. The Mississippi tax law echoed the federal statute.

Gully, the state tax collector, sued to collect the tax. The Bank removed to federal court, arguing that only by virtue of the federal enabling statute was Gully able to maintain the admittedly state-created claim for taxes. On the merits, the Bank argued that the tax violated the statute because it was assessed against the property, not the income, of the predecessor bank. The Fifth Circuit affirmed the district court judgment finding federal question jurisdiction and dismissing on the merits. The Supreme Court, speaking through Justice Cardozo, reversed, finding no jurisdiction.

> How and when a case arises "under the Constitution or laws of the United States" has been much considered in the books. Some tests are well established. To bring a case within the statute, a right or immunity created by the Constitution or laws of the United States must be an element, and an essential one, of the plaintiff's cause of action. The right or immunity must be such that it will be supported if the Constitution or laws of the United States are given

one construction or effect, and defeated if they receive another. A genuine and present controversy, not merely a possible or conjectural one, must exist with reference thereto and the controversy must be disclosed upon the face of the complaint, unaided by the answer or by the petition for removal. Indeed, the complaint itself will not avail as a basis of jurisdiction in so far as it goes beyond a statement of the plaintiff's cause of action and anticipates or replies to a probable defense.

Looking backward we can see that the early cases were less exacting than the recent ones in respect of some of these conditions. If a federal right was pleaded, the question was not always asked whether it was likely to be disputed. This is seen particularly in suits by or against a corporation deriving its charter from an act of Congress. Modern statutes have greatly diminished the importance of those decisions by narrowing their scope. Federal incorporation is now abolished as a ground of federal jurisdiction except where the United States holds more than one-half the stock. Partly under the influence of statutes disclosing a new legislative policy, partly under the influence of more liberal decisions, the probable course of the trial, the real substance of the controversy, has taken on a new significance. "A suit to enforce a right which takes its origin in the laws of the United States is not necessarily, or for that reason alone, one arising under those laws, for a suit does not so arise unless it really and substantially involves a dispute or controversy respecting the validity, construction or effect of such a law, upon the determination of which the result depends." Today, even more clearly than in the past, "the federal nature of the right to be established is decisive—not the source of the authority to establish it."

* * *

This Court has had occasion to point out how futile is the attempt to define a "cause of action" without reference to the context. To define broadly and in the abstract "a case arising under the Constitution or laws of the United States" has hazards of a kindred order. What is needed is something of that common-sense accommodation of judgment to kaleidoscopic situations which characterizes the law in its treatment of problems of causation. One could carry the search for causes backward, almost without end. Instead, there has been a selective process which picks the substantial causes out of the web and lays the other ones aside. As in problems of causation, so here in the search for the underlying law. If we follow the ascent far enough, countless claims of right can be discovered to have their source or their operative limits in the provisions of a federal statute or in the Constitution itself with its circumambient restrictions upon legislative power. To set bounds to the pursuit, the courts have formulated the distinction between controversies that are basic and those that are collateral, between disputes that are necessary and those that are merely possible. We shall be lost in a maze if we put that compass by.

Notes and Questions

1. What restriction does *Gully* place on statutory federal question jurisdiction in addition to that imposed by *Mottley*? Should it be important that the federal enabling statute was the *sine qua non* of Gully's cause of action, even though that claim was state-created?

2. In *Osborn,* Chief Justice Marshall asserted that the potential existence of a federal question not raised by either party made the case a federal question case. Does Justice Cardozo reject that part of *Osborn*? What is the significance of his language about the remoteness of the federal issue?

3. Is there another way to reach the result in *Gully*? If the parties were to contest the federal issue, how would it come up?

MERRELL DOW PHARMACEUTICALS, INC. v. THOMPSON
Supreme Court of the United States, 1986.
478 U.S. 804, 106 S.Ct. 3229, 92 L.Ed.2d 650.

JUSTICE STEVENS delivered the opinion of the Court.

The question presented is whether the incorporation of a federal standard in a state-law private action, when Congress has intended that there not be a federal private action for violations of that federal standard, makes the action one "arising under the Constitution, laws, or treaties of the United States," 28 U.S.C. § 1331.

I

The Thompson respondents are residents of Canada and the MacTavishes reside in Scotland. They filed virtually identical complaints against petitioner, a corporation, that manufactures and distributes the drug Bendectin. The complaints were filed in the Court of Common Pleas in Hamilton County, Ohio. Each complaint alleged that a child was born with multiple deformities as a result of the mother's ingestion of Bendectin during pregnancy. In five of the six counts, the recovery of substantial damages was requested on common-law theories of negligence, breach of warranty, strict liability, fraud, and gross negligence. In Count IV, respondents alleged that the drug Bendectin was "misbranded" in violation of the Federal Food, Drug, and Cosmetic Act (FDCA), because its labeling did not provide adequate warning that its use was potentially dangerous. [Plaintiffs] alleged that the violation of the FDCA "in the promotion" of Bendectin "constitutes a rebuttable presumption of negligence." [They further] alleged that the "violation of said federal statutes directly and proximately caused the injuries suffered" by the two infants.

Petitioner filed a timely petition for removal from the state court to the Federal District Court alleging that the action was "founded, in part, on an alleged claim arising under the laws of the United States." After removal, the two cases were consolidated. Respondents filed a motion to remand to the state forum on the ground that the federal court lacked subject-matter jurisdiction. Relying on our decision in *Smith v. Kansas City Title & Trust Co.,* the District Court held that Count IV of the complaint alleged a cause of action arising under federal law and denied the motion to remand. It then granted petitioner's motion to dismiss on *forum non conveniens* grounds.

The Court of Appeals for the Sixth Circuit reversed. After quoting one sentence from the concluding paragraph in our recent opinion in *Franchise Tax Board v. Construction Laborers Vacation Trust,* and noting "that the FDCA does not create or imply a private right of action for individuals injured as a result of violations of the Act," it explained:

> Federal question jurisdiction would, thus, exist only if plaintiffs' right to relief *depended necessarily* on a substantial question of federal law. Plaintiffs' causes of action referred to the FDCA merely as one available criterion for determining whether Merrell Dow was negligent. Because the jury could find negligence on the part of Merrell Dow without finding a violation of the FDCA, the plaintiffs' causes of action did not depend necessarily upon a question of federal law. Consequently, the causes of action did not arise under federal law and, therefore, were improperly removed to federal court.

We granted certiorari, and we now affirm.

II

Article III of the Constitution gives the federal courts power to hear cases "arising under" federal statutes. That grant of power, however, is not self-executing, and it was not until the Judiciary Act of 1875 that Congress gave the federal courts general federal-question jurisdiction. Although the constitutional meaning of "arising under" may extend to all cases in which a federal question is "an ingredient" of the action, *Osborn v. Bank of the United States,* we have long construed the statutory grant of federal-question jurisdiction as conferring a more limited power.

Under our longstanding interpretation of the current statutory scheme, the question whether a claim "arises under" federal law must be determined by reference to the "well-pleaded complaint." A defense that raises a federal question is inadequate to confer federal jurisdiction. Since a defendant may remove a case only if the claim could have been brought in federal court, moreover, the question for removal jurisdiction must also be determined by reference to the "well-pleaded complaint."

As was true in *Franchise Tax Board,* the propriety of the removal in this case thus turns on whether the case falls within the original "federal question" jurisdiction of the federal courts. There is no "single, precise definition" of that concept; rather, "the phrase 'arising under' masks a welter of issues regarding the interrelation of federal and state authority and the proper management of the federal judicial system."

This much, however, is clear. The "vast majority" of cases that come within this grant of jurisdiction are covered by Justice Holmes' statement that a " 'suit arises under the law that creates the cause of action.' " Thus, the vast majority of cases brought under the general federal-question jurisdiction of the federal courts are those in which federal law creates the cause of action.

We have, however, also noted that a case may arise under federal law "where the vindication of a right under state law necessarily turned on some construction of federal law." Our actual holding in *Franchise Tax Board* demonstrates that this statement must be read with caution; the central issue presented in that case turned on the meaning of the Employee Retirement Income Security Act of 1974, but we nevertheless concluded that federal jurisdiction was lacking.

This case does not pose a federal question of the first kind; respondents do not allege that federal law creates any of the causes of action that they have asserted. This case thus poses what Justice Frankfurter called the "litigation-provoking problem,"—the presence of a federal issue in a state-created cause of action.

In undertaking this inquiry into whether jurisdiction may lie for the presence of a federal issue in a nonfederal cause of action, it is, of course, appropriate to begin by referring to our understanding of the statute conferring federal-question jurisdiction. We have consistently emphasized that, in exploring the outer reaches of § 1331, determinations about federal jurisdiction require sensitive judgments about congressional intent, judicial power, and the federal system.

> If the history of the interpretation of judiciary legislation teaches us anything, it teaches the duty to reject treating such statutes as a wooden set of self-sufficient words * * * . The Act of 1875 is broadly phrased, but it has been continuously construed and limited in the light of the history that produced it, the demands of reason and coherence, and the dictates of sound judicial policy which have emerged from the Act's function as a provision in the mosaic of federal judiciary legislation.

In *Franchise Tax Board,* we forcefully reiterated this need for prudence and restraint in the jurisdictional inquiry: "We have always interpreted what *Skelly Oil* called 'the current of jurisdictional legislation since the Act of March 3, 1875' with an eye to practicality and necessity."

In this case, both parties agree with the Court of Appeals' conclusion that there is no federal cause of action for FDCA violations. For purposes of our decision, we assume that this is a correct interpretation of the FDCA.

* * *

The significance of the necessary assumption that there is no federal private cause of action thus cannot be overstated. For the ultimate import of such a conclusion, as we have repeatedly emphasized, is that it would flout congressional intent to provide a private federal remedy for the violation of the federal statute. We think it would similarly flout, or at least undermine, congressional intent to conclude that the federal courts might nevertheless exercise federal-question jurisdiction and provide remedies for violations of that federal statute solely because the violation of the federal statute is said to be a "rebuttable presumption" or a "proximate cause" under state law, rather than a federal action under federal law.

III

Petitioner advances three arguments to support its position that, even in the face of this congressional preclusion of a federal cause of action for a violation of the federal statute, federal-question jurisdiction may lie for the violation of the federal statute as an element of a state cause of action.

First, petitioner contends that the case represents a straightforward application of the statement in *Franchise Tax Board* that federal-question jurisdiction is appropriate when "it appears that some substantial, disputed question of federal law is a necessary element of one of the well-pleaded state claims." *Franchise Tax Board,* however, did not purport to disturb the long-settled understanding that the mere presence of a federal issue in a state cause of action does not automatically confer federal-question jurisdiction. Indeed, in determining that federal-question jurisdiction was not appropriate in the case before us, we stressed Justice Cardozo's emphasis on principled, pragmatic distinctions: " 'What is needed is something of that common-sense accommodation of judgment to kaleidoscopic situations which characterizes the law in its treatment of causation * * * a selective process which picks the substantial causes out of the web and lays the other ones aside.' "

* * *

Given the significance of the assumed congressional determination to preclude federal private remedies, the presence of the federal issue as an element of the state tort is not the kind of adjudication for which jurisdiction would serve congressional purposes and the federal system.

* * *

We simply conclude that the congressional determination that there should be no federal remedy for the violation of this federal statute is tantamount to a congressional conclusion that the presence of a claimed violation of the statute as an element of a state cause of action is insufficiently "substantial" to confer federal-question jurisdiction.[12]

Second, petitioner contends that there is a powerful federal interest in seeing that the federal statute is given uniform interpretations, and that federal review is the best way of insuring such uniformity. In addition to the significance of the congressional decision to preclude a federal remedy, we do not agree with petitioner's characterization of the federal interest and its implications for federal-question jurisdiction. To the extent that petitioner is arguing that state use and interpretation of the FDCA pose a threat to the order and stability of the FDCA regime, petitioner should be arguing, not that federal courts should be able to review and enforce state FDCA-based causes of action as an aspect of federal-

---

[12] Several commentators have suggested that our § 1331 decisions can best be understood as an evaluation of the nature of the federal interest at stake. *Cf.* Kravitz v. Homeowners Warranty Corp., 542 F.Supp. 317, 320 (E.D.Pa.1982) (Pollak, J.) ("I cannot identify any compelling reasons of federal judicial policy for embracing a case of this kind as a federal question case. The essential Pennsylvania elements of plaintiffs' suit for rescission would be more appropriately dealt with by a Court of Common Pleas than by this court; and, with respect to the lesser-included issue of federal law, Pennsylvania's courts are fully competent to interpret the Magnuson-Moss Warranty Act and the relevant F.T.C. regulations, subject to review by the United States Supreme Court"). Focusing on the nature of the federal interest, moreover, suggests that the widely perceived "irreconcilable" conflict between the finding of federal jurisdiction in *Smith v. Kansas City Title & Trust Co.,* and the finding of no jurisdiction in *Moore v. Chesapeake & Ohio R. Co.* is far from clear. For the difference in results can be seen as manifestations of the differences in the nature of the federal issues at stake. In *Smith,* as the Court emphasized, the issue was the constitutionality of an important federal statute. ("It is * * * apparent that the controversy concerns the constitutional validity of an act of Congress which is directly drawn in question. The decision depends upon the determination of this issue"). In *Moore,* in contrast, the Court emphasized that the violation of the federal standard as an element of state tort recovery did not fundamentally change the state tort nature of the action. (" 'The action fell within the familiar category of cases involving the duty of a master to his servant. This duty is defined by the common law, except as it may be modified by legislation. The federal statute, in the present case, touched the duty of the master at a single point and, save as provided in the statute, the right of the plaintiff to recover was left to be determined by the law of the State' ").

The importance of the nature of the federal issue in federal-question jurisdiction is highlighted by the fact that, despite the usual reliability of the Holmes test as an inclusionary principle, this Court has sometimes found that formally federal causes of action were not properly brought under federal-question jurisdiction because of the overwhelming predominance of state-law issues. *See* Shulthis v. McDougal ("A suit to enforce a right which takes its origin in the laws of the United States is not necessarily, or for that reason alone, one arising under those laws, for a suit does not so arise unless it really and substantially involves a dispute or controversy respecting the validity, construction or effect of such a law, upon the determination of which the result depends. This is especially so of a suit involving rights to land acquired under a law of the United States. If it were not, every suit to establish title to land in the central and western States would so arise, as all titles in those States are traceable back to those laws"); Shoshone Mining Co. v. Rutter ("We pointed out in the former opinion that it was well settled that a suit to enforce a right which takes its origin in the laws of the United States is not necessarily one arising under the Constitution or laws of the United States, within the meaning of the jurisdiction clauses, for if it did every action to establish title to real estate (at least in the newer States) would be such a one, as all titles in those States come from the United States or by virtue of its laws").

question jurisdiction, but that the FDCA pre-empts state-court jurisdiction over the issue in dispute. Petitioner's concern about the uniformity of interpretation, moreover, is considerably mitigated by the fact that, even if there is no original district court jurisdiction for these kinds of action, this Court retains power to review the decision of a federal issue in a state cause of action.

Finally, petitioner argues that, whatever the general rule, there are special circumstances that justify federal-question jurisdiction in this case. Petitioner emphasizes that it is unclear whether the FDCA applies to sales in Canada and Scotland; there is, therefore, a special reason for having a federal court answer the novel federal question relating to the extraterritorial meaning of the Act. We reject this argument. We do not believe the question whether a particular claim arises under federal law depends on the novelty of the federal issue. Although it is true that federal jurisdiction cannot be based on a frivolous or insubstantial federal question, "the interrelation of federal and state authority and the proper management of the federal judicial system," would be ill served by a rule that made the existence of federal-question jurisdiction depend on the district court's case-by-case appraisal of the novelty of the federal question asserted as an element of the state tort. The novelty of an FDCA issue is not sufficient to give it status as a federal cause of action; nor should it be sufficient to give a state-based FDCA claim status as a jurisdiction-triggering federal question.[15]

IV

We conclude that a complaint alleging a violation of a federal statute as an element of a state cause of action, when Congress has determined that there should be no private, federal cause of action for the violation, does not state a claim "arising under the Constitution, laws, or treaties of the United States."

The judgment of the Court of Appeals is affirmed.

It is so ordered.

---

[15] Petitioner also contends that the Court of Appeals opinion rests on a view that federal-question jurisdiction was inappropriate because, whatever the role of the federal issue in the FDCA-related count, the plaintiff could recover on other, strictly state-law claims * * * (noting that "the jury could find negligence on the part of Merrell Dow without finding a violation of the FDCA"). To the extent that the opinion can be read to express such a view, we agree that it was erroneous. If the FDCA-related count presented a sufficient federal question, its relationship to the other, state-law claims would be determined by the ordinary principles of pendent jurisdiction described in [United] *Mine Workers v. Gibbs.* For the reasons that we have stated, however, there is no federal-question jurisdiction even with that possible error corrected.

JUSTICE BRENNAN, with whom JUSTICE WHITE, JUSTICE MARSHALL, and JUSTICE BLACKMUN join, dissenting.

* * *

I believe that the limitation on federal jurisdiction recognized by the Court today is inconsistent with the purposes of § 1331. Therefore, I respectfully dissent.

I

While the majority of cases covered by § 1331 may well be described by Justice Holmes' adage that "[a] suit arises under the law that creates the cause of action," it is firmly settled that there may be federal-question jurisdiction even though both the right asserted and the remedy sought by the plaintiff are state created. The rule as to such cases was stated in what Judge Friendly described as "[t]he path-breaking opinion" in *Smith v. Kansas City Title & Trust Co.*[1]

---

[1] Some commentators have argued that the result in *Smith* conflicts with our decision in *Moore v. Chesapeake & Ohio R. Co.* In *Moore,* the plaintiff brought an action under Kentucky's Employer Liability Act, which provided that a plaintiff could not be held responsible for contributory negligence or assumption of risk where his injury resulted from the violation of any state or federal statute enacted for the safety of employees. The plaintiff in *Moore* alleged that his injury was due to the defendant's failure to comply with the Federal Safety Appliance Act; therefore, an important issue in the adjudication of the state cause of action was whether the terms of the federal law had been violated. The Court could have dismissed the complaint on the ground that the federal issue would arise only in response to a defense of contributory negligence or assumption of risk, and that therefore there was no jurisdiction under the well-pleaded complaint rule. Instead, the Court held that "a suit brought under the state statute which defines liability to employees who are injured while engaged in intrastate commerce, and brings within the purview of the statute a breach of the duty imposed by the federal statute, should [not] be regarded as a suit arising under the laws of the United States and cognizable in the federal court in the absence of diversity of citizenship."

The Court suggests that *Smith* and *Moore* may be reconciled if one views the question whether there is jurisdiction under § 1331 as turning upon "an evaluation of the *nature* of the federal interest at stake." * * * Thus, the Court explains, while in *Smith* the issue was the constitutionality of "an important federal statute," in *Moore* the federal interest was less significant in that "the violation of the federal standard as an element of state tort recovery did not fundamentally change the state tort nature of the action."

In one sense, the Court is correct in asserting that we can reconcile *Smith* and *Moore* on the ground that the "nature" of the federal interest was more significant in *Smith* than in *Moore.* Indeed, as the Court appears to believe, we could reconcile many of the seemingly inconsistent results that have been reached under § 1331 with such a test. But this is so only because a test based upon an *ad hoc* evaluation of the importance of the federal issue is infinitely malleable: at what point does a federal interest become strong enough to create jurisdiction? What principles guide the determination whether a statute is "important" or not? Why, for instance, was the statute in *Smith* so "important" that direct review of a state-court decision (under our mandatory appellate jurisdiction) would have been inadequate? Would the result in *Moore* have been different if the federal issue had been a more important element of the tort claim? The point is that if one makes the test sufficiently vague and general, virtually any set of results can be "reconciled." However, the inevitable—and undesirable—result of a test such as that suggested in the Court's footnote 12 is that federal jurisdiction turns in every case on an appraisal of the federal issue, its importance and its relation to state-law issues. Yet it is precisely because the Court be-

* * *

The continuing vitality of *Smith* is beyond challenge. We have cited it approvingly on numerous occasions, and reaffirmed its holding several times—most recently just three Terms ago by a unanimous Court in *Franchise Tax Board v. Construction Laborers Vacation Trust.*

* * *

There is, to my mind, no question that there is federal jurisdiction over the respondents' fourth cause of action under the rule set forth in *Smith* and reaffirmed in *Franchise Tax Board.* Respondents pleaded that petitioner's labeling of the drug Bendectin constituted "misbranding" in violation of * * * the Federal Food, Drug, and Cosmetic Act (FDCA), and that this violation "directly and proximately caused" their injuries. Respondents asserted in the complaint that this violation established petitioner's negligence *per se* and entitled them to recover damages without more. No other basis for finding petitioner negligent was asserted in connection with this claim. As pleaded, then, respondents' "right to relief depend[ed] upon the construction or application of the Constitution or laws of the United States." *Smith; see also Franchise Tax Board* (there is federal jurisdiction under § 1331 where the plaintiff's right to relief "necessarily depends" upon resolution of a federal question). Furthermore, although petitioner disputes its liability under the FDCA, it concedes that respondents' claim that petitioner violated the FDCA is "colorable, and rests upon a reasonable foundation." *Smith.* Of course, since petitioner must make this concession to prevail in this Court, it need not be accepted at face value. However, independent examination of respondents' claim substantiates the conclusion that it is neither frivolous nor meritless. As stated in the complaint, a drug is "misbranded" under the FDCA if "the labeling or advertising fails to reveal facts material * * * with respect to consequences which may result from the use of the article to which the labeling or advertising relates * * * ." Obviously, the possibility that a mother's ingestion of Bendectin during pregnancy could produce malformed children is material. Peti-

---

lieves that federal jurisdiction would be "ill served" by such a case-by-case appraisal that it rejects petitioner's claim that the difficulty and importance of the statutory issue presented by its claim suffices to confer jurisdiction under § 1331. The Court cannot have it both ways.

My own view is in accord with those commentators who view the results in *Smith* and *Moore* as irreconcilable. That fact does not trouble me greatly, however, for I view *Moore* as having been a "sport" at the time it was decided and having long been in a state of innocuous desuetude. Unlike the jurisdictional holding in *Smith,* the jurisdictional holding in *Moore* has never been relied upon or even cited by this Court. *Moore* has similarly borne little fruit in the lower courts, leading Professor Redish to conclude after comparing the vitality of *Smith* and *Moore* that "the principle enunciated in *Smith* is the one widely followed by modern lower federal courts." Finally, as noted in text, the commentators have also preferred *Smith. Moore* simply has not survived the test of time; it is presently moribund, and, to the extent that it is inconsistent with the well-established rule of the *Smith* case, it ought to be overruled.

tioner's principal defense is that the Act does not govern the branding of drugs that are sold in foreign countries. It is certainly not immediately obvious whether this argument is correct. Thus, the statutory question is one which "discloses a need for determining the meaning or application of [the FDCA]," *T.B. Harms Co. v. Eliscu,* and the claim raised by the fourth cause of action is one "arising under" federal law within the meaning of § 1331.

II

The Court apparently does not disagree with any of this—except, of course, for the conclusion. According to the Court, if we assume that Congress did not intend that there be a private federal cause of action under a particular federal law (and, presumably, *a fortiori* if Congress' decision not to create a private remedy is express), we must also assume that Congress did not intend that there be federal jurisdiction over a state cause of action that is determined by that federal law. Therefore, assuming—only because the parties have made a similar assumption— that there is no private cause of action under the FDCA,[4] the Court holds that there is no federal jurisdiction over the plaintiffs' claim.

* * *

The Court nowhere explains the basis for this conclusion. Yet it is hardly self-evident. Why should the fact that Congress chose not to create a private federal *remedy* mean that Congress would not want there to be federal *jurisdiction* to adjudicate a state claim that imposes liability for violating the federal law? Clearly, the decision not to provide a private federal remedy should not affect federal jurisdiction unless the reasons Congress withholds a federal remedy are also reasons for withholding federal jurisdiction. Thus, it is necessary to examine the reasons for Congress' decisions to grant or withhold both federal jurisdiction and private remedies, something the Court has not done.

A

In the early days of our Republic, Congress was content to leave the task of interpreting and applying federal laws in the first instance to the state courts; with one short-lived exception, Congress did not grant the inferior federal courts original jurisdiction over cases arising under federal law until 1875. The reasons Congress found it necessary to add this

---

[4] It bears emphasizing that the Court does not hold that there is no private cause of action under the FDCA. Rather, it expressly states that "[f]or purposes of our decision, we assume that this is a correct interpretation of the FDCA." The Court simply holds petitioner to its concession that the FDCA provides no private remedy, and decides petitioner's claim on the basis of this concession. I shall do the same. Under the Court's analysis, however, if a party persuaded a court that there is a private cause of action under the FDCA, there would be federal jurisdiction under *Smith* and *Franchise Tax Board* over a state cause of action making violations of the FDCA actionable. Such jurisdiction would apparently exist even if the plaintiff did not seek the federal remedy.

jurisdiction to the district courts are well known. First, Congress recognized "the importance, and even necessity of *uniformity* of decisions throughout the whole United States, upon all subjects within the purview of the constitution." *Martin v. Hunter's Lessee,* (emphasis in original). Concededly, because federal jurisdiction is not always exclusive and because federal courts may disagree with one another, absolute uniformity has not been obtained even under § 1331. However, while perfect uniformity may not have been achieved, experience indicates that the availability of a federal forum in federal-question cases has done much to advance that goal. This, in fact, was the conclusion of the American Law Institute's Study of the Division of Jurisdiction Between State and Federal Courts.

In addition, § 1331 has provided for adjudication in a forum that specializes in federal law and that is therefore more likely to apply that law correctly. Because federal-question cases constitute the basic grist for federal tribunals, "[t]he federal courts have acquired a considerable expertness in the interpretation and application of federal law." By contrast, "it is apparent that federal question cases must form a very small part of the business of [state] courts." As a result, the federal courts are comparatively more skilled at interpreting and applying federal law, and are much more likely correctly to divine Congress' intent in enacting legislation.[6]

These reasons for having original federal-question jurisdiction explain why cases like this one and *Smith*—i.e., cases where the cause of action is a creature of state law, but an essential element of the claim is federal—"arise under" federal law within the meaning of § 1331. Congress passes laws in order to shape behavior; a federal law expresses Congress' determination that there is a federal interest in having individuals or other entities conform their actions to a particular norm established by that law. Because all laws are imprecise to some degree, disputes inevitably arise over what specifically Congress intended to re-

---

[6] Another reason Congress conferred original federal-question jurisdiction on the district courts was its belief that state courts are hostile to assertions of federal rights. Although this concern may be less compelling today than it once was, the American Law Institute reported as recently as 1969 that "it is difficult to avoid concluding that federal courts are more likely to apply federal law sympathetically and understandingly than are state courts." In any event, this rationale is, like the rationale based on the expertise of the federal courts, simply an expression of Congress belief that federal courts are more likely to interpret federal law correctly.

One might argue that this Court's appellate jurisdiction over state-court judgments in cases arising under federal law can be depended upon to correct erroneous state-court decisions and to insure that federal law is interpreted and applied uniformly. However, as any experienced observer of this Court can attest, "Supreme Court review of state courts, limited by docket pressures, narrow review of the facts, the debilitating possibilities of delay, and the necessity of deferring to adequate state grounds of decision, cannot do the whole job." Indeed, having served on this Court for 30 years, it is clear to me that, realistically, it cannot even come close to "doing the whole job" and that § 1331 is essential if federal rights are to be adequately protected.

quire or permit. It is the duty of courts to interpret these laws and apply them in such a way that the congressional purpose is realized. As noted above, Congress granted the district courts power to hear cases "arising under" federal law in order to enhance the likelihood that federal laws would be interpreted more correctly and applied more uniformly. In other words, Congress determined that the availability of a federal forum to adjudicate cases involving federal questions would make it more likely that federal laws would shape behavior in the way that Congress intended.

By making federal law an essential element of a state-law claim, the State places the federal law into a context where it will operate to shape behavior: the threat of liability will force individuals to conform their conduct to interpretations of the federal law made by courts adjudicating the state-law claim. It will not matter to an individual found liable whether the officer who arrives at his door to execute judgment is wearing a state or a federal uniform; all he cares about is the fact that a sanction is being imposed—and may be imposed again in the future—because he failed to comply with the federal law. Consequently, the possibility that the federal law will be incorrectly interpreted in the context of adjudicating the state-law claim implicates the concerns that led Congress to grant the district courts power to adjudicate cases involving federal questions in precisely the same way as if it was federal law that "created" the cause of action. It therefore follows that there is federal jurisdiction under § 1331.

B

The only remaining question is whether the assumption that Congress decided not to create a private cause of action alters this analysis in a way that makes it inappropriate to exercise original federal jurisdiction. According to the Court, "the very reasons for the development of the modern implied remedy doctrine" support the conclusion that, where the legislative history of a particular law shows (whether expressly or by inference) that Congress intended that there be no private federal remedy, it must also mean that Congress would not want federal courts to exercise jurisdiction over a state-law claim making violations of that federal law actionable. These reasons are " 'the increased complexity of federal legislation,' " " 'the increased volume of federal litigation,' " and " 'the desirability of a more careful scrutiny of legislative intent.' "

These reasons simply do not justify the Court's holding. Given the relative expertise of the federal courts in interpreting federal law, the increased complexity of federal legislation argues rather strongly in favor of recognizing federal jurisdiction. And, while the increased volume of litigation may appropriately be considered in connection with reasoned arguments that justify limiting the reach of § 1331, I do not believe that the day has yet arrived when this Court may trim a statute solely because it thinks that Congress made it too broad.

This leaves only the third reason: " 'the desirability of a more careful scrutiny of legislative intent.' " I certainly subscribe to the proposition that the Court should consider legislative intent in determining whether or not there is jurisdiction under § 1331. But the Court has not examined the purposes underlying either the FDCA or § 1331 in reaching its conclusion that Congress' presumed decision not to provide a private federal remedy under the FDCA must be taken to withdraw federal jurisdiction over a private state remedy that imposes liability for violating the FDCA. Moreover, such an examination demonstrates not only that it is consistent with legislative intent to find that there is federal jurisdiction over such a claim, but, indeed, that it is the Court's contrary conclusion that is inconsistent with congressional intent.

The enforcement scheme established by the FDCA is typical of other, similarly broad regulatory schemes. Primary responsibility for overseeing implementation of the Act has been conferred upon a specialized administrative agency, here the Food and Drug Administration (FDA). Congress has provided the FDA with a wide-ranging arsenal of weapons to combat violations of the FDCA * * *. Significantly, the FDA has no independent enforcement authority; final enforcement must come from the federal courts, which have exclusive jurisdiction over actions under the FDCA. Thus, while the initial interpretive function has been delegated to an expert administrative body whose interpretations are entitled to considerable deference, final responsibility for interpreting the statute in order to carry out the legislative mandate belongs to the federal courts.

Given that Congress structured the FDCA so that all express remedies are provided by the federal courts, it seems rather strange to conclude that it either "flout[s]" or "undermine[s]" congressional intent for the federal courts to adjudicate a private state-law remedy that is based upon violating the FDCA. That is, assuming that a state cause of action based on the FDCA is not preempted, it is entirely consistent with the FDCA to find that it "arises under" federal law within the meaning of § 1331. Indeed, it is the Court's conclusion that such a state cause of action must be kept out of the federal courts that appears contrary to legislative intent inasmuch as the enforcement provisions of the FDCA quite clearly express a preference for having federal courts interpret the FDCA and provide remedies for its violation.

* * *

Notes and Questions

1. What are the federal issues in this case? Analytically, how do they fit into the case? How do the majority and the dissent characterize their importance?

2. How persuasive are the distinctions drawn by the majority in footnote 12 among *Smith, Moore,* and *Merrell Dow*?

3. a) The Court concludes, apparently with the dissenters' and the parties' agreement, that Congress did not intend to create private rights of action under the Federal Food, Drug and Cosmetic Act. That conclusion is worth some attention when one studies the recent history of the doctrine of implication of private rights of action, discussed in Chapter 5. Assuming the Court's conclusion is correct, why is that important, given that the Thompsons and MacTavishes did not plead a cause of action under that Act?

b) What role does Congress play in determining jurisdiction in this case? Under what statute is jurisdiction being asserted? For what statute is the majority looking to congressional intent as a determinant of jurisdiction?

c) Assume that Congress did intend a private right of action to exist under the Federal Food, Drug and Cosmetic Act. How then would the majority rule on the jurisdictional challenge? Suppose the plaintiffs, eschewing a federal claim under the FDCA, had pleaded a single count of negligence as a state cause of action, relying for the establishment of negligence only upon the alleged mislabeling of the drug. Would that complaint qualify for federal question jurisdiction?

4. a) Does the Court implicitly suggest that jurisdiction under 28 U.S.C.A. § 1331 is now limited to federal causes of action, expressed or implied? If not, what is the relevance of Congress's presumed lack of intent to create a private right of action? If so, has the Court overruled *Smith* (over its own protest in footnote 12) and returned to *American Well Works*? Since the Court decided *Merrell Dow*, the lower federal courts have diverged on its significance. Several circuits have concluded that if Congress neither explicitly created a federal cause of action nor intended that the courts imply one, federal question jurisdiction cannot exist. *See, e.g., Utley v. Varian Associates, Inc.*, 811 F.2d 1279, 1283 (9th Cir.), *cert. denied* 484 U.S. 824, 108 S.Ct. 89, 98 L.Ed.2d 50 (1987) ("Under *Merrell Dow*, if a federal law does not provide a private right of action, then a state law action based on its violation perforce does not raise a 'substantial' federal question * * * ."). On the other hand, the Second Circuit takes the position that cases like *Smith* are still possible after *Merrell Dow*. In *West 14th Street Commercial Corp. v. 5 West 14th Street Owners Corp.*, 815 F.2d 188 (2d Cir.1987), the court ruled that if the well-pleaded federal question was "decisive," federal question jurisdiction would lie. The court distinguished cases like *Merrell Dow*, in which a federal standard was merely adopted by reference into state law as a standard of conduct, from circumstances where federal law creates the rights and defines the relationships upon which relief depends, even if state law actually creates the cause of action. One commentator has concluded, after an exhaustive study of lower court decisions since *Merrell Dow*, that *Merrell Dow* moves the federal courts far in the direction of *American Well Works*, and undesirably so. Patti Alleva, *Prerogative Lost: The Trouble with Statutory Federal Question Doctrine After* Merrell Dow, 52 OHIO ST.L.J. 1477 (1991). Which approach represents better policy? Which is the better reading of *Merrell Dow*?

b) If the Court has re-adopted the Holmes test, note that the scope of that test may be different from when Justice Holmes announced it. As more fully discussed in Chapter 5, the 1916 Court implied statutory causes of action far more readily than the current Court. *Compare, e.g., Texas & Pac. Ry. v. Rigsby,* 241 U.S. 33, 36 S.Ct. 482, 60 L.Ed. 874 (1916), *with Cort v. Ash,* 422 U.S. 66, 95 S.Ct. 2080, 45 L.Ed.2d 26 (1975), *see infra* at 455, *and California v. Sierra Club,* 451 U.S. 287, 101 S.Ct. 1775, 68 L.Ed.2d 101 (1981), *see infra* at 471. Thus, if the Court has limited § 1331 as suggested, it represents a double restriction on federal question jurisdiction.

5. a) *Christianson v. Colt Industries Operating Corp.,* 486 U.S. 800, 108 S.Ct. 2166, 100 L.Ed.2d 811 (1988), which confirms the identity of the "arising under" tests for general federal question jurisdiction under § 1331 and patent jurisdiction under § 1338, also suggests an explanation for *Merrell Dow* without relying on the Court's new substantiality test. There the unanimous Court noted:

> [It is not] necessarily sufficient that a well-pleaded claim alleges a single theory under which resolution of a patent-law question is essential. If "on the face of a well-pleaded complaint there are * * * reasons completely unrelated to the provisions and purposes of [the patent laws] why the [plaintiff] may or may not be entitled to the relief it seeks," then the claim does not "arise under" those laws. Thus, a claim supported by alternative theories in the complaint may not form the basis for § 1338 jurisdiction unless patent law is essential to *each* of those theories.[9]

[Emphasis added]. In *Merrell Dow,* the plaintiffs alleged ordinary negligence and negligence *per se* by reason of the mislabeling of the drug under the Food, Drug and Cosmetic Act. Their decision to plead ordinary negligence as an alternative theory might have undermined Merrell Dow's assertion of federal jurisdiction. Yet such a view seems inconsistent with footnote 15 in the majority opinion. It is not the existence of a pure state law claim that dooms the assertion of jurisdiction; it is the perceived lack of congressional intent that hybrid cases (state claims with federal components) be heard in the federal forum. The independent existence of a wholly state theory of recovery seems irrelevant.

Christianson may create more problems than it solves. Would the plaintiff there have been better off pleading only the patent law theory of recovery?[10] By doing so, does the plaintiff abandon the state-law theory of recov-

---

[9] It is ironic that Justice Brennan articulated this theory of jurisdictional purity in *Christianson*. Under the Court's early test for pendent jurisdiction, a complaint alleging "two distinct grounds in support of a single cause of action, * * * only one of which presents a federal question, * * *" Hurn v. Oursler, 289 U.S. 238, 246, 53 S.Ct. 586, 589, 77 L.Ed. 1148, 1154 (1933), would have been heard as a federal question case with pendent jurisdiction extended to the non-federal theory of recovery. That issue pattern is precisely what the Court confronted in *Christianson*. In 1966, the Court broadened the test for pendent jurisdiction, finding *Hurn* too restrictive. *See* United Mine Workers v. Gibbs, 383 U.S. 715, 86 S.Ct. 1130, 16 L.Ed.2d 218 (1966). Justice Brennan wrote the Court's opinion.

[10] Other theories may be available in a typical patent case. Patentees commonly license others to manufacture and market the patented invention. When disputes arise, a patentee may sue for breach of the licensing contract or for violation of the patent. *See, e.g.,* Albright v. Teas, 106 U.S. 613, 1 S.Ct. 550, 27 L.Ed. 295 (1882). Since alternative and

ery because of res judicata? The doctrine of claim preclusion, when applicable, bars claims that were or might have been brought in a prior action. A plaintiff might seek to avoid this result by bringing all claims in the state courts in order to avoid the jurisdiction problems. While that tactic would work for some plaintiffs, it is impossible when one of the claims, as in *Christianson,* is a patent claim subject to exclusively federal jurisdiction. Does *Christianson* thus implicitly put to the plaintiff the dilemma of abandoning either the federal patent claim or the state contract claim?

b) Is Justice Brennan's position in *Christianson* incompatible with his dissent in *Merrell Dow*? In the latter, he argued in favor of federal question jurisdiction where the plaintiffs had pleaded several theories of negligence, only one of which depended on federal law. Under his theory in *Merrell Dow,* should he have taken the opposite position in *Christianson*?

6. In other contexts, federal courts have permitted federal rights to be enforced by means of state-created causes of action. *See, e.g., Lowe v. General Motors Corp.,* 624 F.2d 1373, 1379-81 (5th Cir.1980) (state negligence verdict based upon violation of Motor Vehicle Safety Act upheld); *Lukaszewicz v. Ortho Pharmaceutical Corp.,* 510 F.Supp. 961, 964-65 (E.D.Wis.1981) (violation of the Federal Food, Drug and Cosmetic Act established negligence *per se* under Wisconsin law). Both of those cases, however, involved diversity, not federal question jurisdiction. How would the *Merrell Dow* Court decide those cases if the parties were not diverse?

7. In *Bell v. Hood,* 327 U.S. 678, 66 S.Ct. 773, 90 L.Ed. 939 (1946), the Supreme Court considered whether the non-existence of an asserted federal cause of action deprived the federal courts of jurisdiction. Plaintiffs had sued FBI agents who allegedly had violated plaintiffs' Fourth and Fifth Amendment rights. The government argued that neither Amendment contemplated a private right of action for damages, and that the plaintiffs therefore could not state a claim upon which relief could be granted, requiring dismissal under FED.R.CIV.P. 12(b)(6). Consequently, the government argued, the case did not arise under federal law. The Court held that there was subject matter jurisdiction.

> Jurisdiction, therefore, is not defeated as respondents seem to contend, by the possibility that the averments might fail to state a cause of action on which petitioners could actually recover. For it is well settled that the failure to state a proper cause of action calls for a judgment on the merits and not for a dismissal for want of jurisdiction.

The Court acknowledged that if plaintiffs' legal theories were wholly insubstantial and frivolous, jurisdictional dismissal might be proper. It specifically reserved the question of whether there was a federal cause of action against federal officials who violated Fourth Amendment rights. *Bivens v. Six Unknown Named Agents of the Federal Bureau of Narcotics,* 403 U.S. 388, 91 S.Ct. 1999, 29 L.Ed.2d 619 (1971) (see page 440), answered that question affirmatively.

---

even inconsistent pleading is permitted in the federal courts, parties frequently join both types of claim.

Is the jurisdictional theory of *Bell v. Hood* of any use to the parties in *Merrell Dow*? Why or why not? How might one distinguish *Bell* from *Merrell Dow*? What pleading tactic might be employed in a case like *Merrell Dow* to make the case more closely resemble *Bell*?

Bell v. Hood, although now sixty years old, continues to exercise its influence on litigation. In *Arbaugh v. Y&H Corporation*, 546 U.S. 500, 126 S.Ct. 1235, 163 L.Ed.2d 1097 (2006), the plaintiff sought damages under Title VII of the Civil Rights Act of 1964 for her employer's alleged sexual harassment. She prevailed at trial, winning a $40,000 verdict. Two weeks later, when the trial court entered a judgment on the verdict, the defendant moved to dismiss for lack of subject matter jurisdiction, arguing that it did not satisfy the numerosity requirement of Title VII, which exempts employers employing fewer than fifteen persons.[11] The district court reluctantly dismissed, noting that it was "unfair and a waste of judicial resources" to do so but that FED. R. CIV. P. 12(h)(3) compelled dismissal. When the case reached the Supreme Court, Justice Ginsburg's opinion for a unanimous Court found the numerosity requirement to be an element of the plaintiff's cause of action (and therefore suitable for a motion to dismiss for failure to state a claim under FED. R. CIV. P. 12(b)(6)). Such a motion, however, cannot be made after trial, pursuant to FED. R. CIV. P. 12(h)(2). The result was that the defendant's mischaracterization of the defect in the plaintiff's complaint as one of subject matter jurisdiction rather than failure to state a claim, combined with the defendant's tardiness in raising the matter, meant that the plaintiff's judgment would stand.

> [W]hen Congress does not rank a statutory limitation on coverage as jurisdictional, courts should treat the restriction as nonjurisdictional in character. Applying that readily administrable bright line to this case, we hold that the threshold number of employees for application of Title VII is an element of a plaintiff's claim for relief, not a jurisdictional issue.

8. In *Syngenta Crop Protection, Inc. v. Henson*, 537 U.S. 28, 123 S.Ct. 366, 154 L.Ed.2d 368 (2002), Henson had sued several companies in a Louisiana state court, alleging various tort claims. The court stayed his action when he successfully intervened in a similar Alabama federal class action (*Price*). That action ended in a settlement that specified in part that Henson's Louisiana action be dismissed in its entirety with prejudice. The Louisiana court subsequently conducted a hearing to decide whether to dismiss *Henson*. Counsel for defendants did not attend,[12] and Henson's counsel advised the court that the Alabama settlement required dismissal of only some of Henson's claims. The Louisiana court relied on the representation and "invited respondent to amend the complaint and proceed with the ac-

---

[11] It is not clear why the defendant did not raise the numerosity objection sooner, but it is at least possible that it wanted to reap a perceived tactical advantage from the chance it would prevail on the merits, assuming that if it did not like the result, it could always then seek dismissal on subject matter jurisdiction grounds.

[12] Folks, this is why we go to court proceedings even if we "know" what the result must be.

tion."

When defendants learned of the Louisiana court's action, they removed the case under 28 U.S.C. § 1441(a), arguing that federal question jurisdiction existed under the All Writs Act, 28 U.S.C. § 1651, and the supplemental jurisdiction statute, 28 U.S.C. § 1367. The Middle District of Louisiana transferred the case to the Southern District of Alabama, which dismissed on the basis of the *Price* stipulation and sanctioned Henson's counsel. The Eleventh Circuit affirmed the sanctions but vacated the order dismissing Henson's claims on the ground that the district court did not have jurisdiction. Henson's Louisiana action did not qualify for removal as either a diversity or a federal question case. With respect to defendants' argument that the All Writs Act provided a jurisdictional basis for removal so that the federal court could protect the *Price* stipulation and order, the Circuit declined to read § 1651 to permit a jurisdictional result inconsistent with the general removal authorization of § 1441.

A unanimous Supreme Court affirmed, largely echoing the Eleventh Circuit's reasoning. "Section 1441 requires that a federal court have original jurisdiction over an action in order for it to be removed from a state court. The All Writs Act, alone or in combination with the existence of ancillary jurisdiction in a federal court, is not a substitute for that requirement." Does that mean that the defendants were without an effective remedy for Henson's abuse of the Louisiana court? Almost certainly not; the defendants probably retained two options. First, they might apply to the Louisiana court for an order of dismissal on the basis of the federal order in *Price*. Second, they probably could return to the *Price* court and seek an injunction either against the Louisiana court itself or against Henson. Although the Anti-Injunction Act, 28 U.S.C. § 2283 (2001), ordinarily prohibits federal courts from enjoining state court proceedings, Congress does allow a federal court to do so "to protect or effectuate its judgments." Chapter 8 B discusses the Anti-Injunction Act more fully, at pages 746-761.

9. *Steel Company v. Citizens for a Better Environment*, 523 U.S. 83, 118 S.Ct. 1003, 140 L.Ed.2d 210 (1998), takes the jurisdictional issues in *Bell v. Hood* one step further. The Emergency Planning and Community Right-to-Know Act of 1986 (EPCRA) authorizes citizen suits against violators of the Act if the Environmental Protection Agency does not diligently pursue an enforcement proceeding. Plaintiff CBE sued on the basis of the Steel Company's failure timely to file required inventory forms. Before the action began, the Steel Company had filed all of the overdue forms. The Seventh Circuit had decided the case on the merits, relying on a concept of "hypothetical jurisdiction" to reach what it felt was a comparatively simple merits question determinable in favor of the party challenging jurisdiction, thus avoiding the thornier jurisdictional issues. The Court rejected the idea of hypothetical jurisdiction, noting that to decide cases on that basis could lead only to advisory opinions because the courts would be issuing opinions in the absence of jurisdiction. All nine Justices agreed that the action should be dismissed, but they reached that conclusion through different reasoning. The majority held that the plaintiff lacked standing. That aspect of the case is discussed at pages 58-59.

Justice Stevens, concurring in the judgment and joined in part by Justices Souter and Ginsburg, argued that the Court should have dismissed for lack of subject matter jurisdiction. He focused on EPCRA's jurisdictional provision: " 'The district court shall have jurisdiction in actions brought under [§ 326(a)] against an owner or operator of a facility to enforce the requirement concerned and to impose any civil penalty provided for violation of that requirement.' " This wording, he argued, means that "if § 326(a) authorizes citizen suits for wholly past violations, the district court has jurisdiction over these actions; if it does not, the court lacks jurisdiction." Thus, Justice Stevens's view was that the Court faced a choice of answering either of two jurisdictional questions: the Article III standing question or the statutory subject matter jurisdiction question. "[O]ur precedents clearly support the proposition that, given a choice between two jurisdictional questions—one statutory and the other constitutional—the Court has the power to answer the statutory question first." (He also argued that even if one conceptualizes the statutory issue as a 12(b)(6) issue, the Court should decide it in preference to the constitutional question of standing.)

Is Justice Stevens's view compatible with *Bell v. Hood*? He relied on *Bell* for the proposition that "the Court has the power to decide whether a cause of action exists even when it is unclear whether the plaintiff has standing * * * " because it was not clear in *Bell* that the plaintiff's injuries could be redressed.

> The question whether petitioners' injuries [in *Bell*] were redressable—"whether federal courts can grant money recovery for damages said to have been suffered as a result of federal officers violating the Fourth and Fifth Amendments"—was an open one. Nonetheless, * * * the Court held that federal courts have jurisdiction to determine whether a cause of action exists.

Is *Bell* distinguishable from *Steel Company*? Is Justice Stevens suggesting that whenever a statute conferring subject matter jurisdiction refers to a particular cause of action, all of the elements of that cause of action become jurisdictional? What effect would you expect that analysis to have were the Court to adopt it?

10. *Steel Company* dealt with the question of whether the courts could assume jurisdiction for purposes of dismissing a case on its merits, and the Court clearly rejected that sequence of decision. *Ruhrgas AG v. Marathon Oil Company*, 526 U.S. 574, 119 S.Ct. 1563, 143 L.Ed.2d 760 (1999), addressed the proper sequencing of threshold issues. As the Court there noted, many had assumed that questions of subject matter jurisdiction took precedence over any other issues in a case. The Court unanimously held that although that is the customary order of consideration, there is no constitutional or other imperative that makes it so. Where a court confronts a difficult issue of subject matter jurisdiction (here whether a party was fraudulently joined to defeat diversity jurisdiction) and a comparatively easy issue of personal jurisdiction, it may dismiss on the basis of the latter. The Court rejected the Fifth Circuit's conclusion that *Steel Company* required consideration of subject matter jurisdiction before any other issue, distinguishing

instead between threshold and non-threshold bases of disposition. Justice Ginsburg's opinion also dismissed the argument that the Court should first address the statutory subject matter jurisdiction issue and only later reach the constitutional personal jurisdiction issue if necessary, noting that the courts' normal inclination to avoid deciding constitutional questions if possible represents a prudential judgment, not a constitutional requirement. Note that decisions on subject matter jurisdiction and decisions on personal jurisdiction may have different preclusive effect if the plaintiff recommences the litigation in state court. Should that affect the Court's calculus?

GRABLE & SONS METAL PRODUCTS, INC. v. DARUE ENGINEERING & MANUFACTURING

Supreme Court of the United States, 2005.
545 U.S. 308, 125 S.Ct. 2363, 162 L.Ed.2d 390.

JUSTICE SOUTER delivered the opinion of the Court.

* * *

The question is whether want of a federal cause of action to try claims of title to land obtained at a federal tax sale precludes removal to federal court of a state action with non-diverse parties raising a disputed issue of federal title law. We answer no, and hold that the national interest in providing a federal forum for federal tax litigation is sufficiently substantial to support the exercise of federal question jurisdiction over the disputed issue on removal, which would not distort any division of labor between the state and federal courts, provided or assumed by Congress.

I

In 1994, the Internal Revenue Service seized Michigan real property belonging to petitioner Grable & Sons Metal Products, Inc., to satisfy Grable's federal tax delinquency. Title 26 U.S.C. § 6335 required the IRS to give notice of the seizure, and there is no dispute that Grable received actual notice by certified mail before the IRS sold the property to respondent Darue Engineering & Manufacturing. Although Grable also received notice of the sale itself, it did not exercise its statutory right to redeem the property within 180 days of the sale, § 6337(b)(1), and after that period had passed, the Government gave Darue a quitclaim deed.

Five years later, Grable brought a quiet title action in state court, claiming that Darue's record title was invalid because the IRS had failed to notify Grable of its seizure of the property in the exact manner required by § 6335(a), which provides that written notice must be "given by the Secretary to the owner of the property [or] left at his usual place of abode or business." Grable said that the statute required personal service, not service by certified mail.

Darue removed the case to Federal District Court as presenting a federal question, because the claim of title depended on the interpretation of the notice statute in the federal tax law. The District Court declined to remand the case at Grable's behest after finding that the "claim does pose a significant question of federal law," and ruling that Grable's lack of a federal right of action to enforce its claim against Darue did not bar the exercise of federal jurisdiction. On the merits, the court granted summary judgment to Darue, holding that although § 6335 by its terms required personal service, substantial compliance with the statute was enough.

The Court of Appeals for the Sixth Circuit affirmed. On the jurisdictional question, the panel thought it sufficed that the title claim raised an issue of federal law that had to be resolved, and implicated a substantial federal interest (in construing federal tax law). The court went on to affirm the District Court's judgment on the merits. We granted certiorari on the jurisdictional question alone, to resolve a split within the Courts of Appeals on whether *Merrell Dow Pharmaceuticals Inc. v. Thompson* (1986) always requires a federal cause of action as a condition for exercising federal-question jurisdiction. We now affirm.

II

Darue was entitled to remove the quiet title action if Grable could have brought it in federal district court originally, 28 U.S.C. § 1441(a), as a civil action "arising under the Constitution, laws, or treaties of the United States," § 1331. This provision for federal-question jurisdiction is invoked by and large by plaintiffs pleading a cause of action created by federal law (*e.g.,* claims under 42 U.S.C. § 1983). There is, however, another longstanding, if less frequently encountered, variety of federal "arising under" jurisdiction, this Court having recognized for nearly 100 years that in certain cases federal question jurisdiction will lie over state-law claims that implicate significant federal issues. *E.g., Hopkins v. Walker* (1917). The doctrine captures the commonsense notion that a federal court ought to be able to hear claims recognized under state law that nonetheless turn on substantial questions of federal law, and thus justify resort to the experience, solicitude, and hope of uniformity that a federal forum offers on federal issues.

The classic example is *Smith v. Kansas City Title & Trust Co.* (1921), a suit by a shareholder claiming that the defendant corporation could not lawfully buy certain bonds of the National Government because their issuance was unconstitutional. Although Missouri law provided the cause of action, the Court recognized federal-question jurisdiction because the principal issue in the case was the federal constitutionality of the bond issue. *Smith* thus held, in a somewhat generous statement of the scope of the doctrine, that a state-law claim could give rise to federal-question jurisdiction so long as it "appears from the [complaint] that the right to relief depends upon the construction or application of [federal law]."

The *Smith* statement has been subject to some trimming to fit earlier and later cases recognizing the vitality of the basic doctrine, but shying away from the expansive view that mere need to apply federal law in a state-law claim will suffice to open the "arising under" door. As early as 1912, this Court had confined federal-question jurisdiction over state-law claims to those that "really and substantially involv[e] a dispute or controversy respecting the validity, construction or effect of [federal] law." This limitation was the ancestor of Justice Cardozo's later explanation that a request to exercise federal-question jurisdiction over a state action calls for a "common-sense accommodation of judgment to [the] kaleidoscopic situations" that present a federal issue, in "a selective process which picks the substantial causes out of the web and lays the other ones aside." *Gully v. First Nat. Bank in Meridian* (1936). It has in fact become a constant refrain in such cases that federal jurisdiction demands not only a contested federal issue, but a substantial one, indicating a serious federal interest in claiming the advantages thought to be inherent in a federal forum.

But even when the state action discloses a contested and substantial federal question, the exercise of federal jurisdiction is subject to a possible veto. For the federal issue will ultimately qualify for a federal forum only if federal jurisdiction is consistent with congressional judgment about the sound division of labor between state and federal courts governing the application of § 1331. Thus, *Franchise Tax Bd.* explained that the appropriateness of a federal forum to hear an embedded issue could be evaluated only after considering the "welter of issues regarding the interrelation of federal and state authority and the proper management of the federal judicial system." Because arising-under jurisdiction to hear a state-law claim always raises the possibility of upsetting the state-federal line drawn (or at least assumed) by Congress, the presence of a disputed federal issue and the ostensible importance of a federal forum are never necessarily dispositive; there must always be an assessment of any disruptive portent in exercising federal jurisdiction.

These considerations have kept us from stating a "single, precise, all-embracing" test for jurisdiction over federal issues embedded in state-law claims between nondiverse parties. We have not kept them out simply because they appeared in state raiment, as Justice Holmes [dissenting in *Smith*] would have done, but neither have we treated "federal issue" as a password opening federal courts to any state action embracing a point of federal law. Instead, the question is, does a state-law claim necessarily raise a stated federal issue, actually disputed and substantial, which a federal forum may entertain without disturbing any congressionally approved balance of federal and state judicial responsibilities.

III

A

This case warrants federal jurisdiction. Grable's state complaint must specify "the facts establishing the superiority of [its] claim," and

Grable has premised its superior title claim on a failure by the IRS to give it adequate notice, as defined by federal law. Whether Grable was given notice within the meaning of the federal statute is thus an essential element of its quiet title claim, and the meaning of the federal statute is actually in dispute; it appears to be the only legal or factual issue contested in the case. The meaning of the federal tax provision is an important issue of federal law that sensibly belongs in a federal court. The Government has a strong interest in the "prompt and certain collection of delinquent taxes," and the ability of the IRS to satisfy its claims from the property of delinquents requires clear terms of notice to allow buyers like Darue to satisfy themselves that the Service has touched the bases necessary for good title. The Government thus has a direct interest in the availability of a federal forum to vindicate its own administrative action, and buyers (as well as tax delinquents) may find it valuable to come before judges used to federal tax matters. Finally, because it will be the rare state title case that raises a contested matter of federal law, federal jurisdiction to resolve genuine disagreement over federal tax title provisions will portend only a microscopic effect on the federal-state division of labor. *See* n.3, *infra.*

This conclusion puts us in venerable company, quiet title actions having been the subject of some of the earliest exercises of federal-question jurisdiction over state-law claims. In *Hopkins* the question was federal jurisdiction over a quiet title action based on the plaintiffs' allegation that federal mining law gave them the superior claim. Just as in this case, "the facts showing the plaintiffs' title and the existence and invalidity of the instrument or record sought to be eliminated as a cloud upon the title are essential parts of the plaintiffs' cause of action."[3] As in this case again, "it is plain that a controversy respecting the construction and effect of the [federal] laws is involved and is sufficiently real and substantial." This Court therefore upheld federal jurisdiction in *Hopkins*, as well as in * * * similar quiet title matters * * *. Consistent with those cases, the recognition of federal jurisdiction is in order here.

B

Merrell Dow Pharmaceuticals Inc. v. Thompson (1986), on which Grable rests its position, is not to the contrary. *Merrell Dow* considered a state tort claim resting in part on the allegation that the defendant

---

[3] The quiet title cases also show the limiting effect of the requirement that the federal issue in a state-law claim must actually be in dispute to justify federal-question jurisdiction. In *Shulthis v. McDougal* (1912), this Court found that there was no federal question jurisdiction to hear a plaintiff's quiet title claim in part because the federal statutes on which title depended were not subject to "any controversy respecting their validity, construction, or effect." As the Court put it, the requirement of an actual dispute about federal law was "especially" important in "suit[s] involving rights to land acquired under a law of the United States," because otherwise "every suit to establish title to land in the central and western states would so arise [under federal law], as all titles in those States are traceable back to those laws."

drug company had violated a federal misbranding prohibition, and was thus presumptively negligent under Ohio law. The Court assumed that federal law would have to be applied to resolve the claim, but after closely examining the strength of the federal interest at stake and the implications of opening the federal forum, held federal jurisdiction unavailable. Congress had not provided a private federal cause of action for violation of the federal branding requirement, and the Court found "it would * * * flout, or at least undermine, congressional intent to conclude that federal courts might nevertheless exercise federal-question jurisdiction and provide remedies for violations of that federal statute solely because the violation * * * is said to be a * * * 'proximate cause' under state law."

Because federal law provides for no quiet title action that could be brought against Darue,[4] Grable argues that there can be no federal jurisdiction here, stressing some broad language in *Merrell Dow* (including the passage just quoted) that on its face supports Grable's position. But an opinion is to be read as a whole, and *Merrell Dow* cannot be read whole as overturning decades of precedent, as it would have done by effectively adopting the Holmes dissent in *Smith* and converting a federal cause of action from a sufficient condition for federal-question jurisdiction[5] into a necessary one.

In the first place, *Merrell Dow* disclaimed the adoption of any bright-line rule, as when the Court reiterated that "in exploring the outer reaches of § 1331, determinations about federal jurisdiction require sensitive judgments about congressional intent, judicial power, and the federal system." The opinion included a lengthy footnote explaining that questions of jurisdiction over state-law claims require "careful judgments," about the "nature of the federal interest at stake" (emphasis deleted). And as a final indication that it did not mean to make a federal right of action mandatory, it expressly approved the exercise of jurisdiction sustained in *Smith*, despite the want of any federal cause of action available to *Smith*'s shareholder plaintiff. *Merrell Dow* then, did not toss out, but specifically retained the contextual enquiry that had been *Smith*'s hallmark for over 60 years. At the end of *Merrell Dow*, Justice Holmes was still dissenting.

Accordingly, *Merrell Dow* should be read in its entirety as treating the absence of a federal private right of action as evidence relevant to, but not dispositive of, the "sensitive judgments about congressional intent" that § 1331 requires. The absence of any federal cause of action

---

[4] Federal law does provide a quiet title cause of action against the Federal Government. That right of action is not relevant here, however, because the federal government no longer has any interest in the property, having transferred its interest to Darue through the quitclaim deed.

[5] For an extremely rare exception to the sufficiency of a federal right of action, see *Shoshone Mining Co. v. Rutter* (1900).

affected *Merrell Dow's* result two ways. The Court saw the fact as worth some consideration in the assessment of substantiality. But its primary importance emerged when the Court treated the combination of no federal cause of action and no preemption of state remedies for misbranding as an important clue to Congress's conception of the scope of jurisdiction to be exercised under § 1331. The Court saw the missing cause of action not as a missing federal door key, always required, but as a missing welcome mat, required in the circumstances, when exercising federal jurisdiction over a state misbranding action would have attracted a horde of original filings and removal cases raising other state claims with embedded federal issues. For if the federal labeling standard without a federal cause of action could get a state claim into federal court, so could any other federal standard without a federal cause of action. And that would have meant a tremendous number of cases.

One only needed to consider the treatment of federal violations generally in garden variety state tort law. "The violation of federal statutes and regulations is commonly given negligence per se effect in state tort proceedings."[6] RESTATEMENT (THIRD) OF TORTS (proposed final draft) § 14, Comment *a*. A general rule of exercising federal jurisdiction over state claims resting on federal mislabeling and other statutory violations would thus have heralded a potentially enormous shift of traditionally state cases into federal courts. Expressing concern over the "increased volume of federal litigation," and noting the importance of adhering to "legislative intent," *Merrell Dow* thought it improbable that the Congress, having made no provision for a federal cause of action, would have meant to welcome any state-law tort case implicating federal law "solely because the violation of the federal statute is said to [create] a rebuttable presumption [of negligence] * * * under state law." ([I]nternal quotation marks omitted). In this situation, no welcome mat meant keep out. *Merrell Dow's* analysis thus fits within the framework of examining the importance of having a federal forum for the issue, and the consistency of such a forum with Congress's intended division of labor between state and federal courts.

As already indicated, however, a comparable analysis yields a different jurisdictional conclusion in this case. Although Congress also indicated ambivalence in this case by providing no private right of action to Grable, it is the rare state quiet title action that involves contested issues of federal law. Consequently, jurisdiction over actions like Grable's would not materially affect, or threaten to affect, the normal currents of litigation. Given the absence of threatening structural consequences and the clear interest the Government, its buyers, and its delinquents have

---

6 Other jurisdictions treat a violation of a federal statute as evidence of negligence or, like Ohio itself in *Merrell Dow Pharmaceuticals Inc. v. Thompson* (1986), as creating a rebuttable presumption of negligence. RESTATEMENT (THIRD) OF TORTS (proposed final draft) § 14, Comment *c*. Either approach could still implicate issues of federal law.

in the availability of a federal forum, there is no good reason to shirk from federal jurisdiction over the dispositive and contested federal issue at the heart of the state-law title claim.[7]

IV

The judgment of the Court of Appeals, upholding federal jurisdiction over Grable's quiet title action, is affirmed.

It is so ordered.

JUSTICE THOMAS, concurring.

The Court faithfully applies our precedents interpreting 28 U.S.C. § 1331 to authorize federal-court jurisdiction over some cases in which state law creates the cause of action but requires determination of an issue of federal law. In this case, no one has asked us to overrule those precedents and adopt the rule Justice Holmes set forth in *American Well Works Co. v. Layne & Bowler Co.* (1916) limiting § 1331 jurisdiction to cases in which federal law creates the cause of action pleaded on the face of the plaintiff's complaint. In an appropriate case, and perhaps with the benefit of better evidence as to the original meaning of § 1331's text, I would be willing to consider that course.

Jurisdictional rules should be clear. Whatever the virtues of the *Smith* standard, it is anything but clear.

Whatever the vices of the *American Well Works* rule, it is clear. Moreover, it accounts for the " 'vast majority' " of cases that come within § 1331 under our current case law—further indication that trying to sort out which cases fall within the smaller *Smith* category may not be worth the effort it entails. Accordingly, I would be willing in appropriate circumstances to reconsider our interpretation of § 1331.

Notes and Questions

1. *Grable* clears up some questions left after *Merrell Dow*. Or does it? The Court acknowledges, albeit indirectly, that the majority opinion in *Merrell Dow* at the very least gave rise to some substantial misconceptions in the lower federal courts. For example, one might have been tempted after *Merrell Dow* to conclude that a hybrid claim—that is, one with a state-created right of action that necessarily incorporated at least one substantive provision of federal law as an element—could never support federal question jurisdiction without there being a federal right of action. Justice Stevens certainly seemed to imply that when he said,

---

[7] At oral argument Grable's counsel espoused the position that after *Merrell Dow,* federal-question jurisdiction over state-law claims absent a federal right of action could be recognized only where a constitutional issue was at stake. There is, however, no reason in text or otherwise to draw such a rough line. As *Merrell Dow* itself suggested, constitutional questions may be the more likely ones to reach the level of substantiality that can justify federal jurisdiction. But a flat ban on statutory questions would mechanically exclude significant questions of federal law like the one this case presents.

> We *simply* conclude that the congressional determination that there should be no federal remedy for the violation of this federal statute is *tantamount* to a congressional conclusion that the presence of a claimed violation of the statute as an element of a state cause of action is insufficiently "substantial" to confer federal-question jurisdiction.

(Footnote omitted; emphasis added.) And indeed, after *Merrell Dow* many federal courts held that federal courts could not hear hybrid claims under § 1331. *See supra* at 284, Note 4. Well, it now appears that things are not quite as simple as Justice Stevens's statement indicated they were. The statute upon which Grable relied for relief, 26 U.S.C. § 6335, certainly creates no federal cause of action. Indeed, it creates no substantive rights at all, merely entitling tax delinquents to a particular mode of service of the notice of an IRS property seizure.

2. The Court articulates a four-part test to determine whether § 1331 jurisdiction exists over claims created by state law. What are the four parts? Are any of them new, or is the Court merely restating criteria drawn from earlier cases?

3. The Court states that a federal issue must be central to the lawsuit and "substantial" to support federal question jurisdiction and finds that the federal issue *is* substantial in *Grable*. Why? The Court supports its conclusion by adverting to the strong federal interest in the "prompt and certain collection of delinquent taxes." *Grable* is an action between two private parties over ownership of a piece of land. How, exactly, might decision of the case affect government tax collection?

4. Does the Court also seem to assume that a federal court will be more likely than a state court to vindicate an IRS administrative action? A skeptic might observe, "So much for parity." *See supra* at 13-21, *infra* at 640 Note 4(b), 798 Note 8, 1051-1052. In any event, do you agree?

5. By stressing the government's strong interest in collecting taxes, does Justice Souter imply that other federal interests are less important? Does he imply, for example, that the government has no particularly strong interest in controlling the labeling and distribution of drugs that may be harmful, as in *Merrell Dow*? Congress apparently thought there was some significant government interest when it passed the Food, Drug and Cosmetic Act in 1938. Does the Court suggest any principled basis for determining which federal statutes are important enough to support federal question jurisdiction in hybrid cases and which ones are not?

6. a) Does Justice Souter's attempt to distinguish and cabin *Merrell Dow* persuade you? The Sixth Circuit's one-page opinion in *Merrell Dow* suggests an easier way. In *Grable*, the entire case must rise or fall according to the resolution of the federal issue. In *Merrell Dow*, by contrast, the Sixth Circuit pointed out that the plaintiffs had pleaded multiple counts, including one count of common law negligence, and so could prevail on a negligence theory without demonstrating a violation of the Food, Drug and Cosmetic Act. Is that any better?

Consider the Sixth Circuit's approach for a moment. The court said:

Federal question jurisdiction would * * * exist only if plaintiffs' right to relief *depended necessarily* on a substantial question of federal law. Plaintiffs' causes of action referred to the FDCA merely as one available criterion for determining whether Merrell Dow was negligent. Because the jury could find negligence on the part of Merrell Dow without finding a violation of the FDCA, the plaintiffs' causes of action did not depend necessarily upon a question of federal law. Consequently, the causes of action did not arise under federal law and, therefore, were improperly removed to federal court.

On the Sixth Circuit's analysis, would there have been federal question jurisdiction if the *Merrell Dow* plaintiffs had pleaded only Count IV—the FDCA misbranding count—and had omitted the remaining counts, including the count for common law negligence? Then the disposition of the FDCA issue would have been critical to the case. Does the Sixth Circuit's reasoning suggest that the presence of the other counts somehow poisoned federal question jurisdiction that would otherwise have existed? If that were so, what would become of supplemental jurisdiction?

The problem may be that the Sixth Circuit evaluated the case as a whole, not count by count. Note its repeated reference to the plaintiffs' *cause*s of action, as if considering them collectively. As Professor John Oakley has pointed out in his capacity as Reporter for ALI's Judicial Code Revision Project, however, federal question jurisdiction is claim-based, not case-based. *See* AMERICAN LAW INSTITUTE, FEDERAL JUDICIAL CODE REVISION PROJECT 5-7 (2004). If there is federal question jurisdiction with respect to one count, the federal court may also hear the remaining counts if either they have independent jurisdictional bases of their own or if they qualify for supplemental jurisdiction under 28 U.S.C. § 1367. In any event, the character of the other counts does not undercut jurisdiction over the federal question count.

For whatever reason, Justice Stevens's majority opinion in *Merrell Dow* essentially ignored the Sixth Circuit's reasoning. It certainly did not adopt it. Justice Souter, too, implicitly eschews the Circuit's approach.

b) Instead, Justice Souter focuses on numbers. He asserts that finding federal question jurisdiction in *Grable* will result in few additional federal cases, while finding jurisdiction in *Merrell Dow* would have resulted in a flood of new federal filings. Whether his prediction about *Grable* is correct remains to be seen, but he clearly is right that more cases would have arisen under federal law if *Merrell Dow* had come out the other way. Why? If a plaintiff chose to plead a single state cause of action claiming that violation of a federal statutory standard was negligence *per se* rather than making that cause of action one claim among several, decision of the case would necessarily turn on federal law. Perhaps this explains why the *Merrell Dow* Court did not adopt the Sixth Circuit's reasoning.

7. Justice Souter's numbers analysis is pragmatic, but also problematic. One hopes that he is not suggesting that the most important federal issues come up the least often. If a federal issue is substantial (whatever that may mean after *Merrell Dow* and *Grable*), should the federal courts nonetheless

decline to hear a hybrid claim concerning it if one can predict many similar cases arising? Does ubiquity connote lack of substantiality?

8. *Grable* brings forward in time, but does not clear up, a problem that *Merrell Dow* created. The fourth part of the Court's arising-under test is that "the federal issue will ultimately qualify for a federal forum only if federal jurisdiction is consistent with congressional judgment about the sound division of labor between state and federal courts governing the application of § 1331." To which Congress does Justice Souter refer, the Congress that passed the predecessor of § 1331 back in 1875, the last Congress to have re-enacted that section before *Grable* arose (which happened in 1980), or the Congress that passed the tax statute under which Grable claimed its entitlement?

Since there was no Internal Revenue Service in 1875, one might hazard a guess that the Congress that passed the original § 1331 did not spend a lot of time thinking about whether it should include actions where the federal issue was one of proper service under the Internal Revenue Code of 1954. Do you think the Congress sitting in 1980, which recodified § 1331 (removing the previously existing jurisdictional amount, which had always tracked the jurisdictional floor of the diversity statute, § 1332), had a view on whether questions of the propriety of service under the relevant tax statute should suffice for federal question jurisdiction?

In 1954, Congress initially passed the section upon which Darue relied for federal question jurisdiction in removing the case. Congress has subsequently recodified the statute four times, in 1976, 1986, 1988 and 1998. Do you think any of those Congresses had a particular view of whether a dispute about whether there was proper notice under 26 U.S.C. § 6335(a) should come within the jurisdictional ambit of 28 U.S.C. § 1331? Assuming that those Congresses even had such a view, of what importance is it if it did not result in any legislative action with respect to § 1331?

This uncertainty suggests the Court is not really interested in congressional judgment. Yet, "there must always be an assessment of any disruptive portent in exercising federal jurisdiction." Who makes the assessment?

9. *Grable* suggests resolution of an issue that lingered after *Merrell Dow*—whether a state court had jurisdiction to hear a hybrid claim involving a federal statutory standard combined with a state cause of action when the federal statute did not create a private right of action. In *Merrell Dow*, Justice Stevens stated that the import of the lack of a private federal cause of action "is that it would flout congressional intent to provide a private federal remedy for violation of the federal statute." If, as on Justice Stevens's reading, Congress affirmatively did not want private enforcement of the statutory standard, would it flout congressional intent to allow a private remedy in the state courts? Commentators have argued that state courts should be able to hear hybrid claims unless Congress has explicitly preempted state enforcement of the federal statutory provision. *Grable* appears to adopt this standard. Justice Souter states that the *Merrell Dow* Court "treated the combination of no federal cause of action and no preemption of state remedies for misbranding as an important clue to Congress's conception of the

scope of jurisdiction to be exercised under § 1331." Perhaps we read too much into this single sentence, but the implication seems to be that a hybrid claim may go forward in state court even if a federal court cannot hear it.

10. At two points in the opinion, Justice Souter refers to the necessity, when considering jurisdiction over a hybrid claim, of the federal issue being actually in dispute. The first appearance of the idea is in the last sentence of Part II; the second occurs in the third footnote of the opinion. Although he does not cite *Gully v. First National Bank* (*supra* at 270), he probably is echoing Justice Cardozo's admonition that "[a] genuine and present controversy, not merely a possible or conjectural one, must exist with reference" to the federal issue. Do you think Justice Souter is suggesting that if the dispute in a hybrid-claim case exists only with respect to what the facts are and not with respect to what federal law is or how it applies to particular sets of facts, then there is no federal question jurisdiction? Certainly that is not the case when federal law creates the cause of action. In an antitrust dispute, for example, the parties may agree entirely on what the Sherman Act requires and differ only on whether the defendant performed anti-competitive acts. Nonetheless, the federal courts clearly would have jurisdiction in such a case. Justice Souter, however, is quite explicit in Footnote 3 when he adverts to "the requirement that the federal issue in a state-law claim must actually be in dispute to justify federal-question jurisdiction." Is he implying that the courts are to treat federally created claims and hybrid claims differently? What might be the policy justification for such a position?

11. After *Grable*, do we have a clearer idea of the criteria for deciding whether a case arises under federal law? Are the criteria any easier to apply than they were before *Grable*, or are we still looking at the shifting colors of Justice Cardozo's kaleidoscope?

The Court demonstrated the very next year that federal question jurisdiction remains in ferment. *Empire Healthchoice Assurance, Inc. v. McVeigh*, 547 U.S. 677, 126 S.Ct. 2121, 165 L.Ed.2d 131 (2006), involved the federal government's health insurance plan for federal employees. The government contracted with private carriers to administer a variety of health plans funded by government and employee contributions into a special fund under the Federal Employees Health Benefits Act of 1959 (FEHBA). One section of that statute explicitly preempts state law on issues concerning "coverage or benefits" under the plans.[13] It does not create a right of action, nor does it make reference to any subrogation or reimbursement rights of the carriers, although annual contracts between the government and the private insurance carriers oblige the carriers to attempt to recoup amounts paid for employees' medical care. The contracts further provide that employees enrolling in any of the plans agree either to reimburse the carrier for benefit payments if the employee recovers damages from a tort action with respect to the condition or to subrogate the carrier to their claims. A second

---

[13] 5 U.S.C.A. § 8902(m)(1): "The terms of any contract under this chapter which relate to the nature, provision, or extent of coverage or benefits (including payments with respect to benefits) shall supersede and preempt any State or local law, or any regulation issued thereunder, which relates to health insurance or plans."

section of FEHBA explicitly creates federal question jurisdiction for actions against the United States.[14]

The dispute arose when a beneficiary's estate settled a tort action against alleged tortfeasors for more than $3,000,000. Although the carrier knew of the action, it did not participate in it. After the settlement, Empire Healthchoice filed a federal action seeking reimbursement from the estate of the $157,309 it had paid in benefits, and the case arrived in the Supreme Court on the issue of jurisdiction under § 1331.

The Court's analysis is complex because the jurisdictional question turned on whether Empire Healthchoice's reimbursement claim sounded in state law or federal common law, and it is difficult to understand the opinions without being familiar with the Court's recent federal-common-law jurisprudence, which appears in Chapter 5.[15] If one views the reimbursement claim as a function of the contract between the employee and the carrier, then typical analysis would view it as a state law claim (with no federal component) and refuse jurisdiction. If one considers that the employee is a beneficiary of a contract created and controlled by federal law that requires federal law to govern all issues arising under the contract, then the matter may look more like a federal question case.

Five Justices took the former view. Justice Ginsburg's majority opinion noted that Congress had preempted state law in a very limited way, referring only to coverage and benefits and not referring to jurisdiction at all. She contrasted that with Congress's explicit conferral of federal question jurisdiction for actions against the United States. The combination of the majority's refusal to find the federal courts should create federal common law to govern reimbursement claims and Congress's exclusion by implication of federal jurisdiction not involving claims against the United States caused those Justices to rule that the case did not arise under federal law for purposes of § 1331. Finally, referring to § 8902(m)(1), Justice Ginsburg noted that even if one read the preemption provision to require that federal law apply to reimbursement disputes, the Court should not read it simultaneously to confer subject matter jurisdiction on the federal trial court absent some clear indication by Congress that it had had "that atypical intention."[16]

---

[14] 5 U.S.C.A. § 8912: "The district courts of the United States have original jurisdiction, concurrent with the United States Court of Federal Claims, of a civil action or claim against the United States founded on this chapter."

[15] Chapter 5 contains a more complete discussion of the federal common law battle in *Empire Healthchoice, infra* at 429.

[16] The majority summarily rejected Empire's attempt to rely on *Grable*, characterizing that case as "poles apart." There the question involved

> the action of a federal agency (IRS) and its compatibility with a federal statute, the question qualified as "substantial," and its resolution was both dispositive of the case and would be controlling in numerous other cases. Here, the reimbursement claim was triggered, not by the action of any federal department, agency or service, but by the settlement of a personal-injury action launched in state court, and the bottom-line practical issue is the share of that settlement properly payable to Empire.

Justice Breyer wrote for the four dissenters, who included Justice Souter, the author of *Grable*'s majority opinion. He described the reimbursement portions of the contract as "a few scattered islands in a sea of federal contractual provisions." Noting that reimbursed funds must go to the Treasury Department and back into the statutory fund, Justice Breyer argued that the case was pervasively federal and that federal common law should govern. Moreover, he saw the federal government as the real party in interest, which in his view was another reason for federal common law to govern the dispute. That being the case, it was but a short step for him to find jurisdiction under § 1331.[17] At the end of the day, however, he did not have the votes.

C.   THE SPECIAL PROBLEM OF DECLARATORY JUDGMENT CASES

SKELLY OIL CO. v. PHILLIPS PETROLEUM CO.

Supreme Court of the United States, 1950.
339 U.S. 667, 70 S.Ct. 876, 94 L.Ed. 1194.

MR. JUSTICE FRANKFURTER delivered the opinion of the Court.

In 1945, Michigan-Wisconsin Pipe Line Company sought from the Federal Power Commission a certificate of public convenience and necessity, required by § 7(c) of the Natural Gas Act, for the construction and operation of a pipe line to carry natural gas from Texas to Michigan and Wisconsin. A prerequisite for such a certificate is adequate reserves of gas. To obtain these reserves Michigan-Wisconsin entered into an agreement with Phillips Petroleum Company on December 11, 1945, whereby the latter undertook to make available gas from the Hugoton Gas Field, sprawling over Kansas, Oklahoma and Texas, which it produced or purchased from others. Phillips had contracted with petitioners, Skelly Oil Company, Stanolind Oil and Gas Company, and Magnolia Petroleum Company, to purchase gas produced by them in the Hugoton Field for resale to Michigan-Wisconsin. Each contract provided that "in the event Michigan-Wisconsin Pipe Line Company shall fail to secure from the Federal Power Commission on or before [October 1, 1946] a certificate of public convenience and necessity for the construction and operation of its pipe line, Seller [a petitioner] shall have the right to terminate this contract by written notice to Buyer [Phillips] delivered to Buyer at any time after December 1, 1946, but before the issuance of such certificate." The legal significance of this provision is at the core of this litigation.

---

[17] It is quite possible that it should have been a longer step for Justice Breyer. He rather quickly equated his view that federal common law should govern the case with the conclusion that there was § 1331 jurisdiction. Yet, after *Merrell Dow*, that result is far from automatic. Recall that *Merrell Dow* insisted that, at least in the absence of a federally created right of action, the federal question in an otherwise state claim had to be "substantial," a criterion that *Grable* by no means repudiated. Justice Breyer did not acknowledge that part of the jurisdictional test.

The Federal Power Commission, in response to the application of Michigan-Wisconsin, on November 30, 1946, ordered that "A certificate of public convenience and necessity be and it is hereby issued to applicant [Michigan-Wisconsin], upon the terms and conditions of this order," listing among the conditions that there be no transportation or sale of natural gas by means of the sanctioned facilities until all necessary authorizations were obtained from the State of Wisconsin and the communities proposed to be served, that Michigan-Wisconsin should have the approval of the Securities and Exchange Commission for its plan of financing, that the applicant should file for the approval of the Commission a schedule of reasonable rates, and that the sanctioned facilities should not be used for the transportation of gas to Detroit and Ann Arbor except with due regard for the rights and duties of Panhandle Eastern Pipe Line Company, which had intervened before the Federal Power Commission, in its established service for resale in these areas, such rights and duties to be set forth in a supplemental order. It was also provided that Michigan-Wisconsin should have fifteen days from the issue of the supplemental order to notify the Commission whether the certificate "as herein issued is acceptable to it." Finally, the Commission's order provided that for purposes of computing the time within which applications for rehearing could be filed, "the date of issuance of this order shall be deemed to be the date of issuance of the opinions, or of the supplemental order referred to herein, whichever may be later."

News of the Commission's action was released on November 30, 1946, but the actual content of the order was not made public until December 2, 1946. Petitioners severally, on December 2, 1946, gave notice to Phillips of termination of their contracts on the ground that Michigan-Wisconsin had not received a certificate of public convenience and necessity. Thereupon Michigan-Wisconsin and Phillips brought suit against petitioners in the District Court for the Northern District of Oklahoma. Alleging that a certificate of public convenience and necessity, "within the meaning of said Natural Gas Act and said contracts" had been issued prior to petitioners' attempt at termination of the contracts, they invoked the Federal Declaratory Judgment Act for a declaration that the contracts were still "in effect and binding upon the parties thereto." Motions by petitioners to have Michigan-Wisconsin dropped as a party plaintiff were sustained, but motions to dismiss the complaint for want of jurisdiction were denied. The case then went to the merits, and the District Court decreed that the contracts between Phillips and petitioners have not been "effectively terminated and that each of such contracts remain [sic] in full force and effect." The Court of Appeals for the Tenth Circuit affirmed, and we brought the case here, because it raises in sharp form the question whether a suit like this "arises under the Constitution, laws or treaties of the United States," 28 U.S.C. § 1331, so as to enable District Courts to give declaratory relief under the Declaratory Judgment Act.

"[T]he operation of the Declaratory Judgment Act is procedural only." *Aetna Life Ins. Co. v. Haworth.* Congress enlarged the range of remedies available in the federal courts but did not extend their jurisdiction. When concerned as we are with the power of the inferior federal courts to entertain litigation within the restricted area to which the Constitution and Acts of Congress confine them, "jurisdiction" means the kinds of issues which give right of entrance to federal courts. Jurisdiction in this sense was not altered by the Declaratory Judgment Act. Prior to that Act, a federal court would entertain a suit on a contract only if the plaintiff asked for an immediately enforceable remedy like money damages or an injunction, but such relief could only be given if the requisites of jurisdiction, in the sense of a federal right or diversity, provided foundation for resort to the federal courts. The Declaratory Judgment Act allowed relief to be given by way of recognizing the plaintiff's right even though no immediate enforcement of it was asked. But the requirements of jurisdiction—the limited subject matters which alone Congress had authorized the District Courts to adjudicate—were not impliedly repealed or modified.

If Phillips sought damages from petitioners or specific performance of their contracts, it could not bring suit in a United States District Court on the theory that it was asserting a federal right. And for the simple reason that such a suit would "arise" under the State law governing the contracts. Whatever federal claim Phillips may be able to urge would in any event be injected into the case only in anticipation of a defense to be asserted by petitioners. "Not every question of federal law emerging in a suit is proof that a federal law is the basis of the suit." *Gully v. First National Bank in Meridian.* Ever since *Metcalf v. City of Watertown,* it has been settled doctrine that where a suit is brought in the federal courts "upon the sole ground that the determination of the suit depends upon some question of a federal nature, it must appear, at the outset, from the declaration or the bill of the party suing, that the suit is of that character." But "a suggestion of one party that the other will or may set up a claim under the Constitution or laws of the United States does not make the suit one arising under that Constitution or those laws." The plaintiff's claim itself must present a federal question "unaided by anything alleged in anticipation of avoidance of defenses which it is thought the defendant may interpose."

* * *

To be observant of these restrictions is not to indulge in formalism or sterile technicality. It would turn into the federal courts a vast current of litigation indubitably arising under State law, in the sense that the right to be vindicated was State-created, if a suit for a declaration of rights could be brought into the federal courts merely because an anticipated defense derived from federal law. Not only would this unduly swell the volume of litigation in the District Courts but it would also embarrass those courts—and this Court on potential review—in that matters of local law may often be involved, and the District Courts may either have to decide doubtful questions of State law or hold cases pending disposition of such State issues by State courts. To sanction suits for declaratory relief as within the jurisdiction of the District Courts merely because, as in this case, artful pleading anticipates a defense based on federal law would contravene the whole trend of jurisdictional legislation by Congress, disregard the effective functioning of the federal judicial system and distort the limited procedural purpose of the Declaratory Judgment Act. Since the matter in controversy as to which Phillips asked for a declaratory judgment is not one that "arises under the * * * laws * * * of the United States" and since as to Skelly and Stanolind jurisdiction cannot be sustained on the score of diversity of citizenship, the proceedings against them should have been dismissed.

* * *

Notes and Questions

1. What is the precise federal issue in *Skelly Oil*?

2. Declaratory judgment cases presented a new problem in federal question jurisdiction. After *Skelly Oil,* what steps should a court follow in deciding whether a declaratory judgment action arises under federal law?

3. Consider the structure of the complaint in *Skelly Oil.* Is it not likely that it satisfied the various tests for federal question jurisdiction under 28 U.S.C.A. § 1331? In that event, does the case represent another shift in the Court's approach to federal question jurisdiction? If so, should the Court have announced the shift more explicitly? If not, then why does Phillips's well-pleaded complaint that necessarily contains the federal issue not suffice to open the federal courthouse doors?

4. If Skelly Oil had been the plaintiff, seeking a declaration of invalidity of the contract, would it not have been necessary then for it to plead the untimeliness of the issuance of the Federal Power Commission certificate? Would that cause the result to change? Phillips had a potential state claim for breach of contract in the event that Skelly refused to supply the natural gas. By pleading its case as a declaratory judgment case, Phillips sought to create federal question jurisdiction where ordinarily there would have been none. Can the same be said of Skelly Oil as a plaintiff?

5. In connection with the last note, consider *E. Edelmann & Co. v. Triple-A Specialty Co.,* 88 F.2d 852 (7th Cir.), *cert. denied,* 300 U.S. 680, 57 S.Ct. 673, 81 L.Ed. 884 (1937). An alleged patent infringer sued the patentee seeking a declaration of invalidity of the patent or of non-infringement of the patent by plaintiff's device, and an injunction to bar further wrongful allegations of infringement. The Seventh Circuit upheld jurisdiction. In *Franchise Tax Board v. Construction Laborers Vacation Trust,* 463 U.S. 1, 19 n.19, 103 S.Ct. 2841, 2852 n.19, 77 L.Ed.2d 420, 436 n.19 (1983), the Court cited *Edelmann* with approval, "on the theory that an infringement suit by the declaratory judgment defendant would raise a federal question over

which the federal courts have exclusive jurisdiction."

Does *Edelmann* suggest an alternative strategy for the plaintiff in *American Well Works* were the case brought today? What would be the result under an *Edelmann* analysis? Is it consistent with *Skelly Oil*?

FRANCHISE TAX BOARD OF CALIFORNIA v. CONSTRUCTION LABORERS VACATION TRUST
Supreme Court of the United States, 1983.
463 U.S. 1, 103 S.Ct. 2841, 77 L.Ed.2d 420.

JUSTICE BRENNAN delivered the opinion of the Court.

The principal question in dispute between the parties is whether the Employee Retirement Income Security Act of 1974 (ERISA), permits state tax authorities to collect unpaid state income taxes by levying on funds held in trust for the taxpayers under an ERISA-covered vacation benefit plan. The issue is an important one, which affects thousands of federally regulated trusts and all nonfederal tax collection systems, and it must eventually receive a definitive, uniform resolution. Nevertheless, for reasons involving perhaps more history than logic, we hold that the lower federal courts had no jurisdiction to decide the question in the case before us, and we vacate the judgment and remand the case with instructions to remand it to the state court from which it was removed.

I

None of the relevant facts is in dispute. Appellee Construction Laborers Vacation Trust for Southern California (CLVT) is a trust established by an agreement between four associations of employers active in the construction industry in southern California and the Southern California District Council of Laborers, an arm of the District Council and affiliated locals of the Laborers' International Union of North America. The purpose of the agreement and trust was to establish a mechanism for administering the provisions of a collective-bargaining agreement that grants construction workers a yearly paid vacation. The trust agreement expressly proscribes any assignment, pledge, or encumbrance of funds held in trust by CLVT. The Plan that CLVT administers is unquestionably an "employee welfare benefit plan" within the meaning of § 3 of ERISA, and CLVT and its individual trustees are thereby subject to extensive regulation * * * .

Appellant Franchise Tax Board is a California agency charged with enforcement of that State's personal income tax law. California law authorizes appellant to require any person in possession of "credits or other personal property or other things of value, belonging to a taxpayer" "to withhold * * * the amount of any tax, interest, or penalties due from the taxpayer * * * and to transmit the amount withheld to the Franchise Tax Board." Any person who, upon notice by the Franchise Tax Board, fails to comply with its request to withhold and to transmit funds becomes personally liable for the amounts identified in the notice.

In June 1980, the Franchise Tax Board filed a complaint in state court against CLVT and its trustees. Under the heading "First Cause of Action," appellant alleged that CLVT had failed to comply with three levies * * *,[4] concluding with the allegation that it had been "damaged in a sum * * * not to exceed $380.56 plus interest from June 1, 1980." Under the heading "Second Cause of Action," appellant incorporated its previous allegations and added:

> There was at the time of the levies alleged above and continues to be an actual controversy between the parties concerning their respective legal rights and duties. The Board [appellant] contends that defendants [CLVT] are obligated and required by law to pay over to the Board all amounts held * * * in favor of the Board's delinquent taxpayers. On the other hand, defendants contend that section 514 of ERISA preempts state law and that the trustees lack the power to honor the levies made upon them by the State of California.

> [D]efendants will continue to refuse to honor the Board's levies in this regard. Accordingly, a declaration by this court of the parties' respective rights is required to fully and finally resolve this controversy.

In a prayer for relief, appellant requested damages for defendants' failure to honor the levies and a declaration that defendants are "legally obligated to honor all future levies by the Board."

CLVT removed the case to the United States District Court for the Central District of California, and the court denied the Franchise Tax Board's motion for remand to the state court. On the merits, the District Court ruled that ERISA did not pre-empt the State's power to levy on funds held in trust by CLVT. CLVT appealed, and the Court of Appeals reversed. On petition for rehearing, the Franchise Tax Board renewed

---

[4] At several points in 1977 and 1978, appellant issued notices to CLVT requesting it to withhold and to transmit approximately $380 in unpaid taxes, interest, and penalties due from three individuals. CLVT did not dispute that the individuals in question were beneficiaries of its trust or that it was then holding vacation benefit funds for them. In each case, however, it acknowledged receipt of appellant's notice and informed appellant that it had requested an opinion letter from the Administrator for Pension and Welfare Benefit Programs of the United States Department of Labor as to whether it was permitted under ERISA to honor appellant's levy. CLVT also informed appellant that it would withhold the funds from the individual workers until it received an opinion from the Department of Labor, but that it would not transmit the funds to the Franchise Tax Board.

Appellant took no immediate action to enforce its levy, and in January 1980 CLVT finally received the opinion letter it had requested. The opinion letter concluded: "[I]t is the position of the Department of Labor that the process of any state judicial or administrative agency seeking to levy for unpaid taxes or unpaid unemployment insurance contributions upon benefits due a participant or beneficiary under the Plan is pre-empted under ERISA." Accordingly, on January 7, 1980, counsel for CLVT furnished appellant a copy of the opinion letter, informed appellant that CLVT lacked the power to honor appellant's levies, and stated their intention to recommend that CLVT should disburse the funds it had withheld to the employees in question.

its argument that the District Court lacked jurisdiction over the complaint in this case. The petition for rehearing was denied, and an appeal was taken to this Court. We postponed consideration of our jurisdiction pending argument on the merits. We now hold that this case was not within the removal jurisdiction conferred by 28 U.S.C. § 1441, and therefore we do not reach the merits of the preemption question.

II

* * *

For this case—as for many cases where there is no diversity of citizenship between the parties—the propriety of removal turns on whether the case falls within the original "federal question" jurisdiction of the United States district courts * * * .

The most familiar definition of the statutory "arising under" limitation is Justice Holmes' statement, "A suit arises under the law that creates the cause of action." * * *

We have often held that a case "arose under" federal law where the vindication of a right under state law necessarily turned on some construction of federal law, and even the most ardent proponent of the Holmes test has admitted that it has been rejected as an exclusionary principle.

* * *

One powerful doctrine has emerged, however—the "well-pleaded complaint" rule—which as a practical matter severely limits the number of cases in which state law "creates the cause of action" that may be initiated in or removed to federal district court, thereby avoiding more-or-less automatically a number of potentially serious federal-state conflicts.

* * *

For better or worse, under the present statutory scheme as it has existed since 1887, a defendant may not remove a case to federal court unless the *plaintiff's* complaint establishes that the case "arises under" federal law.[9] "[A] right or immunity created by the Constitution or laws

---

[9] The well-pleaded complaint rule applies to the original jurisdiction of the district courts as well as to their removal jurisdiction.

It is possible to conceive of a rational jurisdictional system in which the answer as well as the complaint would be consulted before a determination was made whether the case "arose under" federal law, or in which original and removal jurisdiction were not coextensive. Indeed, until the 1887 amendments to the 1875 Act, the well-pleaded complaint rule was not applied in full force to cases removed from state court; the defendant's petition for removal could furnish the necessary guarantee that the case necessarily presented a substantial question of federal law. Commentators have repeatedly proposed that some mechanism be established to permit removal of cases in which a federal defense may be dispositive. But those proposals have not been adopted.

of the United States must be an element, and an essential one, of the plaintiff's cause of action."

* * *

The rule, however, may produce awkward results, especially in cases in which neither the obligation created by state law nor the defendant's factual failure to comply are in dispute, and both parties admit that the only question for decision is raised by a federal pre-emption defense. Nevertheless, it has been correctly understood to apply in such situations. As we said in *Gully*: "By unimpeachable authority, a suit brought upon a state statute does not arise under an act of Congress or the Constitution of the United States because prohibited thereby."[12]

III

Simply to state these principles is not to apply them to the case at hand. Appellant's complaint sets forth two "causes of action," one of which expressly refers to ERISA; if either comes within the original jurisdiction of the federal courts, removal was proper as to the whole case. Although appellant's complaint does not specifically assert any particular statutory entitlement for the relief it seeks, the language of the complaint suggests (and the parties do not dispute) that appellant's "first cause of action" states a claim under [state law], * * * and its "second cause of action" states a claim under California's Declaratory Judgment Act. As an initial proposition, then, the "law that creates the cause of action" is state law, and original federal jurisdiction is unavailable unless it appears that some substantial, disputed question of federal law is a necessary element of one of the well-pleaded state claims, or that one or the other claim is "really" one of federal law.

A

Even though state law creates appellant's causes of action, its case might still "arise under" the laws of the United States if a well-pleaded complaint established that its right to relief under state law requires resolution of a substantial question of federal law in dispute between the parties. For appellant's first cause of action—to enforce its levy—a straightforward application of the well-pleaded complaint rule precludes original federal-court jurisdiction. California law establishes a set of conditions, without reference to federal law, under which a tax levy may be enforced; federal law becomes relevant only by way of a defense to an obligation created entirely by state law, and then only if appellant has made out a valid claim for relief under state law. The well-pleaded com-

---

[12] Note, however, that a claim of federal pre-emption does not always arise as a defense to a coercive action. *See* n.20, *infra*. And, of course, the absence of original jurisdiction does not mean that there is no federal forum in which a pre-emption defense may be heard. If the state courts reject a claim of federal pre-emption, that decision may ultimately be reviewed on appeal by this Court.

plaint rule was framed to deal with precisely such a situation. As we discuss above, since 1887 it has been settled law that a case may not be removed to federal court on the basis of a federal defense, including the defense of pre-emption, even if the defense is anticipated in the plaintiff's complaint, and even if both parties admit that the defense is the only question truly at issue in the case.

Appellant's declaratory judgment action poses a more difficult problem. Whereas the question of federal pre-emption is relevant to appellant's first cause of action only as a potential defense, it is a necessary element of the declaratory judgment claim. Under [state law], a party with an interest in property may bring an action for a declaration of another party's legal rights and duties with respect to that property upon showing that there is an "actual controversy relating to the legal rights and duties" of the parties. The only questions in dispute between the parties in this case concern the rights and duties of CLVT and its trustees under ERISA. Not only does appellant's request for a declaratory judgment under California law clearly encompass questions governed by ERISA, but appellant's complaint identifies no other questions as a subject of controversy between the parties. Such questions must be raised in a well-pleaded complaint for a declaratory judgment. Therefore, it is clear on the face of its well-pleaded complaint that appellant may not obtain the relief it seeks in its second cause of action ("[t]hat the court declare defendants legally obligated to honor all future levies by the Board upon [CLVT],") without a construction of ERISA and/or an adjudication of its pre-emptive effect and constitutionality—all questions of federal law.

Appellant argues that original federal-court jurisdiction over such a complaint is foreclosed by our decision in *Skelly Oil Co. v. Phillips Petroleum Co.* As we shall see, however, *Skelly Oil* is not directly controlling.

* * *

1. As an initial matter, we must decide whether the doctrine of *Skelly Oil* limits original federal-court jurisdiction under § 1331—and by extension removal jurisdiction under § 1441—when a question of federal law appears on the face of a well-pleaded complaint for a state-law declaratory judgment. Apparently, it is a question of first impression. As the passage quoted above makes clear, *Skelly Oil* relied significantly on the precise contours of the federal Declaratory Judgment Act as well as of § 1331. *Cf.* 339 U.S. at 674 (stressing the need to respect "the limited procedural purpose of the Declaratory Judgment Act"). The Court's emphasis that the Declaratory Judgment Act was intended to affect only the remedies available in a federal district court, not the court's jurisdiction, was critical to the Court's reasoning. Our interpretation of the federal Declaratory Judgment Act in *Skelly Oil* does not apply of its own

force to *state* declaratory judgment statutes, many of which antedate the federal statute.[16]

Yet while *Skelly Oil* itself is limited to the federal Declaratory Judgment Act, fidelity to its spirit leads us to extend it to state declaratory judgment actions as well. If federal district courts could take jurisdiction, either originally or by removal, of state declaratory judgment claims raising questions of federal law, without regard to the doctrine of *Skelly Oil,* the federal Declaratory Judgment Act—with the limitations *Skelly Oil* read into it—would become a dead letter. For any case in which a state declaratory judgment action was available, litigants could get into federal court for a declaratory judgment despite our interpretation of § 2201, simply by pleading an adequate state claim for a declaration of federal law. Having interpreted the Declaratory Judgment Act of 1934 to include certain limitations on the jurisdiction of federal district courts to entertain declaratory judgment suits, we should be extremely hesitant to interpret the Judiciary Act of 1875 and its 1887 amendments in a way that renders the limitations in the later statute nugatory. Therefore, we hold that under the jurisdictional statutes as they now stand[17] federal courts do not have original jurisdiction, nor do they acquire jurisdiction on removal, when a federal question is presented by a complaint for a state declaratory judgment, but *Skelly Oil* would bar jurisdiction if the plaintiff had sought a federal declaratory judgment.

2. The question, then, is whether a federal district court could take jurisdiction of appellant's declaratory judgment claim had it been brought under 28 U.S.C.A. § 2201.[18] The application of *Skelly Oil* to such a suit is somewhat unclear. Federal courts have regularly taken original jurisdiction over declaratory judgment suits in which, if the declaratory judgment defendant brought a coercive action to enforce its

---

[16] California's Declaratory Judgment Act was enacted 13 years before the federal Act. California may well regard its statute as having a more substantive purpose than the federal Act as interpreted in *Skelly Oil.* According to the leading commentator on California procedure: "Declaratory relief is not a special proceeding. It is an action, classified as equitable by reason of the type of relief offered * * *."

[17] It is not beyond the power of Congress to confer a right to a declaratory judgment in a case or controversy arising under federal law—within the meaning of the Constitution or of § 1331—without regard to *Skelly Oil*'s particular application of the well-pleaded complaint rule. The 1969 ALI report strongly criticized the *Skelly Oil* doctrine: "If no other changes were to be made in federal question jurisdiction, it is arguable that such language, and the historical test it seems to embody, should be repudiated." Nevertheless, Congress has declined to make such a change. At this point, any adjustment in the system that has evolved under the *Skelly Oil* rule must come from Congress.

[18] It may seem odd that, for purposes of determining whether removal was proper, we analyze a claim brought under state law, in state court, by a party who has continuously objected to district court jurisdiction over its case, as if that party had been trying to get original federal-court jurisdiction all along. That irony, however, is a more-or-less constant feature of the removal statute, under which a case is removable if a federal district court could have taken jurisdiction had the same complaint been filed.

rights, that suit would necessarily present a federal question.[19] Section 502(a)(3) of ERISA specifically grants trustees of ERISA-covered plans like CLVT a cause of action for injunctive relief when their rights and duties under ERISA are at issue, and that action is exclusively governed by federal law.[20] If CLVT could have sought an injunction under ERISA against application to it of state regulations that require acts inconsistent with ERISA,[21] does a declaratory judgment suit by the State "arise under" federal law?

We think not. We have always interpreted what *Skelly Oil* called "the current of jurisdictional legislation since the Act of March 3, 1875," with an eye to practicality and necessity. "What is needed is something of that common-sense accommodation of judgment to kaleidoscopic situations which characterizes the law in its treatment of problems of causation * * * a selective process which picks the substantial causes out of the web and lays the other ones aside." There are good reasons why the federal courts should not entertain suits by the States to declare the validity of their regulations despite possibly conflicting federal law. States are not significantly prejudiced by an inability to come to federal court for a declaratory judgment in advance of a possible injunctive suit by a person subject to federal regulation. They have a variety of means by which they can enforce their own laws in their own courts, and they do not suffer if the pre-emption questions such enforcement may raise are

---

[19] For instance, federal courts have consistently adjudicated suits by alleged patent infringers to declare a patent invalid, on the theory that an infringement suit by the declaratory judgment defendant would raise a federal question over which the federal courts have exclusive jurisdiction. *See* E. Edelmann & Co. v. Triple-A Specialty Co., 88 F.2d 852 (7th Cir.1937). Taking jurisdiction over this type of suit is consistent with * * * dictum * * * in which we stated only that a declaratory judgment plaintiff could not get original federal jurisdiction if the anticipated lawsuit by the declaratory judgment defendant would *not* "arise under" federal law. It is also consistent with the nature of the declaratory remedy itself, which was designed to permit adjudication of either party's claims of right.

[20] Section 502(a)(3) provides:

> [A civil action may be brought] by a participant, beneficiary, or fiduciary (A) to enjoin any act or practice which violates any provision of this subchapter or the terms of the plan, or (B) to obtain other appropriate equitable relief (i) to redress such violations or (ii) to enforce any provision of this subchapter * * *.

See also n.26, *infra* (federal jurisdiction over suits under § 502 is exclusive, and they are governed entirely by federal common law).

Even if ERISA did not expressly provide jurisdiction, CLVT might have been able to obtain federal jurisdiction under the doctrine applied in some cases that a person subject to a scheme of federal regulation may sue in federal court to enjoin application to him of conflicting state regulations, and a declaratory judgment action by the same person does not necessarily run afoul of the *Skelly Oil* doctrine.

[21] We express no opinion, however, whether a party in CLVT's position could sue under ERISA to enjoin or to declare invalid a state tax levy, despite the Tax Injunction Act, 28 U.S.C. § 1341. To do so, it would have to show either that state law provided no "speedy and efficient remedy" or that Congress intended § 502 of ERISA to be an exception to the Tax Injunction Act.

tested there.[22] The express grant of federal jurisdiction in ERISA is limited to suits brought by certain parties, as to whom Congress presumably determined that a right to enter federal court was necessary to further the statute's purposes.[23] It did not go so far as to provide that any suit *against* such parties must also be brought in federal court when they themselves did not choose to sue. The situation presented by a State's suit for a declaration of the validity of state law is sufficiently removed from the spirit of necessity and careful limitation of district court jurisdiction that informed our statutory interpretation in *Skelly Oil* and *Gully* to convince us that, until Congress informs us otherwise, such a suit is not within the original jurisdiction of the United States district courts. Accordingly, the same suit brought originally in state court is not removable either.

B

CLVT also argues that appellant's "causes of action" are, in substance, federal claims. Although we have often repeated that "the party who brings a suit is master to decide what law he will rely upon," it is an independent corollary of the well-pleaded complaint rule that a plaintiff may not defeat removal by omitting to plead necessary federal questions in a complaint.

CLVT's best argument stems from our decision in *Avco Corp. v. Aero Lodge No. 735*. In that case, the petitioner filed suit in state court alleging simply that it had a valid contract with the respondent, a union, under which the respondent had agreed to submit all grievances to binding arbitration and not to cause or sanction any "work stoppages, strikes, or slowdowns." The petitioner further alleged that the respondent and its officials had violated the agreement by participating in and sanctioning work stoppages, and it sought temporary and permanent injunctions against further breaches. It was clear that, had petitioner invoked it, there would have been a federal cause of action under § 301 of the Labor Management Relations Act, 1947 (LMRA), and that, even in state court, any action to enforce an agreement within the scope of § 301 would be

---

[22] Indeed, as appellant's strategy in this case shows, they may often be willing to go to great lengths to avoid federal-court resolution of a pre-emption question. Realistically, there is little prospect that States will flood the federal courts with declaratory judgment actions; most questions will arise, as in this case, because a State has sought a declaration in state court and the defendant has removed the case to federal court. Accordingly, it is perhaps appropriate to note that considerations of comity make us reluctant to snatch cases which a State has brought from the courts of that State, unless some clear rule demands it.

[23] *Cf.* nn.19, 20, *supra.* Alleged patent infringers, for example, have a clear interest in swift resolution of the federal issue of patent validity—they are liable for damages if it turns out they are infringing a patent, and they frequently have a delicate network of contractual arrangements with third parties that is dependent on their right to sell or license a product. Parties subject to conflicting state and federal regulatory schemes also have a clear interest in sorting out the scope of each government's authority, especially where they face a threat of liability if the application of federal law is not quickly made clear.

controlled by federal law. It was also clear, however, under the law in effect at the time, that independent limits on federal jurisdiction made it impossible for a federal court to grant the injunctive relief petitioner sought.

The Court of Appeals held, and we affirmed, that the petitioner's action "arose under" § 301, and thus could be removed to federal court, although the petitioner had undoubtedly pleaded an adequate claim for relief under the state law of contracts and had sought a remedy available only under state law. The necessary ground of decision was that the preemptive force of § 301 is so powerful as to displace entirely any state cause of action "for violation of contracts between an employer and a labor organization." Any such suit is purely a creature of federal law, notwithstanding the fact that state law would provide a cause of action in the absence of § 301. *Avco* stands for the proposition that if a federal cause of action completely pre-empts a state cause of action any complaint that comes within the scope of the federal cause of action necessarily "arises under" federal law.

CLVT argues by analogy that ERISA, like § 301, was meant to create a body of federal common law, and that "any state court action which would require the interpretation or application of ERISA to a plan document 'arises under' the laws of the United States." ERISA contains provisions creating a series of express causes of action in favor of participants, beneficiaries, and fiduciaries of ERISA-covered plans, as well as the Secretary of Labor.[26] It may be that, as with § 301 as interpreted in *Avco,* any state action coming within the scope of § 502(a) of ERISA would be removable to federal district court, even if an otherwise adequate state cause of action were pleaded without reference to federal law.[27] It does not follow, however, that either of appellant's claims in this case comes within the scope of one of ERISA's causes of action.

The phrasing of § 502(a) is instructive. Section 502(a) specifies which persons—participants, beneficiaries, fiduciaries, or the Secretary of Labor—may bring actions for particular kinds of relief. It neither creates nor expressly denies any cause of action in favor of state governments, to enforce tax levies or for any other purpose. It does not purport

---

[26] The statute further states that "the district courts of the United States shall have exclusive jurisdiction of civil actions under this subchapter brought by the Secretary or by a participant, beneficiary, or fiduciary," except for actions by a participant or beneficiary to recover benefits due, to enforce rights under the terms of a plan, or to clarify rights to future benefits, over which state courts have concurrent jurisdiction. In addition, ERISA's legislative history indicates that, in light of the Act's virtually unique pre-emption provision, "a body of Federal substantive law will be developed by the courts to deal with issues involving rights and obligations under private welfare and pension plans."

[27] Indeed, precedent involving other statutes granting exclusive jurisdiction to the federal courts suggests that, if such an action were not within the class of cases over which state and federal courts have concurrent jurisdiction, the proper course for a federal district court to take after removal would be to dismiss the case altogether, without reaching the merits.

to reach every question relating to plans covered by ERISA. Furthermore, ERISA makes clear that Congress did not intend to preempt entirely every state cause of action relating to such plans. With important, but express limitations, it states that "nothing in this subchapter shall be construed to exempt or relieve any person from any law of any State which regulates insurance, banking, or securities."

Against this background, it is clear that a suit by state tax authorities under a statute like § 18818 does not "arise under" ERISA. Unlike the contract rights at issue in *Avco,* the State's right to enforce its tax levies is not of central concern to the federal statute. For that reason, as in *Gully,* on the face of a well-pleaded complaint there are many reasons completely unrelated to the provisions and purposes of ERISA why the State may or may not be entitled to the relief it seeks.[29] Furthermore, ERISA does not provide an alternative cause of action in favor of the State to enforce its rights, while § 301 expressly supplied the plaintiff in *Avco* with a federal cause of action to replace its pre-empted state contract claim. Therefore, even though the Court of Appeals may well be correct that ERISA precludes enforcement of the State's levy in the circumstances of this case, an action to enforce the levy is not itself preempted by ERISA.

Once again, appellant's declaratory judgment cause of action presents a somewhat more difficult issue. The question on which a declaration is sought—that of the CLVT trustees' "power to honor the levies made upon them by the State of California,"—is undoubtedly a matter of concern under ERISA. It involves the meaning and enforceability of provisions in CLVT's trust agreement forbidding the trustees to assign or otherwise to alienate funds held in trust, and thus comes within the class of questions for which Congress intended that federal courts create federal common law. Under ERISA, a participant, beneficiary, or fiduciary of a plan covered by ERISA may bring a declaratory judgment action in federal court to determine whether the plan's trustees may comply with a state levy on funds held in trust. Nevertheless, CLVT's argument that appellant's second cause of action arises under ERISA fails for the second reason given above. ERISA carefully enumerates the parties entitled to seek relief under § 502; it does not provide anyone other than participants, beneficiaries, or fiduciaries with an express cause of action for a declaratory judgment on the issues in this case. A suit for similar relief by some other party does not "arise under" that provision.

IV

Our concern in this case is consistent application of a system of stat-

---

[29] In theory (looking only at the complaint), it may turn out that the levy was improper under state law, or that in fact the defendant had complied with the levy. Furthermore, a levy on CLVT might be for something like property taxes on real estate it owned. CLVT's trust agreement authorizes its trustees to pay such taxes.

utes conferring original federal-court jurisdiction, as they have been interpreted by this Court over many years. Under our interpretations, Congress has given the lower federal courts jurisdiction to hear, originally or by removal from a state court, only those cases in which a well-pleaded complaint establishes either that federal law creates the cause of action or that the plaintiff's right to relief necessarily depends on resolution of a substantial question of federal law. We hold that a suit by state tax authorities both to enforce its levies against funds held in trust pursuant to an ERISA-covered employee benefit plan, and to declare the validity of the levies notwithstanding ERISA, is neither a creature of ERISA itself nor a suit of which the federal courts will take jurisdiction because it turns on a question of federal law. Accordingly, we vacate the judgment of the Court of Appeals and remand so that this case may be remanded to the Superior Court of the State of California for the County of Los Angeles.

It is so ordered.

Notes and Questions

1. The Court asserts that district courts should treat complaints resting on state declaratory judgment statutes as if they invoked the federal Declaratory Judgment Act, analyzing them under to *Skelly Oil*. What practical reason does the Court offer for requiring this convoluted analytical procedure? Why did *Skelly Oil* articulate the technique it did? Was it a desire to limit the federal case load or was there another, more technical reason? Do the assumptions that caused the *Skelly Oil* Court to decline jurisdiction apply with equal force when a state provision underlies a case?

2. a) Under ERISA, CLVT could have paid the disputed tax levy and then sought, essentially, replevin on the ground that ERISA preempted the state's power to tax. Clearly that would have been a federal question case under the established analysis. Moreover, CLVT could also have commenced an action seeking injunctive relief at the outset of the dispute, and that action would have been not merely federal, but exclusively federal under ERISA. Thus, if one is to look to the potential coercive action of the defendant in determining jurisdiction in a declaratory judgment case, as *Edelmann* suggested, the Franchise Tax Board's declaratory judgment action should have been maintainable in federal court. The Court cited *Edelmann* with approval, but failed to follow it. Why?

b) Moreover, if the Trust had proceeded to seek a declaratory judgment, under the state or federal provisions, *before* paying the disputed tax, that, too, would have been a federal question case under the *Skelly Oil* analysis. Thus, the result in *Franchise Tax* is anomalous, since the Trust would clearly have been able to proceed in federal court had it taken the initiative in the litigation. What rule causes this anomaly? Should the Court abandon the rule of *Skelly Oil* in order to avoid results like this?

c) On the same day as *Franchise Tax*, the Court declared,

A plaintiff who seeks injunctive relief from state regulation, on the ground that such regulation is pre-empted by a federal statute which, by virtue of the Supremacy Clause of the Constitution, must prevail, thus presents a federal question which the federal courts have jurisdiction under 28 U.S.C. § 1331 to resolve.

Shaw v. Delta Airlines, Inc., 463 U.S. 85, 96 n.14, 103 S.Ct. 2890, 2899 n.14, 77 L.Ed.2d 490, 500 n.14 (1983). Is there federal question jurisdiction if such a plaintiff only seeks declaratory relief? Suppose a state agency sued in state court seeking a declaration that the federal statute did not pre-empt. Would *Franchise Tax* prevent removal of the case as a federal question case?

d) In *Textron Lycoming Reciprocating Engine Division, AVCO Corp. v. United Automobile, Aerospace and Agricultural Implement Workers*, 523 U.S. 653, 118 S.Ct. 1626, 140 L.Ed.2d 863 (1998), the Court cast some doubt on the analysis that Justice Brennan discussed in Note 19 and its accompanying text, at least limiting it to cases in which the defense itself, in addition to the anticipated suit by the opposing party, is federal. The Union sought a declaration that Textron's conduct in concluding a collective bargaining agreement amounted to fraud, making the contract voidable at the Union's option. It asserted jurisdiction under § 301(a) of the Labor Management Relations Act, which authorizes the district courts to exercise original jurisdiction over "[s]uits for violation of contracts between an employer and a labor organization * * * ." The Court found that an action seeking to declare a contract voidable was not an action for violation of the contract as the statute requires and so refused jurisdiction. The Union argued

> that in order to determine whether § 301(a) jurisdiction lies over the declaratory-judgment aspect of its suit, we [the Court] must look to the character of the threatened action to which its suit would interpose a defense, which in this case would be Textron's action for breach of the collective-bargaining agreement. It relies on our decision in *Skelly Oil*, which held that a declaratory judgment action asserting a federal defense to a nonfederal claim was not a "civil actio[n] arising under the * * * laws * * * of the United States" within the meaning of the federal question jurisdiction statute, 28 U.S.C. § 1331. This argument makes several assumptions that we do not think can be indulged.

> First, it assumes that facts which were the *converse* of *Skelly Oil—i.e.* a declaratory-judgment complaint raising a *nonfederal* defense to an anticipated *federal* claim—*would* confer § 1331 jurisdiction. That is not clear. It can be argued that anticipating a federal claim in a suit asserting a nonfederal defense no more effectively invokes § 1331 jurisdiction than anticipating a federal defense in a suit asserting a nonfederal claim. * * * Perhaps it was the purpose of the Declaratory Judgment Act to permit such anticipation, see *Franchise Tax Board v. [Construction] Laborers Vacation Trust*, 463 U.S. 1, 19 n.19 (1983), but *Skelly Oil* did not present that issue, and some of its language suggests that the declaratory-judgment plaintiff must himself have a federal claim.[3] No decision of this Court has squarely confronted and explicitly

[3] Prior to [the Declaratory Judgment] Act, a federal court would entertain a suit on a

upheld federal-question jurisdiction on the basis of the anticipated claim against which the declaratory-judgment plaintiff presents a non-federal defense; and neither the Union nor the Government cites such a decision by any other federal court.[4]

Query, however, whether the Court's limited view of the applicability of the technique of *E. Edelmann Co. v. Triple-A Specialty Co.* makes Justice Brennan's silent refusal to use it in *Franchise Tax Board* even more of a conundrum. The CLVT's anticipated suit under ERISA was federal—indeed, exclusively so, just as a patent case is. The Franchise Tax Board's defense to such an action would have been that ERISA did not pre-empt the state tax, clearly a federal matter just as much as an assertion by an alleged patent infringer of the invalidity of the patent. Instead of *Edelmann* being relegated to a footnote in *Franchise Tax*, should it have controlled the decision?

What does it mean to speak of a nonfederal defense to a federal claim? Does federal or state law determine defenses to federal claims? If state law defenses are effective, is it because they are incorporated into federal law, or can state law by its own force limit the circumstances in which federal claims can be enforced? *See, e.g., Dice v. Akron, Canton, and Youngstown R. Co.*, 342 U.S. 359, 72 S.Ct. 312, 96 L.Ed. 398 (1952).

3. The technique of *E. Edelmann Co. v. Triple-A Specialty Co.* apparently is alive and well. In *Holmes Group, Inc. v. Vornado Air Circulation Systems Inc.*, 535 U.S. 826, 122 S.Ct. 1889, 153 L.Ed.2d 13 (2002), the Supreme Court reviewed a case involving arising-under jurisdiction and the exclusivity of the Federal Circuit's jurisdiction over appeals in cases involving patent claims. The plaintiff sought a declaration of non-infringement of defendant's trade dress. The defendant filed a patent infringement counterclaim. The district court, the court of appeals, and the Supreme Court assumed without discussion that the district court had jurisdiction; the only jurisdictional dispute was over whether an appeal lay to the Federal Circuit or the Tenth Circuit from the decision of the district court in Kansas. The Court clearly indicated, however, that the defendant's federal counterclaim did not provide the foundation for the district court's jurisdiction. Perhaps

---

contract only if the plaintiff asked for an immediately enforceable remedy like money damages or an injunction. * * * The Declaratory Judgment Act allowed relief to be given by way of recognizing the plaintiff's right even though no immediate enforcement of it was asked.

> [I]t has been settled doctrine that where a suit is brought in the federal courts "upon the sole ground that the determination of the suit depends upon some question of a federal nature, it must appear, at the outset, from the declaration or the bill of the party suing, that the suit is of that character." But "a suggestion of one party, that the other will or may set up a claim under the Constitution or laws of the United States, does not make the suit one arising under that Constitution or those laws."

[4] In *Franchise Tax Board* we observed, with seeming approval, that "[f]ederal courts have regularly taken original jurisdiction over declaratory judgment suits in which, if the declaratory judgment defendant brought a coercive action to enforce its rights, that suit would necessarily present a federal question." The cases brought forward to support that observation, however, were suits by alleged patent infringers to declare a patent invalid, which of course themselves raise a federal question.

the matter deserves more attention than the federal courts afforded it. In *Skelly Oil*, the Court looked to the plaintiff's hypothetical coercive action to evaluate the jurisdictional worthiness of the declaratory judgment action. In *Holmes Group*, what was the plaintiff's underlying coercive action, and why did it qualify for jurisdiction under § 1331? For that matter, what *was* the plaintiff's cause of action, irrespective of whether it qualified for federal question jurisdiction? Note that this is not a case where the defendant was threatening legal action against plaintiff's customers (as in *American Well Works* and *Edelmann*). Such conduct gives rise to claims of trade libel.

4. In light of the purposes of federal question jurisdiction, should a state or federal court adjudicate the federal issue *Franchise Tax* presents?

5. Apart from reflecting the problems declaratory judgment suits cause, *Franchise Tax* also involves issues of the effect of federal preemption on federal question jurisdiction. The *Franchise Tax* Court rejected the argument that the state law claims before it supported removal because ERISA preempted them. However, the Court reserved decision on whether ERISA preemption converted state-created causes of action "within the scope of § 502(a) of ERISA" into federal claims that would support removal. *Avco Corp. v. Machinists*, 390 U.S. 557, 88 S.Ct. 1235, 20 L.Ed.2d 126 (1968), had held that § 301 of the Labor Management Relations Act had that effect on state claims for breaches of collective bargaining agreements. Four years after *Franchise Tax*, the Court ruled in *Metropolitan Life Ins. Co. v. Taylor*, 481 U.S. 58, 107 S.Ct. 1542, 95 L.Ed.2d 55 (1987), that ERISA had the same effect on some state law claims. Taylor had sustained a work-related injury and received insurance benefits under his employee benefit plan. Subsequently, his employer and Metropolitan Life determined that Taylor was not disabled. Taylor disputed that determination, and his employer terminated him when he did not return to work. Taylor sued his employer and Metropolitan Life in state court against alleging breach of contract and wrongful termination and seeking damages and restoration of all employee benefits. The defendants removed, and the Supreme Court ultimately upheld federal jurisdiction, finding that a suit by a beneficiary seeking to recover benefits from a ERISA-covered plan falls directly under § 502. The Court noted that the language of ERISA's applicable jurisdictional provision closely paralleled the jurisdictional provision of the Labor Management Relations Act that led to *Avco*. Moreover, the Conference Report on ERISA had expressly stated that § 502 actions were to be regarded as arising under federal law in the same manner as those brought under § 301 of the Labor Management Relations Act. Thus, Congress had clearly shown its intent to make such claims removable. Taylor's claims for contract and tort damages were removable to federal court because ERISA had "convert[ed] an ordinary state common law complaint into one stating a federal claim for purposes of the well-pleaded complaint rule." Does *Taylor* overrule *Franchise Tax* by implication?

6. *Franchise Tax Board*'s approval of *Skelly Oil* and "fidelity to its spirit" rests on a shaky foundation. Extensive research by Professor Michael Mushlin indicates that Justice Frankfurter's underlying assumption that the Declaratory Judgment Act of 1934 was not intended to expand federal jurisdiction is unsound. Indeed, there is considerable evidence that Congress

quite explicitly contemplated an increase of cases in the federal courts as a result of the Act. *See* Donald L. Doernberg & Michael B. Mushlin, *The Trojan Horse: How the Declaratory Judgment Act Created a Cause of Action and Expanded Federal Jurisdiction While the Supreme Court Wasn't Looking,* 36 U.C.L.A.L.Rev. 529 (1989). If Congress did intend an expansion of federal jurisdiction, what implications does that have for federal question jurisdiction in general and for the well-pleaded complaint rule in particular?

7. a) Some suggest that the Court's federal question jurisdiction jurisprudence needs to be overhauled. *See, e.g.,* William Cohen, *The Broken Compass: The Requirement that a Case Arise "Directly" under Federal Law,* 115 U.Pa.L.Rev. 890 (1967); AMERICAN LAW INSTITUTE, STUDY OF THE DIVISION OF JURISDICTION BETWEEN STATE AND FEDERAL COURTS (1969). Professor Cohen argues that no "single, all-purpose, neutral analytical concept" explains the Supreme Court decisions on statutory federal question jurisdiction. That should not be surprising. To some extent, the Court has balanced various pragmatic factors in determining whether a particular case warrants original federal court jurisdiction. He contends that the courts should not only engage in such pragmatic balancing but also should do so more openly. The factors he mentions include: "the extent of the caseload increase for federal trial courts if jurisdiction is recognized; the extent to which cases of this class will, in practice, turn on issues of state or federal law; the extent of the necessity for an expert federal tribunal to handle issues of federal law that do arise; the extent of the necessity for a sympathetic federal tribunal in cases of this class." Do the cases reflect such concerns? Should they?

b) Consider again the purposes of federal question jurisdiction. In what sorts of circumstances should litigants be able to take their disputes to the federal trial courts, not only in declaratory judgment cases, but generally? What are the factors that make federal adjudication desirable? In allocating types of cases to the federal courts, bear in mind both policy and practical limitations of the federal courts as a judicial system. To what extent should federalism compel a narrow federal judicial role, at least in cases with some state law components? To what extent should we keep groups of cases out of the federal courts because the federal system is comparatively small? If you were designing a federal question jurisdiction system within the limits of Article III, how would you proceed?

Chapter 4

LEGISLATIVE COURTS

A. INTRODUCTION

The Constitution establishes the limits of the federal judicial power and gives Congress discretion to create federal tribunals inferior to the Supreme Court. Additionally, Article III offers federal judges safeguards from interference by the legislature and executive. First, it provides that they shall have life tenure upon "good behavior." Federal judges can be removed from office only upon impeachment by the House of Representatives and conviction by the Senate for treason, bribery, or other high crimes and misdemeanors. Second, Article III prohibits reductions in their salaries while they are in office.

A literal interpretation of these provisions might suggest that if Congress creates a tribunal with the power to adjudicate federal cases, Article III would protect that court's judges, but these provisions have never been so interpreted. The first Congress, which included many former delegates to the Constitutional Convention, authorized Treasury Department officers to resolve some types of disputes, including claims to veteran's benefits, that were within Article III. Since then, Congress has often created non-Article III tribunals. When the judges of a federal tribunal do not enjoy the protections of Article III, the tribunal is often referred to as an "Article I" or "legislative" court.

The Supreme Court endorsed legislative courts early in the country's history. In *American Insurance Co. v. Canter,* 26 U.S. (1 Pet.) 511, 7 L.Ed. 242 (1828), the Court concluded that Congress could create territorial courts with judges not protected by Article III. The Court reasoned that in legislating for the territories Congress was exercising both state-like and national governmental powers. Consequently, territorial judges were analogous to state judges and were not entitled to the safeguards of Article III. Even today territorial district court judges exercise the same jurisdiction as other federal district judges, but serve only limited terms and are subject to removal by the President for cause.

The jurisdiction of many legislative courts is much more specialized than that of the territorial courts. The jurisdiction of the Tax Court, for example, consists primarily of deciding taxpayers' petitions for redetermination of deficiencies assessed by the Internal Revenue Service. Indeed, it is the only court with the power to review a determination of tax liability by the Service before the payment of the tax. Tax Court judges serve fifteen-year terms and can be removed from office for inefficiency, neglect of duty, or malfeasance. The courts of appeals, Article III courts, have jurisdiction over appeals from the Tax Court.

Modern administrative agencies also operate inconsistently with the literal language of Article III. Congress creates such agencies to administer various federal regulatory schemes. They often adjudicate disputes regarding the application of federal laws and regulations. *Crowell v. Benson,* 285 U.S. 22, 52 S.Ct. 285, 76 L.Ed. 598 (1932), upheld the right of the United States Employees' Compensation Commission to make initial factual determinations in disputes between employers and employees under a federal statutory scheme that required compensation for work-related injuries. The federal district courts could review the Commission's orders. The Supreme Court therefore found that the agency served as an adjunct to the Article III courts, and the scheme was not unconstitutional.

Congress has created Article I courts for several reasons: to keep the number of federal judges small and the appointments prestigious, to limit the number of judges with life tenure and life-time employment, and to insure judicial expertise in specialized areas. This Chapter examines whether these goals are reconcilable with Article III and considers whether there are any limits on Congressional power to use Article I courts. Must their decisions be reviewable by an Article III court? Could every federal case initially be assigned to an administrative agency for fact-finding without violating Article III? Does broad congressional power to create Article I courts imply an inherent weakness of Article III courts?

B.   LIMITS ON LEGISLATIVE COURTS

NORTHERN PIPELINE CONSTRUCTION CO. v. MARATHON PIPE LINE CO.
Supreme Court of the United States, 1982.
458 U.S. 50, 102 S.Ct. 2858, 73 L.Ed.2d 598.

JUSTICE BRENNAN announced the judgment of the Court and delivered an opinion in which JUSTICE MARSHALL, JUSTICE BLACKMUN, and JUSTICE STEVENS joined.

The question presented is whether the assignment by Congress to bankruptcy judges of the jurisdiction granted in 28 U.S.C. § 1471 (1976 ed., Supp. IV) by § 241(a) of the Bankruptcy Act of 1978 violates Art. III of the Constitution.

I

A

In 1978, after almost 10 years of study and investigation, Congress enacted a comprehensive revision of the bankruptcy laws. The Bankruptcy Act of 1978 (Act) made significant changes in both the substantive and procedural law of bankruptcy. It is the changes in the latter that are at issue in this case.

Before the Act, federal district courts served as bankruptcy courts and employed a "referee" system. Bankruptcy proceedings were generally conducted before referees, except in those instances in which the district court elected to withdraw a case from a referee. The referee's final order was appealable to the district court. The bankruptcy courts were vested with "summary jurisdiction"—that is, with jurisdiction over controversies involving property in the actual or constructive possession of the court. And, with consent, the bankruptcy court also had jurisdiction over some "plenary" matters—such as disputes involving property in the possession of a third person.

The Act eliminates the referee system and establishes "in each judicial district, as an adjunct to the district court for such district, a bankruptcy court which shall be a court of record known as the United States Bankruptcy Court for the district." The judges of these courts are appointed to office for 14-year terms by the President, with the advice and consent of the Senate. They are subject to removal by the "judicial council of the circuit" on account of "incompetency, misconduct, neglect of duty or physical or mental disability." In addition, the salaries of the bankruptcy judges are set by statute and are subject to adjustment under the Federal Salary Act.

The jurisdiction of the bankruptcy courts created by the Act is much broader than that exercised under the former referee system. Eliminating the distinction between "summary" and "plenary" jurisdiction, the Act grants the new courts jurisdiction over all "civil proceedings arising under title 11 [the Bankruptcy title] or arising in or related to cases under Title 11." This jurisdictional grant empowers bankruptcy courts to entertain a wide variety of cases involving claims that may affect the property of the estate once a petition has been filed under Title 11. Included within the bankruptcy courts' jurisdiction are suits to recover accounts, controversies involving exempt property, actions to avoid transfers and payments as preferences or fraudulent conveyances, and causes of action owned by the debtor at the time of the petition for bankruptcy. The bankruptcy courts can hear claims based on state law as well as those based on federal law.

The judges of the bankruptcy courts are vested with all of the "powers of a court of equity, law, and admiralty," except that they "may not enjoin another court or punish a criminal contempt not committed in the presence of the judge of the court or warranting a punishment of imprisonment." In addition to this broad grant of power, Congress has allowed bankruptcy judges the power to hold jury trials; to issue declaratory judgments; to issue writs of habeas corpus under certain circumstances; to issue all writs necessary in aid of the bankruptcy court's expanded jurisdiction; and to issue any order, process or judgment that is necessary or appropriate to carry out the provisions of Title 11.

The Act also establishes a special procedure for appeals from orders of bankruptcy courts. The circuit council is empowered to direct the chief judge of the circuit to designate panels of three bankruptcy judges to hear appeals. These panels have jurisdiction of all appeals from final judgments, orders, and decrees of bankruptcy courts, and, with leave of the panel, of interlocutory appeals. If no such appeals panel is designated, the district court is empowered to exercise appellate jurisdiction. The court of appeals is given jurisdiction over appeals from the appellate panels or from the district court. If the parties agree, a direct appeal to the court of appeals may be taken from a final judgment of a bankruptcy court.[5]

B

This case arises out of proceedings initiated in the United States Bankruptcy Court for the District of Minnesota after appellant Northern Pipeline Construction Co. (Northern) filed a petition for reorganization in January 1980. In March 1980, Northern, pursuant to the Act, filed in that court a suit against appellee Marathon Pipe Line Co. (Marathon). Appellant sought damages for alleged breaches of contract and warranty, as well as for alleged misrepresentation, coercion, and duress. Marathon sought dismissal of the suit, on the ground that the Act unconstitutionally conferred Art. III judicial power upon judges who lacked life tenure and protection against salary diminution. The United States intervened to defend the validity of the statute.

The Bankruptcy Judge denied the motion to dismiss. But on appeal the District Court entered an order granting the motion, on the ground that "the delegation of authority in 28 U.S.C. § 1471 to the Bankruptcy Judges to try cases which are otherwise relegated under the Constitution to Article III judges" was unconstitutional. Both the United States and Northern filed notices of appeal in this Court. We noted probable jurisdiction.

II

A

Basic to the constitutional structure established by the Framers was their recognition that "[t]he accumulation of all powers, legislative, executive, and judiciary, in the same hands, whether of one, a few, or many, and whether hereditary, self-appointed, or elective, may justly be pronounced the very definition of tyranny." To ensure against such tyranny, the Framers provided that the Federal Government would consist of three distinct Branches, each to exercise one of the governmental powers recognized by the Framers as inherently distinct. "The Framers regarded the checks and balances that they had built into the tripartite

---

[5] Although no particular standard of review is specified in the Act, the parties in the present cases seem to agree that the appropriate one is the clearly-erroneous standard, employed in old Bankruptcy Rule 810 for review of findings of fact made by a referee.

Federal Government as a self-executing safeguard against the encroachment or aggrandizement of one branch at the expense of the other."

The Federal Judiciary was therefore designed by the Framers to stand independent of the Executive and Legislature—to maintain the checks and balances of the constitutional structure, and also to guarantee that the process of adjudication itself remained impartial. Hamilton explained the importance of an independent Judiciary:

> Periodical appointments, however regulated, or by whomsoever made, would, in some way or other, be fatal to [the courts'] necessary independence. If the power of making them was committed either to the Executive or legislature, there would be danger of an improper complaisance to the branch which possessed it; if to both, there would be an unwillingness to hazard the displeasure of either; if to the people, or to persons chosen by them for the special purpose, there would be too great a disposition to consult popularity, to justify a reliance that nothing would be consulted but the Constitution and the laws.

The Court has only recently reaffirmed the significance of this feature of the Framers' design: "A Judiciary free from control by the Executive and Legislature is essential if there is a right to have claims decided by judges who are free from potential domination by other branches of government."

As an inseparable element of the constitutional system of checks and balances, and as a guarantee of judicial impartiality, Art. III both defines the power and protects the independence of the Judicial Branch. It provides that "The judicial Power of the United States, shall be vested in one supreme Court, and in such inferior Courts as the Congress may from time to time ordain and establish." The inexorable command of this provision is clear and definite: The judicial power of the United States must be exercised by courts having the attributes prescribed in Art. III. Those attributes are also clearly set forth:

> The Judges, both of the supreme and inferior Courts, shall hold their Offices during good Behaviour, and shall, at stated Times, receive for their Services, a Compensation, which shall not be diminished during their Continuance in Office.

The "good Behaviour" Clause guarantees that Art. III judges shall enjoy life tenure, subject only to removal by impeachment. The Compensation Clause guarantees Art. III judges a fixed and irreducible compensation for their services. Both of these provisions were incorporated into the Constitution to ensure the independence of the Judiciary from the control of the Executive and Legislative Branches of government. * * *
The Framers thus recognized:

> Next to permanency in office, nothing can contribute more to

the independence of the judges than a fixed provision for their support * * * . In the general course of human nature, a power over a man's subsistence amounts to a power over his will.

In sum, our Constitution unambiguously enunciates a fundamental principle—that the "judicial Power of the United States" must be reposed in an independent Judiciary. It commands that the independence of the Judiciary be jealously guarded, and it provides clear institutional protections for that independence.

B

It is undisputed that the bankruptcy judges whose offices were created by the Bankruptcy Act of 1978 do not enjoy the protections constitutionally afforded to Art. III judges. The bankruptcy judges do not serve for life subject to their continued "good Behaviour." Rather, they are appointed for 14-year terms, and can be removed by the judicial council of the circuit in which they serve on grounds of "incompetency, misconduct, neglect of duty, or physical or mental disability." Second, the salaries of the bankruptcy judges are not immune from diminution by Congress. In short, there is no doubt that the bankruptcy judges created by the Act are not Art. III judges.

* * *

Appellants suggest two grounds for upholding the Act's conferral of broad adjudicative powers upon judges unprotected by Art. III. First, it is urged that "pursuant to its enumerated Article I powers, Congress may establish legislative courts that have jurisdiction to decide cases to which the Article III judicial power of the United States extends." Referring to our precedents upholding the validity of "legislative courts," appellants suggest that "the plenary grants of power in Article I permit Congress to establish non-Article III tribunals in 'specialized areas having particularized needs and warranting distinctive treatment,'" such as the area of bankruptcy law. Second, appellants contend that even if the Constitution does require that this bankruptcy-related action be adjudicated in an Art. III court, the Act in fact satisfies that requirement. "Bankruptcy jurisdiction was vested in the district court" of the judicial district in which the bankruptcy court is located, "and the exercise of that jurisdiction by the adjunct bankruptcy court was made subject to appeal as of right to an Article III court." Analogizing the role of the bankruptcy court to that of a special master, appellants urge us to conclude that this "adjunct" system established by Congress satisfies the requirements of Art. III. We consider these arguments in turn.

III

Congress did not constitute the bankruptcy courts as legislative courts. Appellants contend, however, that the bankruptcy courts could have been so constituted, and that as a result the "adjunct" system in fact chosen by Congress does not impermissibly encroach upon the judicial power. In advancing this argument, appellants rely upon cases in which we have identified certain matters that "Congress may or may not bring within the cognizance of [Art. III courts], as it may deem proper." But when properly understood, these precedents represent no broad departure from the constitutional command that the judicial power of the United States must be vested in Art. III courts.[15] Rather, they reduce to three narrow situations not subject to that command, each recognizing a circumstance in which the grant of power to the Legislative and Executive Branches was historically and constitutionally so exceptional that the congressional assertion of a power to create legislative courts was consistent with, rather than threatening to, the constitutional mandate of separation of powers. These precedents simply acknowledge that the literal command of Art. III, assigning the judicial power of the United States to courts insulated from Legislative or Executive interference, must be interpreted in light of the historical context in which the Constitution was written, and of the structural imperatives of the Constitution as a whole.

Appellants first rely upon a series of cases in which this Court has upheld the creation by Congress of non-Art. III "territorial courts." This exception from the general prescription of Art. III dates from the earliest days of the Republic, when it was perceived that the Framers intended that as to certain geographical areas, in which no State operated as sovereign, Congress was to exercise the general powers of government. For example, in *American Ins. Co. v. Canter,* the Court observed that Art. IV bestowed upon Congress alone a complete power of government over territories not within the States that constituted the United States. The Court then acknowledged Congress' authority to create courts for those territories that were not in conformity with Art. III. Such courts were

> created in virtue of the general right of sovereignty which exists in the government, or in virtue of that clause which enables Congress to make all needful rules and regulations, respecting the territory belonging to the United States. The jurisdiction with which they are invested * * * is conferred by Congress, in the execution of those general powers which that body possesses over the territories of the United States. Although admiralty jurisdiction can be exercised in the states in those Courts, only, which are established in pursuance of the third article of the Constitution; the same limita-

---

[15] Justice White's dissent finds particular significance in the fact that Congress could have assigned all bankruptcy matters to the state courts. But, of course, virtually all matters that might be heard in Art. III courts could also be left by Congress to state courts. This fact is simply irrelevant to the question before us. Congress has no control over state-court judges; accordingly the principle of separation of powers is not threatened by leaving the adjudication of federal disputes to such judges. The Framers chose to leave to Congress the precise role to be played by the lower federal courts in the administration of justice. But the Framers did not leave it to Congress to define the character of those courts— they were to be independent of the political branches and presided over by judges with guaranteed salary and life tenure.

tion does not extend to the territories. In legislating for them, Congress exercises the combined powers of the general, and of a state government.

The Court followed the same reasoning when it reviewed Congress' creation of non-Art. III courts in the District of Columbia. It noted that there was in the District

> no division of powers between the general and state governments. Congress has the entire control over the district for every purpose of government; and it is reasonable to suppose, that in organizing a judicial department here, all judicial power necessary for the purposes of government would be vested in the courts of justice.

Appellants next advert to a second class of cases—those in which this Court has sustained the exercise by Congress and the Executive of the power to establish and administer courts-martial. The situation in these cases strongly resembles the situation with respect to territorial courts: It too involves a constitutional grant of power that has been historically understood as giving the political Branches of Government extraordinary control over the precise subject matter at issue. Article I, § 8, cls. 13, 14, confer upon Congress the power "[t]o provide and maintain a Navy," and "[t]o make Rules for the Government and Regulation of the land and naval Forces." The Fifth Amendment, which requires a presentment or indictment of a grand jury before a person may be held to answer for a capital or otherwise infamous crime, contains an express exception for "cases arising in the land or naval forces." And Art. II, § 2, cl. 1, provides that "The President shall be Commander in Chief of the Army and Navy of the United States, and of the Militia of the several States, when called into the actual Service of the United States." Noting these constitutional directives, the Court in *Dynes v. Hoover* explained:

> These provisions show that Congress has the power to provide for the trial and punishment of military and naval offences in the manner then and now practiced by civilized nations; and that the power to do so is given without any connection between it and the 3d article of the Constitution defining the judicial power of the United States; indeed, that the two powers are entirely independent of each other.

Finally, appellants rely on a third group of cases, in which this Court has upheld the constitutionality of legislative courts and administrative agencies created by Congress to adjudicate cases involving "public rights."[18] The "public rights" doctrine was first set forth in *Murray's Lessee v. Hoboken Land & Improvement Co.* (1856):

---

[18] Congress' power to create legislative courts to adjudicate public rights carries with it the lesser power to create administrative agencies for the same purpose, and to provide for review of those agency decisions in Art. III courts.

> [W]e do not consider congress can either withdraw from judicial cognizance any matter which, from its nature, is the subject of a suit at the common law, or in equity, or admiralty; nor, on the other hand, can it bring under the judicial power a matter which, from its nature, is not a subject for judicial determination. At the same time there are matters, involving public rights, which may be presented in such form that the judicial power is capable of acting on them, and which are susceptible of judicial determination, but which congress may or may not bring within the cognizance of the courts of the United States, as it may deem proper.

This doctrine may be explained in part by reference to the traditional principle of sovereign immunity, which recognizes that the Government may attach conditions to its consent to be sued. But the public-rights doctrine also draws upon the principle of separation of powers, and a historical understanding that certain prerogatives were reserved to the political Branches of Government. The doctrine extends only to matters arising "between the Government and persons subject to its authority in connection with the performance of the constitutional functions of the executive or legislative departments," and only to matters that historically could have been determined exclusively by those departments. The understanding of these cases is that the Framers expected that Congress would be free to commit such matters completely to nonjudicial executive determination, and that as a result there can be no constitutional objection to Congress' employing the less drastic expedient of committing their determination to a legislative court or an administrative agency.

The public-rights doctrine is grounded in a historically recognized distinction between matters that could be conclusively determined by the Executive and Legislative Branches and matters that are "inherently * * * judicial." For example, the Court in *Murray's Lessee* looked to the law of England and the States at the time the Constitution was adopted, in order to determine whether the issue presented was customarily cognizable in the courts. Concluding that the matter had not traditionally been one for judicial determination, the Court perceived no bar to Congress' establishment of summary procedures, outside of Art. III courts, to collect a debt due to the Government from one of its customs agents.[20] On the same premise, the Court held that the Court of Customs Appeals had been properly constituted by Congress as a legislative court:

> The full province of the court under the act creating it is that of determining matters arising between the Government and others in the executive administration and application of the customs laws

---

[20] Doubtless it could be argued that the need for independent judicial determination is greatest in cases arising between the Government and an individual. But the rationale for the public-rights line of cases lies not in political theory, but rather in Congress' and this Court's understanding of what power was reserved to the Judiciary by the Constitution as a matter of historical fact.

* * * . The appeals include nothing which inherently or necessarily requires judicial determination, but only matters the determination of which may be, and at times has been, committed exclusively to executive officers.

The distinction between public rights and private rights has not been definitively explained in our precedents. Nor is it necessary to do so in the present cases, for it suffices to observe that a matter of public rights must at a minimum arise "between the government and others." In contrast, "the liability of one individual to another under the law as defined" is a matter of private rights. Our precedents clearly establish that only controversies in the former category may be removed from Art. III courts and delegated to legislative courts or administrative agencies for their determination. Private-rights disputes, on the other hand, lie at the core of the historically recognized judicial power.

In sum, this Court has identified three situations in which Art. III does not bar the creation of legislative courts. In each of these situations, the Court has recognized certain exceptional powers bestowed upon Congress by the Constitution or by historical consensus. Only in the face of such an exceptional grant of power has the Court declined to hold the authority of Congress subject to the general prescriptions of Art. III.

We discern no such exceptional grant of power applicable in the cases before us. The courts created by the Bankruptcy Act of 1978 do not lie exclusively outside the States of the Federal Union, like those in the District of Columbia and the Territories. Nor do the bankruptcy courts bear any resemblance to courts-martial, which are founded upon the Constitution's grant of plenary authority over the Nation's military forces to the Legislative and Executive Branches. Finally, the substantive legal rights at issue in the present action cannot be deemed "public rights." Appellants argue that a discharge in bankruptcy is indeed a "public right," similar to such congressionally created benefits as "radio station licenses, pilot licenses, or certificates for common carriers" granted by administrative agencies. But the restructuring of debtor-creditor relations, which is at the core of the federal bankruptcy power, must be distinguished from the adjudication of state-created private rights, such as the right to recover contract damages that is at issue in this case. The former may well be a "public right," but the latter obviously is not. Appellant Northern's right to recover contract damages to augment its estate is "one of private right, that is, of the liability of one individual to another under the law as defined."

Recognizing that the present cases may not fall within the scope of any of our prior cases permitting the establishment of legislative courts, appellants argue that we should recognize an additional situation beyond the command of Art. III, sufficiently broad to sustain the Act. Appellants contend that Congress' constitutional authority to establish "uniform Laws on the subject of Bankruptcies throughout the United States," carries with it an inherent power to establish legislative courts capable of adjudicating "bankruptcy-related controversies."

* * *

Appellants' contention, in essence, is that pursuant to any of its Art. I powers, Congress may create courts free of Art. III's requirements whenever it finds that course expedient. This contention has been rejected in previous cases. Although the cases relied upon by appellants demonstrate that independent courts are not required for all federal adjudications, those cases also make it clear that where Art. III does apply, all of the legislative powers specified in Art. I and elsewhere are subject to it.

The flaw in appellants' analysis is that it provides no limiting principle. It thus threatens to supplant completely our system of adjudication in independent Art. III tribunals and replace it with a system of "specialized" legislative courts. True, appellants argue that under their analysis Congress could create legislative courts pursuant only to some "specific" Art. I power, and "only when there is a particularized need for distinctive treatment." They therefore assert that their analysis would not permit Congress to replace the independent Art. III Judiciary through a "wholesale assignment of federal judicial business to legislative courts." But these "limitations" are wholly illusory. For example, Art. I, § 8, empowers Congress to enact laws, *inter alia,* regulating interstate commerce and punishing certain crimes. Art. I, § 8, cls. 3, 6. On appellants' reasoning Congress could provide for the adjudication of these and "related" matters by judges and courts within Congress' exclusive control. The potential for encroachment upon powers reserved to the Judicial Branch through the device of "specialized" legislative courts is dramatically evidenced in the jurisdiction granted to the courts created by the Act before us. The broad range of questions that can be brought into a bankruptcy court because they are "related to cases under title 11" is the clearest proof that even when Congress acts through a "specialized" court, and pursuant to only one of its many Art. I powers, appellants' analysis fails to provide any real protection against the erosion of Art. III jurisdiction by the unilateral action of the political Branches. In short, to accept appellants' reasoning, would require that we replace the principles delineated in our precedents, rooted in history and the Constitution, with a rule of broad legislative discretion that could effectively eviscerate the constitutional guarantee of an independent Judicial Branch of the Federal Government.

* * *

In sum, Art. III bars Congress from establishing legislative courts to exercise jurisdiction over all matters related to those arising under the bankruptcy laws. The establishment of such courts does not fall within

any of the historically recognized situations in which the general principle of independent adjudication commanded by Art. III does not apply.
Nor can we discern any persuasive reason, in logic, history, or the Constitution, why the bankruptcy courts here established lie beyond the
reach of Art. III.

IV

Appellants advance a second argument for upholding the constitutionality of the Act: that "viewed within the entire judicial framework
set up by Congress," the bankruptcy court is merely an "adjunct" to the
district court, and that the delegation of certain adjudicative functions to
the bankruptcy court is accordingly consistent with the principle that
the judicial power of the United States must be vested in Art. III courts.
As support for their argument, appellants rely principally upon *Crowell
v. Benson* and *United States v. Raddatz,* cases in which we approved the
use of administrative agencies and magistrates as adjuncts to Art. III
courts. The question to which we turn, therefore, is whether the Act has
retained "the essential attributes of the judicial power," in Art. III tribunals.

The essential premise underlying appellants' argument is that even
where the Constitution denies Congress the power to establish legislative courts, Congress possesses the authority to assign certain factfinding functions to adjunct tribunals. It is, of course, true that while the
power to adjudicate "private rights" must be vested in an Art. III court,

> this Court has accepted factfinding by an administrative agency,
> * * * as an adjunct to the Art. III court, analogizing the agency to a
> jury or a special master and permitting it in admiralty cases to per-
> form the function of the special master.

The use of administrative agencies as adjuncts was first upheld in
Crowell v. Benson. The congressional scheme challenged in *Crowell* empowered an administrative agency, the United States Employees' Compensation Commission, to make initial factual determinations pursuant
to a federal statute requiring employers to compensate their employees
for work-related injuries occurring upon the navigable waters of the
United States. The Court began its analysis by noting that the federal
statute administered by the Compensation Commission provided for
compensation of injured employees "irrespective of fault," and that the
statute also prescribed a fixed and mandatory schedule of compensation.
The agency was thus left with the limited role of determining "questions
of fact as to the circumstances, nature, extent and consequences of the
injuries sustained by the employee for which compensation is to be
made." The agency did not possess the power to enforce any of its compensation orders: On the contrary, every compensation order was appealable to the appropriate federal district court, which had the sole
power to enforce it or set it aside, depending upon whether the court determined it to be "in accordance with law" and supported by evidence in

the record. The Court found that in view of these limitations upon the Compensation Commission's functions and powers, its determinations were "closely analogous to findings of the amount of damages that are made, according to familiar practice, by commissioners or assessors." Observing that "there is no requirement that, in order to maintain the essential attributes of the judicial power, all determinations of fact in constitutional courts shall be made by judges," the Court held that Art. III imposed no bar to the scheme enacted by Congress.

Crowell involved the adjudication of congressionally created rights. But this Court has sustained the use of adjunct factfinders even in the adjudication of constitutional rights—so long as those adjuncts were subject to sufficient control by an Art. III district court. In *United States v. Raddatz,* the Court upheld the 1978 Federal Magistrates Act, which permitted district court judges to refer certain pretrial motions, including suppression motions based on alleged violations of constitutional rights, to a magistrate for initial determination. The Court observed that the magistrate's proposed findings and recommendations were subject to *de novo* review by the district court, which was free to rehear the evidence or to call for additional evidence. Moreover, it was noted that the magistrate considered motions only upon reference from the district court, and that the magistrates were appointed, and subject to removal, by the district court.[30] In short, the ultimate decisionmaking authority respecting all pretrial motions clearly remained with the district court. Under these circumstances, the Court held that the Act did not violate the constraints of Art. III.

Together these cases establish two principles that aid us in determining the extent to which Congress may constitutionally vest traditionally judicial functions in non-Art. III officers. First, it is clear that when Congress creates a substantive federal right, it possesses substantial discretion to prescribe the manner in which that right may be adjudicated—including the assignment to an adjunct of some functions historically performed by judges. Thus *Crowell* recognized that Art. III does not require "all determinations of fact [to] be made by judges;" with respect to congressionally created rights, some factual determinations may be made by a specialized factfinding tribunal designed by Congress, without constitutional bar. Second, the functions of the adjunct must be limited in such a way that "the essential attributes" of judicial power are retained in the Art. III court. Thus in upholding the adjunct scheme challenged in *Crowell,* the Court emphasized that "the reservation of full authority to the court to deal with matters of law provides for the appropriate exercise of the judicial function in this class of cases." And in re-

---

[30] Thus in *Raddatz* there was no serious threat that the exercise of the judicial power would be subject to incursion by other branches. "[T]he only conceivable danger of a 'threat' to the 'independence' of the magistrate comes from within, rather than without the judicial department."

fusing to invalidate the Magistrates Act at issue in *Raddatz,* the Court stressed that under the congressional scheme " '[t]he authority—and the responsibility—to make an informed, final determination * * * remains with the judge;' " the statute's delegation of power was therefore permissible, since "the ultimate decision is made by the district court."

These two principles assist us in evaluating the "adjunct" scheme presented in these cases. Appellants assume that Congress' power to create "adjuncts" to consider all cases related to those arising under Title 11 is as great as it was in the circumstances of *Crowell.* But while *Crowell* certainly endorsed the proposition that Congress possesses broad discretion to assign factfinding functions to an adjunct created to aid in the adjudication of congressionally created statutory rights, *Crowell* does not support the further proposition necessary to appellants' argument—that Congress possesses the same degree of discretion in assigning traditionally judicial power to adjuncts engaged in the adjudication of rights not created by Congress. Indeed, the validity of this proposition was expressly denied in *Crowell,* when the Court rejected "the untenable assumption that the constitutional courts may be deprived in all cases of the determination of facts upon evidence even though a constitutional right may be involved," and stated that

> the essential independence of the exercise of the judicial power of the United States in the enforcement of constitutional rights requires that the Federal court should determine * * * an issue [of agency jurisdiction] upon its own record and the facts elicited before it.[34]

Appellants' proposition was also implicitly rejected in *Raddatz.* Congress' assignment of adjunct functions under the Federal Magistrates Act was substantially narrower than under the statute challenged in *Crowell.* Yet the Court's scrutiny of the adjunct scheme in *Raddatz—* which played a role in the adjudication of constitutional rights—was far stricter than it had been in *Crowell.* Critical to the Court's decision to uphold the Magistrates Act was the fact that the ultimate decision was made by the district court.

Although *Crowell* and *Raddatz* do not explicitly distinguish between rights created by Congress and other rights, such a distinction underlies in part *Crowell's* and *Raddatz's* recognition of a critical difference between rights created by federal statute and rights recognized by the Constitution. Moreover, such a distinction seems to us to be necessary in light of the delicate accommodations required by the principle of separation of powers reflected in Art. III. The constitutional system of checks

---

[34] *Crowell's* precise holding, with respect to the review of "jurisdictional" and "constitutional" facts that arise within ordinary administrative proceedings, has been undermined by later cases. But the general principle of *Crowell*—distinguishing between congressionally created rights and constitutionally recognized rights—remains valid.

and balances is designed to guard against "encroachment or aggrandizement" by Congress at the expense of the other branches of government. But when Congress creates a statutory right, it clearly has the discretion, in defining that right, to create presumptions, or assign burdens of proof, or prescribe remedies; it may also provide that persons seeking to vindicate that right must do so before particularized tribunals created to perform the specialized adjudicative tasks related to that right. Such provisions do, in a sense, affect the exercise of judicial power, but they are also incidental to Congress' power to define the right that it has created. No comparable justification exists, however, when the right being adjudicated is not of congressional creation. In such a situation, substantial inroads into functions that have traditionally been performed by the Judiciary cannot be characterized merely as incidental extensions of Congress' power to define rights that it has created. Rather, such inroads suggest unwarranted encroachments upon the judicial power of the United States, which our Constitution reserves for Art. III courts.

We hold that the Bankruptcy Act of 1978 carries the possibility of such an unwarranted encroachment. Many of the rights subject to adjudication by the Act's bankruptcy courts, like the rights implicated in *Raddatz,* are not of Congress' creation. Indeed, the cases before us, which center upon appellant Northern's claim for damages for breach of contract and misrepresentation, involve a right created by state law, a right independent of and antecedent to the reorganization petition that conferred jurisdiction upon the Bankruptcy Court. Accordingly, Congress' authority to control the manner in which that right is adjudicated, through assignment of historically judicial functions to a non-Art. III "adjunct," plainly must be deemed at a minimum. Yet it is equally plain that Congress has vested the "adjunct" bankruptcy judges with powers over Northern's state-created right that far exceed the powers that it has vested in administrative agencies that adjudicate only rights of Congress' own creation.

Unlike the administrative scheme that we reviewed in *Crowell,* the Act vests all "essential attributes" of the judicial power of the United States in the "adjunct" bankruptcy court. First, the agency in *Crowell* made only specialized, narrowly confined factual determinations regarding a particularized area of law. In contrast, the subject-matter jurisdiction of the bankruptcy courts encompasses not only traditional matters of bankruptcy, but also "all civil proceedings arising under title 11 or arising in or related to cases under title 11." Second, while the agency in *Crowell* engaged in statutorily channeled factfinding functions, the bankruptcy courts exercise "all of the jurisdiction" conferred by the Act on the district courts. Third, the agency in *Crowell* possessed only a limited power to issue compensation orders pursuant to specialized procedures, and its orders could be enforced only by order of the district court. By contrast, the bankruptcy courts exercise all ordinary powers of district courts, including the power to preside over jury trials, the power to issue declaratory judgments, the power to issue writs of habeas corpus, and the power to issue any order, process, or judgment appropriate for the enforcement of the provisions of Title 11. Fourth, while orders issued by the agency in *Crowell* were to be set aside if "not supported by the evidence," the judgments of the bankruptcy courts are apparently subject to review only under the more deferential "clearly erroneous" standard. Finally, the agency in *Crowell* was required by law to seek enforcement of its compensation orders in the district court. In contrast, the bankruptcy courts issue final judgments, which are binding and enforceable even in the absence of an appeal. In short, the "adjunct" bankruptcy courts created by the Act exercise jurisdiction behind the facade of a grant to the district courts, and are exercising powers far greater than those lodged in the adjuncts approved in either *Crowell* or *Raddatz*.

We conclude that § 241(a) of the Bankruptcy Act of 1978 has impermissibly removed most, if not all, of "the essential attributes of the judicial power" from the Art. III district court, and has vested those attributes in a non-Art. III adjunct. Such a grant of jurisdiction cannot be sustained as an exercise of Congress' power to create adjuncts to Art. III courts.

V

Having concluded that the broad grant of jurisdiction to the bankruptcy courts * * * is unconstitutional, we must now determine whether our holding should be applied retroactively to the effective date of the Act. Our decision in *Chevron Oil Co. v. Huson* sets forth the three considerations recognized by our precedents as properly bearing upon the issue of retroactivity. They are, first, whether the holding in question "decid[ed] an issue of first impression whose resolution was not clearly foreshadowed" by earlier cases; second, "whether retrospective operation will further or retard [the] operation" of the holding in question; and third, whether retroactive application "could produce substantial inequitable results" in individual cases. In the present cases, all of these considerations militate against the retroactive application of our holding today. It is plain that Congress' broad grant of judicial power to non-Art. III bankruptcy judges presents an unprecedented question of interpretation of Art. III. It is equally plain that retroactive application would not further the operation of our holding, and would surely visit substantial injustice and hardship upon those litigants who relied upon the Act's vesting of jurisdiction in the bankruptcy courts. We hold, therefore, that our decision today shall apply only prospectively.

The judgment of the District Court is affirmed. However, we stay our judgment until October 4, 1982. This limited stay will afford Congress an opportunity to reconstitute the bankruptcy courts or to adopt other valid means of adjudication, without impairing the interim administration of the bankruptcy laws.

* * *

JUSTICE REHNQUIST, with whom JUSTICE O'CONNOR joins, concurring in the judgment.

Were I to agree with the plurality that the question presented by these cases is "whether the assignment by Congress to bankruptcy judges of the jurisdiction granted by § 241(a) of the Bankruptcy Act of 1978 violates Art. III of the Constitution," I would with considerable reluctance embark on the duty of deciding this broad question. But appellee Marathon Pipe Line Co. has not been subjected to the full range of authority granted bankruptcy courts by § 241(a). It was named as a defendant in a suit brought by appellant Northern Pipeline Construction Co. in a United States Bankruptcy Court. The suit sought damages for, inter alia, breaches of contract and warranty. Marathon moved to dismiss the action on the grounds that the Bankruptcy Act of 1978, which authorized the suit, violated Art. III of the Constitution insofar as it established bankruptcy judges whose tenure and salary protection do not conform to the requirements of Art. III.

With the cases in this posture, Marathon has simply been named defendant in a lawsuit about a contract, a lawsuit initiated by appellant Northern after having previously filed a petition for reorganization under the Bankruptcy Act. Marathon may object to proceeding further with this lawsuit on the grounds that if it is to be resolved by an agency of the United States, it may be resolved only by an agency which exercises "[t]he judicial power of the United States" described by Art. III of the Constitution. But resolution of any objections it may make on this ground to the exercise of a different authority conferred on bankruptcy courts by the 1978 Act should await the exercise of such authority.

> This Court, as is the case with all federal courts, "has no jurisdiction to pronounce any statute, either of a State or of the United States, void, because irreconcilable with the Constitution, except as it is called upon to adjudge the legal rights of litigants in actual controversies. In the exercise of that jurisdiction, it is bound by two rules, to which it has rigidly adhered, one, never to anticipate a question of constitutional law in advance of the necessity of deciding it; the other never to formulate a rule of constitutional law broader than is required by the precise facts to which it is to be applied."

Particularly in an area of constitutional law such as that of "Art. III Courts," with its frequently arcane distinctions and confusing precedents, rigorous adherence to the principle that this Court should decide no more of a constitutional question than is absolutely necessary accords with both our decided cases and with sound judicial policy.

From the record before us, the lawsuit in which Marathon was named defendant seeks damages for breach of contract, misrepresentation, and other counts which are the stuff of the traditional actions at common law tried by the courts at Westminster in 1789. There is apparently no federal rule of decision provided for any of the issues in the lawsuit; the claims of Northern arise entirely under state law. No method of adjudication is hinted, other than the traditional common-law mode of judge and jury. The lawsuit is before the Bankruptcy Court only because the plaintiff has previously filed a petition for reorganization in that court.

* * * I need not decide whether these cases in fact support a general proposition and three tidy exceptions, as the plurality believes, or whether instead they are but landmarks on a judicial "darkling plain" where ignorant armies have clashed by night, as Justice White apparently believes them to be. None of the cases has gone so far as to sanction the type of adjudication to which Marathon will be subjected against its will under the provisions of the 1978 Act. To whatever extent different powers granted under that Act might be sustained under the "public rights" doctrine of *Murray's Lessee* and succeeding cases, I am satisfied that the adjudication of Northern's lawsuit cannot be so sustained.

I am likewise of the opinion that the extent of review by Art. III courts provided on appeal from a decision of the bankruptcy court in a case such as Northern's does not save the grant of authority to the latter under the rule espoused in *Crowell v. Benson*. All matters of fact and law in whatever domains of the law to which the parties' dispute may lead are to be resolved by the bankruptcy court in the first instance, with only traditional appellate review by Art. III courts apparently contemplated. Acting in this manner the bankruptcy court is not an "adjunct" of either the district court or the court of appeals.

I would, therefore, hold so much of the Bankruptcy Act of 1978 as enables a Bankruptcy Court to entertain and decide Northern's lawsuit over Marathon's objection to be violative of Art. III of the United States Constitution. Because I agree with the plurality that this grant of authority is not readily severable from the remaining grant of authority to bankruptcy courts under § 241(a), I concur in the judgment. I also agree with the discussion in Part V of the plurality opinion respecting retroactivity and the staying of the judgment of this Court.

CHIEF JUSTICE BURGER, dissenting.

I join Justice White's dissenting opinion, but I write separately to emphasize that, notwithstanding the plurality opinion, the Court does not hold today that Congress' broad grant of jurisdiction to the new bankruptcy courts is generally inconsistent with Art. III of the Constitution. Rather, the Court's holding is limited to the proposition stated by Justice Rehnquist in his concurrence in the judgment—that a "traditional" state common-law action, not made subject to a federal rule of decision, and related only peripherally to an adjudication of bankruptcy under federal law, must, absent the consent of the litigants, be heard by an "Art. III court" if it is to be heard by any court or agency of the United States. This limited holding, of course, does not suggest that there is something inherently unconstitutional about the new bankruptcy courts; nor does it preclude such courts from adjudicating all but a relatively narrow category of claims "arising under" or "arising in or related to cases under" the Bankruptcy Act.

It will not be necessary for Congress, in order to meet the requirements of the Court's holding, to undertake a radical restructuring of the present system of bankruptcy adjudication. The problems arising from today's judgment can be resolved simply by providing that ancillary common-law actions, such as the one involved in these cases, be routed to the United States district court of which the bankruptcy court is an adjunct.

JUSTICE WHITE, with whom THE CHIEF JUSTICE and JUSTICE POWELL join, dissenting.

Article III, § 1, of the Constitution is straightforward and uncomplicated on its face:

> The judicial Power of the United States, shall be vested in one supreme Court, and in such inferior Courts as the Congress may from time to time ordain and establish. The Judges, both of the supreme and inferior Courts, shall hold their Offices during good Behaviour, and shall at stated Times, receive for their Services, a Compensation, which shall not be diminished during their Continuance in Office.

Any reader could easily take this provision to mean that although Congress was free to establish such lower courts as it saw fit, any court that it did establish would be an "inferior" court exercising "judicial Power of the United States" and so must be manned by judges possessing both life tenure and a guaranteed minimal income. This would be an eminently sensible reading and one that, as the plurality shows, is well founded in both the documentary sources and the political doctrine of separation of powers that stands behind much of our constitutional structure.

If this simple reading were correct and we were free to disregard 150 years of history, these would be easy cases and the plurality opinion could end with its observation that "[i]t is undisputed that the bankruptcy judges whose offices were created by the Bankruptcy Act of 1978 do not enjoy the protections constitutionally afforded to Art. III judges." The fact that the plurality must go on to deal with what has been characterized as one of the most confusing and controversial areas of constitutional law itself indicates the gross oversimplification implicit in the plurality's claim that "our Constitution unambiguously enunciates a fundamental principle—that the 'judicial Power of the United States' must be reposed in an independent Judiciary [and] provides clear institutional protections for that independence." While this is fine rhetoric, analytically it serves only to put a distracting and superficial gloss on a difficult question.

That question is what limits Art. III places on Congress' ability to create adjudicative institutions designed to carry out federal policy established pursuant to the substantive authority given Congress elsewhere in the Constitution. Whether fortunate or unfortunate, at this point in the history of constitutional law that question can no longer be answered by looking only to the constitutional text. This Court's cases construing that text must also be considered. In its attempt to pigeonhole these cases, the plurality does violence to their meaning and creates an artificial structure that itself lacks coherence.

I

There are, I believe, two separate grounds for today's decision. First, non-Art. III judges, regardless of whether they are labeled "adjuncts" to Art. III courts or "Art. I judges," may consider only controversies arising out of federal law. Because the immediate controversy in these cases—Northern Pipeline's claim against Marathon—arises out of state law, it may only be adjudicated, within the federal system, by an Art. III court. Second, regardless of the source of law that governs the controversy, Congress is prohibited by Art. III from establishing Art. I courts, with three narrow exceptions. Adjudication of bankruptcy proceedings does not fall within any of these exceptions. I shall deal with the first of these contentions in this section.

The plurality concedes that Congress may provide for initial adjudications by Art. I courts or administrative judges of all rights and duties arising under otherwise valid federal laws. There is no apparent reason why this principle should not extend to matters arising in federal bankruptcy proceedings. The plurality attempts to escape the reach of prior decisions by contending that the bankrupt's claim against Marathon arose under state law. Non-Article III judges, in its view, cannot be vested with authority to adjudicate such issues. It then proceeds to strike down § 241(a) on this ground. For several reasons, the Court's judgment is unsupportable.

* * *

[T]he distinction between claims based on state law and those based on federal law disregards the real character of bankruptcy proceedings. The routine in ordinary bankruptcy cases now, as it was before 1978, is to stay actions against the bankrupt, collect the bankrupt's assets, require creditors to file claims or be forever barred, allow or disallow claims that are filed, adjudicate preferences and fraudulent transfers, and make pro rata distributions to creditors, who will be barred by the discharge from taking further actions against the bankrupt. The crucial point to be made is that in the ordinary bankruptcy proceeding the great bulk of creditor claims are claims that have accrued under state law prior to bankruptcy—claims for goods sold, wages, rent, utilities, and the like. "[T]he word debt as used by the Act is not confined to its technical common law meaning but * * * extends to liabilities arising out of breach of contract * * * to torts * * * and to taxes owing to the United States or state or local governments." Every such claim must be filed and its validity is subject to adjudication by the bankruptcy court. The existence and validity of such claims recurringly depend on state law. Hence, the bankruptcy judge is constantly enmeshed in state-law issues.

The new aspect of the Bankruptcy Act of 1978, in this regard, therefore, is not the extension of federal jurisdiction to state law claims, but its extension to particular kinds of state-law claims, such as contract cases against third parties or disputes involving property in the possession of a third person. Prior to 1978, a claim of a bankrupt against a third party, such as the claim against Marathon in this case, was not within the jurisdiction of the bankruptcy judge. The old limits were based, of course, on the restrictions implicit within the concept of *in rem* jurisdiction; the new extension is based on the concept of *in personam* jurisdiction. "The bankruptcy court is given *in personam* jurisdiction as well as *in rem* jurisdiction to handle everything that arises in a bankruptcy case." The difference between the new and old Acts, therefore, is not to be found in a distinction between state-law and federal-law matters; rather, it is in a distinction between *in rem* and *in personam* jurisdiction. The majority at no place explains why this distinction should have constitutional implications.

* * * [A]ll that can be left of the majority's argument in this regard is that state-law claims adjudicated within the federal system must be heard in the first instance by Art. III judges. I shall argue below that any such attempt to distinguish Art. I from Art. III courts by the character of the controversies they may adjudicate fundamentally misunderstands the historical and constitutional significance of Art. I courts. Initially, however, the majority's proposal seems to turn the separation-of-powers doctrine, upon which the majority relies, on its head: Since state-law claims would ordinarily not be heard by Art. III judges—*i.e.*, they would be heard by state judges—one would think that there is little danger of a diminution of, or intrusion upon, the power of Art. III courts, when such claims are assigned to a non-Art. III court. The plurality misses this obvious point because it concentrates on explaining how it is that federally created rights can ever be adjudicated in Art. I courts—a far more difficult problem under the separation-of-powers doctrine. The plurality fumbles when it assumes that the rationale it develops to deal with the latter problem must also govern the former problem. In fact, the two are simply unrelated and the majority never really explains the separation-of-powers problem that would be created by assigning state law questions to legislative courts or to adjuncts of Art. III courts.

One need not contemplate the intricacies of the separation-of-powers doctrine, however, to realize that the majority's position on adjudication of state-law claims is based on an abstract theory that has little to do with the reality of bankruptcy proceedings. Even prior to the present Act, bankruptcy cases were generally referred to bankruptcy judges, previously called referees. Title 11 U.S.C. § 66 described the jurisdiction of the referees. Their powers included the authority to "consider all petitions referred to them and make the adjudications or dismiss the petitions * * * grant, deny or revoke discharges, determine the dischargeability of debts, and render judgments thereon [and] perform such of the duties as are by this title conferred on courts of bankruptcy, including those incidental to ancillary jurisdiction, and as shall be prescribed by rules or orders of the courts of bankruptcy of their respective districts, except as herein otherwise provided." The bankruptcy judge possessed "complete jurisdiction of the proceedings." The referee would initially hear and decide practically all matters arising in the proceedings, including the allowance and disallowance of the claims of creditors. If a claim was disallowed by the bankruptcy judge and the decision was not reversed on appeal, the creditor was forever barred from further action against the bankrupt. As pointed out above, all of these matters could and usually did involve state-law issues. Initial adjudication of state-law issues by non-Art. III judges is, then, hardly a new aspect of the 1978 Act.

Furthermore, I take it that the Court does not condemn as inconsistent with Art. III the assignment of these functions—*i.e.,* those within the summary jurisdiction of the old bankruptcy courts—to a non-Art. III judge, since, as the plurality says, they lie at the core of the federal bankruptcy power. They also happen to be functions that have been performed by referees or bankruptcy judges for a very long time and without constitutional objection. Indeed, we approved the authority of the referee to allow or disallow claims in *Katchen v. Landy* (1966). There, the referee held that a creditor had received a preference and that his claim could therefore not be allowed. We agreed that the referee had the authority not only to adjudicate the existence of the preference, but also to order that the preference be disgorged. We also recognized that the referee could adjudicate counterclaims against a creditor who files his claim against the estate. The 1973 Bankruptcy Rules make similar provision. Hence, if Marathon had filed a claim against the bankrupt in this case, the trustee could have filed and the bankruptcy judge could have adjudicated a counterclaim seeking the relief that is involved in these cases.

Of course, all such adjudications by a bankruptcy judge or referee were subject to review in the district court, on the record. Bankruptcy Rule 810, transmitted to Congress by this Court, provided that the district court "shall accept the referee's findings of fact unless they are clearly-erroneous." As the plurality recognizes, the 1978 Act provides for appellate review in Art. III courts and presumably under the same "clearly erroneous standard." In other words, under both the old and new Acts, initial determinations of state-law questions were to be made by non-Art. III judges, subject to review by Art. III judges. Why the differences in the provisions for appeal in the two Acts are of unconstitutional dimension remains entirely unclear.

In theory and fact, therefore, I can find no basis for that part of the majority's argument that rests on the state-law character of the claim involved here. Even if, prior to 1978, the referee could not generally participate in cases aimed at collecting the assets of a bankrupt estate, he nevertheless repeatedly adjudicated issues controlled by state law. There is very little reason to strike down § 1471 on its face on the ground that it extends, in a comparatively minimal way, the referees' authority to deal with state-law questions. To do so is to lose all sense of proportion.

II

The plurality unpersuasively attempts to bolster its case for facial invalidity by asserting that the bankruptcy courts are now "exercising powers far greater than those lodged in the adjuncts approved in either *Crowell* or *Raddatz*." In support of this proposition it makes five arguments in addition to the "state-law" issue. Preliminarily, I see no basis for according standing to Marathon to raise any of these additional points. The state-law objection applies to the Marathon case. Only that objection should now be adjudicated.

I also believe that the major premise of the plurality's argument is wholly unsupported: There is no explanation of why *Crowell v. Benson* and *United States v. Raddatz* define the outer limits of constitutional authority. Much more relevant to today's decision are, first, the practice in bankruptcy prior to 1978, which neither the majority nor any authoritative case has questioned, and, second, the practice of today's administrative agencies. Considered from this perspective, all of the plurality's arguments are unsupportable abstractions, divorced from the realities of modern practice.

The first three arguments offered by the plurality focus on the narrowly defined task and authority of the agency considered in *Crowell:* The agency made only "specialized, narrowly confined factual determinations" and could issue only a narrow class of orders. Regardless of whether this was true of the Compensation Board at issue in *Crowell,* it certainly was not true of the old bankruptcy courts, nor does it even vaguely resemble current administrative practice. As I have already said, general references to bankruptcy judges, which was the usual practice prior to 1978, permitted bankruptcy judges to perform almost all of the functions of a bankruptcy court. Referees or bankruptcy judges not only exercised summary jurisdiction but could also conduct adversary proceedings to:

> (1) recover money or property * * * . (2) determine the validity, priority, or extent of a lien or other interest in property, (3) sell prop-

erty free of a lien or other interest for which the holder can be compelled to make a money satisfaction, (4) object to or revoke a discharge, (5) obtain an injunction, (6) obtain relief from a stay * * * (7) determine the dischargeability of a debt.

Although there were some exceptions to the referees' authority, which have been removed by the 1978 Act, the additions to the jurisdiction of the bankruptcy judges were of marginal significance when examined in the light of the overall functions of those judges before and after 1978. In my view, those changes are not sufficient to work a qualitative change in the character of the bankruptcy judge.

The plurality's fourth argument fails to point to any difference between the new and old Bankruptcy Acts. While the administrative orders in *Crowell* may have been set aside by a court if "not supported by the evidence," under both the new and old Acts at issue here, orders of the bankruptcy judge are reviewed under the "clearly-erroneous standard." Indeed, judicial review of the orders of bankruptcy judges is more stringent than that of many modern administrative agencies. Generally courts are not free to set aside the findings of administrative agencies, if supported by substantial evidence. But more importantly, courts are also admonished to give substantial deference to the agency's interpretation of the statute it is enforcing. No such deference is required with respect to decisions on the law made by bankruptcy judges.

Finally, the plurality suggests that, unlike the agency considered in *Crowell,* the orders of a post-1978 bankruptcy judge are final and binding even though not appealed. To attribute any constitutional significance to this, unless the plurality intends to throw into question a large body of administrative law, is strange. More directly, this simply does not represent any change in bankruptcy practice. It was hornbook law prior to 1978 that the authorized judgments and orders of referees, including turnover orders, were final and binding and res judicata unless appealed and overturned:

> The practice before the referee should not differ from that before the judge of the court of bankruptcy and, apart from direct review within the limitation of § 39(c), the orders of the referee are entitled to the same presumption of validity, conclusiveness and recognition in the court of bankruptcy or other courts.

Even if there are specific powers now vested in bankruptcy judges that should be performed by Art. III judges, the great bulk of their functions are unexceptionable and should be left intact. Whatever is invalid should be declared to be such; the rest of the 1978 Act should be left alone. I can account for the majority's inexplicably heavy hand in this case only by assuming that the Court has once again lost its conceptual bearings when confronted with the difficult problem of the nature and role of Art. I courts. To that question I now turn.

III

A

The plurality contends that the precedents upholding Art. I courts can be reduced to three categories. First, there are territorial courts, which need not satisfy Art. III constraints because "the Framers intended that as to certain geographical areas * * * Congress was to exercise the general powers of government." Second, there are courts martial, which are exempt from Art. III limits because of a constitutional grant of power that has been "historically understood as giving the political Branches of Government extraordinary control over the precise subject matter at issue." Finally, there are those legislative courts and administrative agencies that adjudicate cases involving public rights— controversies between the Government and private parties—which are not covered by Art. III because the controversy could have been resolved by the executive alone without judicial review. Despite the plurality's attempt to cabin the domain of Art. I courts, it is quite unrealistic to consider these to be only three "narrow," limitations on or exceptions to the reach of Art. III. In fact, the plurality itself breaks the mold in its discussion of "adjuncts" in Part IV, when it announces that "when Congress creates a substantive federal right, it possesses substantial discretion to prescribe the manner in which that right may be adjudicated." Adjudications of federal rights may, according to the plurality, be committed to administrative agencies, as long as provision is made for judicial review.

The first principle introduced by the plurality is geographical: Art. I courts presumably are not permitted within the States. The problem, of course, is that both of the other exceptions recognize that Art. I courts can indeed operate within the States. The second category relies upon a new principle: Art. I courts are permissible in areas in which the Constitution grants Congress "extraordinary control over the precise subject matter." Preliminarily, I do not know how we are to distinguish those areas in which Congress' control is "extraordinary" from those in which it is not. Congress' power over the Armed Forces is established in Art. I, § 8, cls. 13, 14. There is nothing in those Clauses that creates congressional authority different in kind from the authority granted to legislate with respect to bankruptcy. But more importantly, in its third category, and in its treatment of "adjuncts," the plurality itself recognizes that Congress can create Art. I courts in virtually all the areas in which Congress is authorized to act, regardless of the quality of the constitutional grant of authority. At the same time, territorial courts or the courts of the District of Columbia, which are Art. I courts, adjudicate private, just as much as public or federal, rights.

Instead of telling us what it is Art. I courts can and cannot do, the plurality presents us with a list of Art. I courts. When we try to distinguish those courts from their Art. III counterparts, we find—apart from the obvious lack of Art. III judges—a series of nondistinctions. By the plurality's own admission, Art. I courts can operate throughout the country, they can adjudicate both private and public rights, and they can adjudicate matters arising from congressional actions in those areas in which congressional control is "extraordinary." I cannot distinguish this last category from the general "arising under" jurisdiction of Art. III courts.

The plurality opinion has the appearance of limiting Art. I courts only because it fails to add together the sum of its parts. Rather than limiting each other, the principles relied upon complement each other; together they cover virtually the whole domain of possible areas of adjudication. Without a unifying principle, the plurality's argument reduces to the proposition that because bankruptcy courts are not sufficiently like any of these three exceptions, they may not be either Art. I courts or adjuncts to Art. III courts. But we need to know why bankruptcy courts cannot qualify as Art. I courts in their own right.

* * *

IV

The complicated and contradictory history of the issue before us leads me to conclude that Chief Justice Vinson and Justice Harlan reached the correct conclusion: There is no difference in principle between the work that Congress may assign to an Art. I court and that which the Constitution assigns to Art. III courts. Unless we want to overrule a large number of our precedents upholding a variety of Art. I courts—not to speak of those Art. I courts that go by the contemporary name of "administrative agencies"—this conclusion is inevitable. It is too late to go back that far; too late to return to the simplicity of the principle pronounced in Art. III and defended so vigorously and persuasively by Hamilton in The Federalist Nos. 78-82.

To say that the Court has failed to articulate a principle by which we can test the constitutionality of a putative Art. I court, or that there is no such abstract principle, is not to say that this Court must always defer to the legislative decision to create Art. I, rather than Art. III, courts. Article III is not to be read out of the Constitution; rather, it should be read as expressing one value that must be balanced against competing constitutional values and legislative responsibilities. This Court retains the final word on how that balance is to be struck.

Despite the principled, although largely mistaken, rhetoric expanded by the Court in this area over the years, such a balancing approach stands behind many of the decisions holding Art. I courts.

* * *

I do not suggest that the Court should simply look to the strength of the legislative interest and ask itself if that interest is more compelling than the values furthered by Art. III. The inquiry should, rather, focus equally on those Art. III values and ask whether and to what extent the legislative scheme accommodates them or, conversely, substantially undermines them. The burden on Art. III values should then be measured against the values Congress hopes to serve through the use of Art. I courts.

To be more concrete: *Crowell* suggests that the presence of appellate review by an Art. III court will go a long way toward insuring a proper separation of powers. Appellate review of the decisions of legislative courts, like appellate review of state-court decisions, provides a firm check on the ability of the political institutions of government to ignore or transgress constitutional limits on their own authority. Obviously, therefore, a scheme of Art. I courts that provides for appellate review by Art. III courts should be substantially less controversial than a legislative attempt entirely to avoid judicial review in a constitutional court.

Similarly, as long as the proposed Art. I courts are designed to deal with issues likely to be of little interest to the political branches, there is less reason to fear that such courts represent a dangerous accumulation of power in one of the political branches of government. Chief Justice Vinson suggested as much when he stated that the Court should guard against any congressional attempt "to transfer jurisdiction * * * for the purpose of emasculating" constitutional courts.

V

I believe that the new bankruptcy courts established by the Bankruptcy Act of 1978 satisfy this standard.

First, ample provision is made for appellate review by Art. III courts. Appeals may in some circumstances be brought directly to the district courts. Decisions of the district courts are further appealable to the court of appeals. In other circumstances, appeals go first to a panel of bankruptcy judges and then to the court of appeals. In still other circumstances—when the parties agree—appeals may go directly to the court of appeals. In sum, there is in every instance a right of appeal to at least one Art. III court. Had Congress decided to assign all bankruptcy matters to the state courts, a power it clearly possesses, no greater review in an Art. III court would exist. Although I do not suggest that this analogy means that Congress may establish an Art. I court wherever it could have chosen to rely upon the state courts, it does suggest that the critical function of judicial review is being met in a manner that the Constitution suggests is sufficient.

Second, no one seriously argues that the Bankruptcy Act of 1978 represents an attempt by the political branches of government to aggrandize themselves at the expense of the third branch or an attempt to undermine the authority of constitutional courts in general. Indeed, the congressional perception of a lack of judicial interest in bankruptcy matters was one of the factors that led to the establishment of the bankruptcy courts: Congress feared that this lack of interest would lead to a failure by federal district courts to deal with bankruptcy matters in an expeditious manner. Bankruptcy matters are, for the most part, private adjudications of little political significance. Although some bankruptcies may indeed present politically controversial circumstances or issues, Congress has far more direct ways to involve itself in such matters than through some sort of subtle, or not so subtle, influence on bankruptcy judges. Furthermore, were such circumstances to arise, the Due Process Clause might very well require that the matter be considered by an Art. III judge: Bankruptcy proceedings remain, after all, subject to all of the strictures of that constitutional provision.

Finally, I have no doubt that the ends that Congress sought to accomplish by creating a system of non-Art. III bankruptcy courts were at least as compelling as * * * the ends that have traditionally justified the creation of legislative courts. The stresses placed upon the old bankruptcy system by the tremendous increase in bankruptcy cases were well documented and were clearly a matter to which Congress could respond. I do not believe it is possible to challenge Congress' further determination that it was necessary to create a specialized court to deal with bankruptcy matters. This was the nearly uniform conclusion of all those that testified before Congress on the question of reform of the bankruptcy system, as well as the conclusion of the Commission on Bankruptcy Laws established by Congress in 1970 to explore possible improvements in the system.

The real question is not whether Congress was justified in establishing a specialized bankruptcy court, but rather whether it was justified in failing to create a specialized, Art. III bankruptcy court. My own view is that the very fact of extreme specialization may be enough, and certainly has been enough in the past, to justify the creation of a legislative court. Congress may legitimately consider the effect on the federal judiciary of the addition of several hundred specialized judges: We are, on the whole, a body of generalists. The addition of several hundred specialists may substantially change, whether for good or bad, the character of the federal bench. Moreover, Congress may have desired to maintain some flexibility in its possible future responses to the general problem of bankruptcy. There is no question that the existence of several hundred bankruptcy judges with life tenure would have severely limited Congress' future options. Furthermore, the number of bankruptcies may fluctuate, producing a substantially reduced need for bankruptcy judges. Congress may have thought that, in that event, a bankruptcy specialist should not as a general matter serve as a judge in the countless nonspecialized cases that come before the federal district courts. It would then face the prospect of large numbers of idle federal judges. Finally, Congress may have believed that the change from bankruptcy referees to Art. I judges was far less dramatic, and so less disruptive of the existing bankruptcy and constitutional court systems, than would be a change to Art. III judges.

For all of these reasons, I would defer to the congressional judgment. Accordingly, I dissent.

Notes and Questions

1. Is Congressional power over the territories, the military, and public rights disputes more extraordinary than congressional power over bankruptcy? If not, is there any other explanation for the plurality opinion?

2. When is a legislative court an adjunct to an Article III court? Are there any Article III cases that Congress cannot assign to an adjunct? Could Congress assign all Article III cases to adjuncts?

3. Given that Congress could have left the state-law claims in *Northern Pipeline* to be resolved in state courts, is the independence of Article III courts threatened when Congress instead assigns those claims to Article I courts? Since Congress could abolish diversity jurisdiction, could it assign all diversity cases to Article I courts?

4. Most creditors' claims in bankruptcy proceedings are state law claims. With respect to Congress's power to assign them to legislative courts, are they distinguishable from the state law claims asserted by the bankrupt against Marathon?

5. Justice White's dissent suggests that the Court should balance Article III values against "competing constitutional values and legislative responsibilities" in these cases. Does the text of Article III authorize the Court to conduct such balancing? If not, what is the source of the Court's authority to do so? Is he suggesting that non-constitutional values be balanced against constitutional ones?

6. Though the Supreme Court issued *Northern Pipeline* on June 28, 1982, it stayed the judgment until October 4th of that year to give Congress the opportunity to fix the bankruptcy system the Court found unconstitutional. Subsequently, in light of congressional inaction and upon the Solicitor General's motion, the Court extended the stay to December 24, 1982. The Solicitor General sought another stay, but the Court denied it.

Consequently, the Judicial Conference of the United States published an Emergency Interim Rule, which the federal district courts adopted as a local rule on Christmas Day of 1982. Pursuant to the Rule, the district courts referred bankruptcy proceedings to the bankruptcy courts but retained the power to withdraw them at any time. Generally, the Interim Rule authorized bankruptcy judges to issue enforceable orders and judgments. However, the Rule defined "related proceedings" as those that could have proceeded in a federal or state court in the absence of a bankruptcy petition, and in such proceedings the bankruptcy judge could not enter a judgment or dispositive order. Instead, the bankruptcy judge had to submit findings, conclusions and a proposed judgment or order to the district court, unless the parties consented to entry of the judgment or order by a bankruptcy judge. Proposed orders and judgments were subject to *de novo* review, regardless of whether a notice of appeal had been filed. The Interim Rule subjected final bankruptcy court orders and judgments to *de novo* district court review as well, but only if a timely notice of appeal of the bankruptcy court's decision had been filed. Additionally, the Interim Rule specifically provided that bankruptcy courts had only limited authority to punish criminal contempt and could not conduct jury trials, hear appeals from the decisions of other bankruptcy courts, or enjoin the proceedings of a court. Did the bankruptcy system the Emergency Interim Rule established solve the constitutional problems the Court identified in *Northern Pipeline*? Why or why not?

7. Congress finally responded to *Northern Pipeline*. The Bankruptcy Amendments and Federal Judgeship Act of 1984, Pub.L. No. 98-353, 98 Stat. 333 (1984), establishes a scheme similar to that of the Emergency Interim Rule. The amendments authorize the federal district courts to refer "any or all cases under title 11 and any or all proceedings arising under title 11 or arising in or related to a case under title 11" to bankruptcy judges. However, bankruptcy proceedings are then divided into "core" and "non-core" proceedings, and bankruptcy judges' power to issue final orders or judgments depends upon the classification. In the case of non-core proceedings, the bankruptcy judge must submit proposed findings of fact and conclusions of law to the district court, unless the parties consent to the judge's entry of judgment. The district court then issues final judgments or orders "after considering the bankruptcy judge's proposed findings and conclusions and after reviewing *de novo* those matters to which any party has timely and specifically objected." The statute provides generally for discretionary withdrawal of proceedings from the bankruptcy courts by the district courts and mandates withdrawal in some circumstances. Note that both the Interim Rule and the 1984 Act authorize bankruptcy judges to enter final judgments with the consent of the parties in circumstances in which they could not without the consent. The courts often declare that parties' consent cannot confer subject matter jurisdiction on the federal courts. Are not the limitations Article III imposes on non-Article III tribunals tantamount to limitations on their subject matter jurisdiction? If so, how can the parties' consent determine whether the bankruptcy court has exceeded those limitations?

8. A few years after *Northern Pipeline,* the Court decided *Thomas v. Union Carbide Agricultural Products Co.,* 473 U.S. 568, 105 S.Ct. 3325, 87 L.Ed.2d 409 (1985). The Federal Insecticide, Fungicide, and Rodenticide Act, 7 U.S.C.A. § 136 *et seq.* (FIFRA), requires manufacturers to provide research data to the Environmental Protection Agency (EPA) concerning the health, safety, and environmental effects of products to be registered as pesticides. If an applicant seeks a new registration, permit, or use, FIFRA authorizes the EPA to consider other manufacturers' data, provided the applicant offers compensation to the original data supplier. Prior to 1978, if the parties were unable to agree on compensation, the EPA decided, subject to judicial review. Congress concluded that the EPA lacked the expertise necessary to determine proper compensation and that the burden of doing so impeded the registration process. Consequently, in 1978 Congress amended FIFRA to provide binding arbitration if the parties failed to agree. The arbitrator's decision is subject to judicial review only for fraud, misrepresentation, or other misconduct. Several large chemical companies challenged the

constitutionality of the amendment. They claimed that the imposition of binding arbitration violated Article III because the arbitrators functioned as judicial officers without Article III protections and judicial review was so limited. The eight Justices who addressed the issue rejected the challenge.

The majority pointed out that *Northern Pipeline* did not limit the public rights doctrine to disputes between the federal government and private interests. If it had, the constitutionality of many administrative quasi-judicial activities with respect to wholly private disputes would be open to doubt. *Thomas* found that the doctrine reflects a pragmatic understanding that when Congress adopts a quasi-adjudicative method for resolving controversies that could otherwise be conclusively determined by the political branches, the danger of encroachment on the judicial power is reduced.

Specifically, the Court asserted that the federal right to compensation strongly resembled a public right, even if the United States was not a party. The unrestricted use of data was essential to safeguard public health and therefore served a public purpose. Congress could have authorized the EPA to impose fees on applicants using others' data and subsidized data suppliers. The Court thought that relying instead on arbitrators did not diminish the likelihood of decision-making free from political influence.

Moreover, the Court found that the "near disaster" of the previous scheme and concerns about the danger to public health caused by delays in the registration process had prompted Congress to adopt the arbitration system. It summarized its views thusly:

Congress, acting for a valid legislative purpose pursuant to its powers under Article I, may create a seemingly "private" right that is so closely integrated into a public regulatory scheme as to be a matter appropriate for agency resolution with limited involvement by the Article III judiciary. To hold otherwise would be to erect a rigid and formalistic restraint on the ability of Congress to adopt innovative measures such as negotiation and arbitration with respect to rights created by a regulatory scheme.

Justice Brennan, the author of the plurality opinion in *Northern Pipeline*, concurred on behalf of three members of that group. He agreed with the majority that whether the government was a party did not determine whether a case fell within the public rights doctrine. Because the case involved a federal regulatory scheme that virtually occupied the field and included the active participation of a federal agency in resolving the dispute, he concluded that it was a public rights case.

After *Thomas*, when is a case within the public rights doctrine?

C.   THE MODERN BALANCING TEST

COMMODITY FUTURES TRADING
COMMISSION v. SCHOR
Supreme Court of the United States, 1986.
478 U.S. 833, 106 S.Ct. 3245, 92 L.Ed.2d 675.

JUSTICE O'CONNOR delivered the opinion of the Court.

The question presented is whether the Commodity Exchange Act
(CEA or Act) empowers the Commodity Futures Trading Commission
(CFTC or Commission) to entertain state law counterclaims in reparation proceedings and, if so, whether that grant of authority violates Article III of the Constitution.

I

The CEA broadly prohibits fraudulent and manipulative conduct in
connection with commodity futures transactions. In 1974, Congress
"overhaul[ed]" the Act in order to institute a more "comprehensive regulatory structure to oversee the volatile and esoteric futures trading complex." Congress also determined that the broad regulatory powers of the
CEA were most appropriately vested in an agency which would be relatively immune from the "political winds that sweep Washington." It
therefore created an independent agency, the CFTC, and entrusted to it
sweeping authority to implement the CEA.

Among the duties assigned to the CFTC was the administration of a
reparations procedure through which disgruntled customers of professional commodity brokers could seek redress for the brokers' violations of
the Act or CFTC regulations. Thus, § 14 of the CEA provides that any
person injured by such violations may apply to the Commission for an
order directing the offender to pay reparations to the complainant and
may enforce that order in federal district court. Congress intended this
administrative procedure to be an "inexpensive and expeditious" alternative to existing fora available to aggrieved customers, namely, the courts
and arbitration.

In conformance with the congressional goal of promoting efficient
dispute resolution, the CFTC promulgated a regulation in 1976 which
allows it to adjudicate counterclaims "aris[ing] out of the transaction or
occurrence or series of transactions or occurrences set forth in the complaint." This permissive counterclaim rule leaves the respondent in a
reparations proceeding free to seek relief against the reparations complainant in other fora.

The instant dispute arose in February 1980, when respondents Schor
and Mortgage Services of America, Inc., invoked the CFTC's reparations
jurisdiction by filing complaints against petitioner Conti Commodity
Services, Inc. (Conti), a commodity futures broker, and Richard L. San-
dor, a Conti employee. Schor had an account with Conti which contained

a debit balance because Schor's net futures trading losses and expenses, such as commissions, exceeded the funds deposited in the account. Schor alleged that this debit balance was the result of Conti's numerous violations of the CEA.

Before receiving notice that Schor had commenced the reparations proceeding, Conti had filed a diversity action in Federal District Court to recover the debit balance. Schor counterclaimed in this action, reiterating his charges that the debit balance was due to Conti's violations of the CEA. Schor also moved on two separate occasions to dismiss or stay the District Court action, arguing that the continuation of the federal action would be a waste of judicial resources and an undue burden on the litigants in view of the fact that "[t]he reparations proceedings * * * will fully * * * resolve and adjudicate all the rights of the parties to this action with respect to the transactions which are the subject matter of this action."

Although the District Court declined to stay or dismiss the suit, Conti voluntarily dismissed the federal court action and presented its debit balance claim by way of a counterclaim in the CFTC reparations proceeding. Conti denied violating the CEA and instead insisted that the debit balance resulted from Schor's trading, and was therefore a simple debt owed by Schor.

After discovery, briefing, and a hearing, the Administrative Law Judge (ALJ) in Schor's reparations proceeding ruled in Conti's favor on both Schor's claims and Conti's counterclaims. After this ruling, Schor for the first time challenged the CFTC's statutory authority to adjudicate Conti's counterclaim. The ALJ rejected Schor's challenge, stating himself "bound by agency regulations and published agency policies." The Commission declined to review the decision and allowed it to become final, at which point Schor filed a petition for review with the Court of Appeals for the District of Columbia Circuit. Prior to oral argument, the Court of Appeals, *sua sponte,* raised the question whether CFTC could constitutionally adjudicate Conti's counterclaims in light of *Northern Pipeline Construction Co. v. Marathon Pipe Line Co.,* in which this Court held that "Congress may not vest in a non-Article III court the power to adjudicate, render final judgment, and issue binding orders in a traditional contract action arising under state law, without consent of the litigants, and subject only to ordinary appellate review." *Thomas v. Union Carbide Agricultural Products Co. (Thomas).*

After briefing and argument, the Court of Appeals upheld the CFTC's decision on Schor's claim in most respects, but ordered the dismissal of Conti's counterclaims on the ground that "the CFTC lacks authority (subject matter competence) to adjudicate" common law counterclaims. In support of this latter ruling, the Court of Appeals reasoned that the CFTC's exercise of jurisdiction over Conti's common law counterclaim gave rise to "[s]erious constitutional problems" under *Northern*

Pipeline. The Court of Appeals therefore concluded that, under well-established principles of statutory construction, the relevant inquiry was whether the CEA was " 'fairly susceptible' of [an alternative] construction," such that Article III objections, and thus unnecessary constitutional adjudication, could be avoided.

After examining the CEA and its legislative history, the court concluded that Congress had no "clearly expressed" or "explicit" intention to give the CFTC constitutionally questionable jurisdiction over state common law counterclaims. The Court of Appeals therefore "adopt[ed] the construction of the Act that avoids significant constitutional questions," reading the CEA to authorize the CFTC to adjudicate only those counterclaims alleging violations of the Act or CFTC regulations. Because Conti's counterclaims did not allege such violations, the Court of Appeals held that the CFTC exceeded its authority in adjudicating those claims, and ordered that the ALJ's decision on the claims be reversed and the claims dismissed for lack of jurisdiction.

* * * This Court granted the CFTC's petition for certiorari, vacated the Court of Appeals' judgment, and remanded the case for further consideration in light of *Thomas.* * * *

On remand, the Court of Appeals reinstated its prior judgment. * * * We again granted certiorari and now reverse.

II

* * *

In view of the abundant evidence that Congress both contemplated and authorized the CFTC's assertion of jurisdiction over Conti's common law counterclaim, we conclude that the Court of Appeals' analysis is untenable. The canon of construction that requires courts to avoid unnecessary constitutional adjudication did not empower the Court of Appeals to manufacture a restriction on the CFTC's jurisdiction that was nowhere contemplated by Congress and to reject plain evidence of congressional intent because that intent was not specifically embodied in a statutory mandate. We therefore are squarely faced with the question whether the CFTC's assumption of jurisdiction over common law counterclaims violates Article III of the Constitution.

III

Article III, § 1, directs that the "judicial Power of the United States shall be vested in one supreme Court and in such inferior Courts as the Congress may from time to time ordain and establish," and provides that these federal courts shall be staffed by judges who hold office during good behavior, and whose compensation shall not be diminished during tenure in office. Schor claims that these provisions prohibit Congress from authorizing the initial adjudication of common law counterclaims by the CFTC, an administrative agency whose adjudicatory officers do not enjoy the tenure and salary protections embodied in Article III.

Although our precedents in this area do not admit of easy synthesis, they do establish that the resolution of claims such as Schor's cannot turn on conclusory reference to the language of Article III. Rather, the constitutionality of a given congressional delegation of adjudicative functions to a non-Article III body must be assessed by reference to the purposes underlying the requirements of Article III. This inquiry, in turn, is guided by the principle that "practical attention to substance rather than doctrinaire reliance on formal categories should inform application of Article III."

A

Article III, § 1, serves both to protect "the role of the independent judiciary within the constitutional scheme of tripartite government," and to safeguard litigants' "right to have claims decided before judges who are free from potential domination by other branches of government." Although our cases have provided us with little occasion to discuss the nature or significance of this latter safeguard, our prior discussions of Article III, § 1's guarantee of an independent and impartial adjudication by the federal judiciary of matters within the judicial power of the United States intimated that this guarantee serves to protect primarily personal, rather than structural, interests.

Our precedents also demonstrate, however, that Article III does not confer on litigants an absolute right to the plenary consideration of every nature of claim by an Article III court. Moreover, as a personal right, Article III's guarantee of an impartial and independent federal adjudication is subject to waiver, just as are other personal constitutional rights that dictate the procedures by which civil and criminal matters must be tried. Indeed, the relevance of concepts of waiver to Article III challenges is demonstrated by our decision in *Northern Pipeline*, in which the absence of consent to an initial adjudication before a non-Article III tribunal was relied on as a significant factor in determining that Article III forbade such adjudication.

In the instant cases, Schor indisputably waived any right he may have possessed to the full trial of Conti's counterclaim before an Article III court. Schor expressly demanded that Conti proceed on its counterclaim in the reparations proceeding rather than before the District Court and was content to have the entire dispute settled in the forum he had selected until the ALJ ruled against him on all counts; it was only after the ALJ rendered a decision to which he objected that Schor raised any challenge to the CFTC's consideration of Conti's counterclaim.

Even were there no evidence of an express waiver here, Schor's election to forgo his right to proceed in state or federal court on his claim and his decision to seek relief instead in a CFTC reparations proceeding constituted an effective waiver. Three years before Schor instituted his reparations action, a private right of action under the CEA was explicitly recognized in the Circuit in which Schor and Conti filed suit in District Court. Moreover, at the time Schor decided to seek relief before the CFTC rather than in the federal courts, the CFTC's regulations made clear that it was empowered to adjudicate all counterclaims "aris[ing] out of the same transaction or occurrence or series of transactions or occurrences set forth in the complaint." Thus, Schor had the option of having the common law counterclaim against him adjudicated in a federal Article III court, but, with full knowledge that the CFTC would exercise jurisdiction over that claim, chose to avail himself of the quicker and less expensive procedure Congress had provided him. In such circumstances, it is clear that Schor effectively agreed to an adjudication by the CFTC of the entire controversy by seeking relief in this alternative forum.

B

As noted above, our precedents establish that Article III, § 1, not only preserves to litigants their interest in an impartial and independent federal adjudication of claims within the judicial power of the United States, but also serves as "an inseparable element of the constitutional system of checks and balances." Article III, § 1 safeguards the role of the Judicial Branch in our tripartite system by barring congressional attempts "to transfer jurisdiction [to non-Article III tribunals] for the purpose of emasculating" constitutional courts and thereby preventing "the encroachment or aggrandizement of one branch at the expense of the other." To the extent that this structural principle is implicated in a given case, the parties cannot by consent cure the constitutional difficulty for the same reason that the parties by consent cannot confer on federal courts subject-matter jurisdiction beyond the limitations imposed by Article III, § 2. When these Article III limitations are at issue, notions of consent and waiver cannot be dispositive because the limitations serve institutional interests that the parties cannot be expected to protect.

In determining the extent to which a given congressional decision to authorize the adjudication of Article III business in a non-Article III tribunal impermissibly threatens the institutional integrity of the Judicial Branch, the Court has declined to adopt formalistic and unbending rules. Although such rules might lend a greater degree of coherence to this area of the law, they might also unduly constrict Congress' ability to take needed and innovative action pursuant to its Article I powers. Thus, in reviewing Article III challenges, we have weighed a number of factors, none of which has been deemed determinative, with an eye to the practical effect that the congressional action will have on the constitutionally assigned role of the federal judiciary. Among the factors upon which we have focused are the extent to which the "essential attributes of judicial power" are reserved to Article III courts, and, conversely, the extent to which the non-Article III forum exercises the range of jurisdiction and powers normally vested only in Article III courts, the origins and importance of the right to be adjudicated, and the concerns that drove Congress to depart from the requirements of Article III.

An examination of the relative allocation of powers between the CFTC and Article III courts in light of the considerations given prominence in our precedents demonstrates that the congressional scheme does not impermissibly intrude on the province of the judiciary. The CFTC's adjudicatory powers depart from the traditional agency model in just one respect: the CFTC's jurisdiction over common law counterclaims. While wholesale importation of concepts of pendent or ancillary jurisdiction into the agency context may create greater constitutional difficulties, we decline to endorse an absolute prohibition on such jurisdiction out of fear of where some hypothetical "slippery slope" may deposit us. Indeed, the CFTC's exercise of this type of jurisdiction is not without precedent. Thus, in *RFC v. Bankers Trust Co.* (1943), we saw no constitutional difficulty in the initial adjudication of a state law claim by a federal agency, subject to judicial review, when that claim was ancillary to a federal law dispute. Similarly, in *Katchen v. Landy* (1966), this Court upheld a bankruptcy referee's power to hear and decide state law counterclaims against a creditor who filed a claim in bankruptcy when those counterclaims arose out of the same transaction. We reasoned that, as a practical matter, requiring the trustee to commence a plenary action to recover on its counterclaim would be a "meaningless gesture."

In the instant cases, we are likewise persuaded that there is little practical reason to find that this single deviation from the agency model is fatal to the congressional scheme. Aside from its authorization of counterclaim jurisdiction, the CEA leaves far more of the "essential attributes of judicial power" to Article III courts than did that portion of the Bankruptcy Act found unconstitutional in *Northern Pipeline*. The CEA scheme in fact hews closely to the agency model approved by the Court in *Crowell v. Benson* (1932).

The CFTC, like the agency in *Crowell*, deals only with a "particularized area of law," whereas the jurisdiction of the bankruptcy courts found unconstitutional in *Northern Pipeline* extended to broadly "all civil proceedings arising under title 11 or arising in or related to cases under title 11." CFTC orders, like those of the agency in *Crowell*, but unlike those of the bankruptcy courts under the 1978 Act, are enforceable only by order of the district court. CFTC orders are also reviewed under the same "weight of the evidence" standard sustained in *Crowell*, rather than the more deferential standard found lacking in *Northern Pipeline*. The legal rulings of the CFTC, like the legal determinations of the agency in *Crowell*, are subject to *de novo* review. Finally, the CFTC, unlike the bankruptcy courts under the 1978 Act, does not exercise "all ordinary powers of district courts," and thus may not, for instance, preside over jury trials or issue writs of habeas corpus.

Of course, the nature of the claim has significance in our Article III analysis quite apart from the method prescribed for its adjudication. The counterclaim asserted in this litigation is a "private" right for which state law provides the rule of decision. It is therefore a claim of the kind assumed to be at the "core" of matters normally reserved to Article III courts. Yet this conclusion does not end our inquiry; just as this Court has rejected any attempt to make determinative for Article III purposes the distinction between public rights and private rights, there is no reason inherent in separation of powers principles to accord the state law character of a claim talismanic power in Article III inquiries.

We have explained that "the public rights doctrine reflects simply a pragmatic understanding that when Congress selects a quasi-judicial method of resolving matters that 'could be conclusively determined by the Executive and Legislative Branches,' the danger of encroaching on the judicial powers" is less than when private rights, which are normally within the purview of the judiciary, are relegated as an initial matter to administrative adjudication. Similarly, the state law character of a claim is significant for purposes of determining the effect that an initial adjudication of those claims by a non-Article III tribunal will have on the separation of powers for the simple reason that private, common law rights were historically the types of matters subject to resolution by Article III courts. The risk that Congress may improperly have encroached on the federal judiciary is obviously magnified when Congress "withdraw[s] from judicial cognizance any matter which, from its nature, is the subject of a suit at the common law, or in equity, or admiralty" and which therefore has traditionally been tried in Article III courts, and allocates the decision of those matters to a non-Article III forum of its own creation. Accordingly, where private, common law rights are at stake, our examination of the congressional attempt to control the manner in which those rights are adjudicated has been searching. In this litigation, however, "[l]ooking beyond form to the substance of what" Congress has done, we are persuaded that the congressional authorization of limited CFTC jurisdiction over a narrow class of common law claims as an incident to the CFTC's primary, and unchallenged, adjudicative function does not create a substantial threat to the separation of powers.

It is clear that Congress has not attempted to "withdraw from judicial cognizance" the determination of Conti's right to the sum represented by the debit balance in Schor's account. Congress gave the CFTC the authority to adjudicate such matters, but the decision to invoke this forum is left entirely to the parties and the power of the federal judiciary to take jurisdiction of these matters is unaffected. In such circumstances, separation of powers concerns are diminished, for it seems self-evident that just as Congress may encourage parties to settle a dispute out of court or resort to arbitration without impermissible incursions on the separation of powers, Congress may make available a quasi-judicial mechanism through which willing parties may, at their option, elect to resolve their differences. This is not to say, of course, that if Congress created a phalanx of non-Article III tribunals equipped to handle the entire business of the Article III courts without any Article III supervision or control and without evidence of valid and specific legislative necessities, the fact that the parties had the election to proceed in their forum of choice would necessarily save the scheme from constitutional attack. But this case obviously bears no resemblance to such a scenario, given the degree of judicial control saved to the federal courts, as well as the congressional purpose behind the jurisdictional delegation, the demonstrated need for the delegation, and the limited nature of the delegation.

When Congress authorized the CFTC to adjudicate counterclaims, its primary focus was on making effective a specific and limited federal regulatory scheme, not on allocating jurisdiction among federal tribunals. Congress intended to create an inexpensive and expeditious alternative forum through which customers could enforce the provisions of the CEA against professional brokers. Its decision to endow the CFTC with jurisdiction over such reparations claims is readily understandable given the perception that the CFTC was relatively immune from political pressures, and the obvious expertise that the Commission possesses in applying the CEA and its own regulations. This reparations scheme itself is of unquestioned constitutional validity. It was only to ensure the effectiveness of this scheme that Congress authorized the CFTC to assert jurisdiction over common law counterclaims. Indeed, as was explained above, absent the CFTC's exercise of that authority, the purposes of the reparations procedure would have been confounded.

It also bears emphasis that the CFTC's assertion of counterclaim jurisdiction is limited to that which is necessary to make the reparations procedure workable. The CFTC adjudication of common law counterclaims is incidental to, and completely dependent upon, adjudication of reparations claims created by federal law, and in actual fact is limited to claims arising out of the same transaction or occurrence as the reparations claim.

In such circumstances, the magnitude of any intrusion on the Judicial Branch can only be termed *de minimis.* Conversely, were we to hold that the Legislative Branch may not permit such limited cognizance of common law counterclaims at the election of the parties, it is clear that we would "defeat the obvious purpose of the legislation to furnish a prompt, continuous, expert and inexpensive method for dealing with a class of questions of fact which are peculiarly suited to examination and determination by an administrative agency specially assigned to that task." We do not think Article III compels this degree of prophylaxis.

* * *

C

Schor asserts that Article III, § 1, constrains Congress for reasons of federalism, as well as for reasons of separation of powers. He argues that the state law character of Conti's counterclaim transforms the central question in this litigation from whether Congress has trespassed upon the judicial powers of the Federal Government into whether Congress has invaded the prerogatives of state governments.

At the outset, we note that our prior precedents in this area have dealt only with separation of powers concerns, and have not intimated that principles of federalism impose limits on Congress' ability to delegate adjudicative functions to non-Article III tribunals. This absence of discussion regarding federalism is particularly telling in *Northern Pipeline,* where the Court based its analysis solely on the separation of powers principles inherent in Article III despite the fact that the claim sought to be adjudicated in the bankruptcy court was created by state law.

Even assuming that principles of federalism are relevant to Article III analysis, however, we are unpersuaded that those principles require the invalidation of the CFTC's counterclaim jurisdiction. The sole fact that Conti's counterclaim is resolved by a federal rather than a state tribunal could not be said to unduly impair state interests, for it is established that a federal court could, without constitutional hazard, decide a counterclaim such as the one asserted here under its ancillary jurisdiction, even if an independent jurisdictional basis for it were lacking. Given that the federal courts can and do exercise ancillary jurisdiction over counterclaims such as the one at issue here, the question becomes whether the fact that a federal agency rather than a federal Article III court initially hears the state law claim gives rise to a cognizably greater impairment of principles of federalism.

Schor argues that those Framers opposed to diversity jurisdiction in the federal courts acquiesced in its inclusion in Article III only because they were assured that the federal judiciary would be protected by the tenure and salary provisions of Article III. He concludes, in essence, that to protect this constitutional compact, Article III should be read to absolutely preclude any adjudication of state law claims by federal decisionmakers that do not enjoy the Article III salary and tenure protections. We are unpersuaded by Schor's novel theory, which suffers from a number of flaws, the most important of which is that Schor identifies no historical support for the critical link he posits between the provisions of Article III that protect the independence of the federal judiciary and those provisions that define the extent of the judiciary's jurisdiction over state law claims.

The judgment of the Court of Appeals for the District of Columbia Circuit is reversed, and the cases remanded for further proceedings consistent with this opinion.

It is so ordered.

JUSTICE BRENNAN, with whom JUSTICE MARSHALL joins, dissenting.

* * *

On its face, Article III, § 1, seems to prohibit the vesting of any judicial functions in either the Legislative or the Executive Branch. The Court has, however, recognized three narrow exceptions to the otherwise absolute mandate of Article III: territorial courts, courts-martial, and courts that adjudicate certain disputes concerning public rights. Unlike the Court, I would limit the judicial authority of non-Article III federal tribunals to these few, long-established exceptions and would countenance no further erosion of Article III's mandate.

I

The Framers knew that "[t]he accumulation of all powers, Legislative, Executive, and Judiciary, in the same hands, whether of one, a few, or many, and whether hereditary, self-appointed, or elective, may justly be pronounced the very definition of tyranny." In order to prevent such tyranny, the Framers devised a governmental structure composed of three distinct branches—"a vigorous Legislative Branch," "a separate and wholly independent Executive Branch," and "a Judicial Branch equally independent." The separation of powers and the checks and balances that the Framers built into our tripartite form of government were intended to operate as a "self-executing safeguard against the encroachment or aggrandizement of one branch at the expense of the other." " 'The fundamental necessity of maintaining each of the three general departments of government entirely free from the control or coercive influence, direct or indirect, of either of the others, has often been stressed and is hardly open to serious question.' " The federal judicial power, then, must be exercised by judges who are independent of the Executive and the Legislature in order to maintain the checks and balances that are crucial to our constitutional structure.

The Framers also understood that a principal benefit of the separation of the judicial power from the legislative and executive powers would be the protection of individual litigants from decisionmakers susceptible to majoritarian pressures. Article III's salary and tenure provisions promote impartial adjudication by placing the judicial power of the United States "in a body of judges insulated from majoritarian pressures and thus able to enforce [federal law] without fear of reprisal or public rebuke." As Alexander Hamilton observed, "[t]hat inflexible and uniform adherence to the rights of the Constitution, and of individuals, which we perceive to be indispensable in the Courts of justice can certainly not be expected from Judges who hold their offices by a temporary commission." This is so because

> [i]f the power of making [periodic appointments] was committed either to the Executive or Legislature, there would be danger of an improper complaisance to the branch which possessed it; if to both,

there would be an unwillingness to hazard the displeasure of either; if to the People, or to persons chosen by them for the special purpose, there would be too great a disposition to consult popularity, to justify a reliance that nothing would be consulted but the Constitution and the laws.

"Next to permanency in office," Hamilton added, "nothing can contribute more to the independence of the Judges than a fixed provision for their support" because "a power over a man's subsistencc amounts to a power over his will."

These important functions of Article III are too central to our constitutional scheme to risk their incremental erosion. The exceptions we have recognized for territorial courts, courts-martial, and administrative courts were each based on "certain exceptional powers bestowed upon Congress by the Constitution or by historical consensus." Here, however, there is no equally forceful reason to extend further these exceptions to situations that are distinguishable from existing precedents. The Court, however, engages in just such an extension. By sanctioning the adjudication of state-law counterclaims by a federal administrative agency, the Court far exceeds the analytic framework of our precedents.

* * *

II

* * *

Article III's prophylactic protections were intended to prevent just this sort of abdication to claims of legislative convenience. The Court requires that the legislative interest in convenience and efficiency be weighed against the competing interest in judicial independence. In doing so, the Court pits an interest the benefits of which are immediate, concrete, and easily understood against one, the benefits of which are almost entirely prophylactic, and thus often seem remote and not worth the cost in any single case. Thus, while this balancing creates the illusion of objectivity and ineluctability, in fact the result was foreordained, because the balance is weighted against judicial independence. The danger of the Court's balancing approach is, of course, that as individual cases accumulate in which the Court finds that the short-term benefits of efficiency outweigh the long-term benefits of judicial independence, the protections of Article III will be eviscerated.

Perhaps the resolution of reparations claims such as respondents' may be accomplished more conveniently under the Court's decision than under my approach, but the Framers foreswore this sort of convenience in order to preserve freedom. "The choices we discern as having been made in the Constitutional Convention impose burdens on governmental processes that often seem clumsy, inefficient, even unworkable, but those hard choices were consciously made by men who had lived under a form of government that permitted arbitrary governmental acts to go unchecked. * * * With all the obvious flaws of delay [and] untidiness * * *, we have not yet found a better way to preserve freedom than by making the exercise of power subject to the carefully crafted restraints spelled out in the Constitution."

* * *

The Constitution did not grant Congress the general authority to bypass the Judiciary whenever Congress deems it advisable, any more than it granted Congress the authority to arrogate to itself executive functions.

III

According to the Court, the intrusion into the province of the Federal Judiciary caused by the CFTC's authority to adjudicate state-law counterclaims is insignificant, both because the CFTC shares in, rather than displaces, federal district court jurisdiction over these claims and because only a very narrow class of state-law issues are involved. The "sharing" justification fails under the reasoning used by the Court to support the CFTC's authority. If the administrative reparations proceeding is so much more convenient and efficient than litigation in federal district court that abrogation of Article III's commands is warranted, it seems to me that complainants would rarely, if ever, choose to go to district court in the first instance. Thus, any "sharing" of jurisdiction is more illusory than real.

More importantly, the Court, in emphasizing that this litigation will permit solely a narrow class of state-law claims to be decided by a non-Article III court, ignores the fact that it establishes a broad principle. The decision today may authorize the administrative adjudication only of state-law claims that stem from the same transaction or set of facts that allow the customer of a professional commodity broker to initiate reparations proceedings before the CFTC, but the reasoning of this decision strongly suggests that, given "legislative necessity" and party consent, any federal agency may decide state-law issues that are ancillary to federal issues within the agency's jurisdiction. Thus, while in this litigation "the magnitude of any intrusion on the Judicial Branch" may conceivably be characterized as "*de minimis*," the potential impact of the Court's decision on federal-court jurisdiction is substantial. The Court dismisses warnings about the dangers of its approach, asserting simply that it does not fear the slippery slope, and that this litigation does not involve the creation by Congress of a "phalanx of non-Article III tribunals equipped to handle the entire business of the Article III courts." A healthy respect for the precipice on which we stand is warranted, however, for this reason: Congress can seriously impair Article III's structural and individual protections without assigning away "the entire business of the Article III courts." It can do so by diluting the judicial power of the federal courts. And, contrary to the Court's intimations, dilution of judicial power operates to impair the protections of Article III regardless of whether Congress acted with the "good intention" of providing a more efficient dispute resolution system or with the "bad intention" of strengthening the Legislative Branch at the expense of the Judiciary.

IV

The Court's reliance on Schor's "consent" to a non-Article III tribunal is also misplaced. The Court erroneously suggests that there is a clear division between the separation of powers and the impartial adjudication functions of Article III. The Court identifies Article III's structural, or separation-of-powers, function as preservation of the Judiciary's domain from encroachment by another branch. The Court identifies the impartial adjudication function as the protection afforded by Article III to individual litigants against judges who may be dominated by other branches of government.

In my view, the structural and individual interests served by Article III are inseparable. The potential exists for individual litigants to be deprived of impartial decisionmakers only where federal officials who exercise judicial power are susceptible to congressional and executive pressure. That is, individual litigants may be harmed by the assignment of judicial power to non-Article III federal tribunals only where the Legislative or Executive Branches have encroached upon judicial authority and have thus threatened the separation of powers. The Court correctly recognizes that to the extent that Article III's structural concerns are implicated by a grant of judicial power to a non-Article III tribunal, "the parties cannot by consent cure the constitutional difficulty for the same reason that the parties by consent cannot confer on federal courts subject-matter jurisdiction beyond the limitations imposed by Article III, § 2." Because the individual and structural interests served by Article III are coextensive, I do not believe that a litigant may ever waive his right to an Article III tribunal where one is constitutionally required. In other words, consent is irrelevant to Article III analysis.

V

Our Constitution unambiguously enunciates a fundamental principle—that the "judicial Power of the United States" be reposed in an independent Judiciary. It is our obligation zealously to guard that independence so that our tripartite system of government remains strong and that individuals continue to be protected against decisionmakers subject to majoritarian pressures. Unfortunately, today the Court forsakes that obligation for expediency. I dissent.

Notes and Questions

1. Would the result have been different if the statute required rather than permitted both the federal claims and the state law counterclaims to be asserted in the administrative proceedings? Absent waiver, how does a

court determine if a legislative court violates a litigant's right to have a decision from a judge free from potential influence by the other branches of government?

2. In the federal courts, litigants cannot waive defects in subject matter jurisdiction. Are challenges based upon the lack of Article III safeguards "jurisdictional"?

3. Was CFTC jurisdiction over counterclaims necessary to the effectiveness of the statutory scheme? If so, why was the assertion of counterclaims permissive rather than compulsory?

4. How important are Congress's motives for departing from Article III? Would the result have differed if Congress enacted the scheme in part to reduce the power of the Article III courts?

5. The Court asserts that the state law character of a claim assigned to a legislative court indicates increased danger of encroachment on judicial power. Does it matter that state court judges do not enjoy the safeguards of Article III?

6. Is Justice Brennan correct that, given the consent of the parties, the majority's reasoning would allow any federal agency to decide state law claims that are ancillary to federal issues within the agency's jurisdiction?

7. In the future, will the result of the balancing test be preordained because it weighs the concrete and easily-understood reasons for using legislative courts against the remote and prophylactic concerns of Article III? *See* Martin Redish, *Legislative Courts, Administrative Agencies, and the* Northern Pipeline *Decision,* 1983 DUKE L.J. 197 (1983).

8. Must any adjudication by a legislative court be subject to review by an Article III court for the scheme to be constitutional? Does such review sufficiently protect the values underlying Article III? *See* Richard Fallon, *Of Legislative Courts, Administrative Agencies, and Article III,* 101 HARV.L.REV. 915 (1988) (answering both questions affirmatively).

9. The Bankruptcy Amendments and Federal Judgeship Act of 1984 authorized bankruptcy judges to enter final judgments and orders in core bankruptcy proceedings. The statute specifically defines " proceedings to determine, avoid, or recover fraudulent conveyances" as core proceedings. 28 U.S.C. § 157(2)(H). Does it violate Article III for a bankruptcy judge to enter a final judgment in a suit by a trustee in bankruptcy to recover an allegedly fraudulent monetary transfer from a party who had not submitted a claim against the bankruptcy estate and had not consented to the entry of final judgment by the bankruptcy judge? Does the issue depend upon whether the fraudulent conveyance claim can properly be characterized as one involving "public rights"?

In *Granfinanciera, S.A. v. Nordberg,* 492 U.S. 33, 109 S.Ct. 2782, 106 L.Ed.2d 493 (1989), a bankruptcy trustee sought recovery of $1.7 million that he alleged petitioners had received as a fraudulent transfer of from the bankrupt's corporate predecessor. The defendant petitioners demanded a jury trial. In an opinion by Justice Brennan, the Supreme Court held that the Seventh Amendment gives the petitioners the right to a jury trial even though Congress designated such actions core proceedings in bankruptcy actions. The Court's opinion may help to answer the questions raised above.

The Seventh Amendment generally preserves the right to jury trial in the federal courts "[i]n suits at common law" as it existed in 1791, when the states ratified the Amendment. Thus, the courts determine whether the claim is one that the common law courts or the equity courts of late eighteenth century England would have adjudicated. Consequently, the Court first concluded that in 1791 the trustee would have had to bring his fraudulent conveyance claim for a determinate amount of money in the common law courts and then found that the nature of the relief he sought supported the conclusion that the right he invoked was legal, not equitable. Because those findings suggested that the petitioners did have a right to a jury trial, the Court then turned to whether the Seventh Amendment conferred such a right even though Congress assigned resolution of the claim to a non-Article III tribunal.

The Court then asserted a connection between the Seventh Amendment issue and whether assignment of the claim to a bankruptcy judge violated Article III. "[I]f a statutory cause of action is legal in nature, the question whether the Seventh Amendment permits Congress to assign its adjudication to a tribunal that does not employ juries as factfinders requires the same answer as the question whether Article III allows Congress to assign adjudication of that cause of action to a non-Article tribunal." Though the Court acknowledged that is some circumstances Congress could create statutory claims closely analogous to common law claims and put them outside the protection of the Seventh Amendment by assigning them to non-Article III tribunals, it concluded that the claims had to involve public rights. Citing *Thomas v. Union Carbide Agricultural Products Co.*, discussed in Note 8 on page 350, the opinion noted that the Federal Government does not have to be a party for a case to involve public rights, if the statutory right is closely intertwined with a valid federal regulatory program.

The Court determined, however, that the trustee's right to recover a fraudulent conveyance was private, more closely resembling state law contract claims brought by the bankrupt to increase the estate than creditors' ranked claims to a *pro rata* share of it. Because the right was both private and legal in nature, the Court held that the Seventh Amendment gave the petitioners a right to a jury trial.

Justice Scalia concurred in part of the majority opinion and concurred in the judgment. His major disagreement with the majority was its failure to limit the public-rights doctrine to cases where the Federal Government is a party. He argued that expansion of the doctrine was inconsistent with its origins and that there was no constitutional basis for *Thomas v. Union Carbide Agricultural Products Co.* He also attacked the balancing test announced in *Schor* as "no standard at all," arguing that separation of powers is too important to depend upon such a test. "This central feature of the Constitution must be anchored in rules, not set adrift in some multifactored 'balancing test.' "

Given the apparent connection between the Seventh Amendment and Article III issues, is *Granfinanciera* consistent with *Schor*? Why or why not?

D. MAGISTRATE JUDGES AS ADJUNCTS TO THE DISTRICT COURTS

The Federal Magistrates Act of 1968[1] replaced federal commissioners with magistrates and expanded their responsibilities. It gave them the powers and duties previously held by commissioners and also "such additional duties as are not inconsistent with the Constitution and laws of the United States." The Act presented a non-exhaustive list of "additional duties" that included serving as special masters, presiding over trials of minor criminal offenses with the consent of the accused, and assisting district judges in discovery and other pretrial proceedings. Thereafter, magistrates often conducted hearings and made recommendations to the district court. One provision authorized magistrates to conduct preliminary reviews of petitions for post-conviction relief, and a dispute about its meaning reached the Supreme Court.

Wingo v. Wedding, 418 U.S. 461, 94 S.Ct. 2842, 41 L.Ed.2d 879 (1974), held that the Act authorized magistrates to recommend to district court judges whether to hold evidentiary hearings on habeas petitions, but did not authorize magistrates to conduct the hearings. Congress responded with the Federal Magistrates Act of 1976,[2] overruling *Wingo* by specifying that magistrates could hold the evidentiary hearings and then make recommendations to a district judge. The 1976 amendments also describe in greater detail the role magistrates should play in discovery and other pretrial proceedings. They authorize the district courts to refer to a magistrate for determination any pretrial matter except certain dispositive motions, such as motions for summary judgment or to suppress evidence. The district judge may reconsider the magistrate's decision on a non-dispositive pretrial matter if it is "clearly erroneous or contrary to the law." The court may also refer dispositive motions to a magistrate to conduct an evidentiary hearing, but after the hearing, the magistrate submits proposed findings of fact and a recommended disposition to the district judge. Any party may object to the proposed findings and recommendations; if someone does, the district court must make a *de novo* determination. Whether or not the parties file objections, the district court may accept, reject, or modify the magistrate's findings or recommendations.

Magistrates serve a fixed term of either eight or four years, subject to removal by the district's judges for several reasons, including incompetence. Their salaries can be reduced by act of Congress. Consequently, questions arose as to whether assigning those duties to magistrates violated Article III. In *United States v. Raddatz,* 447 U.S. 667,

---

[1] Act of Oct. 17, 1968, Pub.L. No. 90-578, 82 Stat. 1107.

[2] Act of Oct. 21, 1976, Pub.L. No. 94-577, 90 Stat. 2729.

100 S.Ct. 2406, 65 L.Ed.2d 424 (1980), discussed in *Northern Pipeline,* the Supreme Court upheld the scheme.

Raddatz was charged with unlawfully receiving a firearm. He moved to suppress his incriminating statements. Over the defendant's objection, the district court referred the suppression motion to a magistrate for an evidentiary hearing. The magistrate conducted the hearing, made proposed findings of fact, and recommended that the motion be denied. The defendant objected. The district court reviewed the report, the transcript, and the objections, and heard oral argument before accepting the magistrate's recommendation. On appeal, the defendant argued that the procedure violated Article III. The Supreme Court pointed out that the district court had discretion to authorize the magistrate's hearing and that the entire process was under the district court's control. Because the responsibility and authority for final determination remained with the district judge, the Court found the statutory scheme did not violate Article III.

Raddatz did not end the controversy. The Federal Magistrate Act of 1979[3] again expanded the responsibilities of the magistrates, providing that magistrates specially designated by the district court could conduct all proceedings in civil matters and order entry of judgment, provided the parties consented to the reference. The Supreme Court has not discussed whether this delegation of authority to federal magistrates is constitutional, but the lower federal courts have.

Pacemaker Diagnostic Clinic v. Instromedix, Inc., 725 F.2d 537 (9th Cir. 1984) (en banc) is perhaps the leading case. Pacemaker alleged patent infringement by Instromedix, which counterclaimed to have the patent declared invalid. The parties consented to a trial before a magistrate, who found that the patent was valid and had not been infringed. Both parties appealed, and a court of appeals panel, *sua sponte,* raised the constitutional issue. The panel found a constitutional problem, but the Ninth Circuit, en banc, reversed.

The majority began by asserting that Article III helps delineate the separation of powers and that the separation-of-powers issue has two components. One is the personal right of the litigant to have federal suits tried by Article III judges. The other component is the protection of the integrity and independence of the judiciary in the constitutional structure. The court pointed out that the Supreme Court had held that criminal defendants can waive fundamental constitutional rights. Consequently, it thought it anomalous to hold that a litigant in a civil case cannot waive the personal right to an Article III judge.

Turning to the second component, the court concluded that the provision for trial by magistrate does not threaten the integrity or independence of Article III courts. The court did not see the political

---

[3] Act of Oct. 10, 1979, Pub.L. No. 96-82, 93 Stat. 643.

branches seeking to increase power at the expense of the judiciary. The judiciary maintains substantial control over the magistrate system generally and over cases where there has been references to magistrates for trial. Article III judges control selection and retention of magistrates. Consequently, magistrates are not dependent upon either of the political branches. The statute also authorizes the district court to revoke a reference upon a showing of good cause or extraordinary circumstances. Given these features, and the right of the parties to appeal to an Article III court, the Ninth Circuit found that the power over and the responsibility for such cases remains with the judiciary.

Judge Schroeder dissented vigorously, asserting that magistrates are not the independent decision-makers contemplated by Article III because they depend upon Article III judges for appointment and retention, and upon Congress for their salaries. Yet the provisions upheld by the court allow magistrates to review the constitutionality of actions of the political branches, lessening the judiciary's check upon them. The dissent also argued that the control the district judges have over magistrates destroys the independent decision-making contemplated by Article III. Such control creates a severe conflict of interest for the magistrate who may feel pressed to decide between what is right and what will please the district court. The litigants' consent is irrelevant to these issues because the federal judicial power is conferred and limited by Article III, not by the parties. Finally, Judge Schroeder asserted that in these circumstances, voluntary consent is illusory. Because of crowded dockets, district judges try to channel cases to magistrates, and at least some will try to pressure litigants to consent. Additionally, waiting for adjudication by an Article III judge will mean increased delay and expense and will induce some litigants to consent to trial by magistrates. For these reasons, the dissent concluded the scheme is unconstitutional.

Litigant consent was also an important factor in two Supreme Court cases dealing with magistrates. In *Gomez v. United States,* 490 U.S. 858, 109 S.Ct. 2237, 104 L.Ed.2d 923 (1989), the Court held that the selection of a jury in a felony trial was not one of the "additional duties" a magistrate could receive over the defendant's objection. Focusing upon the language and legislative history of the statute, the Court concluded that Congress did not intend such assignments.

Nonetheless, *Peretz v. United States,* 501 U.S. 923, 111 S.Ct. 2661, 115 L.Ed.2d 808 (1991), interpreted the Act to authorize such assignments *with* the consent of the defendant and held that that did not violate Article III. The Court read *Gomez* narrowly, motivated largely by a desire to interpret the statute to avoid a serious constitutional question. The holding in *Gomez* avoided the question of whether a defendant has a right to demand an Article III judge at every critical stage of a felony trial. In *Peretz,* the defendant's consent significantly changed the constitutional analysis, and the Court had "no trouble" finding no violation of Article III when the district judge permitted a magistrate to conduct *voir dire* with the defendant's consent. Felony defendants lose whatever protection the Constitution provides under Article III if they do not object. Citing *Schor* and cases where criminal defendants have waived other constitutional rights, *Peretz* held that the defendant had waived any personal right to an Article III judge.

In addition, the Court decided that the procedure did not damage the structural protection of the judiciary, pointing to factors very similar to those in *Pacemaker*. Article III judges appoint magistrates and can remove them. The district court has discretion to refer the matter to the magistrate and whether to empanel the jury selected under the magistrate's supervision. Thus, the Court found no danger that Congress was attempting to reduce the power of Article III courts.

The Court did concede that, unlike the provision of the Federal Magistrate Act that *Raddatz* upheld, the provision in *Peretz* did not expressly mandate *de novo* review of the magistrate's rulings during jury selection. Peretz, however, had not sought review of the magistrate's rulings. *Raddatz*, said the Court, establishes that to the extent Article III requires *de novo* review, the parties' failure to request it waives the requirement. Moreover, the Court observed that if a defendant does request review of a magistrate's ruling during jury selection, the statute does not preclude review; it merely does not require it.

In 1990 Congress changed the title "magistrate" to "magistrate judge." Judicial Improvement Act of 1990, Pub. L. No. 101-650, § 321, 104 Stat. 5089 (1990). However, the change in title did not prevent new controversies regarding what their duties should be and in what circumstances they could act. For example, in *Roell v. Withrow*, 538 U.S. 580, 123 S.Ct. 1696, 155 L.Ed.2d 775 (2003), the Court faced the question of whether to infer a party's consent to having a magistrate judge conduct all proceedings and enter a judgment in a civil case from the party's litigation conduct. Though acknowledging that 28 U.S.C. § 636(c)(2) and FRCP 73(b) contemplated advance written consent by the parties, the majority concluded that the statute did not oust the magistrate judge of jurisdiction "so long as the parties have in fact voluntarily consented." The Court noted that interpreting the statute to require written consent as a prerequisite for a magistrate judge's jurisdiction would increase the risk of gamesmanship. A party could appear before a magistrate judge, try the case, and then await the outcome before deciding whether to raise the lack of written consent to vacate the judgment. Consequently, the Court held that "where the litigant or counsel was made aware of the need for consent and the right to refuse it, and still voluntarily appeared to try the case before the Magistrate Judge," there was the necessary consent to establish the magistrate judge's civil jurisdiction. The dissent argued that the majority's interpretation was inconsistent with the plain text of the statute and that its test for implied consent was "rife with ambiguities

Notes and Questions

1. Are the majority's or the dissent's arguments in *Pacemaker* more per-

suasive? Do *Schor* and *Peretz* indicate that *Pacemaker* is rightly or wrongly decided?

2. Does *Schor* necessarily lead to the result in *Peretz*? Is it distinguishable?

Chapter 5

FEDERAL COMMON LAW

A. INTRODUCTION

The determination that a case should or may be heard in the federal courts settles only the question of forum. It does not simultaneously decide what body of law applies to each issue. The court still must choose between federal and state law, an inquiry commonly referred to as a vertical choice-of-law question. If the court decides to use state law (as is generally the case for substantive issues in diversity cases), it then must decide which state's law to use, a horizontal choice-of-law question.[1] Courses on Conflict of Laws ordinarily study horizontal choice-of-law questions, but vertical choice-of-law is primarily the province of Federal Courts.

It is important to realize from the start that choice-of-law inquiries require issue-by-issue analysis. Many cases involve both state and federal law; often state law applies to some issues and federal law to others. One common example occurs in the typical diversity case. After *Erie Railroad v. Tompkins*, 304 U.S. 64, 58 S.Ct. 817, 82 L.Ed. 1188 (1938), state law governs most substantive issues in diversity cases,[2] but federal law will govern many procedural issues, particularly (but not exclusively) when the Federal Rules of Civil Procedure speak directly to the matter. It is not safe to assume that the subject matter jurisdiction provision that brings a case into the federal courts simultaneously decides the law that applies to a particular issue. At best it gives but a hint.

Although many first-year Civil Procedure courses cover *Erie*, many students emerge from the first year of law school with an inaccurate

---

[1] In many cases, where the dispute touches only one state, the answer may be clear, and the horizontal choice-of-law inquiry may never be articulated. Other cases may involve many states, and the inquiry becomes considerably more complex. Erie Railroad v. Tompkins, 304 U.S. 64, 58 S.Ct. 817, 82 L.Ed. 1188 (1938), involved both vertical and horizontal choice-of-law considerations. *Erie* is the progenitor of modern vertical choice-of-law principles. However, the final disposition of the case, which began in the Southern District of New York, depended also upon horizontal choice of law, and the New York federal court applied Pennsylvania substantive law because the accident giving rise to the litigation had occurred in Pennsylvania. At the time, New York adhered to the *lex loci delicti commissi* approach of § 377 of the first Restatement of Conflict of Laws.

[2] *Erie* does not, however, mean that *all* substantive issues in diversity cases will be so governed. *See, e.g.*, Banco Nacional de Cuba v. Sabbatino, 376 U.S. 398, 84 S.Ct. 923, 11 L.Ed.2d 804 (1964), discussed *infra* at 392.

memory of *Erie*. One is apt to remember vaguely that Justice Brandeis, writing for the Court, said that there is no federal common law. He did not say that; he said instead that "[t]here is no federal *general* common law." (Emphasis added.) Justice Brandeis clearly did not contemplate the complete demise of federal common law since on the same day he wrote an opinion holding that federal common law applied to a dispute between states.[3] Federal common law continues to exist and expand.[4]

This chapter explores the principles governing the creation of federal common law. The inquiry proceeds on several levels. First, consider whether state or federal law governs a particular issue. This is the vertical, or *Erie*, choice-of-law question. The answer depends partly on whether there is federal competence in the area, since the federal government has only delegated powers. If there is no federal competence, then clearly state law must govern. If there is federal competence, and Congress has created a rule of decision applicable to the issue, then the Supremacy Clause requires that federal law control, displacing state law. But if there is federal competence, and Congress has not acted, is it appropriate for the federal courts to step in to make common law? The mere fact that the federal government can enter a substantive area is not equivalent to saying that it should or must do so. Perhaps only Congress should establish a federal presence in a substantive area. Some judges and commentators have suggested that, attacking the institutional legitimacy of most judge-made federal law and thus greatly limiting its possible scope. Even for those who accept the legitimacy of federal common law, there are limits. The federal courts could not, for example, create a national health care system out of whole cloth simply because they thought it a good idea and authority to create it could be found somewhere in the Constitution. On the other hand, if a dispute develops between two states over how to apportion water from an interstate stream, neither state can impose its law on the other. Moreover, there is a strong federal interest in peaceful resolution of the conflicts. Consequently, relatively few may object to a federal court fashioning a rule of decision. These poles bound a vast spectrum of possible federal court activity; major amounts of judicial and scholarly time go into attempting to locate the federal courts' proper place on that spectrum.

Second, assuming federal common law should exist, how should the

---

[3] *See* Hinderlider v. LaPlata River & Cherry Creek Ditch Co., 304 U.S. 92, 58 S.Ct. 803, 82 L.Ed. 1202 (1938).

[4] The ensuing discussion presumes the student's familiarity with the early development of the *Erie* doctrine, particularly Guaranty Trust Co. v. York, 326 U.S. 99, 65 S.Ct. 1464, 89 L.Ed. 2079 (1945); Byrd v. Blue Ridge Rural Elec. Co-op., 356 U.S. 525, 78 S.Ct. 893, 2 L.Ed.2d 953 (1958); Hanna v. Plumer, 380 U.S. 460, 85 S.Ct. 1136, 14 L.Ed.2d 8 (1965); Walker v. Armco Steel Corp., 446 U.S. 740, 108 S.Ct. 1978, 64 L.Ed.2d 659 (1980); Stewart Organization. Ricoh Corp., 487 U.S. 22, 108 S.Ct. 2239, 101 L.Ed.2d 22 (1988), and Gasperini v. Center for the Humanities, Inc., 518 U.S. 415, 116 S.Ct. 2211, 135 L.ed.2d 659 (1996). For an excellent discussion of the *Erie* quatrain, see John Hart Ely, *The Irrepressible Myth of* Erie, 87 HARV.L.REV. 693 (1974).

federal courts create it? Are the federal judges simply to make it up, as have common law judges for centuries, or are there resources available to today's federal judges to help decide complex questions that federal common law will govern? In the excerpt that follows *Erie*, Judge Friendly suggests that federal courts create common law in four distinct ways: "spontaneous generation, as in the case of government contracts or interstate controversies, implication of a private federal cause of action from a statute providing other sanctions, construing a jurisdictional grant as a command to fashion federal law, and the normal judicial filling in of statutory interstices." Given the proliferation of state laws, model codes and secondary scholarly sources, federal judges today operate in much less of a vacuum than did their predecessors, both here and in England.

B. THE CORNERSTONE

ERIE RAILROAD CO. v. TOMPKINS
Supreme Court of the United States, 1938.
304 U.S. 64, 58 S.Ct. 817, 82 L.Ed. 1188.

MR. JUSTICE BRANDEIS delivered the opinion of the Court.

The question for decision is whether the oft-challenged doctrine of *Swift v. Tyson* shall now be disapproved.

Tompkins, a citizen of Pennsylvania, was injured on a dark night by a passing freight train of the Erie Railroad Company while walking along its right of way at Hughestown in that State. He claimed that the accident occurred through negligence in the operation, or maintenance, of the train; that he was rightfully on the premises as licensee because on a commonly used beaten footpath which ran for a short distance alongside the tracks; and that he was struck by something which looked like a door projecting from one of the moving cars. To enforce that claim he brought an action in the federal court for southern New York, which had jurisdiction because the company is a corporation of that State. It denied liability; and the case was tried by a jury.

The Erie insisted that its duty to Tompkins was no greater than that owed to a trespasser. It contended, among other things, that its duty to Tompkins, and hence its liability, should be determined in accordance with the Pennsylvania law; that under the law of Pennsylvania, as declared by its highest court, persons who use pathways along the railroad right of way—that is a longitudinal pathway as distinguished from a crossing—are to be deemed trespassers; and that the railroad is not liable for injuries to undiscovered trespassers resulting from its negligence, unless it be wanton or wilful. Tompkins denied that any such rule had been established by the decisions of the Pennsylvania courts; and contended that, since there was no statute of the State on the subject, the railroad's duty and liability is to be determined in federal courts as a matter of general law.

The trial judge refused to rule that the applicable law precluded recovery. The jury brought in a verdict of $30,000; and the judgment entered thereon was affirmed by the Circuit Court of Appeals, which held that it was unnecessary to consider whether the law of Pennsylvania was as contended, because the question was one not of local, but of general, law and that

> upon questions of general law the federal courts are free, in the absence of a local statute, to exercise their independent judgment as to what the law is; and it is well settled that the question of the responsibility of a railroad for injuries caused by its servants is one of general law * * * .

The Erie had contended that application of the Pennsylvania rule was required, among other things, by § 34 of the Federal Judiciary Act of September 24, 1789, which provides: "The laws of the several States, except where the Constitution, treaties, or statutes of the United States otherwise require or provide, shall be regarded as rules of decisions in trials at common law, in the courts of the United States, in cases where they apply."

Because of the importance of the question whether the federal court was free to disregard the alleged rule of the Pennsylvania common law, we granted certiorari.

First, *Swift v. Tyson* held that federal courts exercising jurisdiction on the ground of diversity of citizenship need not, in matters of general jurisprudence, apply the unwritten law of the State as declared by its highest court; that they are free to exercise an independent judgment as to what the common law of the State is—or should be; and that, as there stated by Mr. Justice Story:

> the true interpretation of the thirty-fourth section limited its application to state laws strictly local, that is to say, to the positive statutes of the state, and the construction thereof adopted by the local tribunals, and to rights and titles to things having a permanent locality, such as the rights and titles to real estate, and other matters immovable and intraterritorial in their nature and character. It never has been supposed by us, that the section did apply, or was intended to apply, to questions of a more general nature, not at all dependent upon local statutes or local usages of a fixed and permanent operation, as, for example, to the construction of ordinary contracts or other written instruments, and especially to questions of general commercial law, where the state tribunals are called upon to perform the like functions as ourselves, that is, to ascertain upon general reasoning and legal analogies, what is the true exposition of the contract or instrument, or what is the just rule furnished by the principles of commercial law to govern the case.

The Court in applying the rule of § 34 to equity cases said: "The statute, however, is merely declarative of the rule which would exist in the absence of the statute." The federal courts assumed, in the broad field of "general law," the power to declare rules of decision which Congress was confessedly without power to enact as statutes. Doubt was repeatedly expressed as to the correctness of the construction given § 34, and as to the soundness of the rule which it introduced. But it was the more recent research of a competent scholar, who examined the original document, which established that the construction given to it by the Court was erroneous; and that the purpose of the section was merely to make certain that, in all matters except those in which some federal law is controlling, the federal courts exercising jurisdiction in diversity of citizenship cases would apply as their rules of decision the law of the State, unwritten as well as written.

Criticism of the doctrine became widespread after the decision of *Black & White Taxicab Co. v. Brown & Yellow Taxicab Co.* There, Brown and Yellow, a Kentucky corporation owned by Kentuckians, and the Louisville and Nashville Railroad, also a Kentucky corporation, wished that the former should have the exclusive privilege of soliciting passenger and baggage transportation at the Bowling Green, Kentucky, railroad station; and that the Black and White, a competing Kentucky corporation, should be prevented from interfering with that privilege. Knowing that such a contract would be void under the common law of Kentucky, it was arranged that the Brown and Yellow reincorporate under the law of Tennessee, and that the contract with the railroad should be executed there. The suit was then brought by the Tennessee corporation in the federal court for western Kentucky to enjoin competition by the Black and White; an injunction issued by the District Court was sustained by the Court of Appeals; and this Court, citing many decisions in which the doctrine of *Swift v. Tyson* had been applied, affirmed the decree.

Second. Experience in applying the doctrine of *Swift v. Tyson*, had revealed its defects, political and social; and the benefits expected to flow from the rule did not accrue. Persistence of state courts in their own opinions on questions of common law prevented uniformity; and the impossibility of discovering a satisfactory line of demarcation between the province of general law and that of local law developed a new well of uncertainties.

On the other hand, the mischievous results of the doctrine had become apparent. Diversity of citizenship jurisdiction was conferred in order to prevent apprehended discrimination in state courts against those not citizens of the State. *Swift v. Tyson* introduced grave discrimination by non-citizens against citizens. It made rights enjoyed under the unwritten "general law" vary according to whether enforcement was sought in the state or in the federal court; and the privilege of selecting the court in which the right should be determined was conferred upon the non-citizen. Thus, the doctrine rendered impossible equal protection of the law. In attempting to promote uniformity of law throughout the United States, the doctrine had prevented uniformity in the administration of the law of the State.

The discrimination resulting became in practice far-reaching. This resulted in part from the broad province accorded to the so-called "general law" as to which federal courts exercised an independent judgment. In addition to questions of purely commercial law, "general law" was held to include the obligations under contracts entered into and to be performed within the State, the extent to which a carrier operating within a State may stipulate for exemption from liability for his own negligence or that of his employee; the liability for torts committed within the State upon persons resident or property located there, even where the question of liability depended upon the scope of a property right conferred by the State; and the right to exemplary or punitive damages. Furthermore, state decisions construing local deeds, mineral conveyances, and even devises of real estate were disregarded.

In part the discrimination resulted from the wide range of persons held entitled to avail themselves of the federal rule by resort to the diversity of citizenship jurisdiction. Through this jurisdiction individual citizens willing to remove from their own State and become citizens of another might avail themselves of the federal rule. And, without even change of residence, a corporate citizen of the State could avail itself of the federal rule by re-incorporating under the laws of another State, as was done in the *Taxicab* case.

The injustice and confusion incident to the doctrine of *Swift v. Tyson* have been repeatedly urged as reasons for abolishing or limiting diversity of citizenship jurisdiction. Other legislative relief has been proposed. If only a question of statutory construction were involved, we should not be prepared to abandon a doctrine so widely applied throughout nearly a century. But the unconstitutionality of the course pursued has now been made clear and compels us to do so.

Third. Except in matters governed by the Federal Constitution or by Acts of Congress, the law to be applied in any case is the law of the State. And whether the law of the State shall be declared by its Legislature in a statute or by its highest court in a decision is not a matter of federal concern. There is no federal general common law. Congress has no power to declare substantive rules of common law applicable in a State whether they be local in their nature or "general," be they commercial law or a part of the law of torts. And no clause in the Constitution purports to confer such a power upon the federal courts. As stated by Mr. Justice Field:

> I am aware that what has been termed the general law of the country—which is often little less than what the judge advancing the doctrine thinks at the time should be the general law on a particular subject—has been often advanced in judicial opinions of this

court to control a conflicting law of a State. I admit that learned judges have fallen into the habit of repeating this doctrine as a convenient mode of brushing aside the law of a State in conflict with their views. And I confess that, moved and governed by the authority of the great names of those judges, I have, myself, in many instances, unhesitatingly and confidently, but I think now erroneously, repeated the same doctrine. But, notwithstanding the great names which may be cited in favor of the doctrine, and notwithstanding the frequency with which the doctrine has been reiterated, there stands, as a perpetual protest against its repetition, the Constitution of the United States, which recognizes and preserves the autonomy and independence of the States—dependence in their legislative and independence in their judicial departments. Supervision over either the legislative or the judicial action of the States is in no case permissible except as to matters by the Constitution specifically authorized or delegated to the United States. Any interference with either, except as thus permitted, is an invasion of the authority of the State and, to that extent, a denial of its independence.

The fallacy underlying the rule declared in *Swift v. Tyson* is made clear by Mr. Justice Holmes. The doctrine rests upon the assumption that there is

a transcendental body of law outside of any particular State but obligatory within it unless and until changed by statute, that federal courts have the power to use their judgment as to what the rules of common law are; and that in the federal courts

the parties are entitled to an independent judgment on matters of general law: but law in the sense in which courts speak of it today does not exist without some definite authority behind it. The common law so far as it is enforced in a State, whether called common law or not, is not the common law generally but the law of that State existing by the authority of that State without regard to what it may have been in England or anywhere else * * * .

[T]he authority and only authority is the State, and if that be so, the voice adopted by the State as its own [whether it be of its Legislature or of its Supreme Court] should utter the last word.

Thus the doctrine of *Swift v. Tyson* is, as Mr. Justice Holmes said, "an unconstitutional assumption of powers by courts of the United States which no lapse of time or respectable array of opinion should make us hesitate to correct." In disapproving that doctrine we do not hold unconstitutional § 34 of the Federal Judiciary Act of 1789 or any other Act of Congress. We merely declare that in applying the doctrine this Court and the lower courts have invaded rights which in our opinion are reserved by the Constitution to the several States.

Fourth. The defendant contended that by the common law of Pennsylvania as declared by its highest court the only duty owed to the plaintiff was to refrain from wilful or wanton injury. The plaintiff denied that such is the Pennsylvania law. In support of their respective contentions the parties discussed and cited many decisions of the Supreme Court of the State. The Circuit Court of Appeals ruled that the question of liability is one of general law; and on that ground declined to decide the issue of state law. As we hold this was error, the judgment is reversed and the case remanded to it for further proceedings in conformity with our opinion.

Reversed.

MR. JUSTICE BUTLER, concurring.

* * *

No constitutional question was suggested or argued below or here. And as a general rule, this Court will not consider any question not raised below and presented by the petition. Here it does not decide either of the questions presented but, changing the rule of decision in force since the foundation of the Government, remands the case to be adjudged according to a standard never before deemed permissible.

* * *

While amendments to § 34 have from time to time been suggested, the section stands as originally enacted. Evidently Congress has intended throughout the years that the rule of decision as construed should continue to govern federal courts in trials at common law. The opinion just announced suggests that Mr. Warren's research has established that from the beginning this Court has erroneously construed § 34. But that author's [article] does not purport to be authoritative and was intended to be no more than suggestive. The weight to be given to his discovery has never been discussed at this bar. Nor does the opinion indicate the ground disclosed by the research. In his dissenting opinion in the *Taxicab* case, Mr. Justice Holmes referred to Mr. Warren's work but failed to persuade the Court that "laws" as used in § 34 included varying and possibly ill-considered rulings by the courts of a State on questions of common law. It well may be that, if the Court should now call for argument of counsel on the basis of Mr. Warren's research, it would adhere to the construction it has always put upon § 34. Indeed, the opinion in this case so indicates. For it declares: "If only a question of statutory construction were involved, we should not be prepared to abandon a doctrine so widely applied throughout a century. But the unconstitutionality of the course pursued has now been made clear and compels us to do so." This means that, so far as concerns the rule of decision now condemned, the Judiciary Act of 1789, passed to establish judicial courts to exert the judicial power of the United States, and especially § 34 of that Act as construed, is unconstitutional; that federal courts are now bound to follow decisions of the courts of the State in which the controversies arise; and that Congress is powerless otherwise to ordain. It is hard to foresee the consequences of the radical change so made.

* * *

MR. JUSTICE REED.

I concur in the conclusion reached in this case, in the disapproval of the doctrine of *Swift v. Tyson*, and in the reasoning of the majority opinion except in so far as it relies upon the unconstitutionality of the "course pursued" by the federal courts.

The "doctrine of *Swift v. Tyson*," as I understand it, is that the words "the laws," as used in § 34, line one, of the Federal Judiciary Act of September 24, 1789, do not include in their meaning "the decisions of the local tribunals." Mr. Justice Story, in deciding that point, said: "Undoubtedly, the decisions of the local tribunals upon such subjects are entitled to, and will receive, the most deliberate attention and respect of this Court; but they cannot furnish positive rules, or conclusive authority, by which our own judgments are to be bound up and governed."

To decide the case now before us and to "disapprove" the doctrine of *Swift v. Tyson* requires only that we say that the words "the laws" include in their meaning the decisions of the local tribunals. As the majority opinion shows, by its reference to Mr. Warren's researches and the first quotation from Mr. Justice Holmes, that this Court is now of the view that "laws" includes "decisions," it is unnecessary to go further and declare that the "course pursued" was "unconstitutional," instead of merely erroneous.

The "unconstitutional" course referred to in the majority opinion is apparently the ruling in *Swift v. Tyson* that the supposed omission of Congress to legislate as to the effect of decisions leaves federal courts free to interpret general law for themselves. I am not at all sure whether, in the absence of federal statutory direction, federal courts would be compelled to follow state decisions. There was sufficient doubt about the matter in 1789 to induce the first Congress to legislate. No former opinions of this Court have passed upon it. Mr. Justice Holmes evidently saw nothing "unconstitutional" which required the overruling of *Swift v. Tyson*, for he said in the very opinion quoted by the majority, "I should leave *Swift v. Tyson* undisturbed * * * but I would not allow it to spread the assumed dominion into new fields." *Black & White Taxicab Co. v. Brown & Yellow Taxicab Co.* If the opinion commits this Court to the position that the Congress is without power to declare what rules of substantive law shall govern the federal courts, that conclusion also seems questionable. The line between procedural and substantive law is hazy, but no one doubts federal power over procedure. The Judiciary Article, 3, and the "necessary and proper" clause of Article 1, § 8, may fully authorize legislation, such as this section of the Judiciary Act.

* * *

Notes and Questions

1. If there were no Rules of Decision Act, how would the Court have decided *Erie*? Why? After *Erie*, what does the Rules of Decision Act do?

2. Suppose instead that the Rules of Decision Act made the opposite declaration: that in cases brought in the federal courts, federal law should be applied. Would that have caused any problems?

3. Justice Brandeis tells us that "[e]xcept in matters governed by the Federal Constitution or by Acts of Congress, the law to be applied in any case is the law of the State." A great debate rages around this aspect of *Erie*. The case raises two structural considerations. The first, discussed in most Civil Procedure courses, concerns federalism: the appropriate demarcation of state versus federal power. *Erie* clearly increased state power when it repudiated the legitimacy of federal general common law. The second concerns the allocation of federal power between Congress and the judiciary. Some scholars and judges argue that *Erie* also stands for the idea that the federal courts cannot create common law *even* in areas clearly within the constitutional competence of the federal government, on the theory that separation of powers allows only Congress to create federal law. This view has commanded increasing attention over the last two decades. *See, e.g.,* George D. Brown, *Of Activism and* Erie—*The Implication Doctrine's Implication for the Nature and Role of the Federal Courts,* 69 IOWA L.REV. 617 (1984); Thomas Merrill, *The Common Law Powers of Federal Courts,* 52 U.CHI.L.REV. 1 (1985). Does *Erie* support that idea? Do you think that Justice Brandeis had that in mind?

4. Could Congress have passed a law that would have controlled the result in *Erie*? What part of the Constitution would allow it to do so? If Congress could not, what implications does that have for the separation-of-powers view of *Erie*? Suppose Congress could have legislated but did not. Is that significant in trying to understand *Erie*'s message? What was the Court's view of Congress's power? Should we care?

5. Assuming that the separation-of-powers view is correct, how literally should one take it? In some areas Congress legislates in extraordinarily general terms. For example, the Sherman Antitrust Act merely prohibits "restraint of trade." Over the years, the federal courts have given extensive substantive content to that phrase. Is that practice illegitimate? If so, are there any disadvantages to returning to Congress the burden of defining an unacceptable restraint of trade?

6. Judicial lawmaking considerably antedates the Constitution. The Framers created a new government against the backdrop of hundreds of years of English common law. Is there any evidence that they intended to abandon that system? The new doctrine is rooted in the concept of separation of powers. What precisely does the Constitution say about separation of

powers? What permits or justifies judge-made law?

7. Professor Wilfred Ritz argued strongly that the *Erie* Court and most commentators on the Rules of Decision Act have badly misunderstood Congress's intent. He did not think the Act applied to diversity jurisdiction at all, basing his conclusion upon a variety of factors: the choice of language that refers to state law, the placement of the section in the Judiciary Act of 1789, the congressional debates on the Judiciary Act, and the general structure of state judicial systems at the time.

> [S]ufficient evidence [exists] to demonstrate that Section 34 could not possibly have been intended by Oliver Ellsworth and the other members of the Senate and the House of Representatives in the summer of 1789 to have performed the functions that Professors Warren and Goebel, Justices Story and Brandeis, and the Supreme Court majority in *Erie Railroad Co. v. Tompkins* have attributed to it. It would literally have been unthinkable for the members of the First Congress to have directed national courts sitting in diversity cases to apply the law of the states in which they sat. The necessary conceptual framework was only in the early stages of formation.

> * * *

> Section 34 is a direction to the national courts to apply American law, as distinguished from English law. American law is to be found in the "laws of the several states" viewed as a group of eleven states in 1789, and not viewed separately and individually. It is not a direction to apply the law of a particular state, for if it had been so intended, the section would have referred to the "laws of the respective states."

> * * *

> The section most probably was intended as a temporary measure to provide an applicable American law for national criminal prosecutions, should national criminal prosecutions be brought in the national courts, pending the time that Congress would provide by statute for the definition of national crimes.

> An alternative possibility, although less likely, is that the section was intended as a direction to the national courts to apply American law in all judicial proceedings at common law, both civil and criminal. This application would have included the diversity jurisdiction.

> The one thing that can be said with assurance is that Section 34 was not intended to apply exclusively to diversity proceedings; that it was not intended to direct the application of the law of particular states in diversity proceedings; and that it was not intended to apply to suits in equity. In short, on its historical basis, *Erie* is dead wrong.

WILFRED RITZ, REWRITING THE HISTORY OF THE JUDICIARY ACT OF 1789 79, 148 (1990). It seems unlikely that Professor Ritz's view will overcome the Court's commitment to *Erie* any time soon, considering it took ninety-six years for the Court to overrule *Swift v. Tyson,* 41 U.S. (16 Pet.) 1, 10 L.Ed.

865 (1842), but his work poses interesting questions. If *Erie*'s interpretation of the Rules of Decision Act is incorrect, what law should the federal courts apply in civil litigation? Does Professor Ritz imply that *Swift v. Tyson* was decided correctly? Does *Erie,* even if incorrect about the Rules of Decision Act, have anything to say about the legitimacy of federal common law?

IN PRAISE OF ERIE—AND OF THE NEW FEDERAL COMMON LAW
HENRY J. FRIENDLY
39 N.Y.U.L.REV. 383, 405-07, 421-22 (1964) (footnotes omitted)[a]

[B]y banishing the spurious uniformity of *Swift v. Tyson*—what Mr. Justice Frankfurter was to call "the attractive vision of a uniform body of federal law" but a vision only—and by leaving to the states what ought be left to them, *Erie* led to the emergence of a federal decisional law in areas of national concern that is truly uniform because, under the supremacy clause, it is binding in every forum, and therefore is predictable and useful as its predecessor, more general in subject matter but limited to the federal courts, was not. The clarion yet careful pronouncement of *Erie,* "There is no federal general common law," opened the way to what, for want of a better term, we may call specialized federal common law. I doubt that we sufficiently realize how far this development has gone—let alone where it is likely to go.

Whatever promise Mr. Justice Story's aim to achieve uniformity through the persuasive force of Supreme Court decisions may have had in the fifth decade of the nineteenth century, at least as to commercial law, the prospect had faded long before the fourth decade of the twentieth. The growth of the country multiplied the nation's judicial business far beyond the capacity of any single court to preserve uniformity by the force of example. The trend to making law by statutes struck another blow. Story had excepted from the "general" law which federal courts were free to determine "the positive statutes of the state, and the construction thereof adopted by the local tribunals," as the language of the 34th section [of the Judiciary Act of 1789] rather clearly compelled. Since this exception was held to cover the construction of uniform statutes declaratory of the common law, including the Negotiable Instruments Law, Story's ideal was thereby frustrated in the very area for which it had been most pointedly designed. Finally the increased review of state action as a result of the Fourteenth Amendment and the explosion of federal legislation beginning with Roosevelt I required the Supreme Court to devote the bulk of its time to constitutional law and the interpretation of federal statutes, with the result that, as Judge A.N. Hand noted in 1930, "relatively few cases where rights under the Federal Constitution and statutes are not involved are likely to get beyond the Circuit Court of Appeals" and hence "there is much less chance than

---

[a] Reprinted by permission of New York University Law Review.

formerly of securing or even promoting uniformity through the decisions of the Supreme Court" on issues of "general law." Although the New York Court of Appeals might bow to the superior wisdom of the Supreme Court, speaking through a Mr. Justice Story, on a point of commercial law, one could hardly expect similar deference to a decision of three judges of an intermediate federal court of appeals.

Furthermore, whatever degree of uniformity was attained under *Swift v. Tyson*, reckonability was small. One trouble was that the body of federal "general" law was so meagre. Prediction at the planning stage was nigh impossible since a lawyer could rarely tell whether the issue would be litigated in a state court, where the governing rule was well established, or in a federal court, where it had not been. But the situation was not vastly better even when litigation had begun. On what basis could counsel soundly advise whether the highest court of a state would alter its views on a matter of "general" law to conform to those that had been later expressed by a federal court? In the converse situation, where the litigation was in federal court, how could he fairly prophesy, unless the Supreme Court had already spoken, whether the court would strike out for itself or follow the local view under the "deference" often accorded state decisions?

There was, to be sure, no logical contradiction between federal judges being free to make their own determinations of "general" common law for use only in the federal courts, and also "developing a uniform body of federal decisional rules" which because of their subject are binding in all courts. But the coincidence of the death of the first doctrine and the growth of the second would itself suggest that *Swift v. Tyson* had retarded the development of federal decisional law of the latter type; and other considerations strongly reinforce the inference from chronology alone. Since most cases relating to federal matters were in the federal courts and involved "general" law, the familiar rule of *Swift v. Tyson* usually gave federal judges all the freedom they required in pre-*Erie* days and made it unnecessary for them to consider a more esoteric source of power. *Per contra*, in the rare instance where the issue in such a case was of "local" law in the *Swift v. Tyson* sense, as when the United States was asserting proprietary rights, the Supreme Court seems to have been content to let state law prevail as a sort of quid pro quo, without inquiring whether this was a necessary choice or only a desirable one in the particular case. By focusing judicial attention on the nature of the right being enforced, *Erie* caused the principle of a specialized federal common law, binding in all courts because of its source, to develop within a quarter century into a powerful unifying force. Just as federal courts now conform to state decisions on issues properly for the states, state courts must conform to federal decisions in areas where Congress, acting within powers granted to it, has manifested, be it ever so lightly, an intention to that end. A psychiatrist might say that, having rid itself of subconscious feelings of guilt of federal poaching on state preserves, the Supreme Court became freer to insist on deference to federal decisions by the states where deference was due. As a perceptive judge remarked only three years after *Erie*, "Unto each Caesar, State or federal, is thus rendered that which properly belongs to that particular Caesar, supreme in its distinctive field."

* * *

So, as it seems to me, the Supreme Court in the years since *Erie*, has been forging a new centripetal tool incalculably useful to our federal system. It has employed a variety of techniques—spontaneous generation as in the cases of government contracts or interstate controversies, implication of a private federal cause of action from a statute providing other sanctions, construing a jurisdictional grant as a command to fashion federal law, and the normal judicial filling of statutory interstices. * * * Professor Gilmore thinks the Court has taken these giant steps "almost unconsciously." I doubt that, but it scarcely matters. What does matter is that a not insignificant part of Story's "general law" is already under the sway of the new type of federal common law and that many other parts can readily be brought there if Congress thinks this desirable. We might * * * consider that the Hegelian dialectic has been here at work—with *Swift v. Tyson* the thesis, *Erie* the antithesis, and the new federal common law the synthesis. In less grandiose terms, we can see in this development the thrust and counterthrust so often encountered in the legal as well as the political history of a country wisely addicted to the method of trial and error.

The complementary concepts—that federal courts must follow state decisions on matters of substantive law appropriately cognizable by the states whereas state courts must follow federal decisions on subjects within national legislative power where Congress has so directed—seem so beautifully simple, and so simply beautiful, that we must wonder why a century and a half were needed to discover them, and must wonder even more why anyone should want to shy away once the discovery was made. We may not yet have achieved the best of all possible worlds with respect to the relationship between state and federal law. But the combination of *Erie* with *Clearfield* and *Lincoln Mills* has brought us to a far, far better one than we have ever known before. It thus seems fitting, twenty-five years after the *Erie* decision, to lay this tribute at the feet of Mr. Justice Brandeis and his colleagues, and of the builders, most of them happily still with us, of the new federal common law.

C.   CHOOSING THE APPLICABLE LAW AND DETERMINING ITS CONTENT—FEDERAL INTERESTS OR LACK THEREOF

1. *Spontaneous Generation*

CLEARFIELD TRUST CO. v. UNITED STATES
Supreme Court of the United States, 1943.
318 U.S. 363, 63 S.Ct. 573, 87 L.Ed. 838.

MR. JUSTICE DOUGLAS delivered the opinion of the Court.

On April 28, 1936, a check was drawn on the Treasurer of the United States through the Federal Reserve Bank of Philadelphia to the order of Clair A. Barner in the amount of $24.20. It was dated at Harrisburg, Pennsylvania, and was drawn for services rendered by Barner to the Works Progress Administration. The check was placed in the mail addressed to Barner at his address in Mackeyville, Pa. Barner never received the check. Some unknown person obtained it in a mysterious manner and presented it to the J.C. Penney Co. store in Clearfield, Pa., representing that he was the payee and identifying himself to the satisfaction of the employees of J.C. Penney Co. He endorsed the check in the name of Barner and transferred it to J.C. Penney Co. in exchange for cash and merchandise. Barner never authorized the endorsement nor participated in the proceeds of the check. J.C. Penney Co. endorsed the check over to the Clearfield Trust Co. which accepted it as agent for the purpose of collection and endorsed it as follows: "Pay to the order of Federal Reserve Bank of Philadelphia, Prior Endorsements Guaranteed." Clearfield Trust Co. collected the check from the United States through the Federal Reserve Bank of Philadelphia and paid the full amount thereof to J.C. Penney Co. Neither the Clearfield Trust Co. nor J.C. Penney Co. had any knowledge or suspicion of the forgery. Each acted in good faith. On or before May 10, 1936, Barner advised the timekeeper and the foreman of the W.P.A. project on which he was employed that he had not received the check in question. This information was duly communicated to other agents of the United States and on November 30, 1936, Barner executed an affidavit alleging that the endorsement of his name on the check was a forgery. No notice was given the Clearfield Trust Co. or J.C. Penney Co. of the forgery until January 12, 1937, at which time the Clearfield Trust Co. was notified. The first notice received by Clearfield Trust Co. that the United States was asking reimbursement was on August 31, 1937.

This suit was instituted in 1939 by the United States against the Clearfield Trust Co. * * *. The cause of action was based on the express guaranty of prior endorsements made by the Clearfield Trust Co. J.C. Penney Co. intervened as a defendant. The case was heard on complaint, answer and stipulation of facts. The District Court held that the rights of the parties were to be determined by the law of Pennsylvania and that since the United States unreasonably delayed in giving notice of the forgery to the Clearfield Trust Co., it was barred from recovery. It accordingly dismissed the complaint. On appeal the Circuit Court of Appeals reversed. * * *

We agree with the Circuit Court of Appeals that the rule of *Erie R. Co. v. Tompkins* does not apply to this action. The rights and duties of the United States on commercial paper which it issues are governed by federal rather than local law. When the United States disburses its funds or pays its debts, it is exercising a constitutional function or power. This check was issued for services performed under the Federal Emergency Relief Act of 1935. The authority to issue the check had its origin in the Constitution and the statutes of the United States and was in no way dependent on the laws of Pennsylvania or of any other state. The duties imposed upon the United States and the rights acquired by it as a result of the issuance find their roots in the same federal sources. In absence of an applicable Act of Congress it is for the federal courts to fashion the governing rule of law according to their own standards. * * *

In our choice of the applicable federal rule we have occasionally selected state law. But reasons which may make state law at times the appropriate federal rule are singularly inappropriate here. The issuance of commercial paper by the United States is on a vast scale and transactions in that paper from issuance to payment will commonly occur in several states. The application of state law, even without the conflict of laws rules of the forum, would subject the rights and duties of the United States to exceptional uncertainty. It would lead to great diversity in results by making identical transactions subject to the vagaries of the laws of the several states. The desirability of a uniform rule is plain. And while the federal law merchant, developed for about a century under the regime of *Swift v. Tyson* represented general commercial law rather than a choice of a federal rule designed to protect a federal right, it nevertheless stands as a convenient source of reference for fashioning federal rules applicable to these federal questions.

United States v. National Exchange Bank falls in that category. The Court held that the United States could recover as drawee from one who presented for payment a pension check on which the name of the payee had been forged, in spite of a protracted delay on the part of the United States in giving notice of the forgery. * * * The drawee, whether it be the United States or another, is not chargeable with the knowledge of the signature of the payee.

The *National Exchange Bank* case went no further than to hold that prompt notice of the discovery of the forgery was not a condition precedent to suit. It did not reach the question whether lack of prompt notice might be a defense. We think it may. If it is shown that the drawee on learning of the forgery did not give prompt notice of it and that damage resulted, recovery by the drawee is barred. The fact that the drawee is the United States and the laches those of its employees are not material. The United States as drawee of commercial paper stands in no different light than any other drawee. As stated in *United States v. National Exchange Bank*, "The United States does business on business terms." It is not excepted from the general rules governing the rights and duties of drawees "by the largeness of its dealings and its having to employ agents to do what if done by a principal in person would leave no room for doubt." But the damage occasioned by the delay must be established and not left to conjecture. Cases such as *Market St. Title & Trust Co. v. Chelten Trust Co.* [a Pennsylvania Supreme Court case] place the burden on the drawee of giving prompt notice of the forgery—injury to the defendant being presumed by the mere fact of delay. But we do not think that he who accepts a forged signature of a payee deserves that preferred treatment. It is his neglect or error in accepting the forger's signature which occasions the loss. He should be allowed to shift that loss to the drawee only on a clear showing that the drawee's delay in notifying him of the forgery caused him damage. No such damage has been shown by Clearfield Trust Co. who so far as appears can still recover from J.C. Penney Co. The only showing on the part of the latter is contained in the stipulation to the effect that if a check cashed for a customer is returned unpaid or for reclamation a short time after the date on which it is cashed, the employees can often locate the person who cashed it. It is further stipulated that when J.C. Penney Co. was notified of the forgery in the present case none of its employees was able to remember anything about the transaction or check in question. The inference is that the more prompt the notice the more likely the detection of the forger. But that falls short of a showing that the delay caused a manifest loss. It is but another way of saying that mere delay is enough.

Affirmed.

Notes and Questions

1. On Justice Douglas's reasoning, does federal common law apply whenever the United States is a party and is exercising "a constitutional function"? What cases to which the United States is a party would that formulation exclude from the ambit of federal common law?

2. Should federal common law govern all or most cases in which the federal government is a party?

3. Why should federalism entitle the United States to have federal law applied? What is the constitutional authority upon which the Court relies? Resort to the Supremacy Clause begs the questions. That Clause by its terms applies when there is a clash between federal and state law; here the issue is whether there should be any federal law in the first place.

4. If federal common law applies whenever the United States is a party and exercising a constitutional function, why does the Court bother to discuss the dominant federal interest in uniformity? If the rule calling for fed-

eral common law is a *per se* rule, interest analysis should be irrelevant. If the rule is not absolute, when might the Court consider applying state law in cases to which the United States is a party?

5. How great is the federal interest in uniformity in *Clearfield*? If it is as palpable as the Court suggests, why did Congress not pass a statute embodying a uniform rule? Congress's failure to act poses some interesting problems. Suppose Congress considered such a rule, but the bill failed to pass. Should that affect the result in *Clearfield*? In connection with that problem, consider *Boyle v. United Technologies* at page 406.

6. In *Bank of America National Trust & Savings Association v. Parnell*, 352 U.S. 29, 77 S.Ct. 119, 1 L.Ed.2d 93 (1956), the United States had issued an early call for redemption of some bonds. Bank of America held some bonds that disappeared the day after the call. Four years later, Parnell cashed them at another bank. Bank of America brought a diversity action for conversion against the individuals and banks involved in the presentment and pay-out. The critical issue was whether state or federal law should determine who had the burden of proof on the issue of respondents' good faith in presenting the bonds. The trial court charged the state rule, placing the burden on the presenters to "show[ ] that they acted innocently, honestly, and in good faith * * * ." The Third Circuit reversed in a four-to-three en banc decision, holding that *Clearfield* compelled use of a federal rule requiring Bank of America to show the presenters' lack of good faith.

The Supreme Court reversed, holding that federal law determined whether the bonds were overdue when presented but that state law prescribed the locus of the burden of proof on the issue of good faith in an action between private parties that did not affect the rights and duties of the United States. Justice Frankfurter, writing for the seven-to-two majority, sounded almost miffed at the Third Circuit's handling of the case, noting that "[t]he Court of Appeals misconceived the nature of this litigation in holding that the *Clearfield Trust* case controlled. * * * The basis for this decision was stated with unclouded explicitness * * * ." He then quoted *Clearfield*'s discussion of the vast scale of United States' commercial paper operations and the uncertainty inherent in governing rights and obligations of the United States by state law. The Court allowed that a suit between private parties might nonetheless implicate federal interests properly governed by federal law, but elaborated only by saying that "[f]ederal law of course governs the interpretation of the nature of the rights and obligations created by the Government bonds themselves." Justices Black and Douglas dissented, believing the distinction between suits on government paper by the government versus by private parties to be untenable.

Suppose the majority agreed with the dissenters about the utility of a uniform rule in *Parnell*. Are there any impediments to the Court creating such a rule? Is there federal competence? If not, of course, the matter is simple, but if there is, consider the institutional legitimacy of the Court creating substantive rules in an area that Congress has not entered. Even if Justices Black and Douglas are correct about the difficulties caused by using state law, can one argue that state law must nonetheless govern? What might justify or compel such a position?

7. Lest one think that the United States being a party in an action involving a federal commercial transaction is sufficient to command the use of federal law for all issues, consider *United States v. Yazell*, 382 U.S. 341, 86 S.Ct. 500, 15 L.Ed.2d 404 (1966), in which the United States tried to recoup a Small Business Administration loan made to the Yazells. Texas then had a coverture law shielding a married woman's separate property from contractual alienation in the absence of a court order removing her disability to contract. The government argued that there was a federal interest in collecting the amount due and that such an interest justified having a federal common law rule apply to Mrs. Yazell's capacity to contract.

The Court disagreed. Justice Fortas emphasized that the SBA negotiated all loans individually and had hired local counsel to assist with the Yazells' loan. He noted that the SBA made no attempt to have Mrs. Yazell's disability removed and interpreted its inaction as willingness to operate under the restrictions of Texas law. He found no need for a uniform rule given the individual negotiation of loan contracts and then discussed federalism concerns:

> We do not here consider the question of the constitutional power of the Congress to override state law in these circumstances by direct legislation or by appropriate authorization to an administrative agency coupled with suitable implementing action by the agency. We decide only that this Court, in the absence of specific congressional action, should not decree in this situation that implementation of federal interests requires overriding the particular state rule involved here. Both theory and the precedents of this Court teach us solicitude for state interests, particularly in the field of family and family-property arrangements. They should be overridden by the federal courts only where clear and substantial interests of the National Government, which cannot be served consistently with respect for such state interests, will suffer major damage if the state law is applied.

Notwithstanding that obvious bow to state interests, the Court waffled on what it was actually doing:

> Generally, in the cases applying state law to limit or condition the enforcement of a federal right, the Court has insisted that the state law is being "adopted" as the federal rule. Even so, it has carefully pointed out that this theory would make it possible to "adopt," as the operative "federal" law, differing laws in the different States, depending upon the State where the relevant transaction takes place.

> Although it is unnecessary to decide in the present case whether the Texas law of coverture should apply *ex proprio vigore*—on the theory that the contract here was made pursuant and subject to this provision of state law—or by "adoption" as a federal principle, it is clear that the state rule should govern.

a) Has Congress the authority to pass a statute to govern federal loan transactions? The Court suggested in a footnote that it could. If so, is it significant that Congress had not done so? If not, under what theory is there any federal power to make common law?

b) *Yazell* relied on 28 U.S.C.A. § 1345 for subject matter jurisdiction. That statute confers district court jurisdiction for any action in which the United States is a plaintiff. Does its existence shed any light on the choice-of-law decision? Perhaps Congress intended to signify a federal interest in the application (and development, if necessary) of federal law. But if that is what Congress intended, why did it not say so? Moreover, the jurisdiction conferred by § 1345 is not exclusive. That, too, may suggest either congressional indifference or inattention to the choice-of-law problem.

c) The majority opinion offered an early overview of the convergence of the federalism and separation-of-powers branches of the *Erie* doctrine. Justice Fortas first contrasted Congress's constitutional power to override state concerns with the federal courts' far more limited power to subordinate state to federal interests. He noted that the courts can act only when absolutely necessary to preserve national interests. Congress's authority to act is in Article I, § 8, and Article VI, § 2 of the Constitution. Should the Court have identified the source of authority for the federal courts?

Justice Fortas also emphasized the federalism reasons for allowing state law to govern. If federal law is to displace state law, is it more legitimate for Congress or the federal courts to direct it? Should the criteria that each body might use to make such decisions be different? Why? If you conclude that federal displacement of state law is exclusively or predominantly within Congress's purview, then is the federal courts' role in this respect limited to supremacy inquiries?

d) The majority noted that in cases like *Yazell*, state law generally applies. The Court went on to specify that ordinarily it seems to apply after adoption as federal common law, but concluded with the observation that it was unnecessary to specify why state law was being used. Was it? When would it be necessary, or does the Court mean to say that it is always unnecessary to know whether state law applies because it must or because its content has been incorporated into federal common law? What difference does it make anyway?

8. On occasion, the Court has also recognized the need for federal common law even in diversity cases. *Banco Nacional de Cuba v. Sabbatino,* 376 U.S. 398, 84 S.Ct. 923, 11 L.Ed.2d 804 (1964), arose out of what should have been a simple sugar sale between private entities. The seller conveyed the sugar to the buyer, who loaded it on a ship in Cuba. The Cuban government expropriated the sugar because United States nationals predominantly owned the corporate seller, but allowed the ship to sail when the seller agreed to remit the purchase price to Banco Nacional's predecessor in interest. Demand for payment was duly made in New York. The buyer, rather than remitting the purchase price to Banco Nacional, gave it to Sabbatino, a temporary receiver of the seller's assets in New York. Banco Nacional brought a diversity action against the receiver and the buyer in the Southern District of New York.

The issue was the applicability of the act-of-state doctrine, which prohibits the courts of one country from questioning the legitimacy of acts of a nation within its own territory. The doctrine would have compelled the court to honor Cuba's claim to the proceeds, notwithstanding the expropriation. Under New York's view of international law the seller was entitled to the proceeds. The district and circuit courts followed New York law, but the Supreme Court reversed.

The Court explained that it was necessary for uniform federal law to govern foreign relations cases. Thus, the states could not be left free to interpret international law, nor could federal courts sitting in diversity apply state variants.[5] The Court then ruled that the act of state doctrine applied. Although Congress quickly passed a law establishing a different federal view of the doctrine's applicability, *Sabbatino* stands unchallenged for the proposition that federal common law governs the law of foreign relations in the absence of a federal statute.

Note that the Court's decision compelled use of federal law in *Sabbatino*, a diversity case, notwithstanding *Erie*. *Sabbatino* is a reminder that one cannot answer the choice-of-law inquiry based merely on the type of federal subject matter jurisdiction that the plaintiff invokes. The Court opined that it was highly unlikely that the *Erie* Court considered the sort of situation *Sabbatino* presented. Indeed, *Erie* is distinguishable on the basis of the *Erie* Court's approach. Justice Brandeis stated that there was no federal competence to prescribe the rule of tort law that would govern *Erie*. In *Sabbatino*, by contrast, there is clearly federal competence, both in Congress's power to regulate international commerce, art. I, § 8, cl. 3, and in the President's treaty power, art. II, § 2, cl. 2.

9. Intuitively, preemption and federal common law do not seem linked; one is likely instead to get caught up in the details of the particular competing schemes of substantive law. In fact, Congress rarely specifies that legislation preempts state law.[6] For example, the Court has found preemption in

---

[5] This position was far from a mere recognition at the Supreme Court level of circumstances obtaining in the lower courts. Although eminent commentators had argued against viewing international law as state law, *see, e.g.,* Philip C. Jessup, *The Doctrine of Erie Railroad v. Tompkins Applied to International Law,* 33 AM.J.INT.L. 740 (1939), "[f]ollowing *Erie,* courts assumed that international law was part of state common law and that in diversity cases, federal courts were bound to apply international law as determined by the state courts." Alfred T. Goodwin, *International Law in the Federal Courts,* 20 CAL.W.INT'L.L.J. 157, 161 (1990) (citing *Bergman v. De Sieyes,* 170 F.2d 360, 361 (2d Cir.1948)). In the cited case, Judge Learned Hand observed:

> [S]ince the defendant was served while the cause was in the state court, the law of New York determines its validity, and, although the courts of that state look to international law as a source of New York law, their interpretation of international law is controlling upon us, and we are to follow them so far as they have declared themselves."

[6] Occasionally Congress does specify preemption. *See, e.g.,* Employees Retirement Income Security Act, 29 U.S.C.A. § 41144 (1988) (explicitly preempting state regulation of ERISA-covered employee benefit plans); Cigarette Labeling and Advertising Act, 15 U.S.C.A. § 1334 (1988) (preempting state law cigarette labeling requirements and other state law requirements concerning cigarettes).

the areas of alien registration,[7] anti-subversive legislation,[8] and food labeling.[9] In such circumstances, the Court is making important decisions about the scope of federal law.

The law of preemption is itself federal, and the Supreme Court has created most of it. The Court has identified three types of preemption: explicit, by congressional occupation of the field, and by conflict between state and federal law.[10] In the latter two categories, the federal law of preemption is judge-made, and the preemption inquiry involves balancing sensitive matters of federal and state concern.

Does Congress's occasionally specifying preemption suggest its intent that federal law *not* preempt state law in other circumstances? If so, the Court's actions fly in the face of congressional intent, raising severe separation-of-powers problems. Even if not, should the Court or the legislature decide whether federal law preempts state law in any particular situation?

The courts have recognized the similarity of the preemption inquiry to other areas of common law.[11] "To determine whether a provision of the

---

[7] Hines v. Davidowitz, 312 U.S. 52, 61 S.Ct. 399, 85 L.Ed. 581 (1941). *Hines* ruled that alien registration is so connected with foreign policy as to preclude state registration requirements. The test was whether the state law might impede congressional objectives.

[8] Pennsylvania v. Nelson, 350 U.S. 497, 76 S.Ct. 477, 100 L.Ed. 640 (1956).

[9] Jones v. Rath Packing Co., 430 U.S. 519, 97 S.Ct. 1305, 51 L.Ed.2d 604 (1977). *Jones* held that the states cannot have a food labeling policy more restrictive than that of the federal government.

[10] Northwest Cent. Pipeline Corp. v. State Corp. Comm'n, 489 U.S. 493, 509, 109 S.Ct. 1262, 1273, 103 L.Ed.2d 509, 527 (1989); Pacific Gas & Elec. Co. v. State Energy Resources Conservation & Dev. Comm'n, 461 U.S. 190, 203-04, 103 S.Ct. 1713, 1722, 75 L.Ed.2d 752, 765 (1983).

[11] In Pennsylvania v. Nelson, 350 U.S. 497, 502, 504-05, 76 S.Ct. 477, 480-82, 100 L.Ed. 640, 652-54 (1956), Chief Justice Warren's opinion for the Court articulated three criteria for the courts to use in deciding whether preemption was appropriate:

> First, "[t]he scheme of federal regulation [is] so pervasive as to make reasonable the inference that Congress left no room for the States to supplement it."

> * * *

> Second, the federal statutes "touch a field in which the federal interest is so dominant that the federal system [must] be assumed to preclude enforcement of state laws on the same subject."

> * * *

> Third, enforcement of state * * * acts presents a serious danger of conflict with the administration of the federal program.

This formulation resembles the three-part inquiry in *United States v. Kimbell Foods, Inc.* (following) that determines whether the courts should get the content of federal common law by reference to state law or from some other source. In *Nelson*, the emphasis seems much more on the federal interest than on the state's, but the pendulum may now be swinging the other way. In an echo of its growing reluctance to create common law generally, the Burger Court announced in New York State Dept. of Soc. Serv. v. Dublino, 413 U.S. 405, 93 S.Ct. 2507, 37 L.Ed.2d 688 (1973), its presumption of state competence to legislate in the absence of some clear manifestation from Congress that it intends to preempt

bankruptcy code empowers the federal courts to create federal common law, we apply much the same analysis used to decide whether preemption is necessary." *Justice v. Valley National Bank,* 849 F.2d 1078, 1087 (8th Cir.1988) (citation omitted). The identity, of course, goes both ways. Accordingly, preemption raises the same institutional problems of federalism and separation of powers.

10. The federal courts were also active with respect to determining limitations periods for federal rights of action without congressionally specified limits until Congress created a default federal limitations provision in 28 U.S.C. § 1658 (1990) for federal claims created after the date of § 1658 for which Congress did not otherwise provide a limitation. That law, however, is more interstitial than the areas discussed above. The note on interstitial federal common law at page 499 focuses on this aspect of creating federal common law.

UNITED STATES v. KIMBELL FOODS, INC.
Supreme Court of the United States, 1979.
440 U.S. 715, 99 S.Ct. 1448, 59 L.Ed.2d 711.

MR. JUSTICE MARSHALL delivered the opinion of the Court.

We granted certiorari in these cases to determine whether contractual liens arising from certain federal loan programs take precedence over private liens, in the absence of a federal statute setting priorities. To resolve this question, we must decide first whether federal or state law governs the controversies; and second, if federal law applies, whether this Court should fashion a uniform priority rule or incorporate state commercial law. We conclude that the source of law is federal, but that a national rule is unnecessary to protect the federal interests underlying the loan programs. Accordingly, we adopt state law as the appropriate federal rule for establishing the relative priority of these competing federal and private liens.

I

A

No. 77-1359 involves two contractual security interests in the personal property of O.K. Super Markets, Inc. Both interests were perfected pursuant to Texas' Uniform Commercial Code (UCC). The United States' lien secures a loan guaranteed by the Small Business Administration (SBA). The private lien, which arises from security agreements that preceded the federal guarantee, secures advances respondent made after the federal guarantee.

In 1968, O.K. Super Markets borrowed $27,000 from Kimbell Foods, Inc. (Kimbell), a grocery wholesaler. Two security agreements identified the supermarket's equipment and merchandise as collateral. The

---

state action. Note the parallel with the Court's treatment of implied-right-of-action cases arising under federal statutes. *See infra* pages 455-479.

agreements also contained a standard "dragnet" clause providing that this collateral would secure future advances from Kimbell to O.K. Super Markets. Kimbell properly perfected its security interests by filing financing statements with the Texas Secretary of State according to Texas law.

In February 1969, O.K. Super Markets obtained a $300,000 loan from Republic National Bank of Dallas (Republic). The bank accepted as security the same property specified in Kimbell's 1968 agreements, and filed a financing statement with the Texas Secretary of State to perfect its security interest. The SBA guaranteed 90% of this loan under the Small Business Act, which authorizes such assistance but, with one exception, does not specify priority rules to govern the SBA's security interests.

O.K. Super Markets used the Republic loan proceeds to satisfy the remainder of the 1968 obligation and to discharge an indebtedness for inventory purchased from Kimbell on open account. Kimbell continued credit sales to O.K. Super Markets until the balance due reached $18,258.57 on January 15, 1971. Thereupon, Kimbell initiated state proceedings against O.K. Super Markets to recover this inventory debt.

Shortly before Kimbell filed suit, O.K. Super Markets had defaulted on the SBA-guaranteed loan. Republic assigned its security interest to the SBA in late December 1970, and recorded the assignment with Texas authorities on January 21, 1971. The United States then honored its guarantee and paid Republic $252,331.93 (90% of the outstanding indebtedness) on February 3, 1971. That same day, O.K. Super Markets, with the approval of its creditors, sold its equipment and inventory and placed the proceeds in escrow pending resolution of the competing claims to the funds. Approximately one year later, the state court entered judgment against O.K. Super Markets, and awarded Kimbell $24,445.37, representing the inventory debt, plus interest and attorney's fees.

Kimbell thereafter brought the instant action to foreclose on its lien, claiming that its security interest in the escrow fund was superior to the SBA's. The District Court held for the Government. On determining that federal law controlled the controversy, the court applied principles developed by this Court to afford federal statutory tax liens special priority over state and private liens where the governing statute does not specify priorities. Under these rules, the lien "first in time" is "first in right." However, to be considered first in time, the nonfederal lien must be "choate," that is, sufficiently specific, when the federal lien arises. A state-created lien is not choate until the "identity of the lienor, the property subject to the lien, and the amount of the lien are established." Failure to meet any one of these conditions forecloses priority over the federal lien, even if under state law the nonfederal lien was enforceable for all purposes when the federal lien arose.

Because Kimbell did not reduce its lien to judgment until February

1972, and the federal lien had been created either in 1969, when Republic filed its financing statement, or in 1971, when Republic recorded its assignment, the District Court concluded that respondent's lien was inchoate when the federal lien arose. Alternatively, the court held that even under state law, the SBA lien was superior to Kimbell's claim because the future advance clauses in the 1968 agreements were not intended to secure the debts arising from O.K. Super Market's subsequent inventory purchases.

The Court of Appeals reversed. It agreed that federal law governs the rights of the United States under its SBA loan program and that the "first in time, first in right" priority principle should control the competing claims. However, the court refused to extend the choateness rule to situations in which the Federal Government was not an involuntary creditor of tax delinquents, but rather a voluntary commercial lender. Instead, it fashioned a new federal rule for determining which lien was first in time, and concluded that "in the context of competing state security interests arising under the U.C.C.," the first to meet UCC perfection requirements achieved priority.[9]

The Court of Appeals then considered which lien qualified as first perfected. Disagreeing with the District Court, the court determined that, under Texas law, the 1968 security agreements covered Kimbell's future advances, and that the liens securing those advances dated from the filing of the security agreements before the federal lien arose. But the Court of Appeals did not adopt Texas law. Rather, it proceeded to decide whether the future advances should receive the same treatment under federal common law. After surveying three possible approaches,[10] the court held that Kimbell's future advances dated back to the 1968 agreements, and therefore took precedence over Republic's 1969 loan.

B

At issue in No. 77-1644 is whether a federal contractual security interest in a tractor is superior to a subsequent repairman's lien in the same property. From 1970 to 1972, Ralph Bridges obtained several loans from the Farmers Home Administration (FHA), under the Consolidated Farmers Home Administration Act of 1961. Like the Small Business Act, this statute does not establish rules of priority. To secure the FHA loans, the agency obtained a security interest in Bridges' crops and

---

[9] In so holding, the Court of Appeals refused to formulate a federal doctrine of general applicability, "leav[ing] for another day" questions involving the priority of other nonfederal liens, such as state tax and mechanic's liens.

[10] One approach afforded priority to liens intervening between execution of a security agreement covering future advances and extension of those advances. Another gave priority only to future advances made before the advancing creditor received actual notice of an intervening lien, while a third rule afforded priority regardless of actual notice. The court rejected the first option and found that Kimbell would prevail under either of the other two since it did not have notice of the SBA guarantee.

farm equipment, which it perfected by filing a standard FHA financing statement with Georgia officials on February 2, 1972. Bridges subsequently took his tractor to respondent Crittenden for repairs on numerous occasions, accumulating unpaid repair bills of over $1,600. On December 21, 1973, Bridges again had respondent repair the tractor, at a cost of $543.81. When Bridges could not pay the balance of $2,151.28, respondent retained the tractor and acquired a lien therein under Georgia law.

On May 1, 1975, after Bridges had filed for bankruptcy and had been discharged from his debts,[12] the United States instituted this action against Crittenden to obtain possession of the tractor. The District Court rejected the Government's claim that the FHA's security interest was superior to respondent's, and granted summary judgment for respondent on alternative grounds. First, it held that the agency had not properly perfected its security interest because the financing statement inadequately described the collateral. Second, it found that even if the description were sufficient, both federal and state law accorded priority to respondent's lien.

The Court of Appeals affirmed in part and reversed in part. It first ruled that "the rights and liabilities of the parties to a suit arising from FHA loan transactions must, under the rationale of the *Clearfield Trust* doctrine, be determined with reference to federal law." In fashioning a federal rule for assessing the sufficiency of the FHA's financing statement, the court elected to follow the Model UCC rather than to incorporate Georgia law. And, it determined that the description of the collateral was adequate under the Model UCC to perfect the FHA's security interest.

The Court of Appeals then addressed the priority question and concluded that neither state law nor the first-in-time, first-in-right and choateness doctrines were appropriate to resolve the conflicting claims. In their place, the court devised a special "federal commercial law rule," using the Model UCC and the Tax Lien Act of 1966 as guides. This rule would give priority to repairman's liens over the Government's previously perfected consensual security interests when the repairman continuously possesses the property from the time his lien arises. Applying its rule, the Court of Appeals concluded that Crittenden's lien for only the final $543.81 repair bill took precedence over the FHA's security interest.

II

This Court has consistently held that federal law governs questions involving the rights of the United States arising under nationwide fed-

---

[12] Bridges' bankruptcy did not affect the relative priority of the Government and respondent. The priority rights afforded the United States under § 64a of the Bankruptcy Act do not defeat valid pre-existing liens.

eral programs. As the Court explained in *Clearfield Trust Co. v. United States*:

> When the United States disburses its funds or pays its debts, it is exercising a constitutional function or power * * *. The authority [to do so] had its origin in the Constitution and the statutes of the United States and was in no way dependent on the laws [of any State]. The duties imposed upon the United States and the rights acquired by it * * * find their roots in the same federal sources. In absence of an applicable Act of Congress it is for the federal courts to fashion the governing rule of law according to their own standards. [Citations and footnote omitted.]

Guided by these principles, we think it clear that the priority of liens stemming from federal lending programs must be determined with reference to federal law. The SBA and FHA unquestionably perform federal functions within the meaning of *Clearfield*. Since the agencies derive their authority to effectuate loan transactions from specific Acts of Congress passed in the exercise of a "constitutional function or power," their rights, as well, should derive from a federal source. When Government activities "aris[e] from and bea[r] heavily upon a federal * * * program," the Constitution and Acts of Congress " 'require' otherwise than that state law govern of its own force." In such contexts, federal interests are sufficiently implicated to warrant the protection of federal law.

That the statutes authorizing these federal lending programs do not specify the appropriate rule of decision in no way limits the reach of federal law. It is precisely when Congress has not spoken " 'in an area comprising issues substantially related to an established program of government operation,' " that *Clearfield* directs federal courts to fill the interstices of federal legislation "according to their own standards."

Federal law therefore controls the Government's priority rights. The more difficult task, to which we turn, is giving content to this federal rule.

III

Controversies directly affecting the operations of federal programs, although governed by federal law, do not inevitably require resort to uniform federal rules. Whether to adopt state law or to fashion a nationwide federal rule is a matter of judicial policy "dependent upon a variety of considerations always relevant to the nature of the specific governmental interests and to the effects upon them of applying state law."[21]

---

[21] As explained by one commentator:

> Whether state law is to be incorporated as a matter of federal common law * * * involves the * * * problem of the relationship of a particular issue to a going federal program. The question of judicial incorporation can only arise in an area

Undoubtedly, federal programs that "by their nature are and must be uniform in character throughout the Nation" necessitate formulation of controlling federal rules. Conversely, when there is little need for a nationally uniform body of law, state law may be incorporated as the federal rule of decision. Apart from considerations of uniformity, we must also determine whether application of state law would frustrate specific objectives of the federal programs. If so, we must fashion special rules solicitous of those federal interests. Finally, our choice-of-law inquiry must consider the extent to which application of a federal rule would disrupt commercial relationships predicated on state law.

The Government argues that effective administration of its lending programs requires uniform federal rules of priority. It contends further that resort to any rules other than first in time, first in right and choateness would conflict with protectionist fiscal policies underlying the programs. We are unpersuaded that, in the circumstances presented here, nationwide standards favoring claims of the United States are necessary to ease program administration or to safeguard the Federal Treasury from defaulting debtors. Because the state commercial codes "furnish convenient solutions in no way inconsistent with adequate protection of the federal interest[s]," we decline to override intricate state laws of general applicability on which private creditors base their daily commercial transactions.

A

Incorporating state law to determine the rights of the United States as against private creditors would in no way hinder administration of the SBA and FHA loan programs. In *United States v. Yazell*, this Court rejected the argument, similar to the Government's here, that a need for uniformity precluded application of state coverture rules to an SBA loan contract. Because SBA operations were "specifically and in great detail adapted to state law," the federal interest in supplanting "important and carefully evolved state arrangements designed to serve multiple purposes" was minimal. Our conclusion that compliance with state law would produce no hardship on the agency was also based on the SBA's practice of "individually negotiat[ing] in painfully particularized detail" each loan transaction. These observations apply with equal force here and compel us again to reject generalized pleas for uniformity as substitutes for concrete evidence that adopting state law would adversely affect administration of the federal programs.

* * * FHA regulations expressly incorporate state law. They mandate compliance with state procedures for perfecting and maintaining valid security interests, and highlight those rules that differ from State to State. To ensure that employees are aware of new developments, the

---

which is sufficiently close to a national operation to establish competence in the federal courts to choose the governing law, and yet not so close as clearly to require the application of a single nationwide rule of substance.

FHA also issues "State supplements" to "reflect any State statutory changes in its version of the UCC." Contrary to the Government's claim that the FHA complies only with state procedural rules, the agency's reliance on state law extends to substantive requirements as well. Indeed, applicable regulations suggest that state rules determine the priority of FHA liens when federal statutes or agency regulations are not controlling.

Thus, the agencies' own operating practices belie their assertion that a federal rule of priority is needed to avoid the administrative burdens created by disparate state commercial rules.[28] The programs already conform to each State's commercial standards. By using local lending offices and employees who are familiar with the law of their respective localities, the agencies function effectively without uniform procedures and legal rules.

Nevertheless, the Government maintains that requiring the agencies to assess security arrangements under local law would dictate close scrutiny of each transaction and thereby impede expeditious processing of loans. We disagree. Choosing responsible debtors necessarily requires individualized selection procedures, which the agencies have already implemented in considerable detail. Each applicant's financial condition is evaluated under rigorous standards in a lengthy process. Agency employees negotiate personally with borrowers, investigate property offered as collateral for encumbrances, and obtain local legal advice on the adequacy of proposed security arrangements. In addition, they adapt the terms of every loan to the parties' needs and capabilities. Because each application currently receives individual scrutiny, the agencies can readily adjust loan transactions to reflect state priority rules, just as they consider other factual and legal matters before disbursing Government funds. As we noted in *United States v. Yazell*, these lending programs are distinguishable from "nationwide act[s] of the Federal Government, emanating in a single form from a single source." (Footnote omitted.) Since there is no indication that variant state priority schemes would burden current methods of loan processing, we conclude that considerations of administrative convenience do not warrant adoption of a uniform federal law.

B

The Government argues that applying state law to these lending programs would undermine its ability to recover funds disbursed and

---

[28] The differences between the rules, moreover, are insignificant in comparison with the similarities. All States except Louisiana have enacted Art. 9 of the UCC with minor variations. As Judge Friendly observed:

> When the states have gone so far in achieving the desirable goal of a uniform law governing commercial transactions, it would be a distinct disservice to insist on a different one for the segment of commerce, important but still small in relation to the total, consisting of transactions with the United States.

therefore would conflict with program objectives. In the Government's view, it is difficult "to identify a material distinction between a dollar received from the collection of taxes and a dollar returned to the Treasury on repayment of a federal loan." Therefore, the agencies conclude, just as "the purpose of the federal tax lien statute to insure prompt and certain collection of taxes" justified our imposition of the first-in-time and choateness doctrines in the tax lien context, the federal interest in recovering on loans compels similar legal protection of the agencies' consensual liens. However, we believe significant differences between federal tax liens and consensual liens counsel against unreflective extension of rules that immunize the United States from the commercial law governing all other voluntary secured creditors. These differences persuade us that deference to customary commercial practices would not frustrate the objectives of the lending programs.

That collection of taxes is vital to the functioning, indeed existence, of government cannot be denied. Congress recognized as much over 100 years ago when it authorized creation of federal tax liens. The importance of securing adequate revenues to discharge national obligations justifies the extraordinary priority accorded federal tax liens through the choateness and first-in-time doctrines. By contrast, when the United States operates as a moneylending institution under carefully circumscribed programs, its interest in recouping the limited sums advanced is of a different order. Thus, there is less need here than in the tax lien area to invoke protective measures against defaulting debtors in a manner disruptive of existing credit markets.

To equate tax liens with these consensual liens also misperceives the principal congressional concerns underlying the respective statutes. The overriding purpose of the tax lien statute obviously is to ensure prompt revenue collection. The same cannot be said of the SBA and FHA lending programs. They are a form of social welfare legislation, primarily designed to assist farmers and businesses that cannot obtain funds from private lenders on reasonable terms. We believe that had Congress intended the private commercial sector, rather than taxpayers in general, to bear the risks of default entailed by these public welfare programs, it would have established a priority scheme displacing state law. Far from doing so, both Congress and the agencies have expressly recognized the priority of certain private liens over the agencies' security interests, thereby indicating that the extraordinary safeguards applied in the tax lien area are unnecessary to maintain the lending programs.

The Government's ability to safeguard its interests in commercial dealings further reveals that the rules developed in the tax lien area are unnecessary here, and that state priority rules would not conflict with federal lending objectives.[37] The United States is an involuntary creditor

---

[37] We reject the Government's suggestion that the choateness and first-in-time doc-

of delinquent taxpayers, unable to control the factors that make tax collection likely. In contrast, when the United States acts as a lender or guarantor, it does so voluntarily, with detailed knowledge of the borrower's financial status. The agencies evaluate the risks associated with each loan, examine the interests of other creditors, choose the security believed necessary to assure repayment, and set the terms of every agreement. By carefully selecting loan recipients and tailoring each transaction with state law in mind, the agencies are fully capable of establishing terms that will secure repayment.

The Government nonetheless argues that its opportunity to evaluate the credit worthiness of loan applicants provides minimal safety. Because the SBA and FHA make loans only when private lenders will not, the United States believes that its security interests demand greater protection than ordinary commercial arrangements. We find this argument unconvincing. The lending agencies do not indiscriminately distribute public funds and hope that reimbursement will follow. SBA loans must be "of such sound value or so secured as reasonably to assure repayment." The FHA operates under a similar restriction. Both agencies have promulgated exhaustive instructions to ensure that loan recipients are financially reliable and to prevent improvident loans. The Government therefore is in substantially the same position as private lenders, and the special status it seeks is unnecessary to safeguard the public fisc. Moreover, Congress' admonitions to extend loans judiciously supports the view that it did not intend to confer special privileges on agencies that enter the commercial field. Accordingly, we agree with the Court of Appeals in [Kimbell Foods' case] that "[a]s a quasi-commercial lender, [the Government] does not require * * * the special priority which it compels as sovereign" in its tax-collecting capacity.

The Federal Tax Lien Act of 1966 provides further evidence that treating the United States like any other lender would not undermine federal interests. These amendments modified the Federal Government's preferred position under the choateness and first-in-time doctrines, and recognized the priority of many state claims over federal tax liens. In enacting this legislation, Congress sought to "improv[e] the status of private secured creditors" and prevent impairment of commercial financing transactions by "moderniz[ing] * * * the relationship of Federal tax liens to the interests of other creditors." This rationale has even greater force when the Government acts as a moneylender. We do not suggest that Congress' actions in the tax lien area control our choice of law in the commercial lien context. But in fashioning federal principles to govern areas left open by Congress, our function is to effectuate

---

trines are needed to prevent States from "undercutting" the agencies' liens by creating "arbitrary" rules. Adopting state law as an appropriate federal rule does not preclude federal courts from excepting local laws that prejudice federal interests. The issue here, however, involves commercial rules of general applicability, based on codes that are remarkably uniform throughout the Nation.

congressional policy. To ignore Congress' disapproval of unrestricted federal priority in an area as important to the Nation's stability as taxation would be inconsistent with this function. Thus, without a showing that application of state laws would impair federal operations, we decline to extend to new contexts extraordinary safeguards largely rejected by Congress.

C

In structuring financial transactions, businessmen depend on state commercial law to provide the stability essential for reliable evaluation of the risks involved. However, subjecting federal contractual liens to the doctrines developed in the tax lien area could undermine that stability. Creditors who justifiably rely on state law to obtain superior liens would have their expectations thwarted whenever a federal contractual security interest suddenly appeared and took precedence.[42]

Because the ultimate consequences of altering settled commercial practices are so difficult to foresee, we hesitate to create new uncertainties, in the absence of careful legislative deliberation. Of course, formulating special rules to govern the priority of the federal consensual liens in issue here would be justified if necessary to vindicate important national interests. But neither the Government nor the Court of Appeals advanced any concrete reasons for rejecting well-established commercial rules which have proven workable over time. Thus, the prudent course is to adopt the readymade body of state law as the federal rule of decision until Congress strikes a different accommodation.

IV

Accordingly, we hold that, absent a congressional directive, the relative priority of private liens and consensual liens arising from these Government lending programs is to be determined under nondiscriminatory state laws. * * *

So ordered.

---

[42] The cases under consideration illustrate the substantial new risks that creditors would encounter. Neither the financing statement filed by Republic nor its security agreement mentioned the SBA. To give the federal lien priority in this situation would undercut the reliability of the notice filing system, which plays a crucial role in commercial dealings. Subsequent creditors such as Crittenden and prior creditors such as Kimbell would have no trustworthy means of discovering the undisclosed security interest. Even those creditors aware of a federal agency's lien would have to adjust their lending arrangements to protect against the stringent choateness requirements. In recognition of these burdens, commentators have criticized the doctrine for frustrating private creditors' expectations as well as generating inconsistencies in application.

Considerable uncertainty would also result from the approach used in the opinions below. Developing priority rules on a case-by-case basis, depending on the types of competing private liens involved, leaves creditors without the definite body of law they require in structuring sound business transactions.

Notes and Questions

1. Justice Marshall begins by "conclud[ing] that the source of the law is federal." Why does federal law govern? Is this decision consistent with *United States v. Yazell*, discussed in note 7 at page 391? What view of *Yazell* does the *Kimbell Foods* Court seem to have?

2. In *Butner v. United States,* 440 U.S. 48, 99 S.Ct. 914, 59 L.Ed.2d 136 (1979), a trustee in bankruptcy and a second mortgagee each claimed rents owed the mortgagor during its bankruptcy before a foreclosure sale of the mortgaged property. The issue was whether a federal rule or state law should govern. In similar disputes, the Third and Seventh Circuits had adopted a federal rule giving the mortgagee an automatic security interest in rents upon default and before foreclosure. Five circuits referred to state law; some states accorded mortgagees an automatic security interest while others did not. The *Butner* Court ruled that state law (in that case North Carolina law) should govern. Under that law, a mortgagee was required to take affirmative steps after default to obtain a security interest.

Explaining its decision to endorse the approach of the circuit majority, the Court noted:

> The constitutional authority of Congress to establish "uniform Laws on the subject of Bankruptcies throughout the United States" would clearly encompass a federal statute defining the mortgagee's interest in the rents and profits earned by property in a bankrupt estate. But Congress has not chosen to exercise its power to fashion any such rule. The Bankruptcy Act does include provisions invalidating certain security interests as fraudulent, or as improper preferences over general creditors. Apart from these provisions, however, Congress has generally left the determination of property rights in the assets of a bankrupt's estate to state law.

Butner raises several questions, either alone or in combination with *Kimbell Foods* and *Yazell.*

a) Can Congress overrule the Court's decision in *Butner*? That is, is there federal competence in this area generally, or did the Court mandate the application of state law because it was constitutionally compelled to do so under *Erie*?

b) Assuming *Butner* addresses an area where there is federal competence, if Congress passed a statute embodying the rule that the Third and Seventh Circuits had used before *Butner,* would the Supreme Court be obligated to yield to that rule? If so, why? If not, what institutional problems might the clash between Congress and the Court create?

c) If the Supreme Court must yield to a statute creating a federal substantive rule for cases like *Butner,* is it significant that when the Court decided *Butner* there was no statute? Does the absence of legislation connote Congress's intention that state law not be displaced? Suppose Congress passed a law asserting that state law should govern. Would that control, even if the Supreme Court later decided that the minority circuits had been correct all along and that there were powerful reasons of federal policy that required the protection of a federal substantive rule?

d) In *Erie,* the Court applied state law as a matter of constitutional compulsion; state law applied *because* it was state law, not because its content appealed to the Court as a rule of decision. *Kimbell Foods* explicitly adopted state law as the content of federal common law. Is the same true in *Butner*? Does it make any difference?

e) If *Butner* and *Kimbell Foods* use the same approach to the applicability of state law, why did the Court not consolidate them? They were decided in the same term, though not on the same day. Does the Court's election to treat them separately suggest different approaches? What might justify the difference?

3. After *Kimbell Foods,* what are federal agencies to do in order to protect themselves? Must they now blindly enter commercial transactions and take their chances according to which state or states a particular transaction happens to touch? Does *Kimbell Foods* enshrine unpredictability?

4. The Court considered, but did not adopt, a uniform federal rule. If it had, federal uniformity would have been obtained at the expense of intrastate uniformity, since the uniform federal rule would have diverged from the state rules in at least some jurisdictions. What problems might that create?

BOYLE v. UNITED TECHNOLOGIES CORPORATION

Supreme Court of the United States, 1988.
487 U.S. 500, 108 S.Ct. 2510, 101 L.Ed.2d 442.

JUSTICE SCALIA delivered the opinion of the Court.

This case requires us to decide when a contractor providing military equipment to the Federal Government can be held liable under state tort law for injury caused by a design defect.

I

On April 27, 1983, David A. Boyle, a United States Marine helicopter copilot, was killed when the CH-53D helicopter in which he was flying crashed off the coast of Virginia Beach, Virginia, during a training exercise. Although Boyle survived the impact of the crash, he was unable to escape from the helicopter and drowned. Boyle's father, petitioner here, brought this diversity action in Federal District Court against the Sikorsky Division of United Technologies Corporation (Sikorsky), which built the helicopter for the United States.

At trial, petitioner presented two theories of liability under Virginia tort law that were submitted to the jury. First, petitioner alleged that Sikorsky had defectively repaired a device called the servo in the helicopter's automatic flight control system, which allegedly malfunctioned and caused the crash. Second, petitioner alleged that Sikorsky had defectively designed the copilot's emergency escape system: the escape hatch opened out instead of in (and was therefore ineffective in a submerged craft because of water pressure), and access to the escape hatch handle was obstructed by other equipment. The jury returned a general verdict in favor of petitioner and awarded him $725,000 * * * .

The Court of Appeals reversed and remanded with directions that judgment be entered for Sikorsky. It found, as a matter of Virginia law, that Boyle had failed to meet his burden of demonstrating that the repair work performed by Sikorsky, as opposed to work that had been done by the Navy, was responsible for the alleged malfunction of the flight control system. It also found, as a matter of federal law, that Sikorsky could not be held liable for the allegedly defective design of the escape hatch because, on the evidence presented, it satisfied the requirements of the "military contractor defense," which the court had recognized the same day * * * .

* * *

II

Petitioner's broadest contention is that, in the absence of legislation specifically immunizing Government contractors from liability for design defects, there is no basis for judicial recognition of such a defense. We disagree. In most fields of activity, to be sure, this Court has refused to find federal preemption of state law in the absence of either a clear statutory prescription or a direct conflict between federal and state law. But we have held that a few areas, involving "uniquely federal interests," are so committed by the Constitution and laws of the United States to federal control that state law is preempted and replaced, where necessary, by federal law of a content prescribed (absent explicit statutory directive) by the courts—so-called "federal common law."

The dispute in the present case borders upon two areas that we have found to involve such "uniquely federal interests." We have held that obligations to and rights of the United States under its contracts are governed exclusively by federal law. The present case does not involve an obligation to the United States under its contract, but rather liability to third persons. That liability may be styled one in tort, but it arises out of performance of the contract—and traditionally has been regarded as sufficiently related to the contract that until 1962 Virginia would generally allow design defect suits only by the purchaser and those in privity with the seller.

Another area that we have found to be of peculiarly federal concern, warranting the displacement of state law, is the civil liability of federal officials for actions taken in the course of their duty. We have held in many contexts that the scope of that liability is controlled by federal law. The present case involves an independent contractor performing its obligation under a procurement contract, rather than an official performing his duty as a federal employee, but there is obviously implicated the same interest in getting the Government's work done.[1]

We think the reasons for considering these closely related areas to be of "uniquely federal" interest apply as well to the civil liabilities arising out of the performance of federal procurement contracts * * * .

[I]t is plain that the Federal Government's interest in the procurement of equipment is implicated by suits such as the present one—even though the dispute is one between private parties. It is true that where "litigation is purely between private parties and does not touch the rights and duties of the United States," federal law does not govern. Thus for example, in *Miree v. Dekalb County*, which involved the question whether certain private parties could sue as third-party beneficiaries to an agreement between a municipality and the Federal Aviation Administration, we found that state law was not displaced because "the operations of the United States in connection with FAA grants such as these * * * would [not] be burdened" by allowing state law to determine whether third-party beneficiaries could sue, and because "any federal interest in the outcome of the [dispute] before us '[was] far too speculative, far too remote a possibility to justify the application of federal law to transactions essentially of local concern.' "[2] But the same is not true here. The imposition of liability on Government contractors will directly affect the terms of Government contracts: either the contractor will decline to manufacture the design specified by the Government, or it will raise its price. Either way, the interests of the United States will be directly affected.

That the procurement of equipment by the United States is an area of uniquely federal interest does not, however, end the inquiry. That merely establishes a necessary, not a sufficient, condition for the displacement of state law.[3] Displacement will occur only where, as we have variously described, a "significant conflict" exists between an identifiable

---

[1] The dissent misreads our discussion here to "intimat[e] that the immunity [of federal officials] * * * might extend * * * to nongovernment employees" such as a government contractor. But we do not address this issue, as it is not before us. We cite these cases merely to demonstrate that the liability of independent contractors performing work for the Federal Government, like the liability of federal officials, is an area of uniquely federal interest.

[2] As this language shows, the dissent is simply incorrect to describe *Miree* and other cases as declining to apply federal law despite the assertion of interests "comparable" to those before us here.

[3] We refer here to the displacement of state law although it is possible to analyze it as the displacement of federal-law reference to state law for the rule of decision. Some of our cases appear to regard the area in which a uniquely federal interest exists as being entirely governed by federal law, with federal law deigning to "borro[w]," or "incorporat[e]" or "adopt" state law except where a significant conflict with federal policy exists. We see nothing to be gained by expanding the theoretical scope of the federal preemption beyond its practical effect, and so adopt the more modest terminology. If the distinction between displacement of state law and displacement of federal law's incorporation of state law ever makes a practical difference, it at least does not do so in the present case.

"federal policy or interest and the [operation] of state law," or the application of state law would "frustrate specific objectives" of federal legislation. The conflict with federal policy need not be as sharp as that which must exist for ordinary preemption when Congress legislates "in a field which the States have traditionally occupied." Or to put the point differently, the fact that the area in question is one of unique federal concern changes what would otherwise be a conflict that cannot produce preemption into one that can. But conflict there must be. In some cases, for example where the federal interest requires a uniform rule, the entire body of state law applicable to the area conflicts and is replaced by federal rules. *See, e.g., Clearfield Trust* (rights and obligations of United States with respect to commercial paper must be governed by uniform federal rule). In others, the conflict is more narrow, and only particular elements of state law are superseded. *See, e.g., Little Lake Misere Land Co.* (even assuming state law should generally govern federal land acquisitions, particular state law at issue may not); *Howard v. Lyons* (state defamation law generally applicable to federal official, but federal privilege governs for statements made in the course of federal official's duties).

In *Miree,* the suit was not seeking to impose upon the person contracting with the Government a duty contrary to the duty imposed by the Government contract. Rather, it was the contractual duty *itself* that the private plaintiff (as third-party beneficiary) sought to enforce. Between *Miree* and the present case, it is easy to conceive of an intermediate situation, in which the duty sought to be imposed on the contractor is not identical to one assumed under the contract, but is also not contrary to any assumed. If, for example, the United States contracts for the purchase and installation of an air conditioning unit, specifying the cooling capacity but not the precise manner of construction, a state law imposing upon the manufacturer of such units a duty of care to include a certain safety feature would not be a duty identical to anything promised the Government, but neither would it be contrary. The contractor could comply with both its contractual obligations and the state-prescribed duty of care. No one suggests that state law would generally be preempted in this context.

The present case, however, is at the opposite extreme from *Miree.* Here the state-imposed duty of care that is the asserted basis of the contractor's liability (specifically, the duty to equip helicopters with the sort of escape-hatch mechanism petitioner claims was necessary) is precisely contrary to the duty imposed by the Government contract (the duty to manufacture and deliver helicopters with the sort of escape-hatch mechanism shown by the specifications). Even in this sort of situation, it would be unreasonable to say that there is always a "significant conflict" between the state law and a federal policy or interest. If, for example, a federal procurement officer orders, by model number, a quantity of stock helicopters that happen to be equipped with escape hatches opening outward, it is impossible to say that the Government has a significant interest in that particular feature. That would be scarcely more reasonable than saying that a private individual who orders such a craft by model number cannot sue for the manufacturer's negligence because he got precisely what he ordered.

* * *

There is however, a statutory provision that demonstrates the potential for, and suggests the outlines of, "significant conflict" between federal interests and state law in the context of government procurement. In the Federal Tort Claims Act (FTCA), Congress authorized damages to be recovered against the United States for harm caused by the negligent or wrongful conduct of Government employees, to the extent that a private person would be liable under the law of the place where the conduct occurred. It excepted from this consent to suit, however, "[a]ny claim * * * based upon the exercise or performance or the failure to exercise or perform a discretionary function or duty on the part of a federal agency or an employee of the Government, whether or not the discretion involved be abused."

We think that the selection of the appropriate design for military equipment to be used by our Armed Forces is assuredly a discretionary function within the meaning of this provision. It often involves not merely engineering analysis but judgment as to the balancing of many technical, military, and even social considerations, including specifically the trade-off between greater safety and greater combat effectiveness. And we are further of the view that permitting "second-guessing" of these judgments, through state tort suits against contractors[,] would produce the same effect sought to be avoided by the FTCA exemption. The financial burden of judgments against the contractors would ultimately be passed through, substantially if not totally, to the United States itself, since defense contractors will predictably raise their prices to cover, or to insure against, contingent liability for the Government-ordered designs. To put the point differently: It makes little sense to insulate the Government against financial liability for the judgment that a particular feature of military equipment is necessary when the Government produces the equipment itself, but not when it contracts for the production. In sum, we are of the view that state law which holds Government contractors liable for design defects in military equipment does in some circumstances present a "significant conflict" with federal policy and must be displaced.

We agree with the scope of displacement adopted by the Fourth Circuit here * * *. Liability for design defects in military equipment cannot be imposed, pursuant to state law, when (1) the United States approved reasonably precise specifications; (2) the equipment conformed to those specifications; and (3) the supplier warned the United States about the dangers in the use of the equipment that were known to the supplier but not to the United States. The first two of these conditions assure that the suit is within the area where the policy of the "discretionary function" would be frustrated—*i.e.*, they assure that the design feature in question was considered by a Government officer, and not merely by the contractor itself. The third condition is necessary because, in its absence, the displacement of state tort law would create some incentive for the manufacturer to withhold knowledge of risks, since conveying that knowledge might disrupt the contract but withholding it would produce no liability. We adopt this provision lest our effort to protect discretionary functions perversely impede them by cutting off information highly relevant to the discretionary decision.

We have considered the alternative formulation of the Government contractor defense, urged upon us by petitioner * * *. That would preclude suit only if (1) the contractor did not participate, or participated only minimally, in the design of the defective equipment; *or* (2) the contractor timely warned the Government of the risks of the design and notified it of alternative designs reasonably known by it, *and* the Government, although forewarned, clearly authorized the contractor to proceed with the dangerous design. While this formulation may represent a perfectly reasonable tort rule, it is not a rule designed to protect the federal interest embodied in the "discretionary function" exemption. The design ultimately selected may well reflect a significant policy judgment by Government officials whether or not the contractor rather than those officials developed the design. In addition, it does not seem to us sound policy to penalize, and thus deter, active contractor participation in the design process, placing the contractor at risk unless it identifies all design defects.

III

* * *

[The majority decided that the Court of Appeals' opinion was ambiguous as to whether there was sufficient evidence to send the case to the jury under the correct view of the contractor's defense, so the case was remanded for determination of that question.]

Justice Brennan, with whom Justice Marshall and Justice Blackmun join, dissenting.

Lieutenant David A. Boyle died when the CH-53D helicopter he was copiloting spun out of control and plunged into the ocean. We may assume, for purposes of this case, that Lt. Boyle was trapped under water and drowned because respondent United Technologies negligently designed the helicopter's escape hatch. We may further assume that any competent engineer would have discovered and cured the defects, but that they inexplicably escaped respondent's notice. Had respondent designed such a death trap for a commercial firm, Lt. Boyle's family could sue under Virginia tort law and be compensated for his tragic and unnecessary death. But respondent designed the helicopter for the Federal Government, and that, the Court tells us today, makes all the difference: Respondent is immune from liability so long as it obtained approval of "reasonably precise specifications"—perhaps no more than a rubber-stamp from a federal procurement officer who might or might not have noticed or cared about the defects, or even had the expertise to discover them.

If respondent's immunity "bore the legitimacy of having been prescribed by the people's elected representatives," we would be duty bound to implement their will, whether or not we approved. *United States v. Johnson,* 481 U.S. 681, 703 (1987) (dissenting opinion of Scalia, J.). Congress, however, has remained silent—and conspicuously so, having resisted a sustained campaign by Government contractors to legislate for them some defense.[1] The Court—unelected and unaccountable to the people—has unabashedly stepped into the breach to legislate a rule denying Lt. Boyle's family the compensation that state law assures them. This time the injustice is of this Court's own making.

Worse yet, the injustice will extend far beyond the facts of this case, for the Court's newly discovered Government contractor defense is breathtakingly sweeping. It applies not only to military equipment like the CH-53D helicopter, but (so far as I can tell) to any made-to-order gadget that the Federal Government might purchase after previewing plans—from NASA's Challenger space shuttle to the Postal Service's old mail cars. The contractor may invoke the defense in suits brought not only by military personnel like Lt. Boyle, or Government employees, but by anyone injured by a Government contractor's negligent design, including, for example, the children who might have died had respondent's helicopter crashed on the beach. It applies even if the Government has not intentionally sacrificed safety for other interests like speed or efficiency, and, indeed, even if the equipment is not of a type that is typically considered dangerous; thus, the contractor who designs a Government building can invoke the defense when the elevator cable snaps or the walls collapse. And the defense is invocable regardless of how blatant or easily remedied the defect, so long as the contractor missed it and the specifications approved by the Government, however unreasonably dangerous, were "reasonably precise."

In my view, this Court lacks both authority and expertise to fashion such a rule, whether to protect the Treasury of the United States or the coffers of industry. Because I would leave that exercise of legislative power to Congress, where our Constitution places it, I would reverse the

---

[1] *See, e.g.,* H.R. 4765, 99th Cong., 2d Sess. (1986) (limitations on civil liability of Government contractors); S. 2441, 99th Cong., 2d Sess. (1986) (same). *See also* H.R. 2378, 100th Cong., 1st Sess. (1987) (indemnification of civil liability for Government contractors); H.R. 5883, 98th Cong., 2d Sess. (1984) (same); H.R. 1504, 97th Cong., 1st Sess. (1981) (same); H.R. 5351, 96th Cong., 1st Sess. (1979) (same).

Court of Appeals and reinstate petitioner's jury award.

* * *

II

Congress has not decided to supersede state law here (if anything, it has decided not to) and the Court does not pretend that its newly manufactured "Government contractor defense" fits within any of the handful of "narrow areas" of "uniquely federal interests" in which we have heretofore done so. Rather, the Court creates a new category of "uniquely federal interests" out of a synthesis of two whose origins predate *Erie* itself: the interest in administering the "obligations to and rights of the United States under its contracts," and the interest in regulating the "civil liability of federal officials for actions taken in the course of their duty." This case is, however, simply a suit between two private parties. We have steadfastly declined to impose federal contract law on relationships that are collateral to a federal contract, or to extend the federal employee's immunity beyond federal employees. And the Court's ability to list two, or ten, inapplicable areas of "uniquely federal interest" does not support its conclusion that the liability of Government contractors is so "clear and substantial" an interest that this Court must step in lest state law does "major damage."

A

The proposition that federal common law continues to govern the "obligations to and rights of the United States under its contracts" is nearly as old as *Erie* itself. Federal law typically controls when the Federal Government is a party to a suit involving its rights or obligations under a contract * * *. But it is by now established that our power to create federal common law controlling the Federal Government's contractual rights and obligations does not translate into a power to prescribe rules that cover all transactions or contractual relationships collateral to Government contracts.

In *Miree v. DeKalb County,* for example, the county was contractually obligated under a grant agreement with the Federal Aviation Administration (FAA) to " 'restrict the use of land adjacent to * * * the Airport to activities and purposes compatible with normal airport operations including landing and takeoff of aircraft.' " At issue was whether the county breached its contractual obligation by operating a garbage dump adjacent to the airport, which allegedly attracted the swarm of birds that caused a plane crash. Federal common law would undoubtedly have controlled in any suit by the Federal Government to enforce the provision against the county or to collect damages for its violation. The diversity suit, however, was brought not by the Government, but by assorted private parties injured in some way by the accident. We observed that "the operations of the United States in connection with FAA grants such as these are undoubtedly of considerable magnitude," and that "the United States has a substantial interest in regulating aircraft travel and promoting air travel safety." Nevertheless, we held that state law should govern the claim because "only the rights of private litigants are at issue here," and the claim against the county "will have *no direct effect upon the United States or its treasury,*" (emphasis added).

Miree relied heavily on *Parnell* and *Wallis,* the former involving commercial paper issued by the United States and the latter involving property rights in federal land. In the former case, Parnell cashed certain government bonds that had been stolen from their owner, a bank. It is beyond dispute that federal law would have governed the United States' duty to pay the value bonds upon presentation; we held as much in *Clearfield Trust.* But the central issue in *Parnell,* a diversity suit, was whether the victim of the theft could recover the money paid to Parnell. That issue, we held, was governed by state law, because the "litigation [was] purely between private parties and [did] *not touch the rights and duties of the United States.*" ([E]mphasis added).

The same was true in *Wallis,* which also involved a Government contract—a lease issued by the United States to a private party under the Mineral Leasing Act of 1920—governed entirely by federal law. Again, the relationship at issue in this diversity case was collateral to the Government contract: It involved the validity of contractual arrangements between the lessee and other private parties, not between the lessee and the Federal Government. Even though a federal statute authorized certain assignments of lease rights, and imposed certain conditions on their validity, we held that state law, not federal common law, governed their validity because application of state law would present "no significant threat to any identifiable federal policy or interest."

Here, as in *Miree, Parnell,* and *Wallis,* a Government contract governed by federal common law looms in the background. But here, too, the United States is not a party to the suit and the suit neither "touch[es] the rights and duties of the United States," nor has a "direct effect upon the United States or its Treasury." The relationship at issue is at best collateral to the Government contract. We have no greater power to displace state law governing the collateral relationship in the Government procurement realm than we had to dictate federal rules governing equally collateral relationships in the areas of aviation, Government-issued commercial paper, or federal lands.

That the Government might "have to pay higher prices for what it orders if delivery in accordance with the contract exposes the seller to potential liability" does not distinguish this case. Each of the cases just discussed declined to extend the reach of federal common law despite the assertion of comparable interests that would have affected the terms of the Government contract—whether its price or its substance—just as "*directly*" (or indirectly). Third-party beneficiaries can sue under a county's contract with the FAA, for example, even though—as the

Court's focus on the absence of "*direct* effect on the United States or its Treasury," (emphasis added), suggests—counties will likely pass on the costs to the Government in future contract negotiations. Similarly, we held that state law may govern the circumstances under which stolen federal bonds can be recovered, notwithstanding Parnell's argument that "the value of bonds to the first purchaser and hence their salability by the Government would be materially affected." As in each of the cases declining to extend the traditional reach of federal law of contracts beyond the rights and duties of the Federal Government, "any federal interest in the outcome of the question before us 'is far too speculative, far too remote a possibility to justify the application of federal law to transactions essentially of local concern.'"

B

Our "uniquely federal interest" in the tort liability of affiliates of the Federal Government is equally narrow * * *. Never before have we so much as intimated that the immunity (or the "uniquely federal interest" that justifies it) might extend beyond * * * to cover also nongovernment employees whose authority to act is independent of any source of federal law and that are as far removed from the "functioning of the Federal Government" as is a Government contractor.

The historical narrowness of the federal interest and the immunity is hardly accidental. A federal officer exercises statutory authority, which not only provides the necessary basis for the immunity in positive law, but also permits us confidently to presume that interference with the exercise of discretion undermines congressional will. In contrast, a Government contractor acts independently of any congressional enactment. Thus, immunity for a contractor lacks both the positive law basis and the presumption that it furthers congressional will.

Moreover, even within the category of congressionally authorized tasks, we have deliberately restricted the scope of immunity to circumstances in which "the contributions of immunity to effective government in particular contexts outweigh the perhaps recurring harm to individual citizens," because immunity "contravenes the basic tenet that individuals be held accountable for their wrongful conduct." The extension of immunity to Government contractors skews the balance we have historically struck. On the one hand, whatever marginal effect contractor immunity might have on the "effective administration of policies of government," its "harm to individual citizens" is more severe than in the Government-employee context. Our observation that "there are * * * other sanctions than civil tort suits available to deter the executive official who may be prone to exercise his functions in an unworthy and irresponsible manner," offers little deterrence to the Government contractor. On the other hand, a grant of immunity to Government contractors could not advance "the fearless, vigorous, and effective administration of policies of government" nearly as much as does the current immunity for

Government employees. In the first place, the threat of a tort suit is less likely to influence the conduct of an industrial giant than that of a lone civil servant, particularly since the work of a civil servant is significantly less profitable, and significantly more likely to be the subject of a vindictive lawsuit. In fact, were we to take seriously the Court's assertion that contractors pass their costs—including presumably litigation costs—through, "substantially if not totally, to the United States," the threat of a tort suit should have only marginal impact on the conduct of Government contractors. More importantly, inhibition of the Government official who actually sets Government policy presents a greater threat to the "administration of policies of government," than does inhibition of a private contractor, whose role is devoted largely to assessing the technological feasibility and cost of satisfying the Government's predetermined needs. Similarly, unlike tort suits against Government officials, tort suits against Government contractors would rarely "consume time and energies" that "would otherwise be devoted to governmental service."

In short, because the essential justifications for official immunity do not support an extension to the Government contractor, it is no surprise that we have never extended it that far.

III

[T]he Court invokes the discretionary function exception of the Federal Tort Claims Act (FTCA). The Court does not suggest that the exception has any direct bearing here, for petitioner has sued a private manufacturer (not the Federal Government) under Virginia law (not the FTCA) * * * .

[T]he Court * * * reason[s] that federal common law must immunize Government contractors from state tort law to prevent erosion of the discretionary function exception's *policy* of foreclosing judicial " 'second-guessing' " of discretionary governmental decisions. The erosion the Court fears apparently is rooted not in a concern that suits against Government contractors will prevent them from designing, or the Government from commissioning the design of, precisely the product the Government wants, but in the concern that such suits might preclude the Government from purchasing the desired product at the price it wants: "The financial burden of judgments against the contractors," the Court fears, "would ultimately be passed through, substantially if not totally, to the United States itself."

Even granting the Court's factual premise, which is by no means self-evident, the Court cites no authority for the proposition that burdens imposed on Government contractors, but passed on to the Government, burden the Government in a way that justifies extension of its immunity. However substantial such indirect burdens may be, we have held in other contexts that they are legally irrelevant. * * *

Moreover, the statutory basis on which the Court's rule of federal common law totters is more unstable than any we have ever adopted. In the first place, we rejected an analytically similar attempt to construct federal common law out of the FTCA when we held that the Government's waiver of sovereign immunity for the torts of its employees does not give the Government an implied right of indemnity from them, even though * * * "[t]he financial burden placed on the United States by the Tort Claims Act [could conceivably be] so great that government employees should be required to carry part of the burden." So too here, the FTCA's retention of sovereign immunity for the Government's discretionary acts does not imply a defense for the benefit of contractors who participate in those acts, even though they might pass on the financial burden to the United States. In either case, the most that can be said is that the position "asserted, though the product of a law Congress passed, is a matter on which Congress has not taken a position."

Here, even that much is an overstatement, for the Government's immunity for discretionary functions is not even "a product of" the FTCA. Before Congress enacted the FTCA (when sovereign immunity barred any tort suit against the Federal Government) we perceived no need for a rule of federal common law to reinforce the Government's immunity by shielding also parties who might contractually pass costs on to it. Nor did we (or any other court of which I am aware) identify a special category of "discretionary" functions for which sovereign immunity was so crucial that a government contractor who exercised discretion should share the Government's immunity from state tort law.

* * * There is no more reason for federal common law to shield contractors now that the Government is liable for some torts than there was when the Government was liable for none * * * .

* * *

IV

At bottom, the Court's analysis is premised on the proposition that any tort liability indirectly absorbed by the Government so burdens governmental functions as to compel us to act when Congress has not. That proposition is by no means uncontroversial. The tort system is premised on the assumption that the imposition of liability encourages actors to prevent any injury whose expected cost exceeds the cost of prevention. If the system is working as it should, Government contractors will design equipment to avoid certain injuries (like the deaths of soldiers or Government employees), which would be certain to burden the Government. The Court therefore has no basis for its assumption that tort liability will result in a net burden on the Government (let alone a clearly excessive net burden) rather than a net gain.

Perhaps tort liability is an inefficient means of ensuring the quality of design efforts, but "[w]hatever the merits of the policy" the Court wishes to implement, "its conversion into law is a proper subject for congressional action, not for any creative power of ours." It is, after all, "Congress, not this Court or the other federal courts, [that] is the custodian of the national purse. By the same token [Congress] is the primary and most often the exclusive arbiter of federal fiscal affairs. And these comprehend, as we have said, securing the treasury or the Government against financial losses *however inflicted* * * * ." ([E]mphasis added).

Were I a legislator, I would probably vote against any law absolving multibillion dollar private enterprises from answering for their tragic mistakes, at least if that law were justified by no more than the unsupported speculation that their liability might ultimately burden the United States Treasury. Some of my colleagues here would evidently vote otherwise (as they have here), but that should not matter here. We are judges not legislators, and the vote is not ours to cast.

I respectfully dissent.

JUSTICE STEVENS, dissenting.

When judges are asked to embark on a lawmaking venture, I believe they should carefully consider whether they, or a legislative body, are better equipped to perform the task at hand. There are instances of so-called interstitial lawmaking that inevitably become part of the judicial process. But when we are asked to create an entirely new doctrine—to answer "questions of policy on which Congress has not spoken"—we have a special duty to identify the proper decisionmaker before trying to make the proper decision.

When the novel question of policy involves a balancing of the conflicting interests in the efficient operation of a massive governmental program and the protection of the rights of the individual—whether in the social welfare context, the civil service context, or the military procurement context—I feel very deeply that we should defer to the expertise of the Congress. * * * "The selection of that policy which is most advantageous to the whole involves a host of considerations that must be weighed and appraised. That function is more appropriately for those who write the laws, rather than for those who interpret them."

I respectfully dissent.

Notes and Questions

1. Justice Brennan's dissent cites six bills that Congress did not pass that would have provided some statutory protection for government contractors in United Technologies's position, by either immunizing or indemnifying it. Four contained indemnification provisions. Witnesses in committee hearings suggested two reasons to refuse indemnity: its potential effect on the federal treasury and that it would remove a prime incentive for contractors to maintain high standards. In terms of the legitimacy of federal common law, does it make any difference which of those two reasons underlay Congress's inaction?

2. Justice Scalia's majority opinion does not even acknowledge the bills' existence. Could the majority respond to that evidence and preserve the result in *Boyle*?

3. a) Suppose Congress had passed a statute saying that state law should govern claims against government contractors. Would the majority be able to reach the same result in *Boyle,* or would doing so pose insurmountable separation-of-powers problems?

b) Suppose instead that Congress passed a statute denying government contractors immunity from tort liability arising out of design or manufacturing defects. Would that preclude the result in *Boyle*?

4. Does the majority suggest that in any area that implicates the "interest in getting the Government's work done * * * " there is a unique federal interest that displaces state law? If so, is Justice Brennan correct that the majority displaces not merely state law but also Congress's function? If not, what are the express or implied boundaries of the decision?

5. Justice Scalia says federal common law is appropriate only when there is a unique federal interest and significant conflict between that interest and state law. Does this prove too much? The more significant the conflict, the more likely Congress was aware of it. Could congressional silence then signify that Congress did not want federal law to govern?

6. Would not the most conservative, judicially restrained course of action in *Boyle* have been to refuse the immunity, leaving the ensuing plaintiff's judgment as a spur to Congress to correct the situation if necessary (and to indemnify United Technologies in a private bill, if it saw fit)?

7. Justice Scalia argues with some force the analogy between *Boyle* and the Federal Torts Claims Act's exclusion of governmental liability in suits based on discretionary functions. Is there any difference between the government's waiver of sovereign immunity and a private contractor's liability for negligence? Is Justice Scalia saying that the government's sovereign immunity extends to those with whom the government contracts? Could even Congress do that?

8. a) In *United States v. Standard Oil Co.*, 332 U.S. 301, 67 S.Ct. 1604, 91 L.Ed. 2067 (1947), the Court refused to imply an action on behalf of the United States for its loss because of the incapacitation of a serviceman by the defendant's negligence. The Justices left the determination of federal fiscal policy to Congress, as "custodian of the national purse." Why did it not do so here? What distinguishes *Standard Oil* from *Boyle*? Arguably the impact on the federal treasury is far more direct in *Standard Oil*.

b) *In re "Agent Orange" Product Liability Litigation*, 635 F.2d 987 (2d Cir. 1980), involved consolidated actions by veterans against various American companies to recover for injuries from Agent Orange, a defoliant that defendants had supplied to the military. Plaintiffs urged the court to recognize a federal common law right to recover, arguing that *Clearfield* compelled it. The court responded:

The present litigation is fundamentally different from * * * *Clearfield*

Trust with respect to both uniformity interest and substantive interest in the content of the rules to be applied. Since this litigation is between private parties and no substantial rights or duties of the government hinge on its outcome, there is no federal interest in uniformity for its own sake.

* * *

Thus, the prospect of uniformity is insufficient reason to invoke federal common law in private litigation; and if federal common law were invoked, it would not ensure uniformity since frequently that law takes its substance from local law.

The second fundamental difference between the present litigation and the *Clearfield Trust* type of case is that in the latter, the government's substantive interest in the litigation is essentially monothetic, in that it is concerned only with preserving the federal fisc, whereas here the government has two interests; and here the two interests have been placed in sharp contrast with one another. Thus, the government has an interest in the welfare of its veterans; they have given of themselves in the most fundamental way possible in the national interest. But the government also has an interest in the suppliers of its materiel; imposition, for example, of strict liability as contended for by plaintiffs would affect the government's ability to procure materiel without the exaction of significantly higher prices, or the attachment of onerous conditions, or the demand of indemnification or the like. * * * [U]nlike a simple uniformity interest, neither the government's interest in its veterans nor its interest in its suppliers is content-neutral. Each interest will be furthered only if the federal rule of law to be applied favors that particular group.

The extent to which either group should be favored, and its welfare deemed "paramount" * * * is preeminently a policy determination of the sort reserved in the first instance for Congress. The welfare of veterans and that of military suppliers are clearly federal concerns which Congress should appropriately consider in the setting policy for the governance of the nation, and it is properly left to Congress in the first instance to strike the balance between the conflicting interests of the veterans and the contractors, and thereby identify federal policy.

The majority declined to create the common law cause of action. Since the plaintiffs had predicated jurisdiction on 28 U.S.C.A. § 1331 and, after the court's ruling, had no federal common law with which to present a federal question, the court dismissed the case for want of subject matter jurisdiction.[12]

---

[12] Is the dismissal for want of subject matter jurisdiction consistent with Bell v. Hood, 327 U.S. 678, 66 S.Ct. 773, 90 L.Ed. 939 (1946)? There the plaintiff asserted state claims for trespass and false imprisonment, basing them on the Fourth and Fifth Amendments. The Court held that even if plaintiff's claim eventually failed, the proper dismissal would be for failure to state a claim upon which relief could be granted, not lack of subject matter jurisdiction. *Bell* is discussed in Chapter 3 at page 286.

Chief Judge Feinberg dissented; he saw no federal interest conflict presenting a policy question more appropriately resolved by Congress:

> The allegedly conflicting federal interests are in the welfare of veterans and in the welfare of suppliers of war materiel. But that the plaintiff veterans and the defendant contractors have opposing interests in this litigation hardly means that the paramount federal interest is somehow divided or self-contradictory. The United States has a clear interest in the protection of its soldiers from harm caused by defective war materiel. What other interests does the United States arguably have that might conflict with this clear interest? One such interest might be in seeing that defendants, as suppliers of war materiel, are treated fairly. But that interest cannot be said to conflict with the government's interest in the safety of its soldiers. Another such interest might be in preventing defendants from being driven to bankruptcy by large damage awards to Agent Orange plaintiffs, who have already made claims assertedly greater than defendants' combined liquid assets. This, I take it, is what the majority means by its reference to the federal interest in the "welfare" of defendants. But this interest lies in the future, and in the realm of speculation. There will be time enough to deal with the potential impact of defendants' financial liability if and when they incur any, if it is truly in the interest of the United States to do so. By contrast, plaintiffs' injuries—assuming for the moment that plaintiffs have a viable cause of action—lie in large part in the present, and in the realm of the concrete. The conclusion seems inescapable to me that the United States' interest in the "welfare" of defendants cannot approach, either in magnitude or in quality, its interest in the welfare of the Agent Orange plaintiffs. In short, in the case before us the paramount interests of the United States are in the welfare of its veterans and in their fair and uniform treatment.

Is there a significant difference in approach between *Agent Orange* and *Boyle*? Confronted with possible policy conflicts, should the federal courts do their best to resolve them, leaving it to Congress to adjust the balance if the courts err, or should they effectively throw up their hands and refuse to displace state law by creating federal common law? Or can the approaches in *Agent Orange* and *Boyle* be harmonized? Are the cases sufficiently distinguishable so that creating federal common law in *Boyle* and refusing to do so in *Agent Orange* may both be proper? If so, what is the distinction? If not, which approach better reflects the proper role of the federal courts?

9. *Boyle* demonstrates the dispute over federal courts as common law courts that the New *Erie* doctrine addresses. Justice Brennan argues strenuously that creating a defense in *Boyle* violates separation of powers. The five-member majority seems untroubled by either the abstract possibility that Congress could have acted in the area or by Congress's actual refusal to do so on six occasions. In *Cannon v. University of Chicago*, 441 U.S. 677, 99 S.Ct. 1946, 60 L.Ed.2d 560 (1979), Justice Powell dissented on the ground that policy making should be left to the representative branches of government, not undertaken by the Court. Justice Powell had left the Court before *Boyle*. Justice Kennedy, who replaced him, voted with the majority.

Would Justice Powell have joined the majority? That aside, should the federal courts ever make policy decisions, or should they leave them to the representative branches? If so, does that place an intolerable burden on the legislature to anticipate and keep up with every developing problem in modern society? If not, what principles distinguish legitimate judicial participation in or implementation of policy decisions from that which is illegitimate?

10. *Boyle* aptly illustrates the two themes that pervade this area of federal courts: federalism and separation of powers. With regard to federalism, *Boyle* effectively displaces Virginia law recognizing claims for wrongful death, as Justice Brennan charges in his dissent. Moreover, this is not a situation where pre-existing federal law in some sense preempted state law. Thus, to the extent that the federalism clash exists in *Boyle,* the Court engenders it. That also touches the nerve of separation of powers. Congress could have created this immunity defense but pointedly had not. New *Erie* adherents might argue on a micro level that creating such a defense is the business of the legislature, not the courts, and on a macro level that if a federalism clash is to occur, the representative branches should precipitate it, not the judiciary.

11. A unanimous Court reaffirmed the *Boyle* approach in *Atherton v. Federal Deposit Insurance Corporation,* 519 U.S. 213, 117 S.Ct. 666, 136 L.Ed.2d 656 (1997). The underlying issue was whether there should be a federal common law standard governing the standard of conduct governing officers and directors of federally chartered banks. Congress had specified that officials were liable for "gross negligence" or "similar conduct." The question was whether individual states could impose a stricter standard of conduct. Justice Breyer's opinion rehearsed the Court's post-*Erie* reluctance to create special federal rules of decision and echoed the separation-of-powers theme, noting that the decision to use latent federal power to displace state law "is primarily a decision for Congress." Harking back to a 1966 decision, the Court noted that " 'the guiding principle is that a significant conflict between some federal policy or interest and the use of state law * * * must first be specifically shown.' " Justice Breyer noted that such conflict is "normally" a precondition, citing *inter alia Kimbell Foods.* He did not explain when it might not be a precondition.

In the course of the opinion, the Court rejected the government's talismanic invocation of the need for uniformity, cautioning that "[t]o invoke the concept of 'uniformity,' however, is not to prove its need." In the circumstances, the Court found that there was no need for a federal standard to protect federally-chartered banks from state laws, as in the era of *M'Culloch v. Maryland* (1819), and that a federal uniform standard would come at the expense of intrastate uniformity for state and federal banks. Since 1870, the Court had taken the position that federal banks were subject to state law, and Justice Breyer found no reason to make an exception in this case. "In sum, we can find no significant conflict with, or threat to, a federal interest."

The opinion did not specify whether state law governed of its own force or because the Court adopted it as federal common law, though the former seems more likely. If that is so, has the Court repudiated at least some of

Kimbell Foods? If not, has the Court altered the *Kimbell Foods* balancing test? Although the Court cited *Kimbell Foods* as a precedent for the significant-conflict standard, Justice Marshall's opinion is hardly the sort of ringing endorsement of that standard that either *Boyle* or *Atherton* represents.

Although *Boyle* and *Atherton* mention *Kimbell Foods* favorably, it is not so clear that they are compatible with it. Consider whether the *Kimbell Foods* Court actually found a significant conflict between state law and a federal policy or interest. If you think it did not, then why did the Court hold that federal law governed the disputed priority question? If there was a significant conflict, then how did *Kimbell Foods'* adoption of state law as the content of federal common law ameliorate the conflict?

If finding a significant conflict is a *sine qua non* for the creation of federal common law, will the federal courts be able to continue the practice of adopting state law as the content of federal common law, as *Kimbell Foods* exemplifies?

SEMTEK INTERNATIONAL INCORPORATED v. LOCKHEED MARTIN CORPORATION

Supreme Court of the United States, 2001.
531 U.S. 497, 121 S.Ct. 1021, 149 L.Ed.2d 32.

JUSTICE SCALIA delivered the opinion of the Court.

This case presents the question whether the claim-preclusive effect of a federal judgment dismissing a diversity action on statute-of-limitations grounds is determined by the law of the State in which the federal court sits.

I

Petitioner filed a complaint against respondent in California state court, alleging breach of contract and various business torts. Respondent removed the case to the United States District Court for the Central District of California on the basis of diversity of citizenship, and successfully moved to dismiss petitioner's claims as barred by California's 2-year statute of limitations. In its order of dismissal, the District Court, adopting language suggested by respondent, dismissed petitioner's claims "in [their] entirety on the merits and with prejudice." Without contesting the District Court's designation of its dismissal as "on the merits," petitioner appealed to the Court of Appeals for the Ninth Circuit, which affirmed the District Court's order. Petitioner also brought suit against respondent in the State Circuit Court for Baltimore City, Maryland, alleging the same causes of action, which were not time barred under Maryland's 3-year statute of limitations. Respondent sought injunctive relief against this action from the California federal court under the All Writs Act, 28 U.S.C. § 1651, and removed the action to the United States District Court for the District of Maryland on federal-question grounds (diversity grounds were not available because Lockheed "is a Maryland citizen"). The California federal court denied the relief requested, and the Maryland federal court remanded the case to state court because the federal question arose only by way of defense. Following a hearing, the Maryland state court granted respondent's motion to dismiss on the ground of res judicata. Petitioner then returned to the California federal court and the Ninth Circuit, unsuccessfully moving both courts to amend the former's earlier order so as to indicate that the dismissal was not "on the merits." Petitioner also appealed the Maryland trial court's order of dismissal to the Maryland Court of Special Appeals. The Court of Special Appeals affirmed, holding that, regardless of whether California would have accorded claim-preclusive effect to a statute-of-limitations dismissal by one of its own courts, the dismissal by the California federal court barred the complaint filed in Maryland, since the res judicata effect of federal diversity judgments is prescribed by federal law, under which the earlier dismissal was on the merits and claim preclusive. After the Maryland Court of Appeals declined to review the case, we granted certiorari.

II

Petitioner contends that the outcome of this case is controlled by *Dupasseur v. Rochereau* (1875), which held that the res judicata effect of a federal diversity judgment "is such as would belong to judgments of the State courts rendered under similar circumstances," and may not be accorded any "higher sanctity or effect." Since, petitioner argues, the dismissal of an action on statute-of-limitations grounds by a California state court would not be claim preclusive, it follows that the similar dismissal of this diversity action by the California federal court cannot be claim preclusive. While we agree that this would be the result demanded by *Dupasseur,* the case is not dispositive because it was decided under the Conformity Act of 1872, which required federal courts to apply the procedural law of the forum State in nonequity cases. That arguably affected the outcome of the case.

Respondent, for its part, contends that the outcome of this case is controlled by Federal Rule of Civil Procedure 41(b), which provides as follows:

> Involuntary Dismissal: Effect Thereof. For failure of the plaintiff to prosecute or to comply with these rules or any order of court, a defendant may move for dismissal of an action or of any claim against the defendant. Unless the court in its order for dismissal otherwise specifies, a dismissal under this subdivision and any dismissal not provided for in this rule, other than a dismissal for lack of jurisdiction, for improper venue, or for failure to join a party under Rule 19, operates as an adjudication upon the merits.

Since the dismissal here did not "otherwise specif[y]" (indeed, it specifically stated that it *was* "on the merits"), and did not pertain to the excepted subjects of jurisdiction, venue, or joinder, it. follows, respondent contends, that the dismissal "is entitled to claim preclusive effect."

Implicit in this reasoning is the unstated minor premise that all judgments denominated "on the merits" are entitled to claim-preclusive effect. That premise is not necessarily valid. The original connotation of an "on the merits" adjudication is one that actually "pass[es] directly on the substance of [a particular] claim" before the court. That connotation remains common to every jurisdiction of which we are aware. ("The prototyp[ical] [judgment on the merits is] one in which the merits of [a party's] claim are in fact adjudicated [for or] against the [party] after trial of the substantive issues"). And it is, we think, the meaning intended in those many statements to the effect that a judgment "on the merits" triggers the doctrine of res judicata or claim preclusion.

But over the years the meaning of the term "judgment on the merits" "has gradually undergone change," and it has come to be applied to some judgments (such as the one involved here) that do *not* pass upon the substantive merits of a claim and hence do *not* (in many jurisdictions) entail claim-preclusive effect. That is why the Restatement of Judgments has abandoned the use of the term—"because of its possibly misleading connotations."

In short, it is no longer true that a judgment "on the merits" is necessarily a judgment entitled to claim-preclusive effect; and there are a number of reasons for believing that the phrase "adjudication upon the merits" does not bear that meaning in Rule 41(b). To begin with, Rule 41(b) sets forth nothing more than a default rule for determining the import of a dismissal (a dismissal is "upon the merits," with the three stated exceptions, unless the court "otherwise specifies"). This would be a highly peculiar context in which to announce a federally prescribed rule on the complex question of claim preclusion, saying in effect, "All federal dismissals (with three specified exceptions) preclude suit elsewhere, unless the court otherwise specifies."

And even apart from the purely default character of Rule 41(b), it would be peculiar to find a rule governing the effect that must be accorded federal judgments by other courts ensconced in rules governing the internal procedures of the rendering court itself. Indeed, such a rule would arguably violate the jurisdictional limitation of the Rules Enabling Act: that the Rules "shall not abridge, enlarge or modify any substantive right." In the present case, for example, if California law left petitioner free to sue on this claim in Maryland even after the California statute of limitations had expired, the federal court's extinguishment of that right (through Rule 41(b)'s mandated claim-preclusive effect of its judgment) would seem to violate this limitation.

Moreover, as so interpreted, the Rule would in many cases violate the federalism principle of *Erie R. Co. v. Tompkins* (1938), by engendering " 'substantial' variations [in outcomes] between state and federal litigation" which would "[l]ikely * * * influence the choice of a forum," *Hanna v. Plumer* (1965). With regard to the claim-preclusion issue involved in the present case, for example, the traditional rule is that expiration of the applicable statute of limitations merely bars the remedy and does not extinguish the substantive right, so that dismissal on that ground does not have claim-preclusive effect in other jurisdictions with longer, unexpired limitation periods. Out-of-state defendants sued on stale claims in California and in other States adhering to this traditional rule would systematically remove state-law suits brought against them to federal court—where, unless otherwise specified, a statute-of-limitations dismissal would bar suit everywhere.[43]

Finally, if Rule 41(b) did mean what respondent suggests, we would surely have relied upon it in our cases recognizing the claim-preclusive effect of federal judgments in federal-question cases. Yet for over half a century since the promulgation of Rule 41(b), we have not once done so.

We think the key to a more reasonable interpretation of the meaning of "operates as an adjudication upon the merits" in Rule 41(b) is to be found in Rule 41(a), which, in discussing the effect of voluntary dismissal by the plaintiff, makes clear that an "adjudication upon the merits" is the opposite of a "dismissal without prejudice":

> Unless otherwise stated in the notice of dismissal or stipulation, the dismissal is without prejudice, except that a notice of dismissal operates as an adjudication upon the merits when filed by a plaintiff who has once dismissed in any court of the United States or of any state an action based on or including the same claim.

The primary meaning of "dismissal without prejudice," we think, is dismissal without barring the defendant [*sic*, probably intending "plaintiff"] from returning later, to the same court, with the same underlying claim. That will also ordinarily (though not always) have the consequence of not barring the claim from *other* courts, but its primary meaning relates to the dismissing court itself. Thus, Black's Law Dictionary defines "dismissed without prejudice" as "removed from the court's docket in such a way that the plaintiff may refile the same suit on the same claim," and defines "dismissal without prejudice" as "[a] dismissal that does not bar the plaintiff from refiling the lawsuit within the applicable limitations period."

We think, then, that the effect of the "adjudication upon the merits" default provision of Rule 41(b)—and, presumably, of the explicit order in the present case that used the language of that default provision—is simply that, unlike a dismissal "without prejudice," the dismissal in the

---

[43] Rule 41(b), interpreted as a preclusion-establishing rule, would not have the two effects described in the preceding paragraphs—arguable violation of the Rules Enabling Act and incompatibility with *Erie R. Co. v. Tompkins* (1938)—if the court's failure to specify another-than-on-the-merits dismissal were subject to reversal on appeal whenever it would alter the rule of claim preclusion applied by the State in which the federal court sits. No one suggests that this is the rule, and we are aware of no case that applies it.

present case barred refiling of the same claim in the United States District Court for the Central District of California. That is undoubtedly a necessary condition, but it is not a sufficient one, for claim-preclusive effect in other courts.[44]

III

Having concluded that the claim-preclusive effect, in Maryland, of this California federal diversity judgment is dictated neither by *Dupasseur v. Rochereau,* as petitioner contends, nor by Rule 41(b), as respondent contends, we turn to consideration of what determines the issue. Neither the Full Faith and Credit Clause nor the full faith and credit statute addresses the question. By their terms they govern the effects to be given only to state-court judgments (and, in the case of the statute, to judgments by courts of territories and possessions). And no other federal textual provision, neither of the Constitution nor of any statute, addresses the claim-preclusive effect of a judgment in a federal diversity action.

It is also true, however, that no federal textual provision addresses the claim-preclusive effect of a federal-court judgment in a federal-question case, yet we have long held that States cannot give those judgments merely whatever effect they would give their own judgments, but must accord them the effect that this Court prescribes. The reasoning of that line of cases suggests, moreover, that even when States are allowed to give federal judgments (notably, judgments in diversity cases) no more than the effect accorded to state judgments, that disposition is by direction of *this* Court, which has the last word on the claim-preclusive effect of *all* federal judgments:

> It is true that for some purposes and within certain limits it is only required that the judgments of the courts of the United States shall be given the same force and effect as are given the judgments of the courts of the States wherein they are rendered; but it is equally true that whether a Federal judgment has been given due force and effect in the state court is a Federal question reviewable by this court, which will determine for itself whether such judgment has been given due weight or otherwise. * * *

> When is the state court obliged to give to Federal judgments only the force and effect it gives to state court judgments within its own jurisdiction? Such cases are distinctly pointed out in the opinion of Mr. Justice Bradley in *Dupasseur v. Rochereau* [which stated that

---

[44] We do not decide whether, in a diversity case, a federal court's "dismissal upon the merits" (in the sense we have described), under circumstances where a state court would decree only a "dismissal without prejudice," abridges a "substantive right" and thus exceeds the authorization of the Rules Enabling Act. We think the situation will present itself more rarely than would the arguable violation of the Act that would ensue from interpreting Rule 41(b) as a rule of claim preclusion; and if it is a violation, can be more easily dealt with on direct appeal.

the case was a diversity case, applying state law under state procedure]."

In other words, in *Dupasseur* the State was allowed (indeed, required) to give a federal diversity judgment no more effect than it would accord one of its own judgments only because reference to state law was *the federal rule that this Court deemed appropriate.* In short, federal common law governs the claim-preclusive effect of a dismissal by a federal court sitting in diversity.

It is left to us, then, to determine the appropriate federal rule. And despite the sea change that has occurred in the background law since *Dupasseur* was decided—not only repeal of the Conformity Act but also the watershed decision of this Court in *Erie*—we think the result decreed by *Dupasseur* continues to be correct for diversity cases. Since state, rather than federal, substantive law is at issue there is no need for a uniform federal rule. And indeed, nationwide uniformity in the substance of the matter is better served by having the same claim-preclusive rule (the state rule) apply whether the dismissal has been ordered by a state or a federal court. This is, it seems to us, a classic case for adopting, as the federally prescribed rule of decision, the law that would be applied by state courts in the State in which the federal diversity court sits. As we have alluded to above, any other rule would produce the sort of "forum-shopping * * * and * * * inequitable administration of the laws" that *Erie* seeks to avoid, since filing in, or removing to, federal court would be encouraged by the divergent effects that the litigants would anticipate from likely grounds of dismissal.

This federal reference to state law will not obtain, of course, in situations in which the state law is incompatible with federal interests. If, for example, state law did not accord claim-preclusive effect to dismissals for willful violation of discovery orders, federal courts' interest in the integrity of their own processes might justify a contrary federal rule. No such conflict with potential federal interests exists in the present case. Dismissal of this state cause of action was decreed by the California federal court only because the California statute of limitations so required; and there is no conceivable federal interest in giving that time bar more effect in other courts than the California courts themselves would impose.

* * *

Because the claim-preclusive effect of the California federal court's dismissal "upon the merits" of petitioner's action on statute-of-limitations grounds is governed by a federal rule that in turn incorporates California's law of claim preclusion (the content of which we do not pass upon today), the Maryland Court of Special Appeals erred in holding that the dismissal necessarily precluded the bringing of this action in the Maryland courts. The judgment is reversed, and the case remanded for further proceedings not inconsistent with this opinion.

It is so ordered.

Notes and Questions

1. The Court notes *Dupasseur* as an example of a state giving a federal judgment the same effect as a state judgment, not more, because of the Court's own direction. Is this incompatible with Justice Scalia's opening mention that the Court decided *Dupasseur* pursuant to the Conformity Act of 1872, which prescribed federal courts' use of state procedure? In other words, was it the Court's direction or Congress's that produced the result?

2. Is the Court's adoption of state law as the content of the federal common law rule at odds with its previous insistence in *Boyle* (authored by Justice Scalia) and *Atherton* that the Court should not make federal common law unless it first finds what Justice Scalia called "a significant conflict" between state law and federal interests? If so, should one conclude that the Court has shifted its course on federal common law? If not, how can one reconcile the approach in *Semtek* with that of *Boyle* and *Atherton*? The latter seemed to say that state law remained in place unless some conflict with federal interests required its displacement. What is the conflict here, or indeed, in any case in which the Court directs adoption of state law as the content of federal common law?

3. The Court asserts that because state law provides the rule of decision in *Semtek*, a diversity case, there is no need for a uniform federal rule of preclusion. Is the Court suggesting that the choice of preclusion law depends upon whether the claim being adjudicated reaches the court via federal question or diversity jurisdiction? If so, why? Alternatively, is the determinative factor that "state, rather than federal, substantive law is at issue?" If so, why should that be determinative?

Is there a federal interest in having all federal judgments subject to the same preclusion rules? When federal courts exercise supplemental jurisdiction over state law claims, state law provides the rule of decision. Is there thus no need for uniform federal rules to govern the preclusive effect of a federal court's determination of supplemental state law claims? Or is there a federal interest in having all the claims determined by a court in a single judgment subject to the same preclusion rules?

4. *Empire Healthchoice Assurance, Inc. v. McVeigh*, 547 U.S. 677, 126 S.Ct. 2121, 165 L.Ed.2d 131 (2006), demonstrated how difficult the *Erie*-choice-of-law question remains on the substantive side of the ledger. Joseph McVeigh was a federal employee covered by the Federal Employees Health Benefits Act of 1959 (FEHBA). The federal Office of Personnel Management (OPM) contracted with private carriers for them to provide health insurance plans, and McVeigh was an enrollee of the Empire Healthchoice Plan in New York until his death. Premiums paid by the government and enrollees went into a special Treasury Department fund, from which the carriers paid benefits. McVeigh was badly injured in an accident, and over the course of the remaining four years of his life, Blue Cross paid almost $160,000 in benefits. The health insurance contract to which McVeigh was a party (by reason of his enrolling or accepting services under the plan) provided in part that if a

covered individual wrongfully suffered illness or injury at the hands of another, the carrier was entitled to reimbursement of compensated expenses if there was a recovery from the tortfeasors on any basis ("lawsuit, settlement or otherwise"). (It provided alternatively that if the enrollee elected not to pursue a claim, the carrier was subrogated to the claim.) Reimbursement funds that the carriers received were redeposited in the fund.

McVeigh's surviving wife and child settled claims against the tortfeasors for more than $3,000,000. The carrier asserted a claim for reimbursement and, when McVeigh's wife, as administratrix of his estate, rejected the claim, the carrier sued in the Southern District of New York. The defendant sought dismissal for lack of subject matter jurisdiction, arguing that the case was a simple contract dispute between two private parties. The district and circuit courts agreed, and the case made its way to the Supreme Court, which split five-to-four on the issue. Although the question on which the Court granted certiorari was whether there was jurisdiction under 28 U.S.C. § 1331, that question turned entirely on whether federal or state law should govern the carrier's claim for reimbursement.

Empire's arguments were reminiscent of those heard in cases such as *Kimbell Foods* (*supra* at 395) and *Boyle v. United Technologies, Inc.* (*supra* at 406). It argued first that federal common law governed and second that the Empire Healthchoice Plan itself constituted federal law because it was a contract with the federal government. In support of those positions, Empire argued *à la Boyle* that because resolution of the dispute ultimately would affect the federal treasury and the cost of providing health insurance to federal employees, federal control and uniformity of rules governing reimbursement were essential. Empire also argued that Congress had manifested an interest in uniformity with respect to plan benefits.

Justice Ginsburg's majority opinion disagreed. It noted that the critical factor was Congress's intent to have federal law govern and went on to point out that although the contract that OPM negotiated with its carriers required reimbursement, FEHBA, the statute that authorized the contract contained no such provision. Thus, the majority declined to accept Empire's argument that the federal law created the right to reimbursement and therefore should govern reimbursement disputes.

The majority, adverting to *Boyle*'s two-part test for creating federal common law (unique federal interest plus significant conflict between the application of state law and the identified federal interest), declined to find a significant conflict. It relied on the Second Circuit's majority and concurring opinions, both of which had made clear that the burden with respect to significant conflict rested on the party seeking the creation of federal common law—here Empire—and that there had been no showing of any conflict between New York law that would otherwise govern the reimbursement claim and the unique federal interest that Empire asserted.

In addition, the opinion noted that had Empire been subrogated to McVeigh's entitlement to sue, federal law clearly would not have governed the action. The tortfeasors were strangers to the contract negotiated by OPM with the carriers and to the agreement between the carriers and their insureds. Accordingly, none of those agreements, assuming *arguendo* that federal law governed any dispute connected with them, could apply to the tortfeasors, whose "liability, whether to the insured or the insurer, would be governed not by an agreement to which the tortfeasors are strangers, but by state law, and § 8902(m)(1) would have no sway."

Justice Breyer, writing for the four dissenters, dwelt on the pervasively federal nature of the entire health care program[13] and the fact that the contract under which the reimbursement entitlement arose was between a federal agency and the insurance carriers. In effect, he characterized the federal government as the real party in interest, the carrier merely being its agent with respect both to administering the health plans and to seeking reimbursement for payouts to enrollees who subsequently received compensation from tortfeasors. He relied heavily on *Clearfield* for its holding that federal law governed the United States' duties and rights with regard to federal commercial paper.

In the course of that argument, Justice Breyer cited *Kimbell Foods*. That was a curious case upon which to rely, was it not? After all, notwithstanding that the Court ruled that federal common law had to govern SBA and FHA loans' priority *vis-à-vis* other claims on the debtor, it adopted state law as the content of the federal common law. In the course of doing that, the Court rejected the government's argument that its interest in recoupment of funds required a uniform federal rule, noting that the purpose of the lending programs was not to generate revenue, but rather to provide federal support for people and businesses whom Congress had identified as in need of it. One might make the same argument in response to Justice Breyer. The purpose of the federal health insurance program is not to generate revenue. To be sure, to the extent that the program is able to recoup benefits payments, the fund is better able to make subsequent payments, but the government made the same argument with respect to the SBA and FHA programs in *Kimbell Foods*, to no avail.

***

NOTE ON DISCERNING THE CONTENT OF STATE LAW

Once a federal court has determined that state law governs an issue, because 1) *Erie* says it must as a matter of constitutional imperative, or 2) state law exists in an area of concurrent federal and state power and Congress has not displaced the state law, or 3) state law is to be adopted, as in *Kimbell Foods*, as the appropriate content of federal common law,

---

[13]   He characterized the matter as follows:

> In sum, the statute is federal, the program it creates is federal, the program's beneficiaries are federal employees working throughout the country, the Federal Government pays all relevant costs, and the Federal Government receives all relevant payments. The private carrier's only role in this scheme is to administer the health benefits plan for the federal agency in exchange for a fixed service charge.

the court must then determine what the state law is. That is easy if there is a state statute directly on point or if the highest state court recently issued an opinion. For most cases, however, the federal court has a more difficult task at hand.

The Supreme Court has addressed this issue on several occasions. *Commissioner of Internal Revenue v. Bosch's Estate*, 387 U.S. 456, 87 S.Ct. 1776, 18 L.Ed.2d 886 (1967), summarized the precepts that should guide federal judges. Justice Clark noted that *Erie* requires the federal courts to follow decisions of the highest state courts on issues properly governed by state law. The difficulty arises when the highest court has not spoken and the federal court confronts only lower state court decisions or no decisions at all. In such circumstances, the federal judge should accord some weight to decisions of inferior state courts, but they are not dispositive.

> [E]ven in diversity cases this Court has * * * held that while the decrees of "lower state courts" should be "attributed some weight * * * the decision [is] not controlling * * * " where the highest court of the State has not spoken on the point. [T]his Court further held that "an intermediate appellate state court [decision] * * * is a datum for ascertaining state law which is not to be disregarded by a federal court *unless it is convinced by other persuasive data that the highest court of the state would decide otherwise.*" * * * [T]he underlying substantive rule involved is based on state law and the State's highest court is the best authority on its own law. If there be no decision by that court then federal authorities must apply what they find to be the state law after giving "proper regard" to relevant rulings of other courts of the state. In this respect, [the federal court] may be said to be, in effect, sitting as a state court.

Thus, the federal courts place themselves in the position of inferior state courts and apply essentially the same processes for determining unsettled questions of state law.[14]

---

[14] District court determinations of state law are subject to the normal appellate review process. In Salve Regina College v. Russell, 499 U.S. 225, 111 S.Ct. 1217, 113 L.Ed.2d 190 (1991), the Court ruled that the circuit courts should not defer to district court determinations of state law, but instead should conduct their own *de novo* review of state law under the general principles for determining what state law is.

2.   *Construing a Jurisdictional Grant as a Command to Create Federal Common Law*

TEXTILE WORKERS UNION v. LINCOLN MILLS
Supreme Court of the United States, 1957.
353 U.S. 448, 77 S.Ct. 912, 1 L.Ed.2d 972.

MR. JUSTICE DOUGLAS delivered the opinion of the Court.

Petitioner-union entered into a collective bargaining agreement in 1953 with respondent-employer, the agreement to run one year and from year to year thereafter, unless terminated on specified notices. The agreement provided that there would be no strikes or work stoppages and that grievances would be handled pursuant to a specified procedure. The last step in the grievance procedure—a step that could be taken by either party—was arbitration.

This controversy involves several grievances that concern work loads and work assignments. The grievances were processed through the various steps in the grievance procedure and were finally denied by the employer. The union requested arbitration, and the employer refused. Thereupon the union brought this suit in the District Court to compel arbitration.

The District Court concluded that it had jurisdiction and ordered the employer to comply with the grievance arbitration provisions of the collective bargaining agreement. The Court of Appeals reversed by a divided vote. It held that, although the District Court had jurisdiction to entertain the suit, the court had no authority founded either in federal or state law to grant the relief. The case is here on a petition for a writ of certiorari which we granted because of the importance of the problem and the contrariety of views in the courts.

The starting point of our inquiry is § 301 of the Labor Management Relations Act of 1947, which provides:

> (a) Suits for violation of contracts between an employer and a labor organization representing employees in an industry affecting commerce as defined in this chapter, or between any such labor organizations, may be brought in any district court of the United States having jurisdiction of the parties, without respect to the amount in controversy or without regard to the citizenship of the parties.

> (b) Any labor organization which represents employees in an industry affecting commerce as defined in this chapter and any employer whose activities affect commerce as defined in this chapter shall be bound by the acts of its agents. Any such labor organization may sue or be sued as an entity and in behalf of the employees whom it represents in the courts of the United States. Any money judgment against a labor organization in a district court of the United States shall be enforceable only against the organization as an entity and

against its assets, and shall not be enforceable against any individual member or his assets.

There has been considerable litigation involving § 301 and courts have construed it differently. There is one view that § 301(a) merely gives federal district courts jurisdiction in controversies that involve labor organizations in industries affecting commerce, without regard to diversity of citizenship or the amount in controversy. Under that view § 301(a) would not be the source of substantive law; it would neither supply federal law to resolve these controversies nor turn the federal judges to state law for answers to the questions. Other courts—the overwhelming number of them—hold that § 301(a) is more than jurisdictional—that it authorizes federal courts to fashion a body of federal law for the enforcement of these collective bargaining agreements and includes within that federal law specific performance of promises to arbitrate grievances under collective bargaining agreements. * * * That is our construction of § 301(a), which means that the agreement to arbitrate grievance disputes, contained in this collective bargaining agreement, should be specifically enforced.

From the face of the Act it is apparent that § 301(a) and § 301(b) supplement one another. Section 301(b) makes it possible for a labor organization, representing employees in an industry affecting commerce, to sue and be sued as an entity in the federal courts. Section 301(b) in other words provides the procedural remedy lacking at common law. Section 301(a) certainly does something more than that. Plainly, it supplies the basis upon which the federal district courts may take jurisdiction and apply the procedural rule of § 301(b). The question is whether § 301(a) is more than jurisdictional.

The legislative history of § 301 is somewhat cloudy and confusing. But there are a few shafts of light that illuminate our problem.

The bills, as they passed the House and the Senate, contained provisions which would have made the failure to abide by an agreement to arbitrate an unfair labor practice. This feature of the law was dropped in Conference. As the Conference Report stated, "Once parties have made a collective bargaining contract the enforcement of that contract should be left to the usual processes of the law and not to the National Labor Relations Board."

Both the Senate and the House took pains to provide for "the usual processes of the law" by provisions which were the substantial equivalent of § 301(a) in its present form. Both the Senate Report and the House Report indicate a primary concern that unions as well as employees should be bound to collective bargaining contracts. But there was also a broader concern—a concern with a procedure for making such agreements enforceable in the courts by either party. At one point the Senate Report, states,

We feel that the aggrieved party should also have a right of action in the Federal courts. Such a policy is completely in accord with the purpose of the Wagner Act which the Supreme Court declared was "to compel employers to bargain collectively with their employees to the end that an employment contract, binding on both parties, should be made * * * ."

Congress was also interested in promoting collective bargaining that ended with agreements not to strike.

* * *

Plainly the agreement to arbitrate grievance disputes is the *quid pro quo* for an agreement not to strike. Viewed in this light, the legislation does more than confer jurisdiction in the federal courts over labor organizations. It expresses a federal policy that federal courts should enforce these agreements on behalf of or against labor organizations and that industrial peace can be best obtained only in that way.

To be sure, there is a great medley of ideas reflected in the hearings, reports, and debates on this Act. Yet, to repeat, the entire tenor of the history indicates that the agreement to arbitrate grievance disputes was considered as *quid pro quo* of a no-strike agreement. And when in the House the debate narrowed to the question whether § 301 was more than jurisdictional, it became abundantly clear that the purpose of the section was to provide the necessary legal remedies. Section 302 of the House bill, the substantial equivalent of the present § 301, was being described by Mr. Hartley, the sponsor of the bill in the House:

> Mr. BARDEN. Mr. Chairman, I take this time for the purpose of asking the Chairman a question, and in asking the question I want it understood that it is intended to make a part of the record that may hereafter be referred to as history of the legislation.
>
> It is my understanding that section 302, the section dealing with equal responsibility under collective bargaining contracts in strike actions and proceedings in district courts contemplates not only the ordinary lawsuits for damages but also such other remedial proceedings, both legal and equitable, as might be appropriate in the circumstances; in other words, proceedings could, for example, be brought by the employers, the labor organizations, or interested individual employees under the Declaratory Judgments Act in order to secure declarations from the Court of legal rights under the contract.
>
> Mr. HARTLEY. The interpretation the gentleman has just given of that section is absolutely correct.

It seems, therefore, clear to us that Congress adopted a policy which placed sanctions behind agreements to arbitrate grievance disputes, by implication rejecting the common-law rule against enforcement of executory agreements to arbitrate. We would undercut the Act and defeat its policy if we read § 301 narrowly as only conferring jurisdiction over labor organizations.

The question then is, what is the substantive law to be applied in suits under § 301(a)? We conclude that the substantive law to apply in suits under § 301(a) is federal law, which the courts must fashion from the policy of our national labor laws. The Labor Management Relations Act expressly furnishes some substantive law. It points out what the parties may or may not do in certain situations. Other problems will lie in the penumbra of express statutory mandates. Some will lack express statutory sanction but will be solved by looking at the policy of the legislation and fashioning a remedy that will effectuate that policy. The range of judicial inventiveness will be determined by the nature of the problem. Federal interpretation of the federal law will govern, not state law. But state law, if compatible with the purpose of § 301, may be resorted to in order to find the rule that will best effectuate the federal policy. Any state law applied, however, will be absorbed as federal law and will not be an independent source of private rights.

It is not uncommon for federal courts to fashion federal law where federal rights are concerned. Congress has indicated by § 301(a) the purpose to follow that course here. There is no constitutional difficulty. Article III, § 2, extends the judicial power to cases "arising under * * * the Laws of the United States * * * ." The power of Congress to regulate these labor-management controversies under the Commerce Clause is plain. A case or controversy arising under § 301(a) is, therefore, one within the purview of judicial power as defined in Article III.

* * *

The judgment of the Court of Appeals is reversed and the cause is remanded to that court for proceedings in conformity with this opinion.

Reversed.

MR. JUSTICE FRANKFURTER, dissenting.

The Court has avoided the difficult problems raised by § 301 of the Taft-Hartley Act by attributing to the section an occult content. This plainly procedural section is transmuted into a mandate to the federal courts to fashion a whole body of substantive federal law appropriate for the complicated and touchy problems raised by collective bargaining. * * * I believe that § 301 cannot be so construed, even if constitutional questions cannot be avoided. But the Court has a "clear" and contrary conclusion emerge from the "somewhat," to say the least, "cloudy and confusing legislative history." This is more than can be fairly asked even from the alchemy of construction. Since the Court relies on a few isolated statements in the legislative history which do not support its conclusion, however favoringly read, I have deemed it necessary to set forth in an appendix the entire relevant legislative history of the Taft-Hartley Act and its predecessor, the Case Bill. This legislative history reinforces the natural meaning of the statute as an exclusively procedural provision, affording, that is, an accessible federal forum for suits on agreements between labor organizations and employers, but not enacting federal law for such suits.

* * *

One word more remains to be said. The earliest declaration of unconstitutionality of an act of Congress—by the Justices on circuit—involved a refusal by the Justices to perform a function imposed upon them by Congress because of the non-judicial nature of that function. Since then, the Court has many times declared legislation unconstitutional because it imposed on the Court powers or functions that were regarded as outside the scope of the "judicial power" lodged in the Court by the Constitution.

One may fairly generalize from these instances that the Court has deemed itself peculiarly qualified, with due regard to the contrary judgment of Congress, to determine what is meet and fit for the exercise of "judicial power" as authorized by the Constitution. Solicitude and respect for the confines of "judicial power," and the difficult problem of marking those confines, apply equally in construing precisely what duties Congress has cast upon the federal courts, especially when, as in this case, the most that can be said in support of finding a congressional desire to impose these "legislative" duties on the federal courts is that Congress did not mention the problem in the statute and that, insofar as purpose may be gathered from congressional reports and debates, they leave us in the dark.

The Court, however, sees no problem of "judicial power" in casting upon the federal courts, with no guides except "judicial inventiveness," the task of applying a whole industrial code that is as yet in the bosom of the judiciary. There are severe limits on "judicial inventiveness" even for the most imaginative judges. The law is not a "brooding omnipresence in the sky," and it cannot be drawn from there like nitrogen from the air. These problems created by the Court's interpretation of § 301 cannot "be solved by resort to the established canons of construction that enable a court to look through awkward or clumsy expression, or language wanting in precision, to the intent of the legislature. For the vice of the statute here lies in the impossibility of ascertaining, by any reasonable test, that the legislature meant one thing rather than another * * *." But the Court makes § 301 a mountain instead of a molehill and, by giving an example of "judicial inventiveness," it thereby solves all the constitutional problems that would otherwise have to be faced.

* * *

Notes and Questions

1. Justice Frankfurter has a point; surely if Congress intended to authorize the federal courts to fashion a vast body of substantive labor law, § 301 is a particularly backhanded manner of communicating that. Assuming that was Congress's intent, is the delegation permissible? May Congress assign such wide-ranging exercise of fundamentally legislative power to another branch, or does that circumvent the deliberately cumbersome process Article I describes for enacting a law? On the majority's theory of delegation, there is nothing to stop Congress from assigning legislative power to the President, thus uniting in one branch a legislative process that the Framers prescribed should be separated into two.

2. If Justice Frankfurter is correct that there was no delegation, then can § 301 survive scrutiny under Article III? What is the constitutional basis for a purely jurisdictional statute that confers jurisdiction upon the district courts "without respect to the amount in controversy or without regard to the citizenship of the parties"? If such a statute seems plainly outside the ambit of Article III, § 2, perhaps Congress, presumptively aware of the Court's jurisdictional jurisprudence, would have been unlikely to enact a patently unconstitutional jurisdictional grant and so must have believed there was some "federal question" basis to labor law actions. But does that inference compel or even suggest the further inference that Congress intended to enlist the federal judiciary as additional lawmakers?

3. There is a middle possibility for *Lincoln Mills*. The cryptic reference in § 301 to "an industry affecting commerce" apparently refers to Congress's power to legislate under the Commerce Clause. This, in turn, raises the question of "protective jurisdiction." As Professor Redish points out, the theory exists in two forms, one that would allow a grant of jurisdiction to consider cases involving any area in which Congress can legislate, whether or not it already has, and the other requiring that Congress have already enacted " 'statutes expressing a national policy in the area concerned * * * .' " MARTIN H. REDISH, FEDERAL JURISDICTION: TENSIONS IN THE ALLOCATION OF JUDICIAL POWER 92 (2d ed. 1990) (quoting Paul J. Mishkin, *The Federal "Question" in the District Courts*, 53 COLUM.L.REV. 157, 195 (1953)). Justice Frankfurter's *Lincoln Mills* repudiation of protective jurisdiction is reproduced following *Osborn v. Bank of the United States*, 22 U.S. (9 Wheat.) 738, 6 L.Ed. 204 (1824), in Chapter 3 at pages 237-246. Is protective jurisdiction consistent with the jurisdictional theory of *Osborn* and *Verlinden B.V. v. Central Bank of Nigeria*, 461 U.S. 480, 103 S.Ct. 1962, 76 L.Ed.2d 81 (1983)? If so, on which of the bases described above? If not, can one save the majority's opinion?

4. If the Court's reasoning is supportable, how can one determine which jurisdiction-conferring statutes are intended also as directions to the federal courts to create federal common law and which are not? Should the Court presume that whenever Congress grants jurisdiction but has not enacted a comprehensive legislative scheme, it intends the federal courts to step into the breach?

5. Not all directions to the federal courts to create common law come in

jurisdictional statutes. Federal Rule of Evidence 501 provides:

> Except as otherwise required by the Constitution of the United States or provided by Act of Congress, or in rules prescribed by the Supreme Court pursuant to statutory authority, the privilege of a witness, person, government, State, or political subdivision thereof shall be governed by the principles of the common law as they may be interpreted by the courts of the United States in the light of reason and experience. However, in civil actions and proceedings, with respect to an element of a claim or defense as to which State law supplies the rule of decision, the privilege of a witness, person, government, State or political subdivision thereof shall be determined in accordance with State law.

Pursuant to that authorization, the Supreme Court recognized a new psychotherapist-patient privilege in *Jaffee v. Redmond*, 518 U.S. 1, 116 S.Ct. 1923, 135 L.Ed.2d 337 (1996). This, of course, raises the same delegation difficulties as are present in *Lincoln Mills*, but with an additional twist. The enabling statute that governs the Federal Rules of Evidence, 28 U.S.C. § 2072 (1994), is also the statute that governs the Federal Rules of Civil Procedure; rules proposed by the Supreme Court become effective if not disapproved by Congress by a date certain. *See* 28 U.S.C. § 2076 (1994). However, when the Court first proposed the Federal Rules of Evidence, the privilege provisions would have extended to documents or reports required by statute to be prepared and specifically recognized the following relationships as privileged: lawyer-client, psychotherapist-patient, husband-wife, and clergyman-congregant. Those proposals were sufficiently controversial that Congress disapproved them, substituting Rule 501 above, and further required affirmative approval of any subsequent modification of the rule governing privilege before it may go into effect: "Any such amendment [to the Federal Rules of Evidence] creating, abolishing, or modifying a privilege shall have no force and effect unless it shall be approved by act of Congress." *Id.* Does Congress's restrictive reaction to the original proposals of privileges under the Federal Rules connote its own dissatisfaction with the delegation of common law lawmaking authority generally, or does it represent Congress's faith in its legitimacy? Is the procedure Congress prescribed subject to the same objections as the type of delegation the Court found in *Lincoln Mills*?

Note that the limitations of the privileges prescribed by Rule 501 pose some interesting questions for the federal courts. Suppose, for example, that an individual brings a federal civil rights action against a state governmental actor and joins a parallel state claim with it, as happened in *Jaffee*. The defendant official may claim the new psychotherapist privilege, but state law may not recognize it. Does this mean that the court has to try the claims separately even though there is considerable overlap in their factual predicates? Or, if the claims may be tried together, should the court recognize the privilege?

6. In admiralty and antitrust law, the federal courts have been essentially unrestrained in creating common law. The only mention of admiralty or maritime law in the Constitution is in Article III, which allows federal jurisdiction over such cases. There is no corresponding grant of legislative

power in Article I. Most (but not all) of the law of admiralty is judge-made.[15]

No one has ever seriously questioned the federal courts' power to create such wide-ranging common law, though to be sure the source of authority for doing so is obscure. Justice Story argued in *DeLovio v. Boit,* 7 F.Cas. 418 (C.C.D.Mass.1815), that the constitutional grant of jurisdiction is an implicit command to the federal courts to create the needed body of law. Such a suggestion, however, proves too much. If the grant of admiralty jurisdiction empowers the federal court to create a law of admiralty, why does not the grant of diversity jurisdiction in the same sentence authorize the creation of a federal common law of the type that *Erie* condemned as unconstitutional? In *Southern Pacific Co. v. Jensen,* 244 U.S. 205, 37 S.Ct. 524, 61 L.Ed. 1086 (1917), the Court observed that long-established practice confirmed that the federal courts had adopted the general maritime law and that the Constitution contemplated that they would. Whatever the underlying authority, the federal courts' practice of creating admiralty common law is well established and functions in service of policies of uniformity and strong federal interest that are easily understood..

The basic statutes governing antitrust law, the Sherman Antitrust Act, 15 U.S.C.A. § 1 *et seq.* and the Clayton Act, 15 U.S.C.A. § 15, speak in very broad terms; the federal courts have developed most of the specific governing rules. Antitrust law stands on a footing different from admiralty law, however, because the antitrust statutes are interpreted as intentional, though implicit, delegations of law-making authority from Congress to the federal courts, much as the Court found in *Textile Workers Union v. Lincoln Mills.* The development of common law in this area is distinguishable from *Lincoln Mills* only because here there are at least some substantive statutory provisions expressing congressional goals, whereas in *Lincoln Mills* the statute purported only to be a jurisdictional grant. For institutional legitimacy purposes, does it make any difference whether the courts are trying to determine what Congress meant by "restraint of trade" or are themselves deciding what "restraint of trade" means?

3. Implying Private Rights of Action

BIVENS v. SIX UNKNOWN NAMED AGENTS OF FEDERAL BUREAU OF NARCOTICS

Supreme Court of the United States, 1971.
403 U.S. 388, 91 S.Ct. 1999, 29 L.Ed.2d 619.

MR. JUSTICE BRENNAN delivered the opinion of the Court.

The Fourth Amendment provides that: "The right of the people to be

---

[15] Congress' power to legislate derives from the Necessary and Proper Clause—U.S. CONST. art. I, § 8, cl. 18. In Southern Pacific Co. v. Jensen, 244 U.S. 205, 214-15, 37 S.Ct. 524, 528-29, 61 L.Ed. 1086, 1097-98 (1917), the Court noted that the Necessary and Proper Clause empowers Congress to legislate with respect to all powers vested in any department of the federal government. Since Article III, § 2 brings admiralty cases within the judicial power, the Court reasoned that Congress could legislate in that area even without a specific Article I grant.

secure in their persons, houses, papers, and effects, against unreasonable searches and seizures, shall not be violated * * * ."

In *Bell v. Hood* we reserved the question whether violation of that command by a federal agent acting under color of his authority gives rise to a cause of action for damages consequent upon his unconstitutional conduct. Today we hold that it does.

This case has its origin in an arrest and search carried out on the morning of November 26, 1965. Petitioner's complaint alleged that on that day respondents, agents of the Federal Bureau of Narcotics acting under claim of federal authority, entered his apartment and arrested him for alleged narcotics violations. The agents manacled petitioner in front of his wife and children, and threatened to arrest the entire family. They searched the apartment from stem to stern. Thereafter, petitioner was taken to the federal courthouse in Brooklyn, where he was interrogated, booked, and subjected to a visual strip search.

On July 7, 1967, petitioner brought suit in Federal District Court. In addition to the allegations above, his complaint asserted that the arrest and search were effected without a warrant, and that unreasonable force was employed in making the arrest; fairly read, it alleges as well that the arrest was made without probable cause.[1] Petitioner claimed to have suffered great humiliation, embarrassment, and mental suffering as a result of the agents' unlawful conduct, and sought $15,000 damages from each of them. The District Court, on respondents' motion, dismissed the complaint on the ground, *inter alia*, that it failed to state a cause of action. The Court of Appeals * * * affirmed on that basis. * * * We reverse.

I

Respondents do not argue that petitioner should be entirely without remedy for an unconstitutional invasion of his rights by federal agents. In respondents' view, however, the rights that petitioner asserts—primarily rights of privacy—are creations of state and not of federal law. Accordingly, they argue, petitioner may obtain money damages to redress invasion of these rights only by an action in tort, under state law, in the state courts. In this scheme the Fourth Amendment would serve merely to limit the extent to which the agents could defend the state law tort suit by asserting that their actions were a valid exercise of federal power: if the agents were shown to have violated the Fourth Amendment, such a defense would be lost to them and they would stand before the state law merely as private individuals. Candidly admitting that it

---

[1] Petitioner's complaint does not explicitly state that the agents had no probable cause for his arrest, but it does allege that the arrest was "done unlawfully, unreasonably and contrary to law." Petitioner's affidavit in support of his motion for summary judgment swears that the search was "without cause, consent or warrant," and that the arrest was "without cause, reason or warrant."

is the policy of the Department of Justice to remove all such suits from the state to the federal courts for decision,[4] respondents nevertheless urge that we uphold dismissal of petitioner's complaint in federal court, and remit him to filing an action in the state courts in order that the case may properly be removed to the federal court for decision on the basis of state law.

We think that respondents' thesis rests upon an unduly restrictive view of the Fourth Amendment's protection against unreasonable searches and seizures by federal agents, a view that has consistently been rejected by this Court. Respondents seek to treat the relationship between a citizen and a federal agent unconstitutionally exercising his authority as no different from the relationship between two private citizens. In so doing, they ignore the fact that power, once granted, does not disappear like a magic gift when it is wrongfully used. An agent acting—albeit unconstitutionally—in the name of the United States possesses a far greater capacity for harm than an individual trespasser exercising no authority other than his own. Accordingly, as our cases make clear, the Fourth Amendment operates as a limitation upon the exercise of federal power regardless of whether the State in whose jurisdiction that power is exercised would prohibit or penalize the identical act if engaged in by a private citizen. It guarantees to citizens of the United States the absolute right to be free from unreasonable searches and seizures carried out by virtue of federal authority. And "where federally protected rights have been invaded, it has been the rule from the beginning that courts will be alert to adjust their remedies so as to grant the necessary relief."

First. Our cases have long since rejected the notion that the Fourth Amendment proscribes only such conduct as would, if engaged in by private persons, be condemned by state law. * * * And our recent decisions regarding electronic surveillance have made it clear beyond peradventure that the Fourth Amendment is not tied to the niceties of local trespass laws. In light of these cases, respondents' argument that the Fourth Amendment serves only as a limitation on federal defenses to a state law claim, and not as an independent limitation upon the exercise of federal power, must be rejected.

Second. The interests protected by state laws regulating trespass and the invasion of privacy, and those protected by the Fourth Amendment's guarantee against unreasonable searches and seizures, may be inconsistent or even hostile. Thus, we may bar the door against an un-

---

[4] * * * In light of this, it is difficult to understand our Brother Blackmun's complaint that our holding today "opens the door for another avalanche of new federal cases." In estimating the magnitude of any such "avalanche," it is worth noting that a survey of comparable actions against state officers under 42 U.S.C. § 1983 found only 53 reported cases in 17 years (1951-1967) that survived a motion to dismiss. Increasing this figure by 900% to allow for increases in rate and unreported cases, every federal district judge could expect to try one such case every 13 years.

welcome private intruder, or call the police if he persists in seeking entrance. The availability of such alternative means for the protection of privacy may lead the State to restrict imposition of liability for any consequent trespass. A private citizen, asserting no authority other than his own, will not normally be liable in trespass if he demands, and is granted, admission to another's house. But one who demands admission under a claim of federal authority stands in a far different position. The mere invocation of federal power by a federal law enforcement official will normally render futile any attempt to resist an unlawful entry or arrest by resort to the local police; and a claim of authority to enter is likely to unlock the door as well. "In such cases there is no safety for the citizen, except in the protection of the judicial tribunals, for rights which have been invaded by the officers of the government, professing to act in its name. There remains to him but the alternative of resistance, which may amount to crime." Nor is it adequate to answer that state law may take into account the different status of one clothed with the authority of the Federal Government. For just as state law may not authorize federal agents to violate the Fourth Amendment, neither may state law undertake to limit the extent to which federal authority can be exercised. The inevitable consequence of this dual limitation on state power is that the federal question becomes not merely a possible defense to the state law action, but an independent claim both necessary and sufficient to make out the plaintiff's cause of action.

Third. That damages may be obtained for injuries consequent upon a violation of the Fourth Amendment by federal officials should hardly seem a surprising proposition. Historically, damages have been regarded as the ordinary remedy for an invasion of personal interests in liberty. Of course, the Fourth Amendment does not in so many words provide for its enforcement by an award of money damages for the consequences of its violation. But "it is * * * well settled that where legal rights have been invaded, and a federal statute provides for a general right to sue for such invasion, federal courts may use any available remedy to make good the wrong done." The present case involves no special factors counselling hesitation in the absence of affirmative action by Congress. We are not dealing with a question of "federal fiscal policy," as in *United States v. Standard Oil Co.* In that case we refused to infer from the Government-soldier relationship that the United States could recover damages from one who negligently injured a soldier and thereby caused the Government to pay his medical expenses and lose his services during the course of his hospitalization. Noting that Congress was normally quite solicitous where the federal purse was involved, we pointed out that "the United States [was] the party plaintiff to the suit. And the United States has power at any time to create the liability." Nor are we asked in this case to impose liability upon a congressional employee for actions contrary to no constitutional prohibition, but merely said to be in excess of the authority delegated to him by the Congress. Finally, we cannot accept respondents' formulation of the question as whether the availability of money damages is necessary to enforce the Fourth Amendment. For we have here no explicit congressional declaration that persons injured by a federal officer's violation of the Fourth Amendment may not recover money damages from the agents, but must instead be remitted to another remedy, equally effective in the view of Congress. The question is merely whether petitioner, if he can demonstrate an injury consequent upon the violation by federal agents of his Fourth Amendment rights, is entitled to redress his injury through a particular remedial mechanism normally available in the federal courts.

"The very essence of civil liberty certainly consists in the right of every individual to claim the protection of the laws, whenever he receives an injury." Having concluded that petitioner's complaint states a cause of action under the Fourth Amendment, we hold that petitioner is entitled to recover money damages for any injuries he has suffered as a result of the agents' violation of the Amendment.

II

In addition to holding that petitioner's complaint had failed to state facts making out a cause of action, the District Court ruled that in any event respondents were immune from liability by virtue of their official position. This question was not passed upon by the Court of Appeals, and accordingly we do not consider it here. The judgment of the Court of Appeals is reversed and the case is remanded for further proceedings consistent with this opinion.

So ordered.

MR. JUSTICE HARLAN, concurring in the judgment.

My initial view of this case was that the Court of Appeals was correct in dismissing the complaint, but for reasons stated in this opinion I am now persuaded to the contrary. Accordingly, I join in the judgment of reversal.

* * *

I

I turn first to the contention that the constitutional power of federal courts to accord Bivens damages for his claim depends on the passage of a statute creating a "federal cause of action." Although the point is not entirely free of ambiguity, I do not understand either the Government or my dissenting Brothers to maintain that Bivens' contention that he is entitled to be free from the type of official conduct prohibited by the Fourth Amendment depends on a decision by the State in which he resides to accord him a remedy. Such a position would be incompatible with the presumed availability of federal equitable relief, if a proper showing can be made in terms of the ordinary principles governing equitable remedies. However broad a federal court's discretion concerning equitable remedies, it is absolutely clear—at least after *Erie R. Co. v. Tompkins*—that in a nondiversity suit a federal court's power to grant even equitable relief depends on the presence of a substantive right derived from federal law.

Thus the interest which Bivens claims—to be free from official conduct in contravention of the Fourth Amendment—is a federally protected interest.[3] Therefore, the question of judicial power to grant Bivens damages is not a problem of the "source" of the "right"; instead, the question is whether the power to authorize damages as a judicial remedy for the vindication of a federal constitutional right is placed by the Constitution itself exclusively in Congress' hands.

II

The contention that the federal courts are powerless to accord a litigant damages for a claimed invasion of his federal constitutional rights until Congress explicitly authorizes the remedy cannot rest on the notion that the decision to grant compensatory relief involves a resolution of policy considerations not susceptible of judicial discernment. Thus, in suits for damages based on violations of federal statutes lacking any express authorization of a damage remedy, this Court has authorized such relief where, in its view, damages are necessary to effectuate the congressional policy underpinning the substantive provisions of the statute.[4]

---

[3] The Government appears not quite ready to concede this point. Certain points in the Government's argument seem to suggest that the "state-created right—federal defense" model reaches not only the question of the power to accord a federal damages remedy, but also the claim to any judicial remedy in any court. Thus, we are pointed to Lasson's observation concerning Madison's version of the Fourth Amendment as introduced into the House: "The observation may be made that the language of the proposal did not purport to create the right to be secure from unreasonable search and seizures but merely stated it as a right which already existed." * * *

On this point, the choice of phraseology in the Fourth Amendment itself is singularly unpersuasive. The leading argument against a "Bill of Rights" was the fear that individual liberties not specified expressly would be taken as excluded. This circumstance alone might well explain why the authors of the Bill of Rights would opt for language which presumes the existence of a fundamental interest in liberty, albeit originally derived from the common law.

In truth, the legislative record as a whole behind the Bill of Rights is silent on the rather refined doctrinal question whether the framers considered the rights therein enumerated as dependent in the first instance on the decision of a State to accord legal status to the personal interests at stake. That is understandable since the Government itself points out that general federal-question jurisdiction was not extended to the federal district courts until 1875. The most that can be drawn from this historical fact is that the authors of the Bill of Rights assumed the adequacy of common-law remedies to vindicate the federally protected interest. One must first combine this assumption with contemporary modes of jurisprudential thought which appeared to link "rights" and "remedies" in a 1:1 correlation, before reaching the conclusion that the framers are to be understood today as having created no federally protected interests. And, of course, that would simply require the conclusion that federal equitable relief would not lie to protect those interests guarded by the Fourth Amendment. * * *

[4] The *Borak* case is an especially clear example of the exercise of federal judicial power to accord damages as an appropriate remedy in the absence of any express statutory

If it is not the nature of the remedy which is thought to render a judgment as to the appropriateness of damages inherently "legislative," then it must be the nature of the legal interest offered as an occasion for invoking otherwise appropriate judicial relief. But I do not think that the fact that the interest is protected by the Constitution rather than statute or common law justifies the assertion that federal courts are powerless to grant damages in the absence of explicit congressional action authorizing the remedy. Initially, I note that it would be at least anomalous to conclude that the federal judiciary—while competent to choose among the range of traditional judicial remedies to implement statutory and common-law policies, and even to generate substantive rules governing primary behavior in furtherance of broadly formulated policies articulated by statute or Constitution—is powerless to accord a damages remedy to vindicate social policies which, by virtue of their inclusion in the Constitution, are aimed predominantly at restraining the Government as an instrument of the popular will.

More importantly, the presumed availability of federal equitable relief against threatened invasions of constitutional interests appears entirely to negate the contention that the status of an interest as constitutionally protected divests federal courts of the power to grant damages absent express congressional authorization. Congress provided specially for the exercise of equitable remedial powers by federal courts, in part because of the limited availability of equitable remedies in state courts in the early days of the Republic. And this Court's decisions make clear that, at least absent congressional restrictions, the scope of equitable remedial discretion is to be determined according to the distinctive historical traditions of equity as an institution. The reach of a federal district court's "inherent equitable powers," is broad indeed; nonetheless, the federal judiciary is not empowered to grant equitable relief in the absence of congressional action extending jurisdiction over the subject matter of the suit.

If explicit congressional authorization is an absolute prerequisite to the power of a federal court to accord compensatory relief regardless of the necessity or appropriateness of damages as a remedy simply because of the status of a legal interest as constitutionally protected, then it seems to me that explicit congressional authorization is similarly prerequisite to the exercise of equitable remedial discretion in favor of con-

---

authorization of a federal cause of action. There we "implied"—from what can only be characterized as an "exclusively procedural provision" affording access to a federal forum, *cf.* Textile Workers v. Lincoln Mills, 353 U.S. 448, 462-63 (1957) (Frankfurter, J., dissenting)—a private cause of action for damages for violation of § 14(a) of the Securities Exchange Act of 1934. We did so in an area where federal regulation has been singularly comprehensive and elaborate administrative enforcement machinery had been provided. The exercise of judicial power involved in *Borak* simply cannot be justified in terms of statutory construction, nor did the *Borak* Court purport to do so. The notion of "implying" a remedy, therefore, as applied to cases like *Borak,* can only refer to a process whereby the federal judiciary exercises a choice among traditionally available judicial remedies according to reasons related to the substantive social policy embodied in an act of positive law.

stitutionally protected interests. Conversely, if a general grant of jurisdiction to the federal courts by Congress is thought adequate to empower a federal court to grant equitable relief for all areas of subject-matter jurisdiction enumerated therein, then it seems to me that the same statute is sufficient to empower a federal court to grant a traditional remedy at law. Of course, the special historical traditions governing the federal equity system might still bear on the comparative appropriateness of granting equitable relief as opposed to money damages. That possibility, however, relates, not to whether the federal courts have the power to afford one type of remedy as opposed to the other, but rather to the criteria which should govern the exercise of our power. To that question, I now pass.

III

The major thrust of the Government's position is that, where Congress has not expressly authorized a particular remedy, a federal court should exercise its power to accord a traditional form of judicial relief at the behest of a litigant, who claims a constitutionally protected interest has been invaded, only where the remedy is "essential," or "indispensable for vindicating constitutional rights." While this "essentiality" test is most clearly articulated with respect to damages remedies, apparently the Government believes the same test explains the exercise of equitable remedial powers. It is argued that historically the Court has rarely exercised the power to accord such relief in the absence of an express congressional authorization and that "[i]f Congress had thought that federal officers should be subject to a law different than state law, it would have had no difficulty in saying so, as it did with respect to state officers * * * ." Although conceding that the standard of determining whether a damage remedy should be utilized to effectuate statutory policies is one of "necessity" or "appropriateness," the Government contends that questions concerning congressional discretion to modify judicial remedies relating to constitutionally protected interests warrant a more stringent constraint on the exercise of judicial power with respect to this class of legally protected interests.

These arguments for a more stringent test to govern the grant of damages in constitutional cases seem to be adequately answered by the point that the judiciary has a particular responsibility to assure the vindication of constitutional interests such as those embraced by the Fourth Amendment. To be sure, "it must be remembered that legislatures are ultimate guardians of the liberties and welfare of the people in quite as great a degree as the courts." But it must also be recognized that the Bill of Rights is particularly intended to vindicate the interests of the individual in the face of the popular will as expressed in legislative majorities; at the very least, it strikes me as no more appropriate to await express congressional authorization of traditional judicial relief with regard to these legal interests than with respect to interests protected by federal statutes.

The question then, is, as I see it, whether compensatory relief is "necessary" or "appropriate" to the vindication of the interest asserted. In resolving that question, it seems to me that the range of policy considerations we may take into account is at least as broad as the range of those a legislature would consider with respect to an express statutory authorization of a traditional remedy. In this regard I agree with the Court that the appropriateness of according Bivens compensatory relief does not turn simply on the deterrent effect liability will have on federal official conduct.[8] Damages as a traditional form of compensation for invasion of a legally protected interest may be entirely appropriate even if no substantial deterrent effects on future official lawlessness might be thought to result. Bivens, after all, has invoked judicial processes claiming entitlement to compensation for injuries resulting from allegedly lawless official behavior, if those injuries are properly compensable in money damages. I do not think a court of law—vested with the power to accord a remedy—should deny him his relief simply because he cannot show that future lawless conduct will thereby be deterred.

And I think it is clear that Bivens advances a claim of the sort that, if proved, would be properly compensable in damages. The personal interests protected by the Fourth Amendment are those we attempt to capture by the notion of "privacy"; while the Court today properly points out that the type of harm which officials can inflict when they invade protected zones of an individual's life are different from the types of harm private citizens inflict on one another, the experience of judges in dealing with private trespass and false imprisonment claims supports the conclusion that courts of law are capable of making the types of judgment concerning causation and magnitude of injury necessary to accord meaningful compensation for invasion of Fourth Amendment rights.

On the other hand, the limitations on state remedies for violation of common-law rights by private citizens argue in favor of a federal damages remedy. The injuries inflicted by officials acting under color of law, while no less compensable in damages than those inflicted by private parties, are substantially different in kind, as the Court's opinion today discusses in detail. It seems to me entirely proper that these injuries be compensable according to uniform rules of federal law, especially in light of the very large element of federal law which must in any event control

---

[8] And I think it follows from this point that today's decision has little, if indeed any, bearing on the question whether a federal court may properly devise remedies—other than traditionally available forms of judicial relief—for the purpose of enforcing substantive social policies embodied in constitutional or statutory policies. The Court today simply recognizes what has long been implicit in our decisions concerning equitable relief and remedies implied from statutory schemes; *i.e.,* that a court of law vested with jurisdiction over the subject matter of a suit has the power—and therefore the duty—to make principled choices among traditional judicial remedies. Whether special prophylactic measures— which at least arguably the exclusionary rule exemplifies—are supportable on grounds other than a court's competence to select among traditional judicial remedies to make good the wrong done is a separate question.

the scope of official defenses to liability. Certainly, there is very little to be gained from the standpoint of federalism by preserving different rules of liability for federal officers dependent on the State where the injury occurs.

Putting aside the desirability of leaving the problem of federal official liability to the vagaries of common-law actions, it is apparent that some form of damages is the only possible remedy for someone in Bivens' alleged position. It will be a rare case indeed in which an individual in Bivens' position will be able to obviate the harm by securing injunctive relief from any court. However desirable a direct remedy against the Government might be as a substitute for individual official liability, the sovereign still remains immune to suit. Finally, assuming Bivens' innocence of the crime charged, the "exclusionary rule" is simply irrelevant. For people in Bivens' shoes, it is damages or nothing.

The only substantial policy consideration advanced against recognition of a federal cause of action for violation of Fourth Amendment rights by federal officials is the incremental expenditure of judicial resources that will be necessitated by this class of litigation. There is, however, something ultimately self-defeating about this argument. For if, as the Government contends, damages will rarely be realized by plaintiffs in these cases because of jury hostility, the limited resources of the official concerned, etc., then I am not ready to assume that there will be a significant increase in the expenditure of judicial resources on these claims. Few responsible lawyers and plaintiffs are likely to choose the course of litigation if the statistical chances of success are truly *de minimis*. And I simply cannot agree with my Brother Black that the possibility of "frivolous" claims—if defined simply as claims with no legal merit—warrants closing the courthouse doors to people in Bivens' situation. There are other ways, short of that, of coping with frivolous lawsuits.

On the other hand, if—as I believe is the case with respect, at least, to the most flagrant abuses of official power—damages to some degree will be available when the option of litigation is chosen, then the question appears to be how Fourth Amendment interests rank on a scale of social values compared with, for example, the interests of stockholders defrauded by misleading proxies. Judicial resources, I am well aware, are increasingly scarce these days. Nonetheless, when we automatically close the courthouse door solely on this basis, we implicitly express a value judgment on the comparative importance of classes of legally protected interests. And current limitations upon the effective functioning of the courts arising from budgetary inadequacies should not be permitted to stand in the way of the recognition of otherwise sound constitutional principles.

Of course, for a variety of reasons, the remedy may not often be sought. And the countervailing interests in efficient law enforcement of course argue for a protective zone with respect to many types of Fourth

Amendment violations. But, while I express no view on the immunity defense offered in the instant case, I deem it proper to venture the thought that at the very least such a remedy would be available for the most flagrant and patently unjustified sorts of police conduct. Although litigants may not often choose to seek relief, it is important, in a civilized society, that the judicial branch of the Nation's government stand ready to afford a remedy in these circumstances. It goes without saying that I intimate no view on the merits of petitioner's underlying claim.

For these reasons, I concur in the judgment of the Court.

MR. CHIEF JUSTICE BURGER, dissenting.

I dissent from today's holding which judicially creates a damage remedy not provided for by the Constitution and not enacted by Congress. We would more surely preserve the important values of the doctrine of separation of powers—and perhaps get a better result—by recommending a solution to the Congress as the branch of government in which the Constitution has vested the legislative power. Legislation is the business of the Congress, and it has the facilities and competence for that task—as we do not.

* * *

[Chief Justice Burger's extended argument for overturning the exclusionary rule is omitted.]

* * *

The problems of both error and deliberate misconduct by law enforcement officials call for a workable remedy. Private damage actions against individual police officers concededly have not adequately met this requirement, and it would be fallacious to assume today's work of the Court in creating a remedy will really accomplish its stated objective. There is some validity to the claims that juries will not return verdicts against individual officers except in those unusual cases where the violation has been flagrant or where the error has been complete, as in the arrest of the wrong person or the search of the wrong house. * * * Jurors may well refuse to penalize a police officer at the behest of a person they believe to be a "criminal" and probably will not punish an officer for honest errors of judgment. In any event an actual recovery depends on finding nonexempt assets of the police officer from which a judgment can be satisfied.

I conclude, therefore, that an entirely different remedy is necessary but it is one that in my view is as much beyond judicial power as the step the Court takes today. Congress should develop an administrative or quasi-judicial remedy against the government itself to afford compensation and restitution for persons whose Fourth Amendment rights have been violated. The venerable doctrine of *respondeat superior* in our tort law provides an entirely appropriate conceptual basis for this remedy. * * * Such a statutory scheme would have the added advantage of providing some remedy to the completely innocent persons who are sometimes the victims of illegal police conduct—something that the suppression doctrine, of course, can never accomplish.

A simple structure would suffice. For example, Congress could enact a statute along the following lines:

(a) a waiver of sovereign immunity as to the illegal acts of law enforcement officials committed in the performance of assigned duties;

(b) the creation of a cause of action for damages sustained by any person aggrieved by conduct of governmental agents in violation of the Fourth Amendment or statutes regulating official conduct;

(c) the creation of a tribunal, quasi-judicial in nature or perhaps patterned after the United States Court of Claims, to adjudicate all claims under the statute;

(d) a provision that this statutory remedy is in lieu of the exclusion of evidence secured for use in criminal cases in violation of the Fourth Amendment; and

(e) a provision directing that no evidence, otherwise admissible, shall be excluded from any criminal proceeding because of violation of the Fourth Amendment.

I doubt that lawyers serving on such a tribunal would be swayed either by undue sympathy for officers or by the prejudice against "criminals" that has sometimes moved lay jurors to deny claims. In addition to awarding damages, the record of the police conduct that is condemned would undoubtedly become a relevant part of an officer's personnel file so that the need for additional training or disciplinary action could be identified or his future usefulness as a public official evaluated. Finally, appellate judicial review could be made available on much the same basis that it is now provided as to district courts and regulatory agencies. This would leave to the courts the ultimate responsibility for determining and articulating standards.

Once the constitutional validity of such a statute is established,[7] it can reasonably be assumed that the States would develop their own remedial systems on the federal model. Indeed there is nothing to prevent a State from enacting a comparable statutory scheme without waiting for the Congress. Steps along these lines would move our system toward more responsible law enforcement on the one hand and away from the

---

[7] Any such legislation should emphasize the interdependence between the waiver of sovereign immunity and the elimination of the judicially created exclusionary rule so that if the legislative determination to repudiate the exclusionary rule falls, the entire statutory scheme would fall.

irrational and drastic results of the suppression doctrine on the other. Independent of the alternative embraced in this dissenting opinion, I believe the time has come to re-examine the scope of the exclusionary rule and consider at least some narrowing of its thrust so as to eliminate the anomalies it has produced.

* * *

MR. JUSTICE BLACK, dissenting.

* * * There can be no doubt that Congress could create a federal cause of action for damages for an unreasonable search in violation of the Fourth Amendment. Although Congress has created such a federal cause of action against state officials acting under color of state law, it has never created such a cause of action against federal officials. If it wanted to do so, Congress could, of course, create a remedy against federal officials who violate the Fourth Amendment in the performance of their duties. But the point of this case and the fatal weakness in the Court's judgment is that neither Congress nor the State of New York has enacted legislation creating such a right of action. For us to do so is, in my judgment, an exercise of power that the Constitution does not give us.

Even if we had the legislative power to create a remedy, there are many reasons why we should decline to create a cause of action where none has existed since the formation of our Government. The courts of the United States as well as those of the States are choked with lawsuits. The number of cases on the docket of this Court have reached an unprecedented volume in recent years. A majority of these cases are brought by citizens with substantial complaints—persons who are physically or economically injured by torts or frauds or governmental infringement of their rights; persons who have been unjustly deprived of their liberty or their property; and persons who have not yet received the equal opportunity in education, employment, and pursuit of happiness that was the dream of our forefathers. Unfortunately, there have also been a growing number of frivolous lawsuits, particularly actions for damages against law enforcement officers whose conduct has been judicially sanctioned by state trial and appellate courts and in many instances even by this Court. My fellow Justices on this Court and our brethren throughout the federal judiciary know only too well the time-consuming task of conscientiously poring over hundreds of thousands of pages of factual allegations of misconduct by police, judicial, and corrections officials. Of course, there are instances of legitimate grievances, but legislators might well desire to devote judicial resources to other problems of a more serious nature.

We sit at the top of a judicial system accused by some of nearing the point of collapse. Many criminal defendants do not receive speedy trials and neither society nor the accused are assured of justice when inordinate delays occur. Citizens must wait years to litigate their private civil suits. Substantial changes in correctional and parole systems demand the attention of the lawmakers and the judiciary. If I were a legislator I might well find these and other needs so pressing as to make me believe that the resources of lawyers and judges should be devoted to them rather than to civil damage actions against officers who generally strive to perform within constitutional bounds. There is also a real danger that such suits might deter officials from the proper and honest performance of their duties.

All of these considerations make imperative careful study and weighing of the arguments both for and against the creation of such a remedy under the Fourth Amendment. I would have great difficulty for myself in resolving the competing policies, goals, and priorities in the use of resources, if I thought it were my job to resolve those questions. But that is not my task. The task of evaluating the pros and cons of creating judicial remedies for particular wrongs is a matter for Congress and the legislatures of the States. Congress has not provided that any federal court can entertain a suit against a federal officer for violations of Fourth Amendment rights occurring in the performance of his duties. A strong inference can be drawn from creation of such actions against state officials that Congress does not desire to permit such suits against federal officials. Should the time come when Congress desires such lawsuits, it has before it a model of valid legislation, 42 U.S.C. § 1983, to create a damage remedy against federal officers. Cases could be cited to support the legal proposition which I assert, but it seems to me to be a matter of common understanding that the business of the judiciary is to interpret the laws and not to make them.

I dissent.

MR. JUSTICE BLACKMUN, dissenting.

I, too, dissent. I do so largely for the reasons expressed in Chief Judge Lumbard's thoughtful and scholarly opinion for the Court of Appeals. But I also feel that the judicial legislation, which the Court by its opinion today concededly is effectuating, opens the door for another avalanche of new federal cases. * * * The Fourth Amendment was adopted in 1791, and in all the intervening years neither the Congress nor the Court has seen fit to take this step. I had thought that for the truly aggrieved person other quite adequate remedies have always been available. If not, it is the Congress and not this Court that should act.

Notes and Questions

1. The majority discusses a "dual limitation on state power" as "mak[ing] out the plaintiff's cause of action." Why should the states' inability either to authorize federal agents to violate federal law or to limit federal officials' exercise of authority give rise to a federal cause of action?

2. The majority opinion also mentions "special factors counseling hesita-

tion * * * ," and lists some such factors. The phrase becomes particularly important in cases involving implication of private rights of action in constitutional provisions, especially *Schweiker v. Chilicky*, 487 U.S. 412, 108 S.Ct. 2460, 101 L.Ed.2d 370 (1988), presented at page 480. Is the listing exhaustive and exclusive, or was Justice Brennan merely offering illustrative examples? If the latter, on what principled basis can the Court recognize a new special factor?

3. Justice Harlan argues in part that the Court's established practice of implying private rights of action in federal statutes connotes the propriety of judicial authorization of a damages remedy for a constitutional violation. Has the Court's subsequent retreat from implying causes of action in statutes, exemplified by *Cort v. Ash*, 422 U.S. 66, 95 S.Ct. 2080, 45 L.Ed.2d 26 (1975), *California v. Sierra Club*, 451 U.S. 287, 101 S.Ct. 1775, 68 L.Ed.2d 101 (1981), and *Karahalios v. National Federation of Federal Employees, Local 1263*, 489 U.S. 527, 109 S.Ct. 1282, 103 L.Ed.2d 539 (1989), (discussed later in this Chapter) undermined Justice Harlan's argument?

4. a) Justice Harlan also relies on Congress's grant of equitable power to the federal judiciary and argues that equitable and legal relief must be treated similarly. Upon what grant does he rely? Could it be the uncited All Writs Act, 28 U.S.C.A. § 1651? The statute's wording suggests broad judicial power to craft remedies, but is the argument self-evident? Does it suggest that Congress, although it may have thought it was granting only equitable power, unwittingly granted plenary legal power as well? What is the basis for such a conclusion?

b) If Justice Harlan is not relying on the All Writs Act, then whence the Court's power to create remedies without congressional authorization? Is there some other textual anchor in the Constitution, or is Justice Harlan relying upon a theory of inherent judicial power?

5. Chief Justice Burger, apart from his disapproval of the exclusionary rule, bases his dissent on separation of powers. Justice Black agrees that separation-of-powers concerns counsel against the Court creating the damages remedy. Where does the Constitution discuss separation of powers? Is it implicit in the constitutional scheme that Congress, in addition to being the body with the general legislative power of article I, § 8, is also the exclusive source of enforceability of the Bill of Rights?

6. Suppose Congress decided that the courts should not enforce the Bill of Rights at all. Accepting *arguendo* the Chief Justice's suggestion, if Congress declines to act, are executive violations of the Bill of Rights unredressable, making those provisions hortatory only?

> [A] right without a remedy is not a legal right; it is merely a hope or a wish * * * . In Hohfeldian terms, a right entails a correlative duty to act or refrain from acting for the benefit of another person. Unless a duty can be enforced, it is not really a duty; it is only a voluntary obligation that a person can fulfill or not at his whim.

Donald H. Zeigler, *Rights Require Remedies: A New Approach to the Enforcement of Rights in the Federal Courts*, 38 HASTINGS L.J. 665, 678 (1987).

Professor Zeigler notes Justice Holmes's characterization of the problem: "Legal obligations that 'exist but cannot be enforced are ghosts that are seen in the law but that are elusive to the grasp.' "

7. Suppose, following *Bivens,* Congress were to enact a statute allowing damages against federal officials who violate the Fourth Amendment. If that statute were more limited than the Supreme Court's remedy, what effect would or should the statute have on the judicially-created remedy?

INTRODUCTORY NOTE ON IMPLYING PRIVATE RIGHTS OF ACTION IN FEDERAL STATUTES

Statutes that create new rights or duties often fail to provide private rights of action to enforce them. Almost 300 years ago, the Chief Justice of the King's Bench observed: "If the plaintiff has a right, he must of necessity have a means to vindicate and maintain it, and a remedy if he is injured in the exercise or enjoyment of it; and indeed it is a vain thing to imagine a right without a remedy * * * ." *Ashby v. White*, 92 Eng.Rep. 126, 135-37 (K.B. 1703) (Holt, C.J., dissenting).[16] As Professor Zeigler notes, in the United States during the late nineteenth and early twentieth centuries, state courts routinely created private tort remedies for violations of statutory duties as long as "the statute was intended for the benefit of a class of persons of which the plaintiff was a member rather than for the public generally, and if the harm suffered was of a kind the statute generally was intended to prevent."[17]

Professor Zeigler chronicles the development of implying remedies in statutes in the United States.

> Legislative intent played an important role in the early cases. The requirements that the statute be enacted for the plaintiff's benefit and aimed at preventing the sort of harm that actually occurred ensured that a private remedy was consistent with underlying legislative purposes. * * * [A] court would provide a private remedy even if the legislature was silent on the matter. A court would refuse a private remedy only if the legislature explicitly barred the remedy or made clear its intention to substitute other relief.

> Until quite recently, the federal courts generally followed traditional standards in providing remedies for violation of statutory duties. * * *

> After [*Texas & Pacific Railroad v.*] *Rigsby* [1916], the federal

---

[16] "Subsequently, * * * Chief Justice Holt's dissenting opinion was accepted by the House of Lords and judgment was entered for the plaintiff." Donald H. Zeigler, *Rights Require Remedies: A New Approach to the Enforcement of Rights in the Federal Courts*, 38 HASTINGS L.J. 665, 672 n.44 (1987).

[17] *Id.* at 674.

courts often allowed or "implied" remedies for violations of statutory duties when the statute did not explicitly authorize a private right of action.[18]

In *J.I. Case Company v. Borak,* 377 U.S. 426, 84 S.Ct. 1555, 12 L.Ed.2d 423 (1964), the Court's approach may have reached its high water mark. A unanimous Court implied a private right of action in the Securities Exchange Act for a stockholder seeking recission of a merger or damages because of a misleading proxy statement. The Court noted that although Congress had provided for direct enforcement of the Act only by the Securities Exchange Commission, "[t]o hold that derivative actions are not within the sweep of the section would therefore be tantamount to a denial of private relief. Private enforcement of the proxy rules provides a necessary supplement to Commission action." The Court defended its approach:

> We, therefore, believe that under the circumstances here it is the duty of the courts to be alert to provide such remedies as are necessary to make effective the congressional purpose. * * *

When a federal statute condemns an act as unlawful, the extent and nature of the legal consequences of the condemnation, though left by the statute to judicial determination, are nevertheless federal questions, the answers to which are to be derived from the statute and the federal policy which it has adopted.

Thus, the Court characterized itself as advancing or supporting the legislative policy represented by the statute.

Eleven years after *Borak,* the Court reconsidered implied statutory rights of action in *Cort v. Ash,* 422 U.S. 66, 95 S.Ct. 2080, 45 L.Ed.2d 26 (1975). When a shareholder commenced a derivative action premised on corporate directors' violations of a provision of the federal criminal code prohibiting corporate campaign contributions, the Court (again unanimous) declined to imply a private right of action. Justice Brennan announced a new four-factor test:

> First, is the plaintiff "one of the class for whose *especial* benefit the statute was enacted," *Texas & Pacific R. Co. v. Rigsby,* 241 U.S. 33, 39 (1916) (emphasis supplied)—that is, does the statute create a federal right in favor of the plaintiff? Second, is there any indication of legislative intent, explicit or implicit, either to create such a remedy or to deny one? Third, is it consistent with the underlying purposes of the legislative scheme to imply such a remedy for the plaintiff? And finally, is the cause of action one traditionally relegated to state law, in an area basically the concern of the States, so that it would be inappropriate to infer a cause of action based solely on federal law?

---

[18] *Id.* at 674-76.

The opinion is less than illuminating about why the Justices implied no action. Justice Brennan did note that Ash relied upon a criminal rather than civil statute and that it was thus difficult for him to show that he was a member of a benefited class apart from being a member of society generally, but he also noted that the Court had implied private rights of action in criminal statutes. He did not distinguish those cases. Second, he characterized the primary purpose of the statute as protection of federal election campaigns but acknowledged that protection of stockholders was a secondary concern. Nonetheless, the Court refused to effectuate that secondary purpose at the behest of one of its intended beneficiaries.

Notes and Questions

1. How does the *Cort* test differ from the Court's approach to statutory implication from the 1800's through *Borak* ?

2. Given that Congress did articulate what Justice Brennan characterizes as a "secondary" goal, why is it unworthy of support through a private right of action? Should the Court refuse to support a goal unless it is Congress's "primary" goal? Can Congress have only one "primary" goal? Is it even self-evident that a private right of action would not further the primary goal of protecting federal elections?

3. a) The fourth *Cort* criterion raises several interesting problems. Although the other criteria are embedded in the history of implying private rights of action in statutes, the fourth is new. What values does its introduction serve?

b) Is there not a Janus-like aspect to the fourth criterion? For most of the first century under the Constitution, federal power was extremely limited. Indeed, the Framers feared that the emerging national government would become too strong, hence the Constitution's plan of limited, enumerated powers for the federal government with the balance of governmental authority residing in the states. Only in the last century has the federal government expanded so that national regulation is common. In that light, cannot most issues be seen as "traditionally" relegated to state concern? Still, does the presence of a federal statute at least suggest a strong federal interest in the subject matter? These conflicting perspectives will be present most of the time.

c) The Court is less than consistent applying the fourth criterion to the facts of *Cort*. Having dismissed the "secondary" goal (corporate protection) for purposes of the second criterion, the Court resurrects it in order to discuss the fourth. In asking whether the statute is aimed primarily at an area of traditional state or federal concern, Justice Brennan concludes that state-chartered corporations are within the realm of state interest. Should he ask instead whether protection of the federal electoral process is traditionally a matter of state or federal concern?

4. What should be the relationship of the *Cort* factors to each other? Does a negative answer to any one of them preclude an implied right of action? Should all the factors have equal weight?

CANNON v. UNIVERSITY OF CHICAGO

Supreme Court of the United States, 1979.
441 U.S. 677, 99 S.Ct. 1946, 60 L.Ed.2d 560.

MR. JUSTICE STEVENS delivered the opinion of the Court.

Petitioner's complaints allege that her applications for admission to medical school were denied by the respondents because she is a woman. Accepting the truth of those allegations for the purpose of its decision, the Court of Appeals held that petitioner has no right of action against respondents that may be asserted in a federal court. We granted certiorari to review that holding.

Only two facts alleged in the complaints are relevant to our decision. First, petitioner was excluded from participation in the respondents' medical education programs because of her sex. Second, these education programs were receiving federal financial assistance at the time of her exclusion. These facts, admitted *arguendo* by respondents' motion to dismiss the complaints, establish a violation of § 901(a) of Title IX of the Education Amendments of 1972 (hereinafter Title IX).[2]

---

[2] Petitioner's complaints allege violations of various federal statutes including Title IX. Although the District Court and Court of Appeals ruled adversely on all of these theories, petitioner confined her petition for a writ of certiorari to the Title IX question. On that question, the District Court and Court of Appeals ruled favorably on respondents' motion to dismiss the complaints for failure to state a cause of action. Although respondents sought summary judgment simultaneously with their motion to dismiss, and submitted supporting affidavits, the courts below did not purport to rule on summary judgment or to make factual findings. Accordingly, all of the facts alleged in petitioner's complaints must be taken as true for purposes of review.

According to her complaints, petitioner was qualified to attend both of the respondent medical schools based on both objective (*i.e.,* grade-point average and test scores) and subjective criteria. In fact, both schools admitted some persons to the classes to which she applied despite the fact that those persons had less impressive objective qualifications than she did.

Both medical schools receive federal aid, and both have policies against admitting applicants who are more than 30 years old (petitioner was 39 years old at the time she applied), at least if they do not have advanced degrees. Northwestern Medical School absolutely disqualifies applicants over 35. These policies, it is alleged, prevented petitioner from being asked to an interview at the medical schools, so that she was denied even the opportunity to convince the schools that her personal qualifications warranted her admission in place of persons whose objective qualifications were better than hers. Because the incidence of interrupted higher education is higher among women than among men, it is further claimed, the age and advanced-degree criteria operate to exclude women from consideration even though the criteria are not valid predictors of success in medical schools or in medical practice. As such, the existence of the criteria either makes out or evidences a violation of the medical school's duty under Title IX to avoid discrimination on the basis of sex. Petitioner also claimed that the schools accepted a far smaller percentage of women than their percentage in the general population and in the class of persons with bachelor's degrees. *But cf.* 559 F.2d 1063, 1067, referring to statistics submitted by the University of Chicago in its affidavit accompanying its summary judgment motion indicating that the percentage of women admitted to classes from 1972 to 1975, 18.3%, was virtually identical to the percentage of women applicants. Of course, the dampening impact of a discriminatory rule may undermine the relevance of figures relating to actual applicants.

Upon her rejection by both schools, petitioner sought reconsideration of the decisions by way of written and telephonic communications with admissions officials. Finding these

That section, in relevant part, provides: "No person in the United States shall, on the basis of sex, be excluded from participation in, be denied the benefits of, or be subjected to discrimination under any education program or activity receiving Federal financial assistance * * * ." The statute does not, however, expressly authorize a private right of action by a person injured by a violation of § 901. For that reason, and because it concluded that no private remedy should be inferred, the District Court granted the respondents' motions to dismiss.

The Court of Appeals agreed that the statute did not contain an implied private remedy. Noting that § 902 of Title IX establishes a procedure for the termination of federal financial support for institutions violating § 901, the Court of Appeals concluded that Congress intended that remedy to be the exclusive means of enforcement. It recognized that the statute was patterned after Title VI of the Civil Rights Act of 1964 (hereinafter Title VI), but rejected petitioner's argument that Title VI included an implied private cause of action.

After the Court of Appeals' decision was announced, Congress enacted the Civil Rights Attorney's Fees Awards Act of 1976, which authorizes an award of fees to prevailing private parties in actions to enforce Title IX. The court therefore granted a petition for rehearing to consider whether, in the light of that statute, its original interpretation of Title IX had been correct. After receiving additional briefs, the court concluded that the 1976 Act was not intended to create a remedy that did not previously exist. The court also noted that the Department of Health, Education, and Welfare had taken the position that a private cause of action under Title IX should be implied, but the court disagreed with that agency's interpretation of the Act. In sum, it adhered to its original view.

The Court of Appeals quite properly devoted careful attention to this question of statutory construction. As our recent cases—particularly *Cort v. Ash*—demonstrate, the fact that a federal statute has been violated and some person harmed does not automatically give rise to a private cause of action in favor of that person. Instead, before concluding that Congress intended to make a remedy available to a special class of litigants, a court must carefully analyze the four factors that *Cort* identifies as indicative of such an intent. Our review of those factors per-

---

avenues of no avail, she filed a complaint with the local office of HEW in April 1975, alleging, *inter alia,* violations of Title IX. Three months later, having received only an acknowledgment of receipt of her letter from HEW, petitioner filed suit in the District Court for the Northern District of Illinois against the private defendants. After she amended her complaints to include the federal defendants and requested injunctive relief ordering them to complete their investigation, she was informed that HEW would not begin its investigation of her complaint until early 1976. In June 1976, HEW informed petitioner that the local stages of its investigation had been completed but that its national headquarters planned to conduct a further "in-depth study of the issues raised" because those issues were "of first impression and national in scope." As far as the record indicates HEW has announced no further action in this case.

suades us, however, that the Court of Appeals reached the wrong conclusion and that petitioner does have a statutory right to pursue her claim that respondents rejected her application on the basis of her sex. After commenting on each of the four factors, we shall explain why they are not overcome by respondents' countervailing arguments.

I

First, the threshold question under *Cort* is whether the statute was enacted for the benefit of a special class of which the plaintiff is a member. That question is answered by looking to the language of the statute itself. Thus, the statutory reference to "any employee of any such common carrier" in the 1893 legislation requiring railroads to equip their cars with secure "grab irons or handholds," made "irresistible" the Court's earliest "inference of a private right of action"—in that case in favor of a railway employee who was injured when a grab iron gave way.

Similarly, it was statutory language describing the special class to be benefited by § 5 of the Voting Rights Act of 1965 that persuaded the Court that private parties within that class were implicitly authorized to seek a declaratory judgment against a covered State. The dispositive language in that statute—"no person shall be denied the right to vote for failure to comply with [a new state enactment covered by, but not approved under, § 5]"—is remarkably similar to the language used by Congress in Title IX.

The language in these statutes—which expressly identifies the class Congress intended to benefit—contrasts sharply with statutory language customarily found in criminal statutes, such as that construed in *Cort*, and other laws enacted for the protection of the general public. There would be far less reason to infer a private remedy in favor of individual persons if Congress, instead of drafting Title IX with an unmistakable focus on the benefited class, had written it simply as a ban on discriminatory conduct by recipients of federal funds or as a prohibition against the disbursement of public funds to educational institutions engaged in discriminatory practices.

Unquestionably, therefore, the first of the four factors identified in *Cort* favors the implication of a private cause of action. Title IX explicitly confers a benefit on persons discriminated against on the basis of sex, and petitioner is clearly a member of that class for whose special benefit the statute was enacted.

Second, the *Cort* analysis requires consideration of legislative history. We must recognize, however, that the legislative history of a statute that does not expressly create or deny a private remedy will typically be equally silent or ambiguous on the question. Therefore, in situations such as the present one "in which it is clear that federal law has granted a class of persons certain rights, it is not necessary to show an intention to *create* a private cause of action, although an explicit purpose to *deny* such cause of action would be controlling." *Cort* (emphasis in original). But this is not the typical case. Far from evidencing any purpose to deny a private cause of action, the history of Title IX rather plainly indicates that Congress intended to create such a remedy.

Title IX was patterned after Title VI of the Civil Rights Act of 1964. Except for the substitution of the word "sex" in Title IX to replace the words "race, color, or national origin" in Title VI, the two statutes use identical language to describe the benefited class. Both statutes provide the same administrative mechanism for terminating federal financial support for institutions engaged in prohibited discrimination. Neither statute expressly mentions a private remedy for the person excluded from participation in a federally funded program. The drafters of Title IX explicitly assumed that it would be interpreted and applied as Title VI had been during the preceding eight years.

In 1972 when Title IX was enacted, the critical language in Title VI had already been construed as creating a private remedy. Most particularly, in 1967, a distinguished panel of the Court of Appeals for the Fifth Circuit squarely decided this issue in an opinion that was repeatedly cited with approval and never questioned during the ensuing five years. In addition, at least a dozen other federal courts reached similar conclusions in the same or related contexts during those years. It is always appropriate to assume that our elected representatives, like other citizens, know the law; in this case, because of their repeated references to Title VI and its modes of enforcement, we are especially justified in presuming both that those representatives were aware of the prior interpretation of Title VI and that that interpretation reflects their intent with respect to Title IX.

Moreover, in 1969, this Court had interpreted the comparable language in § 5 of the Voting Rights Act as sufficient to authorize a private remedy.[22] Indeed, during the period between the enactment of Title VI in 1964 and the enactment of Title IX in 1972, this Court had consistently found implied remedies—often in cases much less clear than this.[23] It was *after* 1972 that this Court decided *Cort v. Ash* and the other cases cited by the Court of Appeals in support of its strict construction of the remedial aspect of the statute. We, of course, adhere to the strict approach followed in our recent cases, but our evaluation of congressional action in 1972 must take into account its contemporary legal context. In sum, it is not only appropriate but also realistic to presume that Congress was thoroughly familiar with these unusually important precedents from this and other federal courts and that it expected its

---

[22] In fact, Congress enacted Title IX against a backdrop of three recently issued implied-cause-of-action decisions of this Court involving civil rights statutes with language similar to that in Title IX. In all three, a cause of action was found.

[23] In the decade preceding the enactment of Title IX, the Court decided six implied-cause-of-action cases. In all of them a cause of action was found.

enactment to be interpreted in conformity with them.

It is not, however, necessary to rely on these presumptions. The package of statutes of which Title IX is one part also contains a provision whose language and history demonstrate that Congress itself understood Title VI, and thus its companion, Title IX, as creating a private remedy. Section 718 of the Education Amendments authorizes federal courts to award attorney's fees to the prevailing parties, other than the United States, in private actions brought against public educational agencies to enforce Title VI in the context of elementary and secondary education. The language of this provision explicitly presumes the availability of private suits to enforce Title VI in the education context. For many such suits, no express cause of action was then available; hence Congress must have assumed that one could be implied under Title VI itself. That assumption was made explicit during the debates on § 718. It was also aired during the debates on other provisions in the Education Amendments of 1972 and on Title IX itself, and is consistent with the Executive Branch's apparent understanding of Title VI at the time.

Finally, the very persistence—before 1972 and since, among judges and executive officials, as well as among litigants and their counsel, and even implicit in decisions of this Court—of the assumption that both Title VI and Title IX created a private right of action for the victims of illegal discrimination and the absence of legislative action to change that assumption provide further evidence that Congress at least acquiesces in, and apparently affirms, that assumption. We have no doubt that Congress intended to create Title IX remedies comparable to those available under Title VI and that it understood Title VI as authorizing an implied private cause of action for victims of the prohibited discrimination.

Third, under *Cort*, a private remedy should not be implied if it would frustrate the underlying purpose of the legislative scheme. On the other hand, when that remedy is necessary or at least helpful to the accomplishment of the statutory purpose, the Court is decidedly receptive to its implication under the statute.

Title IX, like its model Title VI, sought to accomplish two related, but nevertheless somewhat different, objectives. First, Congress wanted to avoid the use of federal resources to support discriminatory practices; second, it wanted to provide individual citizens effective protection against those practices. Both of these purposes were repeatedly identified in the debates on the two statutes.

The first purpose is generally served by the statutory procedure for the termination of federal financial support for institutions engaged in discriminatory practices. That remedy is, however, severe and often may not provide an appropriate means of accomplishing the second purpose if merely an isolated violation has occurred. In that situation, the violation might be remedied more efficiently by an order requiring an institution to accept an applicant who had been improperly excluded.

Moreover, in that kind of situation it makes little sense to impose on an individual, whose only interest is in obtaining a benefit for herself, or on HEW, the burden of demonstrating that an institution's practices are so pervasively discriminatory that a complete cut-off of federal funding is appropriate. The award of individual relief to a private litigant who has prosecuted her own suit is not only sensible but is also fully consistent with—and in some cases even necessary to—the orderly enforcement of the statute.

The Department of Health, Education, and Welfare, which is charged with the responsibility for administering Title IX, perceives no inconsistency between the private remedy and the public remedy. On the contrary, the agency takes the unequivocal position that the individual remedy will provide effective assistance to achieving the statutory purposes. The agency's position is unquestionably correct.

Fourth, the final inquiry suggested by *Cort* is whether implying a federal remedy is inappropriate because the subject matter involves an area basically of concern to the States. No such problem is raised by a prohibition against invidious discrimination of any sort, including that on the basis of sex. Since the Civil War, the Federal Government and the federal courts have been the " '*primary* and powerful reliances' " in protecting citizens against such discrimination. *Steffel v. Thompson*, 415 U.S. 452, 464 (emphasis in original), quoting F. Frankfurter & J. Landis, The Business of the Supreme Court 65 (1928). Moreover, it is the expenditure of federal funds that provides the justification for this particular statutory prohibition. There can be no question but that this aspect of the *Cort* analysis supports the implication of a private federal remedy.

In sum, there is no need in this case to weigh the four *Cort* factors; all of them support the same result. Not only the words and history of Title IX, but also its subject matter and underlying purposes, counsel implication of a cause of action in favor of private victims of discrimination.

II

Respondents' principal argument against implying a cause of action under Title IX is that it is unwise to subject admissions decisions of universities to judicial scrutiny at the behest of disappointed applicants on a case-by-case basis. They argue that this kind of litigation is burdensome and inevitably will have an adverse effect on the independence of members of university committees.

This argument is not original to this litigation. It was forcefully advanced in both 1964 and 1972 by the congressional opponents of Title VI and Title IX, and squarely rejected by the congressional majorities that passed the two statutes. In short, respondents' principal contention is not a legal argument at all; it addresses a policy issue that Congress has already resolved.

History has borne out the judgment of Congress. Although victims of discrimination on the basis of race, religion, or national origin have had private Title VI remedies available at least since 1965, respondents have not come forward with any demonstration that Title VI litigation has been so costly or voluminous that either the academic community or the courts have been unduly burdened. Nothing but speculation supports the argument that university administrators will be so concerned about the risk of litigation that they will fail to discharge their important responsibilities in an independent and professional manner.

III

Respondents advance two other arguments that deserve brief mention. Starting from the premise that Title IX and Title VI should receive the same construction, respondents argue (1) that a comparison of Title VI with other Titles of the Civil Rights Act of 1964 demonstrates that Congress created express private remedies whenever it found them desirable; and (2) that certain excerpts from the legislative history of Title VI foreclose the implication of a private remedy.

Even if these arguments were persuasive with respect to Congress' understanding in 1964 when it passed Title VI, they would not overcome the fact that in 1972 when it passed Title IX, Congress was under the impression that Title VI could be enforced by a private action and that Title IX would be similarly enforceable. "For the relevant inquiry is not whether Congress correctly perceived the then state of the law, but rather what its perception of the state of the law was." But each of respondents' arguments is, in any event, unpersuasive.

* * *

IV

When Congress intends private litigants to have a cause of action to support their statutory rights, the far better course is for it to specify as much when it creates those rights. But the Court has long recognized that under certain limited circumstances the failure of Congress to do so is not inconsistent with an intent on its part to have such a remedy available to the persons benefited by its legislation. Title IX presents the atypical situation in which all of the circumstances that the Court has previously identified as supportive of an implied remedy are present. We therefore conclude that petitioner may maintain her lawsuit, despite the absence of any express authorization for it in the statute.

The judgment of the Court of Appeals is reversed, and the case is remanded for further proceedings consistent with this opinion.

It is so ordered.

MR. JUSTICE POWELL, dissenting.

[E]ven under the standards articulated in our prior decisions, it is clear that no private action should be implied here. It is evident from the legislative history reviewed in his dissenting opinion that Congress did not intend to create a private action through Title IX of the Education Amendments of 1972. It also is clear that Congress deemed the administrative enforcement mechanism it did create fully adequate to protect Title IX rights. But as mounting evidence from the courts below suggests, and the decision of the Court today demonstrates, the mode of analysis we have applied in the recent past cannot be squared with the doctrine of the separation of powers. The time has come to reappraise our standards for the judicial implication of private causes of action.[1]

Under Art. III, Congress alone has the responsibility for determining the jurisdiction of the lower federal courts. As the Legislative Branch, Congress also should determine when private parties are to be given causes of action under legislation it adopts. As countless statutes demonstrate, including Titles of the Civil Rights Act of 1964, Congress recognizes that the creation of private actions is a legislative function and frequently exercises it. When Congress chooses not to provide a private civil remedy, federal courts should not assume the legislative role of creating such a remedy and thereby enlarge their jurisdiction.

The facts of this case illustrate the undesirability of this assumption by the Judicial Branch of the legislative function. Whether every disappointed applicant for admission to a college or university receiving federal funds has the right to a civil-court remedy under Title IX is likely to be a matter of interest to many of the thousands of rejected applicants. It certainly is a question of vast importance to the entire higher educational community of this country. But quite apart from the interests of the persons and institutions affected, respect for our constitutional system dictates that the issue should have been resolved by the elected representatives in Congress after public hearings, debate, and legislative decision. It is not a question properly to be decided by relatively uninformed federal judges who are isolated from the political process.

In recent history, the Court has tended to stray from the Art. III and separation-of-powers principle of limited jurisdiction. This, I believe, is evident from a review of the more or less haphazard line of cases that led to our decision in *Cort v. Ash*. The "four factor" analysis of that case is an open invitation to federal courts to legislate causes of action not authorized by Congress. It is an analysis not faithful to constitutional principles and should be rejected. Absent the most compelling evidence of affirmative congressional intent, a federal court should not infer a private cause of action.

---

[1] The phrase "private cause of action" may not have a completely clear meaning. As the term is used herein, I refer to the right of a private party to seek judicial relief from injuries caused by another's violation of a legal requirement. In the context of legislation enacted by Congress, the legal requirement involved is a statutory duty.

I

The implying of a private action from a federal regulatory statute has been an exceptional occurrence in the past history of this Court. A review of those few decisions where such a step has been taken reveals in almost every case special historical circumstances that explain the result, if not the Court's analysis. These decisions suggest that the doctrine of implication applied by the Court today not only represents judicial assumption of the legislative function, but also lacks a principled precedential basis.

* * *

B

It was against this background of almost invariable refusal to imply private actions, absent a complete failure of alternative enforcement mechanisms and a clear expression of legislative intent to create such a remedy, that *Cort v. Ash* was decided. In holding that no private action could be brought to enforce a criminal statute, the Court referred to four factors said to be relevant to determining generally whether private actions could be implied. As Mr. Justice White suggests, these factors were meant only as guideposts for answering a single question, namely, whether Congress intended to provide a private cause of action. The conclusion in that particular case was obvious. But, as the opinion of the Court today demonstrates, the *Cort* analysis too easily may be used to deflect inquiry away from the intent of Congress, and to permit a court instead to substitute its own views as to the desirability of private enforcement.

Of the four factors mentioned in *Cort*, only one refers expressly to legislative intent. The other three invite independent judicial lawmaking. Asking whether a statute creates a right in favor of a private party, for example, begs the question at issue. What is involved is not the mere existence of a legal right, but a particular person's right to invoke the power of the courts to enforce that right. Determining whether a private action would be consistent with the "underlying purposes" of a legislative scheme permits a court to decide for itself what the goals of a scheme should be, and how those goals should be advanced. Finally, looking to state law for parallels to the federal right simply focuses inquiry on a particular policy consideration that Congress already may have weighed in deciding not to create a private action.

That the *Cort* analysis too readily permits courts to override the decision of Congress not to create a private action is demonstrated conclusively by the flood of lower-court decisions applying it. Although from the time *Cort* was decided until today this Court consistently has turned back attempts to create private actions, other federal courts have tended to proceed in exactly the opposite direction. In the four years since we decided *Cort*, no less than 20 decisions by the Courts of Appeals have implied private actions from federal statutes. It defies reason to believe that in each of these statutes Congress absentmindedly forgot to mention an intended private action. Indeed, the accelerating trend evidenced by these decisions attests to the need to re-examine the *Cort* analysis.

II

In my view, the implication doctrine articulated in *Cort* and applied by the Court today engenders incomparably greater problems than the possibility of occasionally failing to divine an unexpressed congressional intent. If only a matter of statutory construction were involved, our obligation might be to develop more refined criteria which more accurately reflect congressional intent. "But the unconstitutionality of the course pursued has now been made clear" and compels us to abandon the implication doctrine of *Cort*.

As the above-cited 20 decisions of the Courts of Appeals illustrate, *Cort* allows the Judicial Branch to assume policymaking authority vested by the Constitution in the Legislative Branch. It also invites Congress to avoid resolution of the often controversial question whether a new regulatory statute should be enforced through private litigation. Rather than confronting the hard political choices involved, Congress is encouraged to shirk its constitutional obligation and leave the issue to the courts to decide.[14] When this happens, the legislative process with its public scrutiny and participation has been bypassed, with attendant prejudice to everyone concerned. Because the courts are free to reach a result different from that which the normal play of political forces would have produced, the intended beneficiaries of the legislation are unable to ensure the full measure of protection their needs may warrant. For the same reason, those subject to the legislative constraints are denied the opportunity to forestall through the political process potentially unnecessary and disruptive litigation. Moreover, the public generally is denied the benefits that are derived from the making of important societal choices through the open debate of the democratic process.

The Court's implication doctrine encourages, as a corollary to the political default by Congress, an increase in the governmental power exercised by the federal judiciary. The dangers posed by judicial arrogation of the right to resolve general societal conflicts have been manifest to

---

[14] Mr. Justice Rehnquist, perhaps considering himself temporarily bound by his position in *University of California Regents v. Bakke,* concurs in the Court's decision today. But writing briefly, he correctly observes "that Congress, at least during the period of the enactment of the several Titles of the Civil Rights Act tended to rely to a large extent on the courts to decide whether there should be a private right of action, rather than determining this question for itself * * *." It does not follow, however, that this Court is obliged to indulge Congress in its refusal to confront these hard questions. In my view, the very reasons advanced by Mr. Justice Rehnquist why "this Court in the future should be extremely reluctant to imply a cause of action" absent specific direction by Congress, apply to this case with special force.

this Court throughout its history.

* * *

It is true that the federal judiciary necessarily exercises substantial powers to construe legislation, including, when appropriate, the power to prescribe substantive standards of conduct that supplement federal legislation. But this power normally is exercised with respect to disputes over which a court already has jurisdiction, and in which the existence of the asserted cause of action is established.[16] Implication of a private cause of action, in contrast, involves a significant additional step. By creating a private action, a court of limited jurisdiction necessarily extends its authority to embrace a dispute Congress has not assigned it to resolve.[17] This runs contrary to the established principle that "[t]he jurisdiction of the federal courts is carefully guarded against expansion by judicial interpretation * * * " and conflicts with the authority of Congress under Art. III to set the limits of federal jurisdiction.

* * *

III

In sum, I believe the need both to restrain courts that too readily have created private causes of action, and to encourage Congress to confront its obligation to resolve crucial policy questions created by the legislation it enacts, has become compelling. Because the analysis suggested by *Cort* has proved inadequate to meet these problems, I would start afresh. Henceforth, we should not condone the implication of any private action from a federal statute absent the most compelling evidence that Congress in fact intended such an action to exist. Where a statutory scheme expressly provides for an alternative mechanism for enforcing the rights and duties created, I would be especially reluctant

---

[16] *See, e.g.,* United States v. Kimbell Foods, Inc., 440 U.S. 715 (1979); Textile Workers v. Lincoln Mills, 353 U.S. 448 (1957); Clearfield Trust Co. v. United States, 318 U.S. 363 (1943).

[17] Because a private action implied from a federal statute has as an element the violation of that statute, the action universally has been considered to present a federal question over which a federal court has jurisdiction under 28 U.S.C. § 1331. Thus, when a federal court implies a private action from a statute, it necessarily expands the scope of its federal-question jurisdiction.

It is instructive to compare decisions implying private causes of action to those cases that have found nonfederal causes of action cognizable by a federal court under § 1331. *E.g., Smith v. Kansas City Title & Trust Co.* Where a court decides both that federal-law elements are present in a state-law cause of action, and that these elements predominate to the point that the action can be said to present a "federal question" cognizable in federal court, the net effect is the same as implication of a private action directly from the constitutional or statutory source of the federal-law elements. To the extent an expansive interpretation of § 1331 permits federal courts to assume control over disputes which Congress did not consign to the federal judicial process, it is subject to the same criticisms of judicial implication of private actions discussed in the text.

ever to permit a federal court to volunteer its services for enforcement purposes. Because the Court today is enlisting the federal judiciary in just such an enterprise, I dissent.

Notes and Questions

1. Is the majority opinion a straight application of the *Cort* test or does it subtly alter the four factors or the manner in which they apply? Is the majority as comfortable with implying rights of action as the Courts that decided *Cort v. Ash* and the cases preceding it appear to have been?

2. In Justice Stevens's analysis of the third *Cort* factor, what does it mean to say that implying a private right of action is "necessary or at least helpful" to the statutory scheme?

3. The Court's treatment of the fourth factor again invites consideration of the protean nature of that inquiry. Note how important characterization is. *Cannon* concerns education, an area of traditional state concern despite recent federal forays into the area. Similarly, although Justice Stevens characterizes *Cannon* as involving sex discrimination rather than education and borrows language from *Steffel v. Thompson*, 415 U.S. 452, 94 S.Ct. 1209, 39 L.Ed.2d 505 (1974) (which involved First Amendment and abstention issues but had nothing to do with education or discrimination), to emphasize federal government primacy in that area, he may overstate his case. Only recently has the federal government become concerned about sex discrimination. *United States v. Yazell*, 382 U.S. 341, 86 S.Ct. 500, 15 L.Ed.2d 404 (1966), at page 391, for example, did not pique the Court's interest in sex discrimination when the Court confronted the Texas law of coverture that, in terms of married women's ability to enter into contracts, effectively made them wards of the state. Indeed, the Court there noted the states' traditional interest in family property arrangements. Have not the states been the primary "governments in interest" not only for education but also for defining the roles of women and men in society?

4. Justice Powell's dissent is the beginning of the Supreme Court's articulated interest in the separation-of-powers view of *Erie*. He begins by observing that implying private rights of action violates separation of powers. But he does suggest that in "compelling" circumstances, where congressional intent is clear, the courts may proceed. If his objection rests on the constitutional doctrine of separation of powers, how is an exception allowable? What evidence would he accept as sufficiently compelling?

5. Justice Powell attributes the federal courts' practice of implying private rights of action to cases where Congress "absentmindedly forgot" to include a private right of action. Is it not possible that Congress assumed that the courts would imply rights of action to provide remedies for substantive rights Congress created, as they traditionally had? Perhaps Congress thought this fulfilled the courts' customary and proper role. On the other hand, perhaps that begs the question of whether that role is compatible with separation of powers.

6. Quoting *Erie*, Justice Powell asserts that implying a private right of action is unconstitutional. Upon which constitutional provisions does he rely

for that conclusion? Is he perhaps guilty of the same sin as Justice Brandeis in *Erie*: failing to specify the particular constitutional language that prohibits the assailed practice?

7. Justice Powell argues that if the courts create private rights of action, the "intended beneficiaries of the legislation" may not receive as much protection as Congress intended, thus frustrating congressional intent. How might that happen?

8. The majority focuses on the relationship between Title VI and Title IX. Does Justice Powell's opinion suggest that the implied right of action in Title VI is also illegitimate? If so, how can he explain Congress's providing a statutory right to recover attorney's fees in Title VI actions? If not, how can he distinguish Title VI from Title IX for implication purposes?

9. Justice Powell is clearly troubled by the idea of federal judges being policy makers and sees implication of private rights of action as one way in which they do that. Is his objection constitutional or prudential?

Is it so clear that implying a private right of action makes policy? Perhaps the policy inheres in the right, not the availability of a particular remedy. Congressional policy against sex discrimination is certainly clear in Title IX. In what sense, then, does the Court make policy when it implies a private right of action to effectuate that congressional policy? Professor Doernberg has argued that "Judicial lethargy in the face of clearly expressed congressional policy may itself be an evisceration of the intent of the legislation, thus violating separation of powers." Donald L. Doernberg, *Juridical Chameleons in the "New* Erie" *Canal*, 1990 UTAH L.REV. 759, 803 n.235. *But see, e.g.*, Thomas W. Merrill, *The Judicial Prerogative*, 12 PACE L.REV. 327 (1992); Martin H. Redish, *Federal Common Law, Political Legitimacy, and the Interpretive Process: An "Institutionalist" Perspective*, 83 NW.L.REV. 761 (1989). It may make little sense to separate the right from the remedy when attempting to ascertain the underlying policy. One can argue that a "policy" underlies almost any decision, as opposed to a purely ministerial act, but then what does the word mean?

10. a) Does Justice Powell's constitutional objection to implying private rights of action apply with equal force to implication in constitutional provisions, as in *Bivens*?

b) Is the Court using similar or different approaches to the implication question in *Cannon* and *Bivens*? To the extent they are similar, is that appropriate? To the extent that they are different, upon what is the difference founded? Why should they not be the same?

11. Finally, Justice Powell argues in footnote 17 that the federal courts impermissibly expand their jurisdiction when they imply private rights of action. He argues that such cases are similar to *Smith v. Kansas City Title & Trust Co.*, 255 U.S. 180, 41 S.Ct. 243, 65 L.Ed. 577 (1921), where the Court found federal question jurisdiction despite the fact that state law created the cause of action. He seems to attack *Smith* and implicitly to urge that the proper jurisdictional standard under 28 U.S.C.A. § 1331 is in *American Well Works Co. v. Layne & Bowler Co.*, 241 U.S. 257, 36 S.Ct. 585,

60 L.Ed. 987 (1916) ("A case arises under the law that creates the cause of action.") This may help to explain his vote in *Merrell Dow Pharmaceuticals, Inc. v. Thompson*, 478 U.S. 804, 106 S.Ct. 3229, 92 L.Ed.2d 650 (1986), decided seven years after *Cannon*, though it leaves the question of why he did not concur in that case to express the view that *Smith* is no longer good law. Justice Stevens's majority opinion emphasized that *Smith* survives *Merrell Dow*. How could Justice Powell join that part of the opinion?

12. The Supreme Court has broadly defined acts of sex discrimination encompassed within the cause of action created in *Cannon*. The Court has held that a student may sue a school district receiving federal funds for the district's deliberate indifference to a teacher's sexual harassment of the student, *Gebser v. Lago Vista Independent Sch. Dist.*, 524 U.S. 274, 118 S.Ct. 1989, 141 L.Ed.2d 277 (1998), or for the sexual harassment of a student by another student, *Davis v. Monroe County Bd. of Educ.*, 526 U.S. 629, 119 S.Ct. 1661, 143 L.Ed.2d 839 (1999). *Jackson v. Birmingham Bd. of Educ.*, 544 U.S. 167, 125 S.Ct. 1497, 161 L.Ed.2d 361 (2005), held the cause of action covers claims of retaliation for complaints of sex discrimination.

CALIFORNIA v. SIERRA CLUB
Supreme Court of the United States, 1981.
451 U.S. 287, 101 S.Ct. 1775, 68 L.Ed.2d 101.

JUSTICE WHITE delivered the opinion of the Court.

Under review here is a decision of the Court of Appeals for the Ninth Circuit holding that private parties may sue under the Rivers and Harbors Appropriation Act of 1899 to enforce § 10 of that Act. An environmental organization and two private citizens (hereafter respondents), seek to enjoin the construction and operation of water diversion facilities which are part of the California Water Project (CWP). They rely upon § 10 of the Act, which prohibits "[t]he creation of any obstruction not affirmatively authorized by Congress, to the navigable capacity of any of the waters of the United States * * * ." Since the Act does not explicitly create a private enforcement mechanism, the initial question presented by these consolidated cases is whether such a private right of action can be implied on behalf of those allegedly injured by a claimed violation of § 10. Petitioner State of California also asks us to decide whether the Act requires permits for the state water allocation projects involved in these cases.

I

The California Water Project consists of a series of water storage and transportation facilities designed primarily to transport water from the relatively moist climate of northern California to the more arid central and southern portions of the State. The water which will be used by the CWP is initially stored behind dams on the Sacramento River and, as needed, released into the Sacramento-San Joaquin Delta. The CWP then diverts a quantity of this water from the Delta and directs it into canals and aqueducts which will carry it south. The project has both federal and state components. The federal component, the Central Valley Project, is designed in part to provide a constant source of water for irrigation to the Central Valley of California. Water for this project is diverted from the Delta by the Tracy Pumping Plant into the 115-mile Delta-Mendota Canal which transports the water to the Mendota Pool in California's Central Valley. The State Water Project supplies water to both central and southern California by way of the California Aqueduct. Water for this project is drawn from the Delta by the Delta Pumping Plant and deposited in the northern terminus of the California Aqueduct, through which it flows to its destinations in central and southern California.

Under the present system the quality of water captured in the north and released into the Delta may be degraded by intruding salt waters from the Pacific Ocean. As a consequence the water which is diverted from the Delta to the Delta-Mendota Canal or the California Aqueduct is potentially of a lesser quality than is the water which is transported to the Delta from storage facilities in the north and from there deposited in the Delta. The State of California has proposed the construction of a 42-mile Peripheral Canal along the eastern edge of the Delta area, which would avoid any mixing of the water from the north with the saline water of the Delta. Instead of depositing water in the Delta, the canal would carry high quality water directly to the Tracy and Delta Pumping Plants.

Respondents commenced the present action in 1971 in the United States District Court for the Northern District of California. Named as defendants were the various federal and state officials who administered the agencies responsible for overseeing the operation, construction, and regulation of the CWP facilities in question. Petitioner water agencies, which had contracted with the State for water from the Delta and which had incurred extensive financial obligations in reliance thereon, were permitted to intervene. The respondents alleged that present and proposed diversions of water from the Delta degraded the quality of Delta water, and that such diversion violated § 10 of the Rivers and Harbors Appropriation Act of 1899. They sought to enjoin further operation or construction of water diversion facilities until the consent of the Army Corps of Engineers was obtained as required by the Act.

The District Court concluded that respondents could avail themselves of a "private cause of action" to enforce § 10 of the Act, and ruled on the merits that approval of the Corps of Engineers was required by § 10 for the Tracy and Delta Pumping Plants and the Peripheral Canal. The Court of Appeals for the Ninth Circuit agreed that a private cause of action to enforce the Act existed. It reversed the District Court as to the Tracy Pumping Plant, however, ruling that Congress has consented to its construction and operation. We granted petitions for certiorari filed by the water agencies and the State of California.

II

Cort v. Ash outlined a "preferred approach for determining whether a private right of action should be implied from a federal statute * * * ." This approach listed four factors thought to be relevant to the inquiry * * * . Combined, these four factors present the relevant inquiries to pursue in answering the recurring question of implied causes of action. Cases subsequent to *Cort* have explained that the ultimate issue is whether Congress intended to create a private right of action, but the four factors specified in *Cort* remain the "criteria through which this intent could be discerned."

Under *Cort*, the initial consideration is whether the plaintiff is a member of a class for " 'whose especial benefit the statute was enacted.' " Without analyzing either the language or legislative history of the Act, the Court of Appeals here concluded that the Act was designed for the especial benefit of private parties who may suffer "special injury" caused by an unauthorized obstruction to a navigable waterway. It was apparently reasoned that since Congress enacted a statute that forbids such obstructions in navigable waters, any person who would be "especially harmed" by an unauthorized obstruction was an especial beneficiary of the Act. But such a definition of "especial" beneficiary makes this factor meaningless. Under this view, a victim of any crime would be deemed an especial beneficiary of the criminal statute's proscription. *Cort* did not adopt such a broad-gauge approach. The question is not simply who would benefit from the Act, but whether Congress intended to confer federal rights upon those beneficiaries.

In ascertaining this intent, the first consideration is the language of the Act. Here, the statute states no more than a general proscription of certain activities; it does not unmistakably focus on any particular class of beneficiaries whose welfare Congress intended to further. Such language does not indicate an intent to provide for private rights of action. "There would be far less reason to infer a private remedy in favor of individual persons if Congress, instead of drafting Title IX (of the Education Amendments of 1972) with an unmistakable focus on the benefited class, had written it simply as a ban on discriminatory conduct by recipients of federal funds or as a prohibition against the disbursement of public funds to educational institutions engaged in discriminatory practices." Section 10 of the Rivers and Harbors Appropriation Act is the kind of general ban which carries with it no implication of an intent to confer rights on a particular class of persons.

Neither the Court of Appeals nor respondents have identified anything in the legislative history suggesting that § 10 was created for the especial benefit of a particular class. On the contrary, the legislative history supports the view that the Act was designed to benefit the public at large by empowering the Federal Government to exercise its authority over interstate commerce with respect to obstructions on navigable rivers caused by bridges and similar structures. In part, the Act was passed in response to this Court's decision in *Willamette Iron Bridge Co. v. Hatch*. There the Court held that there was no federal common law "which prohibits obstructions and nuisances in navigable rivers." Although *Willamette* involved private parties, the clear implication of the Court's opinion was that in the absence of specific legislation no party, including the Federal Government, would be empowered to take any action under federal law with respect to such obstructions. The Act was intended to enable the Secretary of War to take such action.[6] Congress was not concerned with the rights of individuals.

It is not surprising, therefore, that there is no "indication of legislative intent, explicit or implicit, either to create such a remedy or to deny one." The Court of Appeals recognized as much: "The legislative history of the Rivers and Harbors Act of 1899 does not reflect a congressional intent either to afford a private remedy or to deny one." This silence on the remedy question serves to confirm that in enacting the Act, Congress was concerned not with private rights but with the Federal Government's ability to respond to obstructions on navigable waterways.

[T]he focus of the inquiry is on whether Congress intended to create a remedy. The federal judiciary will not engraft a remedy on a statute, no matter how salutary, that Congress did not intend to provide. Here consideration of the first two *Cort* factors is dispositive. The language of the statute and its legislative history do not suggest that the Act was intended to create federal rights for the especial benefit of a class of persons but rather that it was intended to benefit the public at large through a general regulatory scheme to be administered by the then Secretary of War. Nor is there any evidence that Congress anticipated that there would be a private remedy. This being the case, it is unnecessary to inquire further to determine whether the purpose of the statute would be advanced by the judicial implication of a private action or whether such a remedy is within the federal domain of interest. These factors are only of relevance if the first two factors give indication of congressional intent to create the remedy. There being no such indication, the judgment of the Court of Appeals must be reversed.

* * *

It is so ordered.

---

[6] In addition, § 12 of the Act provides criminal penalties for violations of the provisions of various sections of the Act, including the provisions of § 10; and, § 17 of the Act provides that "[t]he Department of Justice shall conduct the legal proceedings necessary to enforce the provisions of [§ 10]." The creation of one explicit mode of enforcement is not dispositive of congressional intent with respect to other complementary remedies. However, here, considering the clear focus of the legislative history on the need to enable the Government to respond to obstructions in navigable waterways, the creation of this enforcement mechanism and the absence of the remedy sought by respondents, certainly reinforces the view that Congress was not concerned with private rights or remedies in designing this legislation.

JUSTICE STEVENS, concurring.

In 1888 this Court reversed a decree enjoining the construction of a bridge over a navigable river. The Court's opinion in that case did not question the right of the private parties to seek relief in a federal court; rather, the Court held that no federal rule of law prohibited the obstruction of the navigable waterway. Congress responded to the *Willamette* case in the Rivers and Harbors Act of 1890 by creating a federal prohibition of such obstructions absent a permit from the Secretary of War. At the time the statute was enacted, I believe the lawyers in Congress simply assumed that private parties in a position comparable to that of the litigants in the *Willamette* case would have a remedy for any injury suffered by reason of a violation of the new federal statute. For at that time the implication of private causes of action was a well-known practice at common law and in American courts. Therefore, in my view, the Members of Congress merely assumed that the federal courts would follow the ancient maxim *"ubi jus, ibi remedium"* and imply a private right of action. Accordingly, if I were writing on a clean slate, I would hold that an implied remedy is available to respondents under this statute.

The slate, however, is not clean. Because the problem of ascertaining legislative intent that is not expressed in legislation is often so difficult, the Court has wisely developed rules to guide judges in deciding whether a federal remedy is implicitly a part of a federal statute. In *Cort v. Ash*, all of my present colleagues subscribed to a unanimous formulation of those rules, and in *Cannon v. University of Chicago*, a majority of the Court joined my attempt to explain the application of those rules in that case. The *Cort v. Ash* analysis is therefore a part of our law.

* * * I believe the Court correctly concludes that application of the *Cort v. Ash* analysis indicates that no private cause of action is available. I think it is more important to adhere to the analytical approach the Court has adopted than to base my vote on my own opinion about what Congress probably assumed in 1890. I therefore join Justice White's opinion for the Court.

JUSTICE REHNQUIST, with whom THE CHIEF JUSTICE, JUSTICE STEWART, and JUSTICE POWELL join, concurring in the judgment.

I agree completely with the conclusion of the Court that in these cases "Congress was not concerned with the rights of individuals" and that "[i]t is not surprising, therefore, that there is no 'indication of legislative intent, explicit or implicit, either to create * * * a [private] remedy or to deny one.' "

I also agree with the Court's analysis where it says: "As recently emphasized, the focus of the inquiry is on whether Congress intended to create a remedy. The federal judiciary will not engraft a remedy on a statute, no matter how salutary, that Congress did not intend to provide." My only difference, and the difference which leads me to write this separate concurrence in the judgment, is that I think the Court's opinion places somewhat more emphasis on *Cort v. Ash* than is warranted in light of several more recent "implied right of action" decisions which limit it. These decisions make clear that the so-called *Cort* factors are merely guides in the central task of ascertaining legislative intent, that they are not of equal weight, and that in deciding an implied-right-of-action case courts need not mechanically trudge through all four of the factors when the dispositive question of legislative intent has been resolved. * * *

Notes and Questions

1. What becomes of the four *Cort* factors after *Sierra Club*? Are they still of any use, or has the Court retreated to asking simply whether Congress intended a private right of action to exist? If the *Cort* factors still exist, reconsider their relationship to each other. Are they of equal weight, or does one negative answer end the inquiry?

2. Justice Stevens's concurrence raises some interesting questions, not the least of which is why he is concurring rather than dissenting. He seems confident that Congress assumed that the federal courts would create a remedy of the type sought. Why does he not vote to create it? His answer is that the Court's newly-adopted analytical approach leads to the conclusion that no private right of action is appropriate. Consider, however, the anomaly his opinion leaves in its wake: the avowed purpose of the Court's analysis is to adhere to legislative intent. Justice Stevens finds that the Court's method of analysis does not lead to a result faithful to legislative intent, yet he applies it anyway. Does that not suggest that there is something wrong with the Court's analytical method, either in its declared purpose or in its application?

3. In *Thompson v. Thompson,* 484 U.S. 174, 108 S.Ct. 513, 98 L.Ed.2d 512 (1988), the plaintiff father sought declaratory and injunctive relief under the Parental Kidnapping Prevention Act (PKPA). The case involved conflicting child custody decrees from different states. The Supreme Court unanimously found that the PKPA could not support an implied cause of action.

The bulk of the analysis is unexceptional, tracking earlier cases and the Court's expression of primary (almost exclusive) reliance upon congressional intent. Because Congress had approached parental kidnapping as a full faith and credit problem, the Court refused to imply a right of action, since the Full Faith and Credit Clause itself creates no cause of action. Justice Marshall's opinion did note, however:

> Our focus on congressional intent does not mean that we require evidence that Members of Congress, in enacting the statute, actually had in mind the creation of a private cause of action. The implied cause of action doctrine would be a virtual dead letter were it limited to correcting drafting errors when Congress simply forgot to codify its evident intention to provide a cause of action.

Justice Scalia concurred in the judgment, and his separate opinion is a powerful echo of Justice Powell's *Cannon* dissent:

> I write separately because in my view the Court is not being faithful to current doctrine in its dictum denying the necessity of an actual congressional intent to create a private right of action, and in referring to *Cort v. Ash* as though its analysis had not been effectively overruled by our later opinions. * * *

> I am at a loss to imagine what congressional intent to create a private right of action might mean, if it does not mean that Congress had in mind the creation of a private right of action.

* * *

> The Court's opinion exaggerates the difficulty of establishing an implied right when it surmises that "[t]he implied cause of action doctrine would be a virtual dead letter were it limited to correcting drafting errors * * * ." That statement rests upon the erroneous premise that one never implies anything except when he forgets to say it expressly.

* * *

> It is, to be sure, not beyond imagination that in a particular case Congress may intend to create a private right of action, but choose to do so by implication. One must wonder, however, whether the good produced by a judicial rule that accommodates this remote possibility is outweighed by its adverse effects. An enactment by implication cannot realistically be regarded as the product of the difficult lawmaking process our Constitution has prescribed.

* * *

> [A]s the likelihood that Congress would leave the matter to implication decreases, so does the justification for bearing the risk of distorting the constitutional process. A legislative act so significant, and so separable from the remainder of the statute, as the creation of a private right of action seems to me so implausibly left to implication that the risk should not be endured.

> If we were to announce a flat rule that private rights of action will not be implied in statutes hereafter enacted, the risk that that course would occasionally frustrate genuine legislative intent would decrease from its current level of minimal to virtually zero.

* * *

> If a change is to be made, we should get out of the business of implied private rights of action altogether.

Since Justice Powell has left the Court, Justice Scalia is not an additional vote for Powell's position. Nonetheless, it is clear that Powell's argument will not soon fade. Do Justices Powell's and Scalia's arguments that the Court ought never to imply causes of action in statutes put Congress on notice that implication is at least unlikely? If so, does a statute's silence take on additional meaning? Consider Note 4 below.

Does the Powell-Scalia view of implied rights of action apply with equal force to implying private rights of action in constitutional provisions?

4. In *Karahalios v. National Federation of Federal Employees, Local 1263*, 489 U.S. 527, 109 S.Ct. 1282, 103 L.Ed.2d 539 (1989), the plaintiff asked the Court to imply a private right of action in a statute, this time the Civil Service Reform Act, for "breach by a union representing federal employees of its statutory duty of fair representation." The Court declined, noting that Congress had created an enforcement scheme in the Federal Labor Relations Authority. The plaintiff argued in vain that his action paralleled cases arising under the National Labor Relations Act, in which the Court had implied a private right of action. The Court distinguished those cases.

a) Of greater importance is the Court's treatment of the implication issue generally. Quoting its own cases from 1979 forward (including *Sierra Club* and *Thompson v. Thompson*), the Court said:

> The "ultimate issue is whether Congress intended to create a private cause of action." Unless such "congressional intent can be inferred from the language of the statute, the statutory structure, or some other source, the essential predicate for implication of a private remedy simply does not exist." It is also an "elemental canon" of statutory construction that where a statute expressly provides a remedy, courts must be especially reluctant to provide additional remedies. In such cases, "[i]n the absence of strong indicia of contrary congressional intent, we are compelled to conclude that Congress provided precisely the remedies it considered appropriate."

How does the Court's approach in *Karahalios* compare with its approach from the 1800's through *Borak, Cort,* and *Cannon?* Would the *Borak* Court have been more likely to imply a private right of action? If so, does the change in the Court's technique raise separation-of-powers issues?

b) The end of the *Karahalios* opinion discussed the significance of the Court's evolving technique of interpreting congressional intent.

> We therefore discern no basis for finding congressional intent to provide petitioner with a cause of action against the union. Congress undoubtedly was aware from our cases such as *Cort v. Ash* that the Court had departed from its prior standard for resolving a claim urging that an implied statutory cause of action should be recognized, and that such issues were being resolved by a straight-forward inquiry into whether Congress intended to provide a private cause of action. Had Congress intended the courts to enforce a federal employees union's duty of fair representation, we would expect to find some evidence of that intent in the statute or its legislative history. We find none. * * * To be sure, courts play a role in CSRA § 7116(b)(8) fair representation cases, but only sitting in review of the FLRA. To hold that the district courts must entertain such cases in the first instance would seriously

undermine what we deem to be the congressional scheme, namely to leave the enforcement of union and agency duties under the Act to the General Counsel and the FLRA and to confine the courts to the role given them under the Act.

The Court's reasoning is not without irony and perhaps not without problems. First, given the Justices' linking the changed approach manifested in *Cort v. Ash* with congressional awareness of the need to be explicit about private rights of action, has *Cort* sowed the seeds of its own destruction?

Second, before *Cort v. Ash,* Congress never suggested dissatisfaction with the Court's method of dealing with statutes that created new rights without explicitly creating remedies. Does Congress's apparent acquiescence connote that the Court should not have changed its technique?

Finally, from the nineteenth century to the present, the Court has discussed congressional intent in deciding whether to imply private rights of action in statutes. Is today's Court taking the same view of congressional intent as did its predecessors?

5. As the foregoing materials show, the Court has not been successful in limiting the inquiry in implied right of action cases solely to the second *Cort* criterion, which examines whether Congress intended to create the cause of action the plaintiff asserts. One of the authors has suggested that it is very difficult to decide whether a cause of action should be implied without considering the rights being asserted and the remedy sought. As a result, the first and third *Cort* criteria tend to creep back into the cases:

The first *Cort* factor continues to be important because the Court must consider the purpose of a cause of action in deciding whether Congress intended to create it. A plaintiff does not come to court asserting a cause of action in the abstract. Instead, a plaintiff asserts that a particular federal statute grants a right that the defendant has violated, and asks the Court to imply a cause of action to enforce that right. The Court must then look at the provision and ask whether "the statute create[s] a federal right in favor of the plaintiff." It is almost impossible to answer the question of whether Congress intended to create a cause of action to enforce the right the plaintiff asserts without deciding whether a statute actually confers the right. Consequently, the first *Cort* factor continues to be central in implied right of action cases, even when the Court does not specifically identify it as such, but instead disguises it as an inquiry into the language of the statute or the legislative history.

Similarly, it is very difficult for the Court to avoid considering the third *Cort* factor—"is it consistent with the underlying purposes of the legislative scheme to imply [a particular] remedy for the plaintiff?"—in deciding implied right of action cases. By definition, the statute does not explicitly create the cause of action, and the legislative history is silent as to whether Congress actually intended to create it. If a statutory provision appears to confer a right on the plaintiff, the Court would have difficulty deciding whether Congress wanted the right to be judicially enforceable without looking at whether it would foster or subvert the underlying statutory purposes to allow such lawsuits. Thus, unless the Court looks at the overall statutory purpose, it denies itself access to the information it needs to answer the question whether Congress intended to create the cause of action.

Donald H. Zeigler, *Rights, Rights of Action, and Remedies: An Integrated Approach*, 76 WASH. L. REV. 67, 110-111 (2001)(footnotes omitted).

SCHWEIKER v. CHILICKY
Supreme Court of the United States, 1988.
487 U.S. 412, 108 S.Ct. 2460, 101 L.Ed.2d 370.

JUSTICE O'CONNOR delivered the opinion of the Court.

This case requires us to decide whether the improper denial of Social Security disability benefits, allegedly resulting from violations of due process by government officials who administered the Federal Social Security program, may give rise to a cause of action for money damages against those officials. We conclude that such a remedy, not having been included in the elaborate remedial scheme devised by Congress, is unavailable.

I

A

Under Title II of the Social Security Act (Act), the Federal Government provides disability benefits to individuals who have contributed to the Social Security program and who, because of a medically determinable physical or mental impairment, are unable to engage in substantial gainful work. * * * Title II, which is administered in conjunction with state welfare agencies, provides benefits only while an individual's statutory disability persists. In 1980, Congress noted that existing administrative procedures provided for reexamination of eligibility "only under a limited number of circumstances." Congress responded by enacting legislation requiring that most disability determinations be reviewed at least once every three years. Although the statute did not require this program for "continuing disability review" (CDR) to become effective before January 1, 1982, the Secretary of Health and Human Services initiated CDR in March 1981.

The administration of the CDR program was at first modeled on the previous procedures for reexamination of eligibility. Under these procedures, an individual whose case is selected for review bears the burden of demonstrating the continuing existence of a statutory disability. The appropriate state agency performs the initial review, and persons who are found to have become ineligible are generally provided with administrative review similar to the review provided to new claimants. Under the original CDR procedures, benefits were usually terminated after a state agency found a claimant ineligible, and were not available during administrative appeals.

Finding that benefits were too often being improperly terminated by state agencies, only to be reinstated by a federal administrative law judge (ALJ), Congress enacted temporary emergency legislation in 1983. This law provided for the continuation of benefits, pending review by an ALJ, after a state agency determined that an individual was no longer disabled. In the Social Security Disability Benefits Reform Act of 1984 (1984 Reform Act), Congress extended this provision until January 1, 1988, and provided for a number of other significant changes in the administration of CDR * * * . In its final form, this legislation was enacted without a single opposing vote in either Chamber.

The problems to which Congress responded so emphatically were widespread. One of the cosponsors of the 1984 Reform Act, who had conducted hearings on the administration of CDR, summarized evidence from the General Accounting Office as follows:

> [T]he message perceived by the State agencies, swamped with cases, was to deny, deny, deny, and, I might add, to process cases faster and faster and faster. In the name of efficiency, we have scanned our computer terminals, rounded up the disabled workers in the country, pushed the discharge button, and let them go into a free [f]all toward economic chaos.

Other legislators reached similar conclusions. ("[T]he Social Security Administration has tried to reduce program cost by terminating the benefits of hundreds of thousands of truly disabled Americans"); [another legislator] allud[ed] to "massive number of beneficiaries who have lost their benefits over the last 3 years even though they are truly disabled and unable to work"). Such conclusions were based, not only on anecdotal evidence, but on compellingly forceful statistics. The Social Security Administration itself apparently reported that about 200,000 persons were wrongfully terminated, and then reinstated, between March 1981 and April 1984. In the first year of CDR, half of those who were terminated appealed the decision, and "an amazing two-thirds of those who appealed were being reinstated."

Congress was also made aware of the terrible effects on individual lives that CDR had produced. The chairman of the Senate's Special Committee on Aging pointed out that "[t]he human dimension of this crisis—the unnecessary suffering, anxiety, and turmoil—has been graphically exposed by dozens of congressional hearings and in newspaper articles all across the country." Termination could also lead to the cut-off of Medicare benefits, so that some people were left without adequate medical care. There is little doubt that CDR led to many hardships and injuries that could never be adequately compensated.

B

Respondents are three individuals whose disability benefits under

Title II were terminated pursuant to the CDR program in 1981 and 1982. Respondents Spencer Harris and Dora Adelerte appealed these determinations through the administrative process, were restored to disabled status, and were awarded full retroactive benefits. Respondent James Chilicky did not pursue these administrative remedies. Instead, he filed a new application for benefits about a year and a half after his benefits were stopped. His application was granted, and he was awarded one year's retroactive benefits; his application for the restoration of the other six months' benefits is apparently still pending. Because the terminations in these three cases occurred before the 1983 emergency legislation was enacted, respondents experienced delays of many months in receiving disability benefits to which they were entitled. All the respondents had been wholly dependent on their disability benefits, and all allege that they were unable to maintain themselves or their families in even a minimally adequate fashion after they were declared ineligible. Respondent James Chilicky was in the hospital recovering from open-heart surgery when he was informed that his heart condition was no longer disabling.

In addition to pursuing administrative remedies, respondents (along with several other individuals who have since withdrawn from the case) filed this lawsuit in the United States District Court for the District of Arizona. They alleged that petitioners * * * had violated respondents' due process rights. The thrust of the complaint, which named petitioners in their official and individual capacities, was that petitioners had adopted illegal policies that led to the wrongful termination of benefits by state agencies. Among the allegations were claims that petitioners improperly accelerated the starting date of the CDR program; illegally refused to acquiesce in decisions of the United States Court of Appeals for the Ninth Circuit; failed to apply uniform written standards in implementing the CDR program; failed to give effect to dispositive evidence in particular cases; and used an impermissible quota system under which state agencies were required to terminate predetermined numbers of recipients. Respondents sought injunctive and declaratory relief, and money damages for "emotional distress and for loss of food, shelter and other necessities proximately caused by [petitioners'] denial of benefits without due process."

* * *

The petition for certiorari presented one question: "Whether a *Bivens* remedy should be implied for alleged due process violations in the denial of social security disability benefits." We granted the petition, and now reverse.

II

A

* * *

In 1971, this Court held that the victim of a Fourth Amendment violation by federal officers acting under color of their authority may bring suit for money damages against the officers in federal court. The Court noted that Congress had not specifically provided for such a remedy and that "the Fourth Amendment does not in so many words provide for its enforcement by an award of money damages for the consequences of its violation." Nevertheless, finding "no special factors counselling hesitation in the absence of affirmative action by Congress," and "no explicit congressional declaration" that money damages may not be awarded, the majority relied on the rule that 'where legal rights have been invaded, and a federal statute provides for a general right to sue for such invasion, federal courts may use any available remedy to make good the wrong done.' "

So-called "*Bivens* actions" for money damages against federal officers have subsequently been permitted under § 1331 for violations of the Due Process Clause of the Fifth Amendment, and Unusual Punishment Clause of the Eighth Amendment. In each of these cases, as in *Bivens* itself, the Court found that there were no "special factors counselling hesitation in the absence of affirmative action by Congress," no explicit statutory prohibition against the relief sought, and no exclusive statutory alternative remedy.

Our more recent decisions have responded cautiously to suggestions that *Bivens* remedies be extended into new contexts. The absence of statutory relief for a constitutional violation, for example, does not by any means necessarily imply that courts should award money damages against the officers responsible for the violation. Thus, we refused—unanimously—to create a *Bivens* action for enlisted military personnel who alleged that they had been injured by the unconstitutional actions of their superior officers and who had no remedy against the Government itself:

> The special nature of military life—the need for unhesitating and decisive action by military officers and equally disciplined responses by enlisted personnel—would be undermined by a judicially created remedy exposing officers to personal liability at the hands of those they are charged to command * * * .

Also, Congress, the constitutionally authorized source of authority over the military system of justice, has not provided a damages remedy for claims by military personnel that constitutional rights have been violated by superior officers. *Any action to provide a judicial response by way of such a remedy would be plainly inconsistent with Congress' authority in this field.*

Taken together, the unique disciplinary structure of the Military Establishment and Congress' activity in the field constitute "special factors" which dictate that it would be inappropriate to provide enlisted military personnel a *Bivens*-type remedy against their superior officers.

([E]mphasis added; citation omitted). *See also United States v. Stanley* (disallowing *Bivens* actions by military personnel "whenever the injury arises out of activity 'incident to service' ").

Similarly, [in *Bush v. Lucas*] we refused—again unanimously—to create a *Bivens* remedy for a First Amendment violation "aris[ing] out of an employment relationship that is governed by comprehensive procedural and substantive provisions giving meaningful remedies against the United States." In that case, a federal employee was demoted, allegedly in violation of the First Amendment, for making public statements critical of the agency for which he worked. He was reinstated through the administrative process, with retroactive seniority and full backpay, but he was not permitted to recover for any loss due to emotional distress or mental anguish, or for attorney's fees. Concluding that the administrative system created by Congress "provides meaningful remedies for employees who may have been unfairly disciplined for making critical comments about their agencies," the Court refused to create a *Bivens* action even though it assumed a First Amendment violation and acknowledged that "existing remedies do not provide complete relief for the plaintiff." The Court stressed that the case involved policy questions in an area that had received careful attention from Congress. Noting that the Legislature is far more competent than the Judiciary to carry out the necessary "balancing [of] governmental efficiency and the rights of employees," we refused to "decide whether or not it would be good policy to permit a federal employee to recover damages from a supervisor who has improperly disciplined him for exercising his First Amendment rights."

In sum, the concept of "special factors counselling hesitation in the absence of affirmative action by Congress" has proved to include an appropriate judicial deference to indications that congressional inaction has not been inadvertent. When the design of a government program suggests that Congress has provided what it considers adequate remedial mechanisms for constitutional violations that may occur in the course of its administration, we have not created additional *Bivens* remedies.

B

The administrative structure and procedures of the Social Security system, which affects virtually every American, "are of a size and extent difficult to comprehend." Millions of claims are filed every year under the Act's disability benefits programs alone, and these claims are handled under "an unusually protective [multi]-step process for the review and adjudication of disputed claims."

The steps provided for under Title II are essentially identical for new claimants and for persons subject to CDR. An initial determination of a claimant's eligibility for benefits is made by a state agency, under federal standards and criteria. Next, a claimant is entitled to *de novo* reconsideration by the state agency, and additional evidence may be presented at that time. If the claimant is dissatisfied with the state agency's decision, review may then be had by the Secretary of Health and Human Services, acting through a Federal ALJ; at this stage, the claimant is again free to introduce new evidence or raise new issues. If the claimant is still dissatisfied, a hearing may be sought before the Appeals Council of the Social Security Administration. Once these elaborate administrative remedies have been exhausted, a claimant is entitled to seek judicial review, including review of constitutional claims. The Act, however, makes no provision for remedies in money damages against officials responsible for unconstitutional conduct that leads to the wrongful denial of benefits. As respondents concede, claimants whose benefits have been fully restored through the administrative process would lack standing to invoke the Constitution under the statute's administrative review provision.

The case before us cannot reasonably be distinguished from *Bush v. Lucas.* Here, exactly as in *Bush,* Congress has failed to provide for "complete relief": respondents have not been given a remedy in damages for emotional distress or for other hardships suffered because of delays in their receipt of Social Security benefits. The creation of a *Bivens* remedy would obviously offer the prospect of relief for injuries that must now go unredressed. Congress, however, has not failed to provide meaningful safeguards or remedies for the rights of persons situated as respondents were. Indeed, the system for protecting their rights is, if anything, considerably more elaborate than the civil service system considered in *Bush.* The prospect of personal liability for official acts, moreover, would undoubtedly lead to new difficulties and expense in recruiting administrators for the programs Congress has established. Congressional competence at "balancing governmental efficiency and the rights of [individuals]" is no more questionable in the social welfare context than it is in the civil service context.

Congressional attention to problems that have arisen in the administration of CDR (including the very problems that gave rise to this case) has, moreover, been frequent and intense. Congress itself required that the CDR program be instituted. Within two years after the program began, Congress enacted emergency legislation providing for the continuation of benefits even after a finding of ineligibility by a state agency. Less than two years after passing that law, and fully aware of the results of extensive investigations of the practices that led to respondents' injuries, Congress again enacted legislation aimed at reforming the administration of CDR; that legislation again specifically addressed the problem that had provoked the earlier emergency legislation. At each step, Congress chose specific forms and levels of protection for the rights of persons affected by incorrect eligibility determinations under CDR. At no point did Congress choose to extend to any person the kind of remedies that respondents seek in this lawsuit. Thus, congressional unwillingness to provide consequential damages for unconstitutional deprivations of a statutory right is at least as clear in the context of this case as it was in *Bush*.

Respondents nonetheless contend that *Bush* should be confined to its facts, arguing that it applies only in the context of what they call "the special nature of federal employee relations." Noting that the parties to this case did "not share the sort of close, collaborative, continuing juridical relationship found in the federal civil service," respondents suggest that the availability of *Bivens* remedies would create less "inconvenience" to the Social Security system than it would in the context of the civil service. The Solicitor General is less sanguine, arguing that the creation of *Bivens* remedy in this context would lead to "a complete disruption of [a] carefully crafted and constantly monitored congressional scheme."

We need not choose between these competing predictions, which have little bearing on the applicability of *Bush* to this case. The decision in *Bush* did not rest on this Court's belief that *Bivens* actions would be more disruptive of the civil service than they are in other contexts where they have been allowed, such as federal law enforcement agencies (*Bivens* itself) or the federal prisons. Rather, we declined in *Bush* " 'to create a new substantive legal liability * * * ' because we are convinced that Congress is in a better position to decide whether or not the public interest would be served by creating it." That reasoning applies as much, or more, in this case as it did in *Bush* itself.

Respondents also suggest that this case is distinguishable from *Bush* because the plaintiff in that case received compensation for the constitutional violation itself, while these respondents have merely received that to which they would have been entitled had there been no constitutional violation. ("Bush's reinstatement was a remedy for the alleged abuse, not just a restoration of something to which he was entitled * * * .") ([F]ailure to create a *Bivens* remedy "would give respondents precisely the same thing whether or not they were victims of constitutional deprivation and would thus leave respondents with no post-deprivation remedy at all for the constitutional violations they allege"). The *Bush* opinion, however, drew no distinction between compensation for a "constitutional wrong" and the restoration of statutory rights that had been unconstitutionally taken away. Nor did it suggest that such labels would matter. Indeed, the Court appeared to assume that civil service employees would get "precisely the same thing whether or not they were victims of constitutional deprivation." * * * *Bush* thus lends no support to the notion that statutory violations caused by unconstitutional conduct necessarily require remedies in addition to the remedies provided generally for such statutory violations. Here, as in *Bush,* it is evident that if we were "to fashion an adequate remedy for every wrong that can be proved in a case * * * [the complaining party] would obviously prevail." In neither case, however, does the presence of alleged unconstitutional conduct that is not separately remedied under the statutory scheme imply that the statute has provided "no remedy" for the constitutional wrong at issue.

* * *

In the end, respondents' various arguments are rooted in their insistent and vigorous contention that they simply have not been adequately recompensed for their injuries. * * *

We agree that suffering months of delay in receiving the income on which one has depended for the very necessities of life cannot be fully remedied by the "belated restoration of back benefits." The trauma to respondents, and thousands of others like them, must surely have gone beyond what anyone of normal sensibilities would wish to see imposed on innocent disabled citizens. Nor would we care to "trivialize" the nature of the wrongs alleged in this case. Congress, however, has addressed the problems created by state agencies' wrongful termination of disability benefits. Whether or not we believe that its response was the best response, Congress is the body charged with making the inevitable compromises required in the design of a massive and complex welfare benefits program. Congress has discharged that responsibility to the extent that it affects the case before us, and we see no legal basis that would allow us to revise its decision.

Because the relief sought by respondents is unavailable as a matter of law, the case must be dismissed. The judgment of the Court of Appeals to the contrary is therefore

Reversed.

JUSTICE BRENNAN, with whom JUSTICE MARSHALL and JUSTICE BLACKMUN join, dissenting.

Respondents are three individuals who, because they are unable to engage in gainful employment as a result of certain disabilities, rely primarily or exclusively on disability benefits awarded under Title II of the Social Security Act for their support and that of their families. Like hundreds of thousands of other such recipients, in the early 1980's they lost this essential source of income following state implementation of a federally mandated "continuing disability review" process (CDR), only to have an administrative law judge (ALJ) ultimately reinstate their benefits after appeal, or to regain them, as respondent James Chilicky did, by filing a new application for benefits. Respondents allege that the initial benefit termination resulted from a variety of unconstitutional actions taken by state and federal officials responsible for administering the CDR program. They further allege, and petitioners do not dispute, that as a result of these deprivations, which lasted from 7 to 19 months, they suffered immediate financial hardship, were unable to purchase food, shelter, and other necessities, and were unable to maintain themselves in even a minimally adequate fashion.

The Court today reaffirms the availability of a federal action for money damages against federal officials charged with violating constitutional rights. " 'Where legal rights have been invaded, and a federal statute provides for a general right to sue for such invasion, federal courts may use any available remedy to make good the wrong done.' " Acknowledging that the trauma respondents and others like them suffered as a result of the allegedly unconstitutional acts of state and federal officials "must surely have gone beyond what anyone of normal sensibilities would wish to see imposed on innocent disabled citizens," the Court does not for a moment suggest that the retroactive award of benefits to which respondents were always entitled remotely approximates full compensation for such trauma. Nevertheless, it refuses to recognize a *Bivens* remedy here because the "design of [the disability insurance] program suggests that Congress has provided what it considers adequate remedial mechanisms for constitutional violations that may occur in the course of its administration."

I agree that in appropriate circumstances we should defer to a congressional decision to substitute alternative relief for a judicially created remedy. Neither the design of Title II's administrative review process, however, nor the debate surrounding its reform contain any suggestion that Congress meant to preclude recognition of a *Bivens* action for persons whose constitutional rights are violated by those charged with administering the program, or that Congress viewed this process as an adequate substitute remedy for such violations. Indeed, Congress never mentioned, let alone debated, the desirability of providing a statutory remedy for such constitutional wrongs. Because I believe legislators of "normal sensibilities" would not wish to leave such traumatic injuries unrecompensed, I find it inconceivable that Congress meant by mere silence to bar all redress for such injuries.

I

In response to the escalating costs of the Title II disability insurance program, Congress enacted legislation in 1980 directing state agencies to review the eligibility of Title II beneficiaries at least once every three years in order to ensure that those receiving benefits continued to qualify for such assistance. Although the CDR program was to take effect January 1, 1982, the then-new administration advanced its starting date to March 1, 1981, and initiated what congressional critics later characterized as a "meat ax approach" to the problem of Social Security fraud.

Respondents allege that in the course of their review proceedings, state and federal officials violated their due process rights by judging their eligibility in light of impermissible quotas, disregarding dispositive favorable evidence, selecting biased physicians, purposely using unpublished criteria and rules inconsistent with statutory standards, arbitrarily reversing favorable decisions, and failing impartially to review adverse decisions.

* * *

Congress responded to the CDR crisis by establishing, for the first time, a statutory standard governing disability review. Designed primarily to end the practice of terminating benefits based on nothing more than a reassessment of old evidence under new eligibility criteria, the medical improvement standard permits the agency to terminate benefits only where substantial evidence demonstrates that one of four specific conditions is met.[1] In addition to establishing these substantive eligibility criteria and directing SSA to revise certain others, Congress enacted several procedural reforms in order to protect recipients from future erroneous deprivations and to ensure that the review process itself would operate in a fairer and more humane manner. The most significant of these protections was a provision allowing recipients to elect to continue to receive benefit payments, subject to recoupment in certain circumstances, through appeal to a federal ALJ, the penultimate stage of administrative review.

II

A

In *Bivens* itself, we noted that, although courts have the authority to provide redress for constitutional violations in the form of an action for money damages, the exercise of that authority may be inappropriate where Congress has created another remedy that it regards as equally effective, or where "special factors counse[l] hesitation [even] in the absence of affirmative action by Congress." Among the "special factors" the Court divines today in our prior cases is "an appropriate deference to indications that congressional inaction has not been inadvertent." De-

---

[1] Under the 1984 standard, the agency may terminate benefits only if 1) substantial evidence demonstrates that the recipient's impairment has medically improved and that he or she is able to engage in substantial gainful activity; 2) new and substantial medical evidence reveals that, although the recipient's condition has not improved medically, he or she has benefitted [sic] from medical or vocational therapy and is able to engage in substantial gainful activity; 3) new or improved diagnostic techniques or evaluations demonstrate that the recipient's impairment is not as disabling as was previously determined and that he or she is able to engage in substantial gainful activity; or 4) substantial evidence, including any evidence previously on record, demonstrates that a prior eligibility determination was erroneous. Congress also barred any further certification of class actions challenging SSA's medical improvement criteria and directed a remand of all such pending actions in order to afford the agency an opportunity to apply the newly prescribed standard.

scribing congressional attention to the numerous problems the CDR process spawned as "frequent and intense," the Court concludes that the very design of that process "suggests that Congress has provided what it considers adequate remedial mechanisms for constitutional violations that may occur in the course of its administration." The cases setting forth the "special factors" analysis upon which the Court relies, however, reveal, by way of comparison, both the inadequacy of Title II's "remedial mechanism" and the wholly inadvertent nature of Congress' failure to provide any statutory remedy for constitutional injuries inflicted during the course of previous review proceedings.

In *Chappell v. Wallace,* where we declined to permit an action for damages by enlisted military personnel seeking redress from their superior officers for constitutional injuries, we noted that Congress, in the exercise of its "plenary constitutional authority over the military, has enacted statutes regulating military life, and has established a comprehensive internal system of justice to regulate military life * * * . The resulting system provides for the review and remedy of complaints and grievances such as [the equal protection claim] presented by respondents." That system not only permits aggrieved military personnel to raise constitutional challenges in administrative proceedings, it authorizes recovery of significant consequential damages, notably retroactive promotions. Similarly, in *Bush v. Lucas,* we concluded that, in light of the "elaborate, comprehensive scheme" governing federal employment relations, recognition of any supplemental judicial remedy for constitutional wrongs was inappropriate. Under that scheme—which Congress has "constructed step-by-step, with careful attention to conflicting policy considerations," over the course of nearly 100 years—"[c]onstitutional challenges * * * are fully cognizable" and prevailing employees are entitled not only to full backpay, but to retroactive promotions, seniority, pay raises, and accumulated leave. Indeed, Congress expressly "intended [to] put the employee 'in the same position he would have been in had the unjustified or erroneous personnel action not taken place.' "

It is true that neither the military justice system nor the federal employment relations scheme affords aggrieved parties full compensation for constitutional injuries; nevertheless, the relief provided in both is far more complete than that available under Title II's review process. Although federal employees may not recover damages for any emotional or dignitary harms they might suffer as a result of a constitutional injury, they, like their military counterparts, are entitled to redress for most economic consequential damages, including, most significantly, consequential damage to their Government careers. Here, by stark contrast, Title II recipients cannot even raise constitutional challenges to agency action in any of the four tiers of administrative review, and if they ultimately prevail on their eligibility claims in those administrative proceedings they can recover no consequential damages whatsoever. The only relief afforded persons unconstitutionally deprived of their disability benefits is retroactive payment of the very benefits they should have received all along. Such an award, of course, fails miserably to compensate disabled persons illegally stripped of the income upon which, in many cases, their very subsistence depends.[4]

The inadequacy of this relief is by no means a product of "the inevitable compromises required in the design of a massive and complex welfare benefits program." In *Chappell* and *Bush,* we dealt with elaborate administrative systems in which Congress anticipated that federal officials might engage in unconstitutional conduct, and in which it accordingly sought to afford injured persons a form of redress as complete as the Government's institutional concerns would allow.

Here, as the legislative history of the 1984 Reform Act makes abundantly clear, Congress did not attempt to achieve a delicate balance between the constitutional rights of Title II beneficiaries on the one hand, and administrative concerns on the other. Rather than fine-tuning "an elaborate remedial scheme that ha[d] been constructed step by step" over the better part of a century, Congress confronted a paralyzing breakdown in a vital social program, which it sought to rescue from near-total anarchy. Although the legislative debate surrounding the 1984 Reform Act is littered with references to "arbitrary," "capricious," and "wrongful" terminations of benefits, it is clear that neither Congress nor anyone else identified unconstitutional conduct by state agencies as the cause of this paralysis. Rather, Congress blamed the systemic problems it faced in 1984 on SSA's determination to control the cost of the disability insurance program by accelerating the CDR process and mandating more restrictive reviews. Legislators explained that, "[b]ecause of the abrupt acceleration of the reviews, * * * [s]tate disability determinations offices were forced to accept a three-fold increase in their workloads," * * * ; yet despite this acceleration, SSA took no steps to "assur[e] that the State agencies had the resources to handle the greatly increased workloads," * * * and instead put "pressure upon [those] agencies to make inaccurate and unfair decisions." * * *

Legislating in a near-crisis atmosphere, Congress saw itself as wrestling with the Executive Branch for control of the disability insurance program. It emphatically repudiated SSA's policy of restrictive, illiberal, and hasty benefit reviews, and adopted a number of prospective measures designed "to prevent further reckless reviews," * * * and to ensure that recipients dependent on disability benefits for their sustenance would be adequately protected in any future review proceedings.

At no point during the lengthy legislative debate, however, did any member of Congress so much as hint that the substantive eligibility cri-

---

[4] The legislative debate over the 1984 Reform Act is replete with anecdotal evidence of recipients who lost their cars and homes, and of some who may even have died as a result of benefit terminations.

teria, notice requirements, and interim payment provisions that would govern future disability reviews adequately redressed the harms that beneficiaries may have suffered as a result of the unconstitutional actions of individual state and federal officials in past proceedings, or that the constitutional rights of those unjustly deprived of benefits in the past had to be sacrificed in the name of administrative efficiency or any other governmental interest. The Court today identifies no legislative compromise, "inevitable" or otherwise, in which lawmakers expressly declined to afford a remedy for such past wrongs. Nor can the Court point to any legislator who suggested that state and federal officials should be shielded from liability for any unconstitutional acts taken in the course of administering the review program, or that exposure to liability for such acts would be inconsistent with Congress' comprehensive and carefully crafted remedial scheme.

* * *

The mere fact, that Congress was aware of the prior injustices and failed to provide a form of redress for them, standing alone, is simply not a "special factor counselling hesitation" in the judicial recognition of a remedy. Inaction, we have repeatedly stated, is a notoriously poor indication of congressional intent, all the more so where Congress is legislating in the face of a massive breakdown calling for prompt and sweeping corrective measures. In 1984, Congress undertook to resuscitate a disability review process that had ceased functioning: that the prospective measures it prescribed to prevent future dislocations included no remedy for past wrongs in no way suggests a conscious choice to leave those wrongs unremedied. I therefore think it altogether untenable to conclude, on the basis of mere legislative silence and inaction, that Congress intended an administrative scheme that does not even take cognizance of constitutional claims to displace a damages action for constitutional deprivations that might arise in the administration of the disability insurance program.

B

Our decisions in *Chappell* and *Bush* reveal yet another flaw in the "special factors" analysis the Court employs today. In both those cases, we declined to legislate in areas in which Congress enjoys a special expertise that the judiciary clearly lacks.

* * *

Ignoring the unique characteristics of the military and civil service contexts that made judicial recognition of a *Bivens* action inappropriate in those cases, the Court today observes that "[c]ongressional competence at 'balancing governmental efficiency and the rights of [individuals]' is no more questionable in the social welfare context than it is in the civil service context * * * ." This observation, however, avails the Court nothing, for in *Bush* we declined to create a *Bivens* action for aggrieved federal employees not because Congress is simply competent to legislate in the area of federal employment relations, but because Congress is far more capable of addressing the special problems that arise in those relations than are courts. Thus, I have no quarrel with the Court's assertion that in *Bush* we did not decline to create a *Bivens* action because we believed such an action would be more disruptive in the civil service context than elsewhere, but because we were " 'convinced that Congress is in a better position to decide whether or not the public interest would be served by creating [such an action.]' " That conviction, however, flowed not from mere congressional competence to legislate in the area of federal employment relations, but from our recognition that we lacked the special expertise Congress had developed in such matters, as well as the ability to evaluate the impact such a right of action would have on the civil service.

The Court's suggestion, therefore, that congressional authority over a given subject is itself a "special factor" that "counsel[s] hesitation [even] in the absence of affirmative action by Congress," is clearly mistaken. In *Davis v. Passman* we recognized a cause of action under the Fifth Amendment's Due Process Clause for a congressional employee who alleged that she had been discriminated against on the basis of her sex, even though Congress is competent to pass legislation governing the employment relations of its own Members. Likewise, in *Carlson v. Green* we created a *Bivens* action for redress of injuries flowing from the allegedly unconstitutional conduct of federal prison officials, notwithstanding the fact that Congress had expressly (and competently) provided a statutory remedy in the Federal Tort Claims Act for injuries inflicted by such officials. In neither case was it necessary to inquire into Congress' competence over the subject matter. Rather, we permitted the claims because they arose in areas in which congressional competence is no greater than that of the courts, and in which, therefore, courts need not fear to tread even in the absence of congressional action.

The same is true here. Congress, of course, created the disability insurance program and obviously may legislate with respect to it. But unlike the military setting, where Congress' authority is plenary and entitled to considerable judicial deference, or the federal employment context, where Congress enjoys special expertise, social welfare is hardly an area in which the courts are largely incompetent to act. The disability insurance program is concededly large, but it does not involve necessarily unique relationships like those between enlisted military personnel and their superior officers, or Government workers and their federal employers. Rather, like the federal law enforcement and penal systems that gave rise to the constitutional claims in *Bivens* and *Carlson,* the constitutional issues that surface in the social welfare system turn on the relationship of the Government and those it governs—the relationship that lies at the heart of constitutional adjudication. Moreover, courts do not lack familiarity or expertise in determining what the dictates of the Due Process Clause are. In short, the social welfare context does not give rise to the types of concerns that make it an area where courts should refrain from creating a damages action even in the absence of congressional action.

* * *

Notes and Questions

1. *Chappell v. Wallace,* 462 U.S. 296, 103 S.Ct. 2362, 76 L.Ed.2d 586 (1983), and *United States v. Stanley,* 483 U.S. 669, 107 S.Ct. 3054, 97 L.Ed.2d 550 (1987), illustrate the Court's increasingly staunch resistance to implying private rights of action. In *Chappell,* cited with apparent approval even by Justice Brennan's dissent, enlisted servicemen sued superior officers claiming that the defendants had discriminated against them by reason of race in making duty assignments, evaluations, and decisions about punishment. In a brief, unanimous opinion, the Court declined to recognize a private constitutional right of action for redress.

Stanley was, if anything, even more dramatic. In 1958, Stanley volunteered for what he was told was a chemical warfare testing program. The Army secretly administered LSD to him, which led to severe, permanent personality changes causing his release from service and dissolution of his marriage. In 1975, Stanley discovered the secret testing when the Army asked him to participate in a follow-up study. He brought a *Bivens* action alleging that the surreptitious dose of LSD violated his constitutional rights. A divided Court refused to allow a private right of action.

Justice O'Connor, later to author the majority opinion in *Chilicky* that relies in part upon *Stanley,* filed a brief, emphatic dissent:

> I * * * agree with the Court that under *Chappell v. Wallace* there is generally no remedy available under *Bivens* for injuries that arise out of the course of activity incident to military service. In *Chappell* this Court unanimously held that enlisted military personnel may not maintain a suit to recover damages from a superior officer for alleged constitutional violations. The "special factors" that we found relevant to the propriety of a *Bivens* action by enlisted personnel against their military superiors "also formed the basis" of this Court's decision in *Feres v. United States* that the [Federal Tort Claims Act] does not extend to injuries arising out of military service. In my view, therefore, *Chappell* and *Feres* must be read together; both cases unmistakably stand for the proposition that the special circumstances of the military mandate that civilian courts avoid entertaining a suit involving harm caused as a result of military service. Thus, no amount of negligence, recklessness, or perhaps even deliberate indifference on the part of the military would justify the entertainment of a *Bivens* action involving actions incident to military service.

> Nonetheless, the *Chappell* exception to the availability of a *Bivens* action applies only to "injuries that 'arise out of or are in the course of ac-

tivity incident to service.' " In my view, conduct of the type alleged in this case is so far beyond the bounds of human decency that as a matter of law it simply cannot be considered a part of the military mission. The bar created by *Chappell*—a judicial exception to an implied remedy for the violation of constitutional rights—surely cannot insulate defendants from liability for deliberate and calculated exposure of otherwise healthy military personnel to medical experimentation without their consent, outside of any combat, combat training, or military exigency, and for no other reason than to gather information on the effect of lysergic acid diethylamide on human beings.

No judicially crafted rule should insulate from liability the involuntary and unknowing human experimentation alleged to have occurred in this case. Indeed, as Justice Brennan observes, the United States military played an instrumental role in the criminal prosecution of Nazi officials who experimented with human subjects during the Second World War, and the standards that the Nuremberg Military Tribunals developed to judge the behavior of the defendants stated that the "voluntary consent of the human subject is absolutely essential * * * to satisfy moral, ethical and legal concepts." If this principle is violated the very least that society can do is to see that the victims are compensated, as best they can be, by the perpetrators. I am prepared to say that our Constitution's promise of due process of law guarantees this much. Accordingly, I would permit James Stanley's *Bivens* action to go forward * * * .

Does the first paragraph suggest that requirements of military expediency effectively trump what would otherwise be enforceable constitutional rights? If so, should conscripted personnel (were there any left) and volunteers stand on the same footing?

Is Justice O'Connor's distinction between "incident to service" and "not part of the military mission" maintainable as a practical matter? Will it not involve the courts and the military in substantial litigation concerning what is and is not "incident" to service?

2. Justice O'Connor gives a dual picture of the remedial structure available to Chilicky. Analogizing *Schweiker* to *Bush v. Lucas*, 462 U.S. 367, 103 S.Ct. 2404, 76 L.Ed.2d 648 (1983), she first describes the structure as "comprehensive," but later recognizes that it is less effective than the damages remedy sought. Are those views reconcilable?

3. Would the Court have implied a private right of action if there had been no comprehensive scheme? If so, then Congress, by passing its remedial scheme, effectively limited the Fifth Amendment in *Schweiker* and the First Amendment in *Bush*. Is that proper? Are the questions of the available remedy and its substantive law source separate from the question of the substantive scope of constitutional amendments?

4. In *Bush v. Lucas*, the majority described the federal courts' common law power to prescribe constitutional remedies as well established. How was it possible for Justice Powell, in light of his *Cannon* dissent, to join the ma-

jority opinion?

5. Is the majority's treatment of *Carlson v. Green*, 446 U.S. 14, 100 S.Ct. 1468, 64 L.Ed.2d 15 (1980), persuasive? Justice O'Connor noted with respect to *Carlson*, that there was "no explicit statutory prohibition against the relief sought, and no exclusive statutory alternative remedy." Is that not true here?

6. a) Justice O'Connor emphasizes *Bush*'s idea that Congress is better equipped to balance governmental efficiency against the rights of individuals. When the asserted individual rights are grounded not in statutes but instead in the Constitution, is that balancing appropriate? If so, is Congress, a majoritarian body the Constitution was intended to restrain, the appropriate institution to conduct such balancing?

b) Justice Brennan disputes the majority's characterization of Congress as having carefully balanced or deliberately compromised the competing interests asserted in *Schweiker*. How direct an indication of congressional consideration of the constitutional issues ought the Court to require? If congressional silence about constitutional rights precludes implication of a remedy, has the standard for implying rights of action in constitutional provisions at least begun to merge with that for implying such rights in statutes? *See* George D. Brown, *Letting Statutory Tails Wag Constitutional Dogs— Have the* Bivens *Dissenters Prevailed?*, 64 IND.L.J. 263 (1989).

7. At the end of Part II A of the majority opinion, Justice O'Connor attempts to summarize the standard the Court will use in considering whether to imply rights of action in constitutional provisions. Is that standard consistent with its expression in *Davis v. Passman*, 442 U.S. 228, 99 S.Ct. 2264, 60 L.Ed.2d 846 (1979), and *Carlson v. Green*, or has it undergone a subtle metamorphosis?

8. Is Congress's intention in creating its remedial scheme important? If the Court disagrees about the adequacy of relief, is it inappropriate to supplement the congressional scheme? If so, under what theory does Congress achieve primacy in interpreting or balancing constitutional guarantees? If not, then why does the Court not refrain from considering the merits of the requested damages remedy?

9. *Correctional Services Corp. v. Malesko*, 534 U.S. 61, 122 S.Ct. 515, 151 L.Ed.2d 456 (2001), seemed to add a new gloss to *Bivens* and *Chilicky*. Petitioner operated a halfway house on behalf of the federal Bureau of Prisons. Respondent, alleged that petitioner negligently injured him by failing to provide him with appropriate medication for his heart condition and by requiring him to walk up five flights of stairs on one occasion, resulting in a heart attack and other injury. He sued the corporation and the individual who had prevented him from using the elevator. The parties assumed that Malesko had alleged a violation of the Eighth Amendment. The district court dismissed the complaint with respect to the corporation, reading *FDIC v. Meyer*, 510 U.S. 471, 114 S.Ct. 996, 127 L.Ed.2d 308 (1994), as holding that a *Bivens* action is available only against individuals. It dismissed with respect to the individual defendant because the statute of limitations had

expired. The Second Circuit reversed with respect to the corporation, finding *Meyer* only declined to expand *Bivens* remedies to embrace federal agencies as well as federal agents. That court ruled that a remedy against a private entity should lie "to accomplish * * * the important *Bivens* goal of providing a remedy for constitutional violations."

The Supreme Court reversed, ruling five-to-four that the *Bivens* remedy does not extend to this action against a private entity acting under color of federal law. Chief Justice Rehnquist's opinion emphasized that the Court has recognized *Bivens* remedies only in situations where the plaintiff had no other avenue of relief. He then characterized *Chilicky* as rejecting even that basis for a *Bivens* remedy. "We therefore rejected the claim that a *Bivens* remedy should be implied simply for want of any other means for challenging a constitutional deprivation in federal court. * * * So long as the plaintiff had an avenue for some redress, bedrock principles of separation of powers foreclosed judicial imposition of a new substantive liability." Finally, the Chief Justice noted that *Meyer* had declared that " 'the purpose of *Bivens* is to deter *the officer*,' not the agency." The deterrent effect of a *Bivens* claim would be lost, the Court reasoned, if individuals could sue the agency rather than the agent. The Court also noted that "federal prisoners in private facilities enjoy a parallel tort remedy that is unavailable to prisoners housed in government facilities." Whereas the *Bivens* Court declined to make a new federal remedy conditional on the non-existence of state tort remedies, the *Malesko* majority did impose that limitation.

Justice Stevens, writing for the four dissenters, viewed the case differently. "[T]he question presented by this case is whether the Court should create an exception to the straightforward application of *Bivens* and *Carlson*, not whether it should extend our cases beyond their 'core premise.' " The dissenters read *Meyer* as a case limited to federal agencies. They also disputed the majority's assertion that alternative remedies were unavailable to Bivens and others similarly situated.

> In *Bivens*, however, even though the plaintiff's suit against the Federal Government under state tort law may have been barred by sovereign immunity, a suit against the officer himself under state tort law was theoretically possible. Moreover, as the Court recognized in *Carlson*, *Bivens* plaintiffs also have remedies available under the FTCA. Thus, the Court is incorrect to portray *Bivens* plaintiffs as lacking any other avenue of relief, and to imply as a result that respondent in this case had a substantially wider array of non-*Bivens* remedies at his disposal than do other *Bivens* plaintiffs.

Is the majority correct that the primary purpose of the *Bivens* decision was to deter individual law enforcement officers from violating people's Fourth Amendment rights? What language in either Justice Brennan's majority or Justice Harlan's concurrence supports that assertion by Chief Justice Rehnquist? Assuming that such deterrence was the primary purpose of *Bivens*, should the majority Justices consider reevaluating their position on the availability of qualified immunity?

With respect to Justice Stevens's opinion, one might ask whether he is a bit too casual in assuming congressional approval of the *Bivens* remedy (or approach). Is it not possible that a disapproving Congress would nonetheless have eschewed an attempt to abolish the *Bivens* cause of action on the ground that the Court was construing the Fourth Amendment and that its decision was therefore not amenable to congressional alteration except by the amendment process of Article V? *Cf. City of Boerne v. Flores*, 521 U.S. 507, 117 S.Ct. 2157, 138 L.Ed.2d 624 (1997). That aside, Congress may never have abolished the remedy, but it has not codified it either, nor has it legislated in any general way to provide individual remedies for constitutional violations at the hands of federal officials.

10. *Alexander v. Sandoval*, 532 U.S. 275, 121 S.Ct. 1511, 149 L.Ed.2d 517 (2001), continued the Court's restrictive approach to implication. The case concerned a Title VI challenge to Alabama's English-only rule that prohibited administering examinations for drivers' licenses in any other language. Plaintiffs argued that the Alabama rule discriminated on the basis of national origin, in violation of a Department of Transportation regulation issued pursuant to § 602 of Title VI, which authorized DOT to effectuate the provisions of § 601. The Court had already construed § 601 to prohibit only intentional (not disparate-impact) discrimination. Plaintiffs asked the Court to imply a private right of action in § 602 to enforce the DOT regulations, but a five-to-four majority declined.

The majority assumed without deciding that even though § 601 prohibited only intentional discrimination, DOT had the authority to issue disparate-impact regulations under § 602. The issue then was whether the Court should imply a private right of action to enforce those regulations. Justice Scalia's opinion for the Court noted particularly the absence of rights-creating language in § 602, the fact that it addressed itself to federal agencies rather than to individuals, and § 602's provision of an enforcement mechanism that federal agencies, not individuals, can invoke. The Court, therefore, was unwilling to find congressional intent that there be a private right of action. In the course of the opinion, Justice Scalia recounted the Court's shift from the comparatively free-implication days preceding *Cort v. Ash* to the Justices' far more restrictive approach since 1975.

The four dissenting Justices focused on that shift as well, arguing that since Congress enacted Title VI before the Court's decision in *Cort v. Ash*, the majority should not apply the heightened standard for finding congressional intent that the Court began to develop more than a decade after Title VI became law. Justice Stevens highlighted the divide on the Court between the Justices who disdain implying private rights of action from those more willing to consider it.

> As the majority narrates our implied right of action jurisprudence, the Court's shift to a more skeptical approach represents the rejection of a common-law judicial activism in favor of a principled recognition of the limited role of a contemporary "federal tribunal." According to its analysis, the recognition of an implied right of action when the text and structure of the statute do not absolutely compel such a conclusion is an act of judicial self-indulgence. * * *

[I]t is the majority's approach that blinds itself to congressional intent. While it remains true that, if Congress intends a private right of action to support statutory rights, "the far better course is for it to specify as much when it creates those rights," its failure to do so does not absolve us of the responsibility to endeavor to discern its intent.

Justice Stevens concluded by noting that from *Cort v. Ash* forward, the Court, although narrowing the circumstances in which it will imply a private right of action, has nonetheless implicitly endorsed the practice by specifying "rules and * * * strategies for this task." And so the battle continues. *See also Willkie v. Robbins*, ___ U.S. ___, 127 S.Ct. 2588, 168 L.Ed.2d 389 (2007) (declining to imply a private right of action in the Fifth Amendment for alleged sustained campaign by Bureau of Land Management, including trespass, threats of cancellation of an existing easement, malicious prosecution, and invasions of privacy, to compel landowner to grant easement).

4. Filling in Statutory Interstices

At the outset, one should remember that Judge Friendly referred to this technique of creating federal common law as "the *normal* judicial filling of statutory interstices." (Emphasis added.) That is an important characterization. Spontaneous generation, while certainly not unheard of, is comparatively rare, and although the Court has cut back dramatically on implying private rights of action in constitutional or statutory provisions and never has done much with construing jurisdictional grants as congressional commands to create common law, interstitial common law is, well, common.

When the courts spontaneously generate federal common law, there is no underlying statutory referent, and on the increasingly rare occasion that they imply a private right of action, the provision containing the underlying right simply does not address the existence *vel non* of a right of action. One might regard those forms of creating federal common law, as well as construing a jurisdictional grant as a congressional command to create common law, to be common law wholesale. Interstitial common law, on the other hand, is definitely retail, dealing essentially with congressional omissions in detailed statutory schemes. Part of the courts' difficulty may be attempting to figure out whether the omission was intentional or inadvertent. Should that make a difference? If so, what difference do you think it should make?

Creating interstitial common law is different from interpreting a statute. In the latter, the courts attribute meaning to particular words or phrases in a statute that, arguably at least, address the topic at hand. In the typical interstitial common law situation, however, the underlying statute is utterly silent. For example, although the Supreme Court had implied private rights of action in § 10(b) of the Securities and Exchange Act of 1934 and Securities and Exchange Commission Rule 10b–5 for investors harmed by reliance on misrepresentations in securities offering memoranda, it had never made clear what limitation period should apply to such actions. The Court confronted that problem in *Lampf, Pleva, Lipkind, Prupis & Pettigrow v. Gilbertson*, 501 U.S. 350, 111 S.Ct. 2773, 115 L.Ed.2d 321 (1991). Its approach is revealing.

The district court, adhering to its circuit's expressed policy, applied the state limitation period applicable to the state law claim most closely analogous to the federal claim. In the district court's view, the analogous state law claim was common law fraud claim. Under state law the applicable limitations period for such claims was two years, but it included a discovery provision that could have the effect of extending prospective plaintiffs' time to sue. The district court dismissed the action on limitations grounds because it felt that the plaintiffs had sufficient notice of problems with the partnerships in which they had invested to give them "inquiry notice" of the fraud, and plaintiffs had not made inquiry sufficient to cause them to file within the basic two-year period. The court of appeals agreed with the district court's selection of the limitation period but reversed and remanded for consideration of unresolved issues of fact as to when the plaintiffs either did discover or reasonably could have discovered the alleged fraud.

In the Supreme Court, the plaintiff-respondents argued that the lower courts were correct in selecting the state limitations period. However, the petitioner contended that a federal law limitation should govern the claim and that the Court should use the limitations scheme that the 1934 Act created for the express causes of action that it contained. Those provisions require actions to be brought within one year of discovery (or reasonable discovery) but in no event more than three years after the actionable conduct. The Solicitor General appeared on behalf of the Securities and Exchange Commission and agreed with the petitioner that the applicable limitations period should come from federal law. Nonetheless, he asked the Court to apply a more-recently-enacted five-year period for a new cause of action that Congress had added to the statute after the *Lampf* litigation began, on the ground that it represented "Congress's most recent views on the accommodation of competing interests, provide[d] the closest federal analogy, and promise[d] to yield the best practical and policy results in 10b-5 litigation."

The Court splintered. Justice Blackmun wrote the opinion of the Court except for a part that rehearsed the Court's long-standing practice of borrowing state limitations periods where Congress has not specified any. Despite recognizing that history as the normal approach, Justice Blackmun pointed out that state-created limitations do not ordinarily reflect legislative consideration of possible federal interests. "[W]hen the operation of a state limitations period would frustrate the policies embraced by the federal enactment, this Court has looked to federal law for a suitable period."

Justice Blackmun prescribed a hierarchical consideration of the question. "First, the court must determine whether a uniform statute of limitations is to be selected." He noted that federal claims often encompass matters that the states would treat under multiple limitations periods[19] and acknowledged that the Court had on occasion chosen from among the various state sources available in order to have a single limitation applicable to the federal claim. "Second, assuming a uniform limitations period is appropriate, the court must decide whether this period should be derived from a state or federal source." To the extent that the federal claim is one likely to touch multiple jurisdictions, that suggests the utility of a federal source in order to avoid forum shopping and extended litigation over limitations. Finally, Justice Blackmun cautioned that "even where geographic considerations counsel federal borrowing [*i.e.*, borrowing a limitation period from a federal source], the * * * presumption of state borrowing requires that a court determine that an analogous federal source truly affords a 'closer fit' with the cause of action * * * than does any available state-law source."

Of course, the case before the Court presented a significant problem: "we are faced with the awkward task of discerning the limitations period that Congress intended courts to apply to a cause of action it really never knew existed." Justice Blackmun found succor in the original statute, in which Congress had created some explicit remedies and specified a limitation on them. "We can imagine no clearer indication of how Congress would have balanced the policy considerations implicit in any limitations provision than the balance struck by the same Congress in limiting similar and related protections." So saying, he adopted the one-and-three-year limitations scheme, in the process rejecting the Government's argument for a five-year period on the ground that the part of the statute that contained it postdated the implied rights of action by nearly half a century and addressed itself to the "specific problem" of insider trading.

Justice Scalia, as is his custom, bemoaned the entire practice of implying private rights of action, but grudgingly conceded that since the Court had created the claim involved in *Lampf* so long ago, it was obliged to answer the question the case presented. Though joining most of the majority opinion, he rejected Justice Blackmun's hierarchical approach, instead stating his preference for either borrowing an appropriate state limitations period or, if the state period was inconsistent with the federal statute's purposes, having no limitation at all. He acknowledged obliquely that having no limitation, while having the benefit of deterring courts from implying additional private rights of action, "would be highly unjust to those who must litigate past inventions." Consequently, he agreed with the other Justices making up the majority that "the most responsible approach, where the enactment that has been the occasion of our creation of a cause of action contains a limitations period

---

[19] For example, a § 1983 action might rest on facts supporting state claims of trespass, assault and battery, conversion, or intentional infliction of emotional harm, each of which, under state law, might have a different limitation period.

for an analogous cause of action, is to use that."

Justice Stevens dissented. Given that the Court initially implied the private right of action more than forty years previously, when it was the practice to borrow state limitations periods for such actions because that was deemed to be the intent of Congress, he felt the Court should do nothing else in the absence of congressional action. In his view, creating limitations periods involved policy considerations that are better left to Congress. Moreover, he did not find anything in the Securities and Exchange Act of 1934 that prompted him "to believe that Congress intended us to depart from our traditional rule and overrule four decades of established law." He therefore would have continued the ordinary practice of borrowing the closest appropriate state limitation period.

Justice O'Connor dissented also. She agreed with Justice Blackmun that a uniform limitation period was appropriate, but disagreed with imposing the three-year period of repose in addition to the one-year discovery rule in *Lampf* itself. "In holding that respondents' suit is time barred under a limitations period that did not exist before today, the Court departs drastically from our established practice and inflicts an injustice on the respondents." She observed that the Court had not previously applied new limitations periods to the cases in which the Court announced them. She pointed out that when the plaintiffs filed suit the federal courts in that circuit had applied state law statutes of limitations for more than thirty years and argued that it was unfair to dismiss their claim because they did not predict the Court's decision.

Finally, Justice Kennedy dissented (though he had also joined Justice O'Connor's dissent). He agreed with the majority that "given that § 10(b) actions are implied under the 1934 Act, it makes sense for us to look to the limitations periods Congress established under the Act." Nonetheless, the Act made three different references to statutes of limitations, and the majority had rejected one. Justice Kennedy also opposed having a three-year repose period at all. He concluded that such an absolute time bar was "inconsistent with the practical realities of § 10(b) litigation and the congressional policies underlying that remedy." Victimized investors may be unable to discover fraudulent schemes within 3 years. "By adopting a 3-year period of repose, the Court makes a § 10(b) action all but a dead letter for injured investors who by no conceivable standard of fairness or practicality can be expected to file suit within three years after the violation occurred." He contended that "[t]he 1-year-from-discovery rule is sufficient to ensure a fair balancing between protecting the legitimate interests of aggrieved investors, yet preventing stale claims."

Lampf demonstrates the difficulties that the courts confront in having multiple sources at their disposal and no legislative guidance in choosing among them. Of course, that statement may be fallacious because it assumes its conclusion. Justice Blackmun and his colleagues felt quite comfortable in concluding that Congress did provide guidance in the 1934 Act. Does the Court's splintered approach in *Lampf* provide ammunition to those who believe that the federal courts are not equipped to be common law courts and should not try to be? Can one make principled distinctions among the Justices' approaches that *Lampf* exemplifies, or are they simply voting their own feelings and attempting, in a rather free-wheeling way, to identify and create good results in a way more commonly associated with legislatures?

Justice Blackmun's opinion in *Lampf* viewed borrowing state limitations periods as "derived from" the Rules of Decision Act. What does that mean? Does the Rules of Decision Act *compel* borrowing? If not, then why is it relevant? If so, how can one justify *Lampf*? Justice Stevens believed the Act "directed" the practice of borrowing state law. Does that belief explain his dissent?

If Congress intends by its silence to have state law govern, is it proper for the Court to decide that state law does not sufficiently protect federal interests? Suppose Congress created a substantive right and a right to sue upon it and specifically included a borrowing position in the new statute. Would it then be appropriate for the Court to conclude that Congress had underestimated the adverse impact of state limitations law on federal interests? In this connection, consider *Lampf*'s conclusion that it is "inappropriate" to believe that Congress would have intended adoption of state law. If Congress's normal intention, manifested by silence, is that the federal courts adopt state law, does it seem the Court should conclude in a particular case that Congress did not so intend, without the statute bearing some evidence of that change of heart?

The majority relied on its finding (feeling?) that the federal rule is a "closer" analogy. Is that appropriate? Whatever happened to *Boyle*'s (and *Atherton*'s) requirement that there be a "significant conflict" between federal and state law before federal common law will displace state law? Given the underlying assumption of congressional intention with respect to limitations, does the significant-conflict test seem even more appropriate, or is the *Boyle* approach inapplicable when a federal court is filling statutory interstices?

Why should we assume that Congress, had it thought explicitly about the question, would have selected the same limitations period for this claim as for other claims under the statute? If the claims are different and the remedies are different, is the assumption supportable? Note that in creating the insider-trading claim, Congress specified a different limitation.

The majority rejected the proffered analogy to § 20A of the Insider Trading Act, but perhaps overlooked the provision's greater significance. That statute explicitly recognized and obviously approved of the implied actions that the courts had recognized. Does this sort of congressional awareness and obvious acquiescence blunt the thrust of the Justices

Powell's and Scalia's anti-implication positions?

Justice Scalia was careful to distinguish common law courts from federal tribunals. Is the distinction justified? As a matter of original intent (leaving to one side the broad issue of whether that sort of approach is appropriate), what sorts of courts are the Framers likely to have contemplated? Why?

The Court decided *James B. Beam Distilling Co. v. Georgia*, 501 U.S. 529, 111 S.Ct. 2439, 115 L.Ed.2d 481 (1991), which made the *Lampf* rule retroactive, the same day as *Lampf*. Thus, cases that had been timely when filed under the pre-*Lampf* rules became untimely, and the courts began to dismiss them. Within six months, Congress overruled *Lampf* for all then-pending cases by restoring state limitations periods for the implied right of action. Congress also included a provision that would have permitted plaintiffs whose cases had been dismissed pursuant to *Lampf* to refile, which raised severe separation-of-powers problems. *Plaut v. Spendthrift Farm, Inc.*, 514 U.S. 211, 115 S.Ct. 1447, 131 L.Ed.2d 328 (1995), declared this aspect of the statute unconstitutional. For more extended discussion of *Plaut* and this part of the controversy, see pages 199-221.

Two things are notable in this exchange. First, although the Court and Congress disagreed about the proper result in these circumstances, the process through which the majority arrived at its decision remains unquestioned. Congress did not dispute the Court's *technique* of balancing federal and state interests; it simply thought the Court had misunderstood the legislature's view of the federal interests involved. Second, the progression from *Lampf* through *Plaut* represents a kind of dialogue between Court and Congress with respect to the proper contours of the law. Even in *Lampf*, the Court tried to discern congressional intent. Congress corrected the Court, but did so in a way that intruded on the functioning of the judiciary as a separate branch, a misstep the Court quickly corrected. The result is that the congressionally preferred rule governs; the only real losers were those plaintiffs whose litigation (appeals included) ended in a final judgment of dismissal on limitations grounds between June 19, 1991, (the date of *Lampf*) and December 19, 1991 (the effective date of the statute).

Many federal statutes that create causes of action do not contain limitations periods. Until recently, a federal court confronted with such a case had three options: 1) inferring that Congress intended there to be no limitations period at all, 2) inferring that Congress intended the courts to borrow some state limitation to use as federal common law, or 3) inferring that Congress intended the federal courts to create a limitations period. The first and third approaches resulted in a uniform, nationwide policy. The second allowed the same generic cause of action to have different limitations in each state. In practice, the Justices at various times have used all three approaches, and each has its difficulties.

Construing the sounds of congressional silence is a difficult enterprise.

County of Oneida v. Oneida Indian Nation, 470 U.S. 226, 105 S.Ct. 1245, 84 L.Ed.2d 169 (1985), considered the Oneidas' 1970 claim for return of lands conveyed to New York in 1795 in violation of a federal statute. The Court found that Congress intended that there be no limitations period. Justice Powell based his conclusion in part on separation of powers and his perception of congressional intent, and rejected the County's argument that the Court should borrow some state limitation. *See also, e.g., Occidental Life Insurance Co. v. EEOC,* 432 U.S. 355, 97 S.Ct. 2447, 53 L.Ed.2d 402 (1977) (holding that there is no limitation period governing the ability of the Equal Employment Opportunity Commission to commence a federal action against an employer).

Wilson v. Garcia, 471 U.S. 261, 105 S.Ct. 1938, 85 L.Ed.2d 254 (1985), exemplified the second technique. There the Court confronted the question of the limitations period to be applied to actions brought under the Civil Rights Act of 1871, 42 U.S.C.A. § 1983. A majority ruled that the personal injury limitations period of the state in which the action was brought govern such actions. The Court noted that "[w]hen Congress has not established a time limitation for a federal cause of action, the settled practice has been to adopt a local time limitation as federal law if it is not inconsistent with federal law or policy to do so." Having decided to borrow state law, the Court also had to choose a state limitations period. It rejected using the period that the state would apply to a state claim on identical facts, explaining that § 1983 claims are subject to such varied characterization that such a practice could lead to great uncertainty and to more than one limitations period applying to a single claim. (For example, on the facts in *Wilson* a state court could have used limitations periods relating to false arrest, false imprisonment, assault and battery, personal injuries, or an action arising under a statute.) The Court concluded that Congress probably would have considered a § 1983 claim most analogous to a claim for personal injuries and directed that each state's personal injury statute govern § 1983 claims brought in that state.[20]

Finally, for some types of claims, the Court has felt that a single, nationwide limitations period is necessary. Sometimes the Court thinks either that state limitations periods are too restrictive to protect important federal interests properly or that using state laws would create unacceptable confusion. *DelCostello v. International Brotherhood of Teamsters,* 462 U.S. 151, 103 S.Ct. 2281, 76 L.Ed.2d 476 (1983), exemplified the first problem. It held that a uniform federal limitations period was

---

[20] In *Graham County Soil & Water Conservation Dist. v. United States,* 545 U.S. 409, 125 S.Ct. 2444, 162 L.Ed.2d 390 (2005), the Court concluded a federal statute was ambiguous as to whether a six-year limitation period applying to existing causes of action should apply to a new cause of action created by congressional amendment to the statute. The Court decided to apply the most closely analogous state limitation period.

necessary to protect fundamental federal labor relations policy in actions by employees against employers for breach of collective bargaining agreements and against unions for breach of the duty of fair representation.

Agency Holding Corp. v. Malley-Duff & Associates, 483 U.S. 143, 107 S.Ct. 2759, 97 L.Ed.2d 121 (1987), illustrated the second. There the Court insisted on a federal limitations period for a civil RICO action because the novel nature of the civil RICO claim, the unlikelihood of finding true analogs in state law, and the fact that such actions may touch many jurisdictions combined to make use of state limitations likely to produce only intolerable uncertainty and extended litigation. Again, the Court looked to the closest federal analogy.

In 1990, Congress limited the development of federal common law in this area. Title 28 U.S.C.A. § 1658 now provides that actions must be commenced within four years of accrual of a claim for any cause of action Congress creates after the effective date of § 1658 that does not otherwise contain a limitation period. Note, however, that Congress did not displace limitations periods adopted by the federal courts for statutory rights existing before 1990. The legislative history suggests that this grandfather treatment reflects Congress's disinclination to "disrupt the settled expectations of a great many parties." On the other hand, Congress could have applied the new limitation generally to all federal causes of action lacking individually-legislated limitations periods, irrespective of when Congress created the cause of action, exempting only cases in which a plaintiff's claim had accrued before the effective date of § 1658. Such an approach would have unified limitations treatment of federal claims without frustrating existing parties' (or potential parties') expectations.

Notwithstanding § 1658, questions regarding appropriate limitations periods continue to arise with respect to federal statutes enacted before 1990. *North Star Steel Company v. Thomas,* 515 U.S. 29, 115 S.Ct. 1927, 132 L.Ed.2d 27 (1995), reiterated *Lampf's* discussion of the hierarchy of selecting limitations periods. Thus, the inquiry continues closely to parallel that in substantive common law cases.

D. CONCLUDING NOTE

Every federal common law case raises federalism and separation-of-powers concerns. In *Clearfield,* for example, the Court's decision to use a federal common law rule created during the reign of *Swift v. Tyson* displaced a contrary Pennsylvania rule, thus potentially raising the hackles of federalism. Should Congress have made that decision? Perhaps the courts freely creating common law to protect court-perceived dominant federal interests implies that the representative branches are not up to the job. New *Erie* theorists argue that practice is illegitimate.

At the extreme, the separation-of-powers view of federal common law means that federal courts can never create common law, clearly something not contemplated by the *Erie* Court. Even Justice Powell, perhaps the Court's most ardent champion of that view, did not advocate so rigid an approach, for although he dissented in *Merrill Lynch, Pierce, Fenner & Smith v. Curran,* 456 U.S. 353, 102 S.Ct. 1825, 72 L.Ed.2d 182 (1982), he did note the possibility of implying a private right of action if there were " 'compelling evidence that Congress in fact intended such an action to exist.' " On the other hand, giving the federal courts effectively unfettered discretion to create common law in any area in which the Constitution permits the federal government to operate may well disrupt the balance of power among the branches of the federal government and has at least the appearance of being anti-majoritarian. Professor Redish, among others, has argued strongly that judicial law-making is incompatible with the nature of our democracy. *See, e.g.,* Martin H. Redish, *Federal Common Law, Political Legitimacy, and the Interpretive Process: An "Institutionalist" Perspective,* 83 NW.L.REV. 761 (1989); Martin H. Redish, *Abstention, Separation of Powers, and the Limits of the Judicial Function,* 94 YALE L.J. 71 (1984).[21]

A middle position may be possible. Perhaps it is permissible from a separation-of-powers standpoint for the federal courts to create common law that implements policies declared in positive law by the representative branches. Thus, each rule of common law would have to find an anchor in legislation declaring or exemplifying the policy the common law rule serves. Implication of a private right of action, as in *Cannon v. University of Chicago,* is then permissible because of the clear policy declaration in Title IX against sex discrimination. Creation of the federal contractors' immunity in *Boyle v. United Technologies,* however, is on considerably shakier ground because there is no apparent anchor in positive law.

Note that the Court's recent emphasis on "significant conflict" as the only legitimate predicate for creating federal common law may, in different circumstances, leave the Justices more or less latitude for creating federal common law than having to find a policy anchor in positive law. *Boyle,* for example, has no such anchor, but the Court found significant conflict and proceeded to fashion federal common law. On the other hand, the Court might have found such an anchor in *United States v. Yazell* (in the federal government's authority to create loan programs through the Small Business Administration), but it found no significant

---

[21] The legitimacy of the creation of federal common law was considered more broadly at the 1992 meeting of the Association of American Law Schools' Section on Federal Courts. Pace Law Review published the papers as a symposium. *See* George D. Brown, *Federal Common Law and the Role of the Federal Courts in Private Law Adjudication—A (New)* Erie *Problem,* 12 PACE L.REV. 229 (1992); Larry Kramer, *The Lawmaking Power of the Federal Courts,* 12 PACE L.REV. 263 (1992); Martha A. Field, *The Legitimacy of Federal Common Law,* 12 PACE L.REV. 303 (1992); Thomas W. Merrill, *The Judicial Prerogative,* 12 PACE L.REV. 327 (1992).

conflict and therefore refused to create federal common law.

Scholars and judges will doubtless continue vigorously to debate the propriety of federal common law. *Erie* opened a Pandora's Box of a sort, but one that may have released something beneficial. The debate about federal common law is merely one aspect of the continuing debate about the contours of the federal system generally. It may be that the debate itself is valuable without any thought of an eventual resolution, because it keeps us keenly aware of the delicate balance that the federal system entails. That there are no easy answers (or, perhaps, any answers at all) may be the good news rather than the bad news.

Chapter 6

THE FEDERAL FORUM, THE FOUR-
TEENTH AMENDMENT,
AND THE CIVIL RIGHTS
ACT OF 1871

A. INTRODUCTION

Two great tensions concerning government have provided enduring and dominant themes for the first two centuries of the United States' existence and are likely to continue to do so indefinitely. The first involves the balance of power between the federal government and the states; United States federalism is a continuing battle between sovereigns about the limits of their sovereignties. The second is created by a similar struggle between government (federal or state) and individuals. The antecedents of both tensions are found in the American colonial period, which was marked by disputes over the distribution of governmental power between the colonies and the crown and by resentment over crown policy with respect to the rights of colonists as individuals.

Earlier chapters have explored the theme of federalism extensively. This chapter continues the focus on federalism, but in the context of state governments' relations with individuals and the federal courts' role in mediating those relationships. The Civil War and its aftermath provoked great federal interest in these relationships, stimulated primarily by problems of African-Americans' attempts to become full, equal participants in American society. Perhaps the most important statute enacted to address the problem is today frequently referred to as "the" Civil Rights Act of 1871, now codified in 42 U.S.C.A. § 1983.[1] Section 1983 is a unique vehicle for exploring the federal courts' functioning *vis-à-vis* the states and Congress. The themes of federalism and government versus

---

[1] The predecessor of § 1983 was not the only civil rights legislation passed by Congress during and just after Reconstruction. Congress also enacted measures that later became 42 U.S.C.A. §§ 1981, 1982, 1984 and 1985 on the civil side, and the predecessors of 18 U.S.C.A. §§ 241, 242 on the criminal side. All of these statutes were and are important, but none has the claim on history of § 1983. The Supreme Court has noted that of the five civil rights measures passed by Congress between 1866 and 1875, "[o]nly § 1 of the Act of April 20, 1871, presently codified as 42 U.S.C. § 1983, achieved measurable success in later years." Zwickler v. Koota, 389 U.S. 241, 247 n. 9, 88 S.Ct. 391, 395 n. 9, 19 L.Ed.2d 444, 449 n. 9 (1967).

individual surface repeatedly in civil rights cases, and with particular poignancy because of the emotionally-charged nature of the government-individual conflict. And, as always, separation-of-powers concerns are often just below the surface. This chapter explores the confluence of those three thematic strands of American history.

B.   THE FOURTEENTH AMENDMENT AND 42 U.S.C.A. § 1983 IN THE REMEDIAL SCHEME

1. *Color of State Law*

MONROE v. PAPE

Supreme Court of the United States, 1961.

365 U.S. 167, 81 S.Ct. 473, 5 L.Ed.2d 492.

MR. JUSTICE DOUGLAS delivered the opinion of the Court.

This case presents important questions concerning the construction of R.S. § 1979, 42 U.S.C. § 1983, which reads as follows:

> Every person who, under color of any statute, ordinance, regulation, custom, or usage, of any State or Territory, subjects, or causes to be subjected, any citizen of the United States or other person within the jurisdiction thereof to the deprivation of any rights, privileges, or immunities secured by the Constitution and laws, shall be liable to the party injured in an action at law, suit in equity, or other proper proceeding for redress.

The complaint alleges that 13 Chicago police officers broke into petitioners' home in the early morning, routed them from bed, made them stand naked in the living room, and ransacked every room, emptying drawers and ripping mattress covers. It further alleges that Mr. Monroe was then taken to the police station and detained on "open" charges for 10 hours, while he was interrogated about a two-day-old murder, that he was not taken before a magistrate, though one was accessible, that he was not permitted to call his family or attorney, that he was subsequently released without criminal charges being preferred against him. It is alleged that the officers had no search warrant and no arrest warrant and that they acted "under color of the statutes, ordinances, regulations, customs and usages" of Illinois and of the City of Chicago. Federal jurisdiction was asserted under R.S. § 1979, which we have set out above, and 28 U.S.C. § 1343 and 28 U.S.C. § 1331.

The City of Chicago moved to dismiss the complaint on the ground that it is not liable under the Civil Rights Acts nor for acts committed in performance of its governmental functions. All defendants moved to dismiss, alleging that the complaint alleged no cause of action under those Acts or under the Federal Constitution. The District Court dismissed the complaint. The Court of Appeals affirmed * * *.

I

* * *

Section 1979 came onto the books as § 1 of the Ku Klux Act of April 20, 1871. It was one of the means whereby Congress exercised the power vested in it by § 5 of the Fourteenth Amendment to enforce the provisions of that Amendment. Senator Edmunds, Chairman of the Senate Committee on the Judiciary, said concerning this section:

> The first section is one that I believe nobody objects to, as defining the rights secured by the Constitution of the United States when they are assailed by any State law or under color of any State law, and it is merely carrying out the principles of the civil rights bill, which has since become a part of the Constitution,

viz., the Fourteenth Amendment.

Its purpose is plain from the title of the legislation, "An Act to enforce the Provisions of the Fourteenth Amendment to the Constitution of the United States, and for other Purposes." Allegation of facts constituting a deprivation under color of state authority of a right guaranteed by the Fourteenth Amendment satisfies to that extent the requirement of R.S. § 1979. So far petitioners are on solid ground. For the guarantee against unreasonable searches and seizures contained in the Fourth Amendment has been made applicable to the States by reason of the Due Process Clause of the Fourteenth Amendment.

II

There can be no doubt at least since *Ex parte Virginia* (1880) that Congress has the power to enforce provisions of the Fourteenth Amendment against those who carry a badge of authority of a State and represent it in some capacity, whether they act in accordance with their authority or misuse it. The question with which we now deal is the narrower one of whether Congress, in enacting § 1979, meant to give a remedy to parties deprived of constitutional rights, privileges and immunities by an official's abuse of his position. We conclude that it did so intend.

It is argued that "under color of" enumerated state authority excludes acts of an official or policeman who can show no authority under state law, state custom, or state usage to do what he did. In this case it is said that these policemen, in breaking into petitioners' apartment, violated the Constitution and laws of Illinois. It is pointed out that under Illinois law a simple remedy is offered for that violation and that, so far as it appears, the courts of Illinois are available to give petitioners that full redress which the common law affords for violence done to a person; and it is earnestly argued that no "statute, ordinance, regulation, custom or usage" of Illinois bars that redress.

The Ku Klux Act grew out of a message sent to Congress by President Grant on March 23, 1871, reading:

> A condition of affairs now exists in some States of the Union rendering life and property insecure and the carrying of the mails and the collection of the revenue dangerous. The proof that such a condition of affairs exists in some localities is now before the Senate. That the power to correct these evils is beyond the control of State authorities I do not doubt; that the power of the Executive of the United States, acting within the limits of existing laws, is sufficient for present emergencies is not clear. Therefore, I urgently recommend such legislation as in the judgment of Congress shall effectually secure life, liberty, and property, and the enforcement of law in all parts of the United States * * * .

The legislation—in particular the section with which we are now concerned—had several purposes. There are threads of many thoughts running through the debates. One who reads them in their entirety sees that the present section had three main aims.

First, it might, of course, override certain kinds of state laws * * * .

Second, it provided a remedy where state law was inadequate. That aspect of the legislation was summed up as follows by Senator Sherman of Ohio:

> * * * [I]t is said the reason is that any offense may be committed upon a negro by a white man, and a negro cannot testify in any case against a white man, so that the only way by which any conviction can be had in Kentucky in those cases is in the United States courts, because the United States courts enforce the United States laws by which negroes may testify.

But the purposes were much broader. The *third* aim was to provide a federal remedy where the state remedy, though adequate in theory, was not available in practice. The opposition to the measure complained that "It overrides the reserved powers of the States," just as they argued that the second section of the bill "[absorbed] the entire jurisdiction of the States over their local and domestic affairs."

This Act of April 20, 1871, sometimes called "the third 'force bill,'" was passed by a Congress that had the Klan "particularly in mind." The debates are replete with references to the lawless conditions existing in the South in 1871. There was available to the Congress during these debates a report, nearly 600 pages in length, dealing with the activities of the Klan and the inability of the state governments to cope with it. This report was drawn on by many of the speakers. It was not the unavailability of state remedies but the failure of certain States to enforce the laws with an equal hand that furnished the powerful momentum behind this "force bill."

* * *

While one main scourge of the evil—perhaps the leading one—was the Ku Klux Klan, the remedy created was not a remedy against it or its members but against those who representing a State in some capacity were unable or unwilling to enforce a state law * * * .

* * *

The debates were long and extensive. It is abundantly clear that one reason the legislation was passed was to afford a federal right in federal courts because, by reason of prejudice, passion, neglect, intolerance or otherwise, state laws might not be enforced and the claims of citizens to the enjoyment of rights, privileges, and immunities guaranteed by the Fourteenth Amendment might be denied by the state agencies.

* * *

Although the legislation was enacted because of the conditions that existed in the South at that time, it is cast in general language and is as applicable to Illinois as it is to the States whose names were mentioned over and again in the debates. It is no answer that the State has a law which if enforced would give relief. The federal remedy is supplementary to the state remedy, and the latter need not be first sought and refused before the federal one is invoked. Hence the fact that Illinois by its constitution and laws outlaws unreasonable searches and seizures is no barrier to the present suit in the federal court.

We had before us in *United States v. Classic* (1941) § 20 of the Criminal Code, which provides a criminal punishment for anyone who "under color of any law, statute, ordinance, regulation, or custom" subjects any inhabitant of a State to the deprivation of "any rights, privileges, or immunities secured or protected by the Constitution or laws of the United States." * * * The right involved in the *Classic* case was the right of voters in a primary to have their votes counted. The laws of Louisiana required the defendants "to count the ballots, to record the result of the count, and to certify the result of the election." But according to the indictment they did not perform their duty. * * * [T]he Court ruled, "Misuse of power, possessed by virtue of state law and made possible only because the wrongdoer is clothed with the authority of state law, is action taken 'under color of' state law." * * *

That view of the meaning of the words "under color of" state law was reaffirmed in *Screws v. United States* (1945). The acts there complained of were committed by state officers in performance of their duties, *viz.,* making an arrest effective. It was urged there, as it is here, that "under color of" state law should not be construed to duplicate in federal law what was an offense under state law. It was said there, as it is here, that the ruling in the *Classic* case as to the meaning of "under color of" state law was not in focus and was ill-advised. It was argued there, as it is here, that "under color of" state law included only action taken by officials pursuant to state law. We rejected that view.

* * *

We conclude that the meaning given "under color of" law in the *Classic* case and in the *Screws* and *Williams* [*v. United States* (1951)] cases was the correct one; and we adhere to it.

In the *Screws* case we dealt with a statute that imposed criminal penalties for acts "wilfully" done. We construed that word in its setting to mean the doing of an act with "a specific intent to deprive a person of a federal right." We do not think that gloss should be placed on § 1979 which we have here. The word "wilfully" does not appear in § 1979. Moreover, § 1979 provides a civil remedy, while in the *Screws* case we dealt with a criminal law challenged on the ground of vagueness. Section 1979 should be read against the background of tort liability that makes a man responsible for the natural consequences of his actions.

So far, then, the complaint states a cause of action. There remains to consider only a defense peculiar to the City of Chicago.

III

The City of Chicago asserts that it is not liable under § 1979. We do not stop to explore the whole range of questions tendered us on this issue at oral argument and in the briefs. For we are of the opinion that Congress did not undertake to bring municipal corporations within the ambit of § 1979.

When the bill that became the Act of April 20, 1871, was being debated in the Senate, Senator Sherman of Ohio proposed an amendment which would have made "the inhabitants of the county, city, or parish" in which certain acts of violence occurred liable "to pay full compensation" to the person damaged or his widow or legal representative. The amendment was adopted by the Senate. The House, however, rejected it. The Conference Committee reported another version. The House rejected the Conference report. In a second conference the Sherman amendment was dropped and in its place § 6 of the Act of April 20, 1871, was substituted. This new section, which is now 42 U.S.C.A. § 1986, dropped out all provision for municipal liability and extended liability in damages to "any person or persons, having knowledge that any" of the specified wrongs are being committed. Mr. Poland, speaking for the House Conferees about the Sherman proposal to make municipalities liable, said: "We informed the conferees on the part of the Senate that the House had taken a stand on that subject and would not recede from it; that that section imposing liability upon towns and counties must go out or we should fail to agree."

The objection to the Sherman amendment stated by Mr. Poland was that "the House had solemnly decided that in their judgment Congress had no constitutional power to impose any obligation upon county and town organizations, the mere instrumentality for the administration of state law." The question of constitutional power of Congress to impose civil liability on municipalities was vigorously debated with powerful arguments advanced in the affirmative.

Much reliance is placed on the Act of February 25, 1871, entitled "An Act prescribing the Form of the enacting and resolving Clauses of Acts and Resolutions of Congress, and Rules for the Construction thereof." Section 2 of this Act provides that "the word 'person' may extend and be applied to bodies politic and corporate." It should be noted, however, that this definition is merely an allowable, not a mandatory, one. It is said that doubts should be resolved in favor of municipal liability because private remedies against officers for illegal searches and seizures are conspicuously ineffective, and because municipal liability will not only afford plaintiffs responsible defendants but cause those defendants to eradicate abuses that exist at the police level. We do not reach those policy considerations. Nor do we reach the constitutional question whether Congress has the power to make municipalities liable for acts of its officers that violate the civil rights of individuals.

The response of the Congress to the proposal to make municipalities liable for certain actions being brought within federal purview by the Act of April 20, 1871, was so antagonistic that we cannot believe that the word "person" was used in this particular Act to include them. Accordingly we hold that the motion to dismiss the complaint against the City of Chicago was properly granted. But since the complaint should not have been dismissed against the officials the judgment must be and is reversed.

Reversed.

MR. JUSTICE HARLAN, whom MR. JUSTICE STEWART joins, concurring.

Were this case here as one of first impression, I would find the "under color of any statute" issue very close indeed. However, in *Classic* and *Screws* this Court considered a substantially identical statutory phrase to have a meaning which, unless we now retreat from it, requires that issue to go for the petitioners here.

From my point of view, the policy of *stare decisis,* as it should be applied in matters of statutory construction, and, to a lesser extent, the indications of congressional acceptance of this Court's earlier interpretation, require that it appear beyond doubt from the legislative history of the 1871 statute that *Classic* and *Screws* misapprehended the meaning of the controlling provision, before a departure from what was decided in those cases would be justified. Since I can find no such justifying indication in that legislative history, I join the opinion of the Court. However, what has been written on both sides of the matter makes some additional observations appropriate.

Those aspects of Congress' purpose which are quite clear in the earlier congressional debates, as quoted by my Brothers Douglas and Frankfurter in turn, seem to me to be inherently ambiguous when applied to the case of an isolated abuse of state authority by an official. One can agree with the Court's opinion that:

> It is abundantly clear that one reason the legislation was passed was to afford a federal right in federal courts because, by reason of prejudice, passion, neglect, intolerance or otherwise, state laws might not be enforced and the claims of citizens to the enjoyment of rights, privileges, and immunities guaranteed by the Fourteenth Amendment might be denied by the state agencies * * *

without being certain that Congress meant to deal with anything other than abuses so recurrent as to amount to "custom, or usage." One can agree with my Brother Frankfurter, in dissent, that Congress had no intention of taking over the whole field of ordinary state torts and crimes, without being certain that the enacting Congress would not have regarded actions by an official, made possible by his position, as far more serious than an ordinary state tort, and therefore as a matter of federal concern. If attention is directed at the rare specific references to isolated abuses of state authority, one finds them neither so clear nor so disproportionately divided between favoring the positions of the majority or the dissent as to make either position seem plainly correct.

* * *

The dissent considers that the "under color of" provision of § 1983 distinguishes between unconstitutional actions taken without state authority, which only the State should remedy, and unconstitutional actions authorized by the State, which the Federal Act was to reach. If so, then the controlling difference for the enacting legislature must have been either that the state remedy was more adequate for unauthorized actions than for authorized ones or that there was, in some sense, greater harm from unconstitutional actions authorized by the full panoply of state power and approval than from unconstitutional actions not so authorized or acquiesced in by the State. I find less than compelling the evidence that either distinction was important to that Congress.

I

If the state remedy was considered adequate when the official's unconstitutional act was unauthorized, why should it not be thought equally adequate when the unconstitutional act was authorized? For if one thing is very clear in the legislative history, it is that the Congress of 1871 was well aware that no action requiring state judicial enforcement could be taken in violation of the Fourteenth Amendment without that enforcement being declared void by this Court on direct review from the state courts. And presumably it must also have been understood that there would be Supreme Court review of the denial of a state damage remedy against an official on grounds of state authorization of the unconstitutional action. It therefore seems to me that the same state remedies would, with ultimate aid of Supreme Court review, furnish identical relief in the two situations * * * .

* * *

Since the suggested narrow construction of § 1983 presupposes that state measures were adequate to remedy unauthorized deprivations of constitutional rights and since the identical state relief could be obtained for state-authorized acts with the aid of Supreme Court review, this narrow construction would reduce the statute to having merely a jurisdictional function, shifting the load of federal supervision from the Supreme Court to the lower courts and providing a federal tribunal for fact findings in cases involving authorized action. Such a function could be justified on various grounds. It could, for example, be argued that the state courts would be less willing to find a constitutional violation in cases involving "authorized action" and that therefore the victim of such action would bear a greater burden in that he would more likely have to carry his case to this Court, and once here, might be bound by unfavorable state court findings. But the legislative debates do not disclose congressional concern about the burdens of litigation placed upon the victims of "authorized" constitutional violations contrasted to the victims of unauthorized violations. Neither did Congress indicate an interest in relieving the burden placed on this Court in reviewing such cases.

The statute becomes more than a jurisdictional provision only if one attributes to the enacting legislature the view that a deprivation of a constitutional right is significantly different from and more serious than a violation of a state right and therefore deserves a different remedy even though the same act may constitute both a state tort and the deprivation of a constitutional right. This view, by no means unrealistic as a common-sense matter, is, I believe, more consistent with the flavor of the legislative history than is a view that the primary purpose of the statute was to grant a lower court forum for fact findings.

* * *

In my view, these considerations put in serious doubt the conclusion that § 1983 was limited to state-authorized unconstitutional acts, on the premise that state remedies respecting them were considered less adequate than those available for unauthorized acts.

II

I think this limited interpretation of § 1983 fares no better when viewed from the other possible premise for it, namely that state-approved constitutional deprivations were considered more offensive than those not so approved. For one thing, the enacting Congress was not unaware of the fact that there was a substantial overlap between the protections granted by state constitutional provisions and those granted by the Fourteenth Amendment. Indeed one opponent of the bill, Senator Trumbull, went so far as to state in a debate with Senators Carpenter and Edmunds that his research indicated a complete overlap in every State, at least as to the protections of the Due Process Clause. Thus, in one very significant sense, there was no ultimate state approval of a large portion of otherwise authorized actions depriving a person of due-process rights. I hesitate to assume that the proponents of the present statute, who regarded it as necessary even though they knew that the provisions of the Fourteenth Amendment were self-executing, would have thought the remedies unnecessary whenever there were self-executing provisions of state constitutions also forbidding what the Fourteenth Amendment forbids. The only alternative is to disregard the possibility that a state court would find the action unauthorized on grounds of the state constitution. But if the defendant official is denied the right to defend in the federal court upon the ground that a state court would find his action unauthorized in the light of the state constitution, it is difficult to contend that it is the added harmfulness of state approval that justifies a different remedy for authorized than for unauthorized actions of state officers. Moreover, if indeed the legislature meant to distinguish between authorized and unauthorized acts and yet did not mean the statute to be inapplicable whenever there was a state constitutional provision which, reasonably interpreted, gave protection similar to that of a provision of the Fourteenth Amendment, would there not have been some explanation of this exception to the general rule? The fact that there is none in the legislative history at least makes more difficult a contention that these legislators were in fact making a distinction between use and misuse of state power.

* * *

These difficulties in explaining the basis of a distinction between authorized and unauthorized deprivations of constitutional rights fortify my view that the legislative history does not bear the burden which *stare decisis* casts upon it. For this reason and for those stated in the opinion of the Court, I agree that we should not now depart from the holdings of the *Classic* and *Screws* cases.

MR. JUSTICE FRANKFURTER, dissenting except insofar as the Court holds that this action cannot be maintained against the City of Chicago.

Abstractly stated, this case concerns a matter of statutory construction. So stated, the problem before the Court is denuded of illuminating concreteness and thereby of its far-reaching significance for our federal system. Again abstractly stated, this matter of statutory construction is one upon which the Court has already passed. But it has done so under circumstances and in settings that negative those considerations of social policy upon which the doctrine of *stare decisis,* calling for the controlling application of prior statutory construction, rests.

* * *

II

[Here Justice Frankfurter discusses the historical importance of protections against governmental overreaching by search and seizure.]

* * *

If the question whether due process forbids this kind of police invasion were before us in isolation, the answer would be quick. If, for example, petitioners had sought damages in the state courts of Illinois and if those courts had refused redress on the ground that the official character of the respondents clothed them with civil immunity, we would be faced with the sort of situation to which the language in the *Wolf* opinion was addressed: "we have no hesitation in saying that were a State affirmatively to sanction such police incursion into privacy it would run counter to the guaranty of the Fourteenth Amendment." If that issue is not reached in this case it is not because the conduct which the record here presents can be condoned. But by bringing their action in a Federal District Court petitioners cannot rest on the Fourteenth Amendment *simpliciter.* They invoke the protection of a specific statute by which Congress restricted federal judicial enforcement of its guarantees to particular enumerated circumstances. They must show not only that their constitutional rights have been infringed, but that they have been infringed "under color of [state] statute, ordinance, regulation, custom, or usage," as that phrase is used in the relevant congressional enactment.

III

* * *

Thus, although this Court has three times found that conduct of state officials which is forbidden by state law may be "under color" of state law for purposes of the Civil Rights Acts, it is accurate to say that that question has never received here the consideration which its importance merits. * * *

"The rule of *stare decisis,* though one tending to consistency and uniformity of decision, is not inflexible." It is true, of course, that the reason for the rule is more compelling in cases involving inferior law, law capable of change by Congress, than in constitutional cases, where this Court—although even in such cases a wise consciousness of the limitations of individual vision has impelled it always to give great weight to prior decisions—nevertheless bears the ultimate obligation for the development of the law as institutions develop.

* * *

IV

This case squarely presents the question whether the intrusion of a city policeman for which that policeman can show no such authority at state law as could be successfully interposed in defense to a state-law action against him, is nonetheless to be regarded as "under color" of state authority within the meaning of R.S. § 1979. Respondents, in breaking into the Monroe apartment, violated the laws of the State of Illinois. Illinois law appears to offer a civil remedy for unlawful searches; petitioners do not claim that none is available. Rather they assert that they have been deprived of due process of law and of equal protection of the laws under color of state law, although from all that appears the courts of Illinois are available to give them the fullest redress which the common law affords for the violence done them, nor does any "statute, ordinance, regulation, custom, or usage" of the State of Illinois bar that redress. Did the enactment by Congress of § 1 of the Ku Klux Act of 1871 encompass such a situation?

* * *

The general understanding of the legislators unquestionably was that, as amended, the Ku Klux Act did "not undertake to furnish redress for wrongs done by one person upon another in any of the States * * * in violation of their laws, unless he also violated some law of the United States, nor to punish one person for an ordinary assault and battery * * *." Even those who—opposing the constitutional objectors—found sufficient congressional power in the Enforcement Clause of the Fourteenth Amendment to give this kind of redress, deemed inexpedient the exercise of any such power: "Convenience and courtesy to the States suggest a sparing use, and never so far as to supplant the State authorities except in cases of extreme necessity, and when the State governments criminally refuse or neglect those duties which are imposed upon them." Extreme Radicals, those who believed that the remedy for the oppressed Unionists in the South was a general expansion of federal judicial jurisdiction so that "loyal men could have the privilege of having their causes, civil and criminal, tried in the Federal courts," were disappointed with the Act as passed.

* * *

The Court now says, however, that "It was not the unavailability of state remedies but the failure of certain States to enforce the laws with an equal hand that furnished the powerful momentum behind this 'force bill.'" Of course, if the notion of "unavailability" of remedy is limited to mean an absence of statutory, paper right, this is in large part true. Insofar as the Court undertakes to demonstrate—as the bulk of its opinion seems to do—that § 1979 was meant to reach some instances of action not specifically authorized by the avowed, apparent, written law inscribed in the statute books of the States, the argument knocks at an open door. No one would or could deny this, for by its express terms the statute comprehends deprivations of federal rights under color of any "statute, ordinance, regulation, *custom, or usage*" of a State. (Emphasis added.) The question is, *what* class of cases other than those involving state statute law were meant to be reached. And, with respect to this question, the Court's conclusion is undermined by the very portions of the legislative debates which it cites. For surely the misconduct of individual municipal police officers, subject to the effective oversight of appropriate state administrative and judicial authorities, presents a situation which differs *toto coelo* from one in which "Immunity is given to crime, and the records of the public tribunals are searched in vain for any evidence of effective redress," or in which murder rages while a State makes "no successful effort to bring the guilty to punishment or afford protection or redress," or in which the "State courts * * * [are] unable to enforce the criminal laws * * * or to suppress the disorders existing," or in which, in a State's "judicial tribunals one class is unable to secure that enforcement of their rights and punishment for their infraction which is accorded to another," or "of * * * hundreds of outrages * * * not one [is] punished," or "the courts of the * * * States fail and refuse to do their duty in the punishment of offenders against the law," or in which a "class of officers charged under the laws with their administration permanently and as a rule refuse to extend [their] protection." These statements indicate that Congress—made keenly aware by the *post-bellum* conditions in the South that States through their authorities could sanction offenses against the individual by settled practice which established state law as truly as written codes—designed § 1979 to reach, as well, official conduct which, because engaged in "permanently and as a rule," or "systematically," came through acceptance by law-administering officers to constitute "custom, or usage" having the cast of law. They do not indicate an attempt to reach, nor does the statute by its terms include, instances of acts in defiance of state law and which no settled state practice, no systematic pattern of official action or inaction, no "custom, or usage, of any State," insulates from effective and adequate reparation by the State's authorities.

Rather, all the evidence converges to the conclusion that Congress by § 1979 created a civil liability enforceable in the federal courts only in instances of injury for which redress was barred in the state courts because some "statute, ordinance, regulation, custom, or usage" sanctioned the grievance complained of. This purpose, manifested even by the so-called "Radical" Reconstruction Congress in 1871, accords with the presuppositions of our federal system. The jurisdiction which Article III of the Constitution conferred on the national judiciary reflected the assumption that the state courts, not the federal courts, would remain the primary guardians of that fundamental security of person and property which the long evolution of the common law had secured to one individual as against other individuals. The Fourteenth Amendment did not alter this basic aspect of our federalism.

Its commands were addressed to the States. Only when the States, through their responsible organs for the formulation and administration of local policy, sought to deny or impede access by the individual to the central government in connection with those enumerated functions assigned to it, or to deprive the individual of a certain minimal fairness in the exercise of the coercive forces of the State, or without reasonable justification to treat him differently than other persons subject to their jurisdiction, was an overriding federal sanction imposed. As between individuals, no corpus of substantive rights was guaranteed by the Fourteenth Amendment, but only "due process of law" in the ascertainment and enforcement of rights and equality in the enjoyment of rights and safeguards that the States afford. This was the base of the distinction between federal citizenship and state citizenship drawn by the *Slaughter-House Cases*. This conception begot the "State action" principle on which, from the time of the *Civil Rights Cases* this Court has relied in its application of Fourteenth Amendment guarantees. As between individuals, that body of mutual rights and duties which constitute the civil personality of a man remains essentially the creature of the legal institutions of the States.

But, of course, in the present case petitioners argue that the wrongs done them were committed not by individuals but by the police as state officials. There are two senses in which this might be true. It might be true if petitioners alleged that the redress which state courts offer them against the respondents is different than that which those courts would offer against other individuals, guilty of the same conduct, who were not the police. This is not alleged. It might also be true merely because the respondents are the police—because they are clothed with an appearance of official authority which is in itself a factor of significance in dealings between individuals. Certainly the night-time intrusion of the man with a star and a police revolver is a different phenomenon than the night-time intrusion of a burglar. The aura of power which a show of authority carries with it has been created by state government. For this reason the national legislature, exercising its power to implement the Fourteenth Amendment, might well attribute responsibility for the intrusion to the State and legislate to protect against such intrusion. The pretense of authority alone might seem to Congress sufficient basis for creating an exception to the ordinary rule that it is to the state tribunals that individuals within a State must look for redress against other individuals within that State. The same pretense of authority might suffice to sustain congressional legislation creating the exception. But until Congress has declared its purpose to shift the ordinary distribution of judicial power for the determination of causes between co-citizens of a State, this Court should not make the shift. Congress has not in § 1979 manifested that intention.

The unwisdom of extending federal criminal jurisdiction into areas of conduct conventionally punished by state penal law is perhaps more obvious than that of extending federal civil jurisdiction into the traditional realm of state tort law. But the latter, too, presents its problems of policy appropriately left to Congress. Suppose that a state legislature or the highest court of a State should determine that within its territorial limits no damages should be recovered in tort for pain and suffering, or for mental anguish, or that no punitive damages should be recoverable. Since the federal courts went out of the business of making "general law," such decisions of local policy have admittedly been the exclusive province of state lawmakers. Should the civil liability for police conduct which can claim no authority under local law, which is actionable as common-law assault or trespass in the local courts, comport different rules? Should an unlawful intrusion by a policeman in Chicago entail different consequences than an unlawful intrusion by a hoodlum? These are matters of policy in its strictly legislative sense, not for determination by this Court. And if it be, as it is, a matter for congressional choice, the legislative evidence is overwhelming that § 1979 is not expressive of that choice. Indeed, its precise limitation to acts "under color" of state statute, ordinance or other authority appears on its face designed to leave all questions of the nature and extent of liability of individuals to the laws of the several States except when a State seeks to shield those individuals under the special barrier of state authority. To extend Civil Rights Act liability beyond that point is to interfere in areas of state policymaking where Congress has not determined to interfere.

* * *

Relevant also are the effects upon the institution of federal constitutional adjudication of sustaining under § 1979 damage actions for relief against conduct allegedly violative of federal constitutional rights, but plainly violative of state law. Permitting such actions necessitates the immediate decision of federal constitutional issues despite the admitted availability of state-law remedies which would avoid those issues. This would make inroads, throughout a large area, upon the principle of federal judicial self-limitation which has become a significant instrument in the efficient functioning of the national judiciary. Self-limitation is not a matter of technical nicety, nor judicial timidity. It reflects the recognition that to no small degree the effectiveness of the legal order depends upon the infrequency with which it solves its problems by resorting to determinations of ultimate power. Especially is this true where the circumstances under which those ultimate determinations must be made are not conducive to the most mature deliberation and decision. If § 1979 is made a vehicle of constitutional litigation in cases where state officers have acted lawlessly at state law, difficult questions of the federal constitutionality of certain official practices—lawful perhaps in some States, unlawful in others—may be litigated between private parties without the participation of responsible state authorities which is obviously desirable to protect legitimate state interests, but also to better guide adjudication by competent record-making and argument.

* * *

Of course, if the States afford less protection against the police, as police, than against the hoodlum—if under authority of state "statute, ordinance, regulation, custom, or usage" the police are specially shielded—§ 1979 provides a remedy which dismissal of petitioners' complaint in the present case does not impair. Otherwise, the protection of the people from local delinquencies and shortcomings depends, as in general it must, upon the active consciences of state executives, legislators and judges. Federal intervention, which must at best be limited to securing those minimal guarantees afforded by the evolving concepts of due process and equal protection, may in the long run do the individual a disservice by deflecting responsibility from the state lawmakers, who hold the power of providing a far more comprehensive scope of protection. Local society, also, may well be the loser, by relaxing its sense of responsibility and, indeed, perhaps resenting what may appear to it to be outside interference where local authority is ample and more appropriate to supply needed remedies.

* * *

This meaning, no doubt, poses difficulties for the case-by-case application of § 1979. Manifestly the applicability of the section in an action for damages cannot be made to turn upon the actual availability or unavailability of a state-law remedy for each individual plaintiff's situation. Prosecution to adverse judgment of a state-court damage claim cannot be made prerequisite to § 1979 relief. In the first place, such a requirement would effectively nullify § 1979 as a vehicle for recovering damages. In the second place, the conclusion that police activity which violates state law is not "under color" of state law does not turn upon the existence of a state tort remedy. Rather, it recognizes the freedom of the States to fashion their own laws of torts in their own way under no threat of federal intervention save where state law makes determinative of a plaintiff's rights the particular circumstance that defendants are acting by state authority. Section 1979 was not designed to cure and level all the possible imperfections of local common-law doctrines, but to provide for the case of the defendant who can claim that some particular dispensation of state authority immunizes him from the ordinary processes of the law.

* * *

V

My Brother Harlan's concurring opinion deserves separate consideration. * * *

To ask why a Congress which legislated to reach a state officer enforcing an unconstitutional law or sanctioned usage did not also legislate to reach the same officer acting unconstitutionally without authority is to abstract this statute from its historical context. The legislative process of the *post-bellum* Congresses which enacted the several Civil Rights Acts was one of struggle and compromise in which the power of the National Government was expanded piece by piece against bitter resistance; the Radicals of 1871 had to yield ground and bargain over detail in order to keep the moderate Republicans in line. This was not an endeavor for achieving legislative patterns of analytically satisfying symmetry. It was a contest of large sallies and small retreats in which as much ground was occupied, at any time, as the temporary coalescences of forces strong enough to enroll a prevailing vote could agree upon. To assume that if Congress reached one situation it would also have reached another situation involving not dissimilar problems—assuming, *arguendo,* that the problems, viewed in intellectual abstraction, are not dissimilar—ignores the temper of the times which produced the Ku Klux Act. This approach would be persuasive only if the two situations, that of a state officer acting pursuant to state authority and that of a state officer acting without state authority, were so entirely similar that they would not, in 1871, have been perceived as two different situations at all * * * .

* * *

In truth, to deprecate the purposes of this 1871 statute in terms of analysis which refers to "merely * * * jurisdictional" effects, to "shifting the load of federal supervision," and to the "administrative burden on the Supreme Court," is to attribute twentieth century conceptions of the federal judicial system to the Reconstruction Congress. If today Congress were to devise a comprehensive scheme for the most effective protection of federal constitutional rights, it might conceivably think in terms of defining those classes of cases in which Supreme Court review of state-court decision was most appropriate, and those in which original federal jurisdiction was most appropriate, fitting all cases into one or the other category. The Congress of 1871 certainly did not think in such terms. Until 1875 there was no original "federal question" jurisdiction in the federal courts, and the ordinary mode of protection of federal constitutional rights was Supreme Court review. In light of the then prevailing notions of the appropriate relative spheres of jurisdiction of state and federal courts of first impression, any allowance of Federal District and Circuit Court competence to adjudicate causes between co-citizens of a State was a very special case, a rarity. To ask why, when such a special case was created to redress deprivations of federal rights under authority of state laws which abridged those rights, a special case was not also created to cover other deprivations of federal rights whose somewhat similar nature might have made the same redress appropriate, disregards the dominant jurisdictional thought of the day and neglects consideration of the fact that redress in a federal trial court was then to be very sparingly afforded. To extend original federal jurisdiction only in the class of cases in which, constitutional violation being sanctioned by state law, state judges would be less likely than federal judges to be sympathetic to a plaintiff's claim, is a purpose quite consistent with the "overflowing protection of constitutional rights" which, assuredly, § 1979 manifests.

Finally, it seems not unreasonable to reject the suggestion that state-sanctioned constitutional violations are no more offensive than violations not sanctioned by the majesty of state authority. Degrees of offensiveness, perhaps, lie largely in the eye of the person offended, but is it implausible to conclude that there is something more reprehensible, something more dangerous, in the action of the custodian of a public building who turns out a Negro pursuant to a local ordinance than in the action of the same custodian who turns out the same Negro, in violation of state law, to vent a personal bias? Or something more reprehensible about the public officer who beats a criminal suspect under orders from the Captain of Detectives, pursuant to a systematic and accepted custom of third-degree practice, than about the same officer who, losing his temper, breaks all local regulations and beats the same suspect? If it be admitted that there is a significant difference between the situation of the individual injured by another individual and who, although the latter is an agent of the State, can claim from the State's judicial or administrative processes the same protection and redress against him as would be available against any other individual, and the situation of one who, injured under the sanction of a state law which shields the offender, is left alone and helpless in the face of the asserted dignity of the State, then, certainly, it was the latter of these two situations—that of the unprotected Southern Negroes and Unionists—about which Congress was concerned in 1871.

* * *

Notes and Questions

1. The *Monroe* Court's expansive interpretation of § 1983 sparked a debate that continues to this day and touches upon federalism, separation of powers, and the content of various constitutional provisions, such as the due process clause of Fourteenth Amendment. Echoes of the debate between Justices Douglas and Harlan on one side and Justice Frankfurter on the other continue to reverberate in § 1983 litigation, and many of the cases turn on the distinctions the debate highlighted, though not always with explicit attribution.

2. *Monroe* dealt with several distinct issues of statutory interpretation, including whether municipalities are "persons" within the meaning of § 1983. Seventeen years later, *Monell v. Department of Social Services*, 436 U.S. 658, 98 S.Ct. 2018, 56 L.Ed.2d 611 (1978) (the next case in this chapter), reversed course and overruled *Monroe*'s unanimous holding that municipalities were not persons within the meaning of the statute and thus not liable under its provisions.

3. A second issue concerned the meaning of the phrase "under color of any statute, ordinance, regulation, custom, or usage, of any State or Territory." The events underlying § 1983 actions fall into three groups: actions authorized by the state, actions not authorized by the state but that do not violate state law, and actions in violation of state law. Even Justice Frankfurter seemed to agree that "under color of state law" includes actions authorized by state law. Should he have conceded that, or could he have taken the position that state judiciaries, bound by the Supremacy Clause, will give full scope to federal civil liberties provisions and are therefore competent to deal with state-authorized behaviors? Should the Court consider the debate about the proper scope of § 1983 according to the social conditions that existed in 1871, when that argument would have been highly suspect, or in light of conditions that exist today? With respect to the other two categories of state actions, do changed social conditions make Justice Frankfurter's argument more appealing?

4. A third issue concerned whether a prospective federal plaintiff must first exhaust any remedies available under state law. The Court noted that Congress meant to provide a federal remedy where state remedies, although adequate in theory, were not available in practice. From this premise the Court concluded that "[t]he federal remedy is supplementary to the state remedy," and no exhaustion of state remedies was required. The Court did not, however, address the question of whether a plaintiff who goes directly to federal court should have to make any showing of the *de jure* or *de facto* unavailability of an adequate state remedy. What do you think?

5. When Congress passed the Civil Rights Act, there was no general federal question jurisdiction, although it was common for Congress to provide federal jurisdiction in individual statutes. Until 1875, only the predecessor of 28 U.S.C.A. § 1343, which was part of the 1871 statute, authorized federal jurisdiction for actions under the Civil Rights Act. Yet that statute did not make civil rights actions exclusively federal. Is that relevant in analyzing Congress's views on § 1983's place in the remedial scheme? Does it suggest that Justice Harlan is correct that the statute was not intended to have merely a jurisdiction-shifting effect? If so, does the possibility of a § 1983 action in the state courts suggest the irrelevance of the existence of state remedies?

6. a) Does a state official act "under color of" state law when he acts either *ultra vires* or in violation of state law? That question arose long before *Monroe* in *Home Telephone and Telegraph Co. v. City of Los Angeles,* 227 U.S. 278, 33 S.Ct. 312, 57 L.Ed. 510 (1913), in which the defendant municipality argued that until the challenged action received the state's *imprimatur,* it was not state action for purposes of the Fourteenth Amendment and hence could not support a federal claim. The Court strongly disapproved the argument, noting "its inherent unsoundness," "its destructive character," and "its departure from the substantially unanimous view which has prevailed from the beginning."

[T]he proposition relied upon presupposes that the terms of the Fourteenth Amendment reach only acts done by State officers which are within the scope of the power conferred by the State. The proposition hence applies to the prohibitions of the Amendment the law of principal and agent governing contracts between individuals and consequently assumes that no act done by an officer of a State is within the reach of the Amendment unless such act can be held to be the act of the State by the application of such law of agency. In other words, the proposition is that the Amendment deals only with the acts of state officers within the strict scope of the public powers possessed by them and does not include an abuse of power by an officer as the result of a wrong done in excess of the power delegated. Here again the settled construction of the Amendment is that it presupposes the possibility of an abuse by a state officer or representative of the powers possessed and deals with such a contingency. It provides, therefore, for a case where one who is in possession of state power uses that power to the doing of the wrongs which the Amendment forbids even although the consummation of the wrong may not be within the powers possessed if the commission of the wrong itself is rendered possible or is efficiently aided by the state authority lodged in the wrongdoer. That is to say, the theory of the Amendment is that where an officer or other representative of a State in the exercise of the authority with which he is clothed misuses the power possessed to do a wrong forbidden by the Amendment, inquiry concerning whether the State has authorized the wrong is irrelevant and the Federal judicial power is competent to afford redress for the wrong by dealing with the officer and the result of his exertion of power.

How is the "under color of state law" issue in *Home Telegraph* different from the issue in *Monroe*? Do the defendants in *Monroe* challenge the holding of *Home Telegraph* or is their argument more narrow? What is the relationship between the "under color of" state law requirement of § 1983 and the state action requirement of the Fourteenth Amendment? Should they be identical? Does the fact that § 1983 is a remedial statute with no substantive content of its own suggest an answer? *See Lugar v. Edmonson Oil Co.,* 457 U.S. 922, 929, 102 S.Ct. 2744, 2749-50, 73 L.Ed.2d 482, 490 (1982).

b) Do professionals employed by the state who owe independent duties to individuals act under color of state law when they breach those duties? In a series of cases involving physicians, the Supreme Court ruled that they do. *See O'Connor v. Donaldson,* 422 U.S. 563, 95 S.Ct. 2486, 45 L.Ed.2d 396 (1975) (prison psychiatrist who also administered a state mental health institution was a state actor); *Estelle v. Gamble,* 429 U.S. 97, 97 S.Ct. 285, 50 L.Ed.2d 251 (1976) (prison doctor who ran the prison hospital was a state actor); *West v. Atkins,* 487 U.S. 42, 108 S.Ct. 2250, 101 L.Ed.2d 40 (1988) (private physician under contract to care for prisoners was a state actor). However, in *Polk County v. Dodson,* 454 U.S. 312, 102 S.Ct. 445, 70 L.Ed.2d 509 (1981), the Court declined to extend that principle to public defenders. What distinction do you think can be drawn between physicians and attorneys employed by the state for purposes of deciding whether they are state actors within the meaning of the Fourteenth Amendment and § 1983?

c) Are private individuals ever state actors? The Court has repeatedly so viewed individuals who conspire with state officials. *See, e.g., Adickes v. S.H. Kress & Co.,* 398 U.S. 144, 90 S.Ct. 1598, 26 L.Ed.2d 142 (1970); *Dennis v. Sparks,* 449 U.S. 24, 101 S.Ct. 183, 66 L.Ed.2d 185 (1980). This rule extends even to federal officials acting in concert with state officials, despite the fact that § 1983 does not reach federal conduct *simpliciter. See, e.g., Cabrera v. Martin,* 973 F.2d 735 (9th Cir. 1992).

d) Finally, how far can Congress legitimately stretch state action? Could it define state action to include conduct by state officials (*e.g.*, police officers) when they are off duty? What criteria should determine whether particular conduct is state action?

7. Although one tends to think of § 1983 as a pure civil rights statute, concerned only with violations of constitutional rights, the statute contains no such limitation. In *Maine v. Thiboutot,* 448 U.S. 1, 100 S.Ct. 2502, 65 L.Ed.2d 555 (1980), the Court gave § 1983 an expansive reading, holding that it is available whenever the plaintiff alleges violation of *any* federal right. Although Maine had argued that the legislative history compelled the conclusion that § 1983 was limited to rights created by the civil rights statutes, the Court found the history less clear on that point and instead relied upon the "plain language" of the statute.

Thiboutot has broad implications and raised the specter of an avalanche of new cases. It also offered prospective federal plaintiffs a way around the Court's recent restrictions on federal courts' discretion to imply private rights of action under federal statutes. *See generally* Chapter 5, Section D, Part 3. Justice Powell's strong dissent in *Thiboutot* focused extensively on this possibility. Of course, the § 1983 remedy in statutory cases, as in constitutional cases, would be limited to state actors.

The primary debate arising from *Thiboutot* has revolved around questions of when a statutory or constitutional provision creates a "right" within the meaning of § 1983. "[A] plaintiff must allege a violation of a federal *right*, not merely a violation of federal *law*." *Blessing v. Freestone*, 520 U.S. 329, 340, 117 S.Ct. 1353, 1359, 137 L.Ed.2d 569, 582 (1997). In *Golden State Transit Corp. v. Los Angeles,* 493 U.S. 103, 110 S.Ct. 444, 107 L.Ed.2d 420 (1989), the Court articulated a three-part test that commands consideration of whether 1) the statutory or constitutional provision creates an obligation binding on a governmental unit or merely expresses a nonbinding preference, 2) the plaintiff's asserted interest is not "too vague and amorphous" and is appropriate for judicial enforcement, and 3) the plaintiff is an intended beneficiary of the provision upon which she relies. The Court ruled that the Supremacy Clause did not create rights enforceable by individuals under § 1983, but that the Labor Management Relations Act, despite its comprehensive scheme of federal regulation, did. *Compare Dennis v. Higgins,* 498 U.S. 439, 111 S.Ct. 865, 112 L.Ed.2d 969 (1991) (holding that the Commerce Clause supports § 1983 claim) *with Pennhurst State School and Hospital v. Halderman,* 451 U.S. 1, 101 S.Ct. 1531, 67 L.Ed.2d 694 (1981) (holding that the Developmentally Disabled Assistance and Bill of Rights Act of 1975 declares policy only, creating no substantive rights in individuals that can be enforced through § 1983). In *Wilder v. Virginia Hospital Asso-*

ciation, 496 U.S. 498, 110 S.Ct. 2510, 110 L.Ed.2d 2455 (1990), the Court asserted that § 1983 is available only when the statute relied upon creates a binding duty. Professor Chemerinsky, among others, has noted the circularity of that test, since the statute will be binding if § 1983 is available to enforce it. *See also Suter v. Artist M.,* 503 U.S. 347, 112 S.Ct. 1360, 118 L.Ed.2d 1 (1992).

In *Blessing*, the Court cautioned the lower courts about simply assuming that federal statutes create enforceable rights, and noted the necessity of identifying such rights with particularity. Title IV-D of the Social Security Act required states to take numerous steps to assist children and custodial parents to collect child support payments. The plaintiffs in *Blessing* alleged that the defendant state official had violated § 1983 by failing to ensure that the state agency he directed was in substantial compliance with the statutory requirements. The Supreme Court concluded that the requirement that a State operate its child support program in substantial compliance with Title IV-D was not intended to benefit individual children and custodial parents. Rather, it was a yardstick by which federal officials could measure a State's system-wide performance to determine whether the Secretary of Health and Human Services should take action under the statute to encourage better compliance. The Court did not rule out, however, the possibility that other provisions of the statute might have created individual rights, and it remanded the case so that the district court could construe the complaint to ascertain the specific rights plaintiffs asserted.

Blessing declares that even if a federal statute creates an enforceable right, there is only a rebuttable presumption that it is enforceable under § 1983. Section 1983 is unavailable if the federal substantive law upon which the plaintiff relies precludes the use of § 1983 either explicitly or implicitly, as, for example, when Congress provides an extensive remedial system, although the Court emphasized that it had inferred such preclusion in only a few instances. *See, e.g., Middlesex County Sewerage Authority v. National Sea Clammers Association,* 453 U.S. 1, 101 S.Ct. 2615, 69 L.Ed.2d 435 (1981) (holding that citizen suit provisions requiring 60 days notice to state and federal officials and to alleged violators, and authorizing only injunctive relief, precluded § 1983 actions for damages and injunctive relief without notice). In *Blessing*, the Supreme Court concluded that the enforcement scheme in Title IV-D was far more limited than those implying preclusion because it contained no private remedy, either judicial or administrative, for an aggrieved person to seek relief.

City of Rancho Palos Verdes v. Abrams, 544 U.S. 113, 125 S.Ct. 1453, 161 L.Ed.2d 316 (2005), appears to make it easier for lower federal courts to conclude that a congressional enforcement system precludes a § 1983 action. The Court restated the governing standards from earlier cases—existence of a statutory right creates a rebuttable presumption the right is enforceable under § 1983, and the presumption can be rebutted only by specific congressional language precluding a § 1983 remedy or by creation of a comprehensive remedial scheme that is incompatible with individual enforcement under § 1983. The Court added, however, that "[T]he provision of an express, private means of redress in the statute itself is ordinarily an indication that

Congress did not intend to leave open a more expansive remedy under § 1983." Thus, although *Blessing* stressed that the Court has inferred preclusion of a § 1983 remedy in only a few instances, *Abrams* appears to make it very easy to rebut the presumption.

Justice Stevens protested on this ground in his concurring opinion. Although he concluded the Court reached the right decision in this case, he stated:

> I do not believe that the Court has properly acknowledged the strength of our normal presumption that Congress intended to preserve, rather than preclude, the availability of § 1983 as a remedy for the enforcement of federal statutory rights. * * * [T]here will be many instances in which § 1983 will be available even though Congress has not explicitly so provided in the text of the statute in question.

2. *Municipalities as Defendants*

MONELL v. DEPARTMENT OF SOCIAL SERVICES
Supreme Court of the United States, 1978.
436 U.S. 658, 98 S.Ct. 2018, 56 L.Ed.2d 611.

Mr. Justice Brennan delivered the opinion of the Court.

Petitioners, a class of female employees of the Department of Social Services and of the Board of Education of the city of New York, commenced this action under 42 U.S.C. § 1983 in July 1971. The gravamen of the complaint was that the Board and the Department had as a matter of official policy compelled pregnant employees to take unpaid leaves of absence before such leaves were required for medical reasons. The suit sought injunctive relief and backpay for periods of unlawful forced leave. Named as defendants in the action were the Department and its Commissioner, the Board and its Chancellor, and the city of New York and its Mayor. In each case, the individual defendants were sued solely in their official capacities.

On cross-motions for summary judgment, the District Court for the Southern District of New York held moot petitioners' claims for injunctive and declaratory relief since the City of New York and the Board, after the filing of the complaint, had changed their policies relating to maternity leaves so that no pregnant employee would have to take leave unless she was medically unable to continue to perform her job. No one now challenges this conclusion. The court did conclude, however, that the acts complained of were unconstitutional. Nonetheless plaintiffs' prayers for backpay were denied because any such damages would come ultimately from the City of New York and, therefore, to hold otherwise would be to "circumven[t]" the immunity conferred on municipalities by *Monroe v. Pape* (1961).

On appeal, petitioners renewed their arguments that the Board of Education was not a "municipality" within the meaning of *Monroe v.*

Pape, and that, in any event, the District Court had erred in barring a damages award against the individual defendants. The Court of Appeals for the Second Circuit rejected both contentions. The court first held that the Board of Education was not a "person" under § 1983 because "it performs a vital governmental function * * *, and, significantly, while it has the right to determine how the funds appropriated to it shall be spent * * *, it has no final say in deciding what its appropriations shall be." The individual defendants, however, were "persons" under § 1983, even when sued solely in their official capacities. Yet, because a damages award would "have to be paid by a city that was held not to be amenable to such an action in *Monroe v. Pape*," a damages action against officials sued in their official capacities could not proceed.

We granted certiorari in this case to consider "[w]hether local governmental officials and/or local independent school boards are "persons" within the meaning of 42 U.S.C. § 1983 when equitable relief in the nature of back pay is sought against them in their official capacities?"

Although, after plenary consideration, we have decided the merits of over a score of cases brought under § 1983 in which the principal defendant was a school board—and, indeed, in some of which § 1983 and its jurisdictional counterpart, 28 U.S.C. § 1343, provided the only basis for jurisdiction—we indicated last Term that the question presented here was open and would be decided "another day." That other day has come and we now overrule *Monroe v. Pape* insofar as it holds that local governments are wholly immune from suit under § 1983.

I

In *Monroe v. Pape,* we held that "Congress did not undertake to bring municipal corporations within the ambit of [§ 1983]." The sole basis for this conclusion was an inference drawn from Congress' rejection of the "Sherman amendment" to the bill which became the Civil Rights Act of 1871, the precursor of § 1983. The Amendment would have held a municipal corporation liable for damage done to the person or property of its inhabitants by *private* persons "riotously and tumultuously assembled." Although the Sherman amendment did not seek to amend § 1 of the Act, which is now § 1983, and although the nature of the obligation created by that amendment was vastly different from that created by § 1, the Court nonetheless concluded in *Monroe* that Congress must have meant to exclude municipal corporations from the coverage of § 1 because " 'the House [in voting against the Sherman amendment] had solemnly decided that in their judgment Congress had no constitutional power to impose any *obligation* upon county and town organizations, the mere instrumentality for the administration of state law.' " This statement, we thought, showed that Congress doubted its "constitutional power * * * to impose *civil liability* on municipalities," and that such doubt would have extended to any type of civil liability.

A fresh analysis of the debate on the Civil Rights Act of 1871, and particularly of the case law which each side mustered in its support, shows, however, that *Monroe* incorrectly equated the "obligation" of which Representative Poland spoke with "civil liability."

A. An Overview

There are three distinct stages in the legislative consideration of the bill which became the Civil Rights Act of 1871. On March 28, 1871, Representative Shellabarger, acting for a House select committee, reported H.R. 320, a bill "to enforce the provisions of the fourteenth amendment to the Constitution of the United States, and for other purposes." H.R. 320 contained four sections. Section 1, now codified as 42 U.S.C. § 1983, was the subject of only limited debate and was passed without amendment. Sections 2 through 4 dealt primarily with the "other purpose" of suppressing Ku Klux Klan violence in the Southern States. The wisdom and constitutionality of these sections—not § 1, now § 1983—were the subject of almost all congressional debate and each of these sections was amended. The House finished its initial debates on H.R. 320 on April 7, 1871, and one week later the Senate also voted out a bill. Again, debate on § 1 of the bill was limited and that section was passed as introduced.

Immediately prior to the vote on H.R. 320 in the Senate, Senator Sherman introduced his amendment. This was not an amendment to § 1 of the bill, but was to be added as § 7 at the end of the bill. Under the Senate rules, no discussion of the amendment was allowed and, although attempts were made to amend the amendment, it was passed as introduced. In this form, the amendment did not place liability on municipal corporations, but made any inhabitant of a municipality liable for damage inflicted by persons "riotously and tumultuously assembled."

The House refused to acquiesce in a number of amendments made by the Senate, including the Sherman amendment, and the respective versions of H.R. 320 were therefore sent to a conference committee. Section 1 of the bill, however, was not a subject of this conference since, as noted, it was passed *verbatim* as introduced in both Houses of Congress.

On April 18, 1871, the first conference committee completed its work on H.R. 320. The main features of the conference committee draft of the Sherman amendment were these: First, a cause of action was given to persons injured by

> any persons riotously and tumultuously assembled together * * * with intent to deprive any person of any right conferred upon him by the Constitution and laws of the United States, or to deter him or punish him for exercising such right, or by reason of his race, color, or previous condition of servitude * * * .

Second, the bill provided that the action would be against the county, city, or parish in which the riot had occurred and that it could be maintained by either the person injured or his legal representative. Third, unlike the amendment as proposed, the conference substitute made the government defendant liable on the judgment if it was not satisfied against individual defendants who had committed the violence. If a municipality were liable, the judgment against it could be collected

> by execution, attachment, mandamus, garnishment, or any other proceeding in aid of execution or applicable to the enforcement of judgments against municipal corporations; and such judgment [would become] a lien as well upon all moneys in the treasury of such county, city, or parish, as upon the other property thereof.

In the ensuing debate on the first conference report, which was the first debate of any kind on the Sherman amendment, Senator Sherman explained that the purpose of his amendment was to enlist the aid of persons of property in the enforcement of the civil rights laws by making their property "responsible" for Ku Klux Klan damage. Statutes drafted on a similar theory, he stated, had long been in force in England and were in force in 1871 in a number of States. Nonetheless there were critical differences between the conference substitute and extant state and English statutes: The conference substitute, unlike most state riot statutes, lacked a short statute of limitations and imposed liability on the government defendant whether or not it had notice of the impending riot, whether or not the municipality was authorized to exercise a police power, whether or not it exerted all reasonable efforts to stop the riot, and whether or not the rioters were caught and punished.

The first conference substitute passed the Senate but was rejected by the House. House opponents, within whose ranks were some who had supported § 1, thought the Federal Government could not, consistent with the Constitution, obligate municipal corporations to keep the peace if those corporations were neither so obligated nor so authorized by their state charters. And, because of this constitutional objection, opponents of the Sherman amendment were unwilling to impose damages liability for nonperformance of a duty which Congress could not require municipalities to perform. This position is reflected in Representative Poland's statement that is quoted in *Monroe.*

Because the House rejected the first conference report a second conference was called and it duly issued its report. The second conference substitute for the Sherman amendment abandoned municipal liability and, instead, made "any person or persons having knowledge [that a conspiracy to violate civil rights was afoot], and having power to prevent or aid in preventing the same," who did not attempt to stop the same, liable to any person injured by the conspiracy. The amendment in this form was adopted by both Houses of Congress and is now codified as 42 U.S.C. § 1986.

The meaning of the legislative history sketched above can most readily be developed by first considering the debate on the report of the first conference committee. This debate shows conclusively that the constitutional objections raised against the Sherman amendment—on which our holding in *Monroe* was based—would not have prohibited congressional creation of a civil remedy against state municipal corporations that infringed federal rights. Because § 1 of the Civil Rights Act does not state expressly that municipal corporations come within its ambit, it is finally necessary to interpret § 1 to confirm that such corporations were indeed intended to be included within the "persons" to whom that section applies.

B. Debate on the First Conference Report

The style of argument adopted by both proponents and opponents of the Sherman amendment in both Houses of Congress was largely legal, with frequent references to cases decided by this Court and the Supreme Courts of the several States. Proponents of the Sherman amendment did not, however, discuss in detail the argument in favor of its constitutionality. Nonetheless, it is possible to piece together such an argument from the debates on the first conference report and those on § 2 of the civil rights bill, which, because it allowed the Federal Government to prosecute crimes "in the States," had also raised questions of federal power. The account of Representative Shellabarger, the House sponsor of H.R. 320, is the most complete.

Shellabarger began his discussion of H.R. 320 by stating that "there is a domain of constitutional law involved in the right consideration of this measure which is wholly unexplored." There were analogies, however. With respect to the meaning of § 1 of the Fourteenth Amendment, and particularly its Privileges or Immunities Clause, Shellabarger relied on the statement of Mr. Justice Washington which defined the privileges protected by Art. IV:

> "What these fundamental privileges are it would perhaps be more tedious than difficult to enumerate. They may, however, be all comprehended under the following general heads: protection by the Government;—
>
> Mark that—
>
> *protection by the Government;* the enjoyment of life and liberty, with the right to acquire and possess property of every kind, and to pursue and obtain happiness and safety * * * ."

Building on his conclusion that citizens were owed protection—a conclusion not disputed by opponents of the Sherman amendment—Shellabarger then considered Congress' role in providing that protection. Here again there were precedents:

> [Congress has always] assumed to enforce, as against the States, and also persons, every one of the provisions of the Constitution. Most of the provisions of the Constitution which restrain and directly relate to the States, such as those in [Art. I, § 10,] relate to

the divisions of the political powers of the State and General Governments * * *. These prohibitions upon political powers of the States are all of such nature that they can be, and even have been, * * * enforced by the courts of the United States declaring void all State acts of encroachment on Federal powers. Thus, and thus sufficiently, has the United States "enforced" these provisions of the Constitution. But there are some that are not of this class. These are where the court secures the rights or the liabilities of persons within the States, as between such persons and the States.

These three are: first, that as to fugitives from justice;[22] second, that as to fugitives from service, (or slaves;)[23] third, that declaring that the "citizens of each State shall be entitled to all the privileges and immunities of citizens in the several States."

And, sir, every one of these—the only provisions where it was deemed that legislation was required to enforce the constitutional provisions—the only three where the rights or liabilities of persons in the States, as between these persons and the States, are directly provided for, Congress has by legislation affirmatively interfered to protect * * * such persons.

Of legislation mentioned by Shellabarger, the closest analog of the Sherman amendment, ironically, was the statute implementing the fugitives from justice and fugitive slave provisions of Art. IV—the Act of Feb. 12, 1793—the constitutionality of which had been sustained in 1842, in *Prigg v. Pennsylvania* (1842). There, Mr. Justice Story, writing for the Court, held that Art. IV gave slaveowners a federal right to the unhindered possession of their slaves in whatever State such slaves might be found. Because state process for recovering runaway slaves might be inadequate or even hostile to the rights of the slaveowner, the right intended to be conferred could be negated if left to state implementation. Thus, since the Constitution guaranteed the right and this in turn required a remedy, Story held it to be a "natural inference" that Congress had the power itself to ensure an appropriate (in the Necessary and Proper Clause sense) remedy for the right.

Building on *Prigg,* Shellabarger argued that a remedy against mu-

---

[22] U.S. CONST., Art. IV, § 2, cl. 2:

> A person charged in any State with Treason, Felony, or other Crime, who shall flee from Justice, and be found in another State, shall on Demand of the executive Authority of the State from which he fled, be delivered up, to be removed to the State having Jurisdiction of the Crime.

[23] *Id.,* cl. 3:

> No Person held to Service or Labour in one State, under the Laws thereof, escaping into another, shall, in Consequence of any Law or Regulation therein, be discharged from such Service or Labour, but shall be delivered up on Claim of the Party to whom such Service or Labour may be due.

nicipalities and counties was an appropriate—and hence constitutional—method for ensuring the protection which the Fourteenth Amendment made every citizen's federal right.[25] This much was clear from the adoption of such statutes by the several States as devices for suppressing riot. Thus, said Shellabarger, the only serious question remaining was "whether, since a county is an integer or part of a State, the United States can impose upon it, as such, *any obligations* to keep the peace in obedience to United States laws." This he answered affirmatively, citing the first of many cases upholding the power of federal courts to enforce the Contract Clause against municipalities.

House opponents of the Sherman amendment—whose views are particularly important since only the House voted down the amendment—did not dispute Shellabarger's claim that the Fourteenth Amendment created a federal right to protection, but they argued that the local units of government upon which the amendment fastened liability were not obligated to keep the peace at state law and further that the Federal Government could not constitutionally require local governments to create police forces, whether this requirement was levied directly, or indirectly by imposing damages for breach of the peace on municipalities. The most complete statement of this position is that of Representative Blair:

> The proposition known as the Sherman amendment * * * is entirely new. It is altogether without a precedent in this country * * *. That amendment claims the power in the General Government to go into the States of this Union and lay such obligations as it may please upon the municipalities, which are the creations of the States alone * * *.
>
> [H]ere it is proposed, not to carry into effect an obligation which rests upon the municipality, but to create that obligation, and that is the provision I am unable to assent to. * * *
>
> [T]here are certain rights and duties that belong to the States, * * * there are certain powers that inhere in the State governments. They create these municipalities, they say what their powers shall be and what their obligations shall be. If the Government of the United States can step in and add to those obligations, may it not utterly destroy the municipality? If it can say that it shall be liable for damages occurring from a riot, * * * where [will] its power * * * stop and what obligations * * * might [it] not lay upon a municipality * * *.
>
> Now, only the other day, the Supreme Court * * * decided [in *Collector v. Day* (1870)] that there is no power in the Government

[25] *See also* [Globe] at 760 (Sen. Sherman) ("If a State may * * * pass a law making a county * * * responsible for a riot in order to deter such crime, then we may pass the same remedies * * *").

of the United States, under its authority to tax, to tax the salary of a State officer. Why? Simply because the power to tax involves the power to destroy, and it was not the intent to give the Government of the United States power to destroy the government of the States in any respect. It was held also in the case of *Prigg* that it is not within the power of the Congress of the United States to lay duties upon a State officer; that we cannot command a State officer to do any duty whatever, as such; and I ask * * * the difference between that and commanding a municipality, which is equally the creature of the State, to perform a duty.

Any attempt to impute a unitary constitutional theory to opponents of the Sherman amendment is, of course, fraught with difficulties, not the least of which is that most Members of Congress did not speak to the issue of the constitutionality of the amendment. Nonetheless, two considerations lead us to conclude that opponents of the Sherman amendment found it unconstitutional substantially because of the reasons stated by Representative Blair: First, Blair's analysis is precisely that of Poland, whose views were quoted as authoritative in *Monroe,* and that analysis was shared in large part by all House opponents who addressed the constitutionality of the Sherman amendment. Second, Blair's exegesis of the reigning constitutional theory of his day, as we shall explain, was clearly supported by precedent—albeit precedent that has not survived—and no other constitutional formula was advanced by participants in the House debates.

Collector v. Day, cited by Blair, was the clearest and, at the time of the debates, the most recent pronouncement of a doctrine of coordinate sovereignty that, as Blair stated, placed limits on even the enumerated powers of the National Government in favor of protecting state prerogatives. There, the Court held that the United States could not tax the income of Day, a Massachusetts state judge, because the independence of the States within their legitimate spheres would be imperiled if the instrumentalities through which States executed their powers were "subject to the control of another and distinct government." Although the Court in *Day* apparently rested this holding in part on the proposition that the taxing "power acknowledges no limits but the will of the legislative body imposing the tax," the Court had in other cases limited other national powers in order to avoid interference with the States.

In *Prigg v. Pennsylvania,* for example, Mr. Justice Story, in addition to confirming a broad national power to legislate under the Fugitive Slave Clause, held that Congress could not "insist that states * * * provide means to carry into effect the duties of the national government." And Mr. Justice McLean agreed that, "[a]s a general principle," it was true "that Congress had no power to impose duties on state officers, as provided in the [Act of Feb. 12, 1793]." Nonetheless he wondered whether Congress might not impose "positive" duties on state officers where a clause of the Constitution, like the Fugitive Slave Clause, seemed to require affirmative government assistance, rather than restraint of government, to secure federal rights.

Had Mr. Justice McLean been correct in his suggestion that, where the Constitution envisioned affirmative government assistance, the States or their officers or instrumentalities could be required to provide it, there would have been little doubt that Congress could have insisted that municipalities afford by "positive" action the protection owed individuals under § 1 of the Fourteenth Amendment whether or not municipalities were obligated by state law to keep the peace. However, any such argument, largely foreclosed by *Prigg,* was made impossible by the Court's holding in *Kentucky v. Dennison* (1861). There, the Court was asked to require Dennison, the Governor of Ohio, to hand over Lago, a fugitive from justice wanted in Kentucky, as required by § 1 of the Act of Feb. 12, 1793, which implemented Art. IV, § 2, cl. 2, of the Constitution. Mr. Chief Justice Taney, writing for a unanimous Court, refused to enforce that section of the Act:

> [W]e think it clear, that the Federal Government, under the Constitution, has no power to impose on a State officer, as such, any duty whatever, and compel him to perform it; for if it possessed this power, it might overload the officer with duties which would fill up all his time, and disable him from performing his obligations to the State, and might impose on him duties of a character incompatible with the rank and dignity to which he was elevated by the State.

The rationale of *Dennison*—that the Nation could not impose duties on state officers since that might impede States in their legitimate activities—is obviously identical to that which animated the decision in *Collector v. Day.* And, as Blair indicated, municipalities as instrumentalities through which States executed their policies could be equally disabled from carrying out state policies if they were also obligated to carry out federally imposed duties. Although no one cited *Dennison* by name, the principle for which it stands was well known to Members of Congress, many of whom discussed *Day* as well as a series of State Supreme Court cases in the mid-1860's which had invalidated a federal tax on the process of state courts on the ground that the tax threatened the independence of a vital state function. Thus, there was ample support for Blair's view that the Sherman amendment, by putting municipalities to the Hobson's choice of keeping the peace or paying civil damages, attempted to impose obligations on municipalities by indirection that could not be imposed directly, thereby threatening to "destroy the government of the States."

If municipal liability under § 1 of the Civil Rights Act of 1871 created a similar Hobson's choice, we might conclude, as *Monroe* did, that Congress could not have intended municipalities to be among the "persons" to which that section applied. But this is not the case.

First, opponents expressly distinguished between imposing an obligation to keep the peace and merely imposing civil liability for damages on a municipality that was obligated by state law to keep the peace, but which had not in violation of the Fourteenth Amendment. Representative Poland, for example, reasoning from Contract Clause precedents, indicated that Congress could constitutionally confer jurisdiction on the federal courts to entertain suits seeking to hold municipalities liable for using their authorized powers in violation of the Constitution—which is as far as § 1 of the Civil Rights Act went:

> I presume * * * that where a State had imposed a duty [to keep the peace] upon [a] municipality * * * an action would be allowed to be maintained against them in the courts of the United States under the ordinary restrictions as to jurisdiction. But the enforcing a liability, existing by their own contract, or by a State law, in the courts, is a very widely different thing from devolving a new duty or liability upon them by the national Government, which has no power either to create or destroy them, and no power or control over them whatever.

Representative Burchard agreed:

> [T]here is not duty imposed by the Constitution of the United States, or usually by State laws, upon a county to protect the people of that county against the commission of the offenses herein enumerated, such as the burning of buildings or any other injury to property or injury to person. Police powers are not conferred upon counties as corporations; they are conferred upon cities that have qualified legislative power. And so far as cities are concerned, where the equal protection required to be afforded by a State is imposed upon a city by State laws, perhaps the United States courts could enforce its performance. But counties * * * do not have any control of the police * * * .

Second, the doctrine of dual sovereignty apparently put no limit on the power of federal courts to enforce the Constitution against municipalities that violated it. Under the theory of dual sovereignty set out in *Prigg,* this is quite understandable. So long as federal courts were vindicating the Federal Constitution, they were providing the "positive" government action required to protect federal constitutional rights and no question was raised of enlisting the States in "positive" action. The limits of the principles announced in *Dennison* and *Day* are not so well defined in logic, but are clear as a matter of history. It must be remembered that the same Court which rendered *Day* also vigorously enforced the Contract Clause against municipalities—an enforcement effort which included various forms of "positive" relief, such as ordering that taxes be levied and collected to discharge federal-court judgments, once a constitutional infraction was found.[40] Thus, federal judicial enforcement

---

[40] Since this Court granted unquestionably "positive" relief in Contract Clause cases,

of the Constitution's express limits on state power, since it was done so frequently, must, notwithstanding anything said in *Dennison* or *Day*, have been permissible, at least so long as the interpretation of the Constitution was left in the hands of the judiciary. Since § 1 of the Civil Rights Act simply conferred jurisdiction on the federal courts to enforce § 1 of the Fourteenth Amendment—a situation precisely analogous to the grant of diversity jurisdiction under which the Contract Clause was enforced against municipalities—there is no reason to suppose that opponents of the Sherman amendment would have found any constitutional barrier to § 1 suits against municipalities.

Finally, the very votes of those Members of Congress, who opposed the Sherman amendment but who had voted for § 1, confirm that the liability imposed by § 1 was something very different from that imposed by the amendment. Section 1 without question could be used to obtain a damages judgment against state or municipal *officials* who violated federal constitutional rights while acting under color of law. However, for *Prigg-Dennison-Day* purposes, as Blair and others recognized, there was no distinction of constitutional magnitude between officers and agents—including corporate agents—of the State: Both were state instrumentalities and the State could be impeded no matter over which sort of instrumentality the Federal Government sought to assert its power. *Dennison* and *Day*, after all, were not suits against municipalities but against *officers,* and Blair was quite conscious that he was extending these cases by applying them to municipal corporations. Nonetheless, Senator Thurman, who gave the most exhaustive critique of § 1—*inter alia,* complaining that it would be applied to state officers—and who opposed both § 1 and the Sherman amendment, the latter on *Prigg* grounds, agreed unequivocally that § 1 was constitutional.[44] Those who voted for § 1 must similarly have believed in its constitutionality despite *Prigg, Dennison,* and *Day.*

-----

it appears that the distinction between the Sherman amendment and those cases was not that the former created a positive obligation whereas the latter imposed only a negative restraint. Instead, the distinction must have been that a violation of the Constitution was the predicate for "positive" relief in the Contract Clause cases, whereas the Sherman amendment imposed damages without regard to whether a local government was in any way at fault for the breach of the peace for which it was to be held for damages. While no one stated this distinction expressly during the debates, the inference is strong that Congressmen in 1871 would have drawn this distinction since it explains why Representatives Poland, Burchard, and Willard could oppose the amendment while at the same time saying that the Federal Government might impose damages on a local government that had defaulted in a state-imposed duty to keep the peace, and it also explains why everyone agreed that a state or municipal officer could constitutionally be held liable under § 1 for violations of the Constitution.

44 In 1880, moreover, when the question of the limits of the *Prigg* principle was squarely presented in *Ex parte* Virginia, this Court held that *Dennison* and *Day* and the principle of federalism for which they stand did not prohibit federal enforcement of § 5 of the Fourteenth Amendment through suits directed to state officers.

C. Debate on § 1 of the Civil Rights Bill

From the foregoing discussion, it is readily apparent that nothing said in debate on the Sherman amendment would have prevented holding a municipality liable under § 1 of the Civil Rights Act for its own violations of the Fourteenth Amendment. The question remains, however, whether the general language describing those to be liable under § 1— "any person"—covers more than natural persons. An examination of the debate on § 1 and application of appropriate rules of construction show unequivocally that § 1 was intended to cover legal as well as natural persons.

Representative Shellabarger was the first to explain the function of § 1:

> [Section 1] not only provides a civil remedy for persons whose former condition may have been that of slaves, but also to all people where, under color of State law, they or any of them may be deprived of rights to which they are entitled under the Constitution by reason and virtue of their national citizenship.

By extending a remedy to all people, including whites, § 1 went beyond the mischief to which the remaining sections of the 1871 Act were addressed. Representative Shellabarger also stated without reservation that the constitutionality of § 2 of the Civil Rights Act of 1866 controlled the constitutionality of § 1 of the 1871 Act, and that the former had been approved by "the supreme courts of at least three States of this Union" and by Mr. Justice Swayne, sitting on circuit, who had concluded: " 'We have no doubt of the constitutionality of every provision of this act.' " Representative Shellabarger then went on to describe how the courts would and should interpret § 1:

> This act is remedial, and in aid of the preservation of human liberty and human rights. All statutes and constitutional provisions authorizing such statutes are liberally and beneficently construed. It would be most strange and, in civilized law, monstrous were this not the rule of interpretation. As has been again and again decided by your own Supreme Court of the United States, and everywhere else where there is wise judicial interpretation, the largest latitude consistent with the words employed is uniformly given in construing such statutes and constitutional provisions as are meant to protect and defend and give remedies for their wrongs to all the people * * * . Chief Justice Jay and also Story say: "Where a power is remedial in its nature there is much reason to contend that it ought to be construed liberally, and it is generally adopted in the interpretation of laws."

The sentiments expressed in Representative Shellabarger's opening speech were echoed by Senator Edmunds, the manager of H.R. 320 in the Senate:

The first section is one that I believe nobody objects to, as defining the rights secured by the Constitution of the United States when they are assailed by any State law or under color of any State law, and it is merely carrying out the principles of the civil rights bill [of 1866], which have since become a part of the Constitution.

[Section 1 is] so very simple and really reenact[s] the Constitution.

And he agreed that the bill "secure[d] the rights of white men as much as of colored men."

In both Houses, statements of the supporters of § 1 corroborated that Congress, in enacting § 1, intended to give a broad remedy for violations of federally protected civil rights. Moreover, since municipalities through their official acts could, equally with natural persons, create the harms intended to be remedied by § 1, and, further, since Congress intended § 1 to be broadly construed, there is no reason to suppose that municipal corporations would have been excluded from the sweep of § 1. One need not rely on this inference alone, however, for the debates show that Members of Congress understood "persons" to include municipal corporations.

Representative Bingham, for example, in discussing § 1 of the bill, explained that he had drafted § 1 of the Fourteenth Amendment with the case of *Barron v. Mayor of Baltimore* (1833) especially in mind. "In [that] case the *city* had taken private property for public use, without compensation * * *, and there was no redress for the wrong * * *." Bingham's further remarks clearly indicate his view that such takings by cities, as had occurred in *Barron,* would be redressable under § 1 of the bill. More generally, and as Bingham's remarks confirm, § 1 of the bill would logically be the vehicle by which Congress provided redress for takings, since that section provided the only civil remedy for Fourteenth Amendment violations and that Amendment unequivocally prohibited uncompensated takings. Given this purpose, it beggars reason to suppose that Congress would have exempted municipalities from suit, insisting instead that compensation for a taking come from an officer in his individual capacity rather than from the government unit that had the benefit of the property taken.

In addition, by 1871, it was well understood that corporations should be treated as natural persons for virtually all purposes of constitutional and statutory analysis. This had not always been so. When this Court first considered the question of the status of corporations, Mr. Chief Justice Marshall, writing for the Court, denied that corporations "as such" were persons as that term was used in Art. III and the Judiciary Act of 1789. By 1844, however, the * * * doctrine was unhesitatingly abandoned: "[A] corporation created by and doing business in a particular state, is to be deemed to all intents and purposes as a person, although an artificial person, * * * capable of being treated as a citizen of that state, as much as a natural person." And only two years before the debates on the Civil Rights Act, the [new] principle was automatically and without discussion extended to municipal corporations. Under this doctrine, municipal corporations were routinely sued in the federal courts and this fact was well known to Members of Congress.

That the "usual" meaning of the word "person" would extend to municipal corporations is also evidenced by an Act of Congress which had been passed only months before the Civil Rights Act was passed. This Act provided that "in all acts hereafter passed * * * the word "person" may extend and be applied to bodies politic and corporate * * * unless the context shows that such words were intended to be used in a more limited sense." Municipal corporations in 1871 were included within the phrase "bodies politic and corporate" and, accordingly, the "plain meaning" of § 1 is that local government bodies were to be included within the ambit of the persons who could be sued under § 1 of the Civil Rights Act. Indeed, a Circuit Judge, writing in 1873 in what is apparently the first reported case under § 1, read the Dictionary Act in precisely this way in a case involving a corporate plaintiff and a municipal defendant.

II

Our analysis of the legislative history of the Civil Rights Act of 1871 compels the conclusion that Congress *did* intend municipalities and other local government units to be included among those persons to whom § 1983 applies. Local governing bodies, therefore, can be sued directly under § 1983 for monetary, declaratory, or injunctive relief where, as here, the action that is alleged to be unconstitutional implements or executes a policy statement, ordinance, regulation, or decision officially adopted and promulgated by that body's officers. Moreover, although the touchstone of the § 1983 action against a government body is an allegation that official policy is responsible for a deprivation of rights protected by the Constitution, local governments, like every other § 1983 "person," by the very terms of the statute, may be sued for constitutional deprivations visited pursuant to governmental "custom" even though such a custom has not received formal approval through the body's official decisionmaking channels. As Mr. Justice Harlan, writing for the Court, said in *Adickes v. S.H. Kress & Co.* (1970): "Congress included customs and usages [in § 1983] because of the persistent and widespread discriminatory practices of state officials * * * . Although not authorized by written law, such practices of state officials could well be so permanent and well settled as to constitute a 'custom or usage' with the force of law."

On the other hand, the language of § 1983, read against the background of the same legislative history, compels the conclusion that Congress did not intend municipalities to be held liable unless action pursuant to official municipal policy of some nature caused a constitutional tort. In particular, we conclude that a municipality cannot be held liable solely because it employs a tortfeasor—or, in other words, a municipality cannot be held liable under § 1983 on a *respondeat superior* theory.

We begin with the language of § 1983 as originally passed:

> *[A]ny person who,* under color of any law, statute, ordinance, regulation, custom, or usage of any State, *shall subject, or cause to be subjected,* any person * * * to the deprivation of any rights, privileges, or immunities secured by the Constitution of the United States, shall, any such law, statute, ordinance, regulation, custom, or usage of the State to the contrary notwithstanding, be liable to the party injured in any action at law, suit in equity, or other proper proceeding for redress * * * .

The italicized language plainly imposes liability on a government that, under color of some official policy, "causes" an employee to violate another's constitutional rights. At the same time, that language cannot be easily read to impose liability vicariously on governing bodies solely on the basis of the existence of an employer-employee relationship with a tortfeasor. Indeed, the fact that Congress did specifically provide that A's tort became B's liability if B "caused" A to subject another to a tort suggests that Congress did not intend § 1983 liability to attach where such causation was absent.

Equally important, creation of a federal law of *respondeat superior* would have raised all the constitutional problems associated with the obligation to keep the peace, an obligation Congress chose not to impose because it thought imposition of such an obligation unconstitutional. To this day, there is disagreement about the basis for imposing liability on an employer for the torts of an employee when the sole nexus between the employer and the tort is the fact of the employer-employee relationship. Nonetheless, two justifications tend to stand out. First is the common-sense notion that no matter how blameless an employer appears to be in an individual case, accidents might nonetheless be reduced if employers had to bear the cost of accidents. Second is the argument that the cost of accidents should be spread to the community as a whole on an insurance theory.

The first justification is of the same sort that was offered for statutes like the Sherman amendment: "The obligation to make compensation for injury resulting from riot is, by arbitrary enactment of statutes, affirmatory law, and the reason of passing the statute is to secure a more perfect police regulation." This justification was obviously insufficient to sustain the amendment against perceived constitutional difficulties and there is no reason to suppose that a more general liability imposed for a similar reason would have been thought less constitutionally objectionable. The second justification was similarly put forward as a justification for the Sherman amendment: "we do not look upon [the Sherman amendment] as a punishment * * * . It is a mutual insurance." Again, this justification was insufficient to sustain the amendment.

We conclude, therefore, that a local government may not be sued under § 1983 for an injury inflicted solely by its employees or agents. Instead, it is when execution of a government's policy or custom, whether made by its lawmakers or by those whose edicts or acts may fairly be said to represent official policy, inflicts the injury that the government as an entity is responsible under § 1983. Since this case unquestionably involves official policy as the moving force of the constitutional violation found by the District Court, we must reverse the judgment below. In so doing, we have no occasion to address, and do not address, what the full contours of municipal liability under § 1983 may be. We have attempted only to sketch so much of the § 1983 cause of action against a local government as is apparent from the history of the 1871 Act and our prior cases, and we expressly leave further development of this action to another day.

* * *

IV

Since the question whether local government bodies should be afforded some form of official immunity was not presented as a question to be decided on this petition and was not briefed by the parties or addressed by the courts below, we express no views on the scope of any municipal immunity beyond holding that municipal bodies sued under § 1983 cannot be entitled to an absolute immunity, lest our decision that such bodies are subject to suit under § 1983 "be drained of meaning."

V

For the reasons stated above, the judgment of the Court of Appeals is

Reversed.

MR. JUSTICE POWELL, concurring.

I join the opinion of the Court, and express these additional views.

Few cases in the history of the Court have been cited more frequently than *Monroe v. Pape,* decided less than two decades ago. Focusing new light on 42 U.S.C. § 1983, that decision widened access to the federal courts and permitted expansive interpretations of the reach of the 1871 measure. But *Monroe* exempted local governments from liability at the same time it opened wide the courthouse door to suits against officers and employees of those entities—even when they act pursuant to express authorization. The oddness of this result, and the weakness of the historical evidence relied on by the *Monroe* Court in support of it, are well demonstrated by the Court's opinion today. Yet the gravity of overruling a part of so important a decision prompts me to write.

I

In addressing a complaint alleging unconstitutional police conduct that probably was unauthorized and actionable under state law, the *Monroe* Court treated the 42d Congress' rejection of the Sherman amendment as conclusive evidence of an intention to immunize local governments from all liability under the statute for constitutional injury. That reading, in light of today's thorough canvass of the legislative history, clearly "misapprehended the meaning of the controlling provision." In this case, involving formal, written policies of the Department of Social Services and the Board of Education of the city of New York that are alleged to conflict with the command of the Due Process Clause, the Court decides "not to reject [wisdom] merely because it comes late."

As the Court demonstrates, the Sherman amendment presented an extreme example of "riot act" legislation that sought to impose vicarious liability on government subdivisions for the consequences of private lawlessness. As such, it implicated concerns that are of marginal pertinence to the operative principle of § 1 of the 1871 legislation—now § 1983— that "any person" acting "under color of" state law may be held liable for affirmative conduct that "subjects, or causes to be subjected, any person * * * to the deprivation of any" federal constitutional or statutory right. Of the many reasons for the defeat of the Sherman proposal, none supports *Monroe*'s observation that the 42d Congress was fundamentally "antagonistic," to the proposition that government entities and natural persons alike should be held accountable for the consequences of conduct directly working a constitutional violation. Opponents in the Senate appear to have been troubled primarily by the proposal's unprecedented lien provision, which would have exposed even property held for public purposes to the demands of § 1983 judgment lienors. The opposition in the House of Representatives focused largely on the Sherman amendment's attempt to impose a peacekeeping obligation on municipalities when the Constitution itself imposed no such affirmative duty and when many municipalities were not even empowered under state law to maintain police forces.

The Court correctly rejects a view of the legislative history that would produce the anomalous result of immunizing local government units from monetary liability for action directly causing a constitutional deprivation, even though such actions may be fully consistent with, and thus not remediable under, state law. No conduct of government comes more clearly within the "under color of" state law language of § 1983. It is most unlikely that Congress intended public officials acting under the command or the specific authorization of the government employer to be *exclusively* liable for resulting constitutional injury.

As elaborated in Part II of today's opinion, the rejection of the Sherman amendment can best be understood not as evidence of Congress' acceptance of a rule of absolute municipal immunity but as a limitation of the statutory ambit to actual wrongdoers, *i.e.,* a rejection of *respondeat superior* or any other principle of vicarious liability. Thus, it has been clear that a public official may be held liable in damages when his actions are found to violate a constitutional right and there is no qualified immunity. Today the Court recognizes that this principle also applies to a local government when implementation of its official policies or established customs inflicts the constitutional injury.

* * *

Mr. Justice Rehnquist, with whom The Chief Justice joins, dissenting.

Seventeen years ago, in *Monroe v. Pape,* this Court held that the 42d Congress did not intend to subject a municipal corporation to liability as a "person" within the meaning of 42 U.S.C. § 1983. Since then, the Congress has remained silent, but this Court has reaffirmed that holding on at least three separate occasions. Today, the Court abandons this long and consistent line of precedents, offering in justification only an elaborate canvass of the same legislative history which was before the Court in 1961. Because I cannot agree that this Court is "free to disregard these precedents," which have been "considered maturely and recently" by this Court, I am compelled to dissent.

I

As this Court has repeatedly recognized, considerations of *stare decisis* are at their strongest when this Court confronts its previous constructions of legislation. In all cases, private parties shape their conduct according to this Court's settled construction of the law, but the Congress is at liberty to correct our mistakes of statutory construction, unlike our constitutional interpretations, whenever it sees fit. The controlling principles were best stated by Mr. Justice Brandeis:

> *Stare decisis* is usually the wise policy, because in most matters it is more important that the applicable rule of law be settled than that it be settled right. * * * This is commonly true even where the error is a matter of serious concern, provided correction can be had by legislation. But in cases involving the Federal Constitution, where correction through legislative action is practically impossible, this court has often overruled its earlier decisions.

Only the most compelling circumstances can justify this Court's abandonment of such firmly established statutory precedents. The best exposition of the proper burden of persuasion was delivered by Mr. Justice Harlan in *Monroe* itself:

> From my point of view, the policy of *stare decisis,* as it should be applied in matters of statutory construction, and, to a lesser extent, the indications of congressional acceptance of this Court's earlier interpretation, require that it appear *beyond doubt* from the legislative history of the 1871 statute that [*United States v.*] *Classic* and *Screws* [*v. United States*] misapprehended the meaning of the controlling provision, before a departure from what was decided in

those cases would be justified." (Emphasis added).

The Court does not demonstrate that any exception to this general rule is properly applicable here. The Court's first assertion, that *Monroe* "was a departure from prior practice," is patently erroneous. * * *

Nor is there any indication that any later Congress has ever approved suit against any municipal corporation under § 1983. Of all its recent enactments, only the Civil Rights Attorney's Fees Awards Act of 1976 explicitly deals with the Civil Rights Act of 1871. The 1976 Act provides that attorney's fees may be awarded to the prevailing party "[i]n any action or proceeding to enforce a provision of sections 1981, 1982, 1983, 1985, and 1986 of this title." There is plainly no language in the 1976 Act which would enlarge the parties suable under those substantive sections; it simply provides that parties who are already suable may be made liable for attorney's fees. As the Court admits, the language in the Senate Report stating that liability may be imposed "whether or not the agency or government is a named party," suggests that Congress did not view its purpose as being in any way inconsistent with the well-known holding of *Monroe.*

The Court's assertion that municipalities have no right to act "on an assumption that they can violate constitutional rights indefinitely," is simply beside the point. Since *Monroe,* municipalities have had the right to expect that they would not be held liable retroactively for their officers' failure to predict this Court's recognition of new constitutional rights. No doubt innumerable municipal insurance policies and indemnity ordinances have been founded on this assumption, which is wholly justifiable under established principles of *stare decisis.* To obliterate those legitimate expectations without more compelling justifications than those advanced by the Court is a significant departure from our prior practice.

I cannot agree with Mr. Justice Powell's view that "[w]e owe somewhat less deference to a decision that was rendered without benefit of a full airing of all the relevant considerations." Private parties must be able to rely upon explicitly stated holdings of this Court without being obliged to peruse the briefs of the litigants to predict the likelihood that this Court might change its mind. To cast such doubt upon each of our cases, from *Marbury v. Madison* (1803) forward, in which the explicit ground of decision "was never actually briefed or argued," would introduce intolerable uncertainty into the law. Indeed, in *Marbury* itself, the argument of Charles Lee on behalf of the applicants—which, unlike the arguments in *Monroe,* is reproduced in the Reports of this Court where anyone can see it—devotes not a word to the question of whether this Court has the power to invalidate a statute duly enacted by the Congress. Neither this ground of decision nor any other was advanced by Secretary of State Madison, who evidently made no appearance. More recent landmark decisions of this Court would appear to be likewise vulnerable under my Brother Powell's analysis. In *Mapp v. Ohio* (1961), none of the parties requested the Court to overrule *Wolf v. Colorado;* it did so only at the request of an *amicus curiae*. That *Marbury, Mapp,* and countless other decisions retain their vitality despite their obvious flaws is a necessary by-product of the adversary system, in which both judges and the general public rely upon litigants to present "all the relevant considerations." While it undoubtedly has more latitude in the field of constitutional interpretation, this Court is surely not free to abandon settled statutory interpretation at any time a new thought seems appealing.

Thus, our only task is to discern the intent of the 42d Congress. That intent was first expounded in *Monroe,* and it has been followed consistently ever since. * * * In these circumstances, it cannot be disputed that established principles of *stare decisis* require this Court to pay the highest degree of deference to its prior holdings. *Monroe* may not be overruled unless it has been demonstrated "beyond doubt from the legislative history of the 1871 statute that [*Monroe*] misapprehended the meaning of the controlling provision." The Court must show not only that Congress, in rejecting the Sherman amendment, concluded that municipal liability was not unconstitutional, but also that, in enacting § 1, it intended to impose that liability. I am satisfied that no such showing has been made.

* * *

III

The decision in *Monroe v. Pape* was the fountainhead of the torrent of civil rights litigation of the last 17 years. Using § 1983 as a vehicle, the courts have articulated new and previously unforeseeable interpretations of the Fourteenth Amendment. At the same time, the doctrine of municipal immunity enunciated in *Monroe* has protected municipalities and their limited treasuries from the consequences of their officials' failure to predict the course of this Court's constitutional jurisprudence. None of the Members of this Court can foresee the practical consequences of today's removal of that protection. Only the Congress, which has the benefit of the advice of every segment of this diverse Nation, is equipped to consider the results of such a drastic change in the law. It seems all but inevitable that it will find it necessary to do so after today's decision.

I would affirm the judgment of the Court of Appeals.

Notes and Questions

1. a) *Monell* notes that there are at least three possible bases for municipal liability: liability for acts directly authorized by the municipality, liability for acts of municipal agents on a *respondeat superior* theory, and liability for the acts of private parties. The majority infers that because Congress rejected the last when it voted down the Sherman Amendment, it

therefore rejected the second also. Does that conclusion follow ineluctably from Congress's rejection of § 7?

b) With respect to *respondeat superior* liability, Justice Brennan appears to resurrect the distinction between authorized and unauthorized acts that Justice Frankfurter urged in *Monroe* but that the *Monroe* majority (which included Justice Brennan) rejected. Is the Court inconsistent or can the two approaches be harmonized? If the former, which approach should the Court embrace?

c) Shortly before *Monell,* the question of *respondeat superior* liability under § 1983 arose in a different context. The plaintiff class in *Rizzo v. Goode,* 423 U.S. 362, 96 S.Ct. 598, 46 L.Ed.2d 561 (1976), alleged widespread excessive use of force by Philadelphia police and challenged the city's lack of effective review procedures for citizen complaints. The primary defendants were the Mayor of Philadelphia, the City Police Commissioner, and the City Managing Director.

> The central thrust of [plaintiffs'] efforts * * * was to lay a foundation for equitable intervention, in one degree or another, because of an assertedly pervasive pattern of illegal and unconstitutional mistreatment by police officers. This mistreatment was said to have been directed at minority citizens in particular and against all Philadelphia residents in general.

> Hearing some 250 witnesses during 21 days of hearings, the District Court was faced with a staggering amount of evidence; each of the 40-odd incidents might alone have been the *pièce de résistance* of a short, separate trial.

The Court denied equitable relief for several reasons. First, and most germane to *Monell,* the Court ruled that § 1983 liability required that the named defendants have played an active part in the constitutional deprivations, either directly or by establishing the policies and practices governing the offending police conduct. "As the facts developed, there was no affirmative link between the occurrence of the various incidents of police misconduct and the adoption of any plan or policy by petitioners—express or otherwise—showing their authorization or approval of such misconduct."

Thus, the majority insisted on a direct, causal connection between each defendant's performance of duty and the deprivation of constitutional rights. The multiple incidents cited by the plaintiffs did not establish the linkage required to cast highly-placed officials in liability. The Court distinguished cases in which high officials were directly linked to pervasive patterns of deprivation of constitutional rights and declined to read § 1983 to allow liability on the basis merely of failure to control or eliminate random police abuses.

The liability that the *Rizzo* plaintiffs sought to establish differs little in structure from *respondeat superior* liability. The only apparent difference is that the supervisory officials in *Rizzo* were not, technically speaking, either the employers or the principals of the individual police officers. The Court's insistence in *Rizzo* on a direct, causal connection to establish individual liability compares closely with its insistence in *Monell* on finding a municipal statute, ordinance, custom, usage or policy in order to establish municipal liability.[2]

2. a) Is it significant that Congress did not repudiate *Monroe*'s holding that municipalities were not § 1983 persons? Had Congress at least acquiesced in the conclusion? Justice Rehnquist's dissent seizes upon Congress's inaction in the face of *Monroe* to argue that *Monroe* should be overruled only if the *Monroe* Court was wrong beyond doubt. Of course, time has an ironic way of affecting such arguments. The Congresses since *Monell* have not repudiated it, despite Justice Rehnquist's prediction that it was "all but inevitable that [Congress] would find it necessary to" address the problem of municipal liability in *Monell*'s wake. *Monell*'s life span now exceeds *Monroe*'s. If municipal liability under § 1983 again is an issue before the Court, should Chief Justice Rehnquist abandon his position in *Monell*?

b) It is possible that Congress disagreed with *Monroe* but also felt it unnecessary to act. Between *Monroe* in 1961 and *Monell* in 1978, lower federal courts routinely implied rights of action against municipalities directly under the Fourteenth Amendment. *See, e.g., Turpin v. Mailet,* 579 F.2d 152, 164 n. 36 (2d Cir.1978) (en banc) ("Indeed, we are not aware of any federal Court of Appeals which has held that a damage action should not be implied from the fourteenth amendment where the municipality itself was responsible for the unconstitutional action.").

c) Assuming the Congresses from 1961 to 1978 either agreed with or acquiesced in *Monroe,* is that fact even relevant to a proper interpretation of § 1983, which the Congress of 1871 enacted? Should the Court as a general rule be concerned with congressional intent as an on-going matter, or only with the intent of the Congress that passes a particular bill?

3. What should be required to attribute an act to a municipality for purposes of establishing § 1983 liability? How much is necessary to establish municipal "custom or usage"? How can one demonstrate the existence of a municipal policy other than one declared in a statute or ordinance? The Court has addressed these issues in a series of cases.

a) *Pembaur v. City of Cincinnati,* 475 U.S. 469, 106 S.Ct. 1292, 89 L.Ed.2d 452 (1986), held that individuals with final authority over a particular matter may establish municipal policy for purposes of § 1983. The county prosecutor directed local police to serve a subpoena by breaking down the office door of a physician thought to be evading service. Though there was no articulated policy to use forcible entry to serve subpoenas generally, the Court held the prosecutor's action sufficient to establish a policy. Thus, an individual decision can be a "policy" even if it is not of general application, and an isolated act may suffice for municipal liability. *But see Board of*

---

[2] *Rizzo* is significant for two other reasons as well. First, the Court found equitable relief inappropriate on standing grounds, for reasons discussed in Chapter 1 at pages 54-55. Second, the Court thought abstention under the doctrine of Younger v. Harris, 401 U.S. 37, 91 S.Ct. 746, 27 L.Ed.2d 669 (1971), was appropriate. Chapter 8 at page 836 discusses this aspect of *Rizzo.*

the County Commissioners v. Brown, at page 555. On the other hand, the Court distinguished between a policy-making body giving discretion to an official and the official having policy-making power. If this distinction seems to the reader difficult to administer, take comfort in the fact that the lower federal courts have not found it any easier. The circuits have, for example, split as to whether police chiefs and sheriffs, city managers, and judges are policy makers for purposes of § 1983.

In *City of St. Louis v. Praprotnik*, 485 U.S. 112, 108 S.Ct. 915, 99 L.Ed.2d 107 (1988), a plurality concluded that whether someone is a "policy maker" is a question of state law, not an issue of fact. A majority adopted that holding in *Jett v. Dallas Independent School District*, 491 U.S. 701, 109 S.Ct. 2702, 105 L.Ed.2d 598 (1989). Thus, the issue of whether someone is a policy maker is for the court, not the jury. The broad policy statements of these decisions, however, do little to help the lower courts determine in particular cases whether an official is a policy maker under state law. What should be the *indicia* of policy making under state law? Does the Court's approach pave the way for the unconstitutional acts of individuals becoming unreachable under federal law?

b) A different question was bound to arise, and did, about when municipal failure to act could be deemed a policy. In *City of Canton v. Harris,* 489 U.S. 378, 109 S.Ct. 1197, 103 L.Ed.2d 417 (1989), police arrested Geraldine Harris when she became upset after receiving a speeding ticket. When the police van arrived at the police station, she was sitting on the floor of the van. Police asked her if she needed medical attention, and she responded incoherently. After police took her inside the station for processing, she twice slumped to the floor, and the police finally left her there to prevent her from falling again. They did not summon medical assistance. After an hour, they released Mrs. Harris, whose family took her by ambulance to a hospital. Physicians diagnosed her as suffering from severe emotional ailments; she remained at the hospital for a week and thereafter received outpatient treatment for a year.

The plaintiff claimed that the City's policy of vesting complete discretion in police station commanders about when detainees should receive medical aid amounted to an actionable failure properly to train city employees. The City argued that it could be found liable only if the underlying policy itself were unconstitutional. The policy stated that a person needing medical care should be taken to a hospital, with the consent of the shift commander. The majority held that failure to train could support an action under § 1983, but "only where the failure to train amounts to deliberate indifference to the rights of persons with whom the police come into contact." The Court emphasized that random unconstitutional behavior by a single employee is not sufficient to cast the municipality in liability.

> Neither will it suffice to prove that an injury or accident could have been avoided if an officer had had better or more training, sufficient to equip him to avoid the particular injury-causing conduct. Such a claim could be made about almost any encounter resulting in injury, yet not condemn the adequacy of the [training] program * * * .

Moreover, for liability to attach in this circumstance the identified deficiency in a city's training program must be closely related to the ultimate injury. Thus in the case at hand, respondent must still prove that the deficiency in training actually caused the police officers' indifference to her medical needs.

The Court then remanded the case for further proceedings.

How might a plaintiff be able to satisfy the Court's failure-to-train standard? Has the Court created an illusory possibility of successful suit, establishing a standard that all but the most dense municipal policy makers will be able to meet? If a municipality proceeds in the face of a known risk (a standard analogous to the *mens rea* of recklessness), is that deliberate indifference, or must a plaintiff show something akin to "knowledge"?

All of the cases in this mold are likely to be fact-intensive. As a practical matter, how can a plaintiff go about proving deliberate indifference? Is it the plaintiff's burden to rummage through the records of municipal proceedings to unearth evidence of municipal awareness of the risks of its training policy, or should the burden (at least of production) of showing the reasonableness of the training policy be placed in the first instance on the municipality? In this respect, consider the Court's views on executive immunities, at pages 576-598.

4. *Monell* left many unanswered questions, some of which later chapters discuss at length. First, is a state, rather than a political subdivision of a state, a "person" within the meaning of 42 U.S.C.A. § 1983? Similarly, are state-level officials § 1983 persons? One might have thought, given *Monell's* partial reliance on the Dictionary Act, that the Court had left the way open also for § 1983 suits against states, but the Court made clear in *Will v. Michigan Department of State Police*, 491 U.S. 58, 109 S.Ct. 2304, 105 L.Ed.2d 45 (1989), that states (and state-level officials sued in their official capacities) are not "persons" within the meaning of § 1983, largely because of the Eleventh Amendment implications of the reverse position. "[I]n enacting § 1983, Congress did not intend to override well-established immunities or defenses under the common law * * * ." *See infra* at 670, Note 3 b).

Second, can local governmental units claim a qualified immunity from suit? *Owen v. City of Independence*, 445 U.S. 622, 100 S.Ct. 1398, 63 L.Ed.2d 673 (1980), held that they cannot. The Court noted that the language of § 1983 makes no mention of immunities, but rather imposes liability on "*every* person" who violates an individual's rights under color of state law. The Justices did recognize that certain immunities were so well established at common law that "Congress would have specifically so provided had it wished their abrogation," and so viewed the statute as having incorporated those immunities. However, the Court held that there was no common law tradition of municipal immunity and that neither history nor policy justified creating one. In the process, the Court rejected the idea that municipalities, as arms of the state when acting in governmental capacities, shared the states' sovereign immunity, holding instead that the passage of § 1983 "abolished whatever vestige of the State's sovereign immunity the municipality possessed." Finally, the Justices refused to insulate municipalities even in cases where they exercised discretionary powers,

The third issue is whether a municipality is subject to punitive damages. *City of Newport v. Fact Concerts, Inc.,* 453 U.S. 247, 101 S.Ct. 2748, 69 L.Ed.2d 616 (1981), answered negatively. The Court reasoned that a municipality cannot have malice independent of that of its officials, and that damages awarded for punitive purposes cannot sensibly be assessed against the municipality itself, particularly since the availability of punitive damages against officials *individually* will provide deterrence without subjecting local governments to potentially crippling awards.

BOARD OF THE COUNTY COMMISSIONERS v. BROWN
Supreme Court of the United States, 1997.
520 U.S. 397, 117 S.Ct. 1382, 137 L.Ed.2d 626.

JUSTICE O'CONNOR delivered the opinion of the Court.

Respondent Jill Brown brought a claim for damages against petitioner Bryan County under Rev. Stat. § 1979, 42 U.S.C. § 1983. She alleged that a county police officer used excessive force in arresting her, and that the county itself was liable for her injuries based on its sheriff's hiring and training decisions. She prevailed on her claims against the county following a jury trial, and the Court of Appeals for the Fifth Circuit affirmed the judgment against the county on the basis of the hiring claim alone. We granted certiorari. We conclude that the Court of Appeals' decision cannot be squared with our recognition that, in enacting § 1983, Congress did not intend to impose liability on a municipality unless *deliberate* action attributable to the municipality itself is the "moving force" behind the plaintiff's deprivation of federal rights.

I

In the early morning hours of May 12, 1991, respondent Jill Brown and her husband were driving from Grayson County, Texas, to their home in Bryan County, Oklahoma. After crossing into Oklahoma, they approached a police checkpoint. Mr. Brown, who was driving, decided to avoid the checkpoint and return to Texas. After seeing the Browns' truck turn away from the checkpoint, Bryan County Deputy Sheriff Robert Morrison and Reserve Deputy Stacy Burns pursued the vehicle. Although the parties' versions of events differ, at trial both deputies claimed that their patrol car reached speeds in excess of 100 miles per hour. Mr. Brown testified that he was unaware of the deputies' attempts to overtake him. The chase finally ended four miles south of the police checkpoint.

After he got out of the squad car, Deputy Sheriff Morrison pointed his gun toward the Browns' vehicle and ordered the Browns to raise their hands. Reserve Deputy Burns, who was unarmed, rounded the corner of the vehicle on the passenger's side. Burns twice ordered respondent Jill Brown from the vehicle. When she did not exit, he used an "arm bar" technique, grabbing respondent's arm at the wrist and elbow, pulling her from the vehicle, and spinning her to the ground. Respondent's knees were severely injured, and she later underwent corrective surgery. Ultimately, she may need knee replacements.

Respondent sought compensation for her injuries under 42 U.S.C. § 1983 and state law from Burns, Bryan County Sheriff B.J. Moore, and the county itself. Respondent claimed, among other things, that Bryan County was liable for Burns' alleged use of excessive force based on Sheriff Moore's decision to hire Burns, the son of his nephew. Specifically, respondent claimed that Sheriff Moore had failed to adequately review Burns' background. Burns had a record of driving infractions and had pleaded guilty to various driving-related and other misdemeanors, including assault and battery, resisting arrest, and public drunkenness. Oklahoma law does not preclude the hiring of an individual who has committed a misdemeanor to serve as a peace officer. At trial, Sheriff Moore testified that he had obtained Burns' driving record and a report on Burns from the National Crime Information Center, but had not closely reviewed either. Sheriff Moore authorized Burns to make arrests, but not to carry a weapon or to operate a patrol car.

* * * Counsel for Bryan County stipulated that Sheriff Moore "was the policy maker for Bryan County regarding the Sheriff's Department." At the close of respondent's case and again at the close of all of the evidence, Bryan County moved for judgment as a matter of law. As to respondent's claim that Sheriff Moore's decision to hire Burns triggered municipal liability, the county argued that a single hiring decision by a municipal policymaker could not give rise to municipal liability under § 1983. The District Court denied the county's motions. * * *

To resolve respondent's claims, the jury was asked to answer several interrogatories. The jury concluded that Stacy Burns had arrested respondent without probable cause and had used excessive force, and therefore found him liable for respondent's injuries. It also found that the "hiring policy" and the "training policy" of Bryan County "in the case of Stacy Burns as instituted by its policymaker, B.J. Moore," were each "so inadequate as to amount to deliberate indifference to the constitutional needs of the Plaintiff." The District Court entered judgment for respondent on the issue of Bryan County's § 1983 liability. The county appealed on several grounds, and the Court of Appeals for the Fifth Circuit * * * held, among other things, that Bryan County was properly found liable under § 1983 based on Sheriff Moore's decision to hire Burns. The court addressed only those points that it thought merited review; it did not address the jury's determination of county liability based on inadequate training of Burns, nor do we. We granted certiorari to decide whether the county was properly held liable for respondent's injuries based on Sheriff Moore's single decision to hire Burns. We now reverse.

II

* * *

The parties join issue on whether, under *Monell* (1978) and subsequent cases, a single hiring decision by a county sheriff can be a "policy" that triggers municipal liability. Relying on our decision in *Pembaur* (1986), respondent claims that a single act by a decisionmaker with final authority in the relevant area constitutes a "policy" attributable to the municipality itself. So long as a § 1983 plaintiff identifies a decision properly attributable to the municipality, respondent argues, there is no risk of imposing *respondeat superior* liability. Whether that decision was intended to govern only the situation at hand or to serve as a rule to be applied over time is immaterial. Rather, under respondent's theory, identification of an act of a proper municipal decisionmaker is all that is required to ensure that the municipality is held liable only for its own conduct. The Court of Appeals accepted respondent's approach.

As our § 1983 municipal liability jurisprudence illustrates, however, it is not enough for a § 1983 plaintiff merely to identify conduct properly attributable to the municipality. The plaintiff must also demonstrate that, through its *deliberate* conduct, the municipality was the "moving force" behind the injury alleged. That is, a plaintiff must show that the municipal action was taken with the requisite degree of culpability and must demonstrate a direct causal link between the municipal action and the deprivation of federal rights.

Where a plaintiff claims that a particular municipal action *itself* violates federal law, or directs an employee to do so, resolving these issues of fault and causation is straightforward. Section 1983 itself "contains no state-of-mind requirement independent of that necessary to state a violation" of the underlying federal right. In any § 1983 suit, however, the plaintiff must establish the state of mind required to prove the underlying violation. Accordingly, proof that a municipality's legislative body or authorized decisionmaker has intentionally deprived a plaintiff of a federally protected right necessarily establishes that the municipality acted culpably. Similarly, the conclusion that the action taken or directed by the municipality or its authorized decisionmaker itself violates federal law will also determine that the municipal action was the moving force behind the injury of which the plaintiff complains.

Sheriff Moore's hiring decision was itself legal, and Sheriff Moore did not authorize Burns to use excessive force. Respondent's claim, rather, is that a single facially lawful hiring decision can launch a series of events that ultimately cause a violation of federal rights. Where a plaintiff claims that the municipality has not directly inflicted an injury, but nonetheless has caused an employee to do so, rigorous standards of culpability and causation must be applied to ensure that the municipality is not held liable solely for the actions of its employee.

In relying heavily on *Pembaur*, respondent blurs the distinction between § 1983 cases that present no difficult questions of fault and causation and those that do. To the extent that we have recognized a cause of action under § 1983 based on a single decision attributable to a municipality, we have done so only where the evidence that the municipality had acted and that the plaintiff had suffered a deprivation of federal rights also proved fault and causation. For example, [two cases] involved formal decisions of municipal legislative bodies. In *Owen*, the city council allegedly censured and discharged an employee without a hearing. In *Fact Concerts*, the city council canceled a license permitting a concert following a dispute over the performance's content. Neither decision reflected implementation of a generally applicable rule. But we did not question that each decision, duly promulgated by city lawmakers, could trigger municipal liability if the decision itself were found to be unconstitutional. Because fault and causation were obvious in each case, proof that the municipality's decision was unconstitutional would suffice to establish that the municipality itself was liable for the plaintiff's constitutional injury.

Similarly, *Pembaur* concerned a decision by a county prosecutor, acting as the county's final decisionmaker to direct county deputies to forcibly enter petitioner's place of business to serve *capiases* upon third parties. Relying on *Owen* (1980) and *Newport* (1981), we concluded that a final decisionmaker's adoption of a course of action "tailored to a particular situation and not intended to control decisions in later situations" may, in some circumstances, give rise to municipal liability under § 1983. In *Pembaur*, it was not disputed that the prosecutor had specifically directed the action resulting in the deprivation of petitioner's rights. The conclusion that the decision was that of a final municipal decisionmaker and was therefore properly attributable to the municipality established municipal liability. No questions of fault or causation arose.

Claims not involving an allegation that the municipal action itself violated federal law, or directed or authorized the deprivation of federal rights, present much more difficult problems of proof. That a plaintiff has suffered a deprivation of federal rights at the hands of a municipal employee will not alone permit an inference of municipal culpability and causation; the plaintiff will simply have shown that the *employee* acted culpably. We recognized these difficulties in *Canton v. Harris* (1989), where we considered a claim that inadequate training of shift supervisors at a city jail led to a deprivation of a detainee's constitutional rights. We held that, quite apart from the state of mind required to establish the underlying constitutional violation—in that case, a violation of due process—a plaintiff seeking to establish municipal liability on the theory that a facially lawful municipal action has led an employee to violate a plaintiff's rights must demonstrate that the municipal action was taken with "deliberate indifference" as to its known or obvious consequences.

A showing of simple or even heightened negligence will not suffice.

We concluded in *Canton* that an "inadequate training" claim could be the basis for § 1983 liability in "limited circumstances." We spoke, however, of a deficient training "program," necessarily intended to apply over time to multiple employees. Existence of a "program" makes proof of fault and causation at least possible in an inadequate training case. If a program does not prevent constitutional violations, municipal decisionmakers may eventually be put on notice that a new program is called for. Their continued adherence to an approach that they know or should know has failed to prevent tortious conduct by employees may establish the conscious disregard for the consequences of their action—the "deliberate indifference"—necessary to trigger municipal liability. * * * In addition, the existence of a pattern of tortious conduct by inadequately trained employees may tend to show that the lack of proper training, rather than a one-time negligent administration of the program or factors peculiar to the officer involved in a particular incident, is the "moving force" behind the plaintiff's injury.

Before trial, counsel for Bryan County stipulated that Sheriff Moore "was the policy maker for Bryan County regarding the Sheriff's Department." Indeed, the county sought to avoid liability by claiming that its Board of Commissioners participated in no policy decisions regarding the conduct and operation of the office of the Bryan County Sheriff. Accepting the county's representations below, then, this case presents no difficult questions concerning whether Sheriff Moore has final authority to act for the municipality in hiring matters. Respondent does not claim that she can identify any pattern of injuries linked to Sheriff Moore's hiring practices. Indeed, respondent does not contend that Sheriff Moore's hiring practices are generally defective. The only evidence on this point at trial suggested that Sheriff Moore had adequately screened the backgrounds of all prior deputies he hired. Respondent instead seeks to trace liability to what can only be described as a deviation from Sheriff Moore's ordinary hiring practices. Where a claim of municipal liability rests on a single decision, not itself representing a violation of federal law and not directing such a violation, the danger that a municipality will be held liable without fault is high. Because the decision necessarily governs a single case, there can be no notice to the municipal decisionmaker, based on previous violations of federally protected rights, that his approach is inadequate. Nor will it be readily apparent that the municipality's action caused the injury in question, because the plaintiff can point to no other incident tending to make it more likely that the plaintiff's own injury flows from the municipality's action, rather than from some other intervening cause.

In *Canton*, we did not foreclose the possibility that evidence of a single violation of federal rights, accompanied by a showing that a municipality has failed to train its employees to handle recurring situations presenting an obvious potential for such a violation, could trigger municipal liability. * * * Respondent purports to rely on *Canton*, arguing that Burns' use of excessive force was the plainly obvious consequence of Sheriff Moore's failure to screen Burns' record. In essence, respondent claims that this showing of "obviousness" would demonstrate both that Sheriff Moore acted with conscious disregard for the consequences of his action and that the Sheriff's action directly caused her injuries, and would thus substitute for the pattern of injuries ordinarily necessary to establish municipal culpability and causation.

The proffered analogy between failure-to-train cases and inadequate screening cases is not persuasive. In leaving open in *Canton* the possibility that a plaintiff might succeed in carrying a failure-to-train claim without showing a pattern of constitutional violations, we simply hypothesized that, in a narrow range of circumstances, a violation of federal rights may be a highly predictable consequence of a failure to equip law enforcement officers with specific tools to handle recurring situations. The likelihood that the situation will recur and the predictability that an officer lacking specific tools to handle that situation will violate citizens' rights could justify a finding that policymakers' decision not to train the officer reflected "deliberate indifference" to the obvious consequence of the policymakers' choice—namely, a violation of a specific constitutional or statutory right. The high degree of predictability may also support an inference of causation—that the municipality's indifference led directly to the very consequence that was so predictable.

Where a plaintiff presents a § 1983 claim premised upon the inadequacy of an official's review of a prospective applicant's record, however, there is a particular danger that a municipality will be held liable for an injury not directly caused by a deliberate action attributable to the municipality itself. Every injury suffered at the hands of a municipal employee can be traced to a hiring decision in a "but-for" sense: But for the municipality's decision to hire the employee, the plaintiff would not have suffered the injury. To prevent municipal liability for a hiring decision from collapsing into *respondeat superior* liability, a court must carefully test the link between the policymaker's inadequate decision and the particular injury alleged.

In attempting to import the reasoning of *Canton* into the hiring context, respondent ignores the fact that predicting the consequence of a single hiring decision, even one based on an inadequate assessment of a record, is far more difficult than predicting what might flow from the failure to train a single law enforcement officer as to a specific skill necessary to the discharge of his duties. * * * "[D]eliberate indifference" is a stringent standard of fault, requiring proof that a municipal actor disregarded a known or obvious consequence of his action. Unlike the risk from a particular glaring omission in a training regimen, the risk from a single instance of inadequate screening of an applicant's background is not "obvious" in the abstract; rather, it depends upon the background of the applicant. A lack of scrutiny may increase the likelihood that an unfit officer will be hired, and that the unfit officer will, when placed in a particular position to affect the rights of citizens, act improperly. But that is only a generalized showing of risk. The fact that inadequate scrutiny of an applicant's background would make a violation of rights more *likely* cannot alone give rise to an inference that a policymaker's failure to scrutinize the record of a particular applicant produced a specific constitutional violation. After all, a full screening of an applicant's background might reveal no cause for concern at all; if so, a hiring official who failed to scrutinize the applicant's background cannot be said to have consciously disregarded an obvious risk that the officer would subsequently inflict a particular constitutional injury.

We assume that a jury could properly find in this case that Sheriff Moore's assessment of Burns' background was inadequate. Sheriff Moore's own testimony indicated that he did not inquire into the underlying conduct or the disposition of any of the misdemeanor charges reflected on Burns' record before hiring him. But this showing of an instance of inadequate screening is not enough to establish "deliberate indifference." In layman's terms, inadequate screening of an applicant's record may reflect "indifference" to the applicant's background. For purposes of a legal inquiry into municipal liability under § 1983, however, that is not the *relevant* "indifference." A plaintiff must demonstrate that a municipal decision reflects deliberate indifference to the risk that a violation of a particular constitutional or statutory right will follow the decision. Only where adequate scrutiny of an applicant's background would lead a reasonable policymaker to conclude that the plainly obvious consequence of the decision to hire the applicant would be the deprivation of a third party's federally protected right can the official's failure to adequately scrutinize the applicant's background constitute "deliberate indifference."

Neither the District Court nor the Court of Appeals directly tested the link between Burns' actual background and the risk that, if hired, he would use excessive force. The District Court instructed the jury on a theory analogous to that reserved in *Canton*. The court required respondent to prove that Sheriff Moore's inadequate screening of Burns' background was "so likely to result in *violations of constitutional rights*" that the Sheriff could "reasonably [be] said to have been deliberately indifferent to the *constitutional needs* of the Plaintiff." The court also instructed the jury, without elaboration, that respondent was required to prove that the "inadequate hiring * * * policy directly caused the Plaintiff's injury."

As discussed above, a finding of culpability simply cannot depend on the mere probability that any officer inadequately screened will inflict any constitutional injury. Rather, it must depend on a finding that this officer was highly likely to inflict the *particular* injury suffered by the plaintiff. The connection between the background of the particular applicant and the specific constitutional violation alleged must be strong. What the District Court's instructions on culpability, and therefore the jury's finding of municipal liability, failed to capture is whether Burns' background made his use of excessive force in making an arrest a plainly obvious consequence of the hiring decision. The Court of Appeals' affirmance of the jury's finding of municipal liability depended on its view that the jury could have found that "inadequate screening of *a deputy* could likely result in the violation of *citizens' constitutional rights*." Beyond relying on a risk of violations of unspecified constitutional rights, the Court of Appeals also posited that Sheriff Moore's decision reflected indifference to "the public's welfare."

Even assuming without deciding that proof of a single instance of inadequate screening could ever trigger municipal liability, the evidence in this case was insufficient to support a finding that, in hiring Burns, Sheriff Moore disregarded a known or obvious risk of injury. To test the link between Sheriff Moore's hiring decision and respondent's injury, we must ask whether a full review of Burns' record reveals that Sheriff Moore should have concluded that Burns' use of excessive force would be a plainly obvious consequence of the hiring decision.[1] On this point, respondent's showing was inadequate. To be sure, Burns' record reflected various misdemeanor infractions. Respondent claims that the record demonstrated such a strong propensity for violence that Burns' application of excessive force was highly likely. The primary charges on which respondent relies, however, are those arising from a fight on a college campus where Burns was a student. In connection with this single incident, Burns was charged with assault and battery, resisting arrest, and public drunkenness.[2] In January 1990, when he pleaded guilty to those charges, Burns also pleaded guilty to various driving-related offenses, including nine moving violations and a charge of driving with a suspended license. In addition, Burns had previously pleaded guilty to being in actual physical control of a vehicle while intoxicated.

---

[1] In suggesting that our decision complicates this Court's § 1983 municipal liability jurisprudence by altering the understanding of culpability, Justice Souter and Justice Breyer misunderstand our approach. We do not suggest that a plaintiff in an inadequate screening case must show a higher degree of culpability than the "deliberate indifference" required in *Canton*; we need not do so, because, as discussed below, respondent has not made a showing of deliberate indifference here. Furthermore, in assessing the risks of a decision to hire a particular individual, we draw no distinction between what is "so obvious" or "so likely to occur" and what is "plainly obvious." The difficulty with the lower courts' approach is that it fails to connect the background of the particular officer hired in this case to the particular constitutional violation the respondent suffered. Ensuring that lower courts link the background of the officer to the constitutional violation alleged does not complicate our municipal liability jurisprudence with degrees of "obviousness," but seeks to ensure that a plaintiff in an inadequate screening case establishes a policymaker's deliberate indifference—that is, conscious disregard for the known and obvious consequences of his actions.

[2] Justice Souter implies that Burns' record reflected assault and battery charges arising from more than one incident. There has never been a serious dispute that a single misdemeanor assault and battery conviction arose out of a single campus fight. Nor did petitioner's expert testify that the record reflected any assault charge without a disposition, although Justice Souter appears to suggest otherwise.

[R]espondent's own expert witness testified that Burns' record reflected a single assault conviction. Petitioner has repeatedly so claimed. Respondent has not once contested this characterization. * * * Involvement in a single fraternity fracas does not demonstrate "a proclivity to violence against the person."

The fact that Burns had pleaded guilty to traffic offenses and other misdemeanors may well have made him an extremely poor candidate for reserve deputy. Had Sheriff Moore fully reviewed Burns' record, he might have come to precisely that conclusion. But unless he would necessarily have reached that decision *because* Burns' use of excessive force would have been a plainly obvious consequence of the hiring decision, Sheriff Moore's inadequate scrutiny of Burns' record cannot constitute "deliberate indifference" to respondent's federally protected right to be free from a use of excessive force.

Justice Souter's reading of the case is that the jury believed that Sheriff Moore in fact read Burns' entire record. That is plausible, but it is also irrelevant. It is not sufficient for respondent to show that Sheriff Moore read Burns' record and therefore hired Burns with knowledge of his background. Such a decision may reflect indifference to Burns' *record*, but what is required is deliberate indifference to a plaintiff's constitutional right. That is, whether Sheriff Moore failed to examine Burns' record, partially examined it, or fully examined it, Sheriff Moore's hiring decision could not have been "deliberately indifferent" unless in light of that record Burns' use of excessive force would have been a plainly obvious consequence of the hiring decision. Because there was insufficient evidence on which a jury could base a finding that Sheriff Moore's decision to hire Burns reflected conscious disregard of an obvious risk that a use of excessive force would follow, the District Court erred in submitting respondent's inadequate screening claim to the jury.

III

Cases involving constitutional injuries allegedly traceable to an ill-considered hiring decision pose the greatest risk that a municipality will be held liable for an injury that it did not cause. In the broadest sense, every injury is traceable to a hiring decision. Where a court fails to adhere to rigorous requirements of culpability and causation, municipal liability collapses into *respondeat superior* liability. As we recognized in *Monell* and have repeatedly reaffirmed, Congress did not intend municipalities to be held liable unless *deliberate* action attributable to the municipality directly caused a deprivation of federal rights. A failure to apply stringent culpability and causation requirements raises serious federalism concerns, in that it risks constitutionalizing particular hiring requirements that States have themselves elected not to impose. Bryan County is not liable for Sheriff Moore's isolated decision to hire Burns without adequate screening, because respondent has not demonstrated that his decision reflected a conscious disregard for a high risk that

Burns would use excessive force in violation of respondent's federally protected right. We therefore vacate the judgment of the Court of Appeals and remand this case for further proceedings consistent with this opinion.

It is so ordered.

JUSTICE SOUTER, with whom JUSTICE STEVENS and JUSTICE BREYER join, dissenting.

* * *

[T]here are * * * three alternatives discernible in our prior cases [for satisfying the requirement that municipalities are liable only when the acts complained of are pursuant to some municipal policy]. It is certainly met when the appropriate officer or entity promulgates a generally applicable statement of policy and the subsequent act complained of is simply an implementation of that policy. *Monell* exemplified these circumstances, where city agencies had issued a rule requiring pregnant employees to take unpaid leaves of absence before any medical need arose.

We have also held the policy requirement satisfied where no rule has been announced as "policy" but federal law has been violated by an act of the policymaker itself. In this situation, the choice of policy and its implementation are one, and the first or only action will suffice to ground municipal liability simply because it is the very policymaker who is acting. * * * It does not matter that the policymaker may have chosen "a course of action tailored [only] to a particular situation and not intended to control decisions in later situations"; if the decision to adopt that particular course of action is intentionally made by the authorized policymaker, "it surely represents an act of official government 'policy' " and "the municipality is equally responsible whether that action is to be taken only once or to be taken repeatedly."

We have, finally, identified a municipal policy in a third situation, even where the policymaker has failed to act affirmatively at all, so long as the need to take some action to control the agents of the Government "is so obvious, and the inadequacy [of existing practice] so likely to result in the violation of constitutional rights, that the policymake[r] * * * can reasonably be said to have been deliberately indifferent to the need." Where, in the most obvious example, the policymaker sits on his hands after repeated, unlawful acts of subordinate officers and that failure "evidences a 'deliberate indifference' to the rights of [the municipality's] inhabitants," the policymaker's toleration of the subordinates' behavior establishes a policy-in-practice just as readily attributable to the municipality as the one-act policy-in-practice described above. Such a policy choice may be inferred even without a pattern of acts by subordinate officers, so long as the need for action by the policymaker is so obvious that the failure to act rises to deliberate indifference.

Deliberate indifference is thus treated, as it is elsewhere in the law, as tantamount to intent, so that inaction by a policymaker deliberately indifferent to a substantial risk of harm is equivalent to the intentional action that setting policy presupposes. * * *

Under this prior law, Sheriff Moore's failure to screen out his 21-year-old great-nephew Burns on the basis of his criminal record, and the decision instead to authorize Burns to act as a deputy sheriff, constitutes a policy choice attributable to Bryan County under § 1983. There is no serious dispute that Sheriff Moore is the designated policymaker for implementing the sheriff's law enforcement powers and recruiting officers to exercise them, or that he "has final authority to act for the municipality in hiring matters." As the authorized policymaker, Sheriff Moore is the county for purposes of § 1983 municipal liability arising from the sheriff's department's exercise of law enforcement authority. As I explain in greater detail below, it was open to the jury to find that the sheriff knew of the record of his nephew's violent propensity, but hired him in deliberate indifference to the risk that he would use excessive force on the job, as in fact he later did. That the sheriff's act did not itself command or require commission of a constitutional violation (like the order to perform an unlawful entry and search in *Pembaur*) is not dispositive under § 1983, for we have expressly rejected the contention that "only unconstitutional policies are actionable" under § 1983, and have never suggested that liability under the statute is otherwise limited to policies that facially violate other federal law. The sheriff's policy choice creating a substantial risk of a constitutional violation therefore could subject the county to liability under existing precedent.[2]

II

At the level of theory, at least, the Court does not disagree, and it assumes for the sake of deciding the case that a single, facially neutral act of deliberate indifference by a policymaker could be a predicate to municipal liability if it led to an unconstitutional injury inflicted by subordinate officers. At the level of practice, however, the tenor of the Court's opinion is decidedly different: it suggests that the trial court insufficiently appreciated the specificity of the risk to which such indifference must be deliberate in order to be actionable; it expresses deep skepticism that such appreciation of risk could ever reasonably be attributed to the policymaker who has performed only a single unsatisfactory, but not facially unconstitutional, act; and it finds the record insufficient to make any such showing in this case. The Court is serially mistaken. This case

---

[2] Given the sheriff's position as law enforcement policymaker, it is simply off the point to suggest, as the Court does, that there is some significance in either the fact that Sheriff Moore's failure to screen may have been a "deviation" from his ordinary hiring practices or that a pattern of injuries resulting from his past practices is absent. *Pembaur* made clear that a single act by a designated policymaker is sufficient to establish a municipal policy, and *Canton* explained, as the Court recognizes, that evidence of a single violation of federal rights can trigger municipal liability under § 1983.

presents no occasion to correct or refine the District Court's jury instructions on the degree of risk required for deliberate indifference; the Court's skepticism converts a newly-demanding formulation of the standard of fault into a virtually categorical impossibility of showing it in a case like this; and the record in this case is perfectly sufficient to support the jury's verdict even on the Court's formulation of the high degree of risk that must be shown.

A

The Court is certainly correct in emphasizing the need to show more than mere negligence on the part of the policymaker, for at the least the element of deliberateness requires both subjective appreciation of a risk of unconstitutional harm, and a risk substantial enough to justify the heightened responsibility that deliberate indifference generally entails. The Court goes a step further, however, in requiring that the "particular" harmful consequence be "plainly obvious" to the policymaker, a characterization of deliberate indifference adapted from dicta * * *. *Canton*, as mentioned above, held that a municipal policy giving rise to liability under § 1983 may be inferred even when the policymaker has failed to act affirmatively at all, so long as a need to control the agents of the Government "is so obvious, and the inadequacy [of existing practice] so likely to result in the violation of constitutional rights, that the policymake[r] * * * can reasonably be said to have been deliberately indifferent to the need." While we speculated in *Canton* that "[i]t could * * * be that the police, in exercising their discretion, so often violate constitutional rights that the need for further training must have been plainly obvious to the city policymakers, who, nevertheless, are 'deliberately indifferent' to the need," we did not purport to be defining the fault of deliberate indifference universally as the failure to act in relation to a "plainly obvious consequence" of harm. Nor did we, in addressing the requisite risk that constitutional violations will occur, suggest that the deliberate indifference necessary to establish municipal liability must be, as the Court says today, indifference to the particular constitutional violation that in fact occurred.

The Court's formulation that deliberate indifference exists only when the risk of the subsequent, particular constitutional violation is a plainly obvious consequence of the hiring decision, while derived from *Canton*, is thus without doubt a new standard. As to the "particular" violation, the Court alters the understanding of deliberate indifference as set forth in Canton, where we spoke of constitutional violations generally. As to "plainly obvious consequence," the Court's standard appears to be somewhat higher, for example, than the standard for "reckless" fault in the criminal law, where the requisite indifference to risk is defined as that which "consciously disregards a substantial and unjustifiable risk that the material element exists or will result * * * [and] involves a gross deviation from the standard of conduct that a law-abiding person would observe in the actor's situation."

That said, it is just possible that our prior understanding of the requisite degree of fault and the standard as the Court now states it may in practice turn out to amount to much the same thing, but I would have preferred an argument addressing the point before ruling on it. There was, however, no such argument here for the simple reason that petitioner never asked that deliberate indifference be defined to occur only when the particular constitutional injury was the plainly obvious consequence of the policymaker's act. Petitioner merely asked the District Court to instruct the jury to determine whether Sheriff Moore acted with "conscious indifference," and made no objection to the District Court's charge that "Sheriff B.J. Moore would have acted with deliberate indifference in adopting an otherwise constitutional hiring policy for a deputy sheriff if the need for closer scrutiny of Stacy Burns' background was so obvious and the inadequacy of the scrutiny given so likely to result in violations of constitutional rights, that Sheriff B.J. Moore can be reasonably said to have been deliberately indifferent to the constitutional needs of the Plaintiff." If, as it appears, today's standard does raise the threshold of municipal liability, it does so quite independently of any issue posed or decided in the trial court.

B

The Court's skepticism that the modified standard of fault can ever be met in a single-act case of inadequate screening without a patently unconstitutional policy, both reveals the true value of the assumption that in theory there might be municipal liability in such a case, and dictates the result of the Court's review of the record in the case before us. It is skepticism gone too far.

It is plain enough that a facially unconstitutional policy is likely to produce unconstitutional injury, and obvious, too, that many facially neutral policy decisions evince no such clear portents. Written standards for hiring law enforcement personnel might be silent on the significance of a prior criminal record without justifying much worry about employing axe-murderers (who are unlikely to apply) or subjecting the public to attacks by someone with a 30-year-old assault conviction (who has probably grown up). But a policymaker need not mandate injury to be indifferent to its risk when obvious, and, because a particular hiring decision may raise a very high probability of harm down the line, it simply ignores the issue before us to lump together in one presumptively benign category every singular administrative act of a policymaker that does not expressly command or constitute unconstitutional behavior. Thus a decision to give law enforcement authority to a scofflaw who had recently engaged in criminal violence presents a very different risk from hiring someone who once drove an overweight truck. While the decision to hire the violent scofflaw may not entail harm to others as unquestionably as an order to "go out and rough-up some suspects," it is a long way from neutral in the risk it creates.

While the Court should rightly be skeptical about predicating municipal or individual liability merely on a failure to adopt a crime-free personnel policy or on a particular decision to hire a guilty trucker, why does it extend that valid skepticism to the quite unsound point of doubting liability for hiring the violent scofflaw? The Court says it fears that the latter sort of case raises a danger of liability without fault. But if the Court means fault generally (as distinct from the blame imputed on classic *respondeat superior* doctrine), it need only recall that whether a particular violent scofflaw is violent enough or scoffing enough to implicate deliberate indifference will depend on applying the highly demanding standard the Court announces: plainly obvious consequence of particular injury. It is the high threshold of deliberate indifference that will ensure that municipalities be held liable only for considered acts with substantial risks. That standard will distinguish single-act cases with only a mild portent of injury from single-act cases with a plainly obvious portent, and from cases in which the harm is only the latest in a series of injuries known to have followed from the policymaker's action. The Court has fenced off the slippery slope.

A second stated reason of the skeptical majority is that, because municipal liability under *Monell* cannot rest on *respondeat superior*, "a court must carefully test the link between the policymaker's inadequate decision and the particular injury alleged." But that is simply to say that the tortious act must be proximately caused by the policymaker. The policy requirement is the restriction that bars straightforward *respondeat superior* liability, and the need to "test the link" is merely the need to apply the law that defines what a cognizable link is. The restriction on imputed fault that saves municipalities from liability has no need of categorical immunization in single-act cases.

In short, the Court's skepticism is excessive in ignoring the fact that some acts of a policymaker present substantial risks of unconstitutional harm even though the acts are not unconstitutional *per se*. And the Court's purported justifications for its extreme skepticism are washed out by the very standards employed to limit liability.

C

For demonstrating the extreme degree of the Court's inhospitality to single-act municipal liability, this is a case on point, for even under the "plainly obvious consequence" rule the evidence here would support the verdict. There is no dispute that before the incident in question the sheriff ordered a copy of his nephew's criminal record. While the sheriff spoke euphemistically on the witness stand of a "driving record," the scope of the requested documentation included crimes beyond motor vehicle violations and the sheriff never denied that he knew this. He admitted that he read some of that record; he said he knew it was "long"; he said he was sure he had noticed charges of driving with a suspended license; and he said that he had taken the trouble to make an independent search for any outstanding warrant for·Burns' arrest. As he put it, however, he somehow failed to "notice" charges of assault and battery or the list of offenses so long as to point either to contempt for law or to incapacity to obey it. Although the jury might have accepted the sheriff's disclaimer, no one who has read the transcript would assume that the jurors gave any credit to that testimony,[4] and it was open to them to find

[4] After Sheriff Moore testified that he knew Burns had been charged with driving while intoxicated, the following exchange with respondent's counsel took place:

Q. And how did you obtain that information?

A. I don't remember now how I got it.

Q. Did you make an inquiry with the proper authorities in Oklahoma to get a copy of Mr. Burns' rap sheet?

A. I run his driving record, yes.

Q. All right. And you can get that rap sheet immediately, can't you?

A. It don't take long.

Q. All right. And did you not see on there where Mr. Burns had been arrested for assault and battery. Did you see that one on there?

A. I never noticed it, no.

Q. Did you notice on there he'd been arrested or charged with [Driving While License Suspended] on several occasions?

* * * *

A. I'm sure I did.

Q. All right. Did you notice on there that he'd been arrested and convicted for possession of false identification?

A. No, I never noticed that.

Q. Did you notice on there where he had been arrested for public drunk?

A. He had a long record.

Q. Did you notice on there where he had been arrested for resisting arrest?

A. No, I didn't.

Q. Did you make any inquiries after you got that information to determine exactly what the disposition of those charges were?

A. No, I didn't.

Q. Did you not make any attempt to find out the status of Mr. Burns' criminal record at that time?

A. As far as him having a criminal record, I don't believe he had a criminal record. It was just all driving and—most of it was, misdemeanors.

Q. Well, did you make any attempts to determine whether or not Mr. Burns was on probation at the time you placed him out there?

A. I didn't know he was on probation, no.

Q. Did you make any effort to find out?

A. I didn't have no idea he was on probation, no.

Q. Well, you saw on his rap sheet where he had been charged with [Driving Under the Influence], didn't you?

A. I had heard about that. I don't remember whether I had seen it on the rap sheet or not.

Q. So you'd heard about it?

* * * *

A. I don't know remember whether I seen it on the rap sheet or heard about it.

Q. All right. Well, whichever way you, it came to your attention, you didn't

that the sheriff was simply lying under oath about his limited perusal. The Court of Appeals noted this possibility, which is more likely than any other reading of the evidence. Law enforcement officers, after all, are not characteristically so devoid of curiosity as to lose interest part way through the criminal record of a subject of personal investigation.

If, as is likely, the jurors did disbelieve the sheriff and concluded he had read the whole record, they certainly could have eliminated any possibility that the sheriff's decision to employ his relative was an act of mere negligence or poor judgment. He did not even claim, for example, that he thought any assault must have been just a youthful peccadillo magnified out of proportion by the criminal charge, or that he had evaluated the assault as merely eccentric behavior in a young man of sound character, or that he was convinced that wild youth had given way to discretion. There being no such evidence of reasonable but mistaken judgment, the jury could readily have found that the sheriff knew his nephew's proven propensities, that he thought the thrust of the evidence was so damaging that he would lie to protect his reputation and the county treasury, and that he simply chose to put a family member on the payroll (the third relative, in fact) disregarding the risk to the public.

At trial, petitioner's expert witness stated during cross-examination that Burns' rap sheet listed repeated traffic violations, including driving while intoxicated and driving with a suspended license, resisting arrest, and more than one charge of assault and battery. The witness further testified that Burns pleaded guilty to assault and battery and other charges 16 months before he was hired by Sheriff Moore.[6] Respondent's

---

check to find out with the proper authorities as to what the disposition of that charge was, did you?

* * * *

A. I don't really know. I can't say.

Q. Did you check to see if Mr. Burns had an arrest warrant out for him?

A. We—I run him through [the National Crime Information Center] and there wasn't—didn't show no warrant, no.

[6] The Court points out that Burns had only one conviction for assault and battery, that respondent has never claimed otherwise, and that her expert witness so testified. This is entirely correct. But the issue here is not what might have been learned by thoroughly investigating Burns' behavior; the issue is the sufficiency of the evidence to support the jury's finding that the sheriff acted with deliberate indifference when he hired Burns. Specifically, assuming the jury found that the sheriff looked at Burns' criminal record, an assumption the Court acknowledges is "plausible," what does the evidence show that the sheriff learned from this examination? The criminal record was not itself introduced into evidence in written form, but it was, in relevant part, read to the jury by petitioner's expert witness Ken Barnes. According to Barnes' testimony, this criminal record's list of numerous charges included four references to assault and battery, two of which the witness said were duplicative, though he conceded this was not necessarily so. The upshot was that if the jury found that the sheriff looked at the written record, it could have found that he read four separate references to assault and battery charges. That is not to say that four assaults necessarily occurred, but only that the record refers four times to such charges before listing one conviction for assault and battery. Barnes also testified that the record does not contain a disposition for all the charges listed, and that a sheriff reviewing such a record should have investigated further to determine the disposition of such charges.

expert witness testified that Burns' arrest record showed a "blatant disregard for the law and problems that may show themselves in abusing the public or using excessive force," and petitioner's own expert agreed that Burns' criminal history should have caused concern. When asked if he would have hired Burns, he replied that it was "doubtful." On this evidence, the jury could have found that the string of arrests and convictions revealed "that Burns had [such] a propensity for violence and a disregard for the law," that his subsequent resort to excessive force was the plainly obvious consequence of hiring him as a law enforcement officer authorized to employ force in performing his duties.

III

The county escapes from liability through the Court's untoward application of an enhanced fault standard to a record of inculpatory evidence showing a contempt for constitutional obligations as blatant as the nepotism that apparently occasioned it. The novelty of this escape shows something unsuspected (by me, at least) until today. Despite arguments that *Monell*'s policy requirement was an erroneous reading of § 1983, I had not previously thought that there was sufficient reason to unsettle the precedent of *Monell*. Now it turns out, however, that *Monell* is hardly settled. That being so, Justice Breyer's powerful call to reexamine § 1983 municipal liability afresh finds support in the Court's own readiness to rethink the matter.

I respectfully dissent.

JUSTICE BREYER, with whom JUSTICE STEVENS and JUSTICE GINSBURG join, dissenting.

In *Monell*, this Court said that municipalities cannot be held liable for constitutional torts under 42 U.S.C. § 1983 "on a *respondeat superior* theory," but they can be held liable "when execution of" a municipality's "policy or custom * * * inflicts the injury." That statement has produced a highly complex body of interpretive law. Today's decision exemplifies the law's complexity, for it distinguishes among a municipal action that "itself violates federal law," an action that "intentionally deprive[s] a plaintiff of a federally protected right," and one that "has caused an employee to do so." It then elaborates this Court's requirement that a consequence be "*so likely*" to occur that a policymaker could "*reasonably be said to have been deliberately indifferent*" with respect to it (emphasis added), with an admonition that the unconstitutional consequence must be "plainly obvious." The majority fears that a contrary view of prior

---

In my judgment, the evidence would have been sufficient (under the majority's test) if it had shown no more than one complaint and conviction for assault and battery, given the mixture of charges of resisting an officer, public drunkenness and multiple traffic offenses over a four-month period ending only sixteen months before Burns was hired. The inference to be drawn would have been that a repeatedly lawless young man had shown a proclivity to violence against the person. But, as it turns out, the evidentiary record is ostensibly more damaging than that.

precedent would undermine *Monell*'s basic distinction. That concern, however, rather than leading us to spin ever finer distinctions as we try to apply *Monell*'s basic distinction between liability that rests upon policy and liability that is vicarious, suggests that we should reexamine the legal soundness of that basic distinction itself.

I believe that the legal prerequisites for reexamination of an interpretation of an important statute are present here. The soundness of the original principle is doubtful. The original principle has generated a body of interpretive law that is so complex that the law has become difficult to apply. Factual and legal changes have divorced the law from the distinction's apparent original purposes. And there may be only a handful of individuals or groups that have significantly relied upon perpetuation of the original distinction. If all this is so, later law has made the original distinction, not simply wrong, but obsolete and a potential source of confusion.

First, consider *Monell*'s original reasoning. The *Monell* "no vicarious liability" principle rested upon a historical analysis of § 1983 and upon § 1983's literal language—language that imposes liability upon (but only upon) any "person." * * * Essentially, the history on which *Monell* relied consists almost exclusively of the fact that the Congress that enacted § 1983 rejected an amendment (called the Sherman amendment) that would have made municipalities vicariously liable for the marauding acts of *private citizens*. That fact, as Justice Stevens and others have pointed out, does not argue against vicarious liability for the act of municipal employees—particularly since municipalities, at the time, were vicariously liable for many of the acts of their employees.

Without supporting history, it is difficult to find § 1983's words "[e]very person" inconsistent with *respondeat superior* liability. In 1871 "bodies politic and corporate," such as municipalities were "person[s]." Section 1983 requires that the "person" either "subjec[t]" or "caus[e]" a different person "to be subjected" to a "deprivation" of a right. As a purely linguistic matter, a municipality, which can act only through its employees, might be said to have "subject[ed]" a person or to have "cause[d]" that person to have been "subjected" to a loss of rights when a municipality's employee acts within the scope of his or her employment. Federal courts on occasion have interpreted the word "person" or the equivalent in other statutes as authorizing forms of vicarious liability.

Second, *Monell*'s basic effort to distinguish between vicarious liability and liability derived from "policy or custom" has produced a body of law that is neither readily understandable nor easy to apply. Today's case provides a good example. The District Court in this case told the jury it must find (1) Sheriff Moore's screening "*so likely* to result in violations of constitutional rights" that he could "*reasonably [be] said to have been deliberately indifferent* to the constitutional needs of the Plaintiff" and (2) that the "inadequate hiring * * * policy directly caused the Plaintiff's injury." ([E]mphasis added). This instruction comes close to repeating this Court's language in *Canton* * * * .

The majority says that the District Court and the Court of Appeals did not look closely enough at the specific facts of this case. It also adds that the harm must be a *"plainly obvious consequence"* of the "decision to hire" Burns. But why elaborate *Canton*'s instruction in this way? The Court's verbal formulation is slightly different; and that being so, a lawyer or judge will ignore the Court's precise words at his or her peril. Yet those words, while adding complexity, do not seem to reflect a difference that significantly helps one understand the difference between "vicarious" liability and "policy." Even if the Court means only that the record evidence does not meet *Canton*'s standard, it will be difficult for juries, and for judges, to understand just why that is so. It will be difficult for them to apply today's elaboration of *Canton*—except perhaps in the limited context of police force hiring decisions that are followed by a recruit's unconstitutional conduct.

Consider some of the other distinctions that this Court has had to make as it has sought to distinguish liability based upon policymaking from liability that is "vicarious." It has proved necessary, for example, to distinguish further, between an exercise of *policymaking authority* and an exercise of *delegated discretionary policy-implementing authority*. Without some such distinction, "municipal liability [might] collaps[e] into *respondeat superior*," for the law would treat similarly (and hold municipalities responsible for) both a police officer's decision about how much force to use when making a particular arrest and a police chief's decision about how much force to use when making a particular *kind* of arrest. But the distinction is not a clear one. It requires federal courts to explore state and municipal law that distributes different state powers among different local officials and local entities. That law is highly specialized; it may or may not say just where policymaking authority lies, and it can prove particularly difficult to apply in light of the Court's determination that a decision can be "policymaking" even though it applies only to a single instance.

It is not surprising that results have sometimes proved inconsistent. * * *

Nor does the location of "policymaking" authority pose the only conceptually difficult problem. Lower courts must also ask decide whether a failure to make policy was "deliberately indifferent," rather than "grossly negligent." And they must decide, for example, whether it matters that some such failure occurred in the officer-training, rather than the officer-hiring, process.

Given the basic *Monell* principle, these distinctions may be necessary, for without them, the Court cannot easily avoid a "municipal liability" that "collaps[es] into *respondeat superior*." But a basic legal principle that requires so many such distinctions to maintain its legal life may not deserve such longevity.

Finally, relevant legal and factual circumstances may have changed in a way that affects likely reliance upon *Monell*'s liability limitation. The legal complexity just described makes it difficult for municipalities to predict just when they will be held liable based upon "policy or custom." Moreover, their potential liability is, in a sense, greater than that of individuals, for they cannot assert the "qualified immunity" defenses that individuals may raise. Further, many States have statutes that appear to, in effect, mimic *respondeat superior* by authorizing indemnification of employees found liable under § 1983 for actions within the scope of their employment. These statutes—valuable to government employees as well as to civil rights victims—can provide for payments from the government that are similar to those that would take place in the absence of *Monell*'s limitations. To the extent that they do so, municipal reliance upon the continuation of *Monell*'s "policy" limitation loses much of its significance.

Any statement about reliance, of course, must be tentative, as we have not heard argument on the matter. We do not know the pattern of indemnification: how often, and to what extent, States now indemnify their employees, and which of their employees they indemnify. I also realize that there may be other reasons, constitutional and otherwise, that I have not discussed that argue strongly for reaffirmation of *Monell*'s holding.

Nonetheless, for the reasons I have set forth, I believe the case for reexamination is a strong one. Today's decision underscores this need. Consequently, I would ask for further argument that would focus upon the continued viability of *Monell*'s distinction between vicarious municipal liability and municipal liability based upon policy and custom.

Notes and Questions

1. The Court tries hard in *Brown* to enforce the mandate of *Monell* that municipalities are liable only for their own misconduct, not that of employees on a *respondeat superior* basis. To that end, it requires plaintiffs to make a two-part showing: first, "that the municipal action was taken with the requisite degree of culpability"; that is, the conduct was "deliberate," and second, the municipality was the "moving force" behind the injury; *i.e.* that there is "direct causal link between the municipal action and the deprivation of federal rights." Counsel for Bryan County stipulated that Sheriff Moore was the policy-maker for the County regarding the Sheriff's Department. Moore clearly acted intentionally in hiring Deputy Stacy Burns, and the plaintiff would not have suffered injury unless Moore had hired Burns. Why, then, does the Court conclude the plaintiff failed to make the required showing? What set of facts do you think would have persuaded the majority that the plaintiff satisfied its two-part test?

2. The Court observes that in a single-case situation, there is no notice to the decisionmaker of the inadequacy of his approach. Yet, elsewhere in

the opinion, Justice O'Connor notes that "[t]he fact that inadequate scrutiny of an applicant's background would make a violation of rights more likely cannot alone give rise to an inference that a policymaker's failure to scrutinize the record of a particular applicant produced a specific constitutional violation." She thus criticizes the plaintiff's argument as too general. Could not one level the same charge at the majority opinion? To borrow from Justice O'Connor, to say that there may be no predictability of inadequacy in the general single-case situation "cannot alone * * * [avoid] to an inference that a policymaker's failure to scrutinize the record of a *particular* applicant produced a specific constitutional violation." (Emphasis added.) Cannot one argue that in *this* case, Sheriff Moore's failure to scrutinize Burns's record should have put him on notice of the likelihood of constitutional violations involving improper use of force? Who, if not a sheriff, should be more aware of the importance of checking someone's criminal information history, particularly if it shows at least one crime of violence, before placing him in a position of significant power and trust that may require the use of state-sanctioned force? Does the Court recharacterize the plaintiff's argument fairly when it refers to lack of scrutiny of applicants' records as tending to promote hiring of unfit officers and denominates that as a "generalized showing of risk," or is it the Court that erects the straw man of generality and then strikes it down in the face of plaintiff's more specific argument?

3. Justice O'Connor concludes by declaring that the particular constitutional violation upon which a plaintiff bases a claim for relief must be a "plainly obvious consequence of the hiring decision," and that the evidence here was insufficient to permit a jury to reach that conclusion. How much evidence is enough to constitute a plainly obvious consequence? Did the Court substitute itself for the jury? Justice Souter sees this case in part as a proximate causation issue. Could a jury reasonably find on the facts of this case that Moore's decision not to scrutinize Burns's rap sheet proximately caused Brown's injury?

4. Does *Brown* announce a new standard for municipal liability? If so, how is it different from the previous one? How specific will a plaintiff have to be in pleading and proving that a municipal decision not itself illegal nonetheless should expose the municipality to liability?

5. Justice O'Connor posits that the consequences of a hiring decision are more difficult to predict than those of a failure-to-train decision with respect to a specific skill. Is the distinction maintainable, or is it just a matter of semantics? Certainly Ms. Brown could argue that one specific skill that a peace officer needs is the ability to restrain himself from using force inappropriately and that Burns's record forecast his inability to do so.

6. Justice Breyer's dissent may be the most far-reaching opinion of all, calling for complete reevaluation of Justice Brennan's majority conclusion in *Monell* that § 1983 does not support any form of *respondeat superior* liability. Is he correct that the law that has sprung from this part of *Monell* is so hopelessly convoluted that reexamination makes sense? Does his opinion suggest that the questions in Notes 1(a, b) on page 550 of the text have taken on new life? How should the pattern of indemnification affect the de-

bate about municipal liability? If indemnification is widespread, does that suggest that there is no need to expand municipal liability because successful plaintiffs already receive compensation from municipalities? Or would widespread indemnification indicate that *respondeat superior* liability exists in fact, if not technically, and that municipality liability doctrine is therefore unnecessarily complex?

3. *Officials' Immunities*

Cases like *Monell* and *Brown* did not concern what immunity, if any, individual officials might have for unlawful conduct while in office. Some immunities, such as those covering judges and other court officials, are well established.   Others, concerning officials in the executive branch, are more problematic.

The Supreme Court has discussed judicial immunity three times in recent years. In *Stump v. Sparkman*, 435 U.S. 349, 98 S.Ct. 1099, 55 L.Ed.2d 331 (1978), the Court reaffirmed the traditional rule that judges enjoy absolute immunity for the performance of judicial acts unless there is a "clear absence of all jurisdiction" to perform the act in question. When Mrs. Sparkman was fifteen years old, her mother brought an *ex parte* proceeding to have her sterilized on the ground that she was "somewhat retarded." The mother told the daughter that the operation was to remove her appendix. Stump, a state judge, approved the petition the same day, without a hearing, notice to the daughter, or appointment of a guardian *ad litem*. The daughter did not discover the truth until years later when she and her husband sought medical assistance for their inability to conceive. The Court ruled that the authority of the state court simply to consider the sterilization petition constituted a complete shield precluding any liability for the judge and denied plaintiffs' claim for damages under 42 U.S.C.A. § 1983. Judicial immunity rests on the notion that the proper administration of justice requires that judges feel free to perform their judicial duties without fear of personal consequences.

Pulliam v. Allen, 466 U.S. 522, 104 S.Ct. 1970, 80 L.Ed.2d 565 (1984), demonstrated that there are some limits to absolute judicial immunity. A five-to-four Court held that absolute judicial immunity does not preclude injunctive relief and that Congress's intent to abrogate traditional immunities by passing 42 U.S.C.A. § 1988 (allowing victorious parties in civil rights actions to collect attorneys' fees) was sufficiently clear to permit awards of such fees against the state judge in *Pulliam*.

Finally, *Forrester v. White*, 484 U.S. 219, 108 S.Ct. 538, 98 L.Ed.2d 555 (1988), considered immunity when a judge acts in a non-judicial capacity. Forrester was a probation officer serving in White's court. White fired her because of her sex. The Court ruled that the judge's supervision of the court's probation officers was non-judicial in nature, so that he was entitled only to the qualified immunity applicable to executive officials under *Harlow v. Fitzgerald* (at page 580), not the absolute immunity that attends judicial decisions.

The Court has also been active with respect to prosecutors' immunity. *Imbler v. Pachtman*, 424 U.S. 409, 96 S.Ct. 984, 47 L.Ed.2d 128, (1976) reaffirmed prosecutors' absolute immunity from civil litigation concerning the initiation of prosecution or the presentation of the state's case. These activities are deemed to be closely associated with the judicial portion of the criminal process and thus "quasi-judicial." Consequently, the Court has found that the policies supporting absolute immunity for judges also supported absolute immunity for prosecutors carrying out these functions. *Imbler* involved a charge that the prosecutor in a prior criminal action had knowingly presented perjured testimony in an attempt to convict. The Court refused to allow the civil suit to proceed, but in *Burns v. Reed*, 500 U.S. 478, 111 S.Ct. 1934, 114 L.Ed.2d 547 (1991), the Justices distinguished between conduct of litigation, still entitled to absolute immunity, and giving legal advice to the police during the course of their investigation. The latter, said the Court, entitles the prosecutor only to qualified immunity. In *Buckley v. Fitzsimmons*, 509 U.S. 259, 113 S.Ct. 2606, 125 L.Ed.2d 209 (1993) the Court held that the *Imbler-Burns* analysis required only qualified immunity for prosecutors alleged to have manufactured evidence prior to the existence of probable cause and to have held an inflammatory press conference to influence the result of a trial, since neither action is part of a prosecutor's functioning as the state's advocate.

Kalina v. Fletcher, 522 U.S. 118, 118 S.Ct. 502, 139 L.Ed.2d 471 (1997), continued the *Imbler-Burns-Buckley* distinction between prosecutorial conduct in which the prosecutor acts as an officer of the court, for which there is absolute immunity, and conduct in which the prosecutor functions in some other capacity. The plaintiff alleged that the prosecutor violated his Fourth Amendment rights by personally attesting to false statements recited in a document filed with the court to procure an arrest warrant. The majority reasoned that no part of prosecutorial judgment could affect "the truth or falsity of the factual statements themselves. Testifying about facts is the function of the witness, not of the lawyer." Thus, the defendant was not entitled to absolute immunity. The absolute immunity for witnesses recognized in *Briscoe v. Lahue*, 460 U.S. 325, 103 S.Ct. 1108, 75 L.Ed.2d 96 (1983), (holding trial witnesses absolutely immune from civil suits based on their testimony even when they gave perjurious testimony) is limited to trial testimony. A state actor—even a prosecutor—who serves as a "complaining witness" by making statements used to obtain an arrest warrant enjoys only a qualified immunity from damages liability.

The Court has long held that state legislators are absolutely immune from damages liability under § 1983 for acts within their legislative capacity. Such immunity is designed to preserve legislative independence and prevent the diversion of the legislators' time and energy from their legislative tasks. In *Bogan v. Scott-Harris*, 523 U.S. 44, 118 S.Ct. 966,

140 L.Ed.2d 79 (1998), the Court held that legislators are also absolutely immune from civil liability for acts performed in a legislative capacity, irrespective of their motive. Plaintiff claimed that the municipality eliminated a department (in which the plaintiff was the sole employee) because of racial animus and in retaliation for plaintiff's exercise of her First Amendment rights. Justice Thomas, writing for a unanimous Court, noted that "[w]hether an act is legislative turns on the nature of the act, rather than on the motive or intent of the official performing it."

The Court recognizes absolute immunity believing that Congress, in enacting § 1983, intended to retain common law immunities rather than eliminate them by implication. The Court notes with great regularity the policies that might have motivated Congress, particularly that if legislators, prosecutors, and judges are subject to liability arising out of the performance of their duties, they will be inhibited by fear of civil suits, whether well-founded or groundless. Is the price paid worth it, or, as Justice Harlan observed in *Bivens v. Six Unknown Named Agents of Federal Bureau of Narcotics*, 403 U.S. 388, 91 S.Ct. 1999, 29 L.Ed.2d 619 (1971), are there better ways to deal with frivolous lawsuits than by dismissing meritorious ones?

In 1996, Congress amended § 1983, which now reads as follows:

> Every person who, under color of any statute, ordinance, regulation, custom, or usage, of any State or Territory or the District of Columbia, subjects, or causes to be subjected, any citizen of the United States or other person within the jurisdiction thereof to the deprivation of any rights, privileges, or immunities secured by the Constitution and laws, shall be liable to the party injured in an action at law, suit in equity, or other proper proceeding for redress, except that in any action brought against a judicial officer for an act or omission taken in such officer's judicial capacity, injunctive relief shall not be granted unless a declaratory decree was violated or declaratory relief was unavailable. For the purposes of this section, any Act of Congress applicable exclusively to the District of Columbia shall be considered to be a statute of the District of Columbia.

42 U.S.C.A. § 1983 (2002). At the same time, Congress restricted the availability of attorney's fees by amending 42 U.S.C.A. § 1988(b) (Supp. 2002):

> In any action or proceeding to enforce a provision of sections 1981, 1981a, 1982, 1983, 1985, and 1986 of this title, * * * the court, in its discretion, may allow the prevailing party, other than the United States, a reasonable attorney's fee as part of the costs, except that in any action brought against a judicial officer for an act or omission taken in such officer's judicial capacity such officer shall not be held liable for any costs, including attorney's fees, unless such action was clearly in excess of such officer's jurisdic-

tion.

These changes significantly alter the rule of *Pulliam v. Allen*, which permitted injunctive suits against judges notwithstanding their otherwise-existing absolute immunity and also permitted recovery of costs and fees by successful plaintiffs. New § 1983 does not, however, establish absolute judicial immunity against prospective relief suits; it instead requires that they commence as declaratory judgment actions, with the possibility of further relief to follow under the authority of 28 U.S.C. § 2202. It does, however, make the effort considerably more expensive for victorious plaintiffs by limiting the possibility of recovering expenses, and may thus, as a practical matter, have the effect of making *Pulliam* a dead letter.

Perhaps these changes are desirable because they lend support to judicial independence and, by analogy, to other factors typically discussed in the context of the qualified immunity the Court has recognized under § 1983, but they do not come without attendant social costs. Is it appropriate to spare judicial officers costs and fees in initial rounds of litigation? If so, do the arguments in favor of doing so hold equally well after a plaintiff, having obtained declaratory relief, must seek further, injunctive relief?

With respect to officials entitled to qualified immunity, the picture is somewhat murkier. The Court considered qualified immunity in the context of § 1983 in *Wood v. Strickland*, 420 U.S. 308, 95 S.Ct. 992, 48 L.Ed.2d 214 (1975). Students challenged the procedure used to expel them from a public high school for "spiking" the punch served at an extracurricular activity attended by parents and students. (As the Court noted, "[t]he punch was served at the meeting, without apparent effect.") All nine Justices agreed that school officials were entitled to a qualified immunity, but the Court split five to four on the nature of the immunity. The majority articulated a standard with both objective and subjective elements:

> Therefore, in the specific context of school discipline, we hold that a school board member is not immune from liability for damages under § 1983 if he knew or reasonably should have known that the action he took within his sphere of official responsibility would violate the constitutional rights of the student affected, or if he took the action with the malicious intention to cause a deprivation of constitutional rights or other injury to the student. That is not to say that school board members are "charged with predicting the future course of constitutional law." A compensatory award will be appropriate only if the school board member has acted with such an impermissible motivation or with such disregard of the student's clearly established constitutional rights that his action cannot reasonably be characterized as being in good faith.

The remaining four Justices, led by Justice Powell (a former member and chairman of the Richmond, Virginia, and Virginia State Boards of Education), concurred and dissented. Justice Powell lamented "impos[ing] a higher standard of care upon public school officials * * * than that heretofore required of any other official." He argued that the majority's concepts of "settled, indisputable law" and "unquestioned constitutional rights" were devoid of reasonably ascertainable meaning, leaving school officials to guess at the law at their peril and raising the possibility that well qualified individuals would hesitate to undertake public responsibilities as a result. "One need only look to the decisions of this Court—to our reversals, our recognition of evolving concepts, and our five-to-four splits—to recognize the hazard of even informed prophecy as to what are 'unquestioned constitutional rights.'" Instead, Justice Powell and his dissenting colleagues would have imposed a much more subjective standard: "whether in light of the discretion and responsibilities of his office, and under all of the circumstances as they appeared at the time, the officer acted reasonably and in good faith."[3] Nine years later, the Court reconsidered the qualified immunity doctrine *vis-à-vis* executive officials, and Justice Powell wrote the opinion for the Court.

HARLOW v. FITZGERALD
Supreme Court of the United States, 1982.
457 U.S. 800, 102 S.Ct. 2727, 73 L.Ed.2d 396.

JUSTICE POWELL delivered the opinion of the Court.

The issue in this case is the scope of the immunity available to the senior aides and advisers of the President of the United States in a suit for damages based upon their official acts.

I

In this suit for civil damages petitioners Bryce Harlow and Alexander Butterfield are alleged to have participated in a conspiracy to violate the constitutional and statutory rights of the respondent A. Ernest Fitzgerald. Respondent avers that petitioners entered the conspiracy in their capacities as senior White House aides to former President Richard M. Nixon.

* * *

Petitioner Butterfield also is alleged to have entered the conspiracy not later than May 1969. Employed as Deputy Assistant to the President and Deputy Chief of Staff to H.R. Haldeman, Butterfield circulated a White House memorandum in that month in which he claimed to have learned that Fitzgerald planned to "blow the whistle" on some "shoddy

---

[3] One might ask, however, whether Justice Powell's concept of reasonableness differed at all from acting in good faith. If not, then he was merely being redundant. If so, however, then one must wonder how Justice Powell would have defined reasonableness and the extent to which it would have been distinct from the majority's "settled, indisputable law."

purchasing practices" by exposing these practices to public view. Fitzgerald characterizes this memorandum as evidence that Butterfield had commenced efforts to secure Fitzgerald's retaliatory dismissal. As evidence that Butterfield participated in the conspiracy to conceal his unlawful discharge and prevent his reemployment, Fitzgerald cites communications between Butterfield and Haldeman in December 1969 and January 1970. After the President had promised at a press conference to inquire into Fitzgerald's dismissal, Haldeman solicited Butterfield's recommendations. In a subsequent memorandum emphasizing the importance of "loyalty," Butterfield counseled against offering Fitzgerald another job in the administration at that time.

For his part, Butterfield denies that he was involved in any decision concerning Fitzgerald's employment status until Haldeman sought his advice in December 1969—more than a month after Fitzgerald's termination had been scheduled and announced publicly by the Air Force. Butterfield states that he never communicated his views about Fitzgerald to any official of the Defense Department. He argues generally that nearly eight years of discovery have failed to turn up any evidence that he caused injury to Fitzgerald.

Together with their codefendant Richard Nixon, petitioners Harlow and Butterfield moved for summary judgment * * *. In denying the motion the District Court upheld the legal sufficiency of Fitzgerald's *Bivens* claim under the First Amendment and his "inferred" statutory causes of action under 5 U.S.C. § 7211 and 18 U.S.C. § 1505. The court found that genuine issues of disputed fact remained for resolution at trial. It also ruled that petitioners were not entitled to absolute immunity.

* * *

II

* * *

Our decisions have recognized immunity defenses of two kinds. For officials whose special functions or constitutional status requires complete protection from suit, we have recognized the defense of "absolute immunity." The absolute immunity of legislators, in their legislative functions, and of judges, in their judicial functions now is well settled. Our decisions also have extended absolute immunity to certain officials of the Executive Branch. These include prosecutors and similar officials, executive officers engaged in adjudicative functions, and the President of the United States.

For executive officials in general, however, our cases make plain that qualified immunity represents the norm. In *Scheuer v. Rhodes* we acknowledged that high officials require greater protection than those with less complex discretionary responsibilities. Nonetheless, we held that a governor and his aides could receive the requisite protection from quali-

fied or good-faith immunity. In *Butz v. Economou* (1978), we extended
the approach of *Scheuer* to high federal officials of the Executive Branch.
* * * [W]e explained that the recognition of a qualified immunity defense
for high executives reflected an attempt to balance competing values:
not only the importance of a damages remedy to protect the rights of
citizens, but also "the need to protect officials who are required to exercise their discretion and the related public interest in encouraging the
vigorous exercise of official authority." Without discounting the adverse
consequences of denying high officials an absolute immunity from private lawsuits alleging constitutional violations * * * we emphasized our
expectation that insubstantial suits need not proceed to trial:

> Insubstantial lawsuits can be quickly terminated by federal courts
> alert to the possibilities of artful pleading. Unless the complaint
> states a compensable claim for relief * * * , it should not survive a
> motion to dismiss. Moreover, the Court recognized in *Scheuer* that
> damages suits concerning constitutional violations need not pro-
> ceed to trial, but can be terminated on a properly supported motion
> for summary judgment based on the defense of immunity * * * . In
> responding to such a motion, plaintiffs may not play dog in the
> manger; and firm application of the Federal Rules of Civil Proce-
> dure will ensure that federal officials are not harassed by frivolous
> lawsuits.

* * *

IV

Even if they cannot establish that their official functions require absolute immunity, petitioners assert that public policy at least mandates
an application of the qualified immunity standard that would permit the
defeat of insubstantial claims without resort to trial. We agree.

A

The resolution of immunity questions inherently requires a balance
between the evils inevitable in any available alternative. In situations of
abuse of office, an action for damages may offer the only realistic avenue
for vindication of constitutional guarantees. It is this recognition that
has required the denial of absolute immunity to most public officers. At
the same time, however, it cannot be disputed seriously that claims frequently run against the innocent as well as the guilty—at a cost not only
to the defendant officials, but to society as a whole. These social costs
include the expenses of litigation, the diversion of official energy from
pressing public issues, and the deterrence of able citizens from acceptance of public office. Finally, there is the danger that fear of being sued
will "dampen the ardor of all but the most resolute, or the most irresponsible [public officials], in the unflinching discharge of their duties."

In identifying qualified immunity as the best attainable accommodation of competing values, we relied on the assumption that this standard would permit "[i]nsubstantial lawsuits [to] be quickly terminated." Yet petitioners advance persuasive arguments that the dismissal of insubstantial lawsuits without trial—a factor presupposed in the balance of competing interests struck by our prior cases—requires an adjustment of the "good faith" standard established by our decisions.

B

Qualified or "good faith" immunity is an affirmative defense that must be pleaded by a defendant official. Decisions of this Court have established that the "good faith" defense has both an "objective" and a "subjective" aspect. The objective element involves a presumptive knowledge of and respect for "basic, unquestioned constitutional rights." The subjective component refers to "permissible intentions." Characteristically the Court has defined these elements by identifying the circumstances in which qualified immunity would *not* be available. Referring both to the objective and subjective elements, we have held that qualified immunity would be defeated if an official *"knew or reasonably should have known* that the action he took within his sphere of official responsibility would violate the constitutional rights of the [plaintiff], or if he took the action *with the malicious intention* to cause a deprivation of constitutional rights or other injury * * * ." ([E]mphasis added).

The subjective element of the good-faith defense frequently has proved incompatible with our admonition in *Butz* that insubstantial claims should not proceed to trial. Rule 56 of the Federal Rules of Civil Procedure provides that disputed questions of fact ordinarily may not be decided on motions for summary judgment. And an official's subjective good faith has been considered to be a question of fact that some courts have regarded as inherently requiring resolution by a jury.

In the context of *Butz'* attempted balancing of competing values, it now is clear that substantial costs attend the litigation of the subjective good faith of government officials. Not only are there the general costs of subjecting officials to the risks of trial—distraction of officials from their governmental duties, inhibition of discretionary action, and deterrence of able people from public service. There are special costs to "subjective" inquiries of this kind. Immunity generally is available only to officials performing discretionary functions. In contrast with the thought processes accompanying "ministerial" tasks, the judgments surrounding discretionary action almost inevitably are influenced by the decisionmaker's experiences, values, and emotions. These variables explain in part why questions of subjective intent so rarely can be decided by summary judgment. Yet they also frame a background in which there often is no clear end to the relevant evidence. Judicial inquiry into subjective motivation therefore may entail broad-ranging discovery and the deposing of numerous persons, including an official's professional colleagues. Inquiries of this kind can be peculiarly disruptive of effective government.

Consistently with the balance at which we aimed in *Butz,* we conclude today that bare allegations of malice should not suffice to subject government officials either to the costs of trial or to the burdens of broad-reaching discovery. We therefore hold that government officials performing discretionary functions generally are shielded from liability for civil damages insofar as their conduct does not violate clearly established statutory or constitutional rights of which a reasonable person would have known.[30]

Reliance on the objective reasonableness of an official's conduct, as measured by reference to clearly established law, should avoid excessive disruption of government and permit the resolution of many insubstantial claims on summary judgment. On summary judgment, the judge appropriately may determine, not only the currently applicable law, but whether that law was clearly established at the time an action occurred. If the law at that time was not clearly established, an official could not reasonably be expected to anticipate subsequent legal developments, nor could he fairly be said to "know" that the law forbade conduct not previously identified as unlawful. Until this threshold immunity question is resolved, discovery should not be allowed. If the law was clearly established, the immunity defense ordinarily should fail, since a reasonably competent public official should know the law governing his conduct. Nevertheless, if the official pleading the defense claims extraordinary circumstances and can prove that he neither knew nor should have known of the relevant legal standard, the defense should be sustained. But again, the defense would turn primarily on objective factors.

* * *

V

The judgment of the Court of Appeals is vacated, and the case is remanded for further action consistent with this opinion.

So ordered.

JUSTICE BRENNAN, with whom JUSTICE MARSHALL, and JUSTICE BLACKMUN join, concurring.

I agree with the substantive standard announced by the Court today, imposing liability when a public-official defendant "knew or should have known" of the constitutionally violative effect of his actions. This standard would not allow the official who actually knows that he was violat-

---

[30] This case involves no issue concerning the elements of the immunity available to state officials sued for constitutional violations under 42 U.S.C. § 1983. We have found previously, however, that it would be "untenable to draw a distinction for purposes of immunity law between suits brought against state officials under § 1983 and suits brought directly under the Constitution against federal officials."

Our decision in no way diminishes the absolute immunity currently available to officials whose functions have been held to require a protection of this scope.

ing the law to escape liability for his actions, even if he could not "reasonably have been expected" to know what he actually did know. Thus the clever and unusually well-informed violator of constitutional rights will not evade just punishment for his crimes. I also agree that this standard applies "across the board," to all "government officials performing discretionary functions." I write separately only to note that given this standard, it seems inescapable to me that some measure of discovery may sometimes be required to determine exactly what a public-official defendant did "know" at the time of his actions. * * *

Notes and Questions

1. Is *Harlow* inconsistent with *Wood v. Strickland* or do they present fundamentally different questions? How did Fitzgerald get into court? Does his basis for proceeding have any implications for the Court's role in evaluating the defendants' claims of immunity?

2. Note that Justice Powell, only three years after decrying the Court's creation of common law in *Cannon v. University of Chicago,* 441 U.S. 677, 99 S.Ct. 1946, 60 L.Ed.2d 560 (1979), candidly recognized that the Court has "extended absolute immunity to certain officials * * * ." Is that something that the author of the *Cannon* dissent ought to cite with approval? Is there a true difference between the practice against which Powell inveighed in *Cannon* and the Court's role with respect to immunities in *Butz v. Economou,* 438 U.S. 478, 98 S.Ct. 2894, 57 L.Ed.2d 895 (1978), and *Nixon v. Fitzgerald,* 457 U.S. 731, 102 S.Ct. 2690, 73 L.Ed.2d 349 (1982)?

3. Justice Powell appears substantially to change his approach from the position he took in *Wood.* There he appeared to rely heavily on the concept of the actor's subjective good faith, whereas in *Harlow* he ostensibly creates an entirely objective standard. What explanation does he give for this change? What shortcoming of the subjective standard does he identify?

4. Leaving to the side for a moment the issue of the appropriate standard for qualified immunity, what values is the Court seeking to serve? Is the goal of the Court's policy to do away with insubstantial claims or to ensure, to the extent possible, that public servants are not deterred from vigorously exercising the powers of their offices by concern over possible litigation?

The *Harlow* Court plainly hoped to simplify qualified immunity law and make the defense easier to adjudicate. Unfortunately, however, *Harlow* raised more questions than it answered. The federal courts have struggled to answer those questions and to clarify how actions against government officials should proceed.

Harlow held that "government officials performing discretionary functions generally are shielded from liability for civil damages insofar as their conduct does not violate clearly established statutory or constitutional rights of which a reasonable person would have known." The

Court anticipated that government defendants would routinely assert this defense and move for summary judgment, thus efficiently curtailing frivolous lawsuits, but the matter was not that simple. If a complaint alleged facts that would constitute a clear violation of federal law if proven, an answer simply denying those allegations plainly would not entitle the defendant to summary judgment. Summary judgment is appropriate only if there is no genuine issue of material fact, and the answer would raise a genuine issue rather than resolve it. Summary judgment might be appropriate if the defendant filed affidavits of eyewitnesses at odds with the plaintiff's story, unless, of course, the plaintiff filed counter-affidavits. Moreover, ambiguity lurked in the *Harlow* standard, thus making it a less effective tool for achieving quick, clean victories. From the defendant's perspective, how murky must the law be to be *not* clearly established? Is it unclear if there is no Supreme Court precedent on point? What if every circuit that has considered the issue has recognized the right, even though the Supreme Court has not ruled on the matter? Can a right be "clearly established" if there is a split in the circuits? Similarly, how does one tell whether a reasonable official should have known that his or her conduct would violate a federal right? Is the defense lost if the official knows generally about the right's existence or only if the official should have known that the conduct in the specific context violated federal law? Finally, it was not clear whether a judge or jury should decide qualified immunity issues. *Harlow*'s plain desire to avoid trial suggested that a judge should decide whether the defense applied. The rule that juries normally decide factual issues, however, suggested that a jury should decide whether the defense applied when its application required resolution of disputed factual questions. Summary judgment for the defendant is appropriate only if no reasonable juror could possibly resolve the material factual issues in the plaintiff's favor.

The Supreme Court recently clarified the proper sequence of inquiry when a defendant raises a qualified immunity defense. In *Wilson v. Layne*, 526 U.S. 603, 119 S.Ct. 1692, 143 L.Ed.2d 818 (1999), and again in *Saucier v. Katz*, 533 U.S. 194, 121 S.Ct. 2151, 150 L.Ed.2d 272 (2001), the Court held that a judge considering the defense must first determine whether the facts alleged would amount to a constitutional violation, and if so, whether the constitutional right was clearly established at the time of the alleged violation. *Wilson* stated that the purpose of deciding the constitutional question first was to spare a defendant not only unwarranted liability but also the unwarranted demands from defending drawn-out litigation. *Saucier* reiterated that the *Harlow* qualified immunity is an immunity from suit, not simply an immunity from liability. It resembles the double jeopardy protection in that it is an entitlement not to face judicial proceedings at all. Consequently, the defense should be resolved at the earliest possible stage of a litigation.

The Court has addressed the central elements of the *Harlow* defense in several cases. *Hope v. Pelzer*, 536 U.S. 730, 122 S.Ct. 2508, 153 L.Ed.2d 666 (2002), considered the circumstances in which a right should be considered clearly established. The Court held that judicial precedent directly on point was unnecessary as long as the defendants had "fair warning" their conduct was unlawful. Alabama had a practice of handcuffing prisoners to "hitching posts" as a disciplinary measure. Hope was handcuffed to a hitching post on two occasions, once for arguing with another inmate, and a second time for using vulgar language that led to a wrestling match with a guard. On the second occasion Hope was attached to the post for seven hours, shirtless in the hot sun, and denied water and toilet breaks. The Court of Appeals held that the use of the hitching post for punitive purposes violated the Eighth Amendment, but granted the defendants immunity because existing judicial precedent, while analogous, were not sufficiently similar to Hope's case. The Supreme Court reversed, holding that the defendants were not entitled to qualified immunity.

The Court began, as mandated in *Saucier*, by deciding whether Hope's allegations, if true, established a constitutional violation. The Court found the Eighth Amendment violation to be "obvious," and then moved to the question of whether the defendants' actions violated clearly established statutory or constitutional rights of which a reasonable person would have known. The Court rejected the Court of Appeals requirement that the facts of previous cases be "materially similar" to the plaintiff's case, stating "[t]his rigid gloss on the qualified immunity standard * * * is not consistent with our cases." While officials must be notice their conduct is unlawful, it is not necessary that the precise misconduct has been so adjudged, as long as the unlawfulness is apparent in light of pre-existing law. The Court then examined existing circuit case law and concluded that because other kinds of severe corporal punishment had been found unconstitutional, defendants should have known their treatment of Hope was unlawful.

Hope v. Pelzer relied heavily on *United States v. Lanier*, 520 U.S. 259, 117 S.Ct. 1219, 137 L.Ed.2d 432 (1997), for its interpretation of "clearly established" law. *Lanier* involved charges pursuant to 18 U.S.C. § 242, the criminal counterpart of § 1983. The defendant judge, charged with sexual assaults, argued both that § 242's incorporation by reference of the state of federal constitutional law was impermissibly vague and that divergent views among the circuits meant that the right concerned could not be clearly established within the meaning of *Harlow*. The Court rejected the vagueness argument and ruled that its own cases do not represent the boundary of the relevant universe of decisional law, even when the circuits are not in agreement:

> Although the Sixth Circuit was concerned, and rightly so, that disparate decisions in various Circuits might leave the law insufficiently certain even on a point widely considered, such a circumstance may be taken into account in deciding whether the warning

is fair enough, without any need for a categorical rule that decisions of the Courts of Appeals and other courts are inadequate as a matter of law to provide it.

The Court also disapproved the defendant's argument that "clearly established" in the context of a criminal charge is a higher standard than in a civil suit, noting:

> the object of the "clearly established immunity standard is not different from that of "fair warning" as it relates to law "made specific" for the purpose of validly applying § 242. The fact that one has a civil and the other a criminal role is of no significance; both serve the same objective, and in effect the qualified immunity test is simply the adaptation of the fair warning standard to give officials (and, ultimately, governments) the same protection from civil liability and its consequences that individuals have traditionally possessed in the face of vague criminal statutes.

Does the Court's linkage of the due-process-notice standard from § 242 and the qualified immunity standard of clarity suggest at least the possibility that the *Harlow* immunity standard has become constitutional in stature? If so, what difference does it make? If not, why should the two rules not have the same hierarchical status?

While *Hope* and *Lanier* may appear pro-plaintiff, *Anderson v. Creighton*, 483 U.S. 635, 107 S.Ct. 3034, 97 L.Ed.2d 523 (1987), and *Saucier* tilt toward defendants on the closely related question of whether a reasonable official must know merely the underlying constitutional rules or know that his conduct in a specific factual context is unlawful. These cases make clear the defense is lost only in the latter situation. The Creightons alleged that FBI agent Anderson and other state and federal law enforcement officials invaded their home without a warrant to search the home and without probable cause. The agents brandished weapons and terrorized the family while searching for a fugitive who was not there, and the agents found no evidence the fugitive had ever been there or that the Creightons or their three young daughters were involved in any type of criminal activity.

When the case reached the Supreme Court, only a *Bivens* claim against Anderson was at issue. Writing for the majority, Justice Scalia argued that "whether an official protected by qualified immunity may be held personally liable for an allegedly unlawful official action generally turns on the 'objective legal reasonableness' of the action * * * assessed in light of the legal rules that were 'clearly established' at the time it was taken." Justice Scalia warned against construing the concept of clearly established right too broadly, noting that if the right in this case were viewed as the Fourth Amendment's proscription against warrantless searches of a dwelling without probable cause, "the test of 'clearly established law' * * * applied at this level of generality * * * would bear no relationship to the 'objective legal reasonableness' that is the touchstone of *Harlow*." The Court continued:

> The contours of the right must be sufficiently clear that a reasonable official would understand that what he is doing violates that right. This is not to say that an official action is protected by qualified immunity unless the very action in question has previously been held unlawful, but it is to say that in light of pre-existing law the unlawfulness must be apparent.

* * *

> The Court of Appeals specifically refused to consider the argument that it was not clearly established that the circumstances with which Anderson was confronted did not constitute probable cause and exigent circumstances. The previous discussion should make clear that this refusal was erroneous. It simply does not follow immediately from the conclusion that it was firmly established that warrantless searches not supported by probable cause and exigent circumstances violate the Fourth Amendment that Anderson's search was objectively legally unreasonable. We have recognized that it is inevitable that law enforcement officials will in some cases reasonably but mistakenly conclude that probable cause is present, and we have indicated that in such cases those officials—like other officials who act in ways they reasonably believe to be lawful—should not be held personally liable. The same is true of their conclusions regarding exigent circumstances.

> It follows from what we have said that the determination whether it was objectively legally reasonable to conclude that a given search was supported by probable cause of exigent circumstances will often require examination of the information possessed by the searching officials. * * * The relevant question in this case, for example is the objective (albeit fact-specific) question whether a reasonable officer could have believed Anderson's warrantless search to be lawful, in light of clearly established law and the information the searching officers possessed.

Three Members of the Court dissented, led by Justice Stevens. He accused the Court of applying *Harlow* far more broadly than that case contemplated. "*Harlow* does not speak to the extent, if any, of an official's insulation from monetary liability when the official concedes that the constitutional right he is charged with violating was deeply etched in our jurisprudence, but argues that he reasonably believed that his particular actions comported with the constitutional command." In such a case, an affirmative defense of reasonable good faith, distinct from *Harlow*, is available to the official at trial. Anderson claimed that a competent officer might have concluded that the particular circumstances constituted "probable cause" and "exigent circumstances," and that his own reasonable belief that the conduct he engaged in was legal was sufficient

to establish immunity. Justice Stevens contended that the factual predicate for such a claim was in the affidavit Anderson filed in support of his
motion for summary judgment and that the Creightons were entitled to
discovery to test its accuracy and completeness. He therefore thought
the Court of Appeals was correct in reversing the grant of summary
judgment.

In the final footnote of its opinion, the majority responded by again
asserting that immunity questions should be resolved at the earliest
possible stage of litigation. Consequently, it directed that the lower
court determine on remand whether a reasonable official could have believed Anderson's actions as alleged by plaintiffs were lawful. If so, then
Anderson would be entitled to summary judgment before discovery. If
not, and if Anderson disputed the Creightons' factual premises, then the
majority conceded that some discovery might be necessary before decision on the summary judgment motion, but cautioned that discovery had
to be tailored specifically to the immunity question.

Given the Court's inquiry into what the "reasonable police officer"
would have done or thought on the facts of the case, will it not be necessary for the district court to permit the plaintiffs to engage in discovery
so that they can make a record of what the facts were? Only then can
the district court make the judgment about whether a reasonable officer
in that position would have thought probable cause and exigent circumstances to exist. By shifting from the question of whether the rule of law
upon which plaintiffs seek to rely is clearly established for *Harlow* purposes to the more fact-based matter of what the reasonable officer would
have done in these circumstances, does not the majority re-introduce the
need for pre-summary-judgment-motion discovery that *Harlow* purports
to be designed to avoid? Given that litigants conduct the vast majority of
discovery to help them to establish facts, not legal theories, why will the
discovery needed here be so much less intrusive than other discovery?

In addition to his argument that the majority misapplied *Harlow*,
Justice Stevens's accused the Court of creating a double-layered standard for reasonableness. His view rested on "the proposition that a warrantless entry into a home without probable cause is always unlawful,"
and he noted that the probable cause standard itself does not require
that the police officer be correct, only that the reasonable person in his
position could believe that the object of the search was in the place
searched. "The concept of probable cause [itself] leaves room for mistakes, provided always that they are mistakes that could have been
made by a reasonable officer." Justice Stevens suggested that it was not
possible for a police officer to be both reasonable (for *Harlow* purposes)
and unreasonable (for probable cause purposes) at the same time.

The upshot of the case was that the Creightons had no federal remedy against the invading officers. Could they have proceeded against the
City of St. Paul for damages resulting from the conduct of the state law

enforcement officials?

To what extent does *Anderson* imply that all applications of the *Harlow* immunity doctrine will now become fact based? Has the Court simply created a special rule for law enforcement officials, or has it performed a more general shift, perhaps opening the door to more discovery generally in cases dealing with immunity as the price of greater substantive protection under the immunity?

Saucier reaffirmed *Anderson*'s determination that trial courts must examine whether a reasonable official would have known his actions violated clearly established law in the specific factual context facing the official at the time. Donald Saucier, a military police officer, was on duty at the Presidio Army base in San Francisco during an event celebrating conversion of the base to a national park. Vice President Albert Gore, Jr. was one of the speakers. When Elliot Katz approached the speaker's platform unfolding a large banner protesting experiments on animals, Saucier and another officer grabbed him and rushed him from the area. Katz brought a *Bivens* action against Saucier, claiming Saucier used excessive force in removing him from the scene. Justice Kennedy, speaking for the Court, said the inquiry into whether a right is clearly established "must be undertaken in light of the specific context of the case, not as a broad general proposition." This approach, he said, "serves to advance understanding of the law and to allow officers to avoid the burden of trial if qualified immunity is applicable."

In the course of the discussion, the Court also reaffirmed *Anderson v. Creighton*'s point that an officer's use of force might be unreasonable for purposes of the Fourth Amendment but still within the scope of the *Harlow* qualified immunity. Rather than remanding to the lower courts for reconsideration based on the proper sequence of inquiry, the Court then proceeded, first to assume that the facts alleged made out a proper excessive force claim and second to examine the facts, declaring that there was no clearly established rule preventing Saucier from acting as he did and that a reasonable officer in his position might well have believed that the degree of force he employed was legitimate given the necessity of protecting the Vice President. Having determined that Saucier was entitled to qualified immunity, the Court remanded, presumably for the lower court to enter an order dismissing the case.

The Court essentially resolved the case on the papers originally filed with respect to Saucier's motion for summary judgment in the district court. Cases like *Saucier* and *Anderson* raise the question of how much latitude a civil rights plaintiff should have to develop a factual record in an attempt to demonstrate that the official acted unreasonably. Does the Court's repeated emphasis on analysis with respect to the particular facts of the case suggest that plaintiffs should be entitled to engage in discovery prior to a defendant's motion for summary judgment? Do you think that is what the Court intends? If so, has the Court eroded much of the protection against the burdens of litigation that it meant in *Harlow* to establish? If not, is the Court's focus on the facts of the individual case slanted in favor of an official-defendant and the allegations that he is able to make supporting the summary judgment motion?

The Court also sought to provide guidance on summary judgment and discovery in cases against government officials in *Crawford-El v. Britton*, 523 U.S. 574, 118 S.Ct. 1584, 140 L.Ed.2d 759 (1998). The plaintiff was a long-term prison inmate who routinely filed lawsuits on behalf of himself and his fellow prisoners. He even managed to give an interview to a newspaper reporter who wrote an article critical of conditions in Lorton Prison. Subsequently, the plaintiff was moved to several other prisons around the country. Boxes containing his personal belongings and legal materials did not catch up with him for several months. He brought suit charging, *inter alia*, that Officer Britton diverted his materials in retaliation for Crawfold-El's exercising his First Amendment rights. The case had a complex procedural history; eventually, the en banc Court of Appeals issued five separate opinions. A majority of the judges required a plaintiff to prove improper motive by clear and convincing evidence where improper motive was an essential element of the plaintiff's claim against a government official. The court reasoned that the heightened proof requirement was a necessary corollary of *Harlow* and would reduce discovery and make cases against officials more amenable to summary judgment.

The Supreme Court reversed, clarifying the relationship between improper motive as an element of the plaintiff's claim and improper motive in the qualified immunity context. In addition, the Court advised how to use existing procedures to achieve expeditious resolution of claims involving examination of officials' state of mind. The Court explained that since *Harlow*, the defendant's intent plays no role in the qualified immunity context: "[A] defense of qualified immunity may not be rebutted by evidence that the defendant's conduct was malicious or otherwise improperly motivated. Evidence concerning a defendant's subjective intent is simply irrelevant to that defense." Evidence of improper motive, however, may be highly relevant to plaintiff's substantive claim; indeed, a charge that defendant acted with improper motive is an essential element of some constitutional claims. Since *Harlow* considered improper motive only in the qualified immunity context, the Court concluded that it provides no support for increasing the plaintiff's burden of proof on the substantive claim.

Although *Harlow* plainly did not compel the Court of Appeals' heightened proof requirement, the Court summarily conceded that some of the purposes underlying *Harlow*'s adoption of an objective standard for qualified immunity would be furthered by the heightened proof requirement. This seems correct. A higher standard of proof would allow weak cases to be terminated more quickly, thus reducing the costs public officials suffer in defending lawsuits. In addition, the higher standard would make it more difficult to survive a summary judgment motion. To make a prima facie case, the plaintiff would be required to submit enough proof from which a reasonable juror could conclude by clear and convincing evidence that the defendant acted with improper motive, rather than merely enough proof from which a reasonable juror could find improper motive by a preponderance. Although the heightened proof standard would support *Harlow*'s purposes, the Court stated "there are countervailing concerns that must be considered before concluding that the balance struck in the context of defining an affirmative defense is also appropriate when evaluating the elements of the plaintiff's cause of action." Because damage actions may be the only realistic remedy when officials abuse their office, serious new limitations on plaintiffs may not be warranted.

The Court gave additional reasons for not changing the law to limit claims that depend on proof of an official's motive. The Court stated that "when intent is an element of a constitutional violation * * * the primary focus is not on any possible animus directed at the plaintiff; rather, it is more specific, such as an intent to disadvantage all members of a class that includes the plaintiff * * * or to deter public comment on a specific issue of public importance." The Court's rationale appears to be that because proof of animus must be relatively specific, an additional heightened proof requirement would impose too great a burden on plaintiffs. In addition, summary judgment may still be appropriate even if a plaintiff alleges a sufficiently specific form of improper motive. The defendant's particular conduct may not be illegal for some other reason, despite the improper motive; alternately, the claim may fail because the plaintiff cannot prove causation.

Finally, the Court distinguished the federal common law created in *Harlow* from that created by the Court of Appeals in imposing a heightened proof requirement by asserting that the absolute and qualified immunity standards of *Harlow* and other cases had a common law pedigree grounded on the Court's efforts to determine the immunity historically granted to officials. The Court of Appeals, by contrast, engaged in improper judicial lawmaking. To "change the burden of proof for an entire category of claims," said the Court, "would stray far from the traditional limits on judicial authority." Is there really a night-and-day difference between creating absolute and qualified immunities and heightening the burden of proof for an element of plaintiff's substantive claim? The Court has assumed that Congress enacted § 1983 against the backdrop of common law immunities, yet there was no discussion of those immunities during the debates on the statute in 1871. Did the Court of Appeals truly stray further from the traditional judicial role than the Supreme Court?

The majority then offered considerable advice to district judges about how to deal with claims of wrongful motive.

The district judge has two primary options prior to permitting any discovery at all. First, the court may order a reply to defendant's or a third party's answer under Federal Rule of Civil Procedure 7(a), or grant the defendant's motion for a more definite statement under Rule 12(e). Thus, the court may insist that the plaintiff "put forward specific, nonconclusory factual allegations" that establish improper motive causing cognizable injury in order to survive a prediscovery motion for dismissal or summary judgment. This option exists even if the official chooses not to plead the affirmative defense of qualified immunity. Second, if the defendant does plead the immunity defense, the district court should resolve that threshold question before permitting discovery. To do so, the court must determine whether, assuming the truth of the plaintiff's allegations, the official's conduct violated clearly established law.

* * * Rule 26 vests the trial judge with broad discretion to tailor discovery narrowly and to dictate the sequence of discovery. * * *

* * * For instance, the court may at first permit the plaintiff to take only a focused deposition of the defendant before allowing any additional discovery. Alternatively, the court may postpone all inquiry regarding the official's subjective motive until discovery has been had on objective factual questions such as whether the plaintiff suffered any injury or whether the plaintiff actually engaged in protected conduct that could be the object of unlawful retaliation. The trial judge can therefore manage the discovery process to facilitate prompt and efficient resolution of the lawsuit, as the evidence is gathered * * * .

Justice Kennedy concurred, finding the majority's balance appropriate under the existing law and noting that what he characterized as Chief Justice Rehnquist's "far-reaching solutions" should spring from the legislative branch, not the judiciary.

The Chief Justice's "far-reaching solutions" referred to by Justice Kennedy flowed from the view that "a government official who is a defendant in a motive-based tort suit is entitled to immunity from suit so long as he can offer a legitimate reason for the action that is being challenged, and the plaintiff is unable to establish, by reliance on objective evidence, that the offered reason is actually a pretext." Chief Justice Rehnquist (joined by Justice O'Connor) was concerned that the majority's approach would effectively strip defendants of the *Harlow* qualified immunity defense by allowing "some measure of intrusion into their subjective worlds." The Chief Justice characterized his proposal as an extension of *Harlow*.

Justice Scalia, joined by Justice Thomas, also dissented, characterizing the Court's entire § 1983 jurisprudence since *Monroe v. Pape* as "bear[ing] scant resemblance to what Congress enacted almost a century earlier." He embraced Justice Frankfurter's view of § 1983 as intended only to encompass actions taken pursuant to governmental authorization. Justice Scalia took the position that even the Chief Justice's proposed test went too far, and offered his own:

> [O]nce the trial court finds that the asserted grounds for the official action were objectively valid (*e.g.* the person fired for alleged incompetence was indeed incompetent), it would not admit any proof that something other than those reasonable grounds was the genuine motive (*e.g.* the incompetent person fired was a Republican). This is, of course, a more severe restriction upon "intent-based" constitutional torts; I am less put off by that consequence than some may be, since I believe that no "intent-based" constitutional tort would have been actionable under the § 1983 that Congress enacted.

Thus, the Douglas-Frankfurter debate from *Monroe v. Pape* is alive and well in the Supreme Court. Is the curtain-raising holding of *Monroe* hanging only by a thin and perhaps-fraying thread?

Does the majority's approach impermissibly allow, as Chief Justice Rehnquist charged, "some intrusion into [the] subjective worlds" of § 1983 defendants? Alternatively, does the Chief Justice's approach (and by extension Justice Scalia's) operate effectively to prevent any motive-based claim from surviving long enough for the plaintiff to engage in any discovery? If so, is that what *Harlow* contemplated? If not, what sorts of claims will survive?

Does Justice Scalia's approach in essence eliminate all constitutional claims where the plaintiff claims the official's justification is merely a pretext? Taking his hypothetical, suppose it were the case that several incompetent people were public employees and the manager fired only the Republicans. Would Justice Scalia's test prevent those employees from obtaining any relief? Suppose the manager stated publicly that the employees were incompetent but were fired only because of their party affiliation or religious belief. Would Justice Scalia find the dismissed employees' plight actionable? Should it be?

Although the Court has extended qualified immunity to public officials confronting § 1983 actions, as in *Wood* and *Harlow*, it has refused other protections. *Leatherman v. Tarrant County Narcotics Intelligence and Coordination Unit*, 507 U.S. 163, 113 S.Ct. 1160, 122 L.Ed.2de 517 (1993), declined to endorse any sort of heightened pleading standard for § 1983 cases against municipalities, Chief Justice Rehnquist holding that the ordinary pleading requirements of the Federal Rules of Civil Procedure apply, unmodified, to such cases.

In *Johnson v. Jones* , 515 U.S. 304, 115 S.Ct. 2151, 132 L.Ed.2d 238 (1995), the Court unanimously declined to apply special appealability standards to § 1983 actions in which summary judgment is refused. Johnson sued five police officers for brutality. Three of the five sought summary judgment, arguing that although there might be evidence of improper behavior by the other two officers, there was none as to the movants. The district court denied the motion, holding that there was sufficient circumstantial evidence to support Jones' contention that the movants had the opportunity to stop the excessive force by their colleagues but failed to do so and noting that its circuit's cases supported liability in such circumstances. The movants appealed, arguing that the plaintiff adduced insufficient evidence in resisting the summary judgment motion. The Seventh Circuit held that it lacked jurisdiction and dismissed the appeal. The Supreme Court affirmed, noting that "the issue here at stake—the existence, or non-existence of a triable issue of fact—is the kind of issue that trial judges, not appellate judges, confront almost daily. Institutionally speaking, appellate judges enjoy no comparative expertise in such matters." The Court also observed that appellate disputes about factual sufficiency could consume large amounts of appellate time and concluded that it would be unwise to commit scarce appellate resources to resolving the factual issue at such a preliminary stage. The Court distinguished *Mitchell v. Forsyth*, 472 U.S. 511, 105 S.Ct. 2806, 86 L.Ed.2d 444 (1985), which had held appealable a denial of summary judgment on the ground that the constitutional principle upon which a § 1983 plaintiff relied was not, in fact, "well established" within the meaning of *Harlow*.

Why do you think the Court permitted interlocutory review in *Forsyth*? Do you think the distinction the Court made in *Johnson v. Jones* between interlocutory reviewability (as in *Mitchell v. Forsyth*) and unreviewability is tenable? Will litigants be able to manipulate the distinction in order to argue that a particular district court order is either appealable or unappealable?

That aside, was the Court's decision correct? If one is to serve the policies and concerns outlined in *Harlow*, does it not make sense to permit interlocutory appeals by defendants of denials of summary judgments? Is a governmental official less likely to be inhibited or interfered with because a district court denial of summary judgment is based upon its differing view of the facts rather than of the law? Of course, one must consider the effect of 28 U.S.C. § 1291, which as a general matter prohibits interlocutory appeals, but the prohibition is not absolute, and the Court has authorized such appeals in a variety of circumstances. May the Court, without violating separation of powers, create an additional category of appealable interlocutory orders in service of policies articulated by the Court that nowhere find expression in statutes?

In *Behrens v. Pelletier*, 516 U.S. 299, 116 S.Ct. 834, 133 L.Ed.2d 773 (1996), the Court took another step down the *Mitchell v. Forsyth* path, holding that not only is "a district court's denial of a claim of qualified immunity, to the extent that it turns on an issue of law, * * * an appealable 'final decision' within the meaning of 28 U.S.C. § 1291," but also that a defendant might have more than one such interlocutory appeal.

The defendant had sought summary judgment on qualified immunity grounds immediately after the complaint was filed and again after discovery. The Ninth Circuit had declined to permit the second appeal, but the Supreme Court disagreed:

> * * * *Mitchell* clearly establishes that an order rejecting the defense of qualified immunity at either the dismissal stage or the summary-judgment stage is a "final" judgment subject to immediate appeal. Since an unsuccessful appeal from a denial of dismissal cannot possibly render the later denial of a motion for summary judgment any less "final," it follows that petitioner's appeal falls within § 1291 and dismissal was improper.

The Court also took the opportunity to attempt to clarify *Johnson v. Jones*.

> *Johnson* held, simply, that determinations of evidentiary sufficiency at summary judgment are not immediately appealable merely because they happen to arise in a qualified-immunity case; if what is at issue in the sufficiency determination is nothing more than whether the evidence could support a finding that particular conduct occurred, the question decided is not truly "separable" from the plaintiff's claim, and hence there is no "final decision" * * *. *Johnson* reaffirmed that summary-judgment determinations are appealable when they resolve a dispute concerning an "abstract issu[e] of law" relating to qualified immunity, typically whether the federal right allegedly infringed was "clearly established."

Does that help?

In *Richardson v. McKnight*, 521 U.S. 399, 117 S.Ct. 2100, 138 L.Ed.2d 540 (1997), a 5-4 majority held that private employees of a company hired to perform a traditional state function are not entitled to the qualified immunity enjoyed by public officials, at least in the circumstances of that case. The majority consisted of Justice Breyer, who wrote the opinion, and Justices Stevens, O'Connor, Souter and Ginsburg. Justice Breyer rejected a purely functional approach to the immunity question, limiting such an approach to the *type* of immunity (absolute or qualified) that follows a judicial determination that there should be *some* immunity. Thus, he refused to recognize any immunity for privately employed prison guards working for a commercial prison management firm. Justice Breyer lauded the market as a control device that makes qualified immunity unnecessary. He argued that overly-aggressive guards unshielded by immunity will ultimately raise prison administration costs and force employers either to leave the market or to train guards to be less aggressive. (He also pointed out that prison management contracts typically are renewable over a relatively short period of time; companies whose personnel do not perform properly face nonrenewal.) In the majority's view, in effect, the combination of privatization and the availability of liability insurance eliminates the "performance-fear factor" that partially undergirds qualified immunity. Justice Breyer did offer three caveats that limit the opinion: the possibility that § 1983 does not reach these defendants at all, the narrowness of the fact pattern that generated the opinion, and the possibility of a good faith defense.

Justice Scalia, speaking for the four dissenters, was not persuaded. Primarily, he saw the matter turning on a purely functional analysis and therefore declined to distinguish privately employed guards from publicly employed guards. He also disparaged the market-pressure theory as illusory, arguing that the political process will interfere with market processes that might otherwise operate. Indeed, he argued that immunity as an incentive to discipline should be the key, though he did not make clear how affording immunity would pressure prison management companies to supervise and control their employees.

4. Note on Protected and Unprotected Interests

The Court has confronted, in addition to the thorny issues of immunity, several others touching upon the scope of § 1983 liability. Note that § 1983 creates neither substantive rights nor subject-matter jurisdiction; it merely creates a private right of action in favor of those who suffer a violation of federal rights found elsewhere in the corpus of federal law. A plaintiff wishing to recover under § 1983 must therefore locate a specific federal right to use as a predicate. That is not always as easy as it might seem.

In *Wisconsin v. Constantineau*, 400 U.S. 433, 91 S.Ct. 507, 27 L.Ed.2d 515 (1971), the plaintiff complained of a city official having "posted" her name pursuant to a state statute, without notice or hearing, making her ineligible to purchase or otherwise to receive alcoholic beverages on the ground that she drank excessively. The Court's majority found that posting violated procedural due process and affirmed the district court's declaration of unconstitutionality. Justice Douglas's opinion noted that "certainly where the State attaches a 'badge of infamy' to the citizen, due process comes into play," and " 'the right to be heard before being condemned to suffer grievous loss of any kind, even though it may not involve the stigma of a criminal conviction, is a principle basic to our society.' " Finally, he observed that

> [w]here a person's good name, reputation, honor, or integrity is at stake because of what the government is doing to him, notice and an opportunity to be heard are essential. "Posting" under the Wisconsin Act may to some be merely the mark of illness, to others it is a stigma, an official branding of a person. The label is a degrading one. Under the Wisconsin Act, [plaintiff was] given no process at all * * *. She may have been the victim of an official's caprice. Only when the whole proceedings leading to the pinning of an unsavory label on a person are aired can oppressive results be prevented.

That being the case, one might have thought that being labeled a thief by state officials would also qualify for relief under § 1983, but *Paul v. Davis*, 424 U.S. 693, 96 S.Ct. 1155, 47 L.Ed.2d 405 (1976), proved the contrary. Davis sued Paul, the police chief of Louisville, Kentucky, because Paul had circulated a flier containing Davis's picture and name (among others) under the caption "Active Shoplifters." At the time, Davis had pleaded "not guilty" to a shoplifting charge; the police court dismissed the charge without trial a few days after the flier appeared. The Court's majority found that Davis stated no claim under § 1983 because it refused to find that what it viewed as defamation rose to the level of infringing any Fourteenth Amendment interest. The majority was explicitly concerned over the possibility of the Fourteenth Amendment becoming what then-Justice Rehnquist characterized as "a font of tort law to be superimposed upon whatever systems may already be administered by the States." Davis had argued that the flier affected his Fourteenth Amendment liberty and property interests because of the stigma of being labeled a thief. The Court, over a vigorous dissent by Justice Brennan,[4] disagreed:

> But the interest in reputation alone which respondent seeks to vindicate in this action in federal court is quite different from the "liberty" or "property" recognized in those decisions. Kentucky law does not extend to respondent any legal guarantee of present enjoyment of reputation which has been altered as a result of petitioners' actions. Rather his interest in reputation is simply one of a number which the State may protect against injury by virtue of its tort law, providing a forum for vindication of those interests by means of damages actions. And any harm or injury to that interest, even where as here inflicted by an officer of the State, does not result in a deprivation of any "liberty" or "property" recognized by state or federal law, nor has it worked any change of respondent's status as theretofore recognized under the State's laws. For these reasons we hold that the interest in reputation asserted in this case is neither "liberty" nor "property" guaranteed against state deprivation without due process of law.

The Court's view of Davis's claim meant, in effect, that for federal constitutional purposes, he was entitled to no process at all prior to having his name thus circulated, although the Court did note that he might have one or more claims under state tort law. One must at least wonder whether the Court's characterization here is completely accurate. If

---

[4] Justice Brennan accused the majority of misreading *Constantineau* by tying the result in that case to deprivation of the "right" to purchase alcoholic beverages and by comparing that case to *Bell v. Burson*, 402 U.S. 535, 91 S.Ct. 1586, 29 L.Ed.2d 90 (1971), in which the Court had required states to hold hearings before revoking or suspending driving privileges, both according to the majority affirmative entitlements granted by state law. Justice Brennan thought the Court clearly based *Constantineau* on the "badge of infamy" reasoning, not on loss of the entitlement to purchase liquor.

Kentucky had had a statute guaranteeing to each person the enjoyment of his good name and reputation, would the majority have to come out differently or to find a different rationale for its result? If so, what of the fact that Kentucky common law did recognize such a right, which provides the underpinning for the state defamation action to which the majority remitted Davis?

More difficult questions were bound to arise. In *Parratt v. Taylor*, 451 U.S. 527, 101 S.Ct. 1908, 68 L.Ed.2d 420 (1981), Nebraska prison inmate Taylor sued prison officials, charging that they negligently deprived him of his property by losing a $23.50 hobby kit sent to Taylor at the prison. The Court could not easily claim that the value of the kit did not represent a Fourteenth Amendment property interest similar to many others the Court had recognized over the years, and so it confronted the specter against which Justice Rehnquist had warned in *Paul v. Davis*. The Court dodged the bullet by noting that not all state interference with property interests violates the Fourteenth Amendment. Only if the deprivation is without due process of law may the complainant invoke the Amendment's protections. The question then, said the Court, is "what process is due?" Given that the predicate for the action was an apparently random act of negligence, Justice Rehnquist noted that pre-deprivation process was impossible as a practical matter and then found that the state's post-deprivation remedy in the form of a state cause of action sounding in negligence was all the process to which Taylor was entitled. Thus, after *Parratt*, negligence could be the basis for a Fourteenth Amendment claim if the state provided insufficient process to vindicate the claimant's life, liberty or property interest.[5] This might have seemed enough to allay the Court's concern that every traffic accident with a state-owned vehicle might become a federal civil rights case, but there was another variation that the Court perhaps had not anticipated, which led several years later to a retreat from *Parratt*.[6]

---

[5] The Court rejected Taylor's claim that because state law 1) permitted suit only against the governmental entity, not against the individuals who actually caused the loss, 2) did not allow punitive damages and 3) did not allow trial by jury, state process was constitutionally defective, noting that "[a]lthough the state remedies may not provide the respondent with all the relief which may have been available if he could have proceeded under § 1983, that does not mean that state remedies are not adequate to satisfy the requirements of due process." *Cf. Schweiker v. Chilicky*, at page 480 (Congress's provision of narrower remedies for wrongful termination than the Court might have implied independently did not render the congressional scheme unconstitutional or entitle plaintiffs to broader remedies under the Fifth Amendment).

[6] In Hudson v. Palmer, 468 U.S. 517, 104 S.Ct. 3194, 82 L.Ed.2d 393 (1984), the Court extended *Parratt*'s reasoning to a case where plaintiff alleged that an individual state official acting deliberately and with malice deprived him of property, finding that pre-deprivation process is unavailable with respect to random and unauthorized actions and that the state's post-deprivation process therefore was adequate. Some years before *Parratt*, the Court had remitted an injured plaintiff to post-deprivation state process even where the official act was neither random nor unauthorized, noting that to require predeprivation process in the circumstances would have a merely marginal effect on the possibility of violations while intruding significantly into an area of state responsibility.

In *Daniels v. Williams*, 474 U.S. 327, 106 S.Ct. 662, 88 L.Ed.2d 662 (1986), the Court faced a situation involving allegedly negligent injury to a state prisoner who had no remedy at state law because of sovereign immunity. On *Parratt*'s reasoning, one might have expected the § 1983 action to go forward, since one would otherwise be forced into saying that the process due for a negligent deprivation of a Fourteenth Amendment interest was none. The Court cut the Gordian knot by revisiting *Parratt*'s rationale.

> Petitioner's claim in this case, which also rests on an alleged Fourteenth Amendment "deprivation" caused by the negligent conduct of a prison official, leads us to reconsider our statement in *Parratt* that "the alleged loss, even though negligently caused, amounted to a deprivation." We conclude that the Due Process Clause is simply not implicated by a negligent act of an official causing unintended loss of or injury to life, liberty, or property.

The upshot in *Daniels*, of course, was that the injured prisoner was left without a remedy of any sort. More importantly, it left negligent harm inflicted by state officials entirely outside the scope of federal constitutional protection.

That said, it is not difficult to sympathize with the Court's dilemma in *Daniels*. If the action were allowed, would it make all traffic accidents involving state vehicles into federal civil rights cases? How can one draw principled distinctions among types of state negligence? *Davidson v. Cannon*, 474 U.S. 344, 106 S.Ct. 668, 88 L.Ed.2d 677 (1986), is more appealing from the prisoner's standpoint. Davidson had warned prison officials of the ill will and the threat from another inmate. As Justice Blackmun argued in dissent, Davidson found himself in a situation where the state had stripped him of the normal ability to defend oneself. State law provided no redress of any sort for him; it denied prisoners relief for harm suffered at the hands of other prisoners. Given that there was no state remedy for the harms that befell Davidson, was the Court implicitly saying that there is no due process liberty interest in bodily integrity at all?

Daniels and *Davidson* do not make clear how much of a mental element must be present for state action to satisfy the Fourteenth Amendment's deprivation component. In *Farmer v. Brennan* (1994), the Court elaborated the mental element required. Petitioner, a preoperative transsexual who displayed what the Court characterized as "feminine characteristics," had been sexually assaulted while incarcerated in a federal prison and commenced a *Bivens* action seeking damages. Justice Souter's opinion noted:

> [t]his case requires us to define the term "deliberate indifference"
> * * * .

> With deliberate indifference lying somewhere between the

poles of negligence at one end and purpose or knowledge at the other, the Courts of Appeals have routinely equated deliberate indifference with recklessness. It is, indeed, fair to say that acting or failing to act with deliberate indifference to a substantial risk of serious harm to a prisoner is the equivalent of recklessly disregarding that risk.

That does not, however, fully answer the pending question about the level of culpability deliberate indifference entails, for the term recklessness is not self-defining. The civil law generally calls a person reckless who acts or (if the person has a duty to act) fails to act in the face of an unjustifiably high risk that is either known or so obvious that it should be known. The criminal law, however, generally permits a finding of recklessness only when a person disregards a risk of harm of which he is aware. The standards proposed by the parties in this case track the two approaches (though the parties do not put it that way): petitioner asks us to define deliberate indifference as what we have called civil-law recklessness, and respondents urge us to adopt an approach consistent with the criminal law.

We reject petitioner's invitation to adopt an objective test for deliberate indifference. We hold instead that a prison official cannot be found liable under the Eighth Amendment for denying an inmate humane conditions of confinement unless the official knows of and disregards an excessive risk to inmate health or safety; the official must both be aware of the facts from which the inference could be drawn that a substantial risk of serious harm exists, and he must also draw the inference. This approach comports best with the text of the Amendment as our cases have interpreted it. The Eighth Amendment does not outlaw cruel and unusual "conditions"; it outlaws cruel and unusual "punishments." * * * [A]n official's failure to alleviate a significant risk that he should have perceived but did not, while no cause for commendation, cannot under our cases be condemned as the infliction of punishment.

A *Bivens* action, of course, is a civil action. Why did the Court depart from the civil concept of recklessness? Does the underlying reason represent a policy judgment that is the Court's to make?

The Court attempted to shed some more light on the state-of-mind component of Fourteenth Amendment deprivations in *County of Sacramento v. Lewis*, 523 U.S. 833, 118 S.Ct. 1708, 140 L.Ed.2d 626 (1998). Plaintiffs' decedent, a passenger on a motorcycle the police were attempting to stop, fell from the motorcycle and died when struck by a police vehicle during the high-speed chase. The Court declined to find a substantive due process violation: "[I]n such circumstances only a purpose to cause harm unrelated to the legitimate object of arrest will satisfy the element of arbitrary conduct shocking to the conscience, necessary for a due process violation." The Court thus rejected the deliberate-indifference standard with regard to substantive due process violations in pursuit cases. Justice Souter's opinion for the Court reasoned that substantive due process focuses on arbitrary government action, and "that only the most egregious official conduct can be said to be 'arbitrary in the constitutional sense * * * .' "

Consider the effect on institutional reform cases the Court's approach in *Parratt, Daniels,* and *Davidson* will have. For example, living conditions at New York's Willowbrook School, an institution for severely mentally handicapped individuals, were described by the district court as "inhumane," and "hazardous to the health, safety, and sanity of the residents." *New York State Association for Retarded Children, Inc. v. Rockefeller* (E.D.N.Y.1973). Suppose those who operated Willowbrook intended no harm to its residents and fully appreciated how bad the conditions were. If they were doing the best job possible given the level of state funding, should a § 1983 action lie, either against the on-the-scene operators of the facility or against the state officials charged with a more general oversight responsibility? If so, how can the officials' conduct be differentiated from that in *Parratt, Daniels,* and *Davidson,* and what should such officials do to avoid potential liability? If not, do residents of such institutions have no enforceable constitutional rights with respect to conditions of confinement? Are conditions in state-operated institutions then beyond constitutional reach as long as the state or its officials do not act maliciously?

After the *Parratt-Davidson* line of cases, one might have thought that in any circumstance where deprivation of a Fourteenth Amendment interest was random and unpredictable, available state post-deprivation process would suffice and preclude resort to a § 1983 action. *Zinermon v. Burch*, 494 U.S. 113, 110 S.Ct. 975, 108 L.Ed.2d 100 (1990), showed that such a prediction would not quite have been accurate, though *Zinermon* today may stand on very shaky ground. Burch sued employees of Florida State Hospital (FSH) complaining that he had been held as a "voluntary patient" for five months although he was not competent to give informed consent to treatment and without having been afforded constitutionally required procedural safeguards. The Court split five to four over the proper disposition of the case. The majority, noting that Burch explicitly did not challenge Florida mental health statutes, which delineated, *inter alia*, the procedures applicable with respect to admission of incompetents. Burch's argument was rather that the FSH officials had failed to follow proper procedure in his case. The Court's majority and dissenters split over the question of whether Burch was entitled to anything more, as a matter of due process, than "an opportunity to sue petitioners in tort for his allegedly unlawful confinement."

Justice Blackmun's majority opinion noted that § 1983 contemplates three classes of claims that may lie under the Fourteenth Amendment's Due Process Clause: 1) claims seeking relief for violation of specific provisions of the Bill of Rights, 2) claims for violation of substantive due process, and 3) claims for violation of procedural due process. With respect to the first two categories, Justice Blackmun noted that *Monroe v. Pape* makes the existence of a state remedy for the alleged violation completely irrelevant to the existence of a § 1983 claim. Claims falling under the third category, however, demand special consideration, since not all deprivations of Fourteenth Amendment interests are unconstitutional. It is in this third category of claim that the question of "what process is due" is critical. The *Parratt* line of cases at least suggested that if the particular violation complained of was random, unauthorized (shades of the Douglas-Frankfurter debate in *Monroe*) and unforeseeable, then state post-deprivation remedies ordinarily satisfy the Due Process Clause. Why not, then, in this case?

The majority distinguished the *Parratt* line by arguing that although a particular case of improper voluntary hospitalization might not be foreseeable, the possibility of such cases arising certainly was. Moreover, Justice Blackmun argued that these were circumstances where it would be possible for the state to establish pre-deprivation procedures to ensure that the state statutory criteria for voluntary and involuntary admissions were satisfied in every case. Thus, the majority found that Florida's delegation of broad authority to individual employees without requiring that some official determine whether the person seeking voluntary admission is competent to give informed consent for the admission to be highly suspect. Avoiding an attack on the Florida statutory scheme, the majority noted:

> It may be permissible constitutionally for a State to have a statutory scheme like Florida's, which gives state officials broad power and little guidance in admitting mental patients. But when those officials fail to provide constitutionally required procedural safeguards to a person whom they deprive of liberty, the state officials cannot then escape liability by invoking *Parratt* and *Hudson*. It is immaterial whether the due process violation Burch alleges is best described as arising from petitioners' failure to comply with state procedures for admitting involuntary patients, or from the absence of a specific requirement that petitioners determine whether a patient is competent to consent to voluntary admission. Burch's suit is neither an action challenging the facial adequacy of a State's statutory procedures, nor an action based only on state officials' random and unauthorized violation of state laws. Burch is not simply attempting to blame the State for misconduct by its employees. He seeks to hold state officials accountable for their abuse of their broadly delegated, uncircumscribed power to effect the deprivation at issue.

The majority thus apparently distinguished the Florida officials' vulnerability to a § 1983 suit for carrying out acts that the state had authorized them to do (in the sense of vesting them with considerable discretion in admissions decisions) from officials' vulnerability to a § 1983 action for carrying out acts that the state had *not* authorized them to do, such as the destruction of legal papers in *Hudson v. Palmer* or the loss of the hobby kit in *Parratt*. Whether this distinction is maintainable rests in the judgment of the reader.

The dissent thought it certainly was not. Justice O'Connor's opinion characterized the events as a random, unauthorized departure from state-mandated admissions procedures and thus found that the existence of state post-deprivation remedies meant that there was no Fourteenth Amendment violation. She accused the majority of overlooking the fact that the complaint did not challenge state procedures; to her, this signified that the complaint regarded Burch's admission as the result of a random, unauthorized act and therefore within the ambit of *Parratt*, *Hudson* and *Daniels*. She and her colleagues feared that the majority's decision would make § 1983 and the Fourteenth Amendment the "font of tort law" about which then-Justice Rehnquist had expressed such concern in his majority opinion in *Paul v. Davis*.

Justice O'Connor's position may ultimately have carried the day. In *Albright v. Oliver*, 510 U.S. 266, 114 S.Ct. 807, 127 L.Ed.2d 114 (1994), an arrestee brought a § 1983 action against a police officer, alleging that the officer had initiated a completely baseless prosecution. The Court declined to recognize a substantive due process right to be free from arrest and prosecution on less than probable cause, concluding that such a right should find its basis in the Fourth Amendment, upon which the plaintiff had not relied. Most important, however, is that Justice Kennedy, joined by Justice Thomas, concurred in the result with a broad statement about the relationship of § 1983 and available state remedies: "In the ordinary case where an injury has been caused not by a state law, policy or procedure, but by a random and unauthorized act that can be remedied by state law, there is no clear basis for intervention under § 1983, at least in a suit based on 'the Due Process Clause of the Fourteenth Amendment *simpliciter*.'" Since Justice Thomas replaced Justice Marshall, a member of the *Zinermon* five-member majority, it appears that *Zinermon* may no longer command five votes. Perhaps more important, however, is those Justices' evident preference for the approach advocated by Justice Frankfurter in *Monroe v. Pape* and the future of federal civil rights litigation when viewed in that light.

Chapter 7

THE ELEVENTH AMENDMENT

A. INTRODUCTION

Few provisions of the Constitution so clearly reflect the federal-state sovereignty conflict as the Eleventh Amendment. A single case, *Chisholm v. Georgia,* 2 U.S. (2 Dall.) 419, 1 L.Ed. 440 (1793), in which the Supreme Court directed a state government to redeem a bond it had issued during the Revolution, almost instantly provoked a national outcry that caused speedy proposal and ratification of the Amendment. It was almost as if the states said in unison to the federal government, "You shall not call us to account for our debts in your courts." To some, *Chisholm* may have brought to life the fears, often expressed during the Constitutional Convention, that the central government would quickly seek to become dominant, destroying states' sovereignty. The colonial experience had sensitized the colonists to the problems of a strong and unresponsive central government. The Articles of Confederation reflected that sensitivity too well: they created so weak a central government that the nation was forced to discard it in only four years. In a very direct way, the Constitutional Convention and the document it created are products of that suspicion of national authority. So, too, is the Eleventh Amendment, and it is well to remember that it reflects, above all, a struggle between governments that continues even today.[1]

A cynic might say that the Amendment is deceptively simple and simply deceptive. There is more to it than meets the eye, but there is also less to it than meets the eye. This Chapter explores that apparent contradiction. Before undertaking *Hans v. Louisiana,* consider the Eleventh Amendment's wording: "The Judicial power of the United States shall not be construed to extend to any suit in law or equity, commenced or prosecuted against one of the United States by Citizens of another State, or by Citizens or Subjects of any Foreign State." What did those who wrote it intend to accomplish? Are the words they chose well-suited

---

[1] Indeed, on the final day of its 1998 Term, the Court announced three cases exemplifying this continuing battle, in the process shifting some of the focus of state sovereign immunity from the Eleventh Amendment to the Tenth. *See* Alden v. Maine, 527 U.S. 706, 119 S.Ct. 2240, 144 L.Ed.2d 636 (1999) (discussed at page 607); College Savings Bank v. Florida Prepaid Postsecondary Education Expense Board, 527 U.S. 627, 119 S.Ct. 2219, 144 L.Ed.2d 575 (1999); Florida Prepaid Postsecondary Education Expense Board v. College Savings Bank, 527 U.S. 666, 119 S.Ct. 2199, 144 L.Ed.2d 605 (1999) (discussed at page 675).

to that goal? Why did they not simply say that no individual could sue a state in a federal court? They did not say that, of course,[2] and so it may not be too surprising to discover that states can, in some circumstances, be defendants in the federal courts. The cases that follow demonstrate the limits of that possibility and of the Eleventh Amendment.

B.   THE BASIC DOCTRINE: MORE THAN MEETS THE EYE

HANS v. LOUISIANA
Supreme Court of the United States, 1890.
134 U.S. 1, 10 S.Ct. 504, 33 L.Ed. 842.

[Hans, a citizen of Louisiana, sought payment on certain state bonds. He alleged that the Louisiana Constitution of 1874, as amended, declared the validity of the bonds and that the state should do nothing to impair them, but that a state constitution adopted five years later did exactly that. He also alleged that Louisiana had levied and collected taxes specifically for the payment of the bonds but had subsequently failed to use those revenues for their intended purpose. Hans sought recovery on the theory that Louisiana's 1879 constitution and its refusal to disburse the tax revenues as above effected an impairment of contract within the meaning of Article I, § 10 of the United States Constitution. Louisiana successfully argued below that the Eleventh Amendment barred the action.]

MR. JUSTICE BRADLEY delivered the opinion of the court.

* * *

[T]he question is presented, whether a State can be sued in a Circuit Court of the United States by one of its own citizens upon a suggestion that the case is one that arises under the Constitution or laws of the United States.

The ground taken is, that under the Constitution, as well as under the act of Congress passed to carry it into effect, a case is within the jurisdiction of the federal courts, without regard to the character of the parties, if it arises under the Constitution or laws of the United States, or, which is the same thing, if it necessarily involves a question under said Constitution or laws. The language relied on is that clause of the 3d article of the Constitution, which declares that "the judicial power of the United States shall extend to all cases in law and equity arising under this Constitution, the laws of the United States, and treaties made, or which shall be made, under their authority;" and the corresponding

---

[2] This is not to say that no one suggested it. As Justice Souter pointed out in his dissent in *Seminole Tribe v. Florida*, Representative Theodore Sedgwick of Massachusetts, later to become Speaker of the House, proposed precisely such an amendment in the aftermath of *Chisholm*, but Congress adopted the Eleventh Amendment instead. *See infra* page 715.

clause of the act conferring jurisdiction upon the Circuit Court * * * . It is said that these jurisdictional clauses make no exception arising from the character of the parties, and, therefore, that a State can claim no exemption from suit, if the case is really one arising under the Constitution, laws or treaties of the United States. It is conceded that where the jurisdiction depends alone upon the character of the parties, a controversy between a State and its own citizens is not embraced within it; but it is contended that though jurisdiction does not exist on that ground, it nevertheless does exist if the case itself is one which necessarily involves a federal question; and with regard to ordinary parties this is undoubtedly true. The question now to be decided is, whether it is true where one of the parties is a State, and is sued as a defendant by one of its own citizens.

That a State cannot be sued by a citizen of another State, or of a foreign state, on the mere ground that the case is one arising under the Constitution or laws of the United States, is clearly established by the decisions of this court in several recent cases. Those were cases arising under the Constitution of the United States, upon laws complained of as impairing the obligation of contracts, one of which was the constitutional amendment of Louisiana complained of in the present case. Relief was sought against state officers who professed to act in obedience to those laws. This court held that the suits were virtually against the States themselves and were consequently violative of the Eleventh Amendment of the Constitution, and could not be maintained. It was not denied that they presented cases arising under the Constitution; but, notwithstanding that, they were held to be prohibited by the amendment referred to.

In the present case the plaintiff in error contends that he, being a citizen of Louisiana, is not embarrassed by the obstacle of the Eleventh Amendment, inasmuch as that amendment only prohibits suits against a State which are brought by the citizens of another State, or by citizens or subjects of a foreign State. It is true, the amendment does so read: and if there were no other reason or ground for abating his suit, it might be maintainable; and then we should have this anomalous result, that in cases arising under the Constitution or laws of the United States, a State may be sued in the federal courts by its own citizens, though it cannot be sued for a like cause of action by the citizens of other States, or of a foreign state; and may be thus sued in the federal courts, although not allowing itself to be sued in its own courts. If this is the necessary consequence of the language of the Constitution and the law, the result is no less startling and unexpected than was the original decision of this court, that under the language of the Constitution and of the judiciary act of 1789, a State was liable to be sued by a citizen of another State, or of a foreign country. That decision was made in the case of *Chisholm v. Georgia,* and created such a shock of surprise throughout the country that, at the first meeting of Congress thereafter, the Eleventh Amendment to the Constitution was almost unanimously proposed, and was in due course adopted by the legislatures of the States. This amendment, expressing the will of the ultimate sovereignty of the whole country, superior to all legislatures and all courts, actually reversed the decision of the Supreme Court. It did not in terms prohibit suits by individuals against the States, but declared that the Constitution should not be construed to import any power to authorize the bringing of such suits. The language of the amendment is that "the judicial power of the United States shall not be construed to extend to any suit in law or equity, commenced or prosecuted against one of the United States by citizens of another State or by citizens or subjects of any foreign state." The Supreme Court had construed the judicial power as extending to such a suit, and its decision was thus overruled. * * * [O]n the succeeding day, the court delivered a unanimous opinion, "that the amendment being constitutionally adopted, there could not be exercised any jurisdiction, in any case, past or future, in which a State was sued by the citizens of another State, or by citizens or subjects of any foreign state."

This view of the force and meaning of the amendment is important. It shows that, on this question of the suability of the States by individuals, the highest authority of this country was in accord rather with the minority than with the majority of the court in the decision of the case of *Chisholm v. Georgia;* and this fact lends additional interest to the able opinion of Mr. Justice Iredell on that occasion. The other justices were more swayed by a close observance of the letter of the Constitution, without regard to former experience and usage; and because the letter said that the judicial power shall extend to controversies "between a State and citizens of another State;" and "between a State and foreign states, citizens or subjects," they felt constrained to see in this language a power to enable the individual citizens of one State, or of a foreign state, to sue another State of the Union in the federal courts. Justice Iredell, on the contrary, contended that it was not the intention to create new and unheard of remedies, by subjecting sovereign States to actions at the suit of individuals, (which he conclusively showed was never done before,) but only, by proper legislation, to invest the federal courts with jurisdiction to hear and determine controversies and cases, between the parties designated, that were properly susceptible of litigation in courts.

Looking back from our present standpoint at the decision in *Chisholm v. Georgia,* we do not greatly wonder at the effect which it had upon the country. Any such power as that of authorizing the federal judiciary to entertain suits by individuals against the States, had been expressly disclaimed, and even resented, by the great defenders of the Constitution whilst it was on its trial before the American people. As some of their utterances are directly pertinent to the question now under consideration, we deem it proper to quote them.

The eighty-first number of the Federalist, written by Hamilton, has the following profound remarks:

It has been suggested that an assignment of the public securities of one State to the citizens of another, would enable them to prosecute that State in the federal courts for the amount of those securities; a suggestion which the following considerations prove to be without foundation:

It is inherent in the nature of sovereignty not to be amenable to the suit of an individual without its consent. This is the general sense and the general practice of mankind; and the exemption, as one of the attributes of sovereignty, is now enjoyed by the government of every State in the Union. Unless, therefore, there is a surrender of this immunity in the plan of the convention, it will remain with the States, and the danger intimated must be merely ideal. The circumstances which are necessary to produce an alienation of state sovereignty were discussed in considering the article of taxation, and need not be repeated here. A recurrence to the principles there established will satisfy us, that there is no color to pretend that the state governments would, by the adoption of that plan, be divested of the privilege of paying their own debts in their own way, free from every constraint but that which flows from the obligations of good faith. The contracts between a nation and individuals are only binding on the conscience of the sovereign, and have no pretension to a compulsive force. They confer no right of action independent of the sovereign will. To what purpose would it be to authorize suits against States for the debts they owe? How could recoveries be enforced? It is evident that it could not be done without waging war against the contracting State; and to ascribe to the federal courts by mere implication, and in destruction of a pre-existing right of the state governments, a power which would involve such a consequence, would be altogether forced and unwarrantable.

The obnoxious clause to which Hamilton's argument was directed, and which was the ground of the objections which he so forcibly met, was that which declared that "the judicial power shall extend to all * * * controversies between a State and citizens of another State, * * * and between a State and foreign states, citizens or subjects." It was argued by the opponents of the Constitution that this clause would authorize jurisdiction to be given to the federal courts to entertain suits against a State brought by the citizens of another State, or of a foreign state. Adhering to the mere letter, it might be so; and so, in fact, the Supreme Court held in *Chisholm v. Georgia;* but looking at the subject as Hamilton did, and as Mr. Justice Iredell did, in the light of history and experience and the established order of things, the views of the latter were clearly right,—as the people of the United States in their sovereign capacity subsequently decided.

But Hamilton was not alone in protesting against the construction put upon the Constitution by its opponents. In the Virginia convention the same objections were raised by George Mason and Patrick Henry, and were met by Madison and Marshall as follows. Madison said:

> Its jurisdiction [the federal jurisdiction] in controversies between a State and citizens of another State is much objected to, and perhaps without reason. It is not in the power of individuals to call any State into court. The only operation it can have is that, if a State should wish to bring a suit against a citizen, it must be brought before the federal court. This will give satisfaction to individuals, as it will prevent citizens on whom a State may have a claim being dissatisfied with the state courts * * *. It appears to me that this [clause] can have no operation but this—to give a citizen a right to be heard in the federal courts; and if a State should condescend to be a party, this court may take cognizance of it.

Marshall, in answer to the same objection, said:

> With respect to disputes between a State and the citizens of another State, its jurisdiction has been decried with unusual vehemence. I hope that no gentleman will think that a State will be called at the bar of the federal court * * *. It is not rational to suppose that the sovereign power should be dragged before a court. The intent is to enable States to recover claims of individuals residing in other States * * *. But, say they, there will be partiality in it if a State cannot be defendant—if an individual cannot proceed to obtain judgment against a State, though he may be sued by a State. It is necessary to be so, and cannot be avoided. I see a difficulty in making a State defendant which does not prevent its being plaintiff.

It seems to us that these views of those great advocates and defenders of the Constitution were most sensible and just; and they apply equally to the present case as to that then under discussion. The letter is appealed to now, as it was then, as a ground for sustaining a suit brought by an individual against a State. The reason against it is as strong in this case as it was in that. It is an attempt to strain the Constitution and the law to a construction never imagined or dreamed of. Can we suppose that, when the Eleventh Amendment was adopted, it was understood to be left open for citizens of a State to sue their own state in the federal courts, whilst the idea of suits by citizens of other states, or of foreign states, was indignantly repelled? Suppose that Congress, when proposing the Eleventh Amendment, had appended to it a *proviso* that nothing therein contained should prevent a State from being sued by its own citizens in cases arising under the Constitution or laws of the United States: can we imagine that it would have been adopted by the States? The supposition that it would is almost an absurdity on its face.

The truth is, that the cognizance of suits and actions unknown to the law, and forbidden by the law, was not contemplated by the Constitution when establishing the judicial power of the United States. Some things, undoubtedly, were made justiciable which were not known as such at the common law; such, for example, as controversies between States as to boundary lines, and other questions admitting of judicial solution. * * *

The suability of a State without its consent was a thing unknown to the law. This has been so often laid down and acknowledged by courts and jurists that it is hardly necessary to be formally asserted. It was fully shown by an exhaustive examination of the old law by Mr. Justice Iredell in his opinion in *Chisholm v. Georgia;* and it has been conceded in every case since, where the question has, in any way been presented, even in the cases which have gone farthest in sustaining suits against the officers or agents of States. In all these cases the effort was to show, and the court held, that the suits were not against the State or the United States, but against the individuals; conceding that if they had been against either the State or the United States, they could not be maintained.

* * *

Undoubtedly a State may be sued by its own consent * * *. But this court decided that the State could repeal that law at any time; that it was not a contract within the terms of the constitution prohibiting the passage of state laws impairing the obligation of a contract. * * *

But besides the presumption that no anomalous and unheard-of proceedings or suits were intended to be raised up by the Constitution—anomalous and unheard of when the Constitution was adopted—an additional reason why the jurisdiction claimed for the Circuit Court does not exist, is the language of the act of Congress by which its jurisdiction is conferred. The words are these: "The circuit courts of the United States shall have original cognizance, concurrent with the courts of the several States, of all suits of a civil nature at common law or in equity, * * * arising under the Constitution or laws of the United States, or treaties," etc.—"Concurrent with the courts of the several States." Does not this qualification show that Congress, in legislating to carry the Constitution into effect, did not intend to invest its courts with any new and strange jurisdictions? The state courts have no power to entertain suits by individuals against a State without its consent. Then how does the Circuit Court, having only concurrent jurisdiction, acquire any such power? It is true that the same qualification existed in the judiciary act of 1789, which was before the court in *Chisholm v. Georgia,* and the majority of the court did not think that it was sufficient to limit the jurisdiction of the Circuit Court. Justice Iredell thought differently. In view of the manner in which that decision was received by the country, the adoption of the Eleventh Amendment, the light of history and the reason of the thing, we think we are at liberty to prefer Justice Iredell's views in this regard.

Some reliance is placed by the plaintiff upon the observations of

Chief Justice Marshall, in *Cohens v. Virginia.* The Chief Justice was there considering the power of review exercisable by this court over the judgments of a state court, wherein it might be necessary to make the State itself a defendant in error. He showed that this power was absolutely necessary in order to enable the judiciary of the United States to take cognizance of all cases arising under the Constitution and laws of the United States. He also showed that making a State a defendant in error was entirely different from suing a State in an original action in prosecution of a demand against it, and was not within the meaning of the Eleventh Amendment; that the prosecution of a writ of error against a State was not the prosecution of a suit in the sense of that amendment, which had reference to the prosecution, by suit, of claims against a State. "Where," said the Chief Justice,

> a State obtains a judgment against an individual, and the court rendering such judgment overrules a defence set up under the Constitution or laws of the United States, the transfer of this record into the Supreme Court for the sole purpose of inquiring whether the judgment violates the Constitution of the United States, can, with no propriety, we think, be denominated a suit commenced or prosecuted against the State whose judgment is so far reexamined. Nothing is demanded from the State. No claim against it of any description is asserted or prosecuted. The party is not to be restored to the possession of any thing * * * . He only asserts the constitutional right to have his defence examined by that tribunal whose province it is to construe the Constitution and laws of the Union * * * . The point of view in which this writ of error, with its citation, has been considered uniformly in the courts of the Union, has been well illustrated by a reference to the course of this court in suits instituted by the United States. The universally received opinion is that no suit can be commenced or prosecuted against the United States; that the judiciary act does not authorize such suits. Yet writs of error, accompanied with citations, have uniformly issued for the removal of judgments in favor of the United States into a superior court * * * . It has never been suggested that such writ of error was a suit against the United States, and, therefore, not within the jurisdiction of the appellate court.

After thus showing by incontestable argument that a writ of error to a judgment recovered by a State, in which the State is necessarily the defendant in error, is not a suit commenced or prosecuted against a State in the sense of the amendment, he added, that if the court were mistaken in this, its error did not affect that case, because the writ of error therein was not prosecuted by "a citizen of another State" or "of any foreign state," and so was not affected by the amendment; but was governed by the general grant of judicial power, as extending "to all cases arising under the Constitution or laws of the United States, without respect to parties."

It must be conceded that the last observation of the Chief Justice does favor the argument of the plaintiff. But the observation was unnecessary to the decision, and in that sense extra judicial, and though made by one who seldom used words without due reflection, ought not to outweigh the important considerations referred to which lead to a different conclusion. With regard to the question then before the court, it may be observed, that writs of error to judgments in favor of the crown, or of the State, had been known to the law from time immemorial; and had never been considered as exceptions to the rule, that an action does not lie against the sovereign.

* * *

It is not necessary that we should enter upon an examination of the reason or expediency of the rule which exempts a sovereign State from prosecution in a court of justice at the suit of individuals. This is fully discussed by writers on public law. It is enough for us to declare its existence. The legislative department of a State represents its polity and its will; and is called upon by the highest demands of natural and political law to preserve justice and judgment, and to hold inviolate the public obligations. Any departure from this rule, except for reasons most cogent, (of which the legislature, and not the courts, is the judge,) never fails in the end to incur the odium of the world, and to bring lasting injury upon the State itself. But to deprive the legislature of the power of judging what the honor and safety of the State may require, even at the expense of a temporary failure to discharge the public debts, would be attended with greater evils than such failure can cause.

The judgment of the Circuit Court is

Affirmed.

MR. JUSTICE HARLAN concurring.

I concur with the court in holding that a suit directly against a State by one of its own citizens is not one to which the judicial power of the United States extends, unless the State itself consents to be sued. Upon this ground alone I assent to the judgment. But I cannot give my assent to many things said in the opinion. The comments made upon the decision in *Chisholm v. Georgia* do not meet my approval. They are not necessary to the determination of the present case. Besides, I am of opinion that the decision in that case was based upon a sound interpretation of the Constitution as that instrument then was.

Notes and Questions

1. a) Would *Hans* be a federal question case today? What is the plaintiff's cause of action? What federal issue is involved in the case, and upon which constitutional provision is it based?

b) The Louisiana Constitution provided that "[t]o secure * * * payment, the judicial power shall be exercised when necessary." Should the Court have considered that language a waiver by Louisiana of Eleventh Amendment or other sovereign immunity protection?

2. a) At the outset, *Hans* confronts the peculiar wording of the Eleventh Amendment. Scholars have echoed and expanded Hans's argument that the Amendment was intended to curtail only party-based jurisdiction. *See, e.g.,* William A. Fletcher, *A Historical Interpretation of the Eleventh Amendment: A Narrow Construction of an Affirmative Grant of Jurisdiction Rather Than a Prohibition Against Jurisdiction,* 35 STAN.L.REV. 1033 (1983); John J. Gibbons, *The Eleventh Amendment and State Sovereign Immunity: A Reinterpretation,* 83 COLUM.L.REV. 1889 (1983). Judge Fletcher, for example, interprets the Eleventh Amendment purely as forbidding diversity cases against the states. Under his theory, any federal question case is maintainable against the states in the federal courts.

Yet, as the Court points out, to accept that argument is to ignore the Amendment's wording when a non-citizen of the defendant state brings a federal-question action. On the other hand, restricting the federal forum to federal question cases brought by a state's citizens would create the anomaly the *Hans* Court noted. Nonetheless, one scholar has argued that the Eleventh Amendment means exactly what it says. *See* Calvin R. Massey, *State Sovereignty and the Tenth and Eleventh Amendments,* 56 U.CHI.L.REV. 61 (1989). Professor Massey suggests that one must read the Tenth and Eleventh Amendments together and that the Eleventh Amendment's primary purpose was to prevent federal suits against states by "outsiders"—primarily British subjects or sympathizers—who might have acquired state paper during the Revolution.

b) Does the Court's argument prove too much? Justice Bradley notes that if the Eleventh Amendment excludes only federal actions against states by non-residents, a resident may bring a federal question action against the state even though a non-resident with the same claim could not. If the anomaly is so plain, and if the Constitution's (and the Eleventh Amendment's) framers were so opposed to federal judicial power being exercised against the states, how did the literal effect of the language manage to escape their attention?

c) Justice Bradley's argument raises a more general question about the Eleventh Amendment. If the drafters intended to preclude all individual actions against states in the federal courts, why did the Amendment not say that? It might have read, "The judicial power shall not be construed to extend to suits against one of the United States." *See infra* page 715 (the Sedgwick proposal made contemporaneously with the consideration of the Eleventh Amendment in Congress). What might have impelled the draftsmen to include wording that seems clearly to contemplate federal suits against a state by its own citizens?

3. a) Is the basis for the decision in *Hans* that the Amendment prohibits the federal courts from hearing the case, or that there is some other immunity doctrine of like effect, or that there is a statutory basis for declining relief? What difference does it make?

b) What is the *Hans* Court's view of the Eleventh Amendment? Is it part of the Constitution's jurisdictional grant to the federal courts, or is it an entitlement of the states individually? What difference does it make?

4. Is *Hans* predominantly a statutory interpretation case? Note the Court's reliance on the federal question jurisdiction statute's language regarding concurrent jurisdiction. The Court reads "concurrent with the courts of the several States" as expressing a limitation on the jurisdictional grant, *i.e.* that Congress intended to grant no jurisdiction broader than that already existing at the state level. Cannot the same language merely indicate that the grant of federal question jurisdiction was not intended to oust the state courts of jurisdiction that they had exercised for eighty-six years? Given the empty legislative history of the 1875 jurisdictional grant, is there any basis for preferring one interpretation over the other?

5. The Court draws heavily upon Justice Iredell's dissenting opinion in *Chisholm v. Georgia,* yet it is far from clear that his dissent directly supports the *Hans* result, much less the more general rule now attributed to *Hans.* In *Chisholm,* the Attorney General of the United States had framed the issue in terms of whether a state could be sued in the federal courts. Justice Iredell was at pains to limit the scope of the issue, though he recognized the difficulty of doing so.

> The particular question then before the Court is, will an action of *assumpsit* lie against a State? This particular question (abstracted from the general one, *viz.* Whether, a State can in any instance be sued?) I took the liberty to propose to the consideration of the Attorney-General * * *. I shall * * * confine myself, as much as possible, to the particular question before the Court, though every thing I have to say upon it will effect [*sic*] every kind of suit, the object of which is to compel the payment of money by a State.

Did Justice Iredell imply by omission that actions against a state for other than monetary relief may stand upon a different footing from cases seeking damages? He noted later that when the Constitution and the Eleventh Amendment were adopted, no individual could maintain an action against a state "for the recovery of money * * * ."

One can read much of Justice Iredell's opinion, however, to allow at least the possibility of federal question cases against states. His discussion of the division of sovereignty between states and federal government and the creation of concurrent judicial power is illuminating.

> Every State in the *Union* in every instance where its sovereignty has not been delegated to the *United States*, I consider to be as completely sovereign, as the *United States* are in respect to the powers surrendered. The *United States* are sovereign as to all the powers of Government actually surrendered: Each State in the *Union* is sovereign as to all the powers reserved. * * * Where certain parties are concerned, although the subject in controversy does not relate to any of the special objects of authority of the general government, wherein the separate sovereignties of the States are blended in one common mass of su-

premacy, yet the general Government has a Judicial Authority in regard to such subjects of controversy, and the Legislature of the *United States*, and their individual sovereignty is in this respect limited. But it is limited no farther than the necessary execution of such authority requires. The authority extends only to the decision of controversies in which a State is a party, and providing laws necessary for that purpose. That surely can refer only to such controversies in which a State *can* be a part; in respect to which, if any question arises, it can be determined, according to the principles I have supported, in no other manner than by a reference either to pre-existent laws, or laws passed under the Constitution and in conformity to it.

Would it be consistent with this view of state immunity to conclude that Congress could authorize federal actions against states concerning any federal power created by the Constitution? If Congress were to create a federal cause of action based on the Commerce Clause, is there anything in Justice Iredell's view of the relationship between states and the federal government that would preclude such a claim against a state in federal court?

6. There are at least four ways in which to read the Eleventh Amendment. First, it may be a general limitation on the subject matter jurisdiction of the federal courts, indicating that their jurisdiction never extends to cases in which a state is a defendant. Note particularly the introductory wording of the Amendment: "The judicial power shall not be construed * * * ." Second, it may constitutionalize a pre-existing common law immunity. Third, it may recognize a common law immunity neither based in nor abrogated by the Constitution or by act of Congress. For example, in *In re New York,* 256 U.S. 490, 497, 41 S.Ct. 588, 589, 65 L.Ed. 1057 (1921), the Court noted that the federal courts cannot entertain a suit by an out-of-stater "because of the Eleventh Amendment; and not even one brought by |a state's| own citizens, because of the fundamental rule of which the Amendment is but an exemplification." Fourth, it may constitute a simple limitation only on the diversity jurisdiction of the federal courts.

a) If the Amendment is a limitation on subject matter jurisdiction, why does the *Hans* Court emphasize that a state may not be sued "without its consent"? After all, parties cannot agree to subject matter jurisdiction that a court does not possess under its constitutive law.

b) With respect to the "fundamental rule" of state immunity exemplified by the Eleventh Amendment, is there not a substantial supremacy problem? What is the source of the fundamental rule? Article VI declares the Constitution and laws passed in conformity with it to be the supreme law. Why would an action based upon a federal statute and brought as a federal question case not prevail over a claim of common law immunity?

c) If the party-based jurisdiction view of the Amendment is correct, what should we make of *Hans*?

7. Whether rightly or wrongly decided, *Hans* is clearly the engine that drives all of the Court's modern Eleventh Amendment jurisprudence. As you proceed through the following cases, keep in mind the role of *Hans* and

its effect on the resolution of particular Eleventh Amendment controversies. Notice also that later Courts may have different views of exactly what *Hans* decided.

GILES v. HARRIS
Supreme Court of the United States, 1903.
189 U.S. 475; 23 S.Ct. 639; 47 L.Ed. 909.

MR. JUSTICE HOLMES delivered the opinion of the Court.

This is a bill in equity brought by a colored man, on behalf of himself "and on behalf of more than five thousand negroes, citizens of the county of Montgomery, Alabama, similarly situated and circumstanced as himself," against the board of registrars of that county. The prayer of the bill is in substance that the defendants may be required to enroll upon the voting lists the name of the plaintiff and of all other qualified members of his race who applied for registration before August 1, 1902, and were refused, and that certain sections of the constitution of Alabama, *viz.*, sections 180, 181, 183, 184, 185, 186, 187 and 188 of article 8, may be declared contrary to the Fourteenth and Fifteenth Amendments of the Constitution of the United States, and void.

The allegations of the bill may be summed up as follows. The plaintiff is subject to none of the disqualifications set forth in the constitution of Alabama and is entitled to vote,—entitled, as the bill plainly means, under the constitution as it is. He applied in March, 1902, for registration as a voter, and was refused arbitrarily on the ground of his color, together with large numbers of other duly qualified negroes, while all white men were registered. The same thing was done all over the State. Under § 187 of article 8 of the Alabama constitution[,] persons registered before January 1, 1903, remain electors for life unless they become disqualified by certain crimes, etc., while after that date severer tests come into play which would exclude, perhaps, a large part of the black race. Therefore, by the refusal, the plaintiff and the other negroes excluded were deprived not only of their votes at an election which has taken place since the bill was filed, but of the permanent advantage incident to registration before 1903. The white men generally are registered for good under the easy test and the black men are likely to be kept out in the future as in the past. This refusal to register the blacks was part of a general scheme to disfranchise them, to which the defendants and the State itself, according to the bill, were parties. The defendants accepted their office for the purpose of carrying out the scheme. The part taken by the State, that is, by the white population which framed the constitution, consisted in shaping that instrument so as to give opportunity and effect to the wholesale fraud which has been practised.

The bill sets forth the material sections of the state constitution, the general plan of which, leaving out details, is as follows: By § 178 of article 8, to entitle a person to vote he must have resided in the State at least two years, in the county one year and in the precinct or ward three months, immediately preceding the election, have paid his poll taxes and have been duly registered as an elector. By § 182, idiots, insane persons and those convicted of certain crimes are disqualified. Subject to the foregoing, by § 180, before 1903 the following male citizens of the State, who are citizens of the United States, were entitled to register, *viz.*: First. All who had served honorably in the enumerated wars of the United States, including those on either side in the "war between the States," Second. All lawful descendants of persons who served honorably in the enumerated wars or in the war of the Revolution. Third. "All persons who are of good character and who understand the duties and obligations of citizenship under a republican form of government." As we have said, according to the allegations of the bill this part of the constitution, as practically administered and as intended to be administered, let in all whites and kept out a large part, if not all, of the blacks, and those who were let in retained their right to vote after 1903, when tests which might be too severe for many of the whites as well as the blacks went into effect. By § 181, after January 1, 1903, only the following persons are entitled to register: First. Those who can read and write any article of the Constitution of the United States in the English language, and who either are physically unable to work or have been regularly engaged in some lawful business for the greater part of the last twelve months, and those who are unable to read and write solely because physically disabled. Second. Owners or husbands of owners of forty acres of land in the State, upon which they reside, and owners or husbands of owners of real or personal estate in the State assessed for taxation at $300 or more, if the taxes have been paid unless under contest. By § 183, only persons qualified as electors can take part in any method of party action. By § 184, persons not registered are disqualified from voting. By § 185, an elector whose vote is challenged shall be required to swear that the matter of the challenge is untrue before his vote shall be received. By § 186, the legislature is to provide for registration after January 1, 1903, the qualifications and oath of the registrars are prescribed, the duties of registrars before that date are laid down, and appeal is given to the county court and Supreme Court if registration is denied. There are further executive details in § 187, together with the above mentioned continuance of the effect of registration before January 1, 1903. By § 188, after the last mentioned date applicants for registration may be examined under oath as to where they have lived for the last five years, the names by which they have been known, and the names of their employers. This, in brief, is the system which the plaintiff asks to have declared void.

Perhaps it should be added to the foregoing statement that the bill was filed in September, 1902, and alleged the plaintiff's desire to vote at an election coming off in November. This election has gone by, so that it is impossible to give specific relief with regard to that. But we are not prepared to dismiss the bill or the appeal on the ground, because to be enabled to cast a vote in that election is not the whole object of the bill.

It is not even the principal object of the relief sought by the plaintiff. The principal object of that is to obtain the permanent advantages of registration as of a date before 1903.

The certificate of the circuit judge raises the single question of the jurisdiction of the court. The plaintiff contends that this jurisdiction is given expressly by Rev. Stat. § 629, cl. 16, coupled with Rev. Stat. § 1979, which provides that every person who, under color of a state "statute, ordinance, regulation, custom, or usage," "subjects, or causes to be subjected, any citizen of the United States or other person within the jurisdiction thereof to the deprivation of any rights, privileges, or immunities secured by the Constitution and laws, shall be liable to the party injured in an action at law, suit in equity, or other proper proceeding for redress."

We assume * * * that § 1979 has not been repealed, and that jurisdiction to enforce its provisions has not been taken away by any later act. But it is suggested that the Circuit Court was right in its ruling that it had no jurisdiction as a court of the United States, because the bill did not aver threatened damage to an amount exceeding two thousand dollars. It is true that * * * the Circuit Courts are given cognizance of suits of a civil nature, at common law or in equity, arising under the Constitution or laws of the United States, in which the matter in dispute exceeds the sum or value of two thousand dollars. We have recognized, too, that the deprivation of a man's political and social rights properly may be alleged to involve damage to that amount, capable of estimation in money. But, assuming that the allegation should have been made in a case like this, the objection to its omission was not raised in the Circuit Court, and as it could have been remedied by amendment, we think it unavailing. The certificate was made *alio intuitu*. There is no pecuniary limit on appeals to this court under section 5 of the act of 1891, and we do not feel called upon to send the case back to the Circuit Court in order that it might permit the amendment. * * *

* * *

It seems to us impossible to grant the equitable relief which is asked. It will be observed in the first place that the language of § 1979 does not extend the sphere of equitable jurisdiction in respect of what shall be held an appropriate subject matter for that kind of relief. The words are "shall be liable to the party injured in an action at law, suit in equity, or other proper proceeding for redress." They allow a suit in equity only when that is the proper proceeding for redress, and they refer to existing standards to determine what is a proper proceeding. The traditional limits of proceedings in equity have not embraced a remedy for political wrongs. But we cannot forget that we are dealing with a new and extraordinary situation, and we are unwilling to stop short of the final considerations which seems to us to dispose of the case.

The difficulties which we cannot overcome are two, and the first is this: The plaintiff alleges that the whole registration scheme of the Alabama constitution is a fraud upon the Constitution of the United States, and asks us to declare it void. But of course he could not maintain a bill for a mere declaration in the air. He does not try to do so, but asks to be registered as a party qualified under the void instrument. If then we accept the conclusion which it is the chief purpose of the bill to maintain, how can we make the court a party to the unlawful scheme by accepting it and adding another voter to its fraudulent lists? If a white man came here on the same general allegations, admitting his sympathy with the plan, but alleging some special prejudice that had kept him off the list, we hardly should think it necessary to meet him with a reasoned answer. But the relief cannot be varied because we think that in the future the particular plaintiff is likely to try to overthrow the scheme. If we accept the plaintiff's allegations for the purposes of his case, he cannot complain. We must accept or reject them. It is impossible simply to shut our eyes, put the plaintiff on the lists, be they honest or fraudulent, and leave the determination of the fundamental question for the future. If we have an opinion that the bill is right on its face, or if we are undecided, we are not at liberty to assume it to be wrong for the purposes of decision. It seems to us that unless we are prepared to say that it is wrong, that all its principal allegations are immaterial and that the registration plan of the Alabama constitution is valid, we cannot order the plaintiff's name to be registered. It is not an answer to say that if all the blacks who are qualified according to the letter of the instrument were registered, the fraud would be cured. In the first place, there is no probability that any way now is open by which more than a few could be registered, but if all could be the difficulty would not be overcome. If the sections of the constitution concerning registration were illegal in their inception, it would be a new doctrine in constitutional law that the original invalidity could be cured by an administration which defeated their intent. We express no opinion as to the alleged fact of their unconstitutionality beyond saying that we are not willing to assume that they are valid, in the face of the allegations and main object of the bill, for the purpose of granting the relief which it was necessary to pray in order that that object should be secured.

The other difficulty is of a different sort, and strikingly reinforces the argument that equity cannot undertake now, any more than it has in the past, to enforce political rights, and also the suggestion that state constitutions were not left unmentioned in § 1979 by accident. In determining whether a court of equity can take jurisdiction, one of the first questions is what it can do to enforce any order that it may make. This is alleged to be the conspiracy of a State, although the State is not and could not be made a party to the bill. *Hans v. Louisiana.* The Circuit Court has no constitutional power to control its action by any direct means. And if we leave the State out of consideration, the court has as little practical power to deal with the people of the State in a body. The bill imports that the great mass of the white population intends to keep the blacks from voting. To meet such an intent something more than ordering the plaintiff's name to be inscribed upon the lists of 1902 will be needed. If the conspiracy and the intent exist, a name on a piece of paper will not defeat them. Unless we are prepared to supervise the voting in that State by officers of the court, it seems to us that all that the plaintiff could get from equity would be an empty form. Apart from damages to the individual, relief from a great political wrong, if done, as alleged, by the people of a state and the State itself, must be given by them or by the legislative and political department of the Government of the United States.

Decree affirmed.

MR. JUSTICE HARLAN dissenting.

By the final judgment in the Circuit Court the bill in this case was dismissed for want of jurisdiction to entertain it and for want of equity; and from that judgment the plaintiffs prayed and were allowed an appeal.

Subsequently an order was made by the Circuit Court certifying that the only question considered and decided was whether upon the bill and demurrer a case was presented of which it had jurisdiction under the Constitution and laws of the United States.

* * *

It is clear that under the act of 1888 a Circuit Court could not take original cognizance of a suit simply because it was one arising under the Constitution or laws of the United States. The value of the matter in dispute in such a case must exceed $2000, exclusive of interest and costs.

The bill makes no allegation whatever as to the value of the matter in dispute, although this court, * * * [has] said: "This" [the question of the value in dispute in cases arising under the Constitution or laws of the United States] "was carefully considered, and it was held that the sum or value named was jurisdictional, and that the Circuit Court could not, under the statute, take original cognizance of a case arising under the Constitution or laws of the United States unless the sum or value of the matter in dispute, exclusive of costs and interest, exceeded two thousand dollars. That decision was reaffirmed." It was added—contrary to the intimation given in the opinion in the present case—that "the conclusion reached is not affected by the fact that the operation of the act of March 3, 1891, was to do away with any pecuniary limitation on appeals directly from the Circuit Courts to this court." Of course, it was not meant by that language that the jurisdiction of the Circuit Courts, so far as the value of the matter in dispute is concerned, was changed as to the case embraced by the fifth section of the act of 1891. The act of 1891 left the original jurisdiction of the Circuit Courts as established by the act of 1888.

1. It cannot be disputed that the present suit is one arising under the Constitution and laws of the United States, and it is clear that the value of the matter in dispute is made by the statute an essential element in the jurisdiction of the Circuit Court in such a case. But it has been suggested that this suit is also embraced by subdivision 16 of § 629 and § 1979 of the Revised Statutes—which provisions this court assumed and now assumes, were not repealed by any subsequent statute, and, therefore, that the value of the matter in dispute is of no consequence. But this suggestion overlooks the declaration of the court * * * to the effect that although the above provisions must be assumed to be still (1899) in force, they refer "to civil rights only." In this view, subdivision 16 of § 629 and § 1979 of the Revised Statutes have no bearing upon the present case, if the rights for the protection of which the present suit was brought are political rights, and not civil rights within the meaning of the statutes relating to "Civil Rights." Consequently the saving clause in the act of 1888 in respect of any jurisdiction or right mentioned in Title 24 of the Revised Statutes, Civil Rights, becomes immaterial in the present case. Whether this be so or not, the court refrains from declaring that the plaintiff could proceed under subdivision 16 of section 629 or section 1979 of the Revised Statutes, without regard to the value of the matter in dispute. If this court thinks that this suit could be maintained under subdivision 16 of § 629 or under § 1979, or under both, without regard to the value of the matter in dispute, I submit that it should have been so adjudged.

* * *

It seems to me that this question as to the value of the matter in dispute was sufficiently raised in the Circuit Court; for the demurrer to the bill was, in part, on the ground that the facts stated did not make a case "within the jurisdiction of the court." But, passing that view, I come to a more serious matter. In cases of which a Circuit Court may take original cognizance, the value of the matter in dispute—which is mentioned in the statute in advance of any reference to the nature of the subject of the action—is as essential to jurisdiction as is the nature of the subject of such dispute. And yet the court says that an objection that the record from the Circuit Court does not show an allegation as to value is unavailing here, even if such allegation ought to have been made. That is a new, and I take leave to say a startling, doctrine. Must not this court upon its own motion decline to pass upon,—indeed, has this court, strictly speaking, jurisdiction to consider and determine,—the merits of a case coming from the Circuit Court, unless it *affirmatively* appears *from the record* that the case is one of which that court could take cognizance? Is not a suit presumably without the jurisdiction of a Circuit Court, unless the record shows it to be one of which that court may take cognizance? Is it of any consequence that the parties did not raise the question of jurisdiction in the Circuit Court? If the record shows nothing more than that the case arises under the Constitution and laws of the

United States, and if it does not affirmatively appear, in some appropriate way, that the value of the matter in dispute is up to the required amount, has this court jurisdiction to consider and determine the merits of the case?

* * *

It will be appropriate to observe that the Circuit Court in effect propounds the question whether it had jurisdiction of this case upon the record before it. That question necessarily involves the inquiry whether subdivision 16 of § 629 and § 1979 of the Revised Statutes were repealed by later acts. But that point is left undecided, the court only assuming that those statutory provisions are still in force, but it does not say whether the suit could be maintained under those sections or under either of them without allegation or proof as to the value of the matter in dispute. Nor does the court distinctly adjudge whether the case is embraced by the act of 1887-88; but simply assuming that the allegation of value should have been made in the bill, it proceeds to consider the case upon its merits. The question of the jurisdiction of the Circuit Court under the acts of Congress, the one certified, is thus left in the air, and the case is examined and disposed of upon its merits just as if jurisdiction of the Circuit Court appeared upon the record. There is no claim that the essential fact of value appears anywhere in the record, either in the bill or otherwise. Consequently, as already said, this court is without power to consider the merits.

* * *

My views may be summed up as follows: 1. This case is embraced by that clause of the act of 1887-88, which provides that the Circuit Court shall have original cognizance "of all suits of a civil nature, * * * where the matter in dispute exceeds, exclusive of interest and costs, the sum or value of two thousand dollars, and arising under the Constitution or laws of the United States." 2. That the sum or value of the matter in dispute in such cases is jurisdictional under the statute. 3. That as it did not appear from the record, in any way, that the matter in dispute exceeded in value the jurisdictional amount, the Circuit Court could not take cognizance of the case or dispose of it upon its merits. 4. That least of all does this court have jurisdiction to determine the merits of this case. 5. That when a case comes here upon a certificate as to the jurisdiction of a Circuit Court, this court may not forbear to decide that question, and determine the merits of the case upon a record which does not show jurisdiction in the Circuit Court.

As these are my views as to the jurisdiction of this court, upon this record, I will not formulate and discuss my views upon the merits of this case. But to avoid misapprehension, I may add that my conviction is that upon the facts alleged in the bill (if the record showed a sufficient value of the matter in dispute) the plaintiff is entitled to relief in respect of his right to be registered as a voter. I agree with Mr. Justice Brewer that it is competent for the courts to give relief in such cases as this.

MR. JUSTICE BREWER dissenting.

I am unable to concur in either the opinion of judgment in this case. The single question is whether the Circuit Court of the United States had jurisdiction. Accepting the statement of facts in the opinion of the majority as sufficiently full, it appears that the plaintiff was entitled to a place on the permanent registry and was denied it by the defendants, the board of registrars in the county in which he lived. No one was allowed to vote who was not registered. He desired to vote at the coming election for representative in Congress. He was deprived of that right by the action of the defendants. Has the Circuit Court jurisdiction to redress such wrong? It is conceded that because of the permanence of the registry the appeal cannot be dismissed, for if registered on the permanent registry the plaintiff can vote at all future elections.

* * *

Although the statute and these decisions thus expressly limit the range of inquiry on a certificate of jurisdiction to the question of jurisdiction, it is held that because there is a constitutional question shown in the pleadings, the certificate may be ignored and the entire case presented to this court for consideration. In other words, although the plaintiff, by his method of appeal, following the provisions of the statute, limited the inquiry to the matter of jurisdiction, this court will ignore such limit and treat the case as coming here on a general appeal, which he did not take. This conclusion seems to me to practically destroy the statute and overrule the prior decisions, for the jurisdiction of Federal courts primarily rests on the Constitution of the United States and the extent of their jurisdiction is determined by its provisions. Hence every case coming up on a certificate of jurisdiction may be held to present a constitutional question and be open for full inquiry in respect to all matters involved.

Neither can I assent to the proposition that the case presented by the plaintiff's bill is not strictly a legal one and entitling a party to a judicial hearing and decision. He alleges that he is a citizen of Alabama, entitled to vote; that he desired to vote at an election for representative in Congress; that without registration he could not vote, and that registration was wrongfully denied him by the defendants. That many others were similarly treated does not destroy his rights or deprive him of relief in the courts. That such relief will be given has been again and again affirmed in both National and state courts.

That the United States Circuit Court has jurisdiction of an action like this seems to me to result inevitably from prior decisions of this court.

* * *

It seems to me nothing need be added to these decisions, and unless they are to be considered as overruled they are decisive of this case.

Mr. Justice Brown also dissents.

Notes and Questions

1. Professor Richard Pildes has noted both *Giles* importance and its obscurity. Noting what he called "the Supreme Court's removal of democracy from the agenda of constitutional law," Richard H. Pildes, *Democracy, Anti-Democracy and the Canon*, 17 CONST. COMMENT. 295, 296 (2000), he went on to observe:

> In this bleak and unfamiliar saga, there is one key moment, one decisive turning point: the 1903 opinion of Justice Oliver Wendell Holmes in *Giles v. Harris*. If canonization requires a ready focal point, this is it for (anti-)democracy in American constitutional law. * * *

> *Giles* has been airbrushed out of the constitutional canon. It is surely one of the most momentous decisions in United States Supreme Court history and one of the most revealing. * * * *Giles* permits the virtual elimination of black citizens from political participation in the South. Yet while extensive attention is devoted to judicial validation of separate but equal segregation, none is devoted to this. Every law student knows *Plessy v. Ferguson*; virtually none know *Giles*. * * * Even the Soviets could admire this success at obscuring all traces of a prior political regime.

> Yet historically, the context of *Giles* is as dramatic as any in American political and constitutional history. Jurisprudentially, the opinion weds legalism with realpolitik into one of the most fascinatingly repellant analyses in the Court's history. And doctrinally, the reverberations of *Giles* resound throughout the century; for notwithstanding the Fourteenth and Fifteenth Amendments, *Giles* carves out from them the category of "political rights" and holds such rights unenforceable. And so they were, until *Baker v. Carr*, sixty years later, with *Giles* enlisted by Justices like Felix Frankfurter in support of constitutional law's insistence that democracy remain off stage.

Id. at 296-98 (footnotes omitted).

2. Justice Holmes's approach to subject matter jurisdiction is an eye opener. From their first year, law students learn that subject matter jurisdiction is always in issue and that the courts will examine it *sua sponte* if the parties do not raise it. *See, e.g., Louisville and Nashville Railroad Company v. Mottley*, 211 U.S. 149 (1908) (at page 249); *Smith v. Kansas City Title & Trust Co.*, 255 U.S. 180 (1921) (at page 265). *Cf.* FED. R. CIV. P 12(h)(3) ("Whenever it appears by suggestion of the parties or otherwise that the court lacks jurisdiction of the subject matter, the court shall dismiss the action."). Of the five cases that *Mottley* cited for that proposition, four antedated *Giles*. Notice that Justice Harlan chastised the majority for taking the position that "the objection * * * was not raised in the Circuit Court, and as

it could have been remedied by amendment, we think it is unavailing." It seems legitimate to wonder why the majority took this surprising approach. Did it simply want to avoid what it regarded as a time-wasting procedure of forcing the plaintiff to amend the complaint by including what Justice Holmes evidently believed to be a *pro forma* allegation of jurisdictional amount? Did it want to reach the other issues that the case presents? If so, why?

3. The majority also argued that plaintiff's attack on the Alabama registration scheme in its entirety left him no platform upon which the Court could fashion relief even if it had no other problems with his request. Is that an accurate representation of the plaintiff's complaint? Was the plaintiff really attacking the structure of the scheme (with its grandfather clause and post-1902 requirements for becoming an elector) or was he attacking the race-based implementation of the scheme? Does it make a difference?

4. The majority also characterized the rights that Giles sought to enforce as "political rights." Do you think the majority meant that Congress intended to erect a distinction between political rights and civil rights and to make only the latter enforceable through § 1983? Is the Fifteenth Amendment relevant to that question?

That aside, Justice Holmes asserts that any remedy for Giles must come through the political branches, not through the courts. Is Holmes saying by implication that such a remedy cannot depend on the judiciary for interpretation and enforcement? Could Giles have argued that the political branches had given him a remedy, in the form of the Fifteenth Amendment and the statutes upon which he relied?

Note the majority's use of *Hans v. Louisiana*. It is as if the Court is sighing mightily and declaring the whole matter out of its hands (*Hans*?). Observe, though, how the combination of *Hans v. Louisiana* and *Giles v. Harris* operated with respect to enforcement of constitutional rights, especially the Civil War Amendments, against unwilling states. *See generally* Edward A. Purcell, Jr., *The Particularly Dubious Case of* Hans v. Louisiana: *An Essay on Law, History, and "Federal Courts,"* 81 N.CAR.L.REV. 1927 (2003). The Supreme Court was not long in addressing the situation. Interestingly, however, the Court addressed the unenforceability problem not in the context of individuals' civil rights against overreaching state governments, but in the then-dominant context of business resisting state control throughout the *Lochner* era. *See Ex parte Young*, 209 U.S. 123, 28 S.Ct. 441, 52 L.Ed. 714 (1908), presented below.

5. It is by now common to refer to the Civil War Amendments as self-executing. *See, e.g., City of Boerne v. Flores*, 521 U.S. 507, 117 S.Ct. 2157, 138 L.Ed.2d 624 (1997) (Fourteenth Amendment); *South Carolina v. Katzenbach*, 383 U.S. 301, 86 S.Ct. 803, 15 L.Ed.2d 769 (1966) (Fifteenth Amendment). Did *Giles* effectively take the position that the Amendments were not self-enforcing, at least with respect to the category of "political rights" that Justice Holmes recognized?

C.　THE BASIC DOCTRINE:　LESS THAN MEETS THE EYE

EX PARTE YOUNG
Supreme Court of the United States, 1908.
209 U.S. 123, 28 S.Ct. 441, 52 L.Ed. 714.

[Justice Peckham delivered for the Court a statement of facts separate from the main body of the opinion.

The state of Minnesota passed some statutes severely restricting rates that railroads operating within the state could charge. The statutes prescribed extraordinarily severe penalties for their violation, including substantial fines and imprisonment of any person connected with a railroad who participated in any manner in charging rates exceeding the statutory authorizations.

Several railroads' shareholders commenced derivative actions in federal court, alleging that the Minnesota statutes were unconstitutional as confiscatory takings under the Fourteenth Amendment's Due Process Clause and as interferences with the Commerce Clause. In addition to joining the railroad corporations and their officers and directors as parties-defendant, the shareholders joined Edward T. Young, the Attorney General of Minnesota. In one of those derivative actions, the court granted injunctive relief against the railroad and its officials, ordering them not to comply with the new rate statutes, and against Young, ordering him to refrain from instituting any enforcement procedure under the challenged statutes. Young had appeared specially in the federal actions, objecting on Eleventh Amendment grounds to the court's jurisdiction.

The day after the court issued the preliminary injunction, Young filed a state mandamus proceeding against the railroad to compel it to comply with the new statutes. The federal court thereupon ordered Young to show cause why he should not be punished for contempt and, upon his reiteration of his Eleventh Amendment jurisdictional objection, found him in contempt and committed him to the custody of the United States marshal. He then applied to the United States Supreme Court for leave to file a petition for a writ of habeas corpus in the Supreme Court as an original proceeding. The Court granted leave and now reviews Young's petition.]

MR. JUSTICE PECKHAM, after making the foregoing statement, delivered the opinion of the court:

* * *

The question of jurisdiction, whether of the circuit court or of this court, is frequently a delicate matter to deal with, and it is especially so in this case, where the material and most important objection to the jurisdiction of the circuit court is the assertion that the suit is, in effect, against one of the states of the Union. It is a question, however, which we are called upon, and which it is our duty to decide. * * *

It is insisted by the petitioner that there is no Federal question presented under the 14th Amendment, because there is no dispute as to the meaning of the Constitution, where it provides that no state shall deprive any person of life, liberty, or property without due process of law; nor deny to any person within its jurisdiction the equal protection of the laws; and whatever dispute there may be in this case is one of fact simply, whether the freight or passenger rates, as fixed by the legislature or by the railroad commission, are so low as to be confiscatory; and that is not a Federal question.

Jurisdiction is given to the circuit court in suits involving the requisite amount, arising under the Constitution or laws of the United States, and the question really to be determined under this objection is whether the acts of the legislature and the orders of the railroad commission, if enforced, would take property without due process of law; and although that question might incidentally involve a question of fact, its solution, nevertheless, is one which raises a Federal question * * *. The sufficiency of rates with reference to the Federal Constitution is a judicial question, and one over which Federal courts have jurisdiction by reason of its Federal nature.

Another Federal question is the alleged unconstitutionality of these acts because of the enormous penalties denounced for their violation, which prevent the railway company, as alleged, or any of its servants or employees, from resorting to the courts for the purpose of determining the validity of such acts. The contention is urged by the complainants in the suit that the company is denied the equal protection of the laws and its property is liable to be taken without due process of law, because it is only allowed a hearing upon the claim of the unconstitutionality of the acts and orders in question, at the risk, if mistaken, of being subjected to such enormous penalties, resulting in the possible confiscation of its whole property, that rather than take such risks the company would obey the laws, although such obedience might also result in the end (though by a slower process) in such confiscation.

Still another Federal question is urged, growing out of the assertion that the laws are, by their necessary effect, an interference with and a regulation of interstate commerce, the grounds for which assertion it is not now necessary to enlarge upon. The question is not, at any rate, frivolous.

We conclude that the circuit court had jurisdiction in the case before it, because it involved the decision of Federal questions arising under the Constitution of the United States.

[The Court then analyzed the merits and concluded that the rate statutes were unconstitutional.]

* * *

We have, therefore, upon this record, the case of an unconstitutional act of the state legislature and an intention by the attorney general of the state to endeavor to enforce its provisions, to the injury of the company * * * . The question that arises is whether there is a remedy that the parties interested may resort to, by going into a Federal court of equity, in a case involving a violation of the Federal Constitution, and obtaining a judicial investigation of the problem, and, pending its solution, obtain freedom from suits, civil or criminal, by a temporary injunction, and, if the question be finally decided favorably to the contention of the company, a permanent injunction restraining all such actions or proceedings.

This inquiry necessitates an examination of the most material and important objection made to the jurisdiction of the circuit court,—the objection being that the suit is, in effect, one against the state of Minnesota, and that the injunction issued against the attorney general illegally prohibits state action, either criminal or civil, to enforce obedience to the statutes of the state. This objection is to be considered with reference to the 11th and 14th Amendments to the Federal Constitution. The 11th Amendment prohibits the commencement or prosecution of any suit against one of the United States by citizens of another state or citizens or subjects of any foreign state. The 14th Amendment provides that no state shall deprive any person of life, liberty, or property without due process of law, nor shall it deny to any person within its jurisdiction the equal protection of the laws.

The case before the circuit court proceeded upon the theory that the orders and acts heretofore mentioned would, if enforced, violate rights of the complainants protected by the latter amendment. We think that whatever the rights of complainants may be, they are largely founded upon that Amendment, but a decision of this case does not require an examination or decision of the question whether its adoption in any way altered or limited the effect of the earlier Amendment. We may assume that each exists in full force, and that we must give to the 11th Amendment all the effect it naturally would have, without cutting it down or rendering its meaning any more narrow than the language, fairly interpreted, would warrant. It applies to a suit brought against a state by one of its own citizens, as well as to a suit brought by a citizen of another state. *Hans v. Louisiana.* It was adopted after the decision of this court in *Chisholm v. Georgia,* where it was held that a state might be sued by a citizen of another state. Since that time there have been many cases decided in this court involving the 11th Amendment, among them being *Osborn v. Bank of United States,* which held that the Amendment applied only to those suits in which the state was a party on the record. In the subsequent case of *Sundry African Slaves v. Madrazo,* that holding was somewhat enlarged, and Chief Justice Marshall, delivering the opinion of the court, while citing *Osborn v. Bank of United States,* said that where the claim was made, as in the case then before the court, against the governor of Georgia as governor, and the demand was made upon him, not personally, but officially (for moneys in the treasury of the state and for slaves in possession of the state government), the state might be considered as the party on the record, and therefore the suit could not be maintained.

Davis v. Gray reiterates the rule of *Osborn v. Bank of United States* so far as concerns the right to enjoin a state officer from executing a state law in conflict with the Constitution or a statute of the United States, when such execution will violate the rights of the complainant.

In *Poindexter v. Greenhow,* it was adjudged that a suit against a tax collector who had refused coupons in payment of taxes, and, under color of a void law, was about to seize and sell the property of a taxpayer for nonpayment of his taxes, was a suit against him personally, as a wrong-doer, and not against the state.

Hagood v. Southern decided that the bill was, in substance, a bill for the specific performance of a contract between the complainants and the state of South Carolina; and, although the state was not in name made a party defendant, yet, being the actual party to the alleged contract the performance of which was sought, and the only party by whom it could be performed, the state was, in effect, a party to the suit, and it could not be maintained for that reason. The things required to be done by the actual defendants were the very things which, when done, would constitute a performance of the alleged contract by the state.

The cases upon the subject were reviewed, and it was held that a bill in equity brought against officers of a state, who, as individuals, have no personal interest in the subject-matter of the suit, and defend only as representing the state, where the relief prayed for, if done, would constitute a performance by the state of the alleged contract of the state, was a suit against the state.

A suit of such a nature was simply an attempt to make the state itself, through its officers, perform its alleged contract, by directing those officers to do acts which constituted such performance. The state alone had any interest in the question, and a decree in favor of plaintiff would affect the treasury of the state.

* * *

The cases above cited do not include one exactly like this under discussion. They serve to illustrate the principles upon which many cases have been decided. We have not cited all the cases, as we have not thought it necessary. But the injunction asked for in the *Ayers* Case was to restrain the state officers from commencing suits under the act of May 12, 1887 (alleged to be unconstitutional), in the name of the state and brought to recover taxes for its use, on the ground that, if such suits were commenced, they would be a breach of a contract with the state. The injunction was declared illegal because the suit itself could not be entertained, as it was one against the state, to enforce its alleged contract. It was said, however, that, if the court had power to entertain such a suit, it would have power to grant the restraining order preventing the commencement of suits. It was not stated that the suit or the injunction was necessarily confined to a case of a threatened direct trespass upon or injury to property.

* * *

In *Smyth v. Ames* (another rate case), it was again held that a suit against individuals, for the purpose of preventing them, as officers of the state, from enforcing, by the commencement of suits or by indictment, an unconstitutional enactment, to the injury of the rights of the plaintiff, was not a suit against a state, within the meaning of the Amendment. [I]n answer to the objection that the suit was really against the state, it was said: "It is the settled doctrine of this court that a suit against individuals, for the purpose of preventing them, as officers of a state, from enforcing an unconstitutional enactment, to the injury of the rights of the plaintiff, is not a suit against the state within the meaning of that Amendment." The suit was to enjoin the enforcement of a statute of Nebraska because it was alleged to be unconstitutional, on account of the rates being too low to afford some compensation to the company, and contrary, therefore, to the 14th Amendment.

* * *

The various authorities we have referred to furnish ample justification for the assertion that individuals who, as officers of the state, are clothed with some duty in regard to the enforcement of the laws of the state, and who threaten and are about to commence proceedings, either of a civil or criminal nature, to enforce against parties affected an unconstitutional act, violating the Federal Constitution, may be enjoined by a Federal court of equity from such action.

* * *

The general discretion regarding the enforcement of the laws when and as he deems appropriate is not interfered with by an injunction which restrains the state officer from taking any steps towards the enforcement of an unconstitutional enactment, to the injury of complainant. In such case no affirmative action of any nature is directed, and the officer is simply prohibited from doing an act which he had no legal right to do. An injunction to prevent him from doing that which he has no legal right to do is not an interference with the discretion of an officer.

It is also argued that the only proceeding which the attorney general could take to enforce the statute, so far as his office is concerned, was one by mandamus, which would be commenced by the state, in its sovereign and governmental character, and that the right to bring such action is a necessary attribute of a sovereign government. It is contended that the complainants do not complain and they care nothing about any action which Mr. Young might take or bring as an ordinary individual, but that he was complained of as an officer, to whose discretion is confided the use of the name of the state of Minnesota so far as litigation is concerned, and that when or how he shall use it is a matter resting in his discretion and cannot be controlled by any court.

The answer to all this is the same as made in every case where an official claims to be acting under the authority of the state. The act to be enforced is alleged to be unconstitutional; and if it be so, the use of the name of the state to enforce an unconstitutional act to the injury of complainants is a proceeding without the authority of, and one which does not affect, the state in its sovereign or governmental capacity. It is simply an illegal act upon the part of a state official in attempting, by the use of the name of the state, to enforce a legislative enactment which is void because unconstitutional. If the act which the state attorney general seeks to enforce be a violation of the Federal Constitution, the officer, in proceeding under such enactment, comes into conflict with the superior authority of that Constitution, and he is in that case stripped of his official or representative character and is subjected in his person to the consequences of his individual conduct. The state has no power to impart to him any immunity from responsibility to the supreme authority of the United States. It would be an injury to complainant to harass it with a multiplicity of suits or litigation generally in an endeavor to enforce penalties under an unconstitutional enactment, and to prevent it ought to be within the jurisdiction of a court of equity. If the question of unconstitutionality, with reference, at least, to the Federal Constitution, be first raised in a Federal court, that court, as we think is shown by the authorities cited hereafter, has the right to decide it, to the exclusion of all other courts.

* * *

It is further objected (and the objection really forms part of the contention that the state cannot be sued) that a court of equity has no jurisdiction to enjoin criminal proceedings, by indictment or otherwise, under the state law. This, as a general rule, is true. But there are exceptions. When such indictment or proceeding is brought to enforce an alleged unconstitutional statute, which is the subject-matter of inquiry in a suit already pending in a Federal court, the latter court, having first obtained jurisdiction over the subject-matter, has the right, in both civil and criminal cases, to hold and maintain such jurisdiction, to the exclusion of all other courts, until its duty is fully performed. But the Federal court cannot, of course, interfere in a case where the proceedings were already pending in a state court.

Where one commences a criminal proceeding who is already party to a suit then pending in a court of equity, if the criminal proceedings are brought to enforce the same right that is in issue before that court, the latter may enjoin such criminal proceedings * * * .

It is further objected that there is a plain and adequate remedy at law open to the complainants, and that a court of equity, therefore, has no jurisdiction in such case. It has been suggested that the proper way to test the constitutionality of the act is to disobey it, at least once, after which the company might obey the act pending subsequent proceedings to test its validity. But in the event of a single violation the prosecutor might not avail himself of the opportunity to make the test, as obedience to the law was thereafter continued, and he might think it unnecessary to start an inquiry. If, however, he should do so while the company was thereafter obeying the law, several years might elapse before there was a final determination of the question, and, if it should be determined that the law was invalid, the property of the company would have been taken during that time without due process of law, and there would be no possibility of its recovery.

Another obstacle to making the test on the part of the company might be to find an agent or employee who would disobey the law, with a possible fine and imprisonment staring him in the face if the act should be held valid. Take the passenger-rate act, for instance: A sale of a single ticket above the price mentioned in that act might subject the ticket agent to a charge of felony, and, upon conviction, to a fine of $5,000 and imprisonment for five years. It is true the company might pay the fine, but the imprisonment the agent would have to suffer personally. It would not be wonderful if, under such circumstances, there would not be a crowd of agents offering to disobey the law. The wonder would be that a single agent should be found ready to take the risk.

* * *

There is nothing in the case before us that ought properly to breed hostility to the customary operation of Federal courts of justice in cases of this character.

The rule to show cause is discharged and the petition for writs of habeas corpus and certiorari is dismissed.

So ordered.

MR. JUSTICE HARLAN, dissenting:

* * *

Let it be observed that the suit instituted by Perkins and Shepard in the circuit court of the United States was, as to the defendant Young, one against him as, and only because he was, attorney general of Minnesota. No relief was sought against him individually, but only in his capacity as attorney general. And the manifest, indeed the avowed and admitted, object of seeking such relief, was to tie the hands of the state so that it could not in any manner or by any mode of proceeding, in its own courts, test the validity of the statutes and orders in question. It would therefore seem clear that within the true meaning of the 11th Amendment the suit brought in the Federal court was one, in legal effect, against the state,—as much so as if the state had been formally named on the record as a party,—and therefore it was a suit to which, under the Amendment, so far as the state or its attorney general was concerned, the judicial power of the United States did not and could not extend. If this proposition be sound it will follow,—indeed, it is conceded that if, so far as relief is sought against the attorney general of Minnesota, this be a suit against the state,—then, the order of the Federal court enjoining that officer from taking any action, suit, step, or proceeding to compel the railway company to obey the Minnesota statute was beyond the jurisdiction of that court and wholly void; in which case, that officer was at liberty to proceed in the discharge of his official duties as defined by the laws of the state, and the order adjudging him to be in contempt for bringing the mandamus proceeding in the state court was a nullity.

The fact that the Federal circuit court had, prior to the institution of the mandamus suit in the state court, preliminarily (but not finally) held the statutes of Minnesota and the orders of its railroad and warehouse commission in question to be in violation of the Constitution of the United States, was no reason why that court should have laid violent hands upon the attorney general of Minnesota, and by its orders have deprived the state of the services of its constitutional law officer in its own courts. Yet that is what was done by the Federal circuit court; for the intangible thing called a state, however extensive its powers, can never appear or be represented or known in any court in a litigated case, except by and through its officers. When, therefore, the Federal court forbade the defendant Young, as attorney general of Minnesota, from taking any action, suit, step, or proceeding whatever looking to the enforcement of the statutes in question, it said in effect to the state of Minnesota:

> It is true that the powers not delegated to the United States by the Constitution, nor prohibited by it to the states, are reserved to the states respectively or to its people, and it is true that, under the Constitution, the judicial power of the United States does not extend to any suit brought against a state by a citizen of another state or by a citizen or subject of a foreign state, yet the Federal court adjudges that you, the state, although a sovereign for many important governmental purposes, shall not appear in your own courts, by your law officer, with the view of enforcing, or even for determining the validity of, the state enactments which the Federal court has, upon a preliminary hearing, declared to be in violation of

the Constitution of the United States.

This principle, if firmly established, would work a radical change in our governmental system. It would inaugurate a new era in the American judicial system and in the relations of the national and state governments. It would enable the subordinate Federal courts to supervise and control the official action of the states as if they were "dependencies" or provinces. It would place the states of the Union in a condition of inferiority never dreamed of when the Constitution was adopted or when the 11th Amendment was made a part of the supreme law of the land. I cannot suppose that the great men who framed the Constitution ever thought the time would come when a subordinate Federal court, having no power to compel a state, in its corporate capacity, to appear before it as a litigant, would yet assume to deprive a state of the right to be represented in its own courts by its regular law officer. That is what the court below did, as to Minnesota, when it adjudged that the appearance of the defendant Young in the state court, as the attorney general of Minnesota, representing his state as its chief law officer, was a contempt of the authority of the Federal court, punishable by fine and imprisonment. Too little consequence has been attached to the fact that the courts of the states are under an obligation equally strong with that resting upon the courts of the Union to respect and enforce the provisions of the Federal Constitution as the supreme law of the land, and to guard rights secured or guaranteed by that instrument. We must assume—a decent respect for the states requires us to assume—that the state courts will enforce every right secured by the Constitution. If they fail to do so, the party complaining has a clear remedy for the protection of his rights; for he can come by writ of error, in an orderly, judicial way, from the highest court of the state to this tribunal for redress in respect of every right granted or secured by that instrument and denied by the state court. The state courts, it should be remembered, have jurisdiction concurrent with the courts of the United States of all suits of a civil nature, at common law or equity, involving a prescribed amount, arising under the Constitution or laws of the United States.

* * *

Whether the Minnesota statutes are or are not violative of the Constitution is not, as already suggested, a question in this habeas corpus proceeding. The essential and only question now before us or that need be decided is whether an order by the Federal court which prevents the state from being represented in its own courts, by its chief law officer, upon an issue involving the constitutional validity of certain state enactments, does not make a suit against the state within the meaning of the 11th Amendment. If it be a suit of that kind, then, it is conceded, the circuit court was without jurisdiction to fine and imprison the petitioner, and he must be discharged, whatever our views may be as to the validity of those state enactments. This must necessarily be so unless the

Amendment has less force and a more restricted meaning now than it had at the time of its adoption, and unless a suit against the attorney general of a state, in his official capacity, is not one against a state under the 11th Amendment when its determination depends upon a question of constitutional power or right under the 14th Amendment. In that view I cannot concur. In my opinion the 11th Amendment has not been modified in the slightest degree as to its scope or meaning by the 14th Amendment, and a suit which, in its essence, is one against the state, remains one of that character and is forbidden even when brought to strike down a state statute alleged to be in violation of that clause of the 14th Amendment, forbidding the deprivation by a state of life, liberty, or property without due process of law.

* * *

Even if it were held that suits to restrain the instituting of actions directly to recover the prescribed penalties would not be suits against the state, it would not follow that we should go further and hold that a proceeding under which the state was, in effect, denied access, by its attorney general, to its own courts, would be consistent with the Eleventh Amendment. * * * [T]o forbid the attorney general of a state (under the penalty of being punished as for contempt) from representing his state in suits of a particular kind, in its own courts, is to forbid the state itself from appearing and being heard in such suits. Neither the words nor the policy of the 11th Amendment will, under our former decisions, justify any order of a Federal court the necessary effect of which will be to exclude a state from its own courts. Such an order, attended by such results, cannot, I submit, be sustained consistently with the powers which the states, according to the uniform declarations of this court, possess under the Constitution. I am justified, by what this court has heretofore declared, in now saying that the men who framed the Constitution, and who caused the adoption of the 11th Amendment, would have been amazed by the suggestion that a state of the Union can be prevented, by an order of a subordinate Federal court, from being represented by its attorney general in a suit brought by it in one of its own courts; and that such a order would be inconsistent with the dignity of the states as involved in their constitutional immunity from the judicial process of the Federal courts (except in the limited cases in which they may constitutionally be made parties in this court), and would be attended by most pernicious results.

I dissent from the opinion and judgment.

Notes and Questions

1. Why does *Young* come out differently from *Hans*? If Hans had named the state treasurer instead of suing Louisiana, would it have made a difference? If the shareholders who brought the original action in *Young* had named Minnesota instead of its attorney general, would the case have followed *Hans*?

2. How does the *Young* Court read *Hans*? Was it an Eleventh Amendment case, an Article III constitutional immunity case, or an unabrogated-common-law immunity case?

3. Note the mechanism that allows the federal proceeding against Young: he is "stripped" of his identity as an official of the state of Minnesota. This raises two substantial problems.

a) Justice Peckham mentions two possible rationales for stripping Minnesota's Attorney General of Eleventh Amendment protection. What are they, and which does the Court choose? Why? Does it make any difference? Keep these questions in mind when you read the note on the Eleventh Amendment and supplemental jurisdiction, *infra* at page 736.

b) Since Young has been stripped of his official identity, how is there any basis under the Fourteenth Amendment for the shareholders' original suit? State action is a predicate for Fourteenth Amendment applicability. Once Young has been stripped, where is the state action? Has the Court created a situation in which any unconstitutional action by a state official is not remediable because the state-action component has been removed?

4. If the Court had upheld Young's claim, would the railroads and their shareholders have had no opportunity to challenge the rate statute other than by violating it and risking substantial penalties? Could the shareholders have brought a state action identical to the federal action?

a) Perhaps Minnesota would not have allowed such an action to proceed, but can a state court refuse to entertain a federal claim that is not exclusively federal? Should a state court be permitted to do so? Does the fact that until 1980 federal question cases, like diversity cases, were subject to a monetary jurisdictional floor suggest an answer?

A special problem exists if states refuse to entertain federal claims against the states themselves. At least in actions against non-state defendants, if the state closes its courts to federal claims, the federal courts may hear them; the same cannot be said for claims against the states. If the Eleventh Amendment prevents such actions in federal court, and the states can close their courts, what of the supposed supremacy of federal law?

In *Testa v. Katt,* 330 U.S. 386, 67 S.Ct. 810, 91 L.Ed. 967 (1947), the Court ruled that states cannot discriminatorily close their courts to federal claims. If a federal claim parallels a state claim (as, for example, a claim pursuant to the Civil Rights Act of 1871 (42 U.S.C. § 1983) may parallel a state tort claim) over which the state's courts have subject matter jurisdiction, the state may not keep the federal claim out. However, if the state does not permit a certain class of claims arising under state law, it may not have to entertain the class of cognate federal claims.

If a state maintains sovereign immunity against suit in its own courts, may it invoke the immunity in the face of a federal question action? One might have thought that the Supremacy Clause compelled a negative answer, but *Alden v. Maine,* 527 U.S. 706, 119 S.Ct. 2240, 144 L.Ed.2d 636 (1999), held (by a five-to-four vote) that the sovereign immunity of states that the Eleventh Amendment reflects is a substantive, not merely a forum, immunity. The plaintiffs sought to recover from Maine based on violations of the federal Fair Labor Standards Act, which clearly applied to states. The majority held that Congress has no Article I power legislation to compel the states (even if they are the proper subject of such legislation) to submit to adjudication of private suits in either state or federal court, relying on the constitutional structure that left the states intact as sovereigns in their own right. At the same time, the Court noted that

> The constitutional privilege of a State to assert its sovereign immunity in its own courts does not confer upon the State a concomitant right to disregard the Constitution or valid federal law. The States and their officers are bound by obligations imposed by the Constitution and by federal statutes that comport with the constitutional design. We are unwilling to assume the States will refuse to honor the Constitution or obey the binding laws of the United States. The good faith of the States thus provides an important assurance that "[t]his Constitution, and the Laws of the United States which shall be made in Pursuance thereof * * * shall be the supreme Law of the Land."

The majority did not comment on the irony of its statement in light of the facts of the case before it, where the plaintiffs alleged precisely such a refusal.[3] The Court did leave open the possibility that the United States, rather than private litigants, might be able to prosecute an enforcement action against Maine, but is the practical effect of *Alden* to leave individuals ostensibly protected by federal law with no way to enforce their entitlement *vis-à-vis* states or state agencies?

b) Assuming that the *Young* shareholders could have proceeded in state court, should they have been compelled to do so? If it is merely a matter of whether their claims were to be heard first in federal or state court, with possible United States Supreme Court review in either event, is the difference significant? This question goes to the heart of the parity debate, which raises several questions.

First, as an empirical matter, are the federal and state courts equal forums of justice on constitutional or other federal claims? Is there any way to determine this issue other than anecdotally? In laboratories one can set up "control cases," but in the judicial system that is rarely possible. If one could determine the question of parity as an empirical matter, and assuming that there is a demonstrable difference, is the difference something that the judicial system ought to acknowledge? Are there unacceptable costs in conceding a lack of parity between the two court systems?

Second, what weight should the plaintiff's choice of forum have in a case challenging official action? In most civil litigation, plaintiffs may choose among forums with jurisdiction over the subject matter and the parties, subject to removal, venue requirements, *forum non conveniens,* and transfer

---

[3] Note, however, that after the original disagreement about the Act's requirements, Maine began to comply. The dispute before the Court concerned only whether Maine should have to make the plaintiffs whole in light of the past transgressions.

within the federal system, considerations that rarely, if ever, avail a *state* defendant anything. The Eleventh Amendment provides another forum-shifting device, one available exclusively to the states. Is it likely that the Congresses that enacted the Fourteenth Amendment, the Civil Rights Act of 1871, and 28 U.S.C. § 1331 contemplated that cases challenging state action on federal constitutional grounds should be brought only in the state court systems of which the Reconstruction Congresses had been so conspicuously suspicious? On the other hand, should the intentions of those nineteenth century Congresses have any weight in interpreting the Eleventh Amendment, enacted decades earlier in the preceding century?

5. Justice Brennan called *Young* one of the most important constitutional cases of the century, undergirding most of the federal courts' involvement in civil rights in the twentieth century. Why did he have this view? What motivated the Court to embark upon the path it followed in *Young* ? If the Court had followed the reasoning of Justice Harlan's dissent instead, what would have been the result—not in *Young* particularly, but in cases challenging state unconstitutional action generally?

6. *Actions by States Against States.* The text of the Eleventh Amendment appears not to preclude suits for money damages in the federal courts by one state against another. Nonetheless, the example of *Hans v. Louisiana* and the cases that have followed it cautions one not to place too much faith in the words themselves. The Court recently clarified the effect of the Eleventh Amendment on state-*versus*-state actions. *Kansas v. Colorado*, 533 U.S. 1, 121 S.Ct. 2023, 150 L.Ed.2d 72 (2001), an original action in the Supreme Court arising out of a dispute under a bi-state water compact, rehearsed cases dating back to 1904 in which the Court had permitted damage actions between state plaintiffs and defendants. However, the Court pointed out that there is an even longer line of authority that prohibits a state from acting as a nominal plaintiff on behalf of individual claimants against another state. Thus, where bondholders assigned state-defaulted bonds to their home state but remained the beneficial owners of the bonds, the state action to recover the bond proceeds from the issuing state would not lie. Similarly, where individuals financed a state-*versus*-state action and the plaintiff state had agreed to divide the litigation proceeds proportionally among the individuals who had suffered losses, the Court had refused to allow the action to proceed. *Kansas v. Colorado* might have appeared to be a middle case. A special master appointed by the Court took evidence and made recommendations to the Court, including one that suggested that the Court award Kansas money damages from Colorado for the latter's depletion of Arkansas River water. The master recommended that the Court calculate damages by Kansas's losses rather than by Colorado's gains from the unlawful depletion. The formula that he used included calculations based on losses by individual Kansas farmers. Colorado objected that this effectively converted the action into one by individuals against a state, with Kansas acting only as a litigation front for its citizens. On this point, a unanimous Court disagreed. Noting that Kansas had financed and retained full control of the litigation, the Court distinguished the action from those where the state proceeded on behalf of individuals rather than in its own interest. Although Kansas's "right to control the disposition of any recovery of damages

is entirely unencumbered," which might mean that Kansas would elect to distribute the damage award to injured individuals, the Court apparently regarded the lack of any formal, identifiable individual interest in or control of the litigation as dispositive. Query whether such a distinction will be effective or whether the Court has simply given potential plaintiff states an extended lesson in structuring litigation to avoid the Eleventh Amendment bar.

7. *Sub- and Extra-State Agencies—Municipalities.* In *Home Telephone and Telegraph Company v. City of Los Angeles,* 227 U.S. 278, 33 S.Ct. 312, 57 L.Ed. 510 (1913), the Court extended the reasoning of *Young* and echoed *Young's* fiction. Upon plaintiff's challenge to a municipal rate ordinance, the City argued that it was entitled to Eleventh Amendment protection and that its action did not become state action until the state had approved it, either legislatively or through judicial endorsement at the highest levels. The Court held that municipalities are not states for Eleventh Amendment purposes but are nonetheless state actors for Fourteenth Amendment purposes. The Court also found that municipal action not authorized by the state was state action for Fourteenth Amendment purposes. This aspect of the case anticipated the Douglas-Frankfurter debate in *Monroe v. Pape,* discussed throughout Chapter 6.

Northern Insurance Co. v. Chatham County, Georgia, 547 U.S. 189, 126 S.Ct. 1689, 164 L.Ed.2d 367 (2006), reaffirmed that sub-state governments cannot avail themselves of the Eleventh Amendment's protection. In addition, a unanimous Court went further. The County did not rely on the Eleventh Amendment, but argued that it was the beneficiary of a "residual immunity" (in the words of the Court of Appeals) that common law had "carved out." The Supreme Court acknowledged that it had extended immunity on occasion to agencies acting as "an arm of the State," but held nonetheless that the County's concession that it was not an arm of the state for Eleventh Amendment purposes was dispositive as to whether it was an arm of the state for common law immunity purposes:

> [T]he County is subject to suit unless it was acting as an arm of the State, as delineated by this Court's precedents, in operating the drawbridge. The County conceded below that it was not entitled to *Eleventh Amendment* immunity, and both the County and the Court of Appeals appear to have understood this concession to be based on the County's failure to qualify as an arm of the State under our precedent. * * * Moreover, the question on which we granted certiorari is premised on the conclusion that the County is not "an 'arm of the state' for *Eleventh Amendment* purposes, and we presume that to be the case. Accordingly, the County's concession and the presumption underlying the question on which we granted review are dispositive.

a) *Home Telephone* raises again questions of interpretive technique when dealing with materials more than a century old. Is it likely that those who passed the Eleventh Amendment so quickly after the shock of *Chisholm v. Georgia* contemplated that actions against states in the federal courts would not lie but that actions against state subdivisions would? Conversely, is it likely that the framers of the Fourteenth Amendment thought that it applied to states but not to municipalities?

With respect to the latter question, consider again the legislative history of § 1983. *Monell v. Department of Social Services*, 436 U.S. 658, 98 S.Ct. 2018, 56 L.Ed.2d 611 (1978) (page 531) interpreted the rejection of the Sherman Amendment as Congress's unwillingness to impose new duties on state governmental subdivisions. Did the Fourteenth Amendment reflect the same understanding? If so, then what function was it to serve? If not, then was it § 1983 or the Amendment itself that imposed the "new duties" that some members of the House of Representatives thought inappropriate?

b) As a practical matter, what would be the effect of accepting Los Angeles's argument that there was no state action until California had given the rate ordinance its *imprimatur*? What are the implications for the role of the inferior federal courts?

c) Does 28 U.S.C.A. § 1343 shed light on the likelihood that the Congress that enacted that jurisdictional statute and the civil rights cause of action in 42 U.S.C.A. § 1983 would have agreed with Los Angeles's interpretation of the state action requirement of the Fourteenth Amendment?

8. *Sub- and Extra-State Agencies—Multistate Agencies.* The Eleventh Amendment shields states from federal suit, but what about agencies formed by compacts among states with congressional consent pursuant to Article I, § 10, cl. 3? *Hess v. Port Authority Trans-Hudson Corporation*, 513 U.S. 30, 115 S.Ct. 394, 130 L.Ed.2d 245 (1994), was the consolidation of two actions against PATH, a wholly-owned subsidiary of the Port Authority of New York and New Jersey, by employees injured on the job, and presented the issue of whether Eleventh Amendment immunity to federal suit extended to that bi-state agency. A five-to-four Court held that it did not. Justice Ginsburg's majority opinion focused on the Port Authority's financial independence from the two states, noting that neither state would be liable for any judgment against the Authority. She also emphasized that states, as separate sovereigns from the federal government, gained protection of their sovereign dignity from the Eleventh Amendment, whereas Compact Clause entities are creations of the states and federal government acting together, making "the federal court[s], in relation to such an enterprise, * * * hardly an instrument of a distant, disconnected sovereign; rather, the federal court is ordained by one of the entity's founders."

The Court relied in part on *Lake Country Estates, Inc. v. Tahoe Regional Planning Agency*, 440 U.S. 391, 99 S.Ct. 1171, 59 L.Ed.2d 401 (1979), in which it had refused Eleventh Amendment immunity to a bi-state agency: "[u]nless there is good reason to believe that the States structured the new agency to enable it to enjoy the special constitutional protection of the States themselves, and that Congress concurred in that purpose." Justice Ginsburg also noted that *Lake Country* contains what she called "indicators of immunity":

The Court in *Lake Country* found "no justification for reading additional meaning into the limited language of the Eleventh Amendment."

Indeed, all relevant considerations in that case weighed against TRPA's plea. The compact called TRPA a "political subdivision," and required that the majority of the governing members be county and city appointees. Obligation of TRPA, the compact directed, "shall not be binding on either State." TRPA's prime function, we noted, was regulation of land use, a function traditionally performed by local governments. Further, the agency's performance of that function gave rise to the litigation. Moreover, rules made by TRPA were "not subject to veto at the state level."

In *Hess*, the Court observed that the indicators pointed in different directions and that "the Eleventh Amendment's twin reasons for being remain our prime guide." The first recognized state dignity by not imposing judgments of "alien" courts. The second, and apparently more important, reason focused "on losses and debts": whether, if the expenditures of the enterprise exceed receipts, a state is obligated for the resulting indebtedness of the enterprise. "When the answer is 'No'—both legally and practically—then the Eleventh Amendment's core concern is not implicated."

Justice O'Connor wrote for the four dissenters. She argued that the Court's reliance on congressional consent in the creation of the Port Authority was a red herring, because Congress was merely concerned with whether the proposed entity would trench upon national power. Once Congress has certified by consenting that there is no such infringement, " 'states [are] in this respect restored to their original inherent sovereignty.' " She also accused the majority of

> substitut[ing] a single overriding criterion [for Eleventh Amendment protection], vulnerability of the state treasury. * * * The Court takes a *sufficient condition* for Eleventh Amendment immunity, and erroneously transforms it into a *necessary* condition. In so doing, the Court seriously reduces the scope of the Eleventh Amendment, thus underprotecting the state sovereignty at which the Eleventh Amendment is principally directed.

The dissenters, by contrast, would have relied on "*indicia* of [state] control":

> New York and New Jersey each select and may remove 6 of the Port Authority's 12 commissioners. The Governors of each State may veto the actions of that State's commissioners. The quorum requirements specify that

> no action of the port authority shall be binding unless taken at a meeting at which at least three of the members from each state are present, and unless a majority of the members from each state present at such meeting but in any event at least three of the members from each state, shall vote in favor thereof.

> Accordingly, each Governor's veto power is tantamount to a full veto power over the actions of the Commission. The Port Authority must make annual reports to the state legislatures, which in turn must approve changes in the Port Authority's rules and any new projects. Each State, and by extension, each State's electorate, exercises ample

authority over the Port Authority.

a) Justice O'Connor also argued that *Hess* is incompatible with the Court's requiring either explicit congressional authorization of suits against the states in federal courts or explicit state consent to such suits to overcome the Eleventh Amendment. *See, e.g., Atascadero State Hospital v. Scanlon*, 473 U.S. 234, 105 S.Ct. 3142, 87 L.Ed.2d 171 (1985), discussed in Note 6 at page 657 and Note 7 at page 672. Is it so obvious that the same standard ought to apply to a bi-state agency of limited purpose? The ostensible purpose of the Eleventh Amendment was to avoid interference with state governments in their sovereign capacities. Does a bi-state agency have a sovereign capacity, or is it more like a corporation simultaneously created by the laws of more than one state? A section of New York law appears both to adopt the corporate analogy and to consent to federal actions, yet the Court did not refer to it:

> The foregoing consent [referring to a statute reciting both states' consent to legal or equitable actions against the Port Authority] is granted upon the condition that venue in any suit, action or proceeding against the port authority shall be laid within a county or *a judicial district, established* by one of said states or *by the United States*, and situated wholly or partially within the port of New York district. The port authority shall be deemed to be a resident of each such county or judicial district for the purpose of such suits, actions or proceedings. Although the port authority is engaged in the performance of governmental functions, the said two states consent to liability on the part of the port authority in such suits, actions or proceedings to the same extent as though it were a private corporation.

N.Y. UNCONSOL. LAWS § 7106 (McKinney 2000) (emphasis added).

b) How could Justice Scalia join the dissenters? After all, the wording of the Eleventh Amendment is quite clear that it protects only "one of the United States." The Port Authority is not one of the states, and Justice Scalia has insisted on other occasions that when the words of a statutory provision are clear, resort to history, legislative or otherwise, is inappropriate. *See, e.g., Pennsylvania v. Union Gas*, 491 U.S. 1, 30, 109 S.Ct. 2273, 2296, 105 L.Ed.2d 1, 26 (1989) ("It is our task, as I see it, not to enter the minds of the Members of Congress—who need have nothing in mind for their votes to be both lawful and effective—but rather to give fair and reasonable meaning to the text of the United States Code * * * .") Has Justice Scalia ignored or forgotten his own counsel, or is the difference that the Court here deals with a constitutional rather than a statutory provision?

c) Given the majority's focus on the source of the funds to pay judgments (echoed in *Edelman v. Jordan*, 451 U.S. 651, 94 S.Ct. 1347, 39 L.Ed.2d 662 (1974), at page 646), would you expect the Eleventh Amendment to bar a federal action nominally against a state agency if the federal government would entirely indemnify the state for any adverse judgment? In *Regents of the State of California v. Doe*, 519 U.S. 425, 117 S.Ct. 900, 137 L.Ed.2d 55 (1997), a unanimous Court held that the state retains its Eleventh Amendment immunity notwithstanding the federal government's undertaking. Is that result incompatible with the Court's analysis in *Hess*? If the money will not come from the state treasury, what purpose does the immunity serve? Is the purpose you identify not applicable in cases like where the money *does* come from the state treasury? In that respect, consider *Milliken v. Bradley*, discussed at page 656.

8. It is easy to get so lost in the intricacies of the constitutional analysis in cases like *Hans v. Louisiana* and *Ex parte Young* that one overlooks their broader implications. On one level, they involve the amenability of states to suit in the federal courts as a matter of constitutional jurisprudence. On a wholly different level, however, they exemplify not just one but two power struggles that typify American society. The first pits the power of the central government against the individual states. The Eleventh Amendment is but one provision of the Constitution that seeks to address that balance, and *Hans* and *Young* reveal the federal judiciary's effort to understand the balance contemplated by the Constitution. The second struggle involves the power of government (here state government) against the individual. The Eleventh Amendment plays a part in that battle, too.

D. EXTENDING AND CABINING THE DOCTRINE: THE LIMITS OF LIMITS

EDELMAN v. JORDAN
Supreme Court of the United States, 1974.
415 U.S. 651, 94 S.Ct. 1347, 39 L.Ed.2d 662.

MR. JUSTICE REHNQUIST delivered the opinion of the Court.

Respondent John Jordan filed a complaint in the United States District Court for the Northern District of Illinois, individually and as a representative of a class, seeking declaratory and injunctive relief against two former directors of the Illinois Department of Public Aid, the director of the Cook County Department of Public Aid, and the comptroller of Cook County. Respondent alleged that these state officials were administering the federal-state programs of Aid to the Aged, Blind, or Disabled (AABD) in a manner inconsistent with various federal regulations and with the Fourteenth Amendment to the Constitution.

AABD is one of the categorical aid programs administered by the Illinois Department of Public Aid pursuant to the Illinois Public Aid Code. Under the Social Security Act, the program is funded by the State and the Federal Governments. The Department of Health, Education, and Welfare (HEW), which administers these payments for the Federal Government, issued regulations prescribing maximum permissible time standards within which States participating in the program had to process AABD applications. Those regulations, originally issued in 1968, required, at the time of the institution of this suit, that eligibility determinations must be made by the States within 30 days of receipt of applications for aid to the aged and blind, and within 45 days of receipt of applications for aid to the disabled. For those persons found eligible, the assistance check was required to be received by them within the applicable time period.

During the period in which the federal regulations went into effect, Illinois public aid officials were administering the benefits pursuant to their own regulations as provided in the Categorical Assistance Manual of the Illinois Department of Public Aid. Respondent's complaint charged that the Illinois defendants, operating under those regulations, were improperly authorizing grants to commence only with the month in which an application was approved and not including prior eligibility months for which an applicant was entitled to aid under federal law. The complaint also alleged that the Illinois defendants were not processing the applications within the applicable time requirements of the federal regulations; specifically, respondent alleged that his own application for disability benefits was not acted on by the Illinois Department of Public Aid for almost four months. Such actions of the Illinois officials were alleged to violate federal law and deny the equal protection of the laws. Respondent's prayer requested declaratory and injunctive relief, and specifically requested "a permanent injunction enjoining the defendants to award to the entire class of plaintiffs all AABD benefits wrongfully withheld."

In its judgment of March 15, 1972, the District Court declared § 4004 of the Illinois Manual to be invalid insofar as it was inconsistent with the federal regulations found in 45 C.F.R. § 206.10(a)(3), and granted a permanent injunction requiring compliance with the federal time limits for processing and paying AABD applicants. The District Court * * * also ordered the state officials to "release and remit AABD benefits wrongfully withheld to all applicants for AABD in the State of Illinois who applied between July 1, 1968 [the date of the federal regulations] and April 16, 1971 [the date of the preliminary injunction issued by the District Court] and were determined eligible * * *."

On appeal to the * * * Seventh Circuit, the Illinois officials contended, *inter alia,* that the Eleventh Amendment barred the award of retroactive benefits, that the judgment of inconsistency between the federal regulations and the provisions of the Illinois Categorical Assistance Manual could be given prospective effect only, and that the federal regulations in question were inconsistent with the Social Security Act itself. The Court of Appeals rejected these contentions and affirmed the judgment of the District Court. Because of an apparent conflict on the Eleventh Amendment issue with the * * * Second Circuit, we granted the petition for certiorari filed by petitioner Joel Edelman, who is the present Director of the Illinois Department of Public Aid, and successor to the former directors sued below. The petition for certiorari raised the same contentions urged by the petitioner in the Court of Appeals. Because we believe the Court of Appeals erred in its disposition of the Eleventh Amendment claim, we reverse that portion of the Court of Appeals decision which affirmed the District Court's order that retroactive benefits be paid by the Illinois state officials.

* * *

The issue [of states' amenability to suit in the federal courts] was squarely presented to the Court in a suit brought at the August 1792 Term by two citizens of South Carolina, executors of a British creditor, against the State of Georgia. After a year's postponement for preparation on the part of the State of Georgia, the Court, after argument, rendered in February 1793, its short-lived decision in *Chisholm v. Georgia*. The decision in that case, that a State was liable to suit by a citizen of another State or of a foreign country, literally shocked the Nation. Sentiment for passage of a constitutional amendment to override the decision rapidly gained momentum, and five years after *Chisholm* the Eleventh Amendment was officially announced by President John Adams. * * *

While the Amendment by its terms does not bar suits against a State by its own citizens, this Court has consistently held that an unconsenting State is immune from suits brought in federal courts by her own citizens as well as by citizens of another State. It is also well established that even though a State is not named a party to the action, the suit may nonetheless be barred by the Eleventh Amendment. "[W]hen the action is in essence one for the recovery of money from the state, the state is the real, substantial party in interest and is entitled to invoke its sovereign immunity from suit even though individual officials are nominal defendants."

Thus the rule has evolved that a suit by private parties seeking to impose a liability which must be paid from public funds in the state treasury is barred by the Eleventh Amendment.

The Court of Appeals in this case, while recognizing that the *Hans* line of cases permitted the State to raise the Eleventh Amendment as a defense to suit by its own citizens, nevertheless concluded that the Amendment did not bar the award of retroactive payments of the statutory benefits found to have been wrongfully withheld. The Court of Appeals held that the above-cited cases, when read in light of this Court's landmark decision in *Ex parte Young,* do not preclude the grant of such a monetary award in the nature of equitable restitution.

Petitioner concedes that *Ex parte Young* is no bar to that part of the District Court's judgment that prospectively enjoined petitioner's predecessors from failing to process applications within the time limits established by the federal regulations. Petitioner argues, however, that *Ex parte Young* does not extend so far as to permit a suit which seeks the award of an accrued monetary liability which must be met from the general revenues of a State, absent consent or waiver by the State of its Eleventh Amendment immunity, and that therefore the award of retroactive benefits by the District Court was improper.

Ex parte Young was a watershed case in which this Court held that the Eleventh Amendment did not bar an action in the federal courts seeking to enjoin the Attorney General of Minnesota from enforcing a statute claimed to violate the Fourteenth Amendment of the United States Constitution. This holding has permitted the Civil War Amendments to the Constitution to serve as a sword, rather than merely as a shield, for those whom they were designed to protect. But the relief awarded in *Ex parte Young* was prospective only; the Attorney General of Minnesota was enjoined to conform his future conduct of that office to the requirement of the Fourteenth Amendment. Such relief is analogous to that awarded by the District Court in the prospective portion of its order under review in this case.

But the retroactive portion of the District Court's order here, which requires the payment of a very substantial amount of money which that court held should have been paid, but was not, stands on quite a different footing. These funds will obviously not be paid out of the pocket of petitioner Edelman.

* * *

The funds to satisfy the award in this case must inevitably come from the general revenues of the State of Illinois, and thus the award resembles far more closely the monetary award against the State itself than it does the prospective injunctive relief awarded in *Ex parte Young*.

The Court of Appeals, in upholding the award in this case, held that it was permissible because it was in the form of "equitable restitution" instead of damages, and therefore capable of being tailored in such a way as to minimize disruptions of the state program of categorical assistance. But we must judge the award actually made in this case, and not one which might have been differently tailored in a different case, and we must judge it in the context of the important constitutional principle embodied in the Eleventh Amendment.[11]

We do not read *Ex parte Young* or subsequent holdings of this Court to indicate that any form of relief may be awarded against a state officer, no matter how closely it may in practice resemble a money judgment

[11] It may be true, as stated by our Brother Douglas in dissent, that "[m]ost welfare decisions by federal courts have a financial impact on the States." But we cannot agree that such a financial impact is the same where a federal court applies *Ex parte Young* to grant prospective declaratory and injunctive relief, as opposed to an order of retroactive payments as was made in the instant case. It is not necessarily true that "[w]hether the decree is prospective only or requires payments for the weeks or months wrongfully skipped over by the state officials, the nature of the impact on the state treasury is precisely the same." This argument neglects the fact that where the State has a definable allocation to be used in the payment of public aid benefits, and pursues a certain course of action such as the processing of applications within certain time periods as did Illinois here, the subsequent ordering by a federal court of retroactive payments to correct delays in such processing will invariably mean there is less money available for payments for the continuing obligations of the public aid system. * * *

payable out of the state treasury, so long as the relief may be labeled "equitable" in nature. The Court's opinion in *Ex parte Young* hewed to no such line. Its citation of *Hagood v. Southern* and *In re Ayers,* which were both actions against state officers for specific performance of a contract to which the State was a party, demonstrate that equitable relief may be barred by the Eleventh Amendment.

As in most areas of the law, the difference between the type of relief barred by the Eleventh Amendment and that permitted under *Ex parte Young* will not in many instances be that between day and night. The injunction issued in *Ex parte Young* was not totally without effect on the State's revenues, since the state law which the Attorney General was enjoined from enforcing provided substantial monetary penalties against railroads which did not conform to its provisions. Later cases from this Court have authorized equitable relief which has probably had greater impact on state treasuries than did that awarded in *Ex parte Young.* * * * But the fiscal consequences to state treasuries in these cases were the necessary result of compliance with decrees which by their terms were prospective in nature. State officials, in order to shape their official conduct to the mandate of the Court's decrees, would more likely have to spend money from the state treasury than if they had been left free to pursue their previous course of conduct. Such an ancillary effect on the state treasury is a permissible and often an inevitable consequence of the principle announced in *Ex parte Young.*

But that portion of the District Court's decree which petitioner challenges on Eleventh Amendment grounds goes much further * * *. It requires payment of state funds, not as a necessary consequence of compliance in the future with a substantive federal-question determination, but as a form of compensation to those whose applications were processed on the slower time schedule at a time when petitioner was under no court-imposed obligation to conform to a different standard. While the Court of Appeals described this retroactive award of monetary relief as a form of "equitable restitution," it is in practical effect indistinguishable in many aspects from an award of damages against the State. It will to a virtual certainty be paid from state funds, and not from the pockets of the individual state officials who were the defendants in the action. It is measured in terms of a monetary loss resulting from a past breach of a legal duty on the part of the defendant state officials.

* * *

Three fairly recent District Court judgments requiring state directors of public aid to make the type of retroactive payment involved here have been summarily affirmed by this Court notwithstanding Eleventh Amendment contentions made by state officers who were appealing from the District Court judgment. *Shapiro v. Thompson* is the only instance in which the Eleventh Amendment objection to such retroactive relief was actually presented to this Court in a case which was orally argued.

The three-judge District Court in that case had ordered the retroactive payment of welfare benefits found by that court to have been unlawfully withheld because of residence requirements held violative of equal protection. This Court, while affirming the judgment, did not in its opinion refer to or substantively treat the Eleventh Amendment argument. Nor, of course, did the summary dispositions of the three District Court cases contain any substantive discussion of this or any other issues raised by the parties.

This case, therefore, is the first opportunity the Court has taken to fully explore and treat the Eleventh Amendment aspects of such relief in a written opinion. *Shapiro v. Thompson* and these three summary affirmances obviously are of precedential value in support of the contention that the Eleventh Amendment does not bar the relief awarded by the District Court in this case. Equally obviously, they are not of the same precedential value as would be an opinion of this Court treating the question on the merits. Since we deal with a constitutional question, we are less constrained by the principle of *stare decisis* than we are in other areas of the law. Having now had an opportunity to more fully consider the Eleventh Amendment issue after briefing and argument, we disapprove the Eleventh Amendment holdings of those cases to the extent that they are inconsistent with our holding today.

The Court of Appeals held in the alternative that even if the Eleventh Amendment be deemed a bar to the retroactive relief awarded respondent in this case, the State of Illinois had waived its Eleventh Amendment immunity and consented to the bringing of such a suit by participating in the federal AABD program. The Court of Appeals relied upon our holdings in *Parden v. Terminal R. Co.* and *Petty v. Tennessee-Missouri Bridge Comm'n* and on the dissenting opinion of Judge Bright in *Employees v. Department of Public Health and Welfare.* While the holding in the latter case was ultimately affirmed by this Court, we do not think that the answer to the waiver question turns on the distinction between *Parden* and *Employees.* Both *Parden* and *Employees* involved a congressional enactment which by its terms authorized suit by designated plaintiffs against a general class of defendants which literally included States or state instrumentalities. Similarly, *Petty v. Tennessee-Missouri Bridge Comm'n* involved congressional approval, pursuant to the Compact Clause, of a compact between Tennessee and Missouri, which provided that each compacting State would have the power "to contract, to sue, and be sued in its own name." The question of waiver or consent under the Eleventh Amendment was found in those cases to turn on whether Congress had intended to abrogate the immunity in question, and whether the State by its participation in the program authorized by Congress had in effect consented to the abrogation of that immunity.

But in this case the threshold fact of congressional authorization to sue a class of defendants which literally includes States is wholly absent.

Thus respondent is not only precluded from relying on this Court's holding in *Employees,* but on this Court's holdings in *Parden* and *Petty* as well.

The Court of Appeals held that as a matter of federal law Illinois had "constructively consented" to this suit by participating in the federal AABD program and agreeing to administer federal and state funds in compliance with federal law. Constructive consent is not a doctrine commonly associated with the surrender of constitutional rights, and we see no place for it here. In deciding whether a State has waived its constitutional protection under the Eleventh Amendment, we will find waiver only where stated "by the most express language or by such overwhelming implications from the text as [will] leave no room for any other reasonable construction." We see no reason to retreat from the Court's statement: "[W]hen we are dealing with the sovereign exemption from judicial interference in the vital field of financial administration a clear declaration of the state's intention to submit its fiscal problems to other courts than those of its own creation must be found."

The mere fact that a State participates in a program through which the Federal Government provides assistance for the operation by the State of a system of public aid is not sufficient to establish consent on the part of the State to be sued in the federal courts. And while this Court has, in cases such as *J.I. Case Co. v. Borak,* authorized suits by one private party against another in order to effectuate a statutory purpose, it has never done so in the context of the Eleventh Amendment and a state defendant. Since *Employees,* where Congress had expressly authorized suits against a general class of defendants and the only thing left to implication was whether the described class of defendants included States, was decided adversely to the putative plaintiffs on the waiver question, surely this respondent must also fail on that issue. The only language in the Social Security Act which purported to provide a federal sanction against a State which did not comply with federal requirements for the distribution of federal monies was found in former 42 U.S.C. § 1384 (now replaced by substantially similar provisions in 42 U.S.C. § 804), which provided for termination of future allocations of federal funds when a participating State failed to conform with federal law.[16] This provision by its terms did not authorize suit against anyone, and standing alone, fell far short of a waiver by a participating State of its Eleventh Amendment immunity.

Our Brother Marshall argues in dissent, and the Court of Appeals held, that although the Social Security Act itself does not create a private cause of action, the cause of action created by 42 U.S.C. § 1983, coupled with the enactment of the AABD program, and the issuance by

---

[16] HEW sought passage of a bill in the 91st Congress, H.R. 16311, § 407(a), which would have given it authority to require retroactive payments to eligible persons denied such benefits. The bill failed to pass the House of Representatives.

HEW of regulations which require the States to make corrective payments after successful "fair hearings" and provide for federal matching funds to satisfy federal court orders of retroactive payments, indicate that Congress intended a cause of action for public aid recipients such as respondent. It is, of course, true that * * * suits in federal court under § 1983 are proper to secure compliance with the provisions of the Social Security Act on the part of participating States. But it has not heretofore been suggested that § 1983 was intended to create a waiver of a State's Eleventh Amendment immunity merely because an action could be brought under that section against state officers, rather than against the State itself. Though a § 1983 action may be instituted by public aid recipients such as respondent, a federal court's remedial power, consistent with the Eleventh Amendment, is necessarily limited to prospective injunctive relief and may not include a retroactive award which requires the payment of funds from the state treasury.

Respondent urges that since the various Illinois officials sued in the District Court failed to raise the Eleventh Amendment as a defense to the relief sought by respondent, petitioner is therefore barred from raising the Eleventh Amendment defense in the Court of Appeals or in this Court. The Court of Appeals apparently felt the defense was properly presented, and dealt with it on the merits. We approve of this resolution, since it has been well settled * * * that the Eleventh Amendment defense sufficiently partakes of the nature of a jurisdictional bar so that it need not be raised in the trial court * * * .

For the foregoing reasons we decide that the Court of Appeals was wrong in holding that the Eleventh Amendment did not constitute a bar to that portion of the District Court decree which ordered retroactive payment of benefits found to have been wrongfully withheld. The judgment of the Court of Appeals is therefore reversed and the cause remanded for further proceedings consistent with this opinion.

So ordered.

MR. JUSTICE DOUGLAS, dissenting.

* * *

In this class action respondent sought to enforce against state aid officials of Illinois provisions of the Social Security Act known as the Aid to the Aged, Blind, or Disabled (AABD) program. The complaint alleges violations of the Equal Protection Clause of the Fourteenth Amendment and also violations of the Social Security Act. Hence § 1983 is satisfied *in haec verba,* for a deprivation of "rights" which are "secured by the Constitution and laws" is alleged. The Court of Appeals, though ruling that the alleged constitutional violations had not occurred, sustained federal jurisdiction because federal "rights" were violated. The main issue tendered us is whether that ruling of the Court of Appeals is consistent with the Eleventh Amendment.

* * *

As the complaint in the instant case alleges violations by officials of Illinois of the Equal Protection Clause of the Fourteenth Amendment, it seems that the case is governed by *Ex parte Young* so far as injunctive relief is concerned. The main thrust of the argument is that the instant case asks for relief which if granted would affect the treasury of the State.

Most welfare decisions by federal courts have a financial impact on the States. Under the existing federal-state cooperative system, a state desiring to participate, submits a "state plan" to HEW for approval; once HEW approves the plan the State is locked into the cooperative scheme until it withdraws. * * * [T]he result in every welfare case coming here is to increase or reduce the financial responsibility of the participating State. In no case when the responsibility of the State is increased to meet the lawful demand of the beneficiary, is there any levy on state funds. Whether the decree is prospective only or requires payments for the weeks or months wrongfully skipped over by the state officials, the nature of the impact on the state treasury is precisely the same.

* * *

It is said however, that the Eleventh Amendment is concerned, not with immunity of States from suit, but with the jurisdiction of the federal courts to entertain the suit. The Eleventh Amendment does not speak of "jurisdiction"; it withholds the "judicial power" of federal courts "to any suit in law or equity * * * against one of the United States * * * ." If that "judicial power," or "jurisdiction" if one prefers that concept, may not be exercised even in "any suit in * * * equity" then *Ex parte Young* should be overruled. But there is none eager to take the step. Where a State has consented to join a federal-state cooperative project, it is realistic to conclude that the State has agreed to assume its obligations under that legislation. There is nothing in the Eleventh Amendment to suggest a difference between suits at law and suits in equity, for it treats the two without distinction. If common sense has any role to play in constitutional adjudication, once there is a waiver of immunity it must be true that it is complete so far as effective operation of the state-federal joint welfare program is concerned.

* * *

As the Court of Appeals in the instant case concluded, Illinois by entering into the joint federal-state welfare plan just as surely "[left] the sphere that is exclusively its own."

It is argued that participation in the program of federal financial assistance is not sufficient to establish consent on the part of the State to be sued in federal courts. But it is not merely participation which supports a finding of Eleventh Amendment waiver, but participation in light of the existing state of the law as exhibited in such decisions as *Shapiro v. Thompson,* which affirmed judgments ordering retroactive payment of benefits. Today's holding that the Eleventh Amendment forbids court-ordered retroactive payments, as the Court recognizes, necessitates an express overruling of several of our recent decisions. But it was against the background of those decisions that Illinois continued its participation in the federal program, and it can hardly be claimed that such participation was in ignorance of the possibility of court-ordered retroactive payments. The decision to participate against the background of precedent can only be viewed as a waiver of immunity from such judgments.

I would affirm the judgment of the Court of Appeals.

MR. JUSTICE BRENNAN, dissenting.

This suit is brought by Illinois citizens against Illinois officials. In that circumstance, Illinois may not invoke the Eleventh Amendment, since that Amendment bars only federal court suits against States by citizens of other States. Rather, the question is whether Illinois may avail itself of the nonconstitutional but ancient doctrine of sovereign immunity as a bar to respondent's claim for retroactive AABD payments. In my view Illinois may not assert sovereign immunity * * *: the States surrendered that immunity in Hamilton's words, "in the plan of the Convention," that formed the Union, at least insofar as the States granted Congress specifically enumerated powers. Congressional authority to enact the Social Security Act, of which AABD is a part, is to be found in art. I, § 8, cl. 1, one of the enumerated powers granted Congress by the States in the Constitution. I remain of the opinion that "because of its surrender, no immunity exists that can be the subject of a congressional declaration or a voluntary waiver," and thus have no occasion to inquire whether or not Congress authorized an action for AABD retroactive benefits, or whether or not Illinois voluntarily waived the immunity by its continued participation in the program against the background of precedents which sustained judgments ordering retroactive payments.

I would affirm the judgment of the Court of Appeals.

Notes and Questions

1. What reading of *Hans* and the Eleventh Amendment does the Court adopt? Is it fair to say that *Hans* now stands for the proposition that the Eleventh Amendment prohibits federal question suits against the states, whether named or sued through their officials?

2. Should *Ex parte Young* have helped the plaintiffs here? The majority argues that the district court's judgment would have its impact only on the state. Yet, in effect, the injunction in *Young* ran only against the state. Young had no personal interest in enforcing the rate statute. Should *Edelman* and *Young* come out the same way? If not, why not?

3. In *Edelman*, even the part of the lower court's decision that the ma-

jority approved would have a direct financial impact on the state. Why does that not violate the Eleventh Amendment? Is the dissent correct that there is no principled distinction between a money judgment based on past conduct and a judgment that compels future disbursement of funds by ordering the state to behave in a certain way?

Milliken v. Bradley, 433 U.S. 267, 97 S.Ct. 2749, 53 L.Ed.2d 745 (1977), approved a district court order that promised to force expenditure of millions of dollars of state funds in a school desegregation case. In dealing with the *Edelman* problem, the Court observed:

> The decree to share the future costs of educational components in this case fits squarely within the prospective-compliance exception reaffirmed by *Edelman.* That exception, which had its genesis in *Ex parte Young,* permits federal courts to enjoin state officials to conform their conduct to requirements of federal law, notwithstanding a direct and substantial impact on the state treasury. The order challenged here does no more than that. The decree requires state officials, held responsible for unconstitutional conduct, in findings which are not challenged, to eliminate a *de jure* segregated school system. More precisely, the burden of state officials is * * * to take the necessary steps "to eliminate from the public schools all vestiges of state-imposed segregation." The educational components, which the District Court ordered into effect prospectively, are plainly designed to wipe out continuing conditions of inequality produced by the inherently unequal dual school system long maintained by Detroit.[1]
>
> * * * That the programs are also "compensatory" in nature does not change the fact that they are part of a plan that operates prospectively to bring about the delayed benefits of a unitary school system. We therefore hold that such prospective relief is not barred by the Eleventh Amendment.

4. *Edelman* did not end the battle over Illinois's administration of this program. Several years later, the plaintiffs returned to the Supreme Court with a new judgment to protect. In *Quern v. Jordan,* 440 U.S. 332, 99 S.Ct. 1139, 59 L.Ed.2d 358 (1979), the lower courts had ordered officials to notify each recipient of AABD funds that officials had unlawfully withheld some funds and that the recipients could file administrative appeals to receive back benefits. The lower court thought this removed the stigma of a federal money judgment against the state. The Seventh Circuit, reversed en banc, disapproving the district court's order because it purported to be a federal-court adjudication of the plaintiffs' right to recover damages from the state, which the Circuit viewed as forbidden by *Edelman.* The Court of Appeals did permit the district court to enter an order 1) advising the plaintiff class of the possibility that funds might be recovered through the state adminis-

---

[1] Unlike the award in *Edelman,* the injunction entered here could not instantaneously restore the victims of unlawful conduct to their rightful condition. Thus, the injunction here looks to the future, not simply to presently compensating victims for conduct and consequences completed in the past.

trative appeals process and 2) furnishing a form that could be used to set the state adjudicative process in motion. The Supreme Court affirmed.

Even that limited relief was narrower than might first appear. In *Green v. Mansour,* 474 U.S. 64, 106 S.Ct. 423, 88 L.Ed.2d 371 (1985), the Court disapproved so-called "notice relief," explaining that it had been allowed in *Quern* only because it was ancillary to prospective relief permitted under what the Court characterized as the narrow exception to states' sovereign immunity recognized by *Ex parte Young.* In *Green* itself, plaintiffs complained of the state's manner of calculating benefits under the federal Aid to Dependent Children program. Before judgment in the lower courts, Congress amended the governing statutes, and "respondent's calculations * * * thereafter conformed to federal law." The Court, noting that injunctive relief was inappropriate, also refused to allow plaintiffs to have declaratory relief of the existence of past violations.

> We think that * * * a declaratory judgment in this situation would be useful in resolving the dispute over the past lawfulness of respondent's action only if it might be offered in state-court proceedings as res judicata on the issue of liability, leaving to the state courts only a form of accounting proceeding whereby damages or restitution would be computed. But the issuance of a declaratory judgment in these circumstances would have much the same effect as a full-fledged award of damages or restitution by the federal court, the latter kinds of relief being of course prohibited by the Eleventh Amendment.

Regarding notice relief of the type *Quern* allowed, the Court observed that without injunctive or declaratory relief, there was nothing to which notice relief could be ancillary. The Court concluded: "Because 'notice relief' is not the type of remedy designed to prevent on-going violations of federal law, the Eleventh Amendment limitation on the Art. III power of federal courts prevents them from ordering it as an independent form of relief."

5. *Edelman* distinguishes several cases, including *Parden* and *Employees,* arguing that Congress intended in those cases to abrogate the states' immunity under the Eleventh Amendment and make them amenable to suit in the federal courts. How can Congress do that? If Congress, in setting up the AABD program, had provided that states could be sued in the federal courts in their own names, would the Court have honored that legislation or declared it unconstitutional as conflicting with the Eleventh Amendment?

6. *Atascadero State Hospital v. Scanlon,* 473 U.S. 234, 105 S.Ct. 3142, 87 L.Ed.2d 171 (1985), demonstrated how rigorously the Court would examine claims of waiver of immunity or consent. Scanlon sought damages under the federal Rehabilitation Act of 1973. A section of the California Constitution provided: "Suits may be brought against the State in such manner and in such courts as shall be directed by law." The Court held the language insufficient to waive the state's Eleventh Amendment immunity: "in order for a state statute or constitutional provision to constitute a waiver of Eleventh Amendment immunity, it must specify the State's intention to subject itself to suit in *federal* court * * * ."

Scanlon also argued that California had consented to federal suit by accepting federal funds under the Rehabilitation Act, which specified that an action would lie against "any recipient," and dealt extensively with states as intended recipients of aid under the Act. The Supreme Court refused the inference. "The Act * * * falls short of manifesting a clear intent to condition participation in the programs funded under the Act on a State's consent to waive its constitutional immunity." (The Court also rejected a third argument, that Congress had stripped participating states of their immunity. Note 7 at page 672 discusses that aspect of the case.)

7. Is a case asserting all federal question claims, some running against a state and some against individuals, removable? If the state, as a defendant, consents to or initiates removal, does that constitute consent to the federal forum that vitiates the Eleventh Amendment bar? *Wisconsin Department of Corrections v. Schacht*, 524 U.S. 381, 118 S.Ct. 2047, 141 L.Ed.2d 364 (1998), confronted both questions. Justice Breyer's opinion for a unanimous Court held that "the presence in an otherwise removable case of a claim that the Eleventh Amendment may bar does not destroy removal jurisdiction that would otherwise exist." In the course of the discussion, the opinion considered whether the Amendment is an immunity or a component of subject matter jurisdiction:

> The Eleventh Amendment, however, does not automatically destroy original jurisdiction. Rather, the Eleventh Amendment grants the State a legal power to assert a sovereign immunity defense should it choose to do so. The State can waive the defense. Nor need a court raise the defect on its own. Unless the State raises the matter, a court can ignore it. * * *

> [W]here original jurisdiction rests upon the Statute's grant of "arising under" jurisdiction, the Court has assumed that the presence of a potential Eleventh Amendment bar with respect to one claim, has not destroyed original jurisdiction over the case. Since a federal court would have original jurisdiction to hear this case had Schacht originally filed it there, the defendants may remove the case from state to federal courts.

> * * *

> [A]t the time of removal [*i.e.*, before the defendant answered], this case fell within the "original jurisdiction of the federal courts. The State's later invocation of the Eleventh Amendment placed the particular claim beyond the power of the federal courts to decide, but it did not destroy removal jurisdiction over the case.

> * * *

> A State's proper assertion of an Eleventh Amendment bar after removal means that the federal court cannot hear the barred claim. But that circumstance does not destroy removal jurisdiction over the remaining claims in the case before us.

The Court's careful parsing of the sequence of events and its reliance on the fact that at the time of removal, the State had asserted no Eleventh Amendment immunity is perhaps surprising, given earlier treatments of the Amendment as a jurisdictional provision. If the Amendment provides only an immunity defense, does that have implications for cases like *Edelman* and *Pennhurst State School & Hospital v. Halderman*, summarized at page 736?

Justice Kennedy, although joining the Court's opinion with its apparent rejection of the waiver theory, also wrote separately to discuss waiver, noting that it should be considered "in some later case." He left little doubt, however, about which way he will lean when that later case arrives.

> By electing to remove, the State created the difficult problem confronted in the Court of Appeals and now here. This is the situation in which law usually says that a party must accept the consequences of its own acts. It would seem simple enough to rule that once a State consents to removal, it may not turn around and say the Eleventh Amendment bars the jurisdiction of the federal court. Consent to removal, it can be argued, is a waiver of the Eleventh Amendment immunity. * * *

> The Court has said the Eleventh Amendment bar may be asserted for the first time on appeal, so a State which is sued in federal court does not waive the Eleventh Amendment simply by appearing and defending on the merits.

> I have my doubts about the propriety of this rule. In permitting the belated assertion of the Eleventh Amendment bar, we allow States to proceed to judgment without facing any real risk of adverse consequences. Should the State prevail, the plaintiff would be bound by principles of res judicata. If the State were to lose, however, it could void the entire judgment simply by asserting its immunity on appeal.

> * * *

> The Court could eliminate the unfairness by modifying our Eleventh Amendment jurisprudence to make it more consistent with our practice regarding personal jurisdiction. Under a rule inferring waiver from the failure to raise an objection at the outset of the proceedings, States would be prevented from gaining an unfair advantage.

> We would not need to make this substantial revision to find waiver in the circumstances here, however. Even if appearing in federal court and defending on the merits is not sufficient to constitute a waiver, a different case may be presented when a State under no compulsion to appear in federal court voluntarily invokes its jurisdiction.

> * * * Since a State which is made a defendant to a state court action is under no compulsion to appear in federal court and, like any other defendant, has the unilateral right to block removal of the case, any appearance the State makes in federal court may well be regarded as voluntary * * *.

Under Justice Kennedy's view, should the Eleventh Amendment simply be another affirmative defense that FED.R.CIV.P. 8(c) requires be asserted or lost? If so, is that a desirable change? If not, what advantages over the usual 8(c) situation will the states retain under Justice Kennedy's formulation?

Justice Kennedy asserts that under current law, the state can avoid an adverse federal judgment by asserting its Eleventh Amendment immunity on appeal. Does that make the federal judgment an advisory opinion? If not, why not? If so, does that mean that the Eleventh Amendment concerns subject matter jurisdiction, thus compelling federal courts to raise the matter *sua sponte*?

9. In *Lapides v. Board of Regents*, 535 U.S. 613, 122 S.Ct. 1640, 152 L.Ed.2d 806 (2002), a unanimous Court took at least one step that Justice Kennedy had urged, holding that the state's decision to join in removal (necessary because under 28 U.S.C. § 1441(a) all defendants must agree for the case to be removable) constituted a waiver of the Eleventh Amendment protection. Thus, *Schacht*'s statement acknowledging the state's entitlement to raise its Eleventh Amendment claim subsequent to removal is no longer accurate.

Justice Breyer's opinion drew a careful distinction between litigation and non-litigation conduct as a source of Eleventh Amendment waiver. Whereas the Court will be extremely reluctant to infer waiver from non-litigation conduct, a state's voluntary invocation of federal jurisdiction will suffice. *Lapides* leaves some interesting questions in its wake, however. The Court emphasized that the case did not involve any federal claims against the state, having only state law claims to which the state had waived immunity state actions. The plaintiff had asserted a § 1983 claim for damages against the individual defendants, but the Court had previously held that states are not "persons" within the meaning of § 1983. If the plaintiff had joined a federal claim against the state, should not the state's removal still constitute a waiver of Eleventh Amendment immunity?

The Court approves waiver by litigation conduct. How far will it extend that idea? In *Ford Motor Co. v. Department of Treasury of Ind.*, 323 U.S. 459, 65 S.Ct. 347, 89 L.Ed. 389 (1945), the plaintiff sued the state originally in the federal court. Had the state then moved for dismissal on Eleventh Amendment grounds, there is little question that it would have prevailed, but it did not. Instead, it litigated the merits and lost, raising its Eleventh Amendment defense only after suffering a loss in the district court and an affirmance in the Seventh Circuit. The *Ford* Court, noting the extreme importance of state sovereign immunity in the federal system, disposed of the case on Eleventh Amendment grounds, refusing to reach the merits and holding that the district court had had no jurisdiction. *Lapides* declared *Ford* overruled "insofar as it would otherwise apply."

After *Lapides*, should a state's decision to eschew its Eleventh Amendment defense in the district court in favor of litigating on the merits represents an acceptance of federal jurisdiction no less significant than that in *Lapides* itself? Sometimes the Court treats the Eleventh Amendment as a provision going to the subject matter jurisdiction of the federal courts (as in *Ford*), and other times it regards it as an immunity that the state can waive (as in *Lapides*). In this respect, one might analogize the Eleventh Amendment to the (non-Eleventh Amendment) defenses of lack of subject matter jurisdiction and lack of personal jurisdiction. As FED.R.CIV.P. 12(h) and many cases make clear, one may raise a subject matter jurisdiction defect at any time, while failure to raise personal jurisdiction in a defendant's first response to the complaint (whether by answer or by Rule 12 motion) is fatal. The former rule proceeds on the theory that the parties may not alter the subject matter jurisdiction of a court by their actions, even by their agreement. The latter rule rests on the estoppel-like principle that one whose litigation conduct is inconsistent with an assertion of the court's lack of jurisdiction over the person has waived any objection. If the Eleventh Amendment only bars the federal courts from exercising jurisdiction over suits against unconsenting states, do states really waive a limitation on the subject matter jurisdiction of the federal courts by consenting to suits, or is the limitation simply inapplicable to such suits? Does treating amenability to suit under the rubric of consent rather than waiver solve the problem or merely change the battleground?

On the other hand, is the characterization critical? The criteria that the Court uses from case to case to arrive at its characterization are anything but clear. With respect to whether the Eleventh Amendment is more akin to subject matter jurisdiction or personal jurisdiction, are *Ford* and *Lapides* fatally inconsistent? If so, given *Lapides*'s unanimity, has the Court made up its mind?

Edelman demonstrated that the stripping theory of *Ex parte Young* would avail individual plaintiffs nothing if they sought damages, even if the damages were characterized as something else such as "equitable restitution." The successors to *Edelman* discussed in Note 4 show how rigorously the Court would enforce the prospective/retroactive distinction. In 1997, the Court decided that even some prospective relief was not exempted from the Eleventh Amendment's proscription.

Idaho v. Coeur d'Alene Tribe, 521 U.S. 261, 117 S.Ct. 2028, 138 L.Ed.2d 438 (1997), involved a dispute between the Tribe and the state over Lake Coeur d'Alene and the water system of which it is a part. The Tribe claimed beneficial interest in the lake and its submerged lands, pursuant to an 1873 Executive Order establishing the Tribe's reservation and ownership by unextinguished aboriginal title. It sought declaratory and injunctive relief and associated costs and attorney's fees. A fractured Court decided that even though the Tribe sought only prospective relief, the Eleventh Amendment prevented the action.

There were three opinions. Justice Kennedy, whom the Chief Justice joined *in toto* and Justices O'Connor, Scalia and Thomas joined in part, held the Tribe's action to be "the functional equivalent of a quiet title action which [*sic*] implicates special sovereignty interests." Tracing the

states' interests in their submerged lands back to colonial times, the majority effectively declared actions involving such land to be special cases, not appropriate for resolution under the usual Eleventh Amendment framework. Justices Souter, with whom Justices Stevens, Ginsburg and Breyer joined, dissented. Standing alone, that may not be so surprising, but it does not stand alone.[4]

Coeur d'Alene's significance, however, may lie in the parts of Justice Kennedy's opinion that only Chief Justice Rehnquist joined. Justice Kennedy characterized the *Ex parte Young* doctrine as having two primary applications: where no state forum is available and when "the case calls for an interpretation of federal law." He pointed out that the Idaho courts could have heard the Tribe's claim, and he characterized the second part of *Ex parte Young* as having the potential to "lead to expansive application of the *Young* exception. It is difficult to say States consented to these types of suits in the plan of the convention." Finally, he argued that there should be no assumption that federal issues necessarily called for federal court interpretation and suggested that the proper approach to the doctrine of *Ex parte Young* was a "case-by-case" balancing. In fact, Justice Kennedy attempted to import into the jurisdictional analysis in *Coeur d'Alene* the far more restrictive "special factors counseling hesitation" that the Court has employed in determining whether to imply private rights of action in constitutional or statutory provisions and that the majority in *Seminole Tribe v. Florida* used as a part of its argument against the application of *Ex parte Young*.

Justices O'Connor, Scalia and Thomas declined to join those sections of Justice Kennedy's opinion. Justice O'Connor appeared to analogize the case to an action for damages when she characterized it as "a private action seeking to divest the State of a property interest." She also distinguished between claims of entitlement to possession (which the Court had previously entertained) and claims of title and immunity to state regulation. She and her concurring colleagues, however, rejected Justice Kennedy's attempt to reformulate *Ex parte Young* more generally. "This approach unnecessarily recharacterizes and narrows much of our *Young* jurisprudence."

Specifically, Justice O'Connor took issue with Justice Kennedy's assertion that unavailability of a state forum was a factor in *Ex parte Young* analysis, arguing that the Court had never articulated such a rationale. In addition, she objected to Justice Kennedy's downplaying of the importance of federal adjudication of important federal matters, highlighting the split between Justice Kennedy's approach and her own.

In any event, as the principal opinion ultimately concedes, in

---

[4] The majority also added to the confusion about the Eleventh Amendment's status: as a component of subject matter jurisdiction or a waivable immunity. *Lapides v. Board of Regents* (2002) may suggest a resolution. *See supra* page 660.

more recent cases *Young* has been applied "[e]ven if there is a prompt and effective remedy in a state forum." When a plaintiff seeks prospective relief to end an ongoing violation of federal rights, ordinarily the Eleventh Amendment poses no bar. Yet the principal opinion unnecessarily questions this basic principle of federal law, finding it "difficult to say States consented to these types of suits in the plan of the convention * * * . For purposes of the Supremacy Clause, it is simply irrelevant whether the claim is brought in state or federal court." We have frequently acknowledged the importance of having federal courts open to enforce and interpret federal rights. There is no need to call into question the importance of having federal courts interpret federal rights— particularly as a means of serving a federal interest in uniformity—to decide this case. Nor does acknowledging the interpretive function of federal courts suggest that state courts are inadequate to apply federal law.

In casting doubt upon the importance of having federal courts interpret federal law, the principal opinion lays the groundwork for its central conclusion: that a case-by-case balancing approach is appropriate where a plaintiff invokes the *Young* exception to the Eleventh Amendment's jurisdictional bar, even when a complaint clearly alleges a violation of federal law and clearly seeks prospective relief. The principal opinion characterizes our modern *Young* cases as fitting this case-by-case model. While it is true that the Court has decided a series of cases on the scope of the *Young* doctrine, these cases do not reflect the principal opinion's approach. Rather, they establish only that a *Young* suit is available where a plaintiff alleges an ongoing violation of federal law, and where the relief sought is prospective rather than retrospective.

Justice O'Connor also objected to several other matters in Justice Kennedy's opinion, criticizing his attempt to tie the availability of the *Ex parte Young* doctrine to the importance of the federal right involved. She argued that the availability of the federal forum under *Young* turned only on whether the relief sought was prospective or retroactive. Finally, she disputed Justice Kennedy's attempt to "import the inquiry employed in *Bivens* into our *Young* jurisprudence," although she acknowledged that *Seminole Tribe*, decided the year before, offered limited support for that notion. Ultimately, Justice O'Connor concurred in the result because "[w]here a plaintiff seeks to divest the State of all regulatory power over submerged lands—in effect, to invoke a federal court's jurisdiction to quiet title to sovereign lands—it simply cannot be said that the suit is not a suit against the State."

Justice Souter's dissent argued that the case fell "squarely within the *Young* doctrine" and that Congress had imposed a jurisdictional obligation to hear such cases. He was quick to acknowledge the importance of Justice O'Connor's break with Justice Kennedy, putting it in terms that Professor Michael Masinter termed "an audible collective sigh of relief":

> Justice O'Connor charts a more limited course that wisely rejects the lead opinion's call for federal jurisdiction contingent on case-by-case balancing * * * .

> While there is reason for great satisfaction that Justice O'Connor's view is the controlling one, it is still true that the effect of the two opinions is to redefine and reduce the substance of federal subject-matter jurisdiction to vindicate federal rights.

Justice Souter viewed *Seminole Tribe* (in which he also dissented) as having left the basic structure of the *Young* doctrine intact, resting instead on the conclusion that in that particular circumstance there was an indication that Congress did not intend the *Young* doctrine to apply.[5] Beyond that, however, he declined to view the property issue as a special case: "[A]n issue of property title is no different from any other legal or constitutional matter that may have to be resolved in deciding whether the officer of an immune government is so acting beyond his authority as to be amenable to suit without necessarily implicating his government."

Justice Souter identified two points of commonality between Justices Kennedy and O'Connor with respect to the non-applicability of *Ex parte Young*. The first was the "functional equivalent" analysis that both subscribed on the basis that the Tribe's success "was an aspersion on the government's claim of title." Regarding that rationale, Justice Souter raised two arguments. He argued first that the Framers could not have intended to leave the individual remediless in such circumstances.

> But a consideration of the alternatives shows why such aspersion was rightly accepted as a fair price to pay for the jurisdiction to consider individual claims of right in [two prior cases], as it has been accepted generally. The one alternative, of settling the matter of title by compelling the State itself to appear in a federal-question suit, is barred by Eleventh Amendment doctrine.[a] The other, of leaving an individual powerless to seek any federal remedy for violation of a federal right, would deplete the federal judicial power to a point the Framers could not possibly have intended, given a history of officer liability riding tandem with sovereign immunity extending back to the Middle Ages.

---

[5] Assuming that *Seminole Tribe* does reflect that view, it creates a problem that Justice Souter did not address in his *Coeur d'Alene* opinion. If *Young* stripping occurs because of supremacy, as Justice Peckham's opinion for the Court certainly indicates and as the majority opinion in *Pennhurst State School & Hosp. v. Halderman* (1984) (*see infra* page 736) confirms, then why is it possible for Congress to declare that that constitutional interest should be disregarded in a particular case?

[a] [AUTHORS' NOTE] Is it significant that Justice Souter did not say that the Eleventh Amendment bars such an action? Keep this in mind when reading *Seminole Tribe, infra* at page 697.

Justice Souter also argued that logic was against the majority's view on this point, pointing out that all *Young* actions are the functional equivalent of actions against the state. In *Young* itself, enforcement of the injunction against Attorney General Young had the same effect as a direct injunction against Minnesota prohibiting enforcement of the disputed rate statute. All successful habeas corpus actions involving state prisoners have the effect of telling the state that it cannot continue to hold them in custody. This had the effect of pointing out the true fiction of *Ex parte Young*: not that an officer can simultaneously be the state (for Fourteenth Amendment purposes) and not be the state (for Eleventh Amendment purposes), but that in allowing the action to proceed against the officer, the federal courts are nonetheless not affecting the state.

Justice Souter also rejected the majority's assertion that the state's special interest in retaining the power to regulate submerged lands was dispositive.

> While this point is no doubt correct, it has no bearing on *Young*'s application in this case. The relevant enquiry, as noted, is whether the state officers are exercising *ultra vires* authority over the disputed submerged lands. If they are, a federal court may enjoin their actions, even though such a ruling would place the land beyond Idaho's regulatory jurisdiction and accordingly deny state officers regulatory authority. Idaho indisputably has a significant sovereign interest in regulating its submerged lands, but it has no legitimate sovereign interest in regulating submerged lands located outside state borders.

In effect, Justice Souter argued that only by determining the merits could the federal courts tell whether they were infringing Idaho's sovereign interest in land.

Justice Souter's minority appears to be fairly stable; it is difficult to anticipate that he or Justice Stevens, Ginsburg or Breyer will abandon the positions that the Eleventh Amendment does not bar federal question cases. On the other hand, a majority of the Court appears to have adopted the functional-equivalent analysis that Justice Kennedy offered as a reason to deny the Tribe relief here. The remaining question is whether Justices O'Connor, Scalia and Thomas will be able to adhere to the middle position that they tried to chart in *Coeur d'Alene* or whether they will be persuaded by Justice Souter's argument that functional equivalence does not distinguish *Coeur d'Alene* from any other case in the *Young* mold. If they find the logic of his position appealing, toward which Justice—Souter or Kennedy—are they likely to move?

FITZPATRICK v. BITZER
Supreme Court of the United States, 1976.
427 U.S. 445, 96 S.Ct. 2666, 49 L.Ed.2d 614.

MR. JUSTICE REHNQUIST delivered the opinion of the Court.

In the 1972 Amendments to Title VII of the Civil Rights Act of 1964, Congress, acting under § 5 of the Fourteenth Amendment, authorized federal courts to award money damages in favor of a private individual against a state government found to have subjected that person to employment discrimination on the basis of "race, color, religion, sex, or national origin." The principal question presented by these cases is whether, as against the shield of sovereign immunity afforded the State by the Eleventh Amendment, *Edelman v. Jordan,* Congress has the power to authorize federal courts to enter such an award against the State as a means of enforcing the substantive guarantees of the Fourteenth Amendment. The Court of Appeals for the Second Circuit held that the effect of our decision in *Edelman* was to foreclose Congress' power. We granted certiorari to resolve this important constitutional question. We reverse.

I

Petitioners in No. 75-251 sued in the United States District Court for the District of Connecticut on behalf of all present and retired male employees of the State of Connecticut. Their amended complaint asserted, *inter alia,* that certain provisions in the State's statutory retirement benefit plan discriminated against them because of their sex, and therefore contravened Title VII of the 1964 Act. Title VII, which originally did not include state and local governments, had in the interim been amended to bring the States within its purview.

The District Court held that the Connecticut State Employees Retirement Act violated Title VII's prohibition against sex-based employment discrimination.[3] It entered prospective injunctive relief in petitioners' favor against respondent state officials. Petitioners also sought an award of retroactive retirement benefits as compensation for losses caused by the State's discrimination, as well as "a reasonable attorney's fee as part of the costs." But the District Court held that both would constitute recovery of money damages from the State's treasury, and were therefore precluded by the Eleventh Amendment and by this Court's decision in *Edelman v. Jordan.*

On petitioners' appeal, the Court of Appeals affirmed in part and reversed in part. It agreed with the District Court that the action, "insofar as it seeks damages, is in essence against the state and as such is subject to the Eleventh Amendment." The Court of Appeals also found that un-

---

[3] Petitioners had also alleged that the retirement plan was contrary to the Equal Protection Clause of the Fourteenth Amendment, but in view of its ruling under Title VII the District Court found no reason to address the constitutional claim.

der the 1972 Amendments to Title VII, "Congress intended to authorize a private suit for backpay by state employees against the state." Notwithstanding this statutory authority, the Court of Appeals affirmed the District Court and held that under *Edelman* a "private federal action for retroactive damages" is not a "constitutionally permissible method of enforcing Fourteenth Amendment rights." It reversed the District Court and remanded as to attorneys' fees, however, reasoning that such an award would have only an "ancillary effect" on the state treasury of the kind permitted under *Edelman*. The petition filed here by the state employees in No. 75-251 contends that Congress does possess the constitutional power under § 5 of the Fourteenth Amendment to authorize their Title VII damage action against the State. The state officials' cross-petition, No. 75-283, argues that under *Edelman* the Eleventh Amendment bars any award of attorneys' fees here because it would be paid out of the state treasury.

II

In *Edelman* this Court held that monetary relief awarded by the District Court to welfare plaintiffs, by reason of wrongful denial of benefits which had occurred previous to the entry of the District Court's determination of their wrongfulness, violated the Eleventh Amendment. Such an award was found to be indistinguishable from a monetary award against the State itself which had been prohibited in *Ford Motor Co. v. Department of Treasury*. It was therefore controlled by that case rather than by *Ex parte Young,* which permitted suits against state officials to obtain prospective relief against violations of the Fourteenth Amendment. *Edelman* went on to hold that the plaintiffs in that case could not avail themselves of the doctrine of waiver expounded in cases such as *Parden v. Terminal R. Co.* and *Employees v. Missouri Public Health Dept.,* because the necessary predicate for that doctrine was congressional intent to abrogate the immunity conferred by the Eleventh Amendment. We concluded that none of the statutes relied upon by plaintiffs in *Edelman* contained any authorization by Congress to join a State as defendant. The Civil Rights Act of 1871 had been held in *Monroe v. Pape* to exclude cities and other municipal corporations from its ambit; that being the case, it could not have been intended to include States as parties defendant. The provisions of the Social Security Act relied upon by plaintiffs were held by their terms not to "authorize suit against anyone," and they, too, were incapable of supplying the predicate for a claim of waiver on the part of the State. All parties in the instant litigation agree with the Court of Appeals that the suit for retroactive benefits by the petitioners is in fact indistinguishable from * * * *Edelman,* since what is sought here is a damages award payable to a private party from the state treasury.

Our analysis begins where *Edelman* ended, for in this Title VII case the "threshold fact of congressional authorization" to sue the State as employer is clearly present. This is, of course, the prerequisite found present in *Parden* and wanting in *Employees.* We are aware of the factual differences between the type of state activity involved in *Parden* and that involved in the present case, but we do not think that difference is material for our purposes. The congressional authorization involved in *Parden* was based on the power of Congress under the Commerce Clause; here, however, the Eleventh Amendment defense is asserted in the context of legislation passed pursuant to Congress' authority under § 5 of the Fourteenth Amendment.

As ratified by the States after the Civil War, that Amendment quite clearly contemplates limitations on their authority.

* * *

The substantive provisions are by express terms directed at the States. Impressed upon them by those provisions are duties with respect to their treatment of private individuals. Standing behind the imperatives is Congress' power to "enforce" them "by appropriate legislation." The impact of the Fourteenth Amendment upon the relationship between the Federal Government and the States, and the reach of congressional power under § 5, were examined at length by this Court in *Ex parte Virginia* (1880). A state judge had been arrested and indicted under a federal criminal statute prohibiting the exclusion on the basis of race of any citizen from service as a juror in a state court. The judge claimed that the statute was beyond Congress' power to enact under either the Thirteenth or the Fourteenth Amendment. The Court first observed that these Amendments "were intended to be, what they really are, limitations of the power of the States and enlargements of the power of Congress." It then addressed the relationship between the language of § 5 and the substantive provisions of the Fourteenth Amendment:

> The prohibitions of the Fourteenth Amendment are directed to the States, and they are to a degree restrictions of State power. It is these which Congress is empowered to enforce, and to enforce against State action, however put forth, whether that action be executive, legislative, or judicial. Such enforcement is no invasion of State sovereignty. No law can be, which the people of the States have, by the Constitution of the United States, empowered Congress to enact * * *. It is said the selection of jurors for her courts and the administration of her laws belong to each State; that they are her rights. This is true in the general [case]. But in exercising her rights, a State cannot disregard the limitations which the Federal Constitution has applied to her power. Her rights do not reach to that extent. Nor can she deny to the general government the right to exercise all its granted powers, though they may interfere with the full enjoyment of rights she would have if those powers had not been thus granted. Indeed, every addition of power to the general government involves a corresponding diminution of the governmental powers of the States. It is carved out of them.

* * *

The argument in support of the petition for a *habeas corpus* ignores entirely the power conferred upon Congress by the Fourteenth Amendment. Were it not for the fifth section of that amendment, there might be room for argument that the first section is only declaratory of the moral duty of the State * * *. But the Constitution now expressly gives authority for congressional interference and compulsion in the cases embraced within the Fourteenth Amendment. It is but a limited authority, true, extending only to a single class of cases; but within its limits it is complete.

Ex parte Virginia's early recognition of this shift in the federal-state balance has been carried forward by more recent decisions * * *.

* * *

It is true that none of these previous cases presented the question of the relationship between the Eleventh Amendment and the enforcement power granted to Congress under § 5 of the Fourteenth Amendment. But we think that the Eleventh Amendment, and the principle of state sovereignty which it embodies, *see Hans v. Louisiana,* are necessarily limited by the enforcement provisions of § 5 of the Fourteenth Amendment. In that section Congress is expressly granted authority to enforce "by appropriate legislation" the substantive provisions of the Fourteenth Amendment, which themselves embody significant limitations on state authority. When Congress acts pursuant to § 5, not only is it exercising legislative authority that is plenary within the terms of the constitutional grant, it is exercising that authority under one section of a constitutional Amendment whose other sections by their own terms embody limitations on state authority. We think that Congress may, in determining what is "appropriate legislation" for the purpose of enforcing the provisions of the Fourteenth Amendment, provide for private suits against States or state officials which are constitutionally impermissible in other contexts.

III

In No. 75-283, the state officials contest the Court of Appeals' conclusion that an award of attorneys' fees in this case would under *Edelman* have only an "ancillary effect" on the state treasury and could therefore be permitted as falling outside the Eleventh Amendment under the doctrine of *Ex parte Young.* We need not address this question, since, given the express congressional authority for such an award in a case brought under Title VII, it follows necessarily from our holding in No. 75-251 that Congress' exercise of power in this respect is also not barred by the Eleventh Amendment. We therefore affirm the Court of Appeals' judgment in No. 75-283 on this basis.

The judgment in No. 75-251 is

Reversed.

The judgment in No. 75-283 is

Affirmed.

Notes and Questions

1. What reading of *Hans, Ex parte Young* and the Eleventh Amendment does the Court adopt?

2. *Fitzpatrick* is indeed an unusual case. In deciding that Congress can act under the Fourteenth Amendment to limit the ambit of the Eleventh, the Court announced a significant shift of power from the states to the federal government. At the outset, the fact that Justice Rehnquist (hardly a proponent of expanded federal power at the expense of state governments) wrote the opinion deserves some thought. Why did he take the position he did?

3. a) The conclusion that the Fourteenth Amendment was intended to limit state power is not surprising. The Amendment was passed by Congress in 1868, at the height of Reconstruction. Does the Court hold that the Fourteenth Amendment itself limits the Eleventh Amendment? After *Fitzpatrick,* can any case asserting a due process violation be brought against a state in the federal courts? If not, how can the Court justify, on the wording of the Fourteenth Amendment and its legislative history, stopping short of that result? If so, is *Edelman* overruled *sub silentio*?

b) *Fitzpatrick,* and *Monell*'s reinterpretation of § 1983 to include municipalities, raised the possibility that § 1983 actions in the federal courts could run also against the states themselves. Congress enacted § 1983 under § 5 of the Fourteenth Amendment, and pursuant to the Court's reasoning in *Fitzpatrick,* it could have abrogated the states' Eleventh Amendment immunity. But in *Quern v. Jordan,* 440 U.S. 332, 99 S.Ct. 1139, 59 L.Ed.2d 358 (1979), the Court announced that it had not, because the Court did not think § 1983's legislative history clearly showed Congress's intent to limit the Eleventh Amendment. The debates on § 1983 did not mention the Eleventh Amendment, and the majority asserted that if the legislators had understood the Civil Rights Act to override the Eleventh Amendment, there would have been a major outcry. Was the majority assuming its conclusion? Dissenting opinions disputed whether the Court should have reached the issue. The Court did reach it, however, and whether the announcement is dictum or not, one must recognize that Supreme Court dicta stand in a special light.

Quern, however, left open the possibility of § 1983 suits against the states in the state courts, since jurisdiction over such actions has never been exclusively federal, and the Eleventh Amendment does not apply in the state courts. In *Will v. Michigan Department of State Police,* 491 U.S. 58, 109 S.Ct. 2304, 105 L.Ed.2d 45 (1989), the Court summoned the ghost of *Monroe v. Pape* and held that states and state officials sued in their official capacities are not "persons" within the meaning of § 1983. It remains to be seen whether *Will* has a longer life-span than did the correlate holding of *Monroe.* Query whether the holding in *Will* was implicit in *Quern* or whether the cases in fact deal with different issues.

Quern and *Will* do not mean that § 1983 is of no use against state officials. *Hafer v. Melo,* 502 U.S. 21, 112 S.Ct. 358, 116 L.Ed.2d 301 (1991), held that state officials sued in their individual capacities may be liable under § 1983, and that the predicate acts may be within or without the officials' authority, provided only that the actions are taken under color of state law. After *Hafer,* what does *Will* accomplish? Has a potential § 1983 plaintiff lost anything as a result of *Will* that *Hafer* did not fully restore?

The Court continues to exclude states from the realm of "persons" unless Congress makes it impossible for the Court to do so. In *Vermont Agency of Natural Resources v. United States ex rel. Stevens,* 529 U.S. 765, 120 S.Ct. 1858, 146 L.Ed.2d 836 (2000), a majority of the Court declined to construe "persons" in the False Claims Act as encompassing states. The majority relied upon the general presumption that sovereigns are unaffected by legislation, disagreeing with Justice Stevens's and Justice Souter's argument that the presumption applies only to legislative acts of the sovereign to be charged. The Court also declined to attribute meaning to "persons" based on the interaction with other sections of the False Claims Act.

By interpreting the False Claims Act as it did, the Court avoided a novel Eleventh Amendment issue. *Vermont Agency* was a *qui tam* action brought by Stevens, the relator. Vermont resisted the action on several grounds, one of them being that the Eleventh Amendment barred the action. That raised the question of whether the relator in some sense assumed the characteristics of the plaintiff United States for Eleventh Amendment purposes. The Eleventh Amendment, of course, has no effect on actions by the federal government against a state. Interestingly, in another section of the opinion, the Court held that the relator assumed the standing of the United States for injury-in-fact and redressability purposes, much as a subrogee has the standing of the subrogor.

Yet the Court's avoidance of the issue raises other questions. To the extent that the Amendment is jurisdictional, as the Court has often said, should the Court have considered an issue of statutory construction before deciding whether it had subject matter jurisdiction at all? The *Ashwander* admonition to avoid decision of constitutional questions whenever possible runs into the principle that a court must first decide its jurisdiction before proceeding to other issues in the case. On the other hand, if one can avoid jurisdictional issues as the Court appears to have done here, why did the Court decide the standing issue, also an Article III matter, before grappling with the statute?

4. Do you think the Constitution-modifying effect of the Fourteenth Amendment is limited to the Eleventh Amendment or can it be applied to other amendments as well? Suppose, for example, Congress decides to attack the problem of "hate speech" by making it a criminal offense. Can such a speech-restricting statute be saved from constitutional infirmity on First Amendment grounds on the basis that it is necessary to secure due process and equal protection of the laws under the Fourteenth Amendment for groups that are the targets of hate speech?

5. Is the *Ex parte Young* fiction necessary to the result in *Fitzpatrick*? If the plaintiffs in *Fitzpatrick* had joined the state of Connecticut as a defendant, would the Court have permitted the suit to proceed?

6. Does § 5 of the Fourteenth Amendment, as interpreted in *Fitzpatrick*, effectively authorize Congress to amend the Constitution, or at least the Eleventh Amendment?

7. In *Atascadero State Hospital v. Scanlon*, 473 U.S. 234, 105 S.Ct. 3142, 87 L.Ed.2d 171 (1985), the Court demonstrated that it will not lightly infer *Fitzpatrick* abrogation. Scanlon argued that when Congress specifically included states as recipients of federal funds under the Rehabilitation Act of 1973 and further provided for private actions against "any recipient" of such funds, it removed the states' Eleventh Amendment immunity to private enforcement actions. The majority disagreed, noting

> the requirement, well established in our cases, that Congress unequivocally express its intention to abrogate the Eleventh Amendment bar to suits against the States in federal court. We * * * affirm that Congress may abrogate the States' constitutionally secured immunity from suit in federal court only by making its intention unmistakably clear in the language of the statute.

The majority thus refused to engage in any inferential, deductive, or interpretive process to decide whether Congress meant to subject the states to private federal suits. Only explicit language in the statute will do.

Justice Brennan dissented, joined by three other Justices. He argued at length that the Court had taken a wrong turn with respect to the Eleventh Amendment in *Hans* and had continued to misunderstand the Amendment's place in the constitutional structure. According to Justice Brennan, the Amendment meant only to preserve in diversity actions a sovereign immunity defense to state-law claims that the states would have enjoyed in their own courts. His position, then and since, has failed to attract the crucial fifth vote, although the Court remains split five-four on the issue with Justices Souter, Ginsburg and Breyer having succeeded to the views of Justices Brennan, Marshall, and Blackmun.

Atascadero demands that Congress be explicit if it intends to limit the states' Eleventh Amendment immunity. Yet the Fourteenth Amendment, the font of congressional power to do so, is itself hardly explicit about its effect on the Eleventh Amendment. Should the Court require legislative implementation to be more explicit than the constitutional authorization, insisting on a specificity that the Constitution appears not to contemplate? Alternatively, should the Court have ruled that the Fourteenth Amendment is insufficiently explicit and thus overruled *Fitzpatrick*?

8. *Raygor v. Regents of the University of Minnesota*, 534 U.S. 533, 122 S.Ct. 999, 152 L.Ed.2d 227 (2002), held that the statute-of-limitations tolling provision of the supplemental jurisdiction statute, 28 U.S.C. § 1367(d), does not apply to a state defendant that has not waived its Eleventh Amendment immunity to federal suit, because there is no "unmistakably clear" language indicating Congress's intention to have the toll apply to states. When you

have read *Seminole Tribe v. Florida*, beginning at page 697, consider whether even an unambiguous declaration by Congress in § 1367(d) would be effective.

9. In *Dellmuth v. Muth,* 491 U.S. 223, 109 S.Ct. 2397, 105 L.Ed.2d 181 (1989), Muth sought damages from the Acting Secretary of Education of Pennsylvania for violations of the federal Education of the Handicapped Act. In a 5-4 decision, the Court upheld the state's Eleventh Amendment immunity claim, noting that Congress had not met *Atascadero*'s standard of explicitness.[6] The Court asserted:

> Legislative history generally will be irrelevant to a judicial inquiry into whether Congress intended to abrogate the Eleventh Amendment. If Congress' intention is "unmistakably clear in the language of the statute," recourse to legislative history will be unnecessary; if Congress' intention is not unmistakably clear, recourse to legislative history will be futile, because by definition the rule of *Atascadero* will not be met.

Justice Brennan, joined by Justices Blackmun, Marshall, and Stevens, dissented, predictably differing with the majority on the issue of the "unmistakability" of Congress's intent, but also noting the following:

> Congress has already had cause to complain of the Court's changing its interpretive rules in mid-course. After the Court held in *Atascadero* that § 504 of the Rehabilitation Act of 1973, * * * contained no "unmistakable language" abrogating Eleventh Amendment immunity, * * * Congress in 1986 enacted an amendment to the Act providing:

> A State shall not be immune under the Eleventh Amendment of the Constitution of the United States from suit in Federal court for a violation of [enumerated provisions of the Rehabilitation Act] or the provisions of any other Federal statute prohibiting discrimination by recipients of Federal financial assistance. 42 U.S.C. § 2000d-7(a)(1) (1982 ed. Supp. IV).

> Congress enacted this provision, the Senate Conference Report tells us, because "[t]he Supreme Court's decision [in *Atascadero*] misinterpreted congressional intent. Such a gap in Section 504 coverage was never intended. It would be inequitable for Section 504 to mandate state compliance with its provisions and yet deny litigants the right to enforce their rights in Federal courts when State or State agency actions are in issue."

---

[6] Congress had provided, *inter alia,* that "it is in the national interest that the Federal government assist State and local efforts to provide programs to meet the education needs of handicapped children in order to assure equal protection of the law," 20 U.S.C.A. § 1400(b)(9) (1982), and had authorized aggrieved parties to "bring a civil action * * * in any State court of competent jurisdiction or in a district court of the United States without regard to the amount in controversy." 20 U.S.C.A. § 1415(e)(2) (1982). Perhaps most important, a 1986 amendment stated that the Act's provision for a *reduction* of attorney's fees did not apply "if the court finds that the State or local educational agency unreasonably protracted the final resolution of the action or proceeding or there was a violation of this section." 20 U.S.C.A. § 1415(e)(4)(G) (1982 ed. Supp. V.)

Do you think this Congress's effort should have precluded subsequent "misinterpretations" by the Court, or was it insufficiently specific about which statutes were included? Did the 1986 amendment implicitly express disapproval of the Court's new interpretive method? If so, should the Court accede, or is Congress stuck with the rules the Court has created? In that respect, consider the following note.

10. a) Some commentators have been critical of this aspect of the Court's Eleventh Amendment jurisprudence. Professors Eskridge and Frickey, discussing the plethora of "clear statement" rules upon which the Court has increasingly insisted, note the following:

> The Eleventh Amendment canon, alive and well but lacking Herculean power in the middle years of the Burger Court, underwent a steroidal transformation in the 1980s. What had once been a presumption-based approach to resolve federal statutory ambiguity—after statutory language, legislative history, and other factors were consulted—became a super-strong clear statement rule focusing on statutory language alone and requiring a very clear statement by Congress. * * *

> Since *Atascadero,* the Court has stuck with this super-strong clear statement rule concerning congressional abrogation of Eleventh Amendment immunity and has applied a similarly strict approach to judging whether a state itself has waived its Eleventh Amendment rights. * * *

William N. Eskridge, Jr. & Philip P. Frickey, *Quasi-Constitutional Law: Clear Statement Rules As Constitutional Lawmaking,* 45 VAND.L.REV. 593, 621-22 (1992).[7] Professors Eskridge and Frickey go on to note that in the context of *Dellmuth,* the Court's approach has had a more profound effect on separation-of-powers concerns than one might appreciate at first glance.

> [T]he Court's new super-strong clear statement rules are extraordinarily countermajoritarian: they not only pose the possibility of ignoring legislative expectations, but they also make it quite hard for Congress to express its expectations even when it is focusing on the issue. Consider the recent case of *Dellmuth v. Muth.* The Court in that case applied the Atascadero super-strong clear statement rule to find that the Education of the Handicapped Act of 1975 (EHA) did not permit damage suits against the states. The decision was countermajoritarian, for the text assumed the viability of such lawsuits, and specific legislative history confirmed the assumption.

> But the decision was more than simply countermajoritarian. It suggested a certain judicial haughtiness and uncooperativeness that is surely inconsistent with the humble due process of lawmaking rationale for the Court's super-strong clear statement rules. For under the Supreme Court's prevailing Eleventh Amendment precedent in 1975, when Congress adopted the statute, the jurisdictional language covering actions against the states plus the specific legislative history were

---

[7] Copyright © 1992 by the Vanderbilt Law Review. Reprinted by permission.

probably enough to rebut the presumption against congressional abrogation of the states' Eleventh Amendment immunity, and were perhaps even strong enough to satisfy a traditional clear statement rule. In 1985, of course, the Court changed its approach to the *Atascadero* super-strong clear statement rule.

Given this shift, Congress in 1986 enacted the following statute: "A State shall not be immune under the Eleventh Amendment * * * from suit in Federal Court for a violation of [statutes protecting people with disabilities, including the EHA]." Congress complained that its intent in the Rehabilitation Act had been thwarted by *Atascadero* and overrode that decision in a way expected to head off state immunity claims under other statutes protecting people with disabilities. Yet in *Dellmuth,* the Court not only held that the EHA of 1975 failed to abrogate state immunity, but cited as evidence the subsequent 1986 statute, which contained the requisite clear statement but did not apply to the case in question. Congress promptly overrode *Dellmuth* in 1990. What is most striking to us is that it took Congress three statutes and fifteen years to accomplish what Congress probably thought it had done in 1975. That is extraordinarily countermajoritarian.

As the *Dellmuth* example illustrates, the countermajoritarian nature of the Court's super-strong clear statement rules is not necessarily mitigated by the possibility of a congressional override. Even when Congress thinks it is overriding the Court, the Court has frustrated Congress's expectations in cases like *Dellmuth.* More important, it is sometimes as difficult to override a Supreme Court statutory decision as it is to override a constitutional one.

Id. at 638–40. When the Court deals with areas in which Congress has acted, are there separation-of-powers concerns that "counsel hesitation" in creating new rules of constitutional interpretation?

Has the *Atascadero* approach effectively created a hierarchy of values with respect to federalism and separation of powers? If not, is there another explanation for Congress having to make three attempts to have its way with respect to the statutes involved in *Dellmuth* and similar cases? If so, what is the authority for the Court to create such a hierarchy?

———

Since *Atascadero* and *Dellmuth,* Congress has demonstrated that it can be sufficiently clear. *See, e.g.,* Copyright Remedy Clarification Act of 1990, 17 U.S.C.A. § 511; Patent and Plant Variety Protection Clarification Act, 7 U.S.C.A. § 2570 (both specifically eliminating Eleventh Amendment protection). One might have anticipated that this would end the interbranch and intersovereign struggle in this respect, but it has not. The Court has responded by declaring substantive limitations on Congress's power.

Florida Prepaid Postsecondary Education Expense Board v. College Savings Bank, 527 U.S. 666, 119 S.Ct. 2219, 144 L.Ed.2d 605 (1999), involved the Patent and Plant Variety Remedy Clarification Act. College Savings Bank alleged that Florida Prepaid had infringed the Bank's patent on a particular method of financing college educations. A five-to-four majority held that Congress's attempt to protect patents against state infringement by legislating pursuant to § 5 of the Fourteenth Amendment was unconstitutional because Congress had insufficient evidence that state infringement of patents was a national problem. The Court therefore ruled that the statute was not "appropriate legislation" within the meaning of § 5.[8]

Kimel v. Florida Board of Regents, 528 U.S. 62, 120 S.Ct. 631, 145 L.Ed.2d 522 (2000), confirmed that the Court will continue to take a critical look at § 5 legislation. The plaintiffs alleged that their state employers discriminated against them on the basis of age, in violation of the Age Discrimination in Employment Act. Although the Court acknowledged that Congress had been sufficiently explicit about abrogating Eleventh Amendment immunity, it nonetheless upheld the states' Eleventh Amendment challenge. Noting that age is not a suspect (or even

---

[8] In reaching this conclusion, the majority distinguished between patent infringement by the states and constitutional violations by the states.

> [A] State's infringement of a patent, though interfering with a patent owner's right to exclude others, does not by itself violate the Constitution. Instead, only where the State provides no remedy, or only inadequate remedies, to injured patent owners for its infringement of their patent could a deprivation of property without due process result.

The Court thus echoed the question it posed in *Parratt v. Taylor* and related cases (*see* pages 600-605): "what process is due?" (In this case, of course, one might be skeptical of the state's ability (let alone its willingness) to provide a remedy for infringement, since patent cases are exclusively federal pursuant to 28 U.S.C. § 1338.) Chief Justice Rehnquist took Congress to task for failing sufficiently to consider what remedies the states might provide, though he did note that Congress "did hear a limited amount of testimony to the effect that the remedies available in some States were uncertain." One might legitimately ask at this point how intensively the Court plans to inject itself into the legislative process or, alternatively, what standard the majority will use to determine when Congress has heard "enough" testimony to justify its legislation. Were a private litigant to ask the Court to invalidate legislation on the ground that Congress had not considered "enough" evidence to justify it, one can only guess at the Justices' reaction.

A related case, *College Savings Bank v. Florida Prepaid Postsecondary Education Expense Board*, 527 U.S. 627, 119 S.Ct. 2199, 144 L.Ed.2d 575 (1999), arose in the context of the Trademark Remedy Clarification Act, which amended the Lanham Act to include states as permissible defendants in trademark actions. The same majority ruled there is no Fourteenth Amendment property interest at all in preventing a competitor from misrepresenting its own product to the detriment of one's trademark. The Court therefore held that Florida Prepaid's alleged misrepresentation did not deprive College Savings Bank of any Fourteenth Amendment property. Consequently, the legislation authorizing federal suit against the state could not survive on the authority of the Amendment.

The Court's approach parallels *Paul v. Davis* (text at 599), where the majority found no cognizable Fourteenth Amendment interest in protecting one's reputation from defamation by the state. That approach had the dual effect of making a § 1983 action unavailable (because there was no federal right upon which to base it) and of making the existence *vel non* of a state remedy irrelevant because there had been no Fourteenth Amendment deprivation for which the state might otherwise have had to provide due process.

quasi-suspect) classification, the Court went on to hold that under the rational-basis test, the presence of a class-based rationale for the classification took the case outside of the Fourteenth Amendment. The majority took the position that it was permissible to use age as a proxy for other characteristics (competence, energy, productivity) in which the state had a legitimate interest, even if the classification was probably not correct in the majority of cases. (This raises fascinating questions about how rational a measuring device is if it malfunctions more often than not, but those are questions for the Constitutional Law course.)

Florida Prepaid and *Kimel* appeared to leave the door open for Congress to legislate provided that it assembled a better legislative record to show that it was addressing a national problem. Just as Congress had adapted to *Atascadero*'s clear-statement rule, it began to legislate in accord with the Court's new demand for more extensive legislative records. And, just as *Dellmuth* showed Congress that it is not as easy to make clear legislative statements as one might think, the Court demonstrated that it would take a rigorous view of whether the legislative record was sufficiently complete.

BOARD OF TRUSTEES OF THE UNIVERSITY OF ALABAMA v. GARRETT

Supreme Court of the United States, 2001.
531 U.S. 356, 121 S.Ct. 955, 148 L.Ed.2d 866.

CHIEF JUSTICE REHNQUIST delivered the opinion of the Court.

We decide here whether employees of the State of Alabama may recover money damages by reason of the State's failure to comply with the provisions of Title I of the Americans with Disabilities Act of 1990 (ADA or Act).[1] We hold that such suits are barred by the Eleventh Amendment.

The ADA prohibits certain employers, including the States, from "discriminat[ing] against a qualified individual with a disability because of the disability of such individual in regard to job application procedures, the hiring, advancement, or discharge of employees, employee compensation, job training, and other terms, conditions, and privileges of employment." To this end, the Act requires employers to "mak[e] rea-

---

[1] Respondents' complaints in the United States District Court alleged violations of both Title I and Title II of the ADA, and petitioners' "Question Presented" can be read to apply to both sections. Though the briefs of the parties discuss both sections in their constitutional arguments, no party has briefed the question whether Title II of the ADA, dealing with the "services, programs, or activities of a public entity," 42 U.S.C. § 12132, is available for claims of employment discrimination when Title I of the ADA expressly deals with that subject. We are not disposed to decide the constitutional issue whether Title II, which has somewhat different remedial provisions from Title I, is appropriate legislation under § 5 of the Fourteenth Amendment when the parties have not favored us with briefing on the statutory question. To the extent the Court granted certiorari on the question whether respondents may sue their state employers for damages under Title II of the ADA, that portion of the writ is dismissed as improvidently granted.

sonable accommodations to the known physical or mental limitations of an otherwise qualified individual with a disability who is an applicant or employee, unless [the employer] can demonstrate that the accommodation would impose an undue hardship on the operation of the [employer's] business."

[R]easonable accommodation may include—

> (A) making existing facilities used by employees readily accessible to and usable by individuals with disabilities; and (B) job restructuring, part-time or modified work schedules, reassignment to a vacant position, acquisition or modification of equipment or devices, appropriate adjustment or modifications of examinations, training materials or policies, the provision of qualified readers or interpreters, and other similar accommodations for individuals with disabilities.

The Act also prohibits employers from "utilizing standards, criteria, or methods of administration * * * that have the effect of discrimination on the basis of disability."

The Act defines "disability" to include "(A) a physical or mental impairment that substantially limits one or more of the major life activities of such individual; (B) a record of such an impairment; or (C) being regarded as having such an impairment." A disabled individual is otherwise "qualified" if he or she, "with or without reasonable accommodation, can perform the essential functions of the employment position that such individual holds or desires."

Respondent Patricia Garrett, a registered nurse, was employed as the Director of Nursing, OB/Gyn/Neonatal Services, for the University of Alabama in Birmingham Hospital. In 1994, Garrett was diagnosed with breast cancer and subsequently underwent a lumpectomy, radiation treatment, and chemotherapy. Garrett's treatments required her to take substantial leave from work. Upon returning to work in July 1995, Garrett's supervisor informed Garrett that she would have to give up her Director position. Garrett then applied for and received a transfer to another, lower paying position as a nurse manager.

Respondent Milton Ash worked as a security officer for the Alabama Department of Youth Services (Department). Upon commencing this employment, Ash informed the Department that he suffered from chronic asthma and that his doctor recommended he avoid carbon monoxide and cigarette smoke, and Ash requested that the Department modify his duties to minimize his exposure to these substances. Ash was later diagnosed with sleep apnea and requested, again pursuant to his doctor's recommendation, that he be reassigned to daytime shifts to accommodate his condition. Ultimately, the Department granted none of the requested relief. Shortly after Ash filed a discrimination claim with the Equal Employment Opportunity Commission, he noticed that his performance evaluations were lower than those he had received on previous occasions.

Garrett and Ash filed separate lawsuits in the District Court, both seeking money damages under the ADA. Petitioners moved for summary judgment, claiming that the ADA exceeds Congress' authority to abrogate the State's Eleventh Amendment immunity. In a single opinion disposing of both cases, the District Court agreed with petitioners' position and granted their motions for summary judgment. The cases were consolidated on appeal to the Eleventh Circuit. The Court of Appeals reversed, adhering to its intervening decision in *Kimel v. State Bd. of Regents* that the ADA validly abrogates the States' Eleventh Amendment immunity.

We granted certiorari, to resolve a split among the Courts of Appeals on the question whether an individual may sue a State for money damages in federal court under the ADA.

I

The ultimate guarantee of the Eleventh Amendment is that nonconsenting States may not be sued by private individuals in federal court.

We have recognized, however, that Congress may abrogate the States' Eleventh Amendment immunity when it both unequivocally intends to do so and "act[s] pursuant to a valid grant of constitutional authority." The first of these requirements is not in dispute here. The question, then, is whether Congress acted within its constitutional authority by subjecting the States to suits in federal court for money damages under the ADA.

Congress may not, of course, base its abrogation of the States' Eleventh Amendment immunity upon the powers enumerated in Article I. In *Fitzpatrick v. Bitzer* (1976), however, we held that "the Eleventh Amendment, and the principle of state sovereignty which it embodies, are necessarily limited by the enforcement provisions of § 5 of the Fourteenth Amendment. As a result, we concluded, Congress may subject nonconsenting States to suit in federal court when it does so pursuant to a valid exercise of its § 5 power. Our cases have adhered to this proposition. Accordingly, the ADA can apply to the States only to the extent that the statute is appropriate § 5 legislation. Section 5 of the Fourteenth Amendment grants Congress the power to enforce the substantive guarantees contained in § 1 by enacting "appropriate legislation." Congress is not limited to mere legislative repetition of this Court's constitutional jurisprudence. "Rather, Congress' power 'to enforce' the Amendment includes the authority both to remedy and to deter violation of rights guaranteed thereunder by prohibiting a somewhat broader swath of conduct, including that which is not itself forbidden by the Amendment's text."

City of Boerne also confirmed, however, the long-settled principle that it is the responsibility of this Court, not Congress, to define the substance of constitutional guarantees. Accordingly, § 5 legislation reaching beyond the scope of § 1's actual guarantees must exhibit "congruence and proportionality between the injury to be prevented or remedied and the means adopted to that end."

II

The first step in applying these now familiar principles is to identify with some precision the scope of the constitutional right at issue. Here, that inquiry requires us to examine the limitations § 1 of the Fourteenth Amendment places upon States' treatment of the disabled. As we did last Term in *Kimel,* we look to our prior decisions under the Equal Protection Clause dealing with this issue.

Under rational-basis review, where a group possesses "distinguishing characteristics relevant to interests the State has the authority to implement," a State's decision to act on the basis of those differences does not give rise to a constitutional violation. "Such a classification cannot run afoul of the Equal Protection Clause if there is a rational relationship between the disparity of treatment and some legitimate governmental purpose." Moreover, the State need not articulate its reasoning at the moment a particular decision is made. Rather, the burden is upon the challenging party to negative " 'any reasonably conceivable state of facts that could provide a rational basis for the classification.' "

Thus, the result of *Cleburne* is that States are not required by the Fourteenth Amendment to make special accommodations for the disabled, so long as their actions toward such individuals are rational. They could quite hardheadedly—and perhaps hardheartedly—hold to job-qualification requirements which do not make allowance for the disabled. If special accommodations for the disabled are to be required, they have to come from positive law and not through the Equal Protection Clause.[5]

III

Once we have determined the metes and bounds of the constitutional right in question, we examine whether Congress identified a history and pattern of unconstitutional employment discrimination by the States against the disabled. Just as § 1 of the Fourteenth Amendment applies only to actions committed "under color of state law," Congress' § 5 authority is appropriately exercised only in response to state transgressions. The legislative record of the ADA, however, simply fails to show that Congress did in fact identify a pattern of irrational state discrimina-

---

[5] It is worth noting that by the time that Congress enacted the ADA in 1990, every State in the Union had enacted such measures. At least one Member of Congress remarked that "this is probably one of the few times where the States are so far out in front of the Federal Government, it's not funny." A number of these provisions, however, did not go as far as the ADA did in requiring accommodation.

tion in employment against the disabled.

Respondents contend that the inquiry as to unconstitutional discrimination should extend not only to States themselves, but to units of local governments, such as cities and counties. All of these, they say, are "state actors" for purposes of the Fourteenth Amendment. This is quite true, but the Eleventh Amendment does not extend its immunity to units of local government. These entities are subject to private claims for damages under the ADA without Congress' ever having to rely on § 5 of the Fourteenth Amendment to render them so. It would make no sense to consider constitutional violations on their part, as well as by the States themselves, when only the States are the beneficiaries of the Eleventh Amendment.

Congress made a general finding in the ADA that "historically, society has tended to isolate and segregate individuals with disabilities, and, despite some improvements, such forms of discrimination against individuals with disabilities continue to be a serious and pervasive social problem." The record assembled by Congress includes many instances to support such a finding. But the great majority of these incidents do not deal with the activities of States.

Respondents in their brief cite half a dozen examples from the record that did involve States. A department head at the University of North Carolina refused to hire an applicant for the position of health administrator because he was blind; similarly, a student at a state university in South Dakota was denied an opportunity to practice teach because the dean at that time was convinced that blind people could not teach in public schools. A microfilmer at the Kansas Department of Transportation was fired because he had epilepsy; deaf workers at the University of Oklahoma were paid a lower salary than those who could hear. The Indiana State Personnel Office informed a woman with a concealed disability that she should not disclose it if she wished to obtain employment.

Several of these incidents undoubtedly evidence an unwillingness on the part of state officials to make the sort of accommodations for the disabled required by the ADA. Whether they were irrational under our decision in *Cleburne* is more debatable, particularly when the incident is described out of context. But even if it were to be determined that each incident upon fuller examination showed unconstitutional action on the part of the State, these incidents taken together fall far short of even suggesting the pattern of unconstitutional discrimination on which § 5 legislation must be based. Congress, in enacting the ADA, found that "some 43,000,000 Americans have one or more physical or mental disabilities." In 1990, the States alone employed more than 4.5 million people. It is telling, we think, that given these large numbers, Congress assembled only such minimal evidence of unconstitutional state discrimination in employment against the disabled.

Even were it possible to squeeze out of these examples a pattern of unconstitutional discrimination by the States, the rights and remedies created by the ADA against the States would raise the same sort of concerns as to congruence and proportionality as were found in *City of Boerne*. For example, whereas it would be entirely rational (and therefore constitutional) for a state employer to conserve scarce financial resources by hiring employees who are able to use existing facilities, the ADA requires employers to "mak[e] existing facilities used by employees readily accessible to and usable by individuals with disabilities." The ADA does except employers from the "reasonable accommodatio[n]" requirement where the employer "can demonstrate that the accommodation would impose an undue hardship on the operation of the business of such covered entity." However, even with this exception, the accommodation duty far exceeds what is constitutionally required in that it makes unlawful a range of alternative responses that would be reasonable but would fall short of imposing an "undue burden" upon the employer. The Act also makes it the employer's duty to prove that it would suffer such a burden, instead of requiring (as the Constitution does) that the complaining party negate reasonable bases for the employer's decision.

The ADA also forbids "utilizing standards, criteria, or methods of administration" that disparately impact the disabled, without regard to whether such conduct has a rational basis. Although disparate impact may be relevant evidence of racial discrimination, such evidence alone is insufficient even where the Fourteenth Amendment subjects state action to strict scrutiny.

The ADA's constitutional shortcomings are apparent when the Act is compared to Congress' efforts in the Voting Rights Act of 1965 to respond to a serious pattern of constitutional violations. In *South Carolina v. Katzenbach*, (1966), we considered whether the Voting Rights Act was "appropriate" legislation to enforce the Fifteenth Amendment's protection against racial discrimination in voting. Concluding that it was a valid exercise of Congress' enforcement power under § 2 of the Fifteenth Amendment, we noted that "[b]efore enacting the measure, Congress explored with great care the problem of racial discrimination in voting."

In that Act, Congress documented a marked pattern of unconstitutional action by the States. State officials, Congress found, routinely applied voting tests in order to exclude African-American citizens from registering to vote. Congress also determined that litigation had proved ineffective and that there persisted an otherwise inexplicable 50-percentage-point gap in the registration of white and African-American voters in some States. Congress' response was to promulgate in the Voting Rights Act a detailed but limited remedial scheme designed to guarantee meaningful enforcement of the Fifteenth Amendment in those areas of the Nation where abundant evidence of States' systematic denial of those rights was identified.

The contrast between this kind of evidence, and the evidence that Congress considered in the present case, is stark. Congressional enactment of the ADA represents its judgment that there should be a "comprehensive national mandate for the elimination of discrimination against individuals with disabilities." Congress is the final authority as to desirable public policy, but in order to authorize private individuals to recover money damages against the States, there must be a pattern of discrimination by the States which violates the Fourteenth Amendment, and the remedy imposed by Congress must be congruent and proportional to the targeted violation. Those requirements are not met here, and to uphold the Act's application to the States would allow Congress to rewrite the Fourteenth Amendment law laid down by this Court in *Cleburne*.[9] Section 5 does not so broadly enlarge congressional authority. The judgment of the Court of Appeals is therefore

Reversed.

JUSTICE BREYER, with whom JUSTICE STEVENS, JUSTICE SOUTER, and JUSTICE GINSBURG join, dissenting.

Section 5, grants Congress the "power to enforce, by appropriate legislation," the Fourteenth Amendment's equal protection guarantee. As the Court recognizes, state discrimination in employment against persons with disabilities might " 'run afoul of the Equal Protection Clause' " where there is no " 'rational relationship between the disparity of treatment and some legitimate governmental purpose.' " In my view, Congress reasonably could have concluded that the remedy before us constitutes an "appropriate" way to enforce this basic equal protection requirement. And that is all the Constitution requires.

I

The Court says that its primary problem with this statutory provision is one of legislative evidence. It says that "Congress assembled only * * * minimal evidence of unconstitutional state discrimination in employment." In fact, Congress compiled a vast legislative record documenting " 'massive, society-wide discrimination' " against persons with disabilities. In addition to the information presented at 13 congressional hearings and its own prior experience gathered over 40 years during which it contemplated and enacted considerable similar legislation Congress created a special task force to assess the need for comprehensive legislation. That task force held hearings in every State, attended by

---

[9] Our holding here that Congress did not validly abrogate the States' sovereign immunity from suit by private individuals for money damages under Title I does not mean that persons with disabilities have no federal recourse against discrimination. Title I of the ADA still prescribes standards applicable to the States. Those standards can be enforced by the United States in actions for money damages, as well as by private individuals in actions for injunctive relief under *Ex parte Young,* (1908). In addition, state laws protecting the rights of persons with disabilities in employment and other aspects of life provide independent avenues of redress.

more than 30,000 people, including thousands who had experienced discrimination first hand. The task force hearings, Congress' own hearings, and an analysis of "census data, national polls, and other studies" led Congress to conclude that "people with disabilities, as a group, occupy an inferior status in our society, and are severely disadvantaged socially, vocationally, economically, and educationally." As to employment, Congress found that "[t]wo-thirds of all disabled Americans between the age of 16 and 64 [were] not working at all," even though a large majority wanted to, and were able to, work productively. And Congress found that this discrimination flowed in significant part from "stereotypic assumptions" as well as "purposeful unequal treatment."

The powerful evidence of discriminatory treatment throughout society in general, including discrimination by private persons and local governments, implicates state governments as well, for state agencies form part of that same larger society. There is no particular reason to believe that they are immune from the "stereotypic assumptions" and pattern of "purposeful unequal treatment" that Congress found prevalent. The Court claims that it "make[s] no sense" to take into consideration constitutional violations committed by local governments. But the substantive obligation that the Equal Protection Clause creates applies to state and local governmental entities alike. Local governments often work closely with, and under the supervision of, state officials, and in general, state and local government employers are similarly situated. Nor is determining whether an apparently "local" entity is entitled to Eleventh Amendment immunity as simple as the majority suggests—it often requires a " 'detailed examination of the relevant provisions of [state] law.' "

In any event, there is no need to rest solely upon evidence of discrimination by local governments or general societal discrimination. There are roughly 300 examples of discrimination by state governments themselves in the legislative record. I fail to see how this evidence "fall[s] far short of even suggesting the pattern of unconstitutional discrimination on which § 5 legislation must be based."

The congressionally appointed task force collected numerous specific examples, provided by persons with disabilities themselves, of adverse, disparate treatment by state officials. They reveal, not what the Court describes as "half a dozen" instances of discrimination, but hundreds of instances of adverse treatment at the hands of state officials—instances in which a person with a disability found it impossible to obtain a state job, to retain state employment, to use the public transportation that was readily available to others in order to get to work, or to obtain a public education, which is often a prerequisite to obtaining employment. State-imposed barriers also frequently made it difficult or impossible for people to vote, to enter a public building, to access important government services, such as calling for emergency assistance, and to find a place to live due to a pattern of irrational zoning decisions similar to the discrimination that we held unconstitutional in *Cleburne.*

As the Court notes, those who presented instances of discrimination rarely provided additional, independent evidence sufficient to prove in court that, in each instance, the discrimination they suffered lacked justification from a judicial standpoint. Perhaps this explains the Court's view that there is "minimal evidence of unconstitutional state discrimination." But a legislature is not a court of law. And Congress, unlike courts, must, and does, routinely draw general conclusions—for example, of likely motive or of likely relationship to legitimate need—from anecdotal and opinion-based evidence of this kind, particularly when the evidence lacks strong refutation. In reviewing § 5 legislation, we have never required the sort of extensive investigation of each piece of evidence that the Court appears to contemplate. Nor has the Court traditionally required Congress to make findings as to state discrimination, or to break down the record evidence, category by category.

Regardless, Congress expressly found substantial unjustified discrimination against persons with disabilities. Moreover, it found that such discrimination typically reflects "stereotypic assumptions" or "purposeful unequal treatment." In making these findings, Congress followed our decision in *Cleburne,* which established that not only discrimination against persons with disabilities that rests upon " 'a bare * * * desire to harm a politically unpopular group,' " violates the Fourteenth Amendment, but also discrimination that rests solely upon "negative attitude[s]," "fea[r]," or "irrational prejudice." Adverse treatment that rests upon such motives is unjustified discrimination in *Cleburne's* terms.

The evidence in the legislative record bears out Congress' finding that the adverse treatment of persons with disabilities was often arbitrary or invidious in this sense, and thus unjustified. A complete listing of the hundreds of examples of discrimination by state and local governments that were submitted to the task force is set forth in Appendix C. Congress could have reasonably believed that these examples represented signs of a widespread problem of unconstitutional discrimination.

II

The Court's failure to find sufficient evidentiary support may well rest upon its decision to hold Congress to a strict, judicially created evidentiary standard, particularly in respect to lack of justification. Justice Kennedy's empirical conclusion—which rejects that of Congress—rests heavily upon his failure to find "extensive litigation and discussion of the constitutional violations," in "*the courts* of the United States." And the Court itself points out that, when economic or social legislation is challenged in court as irrational, hence unconstitutional, the "burden is upon the challenging party to negative any reasonably conceivable state of facts that could provide a rational basis for the classification." Or as Justice Brandeis, writing for the Court, put the matter many years ago,

" 'if any state of facts reasonably can be conceived that would sustain' " challenged legislation, then " 'there is a presumption of the existence of that state of facts, and one who assails the classification must carry the burden of showing * * * that the action is arbitrary.' " Imposing this special "burden" upon Congress, the Court fails to find in the legislative record sufficient indication that Congress has "negative[d]" the presumption that state action is rationally related to a legitimate objective.

The problem with the Court's approach is that neither the "burden of proof" that favors States nor any other rule of restraint applicable to *judges* applies to *Congress* when it exercises its § 5 power. "Limitations stemming from the nature of the judicial process * * * have no application to Congress." *Oregon v. Mitchell* (Brennan, White, and Marshall, JJ., concurring in part and dissenting in part). Rational-basis review— with its presumptions favoring constitutionality—is "a paradigm of *judicial* restraint." (emphasis added). And the Congress of the United States is not a lower court.

Indeed, the Court in *Cleburne* drew this very institutional distinction. We emphasized that "courts have been very reluctant, as they should be in our federal system and with our respect for the separation of powers, to closely scrutinize legislative choices." Our invocation of judicial deference and respect for Congress was based on the fact that "[§]5 of the [Fourteenth] Amendment empowers *Congress* to enforce [the equal protection] mandate." ([E]mphasis added). Indeed, we made clear that the absence of a contrary congressional finding was critical to our decision to apply mere rational-basis review to disability discrimination claims—a "congressional direction" to apply a more stringent standard would have been "controlling." In short, the Court's claim that "to uphold the Act's application to the States would allow Congress to rewrite the Fourteenth Amendment law laid down by this Court in *Cleburne,*" [is] repudiated by *Cleburne* itself.

There is simply no reason to require Congress, seeking to determine facts relevant to the exercise of its § 5 authority, to adopt rules or presumptions that reflect a court's institutional limitations. Unlike courts, Congress can readily gather facts from across the Nation, assess the magnitude of a problem, and more easily find an appropriate remedy. Unlike courts, Congress directly reflects public attitudes and beliefs, enabling Congress better to understand where, and to what extent, refusals to accommodate a disability amount to behavior that is callous or unreasonable to the point of lacking constitutional justification. Unlike judges, Members of Congress can directly obtain information from constituents who have firsthand experience with discrimination and related issues.

Moreover, unlike judges, Members of Congress are elected. When the Court has applied the majority's burden of proof rule, it has explained that we, *i.e.*, the courts, do not " 'sit as a superlegislature to judge the wisdom or desirability of legislative policy determinations.'" To apply a rule designed to restrict courts as if it restricted Congress' legislative power is to stand the underlying principle—a principle of judicial restraint—on its head. But without the use of this burden of proof rule or some other unusually stringent standard of review, it is difficult to see how the Court can find the legislative record here inadequate. Read with a reasonably favorable eye, the record indicates that state governments subjected those with disabilities to seriously adverse, disparate treatment. And Congress could have found, in a significant number of instances, that this treatment violated the substantive principles of justification—shorn of their judicial-restraint-related presumptions—that this Court recognized in *Cleburne*.

III

The Court argues in the alternative that the statute's damages remedy is not "congruent" with and "proportional" to the equal protection problem that Congress found. The Court suggests that the Act's "reasonable accommodation" requirement, and disparate-impact standard, "far excee[d] what is constitutionally required." But we have upheld disparate-impact standards in contexts where they were not "constitutionally required."

And what is wrong with a remedy that, in response to unreasonable employer behavior, requires an employer to make accommodations that are reasonable? Of course, what is "reasonable" in the statutory sense and what is "unreasonable" in the constitutional sense might differ. In other words, the requirement may exceed what is necessary to avoid a constitutional violation. But it is just that power—the power to require more than the minimum that § 5 grants to Congress, as this Court has repeatedly confirmed. As long ago as 1880, the Court wrote that § 5 "brought within the domain of congressional power" whatever "tends to enforce submission" to its "prohibitions" and "to secure to all persons * * * the equal protection of the laws." More recently, the Court added that § 5's "draftsmen sought to grant to Congress, by a specific provision applicable to the Fourteenth Amendment, the same broad powers expressed in the Necessary and Proper Clause, Art. I, § 8, cl. 18."

In keeping with these principles, the Court has said that "[i]t is not for us to review the congressional resolution of * * * the various conflicting considerations—the risk or pervasiveness of the discrimination in governmental services * * *, the adequacy or availability of alternative remedies, and the nature and significance of the state interests that would be affected." "It is enough that we be able to perceive a basis upon which the Congress might resolve the conflict as it did." Nothing in the words "reasonable accommodation" suggests that the requirement has no "tend[ency] to enforce" the Equal Protection Clause, that it is an irrational way to achieve the objective, that it would fall outside the scope of the Necessary and Proper Clause, or that it somehow otherwise exceeds the bounds of the "appropriate."

The Court's more recent cases have professed to follow the long-standing principle of deference to Congress. And even today, the Court purports to apply, not to depart from, these standards. But the Court's analysis and ultimate conclusion deprive its declarations of practical significance. The Court "sounds the word of promise to the ear but breaks it to the hope."

IV

The Court's harsh review of Congress' use of its § 5 power is reminiscent of the similar (now-discredited) limitation that it once imposed upon Congress' Commerce Clause power. The legislation before us, however, does not discriminate against anyone, nor does it pose any threat to basic liberty. And it is difficult to understand why the Court, which applies "minimum 'rational-basis' review" to statutes that *burden* persons with disabilities, subjects to far stricter scrutiny a statute that seeks to *help* those same individuals.

I recognize nonetheless that this statute imposes a burden upon States in that it removes their Eleventh Amendment protection from suit, thereby subjecting them to potential monetary liability. Rules for interpreting § 5 that would provide States with special protection, however, run counter to the very object of the Fourteenth Amendment. By its terms, that Amendment prohibits *States* from denying their citizens equal protection of the laws. U.S. Const., Amdt. 14, § 1. Hence "principles of federalism that might otherwise be an obstacle to congressional authority are necessarily overridden by the power to enforce the Civil War Amendments 'by appropriate legislation.' Those Amendments were specifically designed as an expansion of federal power and an intrusion on state sovereignty." And, ironically, the greater the obstacle the Eleventh Amendment poses to the creation by Congress of the kind of remedy at issue here—the decentralized remedy of private damages actions—the more Congress, seeking to cure important national problems, such as the problem of disability discrimination before us, will have to rely on more uniform remedies, such as federal standards and court injunctions, which are sometimes draconian and typically more intrusive. For these reasons, I doubt that today's decision serves any constitutionally based federalism interest.

The Court, through its evidentiary demands, its non-deferential review, and its failure to distinguish between judicial and legislative constitutional competencies, improperly invades a power that the Constitution assigns to Congress. Its decision saps § 5 of independent force, effectively "confin[ing] the legislative power * * * to the insignificant role of abrogating only those state laws that the judicial branch [is] prepared to adjudge unconstitutional." Whether the Commerce Clause does or does not enable Congress to enact this provision, in my view, § 5 gives Congress the necessary authority.

For the reasons stated, I respectfully dissent.

Notes and Questions

1. Observe at the outset that majority and dissent disagree about the factual record that Congress assembled. Footnote 7 characterizes congressional evidence of discrimination as a "small fraction" of the total record. Justice Breyer, on the other hand, refers to "hundreds of instances of adverse treatment at the hands of state officials." Perhaps majority and dissent approach the problem differently. The majority refuses to approve legislation unless Congress has identified a widespread pattern of state discrimination *in employment cases*. The dissent, on the other hand, appears to have the view that a showing of pervasive state discrimination *against the disabled* in many areas, including but not limited to employment, allows Congress to infer that there may be a pattern of discrimination with respect to employment cases specifically. Which approach is better as a policy matter? Which is more faithful to the Fourteenth Amendment?

2. In connection with Note 1, consider *City of Boerne v. Flores*, in which the Court announced the congruence-and-proportionality test. Does characterization become everything? If Congress's Fourteenth Amendment object is generally to deter or remedy government discrimination against disabled people, whether in the context of employment discrimination or access to public facilities or access to education, should that affect how the Court decides what evidence is relevant for congruence-and-proportionality purposes? Footnote 1 of the majority opinion separates Title I from Title II and declines to consider Title II questions because the parties did not focus on them. (The Court did reach the Title II issue in *Tennessee v. Lane*, 541 U.S. 509, 124 S.Ct. 1978, 158 L.Ed.2d 820 (2004), discussed in Note 7, *infra* at 693.) One might argue, however, that the parties' failure to brief and argue questions with respect to Title II is distinct from the evidence Congress had before it when it enacted the ADA, which is, after all, a single statute that seeks in different sections to affect different kinds of discriminatory conduct. When asking whether a statute satisfies the congruence-and-proportionality test, to what extent should the Court examine the evidence underlying the statute's subsections individually? To the extent that you think the Court's approach proper, consider whether Congress then is on notice to put diverse statutory goals into single sections of the law or, alternatively, how far the Court should go in breaking a statute down into its components. Instead of looking at employment discrimination, for example, the Court might have differentiated further between discrimination that runs against physical versus mental disabilities and then sought an extensive record with respect to each sub-category. Is there anything in the Fourteenth Amendment, particularly in the word "appropriate," that provides guidance on how searching the Court's scrutiny should be?

3. The Chief Justice rejects the respondents' arguments that the Court should consider evidence of sub-state government discrimination against disabled individuals, noting that the Eleventh Amendment does not protect local government units. Does that mean that a quantum of evidence that might satisfy the Court with respect to local government discrimination will

not satisfy it with respect to state discrimination? If that is so, the Eleventh Amendment seems to be modifying the Fourteenth Amendment by heightening the Court's "appropriateness" scrutiny. If earlier provisions of the Constitution can modify later ones in that way, then there seems to be no reason that Congress could not legislate under its Article I powers and curtail the states' Eleventh Amendment immunity, yet the Court (albeit by only a five-to-four margin) has rejected that possibility. *See Seminole Tribe v. Florida, infra* at 697. Should the Eleventh Amendment have anything to do with determining whether Fourteenth Amendment legislation is appropriate?

4. One of the effects of the Court's jurisprudence in this area is to interpret § 5 of the Fourteenth Amendment to provide protection to the states against what the majority clearly sees as congressional overreaching. The Court reads the word "appropriate" to be a limitation on Congress deliberately inserted to insulate the states from federal intrusion. Do you think that is what the 1868 Congress had in mind when it drafted what became the Fourteenth Amendment?

5. Justice Breyer argues that the majority is holding Congress to evidentiary standards that might be appropriate in a courtroom under a clear-and-convincing standard but are not properly applicable to the work of a legislature. He accuses the majority of abandoning the historical pattern of reviewing to see "whether Congress' likely conclusions were reasonable, not whether there was adequate evidentiary support in the record." Are the two as separable as Justice Breyer implies? How can one know whether a conclusion is reasonable without paying attention to the evidence upon which Congress reaches the conclusion?

6. To what extent should the Court's scrutiny of "appropriateness" under the Fourteenth Amendment mirror its jurisprudence on what is "necessary and proper" under Art. I, § 8, cl. 18? The Court has typically been extremely deferential to Congress with respect to the latter. If the standard of review should be different, what in the Constitution and the theory of separation of powers accounts for the difference?

Irrespective of where one's sympathies lie in this debate, it is now clear that Congress must assemble a far more targeted and state-specific legislative record if it wishes to authorize federal suits against the states by individuals. Should the Court read the Eleventh Amendment to require Congress to go beyond the sort of record that ordinarily suffices to support legislation? Note, by the way, the metamorphosis in the Court's approach to such legislation. In the 1980s, in cases like *Atascadero State Hospital v. Scanlon,* the Court's focus was on whether Congress was sufficiently specific that states were subject to suit. Congress learned that lesson, and the Court has now shifted from requiring that sort of specificity in an area of legislative competence to viewing such competence as subdivided for Eleventh Amendment purposes. There is no suggestion in the *Garrett* majority opinion that Congress overstepped itself in applying the Americans with Disabilities Act to county and local governmental units. The legislative record apparently satisfied the normal rational-basis review. With respect to the states, however, the Court appears to have shifted its analysis from whether Congress has competence based on the area being regulated to whether Congress has competence based on the parties to be regulated. Do you think those who wrote the Eleventh Amendment saw it as a limitation on the scope of substantive legislation? In *Fitzpatrick v. Bitzer*, had Congress assembled the sort of legislative record that the Court now demands?

7. *Nevada Department of Human Resources v. Hibbs*, 538 U.S. 721, 123 S. Ct. 1972, 155 L.Ed.2d 953 (2003), demonstrated that the Court's application of the *Garrett* rule to invalidate congressional attempts to subject the states to liability may not be as wide ranging as might have first appeared. The Family and Medical Leave Act (FMLA) of 1993 provided that employees could take up to twelve work weeks (480 hours) of unpaid leave for a variety of reasons, including to care for close family members suffering from the onset of a "serious health condition." Hibbs argued that Nevada had not given him the leave FMLA required. He commenced a federal action seeking damages, an injunction and declaratory relief. The district court granted Nevada's motion for summary judgment on Eleventh Amendment grounds. The Ninth Circuit reversed, and Nevada sought review in the Supreme Court.

Chief Justice Rehnquist wrote the Court's opinion for a six-member majority.[9] Noting that Congress could use its Fourteenth Amendment § 5 legislative power prophylactically rather than simply providing a remedy for direct violations of the Fourteenth Amendment (an assertion originally made in *Kimel* and repeated in *Garrett*), the Chief Justice turned to an examination of the record Congress had assembled to support FMLA. After an exhaustive canvass of the record, he concluded that "the States' record of unconstitutional participation in, and fostering of, gender-based discrimination in the administration of leave benefits is weighty enough to justify the enactment of prophylactic § 5 legislation." (Footnote omitted). The five Justices supporting the opinion went on to find Congress's remedy congruent and proportional, and hence effective to overcome the Eleventh Amendment.

Justice Scalia dissented, arguing that the congressionally created remedy could not survive an Eleventh Amendment challenge by a state that had not itself engaged in gender discrimination. "The constitutional violation that is a prerequisite to 'prophylactic' congressional action to 'enforce' the Fourteenth Amendment is a violation *by the State against which the enforcement action is taken*." He labeled the attempt to apply the remedy against a non-violating state "guilt by association." Justice Scalia argued that Congress cannot, in exercising its Fourteenth Amendment legislative power, treat the states as a collective entity. Implicitly, he said that Congress must find violations by every state in order to fashion a remedy avail-

---

[9] Justice Stevens, although concurring in the result, did not join the opinion. He took the position he had argued in his concurrence in *Pennsylvania v. Union Gas* and repeated in his *Seminole Tribe* dissent, viewing the Eleventh Amendment itself only as a prohibition of the exercise of diversity jurisdiction, not federal question jurisdiction. He acknowledged that the states additionally retained a common law immunity from suit, but again argued that Congress could displace that common law immunity (as it can other parts of the common law) in the proper exercise of its Article I, § 8, legislative powers. He saw no need, therefore, to engage in *Garrett* analysis at all.

able against every state. "Prophylaxis in the sense of extending the remedy beyond the violation is one thing; prophylaxis in the sense of extending the remedy beyond the violator is something else." He did not argue that Congress is powerless unless every state is a violator, but he did take the position that a proper § 5 statute may be unconstitutional as applied to a state with no record of gender discrimination in the workplace.

Justice Kennedy, joined by Justices Scalia and Thomas, wrote an extended dissent making two major points. First, he argued that FMLA is not an appropriate remedial statute within Congress's power under § 5 of the Fourteenth Amendment because it creates an entitlement, a new form of benefit program unrelated to Fourteenth Amendment concerns. He did not say that Congress could not create such an entitlement. In his view, Congress has ample power under the Commerce Clause (not § 5 of the Fourteenth Amendment) to do just what it did in FMLA. The entitlement would be a valid exercise of legislative power, according to Justice Kennedy, but it would not support damages actions against the states because of *Seminole Tribe*. With respect to the Fourteenth Amendment, however, he suggested that Congress was effectively and impermissibly expanding the substantive content of the Equal Protection Clause, in violation of the doctrine of *City of Boerne v. Flores*. "This requirement has special force in the context of the Eleventh Amendment, which protects a State's fiscal integrity from federal intrusion by vesting the States with immunity from private actions for damages pursuant to federal laws." There are two remarkable things about this statement. First, considering that Congress and the States passed the Eleventh Amendment to enable the states to dishonor their debts from the Revolution with impunity and that today it operates to shield states from the consequences of violating individuals' rights, it seems odd to refer to that as "fiscal integrity." Second, *Chisholm*, the impetus for passage of the Eleventh Amendment, involved a damages action under *state*, not federal, law. In addition, Justice Kennedy argued that Congress had insufficient evidence of state gender discrimination with respect to providing family leave. He accused the majority of relying on far too general evidence of gender discrimination by states.

It seems fair to say that the battle lines over *Garrett* invalidation are now relatively clear. The Justices will fight over the quantity of evidence and over its quality, specifically whether the evidence upon which Congress relies relates to the very same conduct that Congress attempts to address in a remedial statute. How much evidence of a widespread pattern of violations will suffice? For that matter, what is a pattern? Presumably if only one or two states are engaging unconstitutional behavior, that would not suffice. Suppose that Congress has evidence that thirty states are acting in a way that would justify legislation under § 5. May Congress then act? If it does, should the Court follow Justice Scalia's suggestion and only permit application of the statute to the thirty violators, or in the name of prophylaxis may Congress prohibit behavior that is not itself unconstitutional (as the Court has acknowledged Congress may do) and apply those prophylactic provisions to states not in violation of any constitutional provision?

With respect to an individual state, should the Court consider a statute unconstitutional as applied if a) Congress had no evidence that the state had ever acted unconstitutionally or b) if the plaintiff is unable to show that the state acted unconstitutionally either with respect to anyone or with respect to him?

Assuming that Congress has evidence of unconstitutional state behavior sufficient to support remedial legislation under § 5, does that legislation *become* unconstitutional as applied if a particular state ceases its unconstitutional behavior or on its face if the states as a whole no longer exhibit a pervasive pattern of constitutional violations?

Finally, *Tennessee v. Lane*, 541 U.S. 509, 124 S.Ct. 1978, 158 L.Ed.2d 820 (2004), also upheld congressional action, this time concerning Title II of the Americans with Disabilities Act. Whereas Title I (involved in *Garrett*) concerned employment discrimination against individuals and involved equal protection only, Title II addressed access to public services, programs and activities. Justice Stevens's opinion for a closely divided Court sketched out the underlying facts:

> Respondents, both of whom are paraplegics who use wheelchairs for mobility, claimed that they were denied access to, and the services of, the state court system by reason of their disabilities. Lane alleged that he was compelled to appear to answer a set of criminal charges on the second floor of a county courthouse that had no elevator. At his first appearance, Lane crawled up two flights of stairs to get to the courtroom. When Lane returned to the courthouse for a hearing, he refused to crawl again or to be carried by officers to the courtroom; he consequently was arrested and jailed for failure to appear. Jones, a certified court reporter, alleged that she has not been able to gain access to a number of county courthouses, and, as a result, has lost both work and an opportunity to participate in the judicial process.

The majority ruled that because the access provisions of Title II implicated fundamental rights applicable to the states through the Fourteenth Amendment (including the Sixth Amendment's Confrontation Clause and fair-cross-section jury entitlement and the First Amendment's contemplation of public access to criminal proceedings), "the sheer volume of evidence demonstrating the nature and extent of unconstitutional discrimination against persons with disabilities in the provision of public services," Congress's Title II response was congruent and proportional and therefore satisfied the Court's test. The four dissenting Justices declined to distinguish *Lane* from *Garrett* and attacked the majority's reliance on evidence much of which, in Chief Justice Rehnquist's words, "does not concern *unconstitutional* action by the *States*. The bulk of the Court's evidence concerns discrimination by nonstate [*sic*] governments, rather than the States themselves."

Thus, there emerges a two-tier analysis. Congress can enact remedial legislation for allowing damages for unconstitutional state conduct. Beyond that, Congress can enact what the Court has called prophylactic legislation that reaches conduct not itself unconstitutional but closely related to the unconstitutional conduct that Congress seeks to deter. Prophylactic legislation, however, must be "congruent and proportional" (under *Boerne* and

Garrett) to the scope and breadth of constitutional violations *by states.* If Congress has not identified a pattern of state constitutional violations, then it cannot enact legislation prohibiting acts that are not unconstitutional under the Fourteenth Amendment.

Title II of the ADA continues to have some Eleventh Amendment teeth. In *United States v. Georgia*, 546 U.S. 151, 126 S.Ct. 877, 163 L.Ed.2d 650 (2006), the Court left the way open for a state prisoner to take advantage of the ADA's provisions. The Court quoted the statute's Eleventh Amendment abrogation provision: "[a] State shall not be immune under the eleventh amendment to the Constitution of the United States from an action in [a] Federal or State court of competent jurisdiction for a violation of this chapter." Justice Scalia's opinion for the Court noted that "We have accepted this * * * statement as an unequivocal expression of Congress's intent to abrogate state sovereign immunity."

The Court remanded the case to allow the plaintiff to amend the complaint as the Eleventh Circuit had strongly suggested he do, but before letting go of the case, the Court remarked on congressional power under the Fourteenth Amendment and simultaneously signaled its interest in a future Eleventh Amendment issue.

> While the Members of this Court have disagreed regarding the scope of Congress's "prophylactic" enforcement powers under § 5 of the Fourteenth Amendment, no on doubts that § 5 grants Congress the power to "enforce * * * the provisions" of the Amendment by creating private remedies against the States for *actual* violations of those provisions. * * * This enforcement power includes the power to abrogate state sovereign immunity by authorizing private suits for damages against the States. Thus, insofar as Title II creates a private cause of action for damages against the States for conduct that *actually* violates the Fourteenth Amendment, Title II validly abrogates state sovereign immunity.

Discussing the remand, the Court pointedly suggested a line of inquiry to the lower courts:

> Once Goodman's complaint is amended, the lower courts will be best situated to determine in the first instance, on a claim-by-claim basis, (1) which aspects of the State's alleged conduct violated Title II[,] (2) to what extent such misconduct also violated the Fourteenth Amendment[,] and (3) insofar as such misconduct violated Title II but did not violate the Fourteenth Amendment, whether Congress's purported abrogation of sovereign immunity as to that class of conduct is nevertheless valid.

Do you think it will be possible for the Court simultaneously to reaffirm Congress's power to act prophylactically under the Fourteenth Amendment and to limit Congress's § 5 power to abrogate the states' Eleventh Amendment immunity? Certainly the Court's phrasing of the third issue suggests that it is entertaining that thought. Another way to look at this is to consider how closely linked § 5's grant of legislative power and § 1's recital of constitutional rights are. If § 5 permits Congress to enact prophylactic legislation, is there any textual basis for the Court to say that Congress may not, at the same time, expose the states to liability for violating that legislation? Conversely, if § 5 does not permit such abrogation, does that necessarily imply that prophylactic legislation is not "appropriate" within the meaning of § 5? Can legislation be "appropriate" for some purposes but not for others? How will the Court make the distinction?

After *Fitzpatrick*, questions arose about whether Congress could limit states' Eleventh Amendment immunity under legislation-authorizing provisions other than Section 5 of the Fourteenth Amendment. A badly fractured Court held in *Pennsylvania v. Union Gas Company*, 491 U.S. 1, 109 S.Ct. 2273, 105 L.Ed.2d 1 (1989), that the Commerce Clause also would support legislation explicitly authorizing suits in the federal courts against states. There was, however, no majority opinion on that issue. Four Justices, led by Justice Brennan, took the view that the Eleventh Amendment merely reflected common law sovereign immunity principles that antedated the Constitution and that Congress therefore could modify those principles. Justice Brennan argued that the states had ceded parts of their sovereignty to the federal government "in the plan of the Convention," and that Article I represented the end result of a zero-sum game, where each power granted to the federal government represented a diminution of state power. Moreover, he argued that the Eleventh Amendment constrained only judicial power, not federal legislative power.

> Because the Commerce Clause withholds power from the States at the same time as it confers it on Congress, and because the congressional power thus conferred would be incomplete without the authority to render States liable in damages, it must be that, to the extent that the States gave Congress the authority to regulate commerce, they also relinquished their immunity where Congress found it necessary, in exercising this authority, to render them liable.

In effect, Justice Brennan's group of four Justices found that that states had consented to be sued in the federal forum whenever Congress authorized such suits in exercise of its Article I powers.

Justice Stevens, though he joined Justice Brennan's opinion, also wrote a separate concurrence noting "the distinction between our two Eleventh Amendments." The first he saw as the party-based jurisdiction amendment that forbids plaintiffs from making states defendants in diversity cases. The second "is the defense of sovereign immunity that the Court has added to the text of the Amendment in cases like *Hans v. Louisiana*." That doctrine, he said, "is not a matter of Eleventh Amendment law at all, but rather is based on a prudential interest in federal-state comity and a concern for 'Our Federalism.'" Thus, he saw no reason why Congress, in the exercise of its Article I powers, could not overrule the Court's prudential doctrine of state sovereign immunity.

Justice Scalia and three other Justices dissented, arguing that the Eleventh Amendment postdated Article I and that Congress could not use Article I powers to modify the immunity it provided. Justice Scalia took direct issue with Justice Brennan's approach, particularly in its effect on *Hans*: "Better to overrule *Hans*, I should think, than to perpetuate the complexities that it creates but eliminate all its benefits to the federal system." Justice Scalia also predicted that *Union Gas* would not survive.

> The Court's holding today can be applauded only by those who think state sovereign immunity so constitutionally insignificant that *Hans* itself might as well be abandoned. It is only the Court's steadfast refusal to accept the fundamental structural importance of that doctrine, reflected in *Hans* and the other cases discussed above, that permits it to regard abrogation through Article I as an open question, and enables the plurality to fight the *Hans-Atascadero* battle all over again—but this time to win it—on the field of the Commerce Clause. It is a particularly unhappy victory, since instead of cleaning up the allegedly muddled Eleventh Amendment jurisprudence produced by *Hans,* the Court leaves that in place, and adds to the clutter the astounding principle that Article III limitations can be overcome by simply exercising Article I powers. It is an unstable victory as well, since that principle is too much at war with itself to endure. We shall either overrule *Hans* in form as well as in fact, or return to its genuine meaning.

Justice White, the ninth Justice, voted for the result urged by Justice Brennan, but refused to join the opinion, noting "I concur in Justice Brennan's conclusion, but not his reasoning," and later, "I agree with the conclusion reached by Justice Brennan * * * that Congress has the authority under Article I to abrogate the Eleventh Amendment immunity of the States, although I do not agree with much of his reasoning." Justice White never, however, articulated his own basis for reaching his conclusion. (Do you think he should have felt some obligation to do so, given that his was the crucial fifth vote on an important constitutional question?) Thus, although the result in *Union Gas* was clear, there was no majority rationale on the critical constitutional point.

Justice Scalia was correct; the situation was inherently unstable. Six years after *Union Gas*, with four of the Justices who participated in that case and voted for the majority result (Justices Blackmun, Brennan, Marshall and White) having retired, the Court granted certiorari in a case raising the issue of whether Congress could limit the states' forum immunity when legislating under the Indian Commerce Clause. In 1996, it issued its opinion.

SEMINOLE TRIBE v. FLORIDA
Supreme Court of the United States, 1996.
517 U.S. 44, 116 S.Ct. 1114, 134 L.Ed.2d 252.

CHIEF JUSTICE REHNQUIST delivered the opinion of the Court.

The Indian Gaming Regulatory Act provides that an Indian tribe may conduct certain gaming activities only in conformance with a valid compact between the tribe and the State in which the gaming activities are located. The Act, passed by Congress under the Indian Commerce Clause, imposes upon the States a duty to negotiate in good faith with an Indian tribe toward the formation of a compact and authorizes a tribe to bring suit in federal court against a State in order to compel performance of that duty. We hold that notwithstanding Congress' clear intent to abrogate the States' sovereign immunity, the Indian Commerce Clause does not grant Congress that power, and therefore § 2710(d)(7) cannot grant jurisdiction over a State that does not consent to be sued. We further hold that the doctrine of *Ex parte Young* may not be used to enforce § 2710(d)(3) against a state official.

I

Congress passed the Indian Gaming Regulatory Act in 1988 in order to provide a statutory basis for the operation and regulation of gaming by Indian tribes. The Act divides gaming on Indian lands into three classes-I, II, and III-and provides a different regulatory scheme for each class. * * * The Act provides that class III gaming is lawful only where it is: (1) authorized by an ordinance or resolution that (a) is adopted by the governing body of the Indian tribe, (b) satisfies certain statutorily prescribed requirements, and (c) is approved by the National Indian Gaming Commission; (2) located in a State that permits such gaming for any purpose by any person, organization, or entity; and (3) "conducted in conformance with a Tribal-State compact entered into by the Indian tribe and the State under paragraph (3) that is in effect."

The "paragraph (3)" to which the last prerequisite of § 2710(d)(1) refers is § 2710(d)(3), which describes the permissible scope of a Tribal-State compact and * * * describes the process by which a State and an Indian tribe begin negotiations toward a Tribal-State compact:

> (A) Any Indian tribe having jurisdiction over the Indian lands upon which a class III gaming activity is being conducted, or is to be conducted, shall request the State in which such lands are located to enter into negotiations for the purpose of entering into a Tribal-State compact governing the conduct of gaming activities. Upon receiving such a request, the State shall negotiate with the Indian tribe in good faith to enter into such a compact.

The State's obligation to "negotiate with the Indian tribe in good faith," is made judicially enforceable by §§ 2710(d)(7)(A)(i) and (B)(i):

> (A) The United States district courts shall have jurisdiction over—

(i) any cause of action initiated by an Indian tribe arising from the failure of a State to enter into negotiations with the Indian tribe for the purpose of entering into a Tribal-State compact under paragraph (3) or to conduct such negotiations in good faith * * * .

(B) (i)   An Indian tribe may initiate a cause of action described in subparagraph (A)(i) only after the close of the 180-day period beginning on the date on which the Indian tribe requested the State to enter into negotiations under paragraph (3)(A).

Sections 2710(d)(7)(B)(ii)-(vii) describe an elaborate remedial scheme designed to ensure the formation of a Tribal-State compact. A tribe that brings an action under § 2710(d)(7)(A)(i) must show that no Tribal-State compact has been entered and that the State failed to respond in good faith to the tribe's request to negotiate; at that point, the burden then shifts to the State to prove that it did in fact negotiate in good faith. If the district court concludes that the State has failed to negotiate in good faith toward the formation of a Tribal-State compact, then it "shall order the State and Indian tribe to conclude such a compact within a 60-day period." If no compact has been concluded 60 days after the court's order, then "the Indian tribe and the State shall each submit to a mediator appointed by the court a proposed compact that represents their last best offer for a compact." The mediator chooses from between the two proposed compacts the one "which best comports with the terms of [the Act] and any other applicable Federal law and with the findings and order of the court," ibid., and submits it to the State and the Indian tribe. If the State consents to the proposed compact within 60 days of its submission by the mediator, then the proposed compact is "treated as a Tribal-State compact entered into under paragraph (3)." If, however, the State does not consent within that 60-day period, then the Act provides that the mediator "shall notify the Secretary [of the Interior]" and that the Secretary "shall prescribe * * * procedures * * * under which class III gaming may be conducted on the Indian lands over which the Indian tribe has jurisdiction."

In September 1991, the Seminole Tribe of Indians, petitioner, sued the State of Florida and its Governor, Lawton Chiles, respondents. Invoking jurisdiction under 25 U.S.C. § 2710(d)(7)(A), as well as 28 U.S.C. §§ 1331 and 1362, petitioner alleged that respondents had "refused to enter into any negotiation for inclusion of [certain gaming activities] in a tribal-state compact," thereby violating the "requirement of good faith negotiation" contained in § 2710(d)(3). Respondents moved to dismiss the complaint, arguing that the suit violated the State's sovereign immunity from suit in federal court. The District Court denied respondents' motion, and the respondents took an interlocutory appeal of that decision.

The Court of Appeals for the Eleventh Circuit reversed the decision of the District Court, holding that the Eleventh Amendment barred petitioner's suit against respondents. The court agreed with the District Court that Congress in § 2710(d)(7) intended to abrogate the States' sovereign immunity, and also agreed that the Act had been passed pursuant to Congress' power under the Indian Commerce Clause. The court disagreed with the District Court, however, that the Indian Commerce Clause grants Congress the power to abrogate a State's Eleventh Amendment immunity from suit, and concluded therefore that it had no jurisdiction over petitioner's suit against Florida. The court further held that *Ex parte Young* does not permit an Indian tribe to force good faith negotiations by suing the Governor of a State. Finding that it lacked subject-matter jurisdiction, the Eleventh Circuit remanded to the District Court with directions to dismiss petitioner's suit.

[W]e granted certiorari in order to consider two questions: (1) Does the Eleventh Amendment prevent Congress from authorizing suits by Indian tribes against States for prospective injunctive relief to enforce legislation enacted pursuant to the Indian Commerce Clause?; and (2) Does the doctrine of *Ex parte Young* permit suits against a State's governor for prospective injunctive relief to enforce the good faith bargaining requirement of the Act? We answer the first question in the affirmative, the second in the negative, and we therefore affirm the Eleventh Circuit's dismissal of petitioner's suit.

* * *

Here, petitioner has sued the State of Florida and it is undisputed that Florida has not consented to the suit. Petitioner nevertheless contends that its suit is not barred by state sovereign immunity. First, it argues that Congress through the Act abrogated the States' sovereign immunity. Alternatively, petitioner maintains that its suit against the Governor may go forward under *Ex parte Young*. We consider each of those arguments in turn.

II

Petitioner argues that Congress through the Act abrogated the States' immunity from suit. In order to determine whether Congress has abrogated the States' sovereign immunity, we ask two questions: first, whether Congress has "unequivocally expresse[d] its intent to abrogate the immunity," and second, whether Congress has acted "pursuant to a valid exercise of power."

* * *

B

Having concluded that Congress clearly intended to abrogate the States' sovereign immunity through § 2710(d)(7), we turn now to consider whether the Act was passed "pursuant to a valid exercise of power." Before we address that question here, however, we think it necessary first to define the scope of our inquiry.

Petitioner suggests that one consideration weighing in favor of finding the power to abrogate here is that the Act authorizes only prospective injunctive relief rather than retroactive monetary relief. But we have often made it clear that the relief sought by a plaintiff suing a State is irrelevant to the question whether the suit is barred by the Eleventh Amendment. We think it follows *a fortiori* from this proposition that the type of relief sought is irrelevant to whether Congress has power to abrogate States' immunity. The Eleventh Amendment does not exist solely in order to "preven[t] federal court judgments that must be paid out of a State's treasury," it also serves to avoid "the indignity of subjecting a State to the coercive process of judicial tribunals at the instance of private parties."

Similarly, petitioner argues that the abrogation power is validly exercised here because the Act grants the States a power that they would not otherwise have, *viz.*, some measure of authority over gaming on Indian lands. It is true enough that the Act extends to the States a power withheld from them by the Constitution. Nevertheless, we do not see how that consideration is relevant to the question whether Congress may abrogate state sovereign immunity. The Eleventh Amendment immunity may not be lifted by Congress unilaterally deciding that it will be replaced by grant of some other authority.

Thus our inquiry into whether Congress has the power to abrogate unilaterally the States' immunity from suit is narrowly focused on one question: Was the Act in question passed pursuant to a constitutional provision granting Congress the power to abrogate? Previously, in conducting that inquiry, we have found authority to abrogate under only two provisions of the Constitution. In *Fitzpatrick*, we recognized that the Fourteenth Amendment, by expanding federal power at the expense of state autonomy, had fundamentally altered the balance of state and federal power struck by the Constitution. We noted that § 1 of the Fourteenth Amendment contained prohibitions expressly directed at the States and that § 5 of the Amendment expressly provided that "The Congress shall have the power to enforce, by appropriate legislation, the provisions of this article." We held that through the Fourteenth Amendment, federal power extended to intrude upon the province of the Eleventh Amendment and therefore that § 5 of the Fourteenth Amendment allowed Congress to abrogate the immunity from suit guaranteed by that Amendment.

In only one other case has congressional abrogation of the States' Eleventh Amendment immunity been upheld. In *Pennsylvania v. Union Gas Co.*, a plurality of the Court found that the Interstate Commerce Clause, Art. I, § 8, cl. 3, granted Congress the power to abrogate state sovereign immunity, stating that the power to regulate interstate commerce would be "incomplete without the authority to render States liable in damages." Justice White added the fifth vote necessary to the result in that case, but wrote separately in order to express that he "[did] not agree with much of [the plurality's] reasoning."

* * *

Both parties make their arguments from the plurality decision in *Union Gas*, and we, too, begin there. We think it clear that Justice Brennan's opinion finds Congress' power to abrogate under the Interstate Commerce Clause from the States' cession of their sovereignty when they gave Congress plenary power to regulate interstate commerce. Respondents' focus elsewhere is misplaced. While the plurality decision states that Congress' power under the Interstate Commerce Clause would be incomplete without the power to abrogate, that statement is made solely in order to emphasize the broad scope of Congress' authority over interstate commerce. Moreover, respondents' rationale would mean that where Congress has less authority, and the States have more, Congress' means for exercising that power must be greater. We read the plurality opinion to provide just the opposite. Indeed, it was in those circumstances where Congress exercised complete authority that Justice Brennan thought the power to abrogate most necessary.

Following the rationale of the *Union Gas* plurality, our inquiry is limited to determining whether the Indian Commerce Clause, like the Interstate Commerce Clause, is a grant of authority to the Federal Government at the expense of the States. The answer to that question is obvious. If anything, the Indian Commerce Clause accomplishes a greater transfer of power from the States to the Federal Government than does the Interstate Commerce Clause. This is clear enough from the fact that the States still exercise some authority over interstate trade but have been divested of virtually all authority over Indian commerce and Indian tribes. Under the rationale of *Union Gas*, if the States' partial cession of authority over a particular area includes cession of the immunity from suit, then their virtually total cession of authority over a different area must also include cession of the immunity from suit. We agree with the petitioner that the plurality opinion in *Union Gas* allows no principled distinction in favor of the States to be drawn between the Indian Commerce Clause and the Interstate Commerce Clause.

Respondents * * * contend that if we find the rationale of the *Union Gas* plurality to extend to the Indian Commerce Clause, then "*Union Gas* should be reconsidered and overruled." Generally, the principle of *stare decisis*, and the interests that it serves, *viz.*, "the evenhanded, predictable, and consistent development of legal principles, * * * reliance on judicial decisions, and * * * the actual and perceived integrity of the judicial process," counsel strongly against reconsideration of our precedent. Nevertheless, we always have treated *stare decisis* as a "principle of policy," and not as an "inexorable command." "[W]hen governing decisions are unworkable or are badly reasoned, 'this Court has never felt constrained to follow precedent.'" Our willingness to reconsider our earlier decisions has been "particularly true in constitutional cases, because in such cases 'correction through legislative action is practically impossible.' "

The Court in *Union Gas* reached a result without an expressed rationale agreed upon by a majority of the Court. We have already seen that Justice Brennan's opinion received the support of only three other Justices. Of the other five, Justice White, who provided the fifth vote for the result, wrote separately in order to indicate his disagreement with the majority's rationale, and four Justices joined together in a dissent that rejected the plurality's rationale. Since it was issued, *Union Gas* has created confusion among the lower courts that have sought to understand and apply the deeply fractured decision.

The plurality's rationale also deviated sharply from our established federalism jurisprudence and essentially eviscerated our decision in *Hans*. It was well established in 1989 when *Union Gas* was decided that the Eleventh Amendment stood for the constitutional principle that state sovereign immunity limited the federal courts' jurisdiction under Article III. The text of the Amendment itself is clear enough on this point * * *. And our decisions since *Hans* had been equally clear that the Eleventh Amendment reflects "the fundamental principle of sovereign immunity [that] limits the grant of judicial authority in Article III." As the dissent in *Union Gas* recognized, the plurality's conclusion-that Congress could under Article I expand the scope of the federal courts' jurisdiction under Article III—"contradict[ed] our unvarying approach to Article III as setting forth the exclusive catalog of permissible federal court jurisdiction."

Never before the decision in *Union Gas* had we suggested that the bounds of Article III could be expanded by Congress operating pursuant to any constitutional provision other than the Fourteenth Amendment. Indeed, it had seemed fundamental that Congress could not expand the jurisdiction of the federal courts beyond the bounds of Article III. The plurality's citation of prior decisions for support was based upon what we believe to be a misreading of precedent. The plurality claimed support for its decision from a case holding the unremarkable, and completely unrelated, proposition that the States may waive their sovereign immunity, and cited as precedent propositions that had been merely assumed for the sake of argument in earlier cases.

The plurality's extended reliance upon our decision in *Fitzpatrick v. Bitzer* that Congress could under the Fourteenth Amendment abrogate the States' sovereign immunity was also, we believe, misplaced. *Fitzpatrick* was based upon a rationale wholly inapplicable to the Interstate Commerce Clause, *viz.*, that the Fourteenth Amendment, adopted well after the adoption of the Eleventh Amendment and the ratification of the Constitution, operated to alter the pre-existing balance between state and federal power achieved by Article III and the Eleventh Amendment. As the dissent in *Union Gas* made clear, *Fitzpatrick* cannot be read to justify "limitation of the principle embodied in the Eleventh Amendment through appeal to antecedent provisions of the Constitution."

In the five [sic] years since it was decided, *Union Gas* has proven to be a solitary departure from established law. Reconsidering the decision in *Union Gas*, we conclude that none of the policies underlying *stare decisis* require our continuing adherence to its holding. The decision has, since its issuance, been of questionable precedential value, largely because a majority of the Court expressly disagreed with the rationale of the plurality. The case involved the interpretation of the Constitution and therefore may be altered only by constitutional amendment or revision by this Court. Finally, both the result in *Union Gas* and the plurality's rationale depart from our established understanding of the Eleventh Amendment and undermine the accepted function of Article III. We feel bound to conclude that *Union Gas* was wrongly decided and that it should be, and now is, overruled.

The dissent makes no effort to defend the decision in *Union Gas* but nonetheless would find congressional power to abrogate in this case. Contending that our decision is a novel extension of the Eleventh Amendment, the dissent chides us for "attend[ing]" to dicta. We adhere in this case, however, not to mere *obiter dicta*, but rather to the well-established rationale upon which the Court based the results of its earlier decisions. When an opinion issues for the Court, it is not only the result but also those portions of the opinion necessary to that result by which we are bound. For over a century, we have grounded our decisions in the oft-repeated understanding of state sovereign immunity as an essential part of the Eleventh Amendment. In *Principality of Monaco v. Mississippi*, the Court held that the Eleventh Amendment barred a suit brought against a State by a foreign state. Chief Justice Hughes wrote for a unanimous Court:

> * * * Manifestly, we cannot rest with a mere literal application of the words of § 2 of Article III, or assume that the letter of the Eleventh Amendment exhausts the restrictions upon suits against non-consenting States. Behind the words of the constitutional provisions are postulates which limit and control. There is the essential postulate that the controversies, as contemplated, shall be found to be of a justiciable character. There is also the postulate that States of the Union, still possessing attributes of sovereignty, shall be immune from suits, without their consent, save where there has been a "surrender of this immunity in the plan of the convention."

It is true that we have not had occasion previously to apply established Eleventh Amendment principles to the question whether Congress has the power to abrogate state sovereign immunity (save in *Union Gas*). But consideration of that question must proceed with fidelity to this century-old doctrine.

The dissent, to the contrary, disregards our case law in favor of a theory cobbled together from law review articles and its own version of historical events. The dissent cites not a single decision since *Hans* (other than *Union Gas*) that supports its view of state sovereign immunity, instead relying upon the now-discredited decision in *Chisholm v. Georgia*. Its undocumented and highly speculative extralegal explanation of the decision in *Hans* is a disservice to the Court's traditional method of adjudication.

The dissent mischaracterizes the *Hans* opinion. That decision found its roots not solely in the common law of England, but in the much more fundamental " 'jurisprudence in all civilized nations.' " The dissent's proposition that the common law of England, where adopted by the States, was open to change by the legislature, is wholly unexceptionable and largely beside the point: that common law provided the substantive rules of law rather than jurisdiction. It also is noteworthy that the principle of state sovereign immunity stands distinct from other principles of the common law in that only the former prompted a specific constitutional amendment.

Hans—with a much closer vantage point than the dissent—recognized that the decision in *Chisholm* was contrary to the well-understood meaning of the Constitution. The dissent's conclusion that the decision in *Chisholm* was "reasonable," certainly would have struck the Framers of the Eleventh Amendment as quite odd. The dissent's lengthy analysis of the text of the Eleventh Amendment is directed at a straw man—we long have recognized that blind reliance upon the text of the Eleventh Amendment is " 'to strain the Constitution and the law to a construction never imagined or dreamed of.' " The text dealt in terms only with the problem presented by the decision in *Chisholm*; in light of the fact that the federal courts did not have federal question jurisdiction at the time the Amendment was passed (and would not have it until 1875), it seems unlikely that much thought was given to the prospect of federal question jurisdiction over the States.

* * *

In overruling *Union Gas* today, we reconfirm that the background principle of state sovereign immunity embodied in the Eleventh Amendment is not so ephemeral as to dissipate when the subject of the suit is an area, like the regulation of Indian commerce, that is under the exclusive control of the Federal Government. Even when the Constitution vests in Congress complete law-making authority over a particular area, the Eleventh Amendment prevents congressional authorization of suits by private parties against unconsenting States. The Eleventh Amendment restricts the judicial power under Article III, and Article I cannot be used to circumvent the constitutional limitations placed upon federal jurisdiction. Petitioner's suit against the State of Florida must be dismissed for a lack of jurisdiction.

III

Petitioner argues that we may exercise jurisdiction over its suit to enforce § 2710(d)(3) against the Governor notwithstanding the jurisdictional bar of the Eleventh Amendment. Petitioner notes that since our decision in *Ex parte Young* we often have found federal jurisdiction over a suit against a state official when that suit seeks only prospective injunctive relief in order to "end a continuing violation of federal law." The situation presented here, however, is sufficiently different from that giving rise to the traditional *Ex parte Young* action so as to preclude the availability of that doctrine.

Here, the "continuing violation of federal law" alleged by petitioner is the Governor's failure to bring the State into compliance with § 2710(d)(3). But the duty to negotiate imposed upon the State by that statutory provision does not stand alone.   * * *   Congress passed § 2710(d)(3) in conjunction with the carefully crafted and intricate remedial scheme set forth in § 2710(d)(7).

Where Congress has created a remedial scheme for the enforcement of a particular federal right, we have, in suits against federal officers, refused to supplement that scheme with one created by the judiciary. *Schweiker v. Chilicky* ("When the design of a Government program suggests that Congress has provided what it considers adequate remedial mechanisms for constitutional violations that may occur in the course of its administration, we have not created additional * * * remedies"). Here, of course, the question is not whether a remedy should be created, but instead is whether the Eleventh Amendment bar should be lifted, as it was in *Ex parte Young*, in order to allow a suit against a state officer. Nevertheless, we think that the same general principle applies: therefore, where Congress has prescribed a detailed remedial scheme for the enforcement against a State of a statutorily created right, a court should hesitate before casting aside those limitations and permitting an action against a state officer based upon *Ex parte Young*.

Here, Congress intended § 2710(d)(3) to be enforced against the State in an action brought under § 2710(d)(7); the intricate procedures set forth in that provision show that Congress intended therein not only to define, but also significantly to limit, the duty imposed by § 2710(d)(3). For example, where the court finds that the State has failed to negotiate in good faith, the only remedy prescribed is an order directing the State and the Indian tribe to conclude a compact within 60 days. And if the parties disregard the court's order and fail to conclude a compact within the 60-day period, the only sanction is that each party then must submit a proposed compact to a mediator who selects the one which best embodies the terms of the Act. Finally, if the State fails to accept the compact selected by the mediator, the only sanction against it is that the mediator shall notify the Secretary of the Interior who then must prescribe regulations governing Class III gaming on the tribal lands at issue. By contrast with this quite modest set of sanctions, an action brought against a state official under *Ex parte Young* would expose that official to the full remedial powers of a federal court, including, presumably, contempt sanctions. If § 2710(d)(3) could be enforced in a suit under *Ex parte Young*, § 2710(d)(7) would have been superfluous; it is difficult to see why an Indian tribe would suffer through the intricate scheme of § 2710(d)(7) when more complete and more immediate relief would be available under *Ex parte Young*.[17]

Here, of course, we have found that Congress does not have authority under the Constitution to make the State suable in federal court under § 2710(d)(7). Nevertheless, the fact that Congress chose to impose upon the State a liability which is significantly more limited than would be the liability imposed upon the state officer under *Ex parte Young* strongly indicates that Congress had no wish to create the latter under § 2710(d)(3). Nor are we free to rewrite the statutory scheme in order to approximate what we think Congress might have wanted had it known that § 2710(d)(7) was beyond its authority. If that effort is to be made, it should be made by Congress, and not by the federal courts. We hold that *Ex parte Young* is inapplicable to petitioner's suit against the Governor of Florida, and therefore that suit is barred by the Eleventh Amendment and must be dismissed for a lack of jurisdiction.

IV

The Eleventh Amendment prohibits Congress from making the State of Florida capable of being sued in federal court. The narrow exception to the Eleventh Amendment provided by the *Ex parte Young* doctrine cannot be used to enforce § 2710(d)(3) because Congress enacted a remedial scheme, § 2710(d)(7), specifically designed for the enforcement of that right. The Eleventh Circuit's dismissal of petitioner's suit is hereby affirmed.

It is so ordered.

JUSTICE STEVENS, dissenting.

This case is about power—the power of the Congress of the United States to create a private federal cause of action against a State, or its Governor, for the violation of a federal right. In *Chisholm v. Georgia*, the entire Court—including Justice Iredell whose dissent provided the blueprint for the Eleventh Amendment—assumed that Congress had such power. In *Hans v. Louisiana*— a case the Court purports to follow today—the Court again assumed that Congress had such power. In *Fitzpatrick v. Bitzer* and *Pennsylvania v. Union Gas Co.* the Court

---

[17] Contrary to the claims of the dissent, we do not hold that Congress cannot authorize federal jurisdiction under *Ex parte Young* over a cause of action with a limited remedial scheme. We find only that Congress did not intend that result in the Indian Gaming Regulatory Act. * * *

squarely held that Congress has such power. In a series of cases beginning with *Atascadero State Hospital v. Scanlon*, the Court formulated a special "clear statement rule" to determine whether specific Acts of Congress contained an effective exercise of that power. Nevertheless, in a sharp break with the past, today the Court holds that with the narrow and illogical exception of statutes enacted pursuant to the Enforcement Clause of the Fourteenth Amendment, Congress has no such power.

The importance of the majority's decision to overrule the Court's holding in *Pennsylvania v. Union Gas Co.* cannot be overstated. The majority's opinion * * * prevents Congress from providing a federal forum for a broad range of actions against States, from those sounding in copyright and patent law, to those concerning bankruptcy, environmental law, and the regulation of our vast national economy.

There may be room for debate over whether, in light of the Eleventh Amendment, Congress has the power to ensure that such a cause of action may be enforced in federal court by a citizen of another State or a foreign citizen. There can be no serious debate, however, over whether Congress has the power to ensure that such a cause of action may be brought by a citizen of the State being sued. Congress' authority in that regard is clear.

As Justice Souter has convincingly demonstrated, the Court's contrary conclusion is profoundly misguided. Despite the thoroughness of his analysis, supported by sound reason, history, precedent, and strikingly uniform scholarly commentary, the shocking character of the majority's affront to a coequal branch of our Government merits additional comment.

I

For the purpose of deciding this case, I can readily assume that Justice Iredell's dissent in *Chisholm* and the Court's opinion in *Hans* correctly stated the law that should govern our decision today. As I shall explain, both of those opinions relied on an interpretation of an Act of Congress rather than a want of congressional power to authorize a suit against the State.

In concluding that the federal courts could not entertain Chisholm's action against the State of Georgia, Justice Iredell relied on the text of the Judiciary Act of 1789, not the State's assertion that Article III did not extend the judicial power to suits against unconsenting States. Justice Iredell argued that, under Article III, federal courts possessed only such jurisdiction as Congress had provided, and that the Judiciary Act expressly limited federal-court jurisdiction to that which could be exercised in accordance with " 'the principles and usages of law.' " He reasoned that the inclusion of this phrase constituted a command to the federal courts to construe their jurisdiction in light of the prevailing common law, a background legal regime which he believed incorporated the doctrine of sovereign immunity.

Because Justice Iredell believed that the expansive text of Article III did not prevent Congress from imposing this common-law limitation on federal-court jurisdiction, he concluded that judges had no authority to entertain a suit against an unconsenting State. At the same time, although he acknowledged that the Constitution might allow Congress to extend federal-court jurisdiction to such an action, he concluded that the terms of the Judiciary Act of 1789 plainly had not done so. * * *

For Justice Iredell then, it was enough to assume that Article III permitted Congress to impose sovereign immunity as a jurisdictional limitation; he did not proceed to resolve the further question whether the Constitution went so far as to prevent Congress from withdrawing a State's immunity. Thus, it would be ironic to construe the *Chisholm* dissent as precedent for the conclusion that Article III limits Congress' power to determine the scope of a State's sovereign immunity in federal court.

* * * There is a special irony in the fact that the error committed by the *Chisholm* majority was its decision that this Court, rather than Congress, should define the scope of the sovereign immunity defense. That, of course, is precisely the same error the Court commits today.

* * *

Justice Brennan has persuasively explained that the Eleventh Amendment's jurisdictional restriction is best understood to apply only to suits premised on diversity jurisdiction, and Justice Scalia has agreed that the plain text of the Amendment cannot be read to apply to federal-question cases. Whatever the precise dimensions of the Amendment, its express terms plainly do not apply to all suits brought against unconsenting States. The question thus becomes whether the relatively modest jurisdictional bar that the Eleventh Amendment imposes should be understood to reveal that a more general jurisdictional bar implicitly inheres in Article III.

The language of Article III certainly gives no indication that such an implicit bar exists. That provision's text specifically provides for federal-court jurisdiction over all cases arising under federal law. Moreover, as I have explained, Justice Iredell's dissent argued that it was the Judiciary Act of 1789, not Article III, that prevented the federal courts from entertaining Chisholm's diversity action against Georgia. Therefore, Justice Iredell's analysis at least suggests that it was by no means a fixed view at the time of the founding that Article III prevented Congress from rendering States suable in federal court by their own citizens. In sum, little more than speculation justifies the conclusion that the Eleventh Amendment's express but partial limitation on the scope of Article III reveals that an implicit but more general one was already in place.

II

The majority appears to acknowledge that one cannot deduce from either the text of Article III or the plain terms of the Eleventh Amendment that the judicial power does not extend to a congressionally created cause of action against a State brought by one of that State's citizens. Nevertheless, the majority asserts that precedent compels that same conclusion. I disagree. * * * The majority suggests that by dismissing the suit, *Hans* effectively held that federal courts have no power to hear federal question suits brought by same-state plaintiffs.

Hans does not hold, however, that the Eleventh Amendment, or any other constitutional provision, precludes federal courts from entertaining actions brought by citizens against their own States in the face of contrary congressional direction. * * * *Hans* instead reflects, at the most, this Court's conclusion that, as a matter of federal common law, federal courts should decline to entertain suits against unconsenting States. Because *Hans* did not announce a constitutionally mandated jurisdictional bar, one need not overrule *Hans*, or even question its reasoning, in order to conclude that Congress may direct the federal courts to reject sovereign immunity in those suits not mentioned by the Eleventh Amendment. Instead, one need only follow it.

* * *

* * * *Hans* itself looked to see whether Congress had displaced the presumption that sovereign immunity obtains. Although the opinion did go to great lengths to establish the quite uncontroversial historical proposition that unconsenting States generally were not subject to suit, that entire discussion preceded the opinion's statutory analysis. Thus, the opinion's thorough historical investigation served only to establish a presumption against jurisdiction that Congress must overcome, not an inviolable jurisdictional restriction that inheres in the Constitution itself.

Indeed, the very fact that the Court characterized the doctrine of sovereign immunity as a "presumption" confirms its assumption that it could be displaced. The *Hans* Court's inquiry into congressional intent would have been wholly inappropriate if it had believed that the doctrine of sovereign immunity was a constitutionally inviolable jurisdictional limitation. Thus, *Hans* provides no basis for the majority's conclusion that Congress is powerless to make States suable in cases not mentioned by the text of the Eleventh Amendment. Instead, *Hans* provides affirmative support for the view that Congress may create federal-court jurisdiction over private causes of action against unconsenting States brought by their own citizens.

* * *

No one has ever suggested that Congress would be powerless to displace the other common-law immunity doctrines that this Court has recognized as appropriate defenses to certain federal claims such as the judicially fashioned *Bivens* remedy. Similarly, our cases recognizing qualified officer immunity in § 1983 actions rest on the conclusion that, in passing that statute, Congress did not intend to displace the common-law immunity that officers would have retained under suits premised solely on the general jurisdictional statute. For that reason, the federal common law of officer immunity that Congress meant to incorporate, not a contrary state immunity, applies in § 1983 cases. There is no reason why Congress' undoubted power to displace those common-law immunities should be either greater or lesser than its power to displace the common-law sovereign immunity defense.

Some of our precedents do state that the sovereign immunity doctrine rests on fundamental constitutional "postulates" and partakes of jurisdictional aspects rooted in Article III. Most notably, that reasoning underlies this Court's holding in *Principality of Monaco v. Mississippi.*

Monaco is a most inapt precedent for the majority's holding today. That case barred a foreign sovereign from suing a State in an equitable state law action to recover payments due on State bonds. It did not, however, involve a claim based on federal law. Instead, the case concerned a purely state law question to which the State had interposed a federal defense. Thus, *Monaco* reveals little about the power of Congress to create a private federal cause of action to remedy a State's violation of federal law.

* * *

Finally, the particular nature of the federal question involved in *Hans* renders the majority's reliance upon its rule even less defensible. *Hans* deduced its rebuttable presumption in favor of sovereign immunity largely on the basis of its extensive analysis of cases holding that the sovereign could not be forced to make good on its debts via a private suit. Because *Hans* * * * involved a suit that attempted to make a State honor its debt, its holding need not be read to stand even for the relatively limited proposition that there is a presumption in favor of sovereign immunity in all federal-question cases.

* * *

III

In reaching my conclusion that the Constitution does not prevent Congress from making the State of Florida suable in federal court for violating one of its statutes, I emphasize that I agree with the majority that in all cases to which the judicial power does not extend—either because they are not within any category defined in Article III or because they are within the category withdrawn from Article III by the Eleventh Amendment—Congress lacks the power to confer jurisdiction on the federal courts. * * *

It was, therefore, misleading for the Court in *Fitzpatrick v. Bitzer* to imply that § 5 of the Fourteenth Amendment authorized Congress to confer jurisdiction over cases that had been withdrawn from Article III by the Eleventh Amendment. Because that action had been brought by Connecticut citizens against officials of the State of Connecticut, jurisdiction was not precluded by the Eleventh Amendment. * * *

* * *

The fundamental error that continues to lead the Court astray is its failure to acknowledge that its modern embodiment of the ancient doctrine of sovereign immunity * * * rests rather on concerns of federalism and comity that merit respect but are nevertheless, in cases such as the one before us, subordinate to the plenary power of Congress.

IV

* * *

While I am persuaded that there is no justification for permanently enshrining the judge-made law of sovereign immunity, I recognize that federalism concerns—and even the interest in protecting the solvency of the States that was at work in *Chisholm* and *Hans*—may well justify a grant of immunity from federal litigation in certain classes of cases. Such a grant, however, should be the product of a reasoned decision by the policymaking branch of our Government. For this Court to conclude that time-worn shibboleths iterated and reiterated by judges should take precedence over the deliberations of the Congress of the United States is simply irresponsible.

* * *

For these reasons, as well as those set forth in Justice Souter's opinion, I respectfully dissent.

JUSTICE SOUTER, with whom JUSTICE GINSBURG and JUSTICE Breyer join, dissenting.

In holding the State of Florida immune to suit under the Indian Gaming Regulatory Act, the Court today holds for the first time since the founding of the Republic that Congress has no authority to subject a State to the jurisdiction of a federal court at the behest of an individual asserting a federal right. Although the Court invokes the Eleventh Amendment as authority for this proposition, the only sense in which that amendment might be claimed as pertinent here was tolerantly phrased by Justice Stevens in his concurring opinion in *Pennsylvania v. Union Gas*. There, he explained how it has come about that we have two Eleventh Amendments, the one ratified in 1795, the other (so-called) invented by the Court nearly a century later in *Hans*. Justice Stevens saw in that second Eleventh Amendment no bar to the exercise of congressional authority under the Commerce Clause in providing for suits on a federal question by individuals against a State, and I can only say that after my own canvass of the matter I believe he was entirely correct in that view, for reasons given below. His position, of course, was also the holding in *Union Gas*, which the Court now overrules and repudiates.

The fault I find with the majority today is not in its decision to reexamine *Union Gas*, for the Court in that case produced no majority for a single rationale supporting congressional authority. Instead, I part company from the Court because I am convinced that its decision is fundamentally mistaken, and for that reason I respectfully dissent.

I

It is useful to separate three questions: (1) whether the States enjoyed sovereign immunity if sued in their own courts in the period prior to ratification of the National Constitution; (2) if so, whether after ratification the States were entitled to claim some such immunity when sued in a federal court exercising jurisdiction either because the suit was between a State and a non-state litigant who was not its citizen, or because the issue in the case raised a federal question; and (3) whether any state sovereign immunity recognized in federal court may be abrogated by Congress.

The answer to the first question is not clear, although some of the Framers assumed that States did enjoy immunity in their own courts. The second question was not debated at the time of ratification, except as to citizen-state diversity jurisdiction; there was no unanimity, but in due course the Court in *Chisholm v. Georgia* answered that a state defendant enjoyed no such immunity. As to federal question jurisdiction, state sovereign immunity seems not to have been debated prior to ratification, the silence probably showing a general understanding at the time that the States would have no immunity in such cases.

The adoption of the Eleventh Amendment soon changed the result in *Chisholm*, not by mentioning sovereign immunity, but by eliminating citizen-state diversity jurisdiction over cases with state defendants. I will explain why the Eleventh Amendment did not affect federal question jurisdiction, a notion that needs to be understood for the light it casts on the soundness of *Hans*'s holding that States did enjoy sovereign immunity in federal question suits. The *Hans* Court erroneously assumed that a State could plead sovereign immunity against a noncitizen suing under federal question jurisdiction, and for that reason held that a State must enjoy the same protection in a suit by one of its citizens. The error of *Hans*'s reasoning is underscored by its clear inconsistency with the Founders' hostility to the implicit reception of common-law doctrine as federal law, and with the Founders' conception of sovereign power as divided between the States and the National Government for the sake of very practical objectives.

The Court's answer today to the third question is likewise at odds with the Founders' view that common law, when it was received into the new American legal systems, was always subject to legislative amendment. In ignoring the reasons for this pervasive understanding at the time of the ratification, and in holding that a nontextual common-law rule limits a clear grant of congressional power under Article I, the Court follows a course that has brought it to grief before in our history, and promises to do so again.

Beyond this third question that elicits today's holding, there is one further issue. To reach the Court's result, it must not only hold the *Hans* doctrine to be outside the reach of Congress, but must also displace the doctrine of *Ex parte Young* that an officer of the government may be ordered prospectively to follow federal law, in cases in which the government may not itself be sued directly. None of its reasons for displacing *Young*'s jurisdictional doctrine withstand scrutiny.

A

The doctrine of sovereign immunity comprises two distinct rules, which are not always separately recognized. The one rule holds that the King or the Crown, as the font of law, is not bound by the law's provisions; the other provides that the King or Crown, as the font of justice, is not subject to suit in its own courts. The one rule limits the reach of substantive law; the other, the jurisdiction of the courts. We are concerned here only with the latter rule, which took its common-law form in the high middle ages. * * *

* * *

Whatever the scope of sovereign immunity might have been in the Colonies * * * or during the period of Confederation, the proposal to establish a National Government under the Constitution drafted in 1787 presented a prospect unknown to the common law prior to the American experience: the States would become parts of a system in which sovereignty over even domestic matters would be divided or parcelled [*sic*] out between the States and the Nation, the latter to be invested with its own judicial power and the right to prevail against the States whenever their respective substantive laws might be in conflict. With this prospect in mind, the 1787 Constitution might have addressed state sovereign immunity by eliminating whatever sovereign immunity the States previously had, as to any matter subject to federal law or jurisdiction; by recognizing an analogue to the old immunity in the new context of federal jurisdiction, but subject to abrogation as to any matter within that jurisdiction; or by enshrining a doctrine of inviolable state sovereign immunity in the text, thereby giving it constitutional protection in the new federal jurisdiction.

The 1787 draft in fact said nothing on the subject, and it was this very silence that occasioned some, though apparently not widespread, dispute among the Framers and others over whether ratification of the Constitution would preclude a State sued in federal court from asserting sovereign immunity as it could have done on any matter of nonfederal law litigated in its own courts. As it has come down to us, the discussion gave no attention to congressional power under the proposed Article I but focused entirely on the limits of the judicial power provided in Article III. And although the jurisdictional bases together constituting the judicial power of the national courts under section 2 of Article III included questions arising under federal law and cases between States and individuals who are not citizens, it was only upon the latter citizen-state diversity provisions that preratification questions about state immunity from suit or liability centered.

[F]or now it is enough to say that there was no consensus on the issue. There was, on the contrary, a clear disagreement, which was left to fester during the ratification period, to be resolved only thereafter. One other point, however, was also clear: the debate addressed only the question whether ratification of the Constitution would, in diversity cases and without more, abrogate the state sovereign immunity or allow it to have some application. We have no record that anyone argued for the third option mentioned above, that the Constitution would affirmatively guarantee state sovereign immunity against any congressional action to the contrary. Nor would there have been any apparent justification for any such argument, since no clause in the proposed (and ratified) Constitution even so much as suggested such a position. It may have been reasonable to contend (as we will see that Madison, Marshall, and Hamilton did) that Article III would not alter States' pre-existing common-law immunity despite its unqualified grant of jurisdiction over diversity suits against States. But then, as now, there was no textual support for contending that Article III or any other provision would "constitutionalize" state sovereign immunity, and no one uttered any such contention.

* * *

C

The Eleventh Amendment, of course, repudiated *Chisholm* and clearly divested federal courts of some jurisdiction as to cases against state parties * * *. There are two plausible readings of this provision's text. Under the first, it simply repeals the Citizen-State Diversity Clauses of Article III for all cases in which the State appears as a defendant. Under the second, it strips the federal courts of jurisdiction in any case in which a state defendant is sued by a citizen not its own, even if jurisdiction might otherwise rest on the existence of a federal question in the suit. Neither reading of the Amendment, of course, furnishes authority for the Court's view in today's case, but we need to choose between the competing readings for the light that will be shed on the *Hans* doctrine and the legitimacy of inflating that doctrine to the point of constitutional immutability as the Court has chosen to do.

The history and structure of the Eleventh Amendment convincingly show that it reaches only to suits subject to federal jurisdiction exclusively under the Citizen-State Diversity Clauses. In precisely tracking the language in Article III providing for citizen-state diversity jurisdiction, the text of the Amendment does, after all, suggest to common sense that only the Diversity Clauses are being addressed. If the Framers had meant the Amendment to bar federal question suits as well, they could not only have made their intentions clearer very easily, but could simply have adopted the first post-*Chisholm* proposal, introduced in the House of Representatives by Theodore Sedgwick of Massachusetts on instructions from the Legislature of that Commonwealth. Its provisions would have had exactly that expansive effect:

> [N]o state shall be liable to be made a party defendant, in any of the judicial courts, established, or which shall be established under the authority of the United States, at the suit of any person or persons, whether a citizen or citizens, or a foreigner or foreigners, or of any body politic or corporate, whether within or without the United States.

With its references to suits by citizens as well as non-citizens, the Sedgwick amendment would necessarily have been applied beyond the Diversity Clauses, and for a reason that would have been wholly obvious to the people of the time. Sedgwick sought such a broad amendment because many of the States, including his own, owed debts subject to collection under the Treaty of Paris. Suits to collect such debts would "arise under" that Treaty and thus be subject to federal question jurisdiction under Article III. * * *

Congress took no action on Sedgwick's proposal, however, and the Amendment as ultimately adopted two years later could hardly have been meant to limit federal question jurisdiction, or it would never have left the states open to federal question suits by their own citizens. To be sure, the majority of state creditors were not citizens, but nothing in the Treaty would have prevented foreign creditors from selling their debt instruments (thereby assigning their claims) to citizens of the debtor State. If the Framers of the Eleventh Amendment had meant it to immunize States from federal question suits like those that might be brought to enforce the Treaty of Paris, they would surely have drafted the Amendment differently.

* * *

In sum, reading the Eleventh Amendment solely as a limit on citizen-state diversity jurisdiction has the virtue of coherence with this Court's practice, with the views of John Marshall, with the history of the Amendment's drafting, and with its allusive language. Today's majority does not appear to disagree, at least insofar as the constitutional text is concerned; the Court concedes, after all, that "the text of the Amendment would appear to restrict only the Article III diversity jurisdiction of the federal courts."

Thus, regardless of which of the two plausible readings one adopts, the further point to note here is that there is no possible argument that the Eleventh Amendment, by its terms, deprives federal courts of jurisdiction over all citizen lawsuits against the States. Not even the Court advances that proposition, and there would be no textual basis for doing so.[12] Because the plaintiffs in today's case are citizens of the State that they are suing, the Eleventh Amendment simply does not apply to them. We must therefore look elsewhere for the source of that immunity by which the Court says their suit is barred from a federal court.[13]

II

The obvious place to look elsewhere, of course, is *Hans v. Louisiana*, and *Hans* was indeed a leap in the direction of today's holding, even though it does not take the Court all the way. The parties in *Hans* raised, and the Court in that case answered, only what I have called the second question, that is, whether the Constitution, without more, permits a State to plead sovereign immunity to bar the exercise of federal question jurisdiction. Although the Court invoked a principle of sovereign immunity to cure what it took to be the Eleventh Amendment's anomaly of barring only those state suits brought by noncitizen plain-

---

[12] The Court does suggest that the drafters of the Eleventh Amendment may not have had federal question jurisdiction in mind, in the apparent belief that this somehow supports its reading. The possibility, however, that those who drafted the Eleventh Amendment intended to deal "only with the problem presented by the decision in *Chisholm*" would demonstrate, if any demonstration beyond the clear language of the Eleventh Amendment were necessary, that the Eleventh Amendment was not intended to address the broader issue of federal question suits brought by citizens. Moreover, the Court's point is built on a faulty foundation. The Court is simply incorrect in asserting that "the federal courts did not have federal question jurisdiction at the time the Amendment was passed." Article III, of course, provided for such jurisdiction, and early Congresses exercised their authority pursuant to Article III to confer jurisdiction on the federal courts to resolve various matters of federal law. In fact, only six years after the passage of the Eleventh Amendment, Congress enacted a statute providing for general federal question jurisdiction. It is, of course, true that this statute proved short-lived (it was repealed by the Act of Mar. 8, 1802, 2 Stat. 132), and that Congress did not pass another statute conferring general federal jurisdiction until 1875, but the drafters of the Eleventh Amendment obviously could not have predicted such things. The real significance of the 1801 act is that it demonstrates the awareness among the Members of the early Congresses of the potential scope of Article III. This, in combination with the pre-Eleventh Amendment statutes that conferred federal question jurisdiction on the federal courts, cast considerable doubt on the Court's suggestion that the issue of federal question jurisdiction never occurred to the drafters of the Eleventh Amendment; on the contrary, just because these early statutes underscore the early Congresses' recognition of the availability of federal question jurisdiction, the silence of the Eleventh Amendment is all the more deafening.

[13] The majority chides me that the "lengthy analysis of the text of the Eleventh Amendment is directed at a straw man." But plain text is the Man of Steel in a confrontation with "background principle[s]" and " 'postulates which limit and control.' " An argument rooted in the text of a constitutional provision may not be guaranteed of carrying the day, but insubstantiality is not its failing. This is particularly true in construing the jurisdictional provisions of Art. III, which speak with a clarity not to be found in some of the more open-textured provisions of the Constitution. That the Court thinks otherwise is an indication of just how far it has strayed beyond the boundaries of traditional constitutional analysis.

tiffs, the *Hans* Court had no occasion to consider whether Congress could abrogate that background immunity by statute. Indeed (except in the special circumstance of Congress's power to enforce the Civil War Amendments), this question never came before our Court until *Union Gas*, and any intimations of an answer in prior cases were mere dicta. In *Union Gas* the Court held that the immunity recognized in *Hans* had no constitutional status and was subject to congressional abrogation. Today the Court overrules *Union Gas* and holds just the opposite. In deciding how to choose between these two positions, the place to begin is with *Hans*'s holding that a principle of sovereign immunity derived from the common law insulates a state from federal question jurisdiction at the suit of its own citizen. A critical examination of that case will show that it was wrongly decided, as virtually every recent commentator has concluded. It follows that the Court's further step today of constitutionalizing *Hans*'s rule against abrogation by Congress compounds and immensely magnifies the century-old mistake of *Hans* itself and takes its place with other historic examples of textually untethered elevations of judicially derived rules to the status of inviolable constitutional law.

A

* * *

Justice Bradley's opinion did not purport to hold that the terms either of Article III or of the Eleventh Amendment barred the suit, but that the ancient doctrine of sovereign immunity that had inspired adoption of the Eleventh Amendment applied to cases beyond the Amendment's scope and otherwise within the federal question jurisdiction. Indeed, Bradley explicitly admitted that "[i]t is true, the amendment does so read [as to permit Hans's suit], and if there were no other reason or ground for abating his suit, it might be maintainable." The Court elected, nonetheless, to recognize a broader immunity doctrine, despite the want of any textual manifestation, because of what the Court described as the anomaly that would have resulted otherwise: the Eleventh Amendment (according to the Court) would have barred a federal question suit by a noncitizen, but the State would have been subject to federal jurisdiction at its own citizen's behest. The State was accordingly held to be free to resist suit without its consent, which it might grant or withhold as it pleased.

Hans thus addressed the issue implicated (though not directly raised) in the preratification debate about the Citizen-State Diversity Clauses and implicitly settled by *Chisholm*: whether state sovereign immunity was cognizable by federal courts on the exercise of federal question jurisdiction. According to *Hans*, and contrary to *Chisholm*, it was. But that is all that *Hans* held. Because no federal legislation purporting to pierce state immunity was at issue, it cannot fairly be said that *Hans* held state sovereign immunity to have attained some constitutional status immunizing it from abrogation.

* * *

Although there was thus no anomaly to be cured by *Hans*, the case certainly created its own anomaly in leaving federal courts entirely without jurisdiction to enforce paramount federal law at the behest of a citizen against a State that broke it. It destroyed the congruence of the judicial power under Article III with the substantive guarantees of the Constitution, and with the provisions of statutes passed by Congress in the exercise of its power under Article I: when a State injured an individual in violation of federal law no federal forum could provide direct relief. Absent an alternative process to vindicate federal law John Marshall saw just what the consequences of this anomaly would be in the early Republic, and he took that consequence as good evidence that the Framers could never have intended such a scheme. * * * And yet that is just what *Hans* threatened to do.

How such a result could have been threatened on the basis of a principle not so much as mentioned in the Constitution is difficult to understand. But history provides the explanation. As I have already said, *Hans* was one episode in a long story of debt repudiation by the States of the former Confederacy after the end of Reconstruction. The turning point in the States' favor came with the Compromise of 1877, when the Republican party agreed effectively to end Reconstruction and to withdraw federal troops from the South in return for Southern acquiescence in the decision of the Electoral Commission that awarded the disputed 1876 presidential election to Rutherford B. Hayes. The troop withdrawal, of course, left the federal judiciary "effectively without power to resist the rapidly coalescing repudiation movement." Contract Clause suits like the one brought by Hans thus presented this Court with "a draconian choice between repudiation of some of its most inviolable constitutional doctrines and the humiliation of seeing its political authority compromised as its judgments met the resistance of hostile state governments." Indeed, Louisiana's brief in *Hans* unmistakably bore witness to this Court's inability to enforce a judgment against a recalcitrant State: "The solemn obligation of a government arising on its own acknowledged bond would not be enhanced by a judgment rendered on such bond. If it either could not or would not make provision for paying the bond, it is probable that it could not or would not make provision for satisfying the judgment." Given the likelihood that a judgment against the State could not be enforced, it is not wholly surprising that the *Hans* Court found a way to avoid the certainty of the State's contempt.

So it is that history explains, but does not honor, *Hans*. The ultimate demerit of the case centers, however, not on its politics but on the legal errors on which it rested. Before considering those errors, it is necessary to address the Court's contention that subsequent cases have read into *Hans* what was not there to begin with, that is, a background principle of sovereign immunity that is constitutional in stature and therefore unalterable by Congress.

* * *

III

Three critical errors in *Hans* weigh against constitutionalizing its holding as the majority does today. The first we have already seen: the *Hans* Court misread the Eleventh Amendment. It also misunderstood the conditions under which common-law doctrines were received or rejected at the time of the Founding, and it fundamentally mistook the very nature of sovereignty in the young Republic that was supposed to entail a State's immunity to federal question jurisdiction in a federal court. While I would not, as a matter of *stare decisis*, overrule *Hans* today, an understanding of its failings on these points will show how the Court today simply compounds already serious error in taking *Hans* the further step of investing its rule with constitutional inviolability against the considered judgment of Congress to abrogate it.

A

There is and could be no dispute that the doctrine of sovereign immunity that *Hans* purported to apply had its origins in the "familiar doctrine of the common law," "derived from the laws and practices of our English ancestors."[26] Although statutes came to affect its importance in the succeeding centuries, the doctrine was never reduced to codification, and Americans took their understanding of immunity doctrine from Blackstone. Here, as in the mother country, it remained a common-law rule.

This fact of the doctrine's common-law status in the period covering the Founding and the later adoption of the Eleventh Amendment should have raised a warning flag to the *Hans* Court and it should do the same for the Court today. For although the Court has persistently assumed that the common law's presence in the minds of the early Framers must have functioned as a limitation on their understanding of the new Nation's constitutional powers, this turns out not to be so at all. One of the characteristics of the Founding generation, on the contrary, was its joinder of an appreciation of its immediate and powerful common-law heri-

---

[26] The Court seeks to disparage the common law roots of the doctrine, and the consequences of those roots which I outline by asserting that *Hans* "found its roots not solely in the common law of England, but in the much more fundamental ' "jurisprudence in all civilized nations." ' " The *Hans* Court, however, relied explicitly on the ground that a suit against the State by its own citizen was "not known * * * at the common law" and was not among the departures from the common law recognized by the Constitution. Moreover, *Hans* explicitly adopted the reasoning of Justice Iredell's dissent in *Chisholm*, and that opinion could hardly have been clearer in relying exclusively on the common law. "The only principles of law * * * which can affect this case," Justice Iredell wrote, "[are] those that are derived from what is properly termed 'the common law,' a law which I presume is the ground-work of the laws in every State in the Union, and which I consider, so far as it is applicable to the peculiar circumstances of the country, and where no special act of Legislation controuls it, to be in force in each State, as it existed in England, (unaltered by any statute) at the time of the first settlement of the country."

tage with caution in settling that inheritance on the political systems of the new Republic. It is not that the Framers failed to see themselves to be children of the common law; as one of their contemporaries put it, "[w]e live in the midst of the common law, we inhale it at every breath, imbibe it at every pore * * * [and] cannot learn another system of laws without learning at the same time another language." But still it is clear that the adoption of English common law in America was not taken for granted, and that the exact manner and extent of the common law's reception were subject to careful consideration by courts and legislatures in each of the new States. An examination of the States' experience with common-law reception * * * demonstrate[s] that our history is entirely at odds with *Hans*'s resort to a common-law principle to limit the Constitution's contrary text.

* * *

2

While the States had limited their reception of English common law to principles appropriate to American conditions, the 1787 draft Constitution contained no provision for adopting the common law at all. This omission stood in sharp contrast to the state constitutions then extant, virtually all of which contained explicit provisions dealing with common-law reception. Since the experience in the States set the stage for thinking at the national level, this failure to address the notion of common-law reception could not have been inadvertent. Instead, the Framers chose to recognize only particular common-law concepts, such as the writ of habeas corpus and the distinction between law and equity by specific reference in the constitutional text. This approach reflected widespread agreement that ratification would not itself entail a general reception of the common law of England.

* * *

B

Given the refusal to entertain any wholesale reception of common law, given the failure of the new Constitution to make any provision for adoption of common law as such, and given the protests already quoted that no general reception had occurred, the *Hans* Court and the Court today cannot reasonably argue that something like the old immunity doctrine somehow slipped in as a tacit but enforceable background principle. The evidence is even more specific, however, that there was no pervasive understanding that sovereign immunity had limited federal question jurisdiction.

1

* * *

The majority sees * * * chiefly in Hamilton's discussion of sovereign immunity in Federalist No. 81, an unequivocal mandate "which would preclude all federal jurisdiction over an unconsenting State." But there is no such mandate to be found.

[T]he immediate context of Hamilton's discussion in Federalist No. 81 has nothing to do with federal question cases. It addresses a suggestion "that an assignment of the public securities of one state to the citizens of another, would enable them to prosecute that state in the federal courts for the amount of those securities." Hamilton is plainly talking about a suit subject to a federal court's jurisdiction under the Citizen-State Diversity Clauses of Article III.

The general statement on sovereign immunity emphasized by the majority then follows, along with a reference back to Federalist No. 32. What Hamilton draws from that prior paper, however, is not a general conclusion about state sovereignty but a particular point about state contracts: "A recurrence to the principles there established will satisfy us, that there is no colour to pretend that the state governments, would by the adoption of that plan, be divested of the privilege of paying their own debts in their own way, free from every constraint but that which flows from the obligations of good faith. The contracts between a nation and individuals are only binding on the conscience of the sovereign, and have no pretensions to a compulsive force. They confer no right of action independent of the sovereign will."

The most that can be inferred from this is, as noted above, that in diversity cases applying state contract law the immunity that a State would have enjoyed in its own courts is carried into the federal court. When, therefore, the *Hans* Court relied in part upon Hamilton's statement, its reliance was misplaced; Hamilton was addressing diversity jurisdiction, whereas *Hans* involved federal question jurisdiction under the Contracts Clause. No general theory of federal question immunity can be inferred from Hamilton's discussion of immunity in contract suits. But that is only the beginning of the difficulties that accrue to the majority from reliance on Federalist No. 81.

Hamilton says that a State is "not * * * amenable to the suit of an individual without its consent * * * [u]nless * * * there is a surrender of this immunity in the plan of the convention." He immediately adds, however, that "[t]he circumstances which are necessary to produce an alienation of state sovereignty, were discussed in considering the article of taxation, and need not be repeated here." The reference is to Federalist No. 32, also by Hamilton, which has this to say about the alienation of state sovereignty:

> [A]s the plan of the Convention aims only at a partial Union or consolidation, the State Governments would clearly retain all the rights of sovereignty which they before had and which were not by that act exclusively delegated to the United States. This exclusive delegation or rather this alienation of State sovereignty would only exist in three cases; where the Constitution in express terms

granted an exclusive authority to the Union; where it granted in one instance an authority to the Union and in another prohibited the States from exercising the like authority; and where it granted an authority to the Union, to which a similar authority in the States would be absolutely and totally contradictory and repugnant. I use these terms to distinguish this last case from another which might appear to resemble it; but which would in fact be essentially different; I mean where the exercise of a concurrent jurisdiction might be productive of occasional interferences in the policy of any branch of administration, but would not imply any direct contradiction or repugnancy in point of constitutional authority.

* * *

The first embarrassment Hamilton's discussion creates for the majority turns on the fact that the power to regulate commerce with Indian Tribes has been interpreted as making "Indian relations * * * the exclusive province of federal law." We have accordingly recognized that "[s]tate laws generally are not applicable to tribal Indians on an Indian reservation except where Congress has expressly provided that State laws shall apply." We have specifically held, moreover, that the states have no power to regulate gambling on Indian lands. In sum, since the States have no sovereignty in the regulation of commerce with the tribes, on Hamilton's view there is no source of sovereign immunity to assert in a suit based on congressional regulation of that commerce. If Hamilton is good authority, the majority of the Court today is wrong.

* * *

Thus, the Court's attempt to convert isolated statements by the Framers into answers to questions not before them is fundamentally misguided. The Court's difficulty is far more fundamental however, than inconsistency with a particular quotation, for the Court's position runs afoul of the general theory of sovereignty that gave shape to the Framers' enterprise. An enquiry into the development of that concept demonstrates that American political thought had so revolutionized the concept of sovereignty itself that calling for the immunity of a State as against the jurisdiction of the national courts would have been sheer illogic.

2

We said * * * that "the States entered the federal system with their sovereignty intact," but we surely did not mean that they entered that system with the sovereignty they would have claimed if each State had assumed independent existence in the community of nations, for even the Articles of Confederation allowed for less than that. While there is no need here to calculate exactly how close the American States came to sovereignty in the classic sense prior to ratification of the Constitution, it is clear that the act of ratification affected their sovereignty in a way different from any previous political event in America or anywhere else.

For the adoption of the Constitution made them members of a novel federal system that sought to balance the States' exercise of some sovereign prerogatives delegated from their own people with the principle of a limited but centralizing federal supremacy.

As a matter of political theory, this federal arrangement of dual delegated sovereign powers truly was a more revolutionary turn than the late war had been. Before the new federal scheme appeared, 18th-century political theorists had assumed that "there must reside somewhere in every political unit a single, undivided, final power, higher in legal authority than any other power, subject to no law, a law unto itself." The American development of divided sovereign powers, which "shatter[ed] * * * the categories of government that had dominated Western thinking for centuries," was made possible only by a recognition that the ultimate sovereignty rests in the people themselves. The people possessing this plenary bundle of specific powers were free to parcel them out to different governments and different branches of the same government as they saw fit.

* * *

Given this metamorphosis of the idea of sovereignty in the years leading up to 1789, the question whether the old immunity doctrine might have been received as something suitable for the new world of federal question jurisdiction is a crucial one. The answer is that sovereign immunity as it would have been known to the Framers before ratification thereafter became inapplicable as a matter of logic in a federal suit raising a federal question. The old doctrine, after all, barred the involuntary subjection of a sovereign to the system of justice and law of which it was itself the font, since to do otherwise would have struck the common-law mind from the Middle Ages onward as both impractical and absurd. But the ratification demonstrated that state governments were subject to a superior regime of law in a judicial system established, not by the State, but by the people through a specific delegation of their sovereign power to a National Government that was paramount within its delegated sphere. When individuals sued States to enforce federal rights, the Government that corresponded to the "sovereign" in the traditional common-law sense was not the State but the National Government, and any state immunity from the jurisdiction of the Nation's courts would have required a grant from the true sovereign, the people, in their Constitution, or from the Congress that the Constitution had empowered. We made a similar point in *Nevada v. Hall*, where we considered a suit against a State in another State's courts:

> This [traditional] explanation [of sovereign immunity] adequately supports the conclusion that no sovereign may be sued in its own courts without its consent, but it affords no support for a claim of immunity in another sovereign's courts. Such a claim necessarily implicates the power and authority of a second sovereign; its source

must be found either in an agreement, express or implied, between the two sovereigns, or in the voluntary decision of the second to respect the dignity of the first as a matter of comity.

Subjecting States to federal jurisdiction in federal question cases brought by individuals thus reflected nothing more than Professor Amar's apt summary that "[w]here governments are acting within the bounds of their delegated 'sovereign' power, they may partake of sovereign immunity; where not, not."

* * *

This sketch of the logic and objectives of the new federal order is confirmed by what we have previously seen of the preratification debate on state sovereign immunity, which in turn becomes entirely intelligible both in what it addressed and what it ignored. It is understandable that reasonable minds differed on the applicability of the immunity doctrine in suits that made it to federal court only under the original Diversity Clauses, for their features were not wholly novel. While they were, of course, in the courts of the new and, for some purposes, paramount National Government, the law that they implicated was largely the old common law (and in any case was not federal law). It was not foolish, therefore, to ask whether the old law brought the old defenses with it. But it is equally understandable that questions seem not to have been raised about state sovereign immunity in federal question cases. The very idea of a federal question depended on the rejection of the simple concept of sovereignty from which the immunity doctrine had developed; under the English common law, the question of immunity in a system of layered sovereignty simply could not have arisen. The Framers' principal objectives in rejecting English theories of unitary sovereignty, moreover, would have been impeded if a new concept of sovereign immunity had taken its place in federal question cases, and would have been substantially thwarted if that new immunity had been held to be untouchable by any congressional effort to abrogate it.[52]

Today's majority discounts this concern. Without citing a single source to the contrary, the Court dismisses the historical evidence regarding the Framers' vision of the relationship between national and state sovereignty, and reassures us that "the Nation survived for nearly two centuries without the question of the existence of [the abrogation] power ever being presented to this Court." But we are concerned here

---

[52] The majority contends that state compliance with federal law may be enforced by other means, but its suggestions are all pretty cold comfort: the enforcement resources of the Federal Government itself are limited; appellate review of state court decisions is contingent upon state consent to suit in state court, and is also called into question by the majority's rationale, and the Court's decision today illustrates the uncertainty that the Court will always permit enforcement of federal law by suits for prospective relief against state officers. Moreover, the majority's position ignores the importance of citizen-suits to enforcement of federal law.

not with the survival of the Nation but the opportunity of its citizens to enforce federal rights in a way that Congress provides. * * * In the end, is it plausible to contend that the plan of the convention was meant to leave the National Government without any way to render individuals capable of enforcing their federal rights directly against an intransigent state?

C

The considerations expressed so far, based on text, *Chisholm*, caution in common-law reception, and sovereignty theory, have pointed both to the mistakes inherent in *Hans* and, even more strongly, to the error of today's holding. Although for reasons of *stare decisis* I would not today disturb the century-old precedent, I surely would not extend its error by placing the common-law immunity it mistakenly recognized beyond the power of Congress to abrogate. In doing just that, however, today's decision declaring state sovereign immunity itself immune from abrogation in federal question cases is open to a further set of objections peculiar to itself. For today's decision stands condemned alike by the Framers' abhorrence of any notion that such common-law rules as might be received into the new legal systems would be beyond the legislative power to alter or repeal, and by its resonance with this Court's previous essays in constitutionalizing common-law rules at the expense of legislative authority.

1

* * * Indeed, the Framers' very insistence that no common-law doctrine would be received by virtue of ratification was focused in their fear that elements of the common law might thereby have been placed beyond the power of Congress to alter by legislation.

* * *

Virtually every state reception provision, be it constitutional or statutory, explicitly provided that the common law was subject to alteration by statute. * * * Just as the early state governments did not leave reception of the common law to implication, then, neither did they receive it as law immune to legislative alteration.

* * *

2

History confirms the wisdom of Madison's abhorrence of constitutionalizing common-law rules to place them beyond the reach of congressional amendment. The Framers feared judicial power over substantive policy and the ossification of law that would result from transforming common law into constitutional law, and their fears have been borne out every time the Court has ignored Madison's counsel on subjects that we generally group under economic and social policy. It is, in fact, remarkable that as we near the end of this century the Court should choose to open a new constitutional chapter in confining legislative judgments on these matters by resort to textually unwarranted common-law rules, for it was just this practice in the century's early decades that brought this Court to the nadir of competence that we identify with *Lochner v. New York*.

It was the defining characteristic of the *Lochner* era, and its characteristic vice, that the Court treated the common-law background (in those days, common-law property rights and contractual autonomy) as paramount, while regarding congressional legislation to abrogate the common law on these economic matters as constitutionally suspect. And yet the superseding lesson that seemed clear after *West Coast Hotel Co. v. Parrish*, that action within the legislative power is not subject to greater scrutiny merely because it trenches upon the case law's ordering of economic and social relationships, seems to have been lost on the Court.

The majority today, indeed, seems to be going *Lochner* one better. When the Court has previously constrained the express Article I powers by resort to common-law or background principles, it has done so at least in an ostensible effort to give content to some other written provision of the Constitution, like the Due Process Clause, the very object of which is to limit the exercise of governmental power. Some textual argument, at least, could be made that the Court was doing no more than defining one provision that happened to be at odds with another. Today, however, the Court is not struggling to fulfill a responsibility to reconcile two arguably conflicting and Delphic constitutional provisions, nor is it struggling with any Delphic text at all. For even the Court concedes that the Constitution's grant to Congress of plenary power over relations with Indian tribes at the expense of any state claim to the contrary is unmistakably clear, and this case does not even arguably implicate a textual trump to the grant of federal question jurisdiction.

* * *

IV

The Court's holding that the States' *Hans* immunity may not be abrogated by Congress leads to the final question in this case, whether federal question jurisdiction exists to order prospective relief enforcing IGRA against a state officer, respondent Chiles, who is said to be authorized to take the action required by the federal law. * * * The answer to this question is an easy yes, the officer is subject to suit under the rule in *Ex parte Young*, and the case could, and should, readily be decided on this point alone.

A

In *Ex parte Young*, this Court held that a federal court has jurisdiction in a suit against a state officer to enjoin official actions violating federal law, even though the State itself may be immune. Under *Young*, "a federal court, consistent with the Eleventh Amendment, may enjoin state officials to conform their future conduct to the requirements of federal law."

* * * Indeed, in the years since *Young* was decided, the Court has recognized only one limitation on the scope of its doctrine: under *Edelman v. Jordan*, *Young* permits prospective relief only and may not be applied to authorize suits for retrospective monetary relief.

It should be no cause for surprise that *Young* itself appeared when it did in the national law. It followed as a matter of course after the *Hans* Court's broad recognition of immunity in federal question cases, simply because "[r]emedies designed to end a continuing violation of federal law are necessary to vindicate the federal interest in assuring the supremacy of that law." *Young* provided, as it does today, a sensible way to reconcile the Court's expansive view of immunity expressed in *Hans* with the principles embodied in the Supremacy Clause and Article III.

* * *

B

This history teaches that it was only a matter of course that once the National Constitution had provided the opportunity for some recognition of state sovereign immunity, the necessity revealed through six centuries or more of history would show up in suits against state officers, just as *Hans* would later open the door to *Ex parte Young* itself. Once, then, the Eleventh Amendment was understood to forbid suit against a State *eo nomine*, the question arose "which suits against officers will be allowed and which will not be." * * * [No cases,] however, erase the fundamental principle of *Osborn* that sovereign immunity would not bar a suit against a state officer.

* * *

Ex parte Young [recognized] * * * the principle that state officers never have authority to violate the Constitution or federal law, so that any illegal action is stripped of state character and rendered an illegal individual act. Suits against these officials are consequently barred by neither the Eleventh Amendment nor *Hans* immunity.

The decision in *Ex parte Young*, and the historic doctrine it embodies, thus plays a foundational role in American constitutionalism, and while the doctrine is sometimes called a "fiction," the long history of its felt necessity shows it to be something much more estimable * * *. The doctrine we call *Ex parte Young* is nothing short of "indispensable to the establishment of constitutional government and the rule of law."

* * *

C

There is no question that by its own terms *Young*'s indispensable rule authorizes the exercise of federal jurisdiction over respondent

Chiles. Since this case does not, of course, involve retrospective relief, *Edelman*'s limit is irrelevant, and there is no other jurisdictional limitation. Obviously, for jurisdictional purposes it makes no difference in principle whether the injunction orders an official not to act, as in *Young*, or requires the official to take some positive step, as in *Milliken* or *Quern*. Nothing, then, in this case renders *Young* unsuitable as a jurisdictional basis for determining on the merits whether the petitioners are entitled to an order against a state official under general equitable doctrine. The Court does not say otherwise, and yet it refuses to apply *Young*. There is no adequate reason for its refusal.

No clear statement of intent to displace the doctrine of *Ex parte Young* occurs in IGRA, and the Court is instead constrained to rest its effort to skirt *Young* on a series of suggestions thought to be apparent in Congress's provision of "intricate procedures" for enforcing a State's obligation under the Act. The procedures are said to implicate a rule against judicial creativity in devising supplementary procedures; it is said that applying *Young* would nullify the statutory procedures; and finally the statutory provisions are said simply to reveal a congressional intent to preclude the application of *Young*.

1

The Court cites *Schweiker v. Chilicky* in support of refraining from what it seems to think would be judicial creativity in recognizing the applicability of *Young*. The Court quotes from *Chilicky* for the general proposition that when Congress has provided what it considers adequate remedial mechanisms for violations of federal law, this Court should not "creat[e]" additional remedies. The Court reasons that Congress's provision in IGRA of "intricate procedures" shows that it considers its remedial provisions to be adequate, with the implication that courts as a matter of prudence should provide no "additional" remedy under *Ex parte Young*.

Chilicky's remoteness from the point of this case is, however, apparent from its facts. In *Chilicky*, Congress had addressed the problem of erroneous denials of certain government benefits by creating a scheme of appeals and awards that would make a successful claimant whole for all benefits wrongly denied. The question was whether this Court should create a further remedy * * * for such harms as emotional distress, when the erroneous denial of benefits had involved a violation of procedural due process. The issue, then, was whether to create a supplemental remedy, backward-looking on the *Bivens* model, running against a federal official in his personal capacity, and requiring an affirmative justification (as *Bivens* does).

The *Bivens* issue in *Chilicky* * * * is different from the *Young* issue here in every significant respect. *Young* is not an example of a novel rule that a proponent has a burden to justify affirmatively on policy grounds in every context in which it might arguably be recognized; it is a general principle of federal equity jurisdiction that has been recognized throughout our history and for centuries before our own history began. *Young* does not provide retrospective monetary relief but allows prospective enforcement of federal law that is entitled to prevail under the Supremacy Clause. It requires, not money payments from a government employee's personal pocket, but lawful conduct by a public employee acting in his official capacity. *Young* would not function here to provide a merely supplementary regime of compensation to deter illegal action, but the sole jurisdictional basis for an Article III court's enforcement of a clear federal statutory obligation, without which a congressional act would be rendered a nullity in a federal court. One cannot intelligibly generalize from *Chilicky*'s standards for imposing the burden to justify a supplementary scheme of tort law, to the displacement of *Young*'s traditional and indispensable jurisdictional basis for ensuring official compliance with federal law when a State itself is immune from suit.

2

Next, the Court suggests that it may be justified in displacing *Young* because *Young* would allow litigants to ignore the "intricate procedures" of IGRA in favor of a menu of streamlined equity rules from which any litigant could order as he saw fit. But there is no basis in law for this suggestion, and the strongest authority to reject it. *Young* did not establish a new cause of action and it does not impose any particular procedural regime in the suits it permits. It stands, instead, for a jurisdictional rule by which paramount federal law may be enforced in a federal court by substituting a non-immune party (the state officer) for an immune one (the State itself). *Young* does no more and furnishes no authority for the Court's assumption that it somehow pre-empts procedural rules devised by Congress for particular kinds of cases that may depend on *Young* for federal jurisdiction.

If, indeed, the Court were correct in assuming that Congress may not regulate the procedure of a suit jurisdictionally dependent on *Young*, the consequences would be revolutionary, for example, in habeas law. It is well established that when a habeas corpus petitioner sues a state official alleging detention in violation of federal law and seeking the prospective remedy of release from custody, it is the doctrine identified in *Ex parte Young* that allows the petitioner to evade the jurisdictional bar of the Eleventh Amendment (or, more properly, the *Hans* doctrine). And yet Congress has imposed a number of restrictions upon the habeas remedy, and this Court has articulated several more. By suggesting that *Ex parte Young* provides a free-standing remedy not subject to the restrictions otherwise imposed on federal remedial schemes (such as habeas corpus), the Court suggests that a state prisoner may circumvent these restrictions by ostensibly bringing his suit under *Young* rather than 28 U.S.C. § 2254. The Court's view implies similar consequences under any number of similarly structured federal statutory schemes.

This, of course, cannot be the law, and the plausible rationale for rejecting the Court's contrary assumption is that Congress has just as much authority to regulate suits when jurisdiction depends on *Young* as it has to regulate when *Young* is out of the jurisdictional picture. If *Young* does not preclude Congress from requiring state exhaustion in habeas cases (and it clearly does not), then *Young* does not bar the application of IGRA's procedures when effective relief is sought by suing a state officer.

3

The Court's third strand of reasoning for displacing *Ex parte Young* is a supposed inference that Congress so intended. Since the Court rests this inference in large part on its erroneous assumption that the statute's procedural limitations would not be applied in a suit against an officer for which *Young* provided the jurisdictional basis, the error of that assumption is enough to show the unsoundness of any inference that Congress meant to exclude *Young*'s application.

* * *

Finally, one must judge the Court's purported inference by stepping back to ask why Congress could possibly have intended to jeopardize the enforcement of the statute by excluding application of *Young*'s traditional jurisdictional rule, when that rule would make the difference between success or failure in the federal court if state sovereign immunity was recognized. Why would Congress have wanted to go for broke on the issue of state immunity in the event the State pleaded immunity as a jurisdictional bar? Why would Congress not have wanted IGRA to be enforced by means of a traditional doctrine giving federal courts jurisdiction over state officers, in an effort to harmonize state sovereign immunity with federal law that is paramount under the Supremacy Clause? There are no plausible answers to these questions.

D

There is, finally, a response to the Court's rejection of *Young* that ought to go without saying. Our long-standing practice is to read ambiguous statutes to avoid constitutional infirmity. This practice alone (without any need for a clear statement to displace *Young*) would be enough to require *Young*'s application. So, too, would the application of another rule, requiring courts to choose any reasonable construction of a statute that would eliminate the need to confront a contested constitutional issue (in this case, the place of state sovereign immunity in federal question cases and the status of *Union Gas*). Construing the statute to harmonize with *Young*, as it readily does, would have saved an act of Congress and rendered a discussion on constitutional grounds wholly unnecessary. This case should be decided on this basis alone.

* * *

Because neither text, precedent, nor history supports the majority's abdication of our responsibility to exercise the jurisdiction entrusted to us in Article III, I would reverse the judgment of the Court of Appeals.

Notes and Questions

1. The majority explicitly adopts Justice Scalia's view of antecedence from his dissent in *Union Gas*, accepting the proposition that since the Eleventh Amendment postdated the Commerce Clause, the latter cannot affect the states' immunity. Yet earlier in the opinion, the Chief Justice, noting the majority's refusal to limit its approach to the words of the Eleventh Amendment, observed that the Court has " 'understood the Eleventh Amendment to stand not so much for what it says, but for the presupposition * * * which it confirms.' " If indeed the Amendment merely confirmed a presupposition, does that not reintroduce the sequencing problem upon which Justice Brennan based his *Union Gas* conclusion: that the Commerce Clause in fact came after the sovereign immunity principle and therefore can modify it in much the same way as the Court (speaking through then-Justice Rehnquist) recognized for § 5 of the Fourteenth Amendment in *Fitzpatrick v. Bitzer*?

2. The historical debate between Chief Justice Rehnquist and Justice Souter about the intentions of those who wrote and ratified the Eleventh Amendment goes to the heart of the Court's modern Eleventh Amendment jurisprudence. Justice Souter, picking up an argument line that Justice Brennan articulated at length in *Atascadero*, takes the diversity view of the Amendment. Chief Justice Rehnquist attempts to undermine Justice Souter's exclusive focus on *Chisholm* and the Eleventh Amendment by arguing that the Eleventh Amendment was but a single manifestation of a generally accepted mosaic of sovereign immunity law. In effect, the Chief Justice accuses the dissent of viewing *Chisholm* and the Amendment as if they existed in a vacuum rather than against the backdrop of general understanding of the immunity of governments to suit without their consent.

On the other hand, one might argue that it is the majority that is unrealistically isolated in its view. Consider that as of 1793 the states had just emerged from a colonial period during which they felt exploited and abused by the centralized power of the Crown. The first national government that they created, under the Articles of Confederation, proved so weak and ineffective that within six years the states convened the Constitutional Convention. Throughout the Convention and the ratification debates and conventions, the single greatest concern was the possibility of federal overreaching and subordination of the states. *Chisholm* came only five years after ratification and ignited a firestorm that resulted in the Eleventh Amendment. How likely is it that with *Chisholm* as a fresh example of their worst fears coming to pass, the states focused on the narrow diversity question *Chisholm* presented and left all other kinds of suits to the general understanding that had just failed to forestall *Chisholm* itself?

Moreover, as Justice Souter points out, Congress did have before it a far broader draft prohibiting individual actions against states. Representative Sedgwick (who would become Speaker in the late 1790s) introduced a version that would have barred all individual actions, irrespective of citizenship. It would clearly have precluded federal question cases, yet Congress did not adopt it. Why not?

Do you think that Chief Justice Rehnquist or Justice Souter has the better of the argument here? As painstaking and detailed as Justice Souter is, does his historical analysis ultimately fail to capture the tenor of the times on the subject of state immunity? On the other hand, perhaps to phrase the question that way assumes the conclusion.

3. Note that the Court's (and the dissents') approach to the immunity question re-emphasizes the importance of determining the ground for the decision in *Hans v. Louisiana*. Was it, as Justice Peckham stated in *Ex parte Young*, a holding that the Eleventh Amendment itself precludes any federal action against an unconsenting state, or was it a recognition of an implicit Article III immunity, or was it a recognition of a common law sovereign immunity that Congress is free to alter in the exercise of its Article I powers but had not altered in *Hans*?

4. Two types of sovereign immunity compete for attention in cases like *Hans, Union Gas,* and *Seminole Tribe*. The Eleventh Amendment itself reflects a forum immunity. It clearly does not speak to whether individuals can sue the states in their own courts on federal claims. But governments often also assert substantive immunity: that a cause of action simply does not lie against them irrespective of the forum. Although nothing in *Seminole Tribe* suggests that the losing plaintiff could not simply replicate its federal action in the Florida courts, *Alden v. Maine*, 527 U.S. 706, 119 S.Ct. 2240, 144 L.Ed.2d 636 (1999), now demonstrates the impossibility of that course. *See supra* page 607. Is there then any way for Congress to provide for enforcement of the substantive state-tribe relationship scheme that IGRA reflects? If not, then what of the Supremacy Clause?

5. Distinguishing between forum sovereign immunity and substantive sovereign immunity may offer a new view of *Hans*. Is it possible that the Eleventh Amendment was intended to tell the federal courts only that they could not ignore a substantive sovereign immunity to state claims that would have precluded plaintiffs like Hans from maintaining an action in the state courts? This, of course, is merely a restatement of the party-based jurisdictional view of the Amendment that Judge Fletcher, among others has advocated, but it may have the advantage of explaining the wording of the Amendment without apparently doing violence to the Supremacy Clause. Does the disappearance of immunity on a supremacy-stripping view of *Ex parte Young* connote that the Eleventh Amendment should merely stand for the preservation of substantive sovereign immunity to state claims?

6. The Court's refusal to permit the plaintiff to proceed against state officials under the aegis of *Ex parte Young* surely is worth some attention. Note that the Court imports the mode of analysis it employed in *Schweiker v. Chilicky* to reach the conclusion that the detailed congressional remedial scheme counsels against the Court permitting what it characterizes as "more

complete and more immediate relief [than] would be available under *Ex parte Young*."

a) The Court thus views *Ex parte Young* as far more than a jurisdictional case for Eleventh Amendment purposes. Yet was it? Cannot one read *Young* merely to say that when a state officer acts incompatibly with federal law, he cannot claim the forum immunity of the Eleventh Amendment? Why should that conclusion necessarily have the additional effect of expanding the scope of relief otherwise available to the plaintiff but for the forum disqualification of the Eleventh Amendment? Is there anything in *Young* that would prevent a federal court, hearing an Indian Gaming Regulatory Act case against a state officer on the jurisdictional theory of *Ex parte Young*, from limiting relief to that specified in the Act?

For an excellent discussion of the potential effects of *Seminole Tribe* on *Ex parte Young*, see Vicki C. Jackson, Seminole Tribe, *the Eleventh Amendment, and the Potential Evisceration of* Ex parte Young, 72 N.Y.U.L.Rev. 495 (1997), and David P. Currie, Ex parte Young *After* Seminole Tribe, 72 N.Y.U.L.Rev. 547 (1997).

b) The majority relies on the existence of a detailed congressionally-mandated remedial scheme to deny relief under *Ex parte Young*, modeling its approach on *Schweiker v. Chilicky*. Yet in that case, the Court essentially told Chilicky that it would not imply a private right of action on his behalf for relief exceeding that available under Congress's remedial scheme. Here, the plaintiff sought precisely the relief that Congress specified. Should that make a difference? (There is, of course, the great irony in *Seminole Tribe* of the Court refusing the Tribe relief by relying on the existence of a congressionally mandated remedial scheme that the Justices had just invalidated.)

7. Fundamentally, the majority seems to assume that the plan of the Convention reflected in the Eleventh Amendment was that the states should never be called to account in the federal courts at the behest of individuals. Yet clearly the Framers understood that states could be made defendants in the federal courts, since Article III explicitly provides state-state jurisdiction. Are those two positions incompatible?

One may be tempted to solve the apparent problem by arguing that federal courts cannot consider states as defendants except as specifically authorized by the Constitution. How, then, can one explain the federal government's ability to sue states in the federal courts? The Court has held that the Eleventh Amendment is unavailing against the United States as plaintiff. *See, e.g., United States v. Mississippi*, 380 U.S. 128, 140, 85 S.Ct. 808, 814-15, 13 L.Ed.2d 717, 725 (1965). Is a state's sovereignty interest (or dignity) any more or less offended according to whether the plaintiff against it in a federal action is the federal government, a foreign government, another state, a citizen from another state, a citizen of the state, or a citizen or subject of another country?

8. Note that despite the departure of most of the Justices supporting the result in *Union Gas*, there still seem to be four votes for overruling *Hans v. Louisiana*. The senior members of the Court are Chief Justice Rehnquist

and Justices Stevens and O'Connor, two of whom have strongly supported *Hans*. As Justice Souter's dissent declares,

> A critical examination of [*Hans*] will show that it was wrongly decided, as virtually every recent commentator has concluded. It follows that the Court's further step today of constitutionalizing *Hans*'s rule against abrogation by Congress compounds and immensely magnifies the century-old mistake of *Hans* itself and takes its place with other historic examples of textually untethered elevations of judicially derived rules to the status of inviolable constitutional law.

It may be too soon to regard the book on *Hans* as closed.

9. The result in *Seminole Tribe* occurred because of a shift of a single vote from the *Union Gas* Court. Justice Thomas, replacing Justice Marshall, joined the four dissenters from *Union Gas* to create the new majority. That circumstance raises the question, with which Chief Justice Rehnquist apparently felt compelled to deal, of the circumstances, if any, in which *stare decisis* ought to compel continuation of a rule with which a current majority of the Court disagrees. Here it does not, the Chief Justice relying in part on the oft-repeated thesis that constitutional rulings are less entitled to *stare decisis* deference than are statutory rulings. Indeed, when the Court overruled *Monroe v. Pape*'s interpretation of § 1983 in *Monell v. Department of Social Services,* then-Justice Rehnquist's opinion sounded like nothing so much as an ode to *stare decisis*, painting a picture of near immutability for the doctrine on the statutory side. Should that be so, or should *stare decisis* function at least similarly in both statutory and constitutional cases?

In another context, Chief Justice Rehnquist noted that cases "decided by the narrowest of margins, over spirited dissents challenging the basic underpinnings of those decisions[,] * * * questioned by Members of the Court in later decisions, and * * * def[ying] consistent application by the lower courts" are candidates for overruling. *Payne v. Tennessee,* 501 U.S. 808, 828-30, 111 S.Ct. 2597, 2610-11, 115 L.Ed.2d 720, 738 (1991). If a few years hence Chief Justice Rehnquist leaves the Court and his successor agrees with Justice Souter's view, should the Court overrule *Seminole Tribe* and reinstate *Union Gas*?

10. After *Seminole Tribe*, one might have thought that the Eleventh Amendment barred any claim against a state sounding in Article I legislation. Certainly that is where Chief Justice Rehnquist's opinion seemed to lead. The impression was, however, at least temporarily misleading. In *Central Virginia Community College v. Katz,* 546 U.S. 356, 126 S.Ct. 990, 163 L.Ed.2d 945 (2006), a five-to-four majority ruled that Congress could also abrogate state immunity under the Bankruptcy Clause of Article I, § 4. Justice Stevens's opinion for the Court discussed at length the Framers' realization of the necessity for a uniform bankruptcy law that transcended state borders, lest bankruptcy relief awarded by a state availed the debtor nothing in any other state. He also noted that bankruptcy jurisdiction, "at its core, is *in rem*." That being the case, the majority argued that the bankruptcy court required plenary power over the debtor's estate, which in turn required being able to recover property of the bankrupt held by someone

else. In effect, the majority said that bankruptcy was a special case, outside of the proscription of Seminole Tribe because the "States agreed in the plan of the Convention not to assert any sovereign immunity defense they might have had in proceedings brought pursuant to 'Laws on the subject of Bankruptcies.'" In *Katz* itself, the trustee in bankruptcy sought to recover payments by the debtor to the College (a state entity) that the trustee believed were voidable preferences under the law of bankruptcy. The Court found that the action could proceed in the federal court.

Justice Thomas, joined by Chief Justice Rehnquist and Justices Scalia and Kennedy, dissented. He recited the Court's Eleventh Amendment jurisprudence, relying heavily on *Seminole Tribe* for the proposition that Congress has no Article I power to abrogate the states' Eleventh Amendment immunity from suit in the federal courts. Justice Thomas referred to the rule as "settled doctrine." That may have been so after *Seminole Tribe* (at least until *Katz*), but his subsequent reference to "long-established principles," all of ten years old when *Katz* came down, seems a bit of a stretch. Recall that the whole idea of Congress affecting the states' Eleventh Amendment immunity only came to light in *Fitzpatrick v. Bitzer* in 1976, in an opinion written by then-Justice Rehnquist that he limited, but did not criticize, in *Seminole Tribe*. The thrust of the dissent was that there is nothing so special about bankruptcy as to justify a jurisdictional result different from the one *Seminole Tribe* otherwise dictated. Indeed, Justice Thomas pointed out that the Framers had similarly recognized the desirability of uniform national treatment of copyright, patent and commerce issued (for the former two providing exclusive federal jurisdiction), but the Court has refused to permit federal actions against states under those clauses. With respect to the majority's reliance on the Framers' concern that bankruptcy relief would be limited by state borders, the dissenters suggested that the Full Faith and Credit Clause addressed that problem fully.[10]

It is difficult to know what to make of *Katz*. Justice Thomas's observations with respect to other areas in which the Framers recognized the desirability of uniform national treatment have some traction. On the other hand, for a trustee in bankruptcy to be unable to marshal all of the assets of the bankrupt's estate because state governments are in possession of some of them makes bankruptcy considerably less useful. To the extent that a

---

[10] Query whether this is really so. If a debtor has property in more than one state, and if bankruptcy is truly an *in rem* proceeding as the majority suggested, how is it possible for the courts of one jurisdiction to exercise jurisdiction over property—particularly real property—located in another jurisdiction? One of the things that is clear about the Full Faith and Credit Clause is that it does not require recognition of a sister-state judgment for which there was no jurisdiction. If a bankruptcy court in one jurisdiction purports to dispose of real property located in another, could the second court refuse full faith and credit? Cases like *Fall v. Eastin*, 215 U.S. 1, 30 S.Ct. 3, 54 L.Ed. 65 (1909) (Washington state court lacked power to transfer to Nebraska land by appointing a commissioner to execute a transfer deed in place of a recalcitrant defendant), seem clearly to say yes. On the other hand, perhaps it is a mistake to regard the federal courts in bankruptcy cases as sitting within particular states. Given the majority's emphasis on the Convention's concern about bankruptcy uniformity, perhaps the relevant jurisdiction for purposes of in rem jurisdiction is the United States as a whole. In that event, the *Fall v. Eastin* objection disappears.

(state) creditor has received impermissible favored treatment from the bankrupt, other creditors lose access to that part of the estate, making settlement terms more onerous and less attractive.

Katz may be an unstable precedent. Justice O'Connor provided the majority's fifth vote shortly before her retirement. Justice Samuel Alito took her place, and it is difficult to glean from his circuit court opinions what his approach to Eleventh Amendment immunity will be. As a Circuit Judge, he hewed closely to the Supreme Court's expressed doctrine without indicating whether he might harbor a more or less expansive view than the Court has articulated over the past thirty years. What he will do now that he is in a position to express his own view remains to be seen; the Court has not decided an Eleventh Amendment case since Justice Alito joined. In the end, *Katz* may rest on ground just as unstable as that under *Pennsylvania v. Union Gas Co.*, which gave way to *Seminole Tribe* in only seven years.

NOTE ON THE ELEVENTH AMENDMENT AND SUPPLEMENTAL JURISDICTION

Ex parte Young held that the Eleventh Amendment does not close the federal forum to actions against state officials for violation of the federal constitution. But what about a federal suits asserting state-law claims against state officials? Even before *Ex parte Young*, federal courts had routinely exercised supplemental (then "pendent") jurisdiction over such claims when they were brought with a related federal claim, and they continued to do so. *See, e.g., Reagan v. Farmers' Loan & Trust*, 154 U.S. 362, 390-91, 14 S.Ct. 1047, 1051-1052, 38 L.Ed. 1014, 1021 (1894) (tortious conduct of state officials under color of state law not protected by Eleventh Amendment); *Johnson v. Lankford*, 245 U.S. 541, 38 S.Ct. 203, 62 L.Ed. 460 (1918) (same rule for claims that state officers violated state statutes). Indeed, the Court often decided such cases solely on the basis of the state law claim when by so doing it could avoid deciding a federal constitutional issue. *See, e.g., Siler v. Louisville & Nashville R. Co.*, 213 U.S. 175, 193, 29 S.Ct. 451, 455, 53 L.Ed. 753, 758 (1909) (enjoining operation of state rate statute based on state law and declining to decide Fourteenth Amendment claim). Given *Fitzpatrick v. Bitzer*'s 1976 ruling that Congress could remove the states' Eleventh Amendment immunity when legislating under the fifth section of the Fourteenth Amendment, the question of whether federal courts could continue to exercise supplemental jurisdiction over nonfederal claims was bound to arise again. In *Pennhurst State School & Hospital v. Halderman*, 465 U.S. 89, 104 S.Ct. 900, 79 L.Ed.2d 67 (1984), the Court repudiated the *Siler* line of cases (overruling at least twenty-eight prior decisions according to Justice Stevens). *Pennhurst* divided the Court five-to-four and saw a major dispute between Justices Powell and Stevens over the nature of federalism and the federal courts' role as mediators of its principles.

Quoting the district court's findings, Justice Powell gave a brief glimpse into that state institution. "Conditions at Pennhurst are not only dangerous, with the residents often physically abused or drugged by staff members, but also inadequate for the 'habilitation' of the retarded. Indeed, the court found that the physical, intellectual, and emotional skills of some residents have deteriorated at Pennhurst." The plaintiff class asserted claims under the Eighth and Fourteenth Amendments, two federal statutes,[11] and the Pennsylvania Mental Health and Mental Retardation Act of 1966, seeking damages and injunctive relief. The district court upheld both of plaintiffs' constitutional claim, their Rehabilitation Act claim and their claim sounding in Pennsylvania law, ordering extensive relief including that Pennsylvania's obligation was to house each member of the plaintiff class in "the least restrictive setting consistent with that individual's needs." The Third Circuit affirmed the judgment, but based its opinion only on the other federal statute and the Pennsylvania statute, without discussing the constitutional issues or the Rehabilitation Act. On the case's first trip to the Supreme Court, the Justices reversed, finding that the federal statute upon which the Third Circuit relied created no substantive rights on which the plaintiffs could sue. It remanded the case specifically so the Third Circuit could consider whether either the Pennsylvania statute, the federal constitutional provisions or the Rehabilitation Act could support the relief granted. The Third Circuit reaffirmed the judgment on the basis of the Pennsylvania statute.

In that second proceeding in the Third Circuit, the state raised an Eleventh Amendment argument for the first time in the litigation. The Court of Appeals rejected it and explained why.

> T]he defendants urge that we may not rely on that Act as support for the order appealed from because the Eleventh Amendment is a bar to federal court consideration of that claim. The contention that neither the district court, this court, nor the Supreme Court has jurisdiction to consider plaintiffs' state law claims has not previously been advanced in this action, and from the dearth of authorities cited in its support, not previously advanced anywhere.

> * * *

> [E]ven if the Commonwealth's unique interpretation of the pendent jurisdiction rule as inapplicable to suits against state offers had any substance, the Court's express mandate that we reconsider the state law issue appears to preclude its adoption in this case by this court.

On the case's second trip to the Supreme Court, a slim majority reversed, finding that the Eleventh Amendment did bar the claim based on

---

[11] The Rehabilitation Act of 1973 and the Developmentally Disabled Assistance and Bill of Rights Act.

state law.[12]

The bottom line of *Pennhurst* is simple: the federal courts cannot exercise supplemental (then pendent) jurisdiction over state law claims against states. The case produced an extended majority opinion by Justice Powell and an equally long and bitter dissent from Justice Stevens.[13] The opinions reveal the deep jurisprudential division on the Court about the Eleventh Amendment and the role of the federal courts *vis-à-vis* the states more generally.

The Justices clashed first over the theory that underlay *Ex parte Young*—the idea that state officials could lose their Eleventh Amendment immunity if they acted unconstitutionally. *See supra* at 639, Note 3(a). Recall that at different points, *Young's* opinion suggested that the loss of immunity occurred either because of supremacy considerations or on the theory that the king (sovereign) can do no wrong and consequently, if an agent of the sovereign commits an unlawful act, he cannot claim that the act is the sovereign's and therefore cannot claim the sovereign's immunity in the face of a civil action.[14] There is certainly strong language in *Young* to support the view that immunity stripping occurs because the state official "comes into conflict with the superior authority of [the] Constitution. . . ." *See supra* at 634. On the other hand, the be-

---

[12] In case the reader is not sure what the term "sandbagging" means, this is it. Justice Stevens reacted angrily to what he viewed as the Court's inconsistency.

> The record demonstrates that the Pennhurst State School and Hospital has been operated in violation of state law. In 1977, after three years of litigation, the District Court entered detailed findings of fact that abundantly support that conclusion. In 1981, after four more years of litigation, this Court ordered the United States Court of Appeals for the Third Circuit to decide whether the law of Pennsylvania provides an independent and adequate ground which can support the District Court's remedial order. The Court of Appeals, sitting en banc, unanimously concluded that it did. This Court does not disagree with that conclusion. Rather, it reverses the Court of Appeals because it did precisely what this Court ordered it to do; the only error committed by the Court of Appeals was its faithful obedience to this Court's command.

[13] The stridency of both opinions is notable. Justice Powell accused Justice Stevens of resting on fiction, emasculating the Eleventh Amendment and being out of touch with reality. Not to be outdone, Justice Stevens suggested that the majority was irrational, did not respect history because it, in Stevens's view, repudiated 28 cases "spanning well over a century of this Court's jurisprudence," was intellectually dishonest and had insufficient respect for federalism. Justice Stevens's opinion had a final rhetorical flourish. The first sentence read, "This case has illuminated the character of an institution." Justice Stevens went on to refer to Pennhurst Hospital's problems as found by the district court. At the end of the opinion, he summed up all of his criticisms of his majority colleagues' approach to the case. He finished with, "As I said at the outset, this case has illuminated the character of an institution," and it is perfectly clear that he is no longer speaking of Pennhurst. In our experience, the number and directness of the rhetorical barbs on both sides is unparalleled.

[14] This phrase is often misunderstood to mean that whatever the sovereign did was perforce lawful. In fact, it meant the opposite—that an unlawful act by one of the king's agents was *not* attributable to the king, and the agent therefore could not take shelter under the king's sovereign immunity.

ginning of the same paragraph offered the king-can-do-no-wrong rationale.

> The answer to all this [the argument that *Young* acted for the state] is the same as made in every case where an official claims to be acting under the authority of the state. The act to be enforced is alleged to be unconstitutional; and if it be so, the use of the name of the state to enforce an unconstitutional act to the injury of complainants is a proceeding without the authority of, and one which does not affect, the state in its sovereign or governmental capacity.

Justice Powell relied on the former statement, Justice Stevens on the latter. In *Pennhurst*, the difference was critical. If supremacy concerns underlay *Ex parte Young* stripping, there clearly were none with respect to state claims, and so the state officials would retain the state's immunity from suit in the federal courts. If the king-can-do-no-wrong approach applied, then an act unlawful under either federal or state law would deprive them of immunity. Justice Powell had the votes.

Exploration of that issue required the Justices also to confront the objectives of the Eleventh Amendment, and they again differed sharply. Justice Powell focused on the states' resentment at having federal *courts* able to issue binding judgments against them, noting the widespread unfavorable reaction to *Chisholm v. Georgia*. Justice Stevens, by contrast, thought that the Amendment reflected post-colonial fears that subjecting the states to federal *law* would erode the states' sovereignty. For Justice Powell, the prime offense to the states was that federal courts were telling them what to do, *i.e.* that the offense was inherent in the messenger. Justice Stevens saw it differently. For him, it would cause far more offense to the states to be compelled to obey federal law than state law, on the theory that they had adopted the state law themselves. For Stevens, the offense inhered in the substance of the law to which the federal courts subjected the states. Which view do you think is empirically correct?

The *Pennhurst* majority opinion is ironic in two ways. First, Justice Powell extols federalism, and yet, as Justice Stevens points out, his position on jurisdiction to hear state claims compels the federal courts to impose federal law on the states in preference to simply requiring them to comply with their own law. The second involves the cautionary principles that Justice Brandeis expressed in his famous concurrence in *Ashwander v. Tennessee Valley Authority*, 297 U.S. 288, 56 S.Ct. 466, 80 L.Ed. 688 (1936), in which he summarized principles of federal judicial restraint to which the Court had long adhered (and continues, for the most part, to honor), including most famously the rule that the Court will avoid deciding a properly presented constitutional question unless there is no other ground on which to decide the case.[15] Justice Powell was a staunch supporter of that view. Nonetheless, his position on the federal courts' power to adjudicate state claims will often compel those courts to decide on federal constitutional grounds rather than on state law grounds.[16]

One might also criticize Justice Stevens's approach. His *Ashwander*-like argument that the federal courts should decide cases on non-constitutional and non-federal grounds whenever possible might lead to disposing of cases like *Pennhurst* on state-law grounds only. Yet, one thing that no one has ever apparently doubted about the Eleventh Amendment is that it intended to eliminate diversity jurisdiction for cases in which states are defendants. Justice Stevens's approach seems to elide that bit of history. Perhaps Justice Powell was correct, although he did not frame his argument on this basis. Nonetheless, given the uproar after *Chisholm*, which was, after all, a diversity case, one might argue that the elimination of diversity jurisdiction is nugatory if the same claims can nonetheless come into federal court under supplemental jurisdiction.

Pennhurst poses some practical problems for counsel. Faced with a case in which the plaintiffs can assert multiple claims, some based in federal law and some in state law, what is counsel to do? If she wants to litigate all of the claims in a single proceeding, she must go to the state courts. If she wants to litigate the federal claims in federal court, she must either abandon the state claims or sue separately on them. Moreover, the sequence of lawsuits is critical. If counsel sues on the state claims in state court than then attempts to sue on the federal claims in federal court, he will be met with a motion to dismiss under Rule 12(b)(6) because the federal claims, which he could have presented to the state court are now either merged with the state court judgment (if plaintiff was successful) or barred by it (if plaintiff was not). *Migra v. Warren City School District*, 465 U.S. 75, 104 S.Ct. 892, 79 L.Ed.2d 56 (1984), makes this clear. Thus, the federal action must proceed to judgment before any state action does.[17] The Court announced *Pennhurst* and *Migra* on the same day. Do you think that is of any significance?

---

[15] "Thus, if a case can be decided on either of two grounds, one involving a constitutional question, the other a question of statutory construction or general law, the Court will decide only the latter." *Siler v. Louisville & Nashville R. Co.*, 213 U.S. 175, 29 S.Ct. 451, 53 L.Ed. 753 (1909) (decided on the basis of state law, avoiding a federal constitutional question).

[16] That may not be so if the plaintiff also has federal statutory support for his claim, but that will often not be the case. *See, e.g. Siler, supra.*

[17] There is no problem of claim preclusion in the state courts. Claim preclusion prohibits litigation of claims that were or might have been litigated in the first action. *Pennhurst* makes clear that the federal courts could not have entertained the state claims.

Federal Maritime Commission v. South Carolina State Ports Authority, 535 U.S. 743, 122 S.Ct. 1864, 152 L.Ed.2d 962 (2002), appears to have extended the states' immunity to federal proceedings in a new direction. The dispute revolved around the defendant Authority's (SCSPA) refusal to open Charleston's port facilities to a cruise ship that permitted gambling on board while in international waters. The company complained that the Authority discriminated in applying its anti-gambling policy, allowing ships from a rival company to use Charleston's berthing facilities.

The company alleged violations of the federal Shipping Act and took its complaint to the Federal Maritime Commission (FMC). FMC referred the complaint to an administrative law judge, who dismissed the complaint on Eleventh Amendment grounds, relying on *Seminole Tribe* for the conclusion that Congress's powerlessness to provide for federal court actions against states pursuant to its Article I powers connoted that FMC, created pursuant to those Article I powers, could not itself subject SCSPA to a federal proceeding at the behest of an individual.

The company did not appeal the ruling, but FMC reviewed it and reached the conclusion that sovereign immunity was not a bar to the proceeding. The Fourth Circuit overturned FMC's conclusion and ordered the case dismissed. The Supreme Court granted FMC's petition for certiorari and affirmed by the predictable five-to-four majority.

Justice Thomas's majority opinion made clear that the Court decided the case not on the basis of the Eleventh Amendment itself, but instead in service of "the sovereign immunity embedded in our constitutional structure and retained by the States when they joined the Union * * * ." It was necessary for him to do so because FMC clearly does not exercise Article III judicial power, and the Court has never pretended that the Eleventh Amendment addresses anything else.[18] That being the case, the majority opinion was at pains to analogize the FMC proceeding to a traditional lawsuit, citing with approval the Fourth Circuit's observation that the proceeding "walks, talks, and squawks very much like a lawsuit."

The majority relied heavily on a carefully selected excerpt from Alexander Hamilton's The Federalist No. 81, in which he stated that "It is inherent in the nature of sovereignty not to be amenable to the suit of an individual *without its consent*." That sentiment, did not stand in isolation. The majority opinion in *Hans* reproduced much of Hamilton's discussion on the point (*see supra* page 611) and demonstrates clearly

---

[18] This is not to say that the Court never pretends anything with respect to the Amendment. It pretends all the time, rewriting both history and psychology to ignore what was going on in the 1790s and to reach the result that a majority of Justices think reflects an appropriate balance of federal and state power, unanchored anywhere in the Constitution. The Court's approach constantly overlooks the adage that repetition does not establish validity.

that he was speaking of the states' sovereign immunity with respect to actions on state debts, *i.e.* state-created contract actions. Lest there be any doubt, consider that the subject of The Federalist No. 81 was a general discussion of Article III, the organization of the Supreme Court and the possibility of having inferior federal courts. The sentence immediately before the quoted language in *Hans* reads: "Though it may rather be a digression from the immediate subject of this paper, I shall take occasion to mention here a supposition which has excited some alarm upon very mistaken grounds." At the conclusion of the aside, Hamilton said: "Let us resume the train of our observations."

It could hardly be clearer, as many distinguished scholars have pointed out, that Hamilton was addressing the possibility of diversity actions in the federal courts. Were that not the case, there would have been no reason to refer to an assignment of the debt to a non-citizen of the defendant state. Hamilton was talking about a state defense to a state claim. If the language (in context) to which Justice Thomas referred suggests anything, it suggests that the diversity interpretation of the Eleventh Amendment is right on target.

Justice Stevens's dissent rejected both of what he characterized as the majority's predicates for its decision. First, to the extent that the majority relied on *Alden v. Maine* and its mention of state dignity as a core value of the doctrine of sovereign immunity, he recalled Justice Souter's *Alden* dissent and continued the argument that neither history nor constitutional structure supported the idea of state immunity from federal law. Second, he disputed the idea that state dignity was a core value of the immunity doctrine that did exist, relying in part on Chief Justice Marshall's statement in *Cohens v. Virginia* (1821) that the Eleventh Amendment existed only to protect states from individual creditors and not to protect a dignity interest in not appearing in another sovereign's courts, for if it were, the Constitution would not have permitted suits against states by other states or by the federal government.

Justice Breyer also dissented, arguing that no constitutional text at all supported the Court's result, given that the Federal Maritime Commission was not a part of the judicial (or legislative) branch at all. He took the position that FMC was executing federal law, "in part by making rules or by adjudicating matters in dispute." For him, the determining factor was that "the Constitution created a Federal Government empowered to enact laws that would bind the States and it empowered that Federal Government to enforce those laws against the States. It also left private individuals perfectly free to complain to the Federal Government about unlawful state activity, and it left the Federal Government free to take subsequent legal action."

More specifically, Justice Breyer asserted that the Court could not legitimately read the words "Judicial power" in the Eleventh Amendment to mean "executive power," though he did note with some acerbity that the Court had read "Citizens of another State" as if it said "citizen of the same State." He rejected a Tenth Amendment approach as well, since in his view the Constitution had delegated the power FMC exercised to the United States, and he accused the majority of reading into the Tenth Amendment a "hidden reservation" with respect to state sovereign immunity. Finally, he argued that the Court's underlying assumption—that state sovereign immunity survived the Constitutional Convention entirely intact—could not survive historical analysis. Moreover, he made clear that the dissenting Justices were not content to let the issue drop. "Today's decision reaffirms the need for continued dissent—unless the consequences of the Court's approach prove anodyne, as I hope, rather than randomly destructive, as I fear."

Finally, consider one additional point about *Federal Maritime Commission*. FMC argued that the action fell within the doctrine of *Ex parte Young* because even if resolved against the state, it would have no adverse impact on the state treasury. Justice Thomas's majority opinion recognized a hierarchy of values within the doctrine of sovereign immunity that the Court expounded, observing that protection of state treasuries was important but noting that "the doctrine's central purpose is to 'accord the States the respect owed them as' joint sovereigns." The Court juxtaposed that assertion with an observation that the federal government can still affect the states using its Article I legislative powers; it simply must enforce such regulations in its own name (including in federal lawsuits) rather than relying on litigation by private entities. This approach leaves several questions open for consideration.

First, if the core value of sovereign immunity doctrine is the states' dignity interest, why does a federal action by an individual seeking only injunctive relief (in the mold of *Ex parte Young*) not pose just as great a threat to the state's dignity as an action seeking damages? Second, why is the dignity interest subordinated if the plaintiff is the federal government or another state? Is the offense to a state's dignity interest determined by the forum in which the adjudication occurs or by the identity of the opposing party? Third, referring to the core concern with states' dignity interests, Justice Thomas noted that "[i]t is for this reason * * * that sovereign immunity applies regardless of whether a private plaintiff's suit is for monetary damages or some other type of relief." Does that statement lay groundwork for substantially limiting the doctrine of *Ex parte Young* or overturning it entirely?

Chapter 8

REFUSING JURISDICTION:
ABSTENTION AND
RELATED DOCTRINES

A. INTRODUCTION

Sometimes a court having jurisdiction of the case and over all of the parties will nonetheless decline to hear it. The basic civil procedure concepts of *forum non conveniens* or transfer of venue are examples. More specialized examples include the federal courts' long-standing refusal to hear domestic relations or probate cases under their diversity jurisdiction.[1] Some jurisdiction-declining rules are created by statute; others by the courts.

A set of doctrines and statutes relating particularly to federal courts has emerged over the two centuries since the Judiciary Act of 1789 created the inferior federal courts. The statutory provisions, which seek to serve the values of federalism, pose some intricate technical problems; the judge-made doctrines raise both substantial federalism and separation-of-powers questions. Section 1983 cases in particular exemplify the federal courts' continuing struggle to accommodate state interests, federal interests, separation-of-powers concerns, and individuals' constitutional rights to be free from government overreaching. The difficulty of this four-part balancing act is nowhere better illustrated than in the statutes and doctrines directing abstention.

All the statutory and common law rules in this area appear against a backdrop of serious issues about the propriety of federal courts refusing cases clearly within their jurisdiction. Nearly two centuries ago, Chief Justice John Marshall said, with characteristic understatement:

> It is most true that this Court will not take jurisdiction if it should not: but it is equally true, that it must take jurisdiction if it should. The judiciary cannot, as the legislature may, avoid a measure because it approaches the confines of the constitution. We cannot pass it by because it is doubtful. With whatever doubts,

---

[1] *See* CHARLES ALAN WRIGHT & MARY KAY KANE, LAW OF FEDERAL COURTS 161-63 (6th ed. 2002).

with whatever difficulties, a case may be attended, we must decide it, if it be brought before us. We have no more right to decline the exercise of jurisdiction which is given, than to usurp that which is not given. The one or the other would be treason to the constitution. Questions may occur which we would gladly avoid; but we cannot avoid them. All we can do is, to exercise our best judgment, and conscientiously to perform our duty.[2]

Whether or not those sentiments were ever the rule in the federal courts, they clearly are not today. In Marshall's terms, the Supreme Court and the inferior federal courts commit treason every day. When Congress has conferred jurisdiction, there is a substantial separation-of-powers question about the legitimacy of judge-made doctrines that implicitly treat jurisdictional statutes not as directives but as offers that can be refused. This section presents an overview of what Marshall might well have regarded as the federal courts' apostasy.[3]

B.   CONGRESSIONAL DOCTRINES OF RESTRAINT

ATLANTIC COAST LINE RAILROAD COMPANY v. BROTHERHOOD OF LOCOMOTIVE ENGINEERS
Supreme Court of the United States, 1970.
398 U.S. 281, 90 S.Ct. 1739, 26 L.Ed.2d 234.

MR. JUSTICE BLACK delivered the opinion of the Court.

Congress in 1793, shortly after the American Colonies became one united Nation, provided that in federal courts "a writ of injunction (shall not) be granted to stay proceedings in any court of a state." Although certain exceptions to this general prohibition have been added, that statute, directing that state courts shall remain free from interference by federal courts, has remained in effect until this time. Today that amended statute provides: "A court of the United States may not grant an injunction to stay proceedings in a State court except as expressly authorized by Act of Congress, or where necessary in aid of its jurisdiction, or to protect or effectuate its judgments." 28 U.S.C. § 2283. Despite the existence of this long standing prohibition, in this case a federal court did enjoin the petitioner, Atlantic Coast Line Railroad Co. (ACL), from invoking an injunction issued by a Florida state court which prohibited certain picketing by respondent Brotherhood of Locomotive Engineers (BLE). The case arose in the following way.

In 1967 BLE began picketing the Moncrief Yard, a switching yard located near Jacksonville, Florida, and wholly owned and operated by ACL. As soon as this picketing began ACL went into federal court seek-

---

[2] Cohens v. Virginia, 19 U.S. (6 Wheat.) 264, 404, 5 L.Ed. 257, 291 (1821).

[3] Chief Justice Marshall would not have been alone. See, for example, Justice Frankfurter's dissent in *Burford v. Sun Oil Co.*, at page 841.

ing an injunction. When the federal judge denied the request, ACL immediately went into state court and there succeeded in obtaining an injunction. No further legal action was taken in this dispute until two years later in 1969, after this Court's decision in *Brotherhood of Railroad Trainmen v. Jacksonville Terminal Co.* In that case the Court considered the validity of a state injunction against picketing by the BLE and other unions at the Jacksonville Terminal, located immediately next to Moncrief Yard. The Court reviewed the factual situation surrounding the Jacksonville Terminal picketing and concluded that the unions had a federally protected right to picket under the Railway Labor Act and that that right could not be interfered with by state court injunctions. Immediately after a petition for rehearing was denied in that case, the respondent BLE filed a motion in state court to dissolve the Moncrief Yard injunction, arguing that under the *Jacksonville Terminal* decision the injunction was improper. The state judge refused to dissolve the injunction, holding that this Court's *Jacksonville Terminal* decision was not controlling. The union did not elect to appeal that decision directly, but instead went back into the federal court and requested an injunction against the enforcement of the state court injunction. The District Judge granted the injunction and upon application a stay of that injunction, pending the filing and disposition of a petition for certiorari, was granted. The Court of Appeals summarily affirmed on the parties' stipulation, and we granted a petition for certiorari to consider the validity of the federal court's injunction against the state court.

In this Court the union contends that the federal injunction was proper either "to protect or effectuate" the District Court's denial of an injunction in 1967, or as "necessary in aid of" the District Court's jurisdiction. Although the questions are by no means simple and clear, and the decision is difficult, we conclude that the injunction against the state court was not justified under either of these two exceptions to the anti-injunction statute. We therefore hold that the federal injunction in this case was improper.

I

Before analyzing the specific legal arguments advanced in this case, we think it would be helpful to discuss the background and policy that led Congress to pass the anti-injunction statute in 1793. While all the reasons that led Congress to adopt this restriction on federal courts are not wholly clear, it is certainly likely that one reason stemmed from the essentially federal nature of our national government. When this Nation was established by the Constitution, each State surrendered only a part of its sovereign power to the national government. But those powers that were not surrendered were retained by the States and unless a State was restrained by "the supreme Law of the Land" as expressed in the Constitution, laws, or treaties of the United States it was free to exercise those retained powers as it saw fit. One of the reserved powers was the maintenance of state judicial systems for the decision of legal controversies. Many of the Framers of the Constitution felt that separate federal courts were unnecessary and that the state courts could be entrusted to protect both state and federal rights. Others felt that a complete system of federal courts to take care of federal legal problems should be provided for in the Constitution itself. This dispute resulted in compromise. One "supreme Court" was created by the Constitution, and Congress was given the power to create other federal courts. In the first Congress this power was exercised and a system of federal trial and appellate courts with limited jurisdiction was created by the Judiciary Act of 1789.

While the lower federal courts were given certain powers in the 1789 Act, they were not given any power to review directly cases from state courts, and they have not been given such powers since that time. Only the Supreme Court was authorized to review on direct appeal the decisions of state courts. Thus from the beginning we have had in this country two essentially separate legal systems. Each system proceeds independently of the other with ultimate review in this Court of the federal questions raised in either system. Understandably this dual court system was bound to lead to conflicts and frictions. Litigants who foresaw the possibility of more favorable treatment in one or the other system would predictably hasten to invoke the powers of whichever court it was believed would present the best chance of success. Obviously this dual system could not function if state and federal courts were free to fight each other for control of a particular case. Thus, in order to make the dual system work and "to prevent needless friction between state and federal courts," it was necessary to work out lines of demarcation between the two systems. Some of these limits were spelled out in the 1789 Act. Others have been added by later statutes as well as judicial decisions. The 1793 anti-injunction Act was at least in part a response to these pressures.

On its face the present Act is an absolute prohibition against enjoining state court proceedings, unless the injunction falls within one of three specifically defined exceptions. The respondents here have intimated that the Act only establishes a "principle of comity," not a binding rule on the power of the federal courts. The argument implies that in certain circumstances a federal court may enjoin state court proceedings even if that action cannot be justified by any of the three exceptions. We cannot accept any such contention. In 1955 when this Court interpreted this statute, it stated: "This is not a statute conveying a broad general policy for appropriate *ad hoc* application. Legislative policy is here expressed in a clear-cut prohibition qualified only by specifically defined exceptions." Since that time Congress has not seen fit to amend the statute and we therefore adhere to that position and hold that any injunction against state court proceedings otherwise proper under general equitable principles must be based on one of the specific statutory exceptions to § 2283 if it is to be upheld. Moreover since the statutory prohibition against such injunctions in part rests on the fundamental constitutional independence of the States and their courts the exceptions should not be enlarged by loose statutory construction. Proceedings in state courts should normally be allowed to continue unimpaired by intervention of the lower federal courts, with relief from error, if any, through the state appellate courts and ultimately this Court.

II

In this case the Florida Circuit Court enjoined the union's intended picketing, and the United States District Court enjoined the railroad "from giving effect to or availing [itself] of the benefits of" that state court order. Both sides agree that although this federal injunction is in terms directed only at the railroad it is an injunction "to stay proceedings in a State court." It is settled that the prohibition of § 2283 cannot be evaded by addressing the order to the parties or prohibiting utilization of the results of a completed state proceeding. Thus if the injunction against the Florida court proceedings is to be upheld, it must be "expressly authorized by Act of Congress," "necessary in aid of (the District Court's) jurisdiction," or "to protect or effectuate (that court's) judgments."

Neither party argues that there is any express congressional authorization for injunctions in this situation and we agree with that conclusion. The respondent union does contend that the injunction was proper either as a means to protect or effectuate the District Court's 1967 order, or in aid of that court's jurisdiction. We do not think that either alleged basis can be supported.

A

The argument based on protecting the 1967 order is not clearly expressed, but in essence it appears to run as follows: In 1967 the railroad sought a temporary restraining order which the union opposed. In the course of deciding that request, the United States District Court determined that the union had a federally protected right to picket Moncrief Yard and that this right could not be interfered with by state courts. When the Florida Circuit Court enjoined the picketing, the United States District Court could, in order to protect and effectuate its prior determination, enjoin enforcement of the state court injunction. Although the record on this point is not unambiguously clear, we conclude that no such interpretation of the 1967 order can be supported.

When the railroad initiated the federal suit it filed a complaint with three counts, each based entirely on alleged violations of federal law. The first two counts alleged violations of the Railway Labor Act, and the third alleged a violation of that Act and the Interstate Commerce Act as well. Each of the counts concluded with a prayer for an injunction against the picketing. Although the union had not been formally served with the complaint and had not filed an answer, it appeared at a hearing on a motion for a temporary restraining order and argued against the issuance of such an order. The union argued that it was a party to a labor dispute with the FEC, that it had exhausted the administrative remedies required by the Railway Labor Act, and that it was thus free to engage in "self-help," or concerted economic activity. Then the union argued that such activity could not be enjoined by the federal court. In an attempt to clarify the basis of this argument the District Judge asked: "You are basing your case solely on the Norris-LaGuardia Act?" The union's lawyer replied: "Right. I think at this point of the argument, since Norris-LaGuardia is clearly in point here." At no point during the entire argument did either side refer to state law, the effects of that law on the picketing, or the possible preclusion of state remedies as a result of overriding federal law. The next day the District Court entered an order denying the requested restraining order. In relevant part that order included these conclusions of law:

> 3. The parties to the BLE-FEC "major dispute," having exhausted the procedures of the Railway Labor Act, are now free to engage in self-help. * * *

> 4. The conduct of the FEC pickets and that of the responding ACL employees are a part of the FEC-BLE major dispute. * * *

> 7. The Norris-LaGuardia Act and the Clayton Act are applicable to the conduct of the defendants here involved.

In this Court the union asserts that the determination that it was "free to engage in self-help" was a determination that it had a federally protected right to picket and that state law could not be invoked to negate that right. The railroad, on the other hand, argues that the order merely determined that the federal court could not enjoin the picketing, in large part because of the general prohibition in the Norris-LaGuardia Act against issuance by federal courts of injunctions in labor disputes. Based solely on the state of the record when the order was entered, we are inclined to believe that the District Court did not determine whether federal law precluded an injunction based on state law. Not only was that point never argued to the court, but there is no language in the order that necessarily implies any decision on that question. In short we feel that the District Court in 1967 determined that federal law could not be invoked to enjoin the picketing at Moncrief Yard, and that the union did have a right "to engage in self-help" as far as the federal courts were concerned. But that decision is entirely different from a decision that the Railway Labor Act precludes state regulation of the picketing as well, and this latter decision is an essential prerequisite for upholding the 1969 injunction as necessary "to protect or effectuate" the 1967 order. Finally we think it highly unlikely that the brief statements in the order conceal a determination of a disputed legal point that later was to divide this Court in a 4-to-3 vote in *Jacksonville Terminal,* in opinions totaling 28 pages. While judicial writing may sometimes be thought cryptic and tightly packed, the union's contention here stretches the content of the words well beyond the limits of reasonableness.

Any lingering doubts we might have as to the proper interpretation of the 1967 order are settled by references to the positions adopted by the parties later in the litigation. In response to the railroad's request for a temporary restraining order from the state court, the union referred to the prior federal litigation, noted that it was part of a "major dispute," that it was covered by § 20 of the Clayton Act and that "[l]abor activity which is within the Clayton Act is 'immunized trade union activities.'" At no point did the union appear to argue that the federal court had already determined that the railroad was precluded from obtaining an injunction under Florida law.

Similarly the union's arguments in 1969 indicate that the 1967 federal order did not determine whether federal law precluded resort to the state courts. When the union tried to dissolve the state court injunction, the argument was based entirely on the controlling effect of the *Jacksonville Terminal* decision on the picketing at Moncrief Yard. The union argued that this Court's "decision is squarely controlling upon [the Moncrief Yard] case which is identical in all material respects." Although the union again mentioned that the federal District Judge had determined in 1967 that it was free to engage in self-help, it never argued that the 1967 order had in effect held with respect to Moncrief Yard what this Court later held was the law with respect to the Jacksonville Terminal situation. The railroad argued that *Jacksonville Terminal* was not controlling, and the Florida judge agreed.[5]

Our reading of this record is not altered by the District Court's 1969 opinion issued when the injunction was granted two years after the 1967 order was entered. In that opinion the court said:

> In its Order of April 26, 1967, this Court found that Plaintiff's Moncrief Yard, the area in question, "is an integral and necessary part of [Florida East Coast Railway Company's] operations." * * * The Court concluded furthermore that Defendants herein "are now free to engage in self-help." * * * The injunction of the state court, if allowed to continue in force, would effectively nullify this Court's findings and delineation of rights of the parties. The categorization of Defendants' activities as "secondary" does not alter this state of affairs. * * * The prohibition of 28 U.S.C. § 2283, therefore, does not deprive this Court of jurisdiction to enter the injunction in this instance.

* * * We think the proper interpretation of that somewhat ambiguous passage can be reached only when it is considered in light of the ar-

---

[5] For purposes of this case only, we will assume, without deciding, that the Florida Circuit Court's decision was wrong in light of our decision in *Jacksonville Terminal*.

guments presented to the District Court by the union. In arguing that an injunction was necessary to protect the 1967 order, the union's lawyer said:

> Now, the basic finding [of that order] is that we are free to engage in such self-help as is permitted under the Railway Labor Act. Now, Your Honor, at that point, did not get to the question of how broad is this right, because the Norris-LaGuardia Act prevented Your Honor from issuing an injunction. Now, how broad, then, is that right? We know, from the [*Jacksonville Terminal*] decision.
> * * *

* * * The lawyer then proceeded to argue that the *Jacksonville Terminal* case had clearly revealed that the right of self-help is beyond state court proscription in these circumstances. At no point during this hearing did the union try to argue, as it now appears to do, that the 1967 order itself had anticipated the *Jacksonville Terminal* decision. Rather the union appears to have argued that the decision of this Court in *Jacksonville Terminal* operated to define the scope of the right to self-help which the District Court had found the union entitled to exercise, and that the state court injunction interfered with that right as so defined. Considered in this light we cannot agree with the dissenting view in this case that the District Court in 1967 "by necessary implication" decided that the union had a federally protected right to picket that "could not be subverted by resort to state proceedings." On the contrary, we read the quoted passage in the 1969 opinion as an indication that the District Court accepted the union's argument and concluded that the *Jacksonville Terminal* decision had amplified its 1967 order, and it was this amplification, rather than the original order itself, that required protection. Such a modification of an earlier order through an opinion in another case is not a "judgment" that can properly be protected by an injunction against state court proceedings.

This record, we think, conclusively shows that neither the parties themselves nor the District Court construed the 1967 order as the union now contends it should be construed. Rather we are convinced that the union in effect tried to get the Federal District Court to decide that the state court judge was wrong in distinguishing the *Jacksonville Terminal* decision. Such an attempt to seek appellate review of a state decision in the Federal District Court cannot be justified as necessary "to protect or effectuate" the 1967 order. The record simply will not support the union's contention on this point.

B

This brings us to the second prong of the union's argument in which it is suggested that even if the 1967 order did not determine the union's right to picket free from state interference, once the decision in *Jacksonville Terminal* was announced, the District Court was then free to enjoin the state court on the theory that such action was "necessary in aid of [the District Court's] jurisdiction." Again the argument is somewhat unclear, but it appears to go in this way: The District Court had acquired jurisdiction over the labor controversy in 1967 when the railroad filed its complaint, and it determined at that time that it did have jurisdiction. The dispute involved the legality of picketing by the union and the *Jacksonville Terminal* decision clearly indicated that such activity was not only legal, but was protected from state court interference. The state court had interfered with that right, and thus a federal injunction was "necessary in aid of its jurisdiction." For several reasons we cannot accept the contention.

First, a federal court does not have inherent power to ignore the limitations of § 2283 and to enjoin state court proceedings merely because those proceedings interfere with a protected federal right or invade an area preempted by federal law, even when the interference is unmistakably clear. This rule applies regardless of whether the federal court itself has jurisdiction over the controversy, or whether it is ousted from jurisdiction for the same reason that the state court is. This conclusion is required because Congress itself set forth the only exceptions to the statute, and those exceptions do not include this situation. Second, if the District Court does have jurisdiction, it is not enough that the requested injunction is related to that jurisdiction, but it must be "necessary in aid of" that jurisdiction. While this language is admittedly broad, we conclude that it implies something similar to the concept of injunctions to "protect or effectuate" judgments. Both exceptions to the general prohibition of § 2283 imply that some federal injunctive relief may be necessary to prevent a state court from so interfering with a federal court's consideration or disposition of a case as to seriously impair the federal court's flexibility and authority to decide that case. Third, no such situation is presented here. Although the federal court did have jurisdiction of the railroad's complaint based on federal law, the state court also had jurisdiction over the complaint based on state law and the union's asserted federal defense as well. *Jacksonville Terminal.* While the railroad could probably have based its federal case on the pendent state law claims as well, it was free to refrain from doing so and leave the state law questions and the related issue concerning preclusion of state remedies by federal law to the state courts. Conversely, although it could have tendered its federal claims to the state court, it was also free to restrict the state complaint to state grounds alone. In short, the state and federal courts had concurrent jurisdiction in this case, and neither court was free to prevent either party from simultaneously pursuing claims in both courts. Therefore the state court's assumption of jurisdiction over the state law claims and the federal preclusion issue did not hinder the federal court's jurisdiction so as to make an injunction necessary to aid that jurisdiction. Nor was an injunction necessary because the state court may have taken action which the federal court was certain was improper under the *Jacksonville Terminal* decision. Again, lower federal courts possess no power whatever to sit in direct review of state court decisions. If the union was adversely affected by the state court's decision, it was free to seek vindication of its federal right in the Florida appellate courts and ultimately, if necessary, in this Court. Similarly if, because of the Florida Circuit Court's action, the union faced the threat of immediate irreparable injury sufficient to justify an injunction under usual equitable principles, it was undoubtedly free to seek such relief from the Florida appellate courts, and might possibly in certain emergency circumstances seek such relief from this Court as well. Unlike the Federal District Court, this Court does have potential appellate jurisdiction over federal questions raised in state court proceedings, and that broader jurisdiction allows this Court correspondingly broader authority to issue injunctions "necessary in aid of its jurisdiction."

III

This case is by no means an easy one. The arguments in support of the union's contentions are not insubstantial. But whatever doubts we may have are strongly affected by the general prohibition of § 2283. Any doubts as to the propriety of a federal injunction against state court proceedings should be resolved in favor of permitting the state courts to proceed in an orderly fashion to finally determine the controversy. The explicit wording of § 2283 itself implies as much, and the fundamental principle of a dual system of courts leads inevitably to that conclusion.

The injunction issued by the District Court must be vacated. Since that court has not yet proceeded to a final judgment in the case, the cause is remanded to it for further proceedings in conformity with this opinion.

Vacated and remanded.

Mr. Justice Brennan, with whom Mr. Justice White joins, dissenting.

My disagreement with the Court in this case is a relatively narrow one. I do not disagree with much that is said concerning the history and policies underlying 28 U.S.C. § 2283. Nor do I dispute the Court's holding * * * that federal courts do not have authority to enjoin state proceedings merely because it is asserted that the state court is improperly asserting jurisdiction in an area preempted by federal law or federal procedures. Nevertheless in my view the District Court has discretion to enjoin the state proceedings in the present case because it acted pursuant to an explicit exception to the prohibition of § 2283, that is, "to protect or effectuate [the District Court's] judgments."

* * *

The thrust of the District Judge's order is that the procedures prescribed by the Railway Labor Act had been exhausted in relation to the BLE-FEC dispute, that BLE was therefore free to engage in self-help tactics, and that it was properly exercising this federal right when it engaged in the picketing that ACL sought to enjoin. This interpretation of the order is supported by the fact that the District Judge relied upon *Brotherhood of Locomotive Engineers v. Baltimore & Ohio R. Co.,* in which this Court held that the parties had exhausted all available procedures under the Railway Labor Act and thus were free to resort to self-help. Furthermore, the District Court invoked § 20 of the Clayton Act, which provides that certain union activities, including striking and peaceful picketing, shall not "be considered or held to be violations of any law of the United States." Thus, contrary to petitioner's contention, the District Court obviously decided considerably more than the threshold question of whether the Norris-LaGuardia Act withdrew jurisdiction to grant federal injunctive relief in the circumstances of this case.

In my view, what the District Court decided in 1967 was that BLE had a federally protected right to picket at the Moncrief Yard and, by necessary implication, that this right could not be subverted by resort to state proceedings. I find it difficult indeed to ascribe to the District Judge the views that the Court now says he held, namely, that ACL, merely by marching across the street to the state court, could render wholly nugatory the District Judge's declaration that BLE had a federally protected right to strike at the Moncrief Yard.

* * *

The Court seeks to bolster its own reading of the District Court's 1967 and 1969 orders by finding them "somewhat ambiguous" and then by referring to the arguments of counsel before that court and the state court both in 1967 and 1969. In the first place, it should be noted that the argument of counsel is not always a sure guide to the interpretation of a subsequent judicial decree or opinion, because it not infrequently happens, in this Court as well as others, that a decision is based on premises not elaborated by counsel. Indeed, occasionally a decision is grounded on a theory not even suggested by counsel's argument.

In any event, I believe that the Court has misinterpreted the argument of counsel in the lower courts. While I do not find the various proceedings below entirely free of confusion with respect to BLE's legal theory, there appear to be at least two strands to its argument. To be sure, BLE did contend, particularly in the state proceedings, that our decision in *Jacksonville Terminal* was controlling on the merits.[2] As I read the record, however, BLE also argued that the state injunction should either

---

[2] It is hardly surprising that BLE emphasized the *Jacksonville Terminal* decision in the state proceedings to dissolve the state injunction, and this reliance is hardly inconsistent with the position that the federal court in 1967 had authoritatively delineated BLE's federally protected right to strike at the Moncrief Yard. BLE may well have thought that its contention that *Jacksonville Terminal* was controlling on the issue of pre-emption would carry more weight with the state court than the alternative position that the protected character of the BLE picketing had been previously determined by the Federal District Court.

be dissolved or enjoined so that it would not interfere with the federal court's 1967 decree. Thus, in moving for a preliminary injunction against the state court proceedings, BLE relied both upon *Jacksonville Terminal* and upon the power of the District Court to issue the injunction "to protect and effectuate the judgment of this Court dated April 26, 1967."

Furthermore, both in support of the motion for a preliminary injunction and during oral argument in the District Court, BLE relied extensively upon *Capital Service, Inc. v. NLRB* and *United Indus. Workers of the Seafarers Int'l Union v. Board of Trustees of Galveston Wharves* ***. A consideration of the factual context of the latter case is instructive in understanding BLE's position below. In *Galveston Wharves* the union fully complied with the pertinent provisions of the Railway Labor Act, but, because the employer had refused to bargain concerning a "major" dispute, the union was free to strike. Meanwhile the employer obtained from a state court an injunction against any picketing on or near its premises. The Federal District Court ordered the parties to bargain and enjoined the employer from giving effect to, or seeking enforcement of, the state court injunction. The Court of Appeals for the Fifth Circuit affirmed the granting of injunctive relief on the ground that this action was within the § 2283 exception relating to the effectuation of federal court judgments. The Court of Appeals held that the union had a right to strike under the Railway Labor Act and that that right could not be frustrated or interfered with by state court injunctions. Similarly, BLE argued below that resort to state equitable proceedings should not be permitted to undermine the District Court's prior determination that BLE had a right to picket at the Moncrief Yard. As its injunction order indicates, the District Court was persuaded by BLE's argument. After the federal injunction was issued, in proceedings brought by ACL to stay the effectiveness of the order, BLE adhered to its position that the state injunction, if not enjoined, would nullify the District Court's 1967 order delineating the rights of the parties. Again BLE relied upon the intervening decision in *Jacksonville Terminal,* but it did so primarily in support of the contention that the 1967 order was proper insofar as it prohibited state court interference with the picketing at the Moncrief Yard. In essence, BLE argued that the 1967 order had correctly anticipated *Jacksonville Terminal.*

In the state courts BLE adopted a position entirely consistent with the foregoing. For example, in opposing ACL's application for a temporary injunction against the picketing, BLE contended that the District Court had previously held that under controlling federal law BLE's right to picket had been established, that this declaration of rights was res judicata in the state proceedings, and consequently that state proscription of the picketing was improper.

In sum, to the extent that the argument of counsel is an interpretive guide to what the District Court actually decided in its 1967 and 1969 orders, the Court's conclusion that the record "conclusively shows that neither the parties themselves nor the District Court construed the 1967 order" to preclude resort to state remedies to prohibit the Moncrief Yard picketing is wholly erroneous. And, quite apart from counsel's argument, it is apparent that the District Judge viewed his own 1967 order as delineating a federally protected right for the BLE picketing in question. Whether the District Court's anticipation of *Jacksonville Terminal* was correct in the circumstances of the present case is not now before us. But if the 1967 order is so understood, it is undeniably clear that the subsequent injunction against the state proceedings was both necessary and appropriate to preserve the integrity of the 1967 order.

* * * Unquestionably § 2283 manifests a general design on the part of Congress that federal courts not precipitately interfere with the orderly determination of controversies in state proceedings. However, this policy of nonintervention is by no means absolute, as the explicit exceptions in § 2283 make entirely clear. Thus, § 2283 itself evinces a congressional intent that resort to state proceedings not be permitted to undermine a prior judgment of a federal court. But that is exactly what has occurred in the present case. Indeed, the federal determination that BLE may picket at the Moncrief Yard has been rendered wholly ineffective by the state injunction. The crippling restrictions that the Court today places upon the power of the District Court to effectuate and protect its orders are totally inconsistent with both the plain language of § 2283 and the policies underlying that statutory provision.

Accordingly, I would affirm the judgment of the Court of Appeals sustaining the District Court's grant of injunctive relief against petitioner's giving effect to, or availing itself of, the benefit of the state court injunction.

Notes and Questions

1. Although the original Anti-Injunction Act was passed in 1793, there is little indication of a specific stimulus for it, unlike the Eleventh Amendment, which was a direct reaction to *Chisholm v. Georgia*, 2 U.S. (2 Dall.) 419, 1 L.Ed. 440 (1793). Professor Charles Warren suggested that *Chisholm* also underlay the Anti-Injunction Act, noting that it was passed only two weeks after *Chisholm*. Charles Warren, *Federal and State Court Interference,* 43 HARV.L.REV. 345, 347-48 (1930). This is at least questionable; *Chisholm* did not involve a federal injunction against a state proceeding, but rather a federal money judgment. Other scholars have argued that the statute was more likely stimulated by complaints from Justices about the rigors of circuit riding and was an effort to reduce the burdens on the federal judiciary. Telford Taylor & Everett Willis, *The Power of Federal Courts to Enjoin Proceedings in State Courts,* 42 YALE L.J. 1169, 1170 (1933). The Supreme Court has been less willing to speculate. "The precise origins of the legislation are shrouded in obscurity." *Mitchum v. Foster,* 407 U.S. 225, 232, 92 S.Ct. 2151, 2156, 32 L.Ed.2d 705, 711 (1972).

2. *Atlantic Coast Line* is difficult to understand unless one grasps the

possible bases for the original district court decision of the Railroad's motion for an injunction. Did the court refuse because federal statutes forbade the requested injunction or because the union enjoyed some positive entitlement? What difference does it make?

3. Although Justice Black spends much of the *Atlantic Coastline* opinion discussing technical questions as to whether the case comes within various exceptions to the Anti-Injunction Act, it is clear that something more fundamental is bothering him. After *Jacksonville Terminal* in 1969, the union asked the state court to dissolve the Moncrief Yard injunction. When the state court refused, the union returned to federal court and asked that court to enjoin enforcement of the state injunction. What is it about this procedural posture that upsets Justice Black? When the district court issued the injunction, what role did it appear to be playing *vis-à-vis* the state trial court? What is wrong with that?

4. The Anti-Injunction Act expresses Congress's general policy against federal interference with state proceedings. It is important to consider separately the three exceptions to the Act's sweep.

a) The "expressly authorized" exception seems straightforward, and indeed might be but for the Supreme Court's application of it. For example, the Federal Interpleader Act, 28 U.S.C.A. § 2361, specifically permits federal courts to enjoin competing state proceedings and to enjoin litigants from initiating potentially competing proceedings. The Court, however, has declined to require that Congress pass "read my lips" statutes that explicitly authorize an injunction against a state proceeding in order to invoke this exception to § 2283. *Amalgamated Clothing Workers v. Richman Brothers,* 348 U.S. 511, 75 S.Ct. 452, 99 L.Ed. 600 (1955), noted that a statute need not specifically refer to § 2283 to qualify as an express authorization.

The most famous decision regarding this exception is undoubtedly *Mitchum v. Foster,* 407 U.S. 225, 92 S.Ct. 2151, 32 L.Ed.2d 705 (1972), which held that the Civil Rights Act of 1871, 42 U.S.C.A. § 1983, must be within the exception because the remedy Congress created "could be frustrated if the federal proceeding were not empowered to enjoin a state court proceeding." The Court elaborated its approach to the Anti-Injunction Act.

> Despite the seemingly uncompromising language of the anti-injunction statute prior to 1948, the Court soon recognized that exceptions must be made to its blanket prohibition if * * * other Acts of Congress were to be given their intended scope. So it was that, in addition to the bankruptcy law exception that Congress explicitly recognized in 1874, the Court through the years found that federal courts were empowered to enjoin state court proceedings, despite the anti-injunction statute, in carrying out the will of Congress under at least six other federal laws. These covered a broad spectrum of congressional action: (1) legislation providing for removal of litigation from state to federal courts, (2) legislation limiting the liability of ship owners, (3) legislation providing for federal interpleader actions, (4) legislation conferring federal jurisdiction over farm mortgages, (5) legislation governing federal habeas corpus proceedings, and (6) legislation providing for control of

prices.

In addition to the exceptions to the anti-injunction statute found to be embodied in these various Acts of Congress, the Court recognized other "implied" exceptions to the blanket prohibition of the anti-injunction statute. One was an "*in rem* " exception, allowing a federal court to enjoin a state court proceeding in order to protect its jurisdiction of a *res* over which it had first acquired jurisdiction. Another was a "relitigation" exception, permitting a federal court to enjoin relitigation in a state court of issues already decided in federal litigation. Still a third exception, more recently developed[,] permits a federal injunction of state court proceedings when the plaintiff in the federal court is the United States itself, or a federal agency asserting "superior federal interests."

In *Toucey v. New York Life Ins. Co.,* the Court in 1941 issued an opinion casting considerable doubt upon the approach to the anti-injunction statute reflected in its previous decisions. The Court's opinion expressly disavowed the "relitigation" exception to the statute, and emphasized generally the importance of recognizing the statute's basic directive "of 'hands off' by the federal courts in the use of the injunction to stay litigation in a state court." The congressional response to *Toucey* was the enactment in 1948 of the anti-injunction statute in its present form in 28 U.S.C. § 2283, which, as the Reviser's Note makes evident, served not only to overrule the specific holding of *Toucey,* but to restore "the basic law as generally understood and interpreted prior to the *Toucey* decision."

We proceed, then, upon the understanding that in determining whether § 1983 comes within the "expressly authorized" exception of the anti-injunction statute, the criteria to be applied are those reflected in the Court's decisions prior to *Toucey.* * * * [I]t is evident that in order to qualify under the "expressly authorized" exception of the anti-injunction statute, a federal law need not contain an express reference to that injunction statute. As the Court has said, "no prescribed formula is required; an authorization need not expressly refer to § 2283." Indeed, none of the previously recognized statutory exceptions contains any such reference. Secondly, a federal law need not expressly authorize an injunction of a state court proceeding in order to qualify as an exception. Three of the six previously recognized statutory exceptions contain no such authorization. Thirdly, it is clear that, in order to qualify as an "expressly authorized" exception to the anti-injunction statute, an Act of Congress must have created a specific and uniquely federal right or remedy, enforceable in a federal court of equity, that could be frustrated if the federal court were not empowered to enjoin a state court proceeding. This is not to say that in order to come within the exception an Act of Congress must, on its face and in every one of its provisions, be totally incompatible with the prohibition of the anti-injunction statute. The test, rather, is whether an Act of Congress, clearly creating a federal right or remedy enforceable in a federal court of equity, could be given its intended scope only by the stay of a state court proceeding.

Thus, after *Mitchum,* the way might have seemed open for the federal court in any action brought under § 1983 to enjoin pending state proceedings. However, the doctrine of *Younger* abstention, discussed later in this chapter, greatly blunts *Mitchum*'s effect.

Professor Redish strongly criticizes *Mitchum,* ridiculing the Court's reasoning. "In what may be one of the most bizarre contortions of Supreme Court analysis, the Court in *Mitchum* found section 1983 to be an 'implied' express exception (an oxymoron if ever there was one) * * * ." Martin H. Redish, *Abstention, Separation of Powers, and the Limits of the Judicial Function,* 94 YALE L.J. 71, 87 (1984). He does recognize, however, that the *Mitchum* interpretation seems firmly entrenched. Martin H. Redish, *Judicial Parity, Litigant Choice, and Democratic Theory: A Comment on Federal Jurisdiction and Constitutional Rights,* 36 U.C.L.A.L.REV. 329, 343 n.53 (1988). If the Court were to change the *Mitchum* interpretation and require explicit language authorizing an injunction against state proceedings, what problem would that cause for Congress?

b) As Justice Black's opinion makes clear, the Court will narrowly construe the jurisdictional exception. Unless a state proceeding threatens in some sense to *defeat* federal jurisdiction, this exception does not apply. Thus, merely parallel litigation in the state courts is insufficient. Only where jurisdiction in one system is fatally incompatible with jurisdiction in the other may an injunction issue. It is well established, for example, that a federal or state court first obtaining jurisdiction by seizure of property may secure its jurisdiction by enjoining a court of the other system from hearing a case involving the same property. *Donovan v. City of Dallas,* 377 U.S. 408, 84 S.Ct. 1579, 12 L.Ed.2d 409 (1964); *Toucey v. New York Life Insurance Co.,* 314 U.S. 118, 62 S.Ct. 139, 86 L.Ed. 100 (1941); *Kline v. Burke Construction Co.,* 260 U.S. 226, 43 S.Ct. 79, 67 L.Ed. 226 (1922). Can you think of another class of cases where a state court, once having had jurisdiction of a case, could be enjoined under this exception if it continued to exercise jurisdiction?

c) The judgments exception is broader than the jurisdictional exception. The exception seeks to prevent harassment of successful federal litigants and to protect the finality of federal judgments. It permits the federal courts to issue injunctions to prevent the state courts from relitigating issues that have already been litigated and decided in federal court. In effect, it permits the federal courts to make sure that their judgments have preclusive effect.

5. In *County of Imperial v. Munoz,* 449 U.S. 54, 101 S.Ct. 289, 66 L.Ed.2d 258 (1980), the Court affirmed that the Anti-Injunction Act does not prevent a federal constitutional challenge to a state statute, even a challenge seeking injunctive relief, merely because state litigation is pending between other parties. Thus, the Anti-Injunction Act has no effect upon a "stranger" to the pending state action. Does the Court's position have the potential of diminishing the protective function of the Act? If so, is that a problem to be addressed by the Court or by Congress?

6. The Anti-Injunction Act's relationship with § 1983 raises questions

about the role of congressional intent in the interpretation of statutes. At the outset, is it likely that the Congress that initially passed the Act would have intended unexpressed exceptions? On the other hand, is it likely that the Reconstruction Congress that passed the Civil Rights Act of 1871 would have made access to the federal courts turn upon whether there was a pending state proceeding? Given that "[t]he very purpose of § 1983 was to interpose the federal courts between the States and the people as guardians of the people's federal rights * * *," *Mitchum v. Foster,* 407 U.S. 225, 242, 92 S.Ct. 2151, 2161-62, 32 L.Ed.2d 705, 717 (1972), is it likely that Congress would have left in place a statute that is premised upon deference to and respect for the state courts? On the other hand, Congress recodified the Act in 1948, specifically overruling the Court's declaration that a federal court could not enjoin a state proceeding to protect its own judgment. Why did it not make clear, one way or the other, whether the Civil Rights Act of 1871 was an exception to the prohibition?

7. Congress passed a much more specific prohibition of federal court interference with state government in the Johnson Act of 1934, 28 U.S.C.A. § 1342, which bars federal injunction of public utility rates. It provides some leeway to the federal courts, since it contains exceptions for cases where the state's order interferes with interstate commerce, where there has not been reasonable notice and an opportunity to be heard prior to setting the rate, and where there is no effective state court remedy.

8. In 1937, Congress passed the Tax Injunction Act, 28 U.S.C.A. § 1341, prohibiting federal judicial interference with the state *executive* function of collecting taxes as long as there is "a plain, speedy and efficient remedy" available in state court. The federalism implications of the Tax Injunction Act are too clear to require discussion, but it does present problems determining what is a tax, what qualifies as an effective state remedy, what federal court actions are unauthorized interference, and whether there are any other exceptions to the general noninterference policy Congress has expressed. For an excellent discussion of these aspects of the statute, see ERWIN CHEMERINSKY, FEDERAL JURISDICTION § 11.3, at 753-64 (5th ed. 2007).

9. Both the Tax Injunction Act and the Johnson Act concern federal judicial interference with state executive functions. Does the fact that Congress specified these two situations connote that federal intervention in all other situations is permissible?

10. If you were designing a policy relating to the ability of federal or state courts directly to affect the operations of branches of the other system, how would you structure it?

C. JUDICIAL DOCTRINES OF RESTRAINT

1. Exhaustion

Monroe v. Pape, 365 U.S. 167, 81, S.Ct. 473, 5 L.Ed.2d 492 (1961) (presented at page 510), held that litigants need not exhaust state judicial remedies before bringing an action in federal court under 42 U.S.C.A. § 1983. But what about state administrative remedies? The next case addresses that issue.

PATSY v. BOARD OF REGENTS
Supreme Court of the United States, 1982.
457 U.S. 496, 102 S.Ct. 2557, 73 L.Ed.2d 172.

JUSTICE MARSHALL delivered the opinion of the Court.

This case presents the question whether exhaustion of state administrative remedies is a prerequisite to an action under 42 U.S.C. § 1983. Petitioner Georgia Patsy filed this action, alleging that her employer, Florida International University (FIU), had denied her employment opportunities solely on the basis of her race and sex. By a divided vote, the United States Court of Appeals for the Fifth Circuit found that petitioner was required to exhaust "adequate and appropriate" administrative remedies, and remanded the case to the District Court to consider the adequacy of the administrative procedures. We granted certiorari, and reverse the decision of the Court of Appeals.

I

Petitioner alleges that even though she is well qualified and has received uniformly excellent performance evaluations from her supervisors, she has been rejected for more than 13 positions at FIU. She further claims that FIU has unlawfully filled positions through intentional discrimination on the basis of race and sex. She seeks declaratory and injunctive relief or, in the alternative, damages.

The United States District Court for the Southern District of Florida granted respondent Board of Regents' motion to dismiss because petitioner had not exhausted available administrative remedies. On appeal, a panel of the Court of Appeals reversed, and remanded the case for further proceedings. The full court then granted respondent's petition for rehearing and vacated the panel decision.

The Court of Appeals reviewed numerous opinions of this Court holding that exhaustion of administrative remedies was not required, and concluded that these cases did not preclude the application of a "flexible" exhaustion rule. After canvassing the policy arguments in favor of an exhaustion requirement, the Court of Appeals decided that a § 1983 plaintiff could be required to exhaust administrative remedies if the following minimum conditions are met: (1) an orderly system of review or appeal is provided by statute or agency rule; (2) the agency can grant relief more or less commensurate with the claim; (3) relief is available within a reasonable period of time; (4) the procedures are fair, are not unduly burdensome, and are not used to harass or discourage those with legitimate claims; and (5) interim relief is available, in appropriate cases, to prevent irreparable injury and to preserve the plaintiff's rights during the administrative process. Where these minimum standards are met, a court must further consider the particular administrative scheme, the nature of the plaintiff's interest, and the values served by the exhaustion doctrine in order to determine whether exhaustion should be required. The Court of Appeals remanded the case to the District Court to determine whether exhaustion would be appropriate in this case.

II

The question whether exhaustion of administrative remedies should ever be required in a § 1983 action has prompted vigorous debate and disagreement. Our resolution of this issue, however, is made much easier because we are not writing on a clean slate. * * *

Respondent suggests that our prior precedents do not control our decision today, arguing that these cases can be distinguished on their facts or that this Court did not "fully" consider the question whether exhaustion should be required. This contention need not detain us long. Beginning with *McNeese v. Board of Education* (1963), we have on numerous occasions rejected the argument that a § 1983 action should be dismissed where the plaintiff has not exhausted state administrative remedies. Respondent may be correct in arguing that several of these decisions could have been based on traditional exceptions to the exhaustion doctrine. Nevertheless, this Court has stated categorically that exhaustion is not a prerequisite to an action under § 1983, and we have not deviated from that position in the 19 years since *McNeese*. Therefore, we do not address the question presented in this case as one of first impression.

III

Respondent argues that we should reconsider these decisions and adopt the Court of Appeals' exhaustion rule. This Court has never announced a definitive formula for determining whether prior decisions should be overruled or reconsidered. However, in *Monell v. New York City Dept. of Social Services,* we articulated four factors that should be considered. Two of these factors—whether the decisions in question misconstrued the meaning of the statute as revealed in its legislative history and whether overruling these decisions would be inconsistent with more recent expressions of congressional intent—are particularly relevant to our decision today.[3] Both concern legislative purpose, which is of paramount importance in the exhaustion context because Congress is vested with the power to prescribe the basic procedural scheme under which claims may be heard in federal courts. Of course, courts play an important role in determining the limits of an exhaustion requirement and may impose such a requirement even where Congress has not ex-

---

[3] The other factors discussed in *Monell*—whether the decisions in question constituted a departure from prior decisions and whether overruling these decisions would frustrate legitimate reliance on their holdings—do not support overruling these decisions. *McNeese* was not a departure from prior decisions—this Court had not previously addressed the application of the exhaustion rule to § 1983 actions. Overruling these decisions might injure those § 1983 plaintiffs who had forgone or waived their state administrative remedies in reliance on these decisions.

pressly so provided. However, the initial question whether exhaustion is required should be answered by reference to congressional intent; and a court should not defer the exercise of jurisdiction under a federal statute unless it is consistent with that intent. Therefore, in deciding whether we should reconsider our prior decisions and require exhaustion of state administrative remedies, we look to congressional intent as reflected in the legislative history of the predecessor to § 1983 and in recent congressional activity in this area.

A

In determining whether our prior decisions misconstrued the meaning of § 1983, we begin with a review of the legislative history to § 1 of the Civil Rights Act of 1871, the precursor to § 1983. Although we recognize that the 1871 Congress did not expressly contemplate the exhaustion question, we believe that the tenor of the debates over § 1 supports our conclusion that exhaustion of administrative remedies in § 1983 actions should not be judicially imposed.

The Civil Rights Act of 1871, along with the Fourteenth Amendment it was enacted to enforce, were crucial ingredients in the basic alteration of our federal system accomplished during the Reconstruction Era. During that time, the Federal Government was clearly established as a guarantor of the basic federal rights of individuals against incursions by state power. As we recognized in *Mitchum v. Foster,* "[t]he very purpose of § 1983 was to interpose the federal courts between the States and the people, as guardians of the people's federal rights—to protect the people from unconstitutional action under color of state law, 'whether that action be executive, legislative, or judicial.' "

At least three recurring themes in the debates over § 1 cast serious doubt on the suggestion that requiring exhaustion of state administrative remedies would be consistent with the intent of the 1871 Congress. First, in passing § 1, Congress assigned to the federal courts a paramount role in protecting constitutional rights. * * *

The 1871 Congress intended § 1 to "throw open the doors of the United States courts" to individuals who were threatened with, or who had suffered, the deprivation of constitutional rights, and to provide these individuals immediate access to the federal courts notwithstanding any provision of state law to the contrary. * * *

A second theme in the debates further suggests that the 1871 Congress would not have wanted to impose an exhaustion requirement. A major factor motivating the expansion of federal jurisdiction through §§ 1 and 2 of the bill was the belief of the 1871 Congress that the state authorities had been unable or unwilling to protect the constitutional rights of individuals or to punish those who violated these rights. Of primary importance to the exhaustion question was the mistrust that the 1871 Congress held for the factfinding processes of state institutions. This Congress believed that federal courts would be less susceptible to local prejudice and to the existing defects in the factfinding processes of the state courts.[9] This perceived defect in the States' factfinding processes is particularly relevant to the question of exhaustion of administrative remedies: exhaustion rules are often applied in deference to the superior factfinding ability of the relevant administrative agency.

A third feature of the debates relevant to the exhaustion question is the fact that many legislators interpreted the bill to provide dual or concurrent forums in the state and federal system, enabling the plaintiff to choose the forum in which to seek relief. * * *

This legislative history supports the conclusion that our prior decisions, holding that exhaustion of state administrative remedies is not a prerequisite to an action under § 1983, did not misperceive the statutory intent: it seems fair to infer that the 1871 Congress did not intend that an individual be compelled in every case to exhaust state administrative remedies before filing an action under § 1 of the Civil Rights Act. We recognize, however, that drawing such a conclusion from this history alone is somewhat precarious: the 1871 Congress was not presented with the question of exhaustion of administrative remedies, nor was it aware of the potential role of state administrative agencies. Therefore, we do not rely exclusively on this legislative history in deciding the question presented here. Congress addressed the question of exhaustion under § 1983 when it recently enacted 42 U.S.C. § 1997e. The legislative history of § 1997e provides strong evidence of congressional intent on this issue.

B

The Civil Rights of Institutionalized Persons Act was enacted primarily to ensure that the United States Attorney General has "legal standing to enforce existing constitutional rights and Federal statutory rights of institutionalized persons." In § 1997e, Congress also created a specific, limited exhaustion requirement for adult prisoners bringing actions pursuant to § 1983. Section 1997e and its legislative history demonstrate that Congress understood that exhaustion is not generally required in § 1983 actions, and that it decided to carve out only a narrow exception to this rule. A judicially imposed exhaustion requirement would be inconsistent with Congress' decision to adopt § 1997e and would usurp policy judgments that Congress has reserved for itself.

* * *

With the understanding that exhaustion generally is not required, Congress decided to adopt the limited exhaustion requirement of § 1997e in order to relieve the burden on the federal courts by diverting certain prisoner petitions back through state and local institutions, and also to

---

[9] Opponents viewed the bill as a declaration of mistrust for state tribunals. Representative McHenry found particularly offensive the removal of the fact-finding function from the local institutions.

encourage the States to develop appropriate grievance procedures. Implicit in this decision is Congress' conclusion that the no-exhaustion rule should be left standing with respect to other § 1983 suits.

A judicially imposed exhaustion requirement would also be inconsistent with the extraordinarily detailed exhaustion scheme embodied in § 1997e. Section 1997e carves out a narrow exception to the general no-exhaustion rule to govern certain prisoner claims, and establishes a procedure to ensure that the administrative remedies are adequate and effective. The exhaustion requirement is expressly limited to § 1983 actions brought by an adult convicted of a crime. Section 1997e(b)(1) instructs the Attorney General to "promulgate minimum standards for the development and implementation of a plain, speedy, and effective system" of administrative remedies, and § 1997e(b)(2) specifies certain minimum standards that must be included. A court may require exhaustion of administrative remedies only if "the Attorney General has certified or the court has determined that such administrative remedies are in substantial compliance with the minimum acceptable standards promulgated under subsection (b)." Before exhaustion may be required, the court must further conclude that it "would be appropriate and in the interests of justice." Finally, in those § 1983 actions meeting all the statutory requirements for exhaustion, the district court may not dismiss the case, but may only "continue such case for a period of not to exceed ninety days in order to require exhaustion." This detailed scheme is inconsistent with discretion to impose, on an *ad hoc* basis, a judicially developed exhaustion rule in other cases.

Congress hoped that § 1997e would improve prison conditions by stimulating the development of successful grievance mechanisms. To further this purpose, Congress provided for the deferral of the exercise of federal jurisdiction over certain § 1983 claims only on the condition that the state prisons develop adequate procedures. This purpose would be frustrated by judicial discretion to impose exhaustion generally: the States would have no incentive to adopt grievance procedures capable of certification, because prisoner § 1983 cases could be diverted to state administrative remedies in any event.

In sum, the exhaustion provisions of the Act make sense, and are not superfluous, only if exhaustion could not be required before its enactment and if Congress intended to carve out a narrow exception to this no-exhaustion rule. The legislative history of § 1997e demonstrates that Congress has taken the approach of carving out specific exceptions to the general rule that federal courts cannot require exhaustion under § 1983. It is not our province to alter the balance struck by Congress in establishing the procedural framework for bringing actions under § 1983.

C

Respondent and the Court of Appeals argue that exhaustion of administrative remedies should be required because it would further various policies. They argue that an exhaustion requirement would lessen the perceived burden that § 1983 actions impose on federal courts; would further the goal of comity and improve federal-state relations by post-poning federal-court review until after the state administrative agency had passed on the issue; and would enable the agency, which presuma-bly has expertise in the area at issue, to enlighten the federal court's ul-timate decision.

As we noted earlier, policy considerations alone cannot justify judi-cially imposed exhaustion unless exhaustion is consistent with congres-sional intent. Furthermore, as the debates over incorporating the ex-haustion requirement in § 1997e demonstrate, the relevant policy con-siderations do not invariably point in one direction, and there is vehe-ment disagreement over the validity of the assumptions underlying many of them. The very difficulty of these policy considerations, and Congress' superior institutional competence to pursue this debate, sug-gest that legislative not judicial solutions are preferable.

Beyond the policy issues that must be resolved in deciding whether to require exhaustion, there are equally difficult questions concerning the design and scope of an exhaustion requirement. These questions include how to define those categories of § 1983 claims in which exhaus-tion might be desirable; how to unify and centralize the standards for judging the kinds of administrative procedures that should be ex-hausted; what tolling requirements and time limitations should be adopted;[17] what is the res judicata and collateral estoppel effect of par-ticular administrative determinations; what consequences should attach to the failure to comply with procedural requirements of administrative proceedings; and whether federal courts could grant necessary interim injunctive relief and hold the action pending exhaustion, or proceed to judgment without requiring exhaustion even though exhaustion might otherwise be required, where the relevant administrative agency is ei-ther powerless or not inclined to grant such interim relief. These and similar questions might be answered swiftly and surely by legislation, but would create costly, remedy-delaying, and court-burdening litigation if answered incrementally by the judiciary in the context of diverse con-stitutional claims relating to thousands of different state agencies.

The very variety of claims, claimants, and state agencies involved in § 1983 cases argues for congressional consideration of the myriad of pol-icy considerations, and may explain why Congress, in deciding whether to require exhaustion in certain § 1983 actions brought by adult prison-ers, carved out such a narrow, detailed exception to the no-exhaustion rule. After full debate and consideration of the various policy argu-ments, Congress adopted § 1997e, taking the largest class of § 1983 ac-tions and constructing an exhaustion requirement that differs substan-

---

[17] Unless the doctrine that statutes of limitations are not tolled pending exhaustion were overruled, a judicially imposed exhaustion requirement might result in the effective repeal of § 1983. Congress avoided this problem in § 1997e by directing the court to merely continue the case for a period not to exceed 90 days.

tially from the *McKart*-type standard urged by respondent and adopted by the Court of Appeals. It is not for us to say whether Congress will or should create a similar scheme for other categories of § 1983 claims or whether Congress will or should adopt an altogether different exhaustion requirement for nonprisoner § 1983 claims.[19]

IV

Based on the legislative histories of both § 1983 and § 1997e, we conclude that exhaustion of state administrative remedies should not be required as a prerequisite to bringing an action pursuant to § 1983. We decline to overturn our prior decisions holding that such exhaustion is not required. The decision of the Court of Appeals is reversed, and the case is remanded for proceedings consistent with this opinion.

It is so ordered.

JUSTICE WHITE, concurring in part.

I fully agree with the Court that our frequent and unequivocal statements on exhaustion cannot be explained or distinguished away as the Fifth Circuit attempted to do. For nearly 20 years and on at least 10 occasions, this Court has clearly held that no exhaustion of administrative remedies is required in a § 1983 suit. Whether or not this initially was a wise choice, these decisions are *stare decisis,* and in a statutory case, a particularly strong showing is required that we have misread the relevant statute and its history. I have no difficulty in concluding that on the issue of exhaustion, unlike the question of municipal immunity faced in *Monell v. New York City Dept. of Social Services,* the Court has not previously misapprehended the meaning of the 1871 debates in rejecting an exhaustion rule in *McNeese v. Board of Education* (1963) and

---

[19] The question was posed from the bench at oral argument whether the Eleventh Amendment might bar this suit on the ground that the Board of Regents is an arm of the State for purposes of the Eleventh Amendment. The District Court dismissed this action on the pleadings, and no Eleventh Amendment issue had been raised. The Board of Regents first raised this issue in its brief to the original panel on appeal, but did not argue it in its brief on rehearing en banc. Neither the original panel nor the en banc court addressed this issue. Although the State mentioned a possible Eleventh Amendment defense in its response in opposition to the petition for certiorari, it did not brief the issue or press it at oral argument. Indeed, counsel for respondent urged that we affirm the Court of Appeals solely on its exhaustion holding. We have noted that "the Eleventh Amendment defense sufficiently partakes of the nature of a jurisdictional bar" that it may be raised by the State for the first time on appeal. However, because of the importance of state law in analyzing Eleventh Amendment questions and because the State may, under certain circumstances, waive this defense, we have never held that it is jurisdictional in the sense that it must be raised and decided by this Court on its own motion. Where, as here, the Board of Regents expressly requested that we address the exhaustion question and not pass on its potential Eleventh Amendment immunity, and, as a consequence, the parties have not briefed the issue, we deem it appropriate to address the issue that was raised and decided below and vigorously pressed in this Court. Nothing in this opinion precludes the Board of Regents from raising its Eleventh Amendment claim on remand. The District Court is in the best position to address in the first instance the competing questions of fact and state law necessary to resolve the Eleventh Amendment issue, and at this stage it has the discretion to permit amendments to the pleadings that might cure any potential Eleventh Amendment problems.

adhering to that position ever since. Our precedents and the legislative history are sufficient to support reversal, and I accordingly join the judgment in all but Part III-B of the opinion of the Court.

In Part III-B, the Court unnecessarily and unwisely ventures further to find support where none may be had. The wisdom of a general no-exhaustion rule in § 1983 suits was not at issue when Congress considered and passed the Civil Rights of Institutionalized Persons Act. As Justice Powell persuasively points out in his dissenting opinion, and as reflected in the title of the Act, congressional attention was narrowly focused on procedures concerning the legal rights of prisoners and other institutionalized persons. Unsurprisingly, the legislation which emerged addressed only the specific problem under investigation; it indicates neither approval of a no-exhaustion rule nor an intent to preclude us from reconsidering the issue.

As the Court acknowledges, the policy arguments cut in both directions. The Court concludes that "the very difficulty of these policy considerations, and Congress' superior institutional competence * * * suggest that legislative not judicial decisions are preferable." To be sure, exhaustion is a statutory issue and the dispositive word on the matter belongs to Congress. It does not follow, however, that, were the issue not foreclosed by earlier decisions, we would be institutionally incompetent to formulate an exhaustion rule. The lack of an exhaustion requirement in § 1983 actions is itself an exception to the general rule, judicially formulated, that exhaustion of administrative remedies is required in a civil action. Unlike other statutory questions, exhaustion is "a rule of judicial administration," and unless Congress directs otherwise, rightfully subject to crafting by judges. Our resolution of this case as governed by *stare decisis,* reinforced by the legislative history of § 1983, should not be taken as undercutting the general exhaustion principle of long standing. The result today is also fully consistent with our decisions that a defendant in a civil or administrative enforcement proceeding may not enjoin and sidetrack that proceeding by resorting to a § 1983 action in federal court, and that a federal action should be stayed pending determination of state-law issues central to the constitutional dispute. On this understanding, I join all but Part III-B of the opinion of the Court.*

---

* In my view, this case does not present a serious Eleventh Amendment issue. The Florida statute authorizing suits against the Board of Regents is clear on its face. I see no reason to read a broad waiver to sue and be sued in "all courts of law and equity" as meaning all but federal courts. Nor am I aware of anything in Florida law that suggests a more limited meaning was intended than indicated by the unequivocal terms of the statute. Certainly, none of our cases have gone so far as to hold that federal courts must be expressly mentioned for an effective Eleventh Amendment waiver. The statutes at issue in cases recited by Justice Powell presented more equivocal embodiments of state intent. * * * Thus, while I do not object to the Court's leaving the Eleventh Amendment issue for further consideration by the lower courts—at least where, as here, there is no logical priority in resolving Eleventh Amendment immunity before exhaustion—I find the issue sufficiently clear to be answered here and now. The statute means what it says.

JUSTICE POWELL, with whom THE CHIEF JUSTICE joins as to Part II, dissenting.

The Court holds that the limitations on federal judicial power embodied in the Eleventh Amendment and in the doctrine of sovereign immunity are not jurisdictional. I consider this holding to be a serious departure from established constitutional doctrine.

I dissent also from the Court's rejection of the rule of "flexible" exhaustion of state administrative remedies developed and stated persuasively by the Court of Appeals for the Fifth Circuit, sitting en banc. In disagreeing with the 17 judges of the Court of Appeals who adopted the flexible exhaustion principle, this Court places mistaken reliance on the Civil Rights of Institutionalized Persons Act. I disagree with both portions of the Court's holding and therefore dissent.

* * *

II. Exhaustion of Remedies.

In view of my belief that this case should be dismissed on jurisdictional grounds, I address the exhaustion question only briefly. Seventeen judges joined in the Court of Appeals' persuasive opinion adopting a rule of "flexible" exhaustion of administrative remedies in § 1983 suits. Other Courts of Appeals have adopted a similar rule. The opinion for the en banc court carefully reviewed the exhaustion doctrine in general and as applied to § 1983 actions. It found that the prior decisions of this Court did not clearly decide the question. And it concluded that the exhaustion of adequate and appropriate state administrative remedies would promote the achievement of the rights protected by § 1983.

I agree with the Court of Appeals' opinion. The requirement that a § 1983 plaintiff exhaust adequate state administrative remedies was the accepted rule of law until quite recently. The rule rests on sound considerations. It does not defeat federal-court jurisdiction, it merely defers it. It permits the States to correct violations through their own procedures, and it encourages the establishment of such procedures. It is consistent with the principles of comity that apply whenever federal courts are asked to review state action or supersede state proceedings.

Moreover, and highly relevant to the effective functioning of the overburdened federal court system, the rule conserves and supplements scarce judicial resources. In 1961, the year that *Monroe v. Pape* was decided, only 270 civil rights actions were begun in the federal district courts. In 1981, over 30,000 such suits were commenced. The result of this unprecedented increase in civil rights litigation is a heavy burden on the federal courts to the detriment of all federal-court litigants, including others who assert that their constitutional rights have been infringed.

The Court argues that past decisions of the Court categorically hold that there is no exhaustion requirement in § 1983 suits. But as the Court of Appeals demonstrates, and as the Court recognizes, many of these decisions can be explained as applications of traditional exceptions to the exhaustion requirement. Other decisions speak to the question in an offhand and conclusory fashion without full briefing and argument. Moreover, a categorical no-exhaustion rule would seem inconsistent with the decision in *Younger v. Harris* prescribing abstention when state criminal proceedings are pending. At least where administrative proceedings are pending, *Younger* would seem to suggest the appropriateness of exhaustion. Yet the Court today adopts a flat rule without exception.

The Court seeks to support its no-exhaustion rule with indications of congressional intent. Finding nothing directly on point in the history of the Civil Rights Act itself, the Court places primary reliance on the recent Civil Rights of Institutionalized Persons Act. This legislation was designed to authorize the Attorney General to initiate civil rights actions on behalf of institutionalized persons. The Act also placed certain limits on the existing authority of the Attorney General to intervene in suits begun by institutionalized persons. In addition, in § 1997e, the Act sets forth an exhaustion requirement but only for § 1983 claims brought by prisoners.

On the basis of the exhaustion provision in § 1997e, and remarks primarily by Representative Kastenmeier, the Court contends that Congress has endorsed a general no-exhaustion rule. The irony in this reasoning should be obvious. A principal concern that prompted the Department of Justice to support, and the Congress to adopt, § 1997e was the vast increase in § 1983 suits brought by state prisoners in federal courts. There has been a year-by-year increase in these suits since the mid-1960s. The increase in fiscal 1981 over fiscal 1980 was some 26%, resulting in a total of 15,639 such suits filed in 1981 as compared with 12,397 in 1980. The 1981 total constituted over 8.6% of the total federal district court civil docket. Although most of these cases present frivolous claims, many are litigated through the courts of appeals to this Court. The burden on the system fairly can be described as enormous with few, if any, benefits that would not be available in meritorious cases if exhaustion of appropriate state administrative remedies were required prior to any federal-court litigation. It was primarily this problem that prompted enactment of § 1997e.

Moreover, it is clear from the legislative history that Congress simply was not addressing the exhaustion problem in any general fashion. The concern focused on the problem of prisoner petitions. The new Act had a dual purpose in this respect. In addition to requiring prior exhaustion of adequate state remedies, Congress wished to authorize the Attorney General to act when necessary to protect the constitutional rights of prisoners, but at the same time minimize the need for federal action of any kind by requiring prior exhaustion.

* * *

In short, in enacting the Civil Rights of Institutionalized Persons Act

Congress was focusing on the powers of the Attorney General, and the particular question of prisoners' suits, not on the general question of exhaustion in § 1983 actions. Also revealing as to the limited purpose of § 1997e is Congress' consistent refusal to adopt legislation imposing a general no-exhaustion requirement. Thus, for example, in 1979, a bill was introduced into the Senate providing: "No court of the United States shall stay or dismiss any civil action brought under this Act on the ground that the party bringing such action failed to exhaust the remedies available in the courts or the administrative agencies of any State." The bill was never reported out of committee.

The requirement that plaintiffs exhaust available and adequate administrative remedies—subject to well-developed exceptions—is firmly established in virtually every area of the law. This is dictated in § 1983 actions by common sense, as well as by comity and federalism, where adequate state administrative remedies are available.

If the exhaustion question were properly before us, I would affirm the Court of Appeals.

Notes and Questions

1. a) *Patsy* remains substantially unchallenged as federal law, despite Justice Powell's dissent. *See, e.g., Wilder v. Virginia Hospital Association*, 496 U.S. 498, 110 S.Ct. 2510, 110 L.Ed.2d 455 (1990), reaffirming the absence of an exhaustion requirement for § 1983 cases, in an opinion by Justice Brennan joined by Justices White, Marshall, Blackmun and Stevens. Chief Justice Rehnquist, joined by Justices O'Connor, Scalia and Kennedy, dissented on another point but did not challenge the majority's reading of *Patsy*.

b) Does *Patsy* govern only federal § 1983 actions, or does it apply as well to § 1983 actions brought in state court? If the former, then an exhaustion requirement is more a function of the court system than of the cause of action. If the latter, there may be significant federalism problems inherent in the federal government telling the states that they cannot indulge their own exhaustion-of-administrative-remedy requirements if a § 1983 case appears in their courts. If state courts were allowed to require exhaustion of administrative remedies in § 1983 actions, would they be likely to do so? If states did impose such a requirement, what impact would that have on plaintiffs' choice of forum?

2. The majority argues that distrust of state fact-finding procedures also underlay the passage of § 1983 and counsels against an exhaustion requirement because of the possible res judicata effect of administrative findings. The Court might achieve the same result by demanding exhaustion but allowing trial *de novo* in the district court if the § 1983 plaintiff was not satisfied with the result of the administrative proceeding. What is the obvious drawback of this solution?

3. a) Justice Powell argues there should be an exhaustion requirement in § 1983 cases. Would it be legitimate for the Court to impose one? Is Justice Powell's position here inconsistent with his argument in *Cannon v. Uni-*

versity of Chicago, 441 U.S. 677, 99 S.Ct. 1946, 60 L.Ed.2d 560 (1979), that the Court should not create federal common law to supplement congressional statutes? After all, Congress has not suggested an exhaustion requirement for civil rights cases.

b) Is it likely that the Congress that created § 1983 or the Congress that enacted 28 U.S.C.A. § 1343 (the civil rights jurisdictional statute that dispensed with the general federal question jurisdiction statute's monetary floor) intended that civil rights plaintiffs, having thus been given a way to avoid state judicial processes, should nonetheless be required to submit to state administrative processes as a condition precedent to invoking the aid of the federal courts?

4. The dissent argues that an exhaustion requirement would encourage the states to develop sound administrative procedures. Would such procedures ultimately result in fewer federal lawsuits? One might argue that the absence of an exhaustion requirement provides more encouragement to develop sound administrative remedies, since in order to avoid federal court "interference," the states must now develop administrative procedures attractive enough to induce potential federal plaintiffs to forgo or defer going to federal court. Is this a realistic argument?

5. The majority says that "[b]eginning with *McNeese v. Board of Education* (1963), we have on numerous occasions rejected the argument that a § 1983 action should be dismissed where the plaintiff has not exhausted state administrative remedies * * * , and we have not deviated from that position in the 19 years since *McNeese*." In the full opinion, the majority cites several cases in the *McNeese* line. Why did the Court of Appeals impose an exhaustion requirement in the face of all this controlling precedent? Why does the Court choose to write a full opinion instead of summarily reversing?

6. The Eleventh Amendment battle among the Justices emerges clearly in *Patsy.* Note the dispute about whether the Amendment is jurisdictional, whether it is waivable, and what is required to waive its protection if a state wishes to do so. Justice White's position is particularly interesting. His footnote rejection of an Eleventh Amendment problem argues that "[t]he statute means what it says." Yet, only three years after *Patsy,* Justice White joined the majority in *Atascadero State Hospital v. Scanlon,* 473 U.S. 234, 105 S.Ct. 3142, 87 L.Ed.2d 171 (1985), holding that California had not waived its Eleventh Amendment immunity despite an apparent California constitutional waiver: "[s]uits may be brought against the State in such manner and in such courts as shall be directed by law." Are Justice White's positions inconsistent?

7. Remember that although the Court has construed § 1983 not to require exhaustion, other statutes may impose an exhaustion requirement with respect to particular kinds of suits. In *Woodford v. Ngo,* 548 U.S. 81, 126 S.Ct. 2378, 165 L.Ed.2d 368 (2006), the Court ruled that the Prison Litigation Reform Act, 110 Stat. 1321-71, as amended, 42 U.S.C. §§ 1997e *et seq.* is in that category. The Act provides, *inter alia*: "No action shall be brought with respect to prison conditions under section 1983 of this title, or any other Federal law, by a prisoner confined in any jail, prison, or other correctional

facility until such administrative remedies as are available are exhausted." Ngo challenged certain administrative actions taken against him by prison officials, actions that he alleged prevented him from participating in religious observances as a Catholic, but he did not file his prison grievance until more than fifteen days later, too late under prison rules. Ngo was unsuccessful in pursuing appellate administrative remedies in the California prison system and thereafter initiated a § 1983 action against the officials. The Court ruled that the PLRA precluded his action, construing the statutory requirement to require "proper" exhaustion, not simply, as Ngo and the dissenters argued, refraining from filing a federal action while administrative remedies remain available.

Justice Stevens, joined by Justices Souter and Ginsburg, dissented. He argued that if the state imposed a fifteen-day statute of limitations on an individual's entitlement to seek vindication of federal constitutional rights against state officials, it "would obviously be unenforceable in a federal court." In his view, the prison's fifteen-day rule effectively accomplished the same thing, and he was loath to conclude that Congress meant to enable states so to limit the time for asserting federal constitutional rights. He also suggested that if Congress had so intended, it would raise constitutional problems under the First Amendment's Petition Clause.

2.   *Abstention: The* Pullman *Doctrine*

RAILROAD COMMISSION v. PULLMAN CO.
Supreme Court of the United States, 1941.
312 U.S. 496, 61 S.Ct. 643, 85 L.Ed. 971.

MR. JUSTICE FRANKFURTER delivered the opinion of the Court.

In those sections of Texas where the local passenger traffic is slight, trains carry but one sleeping car. These trains, unlike trains having two or more sleepers, are without a Pullman conductor; the sleeper is in charge of a porter who is subject to the train conductor's control. As is well known, porters on Pullmans are colored and conductors are white. Addressing itself to this situation, the Texas Railroad Commission after due hearing ordered that "no sleeping car shall be operated on any line of railroad in the State of Texas * * * unless such cars are continuously in the charge of an employee * * * having the rank and position of Pullman conductor." Thereupon, the Pullman Company and the railroads affected brought this action in a federal district court to enjoin the Commission's order. Pullman porters were permitted to intervene as complainants, and Pullman conductors entered the litigation in support of the order. Three judges having been convened, the court enjoined enforcement of the order. From this decree, the case came here directly.

The Pullman Company and the railroads assailed the order as unauthorized by Texas law as well as violative of the Equal Protection, the Due Process and the Commerce Clauses of the Constitution. The intervening porters adopted these objections but mainly objected to the order as a discrimination against Negroes in violation of the Fourteenth Amendment.

The complaint of the Pullman porters undoubtedly tendered a substantial constitutional issue. It is more than substantial. It touches a sensitive area of social policy upon which the federal courts ought not to enter unless no alternative to its adjudication is open. Such constitutional adjudication plainly can be avoided if a definitive ruling on the state issue would terminate the controversy. It is therefore our duty to turn to a consideration of questions under Texas law.

The Commission found justification for its order in a Texas statute which we quote in the margin.[1] It is common ground that if the order is within the Commission's authority its subject matter must be included in the Commission's power to prevent "unjust discrimination * * * and to prevent any and all other abuses" in the conduct of railroads. Whether arrangements pertaining to the staffs of Pullman cars are covered by the Texas concept of "discrimination" is far from clear. What practices of the railroads may be deemed to be "abuses" subject to the Commission's correction is equally doubtful. Reading the Texas statutes and the Texas decisions as outsiders without special competence in Texas law, we would have little confidence in our independent judgment regarding the application of that law to the present situation. The lower court did deny that the Texas statutes sustained the Commission's assertion of power. And this represents the view of an able and experienced circuit judge of the circuit which includes Texas and of two capable district judges trained in Texas law. Had we or they no choice in the matter but to decide what is the law of the state, we should hesitate long before rejecting their forecast of Texas law. But no matter how seasoned the judgment of the district court may be, it cannot escape being a forecast rather than a determination. The last word on the meaning of Article 6445 of the Texas Civil Statutes, and therefore the last word on the statutory authority of the Railroad Commission in this case, belongs neither to us nor to the district court but to the supreme court of Texas. In this situation a federal court of equity is

---

[1] VERNON'S ANNO. TEXAS CIVIL STATUTES, art. 6445:

> Power and authority are hereby conferred upon the Railroad Commission of Texas over all railroads, and suburban, belt and terminal railroads, and over all public wharves, docks, piers, elevators, warehouses, sheds, tracks and other property used in connection therewith in this State, and over all persons, associations and corporations, private or municipal, owning or operating such railroad, wharf, dock, pier, elevator, warehouse, shed, track or other property to fix, and it is hereby made the duty of the said Commission to adopt all necessary rates, charges and regulations, to govern and regulate such railroads, persons, associations and corporations, and to correct abuses and prevent unjust discrimination in the rates, charges and tolls of such railroads, persons, associations and corporations, and to fix division of rates, charges and regulations between railroads and other utilities and common carriers where a division is proper and correct, and to prevent any and all other abuses in the conduct of their business and to do and perform such other duties and details in connection therewith as may be provided by law.

asked to decide an issue by making a tentative answer which may be displaced tomorrow by a state adjudication. The reign of law is hardly promoted if an unnecessary ruling of a federal court is thus supplanted by a controlling decision of a state court. The resources of equity are equal to an adjustment that will avoid the waste of a tentative decision as well as the friction of a premature constitutional adjudication.

An appeal to the chancellor, as we had occasion to recall only the other day, is an appeal to the "exercise of the sound discretion, which guides the determination of courts of equity." The history of equity jurisdiction is the history of regard for public consequences in employing the extraordinary remedy of the injunction. There have been as many and as variegated applications of this supple principle as the situations that have brought it into play. Few public interests have a higher claim upon the discretion of a federal chancellor than the avoidance of needless friction with state policies, whether the policy relates to the enforcement of the criminal law, * * * or the final authority of a state court to interpret doubtful regulatory laws of the state. These cases reflect a doctrine of abstention appropriate to our federal system whereby the federal courts, "exercising a wise discretion," restrain their authority because of "scrupulous regard for the rightful independence of the state governments" and for the smooth working of the federal judiciary * * *. This use of equitable powers is a contribution of the courts in furthering the harmonious relation between state and federal authority without the need of rigorous congressional restriction of those powers.

Regard for these important considerations of policy in the administration of federal equity jurisdiction is decisive here. If there was no warrant in state law for the Commission's assumption of authority there is an end of the litigation; the constitutional issue does not arise. The law of Texas appears to furnish easy and ample means for determining the Commission's authority. Article 6453 of the Texas Civil Statutes gives a review of such an order in the state courts. Or, if there are difficulties in the way of this procedure of which we have not been apprised, the issue of state law may be settled by appropriate action on the part of the State to enforce obedience to the order. In the absence of any showing that these obvious methods for securing a definitive ruling in the state courts cannot be pursued with full protection of the constitutional claim, the district court should exercise its wise discretion by staying its hands.

We therefore remand the cause to the district court, with directions to retain the bill pending a determination of proceedings, to be brought with reasonable promptness, in the state court in conformity with this opinion.

Reversed and remanded.

Notes and Questions

1. The Court does not explicitly state the criteria for *Pullman* absten-

tion, but the circumstances of the case imply three criteria the federal courts should use to decide whether to hear a case or to send the parties to state court for adjudication of state issues before considering whether to decide the federal issues at all. What are the three criteria?

2. *Pullman* attempts to accommodate three important and potentially conflicting principles: 1) federal courts should decide cases within their jurisdiction; 2) courts should avoid adjudication of constitutional questions when possible; and 3) conflict between the federal and state systems should be minimized. The first principle would have warmed Chief Justice Marshall's heart (see the introduction at page 745), and the second echoes Justice Brandeis's famous admonition in *Ashwander v. TVA*, 297 U.S. 288, 346, 56 S.Ct. 466, 482, 80 L.Ed. 688, 710 (1936) (Brandeis, J., concurring). A federal court can accommodate the first two principles by deciding the state law issue itself in a way that avoids the need to consider the federal constitutional question. But would that course of action also accommodate the third principle, or would it increase federal-state friction?

3. Should the federal court abstain under *Pullman* whenever there is a state statute of arguably uncertain meaning or application involved? Consider the following.

a) A state statute imposes on public school teacher a duty to "by precept and example promote respect for the flag and the institutions of the United States of America * * * ." A group of teachers files a federal action seeking a declaration that the statute violates their rights under the First and Fourteenth Amendments. Should the district court abstain? Consider first what specific constitutional entitlements the teachers might argue the statute infringes and then what the state courts might do to ameliorate the asserted constitutional infirmities.

b) A state statute makes it a crime to distribute in quantity any written material relating to an election campaign or issue unless the name and address of the person behind the distribution appears. Individuals wishing anonymously to hand out leaflets critical of a congressman seeking reelection bring a federal challenge to the statute on First and Fourteenth Amendment grounds. Should the district court abstain?

4. a) Federal courts abstain in *Pullman* situations to seek state court clarification of unclear provisions of state law, but they do not abstain in ordinary diversity cases when state law is unclear. *Meredith v. City of Winter Haven*, 320 U.S. 228, 64 S.Ct. 7, 88 L.Ed. 9 (1943) (*see infra* at 853.) Congress has not authorized abstention in either circumstance. Is the Court's decision to abstain in one circumstance but not the other justifiable? What would be the effect on diversity jurisdiction if federal courts routinely abstained when state law was unclear, sending the litigants back to state court? *Pullman* situations, of course, involve the additional goal of avoiding decision of a federal constitutional question. Is that goal important enough to justify abstaining in *Pullman* situations but not in diversity cases?

b) Even if abstention is inappropriate in diversity cases, should the federal courts adopt a more general abstention doctrine for cases coming under the courts' federal question jurisdiction that also involve unsettled questions of state law? If they do, what would be the effect on the exercise of federal question jurisdiction? Should the decision to abstain depend on whether the state court that would hear the case would be deciding questions of its own state's law or the law of some other state?

c) One reason federal courts exercise supplemental jurisdiction over state claims that are related to a plaintiff's federal claims is to avoid discrimination against the federal courts. Because state and federal courts usually have concurrent jurisdiction over federal claims, state courts can hear federal and state claims together. Supplemental jurisdiction allows federal courts to do the same. Without supplemental jurisdiction, a plaintiff who wants to try her federal claim in federal court would be required to bring two actions to present all her claims to courts, thus creating a disincentive to use the federal forum. *Pullman* abstention creates an even greater disincentive. Not only are two lawsuits required, but the plaintiff cannot obtain a federal ruling until the state courts have ruled on the meaning of state law. Why do you think the Court took such different approaches in the supplemental jurisdiction and abstention contexts?

5. Does a court construing a statute have any obligation to interpret it to avoid constitutional infirmity? Does it matter whether it is a state or federal court that is acting?

6. There may be a second way to avoid a federal constitutional question. The state constitution may have a provision that could be interpreted in a way that would avoid the need to decide the federal constitutional question. Should the federal court abstain to allow the state courts the opportunity to dispose of the case under the state constitution? Should the answer turn on whether the federal constitutional provision is one that is widely applied, such as the First Amendment or the Due Process Clause, and the state constitutional provision substantially mirrors the federal provision? If federal courts abstained in such cases, would they abstain more often or less often than they presently abstain? Note that while abstention in such cases would avoid decision of a federal constitutional issue, it would not avoid decision of a state constitutional issue. Thus, the goal of avoiding decision of constitutional issues would be only partly achieved. Is it better to avoid decision of federal than state constitutional issues, or should decision of both be avoided equally when possible? *See generally Examining Board of Engineers v. Flores de Otero,* 426 U.S. 572, 96 S.Ct. 2264, 49 L.Ed.2d 65 (1976); *Wisconsin v. Constantineau,* 400 U.S. 433, 91 S.Ct. 507, 27 L.Ed.2d 515 (1971). *But see Reetz v. Bozanich,* 397 U.S. 82, 90 S.Ct. 788, 25 L.Ed.2d 68 (1970).

7. The Court has modified the third *Pullman* criterion. In place of the requirement that "a definitive ruling on the state issue would terminate the controversy," *Harrison v. NAACP,* 360 U.S. 167, 79 S.Ct. 1025, 3 L.Ed.2d 1152 (1959), decided by a five-to-four vote, found abstention appropriate where "construction by the [state] courts * * * might avoid in whole or in part the necessity for federal constitutional adjudication, or at least materially change the nature of the problem." The dissenters decried what they saw as the expansion of *Pullman* abstention with the concomitant effect of delaying resolution of the dispute that the plaintiff organization had brought to the courts; indeed, Justice Douglas suggested that

Pullman abstention had reached the status of "a delaying tactic." Is the *Harrison* modification sound as a policy matter, or does it make it too easy for the federal courts to perceive a lurking state issue that requires resort to the state courts? Should any statute subject to some interpretation rather than being totally unambiguous provide a predicate for abstention?

Bellotti v. Baird I, 428 U.S. 132, 96 S.Ct. 2857, 49 L.Ed.2d 844 (1976), demonstrates how the modified abstention doctrine works and how developments in state procedural law may affect it. Massachusetts enacted a statute restricting the ability of unmarried women under the age of eighteen to get abortions. Plaintiffs, a group consisting of physicians, counselors and counseling groups, four pregnant, and unmarried minors, filed a class action challenging the statute's restrictions as inconsistent with *Roe v. Wade*, 410 U.S. 113, 93 S.Ct. 705, 35 L.Ed.2d 147 (1973). The parties disputed, *inter alia*, whether the parental notification provisions of the statute meant that the parents had an effective veto and whether a woman could seek judicial authorization for an abortion without first consulting her parents. The majority, in an opinion by Justice Blackmun, who wrote for the Court in *Roe*, remanded the case to the district court with directions that it certify questions on the statute's interpretation to the Supreme Judicial Court of Massachusetts rather than immediately addressing plaintiffs' constitutional challenges.[4] The Court rejected plaintiffs' argument that the state court would inevitably interpret the statute to include a parental veto.

The Massachusetts statute was complex and contained many ambiguities. The district court certified nine questions, and the Supreme Judicial Court returned narrative answers that the United States Supreme Court summarized in a later ruling in the same case. *See Bellotti v. Baird II*, 443 U.S. 622, 99 S.Ct. 3035, 61 L.Ed.2d 797 (1979). Certification is meant to speed up adjudication by providing an efficient way to clarify the meaning of state law. As the *Bellotti* decisions demonstrate, speed is a relative concept. *Bellotti I* began on October 30, 1974, and the district judge issued a temporary order restraining enforcement of the statute. On November 13, 1974, Massachusetts moved alternatively for dismissal, summary judgment, or abstention on *Pullman* grounds; the plaintiffs cross-moved for a preliminary injunction. On April 28, 1975, a three-judge district court declared the statute unconstitutional and enjoined its enforcement, prompting the appeal to the United States Supreme Court that was decided on July 1, 1976. Justice Brennan, as Circuit Justice, issued an order on July 30, 1976, restraining enforcement until the certification of state law questions to the Massachusetts courts was completed. The district court certified its questions to the Supreme Judicial Court of Massachusetts, which responded on January 25, 1977. The district court issued its final opinion

---

[4] Although certification statutes were comparatively rare when *Bellotti* was decided, now forty-eight states and the District of Columbia have them. The procedures under the statutes vary somewhat, but the basic process is the same. The statutes authorize a federal judge faced with an unclear provision of state law to certify questions about the meaning of the law to the state Supreme Court. When the state high court answers the questions, the federal judge can then proceed to decide the case, armed (at least in theory) with a clear understanding of state law.

on February 10, 1977, holding part of the statute unconstitutional and enjoining enforcement. Finally, on July 2, 1979, *Bellotti II* affirmed the district court's decision permanently to enjoin operation of the statute.

Thus, nearly five years elapsed between the initial challenge and the Supreme Court ruling that ended the case. From the time the Supreme Court ordered abstention in 1976 to the district court's receipt of the response to the certified questions and consequent opinion, more than seven months elapsed. While these time periods are not particularly long in the American legal system of the late twentieth century, in the context of a woman seeking abortion, both are obviously too long to permit effective protection of that right without temporary injunctive relief. Such relief was forthcoming in *Bellotti;* in other cases, involving abortion or other issues for which timing is critical, it might not be. Should the availability of temporary relief affect the decision to abstain?

8. *Arizonans for Official English v. Arizona*, 520 U.S. 43, 117 S.Ct. 1055, 137 L.Ed.2d 170 (1997), offers a new view of *Pullman* abstention and of the relationship of the inferior federal courts to the state courts as authoritative interpreters of state law. Justice Ginsburg's opinion for the Court vacated the decision below on the ground of mootness. In the course of the discussion, however, the Court criticized the district court that had found Arizona's "official English" statute facially overbroad. Noting *Pullman* abstention's drawbacks—delay and expense—Justice Ginsburg took the lower courts to task for producing effectively the same result by eschewing Arizona's certification procedure, which Arizona's Attorney General had asked the district court to invoke. The Court clearly suggests that the lower courts govern exercise of their discretion to seek certification according to the standard formerly associated with *Pullman*: whether interpretation of the state law "would avoid or substantially modify the federal constitutional challenge * * * ." One might conclude from this that where a state certification procedure exists, a Court should use that procedure rather than send the parties to a state trial court to begin the cumbersome process of obtaining a ruling from the trial court, an intermediate appellate court, and finally the state Supreme Court. Given the Court's endorsement of certification and criticism of the delay and expense inherent in the process prescribed in *Pullman*, might the Court regard that process as an abuse of discretion if the district court selected it in preference to certification? Or is there some residual use to the *Pullman* process for which certification cannot substitute?

One might have thought that *Pullman* would wither on the vine in the face of the proliferation of state certification statutes, but it has not. Although all but two states now have certification statutes, their terms differ markedly. Nineteen states allow certification from any federal court and from any state court of last resort. Eighteen states will accept certification from any federal court but not from state courts, and eleven states, including California, Florida, Illinois, New York, Pennsylvania and Texas permit certification only from federal appellate courts. To the extent that federal district courts cannot certify questions of state law, *Pullman* abstention remains alive and well.

NOTE ON POST-ABSTENTION PROCEDURE AND TACTICS

When the federal court decides that *Pullman* abstention is appropriate, consider what it and the parties should do. *Pullman* says the lower federal court should jurisdiction pending the plaintiff's resort to the state courts, a procedure that the Court later described as "the better practice," *Zwickler v. Koota,* 389 U.S. 241, 244 n.4, 88 S.Ct. 391, 393 n. 4, 19 L.Ed.2d 444, 448 n.4 (1967), while noting that on occasion it had ordered dismissal rather than retention of jurisdiction.

The parties' task is more difficult. The federal plaintiff presumably should begin a state action seeking construction of the statute. At the outset, should the plaintiff merely argue the statutory construction issue? In *Government and Civil Employees Organizing Committee, CIO v. Windsor,* 353 U.S. 364, 77 S.Ct. 838, 1 L.Ed.2d 894 (1957), the courts twice ordered abstention. An organization of public employees challenged a state statute forbidding them union membership, arguing that it violated the First and Fourteenth Amendments. The district court abstained because it appeared possible for the Alabama courts to find that the organization was not a union within the meaning of the statute. Plaintiffs thereupon sought a construction of the statute from the Alabama courts but did not mention any federal constitutional claims. Upon the Alabama courts' determination that plaintiffs were subject to the statute, they returned to federal court. The Supreme Court then ordered abstention on the ground that the Alabama court, had it known of the federal constitutional objections, might have construed the statute differently. Thus, a plaintiff cannot repair to state court and there remain silent about her federal claims.

Suppose that after abstention, a plaintiff, fortified by her understanding of *Windsor,* argues both state law claims and federal constitutional claims in the state court. If the state court rules against her on all grounds, the doctrine of res judicata precludes her successful return to the federal forum. Once the state court has ruled, is not the plaintiff's proper avenue of redress an appeal to the United States Supreme Court? This would put the plaintiff in a *Pullman* case in a difficult spot. Failure to mention the federal claims to the state court begets renewed abstention under *Windsor.* Presenting the federal claims to the state court threatens to prevent return to the federal district court because of res judicata. *Cf. Migra v. Warren City School District Board of Education,* 465 U.S. 75, 104 S.Ct. 892, 79 L.Ed.2d 56 (1984) (failure to litigate § 1983 claim in state court with transactionally-related state contract claim precludes subsequent litigation in federal court if the state would preclude subsequent litigation).

The Supreme Court addressed this dilemma in *England v. Louisiana State Board of Medical Examiners,* 375 U.S. 411, 84 S.Ct. 461, 11 L.Ed.2d 440 (1964). Plaintiff chiropractors sought a federal determination that the educational requirements of the Louisiana Medical Practice Act were unconstitutional as applied to them. The district court, noting that Louisiana might construe the statute as not applicable to plaintiffs, abstained "until the courts of the State of Louisiana shall have been afforded an opportunity to determine the issues here presented, and retaining jurisdiction to take such steps as may be necessary for the just disposition of the litigation should anything prevent a prompt state court determination." The plaintiffs then proceeded in the Louisiana courts, where, in the words of the United States Supreme Court, they "unreservedly submitted for decision, and briefed and argued, their contention that the Act, if applicable to chiropractors, violated the Fourteenth Amendment." The Louisiana courts ruled against plaintiffs on all grounds.

Plaintiffs did not seek Supreme Court review of the Louisiana decision. Instead, they returned to the district court, where defendants moved to dismiss because the district court could not properly sit in review of the state courts. Plaintiffs countered that they had submitted their claims to the Louisiana courts because *Windsor* required them to do so; indeed, the district court had noted that as the correct procedure, and the Supreme Court observed that commentators had read *Windsor* the same way. The confusion *Windsor* engendered was obvious; the Court refused to keep the plaintiffs out of federal court.

> There are fundamental objections to any conclusion that a litigant who has properly invoked the jurisdiction of a Federal District Court to consider federal constitutional claims can be compelled, without his consent and through no fault of his own, to accept instead a state court's determination of those claims. Such a result would be at war with the unqualified terms in which Congress, pursuant to constitutional authorization, has conferred specific categories of jurisdiction upon the federal courts, and with the principle that "When a Federal court is properly appealed to in a case over which it has by law jurisdiction, it is its duty to take such jurisdiction * * * . The right of a party plaintiff to choose a Federal court where there is a choice cannot be properly denied." Nor does anything in the abstention doctrine require or support such a result. Abstention is a judge-fashioned vehicle for according appropriate deference to the "respective competence of the state and federal court systems." Its recognition of the role of state courts as the final expositors of state law implies no disregard for the primacy of the federal judiciary in deciding questions of federal law. Accordingly, we have on several occasions explicitly recognized that abstention "does not, of course, involve the abdication of federal jurisdiction, but only the postponement of its exercise."[12]

---

[12] The doctrine contemplates only "that controversies involving unsettled questions of state law [may] be decided in the state tribunals preliminary to a federal court's consideration of the underlying federal constitutional questions," "that decision of the federal question be deferred until the potentially controlling state-law issue is authoritatively

It is true that, after a post-abstention determination and rejection of his federal claims by the state courts, a litigant could
seek direct review in this Court. But such review, even when
available by appeal rather than only by discretionary writ of certiorari, is an inadequate substitute for the initial District Court
determination * * * to which the litigant is entitled in the federal
courts. This is true as to issues of law; it is especially true as to
issues of fact. Limiting the litigant to review here would deny
him the benefit of a federal trial court's role in constructing a record and making fact findings. How the facts are found will often
dictate the decision of federal claims. "It is the typical, not the
rare, case in which constitutional claims turn upon the resolution
of contested factual issues." "There is always in litigation a margin of error, representing error in factfinding * * *." Thus in
cases where, but for the application of the abstention doctrine, the
primary fact determination would have been by the District
Court, a litigant may not be unwillingly deprived of that determination. The possibility of appellate review by this Court of a state
court determination may not be substituted, against a party's
wishes, for his right to litigate his federal claims fully in the federal courts. We made this clear only last Term in *NAACP v. But-
ton* when we said that "a party has the right to return to the District Court, after obtaining the authoritative state court construction for which the court abstained, for a final determination of his
claim."

To ensure the party's right to return to federal court, the Court
clarified *Windsor.* That case did not mean a party had to litigate his
federal claims in state court, "but only that he must inform those courts
of what his federal claims are, so that the state statute may be construed 'in light' of those claims." To preserve the right to return, a litigant should "inform the state courts that he is exposing his federal
claims there only for the purpose of complying with *Windsor*, and that
he intends, should the state courts hold against him on the question of
state law, to return to the District Court for disposition of his federal
contentions." The Court also realized a party might want to litigate the
entire case in state court to save time and expense. If this course is
chosen, the party cannot return to federal court.

England may not have been the beacon of clarity that the Court
wished. The Court itself recognized that a party may have trouble in
the "heat of litigation" merely stating, but not asserting or arguing, the
federal constitutional claim. If a party "can persuade the state court
that application of the statute to him would offend the Federal Constitution, he will ordinarily have persuaded it that the statute should not

_____

put to rest," "that federal courts do not decide questions of constitutionality on the basis
of preliminary guesses regarding local law," "that these enactments should be exposed to
state construction or limiting interpretation before the federal courts are asked to decide
upon their constitutionality" * * * .

be construed as applicable to him." If the party crosses the line, however, return to federal court will likely be foreclosed. *San Remo Hotel v. City and County of San Francisco*, 545 U.S. 323, 125 S.Ct. 2491, 162 L.Ed.2d 315 (2005), provides an example. The City of San Francisco imposed restrictions on conversion of hotel units into tourist units because of the "severe shortage" of affordable rental units for elderly, disabled, and low-income persons. In state administrative proceedings, the Hotel claimed these restrictions were unconstitutional and improperly applied to them. Losing in those proceedings, the Hotel filed a state petition for writ of administrative mandamus, which lay dormant for several years.

The Hotel then began a federal suit claiming the City's actions denied them due process and constituted an unlawful taking. The district court granted summary judgment for the City. Perhaps sensing they would not succeed in their appeal to the Ninth Circuit, the Hotel took "the unusual position" that the court should abstain under *Pullman* "because a return to state court could conceivably moot the remaining federal questions." The Ninth Circuit obliged, reminding the Hotel to make the appropriate *England* reservation. When the Hotel reactivated the state court action, however, they did not limit themselves to the issues asserted in the mandamus petition. Instead, they argued their broader federal constitutional claims. The Court held that "[b]y broadening their state action beyond the mandamus petition to include their "substantially advances" claims, petitioners effectively asked the state court to resolve the same federal issues they asked it to reserve. *England* does not support the exercise of any such right."

The Court in *England* also recognized that even if a party does not seek a decision on the federal court claim in state court, a state court may decide it anyway. A state court cannot be prevented from making that decision. While such action muddies the waters, an early, clearly-stated *England* reservation will nonetheless allow a return to federal court. Confusion may also arise because *England* specifically stated that "an explicit reservation is not indispensable" as long as the record makes clear plaintiff did not attempt to actively present the federal claims in state court. When there is no express reservation, confusion is bound to arise over whether the litigant's actions in the state courts are incompatible with returning to federal court.

After *Pullman* abstention, suppose a state court declines to adjudicate because it is being asked for an advisory opinion. Only six states explicitly permit advisory opinions. Sixteen have constitutional or statutory prohibitions of advisory opinions, and in twenty-eight states the judiciary has disapproved of them. Texas had a rule prohibiting its courts from hearing a case that remained on a federal court's docket. In *Harris County Commissioners Court v. Moore,* 420 U.S. 77, 95 S.Ct. 870, 43 L.Ed.2d 32 (1975), the Court directed dismissal so that the state could rule without the shadow of the federal court over it. The Supreme Court explained that upon conclusion of the state litigation, the plaintiff could refile in federal court. Professor Chemerinsky asks rhetorically whether the Supreme Court's attempt to circumvent the states' advisory-opinion rules truly addresses the states' concerns. *See* ERWIN CHEMERINSKY, FEDERAL JURISDICTION § 12.3, at 811-12 (5th ed. 2007). But does referring a case to a state court make the dispute any less real or the state court's decision any less potentially dispositive of the dispute than if the case were pending in the state system?

Suppose a prospective plaintiff anticipates a *Pullman* abstention problem and, to save time, commences his litigation in the state court, mentioning his constitutional concerns but making an explicit *England* reservation of the federal constitutional issues for later federal decision. If the state court decides the case, including the federal issues, can the plaintiff nonetheless go to federal court, or will he run into insurmountable res judicata problems? *Cf. Migra v. Warren City School District Board of Education,* 465 U.S. 75, 104 S.Ct. 892, 79 L.Ed.2d 56 (1984), noted in Chapter 7 at page 740. If so, would the plaintiff do better to begin in federal court and seek abstention so that a state ruling on the state issues may be obtained?

3. *Abstention: The Doctrine of* Younger v. Harris

YOUNGER v. HARRIS
Supreme Court of the United States, 1971.
401 U.S. 37, 91 S.Ct. 746, 27 L.Ed.2d 669.

MR. JUSTICE BLACK delivered the opinion of the Court.

Appellee, John Harris, Jr., was indicted in a California state court, charged with violation of the California Penal Code §§ 11400 and 11401, known as the California Criminal Syndicalism Act * * *. He then filed a complaint in the Federal District Court, asking that court to enjoin the appellant, Younger, the District Attorney of Los Angeles County, from prosecuting him, and alleging that the prosecution and even the presence of the Act inhibited him in the exercise of his rights of free speech and press, rights guaranteed him by the First and Fourteenth Amendments. Appellees Jim Dan and Diane Hirsch intervened as plaintiffs in the suit, claiming that the prosecution of Harris would inhibit them as members of the Progressive Labor Party from peacefully advocating the program of their party, which was to replace capitalism with socialism and to abolish the profit system of production in this country. Appellee Farrell Broslawsky, an instructor in history at Los Angeles Valley College, also intervened claiming that the prosecution of Harris made him uncertain as to whether he could teach about the doctrines of Karl Marx or read from the Communist Manifesto as part of his class work. All claimed that unless the United States court restrained the state prosecution of Harris each would suffer immediate and irreparable injury. A three-judge Federal District Court, convened pursuant to 28 U.S.C. § 2284, held that it had jurisdiction and power to restrain the District

Attorney from prosecuting, held that the State's Criminal Syndicalism Act was void for vagueness and overbreadth in violation of the First and Fourteenth Amendments, and accordingly restrained the District Attorney from "further prosecution of the currently pending action against plaintiff Harris for alleged violation of the Act."

* * * [W]e have concluded that the judgment of the District Court, enjoining appellant Younger from prosecuting under these California statutes, must be reversed as a violation of the national policy forbidding federal courts to stay or enjoin pending state court proceedings except under special circumstances.[2] We express no view about the circumstances under which federal courts may act when there is no prosecution pending in state courts at the time the federal proceeding is begun.

I

Appellee Harris has been indicted, and was actually being prosecuted by California for a violation of its Criminal Syndicalism Act at the time this suit was filed. He thus has an acute, live controversy with the State and its prosecutor. But none of the other parties plaintiff in the District Court, Dan, Hirsch, or Broslawsky, has such a controversy. None has been indicted, arrested, or even threatened by the prosecutor. * * *

* * * Whatever right Harris, who is being prosecuted under the state syndicalism law may have, Dan, Hirsch, and Broslawsky cannot share it with him. If these three had alleged that they would be prosecuted for the conduct they planned to engage in, and if the District Court had found this allegation to be true—either on the admission of the State's district attorney or on any other evidence—then a genuine controversy might be said to exist. But here appellees Dan, Hirsch, and Broslawsky do not claim that they have ever been threatened with prosecution, that a prosecution is likely, or even that a prosecution is remotely possible. They claim the right to bring this suit solely because, in the language of their complaint, they "feel inhibited." We do not think this allegation even if true, is sufficient to bring the equitable jurisdiction of the federal courts into play to enjoin a pending state prosecution. A federal lawsuit to stop a prosecution in a state court is a serious matter. And persons having no fears of state prosecution except those that are imaginary or speculative, are not to be accepted as appropriate plaintiffs in such cases. Since Harris is actually being prosecuted under the challenged laws, however, we proceed with him as a proper party.

---

[2] Appellees did not explicitly ask for a declaratory judgment in their complaint. They did, however, ask the District Court to grant "such other and further relief as to the Court may seem just and proper," and the District Court in fact granted a declaratory judgment. For the reasons stated in our opinion today in *Samuels v. Mackell,* we hold that declaratory relief is also improper when a prosecution involving the challenged statute is pending in state court at the time the federal suit is initiated.

II

Since the beginning of this country's history Congress has, subject to few exceptions, manifested a desire to permit state courts to try state cases free from interference by federal courts. * * * During all this lapse of years from 1793 to 1970 the statutory exceptions to the 1793 congressional enactment have been only three; (1) "except as expressly authorized by Act of Congress"; (2) "where necessary in aid of its jurisdiction"; and (3) "to protect or effectuate its judgments." In addition, a judicial exception to the long-standing policy evidenced by the statute has been made where a person about to be prosecuted in a state court can show that he will, if the proceeding in the state court is not enjoined, suffer irreparable damages. *See Ex parte Young,* 209 U.S. 123 (1908).

The precise reasons for this long-standing public policy against federal court interference with state court proceedings have never been specifically identified but the primary sources of the policy are plain. One is the basic doctrine of equity jurisprudence that courts of equity should not act, and particularly should not act to restrain a criminal prosecution, when the moving party has an adequate remedy at law and will not suffer irreparable injury if denied equitable relief. The doctrine may originally have grown out of circumstances peculiar to the English judicial system and not applicable in this country, but its fundamental purpose of restraining equity jurisdiction within narrow limits is equally important under our Constitution, in order to prevent erosion of the role of the jury and avoid a duplication of legal proceedings and legal sanctions where a single suit would be adequate to protect the rights asserted. This underlying reason for restraining courts of equity from interfering with criminal prosecutions is reinforced by an even more vital consideration, the notion of "comity," that is, a proper respect for state functions, a recognition of the fact that the entire country is made up of a Union of separate state governments, and a continuance of the belief that the National Government will fare best if the States and their institutions are left free to perform their separate functions in their separate ways. This, perhaps for lack of a better and clearer way to describe it, is referred to by many as "Our Federalism," and one familiar with the profound debates that ushered our Federal Constitution into existence is bound to respect those who remain loyal to the ideals and dreams of "Our Federalism." The concept does not mean blind deference to "States' Rights" any more than it means centralization of control over every important issue in our National Government and its courts. The Framers rejected both these courses. What the concept does represent is a system in which there is sensitivity to the legitimate interests of both State and National Governments, and in which the National Government, anxious though it may be to vindicate and protect federal rights and federal interests, always endeavors to do so in ways that will not unduly interfere with the legitimate activities of the States. It should never be forgotten that this slogan, "Our Federalism," born in the early struggling days of our Union of States, occupies a highly important place in our Nation's history and its future.

This brief discussion should be enough to suggest some of the reasons why it has been perfectly natural for our cases to repeat time and time again that the normal thing to do when federal courts are asked to enjoin pending proceedings in state courts is not to issue such injunctions. In *Fenner v. Boykin* (1926), suit had been brought in the Federal District Court seeking to enjoin state prosecutions under a recently enacted state law that allegedly interfered with the free flow of interstate commerce. The Court, in a unanimous opinion made clear that such a suit, even with respect to state criminal proceedings not yet formally instituted, could be proper only under very special circumstances:

> *Ex parte Young* and following cases have established the doctrine that, when absolutely necessary for protection of constitutional rights, courts of the United States have power to enjoin state officers from instituting criminal actions. But this may not be done, except under extraordinary circumstances, where the danger of irreparable loss is both great and immediate. Ordinarily, there should be no interference with such officers; primarily, they are charged with the duty of prosecuting offenders against the laws of the state, and must decide when and how this is to be done. The accused should first set up and rely upon his defense in the state courts, even though this involves a challenge of the validity of some statute, unless it plainly appears that this course would not afford adequate protection.

These principles, made clear in the *Fenner* case, have been repeatedly followed and reaffirmed in other cases involving threatened prosecutions.

In all of these cases the Court stressed the importance of showing irreparable injury, the traditional prerequisite to obtaining an injunction. In addition, however, the Court also made clear that in view of the fundamental policy against federal interference with state criminal prosecutions, even irreparable injury is insufficient unless it is "both great and immediate." Certain types of injury, in particular, the cost, anxiety, and inconvenience of having to defend against a single criminal prosecution, could not by themselves be considered "irreparable" in the special legal sense of that term. Instead, the threat to the plaintiff's federally protected rights must be one that cannot be eliminated by his defense against a single criminal prosecution.

This is where the law stood when the Court decided *Dombrowski v. Pfister* (1965), and held that an injunction against the enforcement of certain state criminal statutes could properly issue under the circumstances presented in that case. * * * The appellants in *Dombrowski* had offered to prove that their offices had been raided and all their files and records seized pursuant to search and arrest warrants that were later summarily vacated by a state judge for lack of probable cause. They also offered to prove that despite the state court order quashing the warrants and suppressing the evidence seized, the prosecutor was continuing to threaten to initiate new prosecutions of appellants under the same statutes, was holding public hearings at which photostatic copies of the illegally seized documents were being used, and was threatening to use other copies of the illegally seized documents to obtain grand jury indictments against the appellants on charges of violating the same statutes. These circumstances, as viewed by the Court sufficiently establish the kind of irreparable injury, above and beyond that associated with the defense of a single prosecution brought in good faith, that had always been considered sufficient to justify federal intervention. Indeed, after quoting the Court's statement in *Douglas* concerning the very restricted circumstances under which an injunction could be justified, the Court in *Dombrowski* went on to say:

> But the allegations in this complaint depict a situation in which defense of the State's criminal prosecution will not assure adequate vindication of constitutional rights. They suggest that a substantial loss of or impairment of freedoms of expression will occur if appellants must await the state court's disposition and ultimate review in this Court of any adverse determination. These allegations, if true, clearly show irreparable injury.

* * * And the Court made clear that even under these circumstances the District Court issuing the injunction would have continuing power to lift it at any time and remit the plaintiffs to the state courts if circumstances warranted * * * .

It is against the background of these principles that we must judge the propriety of an injunction under the circumstances of the present case. Here a proceeding was already pending in the state court, affording Harris an opportunity to raise his constitutional claims. There is no suggestion that this single prosecution against Harris is brought in bad faith or is only one of a series of repeated prosecutions to which he will be subjected. In other words, the injury that Harris faces is solely "that incidental to every criminal proceeding brought lawfully and in good faith," and therefore under the settled doctrine we have already described he is not entitled to equitable relief "even if such statutes are unconstitutional."

* * * It is undoubtedly true, as the Court stated in *Dombrowski,* that "[a] criminal prosecution under a statute regulating expression usually involves imponderables and contingencies that themselves may inhibit the full exercise of First Amendment freedoms." But this sort of "chilling effect," as the Court called it, should not by itself justify federal intervention. In the first place, the chilling effect cannot be satisfactorily eliminated by federal injunctive relief. * * * The chilling effect can, of course, be eliminated by an injunction that would prohibit any prosecution

whatever for conduct occurring prior to a satisfactory rewriting of the statute. But the States would then be stripped of all power to prosecute even the socially dangerous and constitutionally unprotected conduct that had been covered by the statute, until a new statute could be passed by the state legislature and approved by the federal courts in potentially lengthy trial and appellate proceedings. * * *

Moreover, the existence of a "chilling effect," even in the area of First Amendment rights, has never been considered a sufficient basis, in and of itself, for prohibiting state action. Where a statute does not directly abridge free speech, but—while regulating a subject within the State's power—tends to have the incidental effect of inhibiting First Amendment rights, it is well settled that the statute can be upheld if the effect on speech is minor in relation to the need for control of the conduct and the lack of alternative means for doing so. Just as the incidental "chilling effect" of such statutes does not automatically render them unconstitutional, so the chilling effect that admittedly can result from the very existence of certain laws on the statute books does not in itself justify prohibiting the State from carrying out the important and necessary task of enforcing these laws against socially harmful conduct that the State believes in good faith to be punishable under its laws and the Constitution.

Beyond all this is another, more basic consideration. Procedures for testing the constitutionality of a statute "on its face" in the manner apparently contemplated by *Dombrowski,* and for then enjoining all action to enforce the statute until the State can obtain court approval for a modified version, are fundamentally at odds with the function of the federal courts in our constitutional plan. The power and duty of the judiciary to declare laws unconstitutional is in the final analysis derived from its responsibility for resolving concrete disputes brought before the courts for decision; a statute apparently governing a dispute cannot be applied by judges, consistently with their obligations under the Supremacy Clause, when such an application of the statute would conflict with the Constitution. But this vital responsibility, broad as it is, does not amount to an unlimited power to survey the statute books and pass judgment on laws before the courts are called upon to enforce them. Ever since the Constitutional Convention rejected a proposal for having members of the Supreme Court render advice concerning pending legislation it has been clear that, even when suits of this kind involve a "case or controversy" sufficient to satisfy the requirements of Article III of the Constitution, the task of analyzing a proposed statute, pinpointing its deficiencies, and requiring correction of these deficiencies before the statute is put into effect, is rarely if ever an appropriate task for the judiciary. The combination of the relative remoteness of the controversy, the impact on the legislative process of the relief sought, and above all the speculative and amorphous nature of the required line-by-line analysis of detailed statutes ordinarily results in a kind of case that is wholly unsatisfactory for deciding constitutional questions, whichever way they might be decided. In light of this fundamental conception of the Framers as to the proper place of the federal courts in the governmental processes of passing and enforcing laws, it can seldom be appropriate for these courts to exercise any such power of prior approval or veto over the legislative process.

For these reasons, fundamental not only to our federal system but also to the basic functions of the Judicial Branch of the National Government under our Constitution, we hold that the *Dombrowski* decision should not be regarded as having upset the settled doctrines that have always confined very narrowly the availability of injunctive relief against state criminal prosecutions. We do not think that opinion stands for the proposition that a federal court can properly enjoin enforcement of a statute solely on the basis of a showing that the statute "on its face" abridges First Amendment rights. There may, of course, be extraordinary circumstances in which the necessary irreparable injury can be shown even in the absence of the usual prerequisites of bad faith and harassment. For example, * * * "[i]t is of course conceivable that a statute might be flagrantly and patently violative of express constitutional prohibitions in every clause, sentence and paragraph, and in whatever manner and against whomever an effort might be made to apply it." Other unusual situations calling for federal intervention might also arise, but there is no point in our attempting now to specify what they might be. It is sufficient for purposes of the present case to hold, as we do, that the possible unconstitutionality of a statute "on its face" does not in itself justify an injunction against good-faith attempts to enforce it, and that appellee Harris has failed to make any showing of bad faith, harassment, or any other unusual circumstance that would call for equitable relief. Because our holding rests on the absence of the factors necessary under equitable principles to justify federal intervention, we have no occasion to consider whether 28 U.S.C. § 2283, which prohibits an injunction against state court proceedings "except as expressly authorized by Act of Congress" would in and of itself be controlling under the circumstances of this case.

The judgment of the District Court is reversed, and the case is remanded for further proceedings not inconsistent with this opinion.

Reversed.

Notes and Questions

1. As Justice Black notes, this abstention doctrine did not originate with *Younger.* The Court mentions two of its antecedents: *Douglas v. City of Jeannette,* 319 U.S. 157, 63 S.Ct. 877, 87 L.Ed. 1324 (1943), and *Fenner v. Boykin,* 271 U.S. 240, 46 S.Ct. 492, 70 L.Ed. 927 (1926). In fact, the Court's first consideration of the propriety of federal intervention in state criminal proceedings came in *In re Sawyer,* 124 U.S. 200, 8 S.Ct. 482, 31 L.Ed. 402 (1888). Today the doctrine is universally referred to as *Younger* abstention.

For a history of its development up to *Younger,* see Donald H. Zeigler, *An Accommodation of the* Younger *Doctrine and the Duty of the Federal Courts to Enforce Safeguards in the State Criminal Process,* 125 U.PA.L.REV. 266 (1976).

Younger, however, worked a major change in the doctrine, though hardly one to which Justice Black called much attention. Note that the Court's discussion of *Fenner v. Boykin* makes clear that the doctrine there applied to an attempt to enjoin *threatened* prosecutions. *Fenner* did not involve pending criminal prosecutions. In fact, from *In re Sawyer* until *Younger,* the rule of restraint applied only in the context of threatened, not pending actions. Recall that in *Ex parte Young,* the Court said in *dictum,* connoting that it was stating the obvious, "[b]ut the Federal court cannot, of course, interfere in a case where the proceedings were already pending in a state court." *Ex parte Young,* 209 U.S. 123, 169, 28 S.Ct. 441, 457-58, 52 L.Ed. 714, 733 (1908). Thus, before *Younger,* long-standing federal policy barred any federal intervention in a pending state criminal proceeding and permitted equitable relief against threatened state proceedings only in the "extraordinary circumstances" referred to in *Fenner.*

Younger changed that structure dramatically. Near the outset of the opinion, the Court notes that it is reversing the judgment below because it violates the "national policy forbidding federal courts to stay or enjoin *pending* state court proceedings except under special circumstances," (emphasis added), and goes on to say that "[w]e express no view about the circumstances under which federal courts may act when there is no prosecution pending in state courts at the time the federal proceeding is begun." This is serious business, and one might view it as a *de facto* overruling of *Fenner v. Boykin,* despite Justice Black's citation of that case with obvious approval. Before *Younger,* federal intervention in pending state criminal prosecutions was substantially impossible, and federal action against threatened state prosecutions was extremely difficult to secure. After *Younger,* intervention in pending state criminal proceedings was possible, though extremely difficult to secure, and the Court, despite its protest, seemed to be signaling increased possibilities of federal judicial action with respect to threatened state criminal proceedings.

2. The Court rarely decides cases in a vacuum, political *or* doctrinal. *Younger* has an almost symbiotic relationship with *Mitchum v. Foster,* 407 U.S. 225, 92 S.Ct. 2151, 32 L.Ed.2d 705 (1972), decided the year after *Younger. Mitchum, (see also* 758-760) held that 42 U.S.C. § 1983 is a congressionally-authorized exception to 42 U.S.C. § 2283, which bans federal courts from staying state court proceedings except in very limited circumstances. Without *Younger, Mitchum* potentially would have opened the federal courts to thousands of lawsuits by state criminal defendants claiming violation of federal constitutional rights. The issue in *Mitchum* made it impossible for the Court to reach a compromise allowing federal court intervention in extreme cases while denying it in ordinary ones. Section 1983 was either an exception to § 2283 or it was not. If it was, the doors to the federal courthouse were flung open. If not, they were shut tight. As Professor Ann Althouse pointed out, the combination of *Younger* and *Mitchum* did leave the

federal courts able to stay pending state civil proceedings. Ann Althouse, *The Humble and the Treasonous: Judge-Made Jurisdiction Law*, 40 CASE W.RES.L.REV. 1035, 1041-44 (1990). Trading away authority to enjoin criminal proceedings to gain power to enjoin civil proceedings may be desirable, but *Younger*'s dramatic expansion into the civil area after 1971, described below, removes some of the benefit of the bargain that Professor Althouse argues the Court struck in 1971 and 1972.

In *Mitchum*, the unanimous seven-member Court[5] explicitly discussed the relationship among *Younger*, the Anti-Injunction Act, and § 1983 as follows. First, unless the *Younger* Court had viewed § 1983 as an "expressly authorized" exception to the Act, it could have easily and quickly decided *Younger* without discussion of "Our Federalism." Second, if the Anti-Injunction Act applied to § 1983 cases, federal intervention would be impossible even in the extraordinary circumstances *Younger* apparently contemplated, necessitating at least partial overruling of *Younger*. Finally, the legislative debate on § 1983 clearly contemplated the possibility of the Civil Rights Act undergirding federal interference with state proceedings in any branch of state government. As the Court observed, even

> [t]hose who opposed the Act of 1871 clearly recognized that the proponents were extending federal power in an attempt to remedy the state courts' failure to secure federal rights. The debate was not about whether the predecessor of § 1983 extended to actions of state courts, but whether this innovation was necessary or desirable.

At the same time, *Mitchum* endorsed *Younger* abstention. "[W]e do not question or qualify in any way the principles of comity, equity, and federalism that must restrain a federal court when asked to enjoin a state court proceeding. These principles, in the context of state criminal prosecutions, were canvassed at length last Term in *Younger v. Harris* . . . ." In what sense is the Court's position in *Mitchum* inherently inconsistent with its views only a year earlier in *Younger*?

3. *Younger* abstention represents a clash between two of the dominant themes of federal courts jurisprudence: federalism and separation of powers. The federalism aspects of the doctrine are clear; the states are left free to enforce their statutes without federal interference until state proceedings end. On the other hand, there are some unavoidable separation-of-powers problems. There are two authorizations of federal jurisdiction for cases such as Harris's: the general federal-question statute, 28 U.S.C.A. § 1331, and the civil rights jurisdiction statute, 28 U.S.C.A. § 1343. Professor Martin Redish argues strongly that *Younger* violates separation of powers, particularly in light of the congressional intent underlying § 1983 that the Court so clearly recognized in *Mitchum*. Martin H. Redish, *Abstention, Separation of Powers, and the Limits of the Judicial Function*, 94 YALE L.J. 71 (1984). *But see* Michael Wells, *Why Professor Redish Is Wrong About Abstention*, 19 GA.L.REV. 1097 (1985).

---

[5] Justices Powell and Rehnquist were appointed too late to participate.

4. Justice Black discusses *Dombrowski v. Pfister,* 380 U.S. 479, 85 S.Ct. 1116, 14 L.Ed.2d 22 (1965), at some length, distinguishing it from *Younger.* What is left of *Dombrowski* after *Younger*? Has it been limited to its facts? *Younger* does not explicitly overrule *Dombrowski.* Suppose in *Dombrowski* there had been no prior state dismissals. Would the *Younger* Court have allowed federal intervention? Suppose instead that plaintiffs offer to prove that the state prosecution is in retaliation for the exercise of constitutional rights. Does *Younger* permit federal injunctive relief? Does it even permit plaintiffs an evidentiary presentation on the issue? Professor Wingate has addressed some of these questions. C. Keith Wingate, *The Bad Faith Harassment Exception to the* Younger *Doctrine: Exploring the Empty Universe,* 5 REV.LITIG. 123 (1986).

5. a) *Younger* bars an injunction against a state criminal proceeding unless the plaintiff can demonstrate that he will suffer "irreparable injury." While Justice Black does not define irreparable injury, he does say that it is *not* the "cost, anxiety, and inconvenience of having to defend against a single criminal prosecution." Indeed, he speaks of this burden as if it is a comparatively minor aggravation that the good citizen should have to bear. Should the individual prosecuted for a crime under a statute that he alleges is unconstitutional be required to endure the wrenching experience of a criminal proceeding without hope of federal review of his constitutional claim until he has pursued his defense, if necessary, through several levels of state courts, has encumbered assets to post bail, has been held up to the community as a criminal, and perhaps has been imprisoned following conviction pending appeal? On the other hand, how would it affect *Younger* abstention to regard the burden of defending as irreparable injury?

b) Given the limited number of cases the Court hears each year, the practical effect of *Younger* abstention for most cases is that the state courts have not only the first but also the last word on the federal constitutional issues. When *Younger* was decided, federal habeas corpus review was considerably more available to test prisoners' constitutional claims than is now the case. *See generally* Chapter 11. Should *Younger* abstention be reevaluated in light of the current restricted scope of federal habeas review?

c) The Court has taken varying positions about the "cost, anxiety, and inconvenience" of litigation. In the area of official immunities, the Justices have felt that litigation is so burdensome that they were justified in creating federal common law to prevent litigation of all but the clearest abuses of power. *See Harlow v. Fitzgerald,* 457 U.S. 800, 102 S.Ct. 2727, 73 L.Ed.2d 396 (1982), discussed in Chapter 6. True, the *Harlow* Court was concerned with interference with governmental processes, a factor not present when an individual is prosecuted for a crime. On the other hand, it is also true that an official sued for violation of constitutional rights has at his back the defensive resources of the government and may be indemnified in the event of an adverse judgment. *See, e.g.,* WEST'S ANN.CAL.GOV.CODE § 825 (1980); N.Y. GENERAL MUNICIPAL LAW § 50-k (McKinney 1986).

6. In addition to irreparable injury, a plaintiff seeking to avoid abstention must show there is no adequate state remedy for vindicating the plain-

tiff's federal claim. The Court has made clear that any theoretically available state remedy will suffice for *Younger* abstention purposes and that the federal courts have no obligation to evaluate the effectiveness of potential state remedies. *See O'Shea v. Littleton*, 414 U.S. 488, 94 S.Ct. 669, 38 L.Ed.2d 674 (1974). As Professor Owen Fiss has noted, the "adequacy of [the] alternative remedies [in *O'Shea*] was evidently to be presumed from the very fact that Justice White was able to think of them." Owen Fiss, Dombrowski, 86 YALE L.J. 1103, 1154 (1977). Moreover, the presumption of adequacy is essentially irrebuttable. If a federal court dismisses because of *Younger*, litigants cannot return to federal court to show that the judge guessed wrong and that state remedies were unavailing. On occasion, the Court has found there is no adequate remedy at law when state remedies are not even theoretically available or when the plaintiffs can make a clear case the state tribunal will be biased against them.

a) *Gerstein v. Pugh*, 420 U.S. 103, 95 S.Ct. 854, 43 L.Ed.2d 54 (1975), provides an example of the first circumstance. The plaintiff class challenged Florida's procedure in criminal cases generally.

> In Florida, indictments are required only for prosecution of capital offenses. Prosecutors may charge all other crimes by information, without a prior preliminary hearing and without obtaining leave of court. At the time respondents were arrested, a Florida rule seemed to authorize adversary preliminary hearings to test probable cause for detention in all cases. But the Florida courts had held that the filing of an information foreclosed the suspect's right to a preliminary hearing. They had also held that habeas corpus could not be used, except perhaps in exceptional circumstances, to test the probable cause for detention under an information. The only possible methods for obtaining a judicial determination of probable cause were a special statute allowing a preliminary hearing after 30 days, and arraignment, which the District Court found was often delayed a month or more after arrest. As a result, a person charged by information could be detained for a substantial period solely on the decision of a prosecutor.

Plaintiffs argued that they had a constitutional right to a probable cause hearing before imposition of more pretrial detention than necessarily incident to an arrest. They sought declaratory and injunctive relief compelling such hearings. Notwithstanding the pending criminal cases against the members of the plaintiff class, the Supreme Court held abstention inappropriate because there was no Florida procedure to challenge the propriety of the pretrial detention.

> The District Court correctly held that respondents' claim for relief was not barred by the equitable restrictions on federal intervention in state prosecutions. The injunction was not directed at the state prosecutions as such, but only at the legality of the pretrial detention without a judicial hearing, an issue that could not be raised in defense of the criminal prosecution. The order to hold preliminary hearings could not prejudice the conduct of the trial on the merits.

Thus, complete unavailability of a state procedure for raising federal constitutional claims may undercut *Younger* abstention.

b) The Court has also forsworn abstention where the federal plaintiff demonstrates bias in state proceedings otherwise theoretically adequate for raising the federal issues. *See Gibson v. Berryhill,* 411 U.S. 564, 93 S.Ct. 1689, 36 L.Ed.2d 488 (1973). The plaintiffs, licensed optometrists, sought to enjoin hearings charging them with unprofessional conduct by reason of their employment with a corporation. They argued that because the members of the state board of optometry had a pecuniary interest in the outcome, abstention was not warranted. The Court agreed.

7. The Court notes an apparent exception (without examples) to the *Younger* doctrine if a state statute is "flagrantly and patently violative of express constitutional provisions in every clause, sentence and paragraph." Are equity, comity and federalism of any less force then? How is such a case distinguishable in any principled way from one in which the statute is "merely" unconstitutional? Moreover, if the statute is so demonstrably unconstitutional, should not the presumption of the state courts' ability to handle the constitutional issue be stronger rather than weaker?

In *Trainor v. Hernandez,* 431 U.S. 434, 97 S.Ct. 1911, 52 L.Ed.2d 486 (1977), the Court provided an example of what would *not* satisfy this exception. Plaintiffs were public assistance recipients. In state court, Illinois sued to recover payments allegedly wrongfully received and, pursuant to a 100-year old state statute, attached some of plaintiffs' assets. Plaintiffs then sued in federal court, claiming the Illinois statute provided none of the procedural safeguards the Court had held the Due Process Clause to require in four recent cases.[6] The district court found the Illinois procedure clearly unconstitutional, but the Supreme Court reversed, finding that the Illinois scheme was, in some sense, not unconstitutional enough to qualify under the "patently violative" exception. Justice Stevens dissented.

> [T]he Court finds a meaningful difference between a state procedure which is "patently and flagrantly violative of the Constitution" and one that is "flagrantly and patently violative of express constitutional prohibitions in every clause, sentence and paragraph, and in whatever manner and against whomever an effort might be made to apply it."
> * * *
>
> The District Court found the Illinois attachment procedure "patently and flagrantly violative of the constitution." This Court, on the other hand, writes: "It is urged that this case comes within the exception that we said in *Younger* might exist where a state statute is 'flagrantly and patently violative of express constitutional prohibitions in every clause, sentence and paragraph, and in whatever manner and against whomever an effort might be made to apply it.' Even if such a finding was made below, *which we doubt,* it would not have been warranted in

[6] Sniadach v. Family Finance Corp., 395 U.S. 337, 89 S.Ct. 1820, 23 L.Ed.2d 349 (1969); Fuentes v. Shevin, 407 U.S. 67, 92 S.Ct. 1983, 32 L.Ed.2d 556 (1972); Mitchell v. W.T. Grant Co., 416 U.S. 600, 94 S.Ct. 1895, 40 L.Ed.2d 406 (1974); North Georgia Finishing Co., Inc. v. Di-Chem, Inc., 419 U.S. 601, 95 S.Ct. 719, 42 L.Ed.2d 751 (1975).

light of our cases." (Emphasis added).

Since there is no doubt whatsoever as to what the District Court actually said, this Court's expression of doubt can only refer to its uncertainty as to whether a finding that the crux of the statute is patently and flagrantly unconstitutional is sufficient to satisfy the requirement that the statute be patently and flagrantly unconstitutional "in every clause, sentence and paragraph * * * ." It is, therefore, appropriate to consider what is left of this exception to the *Younger* doctrine after today's decision.

The source of this exception is the passage Mr. Justice Black had written some years earlier in *Watson v. Buck,* a case which involved a complicated state antitrust Act. On the basis of its conclusion that certain sections were unconstitutional, a three-judge District Court had enjoined enforcement of the entire Act. This Court reversed, holding: first, that the invalidity of a part of a statute would not justify an injunction against the entire Act; and second, that in any event the eight sections in question were valid.

In his explanation of the first branch of the Court's holding, Mr. Justice Black pointed out that there are few, if any, statutes that are totally unconstitutional in every part. Since *Watson* involved a new statute which had not been construed by any state court, and since such construction might have affected its constitutionality, Mr. Justice Black's comment emphasized the point that an untried state statute should not be invalidated by a federal court before the state court has an opportunity to construe it. This consideration is not present in a case involving an attack on a state statute that has been in use for more than a century. Nothing in *Watson* implies that a limited injunction against an invalid portion of a statute of long standing would be improper.

When he wrote the Court's opinion in *Younger,* Mr. Justice Black quoted the foregoing excerpt from the *Watson* case as an example of a situation in which it would be appropriate for a federal court to enjoin a pending state criminal prosecution. He did not, however, imply that his earlier language rigidly defined the boundaries of one kind of exception from the equitable rationale underlying the *Younger* decision itself.

Today the Court seems to be saying that the "patently and flagrantly unconstitutional" exception to *Younger*-type abstention is unavailable whenever a statute has a legitimate title, or a legitimate severability clause, or some other equally innocuous provision. If this is a fair reading of the Court's opinion, the Court has given Mr. Justice Black's illustrative language definitional significance. In effect, this treatment preserves an illusion of flexibility in the application of a *Younger*-type abstention, but it actually eliminates one of the exceptions from the doctrine. For the typical constitutional attack on a statute focuses on one, or a few, objectionable features. Although, as Mr. Justice Black indicated in *Watson,* it is conceivable that there are some totally unconstitutional statutes, the possibility is quite remote. More importantly, the Court has never explained why all sections of any statute must be considered invalid in order to justify an injunction against a portion that is itself flagrantly unconstitutional. Even if this Court finds the constitutional issue less clear than did the District Court, I do not understand what governmental interest is served by refusing to address the merits at this stage of the proceedings.

8. One of the premises of *Younger* abstention is that the state courts are as able as federal courts to determine federal constitutional claims. That leaves aside the question of whether state courts are equally hospitable to federal claims, particularly when the claims involve possible invalidation of state statutes. Scholars have long debated the supposition of parity. It is ironic, perhaps, that the Court has been eager to presume the states' expertise on matters of state law, but has not been willing to presume corresponding expertise of the federal courts with respect to federal law. *See generally* Burt Neuborne, *The Myth of Parity*, 90 HARV.L.REV. 1105 (1977); Symposium, *Federalism and Parity*, 71 B.U.L.REV. 593 (1991).

9. Is *Younger* a prudential doctrine or constitutionally compelled? For an argument that it is the latter, see Calvin R. Massey, *Abstention and the Constitutional Limits of the Judicial Power of the United States,* 1991 B.Y.U.L.REV. 811.

a) If it is prudential only, then is not the Court violating separation of powers by rejecting what it implicitly treats as an offer of jurisdiction by Congress rather than a command to exercise jurisdiction? In Professor Redish's terms, is it legitimate for the Court, a designedly counter-majoritarian branch of government, to make policy decisions about the wisdom of exercising federal jurisdiction that Congress has conferred? *Younger* abstention is a judicially-created doctrine that effectively overrides legislation conferring jurisdiction, or at least creates judicial exceptions to it. Yet the Court and its members have often inveighed against the propriety of courts considering other than the constitutionality of legislation. "A 'fundamental tenet of judicial review' the late Mr. Justice Jackson said, is that 'not the wisdom or policy of legislation, but only the power of the legislature, is a fit subject for consideration by the courts.' * * * Some 10 years later in *Harisiades v. Shaughnessy,* * * * he added that 'judicially we must tolerate what personally we may regard as a legislative mistake.'" *Granville-Smith v. Granville-Smith,* 349 U.S. 1, 16, 75 S.Ct. 553, 561-62, 99 L.Ed. 773, 783 (1955) (Clark, J., dissenting) (citing ROBERT JACKSON, THE STRUGGLE FOR JUDICIAL SUPREMACY 81 (1941)). The abstention doctrines in particular deal with the day-to-day balance of power between state and federal governments. If the *Younger* doctrine is prudential, then the Court has imposed its vision of what the balance should be. Can Congress remedy the situation if it feels the Court has struck an improper balance?

Arguably, Congress has attempted to remedy the situation, at least if one takes *Mitchum v. Foster* seriously. *Mitchum* held, however questionably, that Congress intended § 1983 cases to fall within the "expressly authorized" exception of the Anti-Injunction Act. Should not that statutory determination of federal policy overcome the federal common law that the Court has created in *Younger*? If so, can *Younger* apply at all to § 1983 cases? If not, then is a federal court's power to determine the propriety of equitable relief hierarchically superior to Congress's legislative power?

b) If the doctrine is constitutionally compelled, several problems arise. First, if *Younger* is a constitutional matter, then should the Court have examined whether the Anti-Injunction Act precluded Harris's action? The Court explicitly did not decide on that basis. Under the *Ashwander* principle of avoiding constitutional decisions, should it have?

Second, if the Constitution compels *Younger* abstention, is *Younger* abstention waivable? The Court has suggested that judges cannot raise it *sua sponte*. *Swisher v. Brady,* 438 U.S. 204, 213 n.11, 98 S.Ct. 2699, 2705 n.11, 57 L.Ed.2d 705, 713 n.11 (1978). That the doctrine is effectively waivable does not necessarily mean that it lacks constitutional stature; many constitutional rights can be waived. On the other hand, given that *Younger* abstention now applies to a vast range of proceedings other than purely criminal matters, and given that the purpose of the doctrine is to safeguard the values of federalism, "it is unclear why consent of the *parties* is sufficient to justify interference." ERWIN CHEMERINSKY, FEDERAL JURISDICTION § 13.4, at 863 (5th ed. 2007).

Third, what is the precise constitutional basis for the tripartite predicate for the *Younger* doctrine—equity, comity and federalism? One can infer principles of federalism (and perhaps comity) from the constitutional structure that establishes the dual government system. Perhaps the only specific reservation in the name of federalism is the Tenth Amendment, often cited as the constitutional underpinning for *Erie v. Tompkins,* 304 U.S. 64, 58 S.Ct. 817, 82 L.Ed. 1188 (1938). It is a great stretch, however, to read the Tenth Amendment as a specific constitutional prohibition of federal injunctions of state proceedings in areas of admitted federal competence. Principles of equity are even more difficult to locate in the Constitution.

Fourth, if *Younger* is constitutionally compelled then its clash with the jurisdiction statutes (28 U.S.C.A. §§ 1331, 1343) is all the more apparent. Should the Court either explicitly construe those statutes not to apply when *Younger* abstention is appropriate or declare those statutes unconstitutional as applied when *Younger* confronts them?

10. *Younger* was only one case of a group now known as the *Younger* sextet, all decided the same day. In *Samuels v. Mackell,* 401 U.S. 66, 91 S.Ct. 764, 27 L.Ed.2d 688 (1971), the Court extended *Younger*'s prohibition to requests for declaratory relief only, noting:

> [O]rdinarily a declaratory judgment will result in precisely the same interference with and disruption of state proceedings that the long-standing policy limiting injunctions was designed to avoid. This is true for at least two reasons. In the first place, the Declaratory Judgment Act provides that after a declaratory judgment is issued the district court may enforce it by granting "[f]urther necessary or proper relief," and therefore a declaratory judgment issued while state proceedings

are pending might serve as the basis for a subsequent injunction against those proceedings to "protect or effectuate" the declaratory judgment, and thus result in a clearly improper interference with the state proceedings. Secondly, even if the declaratory judgment is not used as a basis for actually issuing an injunction, the declaratory relief alone has virtually the same practical impact as a formal injunction would. As we said in the *Wycoff* case:

Is the declaration contemplated here to be res judicata, so that the [state court] cannot hear evidence and decide any matter for itself? If so, the federal court has virtually lifted the case out of the State [court] before it could be heard. If not, the federal judgment serves no useful purpose as a final determination of rights.

We therefore hold that, in cases where the state criminal prosecution was begun prior to the federal suit, the same equitable principles relevant to the propriety of an injunction must be taken into consideration by federal district courts in determining whether to issue a declaratory judgment, and that where an injunction would be impermissible under these principles, declaratory relief should ordinarily be denied as well.

Interestingly, *Samuels* expressed the same reservation about relief in the absence of a pending proceeding as had *Younger:* "We, of course, express no views on the propriety of declaratory relief when no state proceeding is pending at the time the federal suit is begun."

The Court also decided that a federal court cannot order suppression of evidence in a pending state criminal proceeding because such an order might terminate the prosecution as effectively as an injunction. *Perez v. Ledesma,* 401 U.S. 82, 91 S.Ct. 674, 27 L.Ed.2d 701 (1971). In *Boyle v. Landry,* 401 U.S. 77, 91 S.Ct. 758, 27 L.Ed.2d 696 (1971), the Court reversed and remanded with directions to dismiss on the ground that the plaintiffs had not shown even a threatened prosecution and therefore could not show irreparable harm. In *Dyson v. Stein,* 401 U.S. 200, 91 S.Ct. 769, 27 L.Ed.2d 781 (1971) (*per curiam*), and *Byrne v. Karalexis,* 401 U.S. 216, 91 S.Ct. 777, 27 L.Ed.2d 792 (1971) (*per curiam*), cases similar in structure to *Younger* itself, the Court remanded with directions that the district court further consider the injury that the plaintiffs alleged to have suffered.

a) Is the Court's position in *Samuels* tantamount to saying that the Declaratory Judgment Act, 28 U.S.C.A. §§ 2201-2202, was not intended to apply to state criminal proceedings? As Professor Chemerinsky points out, refusal to grant equitable relief is usually justified by the argument that legal relief is available, not by any concept that some other court may be able to decide the same issue as that presented to the court sitting in equity. ERWIN CHEMERINSKY, FEDERAL JURISDICTION § 13.2, at 829 (5th ed. 2007). "It was never a doctrine of equity that a federal court should exercise its judicial discretion to dismiss a suit merely because a state court could entertain it." *Alabama Public Service Commission v. Southern Railway,* 341 U.S. 341, 361, 71 S.Ct. 762, 774, 95 L.Ed. 1002, 1015 (1951). Leaving comity aside, in light of the Court's confident pronouncement in 1951, is there any reason the federal courts should not issue a declaratory judgment in a

Samuels situation?

b) The Court noted that it might allow declaratory relief where it would not allow injunctive relief. Since the preceding paragraph of *Samuels* took some pains to demonstrate the unity of effect of declaratory and injunctive relief on state proceedings, how is it possible that one is permissible and the other not? In what sort of case would the Court permit declaratory, but not injunctive, relief because of *Younger*? The next case addresses that question.

STEFFEL v. THOMPSON
Supreme Court of the United States, 1974.
415 U.S. 452, 94 S.Ct. 1209, 39 L.Ed.2d 505.

MR. JUSTICE BRENNAN delivered the opinion of the Court.

* * * This case presents the important question reserved in *Samuels v. Mackell,* whether declaratory relief is precluded when a state prosecution has been threatened, but is not pending, and a showing of bad-faith enforcement or other special circumstances has not been made.

Petitioner, and others, filed a complaint in the District Court for the Northern District of Georgia, invoking the Civil Rights Act of 1871 * * *. The complaint requested a declaratory judgment that Ga.Code Ann. § 26-1503 (1972) was being applied in violation of petitioner's First and Fourteenth Amendment rights, and an injunction restraining respondents * * * from enforcing the statute so as to interfere with petitioner's constitutionally protected activities.

The parties stipulated to the relevant facts: On October 8, 1970, while petitioner and other individuals were distributing handbills protesting American involvement in Vietnam on an exterior sidewalk of the North DeKalb Shopping Center, shopping center employees asked them to stop handbilling and leave. They declined to do so, and police officers were summoned. The officers told them that they would be arrested if they did not stop handbilling. The group then left to avoid arrest. Two days later petitioner and a companion returned to the shopping center and again began handbilling. The manager of the center called the police, and petitioner and his companion were once again told that failure to stop their handbilling would result in their arrests. Petitioner left to avoid arrest. His companion stayed, however, continued handbilling, and was arrested and subsequently arraigned on a charge of criminal trespass in violation of § 26-1503. Petitioner alleged in his complaint that, although he desired to return to the shopping center to distribute handbills, he had not done so because of his concern that he, too, would be arrested for violation of § 26-1503; the parties stipulated that, if petitioner returned and refused upon request to stop handbilling, a warrant would be sworn out and he might be arrested and charged with a violation of the Georgia statute.[4]

_____

[4] At the District Court hearing, counsel for the police officers indicated that arrests in

After hearing, the District Court denied all relief and dismissed the action, finding that "no meaningful contention can be made that the state has [acted] or will in the future act in bad faith," and therefore "the rudiments of an active controversy between the parties * * * [are] lacking." Petitioner appealed only from the denial of declaratory relief. The Court of Appeals for the Fifth Circuit, one judge concurring in the result, affirmed the District Court's judgment refusing declaratory relief. * * *

We granted certiorari and now reverse.

I

At the threshold we must consider whether petitioner presents an "actual controversy," a requirement imposed by art. III of the Constitution and the express terms of the Federal Declaratory Judgment Act, 28 U.S.C. § 2201.

Unlike three of the appellees in *Younger v. Harris,* petitioner has alleged threats of prosecution that cannot be characterized as "imaginary or speculative." He has been twice warned to stop handbilling that he claims is constitutionally protected and has been told by the police that if he again handbills at the shopping center and disobeys a warning to stop he will likely be prosecuted. The prosecution of petitioner's handbilling companion is ample demonstration that petitioner's concern with arrest has not been "chimerical." In these circumstances, it is not necessary that petitioner first expose himself to actual arrest or prosecution to be entitled to challenge a statute that he claims deters the exercise of his constitutional rights. Moreover, petitioner's challenge is to those specific provisions of state law which have provided the basis for threats of criminal prosecution against him.

Nonetheless, there remains a question as to the continuing existence of a live and acute controversy that must be resolved on the remand we order today. * * * Here, petitioner's complaint indicates that his handbilling activities were directed "against the war in Vietnam and the United States foreign policy in Southeast Asia." Since we cannot ignore the recent developments reducing the Nation's involvement in that part of the world, it will be for the District Court on remand to determine if subsequent events have so altered petitioner's desire to engage in handbilling at the shopping center that it can no longer be said that this case presents "a substantial controversy, between parties having adverse legal interests, of sufficient immediacy and reality to warrant the issuance of a declaratory judgment."

II

We now turn to the question of whether the District Court and the Court of Appeals correctly found petitioner's request for declaratory re-

---

fact would be made if warrants sworn out by shopping center personnel were facially proper.

lief inappropriate.

* * *

Neither *Younger* nor *Samuels* * * * decided the question whether federal intervention might be permissible in the absence of a pending state prosecution. In *Younger,* the Court said: "We express no view about the circumstances under which federal courts may act when there is no prosecution pending in state courts at the time the federal proceeding is begun." Similarly, in *Samuels v. Mackell,* the Court stated: "We, of course, express no views on the propriety of declaratory relief when no state proceeding is pending at the time the federal suit is begun."

These reservations anticipated the Court's recognition that the relevant principles of equity, comity, and federalism "have little force in the absence of a pending state proceeding." When no state criminal proceeding is pending at the time the federal complaint is filed, federal intervention does not result in duplicative legal proceedings or disruption of the state criminal justice system; nor can federal intervention, in that circumstance, be interpreted as reflecting negatively upon the state court's ability to enforce constitutional principles. In addition, while a pending state prosecution provides the federal plaintiff with a concrete opportunity to vindicate his constitutional rights, a refusal on the part of the federal courts to intervene when no state proceeding is pending may place the hapless plaintiff between the Scylla of intentionally flouting state law and the Charybdis of foregoing what he believes to be constitutionally protected activity in order to avoid becoming enmeshed in a criminal proceeding.

When no state proceeding is pending and thus considerations of equity, comity, and federalism have little vitality, the propriety of granting federal declaratory relief may properly be considered independently of a request for injunctive relief. Here, the Court of Appeals held that, because injunctive relief would not be appropriate since petitioner failed to demonstrate irreparable injury—a traditional prerequisite to injunctive relief—it followed that declaratory relief was also inappropriate. Even if the Court of Appeals correctly viewed injunctive relief as inappropriate— a question we need not reach today since petitioner has abandoned his request for that remedy—[12] the court erred in treating the requests for injunctive and declaratory relief as a single issue.

[W]hen no state prosecution is pending and the only question is whether declaratory relief is appropriate[,] * * * the congressional

---

[12] We note that, in those cases where injunctive relief has been sought to restrain an imminent, but not yet pending, prosecution for past conduct, sufficient injury has not been found to warrant injunctive relief. There is some question, however, whether a showing of irreparable injury might be made in a case where, although no prosecution is pending or impending, an individual demonstrates that he will be required to forgo constitutionally protected activity in order to avoid arrest * * * .

scheme that makes the federal courts the primary guardians of constitutional rights, and the express congressional authorization of declaratory relief, afforded because it is a less harsh and abrasive remedy than the injunction, become the factors of primary significance.

The subject matter jurisdiction of the lower federal courts was greatly expanded in the wake of the Civil War. A pervasive sense of nationalism led to enactment of the Civil Rights Act of 1871, empowering the lower federal courts to determine the constitutionality of actions, taken by persons under color of state law, allegedly depriving other individuals of rights guaranteed by the Constitution and federal law.[13] Four years later, in the Judiciary Act of March 3, 1875, Congress conferred upon the lower federal courts, for but the second time in their nearly century-old history, general federal question jurisdiction subject only to a jurisdictional-amount requirement. With this latter enactment, the lower federal courts "ceased to be restricted tribunals of fair dealing between citizens of different states and became the *primary* and powerful reliances for vindicating every right given by the Constitution, the laws, and treaties of the United States." F. Frankfurter & J. Landis, The Business of the Supreme Court 65 (1928) (emphasis added). These two statutes, together with the Court's decision in *Ex parte Young*—holding that state officials who threaten to enforce an unconstitutional state statute may be enjoined by a federal court of equity and that a federal court may, in appropriate circumstances, enjoin future state criminal prosecutions under the unconstitutional Act—have "established the modern framework for federal protection of constitutional rights from state interference."

A "storm of controversy" raged in the wake of *Ex parte Young,* focusing principally on the power of a single federal judge to grant ex parte interlocutory injunctions against the enforcement of state statutes. This uproar was only partially quelled by Congress' passage of legislation requiring the convening of a three-judge district court before a preliminary injunction against enforcement of a state statute could issue, and providing for direct appeal to this Court from a decision granting or denying such relief. From a State's viewpoint the granting of injunctive relief—even by these courts of special dignity—"rather clumsily" crippled state enforcement of its statutes pending further review. Furthermore, plaintiffs were dissatisfied with this method of testing the constitutionality of state statutes, since it placed upon them the burden of demonstrating

---

[13] Sensitiveness to "states' rights", fear of rivalry with state courts and respect for state sentiment, were swept aside by the great impulse of national feeling born of the Civil War. Nationalism was triumphant; in national administration was sought its vindication. The new exertions of federal power were no longer trusted to the enforcement of state agencies.

F. FRANKFURTER & J. LANDIS, THE BUSINESS OF THE SUPREME COURT 64 (1928).

the traditional prerequisites to equitable relief—most importantly, irreparable injury.

To dispel these difficulties, Congress in 1934 enacted the Declaratory Judgment Act. That Congress plainly intended declaratory relief to act as an alternative to the strong medicine of the injunction and to be utilized to test the constitutionality of state criminal statutes in cases where injunctive relief would be unavailable is amply evidenced by the legislative history of the Act * * * .

* * *

First, as Congress recognized in 1934, a declaratory judgment will have a less intrusive effect on the administration of state criminal laws. As was observed in *Perez v. Ledesma* (separate opinion of Brennan, J.):

> Of course, a favorable declaratory judgment may nevertheless be valuable to the plaintiff though it cannot make even an unconstitutional statute disappear. A state statute may be declared unconstitutional *in toto*—that is, incapable of having constitutional applications; or it may be declared unconstitutionally vague or overbroad—that is, incapable of being constitutionally applied to the full extent of its purport. In either case, a federal declaration of unconstitutionality reflects the opinion of the federal court that the statute cannot be fully enforced. If a declaration of total unconstitutionality is affirmed by this Court, it follows that this Court stands ready to reverse any conviction under the statute. If a declaration of partial unconstitutionality is affirmed by this Court, the implication is that this Court will overturn particular applications of the statute, but that if the statute is narrowly construed by the state courts it will not be incapable of constitutional applications. Accordingly, the declaration does not necessarily bar prosecutions under the statute, as a broad injunction would. Thus, where the highest court of a State has had an opportunity to give a statute regulating expression a narrowing or clarifying construction but has failed to do so, and later a federal court declares the statute unconstitutionally vague or overbroad, it may well be open to a state prosecutor, after the federal court decision, to bring a prosecution under the statute if he reasonably believes that the defendant's conduct is not constitutionally protected and that the state courts may give the statute a construction so as to yield a constitutionally valid conviction. Even where a declaration of unconstitutionality is not reviewed by this Court, the declaration may still be able to cut down the deterrent effect of an unconstitutional state statute. The persuasive force of the court's opinion and judgment may lead state prosecutors, courts, and legislators to reconsider their respective responsibilities toward the statute. Enforcement policies or judicial construction may be changed, or the legislature may repeal the statute and start anew. Finally, the federal court judgment may have some res judicata effect, though this point is

not free from difficulty and the governing rules remain to be developed with a view to the proper workings of a federal system. What is clear, however, is that even though a declaratory judgment has "the force and effect of a final judgment," 28 U.S.C. § 2201, it is a much milder form of relief than an injunction. Though it may be persuasive, it is not ultimately coercive; noncompliance with it may be inappropriate, but is not contempt.

Second, engrafting upon the Declaratory Judgment Act a requirement that all of the traditional equitable prerequisites to the issuance of an injunction be satisfied before the issuance of a declaratory judgment is considered would defy Congress' intent to make declaratory relief available in cases where an injunction would be inappropriate. * * * Thus, the Court of Appeals was in error when it ruled that a failure to demonstrate irreparable injury—a traditional prerequisite to injunctive relief, having no equivalent in the law of declaratory judgments—precluded the granting of declaratory relief.

The only occasions where this Court has disregarded these "different considerations" and found that a preclusion of injunctive relief inevitably led to a denial of declaratory relief have been cases in which principles of federalism militated altogether against federal intervention in a class of adjudications. In the instant case principles of federalism not only do not preclude federal intervention, they compel it. Requiring the federal courts totally to step aside when no state criminal prosecution is pending against the federal plaintiff would turn federalism on its head. When federal claims are premised on 42 U.S.C. § 1983 and 28 U.S.C. § 1343(3)—as they are here—we have not required exhaustion of state judicial or administrative remedies, recognizing the paramount role Congress has assigned to the federal courts to protect constitutional rights. But exhaustion of state remedies is precisely what would be required if both federal injunctive and declaratory relief were unavailable in a case where no state prosecution had been commenced.

III

Respondents, however, * * * argue that, although it may be appropriate to issue a declaratory judgment when no state criminal proceeding is pending and the attack is upon the facial validity of a state criminal statute, such a step would be improper where, as here, the attack is merely upon the constitutionality of the statute as applied, since the State's interest in unencumbered enforcement of its laws outweighs the minimal federal interest in protecting the constitutional rights of only a single individual. We reject the argument.

* * *

Indeed, the State's concern with potential interference in the administration of its criminal laws is of lesser dimension when an attack is made upon the constitutionality of a state statute as applied. A declaratory judgment of a lower federal court that a state statute is invalid *in toto*—and therefore incapable of any valid application—or is overbroad or vague—and therefore no person can properly be convicted under the statute until it is given a narrowing or clarifying construction—will likely have a more significant potential for disruption of state enforcement policies than a declaration specifying a limited number of impermissible applications of the statute. While the federal interest may be greater when a state statute is attacked on its face, since there exists the potential for eliminating any broad-ranging deterrent effect on would-be actors, we do not find this consideration controlling. The solitary individual who suffers a deprivation of his constitutional rights is no less deserving of redress than one who suffers together with others.[21]

We therefore hold that, regardless of whether injunctive relief may be appropriate, federal declaratory relief is not precluded when no state prosecution is pending and a federal plaintiff demonstrates a genuine threat of enforcement of a disputed state criminal statute, whether an attack is made on the constitutionality of the statute on its face or as applied. The judgment of the Court of Appeals is reversed, and the case is remanded for further proceedings consistent with this opinion.

It is so ordered.

MR. JUSTICE REHNQUIST, with whom THE CHIEF JUSTICE joins, concurring.

I concur in the opinion of the Court. Although my reading of the legislative history of the Declaratory Judgment Act of 1934 suggests that its primary purpose was to enable persons to obtain a definition of their rights before an actual injury had occurred, rather than to palliate any controversy arising from *Ex parte Young,* Congress apparently was aware at the time it passed the Act that persons threatened with state criminal prosecutions might choose to forgo the offending conduct and instead seek a federal declaration of their rights. Use of the declaratory judgment procedure in the circumstances presented by this case seems consistent with that congressional expectation.

If this case were the Court's first opportunity to deal with this area of law, I would be content to let the matter rest there. But, as our cases abundantly illustrate, this area of law is in constant litigation, and it is an area through which our decisions have traced a path that may accurately be described as sinuous. Attempting to accommodate the principles of the new declaratory judgment procedure with other more established principles—in particular a proper regard for the relationship be-

---

[21] Abstention, a question "entirely separate from the question of granting declaratory or injunctive relief," might be more appropriate when a challenge is made to the state statute as applied, rather than upon its face, since the reach of an uncertain state statute might, in that circumstance, be more susceptible of a limiting or clarifying construction that would avoid the federal constitutional question.

tween the independent state and federal judiciary systems—this Court has acted both to advance and to limit the Act. Because the opinion today may possibly be read by resourceful counsel as commencing a new and less restrictive curve in this path of adjudication, I feel it is important to emphasize what the opinion does and does not say.

To begin with, it seems appropriate to restate the obvious: the Court's decision today deals only with declaratory relief and with threatened prosecutions. The case provides no authority for the granting of any injunctive relief nor does it provide authority for the granting of any relief at all when prosecutions are pending. The Court quite properly leaves for another day whether the granting of a declaratory judgment by a federal court will have any subsequent res judicata effect or will perhaps support the issuance of a later federal injunction. But since possible resolutions of those issues would substantially undercut the principles of federalism reaffirmed in *Younger v. Harris,* and preserved by the decision today, I feel it appropriate to add a few remarks.

First, the legislative history of the Declaratory Judgment Act and the Court's opinion in this case both recognize that the declaratory judgment procedure is an alternative to pursuit of the arguably illegal activity.[1] There is nothing in the Act's history to suggest that Congress intended to provide persons wishing to violate state laws with a federal shield behind which they could carry on their contemplated conduct. Thus I do not believe that a federal plaintiff in a declaratory judgment action can avoid, by the mere filing of a complaint, the principles so firmly expressed in *Samuels.* The plaintiff who continues to violate a state statute after the filing of his federal complaint does so both at the risk of state prosecution and at the risk of dismissal of his federal lawsuit. For any arrest prior to resolution of the federal action would constitute a pending prosecution and bar declaratory relief under the principles of *Samuels.*

Second, I do not believe that today's decision can properly be raised to support the issuance of a federal injunction based upon a favorable declaratory judgment.[2] The Court's description of declaratory relief as "a

[1] The report accompanying the Senate version of the bill stated:

> The procedure has been especially useful in avoiding the necessity, now so often present, of having to act at one's peril or to act on one's own interpretation of his rights, or abandon one's rights because of a fear of incurring damages. So now it is often necessary, in the absence of the declaratory judgment procedure, to violate or purport to violate a statute in order to obtain a judicial determination of its meaning or validity * * *. Persons now often have to act at their peril, a danger which could be frequently avoided by the ability to sue for a declaratory judgment as to their rights or duties.

Petitioner in this case, of course, did cease his handbilling activities after the warning of arrest.

[2] In *Samuels v. Mackell,* the Court expressed concern that a declaratory judgment issued while a state prosecution was pending "might serve as the basis for a subsequent

milder alternative to the injunction remedy," having a "less intrusive effect on the administration of state criminal laws" than an injunction, indicates to me critical distinctions which make declaratory relief appropriate where injunctive relief would not be. It would all but totally obscure these important distinctions if a successful application for declaratory relief came to be regarded, not as the conclusion of lawsuit, but as a giant step toward obtaining an injunction against a subsequent criminal prosecution. The availability of injunctive relief must be considered with an eye toward the important policies of federalism which this Court has often recognized.

If the rationale of cases such as *Younger* and *Samuels* turned in any way upon the relative ease with which a federal district court could reach a conclusion about the constitutionality of a challenged state statute, a preexisting judgment declaring the statute unconstitutional as applied to a particular plaintiff would, of course, be a factor favoring the issuance of an injunction as "further relief" under the Declaratory Judgment Act. But, except for statutes that are "flagrantly and patently violative of express constitutional prohibitions in every clause, sentence and paragraph * * *," the rationale of those cases has no such basis. Their direction that federal courts not interfere with state prosecutions does not vary depending on the closeness of the constitutional issue or on the degree of confidence which the federal court possesses in the correctness of its conclusions on the constitutional point. Those decisions instead depend upon considerations relevant to the harmonious operation of separate federal and state court systems, with a special regard for the State's interest in enforcing its own criminal laws, considerations which are as relevant in guiding the action of a federal court which has previously issued a declaratory judgment as they are in guiding the action of one which has not. While the result may be that injunctive relief is not available as "further relief" under the Declaratory Judgment Act in this particular class of cases whereas it would be in similar cases not involving considerations of federalism, this would be no more a *pro tanto* repeal of that provision of the Declaratory Judgment Act than was *Younger* a *pro tanto* repeal of the All Writs Act, 28 U.S.C. § 1651.

A declaratory judgment is simply a statement of rights, not a binding order supplemented by continuing sanctions. State authorities may choose to be guided by the judgment of a lower federal court, but they are not compelled to follow the decision by threat of contempt or other penalties. If the federal plaintiff pursues the conduct for which he was previously threatened with arrest and is in fact arrested, he may not return the controversy to federal court, although he may, of course, raise the federal declaratory judgment in the state court for whatever value it

---

injunction against those proceedings * * * ." The Court recognized that this chain of litigation would "result in a clearly improper interference with the state proceedings." I believe that such improper interference would be present even though the declaratory judgment itself were issued prior to the time of the federal plaintiff's arrest.

may prove to have.[3] In any event, the defendant at that point is able to present his case for full consideration by a state court charged, as are the federal courts, to preserve the defendant's constitutional rights. Federal interference with this process would involve precisely the same concerns discussed in *Younger* and recited in the Court's opinion in this case.

Third, attempts to circumvent *Younger* by claiming that enforcement of a statute declared unconstitutional by a federal court is *per se* evidence of bad faith should not find support in the Court's decision in this case. As the Court notes, quoting my Brother Brennan's separate opinion in *Perez v. Ledesma,* 401 U.S. 82, 125: "The persuasive force of the [federal] court's opinion and judgment *may* lead state prosecutors, courts, and legislators to reconsider their respective responsibilities toward the statute. Enforcement policies or judicial construction *may* be changed, or the legislature *may* repeal the statute and start anew." (Emphasis added.) This language clearly recognizes that continued belief in the constitutionality of the statute by state prosecutorial officials would not commonly be indicative of bad faith and that such allegations, in the absence of highly unusual circumstances, would not justify a federal court's departure from the general principles of restraint discussed in *Younger.*

If the declaratory judgment remains, as I think the Declaratory Judgment Act intended, a simple declaration of rights without more, it will not be used merely as a dramatic tactical maneuver on the part of any state defendant seeking extended delays. Nor will it force state officials to try cases time after time, first in the federal courts and then in the state courts. I do not believe Congress desired such unnecessary, results, and I do not think that today's decision should be read to sanction them. Rather the Act, and the decision, stand for the sensible proposition that both a potential state defendant, threatened with prosecution but not charged, and the State itself, confronted by a possible violation of its criminal laws, may benefit from a procedure which provides for a declaration of rights without activation of the criminal process. If the federal court finds that the threatened prosecution would depend upon a statute it judges unconstitutional, the State may decide to forgo prosecution of similar conduct in the future, believing the judgment persuasive. Should the state prosecutors not find the decision persuasive enough to justify forbearance, the successful federal plaintiff will at least be able to bolster his allegations of unconstitutionality in the state trial with a decision of the federal district court in the immediate locality.

---

[3] The Court's opinion notes that the possible res judicata effect of a federal declaratory judgment in a subsequent state court prosecution is a question "not free from difficulty." I express no opinion on that issue here. However, I do note that the federal decision would not be accorded the *stare decisis* effect in state court that it would have in a subsequent proceeding within the same federal jurisdiction. Although the state court would not be compelled to follow the federal holding, the opinion might, of course, be viewed as highly persuasive.

The state courts may find the reasoning convincing even though the prosecutors did not. Finally, of course, the state legislature may decide, on the basis of the federal decision, that the statute would be better amended or repealed. All these possible avenues of relief would be reached voluntarily by the States and would be completely consistent with the concepts of federalism discussed above. Other more intrusive forms of relief should not be routinely available.

These considerations should prove highly significant in reaching future decisions based upon the decision rendered today. For the present it is enough to say, as the Court does, that petitioner, if he successfully establishes the existence of a continuing controversy on remand, may maintain an action for a declaratory judgment in the District Court.

Notes and Questions

1. The unanimous decision in *Steffel* may seem generous to potential § 1983 plaintiffs, but it poses substantial practical problems. The potential plaintiff must avoid actual arrest at all costs. Why? Nonetheless, the threat of arrest must be sufficiently real to present a genuine case or controversy. Steffel was fortunate that his unnamed colleague's persistence provided a control case. Suppose the unnamed colleague had not been there or had desisted with Steffel when they were threatened with arrest. Would the Court still have allowed Steffel to proceed? Suppose they had both desisted on the first occasion rather than returning to be warned a second time. Would that have affected the existence of a justiciable case? Should it?

In *Younger,* three of Harris's co-appellants alleged that Harris's arrest deterred them from engaging in similar First Amendment activities. The Court held they lacked standing because "[n]one has been indicted, arrested, or even threatened by the prosecutor." Harris had been arrested for distributing certain leaflets. Co-plaintiffs Dan and Hirsch alleged that they were members of the same political party as Harris and were "inhibited in advocating the program of their political party through peaceful, non-violent means, because of the presence of the Act 'on the books,' and because of the pending criminal prosecution against Harris." *Harris v. Younger,* 281 F.Supp. 507 (C.D.Cal.1968), *rev'd*, 401 U.S. 37, 91 S.Ct. 746, 27 L.Ed.2d 669 (1971). If they had alleged that they wished to distribute the same leaflet as Harris, would the Court have found that they had standing, or would they have had to allege that they wished to do it at the same time and place?

Should any explicit threat be required? There are no empirical data available, but it may be unusual for police confronted with what they believe to be a violation, even a non-violent one, first to warn and only then to arrest if the conduct is not discontinued. Certainly there is no constitutional compulsion for them to do so. Thus, a potential federal plaintiff's ability to avoid the Scylla-Charybdis dilemma to which Justice Brennan referred may be limited as a practical matter by his luck in finding a police officer at least as interested in negotiation as in arrest.

2. The Court notes that Congress intended the Declaratory Judgment Act to be available for challenging state criminal statutes. Does that under-

cut the rationale for *Samuels v. Mackell*? If Congress intended the Declaratory Judgment Act to be used even when a state criminal proceeding was already pending, then is *Samuels* a usurpation, exalting the judicial power to make common law over the congressional power to enact statutes? If Congress did not so intend, is it relevant to inquire how much of a threat of arrest or prosecution Congress thought should justify a declaratory judgment, or is that matter partially or entirely beyond Congress's control?

3. Justice Rehnquist's concurrence raises several interesting questions, having to do both with federalism and separation of powers.

a) He notes that the Court has attempted to reconcile what he calls the "new declaratory judgment procedure with other more established principles" involving primarily federalism. Does he imply that it is peculiarly the function of the federal courts to define what constitutes a "proper regard for the relationship between the independent state and federal judiciary systems"? Suppose the federal courts and Congress differ about what constitutes proper regard. Whose view should prevail?

b) In conjunction with that discussion, Justice Rehnquist notes that the Court has on occasion limited the reach of the Declaratory Judgment Act. On what basis is it permissible for the Court to do that?

c) Although concurring about the availability of declaratory relief in *Steffel,* Justice Rehnquist seems to have a very limited view of the office and effect of a declaratory judgment. If, as he suggests, such a judgment does not support further relief then what has become of 28 U.S.C.A. § 2202, which states: "Further necessary or proper relief based on a declaratory judgment or decree may be granted, after reasonable notice and hearing, against any adverse party whose rights have been determined by such judgment"? Moreover, if the declaratory judgment may not even have res judicata effect, how is it distinguishable from an advisory opinion? Finally, if the effect of declaratory relief is so limited, then is there not less justification for the Court's decision in *Samuels v. Mackell*? But the Court decided *Samuels* on premises directly contradicting Justice Rehnquist's arguments, relying on the possibility of further relief in support of the declaratory judgment that would be as intrusive as an injunction. "Ordinarily, * * * the practical effect of the two forms of relief will be virtually identical * * * ."

4. *Steffel* left open the question of whether plaintiffs threatened with prosecution under an allegedly unconstitutional statute may seek injunctive relief. The Court answered affirmatively, though perhaps not expansively, in *Doran v. Salem Inn, Inc.,* 422 U.S. 922, 95 S.Ct. 2561, 45 L.Ed.2d 648 (1975). A town in New York passed an ordinance prohibiting topless dancing. Three bars sued in federal court to enjoin enforcement. The district court denied an order temporarily restraining enforcement, but set a hearing date for the plaintiffs' motion for a preliminary injunction. In the interim, one bar resumed its activities and received criminal summonses. The district and circuit courts granted preliminary injunctive relief to all three bars. The Supreme Court affirmed in part and reversed in part. With respect to the bar being prosecuted, the Court held that traditional *Younger* principles precluded either declaratory or injunctive relief. With respect to the other

two bars, however, the Court affirmed the preliminary injunction, noting that "they were assuredly entitled to declaratory relief, and since we have previously recognized that '[o]rdinarily * * * the practical effect of [injunctive and declaratory] relief will be virtually identical,' * * * we think that [the two plaintiffs not being prosecuted] were entitled to have their claims for preliminary injunctive relief considered without regard to *Younger's* restrictions." In the year between *Steffel* and *Doran,* Justice Rehnquist seemed to have forgotten his previously-argued position about the impotence of declaratory relief.

Doran may be a very limited case. The circumstances strongly parallel those in *Steffel*: both involved multiple actors some of whom were subsequently charged and some of whom were not. It is not clear, as it was not in *Steffel,* whether the Court would permit an action if there were not such clear proof of a threat of prosecution.

In *Wooley v. Maynard,* 430 U.S. 705, 97 S.Ct. 1428, 51 L.Ed.2d 752 (1977), the Court approved permanent injunctive relief on behalf of an individual threatened with repeated prosecutions. Plaintiff Maynard obscured the New Hampshire state motto, "Live Free or Die," on his license plate. Within a five week period, he was convicted three times of violating a New Hampshire statute that forbade obscuring any letters on a license plate. Though Maynard had not pursued his state appellate remedies, the Court permitted relief, noting that although *Younger* might preclude an attempt to interfere with on-going prosecutions and might therefore require exhaustion of state remedies with respect to the convictions entered, Maynard did not challenge those convictions, but sought instead only to enjoin future prosecutions. The Court also affirmed the district court's conclusion that declaratory relief was insufficient protection for Maynard in view of the repeated prosecutions.

HICKS v. MIRANDA
Supreme Court of the United States, 1975.
422 U.S. 332, 95 S.Ct. 2281, 45 L.Ed.2d 223.

MR. JUSTICE WHITE delivered the opinion of the Court.

* * *

I

On November 23 and 24, 1973, pursuant to four separate warrants issued *seriatim,* the police seized four copies of the film "Deep Throat," each of which had been shown at the Pussycat Theatre in Buena Park, Orange County, Cal. On November 26 an eight-count criminal misdemeanor charge was filed in the Orange County Municipal Court against two employees of the theater, each film seized being the subject matter of two counts in the complaint. Also on November 26, the Superior Court of Orange County ordered appellees[2] to show cause why "Deep

---

[2] The order ran against Vincent Miranda, dba Pussycat Theatre, Walnut Properties,

Throat" should not be declared obscene, an immediate hearing being available to appellees, who appeared that day, objected on state-law grounds to the court's jurisdiction to conduct such a proceeding, purported to "reserve" all federal questions, and refused further to participate. Thereupon, on November 27 the Superior Court held a hearing, viewed the film, took evidence, and then declared the movie to be obscene and ordered seized all copies of it that might be found at the theater. This judgment and order were not appealed by appellees.

Instead, on November 29, they filed this suit in the District Court against appellants—four police officers of Buena Park and the District Attorney and Assistant District Attorney of Orange County. The complaint recited the seizures and the proceedings in the Superior Court, stated that the action was for an injunction against the enforcement of the California obscenity statute, and prayed for judgment declaring the obscenity statute unconstitutional, and for an injunction ordering the return of all copies of the film but permitting one of the films to be duplicated before its return.

A temporary restraining order was requested and denied, the District Judge finding the proof of irreparable injury to be lacking and an insufficient likelihood of prevailing on the merits to warrant an injunction. He requested the convening of a three-judge court, however, to consider the constitutionality of the statute. Such a court was then designated on January 8, 1974.

Service of the complaint was completed on January 14, 1974, and answers and motions to dismiss, as well as a motion for summary judgment, were filed by appellants. Appellees moved for a preliminary injunction. None of the motions was granted and no hearings held, all of the issues being ordered submitted on briefs and affidavits. The Attorney General of California also appeared and urged the District Court to follow *People v. Enskat,* which, after *Miller v. California,* 413 U.S. 15 (1973) (*Miller I*), had upheld the California obscenity statute.

Meanwhile, on January 15, the criminal complaint pending in the Municipal Court had been amended by naming appellees as additional parties defendant and by adding four conspiracy counts, one relating to each of the seized films. Also, on motions of the defendants in that case, two of the films were ordered suppressed on the ground that the two search warrants for seizing "Deep Throat" last issued, one on November 23 and the other on November 24, did not sufficiently allege that the films to be seized under those warrants differed from each other and from the films previously seized, the final two seizures being said to be invalid multiple seizures. Immediately after this order, which was later

---

Inc., and theater employees. Actually, Miranda, who owned the land on which the theatre was located, did business as Walnut Properties, and Pussycat Theatre Hollywood was a California corporation of which Miranda was president and a stockholder. Nothing has been made by the parties of this confusion in identification.

appealed and reversed, the defense and the prosecution stipulated that for purposes of the trial, which was expected to be forthcoming, the four prints of the film would be considered identical and only one copy would have to be proved at trial.

On June 4, 1974, the three-judge court issued its judgment and opinion declaring the California obscenity statute to be unconstitutional for failure to satisfy the requirements of *Miller I* and ordering appellants to return to appellees all copies of "Deep Throat" which had been seized as well as to refrain from making any additional seizures. Appellants' claim that *Younger v. Harris* and *Samuels v. Mackell* required dismissal of the case was rejected, the court holding that no criminal charges were pending in the state court against appellees and that in any event the pattern of search warrants and seizures demonstrated bad faith and harassment on the part of the authorities, all of which relieved the court from the strictures of *Younger v. Harris* and its related cases.

Appellants filed various motions for rehearing, to amend the judgment, and for relief from judgment, also later calling the court's attention to two developments they considered important: First, the dismissal on July 25, 1974, "for want of a substantial federal question" of the appeal in *Miller v. California,* 418 U.S. 915 (*Miller II*), from a judgment of the Superior Court, Appellate Department, Orange County, California, sustaining the constitutionality of the very California obscenity statute which the District Court had declared unconstitutional; second, the reversal by the Superior Court, Appellate Department, of the suppression order which had been issued in the criminal case pending in the Municipal Court, the *per curiam* reversal saying the "requisite prompt adversary determination of obscenity under *Heller v. New York* * * * has been held."

On September 30, the three-judge court denied appellants' motions, reaffirmed its June 4 *Younger v. Harris* ruling and, after concluding it was not bound by the dismissal of *Miller II,* adhered to its judgment that the California statute was invalid under the Federal Constitution. In response to appellants' claim that they were without power to comply with the June 4 injunction, the films being in the possession of the Municipal Court, the court amended the injunctive portion of its order so as to read as follows: "The defendants shall in good faith petition the Municipal Court of the North Orange County Judicial District to return to the plaintiffs three of the four film prints seized from the plaintiffs on November 23 and 24, 1973, in the City of Buena Park." Appeals were taken to this Court from both the judgment of June 4 and the amended judgment of September 30. We postponed further consideration of our jurisdiction to the consideration of the merits of the case.

* * *

III

The District Court committed error in reaching the merits of this case despite the appellants' insistence that it be dismissed under *Younger v. Harris* and *Samuels v. Mackell.* When they filed their federal complaint, no state criminal proceedings were pending against appellees by name; but two employees of the theater had been charged and four copies of "Deep Throat" belonging to appellees had been seized, were being held, and had been declared to be obscene and seizable by the Superior Court. Appellees had a substantial stake in the state proceedings, so much so that they sought federal relief, demanding that the state statute be declared void and their films be returned to them. Obviously, their interests and those of their employees were intertwined; and, as we have pointed out, the federal action sought to interfere with the pending state prosecution. Absent a clear showing that appellees, whose lawyers also represented their employees, could not seek the return of their property in the state proceedings and see to it that their federal claims were presented there, the requirements of *Younger v. Harris* could not be avoided on the ground that no criminal prosecution was pending against appellees on the date the federal complaint was filed. The rule in *Younger v. Harris* is designed to "permit state courts to try state cases free from interference by federal courts," particularly where the party to the federal case may fully litigate his claim before the state court. Plainly, "[t]he same comity considerations apply" where the interference is sought by some, such as appellees, not parties to the state case.

What is more, on the day following the completion of service of the complaint, appellees were charged along with their employees in Municipal Court. Neither *Steffel v. Thompson* nor any other case in this Court has held that for *Younger v. Harris* to apply, the state criminal proceedings must be pending on the day the federal case is filed. Indeed, the issue has been left open; and we now hold that where state criminal proceedings are begun against the federal plaintiffs after the federal complaint is filed but before any proceedings of substance on the merits have taken place in the federal court, the principles of *Younger v. Harris* should apply in full force. Here, appellees were charged on January 15, prior to answering the federal case and prior to any proceedings whatsoever before the three-judge court. Unless we are to trivialize the principles of *Younger v. Harris,* the federal complaint should have been dismissed on the appellants' motion absent satisfactory proof of those extraordinary circumstances calling into play one of the limited exceptions to the rule of *Younger v. Harris* and related cases.[18]

---

[18] Appellees also argue that dismissal under *Younger v. Harris* was not required because *People v. Enskat* had settled the constitutional issue in the state courts with respect to the obscenity statute. But *Younger v. Harris* is not so easily avoided. State courts, like other courts, sometimes change their minds. Moreover, *People v. Enskat* was the decision of an intermediate appellate court of the State, and the Supreme Court of California could have again been asked to pass upon the constitutionality of the California statute. In any

The District Court concluded that extraordinary circumstances had been shown in the form of official harassment and bad faith, but this was also error. The relevant findings of the District Court were vague and conclusory. There were references to the "pattern of seizure" and to "the evidence brought to light by the petition for rehearing"; and the unexplicated conclusion was then drawn that "regardless of the nature of any judicial proceeding," the police were bent on banishing "Deep Throat" from Buena Park. Yet each step in the pattern of seizures condemned by the District Court was authorized by judicial warrant or order; and the District Court did not purport to invalidate any of the four warrants, in any way to question the propriety of the proceedings in the Superior Court,[20] or even to mention the reversal of the suppression order in the Appellate Department of that court. Absent at least some effort by the District Court to impeach the entitlement of the prosecuting officials to rely on repeated judicial authorization for their conduct, we cannot agree that bad faith and harassment were made out. Indeed, such conclusion would not necessarily follow even if it were shown that the state courts were in error on some one or more issues of state or federal law.

In the last analysis, it seems to us that the District Court's judgment rests almost entirely on its conclusion that the California obscenity statute was unconstitutional and unenforceable. But even assuming that the District Court was correct in its conclusion, the statute had not been so condemned in November 1973, and the District Court was not entitled to infer official bad faith merely because it—the District Court— disagreed with *People v. Enskat.* Otherwise, bad faith and harassment would be present in every case in which a state statute is ruled unconstitutional, and the rule of *Younger v. Harris* would be swallowed up by its exception. The District Court should have dismissed the complaint before it and we accordingly reverse its judgment.

So ordered.

MR. JUSTICE STEWART, with whom MR. JUSTICE DOUGLAS, MR. JUSTICE BRENNAN, and MR. JUSTICE MARSHALL join, dissenting.

* * *

In *Steffel v. Thompson,* the Court unanimously held that the principles of equity, comity, and federalism embodied in *Younger v. Harris* and

---

event, the way was open for appellees to present their federal issues to this Court in the event of adverse decision in the California courts.

[20] It has been noted that appellees did not appeal the Superior Court's order of November 27, 1973, declaring "Deep Throat" obscene and ordering all copies of it seized. It may be that under Huffman v. Pursue, Ltd., 420 U.S. 592 (1975), the failure of appellees to appeal the Superior Court order of November 27, 1973, would itself foreclose resort to federal court, absent extraordinary circumstances bringing the case within some exception to *Younger v. Harris.* Appellees now assert, seemingly contrary to their prior statement before Judge Ferguson, that the November 27 order was not appealable. In view of our disposition of the case, we need not pursue the matter further.

Samuels v. Mackell do not preclude a federal district court from entertaining an action to declare unconstitutional a state criminal statute when a state criminal prosecution is threatened but not pending at the time the federal complaint is filed. Today the Court holds that the *Steffel* decision is inoperative if a state criminal charge is filed at any point after the commencement of the federal action "before any proceedings of substance on the merits have taken place in the federal court." Any other rule, says the Court, would "trivialize" the principles of *Younger v. Harris.* I think this ruling "trivializes" *Steffel,* decided just last Term, and is inconsistent with those same principles of equity, comity, and federalism.[1]

There is, to be sure, something unseemly about having the applicability of the *Younger* doctrine turn solely on the outcome of a race to the courthouse. The rule the Court adopts today, however, does not eliminate that race; it merely permits the State to leave the mark later, run a shorter course, and arrive first at the finish line. This rule seems to me to result from a failure to evaluate the state and federal interests as of the time the state prosecution was commenced.

As of the time when its jurisdiction is invoked in a *Steffel* situation, a federal court is called upon to vindicate federal constitutional rights when no other remedy is available to the federal plaintiff. The Court has recognized that at this point in the proceedings no substantial state interests counsel the federal court to stay its hand. Thus, in *Lake Carriers' Assn. v. MacMullan,* we noted that "considerations of equity practice and comity in our federal system have little force in the absence of a pending state proceeding." * * *

Consequently, we concluded [in *Steffel*] that "[r]equiring the federal courts totally to step aside when no state criminal prosecution is pending against the federal plaintiff would turn federalism on its head." In such circumstances, "the opportunity for adjudication of constitutional rights in a federal forum, as authorized by the Declaratory Judgment Act, becomes paramount."

---

[1] There is the additional difficulty that the precise meaning of the rule the Court today adopts is a good deal less than apparent. What are "proceedings of substance on the merits"? Presumably, the proceedings must be both "on the merits" and "of substance." Does this mean, then, that months of discovery activity would be insufficient, if no question on the merits is presented to the court during that time? What proceedings "on the merits" are sufficient is also unclear. An application for a temporary restraining order or a preliminary injunction requires the court to make an assessment about the likelihood of success on the merits. Indeed, in this case, appellees filed an application for a temporary restraining order along with six supporting affidavits on November 29, 1973. Appellants responded on December 3, 1973, with six affidavits of their own as well as additional documents. On December 28, 1973, Judge Lydick denied the request for a temporary restraining order, in part because appellees "have failed totally to make that showing of * * * likelihood of prevailing on the merits needed to justify the issuance of a temporary restraining order." These proceedings, the Court says implicitly, were not sufficient to satisfy the test it announces. Why that should be, even in terms of the Court's holding, is a mystery.

The duty of the federal courts to adjudicate and vindicate federal constitutional rights is, of course, shared with state courts, but there can be no doubt that the federal courts are "the primary and powerful reliances for vindicating every right given by the Constitution, the laws, and treaties of the United States." F. Frankfurter & J. Landis, The Business of the Supreme Court: A Study in the Federal Judicial System 65 (1927). The statute under which this action was brought, 42 U.S.C. § 1983, established in our law "the role of the Federal Government as a guarantor of basic federal rights against state power." Indeed, "[t]he very purpose of § 1983 was to interpose the federal courts between the States and the people." And this central interest of a federal court as guarantor of constitutional rights is fully implicated from the moment its jurisdiction is invoked. How, then, does the subsequent filing of a state criminal charge change the situation from one in which the federal court's dismissal of the action under *Younger* principles "would turn federalism on its head" to one in which failure to dismiss would "trivialize" those same principles?

A State has a vital interest in the enforcement of its criminal law, and this Court has said time and again that it will sanction little federal interference with that important state function. But there is nothing in our decision in *Steffel* that requires a State to stay its hand during the pendency of the federal litigation. If, in the interest of efficiency, the State wishes to refrain from actively prosecuting the criminal charge pending the outcome of the federal declaratory judgment suit, it may, of course, do so. But no decision of this Court requires it to make that choice.

The Court today, however, goes much further than simply recognizing the right of the State to proceed with the orderly administration of its criminal law; it ousts the federal courts from their historic role as the "primary reliances" for vindicating constitutional freedoms. This is no less offensive to "Our Federalism" than the federal injunction restraining pending state criminal proceedings condemned by *Younger v. Harris*. The concept of federalism requires "sensitivity to the legitimate interests of *both* State and National Governments." ([E]mphasis added). *Younger v. Harris* and its companion cases reflect the principles that the federal judiciary must refrain from interfering with the legitimate functioning of state courts. But surely the converse is a principle no less valid.

The Court's new rule creates a reality which few state prosecutors can be expected to ignore. It is an open invitation to state officials to institute state proceedings in order to defeat federal jurisdiction. One need not impugn the motives of state officials to suppose that they would rather prosecute a criminal suit in state court than defend a civil case in a federal forum. Today's opinion virtually instructs state officials to answer federal complaints with state indictments. Today, the State must file a criminal charge to secure dismissal of the federal litigation; perhaps tomorrow an action "akin to a criminal proceeding" will serve the purpose, and the day may not be far off when any state civil action will do.

The doctrine of *Younger v. Harris* reflects an accommodation of competing interests. The rule announced today distorts that balance beyond recognition.

Notes and Questions

1. *Younger v. Harris* held that a federal could not enjoin a pending state criminal proceeding in the absence of special circumstances. Before *Hicks*, a state criminal proceeding was not considered "pending" for *Younger* purposes unless criminal charges were filed against the plaintiff before he began the federal action. After *Hicks*, a state criminal proceeding may be considered pending, thus triggering *Younger* abstention, even if state charges come after the federal suit. How long after initiation of the federal suit does a state prosecutor have to defeat federal jurisdiction by filing state criminal charges? What standard does the Court announce for deciding whether the federal action is far enough along for the federal court to hear it?

a) What is a federal proceeding "of substance on the merits"? In *Hicks*, state criminal charges were filed against the appellees on January 15, 1974, more than six weeks after the federal complaint was filed. What federal proceedings had occurred before January 15, and what papers had the parties filed? Why were these proceedings not "of substance on the merits"? Suppose the district court had granted the temporary restraining order (TRO) enjoining enforcement of the obscenity statute until the court could rule on the appellees' motion for a preliminary injunction. If the California prosecutor had nonetheless initiated the criminal prosecution, would the federal court whose order had just been flouted have been obliged to vacate its order and dismiss the federal action? Or, would the grant of a TRO constitute a proceeding of substance on the merits? Some federal district judges would likely take great offense at being required to abstain in these circumstances. Why? Finally, should determination of whether a proceeding of substance on the merits has occurred depend on whether the court grants or denies plaintiff's TRO motion? Does a difference in outcome mean the proceeding somehow has more or less substance?

b) In *Hawaii Housing Authority v. Midkiff*, 467 U.S. 229, 104 S.Ct. 2321, 81 L.Ed.2d 186 (1984), the Court sidestepped the question of whether the grant of a TRO is a proceeding of substance on the merits, but held that granting a preliminary injunction is. "A federal court action in which a preliminary injunction is granted has proceeded well beyond the 'embryonic state,' and considerations of economy, equity, and federalism counsel against *Younger* abstention at that point." Suppose the federal court denied the preliminary injunction. Would that alter the result for *Younger* abstention purposes? Should it?

c) Suppose the plaintiff seeks neither a TRO nor a preliminary injunction, and the federal suit proceeds. *Hicks* and *Hawaii Housing Authority* give no guidance as to what other pretrial proceedings constitute proceedings of substance on the merits. Pretrial conferences under FED.R.CIV.P. 16, discovery, denial of motions for summary judgment or for failure to state a claim upon which relief may be granted, all might or might not qualify. If the prosecutor can wait until the federal case is far along to decide whether to file criminal charges, the prosecutor has an opportunity to evaluate the federal case, staying with it if a win looks likely or aborting it if not.

2. In *Hicks,* the practical effect of commencement of the prosecution six weeks after Miranda filed his federal action was to cut off his right to proceed in federal court. In other circumstances, however, the Court has recognized "the old and well-established judicially-declared rule that state courts are completely without power to restrain federal-court proceedings in *in personam* actions * * * ." *Donovan v. City of Dallas,* 377 U.S. 408, 412-13, 84 S.Ct. 1579, 1582, 12 L.Ed.2d 409, 413 (1964). The Court also noted that Congress has authorized federal restraint of state proceedings in the limited circumstances described by the Anti-Injunction Act, but observed that Congress has done nothing to alter the rule against state-issued injunctions. Does not the result in *Hicks* have the same effect as a state injunction against a federal action? Does *Hicks* overrule *Donovan* in that respect, at least by implication?

3. Justice Rehnquist strongly foreshadowed *Hicks* in his *Steffel* concurrence when he argued that a federal plaintiff seeking a declaratory judgment could not with impunity continue to violate the state statute. "[A]ny arrest prior to resolution of the federal action would constitute a pending prosecution and bar declaratory relief under the principles of *Samuels.*" The Court only a year later adopted much of Justice Rehnquist's idea, though *Hicks* contains a major variation. Under Justice Rehnquist's formulation, the federal proceeding apparently would have to go to judgment in order to survive the commencement of a state proceeding; *Hicks* requires only that there have been "proceedings of substance." Thus, what on first reading may have seemed a restrictive standard in *Hicks* may actually represent a compromise between Justice Rehnquist and other members of the *Hicks* majority. The ultimate paragraph of Justice White's *Steffel* concurrence, in which he articulates a standard (that the federal action be "sufficiently far along") that sounds much like the opinion he wrote for the Court in *Hicks,* supports that theory.

Justice Rehnquist's formulation leaves another question in its wake. He contemplates a plaintiff who, after filing his federal action, resumes his putatively illegal activity and then is prosecuted. Justice Rehnquist has little sympathy for such an individual and sounds almost as if he resents the impatience he sees in such a course of conduct. Steffel was threatened with prosecution and desisted in favor of filing a federal action, while his companion persisted and was arrested. Suppose Steffel had not resumed his activity during the pendency of the federal action, but that the Georgia police had later arrested him for his conduct before the warning and the arrest of his companion. In Justice Rehnquist's view, would the commencement of that state prosecution serve as a predicate for dismissal of the federal action on the authority of *Younger* and *Hicks*? Should it?

4. Does *Hicks* ultimately reduce or increase federal-state friction?

5. It is important to realize that in the mid-1970's the *Younger* doctrine was expanding on two fronts. One, exemplified in *Hicks,* involves the temporal relationship of federal and state proceedings. All of the cases before *Hicks* involved federal actions begun after state proceedings. But, in *Hicks,* the Court, following several broad hints that it would do so, began to consider whether a later-commenced state proceeding could cut off a federal action. The other, initiated by *Huffman v. Pursue, Ltd.,* the following case, concerns the *type* of state proceeding that qualifies for *Younger* deference.

HUFFMAN v. PURSUE, LTD.
Supreme Court of the United States, 1975.
420 U.S. 592, 95 S.Ct. 1200, 43 L.Ed.2d 482.

MR. JUSTICE REHNQUIST delivered the opinion of the Court.

This case requires that we decide whether our decision in *Younger v. Harris* bars a federal district court from intervening in a state civil proceeding such as this, when the proceeding is based on a state statute believed by the district court to be unconstitutional. * * * Today we do reach the issue, and conclude that in the circumstances presented here the principles of *Younger* are applicable even though the state proceeding is civil in nature.

I

Appellants are the sheriff and prosecuting attorney of Allen County, Ohio. This case arises from their efforts to close the Cinema I Theatre, in Lima, Ohio. Under the management of both its current tenant, appellee Pursue, Ltd., and appellee's predecessor, William Dakota, the Cinema I has specialized in the display of films which may fairly be characterized as pornographic, and which in numerous instances have been adjudged obscene after adversary hearings.

Appellants sought to invoke the Ohio public nuisance statute against appellee. [It] provides that a place which exhibits obscene films is a nuisance, [and] requires closure for up to a year of any place determined to be a nuisance. The statute also provides for preliminary injunctions pending final determination of status as a nuisance, for sale of all personal property used in conducting the nuisance, and for release from a closure order upon satisfaction of certain conditions (including a showing that the nuisance will not be reestablished).

Appellants instituted a nuisance proceeding in the Court of Common Pleas of Allen County against appellee's predecessor, William Dakota. During the course of the somewhat involved legal proceedings which followed, the Court of Common Pleas reviewed 16 movies which had been shown at the theater. The court rendered a judgment that Dakota had engaged in a course of conduct of displaying obscene movies at the Cinema I, and that the theater was therefore to be closed, "for any purpose for a period of one year unless sooner released by Order of [the] Court pursuant to defendant-owners fulfilling the requirements provided in

Section 3767.04 of the Revised Code of Ohio." The judgment also provided for the seizure and sale of personal property used in the theater's operations.

Appellee, Pursue, Ltd., had succeeded to William Dakota's leasehold interest in the Cinema I prior to entry of the state-court judgment. Rather than appealing that judgment within the Ohio court system, it immediately filed suit in the United States District Court for the Northern District of Ohio. The complaint was based on 42 U.S.C. § 1983 and alleged that appellants' use of Ohio's nuisance statute constituted a deprivation of constitutional rights under the color of state law. It sought injunctive relief and a declaratory judgment that the statute was unconstitutional and unenforceable. * * * The District Court concluded that while the statute was not vague, it did constitute an overly broad prior restraint on First Amendment rights insofar as it permanently or temporarily prevented the showing of films which had not been adjudged obscene in prior adversary hearings. Fashioning its remedy to match the perceived constitutional defect, the court permanently enjoined the execution of that portion of the state court's judgment that closed the Cinema I to films which had not been adjudged obscene. The judgment and opinion of the District Court give no indication that it considered whether it should have stayed its hand in deference to the principles of federalism which find expression in *Younger v. Harris.*

On this appeal, appellants raise the *Younger* problem, as well as a variety of constitutional and statutory issues. We need consider only the applicability of *Younger.*

* * *

III

The seriousness of federal judicial interference with state civil functions has long been recognized by this Court. We have consistently required that when federal courts are confronted with requests for such relief, they should abide by standards of restraint that go well beyond those of private equity jurisprudence. For example, *Massachusetts State Grange v. Benton* (1926) involved an effort to enjoin the operation of a state daylight savings act. Writing for the Court, Mr. Justice Holmes cited *Fenner v. Boykin* and emphasized a rule that "should be very strictly observed," "that no injunction ought to issue against officers of a State clothed with authority to enforce the law in question, unless in a case reasonably free from doubt and when necessary to prevent great and irreparable injury."

Although Mr. Justice Holmes was confronted with a bill seeking an injunction against state executive officers, rather than against state judicial proceedings, we think that the relevant considerations of federalism are of no less weight in the latter setting. If anything, they counsel more heavily toward federal restraint, since interference with a state judicial proceeding prevents the state not only from effectuating its substantive policies, but also from continuing to perform the separate function of providing a forum competent to vindicate any constitutional objections interposed against those policies. Such interference also results in duplicative legal proceedings, and can readily be interpreted "as reflecting negatively upon the state courts' ability to enforce constitutional principles."

The component of *Younger* which rests upon the threat to our federal system is thus applicable to a civil proceeding such as this quite as much as it is to a criminal proceeding. *Younger* however, also rests upon the traditional reluctance of courts of equity, even within a unitary system, to interfere with a criminal prosecution. Strictly speaking, this element of *Younger* is not available to mandate federal restraint in civil cases. But whatever may be the weight attached to this factor in civil litigation involving private parties, we deal here with a state proceeding which in important respects is more akin to a criminal prosecution than are most civil cases. The State is a party to the Court of Common Pleas proceeding, and the proceeding is both in aid of and closely related to criminal statutes which prohibit the dissemination of obscene materials. Thus, an offense to the State's interest in the nuisance litigation is likely to be every bit as great as it would be were this a criminal proceeding. Similarly, while in this case the District Court's injunction has not directly disrupted Ohio's criminal justice system, it has disrupted that State's efforts to protect the very interests which underlie its criminal laws and to obtain compliance with precisely the standards which are embodied in its criminal laws.

IV

In spite of the critical similarities between a criminal prosecution and Ohio nuisance proceedings, appellee nonetheless urges that there is also a critical difference between the two which should cause us to limit *Younger* to criminal proceedings. This difference, says appellee, is that whereas a state-court criminal defendant may, after exhaustion of his state remedies, present his constitutional claims to the federal courts through habeas corpus, no analogous remedy is available to one, like appellee, whose constitutional rights may have been infringed in a state proceeding which cannot result in custodial detention or other criminal sanction.

A civil litigant may, of course, seek review in this Court of any federal claim properly asserted in and rejected by state courts. Moreover, where a final decision of a state court has sustained the validity of a state statute challenged on federal constitutional grounds, an appeal to this Court lies as a matter of right. Thus, appellee in this case was assured of eventual consideration of its claim by this Court. But quite apart from appellee's right to appeal had it remained in state court, we conclude that it should not be permitted the luxury of federal litigation of issues presented by ongoing state proceedings, a luxury which, as we have already explained, is quite costly in terms of the interests which *Younger* seeks to protect.

Appellee's argument, that because there may be no civil counterpart to federal habeas it should have contemporaneous access to a federal forum for its federal claim, apparently depends on the unarticulated major premise that every litigant who asserts a federal claim is entitled to have it decided on the merits by a federal, rather than a state, court. We need not consider the validity of this premise in order to reject the result which appellee seeks. Even assuming, *arguendo,* that litigants are entitled to a federal forum for the resolution of all federal issues, that entitlement is most appropriately asserted by a state litigant when he seeks to relitigate a federal issue adversely determined in completed state court proceedings. We do not understand why the federal forum must be available prior to completion of the state proceedings in which the federal issue arises, and the considerations canvassed in *Younger* militate against such a result.

The issue of whether federal courts should be able to interfere with ongoing state proceedings is quite distinct and separate from the issue of whether litigants are entitled to subsequent federal review of state-court dispositions of federal questions. *Younger* turned on considerations of comity and federalism peculiar to the fact that state proceedings were pending; it did not turn on the fact that in any event a criminal defendant could eventually have obtained federal habeas consideration of his federal claims. The propriety of federal-court interference with an Ohio nuisance proceeding must likewise be controlled by application of those same considerations of comity and federalism.

* * *

V

Appellee contends that even if *Younger* is applicable to civil proceedings of this sort, it nonetheless does not govern this case because at the time the District Court acted there was no longer a "pending state court proceeding" as that term is used in *Younger. Younger* and subsequent cases such as *Steffel* have used the term "pending proceeding" to distinguish state proceedings which have already commenced from those which are merely incipient or threatened. Here, of course, the state proceeding had begun long before appellee sought intervention by the District Court. But appellee's point, we take it, is not that the state proceeding had not begun, but that it had ended by the time its District Court complaint was filed.[19]

---

[19] It would ordinarily be difficult to consider this problem, that of the duration of *Younger*'s restrictions after entry of a state trial court judgment, without also considering the res judicata implications of such a judgment. However, appellants did not plead res judicata in the District Court, and it is therefore not available to them here.

Appellee apparently relies on the facts that the Allen County Court of Common Pleas had already issued its judgment and permanent injunction when this action was filed, and that no appeal from that judgment has ever been taken to Ohio's appellate courts. As a matter of state procedure, the judgment presumably became final, in the sense of being nonappealable, at some point after the District Court filing, possibly prior to entry of the District Court's own judgment, but surely after the single judge stayed the state court's judgment. We need not, however, engage in such inquiry. For regardless of when the Court of Common Pleas' judgment became final, we believe that a necessary concomitant of *Younger* is that a party in appellee's posture must exhaust his state appellate remedies before seeking relief in the District Court, unless he can bring himself within one of the exceptions specified in *Younger*.

Virtually all of the evils at which *Younger* is directed would inhere in federal intervention prior to completion of state appellate proceedings, just as surely as they would if such intervention occurred at or before trial. Intervention at the later stage is if anything more highly duplicative, since an entire trial has already taken place, and it is also a direct aspersion on the capabilities and good faith of state appellate courts. Nor, in these state-initiated nuisance proceedings, is federal intervention at the appellate stage any the less a disruption of the State's efforts to protect interests which it deems important. Indeed, it is likely to be even more disruptive and offensive because the State has already won a *nisi prius* determination that its valid policies are being violated in a fashion which justifies judicial abatement.

Federal post-trial intervention, in a fashion designed to annul the results of a state trial, also deprives the States of a function which quite legitimately is left to them, that of overseeing trial court dispositions of constitutional issues which arise in civil litigation over which they have jurisdiction. We think this consideration to be of some importance because it is typically a judicial system's appellate courts which are by their nature a litigant's most appropriate forum for the resolution of constitutional contentions. Especially is this true when, as here, the constitutional issue involves a statute which is capable of judicial narrowing. In short, we do not believe that a State's judicial system would be fairly accorded the opportunity to resolve federal issues arising in its courts if a federal district court were permitted to substitute itself for the State's appellate courts. We therefore hold that *Younger* standards must be met to justify federal intervention in a state judicial proceeding as to which a losing litigant has not exhausted his state appellate remedies.[21]

---

[21] By requiring exhaustion of state appellate remedies for the purposes of applying *Younger* we in no way undermine *Monroe v. Pape.* There we held that one seeking redress under 42 U.S.C. § 1983 for a deprivation of federal rights need not first initiate state proceedings based on related state causes of action. *Monroe v. Pape* had nothing to do with the problem presently before us, that of the deference to be accorded state proceedings

* * *

The District Court should not have entertained this action, seeking pre-appeal interference with a state judicial proceeding, unless appellee established that early intervention was justified under one of the exceptions recognized in *Younger*.[22]

VI

* * *

We therefore think that this case is appropriate for remand so that the District Court may consider whether irreparable injury can be shown * * * and if so, whether that injury is of such a nature that the District Court may assume jurisdiction under an exception to the policy against federal judicial interference with state court proceedings of this kind. The judgment of the District Court is vacated and the cause is remanded for further proceedings consistent with this opinion.

It is so ordered.

MR. JUSTICE BRENNAN, with whom MR. JUSTICE DOUGLAS and MR. JUSTICE MARSHALL join, dissenting.

I dissent. The treatment of the state civil proceeding as one "in aid of and closely related to criminal statutes" is obviously only the first step toward extending to state civil proceedings generally the holding of *Younger v. Harris* that federal courts should not interfere with pending state criminal proceedings except under extraordinary circumstances.[1] Similarly, today's holding that the plaintiff in an action under 42 U.S.C. § 1983 may not maintain it without first exhausting state appellate procedures for review of an adverse state trial court decision is but an obvious first step toward discard of heretofore settled law that such actions may be maintained without first exhausting state judicial remedies.

* * *

[T]oday's extension of *Younger v. Harris* turns the clock back and portends once again the resuscitation of the literal command of the 1793

---

which have already been initiated and which afford a competent tribunal for the resolution of federal issues. Our exhaustion requirement is likewise not inconsistent with * * * cases * * * [that] expressed the doctrine that a federal equity plaintiff challenging state administrative action need not have exhausted his state judicial remedies. Those cases did not deal with situations in which the state judicial process had been initiated.

[22] While appellee had the option to appeal in state courts at the time it filed this action, we do not know for certain whether such remedy remained available at the time the District Court issued its permanent injunction, or whether it remains available now. In any event, appellee may not avoid the standards of *Younger* by simply failing to comply with the procedures of perfecting its appeal within the Ohio judicial system.

[1] The Court reaches the *Younger* issue although appellants did not plead *Younger* in the District Court. Yet the Court implies that *Younger* is not a jurisdictional matter, since we allowed the parties to waive it in *Sosna v. Iowa.* In that circumstance, I address the *Younger* issue solely to respond to the Court's treatment of it.

Anti-Injunction Act—that the state courts should be free from interference by federal injunction even in civil cases. This not only would overrule some 18 decades of this Court's jurisprudence but would heedlessly flout Congress' evident purpose in enacting the 1948 amendment to acquiesce in that jurisprudence.

The extension also threatens serious prejudice to the potential federal-court plaintiff not present when the pending state proceeding is a criminal prosecution. That prosecution does not come into existence until completion of steps designed to safeguard him against spurious prosecution—arrest, charge, information, or indictment. In contrast, the civil proceeding, as in this case, comes into existence merely upon the filing of a complaint, whether or not well founded. To deny by fiat of this Court the potential federal plaintiff a federal forum in that circumstance is obviously to arm his adversary (here the public authorities) with an easily wielded weapon to strip him of a forum and a remedy that federal statutes were enacted to assure him. The Court does not escape this consequence by characterizing the state civil proceeding involved here as "in aid of and closely related to criminal statutes." The nuisance action was brought into being by the mere filing of the complaint in state court, and the untoward consequences for the federal plaintiff were thereby set in train without regard to the connection, if any, of the proceeding to the State's criminal laws.

Even if the extension of *Younger v. Harris* to pending state civil proceedings can be appropriate in any case, and I do not think it can be,[2] it is plainly improper in the case of an action by a federal plaintiff, as in this case, grounded upon 42 U.S.C. § 1983. That statute serves a particular congressional objective long recognized and enforced by the Court. Today's extension will defeat that objective. * * *

Consistently with this congressional objective of the 1871 and 1875 Acts we held in *Monroe v. Pape* that a federal plaintiff suing under § 1983 need not exhaust state administrative or judicial remedies before filing his action under § 1983 in federal district court. "The federal remedy is supplementary to the state remedy, and the latter need not be first sought and refused before the federal one is invoked." The extension today of *Younger v. Harris* to require exhaustion in an action under § 1983 drastically undercuts *Monroe v. Pape* and its numerous progeny— the mere filing of a complaint against a potential § 1983 litigant forces him to exhaust state remedies.

---

[2] Abstention where authoritative resolution by state courts of ambiguities in a state statute is sufficiently likely to avoid or significantly modify federal questions raised by the statute is another matter. Abstention is justified in such cases primarily by the policy of avoidance of premature constitutional adjudication. The federal plaintiff is therefore not dismissed from federal court as he is in *Younger* cases. On the contrary, he may reserve his federal questions for decision by the federal district court and not submit them to the state courts. Accordingly, retention by the federal court of jurisdiction of the federal complaint pending state-court decision, not dismissal of the complaint, is the correct practice.

Mitchum v. Foster, holding that actions under § 1983 are excepted from the operation of the federal anti-injunction statute is also undercut by today's extension of *Younger.* *Mitchum* canvassed the history of § 1983 and concluded that it extended "federal power in an attempt to remedy the state courts' failure to secure federal rights." *Mitchum* prompted the comment that if *Younger v. Harris* were extended to civil cases, "much of the rigidity of section 2283 would be reintroduced, the significance of *Mitchum* for those seeking relief from state civil proceedings would largely be destroyed, and the recognition of section 1983 as an exception to the Anti-Injunction Statute would have been a Pyrrhic victory."[4] Today's decision fulfills that gloomy prophecy. I therefore dissent from the remand and would reach the merits.

Notes and Questions

1. How does *Huffman* extend the *Younger* doctrine? Is the extension substantial or modest? How many cases will it affect?

2. In light of its discussion of the federalism interests *Younger* abstention serves (and note that comity seems to be subsumed as a particular sort of federalism interest), why does the majority feel it necessary to emphasize how closely the state proceedings in *Huffman* are allied to criminal proceedings? Is there anything about criminal proceedings that places them, arguably, in a different light for *Younger* purposes than ordinary civil proceedings to which the state is a party?

3. a) Appellee Pursue lost the nuisance action in the Court of Common Pleas. The state court ordered the theater closed for one year and seizure and sale of certain personal property used in the theater's operation. Pursue then began the federal litigation. Because the state action was over, Pursue argued there was no pending state proceeding, as *Younger* abstention requires. Pursue sought a declaratory judgment that the Ohio nuisance statute was unconstitutional and an injunction against its enforcement. What role was Pursue asking the federal court to play? What is wrong with that? Is Pursue's choice of the federal forum reminiscent of the union's return to federal court in *Atlantic Coast Line R.R. Co. v. Brotherhood of Locomotive Engineers* (page 746) after the state trial judge refused the union's request to dissolve the injunction prohibiting picketing?

b) The majority rejected Pursue's argument, stating that "a party in appellee's posture must exhaust his state appellate remedies before seeking relief in the District Court, unless he can bring himself within one of the exceptions specified in *Younger.*" Assuming Pursue did as directed, would (should) that solve the *Atlantic Coast Line* problem? Note also that in a pure *Younger* case, where the state proceedings are criminal rather than civil-in-aid-of criminal statutes, the defendant cannot proceed to federal district court after his conviction is affirmed by the state supreme court.

c) The majority's suggestion that a federal action is available after ex-

---

[4] Note, *The Supreme Court, 1971 Term,* 86 HARV.L.REV. 50, 217-18 (1972).

haustion of state remedies may also be illusory for another reason. In footnote 19, the Court notes that state officials did not plead res judicata in the federal action, thus waiving the defense. State officials presumably will not make that mistake again. Would res judicata have barred Pursue's federal action, or would the doctrine not apply?

4. Justice Brennan's dissent raises some substantial questions about the effect of *Younger* abstention generally, but also poses some problems about his own positions.

a) Primarily, as he points out, *Mitchum v. Foster* seems to have been overruled as a practical matter. Though the Court may not have reversed its view of § 1983 as an exception to the Anti-Injunction Act, after *Younger*'s extension to civil matters, of what use is *Mitchum* to a litigant who wishes a federal court to enjoin a state court proceeding?

b) Justice Brennan may, however, make a bit too much out of *Huffman*'s effect on *Monroe v. Pape*. There may be many cases in which a potential plaintiff has a choice of remedies—traditional state tort remedies, for example, or an action under § 1983. Where the injured individual would be the plaintiff either in state or federal court, *Huffman* in no sense diminishes his prospect of securing a federal forum. On the other hand, where the prospective federal plaintiff is the defendant in the state court, *Huffman* seems to prevent him from pursuing his federal claim in federal court. Bear in mind, however, that while *Mitchum* dealt with forum-selection, *Monroe* is concerned directly with the existence *vel non* of a cause of action under § 1983, not with the court in which the plaintiff may sue. A prospective § 1983 plaintiff who is the defendant in a state court proceeding (civil or criminal) may still file a § 1983 claim in a state proceeding. That result is at least consistent with *Monroe*.

c) The Justice argues that deference to state criminal proceedings may be justified because the procedural protections afforded the defendant in a criminal action are greater than those in a civil proceeding. Of course, part of the reason for that is that the penalties in a criminal proceeding are so much greater. Yet Justice Brennan does not seem to consider that the lesser threat to the defendant in a civil proceeding may justify greater, not less, state autonomy in evaluating constitutional questions. In any event, why does the permissibility of *Younger* abstention depend on the existence or non-existence of pre-judicial protections for the state defendant?

d) Justice Brennan also argues that *Younger* abstention is never appropriate in civil proceedings, particularly when the federal plaintiff states a § 1983 claim. Does his rationale also suggest that he should oppose *Younger* abstention even with respect to criminal proceedings when the federal challenge relies upon § 1983 (as it virtually always does)? Justice Brennan concurred in *Younger*. Is his position there reconcilable with his dissent here?

5. The majority observes that the district court never considered *Younger* abstention, implying that the court was derelict. On the other hand, as Justice Brennan points out, Ohio did not raise the abstention issue until the case reached the Supreme Court. Does that suggest both that

Younger abstention is, in some sense, an issue having to do with subject matter jurisdiction and that it cannot be waived through failure to raise it? Each suggestion raises problems.

a) If the doctrine is an aspect of subject matter jurisdiction, what of the fact that it is apparently at odds with the subject matter jurisdiction conferred by Congress? Clearly, there are other judge-made subject matter jurisdiction doctrines, most notably the well-pleaded complaint rule and the complete diversity rule, but those at least purport to be constructions of congressional intent in enacting (and recodifying) 28 U.S.C.A. §§ 1331, 1332. *Younger* abstention, by contrast, seems to be at war with two jurisdictional statutes (28 U.S.C.A. §§ 1331, 1343) and a statute creating a federal cause of action (42 U.S.C.A. § 1983) that the Court ruled was specifically designed to permit interference with state proceedings. *See Mitchum v. Foster*, 407 U.S. 225, 92 S.Ct. 2151, 32 L.Ed.2d 705 (1972). *Mitchum* is discussed at pages 758-760 and 792-793. Does the Court's interpretation of *Younger* as quasi-jurisdictional substantially intensify the separation-of-powers problems that seem in any event to inhere in abstention doctrines?

b) Should the Court take the position, even implicitly, that *Younger* protection is not waivable? Suppose the state wants the federal issues litigated in federal court in order to have a federal *imprimatur* of constitutionality on a challenged statute. In some ways, *Younger* abstention operates similarly to a doctrine of personal jurisdiction, limiting the forums in which an non-consenting party can be forced to appear. Defendants who fail to raise defects in personal jurisdiction at the outset of the proceedings waive them. Perhaps *Younger* abstention should work similarly.

6. Could *Huffman* have controlled the result in *Hicks v. Miranda*? The Court cited *Huffman* in note 20 of *Hicks*. Should the Court have relied upon *Huffman* in order to avoid creating new doctrine in *Hicks*?

7. *Huffman* represents the modern *Younger* doctrine's first attempt to protect noncriminal pending state proceedings. The majority seems to recognize how great an extension is involved, because Justice Rehnquist refers to *Younger* and "its civil counterpart which we apply today," implicitly acknowledging that new doctrine has been created rather than old doctrine applied. The dissent's prediction of continuing expansion was to be borne out over the following fifteen years. Indeed, Professors Soifer and Macgill have referred to *Huffman* as "Our Federalism's great leap forward." Aviam Soifer & H.C. Macgill, *The* Younger *Doctrine: Reconstructing Reconstruction*, 55 TEX.L.REV. 1141, 1173 (1977).

a) *Trainor v. Hernandez*, 431 U.S. 434, 97 S.Ct. 1911, 52 L.Ed.2d 486 (1977) (also discussed at pages 796-798), held that *Younger* principles apply with respect to any state judicial proceeding to which the state is a party. A state civil fraud proceeding sought to recover benefits allegedly wrongfully paid. The Illinois courts issued an attachment order directed at some of the respondents' assets, and the respondents commenced a federal action challenging the constitutionality of the attachment statute. In overturning the district court's grant of relief, the Supreme Court drew upon *Huffman* and made clear that any enforcement proceeding brought by the state qualifies for *Younger* abstention, irrespective of any formal linkage with criminal statutes.

b) *Juidice v. Vail,* 430 U.S. 327, 97 S.Ct. 1211, 51 L.Ed.2d 376 (1977), extended *Younger* to a case not involving the state as a party in its sovereign capacity seeking to vindicate important state interests. Judgment creditors obtained contempt citations against their judgment debtors. The debtors brought a federal action arguing that the state's contempt proceedings violated their due process rights. Although the case involved only private parties, the Court held that the state's special interest in the integrity of its judicial proceedings, particularly with respect to contempt, compelled *Younger* abstention.

c) *Moore v. Sims,* 442 U.S. 415, 99 S.Ct. 2371, 60 L.Ed.2d 994 (1979), extended *Younger* to another purely civil proceeding. Texas authorities seized the Sims children on suspicion that the parents were abusive. The parents brought a federal action challenging the Texas procedures, including an allegation that it was not possible for them to obtain a prompt hearing in the state proceedings to recover their children. The district court specifically found that the Texas procedure provided no single forum for timely adjudication of the parents' constitutional claims—that is, that there was no adequate remedy at law. A five-to-four majority reversed. Justice Rehnquist noted that *Younger* abstention was clearly applicable to any civil case in which substantial state interests were involved and further stated that "abstention is appropriate unless state law clearly bars the interposition of the constitutional claim." *Moore*'s tangled procedural history demonstrates how difficult it will be to demonstrate that state remedies are inadequate.

In March, 1976, the Sims children lived with their parents in Montgomery County, Texas, and attended the John G. Osborne Elementary School in the Houston Independent School District, located in Harris County, Texas. On March 25, 1976, the Harris County Child Welfare Unit received a telephone report from the school that Paul Sims was possibly the victim of child abuse. In response to that call, caseworker Rex Downing visited the school and, on the same date, took possession of the three Sims children pursuant to Section 17.01 of Title 2 of the Texas Family Code. The next day, March 26, the Child Welfare Unit instituted a "Suit for the Protection of a Child in an Emergency" pursuant to Chapter 17, which was filed in Juvenile Court Number One of Harris County, Texas, and concerned all three of the Sims children. Also on March 26, 1976, Judge Robert L. Lowry of the Harris County Juvenile Court issued an *ex parte* order pursuant to Section 17.04, which has the effect of removing the children from the custody of their parents. Section 17.05 provides that such an order is of ten days in duration, and, upon the expiration of the order, the court is required to either order the restoration of the children to their parents or direct that a "Suit Affecting the Parent-Child Relationship" be filed.

On March 31, 1976, the plaintiff-parents sought to present to Judge Lowry a motion for modification of the March 26 Order, pursuant to Section 17.06. Although that section requires that a hearing be held on the motion, no hearing was in fact held. Rather, * * * the motion was not presented to Judge Lowry because of his temporary absence and was returned to counsel for the parents. Later on March 31, 1976, counsel for the parents filed with the Juvenile Court Number One, a petition for a writ of habeas corpus * * * .

On April 5, 1976, a hearing was held before Judge Lowry on the parents' petition for a writ of habeas corpus. This was the first time since their seizure that the children were brought before the court for any hearing and the first time the parents were given any opportunity to appear. However, the merits of the dispute were never addressed. At the April 5 hearing, Judge Lowry determined that the children were residents of Montgomery County and, despite their custody in Harris County, transferred the matter to Montgomery County. Later on April 5, at Judge Lowry's direction pursuant to Section 17.05(b)(2), the Harris County Child Welfare Unit filed a "Suit affecting the parent-child relationship" in Harris County. This second petition by the current defendants was filed in the same [c]ause * * * as the original emergency suit filed under Chapter 17. Finally, on April 5, 1976, Judge Lowry issued another *ex parte* temporary order pursuant to Section 11.11. The order directed that the children continue in the possession of the Harris County Child Welfare Unit and purported to set a hearing upon its expiration. However, the order setting the hearing was entered in blank and to date the blanks have never been completed.

On April 6, 1976, the "Suit affecting the parent-child relationship" * * *, which supplanted the emergency suit, and the habeas corpus action * * * were officially transferred to the District Court of Montgomery County and assigned to the docket of Judge Ernest A. Coker, Sr. The transfer was apparently made *sua sponte* under Section 11.06(a) despite the requirement that it be transferred upon a timely motion. It is stipulated that from April 6, 1976, to May 5, 1976, when the first hearing was conducted in this action, no notice, citation or process of any kind was served upon the plaintiff-parents with regard to the Montgomery County cases, nor were they afforded a hearing of any kind before the District Court of Montgomery County. During the entire time, the children remained in the custody of the Harris County Child Welfare Unit.

On April 19, 1976, the plaintiffs filed their Original Complaint in federal court. On May 4, 1976, the plaintiffs filed a motion for leave to file an original petition for a writ of habeas corpus with the Texas Court of Civil Appeals for the 14th District, which was denied on the same date. The next day, the managing judge of the three-judge district court conducted an evidentiary hearing at which the court found that the children were not in the legal custody of the defendants because the *ex parte* temporary order under Chapter 17, dated March 26, and the *ex parte* order under Section 11.11, dated April 5, had both expired. The court ordered that the Sims children be returned to their parents, but did not enjoin the Department of Public Welfare from taking action under state law to properly establish a temporary conservatorship over the children. Therefore, on May 14, 1976, the Department of Public Welfare filed another "Suit affecting the parent-child relationship" in the Juvenile Court of Montgomery County. This action concerned Paul Sims only.

The Juvenile Court on May 14, 1976, established a temporary managing conservatorship for the child and set a hearing for May 21. On May 21, upon the motion of the plaintiffs, the managing judge of the three-judge panel temporarily enjoined the hearing in Montgomery County. Subsequently, after a hearing, the three-judge court extended the restraining order and enjoined any further state proceeding under the challenged statutes pending determination of the plaintiffs' constitutional challenges.

Sims v. State Department of Public Welfare, 438 F.Supp. 1179, 1183-85 (S.D.Tex. 1977), *reversed sub nom. Moore v. Sims,* 442 U.S. 415, 99 S.Ct. 2371, 60 L.Ed.2d 994 (1979) (footnotes omitted).

The dissenting Justices argued that the proceedings in the Texas state courts demonstrated that there was no adequate remedy at law. Some commentators have not been kind to the Court either.

> The Court does not suggest that the course of action pursued by the plaintiffs in seeking return of their children was unreasonable, but only that it indicated insufficient diligence. It is not clear why the many apparently reasonable actions taken by plaintiffs fail to evidence diligent pursuit of state court opportunities, nor is it clear why the Court would have found the question of adequacy "closer" had plaintiffs taken further steps which were likely to be equally inefficacious. Moreover, the Court explains away the delay, confusion, and irregularities in the state's actions as "the predictable byproduct of a new statutory scheme." The Court, however, does not afford the plaintiffs the same consideration when evaluating their actions which were taken pursuant to the same "new statutory scheme."

> By holding that state remedies in *Sims* were adequate to vindicate the plaintiffs' claims, the Court actually may be modifying the adequacy standard. Henceforth, the mere theoretical existence of a state remedy may bar federal relief, no matter how impractical or inadequate such a remedy would be in practice. As Justice Stevens noted in his dissent in *Trainor v. Hernandez:* "Thirty years ago Mr. Justice Rutledge characterized a series of Illinois procedures which effectively foreclosed consideration of the merits of federal constitutional claims as a 'procedural labyrinth * * * made up entirely of blind alleys.' *Marino v. Ragan,* 332 U.S. 561, 567." Texas parents could appropriately apply that characteristic to the state remedies which the Court certifies as adequate in *Moore v. Sims.*

Note, Moore v. Sims: *A Further Expansion of the* Younger *Abstention Doctrine,* 1 PACE L.REV. 149, 177-78 (1980).

d) The Court has also extended *Younger* to state administrative proceedings, noting in *Ohio Civil Rights Commission v. Dayton Christian*

Schools, Inc., 477 U.S. 619, 106 S.Ct. 2718, 91 L.Ed.2d 512 (1986), that past cases suggested that administrative proceedings "judicial in nature" and in which the federal plaintiff "would have a full and fair opportunity to litigate his constitutional claim" qualified for *Younger* abstention. The Justices thus rebuffed Dayton Christian's claim of First Amendment exemption from the state administrative proceeding investigating a claim of sex discrimination filed against Dayton Christian by a former employee. In the course of its opinion, however, the Court subtly shifted the nature of the balance with which *Younger* abstention deals. In prior cases, the focus was on the state's interest in not having its process interrupted by intrusive federal adjudication. In *Dayton Christian*, on the other hand, then-Justice Rehnquist found "that the elimination of prohibited sex discrimination is a sufficiently important state interest to bring the present case within the ambit * * * " of prior *Younger* decisions. Parallel reasoning in *Younger* itself would have had the Court discussing not California's interest in having its criminal process go forward without federal interruption, but rather California's substantive interest in avoiding criminal syndicalism. Similarly, in *Steffel v. Thompson*, the Court would not have focused on the absence of a pending state proceeding with respect to Steffel, but would instead have examined Georgia's interest in combating criminal trespass. Is the shift in emphasis desirable? Does it make abstention more or less likely in the general case?

Middlesex County Ethics Committee v. Garden State Bar Assn., 457 U.S. 423, 102 S.Ct. 2515, 73 L.Ed.2d 46 (1982), which Justice Rehnquist cited in *Dayton Christian*, involved an attorney brought up on disciplinary charges of conduct "prejudicial to the administration of justice" after publicly criticizing a state judge. The attorney filed a federal action attacking the constitutionality of both the regulations under which he was being prosecuted and the proceedings of the Ethics Committee itself. The Court affirmed the district court's decision to abstain. Yet *Middlesex* is not as broad as *Dayton Christian*; the Court emphasized the intimate connection between attorney disciplinary proceedings and the functioning of the state court system. As Professor Chemerinsky notes,

> [B]y itself, the *Middlesex County* decision might be viewed as a narrow expansion of *Younger* abstention principles because bar disciplinary proceedings are a part of the state judicial system. A distinction might be drawn between administrative matters that are handled pursuant to authority delegated by the state judiciary and those that are pending in other state agencies. *Younger* abstention, based on deference to the state judiciary, would be applied to the former, which is a part of the court system, but not the latter.

ERWIN CHEMERINSKY, FEDERAL JURISDICTION § 13.3.4, at 852 (5th ed. 2007). *Dayton Christian* clearly signals the rejection of the proposed distinction.

NOTE ON OTHER DEVELOPMENTS
IN *YOUNGER* ABSTENTION

a) *Dayton Christian* and the cases upon which it relied took the *Younger* doctrine out of the area of strictly judicial proceedings. Yet the Court's exploration of the doctrine's applicability to non-judicial matters did not begin with the administrative agency cases. In two cases in the mid-1970's, the Court suggested that *Younger* abstention might be appropriate with respect to executive actions.

In *O'Shea v. Littleton,* 414 U.S. 488, 94 S.Ct. 669, 38 L.Ed.2d 674 (1974), a coalition of individuals in Cairo, Illinois, brought a civil rights action against the county attorney, his investigator, the local magistrate and the local circuit judge, alleging that their administration of the criminal laws in Cairo was discriminatory against black citizens and was designed to curtail or burden their exercise of First Amendment rights. The Court invoked *Younger* abstention, noting in part that "recognition of the need for a proper balance in the concurrent operation of federal and state courts counsels restraint against the issuance of injunctions against state officers engaged in the administration of the State's criminal laws." Similarly, in *Rizzo v. Goode,* 423 U.S. 362, 96 S.Ct. 598, 46 L.Ed.2d 561 (1976), *see supra* at pages 551-552, individuals and community groups charged that Philadelphia police systematically deprived blacks of their constitutional rights and that the department, through labyrinthine and unresponsive civilian complaint processes, deliberately refused to take appropriate disciplinary action. The Court directed abstention, noting that the federalism values that *Younger* sought to protect were heavily implicated. Neither *O'Shea* nor *Rizzo,* however, has led to a more generalized application of *Younger* outside of adjudicative proceedings, where there is an on-going state proceeding in which the plaintiff can raise his constitutional claims.

b) The *Younger* doctrine's expansion in the judicial context was not quite complete with the decision in *Dayton Christian.* *Pennzoil Company v. Texaco, Inc.,* 481 U.S. 1, 107 S.Ct. 1519, 95 L.Ed.2d 1 (1987), applied *Younger* for the first time to a controversy entirely between private parties not involving the state's contempt power. The case is well-known because of its size; Pennzoil won a verdict in the Texas state courts against Texaco for the latter's tortious interference with a contract for the purchase of stock by Pennzoil from Getty Oil. The original verdict exceeded ten billion dollars, and accumulated prejudgment interest brought the figure to nearly thirteen billion. Under Texas law, the losing party was required to post a bond for the amount of the judgment in order to have execution of the judgment stayed pending appeal. Texaco sued in the United States District Court for the Southern District of New York, seeking an injunction preventing Pennzoil from taking any steps to enforce the judgment, claiming that the Texas procedures for securing a stay of execution pending appeal were unconstitutional because of the bond requirement. The lower courts granted relief, but the Supreme

Court unanimously reversed.

The case generated a majority opinion and five concurrences. The majority found that Texaco had failed to establish that its constitutional objection to the Texas procedure could not be heard in the state courts, particularly because of Texas' "open courts" statute declaring the availability of Texas judicial procedure to every aggrieved litigant. The majority also found a significant state interest in the regular administration of its appellate judicial system without interference from the federal courts, despite Texas' express representation to the Court of Appeals that it had "no interest in the outcome of the state-court adjudication underlying this cause" other than its fair adjudication. Justices Brennan and Marshall argued that *Younger* abstention was, therefore, inappropriate. Justice Brennan found Texaco's Fourteenth Amendment claim without merit, a conclusion with which Justice Marshall concurred but would not have reached. Justice Marshall argued that although abstention was not appropriate, the federal courts had no jurisdiction because of the *Rooker-Feldman* doctrine (*see infra* Chapter 10) that prohibits inferior federal courts from sitting in appellate review of state courts. Justice Scalia took issue with Justice Marshall's application of the *Rooker-Feldman* doctrine; in Justice Scalia's view the federal courts were not being asked to answer any question presented to or decided by the state courts, making *Rooker-Feldman* inapplicable and *Younger* appropriate.

Justices Blackmun and Stevens, each writing a concurring opinion, agreed that state action was involved for purposes of Texaco's § 1983 action, on the theory that Pennzoil's invocation of Texas' judgment-enforcement power effectively made Pennzoil a state actor. Justice Blackmun, however, thought *Younger* abstention inappropriate because Texaco had no adequate remedy at law because of its inability to be heard in the Texas courts without posting the bond. He would have, however, ordered abstention under *Pullman* so that Texas could construe its statute in light of Texaco's due process argument. Justice Stevens, by contrast, found Texaco's due process argument without merit, arguing that nothing in Texas law prevented Texaco from appealing and that the company sought only to avoid untoward business effects that would arise either from allowing execution to begin or from posting a bond to stay execution. In either event, Justice Stevens noted, Texaco's appeal in the Texas courts could go forward unhindered. For him, the true constitutional question presented by the case was whether Texas was constitutionally required to stay execution pending appeal, and that idea he rejected.

The five-member majority's reliance on *Younger* for the result in *Pennzoil* seemed to extend the doctrine to its greatest possible scope. *Pennzoil* is the first case in which the Court applied *Younger* to litigation between private parties where there was no particular state enforcement interest, such as with the contempt proceeding in *Juidice v. Vail.* Scholars wondered whether *Younger* had, in effect, become illimitable when there was any pending state proceeding of any sort. *See, e.g.,* Timothy Kin Lee Hui, Note, *The Ultimate Expansion of the* Younger *Doctrine*: Pennzoil Co. v. Texaco, Inc., 41 Sw.L.J. 1055 (1987); Howard B. Stravitz, Younger *Abstention Reaches a Civil Maturity,* 57 FORDHAM L.REV. 997 (1989). As the *New Orleans Public Service* case was to show, however, reports of the death of federal litigation were somewhat exaggerated.

c) In the early 1970's, New Orleans Public Service, Inc., (NOPSI), a local power company, entered into a plan to construct a nuclear power facility in two parts. As a result of lower-than-expected consumer demand and great cost overruns, the second part of the project was eventually abandoned, leaving behind the question of who was to pay for the first part. Although the Federal Energy Regulatory Commission (FERC) allocates costs and sets rates to be paid by members of "power pools" involved in such projects, local bodies (in this case the New Orleans City Council) have authority with respect to what part of allocated costs may be passed on to consumers and what part must be absorbed by company shareholders.

NOPSI disputed the Council's limited authorization for passing on the project costs. NOPSI sought an additional rate increase, which the Council denied. Thereafter the Council initiated an investigation into the "prudence" of NOPSI's participation in the project. Finally, the Council completed its prudence review and required the company to absorb approximately $135 million of the costs allocated by FERC. NOPSI, having unsuccessfully sought to challenge the Council's action on two previous occasions in federal court, returned to it, arguing there that an earlier Supreme Court decision pre-empted a state inquiry into the prudence of a utility's decision to participate in such a project. Anticipating the possibility of abstention, NOPSI also petitioned a Louisiana court for review of the Council's rate order and also informed the state court of NOPSI's intention to raise its federal pre-emption claim if the federal court again abstained. The district court abstained, and the Fifth Circuit affirmed.

The Supreme Court reversed. *New Orleans Public Service, Inc. v. Council of City of New Orleans*, 491 U.S. 350, 109 S.Ct. 2506, 105 L.Ed.2d 298 (1989).Although it declined NOPSI's request to rule that *Younger* abstention is inappropriate when the underlying federal question is pre-emption, Justice Scalia's opinion for the Court held, nonetheless, that the pending Louisiana court action did not implicate *Younger* abstention. "[I]t has never been suggested that *Younger* requires abstention in deference to a state judicial proceeding reviewing legislative or executive action. Such a broad abstention requirement would make a mockery of the rule that only exceptional circumstances justify a federal court's refusal to decide a case in deference to the States." The Council argued that the Louisiana action was a mere extension of the Council's own proceedings, and that the whole should be treated as a unitary proceeding much as trial and appellate proceedings otherwise are for

Younger purposes. Again the Court balked:

> Respondents' case for abstention still requires, however, that the *Council proceeding* be the sort of proceeding entitled to *Younger* treatment. We think it is not. While we have expanded *Younger* beyond criminal proceedings, and even beyond proceedings in courts, we have never extended it to proceedings that are not "judicial in nature." * * * The Council's proceedings in the present case were not judicial in nature.

Canvassing cases dating back to 1908, Justice Scalia concluded that "the Council's proceedings here were plainly legislative" and did not compel or justify federal abstention. Justice Scalia divided the Louisiana proceedings, however, ruling that the legislative process had to come to an end to permit federal intervention. That, he argued, had happened when the Council issued its final order. The ensuing Louisiana judicial review was "not an extension of the legislative process," so "NOPSI's pre-emption claim was ripe for federal review when the Council's rate order was entered."

Perhaps the most significant part of Justice Scalia's opinion discusses abstention more generally.

> Before proceeding to the merits of the abstention issues, it bears emphasis that the Council does not dispute the District Court's jurisdiction to decide NOPSI's pre-emption claim. Our cases have long supported the proposition that federal courts lack the authority to abstain from the exercise of jurisdiction that has been conferred. For example: "We have no more right to decline the exercise of jurisdiction which is given, than to usurp that which is not given. The one or the other would be treason to the Constitution." * * * Underlying these assertions is the undisputed constitutional principle that Congress, and not the judiciary, defines the scope of federal jurisdiction within the constitutionally permissible bounds.

> That principle does not eliminate, however, and the categorical assertions based upon it do not call into question, the federal courts' discretion in determining whether to grant certain types of relief— a discretion that was part of the common-law background against which the statutes conferring jurisdiction were enacted. Thus, there are some classes of cases in which the withholding of authorized equitable relief because of undue interference with state proceedings is "the normal thing to do." We have carefully defined, however, the areas in which such "abstention" is permissible, and it remains " 'the exception, not the rule.' " As recently as last Term we described the federal courts' obligation to adjudicate claims within their jurisdiction as " 'virtually unflagging.' "

It seems fair to say that Justice Scalia is at least uncomfortable with abstention because of its separation-of-powers overtones and, although there were several concurring opinions, none directly challenged this part of the Court's opinion.

Notes and Questions

1. For those who thought *Younger* abstention a juggernaut, *NOPSI* must have been something of a shock. It is not hard to visualize the Court writing an opinion coming out the other way. Perhaps an even greater shock is the revelation of what apparently has begun to trouble the Court about its abstention jurisprudence: separation of powers.

Professor George Brown sees *NOPSI* as a collision between the twin themes of federalism and separation of powers and, indeed, sums up much of the basic conflict over abstention, federal common law, and federalism.

> *Younger* is different because serious questions of authority and legitimacy are present. The federal plaintiff comes to the district court armed with a federal cause of action—section 1983 plus an underlying provision of federal law, usually the Constitution—and a valid grant of jurisdiction authorizing the tribunal to hear the case. To send her packing, the Court interposes neither the Constitution nor statutory interpretation, but its own notions of comity and federalism. It seems to be flouting the will of Congress in an area over which Congress has clear authority: the jurisdiction of the federal courts. This step is surprising for a Court that often emphasizes the authority of Congress over federal jurisdiction and is generally deferential to the legislative branch.

> *Younger* abstention can thus be viewed solely as a separation of powers issue. It is a separation of powers problem in the literal sense that the Court is making law regarding federal jurisdiction that seems at odds with congressional statutes on the subject. It is also a separation of powers problem in a broader, structural sense. Even if specific legislative language does not resolve all jurisdictional questions, for the Court to develop a body of jurisdictional law is to exceed the judiciary's constitutional bounds and trespass on the legislature's domain. If either of these forms of the critique is valid, the logic of the Court's general position of deference to Congress would require the federalism-based, judge-made doctrine of *Younger* to yield. The critique emerges not as another argument but as an end to an argument.

> So far the Court has largely dealt with the separation of powers problem by ignoring it. The *Younger* cases say little about the source of the Court's authority to renounce jurisdiction based on notions of comity and federalism. How to reconcile this renunciation with federal statutory law is discussed even less. Recent abstention cases suggest, however, that the Court is aware of the separation of powers problem and deeply troubled by it. The Court increasingly has invoked the "virtually unflagging obligation" of the federal courts to exercise the jurisdiction conferred upon them. In *New Orleans Public Service Inc. (NOPSI) v. City Council,* the Court went so far as to state that "[o]ur cases have long supported the proposition that federal courts lack the authority to

abstain from the exercise of the jurisdiction that has been conferred."
It then reversed a lower court's plausible application of *Younger* to
state administrative proceedings. *Younger* is anything but dead, as
the 1987 decision in *Pennzoil Co. v. Texaco,* shows; but the notion of a
"virtually unflagging obligation" of a federal court to exercise the jurisdiction granted cuts against the doctrine.

George D. Brown, *When Federalism and Separation of Powers Collide—
Rethinking* Younger *Abstention,* 59 GEO.WASH.L.REV. 114, 116-17 (1990)
(footnotes omitted).

2. Having expressed separation-of-powers reservations about abstention, the Court was unwilling completely to abandon it. The Court attempted to deal with the separation-of-powers problem by recharacterizing
abstention not as a refusal to exercise jurisdiction conferred by Congress but
rather as a paradigmatically judicial selection of appropriate remedies. Is
that persuasive?

3. Justice Scalia notes that *Younger* abstention has "never" been applied
to nonjudicial proceedings. Is that statement reconcilable with *O'Shea* and
Rizzo, or is it an acknowledgement of the Court's repudiation or at least
abandonment of its dictum in *Rizzo?* Are *Rizzo* and *O'Shea* on the same footing with respect to *Younger* abstention?

4. Justice Scalia's emphatic assertion of the exceptional nature of the
abstention doctrines may be difficult to accept at face value, given particularly the *Younger* doctrine's dramatic expansion after 1971. On the other
hand, perhaps *NOPSI* foretells a reversal of the Court's recent approach to
abstention and a re-evaluation of the balance between separation of powers
and federalism. To the extent that Professor Brown is correct, does the Constitution resolve the battle between federalism and separation of powers? If
so, how? If not, then is the Court, despite the efforts of many of the Justices
over the past several decades to avoid judicial policy-making, cast unavoid-
ably in that role? On what basis should the Court decide how to resolve the
conflict?

4. Burford *and* Thibodaux *Abstention*

BURFORD v. SUN OIL CO.
Supreme Court of the United States, 1943.
319 U.S. 315, 63 S.Ct. 1098, 87 L.Ed. 1424.

MR. JUSTICE BLACK delivered the opinion of the Court.

In this proceeding brought in a federal district court, the Sun Oil Co.
attacked the validity of an order of the Texas Railroad Commission
granting the petitioner Burford a permit to drill four wells on a small
plot of land in the East Texas oil field. Jurisdiction of the federal court
was invoked because of the diversity of citizenship of the parties, and
because of the Companies' contention that the order denied them due
process of law. * * *

Although a federal equity court does have jurisdiction of a particular proceeding, it may, in its sound discretion, whether its jurisdiction is invoked on the ground of diversity of citizenship or otherwise, "refuse to enforce or protect legal rights, the exercise of which may be prejudicial to the public interest"; for it "is in the public interest that federal courts of equity should exercise their discretionary power with proper regard for the rightful independence of state governments in carrying out their domestic policy." While many other questions are argued, we find it necessary to decide only one: Assuming that the federal district court had jurisdiction, should it, as a matter of sound equitable discretion, have declined to exercise that jurisdiction here?

The order under consideration is part of the general regulatory system devised for the conservation of oil and gas in Texas, an aspect of "as thorny a problem as has challenged the ingenuity and wisdom of legislatures." The East Texas field, in which the Burford tract is located, is one of the largest in the United States. It is approximately forty miles long and between five and nine miles wide, and over 26,000 wells have been drilled in it. Oil exists in the pores and crevices of rocks and sand and moves through these channels. A large area of this sort is called a pool or reservoir and the East Texas field is a giant pool. The chief forces causing oil to move are gas and water, and it is essential that the pressures be maintained at a level which will force the oil through wells to the surface. As the gas pressure is dissipated, it becomes necessary to put the well "on the pump" at great expense; and the sooner the gas from a field is exhausted, the more oil is irretrievably lost. Since the oil moves through the entire field, one operator can not only draw the oil from under his own surface area, but can also, if he is advantageously located, drain oil from the most distant parts of the reservoir. The practice of attempting to drain oil from under the surface holdings of others leads to offset wells and other wasteful practices; and this problem is increased by the fact that the surface rights are split up into many small tracts. There are approximately nine hundred operators in the East Texas field alone.

For these, and many other reasons based on geologic realities, each oil and gas field must be regulated as a unit for conservation purposes. The federal government, for the present at least, has chosen to leave the principal regulatory responsibility with the states, but does supplement state control. While there is no question of the constitutional power of the State to take appropriate action to protect the industry and protect the public interest, the State's attempts to control the flow of oil and at the same time protect the interest of the many operators have from time to time been entangled in geological-legal problems of novel nature.

Texas interests in this matter are more than that very large one of conserving gas and oil, two of our most important natural resources. It must also weigh the impact of the industry on the whole economy of the state and must consider its revenue, much of which is drawn from taxes on the industry and from mineral lands preserved for the benefit of its educational and eleemosynary institutions. To prevent "past, present, and imminent evils" in the production of natural gas, a statute was enacted "for the protection of public and private interests against such evils by prohibiting waste and compelling ratable production." The primary task of attempting adjustment of these diverse interests is delegated to the Railroad Commission which Texas has vested with "broad discretion" in administering the law.

The Commission, in cooperation with other oil producing states, has accepted State oil production quotas and has undertaken to translate the amount to be produced for the State as a whole into a specific amount for each field and for each well. These judgments are made with due regard for the factors of full utilization of the oil supply, market demand, and protection of the individual operators, as well as protection of the public interest. As an essential aspect of the control program, the State also regulates the spacing of wells. The legislature has disavowed a purpose of requiring that "the separately owned properties in any pool [should] be unitized under one management, control or ownership" and the Commission must thus work out the difficult spacing problem with due regard for whatever rights Texas recognizes in the separate owners to a share of the common reservoir. At the same time it must restrain waste, whether by excessive production or by the unwise dissipation of the gas and other geologic factors that cause the oil to flow.

Since 1919 the Commission has attempted to solve this problem by its Rule 37. The rule provides for certain minimum spacing between wells, but also allows exceptions where necessary "to prevent waste or to prevent the confiscation of property." The prevention of confiscation is based on the premises that, insofar as these privileges are compatible with the prevention of waste and the achievement of conservation, each surface owner should be permitted to withdraw the oil under his surface area, and that no one else can fairly be permitted to drain his oil away. Hence the Commission may protect his interest either by adjusting his amount of production upward, or by permitting him to drill additional wells. * * *

Additional wells may be required to prevent waste as has been noticed, where geologic circumstances require immediate drilling: "The term 'waste,' as used in oil and gas Rule 37, undoubtedly means the ultimate loss of oil. If a substantial amount of oil will be saved by the drilling of a well that otherwise would ultimately be lost, the permit to drill such well may be justified under one of the exceptions provided in Rule 37 to prevent waste."

The delusive simplicity with which these principles of exception to Rule 37 can be stated should not obscure the actual nonlegal complexities involved in their application. While the surface holder may, subject to qualifications noted, be entitled under current Texas law to the oil under his land, there can be no absolute certainty as to how much oil actually is present, and since the waste and confiscation problems are as a matter of physical necessity so closely interrelated, decision of one of the questions necessarily involves recognition of the other. The sheer quantity of exception cases makes their disposition of great public importance. It is estimated that over two-thirds of the wells in the East Texas field exist as exceptions to the rule, and since each exception may provoke a conflict among the interested parties, the volume of litigation arising from the administration of the rule is considerable. The instant case arises from just such an exception. It is not peculiar that the state should be represented here by its Attorney General, for cases like this, involving "confiscation," are not mere isolated disputes between private parties. Aside from the general principles which may evolve from these proceedings, the physical facts are such that an additional permit may affect pressure on a well miles away. The standards applied by the Commission in a given case necessarily affect the entire state conservation system. Of far more importance than any other private interest is the fact that the over-all plan of regulation, as well as each of its case by case manifestations, is of vital interest to the general public which must be assured that the speculative interests of individual tract owners will be put aside when necessary to prevent the irretrievable loss of oil in other parts of the field. The Commission in applying the statutory standards of course considers the Rule 37 cases as a part of the entire conservation program with implications to the whole economy of the state.[18]

With full knowledge of the importance of the decisions of the Railroad Commission both to the State and to the oil operators, the Texas legislature has established a system of thorough judicial review by its own State courts. The Commission orders may be appealed to a State district court in Travis County, and are reviewed by a branch of the Court of Civil Appeals and by the State Supreme Court. While the constitutional power of the Commission to enforce Rule 37 or to make exceptions to it is seldom seriously challenged, the validity of particular orders from the standpoint of statutory interpretation may present a serious problem, and a substantial number of such cases have been disposed of by the Texas courts which alone have the power to give definite answers to the questions of State law posed in these proceedings.

In describing the relation of the Texas court to the Commission no

---

[18]   The Commission is charged generally with the conservation of oil and gas in their production, storage, transportation. * * * The Commission must make rules, regulations, and orders to accomplish conservation of oil and gas. * * * One of the things that the Commission must do to conserve oil and gas is to see that oil and gas fields are drilled in an orderly and scientific manner. In order to accomplish orderly drilling, the Commission has simply promulgated a rule fixing minimum spacing distances at which wells may be drilled without application, notice, or hearing. Any one desiring to drill a well at a lesser distance must secure a special permit, after notice and hearing.

Gulf Land Co. v. Atlantic Refining Co., 134 Tex. 59, 69, 131 S.W.2d 73, 80 [(1939)].

useful purpose will be served by attempting to label the court's position as legislative, or judicial—suffice it to say that the Texas courts are working partners with the Railroad Commission in the business of creating a regulatory system for the oil industry. The Commission is charged with principal responsibility for fact finding and for policy making and the courts expressly disclaim the administrative responsibility, but on the other hand, the orders of the Commission are tested for "reasonableness" by trial *de novo* before the court, and the Court may on occasion make a careful analysis of all the facts of the case in reversing a Commission order. The court has fully as much power as the Commission to determine particular cases, since after trial *de novo* it can either restrain the leaseholder from proceeding to drill, or, if the case is appropriate, can restrain the Commission from interfering with the leaseholder. The court may even formulate new standards for the Commission's administrative practice and suggest that the Commission adopt them. * * *

To prevent the confusion of multiple review of the same general issues, the legislature provided for concentration of all direct review of the Commission's orders in the State district courts of Travis County. The Texas courts have authoritatively declared the purpose of this restriction: "If an order of the commission, lawful on its face, can be collaterally attacked in the various courts and counties of the state on grounds such as those urged in the instant case, interminable confusion would result." To permit various state courts to pass upon the Commission's rules and orders, "would lead to intolerable confusion. If all district courts of this state had jurisdiction of such matters, different courts of equal dignity might reach different and conflicting conclusions as to the same rule. Manifestly, the jurisdictional provision under discussion was incorporated in the act for the express purpose of avoiding such confusion." Time and experience, say the Texas courts, have shown the wisdom of this rule. Concentration of judicial supervision of Railroad Commission orders permits the state courts, like the Railroad Commission itself, to acquire a specialized knowledge which is useful in shaping the policy of regulation of the ever-changing demands in this field. At the present time, less than ten per cent of these cases come before the federal district court.

The very "confusion" which the Texas legislature and Supreme Court feared might result from review by many state courts of the Railroad Commission's orders has resulted from the exercise of federal equity jurisdiction. As a practical matter, the federal courts can make small contribution to the well organized system of regulation and review which the Texas statutes provide. Texas courts can give fully as great relief, including temporary restraining orders, as the federal courts. Delay, misunderstanding of local law, and needless federal conflict with the State policy, are the inevitable product of this double system of review. The most striking example of misunderstanding has come where the federal court has flatly disagreed with the position later taken by a State court as to State law. In those cases, the federal court attributed a given meaning to the state statute which went to the heart of the control program. The Court of Civil Appeals disagreed, but before ultimate review could be had either in Texas or here, the legislature amended its statutes so that the cases became moot. Had the Texas Civil Appeals decision come first, it would have been unnecessary to make the changes which were made in an effort to stay within the limit thought by the Governor of Texas to have been set by the tone of the federal court's opinion. The Texas legislature later changed the law back to its original state, as clear an example of waste motion as can be imagined. The federal court has been called upon constantly to determine whether the Railroad Commission has acted within the scope of statutory authority, while the important constitutional issues have, as the federal court has repeatedly said, been fairly well settled from the beginning.

These federal court decisions on state law have created a constant task for the Texas Governor, the Texas legislature, and the Railroad Commission. The Governor of Texas, as has been noted above, felt called upon to forge his oil program in the light of the remotest inferences of federal court opinions. In one instance he thought it necessary to declare martial law. Special sessions of the legislature have been occupied with consideration of federal court decisions. Legislation passed under the circumstances of the strain and doubt created by these decisions was necessarily unsatisfactory. The Railroad Commission has had to adjust itself to the permutations of the law as seen by the federal courts. The most recent example was in connection with the *Rowan & Nichols* case in which the Commission felt compelled to adopt a new proration scheme to comply with the demands of a federal court decision which was reversed when it came to this Court.

As has been noted the federal court cases have dealt primarily with the interpretation of state law, some of it state law fairly remote from oil and gas problems. The instant case raised a number of problems of no general significance on which a federal court can only try to ascertain state law. For example, we are asked to determine whether a previous Travis county district court decision makes this case *res adjudicata* and whether another case pending in Travis county deprived the Commission of jurisdiction to consider Burford's application. The existence of these problems throughout the oil regulatory field creates a further possibility of serious delay which can injure the conservation program, for under our decision in *Railroad Commission v. Pullman Co.*, it may be necessary to stay federal action pending authoritative determination of the difficult state questions.

The conflict between federal courts and Texas has lessened appreciably in recent years primarily as a result of the decisions in the *Rowan & Nichols* case. In those cases we assumed that the principal issue in the review of Railroad Commission orders was whether the Commission had confined itself within the boundaries of due process of law, and held that any special relief provided by state statutes must be pursued in a state court. It is now argued that under the decision of the Texas Supreme Court in *Railroad Commission v. Shell Oil Co.*, the courts, whether federal or state, are required to review the Commission's order not for constitutional validity, but for compliance with a standard of "reasonableness" under the state statute which, it is said, is different from the constitutional standard of due process.

The whole cycle of federal-state conflict cannot be permitted to begin again by acceptance of this view. Insofar as we have discretion to do so, we should leave these problems of Texas law to the State court where each may be handled as "one more item in a continuous series of adjustments."

These questions of regulation of the industry by the State administrative agency, whether involving gas or oil prorationing programs or Rule 37 cases, so clearly involves basic problems of Texas policy that equitable discretion should be exercised to give the Texas courts the first opportunity to consider them.

> Few public interests have a higher claim upon the discretion of a federal chancellor and the avoidance of needless friction with state policies, * * *. These cases reflect a doctrine of abstention appropriate to our federal system whereby the federal courts, "exercising a wise discretion," restrain their authority because of "scrupulous regard for the rightful independence of the state governments" and for the smooth working of the federal judiciary * * *. This use of equitable powers is a contribution of the courts in furthering the harmonious relation between state and federal authority without the need of rigorous congressional restriction of those powers.

The state provides a unified method for the formation of policy and determination of cases by the Commission and by the state courts. The judicial review of the Commission's decisions in the state courts is expeditious and adequate. Conflicts in the interpretation of state law, dangerous to the success of state policies, are almost certain to result from the intervention of the lower federal courts. On the other hand, if the state procedure is followed from the Commission to the State Supreme Court, ultimate review of the federal questions is fully preserved here. Under such circumstances, a sound respect for the independence of state action requires the federal equity court to stay its hand.

The decision of the Circuit Court of Appeals is reversed and the judgment of the District Court dismissing the complaint is affirmed for the reasons here stated.

It is so ordered.

MR. JUSTICE FRANKFURTER, joined by MR. JUSTICE ROBERTS and MR. JUSTICE REED, dissenting. THE CHIEF JUSTICE expresses no views as to the desirability, as a matter of legislative policy, of retaining the diversity jurisdiction. In all other respects he concurs in the opinion * * * .

To deny a suitor access to a federal district court under the circumstances of this case is to disregard a duty enjoined by Congress and made manifest by the whole history of the jurisdiction of the United States courts based upon diversity of citizenship between parties. For I am assuming that law declared by this Court, in contradistinction to law declared by Congress, is something other than the manipulation of words to formulate a predetermined result. Judicial law to me implies at least some continuity of intellectual criteria and procedures in dealing with recurring problems.

I believe it to be wholly accurate to say that throughout our history it has never been questioned that a right created by state law and enforceable in the state courts can also be enforced in the federal courts where the parties to the controversy are citizens of different states. The reasons which led Congress to grant such jurisdiction to the federal courts are familiar. It was believed that, consciously or otherwise, the courts of a state may favor their own citizens. Bias against outsiders may become embedded in a judgment of a state court and yet not be sufficiently apparent to be made the basis of a federal claim. To avoid possible discriminations of this sort, so the theory goes, a citizen of a state other than that in which he is suing or being sued ought to be able to go into a wholly impartial tribunal, namely, the federal court sitting in that state. Thus, the basic premise of federal jurisdiction based upon diversity of the parties' citizenship is that the federal courts should afford remedies which are coextensive with rights created by state law and enforceable in state courts.

That is the theory of diversity jurisdiction. Whether it is a sound theory, whether diversity jurisdiction is necessary or desirable in order to avoid possible unfairness by state courts, state judges and juries, against outsiders, whether the federal courts ought to be relieved of the burden of diversity litigation,—these are matters which are not my concern as a judge. They are the concern of those whose business it is to legislate, not mine. I speak as one who has long favored the entire abolition of diversity jurisdiction. But I must decide this case as a judge and not as a legislative reformer.

Aside from the Johnson Act,[1] the many powerful and persistent legislative efforts to abolish or restrict diversity jurisdiction have ever since

[1] The Johnson Act provides that no district court can enjoin the enforcement of any order issued by a state administrative body where the jurisdiction of the court "is based solely upon the ground of diversity of citizenship, or the repugnance of such order to the Constitution of the United States", and "where such order (1) affects rates chargeable by a public utility, (2) does not interfere with interstate commerce, and (3) has been made after reasonable notice and hearing, and where a plain, speedy, and efficient remedy may be had at law or in equity in the courts of such State." * * *

the Civil War been rejected by Congress. Again and again legislation designed to make inroads upon diversity jurisdiction has been proposed to Congress, and on each occasion Congress has deliberately refused to act. * * * We are dealing, then, not with a jurisdiction evolved and shaped by the courts but rather with one explicitly conferred and undeviatingly maintained by Congress.

The only limitations upon the exercise of diversity jurisdiction—apart from that which Congress made in the Johnson Act—are, broadly speaking, those illustrated by *Railroad Comm. v. Rowan & Nichols Oil Co.* In *Rowan & Nichols* the claim based upon state law was derived from a statute requiring proration on a "reasonable basis," and it was not clear from the decisions of the state courts whether such courts might exercise an independent judgment as to what was "reasonable." And in *Pullman* it was also "far from clear" whether state law, as authoritatively defined by the local courts, might not displace the federal questions raised by the bill. Where the controlling state law is so undefined that a federal court attempting to apply such law would be groping utterly in the dark—where "no matter how seasoned the judgment of the district court may be, it cannot escape being a forecast rather than a determination"—a court of equity may "avoid the waste of a tentative decision." * * * Under such circumstances it [is] an affirmation and not a denial of federal jurisdiction * * * to hold the bill pending a seasonable determination of the local issues in a proceeding to be brought in the state courts.

If, in a case of this sort, the state right sought to be enforced in the federal courts depended upon a "forecast rather than a determination" of state law, if the federal court was practically impotent to enforce state law because of its inability to fathom the complexities, legal or factual, of local law, the rule of *Rowan & Nichols* would be applicable. In such a situation the line of demarcation between what belongs to the state administrative body and what to its courts should not be drawn by the federal courts. If it could be shown that the circumstances of this case warranted the application of such a doctrine of abstention, I would gladly join in the decision of the Court. But such a showing has not been attempted, nor, I believe, could it be made.

* * *

It is true that Texas law governing review of Commission orders under Rule 37 has not always been clear and certain, and that there may be parts of the statute and some of the Railroad Commission's Rules, with which we are not now concerned, which, like other legal materials, are not as clear as they might be. But, in a series of recent decisions, the Supreme Court of Texas has not only given precision to the concepts of "waste" and "confiscation of property" employed in Rule 37, it has also defined with clarity the scope of judicial review of Commission action. * * *

In other words, as the Circuit Court of Appeals has said in this case, "We now know the legal requisites of orders and regulations of the Railroad Commission under the conservation laws of Texas."

* * *

And so, the case really reduces itself to this: in the actual application of the standards governing judicial review of Commission orders allowing exceptions under Rule 37—standards which today have been authoritatively and precisely defined—a different result may be obtained if suit is brought in the federal rather than the state courts. And why? Because federal judges are less competent and less fair than state judges in applying the rules that are binding upon both? If this were true here, it would be equally true as applied to almost all types of litigation brought into federal courts to enforce state-created rights. The explanation may perhaps lie in the realm of what has sometimes been called "psychological jurisprudence." In the assessment of evidence and the other elements which enter into a judicial judgment, a federal judge may make judgments different from those which a state judge may make. Federal judges are perhaps to be regarded as men apart—judges who cannot be trusted to judge fairly and impartially. But if this be our premise, why should it not follow that the federal courts are, because of their putative bias, to be denied the right to hear insurance cases, or cases involving controversies between debtors and creditors, landlords and tenants, employers and employees, and all the other complicated controversies arising out of the local law of the forty-eight states?

It is the essence of diversity jurisdiction that federal judges and juries should pass on asserted claims because the result might be different if they were decided by a state court. There may be excellent reasons why Congress should abolish diversity jurisdiction. But, with all deference, it is not a defensible ground for having this Court by indirection abrogate diversity jurisdiction when, as a matter of fact, Congress has persistently refused to restrict such jurisdiction except in the limited area occupied by the Johnson Act. The Congressional premise of diversity jurisdiction is that the possibility of unfairness against outside litigants is to be avoided by providing the neutral forum of a federal court. The Court today is in effect withdrawing this grant of jurisdiction in order to avoid possible unfairness against state interests in the federal courts. That which Congress created to assure impartiality of adjudication is now destroyed to prevent what is deemed to be hostility and bias in adjudication.

Of course, the usual considerations governing the exercise of equity jurisdiction are equally applicable to suits in the federal courts where jurisdiction depends upon the diversity of the parties' citizenship. The chancellor certainly must balance the equities before granting relief; he should stay his hand where another court seized of the controversy can do justice to the claims of the parties; he may refuse equitable relief where the asserted right is doubtful because of the substantive law which he must find as declared by the state. But it is too late in the day to suggest that the chancellor may act on whimsical or purely personal considerations or on private notions of policy regarding the particular suit. It is not for us to say that litigation affecting state laws and state policies ought to be tried only in the state courts. Congress has chosen to confer diversity jurisdiction upon the federal courts. It is not for us to reject that which Congress has made the law of the land simply because of our independent conviction that such legislation is unwise.

* * *

The opinion of the Court cuts deep into our judicial fabric. The duty of the judiciary is to exercise the jurisdiction which Congress has conferred. What the Court is doing today I might wholeheartedly approve if it were done by Congress. But I cannot justify translation of the circumstance of my membership on this Court into an opportunity of writing my private view of legislative policy into law and thereby effacing a far greater area of diversity jurisdiction than Senator Norris, as chairman of the Senate Judiciary Committee, was ever able to persuade Congress itself to do.

Notes and Questions

1. A combination of several factors persuaded the Court to abstain in *Burford*. What are they? It seems unlikely that all of these factors will be present in very many cases, which suggests that *Burford* abstention should be rare. On the other hand, what is the danger in opening the abstention door in this way?

2. Did the decision to abstain in *Burford* avoid "needless friction with state policies"? Why or why not?

3. Sun Oil Company's complaint invoked federal question jurisdiction as well as diversity jurisdiction. In deciding the case, does the Court assume that both grounds for jurisdiction exist? Would abstention be more or less justified in the absence of a substantial federal question? Why does Justice Frankfurter's dissent discuss the policies underlying diversity jurisdiction at length but make no mention of those supporting federal question jurisdiction?

4. Would abstention under *Pullman* or *Younger* have been appropriate? Why or why not?

5. In *Alabama Public Service Comm. v. Southern Railway Co.*, 341 U.S. 341, 71 S.Ct. 762, 95 L.Ed. 1002 (1951), appeared to expand *Burford*. Southern Railway sued in federal court to enjoin the Alabama Public Service Commission and the Attorney General of Alabama from enforcing state laws prohibiting the discontinuance of railroad service. Southern had petitioned the Commission for permission to discontinue the service, but the Commission denied the application, concluding that there was a public need for continued service and that the railroad had not attempted to reduce its losses by using cheaper operating methods. Southern's complaint alleged both that

requiring it to continue to operate the trains at a financial loss constituted confiscation of property in contravention of the Due Process Clause of the Fourteenth Amendment and that there was diversity of citizenship. Alabama law allowed an appeal from any order of the Commission to the Circuit Court of Montgomery County and thereafter to the state supreme court.

The Court cited *Burford* and listed several factors in support of abstention. The case involved "the essentially local problem of balancing the loss to the railroad from continued operation of trains * * * with the public need for that service." In addition, Alabama had concentrated judicial review of Commission orders in the circuit court of Montgomery County, and appellate review of circuit court decisions was relatively broad. The Court concluded with a sweeping endorsement of abstention:

> As adequate state court review of an administrative order based upon predominantly local factors is available to appellee, intervention of a federal court is not necessary for protection of federal rights. Equitable relief may be granted only when the District Court * * * is convinced that the asserted federal right cannot be preserved except by granting the "extraordinary relief of an injunction in the federal courts."

Alabama Public Service bears only a superficial resemblance to *Burford*. Which of the factors present in *Burford* are missing?

6. In *McNeese v. Board of Education*, 373 U.S. 668, 83 S.Ct. 1443, 10 L.Ed.2d 622 (1963), a group of African-American school children sued in an Illinois federal court alleging that officials at the school they attended segregated white and African-American students. Illinois law provided that residents of a school district, if they met certain conditions, could file a complaint with the Superintendent of Public Instruction alleging racial segregation. If, after a hearing, the Superintendent determined the allegations were true, he was to request the state Attorney General to bring suit. The state courts could review the Superintendent's final decision. The Supreme Court noted that there was "no underlying issue of state law controlling" in the case nor was "the federal right in any way entangled in a skein of state law that must be untangled before the federal court can proceed." Additionally, the Court concluded that it was not clear that the state administrative remedy was adequate to preclude the plaintiffs from seeking federal court relief before invoking it. Consequently, the majority rejected the dissent's call for *Burford* abstention.

In *Zablocki v. Redhail*, 434 U.S. 374, 98 S.Ct. 673, 54 L.Ed.2d 618 (1978), plaintiff brought a class action in federal court challenging the constitutionally of a state statute requiring minors' non-custodial parents subject to support orders to obtain a court order allowing them to marry. The statute required that in order to obtain permission to marry, such parents had to demonstrate that they were complying with their support obligation and that their children were not nor were not likely thereafter to become public charges. The Court rejected *Burford* abstention, declaring that "unlike *Burford*" the case did not involve "complex issues of state law, resolution of which would be 'disruptive of state efforts to establish a coherent policy with respect to a matter of substantial public concern.' " After *McNeese* and *Zablocki*, most scholars concluded that *Alabama Public Service Commission* did not portend the broad expansion of the *Burford* doctrine that some of its language may have indicated.

7. Reread the discussion of *New Orleans Public Service, Inc., v. Council of City of New Orleans*, 491 U.S. 350, 109 S.Ct. 2506, 105 L.Ed.2d 298 (1989), at page 838. Was *Burford* abstention appropriate? The Supreme Court held that it was not. The plaintiff's primary claim was that federal law required the Council to reimburse them for wholesale costs that had been allocated by the federal agency. The Court distinguished that claim from one "that a state agency had misapplied its lawful authority or has failed to take into consideration or properly weigh relevant state-law factors." Federal adjudication of the plaintiff's preemption claim would not "disrupt the State's attempt to ensure uniformity in the treatment of an 'essentially local problem.' " The Court refused to view *Burford* as requiring abstention in every case where a complex state administrative process exists or where there is potential for conflict with state regulatory policy.

Plaintiff's alternative claim was that the rate order's nominal basis was a pretext for the Council's determination that the original investment was unwise. The Court acknowledged that adjudication of the pretext claim would require "an inquiry into industry practice, wholesale rates, and power availability," but concluded that because "wholesale electricity is not bought and sold within a predominantly local market," federal adjudication would not disrupt state resolution of local policies. Does *New Orleans Public Service* make the scope of the *Burford* doctrine relatively clear? Why or why not?

8. In the same year as *Burford*, the Court was asked to abstain in a diversity case involving no federal issues at all but where state law was unclear. The Court refused, in an opinion by Chief Justice Stone. *Meredith v. City of Winter Haven*, 320 U.S. 228, 234-35, 64 S.Ct. 7, 11, 88 L.Ed. 9, 13-14 (1943).

> The diversity jurisdiction was not conferred for the benefit of the federal courts or to serve their convenience. Its purpose was generally to afford to suitors an opportunity in such cases, at their option, to assert their rights in the federal rather than in the state courts. In the absence of some recognized public policy or defined principle guiding the exercise of the jurisdiction conferred, which would in exceptional cases warrant its non-exercise, it has from the first been deemed to be the duty of the federal courts, if their jurisdiction is properly invoked, to decide questions of state law whenever necessary to the rendition of a judgment. When such exceptional circumstances are not present, denial of that opportunity by the federal courts merely because the answers to the questions of state law are difficult or uncertain or have not yet been given by the highest court of the state, would thwart the purpose of the jurisdictional act.

> The exceptions relate to the discretionary powers of courts of equity. An appeal to the equity jurisdiction conferred on federal district courts

is an appeal to the sound discretion which guides the determinations of courts of equity. Exercise of that discretion by those, as well as by other courts having equity powers, may require them to withhold their relief in furtherance of a recognized, defined public policy.

The Chief Justice canvassed the justifications for abstention and concluded that none of them applied to pure diversity cases that merely presented difficult or unsettled questions of state law.

Justice Frankfurter, who dissented in *Burford*, wrote for the Court in *Louisiana Power & Light Co. v. City of Thibodaux*, 360 U.S. 25, 79 S.Ct. 1070, 3 L.Ed.2d 1058 (1959), and found abstention warranted. The City instituted state court eminent domain proceedings against petitioner's property. Petitioner removed on the basis of diversity and claimed that the City lacked the power of eminent domain. State law on the question was not clear. The district court stayed its proceeding *sua sponte* to give the state supreme court an opportunity to decide the issue, but the Court of Appeals vacated the stay . The Supreme Court reversed and reinstated the stay. The Court pointed to the special nature of eminent domain proceedings, intimately involved with "sovereign prerogative," asserting that "[t]he considerations that prevailed in conventional equity suits for avoiding the hazards of serious disruption by federal court of state government or needless friction between state and federal authorities are similarly appropriate in a state eminent domain proceeding brought in, or removed to, a federal court." The Court also noted the quandary that faced the district court given the uncertainty of state law. The Court distinguished *Meredith* as a declination of jurisdiction and dismissal, whereas the district court in *Thibodaux* had merely stayed its proceedings to obtain an authoritative ruling on the state law issue from the state court.

Why was the *Pullman* doctrine inapplicable in *Thibodaux*? Was the rationale for abstention in *Thibodaux* analogous to the rationale for abstention in *Burford*? Why or why not? Was Justice Frankfurter's opinion in *Thibodaux* inconsistent with his dissent in *Burford*?

The same day as *Thibodaux*, the Court rejected a district court's decision to abstain in a case involving a state's eminent domain power in *County of Allegheny v. Frank Mashuda Co.*, 360 U.S. 185, 79 S.Ct. 1060, 3 L.Ed.2d 1163 (1959). The County initiated eminent domain proceedings to appropriate plaintiffs' property. A state-court-appointed board assessed the damages owing to plaintiffs, and both sides appealed the board's damages assessment to the state court as provided by state law. The state court proceeding was pending. Plaintiffs then sued in federal court on the basis of diversity, alleging that after the County took possession of the property, it leased it to a private company for a private purpose. State law clearly prohibited taking private property under eminent domain for a private use. Plaintiffs therefore sought a judgment of ouster and damages against the County. The district court dismissed on the ground that federal court interference with state condemnation proceedings was inappropriate. The Supreme Court held that the case presented no exceptional circumstances justifying abstention, declaring "the fact that a case concerns a State's power of eminent domain no more justifies abstention than the fact that it involves any other issue related to sovereignty."

Of course, one distinction between *Thibodaux* and *Frank Mashuda* is that the state law was unclear in *Thibodaux* where the Court upheld abstention, but was clear in *Frank Mashuda*, where the Court rejected it. Was there another distinction between the two cases? Only two justices voted in the majority in both cases, Justices Stewart and Whittaker. Justice Stewart's concurring opinion in *Thibodaux* explains his votes by asserting that in *Frank Mashuda* the Court held it was error for the lower court to dismiss and because the state law was clear there was no reason for the court not to adjudicate the claim promptly. Justice Whittaker was silent. Thus, it is less than crystal clear when abstention under *Thibodaux* is appropriate. Do you think *Thibodaux* abstention is limited to eminent domain cases or are there other state interests sufficiently important to support it?

QUACKENBUSH v. ALLSTATE INSURANCE COMPANY
Supreme Court of the United States, 1996.
517 U.S. 706, 116 S.Ct. 1712, 135 L.Ed.2d 1.

JUSTICE O'CONNOR delivered the opinion of the Court.

In this case, we consider whether an abstention-based remand order is appealable as a final order under 28 U.S.C. § 1291, and whether the abstention doctrine first recognized in *Burford v. Sun Oil Co.* can be applied in a common-law suit for damages.

I

Petitioner, the Insurance Commissioner for the State of California, was appointed trustee over the assets of the Mission Insurance Company and its affiliates (Mission companies) in 1987, after those companies were ordered into liquidation by a California court. In an effort to gather the assets of the defunct Mission companies, the Commissioner filed the instant action against respondent Allstate Insurance Company in state court, seeking contract and tort damages for Allstate's alleged breach of certain reinsurance agreements, as well as a general declaration of Allstate's obligations under those agreements.

Allstate removed the action to federal court on diversity grounds and filed a motion to compel arbitration under the Federal Arbitration Act. The Commissioner sought remand to state court, arguing that the District Court should abstain from hearing the case under *Burford* because its resolution might interfere with California's regulation of the Mission insolvency. Specifically, the Commissioner indicated that Allstate would be asserting its right to set off its own contract claims against the Commissioner's recovery under the contract, that the viability of these setoff claims was a hotly disputed question of state law, and that this question was currently pending before the state courts in another case arising out of the Mission insolvency.

The District Court observed that "California has an overriding interest in regulating insurance insolvencies and liquidations in a uniform and orderly manner," and that in this case "this important state interest could be undermined by inconsistent rulings from the federal and state courts." Based on these observations, and its determination that the setoff question should be resolved in state court, the District Court concluded this case was an appropriate one for the exercise of *Burford* abstention. The District Court did not stay its hand pending the California courts' resolution of the setoff issue, but instead remanded the entire case to state court. The District Court entered this remand order without ruling on Allstate's motion to compel arbitration.

* * * [T]he Court of Appeals for the Ninth Circuit vacated the District Court's decision and ordered the case sent to arbitration. The Ninth Circuit concluded that federal courts can abstain from hearing a case under *Burford* only when the relief being sought is equitable in nature, and therefore held that abstention was inappropriate in this case because the Commissioner purported to be seeking only legal relief.

The Ninth Circuit's holding that abstention-based remand orders are appealable conflicts with the decisions of other courts of appeals, * * * as does its determination that *Burford* abstention can only be exercised in cases in which equitable relief is sought. We granted certiorari to resolve these conflicts, and now affirm on grounds different than those provided by the Ninth Circuit.

II

[The Court considered whether the district court's abstention order was unappealable either under 28 U.S.C. § 1447(d) or 28 U.S.C. § 1291 and concluded that immediate appellate review was permissible.]

III

A

We have often acknowledged that federal courts have a strict duty to exercise the jurisdiction that is conferred upon them by Congress. This duty is not, however, absolute. Indeed, we have held that federal courts may decline to exercise their jurisdiction, in otherwise " 'exceptional circumstances,' " where denying a federal forum would clearly serve an important countervailing interest, for example where abstention is warranted by considerations of "proper constitutional adjudication," "regard for federal-state relations," or "wise judicial administration."

We have thus held that federal courts have the power to refrain from

hearing cases that would interfere with a pending state criminal proceeding or with certain types of state civil proceedings; cases in which
the resolution of a federal constitutional question might be obviated if
the state courts were given the opportunity to interpret ambiguous state
law; cases raising issues "intimately involved with [the states'] sovereign
prerogative," the proper adjudication of which might be impaired by unsettled questions of state law; cases whose resolution by a federal court
might unnecessarily interfere with a state system for the collection of
taxes; and cases which are duplicative of a pending state proceeding.

Our longstanding application of these doctrines reflects "the common-law background against which the statutes conferring jurisdiction
were enacted." And, as the Ninth Circuit correctly indicated, it has long
been established that a federal court has the authority to decline to exercise its jurisdiction when it "is asked to employ its historic powers as a
court of equity." This tradition informs our understanding of the jurisdiction Congress has conferred upon the federal courts, and explains the
development of our abstention doctrines.

* * *

Though we have * * * located the power to abstain in the historic discretion exercised by federal courts "sitting in equity," we have not
treated abstention as a "technical rule of equity procedure." Rather, we
have recognized that the authority of a federal court to abstain from exercising its jurisdiction extends to all cases in which the court has discretion to grant or deny relief. Accordingly, we have not limited the application of the abstention doctrines to suits for injunctive relief, but have
also required federal courts to decline to exercise jurisdiction over certain classes of declaratory judgments, the granting of which is generally
committed to the courts' discretion.

Nevertheless, we have not previously addressed whether the principles underlying our abstention cases would support the remand or dismissal of a common-law action for damages. * * *

[W]e have applied abstention principles to actions "at law" only to
permit a federal court to enter a stay order that postpones adjudication
of the dispute, not to dismiss the federal suit altogether.

Our decisions in *Thibodaux* and *County of Allegheny v. Frank
Mashuda Co.* illustrate the distinction we have drawn between abstention-based remand orders or dismissals and abstention-based decisions
merely to stay adjudication of a federal suit. In *Thibodaux*, a city in
Louisiana brought an eminent domain proceeding in state court, seeking
to condemn for public use certain property owned by a Florida corporation. After the corporation removed the action to federal court on diversity grounds, the Federal District Court decided on its own motion to
stay the case, pending a state court's determination whether the city
could exercise the power of eminent domain under state law. The case

did not arise within the "equity" jurisdiction of the federal courts because the suit sought compensation for a taking, and the District Court lacked discretion to deny relief on the corporation's claim. Nonetheless, the issues in the suit were "intimately involved with [the state's] sovereign prerogative." We concluded that "[t]he considerations that prevailed in conventional equity suits for avoiding the hazards of serious disruption by federal courts of state government or needless friction between state and federal authorities are similarly appropriate in a state eminent domain proceeding brought in, or removed to, a federal court." And based on that conclusion, we affirmed the district court's order staying the case.

County of Allegheny was decided the same day as *Thibodaux*, and like *Thibodaux* it involved review of a District Court order abstaining from the exercise of diversity jurisdiction over a state law eminent domain action. Unlike in *Thibodaux*, however, the District Court in *County of Allegheny* had not merely stayed adjudication of the federal action pending the resolution of an issue in state court, but rather had dismissed the federal action altogether. Based in large measure on this distinction, we reversed the District Court's order.

We were careful to note in *Thibodaux* that the District Court had only stayed the federal suit pending adjudication of the dispute in state court. Unlike the outright dismissal or remand of a federal suit, we held, an order merely staying the action "does not constitute abnegation of judicial duty. On the contrary, it is a wise and productive discharge of it. There is only postponement of decision for its best fruition." We have thus held that in cases where the relief being sought is equitable in nature or otherwise discretionary, federal courts not only have the power to stay the action based on abstention principles, but can also, in otherwise appropriate circumstances, decline to exercise jurisdiction altogether by either dismissing the suit or remanding it to state court. By contrast, while we have held that federal courts may stay actions for damages based on abstention principles, we have not held that those principles support the outright dismissal or remand of damages actions.

* * *

[Here the Court discusses and rejects a parallel between abstention and *forum non conveniens*.]

Federal courts abstain out of deference to the paramount interests of another sovereign, and the concern is with principles of comity and federalism. Dismissal for forum non conveniens, by contrast, has historically reflected a far broader range of considerations, most notably the convenience to the parties and the practical difficulties that can attend the adjudication of a dispute in a certain locality.

B

With these background principles in mind, we consider the contours of the *Burford* doctrine. The principal issue presented in *Burford* was the "reasonableness" of an order issued by the Texas Railroad Commission, which granted "a permit to drill four oil wells on a small plot of land in the East Texas oil field." Due to the potentially overlapping claims of the many parties who might have an interest in a common pool of oil and the need for uniform regulation of the oil industry, Texas endowed the Railroad Commission with exclusive regulatory authority in the area. Texas also placed the authority to review the Commission's orders in a single set of state courts, "[t]o prevent the confusion of multiple review," and to permit an experienced cadre of state judges to obtain "specialized knowledge" in the field. Though Texas had thus demonstrated its interest in maintaining uniform review of the Commission's orders, the federal courts had, in the years preceding *Burford*, become increasingly involved in reviewing the reasonableness of the Commission's orders, both under a constitutional standard imposed under the Due Process Clause and under state law, which established a similar standard.

Viewing the case as "a simple proceeding in equity to enjoin the enforcement of the Commissioner's order," we framed the question presented in terms of the power of a federal court of equity to abstain from exercising its jurisdiction * * * .

Having * * * posed the question in terms of the District Court's discretion, as a court sitting "in equity," to decline jurisdiction, we approved the District Court's dismissal of the complaint on a number of grounds that were unique to that case. We noted, for instance, the difficulty of the regulatory issues presented, stating that the "order under consideration is part of the general regulatory system devised for the conservation of oil and gas in Texas, an aspect of 'as thorny a problem as has challenged the ingenuity and wisdom of legislatures.'" We also stressed the demonstrated need for uniform regulation in the area, citing the unified procedures Texas had established to "prevent the confusion of multiple review," and the important state interests this uniform system of review was designed to serve. Most importantly, we also described the detrimental impact of ongoing federal court review of the Commission's orders, which review had already led to contradictory adjudications by the state and federal courts.

We ultimately concluded in *Burford* that dismissal was appropriate because the availability of an alternative, federal forum threatened to frustrate the purpose of the complex administrative system that Texas had established. We have since provided more generalized descriptions of the *Burford* doctrine, but with the exception of cases that rest only loosely on the *Burford* rationale, we have revisited the decision only infrequently in the intervening 50 years.

In [*New Orleans Public Service, Inc. v. Council of City of New Orleans (NOPSI)*], our most recent exposition of the *Burford* doctrine, we again located the power to dismiss based on abstention principles in the discretionary power of a federal court sitting in equity, and we again illustrated the narrow range of circumstances in which *Burford* can justify the dismissal of a federal action. * * *

We ultimately held that *Burford* did not provide proper grounds for an abstention-based dismissal in *NOPSI* because the "case [did] not involve a state-law claim, nor even an assertion that the federal claims [were] 'in any way entangled in a skein of state law that must be untangled before the federal case can proceed,'" and because there was no serious threat of conflict between the adjudication of the federal claim presented in the case and the State's interest in ensuring uniformity in ratemaking decisions * * * .

These cases do not provide a formulaic test for determining when dismissal under *Burford* is appropriate, but they do demonstrate that the power to dismiss under the *Burford* doctrine, as with other abstention doctrines, derives from the discretion historically enjoyed by courts of equity. They further demonstrate that exercise of this discretion must reflect "principles of federalism and comity." Ultimately, what is at stake is a federal court's decision, based on a careful consideration of the federal interests in retaining jurisdiction over the dispute and the competing concern for the "independence of state action," that the State's interests are paramount and that a dispute would best be adjudicated in a state forum. This equitable decision balances the strong federal interest in having certain classes of cases, and certain federal rights, adjudicated in federal court, against the State's interests in maintaining "uniformity in the treatment of an 'essentially local problem,'" and retaining local control over "difficult questions of state law bearing on policy problems of substantial public import." This balance only rarely favors abstention, and the power to dismiss recognized in *Burford* represents an "'extraordinary and narrow exception to the duty of the District Court to adjudicate a controversy properly before it.'"

C

We turn, finally, to the application of *Burford* in this case. As in *NOPSI*, the federal interests in this case are pronounced, as Allstate's motion to compel arbitration under the Federal Arbitration Act implicates a substantial federal concern for the enforcement of arbitration agreements. With regard to the state interests, however, the case appears at first blush to present nothing more than a run-of-the-mill contract dispute. The Commissioner seeks damages from Allstate for Allstate's failure to perform its obligations under a reinsurance agreement. What differentiates this case from other diversity actions seeking damages for breach of contract, if anything, is the impact federal adjudication of the dispute might have on the ongoing liquidation proceedings in state court: The Commissioner claims that any recovery by Allstate on its setoff claims would amount to an illegal "preference" under state law. This question appears now to have been conclusively answered by the California Supreme Court, although at the time the District Court ruled this question was still hotly contested.

The Ninth Circuit concluded that the District Court's remand order was inappropriate because "*Burford* abstention does not apply to suits seeking solely legal relief." Addressing our abstention cases, the Ninth Circuit held that the federal courts' power to abstain in certain cases is "locat[ed] * * * in the unique powers of equitable courts," and that it derives from equity courts' " 'discretionary power to grant or withhold relief.' " The Ninth Circuit's reversal of the District Court's abstention-based remand order in this case therefore reflects the application of a *per se* rule: "[T]he power of federal courts to abstain from exercising their jurisdiction, at least in *Burford* abstention cases, is founded upon a discretion they possess only in equitable cases."

To the extent the Ninth Circuit held only that a federal court cannot, under *Burford*, dismiss or remand an action when the relief sought is not discretionary, its judgment is consistent with our abstention cases. We have explained the power to dismiss or remand a case under the abstention doctrines in terms of the discretion federal courts have traditionally exercised in deciding whether to provide equitable or discretionary relief, and the Commissioner appears to have conceded that the relief being sought in this case is neither equitable nor otherwise committed to the discretion of the court. In those cases in which we have applied traditional abstention principles to damages actions, we have only permitted a federal court to "withhold action until the state proceedings have concluded;" that is, we have permitted federal courts applying abstention principles in damages actions to enter a stay, but we have not permitted them to dismiss the action altogether.

The *per se* rule described by the Ninth Circuit is, however, more rigid than our precedents require. We have not strictly limited abstention to "equitable cases," but rather have extended the doctrine to all cases in which a federal court is asked to provide some form of discretionary relief. Moreover, as demonstrated by our decision in *Thibodaux*, we have not held that abstention principles are completely inapplicable in damages actions. *Burford* might support a federal court's decision to postpone adjudication of a damages action pending the resolution by the state courts of a disputed question of state law. For example, given the situation the District Court faced in this case, a stay order might have been appropriate: The setoff issue was being decided by the state courts at the time the District Court ruled, and in the interest of avoiding inconsistent adjudications on that point, the District Court might have been justified in entering a stay to await the outcome of the state court litigation.

Like the Ninth Circuit, we review only the remand order which was entered, and find it unnecessary to determine whether a more limited abstention-based stay order would have been warranted on the facts of this case. * * * Nor do we find it necessary to inquire fully as to whether this case presents the sort of "exceptional circumstance" in which *Burford* abstention or other grounds for yielding federal jurisdiction might be appropriate. Under our precedents, federal courts have the power to dismiss or remand cases based on abstention principles only where the relief being sought is equitable or otherwise discretionary. Because this was a damages action, we conclude that the District Court's remand order was an unwarranted application of the *Burford* doctrine. The judgment is affirmed.

It is so ordered.

JUSTICE SCALIA, concurring.

I join the opinion of the Court. I write separately only to respond to Justice Kennedy's concurrence.

Justice Kennedy * * * says that he would "not rule out * * * the possibility that a federal court might dismiss a suit for damages in a case where a serious affront to the interests of federalism could be averted in no other way." I would not have joined today's opinion if I believed it left such discretionary dismissal available. Such action is foreclosed, I think, by the Court's holding, clearly summarized in the concluding sentences of the opinion * * * .

Justice Kennedy's projected horrible of a "serious affront to the interests of federalism" cannot possibly materialize under the Court's holding. There is no "serious affront to the interests of federalism" when Congress lawfully decides to pre-empt state action—which is what our cases hold (and today's opinion affirms) Congress does whenever it instructs federal courts to assert jurisdiction over matters as to which relief is not discretionary.

If the Court today felt empowered to decide for itself when congressionally decreed jurisdiction constitutes a "serious affront" and when it does not, the opinion would have read much differently. Most pertinently, it would not have found it unnecessary "to inquire fully as to whether this case presents the sort of 'exceptional circumstance' in which *Burford* abstention or other grounds for yielding federal jurisdiction might be appropriate." There were certainly grounds for such an inquiry if we thought it relevant. The "[then] unsettled but since resolved question of California law" to which Justice Kennedy refers was only part of the basis for the District Court's decision to remand to state court; the court also pointed more generally to what it thought was the State's "overriding interest in regulating insurance insolvencies and liquidations in a uniform and orderly manner." As the Court's opinion says, it is not necessary to inquire fully into that matter because this was a damages action.

JUSTICE KENNEDY, concurring.

When this suit first was filed, it raised an unsettled but since resolved question of California law concerning the ability of companies in Allstate's position to set off claims held against Mission. The principal reason for the District Court's decision to dismiss the case was the threat posed to the state proceedings by different state and federal rulings on the question. The court's concern was reasonable. States, as a matter of tradition and express federal consent, have an important interest in maintaining precise and detailed regulatory schemes for the insurance industry. The fact that a state court rather than an agency was chosen to implement California's scheme provided more reason, not less, for the federal court to stay its hand.

At the same time, however, we have not considered a case in which dismissal of a suit for damages by extension of the doctrine of *Burford v. Sun Oil Co.* was held to be authorized and necessary. As the Court explains, no doubt the preferred course in such circumstances is to resolve any serious potential for federal intrusion by staying the suit while retaining jurisdiction. We ought not rule out, though, the possibility that a federal court might dismiss a suit for damages in a case where a serious affront to the interests of federalism could be averted in no other way. We need not reach that question here.

Abstention doctrines are a significant contribution to the theory of federalism and to the preservation of the federal system in practice. They allow federal courts to give appropriate and necessary recognition to the role and authority of the States. The duty to take these considerations into account must inform the exercise of federal jurisdiction. Principles of equity thus are not the sole foundation for abstention rules; obligations of comity, and respect for the appropriate balance between state and federal interests, are an important part of the justification and authority for abstention as well. The traditional role of discretion in the exercise of equity jurisdiction makes abstention easiest to justify in cases where equitable relief is sought, but abstention, including dismissal, is a possibility that may yet be addressed in a suit for damages, if fundamental concerns of federalism require us to face the issue.

With these observations, I join the opinion of the Court.

Notes and Questions

1. *Quackenbush* focuses on two key factors in the abstention mix. One is the nature of the relief (discretionary or nondiscretionary) sought in the federal action. How does the Court define each kind of relief? A second factor is the nature of the district court order disposing of the federal case. A court may either dismiss the case entirely or stay the proceeding pending resolution of state law issues in the state courts. An order remanding a case removed from state to federal court back to state court counts as a dismissal for abstention purposes. Disagreeing with the Ninth Circuit, the Court holds that a district court may abstain in a case involving nondiscretionary

relief. What limit does the Court place on the district court order in such cases? What, by contrast, may the district court order when the plaintiff seeks only discretionary relief?

2. The Court's distinction between discretionary and non-discretionary relief has some interesting ripple effects.

a) Note that the Court justifies the abstention doctrines generally as "deference to the paramount interests of another sovereign * * * ." Do the states' paramount interests decline in force when the relief sought is non-discretionary?

b) If it is the discretionary nature of damages that makes an abstention dismissal (or remand) inappropriate, why is a stay more appropriate? If the Court's point is that refusing non-discretionary relief violates separation of powers (a point never explicitly made), does the Court implicitly sanction a "small" violation of separation of powers if it stays a damages action? And if the Court's basis is not separation of powers, what is it?

c) Does the Court's opinion signify that the federal courts have a greater role than Congress in protecting federalism interests when the plaintiff seeks discretionary relief? Why should that be so?

d) Does the clear distinction between cases in which granting relief is discretionary and those in which it is not put the abstention doctrines beyond the reach of Congress? Suppose Congress passed a statute under which granting equitable relief were not discretionary. Would that prevent the federal courts from dismissing or remanding cases brought under the statute?

e) Suppose a plaintiff seeks both damages and injunctive relief. Should the court abstain with respect to only half the case? If the damages part of the case goes forward, will the court's findings in that part of the case affect the state proceeding in favor of which the court ordered abstention as to the equitable part of the case? If so, will abstention have served any purpose?

f) As a practical matter, stay of a damages action may have as great an effect as dismissal or remand, if the stay is for the purpose of permitting some state proceeding to go forward. Under the Full Faith and Credit Statute, 28 U.S.C. § 1738 (1994), the federal court must give the same preclusive effect to a state judgment as would the state. If the federal plaintiff is remitted to the state process for determination of critical issues of fact and law, does it really matter to him whether the order sending him back to the state courts reads "dismissed," "remanded" or "stayed"?

3. At the end of the majority opinion, Justice O'Connor states: "Nor do we find it necessary to inquire fully as to whether this case presents the sort of 'exceptional circumstances' in which *Burford* abstention or other grounds for yielding federal jurisdiction might be appropriate." Does Justice O'Connor cast *Burford* abstention as a broadly applicable doctrine or as one that applies only in narrow circumstances? The relief issue aside, would *Burford* abstention be appropriate?

4. The Court's opinion also may shed light on the stature of the absten-

tion doctrines. Does Justice O'Connor's clarity about the balance that the Court strikes between federal and state interests undermine the notion that the abstention doctrines are constitutionally based? The Constitution's primary balancing between federal and state interests occurs in its enumeration of federal powers in Article I, § 8, and its reservation of state powers in the Tenth Amendment. There is no constitutional provision that speaks of a case-by-case weighing of more amorphous federal and state interests. Thus, although it may be permissible for federal institutions to consider such interests, can it be compulsory that they do so?

5. a) The dispute between Justices Scalia and Kennedy is interesting. Justice Scalia indicates that the Court lacks the power in cases seeking non-discretionary relief to inject its own feelings about the federalism balance into its exercise of jurisdiction. Justice Kennedy clearly finds no such inhibitions, thus implicitly carving out a much greater role for the judiciary in defining the contours of federalism than Justice Scalia sees as permissible.

b) Professors Herbert Wechsler (Herbert Wechsler, *The Political Safeguards of Federalism: The Role of the States in the Composition and Selection of the National Government*, 54 COLUM.L.REV. 543 (1954)) and Jesse Choper (JESSE H. CHOPER, JUDICIAL REVIEW AND THE NATIONAL POLITICAL PROCESS 171-259 (1980)) have suggested that "federalism" ought to be regarded as a non-justiciable political question, off limits to the courts. If that were the case, how would the absence of federalism as a decisional predicate affect the abstention doctrines? How, for that matter, would it affect federal courts doctrine more generally?

5. Colorado River *Abstention*

COLORADO RIVER WATER CONSERVATION DISTRICT v. UNITED STATES
Supreme Court of the United States, 1976.
424 U.S. 800, 96 S.Ct. 1236, 47 L.Ed.2d 483.

MR. JUSTICE BRENNAN delivered the opinion of the Court.

The McCarran Amendment provides that "consent is hereby given to join the United States as a defendant in any suit (1) for the adjudication of rights to the use of water of a river system or other source, or (2) for the administration of such rights, where it appears that the United States is the owner of or is in the process of acquiring water rights by appropriation under State law, by purchase, by exchange, or otherwise, and the United States is a necessary party to such suit." The questions presented by this case concern the effect of the McCarran Amendment upon the jurisdiction of the federal district courts under 28 U.S.C. § 1345 over suits for determination of water rights brought by the United States as trustee for certain Indian tribes and as owner of various non-Indian Government claims.

I

It is probable that no problem of the Southwest section of the Nation is more critical than that of scarcity of water. As southwestern populations have grown, conflicting claims to this scarce resource have increased. To meet these claims, several Southwestern States have established elaborate procedures for allocation of water and adjudication of conflicting claims to that resource. In 1969, Colorado enacted its Water Rights Determination and Administration Act in an effort to revamp its legal procedures for determining claims to water within the State.

Under the Colorado Act, the State is divided into seven Water Divisions, each Division encompassing one or more entire drainage basins for the larger rivers in Colorado. Adjudication of water claims within each Division occurs on a continuous basis. Each month, Water Referees in each Division rule on applications for water rights filed within the preceding five months or refer those applications to the Water Judge of their Division. Every six months, the Water Judge passes on referred applications and contested decisions by Referees. A State Engineer and engineers for each Division are responsible for the administration and distribution of the waters of the State according to the determinations in each Division.

Colorado applies the doctrine of prior appropriation in establishing rights to the use of water. Under that doctrine, one acquires a right to water by diverting it from its natural source and applying it to some beneficial use. Continued beneficial use of the water is required in order to maintain the right. In periods of shortage, priority among confirmed rights is determined according to the date of initial diversion.

The reserved rights of the United States extend to Indian reservations and other federal lands, such as national parks and forests. The reserved rights claimed by the United States in this case affect waters within Colorado Water Division No. 7. On November 14, 1972, the Government instituted this suit in the United States District Court for the District of Colorado, invoking the court's jurisdiction under 28 U.S.C. § 1345. The District Court is located in Denver, some 300 miles from Division 7. The suit, against some 1,000 water users, sought declaration of the Government's rights to waters in certain rivers and their tributaries located in Division 7. In the suit, the Government asserted reserved rights on its own behalf and on behalf of certain Indian tribes, as well as rights based on state law. It sought appointment of a water master to administer any waters decreed to the United States. Prior to institution of this suit, the Government had pursued adjudication of non-Indian reserved rights and other water claims based on state law in Water Divisions 4, 5, and 6, and the Government continues to participate fully in those Divisions.

Shortly after the federal suit was commenced, one of the defendants in that suit filed an application in the state court for Division 7, seeking an order directing service of process on the United States in order to make it a party to proceedings in Division 7 for the purpose of adjudicating all of the Government's claims, both state and federal. On January 3, 1973, the United States was served pursuant to authority of the McCarran Amendment. Several defendants and intervenors in the federal proceeding then filed a motion in the District Court to dismiss on the ground that under the Amendment, the court was without jurisdiction to determine federal water rights. Without deciding the jurisdictional question, the District Court, on June 21, 1973, granted the motion in an unreported oral opinion stating that the doctrine of abstention required deference to the proceedings in Division 7. On appeal, the Court of Appeals for the Tenth Circuit reversed, holding that the suit of the United States was within district-court jurisdiction under 28 U.S.C. § 1345, and that abstention was inappropriate. We granted certiorari to consider the important questions of whether the McCarran Amendment terminated jurisdiction of federal courts to adjudicate federal water rights and whether, if that jurisdiction was not terminated, the District Court's dismissal in this case was nevertheless appropriate. We reverse.

II

We first consider the question of district-court jurisdiction under 28 U.S.C. § 1345. That section provides that the district courts shall have original jurisdiction over all civil actions brought by the Federal Government "[e]xcept as otherwise provided by Act of Congress." It is thus necessary to examine whether the McCarran Amendment is such an Act of Congress excepting jurisdiction under § 1345.

* * *

In view of the McCarran Amendment's language and legislative history, controlling principles of statutory construction require the conclusion that the Amendment did not constitute an exception "provided by Act of Congress" that repealed the jurisdiction of district courts under § 1345 to entertain federal water suits. * * * Accordingly, we hold that the McCarran Amendment in no way diminished federal-district-court jurisdiction under § 1345 and that the District Court had jurisdiction to hear this case.[15]

III

We turn next to the question whether this suit nevertheless was properly dismissed in view of the concurrent state proceedings in Division 7.

* * *

B

Next, we consider whether the District Court's dismissal was appro-

---

[15] The District Court also would have had jurisdiction of this suit under the general federal-question jurisdiction of 28 U.S.C. § 1331. * * * [T]he McCarran Amendment did not affect jurisdiction under § 1331 either.

priate under the doctrine of abstention. We hold that the dismissal cannot be supported under that doctrine in any of its forms.

Abstention from the exercise of federal jurisdiction is the exception, not the rule. "The doctrine of abstention, under which a District Court may decline to exercise or postpone the exercise of its jurisdiction, is an extraordinary and narrow exception to the duty of a District Court to adjudicate a controversy properly before it. Abdication of the obligation to decide cases can be justified under this doctrine only in the exceptional circumstances where the order to the parties to repair to the state court would clearly serve an important countervailing interest." "[I]t was never a doctrine of equity that a federal court should exercise its judicial discretion to dismiss a suit merely because a State court could entertain it." Our decisions have confined the circumstances appropriate for abstention to three general categories.

(a) Abstention is appropriate "in cases presenting a federal constitutional issue which might be mooted or presented in a different posture by a state court determination of pertinent state law." This case, however, presents no federal constitutional issue for decision.

(b) Abstention is also appropriate where there have been presented difficult questions of state law bearing on policy problems of substantial public import whose importance transcends the result in the case then at bar. *Louisiana Power & Light Co. v. City of Thibodaux,* for example, involved such a question. In particular, the concern there was with the scope of the eminent domain power of municipalities under state law. * * * In some cases, however, the state question itself need not be determinative of state policy. It is enough that exercise of federal review of the question in a case and in similar cases would be disruptive of state efforts to establish a coherent policy with respect to a matter of substantial public concern. In *Burford v. Sun Oil Co.,* for example, the Court held that a suit seeking review of the reasonableness under Texas state law of a state commission's permit to drill oil wells should have been dismissed by the District Court. The reasonableness of the permit in that case was not of transcendent importance, but review of reasonableness by the federal courts in that and future cases, where the State had established its own elaborate review system for dealing with the geological complexities of oil and gas fields, would have had an impermissibly disruptive effect on state policy for the management of those fields.[21]

---

[21] We note that *Burford v. Sun Oil Co.,* and *Alabama Pub. Serv. Comm'n v. Southern R. Co.,* differ from *Louisiana Power & Light Co. v. City of Thibodaux,* and *County of Allegheny v. Frank Mashuda Co.,* in that the former two cases, unlike the latter two, raised colorable constitutional claims and were therefore brought under federal-question, as well as diversity jurisdiction. While abstention in *Burford* and *Alabama Public Service* had the effect of avoiding a federal constitutional issue, the opinions indicate that this was not an additional ground for abstention in those cases. We have held, of course, that the opportunity to avoid decision of a constitutional question does not alone justify abstention by a federal court. Indeed, the presence of a federal basis for jurisdiction may raise the level of

The present case clearly does not fall within this second category of abstention. While state claims are involved in the case, the state law to be applied appears to be settled. No questions bearing on state policy are presented for decision. Nor will decision of the state claims impair efforts to implement state policy as in *Burford*. To be sure, the federal claims that are involved in the case go to the establishment of water rights which may conflict with similar rights based on state law. But the mere potential for conflict in the results of adjudications, does not, without more, warrant staying exercise of federal jurisdiction. * * * The potential conflict here, involving state claims and federal claims, would not be such as to impair impermissibly the State's effort to effect its policy respecting the allocation of state waters. Nor would exercise of federal jurisdiction here interrupt any such efforts by restraining the exercise of authority vested in state officers.

(c) Finally, abstention is appropriate where, absent bad faith, harassment, or a patently invalid state statute, federal jurisdiction has been invoked for the purpose of restraining state criminal proceedings, state nuisance proceedings antecedent to a criminal prosecution, which are directed at obtaining the closure of places exhibiting obscene films, or collection of state taxes. Like the previous two categories, this category also does not include this case. We deal here neither with a criminal proceeding, nor such a nuisance proceeding, nor a tax collection. We also do not deal with an attempt to restrain such actions or to seek a declaratory judgment as to the validity of a state criminal law under which criminal proceedings are pending in a state court.

C

Although this case falls within none of the abstention categories, there are principles unrelated to considerations of proper constitutional adjudication and regard for federal-state relations which govern in situations involving the contemporaneous exercise of concurrent jurisdictions, either by federal courts or by state and federal courts. These principles rest on considerations of "[w]ise judicial administration, giving regard to conservation of judicial resources and comprehensive disposition of litigation." Generally, as between state and federal courts, the rule is that "the pendency of an action in the state court is no bar to proceedings concerning the same matter in the Federal court having jurisdiction * * * ." As between federal district courts, however, though no precise rule has evolved, the general principle is to avoid duplicative litigation. This difference in general approach between state-federal concurrent jurisdiction and wholly federal concurrent jurisdiction stems from the virtually unflagging obligation of the federal courts to exercise the jurisdiction given them. Given this obligation, and the absence of weightier considerations of constitutional adjudication and state-federal relations, the circumstances permitting the dismissal of a federal suit due to the pres-

justification needed for abstention.

ence of a concurrent state proceeding for reasons of wise judicial administration are considerably more limited than the circumstances appropriate for abstention. The former circumstances, though exceptional, do
nevertheless exist.

It has been held, for example, that the court first assuming jurisdiction over property may exercise that jurisdiction to the exclusion of other
courts. This has been true even where the Government was a claimant
in existing state proceedings and then sought to invoke district-court
jurisdiction under the jurisdictional provision antecedent to 28 U.S.C.
§ 1345. In assessing the appropriateness of dismissal in the event of an
exercise of concurrent jurisdiction, a federal court may also consider such
factors as the inconvenience of the federal forum, the desirability of
avoiding piecemeal litigation, and the order in which jurisdiction was
obtained by the concurrent forums. No one factor is necessarily determinative; a carefully considered judgment taking into account both the
obligation to exercise jurisdiction and the combination of factors counselling against that exercise is required. Only the clearest of justifications
will warrant dismissal.

Turning to the present case, a number of factors clearly counsel
against concurrent federal proceedings. The most important of these is
the McCarran Amendment itself. The clear federal policy evinced by
that legislation is the avoidance of piecemeal adjudication of water rights
in a river system. This policy is akin to that underlying the rule requiring that jurisdiction be yielded to the court first acquiring control of
property, for the concern in such instances is with avoiding the generation of additional litigation through permitting inconsistent dispositions
of property. This concern is heightened with respect to water rights, the
relationships among which are highly interdependent. Indeed, we have
recognized that actions seeking the allocation of water essentially involve the disposition of property and are best conducted in unified proceedings. The consent to jurisdiction given by the McCarran Amendment bespeaks a policy that recognizes the availability of comprehensive
state systems for adjudication of water rights as the means for achieving
these goals.

As has already been observed, the Colorado Water Rights Determination and Administration Act established such a system for the adjudication and management of rights to the use of the State's waters. As the
Government concedes and as this Court recognized in Eagle County and
Water Div. 5, the Act established a single continuous proceeding for water rights adjudication which antedated the suit in District Court. That
proceeding "reaches all claims, perhaps month by month but inclusively
in the totality." Additionally, the responsibility of managing the State's
waters, to the end that they be allocated in accordance with adjudicated
water rights, is given to the State Engineer.

Beyond the congressional policy expressed by the McCarran

Amendment and consistent with furtherance of that policy, we also find significant (a) the apparent absence of any proceedings in the District Court, other than the filing of the complaint, prior to the motion to dismiss, (b) the extensive involvement of state water rights occasioned by this suit naming 1,000 defendants, (c) the 300-mile distance between the District Court in Denver and the court in Division 7, and (d) the existing participation by the Government in Division 4, 5, and 6 proceedings. We emphasize, however, that we do not overlook the heavy obligation to exercise jurisdiction. We need not decide, for example, whether, despite the McCarran Amendment, dismissal would be warranted if more extensive proceedings had occurred in the District Court prior to dismissal, if the involvement of state water rights were less extensive than it is here, or if the state proceeding were in some respect inadequate to resolve the federal claims. But the opposing factors here, particularly the policy underlying the McCarran Amendment, justify the District Court's dismissal in this particular case.

The judgment of the Court of Appeals is reversed and the judgment of the District Court dismissing the complaint is affirmed for the reasons here stated.

It is so ordered.

MR. JUSTICE STEWART, with whom MR. JUSTICE BLACKMUN and MR. JUSTICE STEVENS concur, dissenting.

The Court says that the United States District Court for the District of Colorado clearly had jurisdiction over this lawsuit. I agree. The Court further says that the McCarran Amendment "in no way diminished" the District Court's jurisdiction. I agree. The Court also says that federal courts have a "virtually unflagging obligation * * * to exercise the jurisdiction given them." I agree. And finally, the Court says that nothing in the abstention doctrine "in any of its forms" justified the District Court's dismissal of the Government's complaint. I agree. These views would seem to lead ineluctably to the conclusion that the District Court was wrong in dismissing the complaint. Yet the Court holds that the order of dismissal was "appropriate." With that conclusion I must respectfully disagree.

In holding that the United States shall not be allowed to proceed with its lawsuit, the Court relies principally on cases reflecting the rule that where "control of the property which is the subject of the suit (is necessary) in order to proceed with the cause and to grant the relief sought, the jurisdiction of one court must of necessity yield to that of the other." But, as those cases make clear, this rule applies only when exclusive control over the subject matter is necessary to effectuate a court's judgment. Here the federal court did not need to obtain *in rem* or *quasi in rem* jurisdiction in order to decide the issues before it. The court was asked simply to determine as a matter of federal law whether federal reservations of water rights had occurred, and, if so, the date and scope

of the reservations. The District Court could make such a determination
without having control of the river.

The rule invoked by the Court thus does not support the conclusion
that it reaches. In the *Princess Lida* [1939] case, for example, the reason
for the surrender of federal jurisdiction over the administration of a
trust was the fact that a state court had already assumed jurisdiction
over the trust estate. But the Court in that case recognized that this
rationale "ha[d] no application to a case in a federal court * * * wherein
the plaintiff seeks merely an adjudication of his right or his interest as a
basis of a claim against a fund in the possession of a state court * * * ."
The Court stressed that "[n]o question is presented in the federal court
as to the right of any person to participate in the res or as to the quantum of his interest in it." Similarly, * * * the Court [has] stressed that
the "object of the suits is to take the property from the depositories and
from the control of the state court, and to vest the property in the United
States. * * * " "The suits are not merely to establish a debt or a right to
share in property, and thus to obtain an adjudication which might be
had without disturbing the control of the state court."

The precedents cited by the Court thus not only fail to support the
Court's decision in this case, but expressly point in the opposite direction. The present suit, in short, is not analogous to the administration of
a trust, but rather to a claim of a "right to participate," since the United
States in this litigation does not ask the court to control the administration of the river, but only to determine its specific rights in the flow of
water in the river. This is an almost exact analogue to a suit seeking a
determination of rights in the flow of income from a trust.

The Court's principal reason for deciding to close the doors of the
federal courthouse to the United States in this case seems to stem from
the view that its decision will avoid piecemeal adjudication of water
rights.[6] To the extent that this view is based on the special considera-

---

[6] The Court lists four other policy reasons for the "appropriateness" of the District
Court's dismissal of this lawsuit. All of those reasons are insubstantial. First, the fact that
no significant proceedings had yet taken place in the federal court at the time of the dismissal means no more than that the federal court was prompt in granting the defendants'
motion to dismiss. At that time, of course, no proceedings involving the Government's
claims had taken place in the state court either. Second, the geographic distance of the
federal court from the rivers in question is hardly a significant factor in this age of rapid
and easy transportation. Since the basic issues here involve the determination of the
amount of water the Government intended to reserve rather than the amount it actually
appropriated on a given date, there is little likelihood that live testimony by water district
residents would be necessary. In any event, the Federal District Court in Colorado is authorized to sit at Durango, the headquarters of Water Division 7. Third, the Government's
willingness to participate in some of the state proceedings certainly does not mean that it
had no right to bring this action, unless the Court has today unearthed a new kind of
waiver. Finally, the fact that there were many defendants in the federal suit is hardly
relevant. It only indicates that the federal court had all the necessary parties before it in
order to issue a decree finally settling the Government's claims. Indeed, the presence of all
interested parties in the federal court made the lawsuit the kind of unified proceeding envisioned by Pacific Live Stock Co. v. Lewis, 241 U.S. 440, 447-49.

tions governing *in rem* proceedings, it is without precedential basis, as the decisions discussed above demonstrate. To the extent that the Court's view is based on the realistic practicalities of this case, it is simply wrong, because the relegation of the Government to the state courts will not avoid piecemeal litigation.

The Colorado courts are currently engaged in two types of proceedings under the State's water-rights law. First, they are processing new claims to water based on recent appropriations. Second, they are integrating these new awards of water rights with all past decisions awarding such rights into one all-inclusive tabulation for each water source. The claims of the United States that are involved in this case have not been adjudicated in the past. Yet they do not involve recent appropriations of water. In fact, these claims are wholly dissimilar to normal state water claims, because they are not based on actual beneficial use of water but rather on an intention formed at the time the federal land use was established to reserve a certain amount of water to support the federal reservations. The state court will, therefore, have to conduct separate proceedings to determine these claims. And only after the state court adjudicates the claims will they be incorporated into the water source tabulations. If this suit were allowed to proceed in federal court the same procedures would be followed, and the federal court decree would be incorporated into the state tabulation, as other federal court decrees have been incorporated in the past. Thus, the same process will occur regardless of which forum considers these claims. Whether the virtually identical separate proceedings take place in a federal court or a state court, the adjudication of the claims will be neither more nor less "piecemeal." Essentially the same process will be followed in each instance.

As the Court says, it is the virtual "unflagging obligation" of a federal court to exercise the jurisdiction that has been conferred upon it. Obedience to that obligation is particularly "appropriate" in this case, for at least two reasons.

First, the issues involved are issues of federal law. A federal court is more likely than a state court to be familiar with federal water law and to have had experience in interpreting the relevant federal statutes, regulations, and Indian treaties. Moreover, if tried in a federal court, these issues of federal law will be reviewable in a federal appellate court, whereas federal judicial review of the state courts' resolution of issues of federal law will be possible only on review by this Court in the exercise of its certiorari jurisdiction.

Second, some of the federal claims in this lawsuit relate to water reserved for Indian reservations. It is not necessary to determine that there is no state-court jurisdiction of these claims to support the proposition that a federal court is a more appropriate forum than a state court for determination of questions of life-and-death importance to Indians.

This Court has long recognized that " '[t]he policy of leaving Indians free from state jurisdiction and control is deeply rooted in the Nation's history.' "

The Court says that "[o]nly the clearest of justifications will warrant dismissal" of a lawsuit within the jurisdiction of a federal court. In my opinion there was no justification at all for the District Court's order of dismissal in this case.

I would affirm the judgment of the Court of Appeals.

Notes and Questions

1. As a preliminary consideration, note the Court's observation that there is no indication, either textual or historical, that Congress intended the McCarran Amendment to limit federal jurisdiction. Justice Brennan quoted *Rosecrans v. United States,* 165 U.S. 257, 262, 17 S.Ct. 302, 304, 41 L.Ed. 708, 710 (1897): "When there are statutes clearly defining the jurisdiction of the courts the force and effect of such provisions should not be disturbed by a mere implication flowing from subsequent legislation." He also quoted *Morton v. Mancari,* 417 U.S. 535, 550, 94 S.Ct. 2474, 2482, 41 L.Ed.2d 290, 300 (1974), a case decided after Chief Justice Burger and Justices Powell and Rehnquist had joined the Court: "In the absence of some affirmative showing of an intention to repeal, the only permissible justification for a repeal by implication is when the earlier and later statutes are irreconcilable." Is that approach consistent with what the Court did in *Merrell Dow Pharmaceuticals v. Thompson,* 478 U.S. 804, 106 S.Ct. 3229, 92 L.Ed.2d 650 (1986), which Chapter 3 presents at page 272? In fairness, one ought to recall that Justice Brennan dissented in *Merrell Dow,* but that is not the case for some of his colleagues in the *Colorado River* majority.

2. Justice Brennan seems to envision abstention as a single doctrine with multiple manifestations, as his discussion in Part III B of the opinion demonstrates. In addition, he implies that what is happening in *Colorado River* is different from abstention when he says, "the circumstances permitting the dismissal of a federal suit due to the presence of a concurrent state proceeding for reasons of wise judicial administration are considerably more limited than the circumstances appropriate for abstention." Why does he characterize *Colorado River* as something other than abstention?

3. Justice Brennan identifies four factors that federal courts should consider in deciding whether interests in wise judicial administration should override the duty to exercise jurisdiction. What are the factors? He states that "[n]o one factor is necessarily determinative" and that "[o]nly the clearest of justifications will warrant dismissal." Does this mean dismissal is appropriate only if all of the factors favor that outcome? Finally, how do the *Colorado River* factors compare with the factors *Pullman, Burford, Thibodaux* and *Younger* abstention use?

4. Does the majority's view of the purpose of the McCarran Amendment prove too much? If Congress passed the Amendment because of concerns about piecemeal litigation and intended the federal courts to yield to avoid duplicative litigation, why did it not simply say so? Should its silence be

construed to mean that it did not intend the federal courts to forswear their power under Article III and the statutory predicate for jurisdiction?

5. There are three other *Colorado River* cases of some import. *Will v. Calvert Fire Insurance Co.,* 437 U.S. 655, 98 S.Ct. 2552, 57 L.Ed.2d 504 (1978), clearly caused more problems than it solved. The Court split four-four-one, with Justice Rehnquist writing a plurality opinion that allowed abstention and stated that "a district court is under no compulsion to exercise * * * jurisdiction where the controversy may be settled more expeditiously in state court." Justice Blackmun concurred based on *Colorado River* principles, but he could not agree with the Rehnquist plurality that the district courts had such broad discretion to abstain. Justice Brennan led a four-member group in dissent, arguing that the analytical framework of *Colorado River* did not permit the wide-ranging discretion visualized by Justice Rehnquist and that abstention was inappropriate on the facts. Nonetheless, "[a]fter *Calvert,* many lower courts believed they had increased authority to abstain to avoid duplicating state court proceedings." ERWIN CHEMERINSKY, FEDERAL JURISDICTION § 14.2, at 848 (5th ed. 2007) (citing Note, *Abstention and Mandamus After* Will v. Calvert Fire Insurance Co., 54 CORNELL L.REV. 566, 585 (1979)).

But then, in *Moses H. Cone Memorial Hospital v. Mercury Construction Corporation,* 460 U.S. 1, 103 S.Ct. 927, 74 L.Ed.2d 765 (1983), the Court seemed to retreat substantially from the position taken by the *Calvert* plurality. The defendant Hospital and the plaintiff disputed amounts due under a construction contract and disputed also the availability of arbitration. The Hospital conceded that the contract provided for arbitration but argued that the arbitration clause had become ineffective because of Mercury's actions. When negotiations broke down, the Hospital sought a state court declaration of non-arbitrability and non-liability. The Hospital later obtained an *ex parte* injunction prohibiting Mercury from "taking any steps toward arbitration." When the injunction was dissolved, Mercury filed in federal court, seeking to compel arbitration. The district court abstained, but an en banc Court of Appeals reversed.

Justice Brennan wrote for a Court unanimous in the view that *Colorado River* abstention was inappropriate.[7] He again stressed the unusual nature of abstention and noted that the *Colorado River* factors were not to be used as a checklist, but were rather simply factors whose weight in any particular case might vary widely in a balancing "heavily weighted in favor of the exercise of jurisdiction."[8] Justice Brennan found no "exceptional circumstances" in *Moses Cone* that justified abstention. Moreover, he placed heavy emphasis on "the fact that federal law provides the rule of decision on the merits * * * "—whether arbitration could be compelled under the United States Ar-

---

[7] Three Members dissented on the question of whether an appeal lay under 28 U.S.C.A. § 1291 to the Court of Appeals from the district court's grant of a *Colorado River* stay.

[8] The six-member majority refused to interpret *Calvert* as modifying the *Colorado River* test, arguing that Justice Rehnquist had spoken for only four Members of the Court in apparently broadening *Colorado River*.

bitration Act—a new factor in the *Colorado River* analysis. The Court's disinclination to abstain was undiminished by the fact that the state proceeding had been commenced first; echoing *Hicks v. Miranda,* 422 U.S. 332, 95 S.Ct. 2281, 45 L.Ed.2d 223 (1975) (page 813), the majority cautioned: "priority should not be measured exclusively by which complaint was filed first, but rather in terms of how much progress has been made in the two actions."

The Court also focused again on the separation-of-powers implications of abstention.

> This refusal to proceed was plainly erroneous in view of Congress' clear intent, in the Arbitration Act, to move the parties to an arbitrable dispute out of court and into arbitration as quickly and easily as possible. The Act provides two parallel devices for enforcing an arbitration agreement: a stay of litigation in any case raising a dispute referable to arbitration and an affirmative order to engage in arbitration. Both of these sections call for an expeditious and summary hearing, with only restricted inquiry into factual issues. Assuming that the state court would have granted prompt relief to Mercury under the Act, there still would have been an inevitable delay as a result of the District Court's stay. The stay thus frustrated the statutory policy of rapid and unobstructed enforcement of arbitration agreements.

Does the Court's reasoning also, perhaps unintentionally, provide some ammunition against the invocation of other forms of abstention?[9]

Moses Cone demonstrates the very limited nature of *Colorado River* abstention, but it also leaves some questions unanswered. It certainly is not clear what factors qualify as sufficiently "exceptional" to justify abstention. In addition, although the presence of a federal issue weighs heavily on the side of exercising federal jurisdiction, the Court stopped short of saying that it ends the abstention inquiry. Moreover, to the extent that a federal issue makes abstention less likely, is the Court implying a lack of confidence in state court competence to deal with federal issues, or is it merely giving more weight to the plaintiff's choice of forum in this context than it has in some other types of abstention? If the former, why should the Court have less confidence here than in other abstention situations? If the latter, why is the plaintiff's forum choice entitled to additional weight here?

Wilton v. Seven Falls Company (1995), suggests that there may be special abstention rules for declaratory judgment cases. The matter arose out of a dispute over some Texas land that contained oil and gas reserves. The Hill Group (one of the disputants) asked London Underwriters, its insurer, to defend and indemnify it, but London Underwriters refused. The Hill Group subsequently lost a $100 million judgment in Texas state court. After receiving notice of the verdict from the Hill

---

[9] It is interesting to note that, given *Moses Cone* and *New Orleans Public Service,* Justices on both wings of the Court (Brennan and Scalia) have now expressed some reservations about abstention doctrines on separation-of-powers grounds.

Group, London Underwriters filed a federal declaratory judgment action based on diversity jurisdiction seeking a determination that its policies did not cover the Hill Group for the Texas judgment. After discussions with the Hill Group, London Underwriters withdrew the action on the condition that the Hill Group give at least two weeks notice if it planned to sue on the policy. When it received the notice, London Underwriters refiled the federal action. Four weeks later, the Hill Group sued in state court, joining parties whose presence made removal impossible. The Hill Group subsequently moved to dismiss or stay the federal action. The Supreme Court endorsed abstention.

The Court emphasized that London Underwriters sought only declaratory relief, characterizing it as a discretionary remedy, with the clear implication that abstention might be appropriate because of the type of relief demanded. Perhaps the Court's argument proves too much, though. Injunctive relief is discretionary also. Should the district courts abstain from deciding federal actions seeking injunctive relief if the federal defendant later files a state action seeking damages?

Finally, the Court roundly criticized London Underwriters for forum shopping. That is a bit odd, for certainly the Court might have leveled the same charge at the Hill Group. After all, London Underwriters chose the federal forum initially. Is every diversity action plaintiff guilty of forum shopping? Moreover, what's wrong with that? The *Erie* Court disapproved forum shopping where it would determine the outcome of the case because of the law the court would apply, but the development of the *Erie* doctrine appears to have pulled the argument's teeth. (London Underwriters, by the way, accused the Hill Group of forum shopping because of the addition of parties (none insured by London Underwriters) who destroyed diversity and thereby rendered the Texas action nonremovable.)

Wilton adds a new twist to the idea underlying *Hicks v. Miranda*. The state court action in *Wilton* began almost four months after the original federal declaratory judgment action and more than one month after commencement of the second. Note that here a later-filed state proceeding was able effectively to cut off a federal court proceeding, just as happened in *Hicks*. Here, as there, there had not been "proceedings of substance on the merits," but in contrast to *Hicks*, the absence of such proceedings may have occurred only because the insured persuaded the insurer to withdraw the original action. Should the parties' agreement have affected the Court's willingness to endorse the stay?

Does any federal declaratory judgment action concerning questions of state law now become an endangered species subject to stay or dismissal (and note that because of res judicata and 28 U.S.C. § 1738 there is little practical difference between them) as a result of a later-filed state action (*à la Hicks*) brought by the declaratory judgment defendant? If so, should the Court extend this vulnerability of federal actions even to coercive cases turning upon state law, thus imperiling diversity jurisdiction more generally? If not, how can the Court distinguish cases like *Wilton*?

One of Congress's primary purposes in passing the Declaratory Judgment Act was to give potential defendants in unfiled but threatened coercive actions a means to precipitate resolution of the dispute. Congress particularly focused on the plight of the alleged patent infringer, but insurance coverage disputes present a similar, if slightly less compelling, question. The alleged patent infringer threatened with suit by the patentee faces the undesirable choice of continuing to market its own device, possibly running up ever-increasing damages if it eventually is unable to prevail in a patent infringement action, or discontinuing its conduct, possibly foregoing substantial profits to which it may have been fully entitled because of unpatentability of the patentee's original device, non-infringement by the alleged infringer's device, or some other reason. In insurance coverage disputes, the insurer does not face a real prospect either of mounting damages or of erroneously discontinuing perfectly lawful, profitable conduct. It does, however, face the dilemma of maintaining its position and losing the opportunity to control the underlying liability litigation or of abandoning its position and providing a defense, with all of the expense that that entails, in a circumstance in which the policy in fact provides no coverage. After *Wilton*, the Declaratory Judgment Act may still have the effect of precipitating judicial resolution of disputes, but not in the form Congress envisioned; the Act may now merely act as a prod to the declaratory judgment defendant to begin its own action.

It is difficult to know whether *Wilton* has greater implications for abstention or for the declaratory judgment remedy. As the majority conceded, the case has none of the traditional *indicia* of abstention, and the Court explicitly refused to abstain under the *Colorado River* doctrine because London Underwriters sought no coercive relief. There are indications that the absence of federal issues motivated the Court. On the other hand, there are no federal issues in diversity cases generally. Could *Wilton* foreshadow a more generalized abstention doctrine in diversity cases? That would present significant separation-of-powers issues given the command of 28 U.S.C.A. § 1332. Then, too, would those issues be any more nettlesome than when the courts abstain in federal question cases under § 1331? The Court's opinion explicitly declined to speculate.

Chapter 9

SUPREME COURT REVIEW OF STATE COURT DECISIONS

A. INTRODUCTION

It is now so common for the Supreme Court to review state court decisions that the phenomenon draws virtually no notice, but it was not always so. Early in the republic's history, the fledgling federal government faced many state challenges to national authority. *Martin v. Hunter's Lessee*, 14 U.S. (1 Wheat.) 304, 4 L.Ed. 97 (1816), was one directed at the Supreme Court. The Virginia Court of Appeals asserted that the United States Supreme Court could not review state court judgments because it would infringe state sovereignty. This challenge and the Court's emphatic rejection of it exemplify the tension of federalism. The Supreme Court derives its power to review state judgments from a combination of article III and the Supremacy Clause. Although that power is now well-established, the clash between federal and state sovereignty stands out in bold relief every time the Court does so. Although *Hunter's Lessee* seemed to resolve whether the states could resist judgments of the Supreme Court, in 1986, then-Attorney General Edwin Meese, Jr., asserted that the Supreme Court does not declare the meaning of the Constitution in any way binding persons not before the Court. Thus, he suggested that declarations of constitutional principle by the Court did not mean that non-parties to the case should alter their behavior accordingly. If that were taken seriously, consider its effect in the context of school desegregation, prayer in schools, search and seizure cases, or almost any other area in which the Court reviews governmental conduct and declares constitutional principle.

There was little debate in the Constitutional Convention about the federal power to review state court decisions. No doubt this is largely owing to the nature of the debate about the federal judicial system generally. Although the Framers agreed there should be a national court at the apex of the judicial system, the Anti-Federalists argued against having any inferior federal courts. They were concerned that an extensive national court system would siphon off too much power from the states and argued that inferior federal courts were unnecessary because the Supreme Court could review state court decisions of federal law. They could hardly have argued in the next breath that there was no Supreme

Court power to review state court decisions. A compromise finally resolved the dispute, permitting inferior federal courts to exist only if the people's and states' representatives in Congress created them. *See* U.S. CONST. art. I, § 8, cl. 9. Recall that until the Seventeenth Amendment, state legislatures chose senators, who were perceived to represent the states directly, not the populace.

Howell v. Mississippi, 543 U.S. 440, 125 S.Ct. 856, 160 L.Ed.2d 873 (2005), reaffirmed the well-established rule that the Supreme Court will not decide a federal issue unless it was fairly presented to the state courts. As in earlier cases, the Court declined to decide whether this rule is jurisdictional or merely prudential. In *Cardinale v. Louisiana,* 394 U.S. 437, 89 S.Ct. 1161, 22 L.Ed.2d 398 (1969), Justice White discussed the policies underlying the rule:

> Questions not raised below are those on which the record is very likely to be inadequate, since it certainly was not compiled with those questions in mind. And in a federal system it is important that state courts be given the first opportunity to consider the applicability of state statutes in light of constitutional challenge, since the statutes may be construed in a way which saves their constitutionality.

The collision between federal and state power may be sharper in this area than in many others. When the federal courts review state legislative or executive action, they act on institutions that do not consider issues from a judicial perspective. Review does not reflect on the competence of those branches to carry out their particular functions, but Supreme Court review of a state court decision may connote that the state judicial system is not up to the adjudicative job, despite the fact that the state judges are themselves sworn to uphold the federal constitution and laws as well as their own, a phenomenon given substantial weight by the Supreme Court in other contexts. For example, the Court routinely asserts in abstention cases that state judges are presumed as dedicated as federal judges to the proper interpretation and application of federal law. *See, e.g., Trainor v. Hernandez,* 431 U.S. 434, 443, 97 S.Ct. 1911, 1917, 52 L.Ed.2d 486 (1977) (reaffirming " 'the principle that state courts have the solemn responsibility equally with the federal courts' to safeguard constitutional rights * * * ") (quoting *Steffel v. Thompson,* 415 U.S. 452, 460-61, 94 S.Ct. 1209, 1216, 39 L.Ed.2d 505 (1974)).

There are three statutory prerequisites for Supreme Court review. First, the Court can review only cases containing federal issues. There would be little reason for the Supreme Court to review state cases presenting only state issues. Certainly the Court lacks any special expertise in matters of state law. Second, Congress has specified that the Court can review only "final" judgments from the state courts. As the law has developed, however, "finality" is as protean a term as any to be found in the law. Third, Congress has specified that only judgments coming from "the highest court * * * of a State in which a decision could be had" are reviewable. This does not mean that the Supreme Court can review cases only from the highest state court. Many states restrict appellate jurisdiction; often cases cannot reach the highest state court. They may nonetheless qualify for Supreme Court review. Perhaps the most famous example is *Thompson v. City of Louisville*, 362 U.S. 199, 80 S.Ct. 624, 4 L.Ed.2d 654 (1960). Upon defendant's conviction for disorderly conduct, no appeal lay to any Kentucky court, so Thompson was able to appeal from the Louisville Police Court directly to the United States Supreme Court. Although the "size" of the jump was unusual, the phenomenon is not.

What is the scope of Supreme Court review? In a case with federal and state issues, which should the Supreme Court review: the federal issues only or all of the issues? Note that Supreme Court adjudication of the state law issues might intensify federal-state friction.

In addition, can the state courts do anything to insulate their decisions from Supreme Court review? The Supreme Court has developed a complex body of doctrine that gives the states substantial latitude to make judgments effectively unreviewable. For example, state courts may decide state issues in a way that makes federal law irrelevant to the disposition of the case.[1] If deciding the federal issue cannot affect the outcome of the case, the Supreme Court generally refuses review.

Finally, remember that there are other federal doctrines and rules that may limit or prevent Supreme Court review of state court decisions, such as standing, ripeness, mootness and the political question doctrine (discussed in detail in Chapter 1). These federal doctrines do not necessarily bind the state courts.

---

[1] *See, e.g.*, State v. Marsala, 216 Conn. 150, 579 A.2d 58 (1990) (rejecting the good-faith exception to the Fourth Amendment's warrant requirement announced in United States v. Leon, 468 U.S. 897, 104 S.Ct. 3405, 82 L.Ed.2d 677 (1984)); People v. Bigelow, 66 N.Y.2d 417, 497 N.Y.S.2d 630, 488 N.E.2d 451 (1985) (same); Commonwealth v. Blood, 400 Mass. 61, 507 N.E.2d 1029 (1987) ("We have often recognized that art. 14 of the Declaration of Rights does, or may, afford more substantive protection to individuals than that which prevails under the Constitution of the United States.") (rejecting the one-party-consent rule for electronic searches of United States v. Caceres, 440 U.S. 741, 99 S.Ct. 1465, 59 L.Ed.2d 733 (1979) and United States v. White, 401 U.S. 745, 91 S.Ct. 1122, 28 L.Ed.2d 453 (1971)); State v. Kimbro, 197 Conn. 219, 496 A.2d 498 (1985) (rejecting the totality-of-the-circumstances test of Illinois v. Gates, 462 U.S. 213, 103 S.Ct. 2317, 76 L.Ed.2d 527 (1983) and adopting as state law the *Aguilar-Spinelli* test formerly used as federal law); People v. Griminger, 71 N.Y.2d 635, 524 N.E.2d 409, 529 N.Y.S.2d 55 (1988) (same). Justice Brennan specifically suggested that states consider further development of state constitutional law. *See* William J. Brennan, *The Bill of Rights and the States: The Revival of State Constitutions as Guardians of Individual Rights*, 61 N.Y.U.L.REV. 535 (1986). On the other hand, such decisions are not unreviewable in any quarter. In California, the proliferation of state constitutional decisions caused voters to pass a referendum measure requiring state courts to construe California law congruently with federal law with respect to the admissibility of evidence in criminal proceedings. *See* CAL. CONST. art. I, § 28(d).

B.   PRELIMINARY JURISDICTIONAL CONSIDERATIONS

Note that 28 U.S.C.A. § 1257, which governs Supreme Court review of state court decisions, now allows review only by writ of certiorari. This is the latest stage in two centuries of change. Review in the Supreme Court was originally only by writ of error, a nondiscretionary device. The Judiciary Act of 1789 allowed review only in three circumstances.[2] The first two were: 1) when a state court invalidated a federal statute, treaty or authority, and 2) when a state court upheld state law in the face of a supremacy challenge. By clear implication, the Supreme Court could not review cases where federal law was upheld or state laws stricken, apparently on the theory that review was unnecessary to protect federal interests. The third category allowed review

> where is drawn in question the construction of any clause of the Constitution, or of a treaty or statute of the Constitution, or of a treaty or statute of, or commission held under the United States, and the decision is against the title, right, privilege or exemption specially set up or claimed by either party * * * .

In short, this category involved the bulk of federal question cases. Note, however, that review of federal questions in the Supreme Court was not subject to the well-pleaded complaint rule, as original and removal jurisdiction now are in the district court; the statute specifically provided that either party could raise the federal matter. Accordingly, a federal question arising anywhere in a case qualified the case for eventual Supreme Court review.[3] Why do you think the Court does not apply the *Mottley* rule in this context? Recall the practical reasons for the *Mottley* rule in cases the federal courts heard after enactment of the general federal-question statute in 1875. Do they apply to review under § 1257? In addition, if the *Mottley* rule did apply, how would that affect the federal courts' power to ensure the uniformity of federal law?

In 1914, Congress provided review by certiorari for cases that were the converse of the three categories noted above: those where the state court had decided *in favor of* federal law by refusing to declare federal law unconstitutional, by invalidating a state statute on supremacy grounds, or by upholding a claimed federal right or construction. Unlike the writ of error, the writ of certiorari is wholly discretionary. In 1916, all federal question cases (the old category 3 from the Judiciary Act of 1789) were moved from the writ of error category into the certiorari category, irrespective of whether the state court decided for or against

[2] The Judiciary Act language authorizing Supreme Court review of state court decisions appears at the beginning of *Murdock v. City of Memphis*, at page 884.

[3] This explains how Louisville & Nashville Railroad v. Mottley, 211 U.S. 149, 29 S.Ct. 42, 53 L.Ed. 126 (1908), after being dismissed as an original federal action for want of subject matter jurisdiction, could reach the Supreme Court for substantive review after being recommenced in the state courts. *See* Louisville & Nashville Railroad v. Mottley, 219 U.S. 467, 31 S.Ct. 265, 55 L.Ed. 297 (1911).

the claimed federal entitlement. In 1928, Congress substituted review by appeal for review by writ of error, a structure that lasted until the latest revision of § 1257 in 1988, when Congress eliminated all review as of right in favor of review by certiorari.

Review by appeal no longer exists, but it commands one last bit of attention. Although cases reviewable by appeal or writ of error were entitled to review "as of right," they did not all receive full hearings. Often the Court summarily affirmed or dismissed the appeal without hearing oral argument or even getting briefs from the parties beyond those seeking the appellate review. Such dismissals were termed "for want of a substantial federal question" and operated as decisions on the merits, unlike denials of certiorari.[4] For example, in *Zucht v. King*, 260 U.S. 174, 43 S.Ct. 24, 67 L.Ed. 194 (1922), a challenge to a San Antonio ordinance requiring children in public schools to be vaccinated, the Court dismissed a writ of error because, "[l]ong before this suit was instituted, *Jacobson v. Massachusetts* [1905] had settled that it is within the police power of a state to provide for compulsory vaccination." The Court thus declared the federal issue that Zucht presented "insubstantial"[5] and dismissed the case without a full appeal.

Section 1257's terms did limit appeal as of right to cases presenting a substantial federal issue. Did the substantiality requirement give the Court unauthorized power summarily to dismiss any case where the appellant sought to overturn existing precedent? Could the Court have turned aside review of the state court challenge to *Plessy v. Ferguson*, 163 U.S. 537, 16 S.Ct. 1138, 41 L.Ed. 256 (1896), that was included in the four cases consolidated for review as *Brown v. Board of Education*, 347 U.S. 483, 74 S.Ct. 686, 98 L.Ed. 873 (1954)? What important practical reason underlay imposition of the substantiality requirement?

---

[4] In practice, it mattered little whether review was by appeal (as of right) or by certiorari (discretionary). Statistically, the odds of getting full review by appeal were only slightly better than those for certiorari. But summary decisions on the merits have precedential effect; denials of certiorari do not, although that difference was muted somewhat by the Court's assertion in Edelman v. Jordan, 415 U.S. 651, 670-71, 94 S.Ct. 1347, 1359, 39 L.Ed.2d 662 (1974), that summary dispositions lack the *stare decisis* impact of full hearings.

[5] The Court also noted that although the issue of the state's power to compel vaccination generally was unreviewable, Zucht's allegations of discrimination were, albeit by certiorari and not by appeal. That being the case, why did the Court not decide to treat the writ of error as a petition for certiorari, as it has on other occasions? *E.g., Longest v. Langford,* 274 U.S. 499, 501, 47 S.Ct. 668, 668, 71 L.Ed. 1170, 1171 (1927) ("While we cannot take jurisdiction on the writ of error so improvidently allowed, we can, under section 237(c) of the Judicial Code, treat the papers whereon the writ was allowed as a petition for certiorari and as if presented to this court at the time they were presented to the judge who allowed the writ."). *Accord, Mississippi Band of Choctaw Indians v. Holyfield,* 490 U.S. 30, 109 S.Ct. 1597, 104 L.Ed.2d 29 (1989).

MURDOCK v. CITY OF MEMPHIS

Supreme Court of the United States, 1875.
87 U.S. (20 Wall.) 590, 22 L.Ed. 429.

THE TWENTY-FIFTH SECTION OF THE ACT OF 1789.

That a final judgment or decree in any suit, in the highest court of *law or equity* of a State in which a decision in the suit could be had, where is drawn in question the validity of a treaty or statute of, or an authority exercised under the United States, and the decision is against their validity; or where is drawn in question the validity of a statute of, or an authority exercised under any State, on the ground of their being repugnant to the Constitution, treaties, or laws of the United States, and the decision is in favor of such their validity, *or where is drawn in question the construction of any clause* of the Constitution, or of a treaty or statute of, or commission held under the United States, and the decision is against the title, right, privilege or *exemption* specially set up or claimed by either party, under such clause of the said Constitution, treaty, statute, or commission, may be reexamined and reversed or affirmed in the Supreme Court of the United States upon a writ of error, the citation being signed by the chief justice, or judge, or chancellor of the court rendering or passing the judgment or decree complained of, or by a justice of the Supreme Court of the United States, in the same manner and under the same regulations, and the writ shall have the same effect as if the judgment or decree complained of had been rendered or passed in a *Circuit Court,* and the proceeding upon the re-

THE SECOND SECTION OF THE ACT OF 1867.

That a final judgment or decree in any suit in the highest court of a State in which a decision in the suit could be had, where is drawn in question the validity of a treaty or statute of or an authority exercised under the United States, and the decision is against their validity, or where is drawn in question the validity of a statute of or an authority exercised under any State, on the ground of their being repugnant to the Constitution, treaties, or laws of the United States, and the decision is in favor of such their validity, or where any title, right, privilege, or *immunity is claimed* under the Constitution, or any treaty or statute of, or commission held, or *authority exercised*, under the United States, and the decision is against the title, right, privilege, or immunity specially set up or claimed by either party under such Constitution, treaty, statute, commission, or *authority,* may be reexamined and reversed or affirmed in the Supreme Court of the United States, upon a writ of error, the citation being signed by the chief justice, or judge, or chancellor of the court rendering or passing the judgment or decree complained of, or by a justice of the Supreme Court of the United States, in the same manner, and under the same regulations, and the writ shall have the same effect as if the judg-

versal shall also be the same, except that the Supreme Court, *instead of remanding the cause for a final decision, as before provided, may at their discretion, if the cause shall have been once remanded before, proceed to a final decision of the same and award execution. But no other error shall be assigned or regarded as a ground of reversal in any such case as aforesaid than such as appears on the face of the record and immediately respects the before-mentioned questions of validity or construction of the said Constitution, treaties, statutes, commissions, or authorities in dispute.*

ment or decree complained of had been rendered or passed *in a court of the United States;* and the proceeding upon the reversal shall also be the same, *except that the Supreme Court may, at their discretion, proceed to a final decision of the same, and award execution or remand the same to an inferior court.*

Murdock filed a bill in one of the courts of chancery of Tennessee, against the city of Memphis, in that State. The bill and its exhibits made this case:

In July, 1844,—Congress having just previously authorized the establishment of a naval depot in that city, and appropriated a considerable sum of money for the purpose—the ancestors of Murdock—by ordinary deed of bargain and sale, without any covenants or declaration of trust on which the land was to be held by the city, but referring to the fact of "the location of the naval depot lately established by the United States at said town"—conveyed to the city certain land described in and near its limits "for the location of the naval depot aforesaid."

By the same instrument (a quadrupartite one) both the grantors and the city conveyed the same land to one Wheatley, in fee, in trust for the grantors and their heirs, "in case the same shall not be appropriated by the United States for that purpose."

On the 14th of September, 1844, the city of Memphis, in consideration of the sum of $20,000 paid by the United States, conveyed the said land to the United States with covenant of general warranty; there being, however, in this deed to the United States no designation of any purpose to which the land was to be applied, nor any conditions precedent or subsequent, or of any kind whatsoever.

The United States took possession of the land for the purpose of the erection of a naval depot upon it, erected buildings, and made various expenditures and improvements for the said purpose; but in about ten years after, by an act of August 5th, 1854, transferred the land back to the city. The act was in these words: "All the grounds and appurtenances thereunto belonging, known as the Memphis Navy Yard, in

Shelby County, Tennessee, be, and the same is hereby, ceded to the mayor and aldermen of the city of Memphis, *for the use and benefit of said city.*"

There was no allegation in the bill that the city was in any way instrumental in procuring this transfer or the abandonment of the site as a naval depot; on the contrary, it is averred that the city authorities endeavored to prevent both.

The bill charged that by the failure of the United States to appropriate the land for a naval depot, and the final abandonment by the United States of any intention to do so, the land came within the clause of the deed of July, 1844, conveying it to Wheatley in trust; or if not, that it was held by the city in trust for the original grantors, and the prayer sought to subject it to said trusts.

The answer, denying the construction put upon the deed of 1844, which established a trust, asserted that the land had been appropriated by the United States as a naval depot within the meaning and intent of the deed of July, 1844, and that the subsequent perpetual occupation of it was not a condition subsequent; and consequently that the abandonment of it as a naval depot was not a breach of a condition such as divested the title so conveyed by the deed.

It pleaded the statute of limitations. It also demurred to the bill as seeking to enforce a forfeiture for breach of condition subsequent.

The court sustained the demurrer, and also decreed that the city had a perfect title to the property against the complainants both under the act of Congress and the statute of limitations, and dismissed the bill. The Supreme Court of Tennessee affirmed this decree.

That court was also of opinion, and so declared itself to be, that the act of Congress "cedes the property in controversy in this cause to the mayor and aldermen of the city of Memphis, for the use of the city only, and not in trust for the complainant; and that the complainant takes no benefit under the said act."

The complainant thereupon sued out a writ of error to this court.

* * *

MR. JUSTICE MILLER (now, January 11th, 1875) delivered the opinion of the court.

In the year 1867 Congress passed an act, approved February 5th, entitled an act to amend "An act to establish the judicial courts of the United States, approved September the 24th, 1789." This act consisted of two sections, the first of which conferred upon the Federal courts and upon the judges of those courts additional power in regard to writs of habeas corpus, and regulated appeals and other proceedings in that class of cases. The second section was a reproduction, with some changes, of the twenty-fifth section of the act of 1789, to which, by its title, the act of 1867 was an amendment, and it related to the appellate jurisdiction of this court over judgments and decrees of State courts.

The difference between the twenty-fifth section of the act of 1789 and the second section of the act of 1867 did not attract much attention, if any, for some time after the passage of the latter. Occasional allusions to its effect upon the principles long established by this court under the former began at length to make their appearance in the briefs and oral arguments of counsel, but were not found to be so important as to require any decision of this court on the subject.

* * * [T]he proposition has been urged upon the court that the latter act worked a total repeal of the twenty-fifth section of the former, and introduced a rule for the action of this court in the class of cases to which they both referred, of such extended operation and so variant from that which had governed it heretofore that the subject received the serious consideration of the court. * * *

The proposition is that by a fair construction of the act of 1867 this court must, when it obtains jurisdiction of a case decided in a State court, by reason of one of the questions stated in the act, proceed to decide every other question which the case presents which may be found necessary to a final judgment on the whole merits. * * *

When the case standing at the head of this opinion came on to be argued, it was insisted by counsel for defendants in error that none of the questions were involved in the case necessary to give jurisdiction to this court, either under the act of 1789 or of 1867, and that if they were, there were other questions exclusively of State court cognizance which were sufficient to dispose of the case, and that, therefore, the writ of error should be dismissed.

Counsel for plaintiffs in error, on the other hand, argued that not only was there a question in the case decided against them which authorized the writ of error from this court under either act, but that this court having for this reason obtained jurisdiction of the case, should re-examine all the questions found in the record, though some of them might be questions of general common law or equity, or raised by State statutes, unaffected by any principle of Federal law, constitutional or otherwise.

When, after argument, the court came to consider the case in consultation, it was found that it could not be disposed of without ignoring or deciding some of these propositions, and it became apparent that the time had arrived when the court must decide upon the effect of the act of 1867 on the jurisdiction of this court as it had been supposed to be established by the twenty-fifth section of the act of 1789.

* * *

The questions propounded by the court for discussion by counsel were these:

1. Does the second section of the act of February 5th, 1867, repeal all or any part of the twenty-fifth section of the act of 1789, commonly called the Judiciary Act?

2. Is it the true intent and meaning of the act of 1867, above referred to, that when this court has jurisdiction of a case, by reason of any of the questions therein mentioned, it shall proceed to decide all the questions presented by the record which are necessary to a final judgment or decree?

3. If this question be answered affirmatively, does the Constitution of the United States authorize Congress to confer such a jurisdiction on this court?

1. The act of 1867 has no repealing clause nor any express words of repeal. If there is any repeal, therefore, it is one of implication * * * .

* * *

The * * * twenty-fifth section of the act of 1789 is technically repealed, and * * * the second section of the act of 1867 has taken its place. What of the statute of 1789 is embraced in that of 1867 is of course the law now and has been ever since it was first made so. What is changed or modified is the law as thus changed or modified. That which is omitted ceased to have any effect from the day that the substituted statute was approved.

* * *

2. The affirmative of the second question propounded above is founded upon the effect of the omission or repeal of the last sentence of the twenty-fifth section of the act of 1789. That clause in express terms limited the power of the Supreme Court in reversing the judgment of a State court, to errors apparent on the face of the record and which respected questions, that for the sake of brevity, though not with strict verbal accuracy, we shall call Federal questions, namely, those in regard to the validity or construction of the Constitution, treaties, statutes, commissions, or authority of the Federal government.

The argument may be thus stated: 1. That the Constitution declares that the judicial power of the United States shall extend to cases of a character which includes the questions described in the section, and that by the word case, is to be understood all of the case in which such a question arises. 2. That by the fair construction of the act of 1789 in regard to removing those cases to this court, the power and the duty of re-examining the whole case would have been devolved on the court, but for the restriction of the clause omitted in the act of 1867; and that the same language is used in the latter act regulating the removal, but omitting the restrictive clause. And, 3. That by re-enacting the statute in the same terms as to the removal of cases from the State courts, without the restrictive clause, Congress is to be understood as conferring the power which the clause prohibited.

We will consider the last proposition first.

What were the precise motives which induced the omission of this clause it is impossible to ascertain with any degree of satisfaction. In a legislative body like Congress, it is reasonable to suppose that among those who considered this matter at all, there were varying reasons for consenting to the change. No doubt there were those who, believing that the Constitution gave no right to the Federal judiciary to go beyond the line marked by the omitted clause, thought its presence or absence immaterial; and in a revision of the statute it was wise to leave it out, because its presence implied that such a power was within the competency of Congress to bestow. There were also, no doubt, those who believed that the section standing without that clause did not confer the power which it prohibited, and that it was, therefore, better omitted. It may also have been within the thought of a few that all that is now claimed would follow the repeal of the clause. But if Congress, or the framers of the bill, had a clear purpose to enact affirmatively that the court *should consider* the class of errors which that clause forbid, nothing hindered that they should say so in positive terms; and in reversing the policy of the government from its foundation in one of the most important subjects on which that body could act, it is reasonably to be expected that Congress would use plain, unmistakable language in giving expression to such intention.

There is, therefore, no sufficient reason for holding that Congress, by repealing or omitting this restrictive clause, intended to enact affirmatively the thing which that clause had prohibited.

* * *

If the invariable effect of a writ of error to a Circuit Court of the United States is to require of this court to examine and pass upon all the errors of the inferior court, and if re-examination of the judgment of the court in the same manner and under the same regulations, means that in the re-examination everything is to be considered which could be considered in [a writ to the Circuit Court, and nothing else, then the inference] which is drawn from these premises would seem to be correct.

* * *

There is, therefore, nothing in the language of the act, as far as we have criticized it, which in express terms defines the extent of the re-examination which this court shall give to such cases.

But we have not yet considered the most important part of the statute, namely, that which declares that it is only upon the existence of certain questions in the case that this court can entertain jurisdiction at all. Nor is the mere existence of such a question in the case sufficient to give jurisdiction—the question must have been *decided* in the State court. Nor is it sufficient that such a question was raised and was decided. It must have been decided in a certain way, that is, against the right set up under the Constitution, laws, treaties, or authority of the United States. The Federal question may have been erroneously decided. It may be quite apparent to this court that a wrong construction has been given to the Federal law, but if the right claimed under it by plaintiff in error has been conceded to him, this court cannot entertain jurisdiction of the case, so very careful is the statute, both of 1789 and of 1867, to narrow, to limit, and define the jurisdiction which this court exercises over the judgments of the State courts. Is it consistent with this extreme caution to suppose that Congress intended, when those cases came here, that this court should not only examine those questions, but all others found in the record—questions of common law, of State statutes, of controverted facts, and conflicting evidence? Or is it the more reasonable inference that Congress intended that the case should be brought here that *those questions* might be decided and *finally* decided by the court established by the Constitution of the Union, and the court which has always been supposed to be not only the most appropriate but the only proper tribunal for their final decision? No such reason nor any necessity exists for the decision by this court of other questions in those cases. The jurisdiction has been exercised for nearly a century without serious inconvenience to the due administration of justice. The State courts are the appropriate tribunals, as this court has repeatedly held, for the decision of questions arising under their local law, whether statutory or otherwise. And it is not lightly to be presumed that Congress acted upon a principle which implies a distrust of their integrity or of their ability to construe those laws correctly.

Let us look for a moment into the effect of the proposition contended for upon the cases as they come up for consideration in the conference-room. If it is found that no such question is raised or decided in the court below, then all will concede that it must be dismissed for want of jurisdiction. But if it is found that the Federal question was raised and was decided against the plaintiff in error, then the first duty of the court obviously is to determine whether it was correctly decided by the State court. Let us suppose that we find that the court below was right in its decision on that question. What, then, are we to do? Was it the intention of Congress to say that while you can only bring the case here on account of this question, yet when it is here, though it may turn out that the plaintiff in error was wrong on that question, and the judgment of the court below was right, though he has wrongfully dragged the defendant into this court by the allegation of an error which did not exist, and without which the case could not rightfully be here, he can still insist on an inquiry into all the other matters which were litigated in the case?

This is neither reasonable nor just.

In such case both the nature of the jurisdiction conferred and the nature and fitness of things demand that, no error being found in the matter which authorized the re-examination, the judgment of the State court should be affirmed, and the case remitted to that court for its further enforcement.

The whole argument we are combating, however, goes upon the assumption that when it is found that the record shows that one of the questions mentioned has been decided against the claim of the plaintiff in error, this court has jurisdiction, and that jurisdiction extends to the whole case. We are of opinion that upon a fair construction of the whole language of the section the jurisdiction conferred is limited to the decision of the questions mentioned in the statute, and, as a necessary consequence of this, to the exercise of such powers as may be necessary to cause the judgment in that decision to be respected.

We will now advert to one or two considerations apart from the mere language of the statute, which seem to us to give additional force to this conclusion.

It has been many times decided by this court, on motions to dismiss this class of cases for want of jurisdiction, that if it appears from the record that the plaintiff in error raised and presented to the court by pleadings, prayer for instruction, or other appropriate method, one of the questions specified in the statute, and the court ruled against him, the jurisdiction of this court attached, and we must hear the case on its merits. Heretofore these merits have been held to be to determine whether the propositions of law involved in the specific Federal question were rightly decided, and if not, did the case of plaintiff in error, on the pleadings and evidence, come within the principle ruled by this court. This has always been held to be the exercise of the jurisdiction and re-examination of the case provided by the statute. But if when we once get jurisdiction, everything in the case is open to re-examination, it follows that every case tried in any State court, from that of a justice of the peace to the highest court of the State, may be brought to this court for final decision on all the points involved in it.

* * *

The twenty-fifth section of the act of 1789 has been the subject of innumerable decisions, some of which are to be found in almost every volume of the reports from that year down to the present. These form a system of appellate jurisprudence relating to the exercise of the appellate power of this court over the courts of the States. That system has been based upon the fundamental principle that this jurisdiction was limited to the correction of errors relating solely to Federal law. And though it may be argued with some plausibility that the reason of this is to be found in the restrictive clause of the act of 1789, which is omitted in the act of 1867, yet an examination of the cases will show that it rested quite as much on the conviction of this court that without that clause and on general principles the jurisdiction extended no further. It requires a very bold reach of thought, and a readiness to impute to Congress a radical and hazardous change of a policy vital in its essential nature to the independence of the State courts, to believe that that body contemplated, or intended, what is claimed, by the mere omission of a clause in the substituted statute, which may well be held to have been superfluous, or nearly so, in the old one.

Another consideration, not without weight in seeking after the intention of Congress, is found in the fact that where that body has clearly shown an intention to bring the whole of a case which arises under the constitutional provision as to its subject-matter under the jurisdiction of a Federal court, it has conferred its cognizance on Federal courts of original jurisdiction and not on the Supreme Court.

* * *

And we think it equally clear that it has been the counterpart of the same policy to vest in the Supreme Court, as a court of *appeal* from the State courts, a jurisdiction limited to the questions of a Federal character which might be involved in such cases.

* * *

There may be some plausibility in the argument that these rights cannot be protected in all cases unless the Supreme Court has final control of the whole case. But the experience of eighty-five years of the administration of the law under the opposite theory would seem to be a satisfactory answer to the argument. It is not to be presumed that the State courts, where the rule is clearly laid down to them on the Federal question, and its influence on the case fully seen, will disregard or overlook it, and this is all that the rights of the party claiming under it require. Besides, by the very terms of this statute, when the Supreme Court is of opinion that the question of Federal law is of such relative importance to the whole case that it should control the final judgment, that court is authorized to render such judgment and enforce it by its own process. It cannot, therefore, be maintained that it is in any case necessary for the security of the rights claimed under the Constitution, laws, or treaties of the United States that the Supreme Court should examine and decide other questions not of a Federal character.

And we are of opinion that the act of 1867 does not confer such a jurisdiction.

This renders unnecessary a decision of the question whether, if Congress had conferred such authority, the act would have been constitutional. It will be time enough for this court to inquire into the existence of such a power when that body has attempted to exercise it in language which makes such an intention so clear as to require it.

* * *

It is proper, in this first attempt to construe this important statute as amended, to say a few words on another point. What shall be done by this court when the question has been found to exist in the record, and to have been decided against the plaintiff in error, and *rightfully* decided, we have already seen, and it presents no difficulties.

But when it appears that the Federal question was decided erroneously against the plaintiff in error, we must then reverse the case undoubtedly, if there are no other issues decided in it than that. It often has occurred, however, and will occur again, that there are other points in the case than those of Federal cognizance, on which the judgment of the court below may stand; those points being of themselves sufficient to control the case.

Or it may be, that there are other issues in the case, but they are not of such controlling influence on the whole case that they are alone sufficient to support the judgment.

It may also be found that notwithstanding there are many other questions in the record of the case, the issue raised by the Federal question is such that its decision must dispose of the whole case.

In the two latter instances there can be no doubt that the judgment of the State court must be reversed, and under the new act this court can either render the final judgment or decree here, or remand the case to the State court for that purpose.

But in the other cases supposed, why should a judgment be reversed for an error in deciding the Federal question, if the same judgment must be rendered on the other points in the case? And why should this court reverse a judgment which is right on the whole record presented to us; or where the same judgment will be rendered by the court below, after they have corrected the error in the Federal question?

We have already laid down the rule that we are not authorized to examine these other questions for the purpose of deciding whether the State court ruled correctly on them or not. We are of opinion that on these subjects not embraced in the class of questions stated in the statute, we must receive the decision of the State courts as conclusive.

But when we find that the State court has decided the Federal question erroneously, then to prevent a useless and profitless reversal, which can do the plaintiff in error no good, and can only embarrass and delay the defendant, we must so far look into the remainder of the record as to see whether the decision of the Federal question alone is sufficient to dispose of the case, or to require its reversal; or on the other hand, whether there exist other matters in the record actually decided by the State court which are sufficient to maintain the judgment of that court, notwithstanding the error in deciding the Federal question. In the latter case the court would not be justified in reversing the judgment of the State court.

But this examination into the points in the record other than the Federal question is not for the purpose of determining whether they were correctly or erroneously decided, but to ascertain if any such have been decided, and their sufficiency to maintain the final judgment, as decided by the State court.

Beyond this we are not at liberty to go, and we can only go this far to prevent the injustice of reversing a judgment which must in the end be reaffirmed, even in this court, if brought here again from the State court after it has corrected its error in the matter of Federal law.

Finally, we hold the following propositions on this subject as flowing from the statute as it now stands:

1. That it is essential to the jurisdiction of this court over the judgment of a State court, that it shall appear that one of the questions mentioned in the act must have been raised, and presented to the State court.

2. That it must have been decided by the State court, or that its decision was necessary to the judgment or decree, rendered in the case.

3. That the decision must have been against the right claimed or asserted by plaintiff in error under the Constitution, treaties, laws, or authority of the United States.

4. These things appearing, this court has jurisdiction and must examine the judgment so far as to enable it to decide whether this claim of right was correctly adjudicated by the State court.

5. If it finds that it was rightly decided, the judgment must be affirmed.

6. If it was erroneously decided against plaintiff in error, then this court must further inquire, whether there is any other matter or issue adjudged by the State court, which is sufficiently broad to maintain the judgment of that court, notwithstanding the error in deciding the issue raised by the Federal question. If this is found to be the case, the judgment must be affirmed without inquiring into the soundness of the decision on such other matter or issue.

7. But if it be found that the issue raised by the question of Federal law is of such controlling character that its correct decision is necessary to any final judgment in the case, or that there has been no decision by the State court of any other matter or issue which is sufficient to maintain the judgment of that court without regard to the Federal question, then this court will reverse the judgment of the State court, and will either render such judgment here as the State court should have rendered, or remand the case to that court, as the circumstances of the case may

require.

Applying the principles here laid down to the case now before the court, we are of opinion that this court has jurisdiction, and that the judgment of the Supreme Court of Tennessee must be affirmed.

* * *

The plaintiffs in error, by their bill, allege that the title was originally conveyed to the city of Memphis, in trust, for certain purposes, including that of having a navy yard built on it by the United States; that when the title reverted to the city by reason of the abandonment of the place as a navy yard by the United States, and the act of Congress aforesaid, the city received the title in trust for the original grantors, who are the plaintiffs, or who are represented by plaintiffs. A demurrer to the bill was filed. Also an answer denying the trust and pleading the statute of limitations. On the hearing the bill was dismissed, and this decree was affirmed by the Supreme Court of the State. The complainants, in their bill, and throughout the case, insisted that the effect of the act of 1854 was to vest the title in the mayor or aldermen of the city in trust for them.

* * *

But we need not consume many words to prove that neither by the deed of the city to the United States, which is an ordinary deed of bargain and sale for a valuable consideration, nor from anything found in the act of 1854, is there any such trust to be inferred. The act, so far from recognizing or implying any such trust, cedes the property to the mayor and aldermen *for the use of the city.* We are, therefore, of opinion that this, the only Federal question in the case, was rightly decided by the Supreme Court of Tennessee.

But conceding this to be true, the plaintiffs in error have argued that the court having jurisdiction of the case must now examine it upon all the questions which affect its merits; and they insist that the conveyance by which the city of Memphis received the title previous to the deed from the city to government, and the circumstances attending the making of the former deed are such, that when the title reverted to the city, a trust was raised for the benefit of plaintiffs.

After what has been said in the previous part of this opinion, we need discuss this matter no further. The claim of right here set up is one to be determined by the general principles of equity jurisprudence, and is unaffected by anything found in the Constitution, laws, or treaties of the United States. Whether decided well or otherwise by the State court, we have no authority to inquire. According to the principles we have laid down as applicable to this class of cases, the judgment of the Supreme Court of Tennessee must be

Affirmed.

MR. JUSTICE CLIFFORD, with whom concurred MR. JUSTICE SWAYNE, dissenting:

I dissent from so much of the opinion of the court as denies the jurisdiction of this court to determine the whole case, where it appears that the record presents a Federal question and that the Federal question was erroneously decided to the prejudice of the plaintiff in error; as in that state of the record it is, in my judgment, the duty of this court, under the recent act of Congress, to decide the whole merits of the controversy, and to affirm or reverse the judgment of the State court. Tested by the new law it would seem that it must be so, as this court cannot in that state of the record dismiss the writ of error, nor can the court reverse the judgment without deciding every question which the record presents.

Where the Federal question is rightly decided the judgment of the State court may be affirmed, upon the ground that the jurisdiction does not attach to the other questions involved in the merits of the controversy; but where the Federal question is erroneously decided the whole merits must be decided by this court, else the new law, which it is admitted repeals the twenty-fifth section of the Judiciary Act, is without meaning, operation, or effect, except to repeal the prior law.

Sufficient proof of the fact that the new law was not intended to be without meaning and effective operation is found in the fact that the provision in the old law which restricts the right of the plaintiff in error or appellant to assign for error any matter except such as respects one of the Federal questions enumerated in the twenty-fifth section of the Judiciary Act, is wholly omitted in the new law.

MR. JUSTICE BRADLEY, dissenting:

I feel obliged to dissent from the conclusion to which a majority of the court has come on the public question in this cause, but shall content myself with stating briefly the grounds of that dissent, without entering into any prolonged argument on the subject.

* * *

[S]upposing, as the majority of the court holds, that it has jurisdiction, I cannot concur in the conclusion that we can only decide the Federal question raised by the record. If we have jurisdiction at all, in my judgment we have jurisdiction of the *case,* and not merely of a *question* in it. The act of 1867, and the twenty-fifth section of the Judiciary Act both provide that a final judgment or decree in any suit in the highest court of a State, where is drawn in question certain things relating to the Constitution or laws of the United States, or to rights or immunities claimed under the United States, and the decision is adverse to such Constitution, laws, or rights, may be re-examined and reversed or affirmed in the Supreme Court of the United States upon a writ of error. Had the original act stopped here there could have been no difficulty.

This act derives its authority and is intended to carry into effect, at least in part, that clause of the Constitution which declares that the judicial power shall extend to all cases, in law and equity, arising under this Constitution, the laws of the United States, and treaties made under their authority—not to all *questions,* but to all *cases.* This word "cases," in the residue of the section, has frequently been held to mean suits, actions, embracing the whole cases, not mere questions in them; and that is undoubtedly the true construction. The Constitution, therefore, would have authorized a revision by the judiciary of the United States of all *cases* decided in State courts in which questions of United States law of Federal rights are necessarily involved. Congress in carrying out that clause could have so ordained. And the law referred to, had it stopped at the point to which I have quoted it above, would clearly have been understood as so ordaining. But the twenty-fifth section of the Judiciary Act went on to declare that in such cases no other error should be assigned or regarded as a ground of reversal than such as immediately respected the question referred to as the ground of jurisdiction. It having been early decided that Congress had power to regulate the exercise of the appellate jurisdiction of the Supreme Court, the court has always considered itself bound by this restriction, and as authorized to reverse judgments of State courts only for errors in deciding the Federal questions involved therein.

Now, Congress, in the act of 1867, when revising the twenty-fifth section of the Judiciary Act, whilst following the general frame and modes of expression of that section, omitted the clause above referred to, which restricted the court to a consideration of the Federal questions. This omission cannot be regarded as having no meaning. The clause by its presence in the original act meant something, and effected something. It had the effect of restricting the consideration of the court to a certain class of questions as a ground of reversal, which restriction would not have existed without it. The omission of the clause, according to a well-settled rule of construction, must necessarily have the effect of removing the restriction which it effected in the old law.

In my judgment, therefore, if the court had jurisdiction of the case, it was bound to consider not only the Federal question raised by the record, but the whole case. As the court, however, has decided otherwise, it is not proper that I should express any opinion on the merits.

Notes and Questions

1. All of the questions this case raises turn on Congress's intent in deleting the final sentence of § 25 of the Judiciary Act of 1789, which clearly limited review to matters of federal law. Consider whether the Court's assignment of meaning (or, rather, lack of meaning) to the deletion is historically sound. After all, the amendment did not occur in a vacuum; it came in 1867, when Reconstruction was at its peak. Federal distrust of the reconstituted Southern governments was enormous. The elections of 1866 completely repudiated President Andrew Johnson's efforts at moderate reconstruction;

Radical Republicans swept into office. Although the Radical Republicans did not agree as to all particulars, "they did all agree * * * that the existing state governments in the South—with the exception of Tennessee's—must be set aside and replaced for the time being by direct federal rule." ERIC L. MCKITRICK, ANDREW JOHNSON AND RECONSTRUCTION 456 (1960). There were frequent reports of miscarriages of justice in southern courts. The amendment to the 1789 Act passed in February 1867 while Congress debated establishing military reconstruction in the South. Although Justice Miller asserts that "it is not lightly to be presumed that Congress acted upon a principle which implies a distrust of [state courts'] integrity[,] * * *" given the times, the Court's view of Congress's likely intent is at least questionable.

2. Suppose the 1789 Act had not contained the sentence Congress struck in 1867. Would the Court still have ruled that Congress should "use plain, unmistakable language * * *" to allow review of state law issues?

3. *Murdock* declined to consider whether Congress could constitutionally extend the Supreme Court's jurisdiction to all issues raised in an appeal. Has Congress the power to do that? Consider the following arguments pro and con:

> One can make a very strong affirmative argument. The Supreme Court says that the arising under jurisdiction [of Article III] is coextensive in the original, removal, and appellate modes. In *Martin v. Hunter's Lessee* [1816], the Court said that the difference between removal and appellate jurisdiction was merely one of timing. When an action is removed to a lower federal court, the court adjudicates the entire case, not just the federal issue involved. If all issues can be adjudicated in a removed case, and removal and appellate jurisdiction are coextensive, then the Supreme Court should be able to hear all issues in cases on appeal.
>
> Moreover, in discussing the arising under jurisdiction, the Court refers uniformly to "cases," rather than to "issues" or "claims." This suggests that once jurisdiction over a case attaches, the federal courts have authority to decide the entire case, and not just the federal issues therein. The Court made this inference explicit in *Osborn v. Bank of United States* [1824] and *Tennessee v. Davis* [1879]. In discussing the original jurisdiction, the *Osborn* Court asserted that once federal jurisdiction attached, "then all the other questions must be decided as incidental to this, which gives that jurisdiction." The Court reasoned that because so few cases involve only federal issues, to hold otherwise would effectively cripple the original jurisdiction of the lower federal courts. In discussing the removal jurisdiction, the *Davis* Court stated: "Nor is it any objection that questions are involved which are not at all of a Federal character. If one of the latter exist, if there be a single such ingredient in the mass, it is sufficient."
>
> The modern Supreme Court cases and the federal statute authorizing supplemental jurisdiction also support the argument that Congress can authorize the Supreme Court to hear all issues in cases appealed from state court. In *United Mine Workers v. Gibbs* [1966], the Su-

preme Court held that Article III allows the federal courts to hear a state claim along with a federal claim when the two claims "derive from a common nucleus of operative fact," thus "permit[ting] the conclusion that the entire action before the court comprises but one constitutional 'case.' " Congress codified *Gibbs* and further extended supplemental jurisdiction to state claims involving additional parties so long as the claims form part "of the same case or controversy." The authority to exercise supplemental jurisdiction over state claims supports the argument here in two ways. First, if the lower federal courts have the power to hear state claims in a case arising under federal law, it is difficult to see why the Supreme Court should not have the same power in a case coming to it from a state court. In addition, Article III's grant of appellate jurisdiction to the Supreme Court in cases arising under federal law applies both to cases reaching it from the lower federal courts and from state courts. Since the Supreme Court has the power to adjudicate pendent state claims in a case that reaches it from a lower federal court, it is difficult to see why the Court could not adjudicate the state claims if the same case came up on appeal from a state court.

In sum, one can make a very strong argument that Congress could constitutionally extend jurisdiction to all issues in an appeal. One counterargument has some merit, however. The states' highest courts are supposed to have the final word on the meaning of state law. If the Supreme Court takes a case on appeal from a state's high court and reverses based on a different interpretation of state law, state authority plainly is compromised. Of course, the federal courts (including the Supreme Court) decide issues of state law when exercising supplemental jurisdiction and in diversity cases, and they sometimes decide wrongly. The state courts are not bound in later cases by these misreadings of state law. Presumably, the state courts also could ignore misinterpretations by the Supreme Court in cases heard on appeal from the state courts. Nonetheless, the federal-state conflict seems potentially more acute in an appeal, because the Supreme Court might tell a state's high court that it is misinterpreting state law in the very case both courts are hearing.

Donald H. Zeigler, *Twins Separated at Birth: A Comparative History of the Civil and Criminal Arising Under Jurisdiction of the Federal Courts and Some Proposals for Change*, 19 VT. L. REV. 673, 729-30 n.285 (1995) (citations omitted or modified).

Although the arguments supporting Congress' power to extend jurisdiction to all issues raised in an appeal seem quite strong, it does not necessarily follow that Congress should exercise the power. In assessing this issue, consider whether the policies supporting supplemental jurisdiction at the district court level would apply with the same force in § 1257 cases.

4. Congress originally required not only that a federal question be present, but also that the state court have decided the federal question in a way that would have a direct, adverse effect on federal interests if the state court

had erred. Congress provided no review, however, when the state court upheld a federal law or overturned a state law in the face of a federal law challenge. What if the state court interpreted federal law too broadly? Since the
balance of federal and state power constantly affects delicate federalism interests, there may be a federal interest in not having state courts give federal rights unintended scope. Perhaps this is why Congress removed these
limitations on the Court's appellate jurisdiction in 1914.

5. a) Consider numbers four, five, and six of Justice Miller's list of
propositions. If the state court decided an issue of federal law, he asserts
that the Supreme Court must decide whether the state court decided the
issue correctly. If it did, the Supreme Court should affirm. If the state court
decided incorrectly, then the Supreme Court should see whether the state
court also decided some issue of state law that requires affirmance "notwithstanding the error in deciding the issue raised by the federal question." If
this is so, the Court should affirm without reviewing the state court decision
on the state law issue. Is this not an inefficient procedure? If state law will
control the decision in any event, why should the Court gratuitously decide
whether the state court erred on the non-controlling federal issue? What
would be a better way to proceed?

b) In accord with Justice Miller's propositions, the Court examines
whether the Tennessee courts properly construed the federal statute that
reconveyed the land to Memphis. The Court concludes the Tennessee courts
decided the federal issue correctly and therefore affirms without reviewing
any state law questions. What, then, is the binding effect of propositions six
and seven, which explain how the Court should proceed when a state court
wrongly decides the federal issue?

c) What is the status of the rule that the Supreme Court will not reverse
a state court judgment based on an erroneous interpretation of federal law if
there is a state law ground sufficient to maintain the judgment notwithstanding the state court's error? Is the rule a constitutional imperative, a
statutory prescription, or a prudential rule of the Court's own making? If
the first, what provision of the Article III prevents the Court from ruling on
the disputed federal issue? If the second, what part of the statute authorizing review dictates the rule the Court announces? If the last, what is the
source of authority for the Court to prescribe such a rule?

d) One intriguing question about *Murdock* is whether expiration of the
statute of limitations would have required affirmance even if the state courts
had decided the federal question wrongly. The answer lies in the opinions of
the Justices of the Tennessee Supreme Court. The majority ruled for the
City on the federal issue and then said: "The views we have expressed render it unnecessary to express an opinion as to many points raised in argument." Dissenting, Justice Hawkins made it plain that the court did not
decide the limitations question. He would have ruled for the complainants
on the federal issue, which, he said, would have made it necessary to reach
the limitations question, but since the majority ruled against the complainants on the merits, he agreed it was not necessary to reach it. *Murdock v.
The Mayor and Aldermen of Memphis*, 47 Tenn. 483, 507-08 (1870). Even if

the Tennessee Supreme Court had decided the federal issue erroneously, its determination to decide the case on the federal question and not on that statute of limitations ground would have brought it within the rule discussed in *Orr v. Orr* (1979), *infra* at 956, where the Court held that its jurisdiction is secure if the state court actually decides a case on the federal issue, even though it might have disposed of the case on state law grounds.

C. INSULATING STATE DECISIONS FROM SUPREME COURT REVIEW

1. *With Substantive Law*

a. Adequacy, Independence and Certainty

FOX FILM CORP. v. MULLER
Supreme Court of the United States, 1935.
296 U.S. 207, 56 S.Ct. 183, 80 L.Ed. 158.

MR. JUSTICE SUTHERLAND delivered the opinion of the Court.

This is an action brought in a Minnesota state court of first instance by the Film Corporation against Muller, to recover damages for an alleged breach of two contracts by which Muller was licensed to exhibit certain moving picture films belonging to the corporation. Muller answered, setting up the invalidity of the contracts under the Sherman Anti-trust Act. It was and is agreed that these contracts are substantially the same as the one involved in *United States v. Paramount Famous Lasky Corp.*, 34 F.2d 984, *aff'd* 282 U.S. 30; that petitioner was one of the defendants in that action; and that the "arbitration clause," paragraph 18 of each of the contracts sued upon, is the same as that held in that case to be invalid. In view of the disposition which we are to make of this writ, it is not necessary to set forth the terms of the arbitration clause or the other provisions of the contract.

The court of first instance held that each contract sued upon violated the Sherman Anti-trust Act, and dismissed the action. In a supplemental opinion that court put its decision upon the grounds, first, that the arbitration plan is so connected with the remainder of the contract that the entire contract is tainted, and, second, that the contract violates the Sherman Anti-trust law. The state supreme court affirmed. We granted certiorari, but, when the case was called for argument, it appeared that no final judgment had been entered and the writ was dismissed as improvidently granted. The case was then remanded to the state supreme court; and, the judgment having been made final, and again affirmed by the state supreme court on the authority of its previous opinion, we allowed the present writ.

In its opinion, the state supreme court, after a statement of the case, said: "The question presented on this appeal is whether the arbitration clause is severable from the contract, leaving the remainder of the contract enforceable, or not severable, permeating and tainting the whole contract with illegality and making it void."

That court then proceeded to refer to and discuss a number of decisions of state and federal courts, some of which took the view that the arbitration clause was severable, and others that it was not severable, from the remainder of the contract. After reviewing the opinion and decree of the federal district court in the *Paramount* case, the lower court reached the conclusion that the holding of the federal court was that the entire contract was illegal; and upon that view and upon what it conceived to be the weight of authority, held the arbitration plan was inseparable from the other provisions of the contract. Whether this conclusion was right or wrong we need not determine. It is enough that it is, at least, not without fair support.

Respondent contends that the question of severability was alone decided and that no federal question was determined by the lower court. This contention petitioner challenges, and asserts that a federal question was involved and decided. We do not attempt to settle the dispute; but, assuming for present purposes only that petitioner's view is the correct one, the case is controlled by the settled rule that where the judgment of a state court rests upon two grounds, one of which is federal and the other non-federal in character, our jurisdiction fails if the non-federal ground is independent of the federal ground and adequate to support the judgment. This rule had become firmly fixed * * * and has been reiterated in a long line of cases since that time.

Whether the provisions of a contract are non-severable, so that if one be held invalid the others must fall with it, is clearly a question of general and not of federal law. The invalidity of the arbitration clause which the present contracts embody is conceded. It was held invalid by the federal district court in the *Paramount* case, and its judgment was affirmed here. The question, therefore, was foreclosed; and was not the subject of controversy in the state courts. In that situation, the primary question to be determined by the court below was whether the concededly invalid clause was separable from the other provisions of the contract. The ruling of the state supreme court that it was not, is sufficient to conclude the case without regard to the determination, if, in fact, any was made, in respect of the federal question. It follows that the non-federal ground is adequate to sustain the judgment.

The rule announced * * * to the effect that our jurisdiction attaches where the non-federal ground is so interwoven with the other as not to be an independent matter, does not apply. The construction put upon the contracts did not constitute a preliminary step which simply had the effect of bringing forward for determination the federal question, but was a decision which automatically took the federal question out of the case if otherwise it would be there. The non-federal question in respect of the construction of the contracts, and the federal question in respect of their validity under the Anti-trust Act, were clearly independent of one another. The case, in effect, was disposed of before the federal question said to be involved was reached. A decision of that question then became unnecessary; and whether it was decided or not, our want of jurisdiction is clear.

Writ dismissed for want of jurisdiction.

Notes and Questions

1. Justice Sutherland notes that the parties agree that the contracts in *Fox Film* and *Paramount* are identical. Moreover, he notes that Fox Film is not challenging the ruling in *Paramount*. What, then, is the federal question that Fox Film insists is present for decision?

2. In turn, what is the non-federal question that Muller claims prevents the Supreme Court from considering the case?

3. Recall that *Murdock* said that the Court would first determine whether the state court correctly decided the federal issue and, if it did not, then determine whether the state court's decision of state issues would nonetheless require affirmance. Does the Court follow that sequence in *Fox*?

4. a) The Court dismisses the writ of certiorari for "want of jurisdiction." Why does an adequate and independent state ground for the decision below mean that the Court lacks jurisdiction? What constitutional or statutory provisions preclude jurisdiction?

b) Note that the issues here involve substantive law. Keep in mind your answer to the preceding part of this note when you read *Herndon v. Georgia, infra* at 946, to see whether the same rationale applies when the asserted state ground for decision is procedural rather than substantive.

DELAWARE v. PROUSE
Supreme Court of the United States, 1979.
440 U.S. 648, 99 S.Ct. 1391, 59 L.Ed.2d 660.

MR. JUSTICE WHITE delivered the opinion of the Court.

The question is whether it is an unreasonable seizure under the Fourth and Fourteenth Amendments to stop an automobile, being driven on a public highway, for the purpose of checking the driving license of the operator and the registration of the car, where there is neither probable cause to believe nor reasonable suspicion that the car is being driven contrary to the laws governing the operation of motor vehicles or that either the car or any of its occupants is subject to seizure or detention in connection with the violation of any other applicable law.

I

At 7:20 p.m. on November 30, 1976, a New Castle County, Delaware, patrolman in a police cruiser stopped the automobile occupied by respondent. The patrolman smelled marihuana smoke as he was walking toward the stopped vehicle, and he seized marihuana in plain view on

the car floor. Respondent was subsequently indicted for illegal possession of a controlled substance. At a hearing on respondent's motion to
suppress the marihuana seized as a result of the stop, the patrolman
testified that prior to stopping the vehicle he had observed neither traffic
or equipment violations nor any suspicious activity, and that he made
the stop only in order to check the driver's license and registration. The
patrolman was not acting pursuant to any standards, guidelines, or procedures pertaining to document spot checks, promulgated by either his
department or the State Attorney General. Characterizing the stop as
"routine," the patrolman explained, "I saw the car in the area and wasn't
answering any complaints, so I decided to pull them off." The trial court
granted the motion to suppress, finding the stop and detention to have
been wholly capricious and therefore violative of the Fourth Amendment.

The Delaware Supreme Court affirmed, noting first that "[t]he issue
of the legal validity of systematic, roadblock-type stops of a number of
vehicles for license and vehicle registration check is *not* now before the
Court." The court held that "a random stop of a motorist in the absence
of specific articulable facts which justify the stop by indicating a reasonable suspicion that a violation of the law has occurred is constitutionally
impermissible and violative of the Fourth and Fourteenth Amendments
to the United States Constitution." We granted certiorari to resolve the
conflict between this decision, which is in accord with decisions in five
other jurisdictions, and the contrary determination in six jurisdictions
that the Fourth Amendment does not prohibit the kind of automobile
stop that occurred here.

II

Because the Delaware Supreme Court held that the stop at issue not
only violated the Federal Constitution but also was impermissible under
art. I, § 6, of the Delaware Constitution, it is urged that the judgment
below was based on an independent and adequate state ground and that
we therefore have no jurisdiction in this case. At least, it is suggested,
the matter is sufficiently uncertain that we should remand for clarification as to the ground upon which the judgment rested. Based on our
reading of the opinion, however, we are satisfied that even if the State
Constitution would have provided an adequate basis for the judgment,
the Delaware Supreme Court did not intend to rest its decision independently on the State Constitution and that we have jurisdiction of this
case.

As we understand the opinion below, art. I, § 6, of the Delaware Constitution will automatically be interpreted at least as broadly as the
Fourth Amendment;[4] that is, every police practice authoritatively de-

---

[4] The court stated: "The Delaware Constitution Article I, § 6 is substantially similar
to the Fourth Amendment and a violation of the latter is necessarily a violation of the former." 382 A.2d at 1362, citing State v. Moore, 55 Del. 356, 187 A.2d 807 (1963).

termined to be contrary to the Fourth and Fourteenth Amendments will, without further analysis, be held to be contrary to art. I, § 6. This approach, which is consistent with previous opinions of the Delaware Supreme Court,[5] was followed in this case. The court analyzed the various decisions interpreting the Federal Constitution, concluded that the Fourth Amendment foreclosed spot checks of automobiles, and summarily held that the State Constitution was therefore also infringed. This is one of those cases where "at the very least, the [state] court felt compelled by what it understood to be federal constitutional considerations to construe * * * its own law in the manner it did." Had state law not been mentioned at all, there would be no question about our jurisdiction, even though the state Constitution might have provided an independent and adequate state ground. The same result should follow here where the state constitutional holding depended upon the state court's view of the reach of the Fourth and Fourteenth Amendments. If the state court misapprehended federal law, "[i]t should be freed to decide * * * these suits according to its own local law."

* * *

VII

Accordingly, we hold that except in those situations in which there is at least articulable and reasonable suspicion that a motorist is unlicensed or that an automobile is not registered, or that either the vehicle or an occupant is otherwise subject to seizure for violation of law, stopping an automobile and detaining the driver in order to check his driver's license and the registration of the automobile are unreasonable under the Fourth Amendment. This holding does not preclude the State of Delaware or other States from developing methods for spot checks that involve less intrusion or that do not involve the unconstrained exercise of discretion. Questioning of all oncoming traffic at roadblock-type stops is one possible alternative. We hold only that persons in automobiles on public roadways may not for that reason alone have their travel and privacy interfered with at the unbridled discretion of police officers. The judgment below is affirmed.

So ordered.

Moore was decided less than two years after Mapp v. Ohio, 367 U.S. 643 (1961), applied to the States the limitations previously imposed only on the Federal Government. In setting forth the approach reiterated in the opinion below, *Moore* noted not only the common purposes and wording of the Fourth Amendment and the state constitutional provision, but also the overriding effect of the former.

[5] We have found only one case decided after *State v. Moore* in which the court relied solely on state law in upholding the validity of a search or seizure, and that case involved not only Del. Const. art. I, § 6, but also state statutory requirements for issuance of a search warrant. Moreover, every case holding a search or seizure to be contrary to the state constitutional provision relies on cases interpreting the Fourth Amendment and simultaneously concludes that the search or seizure is contrary to that provision.

Notes and Questions

1. Justice White notes that the Delaware Supreme Court has stated that conduct forbidden by the Fourth Amendment is also forbidden by art. I, § 6 of the Delaware Constitution. He argues that this supports his conclusion that the provisions are co-extensive. But does not the Delaware Supreme Court thus simply state the constitutional imperative? If the Delaware Constitution authorized searches the Fourth Amendment prohibits, the state provision would be unconstitutional under the Supremacy Clause. Why does the Delaware court's statement of the obvious lend support to the Supreme Court's position?

2. a) Is the Court implicitly saying that the Delaware Supreme Court would have been better off to have written the very same opinion but without reference to federal law if it wanted Delaware law to control the case?

b) Is there any way for a state court to cite federal and state constitutions and still use the adequate and independent state ground rule to insulate its decision from Supreme Court review?

c) If state law provides a complete ground for decision, why would a state court ever cite apparently superfluous federal law?

3. Suppose the Supreme Court decided that the police conduct in *Prouse* did not violate the Fourth Amendment. Should the Court then remand to the trial court, or should the Delaware Supreme Court have an opportunity to construe the Delaware Constitution more broadly than the Fourth Amendment, obviating the need for a trial?

MINNESOTA v. NATIONAL TEA CO.
Supreme Court of the United States, 1940.
309 U.S. 551, 60 S.Ct. 676, 84 L.Ed. 920.

MR. JUSTICE DOUGLAS delivered the opinion of the Court.

In 1933 Minnesota enacted a chain store tax[,] one item of which was a tax on gross sales. The gross sales tax was graduated: one-twentieth of one per cent was applied on that portion of gross sales not in excess of $100,000; and larger percentages were applied as the volume of gross sales increased, until one per cent was exacted on that portion of gross sales in excess of $1,000,000. Respondents (chain stores conducting retail businesses in Minnesota) paid under protest the gross sales tax demanded by the Minnesota Tax Commission for the years 1933 and 1934 and thereafter sued in the state court for refunds. Judgments granting refunds were affirmed by the Supreme Court of Minnesota. * * *

At the threshold * * * we are met with a question which is decisive of the present petition. That is the question of jurisdiction.

The Supreme Court of Minnesota discussed not only the equal protection clause of the Fourteenth Amendment of the federal constitution but also art. 9, § 1 of the Minnesota constitution which provides: "Taxes shall be uniform upon the same class of subjects * * * ." It said that "these provisions of the Federal and State Constitutions impose identical restrictions upon the legislative power of the state in respect to classification for purposes of taxation." It stated that the "question is * * * whether the imposition of a graduated gross sales tax upon all those engaged in conducting chain stores is discriminatory as between such owners, thus violating the constitutional requirement of uniformity." It quoted the conclusion of the lower Minnesota court that the statute violated both the federal and the state constitution. It then adverted briefly to three of its former decisions which had interpreted art. 9, § 1 of the Minnesota constitution and quoted from one of them.[3] It merely added: "So much for our own cases"; and proceeded at once to a discussion of cases based solely on the Fourteenth Amendment of the federal constitution. While its discussion of art. 9, § 1 of the Minnesota constitution was in general terms, its analysis of the Fourteenth Amendment was specifically related to chain store taxation. It distinguished decisions of this Court which held that the number of stores in a given chain affords an appropriate basis for classification for imposition of progressively higher taxes. It then stated that the "precise question here presented" had been directly passed upon adversely to the state's contention in five cases. It added that the tax here involved was on all fours with that struck down by this Court. * * * And it concluded with the following statement:

> We think the five cases to which we have referred have so definitely and finally disposed of the legal problem presented as to make it needless for us to analyze or discuss the great number of other tax cases where the same constitutional question was involved. These being the only cases to which our attention has been called *directly deciding the question presented* we are of opinion that we should follow them and *that it is our duty so to do.* [Italics added.]

Respondents contend that the court held the statute invalid for violation not only of the federal constitution but also of the state constitution. Hence they seek to invoke the familiar rule that where a judgment of a state court rests on two grounds, one involving a federal question

---

[3] This reference to Minnesota constitutional law was limited to the following:

Our cases hold (and that is the general rule) that the legislature

> has a wide discretion in classifying property for the purposes of taxation, but the classification must be based on differences which furnish a reasonable ground for making a distinction between the several classes. The differences must not be so wanting in substance that the classification results in permitting one to escape a burden imposed on another under substantially similar circumstances and conditions. The rule of uniformity, established by the Constitution, requires that all similarly situated shall be treated alike.

State v. Minnesota Farmers Mut. Ins. Co., 145 Minn. 231, 234, 176 N.W. 756, 757; State ex rel. Mudeking v. Parr, 109 Minn. 147, 152, 123 N.W. 408, 134 A.S.R. 759; In re Improvement of Third Street, 185 Minn. 170, 240 N.W. 355.

and the other not, this Court will not take jurisdiction. In support of this position they point to the court's discussion of the Minnesota constitution and to the fact that the syllabus states that such a tax is violative of both the federal and state constitutions.[6] But as to the latter we are not referred to any Minnesota authority which, as in some states, makes the syllabi the law of the case. And as to the former the opinion is quite inconclusive. For the opinion as a whole leaves the impression that the court probably felt constrained to rule as it did because of the five decisions which it cited and which held such gross sales taxes unconstitutional by reason of the Fourteenth Amendment. That is at least the meaning, if the words used are taken literally. For if, as stated by the court, the "precise question here presented" was ruled by those five cases, that question was a federal one. And in that connection it is perhaps significant that the court stated not only that it "should follow" those decisions but that "it is our duty so to do."

Enough has been said to demonstrate that there is considerable uncertainty as to the precise grounds for the decision. That is sufficient reason for us to decline at this time to review the federal question asserted to be present, consistently with the policy of not passing upon questions of a constitutional nature which are not clearly necessary to a decision of the case.

But that does not mean that we should dismiss the petition. This Court has frequently held that in the exercise of its appellate jurisdiction it has the power not only to correct errors of law in the judgment under review but also to make such disposition of the case as justice requires. That principle has been applied to cases coming from state courts where supervening changes had occurred since entry of the judgment, where the record failed adequately to state the facts underlying a decision of the federal question, and where the grounds of the state decision were obscure. That principle was also applied where it was said:

> * * * if the state court did in fact intend alternatively to base its decision upon the state statute and upon an immunity it thought granted by the Constitution as interpreted by this Court, these two grounds are so interwoven that we are unable to conclude that the judgment rests upon an independent interpretation of the state law.

The procedure in those cases was to vacate the judgment and to remand the cause for further proceedings, so that the federal question might be dissected out or the state and federal questions clearly separated.

In this type of case we deem it essential that this procedure be followed. It is possible that the state court employed the decisions under

---

[6] By statute the court is required to prepare the syllabus.

the federal constitution merely as persuasive authorities for its independent interpretation of the state constitution. If that were true, we would have no jurisdiction to review. On the other hand we cannot be content with a dismissal of the petition where there is strong indication, as here, that the federal constitution as judicially construed controlled the decision below.

If a state court merely said that the Fourteenth Amendment, as construed by this Court, is the "supreme law of the land" to which obedience must be given, our jurisdiction would seem to be inescapable. And that would follow though the state court might have given, if it had chosen, a different construction to an identical provision in the state constitution. But the Minnesota Supreme Court did not take such an unequivocal position. On the other hand, it did not declare its independence of the decisions of this Court, when the state constitutional provision avowedly had identity of scope with the relevant clause of the Fourteenth Amendment. In the latter respect this case differs from *New York City v. Central Savings Bank.* The cases in which the New York Court of Appeals professes to go on both the state and federal due process clauses clearly rest upon an adequate non-federal ground. For that court has ruled that its own conception of due process governs, though the same phrase in the federal constitution may have been given different scope by decisions of this Court. The instant case therefore presents an intermediate situation * * * .

It is important that this Court not indulge in needless dissertations on constitutional law. It is fundamental that state courts be left free and unfettered by us in interpreting their state constitutions. But it is equally important that ambiguous or obscure adjudications by state courts do not stand as barriers to a determination by this Court of the validity under the federal constitution of state action. Intelligent exercise of our appellate powers compels us to ask for the elimination of the obscurities and ambiguities from the opinions in such cases. Only then can we ascertain whether or not our jurisdiction to review should be invoked. Only by that procedure can the responsibility for striking down or upholding state legislation be fairly placed. For no other course assures that important federal issues, such as have been argued here, will reach this Court for adjudication; that state courts will not be the final arbiters of important issues under the federal constitution; and that we will not encroach on the constitutional jurisdiction of the states. This is not a mere technical rule nor a rule for our convenience. It touches the division of authority between state courts and this Court and is of equal importance to each. Only by such explicitness can the highest courts of the states and this Court keep within the bounds of their respective jurisdictions.

For these reasons we vacate the judgment of the Supreme Court of Minnesota and remand the cause to that court for further proceedings.

Judgment vacated.

MR. CHIEF JUSTICE HUGHES, dissenting:

I think that sound principle governing the exercise of our jurisdiction requires the dismissal of the writ. I see no reason to doubt that the Supreme Court of Minnesota held that the tax in question was laid in violation of the uniformity clause of the State Constitution. Not only is that shown, as it seems to me, from the court's discussion of that question, but it conclusively appears from the syllabus which definitely states that the tax is "violative of art. 9, § 1, of our state constitution." Minnesota requires that in all cases decided by the Supreme Court it shall give its decision in writing, "together with headnotes, briefly stating the points decided." In obedience to the statute, the court has thus given explicitly in its syllabus its own deliberate construction of what it has decided.

The decision thus rested upon an adequate non-federal ground and in accordance with long-established doctrine we are without jurisdiction.

This is not a case where the record leaves us in uncertainty as to what has actually been determined by the state court. Nor have there been supervening changes since the entry of the judgment. I find no warrant for vacating the judgment on either of these grounds.

The fact that provisions of the state and federal constitutions may be similar or even identical does not justify us in disturbing a judgment of a state court which adequately rests upon its application of the provision of its own constitution. That the state court may be influenced by the reasoning of our opinions makes no difference. The state court may be persuaded by majority opinions in this Court or it may prefer the reasoning of dissenting judges, but the judgment of the state court upon the application of its own constitution remains a judgment which we are without jurisdiction to review. Whether in this case we thought that the state tax was repugnant to the federal constitution or consistent with it, the judgment of the state court that the tax violated the state constitution would still stand. It cannot be supposed that the Supreme Court of Minnesota is not fully conscious of its independent authority to construe the constitution of the State, whatever reasons it may adduce in so doing. As the Minnesota court said in [another case], after referring to the question presented under the federal constitution, "Our interpretation of our own constitution is of course final."

The disposition of this case is directly within our recent and unanimous ruling in *New York City v. Central Savings Bank.* In that case, the Court of Appeals of New York had decided that a state statute was repugnant to the due process clause of the state constitution, that clause being the same as the due process clause of the Fourteenth Amendment which the court held had also been violated. We declined jurisdiction upon the ground that the judgment of the state court in applying the state constitution rested upon an adequate non-federal ground, despite the reliance upon our decisions.

Questions

Are *Prouse* and *National Tea* distinguishable? How do the federal and state constitutional provisions compare to each other in each case? Are they more similar in one case than in the other? In which case is the Court better able to determine whether the state court based its ruling on an adequate and independent state ground? How does the answer to that question help to explain the different outcomes?

MICHIGAN v. LONG

Supreme Court of the United States, 1983.
463 U.S. 1032, 103 S.Ct. 3469, 77 L.Ed.2d 1201.

JUSTICE O'CONNOR delivered the opinion of the Court.

In *Terry v. Ohio* we upheld the validity of a protective search for weapons in the absence of probable cause to arrest because it is unreasonable to deny a police officer the right "to neutralize the threat of physical harm," when he possesses an articulable suspicion that an individual is armed and dangerous. We did not, however, expressly address whether such a protective search for weapons could extend to an area beyond the person in the absence of probable cause to arrest. In the present case, respondent David Long was convicted for possession of marihuana found by police in the passenger compartment and trunk of the automobile that he was driving. The police searched the passenger compartment because they had reason to believe that the vehicle contained weapons potentially dangerous to the officers. We hold that the protective search of the passenger compartment was reasonable under the principles articulated in *Terry* and other decisions of this Court. We also examine Long's argument that the decision below rests upon an adequate and independent state ground, and we decide in favor of our jurisdiction.

* * *

II

Before reaching the merits, we must consider Long's argument that we are without jurisdiction to decide this case because the decision below rests on an adequate and independent state ground. The court below referred twice to the State Constitution in its opinion, but otherwise relied exclusively on federal law.[3] Long argues that the Michigan courts have provided greater protection from searches and seizures under the State Constitution than is afforded under the Fourth Amendment, and

---

[3] On the first occasion, the court merely cited in a footnote both the State and Federal Constitutions. On the second occasion, at the conclusion of the opinion, the court stated: "We hold, therefore, that the deputies' search of the vehicle was proscribed by the Fourth Amendment to the United States Constitution and art. 1, § 11 of the Michigan Constitution."

the references to the State Constitution therefore establish an adequate and independent ground for the decision below.

It is, of course, "incumbent upon this Court * * * to ascertain for itself * * * whether the asserted non-federal ground independently and adequately supports the judgment." *Abie State Bank v. Bryan* (1931). Although we have announced a number of principles in order to help us determine whether various forms of references to state law constitute adequate and independent state grounds,[4] we openly admit that we have thus far not developed a satisfying and consistent approach for resolving this vexing issue. In some instances, we have taken the strict view that if the ground of decision was at all unclear, we would dismiss the case. In other instances, we have vacated or continued a case in order to obtain clarification about the nature of a state court decision. In more recent cases, we have ourselves examined state law to determine whether state courts have used federal law to guide their application of state law or to provide the actual basis for the decision that was reached. In *Oregon v. Kennedy,* we rejected an invitation to remand to the state court for clarification even when the decision rested in part on a case from the state court, because we determined that the state case itself rested upon federal grounds. We added that "[e]ven if the case admitted of more doubt as to whether federal and state grounds for decision were intermixed, the fact that the state court relied to the extent it did on federal grounds requires us to reach the merits."

This *ad hoc* method of dealing with cases that involve possible adequate and independent state grounds is antithetical to the doctrinal consistency that is required when sensitive issues of federal-state relations are involved. Moreover, none of the various methods of disposition that we have employed thus far recommends itself as the preferred method that we should apply to the exclusion of others, and we therefore determine that it is appropriate to reexamine our treatment of this jurisdictional issue in order to achieve the consistency that is necessary.

The process of examining state law is unsatisfactory because it requires us to interpret state laws with which we are generally unfamiliar, and which often, as in this case, have not been discussed at length by the

---

[4] For example, we have long recognized that "where the judgment of a state court rests upon two grounds, one of which is federal and the other non-federal in character, our jurisdiction fails if the non-federal ground is independent of the federal ground and adequate to support the judgment." We may review a state case decided on a federal ground even if it is clear that there was an available state ground for decision on which the state court could properly have relied. Also, if, in our view, the state court " 'felt compelled by what it understood to be federal constitutional considerations to construe * * * its own law in the manner it did,' " then we will not treat a normally adequate state ground as independent, and there will be no question about our jurisdiction.

Finally, "where the non-federal ground is so interwoven with the [federal ground] as not to be an independent matter, or is not of sufficient breadth to sustain the judgment without any decision of the other, our jurisdiction is plain."

parties. Vacation and continuance for clarification have also been unsatisfactory both because of the delay and decrease in efficiency of judicial administration,[5] and, more important, because these methods of disposition place significant burdens on state courts to demonstrate the presence or absence of our jurisdiction. Finally, outright dismissal of cases is clearly not a panacea because it cannot be doubted that there is an important need for uniformity in federal law, and that this need goes unsatisfied when we fail to review an opinion that rests primarily upon federal grounds and where the independence of an alleged state ground is not apparent from the four corners of the opinion. We have long recognized that dismissal is inappropriate "where there is strong indication * * * that the federal constitution as judicially construed controlled the decision below."

Respect for the independence of state courts, as well as avoidance of rendering advisory opinions, have been the cornerstones of this Court's refusal to decide cases where there is an adequate and independent state ground. It is precisely because of this respect for state courts, and this desire to avoid advisory opinions, that we do not wish to continue to decide issues of state law that go beyond the opinion that we review, or to require state courts to reconsider cases to clarify the grounds of their decisions. Accordingly, when, as in this case, a state court decision fairly appears to rest primarily on federal law, or to be interwoven with the federal law, and when the adequacy and independence of any possible state law ground is not clear from the face of the opinion, we will accept as the most reasonable explanation that the state court decided the case the way it did because it believed that federal law required it to do so. If a state court chooses merely to rely on federal precedents as it would on the precedents of all other jurisdictions, then it need only make clear by a plain statement in its judgment or opinion that the federal cases are being used only for the purpose of guidance, and do not themselves compel the result that the court has reached. In this way, both justice and judicial administration will be greatly improved. If the state court decision indicates clearly and expressly that it is alternatively based on bona fide separate, adequate, and independent grounds, we, of course, will not undertake to review the decision.

This approach obviates in most instances the need to examine state law in order to decide the nature of the state court decision, and will at the same time avoid the danger of our rendering advisory opinions.[6] It

---

[5] Indeed, *Dixon v. Duffy* is also illustrative of another difficulty involved in our requiring state courts to reconsider their decisions for purposes of clarification. In *Dixon*, we continued the case on two occasions in order to obtain clarification, but none was forthcoming: "[T]he California court advised petitioner's counsel informally that it doubted its jurisdiction to render such a determination." We then vacated the judgment of the state court, and remanded.

[6] There may be certain circumstances in which clarification is necessary or desirable, and we will not be foreclosed from taking the appropriate action.

also avoids the unsatisfactory and intrusive practice of requiring state courts to clarify their decisions to the satisfaction of this Court. We believe that such an approach will provide state judges with a clearer opportunity to develop state jurisprudence unimpeded by federal interference, and yet will preserve the integrity of federal law. "It is fundamental that state courts be left free and unfettered by us in interpreting their state constitutions. But it is equally important that ambiguous or obscure adjudications by state courts do not stand as barriers to a determination by this Court of the validity under the federal constitution of state action."

The principle that we will not review judgments of state courts that rest on adequate and independent state grounds is based, in part, on "the limitations of our own jurisdiction."[7] The jurisdictional concern is that we not "render an advisory opinion, and if the same judgment would be rendered by the state court after we corrected its views of federal laws, our review could amount to nothing more than an advisory opinion." Our requirement of a "plain statement" that a decision rests upon adequate and independent state grounds does not in any way authorize the rendering of advisory opinions. Rather, in determining, as we must, whether we have jurisdiction to review a case that is alleged to rest on adequate and independent state grounds, we merely assume that there are no such grounds when it is not clear from the opinion itself that the state court relied upon an adequate and independent state ground and when it fairly appears that the state court rested its decision primarily on federal law.[8]

---

[7] In *Herb v. Pitcairn,* the Court also wrote that it was desirable that state courts "be asked rather than told what they have intended." It is clear that we have already departed from that view in those cases in which we have examined state law to determine whether a particular result was guided or compelled by federal law. Our decision today departs further from *Herb* insofar as we disfavor further requests to state courts for clarification, and we require a clear and express statement that a decision rests on adequate and independent state grounds. However, the "plain statement" rule protects the integrity of state courts for the reasons discussed above. The preference for clarification expressed in *Herb* has failed to be a completely satisfactory means of protecting the state and federal interests that are involved.

[8] It is not unusual for us to employ certain presumptions in deciding jurisdictional issues. For instance, although the petitioner bears the burden of establishing our jurisdiction, we have held that the party who alleges that a controversy before us has become moot has the "heavy burden" of establishing that we lack jurisdiction. That is, we presume in those circumstances that we have jurisdiction until some party establishes that we do not for reasons of mootness.

We also note that the rule that we announce today was foreshadowed by our opinions in Delaware v. Prouse, 440 U.S. 648 (1979), and Zacchini v. Scripps-Howard Broadcasting Co., 433 U.S. 562 (1977). In these cases, the state courts relied on both state and federal law. We determined that we had jurisdiction to decide the cases because our reading of the opinions led us to conclude that each court "felt compelled by what it understood to be federal constitutional considerations to construe and apply its own law in the manner it did." In *Delaware,* we referred to prior state decisions that confirmed our understanding of the opinion in that case, but our primary focus was on the face of the opinion. In *Zacchini,* we relied entirely on the syllabus and opinion of the state court.

Our review of the decision below under this framework leaves us unconvinced that it rests upon an independent state ground. Apart from its two citations to the State Constitution, the court below relied exclusively on its understanding of *Terry* and other federal cases. Not a single state case was cited to support the state court's holding that the search of the passenger compartment was unconstitutional.[9] Indeed, the court declared that the search in this case was unconstitutional because "[t]he Court of Appeals erroneously applied the principles of *Terry v. Ohio* * * * to the search of the interior of the vehicle in this case." The references to the State Constitution in no way indicate that the decision below rested on grounds in any way independent from the state court's interpretation of federal law. Even if we accept that the Michigan Constitution has been interpreted to provide independent protection for certain rights also secured under the Fourth Amendment, it fairly appears in this case that the Michigan Supreme Court rested its decision primarily on federal law.

Rather than dismissing the case, or requiring that the state court reconsider its decision on our behalf solely because of a mere possibility that an adequate and independent ground supports the judgment, we find that we have jurisdiction in the absence of a plain statement that the decision below rested on an adequate and independent state ground. It appears to us that the state court "felt compelled by what it understood to be federal constitutional considerations to construe * * * its own law in the manner it did." *Zacchini v. Scripps-Howard Broadcasting Co.*[10]

In dissent, Justice Stevens proposes the novel view that this Court should never review a state court decision unless the Court wishes to vindicate a federal right that has been endangered. The rationale of the dissent is not restricted to cases where the decision is arguably supported by adequate and independent state grounds. Rather, Justice Stevens appears to believe that even if the decision below rests exclusively on federal grounds, this Court should not review the decision as long as there is no federal right that is endangered.

The state courts handle the vast bulk of all criminal litigation in this country. In 1982, more than 12 million criminal actions (excluding juvenile and traffic charges) were filed in the 50 state court systems and the District of Columbia. By comparison, approximately 32,700 criminal suits were filed in federal courts during that same year. The state courts are required to apply federal constitutional standards, and they necessarily create a considerable body of "federal law" in the process. It is not surprising that this Court has become more interested in the application and development of federal law by state courts in the light of the recent significant expansion of federally created standards that we have imposed on the States.

[9] At oral argument, Long argued that the state court relied on its decision in *People v. Reed*. However, the court cited that case only in the context of a statement that the State did not seek to justify the search in this case "by reference to other exceptions to the warrant requirement." The court then noted that *Reed* held that " '[a] warrantless search and seizure is unreasonable *per se* and violates the Fourth Amendment of the United States Constitution and Art. 1, § 11 of the state constitution unless shown to be within one of the exceptions to the rule.' "

[10] There is nothing unfair about requiring a plain statement of an independent state ground in this case. Even if we were to rest our decision on an evaluation of the state law relevant to Long's claim, as we have sometimes done in the past, our understanding of

* * *

[The Court's discussion of the merits of the Fourth Amendment issue is omitted. The majority ruled that the police conduct in this case did not violate Long's Fourth Amendment rights.]

V

The judgment of the Michigan Supreme Court is reversed, and the case is remanded for further proceedings not inconsistent with this opinion.

It is so ordered.

JUSTICE STEVENS, dissenting.

The jurisprudential questions presented in this case are far more important than the question whether the Michigan police officer's search of respondent's car violated the Fourth Amendment. The case raises profoundly significant questions concerning the relationship between two sovereigns—the State of Michigan and the United States of America.

The Supreme Court of the State of Michigan expressly held "that the deputies' search of the vehicle was proscribed by the Fourth Amendment to the United States Constitution and *art. 1, § 11 of the Michigan Constitution.*" The state law ground is clearly adequate to support the judgment, but the question whether it is independent of the Michigan Supreme Court's understanding of federal law is more difficult. Four possible ways of resolving that question present themselves: (1) asking the

---

Michigan law would also result in our finding that we have jurisdiction to decide this case. Under state search-and-seizure law, a "higher standard" is imposed under art. 1, § 11, of the 1963 Michigan Constitution. If, however, the item seized is, *inter alia,* a "narcotic drug * * * seized by a peace officer outside the curtilage of any dwelling house in this state," art. 1, § 11, of the 1963 Michigan Constitution, then the seizure is governed by a standard identical to that imposed by the Fourth Amendment.

  Long argues that under the current Michigan Comp. Laws § 333.7107 (1979), the definition of a "narcotic" does not include marihuana. The difficulty with this argument is that Long fails to cite any authority for the proposition that the term "narcotic" as used in the Michigan Constitution is dependent on current statutory definitions of that term. Indeed, it appears that just the opposite is true. The Michigan Supreme Court has held that constitutional provisions are presumed "to be interpreted in accordance with existing laws and legal usages of the time" of the passage of the provision. If the state legislature were able to change the interpretation of a constitutional provision by statute, then the legislature would have "the power of outright repeal of a duly-voted constitutional provision." Applying these principles, the Michigan courts have held that a statute passed subsequent to the applicable state constitutional provision is not relevant for interpreting its Constitution, and that a definition in a legislative Act pertains only to that Act. At the time that the 1963 Michigan Constitution was enacted, it is clear that marihuana was considered a narcotic drug. Indeed, it appears that marihuana was considered a narcotic drug in Michigan until 1978, when it was removed from the narcotic classification. We would conclude that the seizure of marihuana in Michigan is not subject to analysis under any "higher standard" than may be imposed on the seizure of other items. In the light of our holding in *Delaware v. Prouse* that an interpretation of state law in our view compelled by federal constitutional considerations is not an independent state ground, we would have jurisdiction to decide the case.

Michigan Supreme Court directly, (2) attempting to infer from all possible sources of state law what the Michigan Supreme Court meant, (3) presuming that adequate state grounds are independent unless it clearly appears otherwise, or (4) presuming that adequate state grounds are not independent unless it clearly appears otherwise. This Court has, on different occasions, employed each of the first three approaches; never until today has it even hinted at the fourth. In order to "achieve the consistency that is necessary," the Court today undertakes a reexamination of all the possibilities. It rejects the first approach as inefficient and unduly burdensome for state courts, and rejects the second approach as an inappropriate expenditure of our resources. Although I find both of those decisions defensible in themselves, I cannot accept the Court's decision to choose the fourth approach over the third—to presume that adequate state grounds are intended to be dependent on federal law unless the record plainly shows otherwise. I must therefore dissent.

If we reject the intermediate approaches, we are left with a choice between two presumptions: one in favor of our taking jurisdiction, and one against it. Historically, the latter presumption has always prevailed. The rule, as succinctly stated in *Lynch,* was as follows: "Where the judgment of the state court rests on two grounds, one involving a federal question and the other not, or if it does not appear upon which to two grounds the judgment was based, and the ground independent of a federal question is sufficient in itself to sustain it, this Court will not take jurisdiction."

The Court today points out that in several cases we have weakened the traditional presumption by using the other two intermediate approaches identified above. Since those two approaches are now to be rejected, however, I would think that *stare decisis* would call for a return to historical principle. Instead, the Court seems to conclude that because some precedents are to be rejected, we must overrule them all.

Even if I agreed with the Court that we are free to consider as a fresh proposition whether we may take presumptive jurisdiction over the decisions of sovereign States, I could not agree that an expansive attitude makes good sense. It appears to be common ground that any rule we adopt should show "respect for state courts, and [a] desire to avoid advisory opinions." And I am confident that all Members of this Court agree that there is a vital interest in the sound management of scarce federal judicial resources. All of those policies counsel against the exercise of federal jurisdiction. They are fortified by my belief that a policy of judicial restraint—one that allows other decisional bodies to have the last word in legal interpretation until it is truly necessary for this Court to intervene—enables this Court to make its most effective contribution to our federal system of government.

The nature of the case before us hardly compels a departure from tradition. These are not cases in which an American citizen has been deprived of a right secured by the United States Constitution or a federal statute. Rather, they are cases in which a state court has upheld a citizen's assertion of a right, finding the citizen to be protected under both federal and state law. The complaining party is an officer of the State itself, who asks us to rule that the state court interpreted federal rights too broadly and "overprotected" the citizen.

Such cases should not be of inherent concern to this Court. The reason may be illuminated by assuming that the events underlying this case had arisen in another country, perhaps the Republic of Finland. If the Finnish police had arrested a Finnish citizen for possession of marihuana, and the Finnish courts had turned him loose, no American would have standing to object. If instead they had arrested an American citizen and acquitted him, we might have been concerned about the arrest but we surely could not have complained about the acquittal, even if the Finnish court had based its decision on its understanding of the United States Constitution. That would be true even if we had a treaty with Finland requiring it to respect the rights of American citizens under the United States Constitution. We would only be motivated to intervene if an American citizen were unfairly arrested, tried, and convicted by the foreign tribunal.

In this case the State of Michigan has arrested one of its citizens and the Michigan Supreme Court has decided to turn him loose. The respondent is a United States citizen as well as a Michigan citizen, but since there is no claim that he has been mistreated by the State of Michigan, the final outcome of the state processes offended no federal interest whatever. Michigan simply provided greater protection to one of its citizens than some other State might provide or, indeed, than this Court might require throughout the country.

I believe that in reviewing the decisions of state courts, the primary role of this Court is to make sure that persons who seek to vindicate federal rights have been fairly heard. That belief resonates with statements in many of our prior cases. In *Abie State Bank v. Bryan,* the Supreme Court of Nebraska had rejected a federal constitutional claim, relying in part on the state law doctrine of laches. Writing for the Court in response to the Nebraska Governor's argument that the Court should not accept jurisdiction because laches provided an independent ground for decision, Chief Justice Hughes concluded that this Court must ascertain for itself whether the asserted nonfederal ground independently and adequately supported the judgment "in order that constitutional guaranties may appropriately be enforced." He relied on [an] opinion in which Justice Holmes had made it clear that the Court engaged in such an inquiry so that it would not "be possible for a State to impose an unconstitutional burden" on a private party. And both [cases] rely on [a case] in which the Court explained its duty to review the findings of fact of a state court "where a Federal right has been denied."

Until recently we had virtually no interest in cases of this type. Thirty years ago, this Court reviewed only one. Indeed, that appears to have been the only case during the entire 1953 Term in which a State even sought review of a decision by its own judiciary. Fifteen years ago, we did not review any such cases, although the total number of requests had mounted to three. Some time during the past decade, perhaps about the time of the 5-to-4 decision in *Zacchini v. Scripps-Howard Broadcasting Co.,* our priorities shifted. The result is a docket swollen with requests by States to reverse judgments that their courts have rendered in favor of their citizens. I am confident that a future Court will recognize the error of this allocation of resources. When that day comes, I think it likely that the Court will also reconsider the propriety of today's expansion of our jurisdiction.

The Court offers only one reason for asserting authority over cases such as the one presented today: "an important need for uniformity in federal law [that] goes unsatisfied when we fail to review an opinion that rests primarily upon federal grounds and where the independence of an alleged state grounds is not apparent from the four corners of the opinion." Of course, the supposed need to "review an opinion" clashes directly with our oft-repeated reminder that "our power is to correct wrong judgments, not to revise opinions." The clash is not merely one of form: the "need for uniformity in federal law" is truly an ungovernable engine. That same need is no less present when it is perfectly clear that a state ground is both independent and adequate. In fact, it is equally present if a state prosecutor announces that he believes a certain policy of non-enforcement is commanded by federal law. Yet we have never claimed jurisdiction to correct such errors, no matter how egregious they may be, and no matter how much they may thwart the desires of the state electorate. We do not sit to expound our understanding of the Constitution to interested listeners in the legal community; we sit to resolve disputes. If it is not apparent that our views would affect the outcome of a particular case, we cannot presume to interfere.[4]

---

[4] In this regard, one of the cases overruled today deserves comment. In *Minnesota v. National Tea Co.,* the Court considered a case much like this one—the Minnesota Supreme Court had concluded that both the Fourteenth Amendment to the United States Constitution and art. 9, § 1, of the Minnesota Constitution prohibited a graduated income tax on chain store income. The state court stated that "th[e] provisions of the Federal and State Constitutions impose identical restrictions upon the legislative power of the state in respect to classification for purposes of taxation," and "then adverted briefly to three of its former decisions which had interpreted" the state provision. It then proceeded to conduct a careful analysis of the Federal Constitution. It could justly be said that the decision rested primarily on federal law. The majority of the Court reasoned as follows:

> Enough has been said to demonstrate that there is considerable uncertainty as to the precise grounds for the decision. That is sufficient reason for us to decline at this time to review the federal question asserted to be present, consistently with the policy of not passing upon questions of a constitutional nature which are not clearly necessary to a decision of the case.

The Court therefore remanded to the state court for clarification.

Finally, I am thoroughly baffled by the Court's suggestion that it must stretch its jurisdiction and reverse the judgment of the Michigan Supreme Court in order to show "[r]espect for the independence of state courts." Would we show respect for the Republic of Finland by convening a special sitting for the sole purpose of declaring that its decision to release an American citizen was based upon a misunderstanding of American law?

I respectfully dissent.

Notes and Questions

1. The majority and the dissent agree that the Supreme Court has applied three different approaches when it is not clear from the face of an opinion whether the state court decision rests on an adequate and independent state ground. The majority, however, in an opinion by Justice O'Connor, rejects the traditional approaches and adopts a new one:

> W]hen * * * "a state court decision fairly appears to rest primarily on federal law * * * and when the adequacy and independence of any possible state law ground is not clear from the face of the opinion, we will accept as the most reasonable explanation that the state court decided the case the way it did because it believed that federal law required it to do so."

Justice O'Connor then asserts that the new standard will "avoid the danger of our rendering advisory opinions." It seems clear, however, that advisory opinions are more likely under the new standard than under any of the traditional approaches. Why?

2. In footnote 6 of the majority opinion, Justice O'Connor holds open the possibility of the Court using the *National Tea* approach to seek clarification in appropriate circumstances. The Court followed this course in *Bush v. Palm Beach County Canvassing Board,* 531 U.S. 70, 121 S.Ct. 471, 148 L.Ed.2d 366 (2000). Then-Governor George Bush sought review in the United States Supreme Court of an order of the Florida Supreme Court in-

---

Today's Court rejects that approach as intruding unduly on the state judicial process. One might therefore expect it to turn to Chief Justice Hughes' dissenting opinion in *National Tea.* In a careful statement of the applicable principles, he made an observation that I find unanswerable:

> The fact that provisions of the state and federal constitutions may be similar or even identical does not justify us in disturbing a judgment of a state court which adequately rests upon its application of the provisions of its own constitution. That the state court may be influenced by the reasoning of our opinions makes no difference. The state court may be persuaded by majority opinions in this Court or it may prefer the reasoning of dissenting judges, but the judgment of the state court upon the application of its own constitution remains a judgment which we are without jurisdiction to review. Whether in this case we thought that the state tax was repugnant to the federal constitution or consistent with it, the judgment of the state court that the tax violated the state constitution would still stand. It cannot be supposed that the Supreme Court of Minnesota is not fully conscious of its independent authority to construe the constitution of the State, whatever reasons it may adduce in so doing.

Sec. C   **INSULATING STATE DECISIONS**   **921**

terpreting Florida election statutes to permit manual recounts of ballots and extending the time in which such recounts could occur beyond the time that the Florida Secretary of State had determined. Bush argued that the Florida decision ran afoul of two federal constitutional provisions. A *per curiam* Court concluded that

> After reviewing the opinion of the Florida Supreme Court, we find "that there is considerable uncertainty as to the precise grounds for the decision." *Minnesota v. National Tea Co.*, 309 U.S. 551, 555, 60 S.Ct. 676, 84 L.Ed. 920 (1940). This is sufficient reason for us to decline at this time to review the federal questions asserted to be present. * * *

> Specifically, we are unclear as to the extent to which the Florida Supreme Court saw the Florida Constitution as circumscribing the legislature's authority under Art. II, § 1, cl. 2. We are also unclear as to the consideration the Florida Supreme Court accorded to 3 U.S.C. § 5. The judgment of the Supreme Court of Florida is therefore vacated, and the case is remanded for further proceedings not inconsistent with this opinion.

Why do you think the Court chose to follow the *National Tea* approach? Does the Court suspect there might be an adequate and independent state ground, or is it just uncertain how the Florida Supreme Court decided the federal law issues or how it gauged the impact of federal law on state law? *Bush v. Palm Beach*'s more famous sibling, *Bush v. Gore*, 531 U.S. U.S. 98, 121 S.Ct. 525, 148 L.Ed.2d 388 (2000), shows the Court was not reluctant to enter this particular political thicket. One hopes that the 2000 federal election dispute is *sui generis*. If so, *Bush v. Palm Beach* may tell us little about whether the *National Tea* approach is staging a comeback.

3. a) Justice O'Connor asserts that the Court itself has the responsibility to determine whether a state judgment rests on an adequate and independent state ground. Is the new *Michigan v. Long* approach adequate to fulfill that responsibility? Are any of the traditional approaches likely to do a better job?

b) Chief Justice Burger, Justice Powell and then-Justice Rehnquist all join Justice O'Connor's opinion. These Justices generally favor narrow construction of federal jurisdictional statutes, yet here they embrace a rule that seems to expand the Supreme Court's jurisdiction. Why do you think they support this expansion?

4. As Justice O'Connor appears to acknowledge, her analytical method requires the Court to presume jurisdiction in unclear cases. Footnote 8 suggests that she realizes there may be some problem with that presumption, which elides the normal burden of the party invoking federal jurisdiction to establish it. *Cf.* Fed.R.Civ.P. 8(a)(1). She argues that presumptions of jurisdiction are not unusual, citing *County of Los Angeles v. Davis*, 440 U.S. 625, 99 S.Ct. 1379, 59 L.Ed.2d 642 (1979), which discussed the burden of a party asserting mootness to establish it. She may, however, read too much into *Davis* in using it as an example of a presumption of jurisdiction. *Davis* said in pertinent part, "jurisdiction, properly acquired, may abate if the case be-

comes moot * * * ." That implies that the party seeking review must establish jurisdiction as a threshold matter, and that the burden of defeating jurisdiction on mootness grounds exists only after the appealing party establishes jurisdiction. That is different from *Long,* where the presumption establishes jurisdiction in the first instance.

5. In *Caldwell v. Mississippi,* 472 U.S. 320, 105 S.Ct. 2633, 86 L.Ed.2d 231 (1985), the Court applied *Long* to a case involving the adequacy and independence of a state procedural ground, presuming in the absence of a clear statement of reliance on state law that federal law drove the state decision. Is the effect of the *Long* presumption the same when the underlying state ground is procedural as when it is substantive? Consider *Herndon v. Georgia* and *Henry v. Mississippi,* at pages 946–972.

6. Justice Stevens asserts there is no federal interest in reviewing cases when state courts may have construed federal rights too broadly.

a) Is he correct, or is Justice O'Connor persuasive that there is some federal interest in avoiding the accumulation of decisions that misapply federal constitutional principles, even those favoring individuals' claims against state governments?

b) Does Justice Stevens's approach raise questions reminiscent of the separation-of-powers view of the *Erie* doctrine about the proper role of the Supreme Court? He seems to engage in some sort of interest analysis or balancing to determine whether to exercise jurisdiction, asserting that where the only danger is overbroad construction of federal rights, the Court ought to decline jurisdiction. Would that be appropriate or an abdication (or nullification) of reviewing power conferred by Congress? Suppose, as Justice O'Connor suggests, a state court decided a criminal case clearly and exclusively on the basis of its perception of federal constitutional law, vacating a conviction in all other respects proper. Does Justice Stevens truly mean the Court lacks jurisdiction to review that decision?

c) Justice Stevens has stuck to his guns on this issue. In *Brigham City v. Stuart,* 547 U.S. 398, ___, 126 S.Ct. 1943, 1949–50, 164 L.Ed.2d 650, 660 (2006) (footnote omitted), he reiterated his *Long* argument regarding the impropriety of the Court taking the case for review:

> This is an odd flyspeck of a case. The charges that have been pending against respondents for the past six years are minor offenses—intoxication, contributing to the delinquency of a minor, and disorderly conduct—two of which could have been proved by evidence that was gathered by the responding officers before they entered the home. The maximum punishment for these crimes ranges between 90 days and 6 months in jail. And the Court's unanimous opinion restating well-settled rules of federal law is so clearly persuasive that it is hard to imagine the outcome was ever in doubt.

> Under these circumstances, the only difficult question is which of the following is the most peculiar: (1) that the Utah trial judge, the intermediate state appellate court, and the Utah Supreme Court all found a Fourth Amendment violation on these facts; (2) that the prose-

cution chose to pursue this matter all the way to the United States Supreme Court; or (3) that this Court voted to grant the petition for a writ of certiorari.

A possible explanation for the first is that the suppression ruling was correct as a matter of Utah law, and neither trial counsel nor the trial judge bothered to identify the Utah Constitution as an independent basis for the decision because they did not expect the prosecution to appeal. The most plausible explanation for the latter two decisions is that they were made so police officers in Utah may enter a home without a warrant when they see ongoing violence—we are, of course, reversing the Utah Supreme Court's conclusion to the contrary. But that purpose, laudable though it may be, cannot be achieved in this case. Our holding today addresses only the limitations placed by the Federal Constitution on the search at issue; we have no authority to decide whether the police in this case violated the Utah Constitution.

The Utah Supreme Court, however, has made clear that the Utah Constitution provides greater protection to the privacy of the home than does the Fourth Amendment. And it complained in this case of respondents' failure to raise or adequately brief a state constitutional challenge, thus preventing the state courts from deciding the case on anything other than Fourth Amendment grounds. "[S]urpris[ed]" by "[t]he reluctance of litigants to take up and develop a state constitutional analysis," the court expressly invited future litigants to bring challenges under the Utah Constitution to enable it to fulfill its "responsibility as guardians of the individual liberty of our citizens" and "undertak[e] a principled exploration of the interplay between federal and state protections of individual rights." The fact that this admonishment and request came from the Utah Supreme Court in this very case not only demonstrates that the prosecution selected the wrong case for establishing the rule it wants, but indicates that the Utah Supreme Court would probably adopt the same rule as a matter of state constitutional law that we reject today under the Federal Constitution.

Whether or not that forecast is accurate, I can see no reason for this Court to cause the Utah courts to redecide the question as a matter of state law. Federal interests are not offended when a single State elects to provide greater protection for its citizens than the Federal Constitution requires.

Does Justice Stevens undermine his own argument with respect to this particular case? He appears to concede that the Utah Supreme Court did not decide *Stuart* on the basis of the Utah Constitution. That being the case, should he concern himself with what that court might have done if Stuart's attorney had argued the case differently? Note that, in contrast to *Long*, this was not a case in which Justice Stevens could have argued for a remand for clarification of the basis for the state court's decision (a procedure that *Long* disapproved anyway), because the ground for the decision was apparent.

In *Kansas v. Marsh*, 548 U.S. 163, 126 S.Ct. 2516, 165 L.Ed.2d 429 (2006), the Kansas Supreme Court had found a part of the capital sentencing statute to be facially unconstitutional under the Eighth and Fourteenth Amendments and had reversed Marsh's capital murder conviction and remanded for a new trial. The Supreme Court reviewed the case (raising finality questions discussed *infra* at page 990) and reversed.

Undeterred by *Stuart* (and *Long*), Justice Stevens continued the battle.

> [T]he State of Kansas petitioned us to review a ruling of its own Supreme Court on the grounds that the Kansas court had granted more protection to a Kansas litigant than the Federal Constitution required. A policy of judicial restraint would allow the highest court of the State to be the final decisionmaker in a case of this kind.

Of course, by phrasing the matter in this way, Justice Stevens also makes clear that the Kansas court granted *less* protection to a Kansas litigant's— the state's—position by its misinterpretation of the Constitution. It seems appropriate at least to wonder whether in *Long*, *Stuart* and *Marsh*, Justice Stevens envisions a "heads I win; tails you lose" situation with respect to states' entitlement to have convictions vacated, if at all, at least by proper interpretation of the invalidating federal standard.

So it seemed to Justice Scalia. "While it might be appropriate for Congress to place such a thumb on the scales of our power to review, it seems to me a peculiar mode of decisionmaking for judges sworn to 'impartially discharge * * * all the duties' of their office." In addition, Justice Scalia identified federalism interests that he felt Justice Stevens's approach overlooked.

> When state courts erroneously invalidate actions taken by the people of a State (through initiative or through normal operation of the political branches of their state government) on *state-law* grounds, it is generally none of our business; and our displacing of those judgments would indeed be an intrusion upon state autonomy. But when state courts erroneously invalidate such actions because they believe federal law requires it—and *especially* when they do so because they believe the Federal *Constitution* requires it—review by this Court, far from *undermining* state autonomy, is the only possible way to *vindicate* it. When a federal constitutional interdict against the duly expressed will of the people of a State is erroneously pronounced by a State's highest court, no authority in the State—not even a referendum agreed to by all its citizens—can undo the error. Thus, a general presumption against such review displays not respect for the States, but a complacent willingness to allow judges to strip the people of the power to govern themselves. When we correct a state court's federal errors, *we return power to the State, and to its people*.

Who has the better side of this debate? Justice Stevens, repeating his own question from an earlier case, asked "what harm would have been done to the administration of justice by state courts if the [Kansas] court had been left undisturbed in its determination[?]" Is he taking the position that misinterpretation of the Constitution that directly determines the result in a case is harmless error?

7. Professor Welsh argues that the Court should not confuse the possible persuasive influence of federal constitutional decisions upon state law with state law's "constitutional dependence" upon the Constitution. Robert Welsh, *Reconsidering the Constitutional Relationship Between State and Federal Courts: A Critique of* Michigan v. Long, 59 NOTRE DAME L.REV. 1118, 1129-30 (1984). Thus, he argues, the fact that state courts may find Supreme Court interpretations persuasive does not permit the inference that the state courts feel constitutionally compelled to follow the federal Constitution's lead. His argument echoes the Oregon Supreme Court:

> This court like others has high respect for the opinions of the Supreme Court, particularly when they provide insight into the origins of provisions common to the state and federal bills of rights rather than only a contemporary "balance" of pragmatic considerations about which reasonable people may differ over time and among the several states. It is therefore to be expected that counsel and courts often will refer to federal decisions, or to commentary based on such decisions, even in debating an undecided issue under state law. Lest there be any doubt about it, when this court cites federal opinions in interpreting a provision of Oregon law, it does so because it finds the views there expressed persuasive, not because it considers itself bound to do so by its understanding of federal doctrines.

State v. Kennedy, 295 Or. 260, 267, 666 P.2d 1316, 1321 (1983). Is there a difference between a state following federal constitutional interpretation when construing its own constitution because the state feels compelled to do so and a state following the federal lead because it recognizes it as good policy? If so, should that make a difference in the way the Court decides cases like *Michigan v. Long* or *Delaware v. Prouse*?

8. a) In what must surely be one of the most famous concurring opinions in Court history, Justice Brandeis set forth his understanding of the Court's obligations when confronted with constitutional questions:

> The Court [has] developed, for its own governance in the cases confessedly within its jurisdiction, a series of rules under which it has avoided passing upon a large part of all the constitutional questions pressed upon it for decision. They are:
>
> * * *
>
> 2. The Court will not "anticipate a question of constitutional law in advance of the necessity of deciding it." "It is not the habit of the court to decide questions of a constitutional nature unless absolutely necessary to a decision of the case." * * *
>
> 4. The Court will not pass upon a constitutional question although properly presented by the record, if there is also present some other ground upon which the case may be disposed of. This rule has found most varied application. Thus, if a case can be decided on either of two grounds, one involving a constitutional question, the other a question

of statutory construction or general law, the Court will decide only the latter. Appeals from the highest court of a state challenging its decision of a question under the Federal Constitution are frequently dismissed because the judgment can be sustained on an independent state ground.

Ashwander v. TVA, 297 U.S. 288, 346-47, 56 S.Ct. 466, 483, 80 L.Ed. 688 (1936) (Brandeis, J., concurring). There the Court confronted a challenge to a federal statute, and separation-of-powers considerations heavily influenced the concurrence. Nonetheless, do not those principles, which the Court cites approvingly in many contexts, suggest some difficulty with the new approach *Long* articulates? Where the grounds of the state court's decision are at least arguably unclear, does the Court risk unnecessary constitutional decisions by proceeding? If so, does the decision to proceed have federalism implications?

b) On the other hand, in cases like *Prouse* or *Long*, the state court has already made a constitutional decision that is necessary to resolve the controversy. Assuming *arguendo* that the *Ashwander* principles apply to Supreme Court review of state court decisions, do they apply with equal force when declining jurisdiction merely substitutes a state constitutional decision for a federal one? In another context, the federal courts have not held back. The doctrine of *Railroad Commission v. Pullman Co.*, 312 U.S. 496, 61 S.Ct. 643, 85 L.Ed. 971 (1941) (at pages 774-785), requires federal courts to abstain from deciding a federal constitutional challenge to a state statute if construing the statute may obviate or substantially modify the constitutional issue. Nonetheless, the Court has held that abstention is inappropriate in favor of a state constitutional provision that mirrors the federal provision. *See, e.g., Wisconsin v. Constantineau*, 400 U.S. 433, 91 S.Ct. 507, 27 L.Ed.2d 515 (1971); *Zwickler v. Koota*, 389 U.S. 241, 88 S.Ct. 391, 19 L.Ed.2d 444 (1967). Perhaps the Court's willingness to proceed with federal constitutional adjudication supports Justice O'Connor's position that the state courts should have the burden of stating clearly their reliance on state constitutional grounds.

b. Limits: Of State Incorporation of Federal and Federal Incorporation of State Law

STANDARD OIL v. JOHNSON
Supreme Court of the United States, 1942.
316 U.S. 481, 62 S.Ct. 1168, 86 L.Ed. 1611.

MR. JUSTICE BLACK delivered the opinion of the Court.

The California Motor Vehicle Fuel License Tax Act imposes a license tax, measured by gallonage, on the privilege of distributing any motor vehicle fuel. Section 10 states that the Act is inapplicable "to any motor vehicle fuel sold to the government of the United States or any department thereof for official use of said government." The appellant, a "distributor" within the meaning of the Act, sold gasoline to the United States Army Post Exchanges in California. The State levied a tax, and the appellant paid it under protest. The appellant then filed this suit in the Superior Court of Sacramento County seeking to recover the payment on two grounds: (1) that sales to the Exchanges were exempt from tax under § 10; (2) that, if construed and applied to require payment of the tax on such sales, the Act would impose a burden upon instrumentalities or agencies of the United States contrary to the Federal Constitution. Holding against the appellant on both grounds, the trial court rendered judgment for the State. The Supreme Court of California affirmed * * * . Since validity of the state statute as construed was drawn in question on the ground of its being repugnant to the Constitution, we think the case is properly here on appeal under § 237(a) of the Judicial Code.

Since § 10 of the California Act made the tax inapplicable "to any motor vehicle fuel sold to the government of the United States or any department thereof," it was necessary for the Supreme Court of California to determine whether the language of this exemption included sales to post exchanges. If the court's construction of § 10 of the Act had been based purely on local law, this construction would have been conclusive, and we should have to determine whether the statute so construed and applied is repugnant to the Federal Constitution. But in deciding that post exchanges were not "the government of the United States or any department thereof," the court did not rely upon the law of California. On the contrary, it relied upon its determination concerning the relationship between post exchanges and the Government of the United States, a relationship which is controlled by federal law. For post exchanges operate under regulations of the Secretary of War pursuant to federal authority. These regulations and the practices under them establish the relationship between the post exchange and the United States Government, and together with the relevant statutory and constitutional provisions from which they derive, afford the data upon which the legal status of the post exchange may be determined. It was upon a determination of a federal question, therefore, that the Supreme Court of California rested its conclusion that, by § 10, sales to post exchanges were not exempted from the tax. Since this determination of a federal question was by a state court, we are not bound by it. We proceed to consider whether it is correct.

On July 25, 1895, the Secretary of War, under authority of Congressional enactments promulgated regulations providing for the establishment of post exchanges. These regulations have since been amended from time to time and the exchange has become a regular feature of Army posts. That the establishment and control of post exchanges have been in accordance with regulations rather than specific statutory directions does not alter their status, for authorized War Department regulations have the force of law.

Congressional recognition that the activities of post exchanges are governmental has been frequent. Since 1903, Congress has repeatedly made substantial appropriations to be expended under the direction of the Secretary of War for construction, equipment, and maintenance of suitable buildings for post exchanges. In 1933 and 1934, Congress ordered certain moneys derived from disbanded exchanges to be handed over to the Federal Treasury. And in 1936, Congress gave consent to state taxation of gasoline sold by or through post exchanges, when the gasoline was not for the exclusive use of the United States.

The commanding officer of an Army Post, subject to the regulations and the commands of his own superior officers, has complete authority to establish and maintain an exchange. He details a post exchange officer to manage its affairs. This officer and the commanding officers of the various company units make up a council which supervises exchange activities. None of these officers receives any compensation other than his regular salary. The object of the exchanges is to provide convenient and reliable sources where soldiers can obtain their ordinary needs at the lowest possible prices. Soldiers, their families, and civilians employed on military posts here and abroad can buy at exchanges. The Government assumes none of the financial obligations of the exchange. But government officers, under government regulations, handle and are responsible for all funds of the exchange which are obtained from the companies or detachments composing its membership. Profits, if any, do not go to individuals. They are used to improve the soldiers' mess, to provide various types of recreation, and in general to add to the pleasure and comfort of the troops.

From all of this, we conclude that post exchanges as now operated are arms of the Government deemed by it essential for the performance of governmental functions. They are integral parts of the War Department, share in fulfilling the duties entrusted to it, and partake of whatever immunities it may have under the Constitution and federal statutes. In concluding otherwise, the Supreme Court of California was in error.

Whether the California Supreme Court would have construed the Motor Vehicle Fuel License Act as applicable to post exchanges if it had decided the issue of legal status of post exchanges in accordance with this opinion, we have no way of knowing. Hence, a determination here of the constitutionality of such an application of the Act is not called for by the state of the record. Accordingly, we reverse the judgment and remand the cause to the court below for further proceedings not inconsistent with this opinion.

Reversed.

Notes and Questions

1. By structuring the inquiry as it does, the Court manages to avoid adjudicating the constitutionality of the California statute. Are there other values served by the Court's review of California's understanding of the federal law incorporated into the state statute?

2. Suppose California interpreted federal law too broadly. Should the Supreme Court still review, or should it adopt Justice Stevens's philosophy from *Michigan v. Long* that the federal government has no need to limit an overbroad deference to federal interests, real or imaginary?

3. Reread Note 2 following *Michigan v. Long*, at page 920. In discussing its power to review the Florida decision, the Court said:

> As a general rule, this Court defers to a state court's interpretation of a state statute. But in the case of a law enacted by a state legislature applicable not only to elections to state offices, but also to the selection of Presidential electors, the legislature is not acting solely under the authority given it by the people of the State, but by virtue of a direct grant of authority made under Art. II, § 1, cl. 2, of the United States Constitution.

As an aside, is the Court entirely accurate in characterizing its normal approach as "deferring" to state courts? *Murdock v. Memphis* appears to stand for the proposition that on appeals from state courts, those courts speak with final authority on the *meaning* of state law, and the Supreme Court is without power to review such determinations except for constitutional infirmity. Is the Court suggesting that its deference is a matter of policy more than of jurisdiction? As in *Standard Oil v. Johnson*, since the proper interpretation of state law depended on the meaning of federal law incorporated in federal law, either explicitly or by necessary implication, the Supreme Court had authority to review the federal issues.

4. *Reconstruction Finance Corporation v. Beaver County*, 328 U.S. 204, 66 S.Ct. 992, 90 L.Ed. 1172 (1946), presented the converse of *Standard Oil*. The County taxed machinery in a defense plant RFC, a federal corporation, operated. A federal statute prohibited state taxation of the corporation's personal property but did not define personal property, leaving state definitions to fill the vacuum. The Pennsylvania Supreme Court upheld the tax on the theory that the machinery was real, not personal, property.

The United States Supreme Court affirmed, accepting Pennsylvania's definition of personal property. Notice the importance of the *Erie* choice-of-law question. Congress used the term "real property" but did not define it. This implicitly raised the question of whether state or federal law should give content to the term. The Court reasoned that Congress knew and intended that state definitions would apply. (Is it likely that Congress even thought about this sort of problem?) The Court, however, did not give the states *carte blanche;* it held that the state rules could be adopted as the content of federal common law as long as the state law did not discriminate against the federal government (which presumably would take the matter outside of the intent of Congress) or patently run counter to the federal Act.

Reconstruction Finance is important as a matter of federal common law, but it also significant for Supreme Court review. Ordinarily, state courts speak with final authority (*ex cathedra*) on matters of state law; thus the Supreme Court cannot review. *Reconstruction Finance* cautions that when state law has been adopted as federal common law, state-court authoritativeness is compromised, though not discarded entirely.

Thus, in *Standard Oil,* the federal government gets the last word on federal law incorporated in state law, and, in *Reconstruction Finance,* the states usually, but not always, get the last word on state law incorporated in federal law. This arrangement is not quite symmetrical; there are no conditions on the federal government's ability to impose its own view of federal law used by the states. What accounts for the asymmetry?

c. Limits: Supreme Court Review of Findings of Fact

WARD v. BOARD OF COUNTY COMMISSIONERS
Supreme Court of the United States, 1920.
253 U.S. 17, 40 S.Ct. 419, 64 L.Ed. 751.

MR. JUSTICE VAN DEVANTER delivered the opinion of the Court.

This is a proceeding by and on behalf of Coleman J. Ward and sixty-six other Indians to recover moneys alleged to have been coercively collected from them by Love County, Oklahoma, as taxes on their allotments, which under the laws and Constitution of the United States were nontaxable. The county commissioners disallowed the claim and the claimants appealed to the district court of the county. There the claimants' petition was challenged by a demurrer, which was overruled and the county elected not to plead further. A judgment for the claimants followed, and this was reversed by the Supreme Court. The case is here on writ of certiorari.

The claimants, who were members of the Choctaw Tribe and wards of the United States, received their allotments out of the tribal domain under a congressional enactment of 1898, which subjected the right of alienation to certain restrictions and provided that "the lands allotted shall be nontaxable while the title remains in the original allottee, but not to exceed twenty-one years from date of patent." * * * In the act of 1906, enabling Oklahoma to become a state, Congress made it plain that no impairment of the rights of property pertaining to the Indians was intended, * * * and the state included in its Constitution a provision exempting from taxation "such property as may be exempt by reason of treaty stipulations, existing between the Indians and the United States government, or by federal laws, during the force and effect of such treaties or federal laws." * * * Afterwards Congress, by an act of 1908, removed the restrictions on alienation as to certain classes of allottees, including the present claimants, and declared that all land from which the restrictions were removed "shall be subject to taxation, * * * as though it were the property of other persons than allottees."

Following the last enactment the officers of Love and other counties began to tax the allotted lands from which restrictions on alienation were removed, and this met with pronounced opposition on the part of the Indian allottees, who insisted, as they had been advised, that the tax exemption was a vested property right which could not be abrogated or destroyed consistently with the Constitution of the United States. Suits were begun in the state courts to maintain the exemption and enjoin the threatened taxation, one of the suits being prosecuted by some 8,000 allottees against the officers of Love and other counties. The suits were resisted, and the state courts, being of opinion that the exemption had been repealed by Congress, sustained the power to tax. The cases were then brought here, and this court held that the exemption was a vested property right which Congress could not repeal consistently with the Fifth Amendment, that it was binding on the taxing authorities in Oklahoma, and that the state courts had erred in refusing to enjoin them from taxing the lands.

While those suits were pending the officers of Love County, with full knowledge of the suits, and being defendants in one, proceeded with the taxation of the allotments, demanded of these claimants that the taxes on their lands be paid to the county, threatened to advertise and sell the lands unless the taxes were paid, did advertise and sell other lands similarly situated, and caused these claimants to believe that their lands would be sold if the taxes were not paid. So, to prevent such a sale and to avoid the imposition of a penalty of eighteen per cent., for which the local statute provided, these claimants paid the taxes. They protested and objected at the time that the taxes were invalid, and the county officers knew that all the allottees were pressing the objection in the pending suits.

As a conclusion from these facts the claimants asserted that the taxes were collected by Love County by coercive means, that their collection was in violation of a right arising out of a law of Congress and protected by the Constitution of the United States, and that the county was accordingly bound to repay the moneys thus collected. The total amount claimed is $7,833.35, aside from interest.

* * *

In reversing the judgment which the district court had given for the claimants the [state] Supreme Court held, first, that the taxes were not collected by coercive means, but were paid voluntarily, and could not be recovered back as there as there was no statutory authority therefor; and, secondly, that there was no statute making the county liable for taxes collected and then paid over to the state and municipal bodies other than the county—which it was assumed was true of a portion of these taxes—and that the petition did not show how much of the taxes was retained by the county, or how much paid over to the state and other municipal bodies, and therefore it could not be the basis of any judgment against the county.

The county challenges our jurisdiction by a motion to dismiss the writ of certiorari and by way of supporting the motion insists that the Supreme Court put its judgment entirely on independent nonfederal grounds which were broad enough to sustain the judgment.

As these claimants had not disposed of their allotments and twenty-one years had not elapsed since the date of the patents, it is certain that the lands were nontaxable. This was settled in *Choate v. Trapp,* and the other cases decided with it; and it also was settled in those cases that the exemption was a vested property right arising out of a law of Congress and protected by the Constitution of the United States. This being so, the state and all its agencies and political subdivisions were bound to give effect to the exemption. It operated as a direct restraint on Love County, no matter what was said in local statutes. The county did not respect it, but, on the contrary, assessed the lands allotted to these claimants, placed them on the county tax roll, and there charged them with taxes like other property. If a portion of the taxes was to go to the state and other municipal bodies after collection—which we assume was the case—it still was the county that charged the taxes against these lands and proceeded to collect them. Payment of all the taxes was demanded by the county, and all were paid to it in the circumstances already narrated.

We accept so much of the [state] Supreme Court's decision as held that, if the payment was voluntary, the moneys could not be recovered back in the absence of a permissive statute, and that there was no such statute. But we are unable to accept its decision in other respects.

The right to the exemption was a federal right, and was specially set up and claimed as such in the petition. Whether the right was denied, or not given due recognition, by the Supreme Court is a question as to which the claimants were entitled to invoke our judgment, and this they have done in the appropriate way. It therefore is within our province to inquire not only whether the right was denied in express terms, but also whether it was denied in substance and effect, as by putting forward nonfederal grounds of decision that were without any fair or substantial support. Of course, if nonfederal grounds, plainly untenable, may be thus put forward successfully, our power to review easily may be avoided. With this qualification, it is true that a judgment of a state court, which is put on independent nonfederal grounds broad enough to sustain it, cannot be reviewed by us. But the qualification is a material one and cannot be disregarded without neglecting or renouncing a jurisdiction conferred by law and designed to protect and maintain the supremacy of the Constitution and the laws made in pursuance thereof.

The facts set forth in the petition, all of which were admitted by the demurrer whereon the county elected to stand, make it plain, as we think, that the finding or decision that the taxes were paid voluntarily was without any fair or substantial support. The claimants were Indians just emerging from a state of dependency and wardship. Through the pending suits and otherwise they were objecting and protesting that the taxation of their lands was forbidden by a law of Congress. But, notwithstanding this, the county demanded that the taxes be paid, and by threatening to sell the lands of these claimants and actually selling other lands similarly situated made it appear to the claimants that they must choose between paying the taxes and losing their lands. To prevent a sale and to avoid the imposition of a penalty of eighteen per cent. they yielded to the county's demand and paid the taxes, protesting and objecting at the time that the same were illegal. The moneys thus collected were obtained by coercive means—by compulsion. The county and its officers reasonably could not have regarded it otherwise; much less the Indian claimants. * * *

As the payment was not voluntary, but made under compulsion, no statutory authority was essential to enable or require the county to refund the money. It is a well-settled rule that "money got through imposition" may be recovered back; and, as this court has said on several occasions, "the obligation to do justice rests upon all persons, natural and artificial, and if a county obtains the money or property of others without authority, the law, independent of any statute, will compel restitution or compensation." To say that the county could collect these unlawful taxes by coercive means and not incur any obligation to pay them back is nothing short of saying that it could take or appropriate the property of these Indian allottees arbitrarily and without due process of law. Of course this would be in contravention of the Fourteenth Amendment * * * .

If it be true, as the [state] Supreme Court assumed, that a portion of the taxes was paid over, after collection, to the state and other municipal bodies, we regard it as certain that this did not alter the county's liability to the claimants. The county had no right to collect the money, and it took the same with notice that the rights of all who were to share in the taxes were disputed by these claimants and were being contested in the pending suits. In these circumstances it could not lessen its liability by paying over a portion of the money to others whose rights it knew were disputed and were no better than its own. * * * In legal contemplation it received the money for the use and benefit of the claimants and should respond to them accordingly.

* * *

Motion to dismiss denied.

Judgment reversed.

Notes and Questions

1. How much latitude should the Supreme Court have to ignore state court findings? Is it enough for the Court merely to disagree about the inferences to be made from the record, or must the Court be willing to rule that the state courts' findings were, in effect, a sham designed to circumvent Supreme Court review?

2. With respect to the standard of review, consider *Thompson v. City of Louisville,* 362 U.S. 199, 80 S.Ct. 624, 4 L.Ed.2d 654 (1960). The Court reversed the defendant's conviction for disorderly conduct and loitering on the ground that the conviction was "so totally devoid of evidentiary support as to

render [it] unconstitutional * * * ." Does *Ward* adopt the same standard? The *Thompson* Court insisted that the case was not one of evidentiary insufficiency, but instead involved whether there was any evidence at all to support the conviction. Should one view *Ward* differently because it involves only the question of whether the tax payments were made "voluntarily"? *Thompson* was a due process case, not involving Supreme Court review of a purportedly adequate and independent state ground. Should the difference in characterization determine the standard applied?

3. Note that this area magnifies the federalism problems inherent in Supreme Court review of state court decisions. It is one thing for the Court to reverse a state decision because the state courts misapprehend the meaning or application of federal law to a complex matter; it is quite another for the Court to tell the state court that it did not realistically evaluate the facts. Should the Court do that? If so, what standards should govern when the practice is permissible? Bear in mind the obvious desirability of keeping overt clashes between state and federal courts to a minimum. If not, what can be done about a state court decision that, while careful, is manifestly disingenuous?

FISKE v. KANSAS
Supreme Court of the United States, 1927.
274 U.S. 380, 47 S.Ct. 655, 71 L.Ed. 1108.

MR. JUSTICE SANFORD delivered the opinion of the Court.

The plaintiff in error was tried and convicted in the District Court of Rice County, Kansas, upon an information charging him with violating the Criminal Syndicalism Act of that State * * * . The judgment was affirmed by the Supreme Court of the State, * * *; and this writ of error was allowed by the Chief Justice of that court.

The only substantial Federal question presented to and decided by the State court, and which may therefore be re-examined by this Court, is whether the Syndicalism Act as applied in this case is repugnant to the due process clause of the Fourteenth Amendment.

The relevant provisions of the Act are:

> Section 1. "Criminal syndicalism" is hereby defined to be the doctrine which advocates crime, physical violence, arson, destruction of property, sabotage, or other unlawful acts or methods, as a means of accomplishing or effecting industrial or political ends, or as a means of effecting industrial or political revolution, or for profit. * * *

> Sec. 3. Any person who, by word of mouth, or writing, advocates, affirmatively suggests or teaches the duty, necessity, propriety or expediency of crime, criminal syndicalism, or sabotage, * * * is guilty of a felony. * * *

The information charged that the defendant did

by word of mouth and by publicly displaying and circulating certain books and pamphlets and written and printed matter, advocate, affirmatively suggest and teach the duty, necessity, propriety and expediency of crime, criminal syndicalism, and sabotage by * * * knowingly and feloniously persuading, inducing and securing [certain persons] to sign an application for membership in * * * and by issuing to [them] membership cards [in a certain Workers' Industrial Union,] a branch of and component part of the Industrial Workers of the World organization, said defendant then and there knowing that said organization unlawfully teaches, advocates and affirmatively suggests:

That the working class and the employing class have nothing in common, and that there can be no peace so long as hunger and want are found among millions of working people and the few who make up the employing class have all the good things of life. [And that] Between these two classes a struggle must go on until the workers of the World organize as a class, take possession of the earth and the machinery of production and abolish the wage system. [And that]: Instead of the conservative motto, "A fair day's wages for a fair day's work," we must inscribe on our banner the revolutionary watchword, "Abolition of the wage system." By organizing industrially we are forming the structure of the new society within the shell of the old.

The defendant moved to quash the information as insufficient, for the reason, among others, that it failed to specify the character of the organization in which he was alleged to have secured members. This was overruled.

On the trial the State offered no evidence as to the doctrines advocated, suggested or taught by the Industrial Workers of the World organization other than a copy of the preamble to the constitution of that organization containing the language set forth and quoted in the information. The defendant, who testified in his own behalf, stated that he was a member of that organization and understood what it taught; that while it taught the matters set forth in this preamble it did not teach or suggest that it would obtain industrial control in any criminal way or unlawful manner, but in a peaceful manner; that he did not believe in criminal syndicalism or sabotage, and had not at any time advocated, suggested or taught the duty, necessity, propriety and expediency of crime, criminal syndicalism or sabotage, and did not know that they were advocated, taught or suggested by the organization; and that in taking the applications for membership in the organization, which contained the preamble to the constitution, he had explained the principles of the organization so far as he knew them by letting the applicants read this preamble.

The jury was instructed that before the defendant could be convicted they must be satisfied from the evidence, beyond a reasonable doubt, that the Industrial Workers of the World was an organization that taught criminal syndicalism as defined by the Syndicalism Act.

The defendant moved in arrest of judgment upon the ground, among others, that the evidence and the facts stated did not constitute a public offense and substantiate the charges alleged in the information. And he also moved for a new trial upon the grounds, among others, that the verdict was contrary to the law and the evidence and wholly unsupported by the evidence. Both of these motions were overruled.

On the appeal to the Supreme Court of the State, among the errors assigned were, generally, that the court erred in overruling his motions to quash the information, his demurrer to the evidence—which does not appear in the record—and his motions in arrest of judgment and for a new trial; and specifically, that the "court erred in refusing to quash the information, in overruling the demurrer to the evidence, and in overruling the motion in arrest of judgment, because the information and the cause of action attempted to be proved were based upon" the Kansas Syndicalism Act, "which, in so far as it sustains this prosecution is in violation * * * of the Constitution of the United States and especially of the Fourteenth Amendment" including the due process clause thereof.

The Supreme Court of the State, in its opinion, said:

> The information does not in set phrase allege that the association known as the Industrial Workers of the World advocates, affirmatively suggests or teaches criminal syndicalism, but when read as a whole it clearly signifies this, and also that the language quoted (which the evidence shows to be taken from the preamble of the constitution of that organization) was employed to express that doctrine * * * . The language quoted from the I.W.W. preamble need not—in order to sustain the judgment—be held necessarily and as a matter of law, to advocate, teach or even affirmatively suggest physical violence as a means of accomplishing industrial or political ends. It is open to that interpretation and is capable of use to convey that meaning * * * . The jury were not required to accept the defendant's testimony as a candid and accurate statement. There was room for them to find, as their verdict shows they did, that the equivocal language of the preamble and of the defendant in explaining it to his prospects was employed to convey and did convey the sinister meaning attributed to it by the state. A final contention is that the statute * * * is obnoxious to the due process of law clause of the Fourteenth Amendment to the Federal Constitution. Statutes penalizing the advocacy of violence in bringing about governmental changes do not violate constitutional guarantees of freedom of speech.

A decision of a State court applying and enforcing a State statute of general scope against a particular transaction as to which there was a distinct and timely insistence that if so applied, the statute was void under the Federal Constitution, necessarily affirms the validity of the statute as so applied, and the judgment is, therefore, reviewable by writ of error * * * . The inquiry then is whether the statute is constitutional as applied and enforced in respect of the situation presented.

And this Court will review the finding of facts by a State court where a Federal right has been denied as the result of a finding shown by the record to be without evidence to support it; or where a conclusion of law as to a Federal right and a finding of fact are so intermingled as to make it necessary, in order to pass upon the Federal question, to analyze the facts.

Here the State court held the Syndicalism Act not to be repugnant to the due process clause as applied in a case in which the information in effect charged the defendant with violation of the Act in that he had secured members in an organization which taught, advocated and affirmatively suggested the doctrines set forth in the extracts from the preamble to its constitution, and in which there was no evidence that the organization, taught, advocated or suggested any other doctrines. No substantial inference can, in our judgment, be drawn from the language of this preamble, that the organization taught, advocated or suggested the duty, necessity, propriety, or expediency of crime, criminal syndicalism, sabotage, or other unlawful acts or methods. There is no suggestion in the preamble that the industrial organization of workers as a class for the purpose of getting possession of the machinery of production and abolishing the wage system, was to be accomplished by any other than lawful methods; nothing advocating the overthrow of the existing industrial or political conditions by force, violence or unlawful means. And standing alone, as it did in this case, there was nothing which warranted the court or jury in ascribing to this language, either as an inference of law or fact, "the sinister meaning attributed to it by the state." In this respect the language of the preamble is essentially different from that of the manifesto involved in *Gitlow v. New York,* and lacks the essential elements which brought that document under the condemnation of the law. And it is not as if the preamble were shown to have been followed by further statements or declarations indicating that it was intended to mean, and to be understood as advocating, that the ends outlined therein would be accomplished or brought about by violence or other related unlawful acts or methods.

The result is that the Syndicalism Act has been applied in this case to sustain the conviction of the defendant, without any charge or evidence that the organization in which he secured members advocated any crime, violence or other unlawful acts or methods as a means of effecting industrial or political changes or revolution. Thus applied the Act is an arbitrary and unreasonable exercise of the police power of the State, unwarrantably infringing the liberty of the defendant in violation of the due process clause of the Fourteenth Amendment. The judgment is accordingly reversed, and the case is remanded for further proceedings not inconsistent with this opinion.

Reversed.

Notes and Questions

1. a) What scope of review of facts does the Court describe? When will the Court review the facts and permit itself to make findings at variance with those below? Of the patterns that Chief Justice Hughes says justify Supreme Court review of the facts, into which does *Fiske* fit?

b) How does the standard the Court suggests compare with the standard for granting judgment as a matter of law following a jury verdict? Should the Court review the facts only when it is persuaded that no rational finder of fact could have concluded as the court or jury did below, or is some more relaxed standard appropriate? If so, what standard? If not, then should Supreme Court review of the facts be available only if the party seeking review timely made and preserved a motion for judgment as a matter of law?

2. Whenever the Court is prepared to examine the factual record, should it merely indicate its dissatisfaction with the fact-finding below and remand for further consideration of the facts? Or should the Court feel free to substitute its own findings based on the record for those certified by the highest state court?

NORRIS v. ALABAMA
Supreme Court of the United States, 1935.
294 U.S. 587, 55 S.Ct. 579, 79 L.Ed. 1074.

MR. CHIEF JUSTICE HUGHES delivered the opinion of the Court.

Petitioner, Clarence Norris, is one of nine negro boys who were indicted in March, 1931, in Jackson county, Ala., for the crime of rape. On being brought to trial in that county, eight were convicted. The Supreme Court of Alabama reversed the conviction of one of these and affirmed that of seven, including Norris. This Court reversed the judgments of conviction upon the ground that the defendants had been denied due process of law in that the trial court had failed in the light of the circumstances disclosed, and of the inability of the defendants at that time to obtain counsel, to make an effective appointment of counsel to aid them in preparing and presenting their defense.

After the remand, a motion for change of venue was granted and the cases were transferred to Morgan county. Norris was brought to trial in November, 1933. At the outset, a motion was made on his behalf to quash the indictment upon the ground of the exclusion of negroes from juries in Jackson county where the indictment was found. A motion was also made to quash the trial venire in Morgan county upon the ground of the exclusion of negroes from juries in that county. In relation to each county, the charge was of long-continued, systematic, and arbitrary exclusion of qualified negro citizens from service on juries, solely because of their race and color, in violation of the Constitution of the United States.

The state joined issue on this charge and after hearing the evidence, which we shall presently review, the trial judge denied both motions, and exception was taken. The trial then proceeded and resulted in the conviction of Norris who was sentenced to death. On appeal, the Supreme Court of the state considered and decided the federal question which Norris had raised and affirmed the judgment. We granted a writ of certiorari.

First. There is no controversy as to the constitutional principle involved. That principle, long since declared, was not challenged, but was expressly recognized, by the Supreme Court of the state. Summing up precisely the effect of earlier decisions, this Court thus stated the principle in relation to exclusion from service on grand juries:

> Whenever by any action of a state, whether through its Legislature, through its courts, or through its executive or administrative officers, all persons of the African race are excluded, solely because of their race or color, from serving as grand jurors in the criminal prosecution of a person of the African race, the equal protection of the laws is denied to him, contrary to the Fourteenth Amendment of the Constitution of the United States.

* * * The principle is equally applicable to a similar exclusion of negroes from service on petit juries. * * * And although the state statute defining the qualifications of jurors may be fair on its face, the constitutional provision affords protection against action of the state through its administrative officers in effecting the prohibited discrimination. * * *

The question is of the application of this established principle to the facts disclosed by the record. That the question is one of fact does not relieve us of the duty to determine whether in truth a federal right has been denied. When a federal right has been specially set up and claimed in a state court, it is our province to inquire not merely whether it was denied in express terms but also whether it was denied in substance and effect. If this requires an examination of evidence, that examination must be made. Otherwise, review by this Court would fail of its purpose in safeguarding constitutional rights. Thus, whenever a conclusion of law of a state court as to a federal right and findings of fact are so intermingled that the latter control the former, it is incumbent upon us to analyze the facts in order that the appropriate enforcement of the federal right may be assured. * * *

Second. The evidence on the motion to quash the indictment. In 1930, the total population of Jackson county, where the indictment was found, was 36,881, of whom 2,688 were negroes. The male population over twenty-one years of age numbered 8,801, and of these 666 were negroes.

The qualifications of jurors were thus prescribed by the state statute:

> The jury commission shall place on the jury roll and in the jury

box the names of all male citizens of the county who are generally reputed to be honest and intelligent men, and are esteemed in the community for their integrity, good character and sound judgment, but no person must be selected who is under twenty-one or over sixty-five years of age, or, who is an habitual drunkard, or who, being afflicted with a permanent disease or physical weakness is unfit to discharge the duties of a juror, or who cannot read English, or who has ever been convicted of any offense involving moral turpitude. If a person cannot read English and has all the other qualifications prescribed herein and is a freeholder or householder, his name may be placed on the jury roll and in the jury box.

* * *

Defendant adduced evidence to support the charge of unconstitutional discrimination in the actual administration of the statute in Jackson county. The testimony, as the state court said, tended to show that "in a long number of years no negro had been called for jury service in that county." It appeared that no negro had served on any grand or petit jury in that county within the memory of witnesses who had lived there all their lives. Testimony to that effect was given by men whose ages ran from fifty to seventy-six years. Their testimony was uncontradicted. It was supported by the testimony of officials. The clerk of the jury commission and the clerk of the circuit court had never known of a negro serving on a grand jury in Jackson county. The court reporter, who had not missed a session in that county in twenty-four years, and two jury commissioners testified to the same effect. One of the latter, who was a member of the commission which made up the jury roll for the grand jury which found the indictment, testified that he had "never known of a single instance where any negro sat on any grand or petit jury in the entire history of that county."

That testimony in itself made out a *prima facie* case of the denial of the equal protection which the Constitution guarantees * * * . The case thus made was supplemented by direct testimony that specified negroes, thirty or more in number, were qualified for jury service. Among these were negroes who were members of school boards, or trustees, of colored schools, and property owners and householders. It also appeared that negroes from that county had been called for jury service in the federal court. Several of those who were thus described as qualified were witnesses. While there was testimony which cast doubt upon the qualifications of some of the negroes who had been named, and there was also general testimony by the editor of a local newspaper who gave his opinion as to the lack of "sound judgment" of the "good negroes" in Jackson county, we think that the definite testimony as to the actual qualifications of individual negroes, which was not met by any testimony equally direct, showed that there were negroes in Jackson county qualified for jury service.

The question arose whether names of negroes were in fact on the jury roll. The books containing the jury roll for Jackson county for the year 1930-31 were produced. They were produced from the custody of a member of the jury commission which, in 1931, had succeeded the commission which had made up the jury roll from which the grand jury in question had been drawn. On the pages of this roll appeared the names of six negroes. They were entered, respectively, at the end of the precinct lists which were alphabetically arranged. The genuineness of these entries was disputed. It appeared that after the jury roll in question had been made up, and after the new jury commission had taken office, one of the new commissioners directed the new clerk to draw lines after the names which had been placed on the roll by the preceding commission. These lines, on the pages under consideration, were red lines, and the clerk of the old commission testified that they were not put in by him. The entries made by the new clerk, for the new jury roll, were below these lines.

The names of the six negroes were in each instance written immediately above the red lines. An expert of long experience testified that these names were superimposed upon the red lines, that is, that they were written after the lines had been drawn. The expert was not cross-examined and no testimony was introduced to contradict him.[1] In denying the motion to quash, the trial judge expressed the view that he would not "be authorized to presume that somebody had committed a crime" or to presume that the jury board "had been unfaithful to their duties and allowed the books to be tampered with." His conclusion was that names of negroes were on the jury roll.

We think that the evidence did not justify that conclusion. The Supreme Court of the state did not sustain it. That court observed that the charge that the names of negroes were fraudulently placed on the roll did not involve any member of the jury board, and that the charge "was, by implication at least, laid at the door of the clerk of the board." The court, reaching its decision irrespective of that question, treated that phase of the matter as "wholly immaterial" and hence passed it by "without any expression of opinion thereon."

The state court rested its decision upon the ground that even if it were assumed that there was no name of a negro on the jury roll, it was not established that race or color caused the omission. The court pointed out that the statute fixed a high standard of qualifications for jurors * * * and that the jury commission was vested with a wide discretion. The court adverted to the fact that more white citizens possessing age qualifications had been omitted from the jury roll than the entire negro population of the county, and regarded the testimony as being to the effect

---

[1] The books containing the jury roll in question were produced on the argument at this bar and were examined by the Court.

that "the matter of race, color, politics, religion or fraternal affiliations" had not been discussed by the commission and had not entered into their consideration, and that no one had been excluded because of race or color.

The testimony showed the practice of the jury commission. One of the commissioners who made up the jury roll in question, and the clerk of that commission, testified as to the manner of its preparation. The other two commissioners of that period did not testify. It was shown that the clerk, under the direction of the commissioners, made up a preliminary list which was based on the registration list of voters, the polling list and the tax list, and apparently also upon the telephone directory. The clerk testified that he made up a list of all male citizens between the ages of twenty-one and sixty-five years without regard to their status or qualifications. The commissioner testified that the designation "col." was placed after the names of those who were colored. In preparing the final jury roll, the preliminary list was checked off as to qualified jurors with the aid of men whom the commissioners called in for that purpose from the different precincts. And the commissioner testified that in the selections for the jury roll no one was "automatically or systematically" excluded, or excluded on account of race or color; that he "did not inquire as to color," that was not discussed.

But, in appraising the action of the commissioners, these statements cannot be divorced from other testimony. As we have seen, there was testimony, not overborne or discredited, that there were in fact negroes in the county qualified for jury service. That testimony was direct and specific. After eliminating those persons as to whom there was some evidence of lack of qualifications, a considerable number of others remained. The fact that the testimony as to these persons, fully identified, was not challenged by evidence appropriately direct, cannot be brushed aside. There is no ground for an assumption that the names of these negroes were not on the preliminary list. The inference to be drawn from the testimony is that they were on that preliminary list, and were designated on that list as the names of negroes, and that they were not placed on the jury roll. There was thus presented a test of the practice of the commissioners. Something more than mere general asseverations was required. Why were these names excluded from the jury roll? Was it because of the lack of statutory qualifications? Were the qualifications of negroes actually and properly considered?

The testimony of the commissioner on this crucial question puts the case in a strong light. That testimony leads to the conclusion that these or other negroes were not excluded on account of age, or lack of esteem in the community for integrity and judgment, or because of disease or want of any other qualification. The commissioner's answer to specific inquiry upon this point was that negroes were "never discussed." We give in the margin quotations from his testimony.[2]

We are of the opinion that the evidence required a different result from that reached in the state court. We think that the evidence that for a generation or longer no negro had been called for service on any jury in Jackson county, that there were negroes qualified for jury service, that according to the practice of the jury commission their names would normally appear on the preliminary list of male citizens of the requisite age but that no names of negroes were placed on the jury roll, and the testimony with respect to the lack of appropriate consideration of the qualifications of negroes, established the discrimination which the Constitution forbids. The motion to quash the indictment upon that ground should have been granted.

Third. The evidence on the motion to quash the trial venire. The population of Morgan county, where the trial was had, was larger than that of Jackson county, and the proportion of negroes was much greater. The total population of Morgan county in 1930 was 46,176, and of this

---

[2] Q. Did you ever exclude from the jury rolls any negroes because you found first, he was a man under twenty-one years old or over sixty-five, and he was excluded by reason of his age; secondly because he was a person who wasn't esteemed in the community for being a decent and honorable citizen, for good sound common sense and judgment, did you ever see or hear of them not going to take that negro because he wasn't esteemed in the community for good sense and judgment?

A. No, sir.

Q. Did you ever have occasion to say, I can't take that negro because he is a fellow that has a disease which may affect or does affect, his mentality, did you ever say that to yourself, with reference to any particular negro?

A. No, sir, negroes was never discussed.

Q. Did you ever say to yourself as a jury commissioner in compiling those lists, I am not going to take that negro because he has been convicted before of a crime involving moral turpitude, have you ever excluded a negro on that ground, did you ever find any negro that came within that category, under your personal knowledge in Jackson County?

A. I couldn't recall any, no, sir, I don't know.

Q. Have you ever known of any negro in Jackson County who was excluded by reason of the fact that he could not read English, and that negro at the same time wasn't a free holder or house holder, did you ever say I can't take that negro because he is prohibited under the rules from serving by reason of that provision?

A. No, sir.

Q. Or anybody in your presence?

A. It never was discussed.

Q. You had been a jury commissioner how long?

A. I was on it under Bibb Graves administration, 1928, 1929, 1930.

Q. Three years?

A. Yes, sir.

Q. And you never had occasion to exclude any negro in Jackson County by reason of the disqualifying provisions I have just called to your attention?

A. Not to my personal knowledge, no, sir.

number 8,311 were negroes.

Within the memory of witnesses, long resident there, no negro had ever served on a jury in that county or had been called for such service. Some of these witnesses were over fifty years of age and had always lived in Morgan county. Their testimony was not contradicted. A clerk of the circuit court, who had resided in the county for thirty years, and who had been in office for over four years, testified that during his official term approximately 2,500 persons had been called for jury service and that not one of them was a negro; that he did not recall "ever seeing any single person of the colored race serve on any jury in Morgan County."

There was abundant evidence that there were a large number of negroes in the county who were qualified for jury service. Men of intelligence, some of whom were college graduates, testified to long lists (said to contain nearly 200 names) of such qualified negroes, including many business men, owners of real property and householders. When defendant's counsel proposed to call many additional witnesses in order to adduce further proof of qualifications of negroes for jury service, the trial judge limited the testimony, holding that the evidence was cumulative.

We find no warrant for a conclusion that the names of any of the negroes as to whom this testimony was given, or of any other negroes, were placed on the jury rolls. No such names were identified. The evidence that for many years no negro had been called for jury service itself tended to show the absence of the names of negroes from the jury rolls, and the state made no effort to prove their presence. The trial judge limited the defendant's proof "to the present year, the present jury roll." The sheriff of the county, called as a witness for defendants, scanned the jury roll and after "looking over every single name on that jury roll, from A to Z," was unable to point out "any single negro on it."

For this long-continued, unvarying, and wholesale exclusion of negroes from jury service we find no justification consistent with the constitutional mandate. We have carefully examined the testimony of the jury commissioners upon which the state court based its decision. One of these commissioners testified in person and the other two submitted brief affidavits. By the state act * * * in force at the time the jury roll in question was made up, the clerk of the jury board was required to obtain the names of all male citizens of the county over twenty-one and under sixty-five years of age, and their occupation, place of residence, and place of business * * *. The qualifications of those who were to be placed on the jury roll were the same as those prescribed by the earlier statute which we have already quoted * * *. The member of the jury board, who testified orally, said that a list was made up which included the names of all male citizens of suitable age; that black residents were not excluded from this general list; that in compiling the jury roll he did not consider race or color; that no one was excluded for that reason; and that he had placed on the jury roll the names of persons possessing the qualifications under the statute. The affidavits of the other members of the board contained general statements to the same effect.

We think that this evidence failed to rebut the strong *prima facie* case which defendant had made. That showing as to the long-continued exclusion of negroes from jury service, and as to the many negroes qualified for that service, could not be met by mere generalities. If, in the presence of such testimony as defendant adduced, the mere general assertions by officials of their performance of duty were to be accepted as in adequate justification for the complete exclusion of negroes from jury service, the constitutional provision—adopted with special reference to their protection—would be but a vain and illusory requirement. The general attitude of the jury commissioner is shown by the following extract from his testimony:

> I do not know of any negro in Morgan County over twenty-one and under sixty-five who is generally reputed to be honest and intelligent and who is esteemed in the community for his integrity, good character and sound judgment, who is not an habitual drunkard, who isn't afflicted with a permanent disease or physical weakness which would render him unfit to discharge the duties of a juror, and who can read English, and who has never been convicted of a crime involving moral turpitude.

In the light of the testimony given by defendant's witnesses, we find it impossible to accept such a sweeping characterization of the lack of qualifications of negroes in Morgan county. It is so sweeping, and so contrary to the evidence as to the many qualified negroes, that it destroys the intended effect of the commissioner's testimony.

In *Neal v. Delaware,* decided over fifty years ago, this Court observed that it was a "violent presumption," in which the state court had there indulged, that the uniform exclusion of negroes from juries, during a period of many years, was solely because, in the judgment of the officers, charged with the selection of grand and petit jurors, fairly exercised, "the black race in Delaware were utterly disqualified by want of intelligence, experience, or moral integrity, to sit on juries." Such a presumption at the present time would be no less violent with respect to the exclusion of the negroes of Morgan county. And, upon the proof contained in the record now before us, a conclusion that their continuous and total exclusion from juries was because there were none possessing the requisite qualifications, cannot be sustained.

We are concerned only with the federal question which we have discussed, and in view of the denial of the federal right suitably asserted, the judgment must be reversed and the cause remanded for further proceedings not inconsistent with this opinion.

It is so ordered.

Notes and Questions

1. Does the Court implicitly take the position that a witness can be incredible as a matter of law, thus allowing appellate review of what otherwise is a matter only for the fact-finder?

2. Chief Justice Hughes describes an apparently broad standard for allowing review of facts found in the state courts. Ordinarily do not the facts of a case control the success or failure of assertions of rights, federal or otherwise? Has the Court just described a standard of review without effective limitation?

3. Should the Court regularly review the facts to see whether they are fairly supported by the record? If not, cannot the lower courts effectively prevent Supreme Court review by manipulating the facts? *Ward v. Love County,* of course, suggests that there are limits to the Court's patience with lower court dissembling. But does *Ward* merely suggest that the state courts must be a bit subtle about insulating the record?

2. *With Procedural Law*

HERNDON v. GEORGIA
Supreme Court of the United States, 1935.
295 U.S. 441, 55 S.Ct. 794, 79 L.Ed. 1530.

MR. JUSTICE SUTHERLAND delivered the opinion of the Court.

Appellant was sentenced to a term of imprisonment upon conviction by a jury in a Georgia court of first instance of an attempt to incite insurrection by endeavoring to induce others to join in combined resistance to the authority of the state to be accomplished by acts of violence, in violation of § 56 of the Penal Code of Georgia.[1] The supreme court of the state affirmed the judgment. On this appeal, the statute is assailed as contravening the due process clause of the Fourteenth Amendment in certain designated particulars. We find it unnecessary to review the points made, since this court is without jurisdiction for the reason that no federal question was seasonably raised in the court below or passed upon by that court.

It is true that there was a preliminary attack upon the indictment in the trial court on the ground, among others, that the statute was in violation "of the Constitution of the United States," and that this contention was overruled. But, in addition to the insufficiency of the specification, the adverse action of the trial court was not preserved by exceptions

---

[1] "§ 56. Any attempt, by persuasion or otherwise, to induce others to join in any combined resistance to the lawful authority of the State shall constitute an attempt to incite insurrection."

"Insurrection" is defined by the preceding section. "§ 55. Insurrection shall consist in any combined resistance to the lawful authority of the State, with intent to the denial thereof, when the same is manifested, or intended to be manifested, by acts of violence."

pendente lite or assigned as error in due time in the bill of exceptions, as the settled rules of the state practice require. In that situation, the state supreme court declined to review any of the rulings of the trial court in respect of that and other preliminary issues; and this determination of the state court is conclusive here.

The federal question was never properly presented to the state supreme court unless upon motion for rehearing; and that court then refused to consider it. The long-established general rule is that the attempt to raise a federal question after judgment, upon a petition for rehearing, comes too late, unless the court actually entertains the question and decides it.

Petitioner, however, contends that the present case falls within an exception to the rule—namely, that the question respecting the validity of the statute as applied by the lower court first arose from its unanticipated act in giving to the statute a new construction which threatened rights under the Constitution. There is no doubt that the federal claim was timely if the ruling of the state court could not have been anticipated and a petition for rehearing presented the first opportunity for raising it. The whole point, therefore, is whether the ruling here assailed should have been anticipated.

The trial court instructed the jury that the evidence would not be sufficient to convict the defendant if it did not indicate that his advocacy would be acted upon immediately; and that—"In order to convict the defendant, * * * it must appear clearly by the evidence that immediate serious violence against the State of Georgia was to be expected or was advocated." Petitioner urges that the question presented to the state supreme court was whether the evidence made out a violation of the statute as thus construed by the trial court, while the supreme court construed the statute as not requiring that an insurrection should follow instantly or at any given time, but that "it would be sufficient that he [the defendant] intended it to happen at any time, as a result of his influence, by those whom he sought to incite," and upon that construction determined the sufficiency of the evidence against the defendant. If that were all, the petitioner's contention that the federal question was raised at the earliest opportunity well might be sustained; but it is not all.

The verdict of the jury was returned on January 18, 1933, and judgment immediately followed. On July 5, 1933, the trial court overruled a motion for new trial. The original opinion was handed down and the judgment of the state supreme court entered May 24, 1934, the case having been in that court since the preceding July.

On March 18, 1933, several months prior to the action of the trial court on the motion for new trial, the state supreme court had decided *Carr v. State.* In that case § 56 of the Penal Code, under which it arose, was challenged as contravening the Fourteenth Amendment. The court in substance construed the statute as it did in the present case. In the course of the opinion it said:

> It [the state] can not reasonably be required to defer the adoption of measures for its own peace and safety until the revolutionary utterances lead to actual disturbances of the public peace or imminent and immediate danger of its own destruction; but it may, in the exercise of its judgment, suppress the threatened danger in its incipiency * * * .

> Manifestly, the legislature has authority to forbid the advocacy of a doctrine designed and intended to overthrow the government, without waiting until there is a present and imminent danger of the success of the plan advocated. If the State were compelled to wait until the apprehended danger became certain, then its right to protect itself would come into being simultaneously with the overthrow of the government, when there would be neither prosecuting officers nor courts for the enforcement of the law.

The language contained in the subquotation is taken from *People v. Lloyd* [an Illinois case] and is quoted with approval by this court in *Gitlow v. New York.*

In the present case, following the language quoted at an earlier point in this opinion to the effect that it was sufficient if the defendant intended an insurrection to follow at any time, etc., the court below, in its original opinion, added—"It was the intention of this law to arrest at its incipiency any effort to overthrow the state government, where it takes the form of an actual attempt to incite others to insurrection." The phrase "at any time" is not found in the foregoing excerpt from the *Carr* case, but it is there in effect, when the phrase is given the meaning disclosed by the context, as that meaning is pointed out by the court below in its opinion denying the motion for a rehearing, when it said that the phrase was necessarily intended to mean within a reasonable time—"that is, within such time as one's persuasion or other adopted means might reasonably be expected to be directly operative in causing an insurrection."

Appellant, of course, cannot plead ignorance of the ruling in the *Carr* case, and was therefore bound to anticipate the probability of a similar ruling in his own case, and preserve his right to a review here by appropriate action upon the original hearing in the court below. It follows that his contention that he raised the federal question at the first opportunity is without substance, and the appeal must be dismissed for want of jurisdiction.

Dismissed.

MR. JUSTICE CARDOZO, dissenting.

The appellant has been convicted of an attempt to incite insurrection in violation of § 56 of the Penal Code of Georgia. He has been convicted after a charge by the trial court that to incur a verdict of guilt he must have advocated violence with the intent that his advocacy should be acted on immediately and with reasonable grounds for the expectation that the intent would be fulfilled. The appellant did not contend then, nor does he contend now, that a statute so restricted would involve an unconstitutional impairment of freedom of speech. However, upon appeal from the judgment of conviction the Supreme Court of Georgia repudiated the construction adopted at the trial and substituted another. Promptly thereafter the appellant moved for a rehearing upon the ground that the substituted meaning made the statute unconstitutional, and in connection with that motion invoked the protection of the Fourteenth Amendment. A rehearing was denied with an opinion which again construed the statute and again rejected the construction accepted in the court below. Now in this court the appellant renews his plaint that the substituted meaning makes the statute void. By the judgment just announced the court declines to hear him. It finds that he was tardy in asserting his privileges and immunities under the Constitution of the United States, and disclaiming jurisdiction dismisses his appeal.

I hold the view that the protection of the Constitution was seasonably invoked and that the court should proceed to an adjudication of the merits. Where the merits lie I do not now consider, for in the view of the majority the merits are irrelevant. My protest is confined to the disclaimer of jurisdiction. The settled doctrine is that when a constitutional privilege or immunity has been denied for the first time by a ruling made upon appeal, a litigant thus surprised may challenge the unexpected ruling by a motion for rehearing, and the challenge will be timely. Within that settled doctrine the cause is rightly here.

Though the merits are now irrelevant, the controversy must be so far explained as to show how a federal question has come into the record. The appellant insists that words do not amount to an incitement to revolution, or to an attempt at such incitement, unless they are of such a nature and are used in such circumstances as to create "a clear and present danger" (*Schenck v. United States*) of bringing the prohibited result to pass. He insists that without this limitation a statute so lacking in precision as the one applied against him here is an unconstitutional restraint upon historic liberties of speech. For present purposes it is unimportant whether his argument be sound or shallow. At least it has color of support in words uttered from this bench, and uttered with intense conviction. The court might be unwilling, if it were to pass to a decision of the merits, to fit the words so uttered within the framework of this case. What the appellant is now asking of us is an opportunity to be heard. That privilege is his unless he has thrown it away by silence and acquiescence when there was need of speech and protest.

We are told by the state that the securities of the Constitution should have been invoked upon the trial. The presiding judge should have been warned that a refusal to accept the test of clear and present danger would be a rejection of the restraints of the Fourteenth Amendment. But the trial judge had not refused to accept the test proposed; on the contrary, he had accepted it and even gone a step beyond. In substance he had charged that even a present "danger" would not suffice, if there was not also an expectation, and one grounded in reason, that the insurrection would begin at once. It is novel doctrine that a defendant who has had the benefit of all he asks, and indeed of a good deal more, must place a statement on the record that if some other court at some other time shall read the statute differently, there will be a denial of liberties that at the moment of the protest are unchallenged and intact. Defendants charged with crime are as slow as are men generally to borrow trouble of the future.

We are told, however, that protest, even if unnecessary at the trial, should have been made by an assignment of error or in some other appropriate way in connection with the appeal, and this for the reason that by that time, if not before, the defendant was chargeable with knowledge as a result of two decisions of the highest court of Georgia that the statute was destined to be given another meaning. The decisions relied upon are *Carr v. State* (No. 1) and *Carr v. State* (No. 2). The first of these cases was decided in November, 1932, before the trial of the appellant, which occurred in January, 1933. The second was decided in March, 1933, after the appellant had been convicted, but before the denial or submission of his motion for a new trial. Neither is decisive of the question before us now.

Carr v. State, No. 1, came up on demurrer to an indictment. The prosecution was under § 58 of the Penal Code, which makes it a crime to circulate revolutionary documents.[*] All that was held was that upon the face of the indictment there had been a wilful incitement to violence, sufficient, if proved, to constitute a crime. The opinion contains an extract covering about four pages from the opinion of this court in *Gitlow v. New York.* Imbedded in that long quotation are the words now pointed to by the state as decisive of the case at hand. They are the words of Sanford, J., writing for this court. "The immediate danger is none the less real and substantial, because the effect of a given utterance cannot be accurately foreseen." A state "cannot reasonably be required to defer the adoption of measures for its own peace and safety until the revolutionary utterances lead to actual disturbances of the public peace or imminent and immediate danger of its own destruction; but it may, in the exercise of its judgment, suppress the threatened danger in its incipiency."

---

[*] § 58. If any person shall bring, introduce, print, or circulate, or cause to be introduced, circulated, or printed, or aid or assist, or be in any manner instrumental in bringing, introducing, circulating, or printing within this State any paper, pamphlet, circular, or any writing, for the purpose of inciting insurrection, riot, conspiracy, or resistance against the lawful authority of the State, or against the lives of the inhabitants thereof, or any part of them, he shall be punished by confinement in the penitentiary for not less than five nor longer than twenty years.

To learn the meaning of these words in their application to the Georgia statute we must read them in their setting. Sanford, J., had pointed out that the statute then before him, the New York criminal anarchy act, forbade the teaching and propagation by spoken word or writing of a particular form of doctrine, carefully defined and after such definition denounced on reasonable grounds as fraught with peril to the state. There had been a determination by the state through its legislative body that such utterances "are so inimical to the general welfare and involve such danger of substantive evil that they may be penalized in the exercise of its police power." In such circumstances "the question whether any specific utterance coming within the prohibited class is likely, in and of itself, to bring about the substantive evil, is not open to consideration. It is sufficient that the statute itself be constitutional and that the use of the language comes within its prohibition." In effect the words had been placed upon an expurgatory index. At the same time the distinction was sharply drawn between statutes condemning utterances identified by a description of their meaning and statutes condemning them by reference to the results that they are likely to induce.

> It is clear that the question in such cases [*i.e.* where stated doctrines are denounced] is entirely different from that involved in those cases where the statute merely prohibits certain acts involving the danger of substantive evil, without any reference to language itself, and it is sought to apply its provisions to language used by the defendant for the purpose of bringing about the prohibited results.

The effect of all this was to leave the question open whether in cases of the second class, in cases, that is to say, where the unlawful quality of words is to be determined not upon their face but in relation to their consequences, the opinion in *Schenck v. United States,* supplies the operative rule. The conduct charged to this appellant—in substance an attempt to enlarge the membership of the Communist party in the city of Atlanta—falls, it will be assumed, within the second of these groupings, but plainly is outside the first. There is no reason to believe that the Supreme Court of Georgia, when it quoted from the opinion in Gitlow's case, rejected the restraints which the author of that opinion had placed upon his words. For the decision of the case before it there was no need to go so far. Circulation of documents with intent to incite to revolution had been charged in an indictment. The state had the power to punish such an act as criminal, or so the court had held. How close the nexus would have to be between the attempt and its projected consequences was matter for the trial.

Carr v. State, No. 2, like the case under review, was a prosecution under Penal Code, § 56 (not § 58), and like *Carr v. State,* No. 1, came up on demurrer. All that the court held was that when attacked by demurrer the indictment would stand. This appears from the headnote, drafted by the court itself. After referring to this headnote, the court states that it may be "useful and salutary" to repeat what it had written in *Carr v. State,* No. 1. Thereupon it quotes copiously from its opinion in that case including the bulk of the same extracts from *Gitlow v. New York.* The extracts show upon their face that they have in view a statute denouncing a particular doctrine and prohibiting attempts to teach it. They give no test of the bond of union between an idea and an event.

What has been said as to the significance of the opinions in the two cases against Carr has confirmation in what happened when appellant was brought to trial. The judge who presided at that trial had the first of those opinions before him when he charged the jury, or so we may assume. He did not read it as taking from the state the burden of establishing a clear and present danger that insurrection would ensure as a result of the defendant's conduct. This is obvious from the fact that in his charge he laid that very burden on the state with emphasis and clarity. True, he did not have before him the opinion in prosecution No. 2, for it had not yet been handed down, but if he had seen it, he could not have gathered from its quotation of the earlier case that it was announcing novel doctrine.

From all this it results that Herndon, this appellant, came into the highest court of Georgia without notice that the statute defining his offense was to be given a new meaning. There had been no rejection, certainly no unequivocal rejection, of the doctrine of *Schenck v. United States,* which had been made the law of the case by the judge presiding at his trial. For all that the record tells us, the prosecuting officer acquiesced in the charge, and did not ask the appellate court to apply a different test. In such a situation the appellant might plant himself as he did on the position that on the case given to the jury his guilt had not been proved: He was not under a duty to put before his judges the possibility of a definition less favorable to himself, and make an argument against it, when there had been no threat of any change, still less any forecast of its form or measure. He might wait until the law of the case had been rejected by the reviewing court before insisting that the effect would be an invasion of his constitutional immunities. If invasion should occur, a motion for rehearing diligently pressed thereafter would be seasonable notice. * * * It is the doctrine that must prevail if the great securities of the Constitution are not to be lost in a web of procedural entanglements.

New strength is given to considerations such as these when one passes to a closer view of just what the Georgia court did in its definition of the statute. We have heard that the meaning had been fixed by what had been held already in *Carr v. State,* and that thereby the imminence of the danger had been shown to be unrelated to innocence or guilt. But if that is the teaching of those cases, it was discarded by the very judgment now subjected to review. True, the Georgia court, by its first opinion in the case at hand, did prescribe a test that, if accepted, would bar the consideration of proximity in time. "It is immaterial whether the authority of the state was in danger of being subverted or that an insurrection actually occurred or was impending." "Force must have been contemplated, but * * * the statute does not include either its occurrence or its imminence as an ingredient of the particular offense charged." It would not be "necessary to guilt that the alleged offender should have intended that an insurrection should follow instantly, or at any given time, but it would be sufficient that he intended it to happen at any time, as a result of his influence, by those whom he sought to incite." On the motion for a rehearing the Georgia court repelled with a little heat the argument of counsel that these words were to be taken literally, without "the usual reasonable implications." "The phrase 'at any time,' as criticized in the motion for rehearing, was not intended to mean at any time in the indefinite future, or at any possible later time, however remote." "On the contrary the phrase 'at any time' was necessarily intended, and should have been understood, to mean within a reasonable time; that is, within such time as one's persuasion or other adopted means might reasonably be expected to be directly operative in causing an insurrection." "Under the statute as thus interpreted, we say, as before, that the evidence was sufficient to authorize the conviction."

Here is an unequivocal rejection of the test of clear and present danger, yet a denial also of responsibility without boundaries in time. True, in this rejection, the court disclaimed a willingness to pass upon the question as one of constitutional law, assigning as a reason that no appeal to the Constitution had been made upon the trial or then considered by the judge. Such a rule of state practice may have the effect of attaching a corresponding limitation to the jurisdiction of this court where fault can fairly be imputed to an appellant for the omission to present the question sooner. No such consequence can follow where the ruling of the trial judge has put the Constitution out of the case and made an appeal to its provisions impertinent and futile. In such circumstances, the power does not reside in a state by any rule of local practice to restrict the jurisdiction of this court in the determination of a constitutional question brought into the case thereafter. If the rejection of the test of clear and present danger was a denial of fundamental liberties, the path is clear for us to say so.

What was brought into the case upon the motion for rehearing was a standard wholly novel, the expectancy of life to be ascribed to the persuasive power of an idea. The defendant had no opportunity in the state court to prepare his argument accordingly. He had no opportunity to argue from the record that guilt was not a reasonable inference, or one permitted by the Constitution, on the basis of that test any more than on the basis of others discarded as unfitting. The argument thus shut out is submitted to us now. Will men "judging in calmness" (Brandeis, J.) say of the defendant's conduct as shown forth in the pages of this record that it was an attempt to stir up revolution through the power of his persuasion and within the time when that persuasion might be expected to endure? If men so judging will say yes, will the Constitution of the United

States uphold a reading of the statute that will lead to that response? Those are the questions that the defendant lays before us after conviction of a crime punishable by death in the discretion of the jury. I think he should receive an answer.

Notes and Questions

1. *Herndon* makes clear that procedural default in state court, such as failure to raise a federal issue in a timely manner, can constitute an adequate and independent state ground barring Supreme Court review of the federal issue. This bar does not apply if the state court actually decides the federal issue notwithstanding the procedural default. It may also not apply if the state court gives a new interpretation to a state statute that raises a federal issue for the first time. If the party seeking United States Supreme Court review could not have anticipated the new interpretation, then an objection based on federal law is timely made, and the Supreme Court may hear it. "The whole point, therefore," says Justice Sutherland, "is whether the ruling here assailed should have been anticipated."

It is difficult to understand the battle between Justices Sutherland and Cardozo on this question without understanding more fully what the two *Carr* cases were about. *Carr v. State* (No. 1), 176 Ga. 55, 166 S.E. 827 (1932), decided before Herndon's trial, involved, as Justice Cardozo points out, a different statute from the one in *Herndon*. The Georgia Supreme Court heard the case on appeal from the trial court's overruling of a demurrer to the indictment that argued, *inter alia,* that the statute was void for vagueness and violated both the free speech provision of the Georgia Civil Code and the due process and privileges-and-immunities provisions of the Fourteenth Amendment.

The Georgia Supreme Court quoted from *Gitlow v. New York,* 268 U.S. 652, 45 S.Ct. 625, 69 L.Ed. 1138 (1925), four and one-half pages discussing the difference between abstract advocacy of the doctrine of forcible overthrow of the government and advocacy of concrete action directed to that end. The Supreme Court had noted that the state "cannot reasonably be required to defer the adoption of measures for its own peace and safety until the revolutionary utterances lead to actual disturbances of the public peace or imminent and immediate danger of its own destruction; but it may, in the exercise of its judgment, suppress the threatened danger in its incipiency." *Gitlow* did not, however, explicitly repudiate the clear-and-present-danger test of *Schenck v. United States,* 249 U.S. 47, 39 S.Ct. 247, 63 L.Ed. 470 (1919), instead finding it inapplicable on the facts. *Gitlow* seemed to say that *Schenck* applied only when the legislature had not prohibited particular utterances but had sought instead only to prohibit certain acts without focusing on speech that might stimulate or accompany such acts. JOHN E. NOWAK & RONALD D. ROTUNDA, CONSTITUTIONAL LAW § 16.13, at 1170 (7th ed. 2004). The Georgia Supreme Court held that the indictment in *Carr I* was sufficient to withstand the demurrer.

Justice Cardozo argued that *Carr I* did not clearly announce a First Amendment standard different from *Schenck*. Certainly the opinion focused on the difference between doctrinal advocacy in principle and advocacy intended to spur people to action, not on the related but separate question of the temporal connection between advocacy and event that *Schenck* addressed. Moreover, the *Carr* statute was far more specific about the precise prohibited speech (and thus within *Gitlow* and outside of *Schenck*) than the *Herndon* statute. *Carr I* was far from clear that it repudiated *Schenck* for all purposes, and it requires some stretching to conclude that even if the Georgia Supreme Court intended that with respect to the statute involved in *Carr I,* that would also have been its intention in construing a different statute.

The trial court used the *Schenck* clear-and-present-danger standard in charging the jury. Even if one assumes that Herndon's counsel was familiar with *Carr I* and suspected that it might have announced a standard less strict than *Schenck*, what could he have done at that point? Could he have put a federal constitutional objection to *Carr I* on the record? What obvious danger to his client would that have posed?

Carr v. State (No. 2), 176 Ga. 747, 169 S.E. 201 (1933), was decided after Herndon's trial, but before his motion for a new trial was considered. Although *Carr II* at least concerned the same statute as *Herndon,* there the repudiation of *Schenck* is even less clear. The Georgia Supreme Court did, however, say that "[t]here is no constitutional right to advocate the overthrow of this government by force," apparently eschewing any requirement of a likely temporal connection between advocacy and event. The Georgia court also implied that it thought the immediacy of the connection between advocacy and event was less important than had the Court in *Schenck*.

What should Herndon have done then? The trial court had apparently adopted a view of the statute that satisfied *Schenck*. In his motion for a new trial should the defendant have urged the trial court, in reliance on *Carr II,* to adopt a broader view of § 56 that would make it easier to convict him on retrial? Is that a realistic position to expect counsel to take?

2. This aspect of *Herndon* raises an interesting ethical question concerning the obligation of counsel to be candid with the court. Counsel has an obligation to notify the court that it is proceeding upon a manifestly erroneous view of the law in contravention of clear authority, even if the court's error helps counsel's client. How far does that obligation extend? How "manifest" must the court's error be in order to bring to bear counsel's ethical obligation? Note the conflict here between counsel's obligation zealously to represent the client's interests and the obligation to deal candidly with the court. To be sure, counsel cannot conceal from the court a case on all fours and incompatible with the client's position. Does that mean, however, that candor requires counsel to raise and then rebut all arguments that might reasonably be made against the client's position?

3. As a practical matter, even if counsel had so informed the trial court, would it have made any difference? Upon hearing counsel's argument that the Georgia Supreme Court's interpretation of § 56 in *Carr II* was unconstitutional, could the trial court have invalidated the statute or reinterpreted it? Was the Georgia Supreme Court saying to Herndon that it was his obligation futilely to raise the constitutional point in the trial court to preserve

it for review by the Georgia Supreme Court? What does such a course gain?

4. The fact that the Georgia Supreme Court announced a further clarification of the state statute on the motion for rehearing strengthens Justice Cardozo's argument that the *Carr* cases had not announced a clear change in the law. What was the clarification? How did that affect Herndon's ability to have made a coherent objection to the state statute in the trial court?

5. *Herndon* is the first case in this chapter in which a *procedural* default is asserted as an adequate and independent state ground precluding Supreme Court review. Justice Sutherland says the Court lacks jurisdiction to review. Why is that so? The adequate-and-independent-state-ground rule operates differently depending on whether the state ground alleged to bar Supreme Court review is substantive or procedural. *Henry v. Mississippi*, which appears immediately following the note on *Orr v. Orr*, explores the difference.

NOTE ON *ORR V. ORR*.[6]

Orr demonstrates that only a state ground upon which the state court actually relies precludes review by the United States Supreme Court. The appellant in *Orr* was a husband who, as a part of a divorce proceeding in Alabama, had agreed to pay alimony. When he fell into arrears, his former wife began a contempt proceeding. The defendant argued that Alabama's statute, which allowed alimony only to wives, violated the Equal Protection Clause.

The Court considered three preliminary issues. First, the Justices inquired whether the husband had standing despite having requested no alimony from the wife; they held that he did. Second, the Court asked whether the challenge was timely, since he had never raised the constitutional question in the initial divorce proceeding. The Court noted that the timing issue might have provided an adequate and independent state (procedural) ground, but the wife had never raised it, and the Alabama Supreme Court had decided the husband's claim on its merits. "[T]he elementary rule is that it is irrelevant to inquire * * * *when* a Federal question was raised in a court below when it appears that such a question was actually considered and decided." (Emphasis added). Third, the Court considered whether the husband should be bound, as a matter of state contract law, by his stipulation to pay alimony. That could have constituted an adequate and independent state substantive ground, but since the objection was neither raised nor relied upon in the Alabama courts, the Supreme Court refused to consider it.

> "Where a state court does not decide against a petitioner or appellant upon an independent state ground, but deeming the federal question before it, actually entertains and decides that question adversely to the federal right asserted, this Court has jurisdiction

---

[6] 440 U.S. 268, 99 S.Ct. 1102, 59 L.Ed.2d 306 (1979)

to review the judgment if, as here, it is a final judgment. We cannot refuse jurisdiction because the state court might have based its decision, consistently with the record, upon an independent and adequate non-federal ground."

A party may thus be saved from his (or his attorney's) folly if the highest state court bypasses potentially adequate and independent state grounds and decides the federal issues presented.

HENRY v. MISSISSIPPI.
Supreme Court of the United States, 1965.
379 U.S. 443, 85 S.Ct. 564, 13 L.Ed.2d 408.

MR. JUSTICE BRENNAN delivered the opinion of the Court.

Petitioner was convicted of disturbing the peace, by indecent proposals to and offensive contact with an 18-year-old hitchhiker to whom he is said to have given a ride in his car. The trial judge charged the jury that "you cannot find the defendant guilty on the unsupported and uncorroborated testimony of the complainant alone." The petitioner's federal claim derives from the admission of a police officer's testimony, introduced to corroborate the hitchhiker's testimony. The Mississippi Supreme Court held that the officer's testimony was improperly admitted as the fruit of "an unlawful search and was in violation of § 23, Miss. Constitution 1890." The tainted evidence tended to substantiate the hitchhiker's testimony by showing its accuracy in a detail which could have been seen only by one inside the car. In particular, it showed that the right-hand ash tray of the car in which the incident took place was full of Dentyne chewing gum wrappers, and that the cigarette lighter did not function. The police officer testified that after petitioner's arrest he had returned to the petitioner's house and obtained the permission of petitioner's wife to look in petitioner's car. The wife provided the officer with the keys * * * . He testified that he tried the lighter and it would not work, and also that the ashtray "was filled with red dentyne chewing gum wrappers."

The Mississippi Supreme Court first filed an opinion which reversed petitioner's conviction and remanded for a new trial. The court held that the wife's consent to the search of the car did not waive petitioner's constitutional rights, and noted that the "[t]estimony of the State's witness * * * is, in effect, uncorroborated without the evidence disclosed by the inspection of defendant's automobile." Acting in the belief that petitioner had been represented by nonresident counsel unfamiliar with local procedure, the court reversed despite petitioner's failure to comply with the Mississippi requirement that an objection to illegal evidence be made at the time it is introduced. The court noted that petitioner had moved for a directed verdict at the close of the State's case, assigning as one ground the use of illegally obtained evidence; it did not mention petitioner's renewal of his motion at the close of all evidence.

After the first opinion was handed down, the State filed a Suggestion of Error, pointing out that petitioner was in fact represented at his trial by competent local counsel, as well as by out-of-state lawyers. Thereupon the Mississippi Supreme Court withdrew its first opinion and filed a new opinion in support of a judgment affirming petitioner's conviction. The new opinion is identical with the first save for the result, the statement that petitioner had local counsel, and the discussion of the effect of failure for whatever reason to make timely objection to the evidence[:] "In such circumstances, even if honest mistakes of counsel in respect to policy or strategy or otherwise occur, they are binding upon the client as a part of the hazards of courtroom battle." Moreover, the court reasoned, petitioner's cross-examination of the State's witness before the initial motion for directed verdict, and introduction of other evidence of the car's interior appearance afterward, "cured" the original error and estopped petitioner from complaining of the tainted evidence. * * * We vacate the judgment of conviction and remand for a hearing on the question whether the petitioner is to be deemed to have knowingly waived decision of his federal claim when timely objection was not made to the admission of the illegally seized evidence.

It is, of course, a familiar principle that this Court will decline to review state court judgments which rest on independent and adequate state grounds, even where these judgments also decide federal questions. The principle applies not only in cases involving state substantive grounds, but also in cases involving state procedural grounds. But it is important to distinguish between state substantive grounds and state procedural grounds. Where the ground involved is substantive, the determination of the federal question cannot affect the disposition if the state court decision on the state law question is allowed to stand. Under the view taken in *Murdock* of the statutes conferring appellate jurisdiction on this Court, we have no power to revise judgments on questions of state law. Thus, the adequate nonfederal ground doctrine is necessary to avoid advisory opinions.

These justifications have no application where the state ground is purely procedural. A procedural default which is held to bar challenge to a conviction in state courts, even on federal constitutional grounds, prevents implementation of the federal right. Accordingly, we have consistently held that the question of when and how defaults in compliance with state procedural rules can preclude our consideration of a federal question is itself a federal question. As Mr. Justice Holmes said:

> When as here there is a plain assertion of federal rights in the lower court, local rules as to how far it shall be reviewed on appeal do not necessarily prevail. * * * Whether the right was denied or not given due recognition by the [state court] * * * is a question as to which the plaintiffs are entitled to invoke our judgment.

Only last Term, we reaffirmed this principle, holding that a state appellate court's refusal, on the ground of mootness, to consider a federal claim, did not preclude our independent determination of the question of mootness; that is itself a question of federal law which this Court must ultimately decide. These cases settle the proposition that a litigant's procedural defaults in state proceedings do not prevent vindication of his federal rights unless the State's insistence on compliance with its procedural rule serves a legitimate state interest. In every case we must inquire whether the enforcement of a procedural forfeiture serves such a state interest. If it does not, the state procedural rule ought not be permitted to bar vindication of important federal rights.[3]

The Mississippi rule requiring contemporaneous objection to the introduction of illegal evidence clearly does serve a legitimate state interest. By immediately apprising the trial judge of the objection, counsel gives the court the opportunity to conduct the trial without using the tainted evidence. If the objection is well taken the fruits of the illegal search may be excluded from jury consideration, and a reversal and new trial avoided. But on the record before us it appears that this purpose of the contemporaneous-objection rule may have been substantially served by petitioner's motion at the close of the State's evidence asking for a directed verdict because of the erroneous admission of the officer's testimony. For at this stage the trial judge could have called for elaboration of the search and seizure argument and, if persuaded, could have stricken the tainted testimony or have taken other appropriate corrective action. For example, if there was sufficient competent evidence without this testimony to go to the jury, the motion for a directed verdict might have been denied, and the case submitted to the jury with a properly worded appropriate cautionary instruction.[4] In these circumstances, the delay until the close of the State's case in presenting the objection cannot be said to have frustrated the State's interest in avoiding delay and waste of time in the disposition of the case. If this is so, and enforcement of the rule here would serve no substantial state interest, then settled principles would preclude treating the state ground as adequate; giving effect to the contemporaneous-objection rule for its own

---

[3] This will not lead inevitably to a plethora of attacks on the application of state procedural rules; where the state rule is a reasonable one and clearly announced to defendant and counsel, application of the waiver doctrine will yield the same result as that of the adequate nonfederal ground doctrine in the vast majority of cases.

[4] The view of the Mississippi court in its first opinion seems to have been that there was insufficient evidence apart from the tainted testimony to support the conviction. Hence, appropriate corrective action as a matter of state law might have included granting petitioner's motion. We have not overlooked the fact that the first opinion remanded for a new trial, although the usual practice of the Mississippi Supreme Court where a motion for directed verdict, renewed at the close of all the evidence, is improperly denied is to dismiss the prosecution. The opinion offers no explanation of the mandate; the answer is probably that the court refers only to the motion at the end of the State's case, and overlooks the fact that it was renewed at the close of all the evidence, just as it overlooks the presence of local counsel. If the motion were not renewed, the appellate court could not dismiss the prosecution.

sake "would be to force resort to an arid ritual of meaningless form."

We have no reason, however, to decide that question now or to express any view on the merits of petitioner's substantial constitutional claim.[6] For even assuming that the making of the objection on the motion for a directed verdict satisfied the state interest served by the contemporaneous-objection rule, the record suggests a possibility that petitioner's counsel deliberately bypassed the opportunity to make timely objection in the state court, and thus that the petitioner should be deemed to have forfeited his state court remedies. Although the Mississippi Supreme Court characterized the failure to object as an "honest mistake," the State, in the brief in support of its Suggestion of Error in the Supreme Court of Mississippi asserted its willingness to agree that its Suggestion of Error "should not be sustained if either of the three counsel [for petitioner] participating in this trial would respond hereto with an affidavit that he did not know that at some point in a trial in criminal court in Mississippi that an objection to such testimony must have been made." The second opinion of the Mississippi Supreme Court does not refer to the State's proposal and thus it appears that the Court did not believe that the issue was properly presented for decision. Another indication of possible waiver appears in an affidavit attached to the State's brief in this Court; there, the respondent asserted that one of petitioner's lawyers stood up as if to object to the officer's tainted testimony, and was pulled down by co-counsel. Again, this furnishes an insufficient basis for decision of the waiver questions at this time. But, together with the proposal in the Suggestion of Error, it is enough to justify an evidentiary hearing to determine whether petitioner "after consultation with competent counsel or otherwise, understandingly and knowingly forewent the privilege of seeking to vindicate his federal claims in the state courts, whether for strategic, tactical, or any other reasons that can fairly be described as the deliberate by-passing of state procedures * * * ."

The evidence suggests reasons for a strategic move. Both the complaining witness and the police officer testified that the cigarette lighter in the car did not work. After denial of its motion for a directed verdict the defense called a mechanic who had repaired the cigarette lighter. The defense might have planned to allow the complaining witness and the officer to testify that the cigarette lighter did not work, and then, if the motion for directed verdict were not granted, to discredit both wit-

---

[6] Thus, consistently with the policy of avoiding premature decision on the merits of constitutional questions, we intimate no view whether the pertinent controlling federal standard governing the legality of a search or seizure is the same as the Mississippi standard applied here, which holds that the wife's consent cannot validate a search as against her husband. Nor do we rule at this time on the question whether petitioner's cross-examination of the officer, before raising any objection, "cured" the effect of the inadmissible testimony; this Court has not yet ruled on the role of harmless error in search and seizure cases. Of course, nothing occurring after the judge's refusal to honor petitioner's objection could have this curative effect.

nesses by showing that it did work, thereby persuading the jury to acquit. Or, by delaying objection to the evidence, the defense might have hoped to invite error and lay the foundation for a subsequent reversal. If either reason motivated the action of petitioner's counsel, and their plans backfired, counsel's deliberate choice of the strategy would amount to a waiver binding on petitioner and would preclude him from a decision on the merits of his federal claim either in the state courts or here. Although trial strategy adopted by counsel without prior consultation with an accused will not, where the circumstances are exceptional, preclude the accused from asserting constitutional claims, we think that the deliberate bypassing by counsel of the contemporaneous-objection rule as a part of trial strategy would have that effect in this case.

Only evidence extrinsic to the record before us can establish the fact of waiver, and the State should have an opportunity to establish that fact. * * * [A] dismissal on the basis of an adequate state ground would not end this case; petitioner might still pursue vindication of his federal claim in a federal habeas corpus proceeding in which the procedural default will not alone preclude consideration of his claim, at least unless it is shown that petitioner deliberately bypassed the orderly procedure of the state courts.[a]

Of course, in so remanding we neither hold nor even remotely imply that the State must forgo insistence on its procedural requirements if it finds no waiver. Such a finding would only mean that petitioner could have a federal court apply settled principles to test the effectiveness of the procedural default to foreclose consideration of his constitutional claim. If it finds the procedural default ineffective, the federal court will itself decide the merits of his federal claim, at least so long as the state court does not wish to do so. By permitting the Mississippi courts to make an initial determination of waiver, we serve the causes of efficient administration of criminal justice, and of harmonious federal-state judicial relations. Such a disposition may make unnecessary the processing of the case through federal courts already laboring under congested dockets, or it may make unnecessary the relitigation in a federal forum of certain issues. * * * Therefore, the judgment is vacated and the case is remanded to the Mississippi Supreme Court for further proceedings not inconsistent with this opinion.

It is so ordered.

MR. JUSTICE BLACK, dissenting.

Petitioner contends that his conviction was based in part on evidence obtained by an allegedly unlawful search in violation of the United States Constitution. I would decide this federal question here and now.

---

[a] [AUTHORS' NOTE] The Court has since overruled the standard for review on habeas corpus expressed here. *See* Coleman v. Thompson, 501 U.S. 722, 111 S.Ct. 2546, 115 L.Ed.2d 640 (1991), presented at page 1164 in Chapter 11.

I do not believe that the Mississippi procedural trial rule relied on by the State can shut off this Court's review, nor do I find a particle of support for the Court's suggestion that petitioner knowingly waived his right to have this constitutional question decided by the state trial court.

As far as the issue of waiver is concerned, I agree with the Mississippi Supreme Court, which considered the failure to object one of the "honest mistakes" which any lawyer might make, since I believe that the record is completely barren of evidence to support a finding of a conscious and intentional waiver of petitioner's due process right to have the trial court decide whether evidence used against him had been unconstitutionally seized. Therefore I would not remand for a hearing by the State Supreme Court or the trial court on the issue of waiver.[2] And even if I considered that a real issue of waiver had been shown and was properly before us, I would decide it here. I cannot agree to the Court's judgment remanding the case to the state courts for a hearing on that issue alone, thereby giving the State a chance to supplement the trial record to save its conviction from constitutional challenge in a summary hearing before a court without a jury. * * *

Nor do I believe that Mississippi's procedural rule concerning the stage of a trial at which constitutional objections should be made is the kind of rule that we should accept as an independent, adequate ground for the State Supreme Court's refusal to decide the constitutional question raised by petitioner. * * * [T]his Court held that where a State allows constitutional questions "to be raised at a late stage and be determined by its courts as a matter of discretion, we are not concluded from assuming jurisdiction and deciding whether the state court action in the particular circumstances is, in effect, an avoidance of the federal right." No Mississippi court opinions or state statutes have been called to our attention that I read as denying power of the State Supreme Court, should that court wish to do so, to consider and determine constitutional questions presented at the time this one was. In fact, as I understand counsel for the State, the Supreme Court of Mississippi does have power in its discretion to consider such questions regardless of when they are presented. As that court has said most persuasively: "Constitutional rights in serious criminal cases rise above mere rules of procedure. * * * Errors affecting fundamental rights are exceptions to the rule that questions not raised in the trial court cannot be raised for the first time on appeal."

---

[2] I think that the very "evidence" cited in the Court's opinion points up the fact that there was no evidence from which it can be inferred that a conscious waiver was made. I can find no support, as the Court does, from an affidavit filed for the first time as an appendix to the State's brief in this Court, stating that the district attorney who tried the case had seen one of petitioner's counsel start to rise from his chair when the evidence from the search was introduced, but that another of petitioner's counsel gave a "jerk on the coat tail" of the lawyer, "returning him to his seat." It is hard for me to see how one could infer from this "jerk on the coat tail" even a suspicion that petitioner had consciously and knowingly waived his right to object to the evidence offered against him.

After stating this to be the rule it followed, and citing a number of its past decisions which stated and applied the same rule, the highest court of Mississippi, in the opinion quoted from, because of that rule reversed a conviction obtained through the use of unconstitutionally seized evidence, even though as in the present case there had been no objection made at the time the evidence was presented. The court noted that it had applied this same rule in other cases where proper objection had not been made at the trial * * * . In all of those cases the defendant appears to have been represented by local counsel. Yet this Court now apparently holds that the state court may, if it chooses to do so, depart from its prior cases and apply a new, stricter rule against this defendant and thereby prevent this Court from reviewing the case to see that his federal constitutional rights were safeguarded. I do not believe the cherished federal constitutional right of a defendant to object to unconstitutionally seized evidence offered against him can be cut off irrevocably by state-court discretionary rulings which might be different in particular undefined circumstances in other cases. I think such a procedural device for shutting off our review of questions involving constitutional rights is too dangerous to be tolerated.

For these reasons I dissent from the disposition of this case.

MR. JUSTICE HARLAN, with whom MR. JUSTICE CLARK and MR. JUSTICE STEWART join, dissenting.

Flying banners of federalism, the Court's opinion actually raises storm signals of a most disquieting nature. While purporting to recognize the traditional principle that an adequate procedural, as well as substantive, state ground of decision bars direct review here of any federal claim asserted in the state litigation, the Court, unless I wholly misconceive what is lurking in today's opinion, portends a severe dilution, if not complete abolition, of the concept of "adequacy" as pertaining to state procedural grounds.

In making these preliminary observations I do not believe I am seeing ghosts. For I cannot account for the remand of this case in the face of what is a demonstrably adequate state procedural ground of decision by the Mississippi Supreme Court except as an early step toward extending in one way or another the doctrine of *Fay v. Noia*, to direct review. In that case, decided only two Terms ago, the Court turned its back on history * * * and did away with the adequate state ground doctrine in federal habeas corpus proceedings.

Believing that any step toward extending *Noia* to direct review should be flushed out and challenged at its earliest appearance in an opinion of this Court, I respectfully dissent.

I

The Mississippi Supreme Court did not base its ultimate decision upon petitioner's federal claim that his wife's consent could not validate an otherwise improper police search of the family car, but on the procedural ground that petitioner (who was represented by three experienced lawyers) had not objected at the time the fruits of this search were received in evidence. This Court now strongly implies, but does not decide (in view of its remand on the "waiver" issue) that enforcement of the State's "contemporaneous-objection" rule was inadequate as a state ground of decision because the petitioner's motion for a directed verdict of acquittal afforded the trial judge a satisfactory opportunity to take "appropriate corrective action" with reference to the allegedly inadmissible evidence. Thus, it is suggested, this may be a situation where "giving effect to the contemporaneous-objection rule for its own sake 'would be to force resort to an arid ritual of meaningless form.' "

From the standpoint of the realities of the courtroom, I can only regard the Court's analysis as little short of fanciful. The petitioner's motion for a verdict could have provoked one of three courses of action by the trial judge, none of which can reasonably be considered as depriving the State's contemporaneous-objection rule of its capacity to serve as an adequate state ground.

1. The trial judge might have granted the directed verdict. But had this action been appropriate, the Supreme Court of Mississippi, in its first opinion, would have ordered the prosecution dismissed. Since it did not, and the matter is entirely one of state law, further speculation by this Court should be foreclosed.[1]

2. The trial judge might have directed a mistrial. The State's interest in preventing mistrials through the contemporaneous-objection requirement is obvious.

3. The remaining course of action is the example given by the Court; the trial judge could have denied the motion for a directed verdict, but, *sua sponte*, called for elaboration of the argument, determined that the search of the automobile was unconstitutional, and given cautionary instructions to the jury to disregard the inadmissible evidence when the case was submitted to it.

The practical difficulties with this approach are manifestly sufficient to show a substantial state interest in their avoidance, and thus to show an "adequate" basis for the State's adherence to the contemporaneous-objection rule. To make my point I must quote the motion for di-

---

[1] The court, as a matter of state law, could have found (a) that there was sufficient corroborative evidence, (b) that none was necessary, or (c) that retrial was necessary to prevent defendants in criminal cases from hanging back until the completion of the State's case and then for the first time moving to strike a piece of evidence crucial to getting the case to the jury.

The Court's suggestion that we may proceed on the speculation that the Mississippi Supreme Court "overlooked" the renewal of the motion for directed verdict made at the completion of the case hardly requires comment.

rected verdict in full.

Atty Carter: We're going to make a motion, your Honor, for a directed verdict in this case. We are going to base our motion on several grounds. First, we think that this whole process by which this defendant was brought or attempted to be brought into the jurisdiction of this Court is illegal and void. There is nothing in the record in this case to show that the warrant that was issued against this defendant was based upon—it must be based in this State and any other State on an affidavit, on a proper affidavit or a proper complaint by any party. True, there is some testimony that some affidavit was made, and the complaining witness said so, but in the record in this case which is before the Court, no such affidavit is present and there is a verification from the Justice of the Peace that no such affidavit is present in this case; therefore, we contend that the warrant under which this defendant was subjected to arrest was illegal and without force and effect. Secondly, we contend that the warrant having been issued and the testimony of this Mr. Collins on the stand to the effect that after he had placed this man under arrest, he then proceeded to go and search his car, and clearly, this is a violation of his rights under the Fourth Amendment, and it is unlawful search and seizure so the evidence that they have secured against this defendant is illegal and unlawful. Finally, we contend that on the basis of these facts that the affidavit under which the defendant was tried before the Justice of the Peace Court, as we contended yesterday, based upon the statement that was sworn to by the County Attorney, not on information and belief, but directly that this is void and defective and could give the Justice of the Peace no jurisdiction in this case. We contend under these circumstances that the state—that this is an illegal process; that this man's rights have been violated under the Fourteenth Amendment, and finally, we contend that the State has failed to prove beyond a reasonable doubt to any extent to implicate this man in this case. Now, on these basis [sic] we contend that this whole process is illegal and void, and that it has permeated and contended [sic, apparently intending "contaminated"2] the whole process insofar as the jurisdiction of this Court is concerned or jurisdiction over this individual is concerned; therefore, he should be released, and we move for a directed verdict.

Court: Motion overruled. Bring the jury back.

The motion was renewed at the completion of the defense in the following language:

Atty Carter: Your Honor, at this time at the close of the case we want to make a motion for a directed verdict. We base it on the grounds and the reasons which we set forth in our motion for a directed verdict at the close of the State's case. We make it now at

the close of the entire case on those grounds and on the grounds
that the evidence has not shown beyond any reasonable doubt under the law that the defendant is guilty of the charge. We therefore
make a motion for a directed verdict at this time.

Court: Motion is overruled.

The single sentence in the first motion is the only direct reference to
the search and seizure question from beginning to end of the trial.

As every trial lawyer of any experience knows, motions for directed
verdicts are generally made as a matter of course at the close of the
prosecution's case, and are generally denied without close consideration
unless the case is clearly borderline. It is simply unrealistic in this context to have expected the trial judge to pick out the single vague sentence from the directed verdict motion and to have acted upon it with the
refined imagination the Court would require of him. Henry's three lawyers apparently regarded the search and seizure claim as make-weight.
They had not mentioned it earlier in the trial and gave no explanation
for their laxity in raising it. And when they did mention it, they did so
in a cursory and conclusional sentence placed in a secondary position in
a directed verdict motion. The theory underlying the search and seizure
argument—that a wife's freely given permission to search the family car
is invalid—is subtle to say the very least, and as the matter was presented to the trial judge it would have been extraordinary had he caught
it, or even realized that there was a serious problem to catch. But this is
not all the Court would require of him. He must, in addition, realize
that despite the inappropriateness of granting the directed verdict requested of him, he could partially serve the cause of the defense by taking it upon himself to frame and give cautionary instructions to the jury
to disregard the evidence obtained as fruits of the search.[2]

Contrast with this the situation presented by a contemporaneous objection. The objection must necessarily be directed to the single question
of admissibility; the judge must inevitably focus on it; there would be no
doubt as to the appropriate form of relief, and the effect of the trial
judge's decision would be immediate rather than remote. Usually the
proper timing of an objection will force an elaboration of it. Had objection been made in this case during the officer's testimony about the
search, it would have called forth of its own force the specific answer
that the wife had given her permission and, in turn, the assertion that
the permission was ineffective. The issue, in short, would have been ad-

---

[2] Furthermore, even if counsel had fully elaborated the argument and had made it in
the context of a motion to strike rather than a motion for directed verdict, the trial judge
could properly have exercised his discretion (as the Mississippi Supreme Court did) and
denied any relief. This power is recognized in trial judges in the federal system in order to
prevent the 'ambushing' of a trial through the withholding of an objection that should have
been made when questionable evidence was first introduced. Federalism is turned upside
down if it is denied to judges in the state systems.

vertently faced by the trial judge and the likelihood of achieving a correct result maximized.

Thus the state interest which so powerfully supports the contemporaneous-objection rule is that of maximizing correct decisions and concomitantly minimizing errors requiring mistrials and retrials. The alternative for the State is to reverse a trial judge who, from a long motion, fails to pick out and act with remarkable imagination upon a single vague sentence relating to admissibility of evidence long since admitted. A trial judge is a decision-maker, not an advocate. To force him out of his proper role by requiring him to coax out the arguments and imaginatively reframe the requested remedies for the counsel before him is to place upon him more responsibility than a trial judge can be expected to discharge.

There was no "appropriate corrective action" that could have realistically satisfied the purposes of the contemporaneous-objection rule. Without question the State had an interest in maintaining the integrity of its procedure, and thus without doubt reliance on the rule in question is 'adequate' to bar direct review of petitioner's federal claim by this Court.[3]

II

The real reason for remanding this case emerges only in the closing pages of the Court's opinion. It is pointed out that even were the contemporaneous-objection rule considered to be an adequate state ground, this would not, under *Fay v. Noia*, preclude consideration of Henry's federal claim in federal habeas corpus unless it were made to appear that Henry had deliberately waived his federal claim in the state proceedings. It is then said that in the interest of "efficient administration of criminal justice" and "harmonious" relations between the federal and state judiciaries the Mississippi courts should be given the opportunity to pass, in the first instance, on the waiver issue; the prospect is entertained that such action on the part of this Court will encourage the States to grasp the "opportunity" afforded by * * * providing "state procedures, direct or collateral, for a full airing of federal claims." It is "suggested" that were this to be done "irritation" and "friction" respecting the exercise of federal habeas corpus power vis-à-vis state convictions "might be ameliorated."

What does all this signify? The States are being invited to voluntarily obliterate all state procedures, however conducive they may be to the

---

[3] As the first opinion by the Mississippi Supreme Court shows, there is discretion in certain circumstances to lower the procedural bar. It does not follow that this Court is completely free to exercise that discretion. Even in cases from lower federal courts we do so only if there has been an abuse. If, in order to insulate its decisions from reversal by this Court, a state court must strip itself of the discretionary power to differentiate between different sets of circumstances, the rule operates in a most perverse way.

orderly conduct of litigation, which might thwart state-court consideration of federal claims. But what if the States do not accept the invitation? Despite the Court's soft-spoken assertion that "settled principles"
will be applied in the future, I do not think the intimation will be missed
by any discerning reader of the Court's opinion that at the least a substantial dilution of the adequate state-ground doctrine may be expected.
A contrary prediction is belied by the implication of the opinion that under "settled principles," the contemporaneous-objection rule relied upon
in this case could be declared inadequate.

To me this would not be a move toward "harmonious" federalism;
any further disrespect for state procedures, no longer cognizable at all in
federal habeas corpus, would be the very antithesis of it. While some
may say that, given *Fay v. Noia*, what the Court is attempting to do is
justifiable as a means of promoting "efficiency" in the administration of
criminal justice, it is the sort of efficiency which, though perhaps appropriate in some watered-down form of federalism, is not congenial to the
kind of federalism I had supposed was ours. I venture to say that to all
who believe the federal system as we have known it to be a priceless aspect of our Constitutionalism, the spectre implicit in today's decision will
be no less disturbing than what the Court has already done in *Fay v.
Noia*.

Believing that the judgment below rests on an adequate independent
state ground, I would dismiss the writ issued in this case as improvidently granted.

Notes and Questions

1. *Henry v. Mississippi* was certainly not the ordinary case; it had great
political and social significance not reflected in the record. After the Court's
decision above, the Mississippi Supreme Court, perhaps contrary to the
United States Supreme Court's hopes, declined to find that the directed verdict motion sufficiently satisfied the state's interest to permit litigation of
the federal issue and specifically found that there had been a deliberate and
knowing waiver of the Fourth Amendment claim. Henry again sought review, but the Supreme Court denied the petition for certiorari while append-
ing an unusual note that Henry was free to seek federal habeas corpus relief,
which he subsequently did.

> The intransigence of the Mississippi Supreme Court and the desire of
> the U.S. Supreme Court to intervene is more understandable when one
> notes that Aaron Henry was not an ordinary criminal defendant.
> Henry, in fact, was the president of the local NAACP chapter. The
> prosecution was in Mississippi and the year was 1962. There is some
> question as to whether Henry was being singled out for prosecution.

Robert Jerome Glennon, *The Jurisdictional Legacy of the Civil Rights Movement*, 61 TENN.L.REV. 869, 899 (1994) (citation omitted).

2. Suppose federal law made the wife's consent to the inspection of the
automobile effective as to the husband. Could Mississippi take a contrary

position? Assuming that Mississippi did so, would that have any effect on the appealability of the case?

3. The Court notes that the adequate and independent state ground rule applies whether the state ground is substantive or procedural; however, the rule applies differently in the two contexts. What are the differences? The Court appears to say the rule is jurisdictional in one context but not in the other. In which context is it jurisdictional? When the rule is not jurisdictional, does the Court's refusal to hear the case amount to another abstention doctrine? The Court goes on to state that "the question of when and how defaults in compliance with state procedural rules can preclude our consideration of a federal question is itself a federal question." If the state procedural default constitutes an "adequate" ground, the Court will not review the federal question. What test does the Court announce for assessing whether a state ground is adequate?

4. a) Discussing the contemporaneous-objection rule, Justice Brennan notes that it "clearly does serve a legitimate state interest," but observes that Henry's motion for directed verdict "substantially serve[s]" the purpose. Who ought to make the judgment of whether an alternate procedure sufficiently protects the state's interest? Does the majority imply either that the state is obligated to adopt the least restrictive rules possible to protect its interests or that if litigants devise their own ways to protect the state's interest, the state must accept them?

b) This is a point that draws Justice Harlan's attention in dissent. Who should judge whether a rule appropriately serves a state interest? On what basis, if any, should the Supreme Court decide that a state procedural rule is inappropriate? Does the Court owe any deference to the state's perception of its own interests and selection of rules to protect them?

c) To extrapolate from the majority's approach, suppose a state procedural rule prevents appellate consideration within the state court system of an issue of state law upon which the appealing party wishes to rely. Could the aggrieved party seek United States Supreme Court review on the theory that the state procedural rule did not serve any legitimate state interest and was therefore unconstitutional?

5. In *Michel v. Louisiana*, 350 U.S. 91, 76 S.Ct. 158, 100 L.Ed. 83 (1955), the Court considered whether to review a case where the substantive constitutional challenge involved the composition of the grand jury pool. Louisiana law required defendants to raise challenges to the composition of the grand jury "before the expiration of the third judicial day following the end of the grand jury's term or before trial, whichever is earlier." The defendants in *Michel* had not filed timely challenges. The Court characterized the issue before it as follows: "In these cases, we are asked to decide whether this statute as applied violates the Fourteenth Amendment." This challenge to the adequacy of the state procedural rule is of a different nature than the challenge to adequacy of the procedural rule in *Henry*. How are the challenges different? Does *Henry* overrule *Michel*, or can the different kinds of challenges coexist?

6. Justice Black's dissent raises a different question. He notes that Mississippi's Supreme Court has discretion to waive compliance with the rule and has done so on occasion in the past. Does he implicitly take the position that having exercised such discretion, the Mississippi Supreme Court has made the contemporaneous-objection rule unavailable as a basis for resisting review in the United States Supreme Court? Must the state's courts take an all-or-nothing position with respect to such rules?

7. The Court tends to follow a two-step inquiry when the respondent seeks to block Supreme Court review based on a state procedural default. First, is there an independent state procedural ground[8] that is adequate to support the judgment? If not, then the Court may proceed to hear the petitioner's federal claims.[7] If the answer is "Yes," the Court moves to the second inquiry: Do circumstances exist that will excuse the petitioner's non-compliance with the state procedural rule?

a) As to the first inquiry, *Henry* took a very searching look at the adequacy of the Mississippi contemporaneous objection rule, observing that raising the Fourth Amendment claim in a motion for a directed verdict would serve the legitimate state interest equally well. This portion of Justice Brennan's opinion plainly is strained. In fact, *Henry* did not usher in a new era of aggressive examination of the adequacy of state procedural rules. On occasion, the Court found state court reliance on a procedural rule to bar a constitutional claim to be an inadequate ground. For example, in *Douglas v. Alabama*, 380 U.S. 415, 85 S.Ct. 1074, 13 L.Ed.2d 934 (1965), the Court found an Alabama rule requiring multiple objections to the admission of a confession inadequate to bar Supreme Court review. But such cases were rare. The Court was much more likely to stress the importance of state contemporaneous objection rules.

Recently, however, the Court appeared to adopt *Henry*'s approach in a different context in *Lee v. Kemna*, 534 U.S. 362, 122 S.Ct. 877, 151 L.Ed.2d 820 (2002). There a state prisoner seeking federal habeas corpus relief had been denied an overnight continuance in his murder trial when his subpoenaed alibi witnesses disappeared from the courthouse. The trial court refused the continuance because of other schedule commitments. The state appellate courts had upheld the denial, but only on the ground that the defendant had not complied with the state rule requiring such requests to be in writing and with a certain amount of detail. Neither the trial court nor the prosecutor had raised either concern. The inferior federal courts denied relief, but a majority of the Supreme Court held that the procedural default noted for the first time at the appellate level should not bar review. The Court freely acknowledged that the state rules served a legitimate state interest, but it also noted that the manner in which the defendant had sought

[8] The independence of the state law ground is rarely an issue when the state ground is procedural. Independence is more likely to be an issue when the state ground is substantive, as *Fox Film Corp. v. Muller*, at page 901, shows.

[7] *Henry* suggests a caveat. Even if a state procedural ground is inadequate to support the state court judgment, Supreme Court review of the federal claim may be inappropriate if the party seeking review has taken some other action to waive the claim.

the continuance gave the trial court the relevant information at the relevant time. (The latter might distinguish the case from *Henry*). At the same time, the majority explicitly denied that it relied on *Henry* in reaching the result, a claim that Justice Kennedy, in dissent, could not accept.

Despite the majority's insistence that *Henry* did not underlie the decision, the fact remains that the Court did evaluate concededly legitimate state procedural rules on an as-applied basis, just as the *Henry* Court did. Moreover, Note 16 of the majority opinion appears to approve the as-applied approach that the Court used in *Henry* and later endorsed in *Osborne v. Ohio*, 495 U.S. 103, 110 S.Ct. 1691, 109 L.Ed.2d 298 (1990). The Court seemed at pains only to distance itself from *Henry*'s permitting later events to substitute for actions that the defendant should have taken earlier. (In some ways, *Lee* seems more defensible than *Henry*, since Lee moved timely for the continuance whereas Henry did not lodge a contemporaneous objection to the introduction of the evidence from the search.) Although the majority did not use the term, it appeared implicitly to find the facially legitimate state rules unconstitutional as applied to Lee's case, just as the *Henry* majority seemed to reach the same sort of conclusion. The open question now may be whether *Lee* signifies that the Court will take a more searching look at procedural defaults to ensure that application of the state rules in the case in fact serves the legitimate state interest that the rules, considered in the abstract, address.

b) *Henry* appears to suggest that the standards for assessing the second inquiry—whether to excuse a failure to obey a state rule found adequate to support the judgment—may be quite lax. Two years before *Henry*, *Fay v. Noia*, 372 U.S. 391, 83 S.Ct. 822, 9 L.Ed.2d 837 (1963), held that a state procedural default would not bar federal court review of a state judgment in a habeas corpus case unless the applicant "deliberately by-passed the orderly procedures of the state courts and in so doing * * * forfeited his state court remedies." To Justice Harlan's distress, Justice Brennan seemed to imply that the habeas standard would also apply in § 1257 cases.

Coleman v. Thompson, 501 U.S. 722, 111 S.Ct. 2546, 115 L.Ed.2d 640 (1991), imposes a much stricter standard for excusing procedural default in habeas cases and it probably also applies in § 1257 cases. *Coleman* explicitly overruled *Fay v. Noia*'s deliberate by-pass standard and replaced it with the so-called cause-and-prejudice standard. Under this new standard, a federal habeas court will excuse non-compliance with a state procedural rule only if the petitioner shows good cause for not complying with the rule and that the result of his case would have been different if the state court had considered his constitutional claim. Although the Court did not specifically address whether the cause-and-prejudice standard would apply to § 1257 cases, it is hard to see why it should not. The conclusion that it does apply is strengthened by the Court's reminder in *Coleman* that it applies the standards of *Michigan v. Long*, a § 1257 case, to habeas cases. Treating like cases alike should work both ways.

If the cause-and-prejudice standard applies to Supreme Court review of state court decisions, the petitioner in a case like *Michel* would have to persuade the Court that there was a good reason underlying the failure to comply with the three-day rule *and* that if the court heard the grand jury challenge, no conviction would have ensued. Similarly, in *Henry,* the Court might defer the inquiry into the "legitimate state interest" until the petitioner satisfies the cause-and-prejudice inquiry *Coleman* now mandates. It is not yet clear whether the Court will adopt a similar standard in civil cases, but the breadth of *Coleman*'s language at least suggests that it will. Does such a standard mean that a state procedural default almost inevitably bars subsequent consideration of the federal constitutional claim?

There have been three broad categories of cases in which a state procedural default does not preclude Supreme Court review. The first, discussed in *Michel,* involves state procedural rules that are themselves unconstitutional, ordinarily because they deny due process of law. The second, hinted at in *Michel,* involves state procedural rules that, while constitutional on their face, are applied haphazardly or discriminatorily. As recently as 1991, the Court reaffirmed its view of such rules, noting that a state procedural rule must be "firmly established and regularly followed" if it is to bar review. *Ford v. Georgia,* 498 U.S. 411, 424, 111 S.Ct. 850, 857, 112 L.Ed.2d 935, 949 (1991). The third, exemplified by *Henry,* concerns circumstances in which the Court finds either that the state procedural rule serves no legitimate state interest or that the legitimate state interest the rule does represent may be satisfied in other ways. What effect do you think *Coleman* will have on each of these three categories?

8. Counsel's rigorous adherence to state timing rules may also present problems. Where a state allows a comparatively short time in which to make certain motions (*e.g.* a state rule potentially requiring objections to the composition of a grand jury panel to be filed within three days of indictment, (as in *Michel v. Louisiana*), what is counsel's best course upon entering a complex case? If the state has a counterpart to FED.R.CIV.P. 11, which requires counsel to make a reasonable inquiry into the basis for a motion, does that affect the answer? Should existence of a counterpart affect the Court's analysis in procedural default cases?

3. With the Final Judgment Rule

COX BROADCASTING CORP. v. COHN
Supreme Court of the United States, 1975.
420 U.S. 469, 95 S.Ct. 1029, 43 L.Ed.2d 328.

MR. JUSTICE WHITE delivered the opinion of the Court.

The issue before us in this case is whether, consistently with the First and Fourteenth Amendments, a State may extend a cause of action for damages for invasion of privacy caused by the publication of the name of a deceased rape victim which was publicly revealed in connection with the prosecution of the crime.

I

In August 1971, appellee's 17-year-old daughter was the victim of a rape and did not survive the incident. Six youths were soon indicted for murder and rape. Although there was substantial press coverage of the crime and of subsequent developments, the identity of the victim was not disclosed pending trial, perhaps because of Ga.Code Ann. § 26-9901 (1972), which makes it a misdemeanor to publish or broadcast the name or identity of a rape victim. In April 1972, some eight months later, the six defendants appeared in court. Five pleaded guilty to rape or attempted rape, the charge of murder having been dropped. The guilty pleas were accepted by the court, and the trial of the defendant pleading not guilty was set for a later date.

In the course of the proceedings that day, appellant Wassell, a reporter covering the incident for his employer, learned the name of the victim from an examination of the indictments which were made available for his inspection in the courtroom.[3] That the name of the victim appears in the indictments and that the indictments were public records available for inspection are not disputed. Later that day, Wassell broadcast over the facilities of station WSB-TV, a television station owned by appellant Cox Broadcasting Corp., a news report concerning the court proceedings. The report named the victim of the crime and was repeated the following day.[5]

In May 1972, appellee brought an action for money damages against appellants, relying on § 26-9901 and claiming that his right to privacy had been invaded by the television broadcasts giving the name of his deceased daughter. Appellants admitted the broadcasts but claimed that they were privileged under both state law and the First and Fourteenth

---

[3] Wassell has described the way in which he obtained the information reported in the broadcast as follows:

> The information on which I prepared the said report was obtained from several sources. First, by personally attending and taking notes of the said trial and the subsequent transfer of four of the six defendants to the Fulton County Jail, I obtained personal knowledge of the events that transpired during the trial of this action and the said transfer of the defendants. Such personal observations and notes were the primary and almost exclusive source of the information upon which the said news report was based. Secondly, during a recess of the said trial, I approached the clerk of the court, who was sitting directly in front of the bench, and requested to see a copy of the indictments. In open court, I was handed the indictments, both the murder and the rape indictments, and was allowed to examine fully this document. As is shown by the said indictments * * * the name of the said Cynthia Cohn appears in clear type. Moreover, no attempt was made by the clerk or anyone else to withhold the name and identity of the victim from me or from anyone else and the said indictments apparently were available for public inspection upon request.

[5] The relevant portion of the transcript of the televised report reads as follows:

> Six youths went on trial today for the murder-rape of a teenaged girl.
>
> The six Sandy Springs High School boys were charged with murder and rape in the death of seventeen year old Cynthia Cohn following a drinking party last August 18th.
>
> The tragic death of the high school girl shocked the entire Sandy Springs community. Today the six boys had their day in court.

Amendments. The trial court, rejecting appellants' constitutional claims and holding that the Georgia statute gave a civil remedy to those injured by its violation, granted summary judgment to appellee as to liability, with the determination of damages to await trial by jury.

On appeal, the Georgia Supreme Court, in its initial opinion, held that the trial court had erred in construing § 26-9901 to extend a civil cause of action for invasion of privacy and thus found it unnecessary to consider the constitutionality of the statute. The court went on to rule, however, that the complaint stated a cause of action "for the invasion of the appellee's right of privacy, or for the tort of public disclosure"—a "common law tort exist[ing] in this jurisdiction without the help of the statute that the trial judge in this case relied on." Although the privacy invaded was not that of the deceased victim, the father was held to have stated a claim for invasion of his own privacy by reason of the publication of his daughter's name. The court explained, however, that liability did not follow as a matter of law and that summary judgment was improper; whether the public disclosure of the name actually invaded appellee's "zone of privacy," and if so, to what extent, were issues to be determined by the trier of fact. Also, "in formulating such an issue for determination by the fact-finder, it is reasonable to require the appellee to prove that the appellants invaded his privacy with wilful or negligent disregard for the fact that reasonable men would find the invasion highly offensive." The Georgia Supreme Court did agree with the trial court, however, that the First and Fourteenth Amendments did not, as a matter of law, require judgment for appellants. The court concurred with the statement [of the California Supreme Court] that "the rights guaranteed by the First Amendment do not require total abrogation of the right to privacy. The goals sought by each may be achieved with a minimum of intrusion upon the other."

Upon motion for rehearing the Georgia court countered the argument that the victim's name was a matter of public interest and could be published with impunity by relying on § 26-9901 as an authoritative declaration of state policy that the name of a rape victim was not a matter of public concern. This time the court felt compelled to determine the constitutionality of the statute and sustained it as a "legitimate limitation on the right of freedom of expression contained in the First Amendment." The court could discern "no public interest or general concern about the identity of the victim of such a crime as will make the right to disclose the identity of the victim rise to the level of First Amendment protection."

We postponed decision as to our jurisdiction over this appeal to the hearing on the merits. We conclude that the Court has jurisdiction, and reverse the judgment of the Georgia Supreme Court.

II

Appellants invoke the appellate jurisdiction of this Court under 28

U.S.C. § 1257(2) and, if that jurisdictional basis is found to be absent, through a petition for certiorari under 28 U.S.C. § 2103. Two questions concerning our jurisdiction must be resolved: (1) whether the constitutional validity of § 26-9901 was "drawn in question," with the Georgia Supreme Court upholding its validity, and (2) whether the decision from which this appeal has been taken is a "[f]inal judgment or decree."

A

Appellants clearly raised the issue of the constitutionality of § 26-9901 in their motion for rehearing in the Georgia Supreme Court. In denying that motion that court held: "A majority of this court does not consider this statute to be in conflict with the First Amendment." Since the court relied upon the statute as a declaration of the public policy of Georgia that the disclosure of a rape victim's name was not to be protected expression, the statute was drawn in question in a manner directly bearing upon the merits of the action, and the decision in favor of its constitutional validity invokes this Court's appellate jurisdiction.

B

Since 1789, Congress has granted this Court appellate jurisdiction with respect to state litigation only after the highest state court in which judgment could be had has rendered a "[f]inal judgment or decree." Title 28 U.S.C. § 1257 retains this limitation on our power to review cases coming from state courts. The Court has noted that "[considerations] of English usage as well as those of judicial policy" would justify an interpretation of the final-judgment rule to preclude review "where anything further remains to be determined by a State court, no matter how dissociated from the only federal issue that has finally been adjudicated by the highest court of the State." *Radio Station WOW, Inc. v. Johnson.* But the Court there observed that the rule had not been administered in such a mechanical fashion and that there were circumstances in which there has been "a departure from this requirement of finality for federal appellate jurisdiction."

These circumstances were said to be "very few," but as the cases have unfolded, the Court has recurringly encountered situations in which the highest court of a State has finally determined the federal issue present in a particular case, but in which there are further proceedings in the lower state courts to come. There are now at least four categories of such cases in which the Court has treated the decision on the federal issue as a final judgment for the purposes of 28 U.S.C. § 1257 and has taken jurisdiction without awaiting the completion of the additional proceedings anticipated in the lower state courts. In most, if not all, of the cases in these categories, these additional proceedings would not require the decision of other federal questions that might also require review by the Court at a later date,[6] and immediate rather than delayed review would be the best way to avoid "the mischief of economic waste and of delayed justice," as well as precipitate interference with state litigation.[7] In the cases in the first two categories considered below, the federal issue would not be mooted or otherwise affected by the proceedings yet to be had because those proceedings have little substance, their outcome is certain, or they are wholly unrelated to the federal question. In the other two categories, however, the federal issue would be mooted if the petitioner or appellant seeking to bring the action here prevailed on the merits in the later state-court proceedings, but there is nevertheless sufficient justification for immediate review of the federal question finally determined in the state courts.

In the first category are those cases in which there are further proceedings—even entire trials—yet to occur in the state courts but where for one reason or another the federal issue is conclusive or the outcome of further proceedings preordained. In these circumstances, because the case is for all practical purposes concluded, the judgment of the state court on the federal issue is deemed final. In *Mills v. Alabama,* for example, a demurrer to a criminal complaint was sustained on federal constitutional grounds by a state trial court. The State Supreme Court reversed, remanding for jury trial. This Court took jurisdiction on the reasoning that the appellant had no defense other than his federal claim and could not prevail at trial on the facts or any nonfederal ground. To dismiss the appeal "would not only be an inexcusable delay of the benefits Congress intended to grant by providing for appeal to this Court, but it would also result in a completely unnecessary waste of time and energy in judicial systems already troubled by delays due to congested dockets."[8]

---

[6] Eminent domain proceedings are of the type that may involve an interlocutory decision as to a federal question with another federal question to be decided later. "For in those cases the federal constitutional question embraces not only a taking, but a taking on payment of just compensation. A state judgment is not final unless it covers both aspects of that integral problem."

[7] Gillespie v. United States Steel Corp., 379 U.S. 148 (1964), arose in the federal courts and involved the requirement of 28 U.S.C. § 1291 that judgments of district courts be final if they are to be appealed to the courts of appeals. In the course of deciding that the judgment of the District Court in the case had been final, the Court indicated its approach to finality requirements:

> And our cases long have recognized that whether a ruling is "final" within the meaning of § 1291 is frequently so close a question that decision of that issue either way can be supported with equally forceful arguments, and that it is impossible to devise a formula to resolve all marginal cases coming within what might well be called the "twilight zone" of finality. Because of this difficulty this Court has held that the requirement of finality is to be given a "practical rather than a technical construction." [We also] pointed out that in deciding the question of finality the most important competing considerations are "the inconvenience and costs of piecemeal review on the one hand and the danger of denying justice by delay on the other."

[8] * * * In the *Richfield* case the Court said with respect to finality:

Second, there are cases such as *Radio Station WOW,* and *Brady v. Maryland* in which the federal issue, finally decided by the highest court in the State, will survive and require decision regardless of the outcome of future state-court proceedings. In *Radio Station WOW,* the Nebraska Supreme Court directed the transfer of the properties of a federally licensed radio station and ordered an accounting, rejecting the claim that the transfer order would interfere with the federal license. The federal issue was held reviewable here despite the pending accounting on the "presupposition * * * that the federal questions that could come here have been adjudicated by the State court, and that the accounting which remains to be taken could not remotely give rise to a federal question * * * that may later come here * * *." The judgment rejecting the federal claim and directing the transfer was deemed "dissociated from a provision for an accounting even though that is decreed in the same order." Nothing that could happen in the course of the accounting, short of settlement of the case, would foreclose or make unnecessary decision on the federal question. Older cases in the Court had reached the same result on similar facts. * * *[9]

In the third category are those situations where the federal claim has been finally decided, with further proceedings on the merits in the state courts to come, but in which later review of the federal issue cannot be had, whatever the ultimate outcome of the case. Thus, in these cases, if the party seeking interim review ultimately prevails on the merits, the federal issue will be mooted; if he were to lose on the merits, however, the governing state law would not permit him again to present his federal claims for review. The Court has taken jurisdiction in these circumstances prior to completion of the case in the state courts. *California v. Stewart* (decided with *Miranda v. Arizona*), epitomizes this category. There the state court reversed a conviction on federal constitutional grounds and remanded for a new trial. Although the State might have prevailed at trial, we granted its petition for certiorari and affirmed, explaining that the state judgment was "final" since an acquittal of the defendant at trial would preclude, under state law, an appeal by the State.

A recent decision in this category is *North Dakota State Board of Pharmacy v. Snyder's Drug Stores, Inc.,* in which the Pharmacy Board rejected an application for a pharmacy operating permit relying on a

---

The designation given the judgment by state practice is not controlling. The question is whether it can be said that "there is nothing more to be decided" that there has been "an effective determination of the litigation." That question will be resolved not only by an examination of the entire record but, where necessary, by resort to the local law to determine what effect the judgment has under the state rules of practice.

[9] In *Brady v. Maryland,* the Maryland courts had ordered a new trial in a criminal case but on punishment only, and the petitioner asserted here that he was entitled to a new trial on guilt as well. We entertained the case, saying that the federal issue was separable and would not be mooted by the new trial on punishment ordered in the state courts.

state statute specifying ownership requirements which the applicant did not meet. The State Supreme Court held the statute unconstitutional and remanded the matter to the Board for further consideration of the application, freed from the constraints of the ownership statute. The Board brought the case here, claiming that the statute was constitutionally acceptable under modern cases. After reviewing the various circumstances under which the finality requirement has been deemed satisfied despite the fact that litigation had not terminated in the state courts, we entertained the case over claims that we had no jurisdiction. The federal issue would not survive the remand, whatever the result of the state administrative proceedings. The Board might deny the license on state-law grounds, thus foreclosing the federal issue, and the Court also ascertained that under state law the Board could not bring the federal issue here in the event the applicant satisfied the requirements of state law except for the invalidated ownership statute. Under these circumstances, the issue was ripe for review.

Lastly, there are those situations where the federal issue has been finally decided in the state courts with further proceedings pending in which the party seeking review here might prevail on the merits on non-federal grounds, thus rendering unnecessary review of the federal issue by this Court, and where reversal of the state court on the federal issue would be preclusive of any further litigation on the relevant cause of action rather than merely controlling the nature and character of, or determining the admissibility of evidence in, the state proceedings still to come. In these circumstances, if a refusal immediately to review the state-court decision might seriously erode federal policy, the Court has entertained and decided the federal issue, which itself has been finally determined by the state courts for purposes of the state litigation.

In *Construction Laborers v. Curry,* the state courts temporarily enjoined labor union picketing over claims that the National Labor Relations Board had exclusive jurisdiction of the controversy. The Court took jurisdiction for two independent reasons. First, the power of the state court to proceed in the face of the preemption claim was deemed an issue separable from the merits and ripe for review in this Court, particularly "when postponing review would seriously erode the national labor policy requiring the subject matter of respondents' cause to be heard by the * * * Board, not by the state courts." Second, the Court was convinced that in any event the union had no defense to the entry of a permanent injunction other than the preemption claim that had already been ruled on in the state courts. Hence the case was for all practical purposes concluded in the state tribunals.

In *Mercantile National Bank v. Langdeau,* two national banks were sued, along with others, in the courts of Travis County, Tex. The claim asserted was conspiracy to defraud an insurance company. The banks as a preliminary matter asserted that a special federal venue statute immunized them from suit in Travis County and that they could properly be sued only in another county. Although trial was still to be had and the banks might well prevail on the merits, the Court, relying on *Curry*, entertained the issue as a "separate and independent matter, anterior to the merits and not enmeshed in the factual and legal issues comprising the plaintiff's cause of action." Moreover, it would serve the policy of the federal statute "to determine now in which state court appellants may be tried rather than to subject them * * * to long and complex litigation which may all be for naught if consideration of the preliminary question of venue is postponed until the conclusion of the proceedings."

Miami Herald Publishing Co. v. Tornillo is the latest case in this category. There a candidate for public office sued a newspaper for refusing, allegedly contrary to a state statute, to carry his reply to the paper's editorial critical of his qualifications. The trial court held the act unconstitutional, denying both injunctive relief and damages. The State Supreme Court reversed, sustaining the statute against the challenge based upon the First and Fourteenth Amendments and remanding the case for a trial and appropriate relief, including damages. The newspaper brought the case here. We sustained our jurisdiction, relying on the principles elaborated in the *North Dakota* case and observing:

> Whichever way we were to decide on the merits, it would be intolerable to leave unanswered, under these circumstances, an important question of freedom of the press under the First Amendment; an uneasy and unsettled constitutional posture of § 104.38 could only further harm the operation of a free press.[12]

In light of the prior cases, we conclude that we have jurisdiction to review the judgment of the Georgia Supreme Court rejecting the challenge under the First and Fourteenth Amendments to the state law authorizing damage suits against the press for publishing the name of a rape victim whose identity is revealed in the course of a public prosecution. The Georgia Supreme Court's judgment is plainly final on the federal issue and is not subject to further review in the state courts. Appellants will be liable for damages if the elements of the state cause of action are proved. They may prevail at trial on nonfederal grounds, it is true, but if the Georgia court erroneously upheld the statute, there should be no trial at all. Moreover, even if appellants prevailed at trial and made unnecessary further consideration of the constitutional question, there would remain in effect the unreviewed decision of the State Supreme Court that a civil action for publishing the name of a rape victim disclosed in a public judicial proceeding may go forward despite the First and Fourteenth Amendments. Delaying final decision of the First

---

[12] The import of the Court's holding in *Tornillo* is underlined by its citation of the concurring opinion in *Mills v. Alabama*. There, Mr. Justice Douglas, joined by Mr. Justice Brennan, stated that even if the appellant had a defense and might prevail at trial, jurisdiction was properly noted in order to foreclose unwarranted restrictions on the press should the state court's constitutional judgment prove to be in error.

Amendment claim until after trial will "leave unanswered * * * an important question of freedom of the press under the First Amendment," "an uneasy and unsettled constitutional posture [that] could only further harm the operation of a free press." On the other hand, if we now hold that the First and Fourteenth Amendments bar civil liability for broadcasting the victim's name, this litigation ends. Given these factors—that the litigation could be terminated by our decision on the merits[13] and that a failure to decide the question now will leave the press in Georgia operating in the shadow of the civil and criminal sanctions of a rule of law and a statute the constitutionality of which is in serious doubt—we find that reaching the merits is consistent with the pragmatic approach that we have followed in the past in determining finality.

Reversed.

MR. JUSTICE REHNQUIST, dissenting.

Because I am of the opinion that the decision which is the subject of this appeal is not a "final" judgment or decree, as that term is used in 28 U.S.C. § 1257, I would dismiss this appeal for want of jurisdiction.

Radio Station WOW, Inc. v. Johnson established that in a "very few" circumstances review of state-court decisions could be had in this Court even though something "further remain[ed] to be determined by a State court." Over the years, however, and despite vigorous protest by Mr. Justice Harlan, this Court has steadily discovered new exceptions to the finality requirement, such that they can hardly any longer be described as "very few." Whatever may be the unexpressed reasons for this process of expansion, it has frequently been the subject of no more formal an express explanation than cursory citations to preceding cases in the line. * * * Although the Court's opinion today does accord detailed consideration to this problem, I do not believe that the reasons it expresses can support its result.

---

[13] Mr. Justice Rehnquist is correct in saying that this factor involves consideration of the merits in determining jurisdiction. But it does so only to the extent of determining that the issue is substantial and only in the context that if the state court's final decision on the federal issue is incorrect, federal law forecloses further proceedings in the state court. That the petitioner who protests against the state court's decision on the federal question might prevail on the merits on nonfederal grounds in the course of further proceedings anticipated in the state court and hence obviate later review of the federal issue here is not preclusive of our jurisdiction. *Curry, Langdeau, North Dakota State Board of Pharmacy, California v. Stewart,* decided with *Miranda v. Arizona,* and *Miami Herald Publishing Co. v. Tornillo,* make this clear. In those cases, the federal issue having been decided, arguably wrongly, and being determinative of the litigation if decided the other way, the finality rule was satisfied.

The author of the dissent, a member of the majority in *Tornillo,* does not disavow that decision. He seeks only to distinguish it by indicating that the First Amendment issue at stake there was more important and pressing than the one here. This seems to embrace the thesis of that case and of this one as far as the approach to finality is concerned, even though the merits and the avoidance doctrine are to some extent involved.

I

The Court has taken what it terms a "pragmatic" approach to the finality problem presented in this case. In so doing, it has relied heavily on *Gillespie v. United States Steel Corp.* As the Court acknowledges, *Gillespie* involved 28 U.S.C. § 1291, which restricts the appellate jurisdiction of the federal courts of appeals to "final decisions of the district courts." Although acknowledging this distinction, the Court accords it no importance and adopts *Gillespie*'s approach without any consideration of whether the finality requirement for this Court's jurisdiction over a "judgment or decree" of a state court is grounded on more serious concerns than is the limitation of court of appeals jurisdiction to final "decisions" of the district courts.[3] I believe that the underlying concerns are different, and that the difference counsels a more restrictive approach when § 1257 finality is at issue.

According to *Gillespie,* the finality requirement is imposed as a matter of minimizing "the inconvenience and costs of piecemeal review." This proposition is undoubtedly sound so long as one is considering the administration of the federal court system. Were judicial efficiency the only interest at stake there would be less inclination to challenge the Court's resolution in this case, although, as discussed below, I have serious reservations that the standards the Court has formulated are effective for achieving even this single goal. The case before us, however, is an appeal from a state court, and this fact introduces additional interests which must be accommodated in fashioning any exception to the literal application of the finality requirement. I consider § 1257 finality to be but one of a number of congressional provisions reflecting concern that uncontrolled federal judicial interference with state administrative and judicial functions would have untoward consequences for our federal system.[4] This is by no means a novel view of the § 1257 finality re-

---

[3] The textual distinction between §§ 1291 and 1257, the former referring to "final decisions," while the latter refers to "final judgments or decrees," first appeared in the Evarts Act, Act of Mar. 3, 1891, which created the courts of appeals. Section 6 of that Act provided that courts of appeals should exercise appellate jurisdiction over "final decision" of the federal trial courts. The House version of the Act had referred to "final judgment or decree," but the Senate Judiciary Committee changed the wording without formal explanation. Perhaps significance can be attached to the fact that under the House bill the courts of appeals would have been independent of the federal trial courts, being manned by full-time appellate judges; the Senate version, on the other hand, generally provided that court of appeals duties would be performed by the trial judges within each circuit.

The first Judiciary Act, Act of Sept. 24, 1789, used the terms "judgment" and "decree" in defining the appellate jurisdiction of both the Supreme Court, § 25, and the original circuit courts.

[4] *See, e.g.,* 28 U.S.C. § 1341 (limitation on power of district courts to enjoin state taxing systems); 28 U.S.C. § 1739 (requiring that state judicial proceedings be accorded full faith and credit in federal courts); 28 U.S.C. §§ 2253-2254 (prescribing various restrictions on federal habeas corpus for state prisoners); 28 U.S.C. § 2281 (three-judge district court requirement); 28 U.S.C. § 2283 (restricting power of federal courts to enjoin state-court proceedings).

quirement. In *Radio Station WOW, Inc. v. Johnson,* Mr. Justice Frankfurter's opinion for the Court explained the finality requirement as follows:

> This requirement has the support of considerations generally applicable to good judicial administration. It avoids the mischief of economic waste and of delayed justice. Only in very few situations, where intermediate rulings may carry serious public consequences, has there been a departure from this requirement of finality for federal appellate jurisdiction. *This prerequisite to review derives added force when the jurisdiction of this Court is invoked to upset the decision of a State court.* Here we are in the realm of potential conflict between the courts of two different governments. And so, ever since 1789, Congress has granted this Court the power to intervene in State litigation only after "the highest court of a State in which a decision in the suit could be had" has rendered a "final judgment or decree." § 237 of the Judicial Code, 28 U.S.C. § 344(a). *This requirement is not one of those technicalities to be easily scorned. It is an important factor in the smooth working of our federal system.* [Emphasis added.]

In *Republic Gas Co. v. Oklahoma,* Mr. Justice Frankfurter, speaking for the Court, again expressed this view:

> This prerequisite for the exercise of the appellate powers of this Court is especially pertinent when a constitutional barrier is asserted against a State court's decision on matters peculiarly of local concern. Close observance of this limitation upon the Court is not regard for a strangling technicality. History bears ample testimony that it is an important factor in securing harmonious State-federal relations.

That comity and federalism are significant elements of § 1257 finality has been recognized by other members of the Court as well, perhaps most notably by Mr. Justice Harlan. [H]e argued that one basis of the finality rule was that it foreclosed "this Court from passing on constitutional issues that may be dissipated by the final outcome of a case, thus helping to keep to a minimum undesirable federal-state conflicts." One need cast no doubt on the Court's decision in such cases as *Langdeau* to recognize that Mr. Justice Harlan was focusing on a consideration which should be of significance in the Court's disposition of this case.

"Harmonious state-federal relations" are no less important today * * * . Indeed, we have in recent years emphasized and re-emphasized the importance of comity and federalism in dealing with a related problem, that of district court interference with ongoing state judicial proceedings. Because these concerns are important, and because they provide "added force" to § 1257's finality requirement, I believe that the Court has erred by simply importing the approach of cases in which the only concern is efficient judicial administration.

II

But quite apart from the considerations of federalism which counsel against an expansive reading of our jurisdiction under § 1257, the Court's holding today enunciates a virtually formless exception to the finality requirement, one which differs in kind from those previously carved out. By contrast, *Construction Laborers v. Curry* and *Mercantile National Bank v. Langdeau* are based on the understandable principle that where the proper forum for trying the issue joined in the state courts depends on the resolution of the federal question raised on appeal, sound judicial administration requires that such a question be decided by this Court, if it is to be decided at all, sooner rather than later in the course of the litigation. *Organization for a Better Austin v. Keefe* and *Mills v. Alabama* rest on the premise that where as a practical matter the state litigation has been concluded by the decision of the State's highest court, the fact that in terms of state procedure the ruling is interlocutory should not bar a determination by this Court of the merits of the federal question.

Still other exceptions, as noted in the Court's opinion, have been made where the federal question decided by the highest court of the State is bound to survive and be presented for decision here regardless of the outcome of future state-court proceedings, and for the situation in which later review of the federal issue cannot be had, whatever the ultimate outcome of the subsequent proceedings directed by the highest court of the State. While the totality of these exceptions certainly indicates that the Court has been willing to impart to the language "final judgment or decree" a great deal of flexibility, each of them is arguably consistent with the intent of Congress in enacting § 1257, if not with the language it used, and each of them is relatively workable in practice.

To those established exceptions is now added one so formless that it cannot be paraphrased, but instead must be quoted:

> Given these factors—that the litigation could be terminated by our decision on the merits and that a failure to decide the question now will leave the press in Georgia operating in the shadow of the civil and criminal sanctions of a rule of law and a statute the constitutionality of which is in serious doubt—we find that reaching the merits is consistent with the pragmatic approach that we have followed in the past in determining finality.

There are a number of difficulties with this test. One of them is the Court's willingness to look to the merits. It is not clear from the Court's opinion, however, exactly how great a look at the merits we are to take. On the one hand, the Court emphasizes that if we reverse the Supreme Court of Georgia the litigation will end, and it refers to cases in which the federal issue has been decided "arguably wrongly." On the other hand, it claims to look to the merits "only to the extent of determining that the issue is substantial." If the latter is all the Court means, then the inquiry is no more extensive than is involved when we determine whether a case is appropriate for plenary consideration; but if no more is meant, our decision is just as likely to be a costly intermediate step in the litigation as it is to be the concluding event. If, on the other hand, the Court really intends its doctrine to reach only so far as cases in which our decision in all probability will terminate the litigation, then the Court is reversing the traditional sequence of judicial decisionmaking. Heretofore, it has generally been thought that a court first assumed jurisdiction of a case, and then went on to decide the merits of the questions it presented. But henceforth in determining our own jurisdiction we may be obliged to determine whether or not we agree with the merits of the decision of the highest court of a State.

Yet another difficulty with the Court's formulation is the problem of transposing to any other case the requirement that "failure to decide the question now will leave the press in Georgia operating in the shadow of the civil and criminal sanctions of a rule of law and a statute the constitutionality of which is in serious doubt." Assuming that we are to make this determination of "serious doubt" at the time we note probable jurisdiction of such an appeal, is it enough that the highest court of the State has ruled against any federal constitutional claim? If that is the case, then because § 1257 by other language imposes that requirement, we will have completely read out of the statute the limitation of our jurisdiction to a "final judgment or decree." Perhaps the Court's new standard for finality is limited to cases in which a First Amendment freedom is at issue. The language used by Congress, however, certainly provides no basis for preferring the First Amendment, as incorporated by the Fourteenth Amendment, to the various other Amendments which are likewise "incorporated," or indeed for preferring any of the "incorporated" Amendments over the due process and equal protection provisions which are embodied literally in the Fourteenth Amendment.

Another problem is that in applying the second prong of its test, the Court has not engaged in any independent inquiry as to the consequences of permitting the decision of the Supreme Court of Georgia to remain undisturbed pending final state-court resolution of the case. This suggests that in order to invoke the benefit of today's rule, the "shadow" in which an appellant must stand need be neither deep nor wide. In this case nothing more is at issue than the right to report the name of the victim of a rape. No hindrance of any sort has been imposed on reporting the fact of a rape or the circumstances surrounding it. Yet the Court unquestioningly places this issue on a par with the core First Amendment interest involved in *Miami Herald Publishing Co. v. Tornillo* and *Mills v. Alabama,* that of protecting the press in its role of providing uninhibited political discourse.

But the greatest difficulty with the test enunciated today is that it totally abandons the principle that constitutional issues are too important to be decided save when absolutely necessary, and are to be avoided if there are grounds for decision of lesser dimension.[6] The long line of cases which established this rule makes clear that it is a principle primarily designed, not to benefit the lower courts, or state-federal relations, but rather to safeguard this Court's own process of constitutional adjudication.

* * *

In this case there has yet to be an adjudication of liability against appellants, and unlike the appellant in *Mills v. Alabama,* they do not concede that they have no nonfederal defenses. Nonetheless, the Court rules on their constitutional defense. Far from eschewing a constitutional holding in advance of the necessity for one, the Court construes § 1257 so that it may virtually rush out and meet the prospective constitutional litigant as he approaches our doors.

III

This Court is obliged to make preliminary determinations of its jurisdiction at the time it votes to note probable jurisdiction. At that stage of the proceedings, prior to briefing on the merits or oral argument, such determinations must of necessity be based on relatively cursory acquaintance with the record of the proceedings below. The need for an understandable and workable application of a jurisdictional provision such as § 1257 is therefore far greater than for a similar interpretation of statutes dealing with substantive law.[7] We, of course, retain the authority to dismiss a case for want of a final judgment after having studied briefs on the merits and having heard oral argument, but I can recall not a single instance of such a disposition during the last three Terms of the Court. While in theory this may be explained by saying that during these Terms we have never accorded plenary consideration to a § 1257 case which was not a "final judgment or decree," I would guess it just as accurate to say that after the Court has studied briefs and heard oral argument, it has an understandable tendency to proceed to a decision on the merits in preference to dismissing for want of jurisdiction. It is thus especially disturbing that the rule of this case, unlike the more workable and straightforward exceptions which the Court has previously formulated, will seriously compound the already difficult task of accurately determining, at a preliminary stage, whether an appeal from a state-court judgment is a "final judgment or decree."

A further aspect of the difficulties which the Court is generating is il-

---

[6] One important distinction between this case and *Construction Laborers v. Curry* has already been discussed. Another is that the federal issue here is constitutional, whereas that in *Curry* was statutory.

[7] *Cf. United States v. Sisson:* "Clarity is to be desired in any statute, but in matters of jurisdiction it is especially important. Otherwise the courts and the parties must expend great energy, not on the merits of dispute settlement, but on simply deciding whether a court has the power to hear a case."

lustrated by a petition for certiorari recently filed in this Court, *Time, Inc. v. Firestone.* The case was twice before the Florida Supreme Court. That court's first decision was rendered in December 1972; it rejected Time's First Amendment defense to a libel action, and remanded for further proceedings on state-law issues. The second decision was rendered in 1974, and dealt with the state-law issues litigated on remand. Before this Court, Time seeks review of the First Amendment defense rejected by the Florida Supreme Court in December 1972. Under the Court's decision today, one could conclude that the 1972 judgment was itself a final decision from which review might have been had. If it was, then petitioner Time is confronted by 28 U.S.C. § 2101(c), which restricts this Court's jurisdiction over state civil cases to those in which review is sought within 90 days of the entry of a reviewable judgment.

I in no way suggest either my own or the Court's views on our jurisdiction over *Time, Inc. v. Firestone.* This example is simply illustrative of the difficulties which today's decision poses not only for this Court, but also for a prudent counsel who is faced with an adverse interlocutory ruling by a State's highest court on a federal issue asserted as a dispositive bar to further litigation. I suppose that such counsel would be unwilling to presume that this Court would flout both the meaning of words and the command of Congress by employing loose standards of finality to obtain jurisdiction, but strict ones to prevent its loss. He thus would be compelled to judge his situation in light of today's formless, unworkable exception to the finality requirement. I would expect him frequently to choose to seek immediate review in this Court, solely as a matter of assuring that his federal contentions are not lost for want of timely filing. The inevitable result will be totally unnecessary additions to our docket and serious interruptions and delays of the state adjudicatory process.

Although unable to persuade my Brethren that we do not have in this case a final judgment or decree of the Supreme Court of Georgia, I nonetheless take heart from the fact that we are concerned here with an area in which "*stare decisis* has historically been accorded considerably less than its usual weight." I would dismiss for want of jurisdiction.

Notes and Questions

1. To understand fully the Court's four categories of non-final cases that will be treated as final for purposes of 28 U.S.C.A. § 1257, it is necessary not only to identify the general criteria for each category but also to review carefully the examples the Court gives of each to see exactly how the federal issue arises and what is likely to happen to it in further state court proceedings. *Cox's* analysis raises many questions about the functioning of the federal courts generally. As a preliminary matter, consider the purposes of the finality requirement. The Court most often mentions judicial efficiency—the need to conserve judicial time, but particularly federal judicial time. The Court believes there times when that goal may be better served by allowing review of a nonfinal judgment—times when the "custom is more honored in

the breach than in the observance." WILLIAM SHAKESPEARE, HAMLET, act I, sc. iv, lines 17-18.

2. Does the Court subdivide the fourth category into three parts? It first cites *Construction Laborers v. Curry*. The Court argued intervention was justified because of the need to avoid erosion of important federal policy. Then it reviews *Mercantile National Bank v. Langdeau* as an example of deciding a preliminary matter to avoid complex, costly, and potentially futile litigation. Finally, the Court cites *Miami Herald Publishing Co. v. Tornillo* as exemplifying cases where important federal issues, though they may well survive further state court litigation, ought not to be left unsettled in the interim. Are these three cases fungible or do they represent different concerns that may call for a common solution?

3. The Court notes its long-standing "pragmatic" approach to determining what "final" means. Does "final" mean the same thing in all four categories? By definition, does the fourth category, in any of its manifestations, involve judgments that are demonstrably not final?

4. With respect to the fourth category, are there any discernible limits to the Court's asserted ability to review federal issues that it considers important, or is that category a roving commission for the court to seek out issues to which at least four Justices wish to speak? *Cox* notes that "if Georgia erroneously upheld the statute, there should be no trial at all." Accepting the characterization as an indication that summary disposition in defendant's favor would be appropriate, either by summary judgment or under FED. R. CIV. P. 12(b)(6), does *Cox* mean that any erroneous denial of a defendant's federally-based motion for summary disposition is reviewable under § 1257? If not, how is this case different from any other case where a legal issue disposes of the plaintiff's claim?

5. Applying the *Cox* categories, especially the fourth, can be difficult. In *Nike, Inc. v. Kasky*, 539 U.S. 654, 123 S.Ct. 2554, 156 L.Ed.2d 580 (2003) (dismissing the writ of certiorari as improvidently granted), Justices Stevens and Breyer battled over how far the *Cox* pattern extended. The underlying issue was whether certain statements that Nike had made were entitled to First Amendment protection as noncommercial speech or only as commercial speech, which might have left Nike vulnerable to an adverse judgment under California's Unfair Competition Law and its False Advertising Law. When Kasky appealed the lower state courts' ruling that Nike's speech was entitled to full First Amendment protection as "part of a public dialogue on a matter of public concern within the core area of expression protected by the First Amendment," which led them to dismiss the action, the California Supreme Court had reversed, finding that the speech was commercial, entitled to less embracing First Amendment protection, and that Nike therefore had to go to trial on whether its speech had been false and misleading within the meaning of the California statutes. Nike sought Supreme Court review, and the Court originally granted certiorari.

Ultimately, the Court dismissed the writ. The case raised a critical issue of whether the Supreme Court had statutory jurisdiction to review under 28 U.S.C. § 1257. The California Supreme Court's ruling that Nike's speech was commercial was not a final defeat for Nike; Kasky might have been unable to demonstrate that the speech satisfied the California criteria for liability, so Nike might have prevailed. Even had it lost, it might have preserved the First Amendment question that it had lost on the interlocutory appeal in California and ultimately sought to present it to the United States Supreme Court. These circumstances make *Nike* look rather like *Cox*. Had Cox been required to go to trial, it might have won, as the Georgia Supreme Court had observed, on the issue of whether the publication had invaded the victim's father's zone of privacy. Ultimately, had Cox lost, it might have sought review in the United States Supreme Court.

That parallel did not satisfy Justices Stevens and Ginsburg, who concurred in the dismissal of the writ. Justice Stevens's opinion distinguished *Nike* from *Cox* on the ground that the First Amendment issue in *Nike* involved multiple statements made at different times and in different circumstances, and it criticized Nike's argument as assuming that all of the speech involved was classifiable uniformly as commercial or noncommercial. "[E]ven if we were to decide the First Amendment issues presented to us today, more First Amendment issues might well remain in this case, making piecemeal review of the Federal First Amendment issues likely." This caused Justice Stevens to view the state judgment as insufficiently final to support the exercise of Supreme Court jurisdiction and to conclude that it was not sufficiently likely that a decision by the Court could end the litigation on Kasky's claim, because he saw several possible decisions on the merits of the First Amendment questions.

Justices Breyer and O'Connor dissented from the dismissal. Justice Breyer identified four criteria from *Cox* (final decision of the federal issue at the state level, possibility of the party seeking review prevailing on nonfederal grounds that would prevent Supreme Court consideration of the federal issue, "reversal of the state court on the federal issue [being] preclusive of any further litigation on the relevant cause of action rather than merely controlling the nature and character of, or determination the admissibility of evidence in, the state proceedings still to come," (internal quotation marks omitted) and erosion of important federal policy as a result of refusal to review) and concluded that *Nike* satisfied each. The primary areas of dispute with Justice Stevens were the first and third criteria. Justice Breyer conceded that it was conceivable that additional First Amendment issues would arise in the course of further litigation, but he took the position that every case in the fourth category, particularly including *Cox* itself, presented that possibility.

With respect to the third criterion, Justice Breyer noted that some potential decisions by the Court would leave Kasky's claim alive, thus not satisfying the criterion, but he was not willing to conclude that "outright reversal [which would have ended the litigation] is not a very realistic possibility." He argued that the line between commercial and noncommercial speech was not sharp or bright and speculated that the Court might well conclude that even if some commercial speech were mixed with some noncommercial speech, the First Amendment required a protective rule with a broad embrace. One may agree or disagree with either Justice about the proper decision on the merits of the First Amendment question(s), but perhaps that misses the point, at least for present purposes.

To what extent do you think the Justices' forecast of how the Court might decide the merits of the federal issue should be relevant to the question of whether the Court can exercise jurisdiction over cases in the *Cox* category? Should the mere theoretical possibility of a litigation-ending decision be sufficient to satisfy the third criterion that Justice Breyer described, or is it appropriate (or even mandatory) that the Justices making the decision on certiorari engage in some sort of determination of the probabilities of one or another result? If the former, does that approach underscore the separation-of-powers problems that underlie the Court's decidedly non-literal interpretation of § 1257's finality requirement? If the latter, what sorts of standards can you suggest for the Court to use?

6. Is the Court's treatment of the finality issue consistent with its oft-repeated insistence that constitutional issues be decided only when unavoidable? *See, e.g., Ashwander v. TVA*, 297 U.S. 288, 56 S.Ct. 466, 80 L.Ed. 688 (1936) (Brandeis, J., concurring), which Justice Rehnquist cites in his dissent.

In *Nike, Inc. v. Kasky*, 539 U.S. 654, 123 S.Ct. 2554, 156 L.Ed.2d 580 (2003) (dismissing the writ of certiorari as improvidently granted), Justices Stevens and Breyer also clashed over application of the prudential rule derived from *Ashwander v. TVA*, 297 U.S. 288, 56 S.Ct. 466, 80 L.Ed. 688 (1936) (Brandeis, J., concurring), which counsels that the Court should strain to avoid deciding constitutional questions when possible. Justice Stevens took the position that the very novelty and indeterminateness of the First Amendment questions presented argued powerfully for avoiding them unless it was absolutely necessary at some future point (presumably after Nike had lost at trial) to decide them. Justice Breyer argued that prudence was on the side of the Court deciding the issue, largely because

> waiting extracts a heavy First Amendment price. If this suit goes forward, both Nike and other potential speakers, out of reasonable caution or even an excess of caution, may censor their own expression well beyond what the law may constitutionally demand. That is what a "chilling effect" means. It is present here.

For Justice Breyer, the novelty and indeterminateness of the First Amendment questions provided a strong reason to go forward rather than to refuse review.

Should the existence of both the third and fourth categories of review of non-final state court judgments cause the Court to reexamine more generally its position on the *Ashwander* rule? In the third category, it is entirely certain that the federal issues will *not* survive for presentation to the Court; that is the criterion for allowing review. Are the third criterion and *Ashwander* irreconcilably in conflict? With respect to the fourth category, by definition it *may be* possible for the Court to avoid deciding the federal issues. Is not that enough to demonstrate that decision is not unavoidable? Perhaps the Court should undertake to articulate standards or some sort of balancing test to describe when the nature of the federal issues presented is such that the federal courts should ignore *Ashwander*'s counsel. Can you suggest any such standards that will not have the effect of gutting the rule?

7. Justice Rehnquist's dissent in *Cox* deserves considerable attention. Note that he has a variety of objections to the Court's reviewing cases before they have been entirely terminated in the state courts.

a) Does his objection to the rationale and result of *Cox* apply to each category of nonfinal final review described by the majority?

b) Is it appropriate for the Court to rely on cases construing 28 U.S.C.A. § 1291, which concerns finality for purposes of appeals from federal district courts to the United States Court of Appeals? Justice Rehnquist argues powerfully that federalism concerns that have no force within the federal judicial system may counsel strongly against permitting review of non-final state court judgments.

c) Does Justice Rehnquist's argument about the impropriety of the Court's interpretation of "final judgment" in § 1257 take on additional force in light of the 1988 amendment to the Rules Enabling Act, 28 U.S.C.A. § 2072, that allows the Supreme Court to prescribe rules that "may define when a ruling of a district court is final for the purposes of appeal under section 1291 of this title"?

d) Justice Rehnquist raises an interesting tactical point about the timing of review. If the Court will consider cases, particularly in the fourth category, when state proceedings have not ended, does that place an obligation upon counsel promptly to seek Supreme Court review whenever a federal issue is adversely decided? If the case is reviewable at that point, does that not start the clock ticking for purposes of the timely appeal rule embodied in 28 U.S.C.A. § 2101(c)? If so, will it not generate a great deal of appellate litigation, most of it addressing not the merits but instead the question of interlocutory appealability of the federal issue?

For example, suppose Cox Broadcasting had not sought immediate review in the United States Supreme Court, but instead had gone back to the trial court to defend on the merits. If after subsequent state proceedings Cox eventually sought Supreme Court review, perhaps nine months or a year after the original Georgia Supreme Court decision rejecting Cox's First Amendment challenge, could Cohn have resisted jurisdiction by arguing that the case became appealable after that ruling and that Cox had waived its right to Supreme Court review by not seeking review within ninety days? Were Cox's counsel therefore wise to seek review when they did? Would counsel in other cases be well-advised to follow a similarly conservative course?

The former Chief Justice's objections notwithstanding, the *Cox* doctrine appears to be alive and well. In *Kansas v. Marsh*, 548 U.S. 163, 126 S.Ct. 2516, 165 L.Ed.2d 429 (2006), the Court reviewed a case in the third *Cox* category, citing *Cox* with approval. Although the Court split 5-4 on the merits, none of the Justices argued that review was inappropriate because of the finality requirement of 28 U.S.C. § 1257.

8. Is there an unrealized separation-of-powers question underlying the debate in *Cox* as well? Justice Rehnquist notes with some force the federalism concerns implicated by the Court's willingness to review nonfinal cases. Is the Court also ignoring legislatively-imposed limits on its power when it construes "[f]inal judgments or decrees" to mean only that "the judgment of the state court on the federal issue is deemed final"? If Congress meant to allow interlocutory review from conclusive determinations of federal issues, why did it not say so? On the other hand, if Congress does not at least acquiesce in the construction of § 1257, why has it never objected, despite having amended or recodified § 1257 several times?

Chapter 10

THE *ROOKER-FELDMAN* DOCTRINE

A. INTRODUCTION

Martin v. Hunter's Lessee[1] clearly illustrates the states' resistance to the idea that the Supreme Court of the United States could review the judgments of state courts. Given the great concern in the post-colonial period about the potential evils of centralized government, manifested scarcely thirty years before *Martin* in the Articles of Confederation and then in the Constitutional Convention, the surprise might have been if the states had acquiesced too readily. The relationship of federal courts to state courts was thus one of the early battlegrounds of federalism.

Imagine, if you will, what the reaction of the states might have been to the idea that even the inferior federal courts could review state court judgments. In one way, *Ex parte Young*[2] and its immediate aftermath demonstrate that the issue was very much alive at the beginning of the twentieth century, as it remains today. Shortly after the Court's decision, there was a movement to remove cases challenging the constitutionality of state statutes from the jurisdiction of the district courts. In response, Congress passed the Three-Judge-Court Act,[3] which provided that a three-judge district court comprised of one circuit judge and two district judges should hear constitutional challenges to a state statute. The legislative history of that statute makes clear that Congress intended it to avoid the specter of a single district judge overturning a state statutory scheme (as had happened in *Ex parte Young*).[4] As one

---

[1] 14 U.S. (1 Wheat.) 304, 4 L.Ed. 97 (1816).

[2] 209 U.S. 123, 28 S.Ct. 441, 52 L.Ed. 714 (1908). Chapter 7 presents and discusses *Young* at pages 629-638.

[3] Act of June 18, 1910, ch. 309, § 17, 36 Stat. 557.

[4] Writing for the majority in Swift & Company v. Wickham, 382 U.S. 111, 86 S.Ct. 258, 15 L.Ed.2d 194 (1965), Justice Harlan noted:

> The three-judge district court is a unique feature of our jurisprudence, created to alleviate a specific discontent within the federal system. * * * [It was] passed to assuage growing popular displeasure with the frequent grants of injunctions by federal courts against the operation of state legislation regulating railroads and utilities in particular. * * * The advent of the Granger and labor movements in the late nineteenth century, and the acceleration of state social legislation especially through the creation of regulatory bodies met with opposition in the federal judiciary. [T]his Court held that the setting of rates not permitting a

district court put it, Congress's goal was "protecting the states from the imprudent exercise of federal injunctive power."[5] The Act, provided, *inter alia*, that the losing party in such a case could appeal directly to the Supreme Court.[6] The Act lasted, largely unchanged, until Congress substantially narrowed it in 1976, limiting its applicability to congressional or statewide legislative apportionment cases or other cases in which legislation might direct use of such a court.[7]

The problem of inferior federal court review of state court decisions, however, came cloaked, as it were. No one would have thought of filing a notice of appeal with a state's highest court seeking appellate review in the federal district court. There are other ways, nonetheless, that one may ask one court to do something that affects the judgment of another. The question then becomes one of deciding when something not called an appeal nonetheless functions as one. The Supreme Court turned to that problem in 1923.

B. THE BASIC DOCTRINE

ROOKER v. FIDELITY TRUST CO.
Supreme Court of the United States, 1923.
263 U.S. 413, 44 S.Ct. 149, 68 L.Ed. 362.

MR. JUSTICE VAN DEVANTER delivered the opinion of the Court.

This is a bill in equity to have a judgment of a circuit court in Indiana, which was affirmed by the Supreme Court of the state, declared null and void, and to obtain other relief dependent on that outcome. An effort to have the judgment reviewed by this court on writ of error had failed because the record did not disclose the presence of any question constituting a basis for such a review. The parties to the bill are the same as in the litigation in the state court, but with an addition of two defendants whose presence does not need special notice. All are citizens of the same state. The grounds advanced for resorting to the District Court are that the judgment was rendered and affirmed in contravention

---

fair return violated the Due Process Clause of the Fourteenth Amendment. Ex parte Young established firmly the corollary that inferior federal courts could enjoin state officials from enforcing such unconstitutional state laws. * * * The sponsor of the bill establishing the three-judge procedure for these cases, Senator Overman of North Carolina, noted:

> Whenever one judge stands up in a State and enjoins the governor and the attorney-general, the people resent it, and public sentiment is stirred, as it was in my State, when there was almost a rebellion, whereas if three judges declare that a state statute is unconstitutional the people would rest easy under it.

Id. at 116-18, 86 S.Ct. at 261-63, 15 L.Ed.2d at 199-200.

[5] Webber v. White, 422 F. Supp. 416, 425 (N.D. Tex. 1976).

[6] Swift & Company v. Wickham, 382 U.S. at 119, 86 S.Ct. at 263, 15 L.Ed.2d at 201.

[7] *See* 28 U.S.C. § 2284 (2000).

of the contract clause of the Constitution of the United States and the due process of law and equal protection clauses of the Fourteenth Amendment, in that it gave effect to a state statute alleged to be in conflict with those clauses and did not give effect to a prior decision in the same cause by the Supreme Court of the State which is alleged to have become the "law of the case." The District Court was of opinion that the suit was not within its jurisdiction as defined by Congress, and on that ground dismissed the bill. The plaintiffs have appealed directly to this court under section 238 of the Judicial Code.

The appellees move that the appeal be dismissed, or in the alternative that the decree be affirmed.

The appeal is within the first clause of section 238, so the motion to dismiss must be overruled. But the suit is so plainly not within the District Court's jurisdiction as defined by Congress that the motion to affirm must be sustained.

It affirmatively appears from the bill that the judgment was rendered in a cause wherein the circuit court had jurisdiction of both the subject-matter and the parties, that a full hearing was had therein, that the judgment was responsive to the issues, and that it was affirmed by the Supreme Court of the state on an appeal by the plaintiffs. If the constitutional questions stated in the bill actually arose in the cause, it was the province and duty of the state courts to decide them; and their decision, whether right or wrong, was an exercise of jurisdiction. If the decision was wrong, that did not make the judgment void, but merely left it open to reversal or modification in an appropriate and timely appellate proceeding. Unless and until so reversed or modified, it would be an effective and conclusive adjudication. Under the legislation of Congress, no court of the United States other than this court could entertain a proceeding to reverse or modify the judgment for errors of that character. To do so would be an exercise of appellate jurisdiction. The jurisdiction possessed by the District Courts is strictly original. Besides, the period within which a proceeding might be begun for the correction of errors such as are charged in the bill had expired before it was filed, and * * * after that period elapses an aggrieved litigant cannot be permitted to do indirectly what he no longer can do directly.

Some parts of the bill speak of the judgment as given without jurisdiction and absolutely void; but this is merely mistaken characterization. A reading of the entire bill shows indubitably that there was full jurisdiction in the state courts and that the bill at best is merely an attempt to get rid of the judgment for alleged errors of law committed in the exercise of that jurisdiction.

In what has been said we have proceeded on the assumption that the constitutional questions alleged to have arisen in the state courts respecting the validity of a state statute and the effect to be given to a prior decision in the same cause by the Supreme Court of the state were questions of substance, but we do not hold that they were such—the assumption being indulged merely for the purpose of testing the nature of the bill and the power of the District Court to entertain it.

* * *

Decree affirmed.

Notes and Questions

1. Why did the district court not simply refuse to act on the ground that the state court's judgment was entitled to res judicata effect, preventing a collateral attack?

When the Indiana legislature enacted the statute that the plaintiff challenged in this litigation, could the plaintiff have sued to enjoin enforcement of the statute (assuming that the plaintiff could satisfy justiciability requirements)? Would such an action have been an appeal? Is there a difference in effect between such an approach and what actually happened in the case?

2. Since its original enactment in 1793, the Anti-Injunction Act, 28 U.S.C. § 2283 (2000), has signaled Congress's intense concern that federal courts not interfere with state judicial proceedings by staying them, except in three circumstances.[8] Is it significant that for more than a century before *Rooker* reached the Supreme Court, Congress had forbidden stays but had not forbidden collateral attacks on state court judgments when the state litigation was no longer pending?

3. Where does federal habeas corpus for state prisoners fit into this structure? Is a habeas challenge to state confinement, brought pursuant to 28 U.S.C. § 2254, an appeal within the meaning of *Rooker*? If not, how can one differentiate a case in that procedural posture from *Rooker* itself? If so, how can habeas proceed in the federal courts? The federal courts have been saying for a long time that federal habeas corpus is an exception to the *Rooker-Feldman* doctrine because 28 U.S.C. § 2241 is a grant of jurisdiction to the federal courts. *See, e.g., Zadvydas v. Davis*, 533 U.S. 678, 687, 121 S.Ct. 2491, 2497, 150 L.Ed.2d 653, 664-65 (2001). Take a look at § 2241. Does it sound like a jurisdiction-vesting statute in the manner of 28 U.S.C. §§ 1330-1338? Does Congress's conferring the power to issue a writ represent a jurisdictional grant or merely provision of a specific remedy? If the former, does the All Writs Act, 28 U.S.C. § 1651 (2000) become a font of jurisdiction? If not, whence the district courts' jurisdiction to entertain habeas cases? If one were to read § 2241 as not vesting jurisdiction, but rather limiting the courts' ability to issue the writ under jurisdiction conferred elsewhere (§ 1331, for example), would that make any difference for *Rooker-Feldman* purposes? Assuming § 2241 is a grant of jurisdiction, does that necessarily resolve the matter? Does Congress have the power under Article

---

[8] Chapter 8 A discusses the Anti-Injunction Act. Note that in the *Atlantic Coast Line* case presented in that chapter, *supra* at 746, the Court construed the three exceptions to the Act's prohibition quite narrowly.

III to grant the inferior federal courts appellate jurisdiction over state court decisions?

4. *Rooker* is, despite some questions, a fairly straightforward case. It contained, however, hidden problems inherent in the idea that something not styled an appeal might nonetheless be an appeal. It forced the courts to consider, *inter alia*, what sorts of decisions were "judicial" in nature. The Supreme Court waited only sixty years to reach that issue.

DISTRICT OF COLUMBIA COURT OF APPEALS v. FELDMAN
Supreme Court of the United States, 1983.
460 U.S. 462, 103 S.Ct. 1303, 75 L.Ed.2d 206.

JUSTICE BRENNAN delivered the opinion of the Court.

We must decide in these cases what authority the United States District Court for the District of Columbia and the United States Court of Appeals for the District of Columbia Circuit have to review decisions of the District of Columbia Court of Appeals in bar admission matters. The United States Court of Appeals for the District of Columbia Circuit, reversing the United States District Court, held that the District Court had jurisdiction to review the District of Columbia Court of Appeals' denials of the respondents' requests for waivers of a bar admission rule that requires applicants to have graduated from an approved law school. We vacate the decision of the United States Court of Appeals for the District of Columbia Circuit and remand the case for proceedings consistent with this opinion.

I

We have discussed in detail in earlier opinions the changes in the structure of the District of Columbia court system effected by the District of Columbia Court Reform and Criminal Procedure Act of 1970. For purposes of this case, three provisions of that legislation are crucial. One provision made "final judgments and decrees of the District of Columbia Court of Appeals * * * reviewable by the Supreme Court of the United States in accordance with section 1257 of title 28, United States Code." Another provision amended 28 U.S.C. § 1257 to specify that the term "highest court of a state" as used in § 1257 includes the District of Columbia Court of Appeals. These provisions make the judgments of the District of Columbia Court of Appeals, like the judgments of state courts, directly reviewable in this Court. Cases no longer have to proceed from the local courts to the United States Court of Appeals and then to this Court under 28 U.S.C. § 1254. The third provision authorized the District of Columbia Court of Appeals to "make such rules as it deems proper respecting the examination, qualification, and admission of persons to membership in its bar, and their censure, suspension, and expulsion." This provision divested the United States District Court of its former authority to supervise admission to the District of Columbia bar.

Pursuant to its new rulemaking authority, the District of Columbia Court of Appeals adopted, as part of its general rules, Rule 46 I (1973), which governs admission to the bar. Rule 46 I(b)(3) states:

> (3) Proof of Legal Education. An applicant who has graduated from a law school that at the time of graduation was approved by the American Bar Association or who shall be eligible to be graduated from an approved law school within 60 days of the date of the examination will be permitted to take the bar examination. Under no circumstances shall an applicant be admitted to the bar without having first submitted to the Secretary to the Committee [on Admissions] a certificate verifying that he has graduated from an approved law school.[1]

Neither of the respondents graduated from an approved law school. Their efforts to avoid the operation of Rule 46 I(b)(3) form the foundation of this case.

A

Respondent Feldman did not attend law school. Instead, he pursued an alternative path to a legal career provided by the State of Virginia involving a highly structured program of study in the office of a practicing attorney. In addition to his work and study at a law firm in Charlottesville, Virginia, Feldman formally audited classes at the University of Virginia School of Law. For the final six months of his alternative course of study, Feldman served as a law clerk to a United States District Judge.

Having passed the Virginia bar examination, Feldman was admitted to that state's bar in April, 1976. In March of that year he had begun working as a staff attorney for the Baltimore, Maryland Legal Aid Bureau. He continued in that job until January, 1977. Like the District of Columbia, Maryland has a rule limiting access to the bar examination to graduates of ABA-approved law schools, but the Maryland Board of Law Examiners waived the rule for Feldman. Feldman passed the Maryland examination and later was admitted to that state's bar.

In November, 1976 Feldman applied to the Committee on Admissions of the District of Columbia Bar for admission to the District bar under a rule which, prior to its recent amendment, allowed a member of a bar in another jurisdiction to seek membership in the District bar without examination. In January, 1977 the Committee denied Feldman's application on the ground that he had not graduated from an approved law school. Initially, the Committee stated that waivers of

---

[1] Under Rule 46 I(b)(4), a graduate of an unaccredited law school "may be permitted admission to an examination only after receiving credit for 24 semester hours of study in a law school that at the time of study was approved by the American Bar Association and with Committee approval."

Rule 46 I(b)(3), or exceptions to it, were not authorized. Following further contact with the Committee, however, Feldman was granted an informal hearing. After the hearing, the Committee reaffirmed its denial of Feldman's application and stated that only the District of Columbia Court of Appeals could waive the requirement of graduation from an approved law school.

In June, 1977 Feldman submitted to the District of Columbia Court of Appeals a petition for admission to the bar without examination. Alternatively, Feldman requested that he be allowed to sit for the bar examination. In his petition, Feldman described his legal training, work experience, and other qualifications. He suggested that his professional training and education were "equal to that received by those who have attended an A.B.A. approved law school." In view of his training, experience, and success in passing the bar examinations in other jurisdictions, Feldman stated that "the objectives of the District of Columbia's procedures and requirements for admission to the Bar will not be frustrated by granting this petition."

The District of Columbia Court of Appeals did not act on Feldman's petition for several months. In March, 1978, Feldman's counsel wrote to the Chief Judge of the District of Columbia Court of Appeals to urge favorable action on Feldman's petition. The letter stated that Feldman had "abundantly demonstrated his fitness to practice law" and suggested that "it would be a gross injustice to exclude him from the Bar without even considering his individual qualifications." The letter went on to state that "in the unique circumstances of his case, barring Mr. Feldman from the practice of law merely because he has not graduated from an accredited law school would raise important questions under the United States Constitution and the federal antitrust laws—questions that Mr. Feldman is prepared to pursue in the United States District Court if necessary." In support of Feldman's position, the letter again stressed the strength of his training and the breadth of his experience. While acknowledging that a strict reading of Rule 46 I(b)(3) prevented Feldman from taking the bar examination, Feldman's counsel suggested that the court was not precluded from considering "Mr. Feldman's application on its merits." The court has plenary power to regulate the licensing of attorneys, which, in the view of Feldman's counsel, includes the discretion to waive the requirements of Rule 46 in a deserving case. In view of Feldman's "unusually high qualifications for admission" his case provided "an ideal occasion for the exercise of such discretion."

Feldman's counsel also pointed out that the court had granted waivers of the rule in the past and suggested that a "failure to consider Mr. Feldman's application would be highly arbitrary and would raise serious questions about the fairness and even-handedness of the Court's policies regarding bar admissions." He went on to state that "serious questions under the United States Constitution are raised by any bar admissions procedure which automatically rejects applicants who have not graduated from an A.B.A. accredited law school, without any opportunity to show that their experience and education provide equivalent evidence of their fitness to practice law." Feldman's counsel cited case authority in support of his position. Finally, Feldman's counsel stated that "the federal antitrust laws provide an alternative basis for questioning the legality of a bar admissions procedure which presumes applicants to be unqualified if they lack a law degree and denies them any opportunity to show that their individual training and experience still qualify them to practice law." Feldman's counsel also cited cases in support of this position.

In late March, 1978, the Chief Judge of the District of Columbia Court of Appeals responded to the letter from Feldman's counsel. The Chief Judge stated that while the Committee on Admissions had recognized Mr. Feldman's "exceptional opportunity for training" and his fine personal qualities, the purpose of the rule at issue was "to prevent the Committee and the Court from assuming the practicably impossible task of making separate subjective evaluations of each applicant's training and education; hence, an objective and reasonable standard as prescribed by the rule must be utilized." In this light, the court decided not to waive the rule and upheld the Committee's denial of Feldman's application.

On March 30, 1978, the District of Columbia Court of Appeals issued a *per curiam* order denying Feldman's petition. The order stated simply that "[o]n consideration of the petition of Marc Feldman to waive the provisions of Rule 46 of the General Rules of this Court, it is ORDERED that applicant's petition is denied."

In May, 1978, Feldman filed a complaint in the United States District Court for the District of Columbia challenging the District of Columbia Court of Appeals' refusal to waive Rule 46 I(b)(3) on his behalf.[2] The complaint stated that the "defendants' refusal to consider plaintiff's individual qualifications to practice law is unlawful in view of his demonstrated fitness and competence, as well as the prior admission to the D.C. bar of several other individuals who did not attend an accredited law school." Feldman sought "a declaration that defendants' actions have violated the Fifth Amendment to the Constitution and the Sherman Act, and * * * an injunction requiring defendants either to grant plaintiff immediate admission to the District of Columbia bar or to permit him to sit for the bar examination as soon as possible."

The District Court granted the defendants' motion to dismiss on the ground that it lacked subject matter jurisdiction over the action. The court found that the District of Columbia Court of Appeals' order deny-

---

[2] The complaint named as defendants the District of Columbia Court of Appeals, the Chief Judge of the District of Columbia Court of Appeals in his official capacity, the Committee on Admissions, and the Chairman and Secretary of that Committee.

ing Feldman's petition was a judicial act "which fully encompassed the constitutional and statutory issues raised." The court stated that if it were "to assume jurisdiction over the subject matter of this lawsuit, it would find itself in the unsupportable position of reviewing an order of a jurisdiction's highest court."

* * *

B

[Hickey, the second respondent, similarly sought permission to sit for the bar examination, and the Court detailed his qualifications and experience. The details of Hickey's background are not important for our purposes. The only significant potential difference is that Hickey was apparently not represented by counsel and advanced only policy arguments in favor of his application, not raising his Fifth Amendment and antitrust arguments until he filed his complaint in the United States District Court.]

C

Both Hickey and Feldman appealed the dismissals of their complaints to the United States Court of Appeals for the District of Columbia Circuit. The District of Columbia Circuit affirmed the dismissals of Hickey's and Feldman's antitrust claims on the ground that they were insubstantial.[11] The court, however, concluded that the waiver proceedings in the District of Columbia Court of Appeals "were not judicial in the federal sense, and thus did not foreclose litigation of the constitutional contentions in the District Court." The court therefore reversed the dismissals of the constitutional claims and remanded them for consideration on the merits.

Although the District of Columbia Circuit acknowledged that "review of a final judgment of the highest judicial tribunal of a state is vested solely in the Supreme Court of the United States," (footnote omitted), and that the United States District Court therefore is without authority to review determinations by the District of Columbia Court of Appeals in judicial proceedings, the court found that the District Court has jurisdiction over these cases because the proceedings in the District of Columbia Court of Appeals "were not judicial * * *." The court based this conclusion on a finding that neither Feldman nor Hickey asserted in their waiver petitions "any sort of *right* to be admitted to the District of Columbia bar, or even to take the examination therefor." ([E]mphasis in original). Feldman and Hickey simply sought an exemption from the rule. In particular, Hickey did not present any legal arguments nor did "he demand admission to the examination as a matter of legal entitlement." He "merely asked the court to exercise its administrative discre-

---

[11] We denied respondents' cross-petitions for certiorari from the disposition of the antitrust claims. Those claims, therefore, are not before us.

tion to permit him to take the test." This amounted to a request that the court "make a policy decision equating his personal qualities with accredited legal education, not an adjudication requiring resort to legal principles." ([F]ootnote omitted).

The District of Columbia Circuit found Feldman's case more difficult, but still concluded that the proceedings on his waiver petition were not judicial in nature because the "claim-of-right element" was lacking. Feldman's petition did not "claim that a refusal of his waiver request would deny him any right at all." Instead, the petition "invoked the administrative discretion of [the court], simply asking that it temper its rule in his favor, for personal and not legal reasons." The District of Columbia Circuit rejected the argument that the letter from Feldman's counsel, which raised certain legal arguments, changed the nature of the proceedings. The District of Columbia Circuit stated: "We are unable to discern in the letter any desire that the court consider Feldman's legal criticisms of the rule on their merits, or hand down a decision dealing with them. The letter made unmistakably clear that these criticisms would be litigated, if at all, in the District Court * * * ." ([F]ootnotes omitted).[12]

II

The District of Columbia Circuit properly acknowledged that the United States District Court is without authority to review final determinations of the District of Columbia Court of Appeals in judicial proceedings. Review of such determinations can be obtained only in this Court. A crucial question in this case, therefore, is whether the proceedings before the District of Columbia Court of Appeals were judicial in nature.[13]

---

[12] The District of Columbia Circuit rejected the petitioners' alternative argument that consideration of the legal issues Feldman sought to raise in District Court was barred by principles of res judicata. The court did so on the ground that the proceedings in the District of Columbia Court of Appeals were non-judicial in nature.

In an opinion concurring in part and dissenting in part, Judge Robb expressed the view that the District Court had no jurisdiction to review the orders of the District of Columbia Court of Appeals. He noted that the District of Columbia Court of Appeals has the status of a state supreme court and stated:

> The adverse decisions in the appellants' cases were reviewable in the Supreme Court of the United States. Although the appellants cast their petitions to the Court of Appeals in terms of requests for waivers, the petitions in essence were demands that the court declare the petitioners qualified to sit for the bar examination. Those demands were denied by en banc orders of the Court of Appeals. The denials were judicial acts and as such were reviewable on writ of certiorari to the Supreme Court. They were not reviewable in the District Court."

[13] As the District of Columbia Circuit recognized, it is a question of federal law whether "a particular proceeding before another tribunal was truly judicial" for purposes of ascertaining the jurisdiction of a federal court.

A

This Court has considered the distinction between judicial and administrative or ministerial proceedings on several occasions. In *Prentis v. Atlantic Coast Line* (1908), a railroad challenged in federal court the constitutionality of rail passenger rates set by the state corporation commission. The question presented by the case was whether the federal court was free to enjoin implementation of the rate order. In considering this question, we assumed that the state corporation commission was, at least for some purposes, a court. We held, however, that the federal court could enjoin implementation of the rate order because the commission had acted in a legislative as opposed to a judicial capacity in setting the rates. In reaching this conclusion, we stated:

> A judicial inquiry investigates, declares and enforces liabilities as they stand on present or past facts and under laws supposed already to exist. That is its purpose and end. Legislation on the other hand looks to the future and changes existing conditions by making a new rule to be applied thereafter to all or some part of those subject to its power. The establishment of a rate is the making of a rule for the future, and therefore is an act legislative not judicial in kind * * *

We went on to suggest that the nature of a proceeding "depends not upon the character of the body but upon the character of the proceedings."

In *In re Summer,* (1945), we considered the petitioner's challenge to the constitutionality of a state Supreme Court's refusal to admit him to the practice of law. At the outset, we noted that the record was not in the "customary form" because the state court had not treated the proceeding as "judicial." In fact, the state court contested our certiorari jurisdiction on the ground that the state court proceedings had not been judicial in nature and that no case or controversy therefore existed in this Court under Article III of the Federal Constitution. In considering this contention, we conceded that the state court proceeding might not have been judicial under state law and that the denial of the petitioner's application for admission to the bar was treated "as a ministerial act which is performed by virtue of the judicial power, such as the appointment of a clerk or bailiff or the specification of the requirements of eligibility or the course of study for applicants for admission to the bar, rather than a judicial proceeding." We stated, however, that in determining the nature of the proceedings "we must for ourselves appraise the circumstances of the refusal."

In conducting this appraisal, we first stated:

> A case arises, within the meaning of the Constitution, when any question respecting the Constitution, treaties or laws of the United States has assumed "such a form that the judicial power is capable

of acting on it." * * * A declaration on rights as they stand must be sought, not on rights which may arise in the future, and there must be an actual controversy over an issue, not a desire for an abstract declaration of the law. The form of the proceeding is not significant. It is the nature and effect which is controlling.

Applying this standard, we noted that the state court had concluded that the report of the Committee on Character and Fitness, which refused to issue a favorable certificate, should be sustained. The state court, therefore, considered the petitioner's petition "on its merits." Although "no entry was placed by the Clerk in the file, on a docket, or in a judgment roll," we found that the state court had taken "cognizance of the petition and passed an order which [was] validated by the signature of the presiding officer." ([F]ootnote omitted). We stated:

> Where relief is thus sought in a state court against the action of a committee, appointed to advise the court, and the court takes cognizance of the complaint without requiring the appearance of the committee or its members, we think the consideration of the petition by the Supreme Court, the body which has authority itself by its own act to give the relief sought, makes the proceeding adversary in the sense of a true case or controversy.

> A claim of a present right to admission to the bar of a state and a denial of that right is a controversy. When the claim is made in a state court and a denial of the right is made by judicial order, it is a case which may be reviewed under Article III of the Constitution when federal questions are raised and proper steps taken to that end, in this Court. ([F]ootnote omitted).

B

These precedents clearly establish that the proceedings in the District of Columbia Court of Appeals surrounding Feldman's and Hickey's petitions for waiver were judicial in nature. The proceedings were not legislative, ministerial, or administrative. The District of Columbia Court of Appeals did not "loo[k] to the future and chang[e] existing conditions by making a new rule to be applied thereafter to all or some part of those subject to its power." Nor did it engage in rulemaking or specify "the requirements of eligibility or the course of study for applicants for admission to the bar * * *." Nor did the District of Columbia Court of Appeals simply engage in ministerial action. Instead, the proceedings before the District of Columbia Court of Appeals involved a "judicial inquiry" in which the court was called upon to investigate, declare, and enforce "liabilities as they [stood] on present or past facts and under laws supposed already to exist."

In his petition to the District of Columbia Court of Appeals, discussed in detail above, Feldman contended that he possessed "the requisite fitness and good moral character necessary to practice law in this jurisdiction." In support of his position, he described in detail his legal training and experience. He asserted that his professional education and training were "equal to that received by those who have attended an A.B.A. approved law school." He further argued that granting his petition would not frustrate the objectives of the District of Columbia's procedures and requirements for admission to the bar. In his later letter, Feldman pointed out that the court's former practice of granting waivers to graduates of unaccredited law schools raised questions about the fairness of denying his petition. He also made explicit legal arguments against the rule based both on the Constitution and on the federal antitrust laws. All of this was done against the background of an existing rule.

In essence, Feldman argued on policy grounds that the rule should not be applied to him because he had fulfilled the spirit, if not the letter, of Rule 46 I(b)(3). Alternatively, he argued in his letter that the rule was invalid. In short, he was seeking "a declaration on rights as they [stood] * * * not on rights which [might] arise in the future * * * ." This required the District of Columbia Court of Appeals to determine in light of existing law and in light of Feldman's qualifications and arguments whether Feldman's petition should be granted. The court also had before it legal arguments against the validity of the rule. When it issued a *per curiam* order denying Feldman's petition, it determined as a legal matter that Feldman was not entitled to be admitted to the bar without examination or to sit for the bar examination. The court had adjudicated Feldman's "claim of a present right to admission to the bar," and rejected it. This is the essence of a judicial proceeding.

The same conclusion obtains with respect to the proceedings on Hickey's petition for waiver.

* * *

Admittedly, the proceedings in both Feldman's and Hickey's case did not assume the form commonly associated with judicial proceedings. As we said in *In re Summers,* however, "the form of the proceeding is not significant. It is the nature and effect which is controlling."[15]

III

A

A determination that the proceedings on Feldman's and Hickey's petitions were judicial does not finally dispose of this case. As we have noted, a United States District Court has no authority to review final judgments of a state court in judicial proceedings. Review of such judgments may be had only in this Court. Therefore, to the extent that

---

[15] Our conclusion that the proceedings before the District of Columbia Court of Appeals were judicial in nature is consistent with our grants of certiorari to review state court decisions on bar-related matters in [eight cases from 1957 to 1982].

Hickey and Feldman sought review in District Court of the District of Columbia Court of Appeals' denial of their petitions for waiver the District Court lacked subject matter jurisdiction over their complaints. Hickey and Feldman should have sought review of the District of Columbia Court of Appeals' judgments in this Court.[16] To the extent that Hickey and Feldman mounted a general challenge to the constitutionality of Rule 46 I(b)(3), however, the District Court did have subject matter jurisdiction over their complaints.

The difference between seeking review in a federal district court of a state court's final judgment in a bar admission matter and challenging the validity of a state bar admission rule has been recognized in the lower courts and, at least implicitly, in the opinions of this Court.

* * *

B

Applying this standard to the respondents' complaints, it is clear that their allegations that the District of Columbia Court of Appeals acted arbitrarily and capriciously in denying their petitions for waiver and that the court acted unreasonably and discriminatorily in denying their petitions in view of its former policy of granting waivers to graduates of unaccredited law schools, required the District Court to review a final judicial decision of the highest court of a jurisdiction in a particular case. These allegations are inextricably intertwined with the District of

---

[16] It is possible that review of a state court decision by this Court could be barred by a petitioner's failure to raise his constitutional claims in the state courts. * * * The United States Court of Appeals for the Fifth Circuit has relied on this limit on our certiorari jurisdiction to hold that a federal district court has jurisdiction over constitutional claims asserted by a plaintiff who has been denied admission to a state bar in a state court judicial proceeding if he failed to raise his constitutional claims in the state court.

The Fifth Circuit Court of Appeals' reasoning * * * is flawed. As we noted "lower federal courts possess no power whatever to sit in direct review of state court decisions." If the constitutional claims presented to a United States District Court are inextricably intertwined with the state court's denial in a judicial proceeding of a particular plaintiff's application for admission to the state bar, then the District Court is in essence being called upon to review the state court decision. This the District Court may not do. Moreover, the fact that we may not have jurisdiction to review a final state court judgment because of a petitioner's failure to raise his constitutional claims in state court does not mean that a United States District Court should have jurisdiction over the claims. By failing to raise his claims in state court a plaintiff may forfeit his right to obtain review of the state court decision in any federal court. This result is eminently defensible on policy grounds. We have noted the competence of state courts to adjudicate federal constitutional claims. * * * [O]ne of the policies underlying the requirement that constitutional claims be raised in state court as a predicate to our certiorari jurisdiction is the desirability of giving the state court the first opportunity to consider a state statute or rule in light of federal constitutional arguments. A state court may give the statute a saving construction in response to those arguments.

Finally, it is important to note in the context of this case the strength of the state interest in regulating the state bar. * * * "[T]he interest of the States in regulating lawyers is especially great since lawyers are essential to the primary governmental function of administering justice, and have historically been 'officers of the courts.'"

Columbia Court of Appeals' decisions, in judicial proceedings, to deny the respondents' petitions. The District Court, therefore, does not have jurisdiction over these elements of the respondents' complaints.

The remaining allegations in the complaints, however, involve a general attack on the constitutionality of Rule 46 I(b)(3). The respondents' claims that the rule is unconstitutional because it creates an irrebuttable presumption that only graduates of accredited law schools are fit to practice law, discriminates against those who have obtained equivalent legal training by other means, and impermissibly delegates the District of Columbia Court of Appeals' power to regulate the bar to the American Bar Association, do not require review of a judicial decision in a particular case. The District Court, therefore, has subject matter jurisdiction over these elements of the respondents' complaints.

In deciding that the District Court has jurisdiction over those elements of the respondents' complaints that involve a general challenge to the constitutionality of Rule 46 I(b)(3), we expressly do not reach the question of whether the doctrine of res judicata forecloses litigation on these elements of the complaints. We leave that question to the District Court on remand.

IV

The judgment of the District of Columbia Circuit is vacated and the cases are remanded to the District Court for further proceedings consistent with this opinion.

So ordered.

JUSTICE STEVENS, dissenting.

There are many crafts in which the State performs a licensing function. That function is important, not only to those seeking access to a gainful occupation but to the members of the public served by the profession as well. State- created rules governing the grant or denial of licenses must comply with constitutional standards and must be administered in accordance with due process of law. Given these acknowledged constitutional limitations on action by the State, it should be beyond question that a federal district court has subject matter jurisdiction over an individual's lawsuit raising federal constitutional challenges either to licensing rules themselves or to their application in his own case. Curiously, however, the Court today ignores basic jurisdictional principles when it decides a jurisdictional issue affecting the licensing of members of the legal profession.

The Court holds that respondents may make a general constitutional attack on the rules governing the admission of lawyers to practice in the District of Columbia. I agree. But the Court also concludes that a United States District Court has no subject matter jurisdiction over a claim that those rules have been administered in an unconstitutional manner. According to the Court's opinion, respondents' contentions that bar admission rules have been unconstitutionally applied to them by the District of Columbia Court of Appeals somehow constitute impermissible attempts to secure appellate review of final judgments of that court. There are two basic flaws in the Court's analysis.

First, neither Feldman nor Hickey requested the District of Columbia Court of Appeals to pass on the validity of Rule 46 I(b)(3) or to grant them admission to the bar or the bar examination as a matter of right. Rather, each of them asked the court to waive the requirements of the rule for a variety of reasons. I would not characterize the court's refusal to grant a requested waiver as an adjudication. Unlike the decision of the Supreme Court of Illinois reviewed in *In re Summers,* the order of the District of Columbia Court of Appeals did not determine a claim of right, nor did it even apply standard equitable principles to a prayer for relief. Rather, that court performed no more and no less than the administrative function of a licensing board. As the United States Court of Appeals wrote, Hickey asked the court "to make a policy decision equating his personal qualities with accredited legal education, not an adjudication requiring resort to legal principles," and Feldman "invoked the administrative discretion of that body, simply asking that it temper its rule in his favor, for personal and not legal reasons." Rejection of those petitions was not "adjudicative" and was therefore not susceptible to certiorari review in this Court.

Second, even if the refusal to grant a waiver were an adjudication, the federal statute that confers jurisdiction upon the United States District Court to entertain a constitutional challenge to the rules themselves also authorizes that court to entertain a collateral attack upon the unconstitutional application of those rules. The Court's opinion fails to distinguish between two concepts: appellate review and collateral attack. If a challenge to a state court's decision is brought in United States District Court and alleges violations of the United States Constitution, then by definition it does not seek appellate review. It is plainly within the federal-question jurisdiction of the federal court. There may be other reasons for denying relief to the plaintiff—such as failure to state a cause of action, claim or issue preclusion, or failure to prove a violation of constitutional rights.[2] But it does violence to jurisdictional concepts for this Court to hold, as it does, that the federal district court has no *jurisdiction* to conduct independent review of a specific claim that a licensing body's action did not comply with federal constitutional standards. The fact that the licensing function in the legal profession is con-

---

[2] Constitutional challenges to specific licensing actions may, of course, fail on the merits. But in my view, if plaintiffs challenging a bar admissions decision by a state court prove facts comparable to the allegations made by the appellants in *Yick Wo v. Hopkins* (1886), they would clearly be entitled to relief in the United States District Court. If they were seeking admission to any other craft regulated by the state, they would unquestionably have such a right.

trolled by the judiciary is not a sufficient reason to immunize allegedly unconstitutional conduct from review in the federal courts.

I therefore respectfully dissent.

Notes and Questions

1. What is the basis for the *Rooker-Feldman* doctrine? Does the Constitution compel it? Is it a creature of statute? Is it federal common law? Does the answer make any difference?

2. Suppose a state permits collateral attacks on judgments. In such circumstances, if the party entitled to make a collateral attack in the state courts instead mounts one in federal court, do the premises on which the *Rooker-Feldman* doctrine relies still counsel the federal court to refuse to entertain the case?

3. In *Federal Maritime Commission v. South Carolina State Ports Authority*, 535 U.S. 743, 122 S.Ct. 1864, 152 L.Ed.2d 962 (2002), a case involving Eleventh Amendment immunity from federal suit, the Court characterized a proceeding before a federal executive branch agency brought by a private company as within the state's sovereign immunity protection, quoting with approval the Fourth Circuit's declaration that the proceeding " 'walks, talks, and squawks very much like a lawsuit' and that '[i]ts placement within the Executive Branch cannot blind us to the fact that the proceeding is truly an adjudication.' " Do the proceedings involving Feldman's and Hickey's applications to the District of Columbia bar qualify as judicial proceedings under the Court's new Duck Test?

a) The Court makes much of the fact that Feldman's attorney spoke the language of the law in specifying constitutional and other legal problems he thought attended refusal to allow his client to become a member of the District of Columbia bar or even to sit for the examination. Is an application for a driver's license a judicial proceeding within the meaning of the *Rooker-Feldman* rule? If so, was it unnecessary for the Court to call attention to the nature of counsel's argument on Feldman's behalf? If not, does it become one if counsel for a driver-applicant states in a letter to the commissioner of motor vehicles that denying a license to his client violates one or more constitutional or statutory provisions?

b) The Court notes that Hickey's application "did not present any legal arguments nor did 'he demand admission to the examination as a matter of legal entitlement.' " Should that put Hickey on different footing from Feldman? Does that alter whether the proceedings of the District of Columbia Court of Appeals on applications to sit for the bar examination (or to be admitted without having taken the bar examination) are "judicial"?

4. The Court's discussion of *Prentis* raises an interesting possibility. There the Court allowed the railroad to challenge conditions of operation (rates) set by the state corporation commission. If Feldman and Hickey had restructured their challenges, going directly to the district court and arguing that the District of Columbia requirement that all applicants have attended ABA-approved law schools was unconstitutional on its face, would they have

been entitled to a hearing on the merits? Was their mistake in presenting too particularized a case to the federal courts? Or, if they had adopted this alternative approach, would they also have been entitled to a determination of whether the requirement was unconstitutional as applied to them?

5. *In re Summers* appeared to pit the United States Supreme Court against the Supreme Court of Illinois, the latter declaring that its bar admission proceedings were not judicial, and the former ruling that state courts could not make such a determination for purposes of *federal law*.

> The return of the [Illinois Supreme Court] states that the correspondence and communications of petitioner with the Justices were not spread upon the records of the Supreme Court of Illinois and that under the law of Illinois this petition for admission to the bar does not constitute a case or controversy or a judicial proceeding but is a mere application for appointment as an officer of the court. We of course accept this authoritative commentary upon the law of Illinois as establishing for that state the non-judicial character of an application for admission to the bar. We take it that the law of Illinois treats the action of the Supreme Court on this petition as a ministerial act which is performed by virtue of the judicial power, such as the appointment of a clerk or bailiff or the specification of the requirements of eligibility or the course of study for applicants for admission to the bar, rather than a judicial proceeding.

> For the purpose of determining whether the action of the Supreme Court of Illinois is a judgment in a judicial proceeding which involves a case or controversy reviewable in this Court under Article III, Sec. 2, Cl. 1, of the Constitution of the United States, we must for ourselves appraise the circumstances of this refusal.

In re Summers, 325 U.S. 561, 565–66, 65 S.Ct. 1307, 1310–11, 89 L.Ed.2d 1795, 1799–1800 (1945) (footnotes omitted). Thus, whether the Illinois Supreme Court's proceedings were judicial for *Rooker* purposes was a question of federal, not state law. One should note that the *Summers* Court did not cite *Rooker*. More than that, the Court engaged in the quoted discussion as a way of demonstrating that it *could* reach and decide the merits (which, by the way, involved the Court's affirming Illinois's refusal to admit Summers to the practice of law because he was a conscientious objector and a pacifist). Nonetheless, does the language of that Court imply that the *Rooker-Feldman* doctrine is a matter of constitutional imperative? To the extent that the doctrine exists to protect the dignity of state courts against intrusion by the inferior federal courts, should it be relevant that the state courts themselves characterize a proceeding as non-judicial?

As *Rooker* and *Feldman* suggest, a doctrine comparatively simple to state ("The inferior federal courts cannot hear appeals of state court decisions.") nonetheless presents considerable difficulties of application. The following materials elaborate some the difficulties that the lower federal courts have experienced.

C. PROBLEMS OF INTERPRETATION

1. *The Source of the Injury: Independent Act or State Court Judgment?*

EXXON MOBIL CORPORATION v. SAUDI BASIC INDUSTRIES CORPORATION

Supreme Court of the United States, 2005.
544 U.S. 280, 125 S.Ct. 1517, 161 L.Ed.2d 454.

JUSTICE GINSBURG delivered the opinion of the Court.

This case concerns what has come to be known as the *Rooker-Feldman* doctrine, applied by this Court only twice, first in *Rooker v. Fidelity Trust Co.* (1923), then, 60 years later, in *District of Columbia Court of Appeals v. Feldman* (1983). Variously interpreted in the lower courts, the doctrine has sometimes been construed to extend far beyond the contours of the *Rooker* and *Feldman* cases, overriding Congress' conferral of federal-court jurisdiction concurrent with jurisdiction exercised by state courts, and superseding the ordinary application of preclusion law pursuant to 28 U.S.C. § 1738.

Rooker was a suit commenced in Federal District Court to have a judgment of a state court, adverse to the federal court plaintiffs, "declared null and void." In *Feldman,* parties unsuccessful in the District of Columbia Court of Appeals (the District's highest court) commenced a federal-court action against the very court that had rejected their applications. Holding the federal suits impermissible, we emphasized that appellate jurisdiction to reverse or modify a state-court judgment is lodged, initially by § 25 of the Judiciary Act of 1789 and now by 28 U.S.C. § 1257, exclusively in this Court. Federal district courts, we noted, are empowered to exercise original, not appellate, jurisdiction. Plaintiffs in *Rooker* and *Feldman* had litigated and lost in state court. Their federal complaints, we observed, essentially invited federal courts of first instance to review and reverse unfavorable state-court judgments. We declared such suits out of bounds, *i.e.,* properly dismissed for want of subject-matter jurisdiction.

The *Rooker-Feldman* doctrine, we hold today, is confined to cases of the kind from which the doctrine acquired its name: cases brought by state-court losers complaining of injuries caused by state-court judgments rendered before the district court proceedings commenced and inviting district court review and rejection of those judgments. *Rooker-Feldman* does not otherwise override or supplant preclusion doctrine or augment the circumscribed doctrines that allow federal courts to stay or dismiss proceedings in deference to state-court actions.

In the case before us, the Court of Appeals for the Third Circuit misperceived the narrow ground occupied by *Rooker-Feldman*, and consequently erred in ordering the federal action dismissed for lack of subject-matter jurisdiction. We therefore reverse the Third Circuit's judgment.

I

In *Rooker v. Fidelity Trust Co.,* the parties defeated in state court turned to a Federal District Court for relief. Alleging that the adverse state-court judgment was rendered in contravention of the Constitution, they asked the federal court to declare it "null and void." This Court noted preliminarily that the state court had acted within its jurisdiction. If the state-court decision was wrong, the Court explained, "that did not make the judgment void, but merely left it open to reversal or modification in an appropriate and timely appellate proceeding." Federal district courts, the *Rooker* Court recognized, lacked the requisite appellate authority, for their jurisdiction was "strictly original." Among federal courts, the *Rooker* Court clarified, Congress had empowered only this Court to exercise appellate authority "to reverse or modify" a state-court judgment. Accordingly, the Court affirmed a decree dismissing the suit for lack of jurisdiction.

Sixty years later, the Court decided *District of Columbia Court of Appeals v. Feldman.* The two plaintiffs in that case, Hickey and Feldman, neither of whom had graduated from an accredited law school, petitioned the District of Columbia Court of Appeals to waive a court Rule that required D.C. bar applicants to have graduated from a law school approved by the American Bar Association. After the D.C. court denied their waiver requests, Hickey and Feldman filed suits in the United States District Court for the District of Columbia. The District Court and the Court of Appeals for the District of Columbia Circuit disagreed on the question whether the federal suit could be maintained, and we granted certiorari.

Recalling *Rooker,* this Court's opinion in *Feldman* observed first that the District Court lacked authority to review a final judicial determination of the D.C. high court. "Review of such determinations," the *Feldman* opinion reiterated, "can be obtained only in this Court." The "crucial question," the Court next stated, was whether the proceedings in the D.C. court were "judicial in nature." Addressing that question, the Court concluded that the D.C. court had acted both judicially and legislatively.

In applying the accreditation Rule to the Hickey and Feldman waiver petitions, this Court determined, the D.C. court had acted judicially. As to that adjudication, *Feldman* held, this Court alone among federal courts had review authority. Hence, "to the extent that Hickey and Feldman sought review in the District Court of the District of Columbia Court of Appeals' denial of their petitions for waiver, the District Court lacked subject-matter jurisdiction over their complaints." But that determination did not dispose of the entire case, for in promulgating the bar admission rule, this Court said, the D.C. court had acted legislatively, not judicially. "Challenges to the constitutionality of state bar rules," the Court elaborated, "do not necessarily require a United States district court to review a final state-court judgment in a judicial proceeding." Thus, the Court reasoned, 28 U.S.C. § 1257 did not bar District Court proceedings addressed to the validity of the accreditation Rule itself. The Rule could be contested in federal court, this Court held, so long as plaintiffs did not seek review of the Rule's application in a particular case.

The Court endeavored to separate elements of the Hickey and Feldman complaints that failed the jurisdictional threshold from those that survived jurisdictional inspection. Plaintiffs had urged that the District of Columbia Court of Appeals acted arbitrarily in denying the waiver petitions of Hickey and Feldman, given that court's "former policy of granting waivers to graduates of unaccredited law schools." That charge, the Court held, could not be pursued, for it was "inextricably intertwined with the District of Columbia Court of Appeals' decisions, in judicial proceedings, to deny [plaintiffs'] petitions."[1]

On the other hand, the Court said, plaintiffs could maintain

> claims that the [bar admission] rule is unconstitutional because it creates an irrebuttable presumption that only graduates of accredited law schools are fit to practice law, discriminates against those who have obtained equivalent legal training by other means, and impermissibly delegates the District of Columbia Court of Appeals' power to regulate the bar to the American Bar Association,"

for those claims "do not require review of a judicial decision in a particular case." The Court left open the question whether the doctrine of res judicata foreclosed litigation of the elements of the complaints spared from dismissal for want of subject-matter jurisdiction.

Since *Feldman*, this Court has never applied *Rooker-Feldman* to dismiss an action for want of jurisdiction. The few decisions that have mentioned *Rooker* and *Feldman* have done so only in passing or to explain why those cases did not dictate dismissal. *See Verizon Md. Inc. v. Public Serv. Comm'n of Md.* (2002) (*Rooker-Feldman* does not apply to a suit seeking review of state agency action); *Johnson v. De Grandy* (1994) (*Rooker-Feldman* * * * has no application to a federal suit brought by a nonparty to the state suit.); *Howlett v. Rose* (1990) (citing *Rooker* and *Feldman* for "the rule that a federal district court cannot entertain an original action alleging that a state court violated the Constitution by giving effect to an unconstitutional state statute"); *ASARCO Inc. v. Kadish* (1989) (If, instead of seeking review of an adverse state supreme court decision in the Supreme Court, petitioners sued in federal district court, the federal action would be an attempt to obtain direct review of

---

[1] Earlier in the opinion the Court had used the same expression. In a footnote, the Court explained that a district court could not entertain constitutional claims attacking a state-court judgment, even if the state court had not passed directly on those claims, when the constitutional attack was "inextricably intertwined" with the state court's judgment.

the state supreme court decision and would "represent a partial inroad on *Rooker-Feldman*'s construction of 28 U.S.C. § 1257.");[2] *Pennzoil Co. v. Texaco Inc.* (1987) (abstaining under *Younger v. Harris* (1971), rather than dismissing under *Rooker-Feldman*, in a suit that challenged Texas procedures for enforcing judgments); [*id.*] (Scalia, J., concurring) (The "so-called *Rooker-Feldman* doctrine" does not deprive the Court of jurisdiction to decide Texaco's challenge to the Texas procedures); *id.* (Brennan, J., concurring in judgment) (*Rooker* and *Feldman* do not apply; Texaco filed its federal action to protect its "right to a meaningful opportunity for appellate review, not to challenge the merits of the Texas suit."). *But cf.* (Marshall, J., concurring in judgment) (*Rooker-Feldman* would apply because Texaco's claims necessarily called for review of the merits of its state appeal). *See also Martin v. Wilks* (1989) (Stevens, J., dissenting) (it would be anomalous to allow courts to sit in review of judgments entered by courts of equal, or greater, authority (citing *Rooker* and *Feldman*)).

II

In 1980, two subsidiaries of petitioner Exxon Mobil Corporation (then the separate companies Exxon Corp. and Mobil Corp.) formed joint ventures with respondent Saudi Basic Industries Corp. (SABIC) to produce polyethylene in Saudi Arabia. Two decades later, the parties began to dispute royalties that SABIC had charged the joint ventures for sublicenses to a polyethylene manufacturing method.

SABIC preemptively sued the two ExxonMobil subsidiaries in Delaware Superior Court in July 2000 seeking a declaratory judgment that the royalty charges were proper under the joint venture agreements. About two weeks later, ExxonMobil and its subsidiaries countersued SABIC in the United States District Court for the District of New Jersey, alleging that SABIC overcharged the joint ventures for the sublicenses. ExxonMobil invoked subject-matter jurisdiction in the New Jersey action under 28 U.S.C. § 1330, which authorizes district courts to adjudicate

---

[2] Respondent Saudi Basic Industries Corp. urges that *ASARCO Inc. v. Kadish*, expanded *Rooker-Feldman's* jurisdictional bar to include federal actions that simply raise claims previously litigated in state court. This is not so. In *ASARCO*, the petitioners (defendants below in the state-court action) sought review in this Court of the Arizona Supreme Court's invalidation of a state statute governing mineral leases on state lands. This Court dismissed the suggestion of the United States that the petitioners should have pursued their claim as a new action in federal district court. Such an action, we said, "in essence, would be an attempt to obtain direct review of the Arizona Supreme Court's decision in the lower federal courts" in contravention of 28 U.S.C. § 1257. The injury of which the petitioners (the losing parties in state court) could have complained in the hypothetical federal suit would have been caused by the state court's invalidation of their mineral leases, and the relief they would have sought would have been to undo the state court's invalidation of the statute. The hypothetical suit in *ASARCO*, therefore, shares the characteristics of the suits in *Rooker* and *Feldman, i.e.,* loser in state court invites federal district court to overturn state-court judgment.

actions against foreign states.[4]

In January 2002, the ExxonMobil subsidiaries answered SABIC's state-court complaint, asserting as counterclaims the same claims ExxonMobil had made in the federal suit in New Jersey. The state suit went to trial in March 2003, and the jury returned a verdict of over $400 million in favor of the ExxonMobil subsidiaries. SABIC appealed the judgment entered on the verdict to the Delaware Supreme Court.

Before the state-court trial, SABIC moved to dismiss the federal suit, alleging, *inter alia,* immunity under the Foreign Sovereign Immunities Act of 1976. The Federal District Court denied SABIC's motion to dismiss. SABIC took an interlocutory appeal, and the Court of Appeals heard argument in December 2003, over eight months after the state-court jury verdict.

The Court of Appeals, on its own motion, raised the question whether "subject matter jurisdiction over this case fails under the *Rooker-Feldman* doctrine because ExxonMobil's claims have already been litigated in state court." The court did not question the District Court's possession of subject-matter jurisdiction at the outset of the suit, but held that federal jurisdiction terminated when the Delaware Superior Court entered judgment on the jury verdict. The court rejected ExxonMobil's argument that *Rooker-Feldman* could not apply because ExxonMobil filed its federal complaint well before the state-court judgment. The only relevant consideration, the court stated, "is whether the state judgment precedes a federal judgment on the same claims." If *Rooker-Feldman* did not apply to federal actions filed prior to a state-court judgment, the Court of Appeals worried, "we would be encouraging parties to maintain federal actions as 'insurance policies' while their state court claims were pending." Once ExxonMobil's claims had been litigated to a judgment in state court, the Court of Appeals held, *Rooker-Feldman* "preclude[d][the] federal district court from proceeding." ([I]nternal quotation marks omitted).

ExxonMobil, at that point prevailing in Delaware, was not seeking to overturn the state-court judgment. Nevertheless, the Court of Appeals hypothesized that, if SABIC won on appeal in Delaware, ExxonMobil would be endeavoring in the federal action to "invalidate" the state-court judgment, "the very situation," the court concluded, "contemplated by *Rooker-Feldman's* 'inextricably intertwined' bar."

We granted certiorari to resolve conflict among the Courts of Appeals over the scope of the *Rooker-Feldman* doctrine. We now reverse the judgment of the Court of Appeals for the Third Circuit.

---

[4] SABIC is a Saudi Arabian corporation, 70% owned by the Saudi Government and 30% owned by private investors.

III

Rooker and *Feldman* exhibit the limited circumstances in which this Court's appellate jurisdiction over state-court judgments, 28 U.S.C. § 1257, precludes a United States district court from exercising subject-matter jurisdiction in an action it would otherwise be empowered to adjudicate under a congressional grant of authority, *e.g.,* § 1330 (suits against foreign states), § 1331 (federal question), and § 1332 (diversity). In both cases, the losing party in state court filed suit in federal court after the state proceedings ended, complaining of an injury caused by the state-court judgment and seeking review and rejection of that judgment. Plaintiffs in both cases, alleging federal-question jurisdiction, called upon the District Court to overturn an injurious state-court judgment. Because § 1257, as long interpreted, vests authority to review a state court's judgment solely in this Court, the District Courts in *Rooker* and *Feldman* lacked subject-matter jurisdiction.[8]

When there is parallel state and federal litigation, *Rooker-Feldman* is not triggered simply by the entry of judgment in state court. This Court has repeatedly held that "the pendency of an action in the state court is no bar to proceedings concerning the same matter in the Federal court having jurisdiction." Comity or abstention doctrines may, in various circumstances, permit or require the federal court to stay or dismiss the federal action in favor of the state-court litigation. But neither *Rooker* nor *Feldman* supports the notion that properly invoked concurrent jurisdiction vanishes if a state court reaches judgment on the same or related question while the case remains *sub judice* in a federal court.

Disposition of the federal action, once the state-court adjudication is complete, would be governed by preclusion law. The Full Faith and Credit Act * * * requires the federal court to "give the same preclusive effect to a state-court judgment as another court of that State would give." Preclusion, of course, is not a jurisdictional matter. In parallel litigation, a federal court may be bound to recognize the claim- and issue-preclusive effects of a state-court judgment, but federal jurisdiction over an action does not terminate automatically on the entry of judgment in the state court.

Nor does § 1257 stop a district court from exercising subject-matter jurisdiction simply because a party attempts to litigate in federal court a matter previously litigated in state court. If a federal plaintiff "present[s] some independent claim, albeit one that denies a legal conclusion that a state court has reached in a case to which he was a party * * * , then there is jurisdiction and state law determines whether the defendant prevails under principles of preclusion."

---

[8] Congress, if so minded, may explicitly empower district courts to oversee certain state-court judgments and has done so, most notably, in authorizing federal habeas review of state prisoners' petitions.

This case surely is not the "paradigm situation in which *Rooker-Feldman* precludes a federal district court from proceeding." ExxonMobil plainly has not repaired to federal court to undo the Delaware judgment in its favor. Rather, it appears ExxonMobil filed suit in Federal District Court (only two weeks after SABIC filed in Delaware and well before any judgment in state court) to protect itself in the event it lost in state court on grounds (such as the state statute of limitations) that might not preclude relief in the federal venue.[9] *Rooker-Feldman* did not prevent the District Court from exercising jurisdiction when ExxonMobil filed the federal action, and it did not emerge to vanquish jurisdiction after ExxonMobil prevailed in the Delaware courts.

* * *

For the reasons stated, the judgment of the Court of Appeals for the Third Circuit is reversed, and the case is remanded for further proceedings consistent with this opinion.

It is so ordered.

Notes and Questions

1. Does the Court effectively say that if the object of a federal action when filed is not to overturn an existing state court judgment, *Rooker-Feldman* has no application? In *Garry v. Geils*, 82 F.3d 1362 (7th Cir. 1996), the court noted just such a distinction:

> If the injury alleged resulted from the state court judgment itself, *Rooker-Feldman* directs that the lower federal courts lack jurisdiction. If the injury alleged is distinct from that judgment, *i.e.*, the party maintains an injury apart from the loss in state court and not "inextricably intertwined" with the state judgment, res judicata may apply, but *Rooker-Feldman* does not.

Has *Exxon Mobil* embraced the Seventh Circuit's view? If it has, does that not connote at least that *Rooker-Feldman* can never apply unless there is a state court judgment that antedates commencement of the federal action?

2. *Exxon Mobil* seems once again to raise the question (*see infra* at 1043, Note 3) of whether *Rooker-Feldman* is simply a redundant doctrine given the Full Faith and Credit Statute, which requires federal courts to give preclusive effect to state court judgments. Is the answer a technical rather than a practical one? Recall that preclusion is not jurisdictional; that is why it appears as an affirmative defense that the party relying on it must plead pursuant to FED. R. CIV. P. 8(c). Does *Rooker-Feldman* exist because the Court has characterized it as going to the subject matter jurisdiction of the inferior federal courts and thus as a threshold matter? Does that difference in treatment underscore the dividing point suggested in Note 1 above: that if

---

[9] The Court of Appeals criticized ExxonMobil for pursuing its federal suit as an "insurance policy" against an adverse result in state court. There is nothing necessarily inappropriate, however, about filing a protective action.

there is a state court judgment when the federal action begins, *Rooker-Feldman* may apply, but otherwise preclusion principles will have to do?

3. The *Feldman* Court rejected part of the plaintiffs' challenge (based on alleged arbitrariness in granting waivers to graduates of unaccredited schools) because it was "inextricably intertwined" with the judicial decisions that aggrieved the plaintiffs. Is Exxon Mobil's action here "inextricably intertwined" with the Delaware action that SABIC began and in which Exxon Mobil counterclaimed? Does one even need to ask the preceding question? Note that the Court, although mentioning that part of the *Feldman* opinion more than once, never analyzes *Exxon Mobil* on that basis. Why not?

4. Given *Exxon Mobil*'s approach, is there anything left for the "inextricably intertwined" language from *Feldman* to do or has the Court read it out of the calculus? Does *Facio v. Jones* (*infra* at 1044) predict an answer?

Some courts think that the inextricably-intertwined criterion continues to have teeth. In *Industrial Communications and Electronics, Inc. v. Monroe County*, 134 Fed.Appx. 314 (11th Cir. 2005), the court set out a four-part test for determining whether *Rooker-Feldman* bars a federal action:

> (1) the party in federal court is the same as the party in state court; (2) the prior state court ruling was a final or conclusive judgment on the merits; (3) the party seeking relief in federal court had a reasonable opportunity to raise its federal claims in the state court proceeding; and (4) the issue before the federal court was either adjudicated by the state court or was inextricably intertwined with the state court's judgment.

The court suggested that a claim is inextricably intertwined if the federal plaintiff had "a reasonable opportunity to raise it during the state court proceeding." Thus, although the Supreme Court was careful to distinguish between *Rooker-Feldman* and res judicata, it appears that the latter concept is useful for determining whether *Rooker-Feldman* prevents assertion of a claim not raised in earlier state court proceedings.

5. Suppose a state court issued a preliminary injunction in an on-going case. After *Exxon Mobil*, would the *Rooker-Feldman* doctrine prevent a federal district court from hearing a challenge to the preliminary injunction, assuming that the state case has not reached final judgment? The Court discusses *Rooker-Feldman* in terms of "state court losers." Is the party against whom a preliminary injunction operates a state court loser? On the other hand, the Court also refers to situations in which the federal action begins "after the state proceedings ended [*supra* page 1016]." Might that suggest that the *Rooker-Feldman* doctrine would not prevent review of interlocutory orders in pending state actions?

6. Since *Exxon Mobil*, lower federal courts have been careful to limit *Rooker-Feldman* to the paradigmatic situation of the loser in the state court challenging that court's judgment in a federal proceeding commenced after the state court decision. *See, e.g., Nivens v. Gilchrist*, 444 F.3d 237 (4th Cir. 2006) (*Younger* abstention, not *Rooker-Feldman*, is appropriate course where federal plaintiffs seek federal judicial action with respect to on-going state

prosecution); *Parejko v. Dunn County Circuit Court*, 408 F.Supp.2d 704 (W.D.Wis. 2006) (same).

7. For a thoughtful discussion of the issues that *Exxon Mobil* raises without resolving, see Thomas D. Rowe, Jr. & Edward L. Baskauskas, *"Inextricably Intertwined" Explicable at Last?:* Rooker-Feldman *Analysis After the Supreme Court's* Exxon Mobil *Decision*, 2006 FED.CTS.L.REV. 1 (2006).

2. *The Type of Relief Sought*

CENTIFANTI v. NIX
United States Court of Appeals for the Third Circuit, 1989.
865 F.2d 1422.

COWEN, Circuit Judge.

J. Benedict Centifanti appeals the order of the district court dismissing his complaint for lack of subject matter jurisdiction and denying his motion for leave to amend the complaint. Centifanti filed a complaint under 42 U.S.C. § 1983 (1982) against the Chief Justice and the Justices of the Supreme Court of Pennsylvania ("the Justices" or "Justice Nix"), following the Court's denial of his petition for reinstatement to the bar of the Supreme Court of Pennsylvania. The complaint alleged various constitutional defects in the procedural rules under which the Supreme Court considers petitions for the reinstatement of suspended attorneys.

We hold that the complaint, properly framed, raises a permissible general constitutional challenge to state rules, and does not improperly seek review of a state court decision. Therefore, we will reverse the district court's dismissal of the complaint for lack of subject matter jurisdiction. We will also reverse the district court's denial of Centifanti's motion for leave to amend his complaint to eliminate improper factual detail contained in the complaint. * * * Finally, we conclude that Centifanti's suit is not barred by either the statute of limitations or the doctrine of res judicata.

I.

BACKGROUND

Before discussing the facts of this case, we briefly examine the relevant provisions of the Pennsylvania Rules of Disciplinary Enforcement ("R.D.E."), which govern the investigation and sanction of attorney misconduct. The Rules designate the Supreme Court of Pennsylvania as the ultimate decisionmaker on matters of attorney discipline. The Rules provide for a Disciplinary Board and hearing committees which make findings and submit recommendations to the Supreme Court.

The Disciplinary Board has "the power and the duty * * * [t]o consider and investigate the conduct of any person subject to these rules * * *." More specifically, the Board has the authority to appoint three or more hearing committees within each disciplinary district, and to assign formal charges to a hearing committee. The Board is also authorized "[t]o review the conclusions of hearing committees with respect to formal charges and to prepare and forward its own findings and recommendations, together with the record of the proceeding before the hearing committee, to the Supreme Court." Hearing committees, in turn, are authorized to conduct hearings into formal charges of misconduct upon assignment by the Board, to submit their conclusions (together with the record of the hearing) to the Board, and to review and approve or modify recommendations by Disciplinary Counsel for dismissals, informal admonitions, private reprimands and institution of formal charges.

With regard to decisions on initial disciplinary actions, R.D.E. 208(e)(5) provides that the Supreme Court "shall review the record, where appropriate consider oral argument, and enter an order." R.D.E. 208(e)(4) states, however, that "[e]xcept as provided in [R.D.E. 208](e)(2) and (e)(3), respondent-attorney will not be afforded the right of oral argument." R.D.E. 208(e)(2) provides that if the Board recommends disbarment, the attorney may submit to the Supreme Court a request to present oral argument. R.D.E. 208(e)(3) provides that if the Board recommends a sanction less than disbarment, the Court may issue a rule to show cause why an order of disbarment should not be entered, if the Court so decides after considering the Board's recommendation. In the latter case, the attorney "shall have the absolute right upon request for oral argument." R.D.E. 208(e)(3).

R.D.E. 218(a) provides that "[n]o attorney suspended for a period exceeding three months * * * may resume practice until reinstated by order of the Supreme Court after petition therefor pursuant to these rules." R.D.E. 218(b) provides that, with exceptions which are not germane here, "[a] person who has been disbarred may not apply for reinstatement until the expiration of at least five years from the effective date of the disbarment * * * ." With regard to reinstatement petitions of disbarred or suspended attorneys, R.D.E. 218(c)(6) states: "The Supreme Court shall review the record [of the hearing committee and Disciplinary Board] and enter an appropriate order. Unless otherwise ordered, matters arising under this rule will be considered without oral argument."

Centifanti is an attorney admitted to the bar of the Supreme Court of Pennsylvania in 1972. In 1980, by order of the Supreme Court of Pennsylvania, Centifanti was retroactively suspended from the practice of law for five years, resulting from a plea of *nolo contendere* to two charges of aggravated assault on his wife in 1976.

On August 10, 1983, having successfully completed his criminal probation, Centifanti filed a petition for reinstatement with the Disciplinary Board of the Supreme Court of Pennsylvania. Following the completion of hearings, a hearing committee of the Disciplinary Board submitted a report to the Board unanimously recommending that Centifanti's petition for reinstatement be granted.

Upon review, the Disciplinary Board remanded the petition to the hearing committee to consider certain factual questions which it believed were presented by the record and to consider independent medical testimony concerning Centifanti's mental health. The hearing committee reviewed additional evidence and again unanimously recommended reinstatement. On review of the record, the Disciplinary Board issued an opinion recommending Centifanti's reinstatement by a vote of eight to one.

Centifanti filed an application for leave to file a brief in support of his petition for reinstatement with the Supreme Court of Pennsylvania. By letter dated July 9, 1986, the Court, with one Justice dissenting, denied the petition for reinstatement to the Bar as well as the application for leave to file a brief. The decision was unaccompanied by an opinion or statement of reasons.

On January 2, 1987, Centifanti filed a complaint in the district court alleging a cause of action under 42 U.S.C. § 1983 against the Chief Justice and the Justices of the Supreme Court of Pennsylvania. The complaint alleges that the court-promulgated procedural rules governing attorney reinstatement violate the due process and equal protection clauses of the fourteenth amendment to the United States Constitution. Although we do not decide the merits of Centifanti's constitutional claims in this opinion, an understanding of these claims is necessary to resolve the jurisdictional issue in this case. The complaint, fairly read, essentially alleges the following due process defects in the rules:

1) that the rules fail to provide for a hearing before the Justices prior to action on a petition for reinstatement, following favorable action on the petition by the hearing committee and the Disciplinary Board;

2) that the rules fail to allow petitioners to submit briefs to the Justices in support of the recommendation of the Disciplinary Board that petitioners be reinstated, or to address any concerns or comments expressed by the Board;

3) that the rules fail to provide notification to petitioners, following favorable action by the Board, that the Justices may believe that reinstatement may not be in order, and fail to allow petitioners a hearing before the Justices and to submit a brief addressing any concerns the Justices may have; and

4) that the rules fail to require issuance of a statement of reasons when the Justices reject a petition for reinstatement which had been favorably acted upon by the Board.

Centifanti's complaint also alleges that the rules violate the constitutional guarantee of equal protection. The complaint notes that the rules provide that attorneys suspended for more than three months may not resume practice without first formally petitioning for reinstatement and obtaining the approval of a hearing committee, the Disciplinary Board and the Justices. Yet, although such attorneys are subject to *"de facto* disbarment,"* they are not afforded the same procedural safeguards as attorneys who are formally disbarred.

In a memorandum opinion and order dated June 1, 1988, the district court dismissed Centifanti's complaint for lack of subject matter jurisdiction, and also denied his application for leave to amend the complaint. The court considered Centifanti's complaint to be identical in effect to the complaint filed in *Stern v. Nix,* in which this Court held that the district court lacked subject matter jurisdiction over the complaint. The district court viewed Centifanti's complaint as an attempt to obtain improper review of the decision of the highest court of a state, rather than a permissible generalized constitutional challenge to a state law. The district court also determined that his "proposal to amend the complaint by deleting much of the personal detail does not alter the fundamental nature of this action which is, as it has always been, to challenge the Pennsylvania Supreme Court's judgment." ([F]ootnote omitted). Centifanti appeals to this Court.

II.

THE APPLICABLE LAW

Congress has provided that "[f]inal judgments or decrees rendered by the highest court of a State in which a decision could be had, may be reviewed by the Supreme Court * * * ." In *Rooker v. Fidelity Trust Co.,* the Supreme Court held that section 1257 provides that *only* the Supreme Court, and not lower federal courts, may review decisions of the highest court of a state.

In *District of Columbia Court of Appeals v. Feldman,* the Court reaffirmed its holding in *Rooker,* stating that a district court has "no authority to review final judgments of a state court in judicial proceedings" and "[r]eview of such judgments may be had only in this Court."[3] The Court in *Feldman* also added an important qualification to this rule, however,

---

[3] After an extensive analysis, the *Feldman* Court found the state court proceedings to be "judicial," rather than legislative, ministerial or administrative, and thus subject to the proscription against appeal in the lower federal courts. The Court stated that " '[a] judicial inquiry investigates, declares and enforces liabilities as they stand on present or past facts and under laws supposed already to exist * * * . Legislation on the other hand looks to the future and changes existing conditions by making a new rule to be applied thereafter to all or some part of those subject to its power.' "

Another court has aptly noted: "Following the decision in *Feldman,* courts have consistently found state court decisions regarding the application of bar rules to be judicial rather than ministerial, even when the decisions are made not by the state's supreme court, but by a committee appointed by that court. The determination in these cases turns on whether the state court or its designee considers a present claim of right by applying the terms of a rule to the facts of a petitioner's case."

The parties in the instant case do not appear to dispute that when the Pennsylvania Supreme Court decided Centifanti's petition, it was applying existing rules to the facts to reach a decision and was thus acting in a judicial capacity.

in the following discussion:

> We have recognized that state supreme courts may act in a nonjudicial capacity in promulgating rules regulating the bar. Challenges to the constitutionality of state bar rules, therefore, do not necessarily require a United States district court to review a final state-court judgment in a judicial proceeding. Instead, the district court may simply be asked to assess the validity of a rule promulgated in a nonjudicial proceeding. If this is the case, the district court is not reviewing a state court judicial decision. In this regard, 28 U.S.C. § 1257 does not act as a bar to the district court's consideration of the case and because the proceedings giving rise to the rule are nonjudicial the policies prohibiting United States district court review of final state-court judgments are not implicated. *United States district courts, therefore, have subject-matter jurisdiction over general challenges to state bar rules, promulgated by state courts in nonjudicial proceedings, which do not require review of a final state-court judgment in a particular case.*

([E]mphasis added) (citations omitted).

* * *

The *Feldman* Court held that the district court lacked subject matter jurisdiction over those claims which alleged that the denial by the state court of the attorneys' petitions for waiver was arbitrary and capricious, but that it *did* have subject matter jurisdiction over those claims which raised general challenges to the constitutionality of the rules.

The Court in *Feldman* recognized the occasional difficulty in distinguishing between a general challenge to court-promulgated attorney disciplinary or admission rules, and a specific challenge to a particular decision involving these rules by a state supreme court. The Court suggested that "[i]f the constitutional claims presented to a United States district court are *inextricably intertwined* with the state court's denial in a judicial proceeding of a particular plaintiff's application for admission to the state bar, then the district court is in essence being called upon to review the state-court decision * * * [which] the district court may not do." ([E]mphasis added).

We recently had occasion to apply the so-called *Rooker-Feldman* doctrine in *Stern v. Nix.*[6] Stern, a Pennsylvania attorney, was the subject of a disciplinary investigation by state bar authorities. A hearing committee of the Disciplinary Board recommended a private reprimand as a sanction against Stern for his misbehavior. The Disciplinary Board on review recommended the higher sanction of public censure. The Su-

---

[6] The *Stern* decision was decided by a panel of Second Circuit judges sitting as a panel of the Court of Appeals for the Third Circuit, by designation of the Chief Justice of the United States. All the judges of this Court had recused themselves on the appeal.

preme Court rejected the factual findings of both the committee and the Board, which the disciplinary rules allowed it to do, and imposed the penalty of disbarment.

Stern then filed a section 1983 action in federal district court against the Justices of the Supreme Court, challenging the combined effect of two state court rules. The first rule was a court-made rule which provides that the Pennsylvania Supreme Court may review *de novo* attorney disciplinary hearings without being bound by the findings of the hearing committee or the Disciplinary Board. The second rule was a Pennsylvania Rule of Disciplinary Enforcement which provided that attorneys facing disciplinary charges had the right to oral argument before the Supreme Court, but made no provision for an evidentiary hearing before the Court. Stern challenged the Supreme Court's practice of rejecting administrative findings of fact without conducting an evidentiary hearing.

The district court denied the Justices' motion to dismiss the action on the basis of lack of subject matter jurisdiction, but also denied the injunction requested by Stern. On appeal, we held that the district court lacked subject matter jurisdiction over Stern's complaint, because the complaint sought reversal of the decision of the Supreme Court of Pennsylvania, in contravention of *Rooker-Feldman*.

We based our decision in *Stern* on our determination that the remedy sought would, if granted, force the district court to review the merits of the state court's decision, for two reasons. First, Stern sought a permanent injunction preventing the state court from disbarring him and others without a hearing. We noted that this remedy, if granted, would effectively reverse the state court judgment, and thus improperly review that judgment.

Second, Stern also requested a temporary restraining order and a preliminary injunction. We noted that both of these remedies "required him to demonstrate the likelihood of success on the merits and irreparable harm to *himself*, thus shifting the focus to the actions of the Supreme Court of Pennsylvania in his particular case." *Id.* (emphasis in original). Thus we concluded that Stern's complaint, although couched in terms of a general challenge to the constitutionality of the state rules, was in reality an attempt to obtain reversal of the state court judgment which disbarred him.[7]

---

[7] Our decision in *Stern* was also influenced by the excessive factual detail in Stern's complaint. We noted that "[t]he complaint and the stipulation of facts contained extensive exposition of the specific facts in Stern's case, which hardly would have been necessary if the district court were being asked only to 'assess the validity' of the rule in its general application." ([Q]uoting *Feldman*.)

III.

DISCUSSION

A. *Subject Matter Jurisdiction*

We must determine on which side of the *Rooker-Feldman* line Centifanti's complaint falls. * * *

Our first task is to characterize the precise object of Centifanti's constitutional challenge. In *Feldman,* the appellants challenged the decisions of a state court not to waive bar application requirements in their cases, but they also made a general challenge to the constitutionality of those requirements. The Supreme Court emphasized the fundamental difference between the two types of challenges. Here Centifanti challenges the constitutionality of the Pennsylvania rules as they exist, rather than the state court's application of them to deny his petition. As in *Feldman,* Centifanti's claims reflect "general challenges to state bar rules, promulgated by [a] state court[ ] in nonjudicial proceedings, which do not require review of a final state-court judgment in a particular case." Thus, Centifanti's complaint is in the nature of those *Feldman*-type claims (general challenges to the constitutionality of state supreme court rules) over which the district court has jurisdiction, and does not run afoul of the prohibition against appeals of state court decisions to lower federal courts.

As in *Stern,* examining the nature of the specific relief requested will aid us in determining what is being challenged and, thus, whether the district court has subject matter jurisdiction. In his due process claim, Centifanti requests a declaratory judgment that "the rules and procedures for considering petitions for reinstatement of suspended attorneys are unconstitutional." This would not require the district court to review the state supreme court decision. The declaratory judgment Centifanti seeks is prospective and directed toward "the rules and procedures for considering [future] petitions for reinstatement," rather than toward the decision of the state supreme court on Centifanti's prior petition. In *Stern,* we noted that Stern requested a declaratory judgment as well as injunctive relief, and we expressed no jurisdictional difficulty with the former.[8]

---

[8] In fact, we strongly implied in *Stern* that a challenge seeking declaratory relief did *not* violate the *Rooker-Feldman* doctrine. Stern had argued that his case was similar to a case from another circuit in which the court of appeals held that the district court had jurisdiction over a challenge to a state's procedural rule governing attorney discipline. We rejected Stern's comparison, noting that [that case], the plaintiff requested *only declaratory relief* and a hearing, *not an injunction.* ([E]mphasis added).

Of course, the substance and not the form of the requested relief is ultimately controlling. For example, a federal court would not have jurisdiction over a complaint seeking a "declaration" that a state court's decision not to waive a bar application requirement was arbitrary and capricious. This certainly would raise a retrospective challenge to a state court decision.

Centifanti also sought "injunctive relief directing the Defendant Justices to afford plaintiff and all similarly situated future petitioners for reinstatement Due Process prior to denial of their petitions," including the right to a hearing before the Justices, and the right to submit briefs to them and to receive a statement of reasons from them. Centifanti's request for a permanent injunction differs significantly from the injunction sought in *Stern.* Stern sought an injunction restraining the state supreme court from disbarring him and similarly situated attorneys unless the court, in cases where it plans to reject the findings of the hearing committee ("which of course would include Stern's case," we noted), first grants an evidentiary hearing. We considered this an improper attempt to enjoin, albeit conditionally, the enforcement of the state supreme court judgment disbarring Stern.

In contrast to the injunction sought in *Stern,* Centifanti seeks to enjoin the Justices to direct that they "afford *plaintiff and all similarly situated future petitioners for reinstatement* Due Process prior to the denial of their petitions." ([E]mphasis added). Centifanti argues, and we agree, that the complaint's joint reference to Centifanti "and all similarly situated future petitioners" indicates that he seeks *prospective* relief. He does not request the district court to interfere in any way with the decision of the Pennsylvania Supreme Court to deny his petition, or with the enforcement of that decision. Instead, he requests an injunction ordering the state court to correct alleged constitutional defects in the procedural rules applied in reaching that decision. Although such relief, if granted, could affect *future* decisions of the state supreme court, it would not require review of a past decision. Thus, we hold that the district court has subject matter jurisdiction over the due process claim.

Centifanti's requests for injunctive relief in his equal protection claim * * * are framed in terms identical to his due process claim. That is, they seek prospective relief in the form of ordering the Justices to remedy the alleged defects for the purposes of future reinstatement proceedings. Thus, the analysis we have set forth above of his due process claim applies as well to these additional constitutional challenges.

We must also determine whether Centifanti's claims are "inextricably intertwined" with the merits of the state court's denial of Centifanti's petition. In his concurring opinion in *Pennzoil Co. v. Texaco, Inc.,* Justice Marshall addressed the problem of determining when a constitutional claim is "inextricably intertwined" with the particular decision of a state court:

> While the question whether a federal constitutional challenge is inextricably intertwined with the merits of a state-court judgment may sometimes be difficult to answer, it is apparent, as a first step, that the federal claim is inextricably intertwined with the state-court judgment if the federal claim succeeds only to the extent that the state court wrongly decided the issues before it.

Where federal relief can only be predicated upon a conviction that the state court was wrong, it is difficult to conceive the federal proceeding as, in substance, anything other than a prohibited appeal of the state-court judgment.

In the instant case, the district court could hold that the state rules in question violate the Constitution, without holding that the Pennsylvania Supreme Court erred in denying Centifanti's petition for reinstatement. Thus, the federal claim is not inextricably intertwined with the state court judgment.

B. *Amendment of the Complaint*

In order for the district court to have subject matter jurisdiction over Centifanti's complaint, the complaint must challenge the *rules* promulgated by the court, rather than the court's *decision* on Centifanti's petition for reinstatement. Thus, Centifanti's complaint need only contain enough factual detail to enable him to establish standing to bring an action pursuant to 42 U.S.C. § 1983 challenging the state supreme court rules.

Centifanti includes in his complaint far more detail than is necessary to mount a general constitutional challenge to the Pennsylvania rules. He describes his productivity since his suspension from the practice of law, his rehabilitation from an alcohol problem, his completion of probation, and his numerous character references. He also describes the hearing committee's and Disciplinary Board's strong recommendations for reinstatement. However, the facts alleged are simply outside the scope of and irrelevant to a federal district court's review of state court-promulgated rules. The excessive detail undermines the validity of Centifanti's general constitutional challenge, and his complaint begins to resemble an attempt to seek improper review of the state supreme court decision.

In his supplemental response to defendant's motion for summary judgment, Centifanti moved, in the alternative, for leave to amend his complaint to eliminate the improper factual detail from the complaint. The district court denied the motion, stating that "plaintiff's proposal to amend the complaint by deleting much of the personal detail does not alter the fundamental nature of this action which is, as it has always been, to challenge the Pennsylvania Supreme Court's judgment." ([F]ootnote omitted).

* * *

The district court determined that it lacked subject matter jurisdiction over Centifanti's complaint under the *Rooker-Feldman* doctrine. Based on this conclusion, it denied the motion to amend the complaint, asserting simply that an amendment would not cure the jurisdictional defect, and thus by implication, that the amendment would not survive a motion to dismiss. Because we hold that the district court has subject matter jurisdiction over the complaint, we determine that the amendment would survive a motion to dismiss for lack of subject matter jurisdiction. The district court abused its discretion in denying the motion for leave to amend the complaint, and we will reverse the district court's order.[11]

* * *

D. *Statute of Limitations and Res Judicata*

The district court, having decided that it lacked jurisdiction over the instant matter and having denied leave to amend the complaint, expressly did not reach the Justices' claims that the proposed amended complaint would be barred by Pennsylvania's two year statute of limitations for tort actions and by principles of issue and claim preclusion. We address these two questions now.

With regard to the statute of limitations, the Justices argue that Centifanti's cause of action accrued in 1983, when Centifanti filed his petition for reinstatement. They note that Centifanti's section 1983 action was brought in 1987, beyond the two-year statute of limitations for tort actions—and thus for section 1983 actions—in Pennsylvania. The Justices argue that because Centifanti is alleging a general infirmity in the state supreme court rules rather than a defect in the decision on his petition, Centifanti did not have to wait until his petition was denied to bring suit.

We find the Justices' arguments unpersuasive. First, we observe that Centifanti remains suspended from the practice of law, and thus he alleges what is in essence a continuing wrong. His cause of action continues to accrue on each day of the alleged wrong. Second, even if we did not determine that the cause of action continued to accrue each day, we would nevertheless find the complaint not barred by the statute of limitations. Although we agree with the Justices that Centifanti is alleging a defect in the rules and not in the state court's decision, this does not mean that the cause of action accrued as soon as he filed his reinstatement petition. Centifanti did not have standing to challenge the rules until he had suffered or was about to suffer an actual injury. This did not occur until the Pennsylvania Supreme Court denied his petition in July of 1986, or at least until the hearing committee and the Disciplinary Board recommended his reinstatement. He filed his complaint in the federal district court in January of 1987, well within two years of both the Court's denial and the Board's recommendation.

---

[11] We recognize that in *Stern* the excessive factual detail in the complaint was a factor in our characterizing that complaint as an attempt at improper review of the state court decision. In that case, however, we did not have occasion to address the issue of amending the defective complaint, as Stern apparently did not file an amended complaint or move for leave to do so. Moreover, our decision in *Stern* was based primarily on the retrospective nature of the specific injunction sought, as discussed above. Thus, *Stern* does not prevent us from reversing the district court on its denial of the motion to amend.

The Justices also argue that Centifanti could have raised his constitutional claims in the reinstatement proceeding in the state supreme court, or before the hearing committee or Disciplinary Board, and that his failure to do so bars the district court from hearing those claims under the doctrine of res judicata. In *Feldman,* the Supreme Court expressly declined to reach the issue of res judicata. The Justices cite several cases in their brief which hold that res judicata may apply to an attorney's constitutional challenges to procedural rules where the claims could have been but were not litigated in the state-court attorney disciplinary proceedings.

Centifanti does not dispute that res judicata *may* apply in such cases, but he argues that he did not have a realistic opportunity to raise his federal constitutional claims in the state court proceeding. We agree that on the record before us and in the factual context of his particular application for reinstatement, Centifanti did not have a realistic opportunity to fully and fairly litigate these issues. Thus, we determine that he is not barred by res judicata from bringing his constitutional claims in the district court.

IV.

CONCLUSION

For the reasons discussed, we will reverse the district court's order dismissing the complaint for lack of subject matter jurisdiction. We will also reverse the court's order denying Centifanti leave to amend his complaint to delete the improper factual detail. * * * Finally, we determine that neither the statute of limitations nor res judicata preclude this action.

Costs taxed against appellees.

Notes and Questions

1. Centifanti is attempting to have the federal courts declare unconstitutional the Pennsylvania Supreme Court's rules for adjudicating applications for reinstatement to the bar. Was the injury of which Centifanti complains suffered at the hands of the Pennsylvania Supreme Court's judgment or from some independent source? Does the *Rooker-Feldman* doctrine aim to protect state courts or state judgments from federal judicial interference?

2. a) If Centifanti gets relief, clearly it will affect the efficacy of the Pennsylvania Supreme Court's previous orders denying him leave to file a brief or have an evidentiary hearing. Why does *that* not violate *Rooker-Feldman?*

b) Is it really possible for the federal court to say that the rules denying Centifanti reinstatement were unconstitutional without saying that the Pennsylvania Supreme Court committed constitutional error in reaching its decision under those rules? Is the difference that the court here is making no effort to give its ruling coercive effect with respect to the state courts? If the ruling can have no coercive effect at all, then does it amount to an advisory opinion?

c) Does the court's distinction between declaratory and injunctive relief hold up? See particularly Note 8 in the opinion. In the *Younger* abstention context, the Supreme Court has noted that a declaratory judgment may interfere with state judicial proceedings just as much as an injunction. (Note 10 on page 799 discusses *Samuels v. Mackell*, the case decided with *Younger v. Harris* in which the Court declined to allow a plaintiff to evade *Younger*'s admonition against enjoining pending state criminal proceedings by seeking declaratory relief instead.) For that matter, the second section of the Declaratory Judgment Act, 28 U.S.C. § 2202, explicitly authorizes "* * * further necessary or proper relief based on a declaratory judgment * * *." Under the Third Circuit's reasoning, could Stern have accomplished in two steps what the court forbade him to do in one? On the other hand, if one takes the position that the successful declaratory judgment plaintiff cannot avail himself of § 2202 without running afoul of *Rooker-Feldman*, then is there an insurmountable standing problem under the doctrine of *Simon v. Eastern Kentucky Welfare Rights Organization*, 426 U.S. 26, 96 S.Ct. 1917, 48 L.Ed.2d 450 (1976), because the relief requested will not redress the plaintiff's injury?

3. a) Why is Centifanti's claim not subject to the same objections as Stern's? He is in court only because of the adverse decision. If the Pennsylvania Supreme Court had not acted on his application when he filed the federal suit, or if he had not yet sought reinstatement, would his case be justiciable under Article III?

b) Is the real difference between *Centifanti* and *Stern* the fact that Stern was trying to undo a state court judgment that had expelled him from the bar, whereas Centifanti was trying to set up a future application for reentry?

4. Is it only Centifanti's on-going entitlement to apply for reinstatement that enables him to evade the *Rooker-Feldman* bar that Stern encountered? If so, should one conclude that only "applications" cases can survive a *Rooker-Feldman* attack?

5. Would Stern have been better off for *Rooker-Feldman* purposes if he mounted his federal challenge to Pennsylvania's *de novo* and no-evidentiary-hearing rules while his state proceeding was still before the state's Rule of Disciplinary Enforcement Board? Then there would have been no state court judgment. On the other hand, would Stern then have faced insurmountable problems under either the Anti-Injunction Act, 28 U.S.C. § 2283 (*see* pages 746-761 of the text) or under the *Younger* abstention doctrine (*see* pages 785-841 of the text)?

6. Why did Centifanti move to amend his complaint? Under the Federal Rules, the courts do not dismiss a complaint simply because of surplusage. The Third Circuit notes that "[t]he excessive detail undermines the validity of Centifanti's general constitutional challenge, and his complaint begins to resemble an attempt to seek improper review of the state supreme court decision." Does the court's handling of this issue suggest that *Rooker-Feldman*

(and hence subject matter jurisdiction) may simply be a matter of artful pleading? In this regard, see particularly Note 11 in the opinion. Does the court imply that *Stern* might have come out differently had the plaintiff there amended his complaint? While it would be difficult to overstate the potential benefits of attorneys learning when to keep their mouths shut, in determining the applicability of *Rooker-Feldman* should the courts focus on the complaint's language or the effect of a federal judgment on an earlier state judgment?

3. *Appeal vs. Collateral Attack vs. Independent Action*

KAMILEWICZ v. BANK OF BOSTON CORPORATION
United States Court of Appeals for the Seventh Circuit, 1996.
92 F.3d 506.

TERENCE T. EVANS, Circuit Judge.

A class action in Alabama cost Dexter Kamilewicz $91.33 in attorney fees to recover $2.19 on the merits. When he learned of this news, he and the other plaintiffs (his wife and Martha Preston) sued the class action attorneys (as well as certain defendants in the Alabama action) in the District Court for the Northern District of Illinois. There, to add to their chagrin, they ran up against another obstacle—the *Rooker-Feldman* doctrine. This is their appeal from an order dismissing their federal case for lack of subject matter jurisdiction.

Kamilewicz and the other plaintiffs have had mortgages serviced by BancBoston Mortgage Corporation, one of the defendants. They were among an estimated 715,000 members of a class in a nationwide class action filed in the circuit court for Mobile County, Alabama. The suit—*Hoffman, et al. v. BancBoston Mortgage Corp.*—challenged the manner in which BancBoston calculated the amount of surplus each member of the class was required to maintain in their escrow accounts. Deposits to the escrow accounts were paid as part of the class members' monthly mortgage payments. There was no question regarding the ultimate ownership of the surplus; it belonged to the mortgagor and was to be returned when the mortgage debt was satisfied. The issue in the lawsuit was the propriety of BancBoston's holding the surplus until the time it would be returned to the mortgagor.

In October 1993, the Alabama court granted partial summary judgment in favor of the plaintiff class. The court found that BancBoston's practice was, in fact, inconsistent with the terms of the mortgages. Then in October 1995, counsel for the class prepared a notice of a proposed settlement of the suit. The notice stated that the settlement was "fair, reasonable, adequate, and in the best interests of the class" and that the attorney fees sought were "reasonable" and would "not exceed one-third of the economic benefit" to the class. Bank of Boston—one of the defendants—objected to the notice because it failed to advise the class that there were "substantial adverse effects" to the proposed settlement.

Those perceived adverse effects were that if BancBoston were ordered to refund the escrow surplus and if the attorneys for the class were to seek attorney fees out of the refund, some class members would suffer an out-of-pocket loss as a result of the lawsuit. It should be noted here that the Bank of Boston and BancBoston had offered, prior to the grant of partial summary judgment in 1993, to settle the litigation. As part of that proposed settlement, the bank and BancBoston would have had to pay $500,000 in attorney fees out of the banks' own funds, and the entire amount of the escrow refund would have gone to the class members.

Nevertheless, the Alabama court approved the proposed notice and held a fairness hearing on January 10 and 11, 1994. On January 24, 1994, the court approved the settlement under which the class members received one-time interest payments ranging from $0.00 to $8.76. The court also found the attorney fees reasonable. The fee award was a percentage of the escrow accounts, or, the complaint in the present case asserts, in excess of $14 million. The fact may be that the award was closer to $8,500,000, but because in either event we are talking about significant amounts of money, the actual amount is not material and, of course, the allegations of the complaint are accepted as true at this point in the litigation. Under the settlement, BancBoston deducted attorney fees from the class members' escrow accounts. The deduction was recorded on the 1994 annual tax and interest statements as a "miscellaneous disbursement." In most cases, the "miscellaneous disbursement" was more—far more—than the interest refund. It was this statement that, understandably, caught Mr. Kamilewicz's eye.

Unhappy with the peculiar result of the class action suit in Alabama, Mr. and Mrs. Kamilewicz and Ms. Preston filed the present federal class action against the bank and the mortgage company, and the plaintiffs' attorneys in the Alabama action. The complaint contained allegations of violations of the Racketeer Influenced and Corrupt Organizations Act, 18 U.S.C. § 1962, and of the Civil Rights Act, 42 U.S.C. § 1983, as well as claims of common law fraud, negligent misrepresentation, attorney malpractice, breach of fiduciary duty, and conversion. In turn, the defendants in the federal case filed a motion with the Alabama court seeking an order directed to the Kamilewicz plaintiffs to show cause why they were not bound by the January 1994 order of that court. A hearing was scheduled in Alabama, to which the Kamilewicz plaintiffs sent an attorney for the purpose of stating that they would not participate in the hearing because they contested whether Alabama had personal jurisdiction over them. On January 30, 1996, the Alabama court reaffirmed the order of settlement.

Meanwhile, back in Chicago, on December 15, 1995, Judge Paul Plunkett of the Northern District of Illinois had entered his order dismissing the federal case for lack of subject matter jurisdiction. He found that even though the federal case was "dressed up" as a claim for RICO damages or for attorney malpractice, it was, nevertheless, a collateral attack on a state court judgment which would require that he consider issues "inextricably intertwined" with the state court case. This he was prohibited to do, he concluded, under the doctrine known as *Rooker-Feldman*.

* * * [W]e find ourselves in agreement with the district court.

We first note that the exact ground on which the plaintiffs and, for that matter, the Amici, who are attorneys general from several states, stand in this appeal is a little like shifting sand. The plaintiffs argue that the judgment of the Alabama court is null and void because the court did not have personal jurisdiction over them and that the special protections required for class actions—notice, adequate representation, etc.—were not complied with. However, they also say that they are not seeking to overturn the Alabama judgment. Then, they state that where the district court went wrong was to use a state court judgment which was "null and void" as the basis for the *Rooker-Feldman* bar. In addition, plaintiffs veer into a claim that the January 30, 1996, Alabama court order cannot be a basis for the *Rooker-Feldman* bar because there was no personal jurisdiction over them, and furthermore that fraud claims are somehow outside the *Rooker-Feldman* bar. The Amici say that they do not want to establish an exception to the general rule that absent class members may be bound by a nationwide class action settlement, but that on the unusual—and egregious—facts of this case, the Kamilewicz action should be allowed to proceed.

The *Rooker-Feldman* doctrine * * * is a recognition of the principle that the inferior federal courts generally do not have the power to exercise appellate review over state court decisions. In *Rooker,* the Supreme Court stated that because the jurisdiction of the federal district courts was strictly original, those courts cannot reverse or modify a state court judgment—even if that judgment is wrong. Only the Supreme Court has that power. *Feldman* involved proceedings denying him a waiver of a bar admission rule which required that applicants have graduated from an approved law school. The first issue was whether the action constituted a judicial proceeding. The Court determined that it was in fact such a proceeding and that a district court "has no authority to review final judgment of a state court in judicial proceedings."

It becomes necessary to our analysis, then, to determine whether what the federal court was asked to do in this case was, essentially, review a decision of a state court. Our cases offer means by which that determination is made. We ask whether the federal plaintiff seeks to set aside a state court judgment or whether he is, in fact, presenting an independent claim. Put another way, if the injury which the federal plaintiff alleges resulted from the state court judgment itself, then *Rooker-Feldman* controls, and the lower federal courts lack jurisdiction over the claim. It does not matter that the state court judgment might be erroneous or even unconstitutional. Nor does it matter that the time for appeal to the United States Supreme Court may have passed.

In addition, the state and federal cases also do not need to be directly on point. The Court found a lack of jurisdiction in *Feldman* itself when the federal constitutional claims were "inextricably intertwined," with the state court judgment. As we have explained, lower federal courts might be engaging in impermissible appellate review even when asked to entertain a claim that was not argued in the state court but was "inextricably intertwined" with the state court judgment.

Our cases have attempted to make the analysis of this issue easier by offering a sometimes helpful tip. That tip is that often, if a federal plaintiff was the plaintiff in the state court action, the doctrine he must contend with is res judicata, not *Rooker-Feldman*. On the other hand, if the federal plaintiff was the defendant in state court, *Rooker-Feldman* is the applicable doctrine. *Homola v. McNamara* (7th Cir.1995); *Nesses v. Shepard* (7th Cir.1995). The tip, however, is merely that, and allows exceptions. * * * [B]oth the *Rooker* and *Feldman* plaintiffs were also plaintiffs in the state judicial proceedings. Although it may be that the federal plaintiff's position as either a plaintiff or a defendant in the state court proceeding will "usually coalesce with the source-of-the-injury standard," as we said in *Garry,* it may not always do so, and the important issue remains the source of the injury: the issue is whether the federal plaintiff is injured by the state court judgment or by a prior injury at the hands of the defendant.

How does all of this theory apply to the case before us? As a preliminary matter, we note that the Alabama court specifically found the settlement to be fair and approved the fees. In his order of January 24, 1994, the state judge found that the notice complied with all requirements of due process, that the consent decree was fair and reasonable, and that the attorney fees were reasonable.

Plaintiffs seem to be urging us to reach the conclusion that we can overturn the decision of the Alabama court insofar as it involved a determination that procedural due process was complied with. As support for this proposition, they rely on decisions which hold that a party can attack a *default* judgment against him if it is entered by a court without personal jurisdiction over him. We see significant differences between default judgments and the judgment under attack here. We reject the plaintiffs' far-reaching proposed exception to the *Rooker-Feldman* doctrine.

Another argument which seems slightly off-center is that the January 30, 1996, order, finding the allegations of fraud "baseless," is not subject to a *Rooker-Feldman* bar because it was entered in the absence of personal jurisdiction over the plaintiffs and it was entered after the federal lawsuit was filed. This argument is tied to the claim that the plaintiffs were precluded from litigating their fraud claim in the state court, and thus were required to—or had a right to—litigate it in federal court.

The January 30 order itself is not material to the issues before us. It is not necessary to rely on it to determine that the federal lawsuit was properly dismissed. The fact is that the proper court for an assertion of fraud in the procurement of a judgment is the one which rendered the judgment. As we stated in *Homola*:

> Relief in civil cases differs from that in criminal cases in two principal respects. First, the civil time limits are shorter (in federal litigation, for example, a claim of fraud on the court, Homola's theme, must be made within one year). Second, the losing party cannot move to a new forum but must present his argument to the court that rendered the judgment. Homola has tried to shift not only courts but also jurisdictions, asking a federal judge to award relief for wrongs committed in state court. Instead of saying that there was no constitutional flaw in the state proceedings, the district court should have refused to entertain the claims, sending Homola back where he belongs—the original courts.

Alabama has a procedure by which a litigant can assert an independent action for fraud upon the court within three years of the entry of the fraudulently induced judgment. In addition, the Alabama court retained continuing jurisdiction over the class action. It is not for the federal court to decide these issues.

* * *

The Kamilewiczes were class member/plaintiffs in the Alabama suit. The part of the judgment they are unhappy with is the approval of the settlement as to the fees to be paid to their attorneys—fees which were assessed against them. The district court concluded that the *Kamilewicz* plaintiffs were in the position of defendants in this aspect of the state court proceedings. That conclusion has some support in logic and bolsters a finding of a *Rooker-Feldman* bar. More important, however, is the fact that the plaintiffs' injuries are a result of the state court judgment. Their claim in federal court is a multi-pronged attack on the approval of the settlement regarding the attorney fees issue. Regardless of which of the specific federal claims the district court were to consider, it would run directly into the state court finding, entered after a two-day fairness hearing—that the fees were reasonable. The federal claims are "inextricably intertwined" with the state court judgment, whether that judgment is right or wrong.

We won't deny that the Alabama judgment seems questionable on the surface. How can it be right that a plaintiff should recover less than $10 and have to pay nearly $100 in fees? But how can we—or the district court—know that we would have ruled another way? To determine that, we would have to go through the steps already taken in the state court—precisely what lower federal courts are not allowed to do under *Rooker-Feldman*. And perhaps if we undertook that analysis we would find that some less tangible economic benefit to the class justified the settlement.

That the facts seem at least superficially egregious brings us to the arguments of Amici that on facts such as these an exception of some undefined sort should be carved out, and that if the plaintiff class was actually in the position of defendants on the attorney fees issue, then even under *Phillips Petroleum Co. v. Shutts*, 472 U.S. 797, 105 S.Ct. 2965, 86 L.Ed.2d 628 (1985), perhaps personal jurisdiction was lacking in the Alabama court. We decline to take the step urged by the Amici.

In *Shutts,* the Court loosened somewhat the requirements for assertion of personal jurisdiction over members of a plaintiff class and determined that due process would be satisfied if there was notice, an opportunity to appear in person or by counsel, an opportunity to opt out of the class, and adequate representation. The rationale was, in part, that absent plaintiffs ordinarily do not face the same exposure as defendants. Amici argue that if on the attorney fees issue the *Kamilewicz* plaintiffs were actually in the position of defendants, then due process requires that issues of personal jurisdiction be assessed under the traditional minimum contacts analysis of *International Shoe Co. v. Washington* (1945).

Even were we to accept the argument, it does not change the fact that lower federal courts cannot review decisions of the state court. Here, the state court approved the settlement, including the fees. The Supreme Court of Alabama or the United States Supreme Court could reverse the decision were either so inclined. The federal district court, on the other hand, cannot review the Alabama decision. We also note the obvious—that the posture of the Alabama case is not unique. In class actions, often the fees are a percentage of the award granted to the plaintiff class. The argument of Amici, if accepted, could have ramifications far beyond this case.

Because we agree that *Rooker-Feldman* bars this action, the judgment of the district court is AFFIRMED.

KAMILEWICZ v. BANK OF BOSTON CORPORATION
United States Court of Appeals for the Seventh Circuit, 1996.
100 F.3d 1348.

ON PETITION FOR REHEARING WITH SUGGESTION
FOR REHEARING EN BANC

ORDER

A panel decided this case on August 8, 1996. On August 22, 1996, the plaintiffs-appellants filed a petition for rehearing and suggestion for rehearing en banc. Subsequently, the judges on the panel voted to deny the petition for rehearing, and a vote was requested on the suggestion for rehearing en banc. A majority of the active members of the court have voted to deny rehearing en banc. Chief Judge Posner and Circuit Judges Easterbrook, Manion, Rovner, and Diane P. Wood voted to grant rehearing en banc.

IT IS THEREFORE ORDERED that the petition for rehearing is hereby DENIED. Because a majority of judges voted to deny rehearing en banc, the suggestion to do so is also DENIED.

EASTERBROOK, CIRCUIT JUDGE, with whom POSNER, CHIEF JUDGE, and MANION, ROVNER, and DIANE P. WOOD, Circuit Judges, join, dissenting from the denial of rehearing en banc.

A class action contending that the Bank of Boston and its affiliates (collectively, the Bank) did not promptly post interest to real estate escrow accounts was filed in Alabama by a Chicago law firm. Settlement ensued, and the class members learned only what the notice told them. Few opted out or objected, because the maximum award to any class member was less than $9. Any recovery, however small, seemed preferable to initiating a separate suit or even bearing the costs of protesting the settlement's terms. After the state judge approved the pact, the Bank carried out its part: it disbursed more than $8 million to the class attorneys in legal fees and credited most accounts with paltry sums. Problem: the fees, equal to 5.32 percent of the balance in each account, were debited to the accounts. For many accounts the debit exceeded the credit. Dexter J. Kamilewicz, for example, received a credit of $2.19 and a debit of $91.33, for a loss of $89.14.

Outraged account holders hired new lawyers to sue their "champions" from the state case for malpractice, breach of fiduciary duty, indeed for fraud. Defendants insist that most members of the class emerged with net benefits, but they do not deny that many suffered net losses—and that these impending losses, known to those who negotiated the settlement, were not disclosed to the class members. Kamilewicz believes that even when the credit exceeded the debit the account holder lost, because the credit would have been made when the mortgage terminated and the escrowed sum was released; the real economic benefit was not the amount of the credit but the interest that could be earned from investing the payment sooner.

Kamilewicz and the other representative plaintiffs sued not only the lawyers for the plaintiff class in *Hoffman* but also the Bank and the Bank's lawyers. Everything the Bank did to affect Kamilewicz's interests was authorized by the judgment based on the settlement, so the Bank's inclusion in the case marked an effort to obtain collateral review of the state court's judgment. Kamilewicz argued that the judgment is void with respect to account holders who live outside Alabama—for what right does Alabama have to instruct financial institutions in Florida to debit the accounts of citizens of Maine and other states? (Despite its name, BancBoston's headquarters are in Florida, and the Kamilewiczes hail from Maine.) Class members are not bound when a state court exceeds its jurisdiction. The Attorneys General of Florida, Maine, and seven other states have filed a brief as amicus curiae to protest their citizens' treatment by Alabama. According to Kamilewicz, the Alabama judgment is doubly flawed, because the notice was so misleading that it denied the class members due process of law. A deficient notice means that the class members' right to opt out was defeated, which has jurisdictional consequences of its own. Lack of jurisdiction and unconstitutional procedures are recognized grounds for disregarding a judgment in a class action. But by asking for collateral review of a judgment, the Kamilewicz class invited the response: "In federal court?" Under the *Rooker-Feldman* doctrine, * * * the Supreme Court of the United States is the only federal court authorized to review a state court's judgment in civil litigation. Defendants invoked this rule and argued that the Kamilewicz class could obtain relief only from a state court. The district court agreed and dismissed the entire complaint for want of jurisdiction, and a panel of this court affirmed.

Suppose A sues B in a state that lacks any connection to B or to the dispute. B refuses to appear and the court enters a default judgment, which A attempts to collect using the processes of the federal court under the diversity jurisdiction. Would the court really direct B to pay, without inquiring into the jurisdiction of the state court? Certainly not in the fifth circuit, which has held that the *Rooker-Feldman* doctrine permits the kinds of collateral attacks that any state court of general jurisdiction could entertain. ("Any" is an important qualifier, for reasons discussed in *Homola v. McNamara* (7th Cir. 1995), and *Harris Trust & Savings Bank v. Ellis* (7th Cir. 1987).) When *Hansberry v. Lee* (1940) held that a judgment rendered without personal jurisdiction over members of the class is not entitled to full faith and credit, the Justices did not add: "except in federal court." Granted, the defendants in today's case are not trying to execute a judgment; they want to fend off a challenge to the status quo. But the difference between offensive and defensive use of a judgment is not important to the panel's conclusion, or to mine—which is that a judgment that is not entitled to full faith and credit does not acquire extra force via the *Rooker-Feldman* doctrine.

Collateral attacks based on lack of personal or subject-matter jurisdiction are proper, no less in class actions than in other cases—indeed, they are especially appropriate where class members are stunned to find that, although aligned as plaintiffs, they are net losers, just as if the original defendants had filed and prevailed on a counterclaim of which they received no notice and over which the state court had no jurisdiction. In effect, though not in name, this was a defendant class, attempting (unbeknownst to its members) to fend off predatory lawyers' claims to the balances in the escrow accounts. The substantial jurisdictional problems entailed by defendant classes, were aggravated by the class members' ignorance of their exposure.

In *Matsushita Electric Industrial Co. v. Epstein* (1996), members of a class in a securities case filed in state court initiated an independent action in federal court for the purpose of attacking the terms on which the state case had been settled. They argued that the state court lacked jurisdiction to resolve claims based on federal securities law. Ultimately they lost—but not on *Rooker-Feldman* grounds. The Supreme Court concluded that state judges may accept and enforce settlements of federal claims. This it held on the merits. It did not mention the possibility that the federal court lacked jurisdiction, which I think signifies how obvious it was to all concerned that the *Rooker-Feldman* doctrine is inapplicable. If it was inapplicable in *Matsushita,* it is inapplicable here too. I grant that *Matsushita* did not "hold" this, because it did not discuss jurisdiction. Shared assumptions are revealing nonetheless. And in today's case as in *Matsushita* the aggrieved class members may choose a new forum; they need not return to a court whose lack of jurisdiction is the basis of their position. None of this is to say that the Alabama court actually lacked jurisdiction, or that the notice was inadequate; to get anywhere against the Bank the Kamilewicz class must establish these things; but under the panel's approach the state court's judgment blocks federal litigation even if it lacked jurisdiction.

Next consider plaintiffs' claim against the *Hoffman* class counsel, which is not a collateral attack on a judgment. It takes the judgment as a given—indeed, it is only so long as the judgment stands that the litigant has a compensable loss. Neither state nor federal law requires a malpractice suit to be filed in the same court that handled the initial litigation. The *Rooker-Feldman* doctrine therefore does not apply to malpractice suits, which may be litigated in federal courts without regard to the location of the initial case. If the panel is right, no malpractice suit growing out of state litigation in which the judge awarded attorneys' fees—maybe no malpractice suit, period—may be brought in federal court, even if all requirements of the diversity jurisdiction have been satisfied. This holding is sufficiently troubling and affects so many other cases that it is worth the time of our court to consider the subject en banc.

The *Rooker-Feldman* doctrine has two rationales: first, that the decision of a state court reached after notice and opportunity for hearing is not an independent violation of the Constitution, and therefore is not actionable under 42 U.S.C. § 1983; second, that by virtue of 28 U.S.C. § 1257 only the Supreme Court may review the decision of a state court in civil litigation. The rationales of the doctrine identify important limits: the first theme is irrelevant to a malpractice suit, and the second is beside the point, because the plaintiff does not seek review of the decision. The original parties' entitlements *vis-à-vis* each other are fixed by the judgment. The contest now is between the litigant and his lawyer. We have emphasized this distinction many times—not only in malpractice cases, but also when the loser tries to get relief from judgment because of the lawyer's incompetence.

Consider a related sequence of litigation. A sells a painting to B, and before delivering the painting to B sells it again to C. Then A learns that the painting has increased in value and holds onto it. B sues A in state court for specific performance and prevails. Next C sues A for damages. Surely the *Rooker-Feldman* doctrine does not foreclose C from using federal court. C's suit does not attack the judgment (B keeps the painting); C wasn't even a party to B v. A; and the cause of C's loss wasn't the judgment, but A's double dealing. So too with malpractice litigation: it is a suit against a nonparty (the lawyer) alleging harm from incompetent or deceitful acts. That the lawyer's misconduct occurred in a judicial proceeding doesn't insulate the lawyer from liability, even when the *Rooker-Feldman* doctrine insulates the *judgment*.

The Supreme Court's most recent discussion of the *Rooker-Feldman* doctrine strongly implies that it does not bar malpractice litigation. *Johnson v. De Grandy* (1994), holds that the *Rooker-Feldman* doctrine does not bar voting rights litigation filed by the United States, even though the districts being challenged were approved by a state court in adversarial litigation. The Court observed that the United States was not a party to the state case and therefore could not have presented its claim by petition for certiorari under § 1257; the inability to do so meant that it could litigate independently. We, too, have held that the *Rooker-Feldman* doctrine does not affect suits by or against persons who were not parties to the initial case. It may apply when the non-parties occupy positions functionally identical to the parties (for example, when a person whose property has been condemned by a city retaliates with a suit against the mayor), but the class attorneys are not the Bank's alter egos. The attorneys representing the *Hoffman* class were not parties to the Alabama case. Neither were the class members. Absent class members are represented by the named plaintiffs and their lawyers, but they aren't parties, a point reflected in federal litigation by disregarding their citizenship. They are ignored in negotiating settlements as well. A real party's lack of assent means that there is no settlement; but the missing class members don't sign the settlement, and their objection is not dispositive. It is crammed down the throats of objectors, which cannot be done to real parties. What is more, the members of the Kamilewicz class could not have presented their malpractice arguments to the Supreme Court by petition for certiorari under § 1257: they did not discover the malpractice until later (it was not reflected in the record of the state proceeding); it was not litigated in the *Hoffman* case; class members can't seek appellate review without intervening, which further illustrates their non-party status; and of course malpractice is not a federal claim, so it is outside the scope of § 1257. For some purposes missing class members are treated *like* parties, but only if the named plaintiffs adequately represent the interests of the class, and only if the unnamed members of the class receive adequate notice and elect not to opt out—which in this case is the very thing in dispute! It gets the cart before the horse to reject, as barred by a judgment, an effort by the absent class members to show that they were not properly brought into the state case and therefore are not affected by the judgment.

From all of this it follows that a malpractice action is not affected by the *Rooker-Feldman* doctrine. Does the fairness hearing required to approve the settlement of a class action make a difference? I think not. For the reasons just explained, absent class members (*especially* those who deny the state court's jurisdiction over them) are not parties and cannot be treated as bound by the findings implicit in the approval of the settlement and the award of fees to attorneys. The panel implied approval of the district court's conclusion that the class members were effectively defendants resisting financial demands by the attorneys, which makes the jurisdictional shortcoming clear and establishes that the judgment is not entitled to full faith and credit.

All jurisdictional doubts to one side, a settlement followed by a fairness hearing remains more like a contract than like litigation. Accordingly there is even less reason to apply the *Rooker-Feldman* doctrine than in a normal malpractice case, where the loss ensues from a genuine contest. Representative plaintiffs and their lawyers may be imperfect agents of the other class members—may even put one over on the court, in a staged performance. The lawyers support the settlement to get fees; the defendants support it to evade liability; the court can't vindicate the class's rights because the friendly presentation means that it lacks essential information. This possibility, a staple of the literature about class actions, enjoys judicial recognition. Recall that even the active opposition of class members does not automatically block the settlement, which therefore rests on the *lawyers'* consent, not the litigants' agreement or the legal decision of a court.

The Kamilewicz class asserts that it suffered harm from the *Hoffman* class lawyers' breach of their duties of care and loyalty in negotiating the settlement, which was concealed from the Alabama judge (and the class) by a further breach of the duty of loyalty in drafting the notice about the settlement. The notice not only didn't alert the absent class members to the impending loss but also pulled the wool over the state judge's eyes. Suing faithless agents is far from the core of the *Rooker-Feldman* doctrine, which should not be extended to block suits like this. "Were [plaintiff] merely claiming that the decision of the state court was incorrect, even that it denied him some constitutional right, the doctrine would indeed bar his claim. But if he claims, as he does, that people involved in the decision violated some independent right of his * * * then he can, without being blocked by the *Rooker-Feldman* doctrine, sue to vindicate that right."

The panel's decision is important. If I am right that the state court's award of attorneys' fees does not matter, then the decision logically bars all malpractice and related fiduciary-duty suits arising out of state litigation. We have entertained many, without seeing jurisdictional problems. And even if I am wrong about the sweep of the panel's decision, the issue is recurrent. * * * If the *Rooker-Feldman* doctrine applies to suits by the absent class members because a malpractice action is a collateral attack on the order approving the settlement and awarding attorneys' fees, then the law of preclusion (res judicata) should bar malpractice actions in any court, state or federal, and without regard to which judicial system handled the first case. Yet no one thinks that. A malpractice suit is an independent action. A (potential) defense of issue preclusion is defeated by the very theory of the claim: that the first judgment is unreliable because of the attorney's bungling. The bungler cannot point to the adverse judgment produced by his own incompetence to ward off the client's demand. The Kamilewicz class may fail in its proof, or it may encounter other obstacles, but the *Rooker- Feldman* doctrine does not close the door of the federal courthouse.

Notes and Questions

1. As Judge Easterbrook points out, one can attack a state court default judgment collaterally on jurisdictional grounds in a federal court enforcement proceeding. When a defendant receives a summons and fails to appear, he may resist a subsequent enforcement action on the ground that the state court lacked jurisdiction over him, either because the court had no basis upon which to exercise jurisdiction or because the summons was defective. (There are other possible attacks as well, but they are not relevant here.) In *Kamilewicz*, the plaintiffs had received a notice that they ignored and that they now claim conferred no jurisdiction on the Alabama court because both the notice itself and the representation of the class did not comport with the constitutional standards that *Phillips Petroleum Co. v. Shutts*, 472 U.S. 797, 105 S.Ct. 2965, 86 L.Ed.2d 628 (1985), articulated. Is their position truly distinguishable from that of a defaulting defendant? Note that the Seventh Circuit's panel concedes that for purposes of the fee awards, the nominal plaintiffs were in fact in the position of defendants.

2. The plaintiffs' position is aggravated here because under the terms of the settlement, the attorneys essentially got automatic enforcement of the

judgment. If the attorneys had had to bring an enforcement action against the plaintiffs to recover the fees (and before you say that it would not be worth their while for such small individual amounts, remember that they just represented a plaintiff class in exactly such a case), would the plaintiffs have been allowed to resist on jurisdictional grounds? Does the difference between a case in which the plaintiffs can resist and one in which they cannot simply depend on which side of the "*v.*" the plaintiffs find themselves?

3. Given the Alabama court's determination that the attorneys' fees were reasonable, is there anything that *Rooker-Feldman* accomplishes here that res judicata would not do just as well? Does *Rooker-Feldman* ever accomplish anything beyond the reach of the preclusion doctrines? *See* Suzanna Sherry, *Judicial Federalism in the Trenches: The* Rooker-Feldman *Doctrine in Action*, 74 NOTRE DAME L. REV. 1085 (1999).

4. Judge Evans notes that the Alabama judgment may be "questionable" but says that the federal courts are in no position to evaluate it without reopening and relitigating the Alabama case. Are the plaintiffs asking the federal courts to evaluate the fairness of the Alabama proceedings or the fee award on the merits, or are they raising jurisdictional objections relying on *Shutts*?

5. Is there a meaningful distinction between attacking a judgment and attacking the correctness of a judgment? The plaintiffs here seek to file a malpractice claim against the attorneys. Malpractice claims generally do not have to be brought in the same court in which the alleged malpractice occurred. Why should this one? If the attorneys had not applied for a fee award from the Alabama court, would the malpractice action lie for *Rooker-Feldman* purposes? Suppose at the conclusion of a trial, the state judge tells a party's counsel that she has done "an excellent job." Would *Rooker-Feldman* then say that the federal courts are without jurisdiction to entertain a malpractice action from the unappreciative client?

6. Should the panel have dealt with *Matsushita*? Is Judge Easterbrook correct that it is apposite? Granted, *Matsushita* did not discuss *Rooker-Feldman*. Nonetheless, since the courts have emphasized that the doctrine goes to subject matter jurisdiction, and since a court can raise subject matter jurisdiction questions *sua sponte* (*see, e.g.*, *Louisville & Nashville Railroad v. Mottley* and *Smith v. Kansas City Title & Trust Co.*), does the fact that the Court decided the case on the merits allow us to conclude that it found no subject matter jurisdiction problem?

7. Is Judge Easterbrook's "painting" hypothetical apposite? Are the plaintiffs here analogous to B or C (or to both)? Does the hypothetical suggest that Judge Evans is correct that the plaintiffs are attacking the Alabama court's judgment of fairness?

8. Note that the lawyers will receive the money from the escrow accounts, which is all that the Alabama court ordered. The plaintiffs are not seeking an injunction against the disbursement; they seek damages in a separate action for claims not adjudicated in the first action. Should that make a difference for *Rooker-Feldman* purposes?

9. Is it really true, as Judge Easterbrook says, that absent class members are not parties to the action even though they have received service? If that is correct, then how can a judgment bind them? Is it possible to view someone as a party for some purposes and not for others? Are the provisions of Federal Rule of Civil Procedure 23 relevant insofar as they talk about intervention for absent class members?

10. Is *DeGrandy* helpful to the plaintiffs? Are they in a position analogous to the United States in that case? In this connection, consider *Devlin v. Scardelletti*, 536 U.S. 1, 122 S.Ct. 2005, 153 L.Ed.2d 27 (2002), in which the Court ruled that an unnamed class member who was denied intervention can state objections to a proposed settlement and then appeal from an unfavorable ruling without intervening, provided that the appeal also challenges denial of the motion to intervene.

4. Threading the Needle: Rooker-Feldman and Standing

FACIO v. JONES
United States Court of Appeals for the Tenth Circuit, 1991.
929 F.2d 541

EBEL, Circuit Judge.

This is an appeal and cross-appeal from a judgment of the federal district court under 42 U.S.C. § 1983 which declared unconstitutional the Utah state rule requiring that a default judgment debtor show a meritorious defense before the default judgment against him could be vacated. The district court also granted plaintiff costs and attorney's fees under 42 U.S.C. § 1988. In addition, plaintiff cross-appeals the district court's denial of a request for attorney's fees against the state court judge. We do not reach the merits of this appeal because we find that the district court lacked subject matter jurisdiction to hear the original case.

FACTS

Gary Facio, the plaintiff below, wrote a bad check. Mr. Facio received notice that the check had bounced and thereafter sent a money order to cover the debit and expenses. For reasons not entirely clear, one appellant, Collection Agency Management, nevertheless instituted a civil action against Mr. Facio in a Utah state court based on the bad check. Although Mr. Facio was validly served with process and thus had received notice of that litigation, he failed to answer because he apparently believed that the money order had settled the controversy. Ultimately, a default judgment was entered against him. Mr. Facio then filed a motion to set aside the default judgment pursuant to Utah Rules of Civil Procedure 55(c) and 60(b). The state court judge—the Honorable Maurice Jones—denied the motion because Mr. Facio failed to present proof of a meritorious defense as required by the Utah Supreme Court's interpretation of Rules 55(c) and 60(b). Eventually, the judgment was satisfied through garnishment of Mr. Facio's wages and bank account.

Thereafter, Mr. Facio filed suit in federal district court. He sought

> declaratory relief under 42 U.S.C. § 1983 for deprivation of property without due process of law in violation of the Fourteenth Amendment * * *. Specifically, plaintiff contend[ed] that Judge Jones' application of Utah Rules of Civil Procedure 55(c) and 60(b) [was] unconstitutional to the extent that a defendant [was] required to offer proof of a meritorious defense * * *. By pendant [*sic*] claim, plaintiff challenge[d] the validity of the default and default judgment entered against him.

The district court agreed with Mr. Facio, finding that the Utah procedural requirement that a meritorious defense be presented before a default judgment could be set aside was unconstitutional. The district court set aside the default judgment and ordered costs to be paid by both Judge Jones and the collection agency and attorney's fees to be paid by the collection agency only. Judge Jones and the collection agency appealed. Mr. Facio cross-appealed, claiming that the district court did not articulate reasons sufficient to exempt Judge Jones from paying attorney's fees.

DISCUSSION

The district court considered the possibility that it did not have jurisdiction over the case. In particular, the court referred to the Tenth Circuit case of *Razatos v. Colorado Supreme Court,* 746 F.2d 1429 (10th Cir.1984), *cert. denied,* 471 U.S. 1016, 105 S.Ct. 2019, 85 L.Ed.2d 301 (1985) for the proposition that "[i]t is clearly established law that the Supreme Court has the exclusive power to review state court decisions. However, federal trial courts can adjudicate civil rights complaints such as that brought by plaintiff without directly reviewing state court decisions." We disagree with that conclusion as it applies to the particular facts of this case. We hold that the district court did not have jurisdiction to consider Mr. Facio's lawsuit and, therefore, we do not reach the merits on appeal.

In his federal action, Mr. Facio seeks two types of relief. First, he wants the default judgment against him set aside. Second, he asks the federal courts to declare the Utah Rules of Civil Procedure 55(c) and 60(b) unconstitutional as applied by the Utah courts.

To the extent that Mr. Facio sought to have the federal district court set aside a state default judgment, the federal court lacked jurisdiction to grant that relief. * * * Any such federal review has to be addressed directly to the United States Supreme Court from the state's highest court pursuant to 28 U.S.C. § 1257.

Mr. Facio also seeks a second form of relief that would have the federal court declare the Utah default rules unconstitutional as applied. However, *Feldman* not only prohibited direct review of state judgments by lower federal courts, but it also prohibited those federal courts from issuing any declaratory relief that is "inextricably intertwined" with the state court judgment. We believe that Mr. Facio's request for declaratory relief is inextricably intertwined with his request to vacate and to set aside the default judgment. In this case, the two forms of relief are so intertwined, in fact, that if Mr. Facio is not able to set aside the default judgment against him, he would lack standing to assert his second claim, which is the request that the federal court declare Utah's default judgment procedures unconstitutional. Unless Mr. Facio's default judgment is upset, his only interest in Utah's default judgment procedures is prospective and hypothetical in nature. He cannot establish a sufficient interest in the future application of those procedures to him to establish a constitutional case or controversy.

Because Mr. Facio's threshold ability to establish standing with regard to his claim for declaratory relief is dependent upon his ability to upset the default judgment against him, that presents a classic case of an inextricably intertwined relationship between the two requested types of relief. * * * For instance, this court * * * refused to allow a plaintiff to hide behind the language of a general attack on state procedures while bringing what was in reality a claim to overturn a state court decision. We stated * * * in a holding that is equally applicable here, that "[w]here a constitutional issue could have been reviewed on direct appeal by the state appellate courts, a litigant may not seek to reverse or modify the state court judgment by bringing a constitutional claim under 42 U.S.C. § 1983."

If the two forms of relief Mr. Facio seeks are separated and the request for declaratory relief is looked at in isolation, Mr. Facio lacks standing to assert that claim. He has not demonstrated any real chance of being subjected in the future to Utah's procedures for reversing default judgments. Indeed, after separating out Mr. Facio's impermissible request that the federal district court overturn the state judgment against him, his situation is indistinguishable from that of any other citizen of Utah who, without any palpable chance of being subjected to those procedures in the future, might desire to challenge that state's default judgment rule.

Our analysis is consistent with, and well-grounded in, Supreme Court cases which have held that while a plaintiff who has been constitutionally injured can bring a § 1983 action to recover damages, that same plaintiff cannot maintain a declaratory or injunctive action unless he or she can demonstrate a good chance of being likewise injured in the future. * * *

In [*City of Los Angeles v.*] *Lyons* [1983], a citizen brought suit under § 1983 in federal district court, alleging that Los Angeles police officers had unconstitutionally applied a dangerous "chokehold" to his neck. Plaintiff sought damages and also requested an injunction that would have prevented the police from using chokeholds in similar situations.

The Court found that although Lyons had allegedly suffered actual harm—and could presumably recover damages under § 1983—he could not "demonstrate a case or controversy with the City that would justify the equitable relief sought" because "standing to seek the injunction requested depended on whether he was likely to suffer future injury from the use of the chokeholds by police officers."

* * *

The cases of *Feldman* and *Razatos* involved plaintiffs who had been denied admission to a particular state's bar, and therefore wanted to have the allegedly unconstitutional law invalidated so that they could practice law in the state or district. But in each case, it was clear that even though the federal district court could not reverse the adverse state court judgment that had been rendered against the plaintiffs, the plaintiffs still had standing because they could reapply to the state's bar. In other words, even though the individual state court decisions stood against them, they each still had an interest in practicing law in the state or district involved and therefore had standing to assert that the restrictive bar admission rules should be declared unconstitutional. Thus, in each of those cases the federal court had before it a real case or controversy.

In contrast, if Mr. Facio's default judgment stands—and it must because it is final under state law and under 28 U.S.C. § 1257 the federal district court has no jurisdiction to review it—he cannot demonstrate any continuing interest in having Utah's default judgment rules set aside. The default against him is final, whether or not the default judgment rules may later be held unconstitutional. Any ruling now that Utah's procedures to vacate default judgments are unconstitutional could not undo the judgment against Mr. Facio anymore than it would undo the countless other default judgments that presumably have been entered in Utah pursuant to this rule and have long since become final.

Unable to attack the final default judgment rendered against him and without any evidence that he will again be subject to Utah's default provisions, Mr. Facio is left with no interest greater than that of any other citizen of Utah. Accordingly, Mr. Facio's action must be dismissed; the federal courts have "no jurisdiction to pronounce any statute, either of a State or of the United States, void, because irreconcilable with the Constitution, except as it is called upon to adjudge the legal rights of litigants in actual controversies."

We should add that any concern about whether the *Feldman* rule effectively isolates state court decisions from federal review is unfounded. First, there is the obvious alternative open to litigants—and it was open to Mr. Facio—to appeal the state court decision through the state courts and then to seek certiorari review by the United States Supreme Court. Second, it may be possible for some litigants (as, perhaps, credit companies) to demonstrate that the repeated application of default judgment rules operate to their continuing harm even though a particular case may be final. Thus, they may be able to attack the rule *if* they are able to establish that the particular rule sufficiently impedes their future action. However, Mr. Facio cannot demonstrate that requirement because for him this was a one-shot case. Indeed, the Supreme Court has stated that "[p]ast exposure to illegal conduct does not in itself show a present case or controversy regarding injunctive relief * * * if unaccompanied by any continuing, present adverse effects."

The *Feldman* rule is soundly and clearly based in the language of 28 U.S.C. § 1257 and in the public policy of federalism. Federal district courts are specifically proscribed from the business of reviewing state court judgments. Mr. Facio's request for an order reversing his final default judgment was outside the district court's jurisdiction. Likewise, his request for declaratory relief was hopelessly intertwined with his claim for retrospective relief. If the different remedies Mr. Facio seeks *are* separated, then he is left with no case or controversy to challenge the future application of that rule.

Thus, the district court did not have jurisdiction to consider Mr. Facio's claims. The district court order is hereby vacated and the matter is remanded with instructions that the action be dismissed for lack of jurisdiction.

Notes and Questions

1. Would (should) it make any difference in the disposition of this case if Utah law allows Facio to make an additional application in a state court to have the default judgment vacated? If so, why?

2. Assume (as the court implies) that the creditor knew the money order had satisfied the debt represented by the bounced check before the creditor sued on the check. If Utah allowed a tort action for either wrongful civil proceedings (a civil equivalent of the tort of malicious prosecution) or for abuse of process, would Facio be able to pursue such a suit against the creditor in federal court (assuming that subject matter jurisdiction was not a problem) despite *Rooker-Feldman*? If not, why not? If so, then did Facio's counsel blunder by not including such a count in Facio's complaint?

3. Note that if Facio brought an abuse-of-process action independent of any other claim (such as one to set aside the Utah default judgment), the Utah judgment would remain intact and in effect, irrespective of the outcome of the abuse claim. Does *Rooker-Feldman* compel dismissal of any federal case that might tend do undo the practical effect of a state judgment, or does it only bar actions that would act upon the state judgment itself?

The Anti-Injunction Act, 28 U.S.C. § 2283, allows a federal court to enjoin state courts from proceeding with cases if necessary "to protect or effectuate its judgments." This is known as the "relitigation exception" and allows the federal courts to prevent state courts from relitigating claims or issues already decided in federal court. ERWIN CHEMERINSKY, FEDERAL COURTS § 11.2.4, at 749-52 (5th ed. 2007). Does that shed any light on how narrowly or broadly the federal courts should interpret *Rooker-Feldman*?

If Congress thought it necessary in the Anti-Injunction Act to create *res-judicata*-by-injunction (and that in cases in which the state trial courts certainly lack appellate jurisdiction with respect to federal judgments), should one conclude that Congress would regard res judicata as a sufficient protection for state judgments in federal courts, given the Full Faith and Credit Act, 28 U.S.C. § 1738? If so, does that suggest whether Congress would simultaneously have contemplated regulating this particular kind of federal court behavior through the various subject matter jurisdictional statutes? To put it another way, if the federal jurisdictional statutes create res judicata protection for state judgments, should one assume that Congress enacted a superfluous res judicata protection in § 1738?

4. Is the court's use of *City of Los Angeles v. Lyons* apt? If it is not, where does the analogy break down? If it is, does that not raise again the question of what *Rooker-Feldman* adds to the effects of § 1738 and justiciability doctrine? Now, one might say that *Rooker-Feldman*, insofar as one regards it as jurisdictional, in some sense preempts the effect of § 1738 because the courts decide subject matter jurisdiction issues before other issues, but one cannot raise the same point with respect to standing, which also goes to subject matter jurisdiction under Article III, § 2.

In some sense, there may be a sequencing problem in reconciling 28 U.S.C. § 1331 (and other subject matter jurisdiction statutes) as seen through the eyes of the *Rooker-Feldman* doctrine and 28 U.S.C. § 1738. If those jurisdictional statutes necessarily include the *Rooker-Feldman* concept because they do not authorize the inferior courts to hear appeals from the state courts, why did Congress think it necessary also to enact the Full Faith and Credit Act, § 1738, which ostensibly accomplishes the same thing. If, on the other hand, those jurisdictional statutes do not include the *Rooker-Feldman* concept, then the need for § 1738 is clear, but the foundation for the Court's articulation of *Rooker-Feldman* is gone.

5. At bottom, what is it that the *Rooker-Feldman* doctrine should protect? Should it guard only against federal actions that by their terms might prevent enforcement of all or parts of state court judgments (such an action to set aside a judgment)? On the other hand, should it forbid any federal action that might have the practical (but not legal) effect of making the relief afforded by a state judgment less satisfying to the state court victor than it might otherwise have been? In *Kamilewicz*, for example, if the plaintiffs pursued a malpractice action against the class attorneys, that would not deprive the state judgment for attorneys fees of any force; the attorneys would still get the fees from the escrow accounts. They might, of course, be less than satisfied with that multimillion dollar fee if the *Kamilewicz* class succeeded in recovering from them an even larger sum as malpractice damages. Should that rise to the level of *Rooker-Feldman*?

6. You can now see why the doctrine is creating such consternation in the inferior federal courts. There is an almost Zen-like quality to the doctrine: when is something that is not an appeal actually an appeal? This parallels a common question in the area of Supreme Court review of state

court decisions under 28 U.S.C. § 1257: when is a non-final state court ruling in a case final within the meaning of § 1257? *Cox Broadcasting Corp. v. Cohn*, presented at page 972, discusses that issue. Then-Justice Rehnquist dissented vigorously from the majority's conclusion that four categories of cases from the state courts were final for § 1257 purposes even though there were further state court proceedings to come. He argued that "final" actually means "final," but was not able to persuade his colleagues. In the *Rooker-Feldman* context, could one argue that "appeal" means "appeal," so that the jurisdictional base for the doctrine crumbles? If *Rooker-Feldman* is not based in the jurisdictional statutes, is there any other justification for it?

7. For some excellent scholarly consideration of the *Rooker-Feldman* doctrine, see the symposium issue of Notre Dame Law Review that includes papers presented to the Federal Courts section at the 1999 Annual Meeting of the Association of American Law Schools: Thomas D. Rowe, Jr., Rooker-Feldman: *Worth Only the Powder to Blow It Up?*, 74 NOTRE DAME L. REV. 1081 (1999); Suzanna Sherry, *Judicial Federalism in the Trenches: The* Rooker-Feldman *Doctrine in Action*, 74 NOTRE DAME L. REV. 1085 (1999); Barry Friedman & James E. Gaylord, Rooker-Feldman *from the Ground Up*, 74 NOTRE DAME L. REV. 1129 (1999); Susan Bandes, *The* Rooker-Feldman *Doctrine: Evaluating Its Jurisdictional Status*, 74 NOTRE DAME L. REV. 1175 (1999); Jack M. Beermann, *Comments on* Rooker-Feldman *or Let State Law Be Our Guide*, 74 NOTRE DAME L. REV. 1209 (1999).

Chapter 11

FEDERAL HABEAS CORPUS

A. INTRODUCTION

"Habeas corpus" is Latin for "you have the body."[1] Although the writ of habeas corpus took different forms at common law, this chapter concerns only the writ of *habeas corpus ad subjiciendum*, known as the Great Writ. A person claiming to be held in custody in violation of federal law may petition a federal court to issue a writ of habeas corpus to inquire into the legality of the detention. Most often, the custody is the result of a state criminal conviction, but the proceeding is not a direct appeal of the conviction.[2] Instead, it is a separate civil lawsuit called a "collateral proceeding." With the exception of the enemy combatant detention cases, all of the cases in this Chapter concern state criminal convictions.

Habeas corpus is a remarkably appropriate finale for studying the federal courts as an institution. The enduring themes of federalism and separation of powers figure heavily in the jurisprudence of The Great Writ, and the manner in which federal habeas corpus operates connotes much about the oft-debated subject of parity. Although habeas corpus lies to challenge civil or criminal custody, the huge majority of the cases (and all that attract public attention) involve criminal cases.[3] That is one of the things that makes habeas corpus a focal point of emotional and political attention in a society so preoccupied with the problem of crime. As Professor William Hellerstein once observed, "You're selling a product nobody wants to buy: reversal of a criminal conviction." That observation, although made in the context of direct rather than collateral attack on a conviction, illustrates one of the things that has made federal habeas corpus an especially hot topic over the past two decades.

How one feels about federal habeas corpus will depend, in no small part, on one's view of the appropriate role of the federal courts and how those courts, particularly the inferior federal courts, should relate to the states generally and to the state judiciaries in particular. Although a

---

[1] BLACK'S LAW DICTIONARY 728 (8th ed. 2004).

[2] As Chapter 10 discussed, as a formal matter inferior federal courts may not review state court decisions.

[3] *See, e.g.*, ERWIN CHEMERINSKY, FEDERAL JURISDICTION § 15.1, at 896 (5th ed. 2007).

habeas proceeding is not an appeal, the inferior federal courts in effect sit in review of state courts' conduct of criminal cases.

> [T]he availability of federal habeas as a sequel to state court consideration of the same claim does, in the nature of things, place a district court in position to second-guess the state court. In this practical sense, postconviction federal habeas has an undeniable appellate flavor. The great intellectual challenge has always been to reconcile the theoretical (original) nature of the federal courts' jurisdiction * * * with the practical (appellate) character of the federal courts' function when the state courts have previously adjudicated prisoners' claims.[4]

When a federal court grants habeas corpus relief, it often vacates a conviction.[5] Although technically the relief runs against the custodian, not the court that issued the order of confinement,[6] the emotional and political impact is little different from true appellate reversal. The federalism and parity implications are obvious. When a federal court orders habeas relief for a state prisoner, it imposes its own view of federal law, almost always displacing a contrary state court view, in an area of intense state concern. In an individual case, one might simply regard the doctrine as another error-correcting mechanism. The existence of federal habeas itself, however, connotes to some the underlying judgment that state courts are institutionally not quite up to the job of properly interpreting and applying federal constitutional principles.

The separation-of-powers issues raised by habeas corpus are not always as apparent as the federalism concerns. Nonetheless, there is tension between Congress and the federal courts over habeas. It appears most often in judges' statements appearing to chafe over the congressionally imposed responsibility to hear habeas cases. Consider Justice Frankfurter's comments in *Brown v. Allen*, 344 U.S. 443, 73 S.Ct. 437, 97 L.Ed. 469 (1953):

> Congress could have left the enforcement of federal constitutional rights governing the administration of criminal justice in the States exclusively to the State courts. These tribunals are under

---

[4] Larry W. Yackle, *A Primer on the New Habeas Corpus Statute*, 44 BUFF. L. REV. 381, 403 (1996).

[5] Even vacating a conviction, moreover, does not necessarily compel release of the prisoner. Often, the state retries the defendant successfully.

There have been cases, however, in which habeas corpus relief goes to the sentence a prisoner has received (usually the death penalty), not to the validity of the conviction. To some extent, the Antiterrorism and Effective Death Penalty Act appears to restrict such relief, at least when the prisoner seeks it in a second or successive petition. See 28 U.S.C. § 2244(b)(2)(B).

[6] It would be unthinkable, for example, for a federal court granting habeas corpus relief to attempt to return the case to the state courts with instructions, as is common when an appellate court reverses a lower court.

the same duty as the federal courts to respect rights under the United States Constitution. * * * It is not for us to determine whether this power should have been vested in the federal courts. As Mr. Justice Bradley, with his usual acuteness, commented not long after the passage of [the 1867 statute authorizing the federal courts to hear habeas petitions from state prisoners], "although it may appear unseemly that a prisoner, after conviction in a state court, should be set at liberty by a single judge on habeas corpus, there seems to be no escape from the law." His feeling has been recently echoed in a proposal of the Judicial Conference of Senior Circuit Judges that these cases be heard by three-judge courts. But the wisdom of such a modification in the law is for Congress to consider, particularly in view of the effect of the expanding concept of due process upon enforcement by the States of their criminal laws. It is for this Court to give fair effect to the habeas corpus jurisdiction as enacted by Congress.

In the late 1980's, Chief Justice Rehnquist openly lobbied Congress to restrict the writ, and Congress finally responded in the Antiterrorism and Effective Death Penalty Act of 1996 (AEDPA). Judicial actions, whether expanding or contracting the writ, take place in an area of extensive legislation; modification of the rules concerning the availability of habeas corpus inevitably involves that statutory structure. The cases that follow demonstrate the Justices' frequent awareness of the separation-of-powers implications of their actions.

The dispute over whether prisoners detained at Guantanamo Bay, Cuba, may seek federal habeas relief has exacerbated tensions between the legislative and judicial branches. *Rasul v. Bush*, 542 U.S. 466, 124 S.Ct. 2686, 159 L.Ed.2d 548 (2004), held that the federal courts had jurisdiction to hear petitions by foreign nationals detained there. Congress responded by enacting the Detainee Treatment Act of 2005,[7] withdrawing jurisdiction in such cases. *Hamdan v. Rumsfeld*, __ U.S. __, 126 S.Ct. 2749, 165 L.Ed.2d 723 (2006), held that the effective-date provision of the Act did not apply to pending habeas petitions, prompting Congress to pass the Military Commissions Act of 2006,[8] which unequivocally withdrew jurisdiction over any habeas petition, pending or future, brought by an alien "who has been determined by the United States to have been properly detained as an enemy combatant or is awaiting such determination." In *Boumediene v. Bush*, 476 F.3d 981 (D.C. Cir.), *cert. granted*, ___ U.S.___, 127 S.Ct. 3078, 168 L.Ed.2d 755 (2007), the United States Court of Appeals for the District of Columbia held by a two-one vote that the 2006 Act does not violate the Suspension Clause of the

[7] Pub. L. 109-148, 119 Stat. 2739 (2005).

[8] Pub. L. No. 109-366, 120 Stat. 2600 (2006).

Constitution.[9]

Habeas corpus came to the American colonies from England. The Constitution provides: "The Privilege of the Writ of Habeas Corpus shall not be suspended unless when in Cases of Rebellion or Invasion the public Safety may require it."[10] The Judiciary Act of 1789 made the writ available to federal prisoners. After some piecemeal extension of the writ to state prisoners,[11] in 1867 Congress authorized federal courts to issue writs of habeas corpus in "all cases where any person may be restrained of his or her liberty in violation of the constitution, or of any treaty or law of the United States."[12] This statute, as many others adopted during Reconstruction, aimed at reforming Southern criminal and civil justice systems that were being used systematically to re-enslave the freed African-Americans and to harass whites serving in the Union Army or the Freedmen's Bureau.[13] Given the depth of Congress' anger and frustration with the South in the aftermath of the Civil War, it is not surprising that legislators openly favored broad construction of the statute during the limited debate on the measure.

Scholars disagree about the actual scope of habeas corpus both before and after the Civil War. Paul M. Bator contends that habeas was limited to deciding whether the convicting court had subject matter jurisdiction and proper jurisdiction over the defendant's person,[14] while Gary Peller concludes that federal courts exercised a broader power to review constitutional errors.[15] Recently, Ann Woolhandler presented a more nuanced, middle view:

> [T]he federal habeas remedy was not uniformly available to address all constitutional wrongs arising in criminal cases in the nineteenth century. Nevertheless, the scope of habeas review reflected the Court's gradual willingness to address ad hoc or random acts of official illegality (that is, official action not specifically authorized by legislation) as constitutional violations rather than common law violations, and to provide federal remedies for such

---

[9] "The Privilege of the Writ of Habeas Corpus shall not be suspended, unless when in cases of Rebellion or Invasion the public Safety may require it." U.S. CONST. art. 1, § 9, cl. 2.

[10] U.S. CONST. art. 1, § 9, cl. 2.

[11] The Force Act of 1833, for example, made the writ available to federal officials held in state custody. Act of Mar. 2, 1833, c. 57, § 3, 4 Stat. 633.

[12] Habeas Corpus Act of 1867, ch. 28, 14 Stat. 385.

[13] See generally, Donald H. Zeigler, *A Reassessment of the* Younger *Doctrine in Light of the Legislative History of Reconstruction*, 1983 DUKE L.J. 987, 990–1020.

[14] Paul M. Bator, *Finality in Criminal Law and Federal Habeas Corpus for State Prisoners*, 76 HARV.L.REV. 441 (1963).

[15] Gary Peller, *In Defense of Federal Habeas Corpus Relitigation*, 16 HARV.C.R.-C.L. L. REV. 579 (1982).

abuses.[16]

Frank v. Mangum, 237 U.S. 309, 35 S.Ct. 582, 59 L.Ed. 969 (1915), expanded the scope of habeas corpus by authorizing federal courts to examine whether the petitioner had been given a fair and adequate opportunity to raise and litigate his constitutional claims in state court. If such "corrective process" was not given, the federal claim could be heard on the merits. While *Frank* took a step in expanding habeas, *Brown v. Allen* (1953) took a giant leap. *Brown* held that federal courts generally must review federal constitutional claims by way of habeas so long as the petitioner exhausted available means of presenting the claims to the state court.[17] *Brown* also reaffirmed that ordinary principles of res judicata do not apply in habeas corpus cases. This seemingly technical point is actually of enormous importance. What would be the impact on the scope of the writ if res judicata did apply? *Daniels v. Allen*, 345 U.S. 946, 73 S.Ct. 827, 97 L.Ed. 1370 (1953), a companion case to *Brown*, held that habeas corpus would not lie if the petitioner was unable to present his claims to state trial and appellate courts because of his own failure to comply with state procedural requirements.

Three 1963 cases—*Fay v. Noia*, 372 U.S. 391, 83 S.Ct. 822, 9 L.Ed.2d 837 (1963); *Townsend v. Sain*, 372 U.S. 293, 83 S.Ct. 745, 9 L.Ed.2d 770 (1963); *Sanders v. United States*, 373 U.S. 1, 83 S.Ct. 1068, 10 L.Ed.2d 148 (1963)—marked the high-water point in federal habeas corpus jurisdiction. In *Noia* three men were convicted of felony murder in a New York State court. The only evidence against each man was his confession. Noia's co-defendants appealed and eventually their convictions were overturned because their confessions were coerced. Although Noia's confession was also, the district court denied his application for federal habeas relief because he had failed to exhaust state remedies. (Noia did attempt a collateral attack on his conviction in state court, but the New York Court of Appeals held a collateral attack could not substitute for a direct appeal.) The Supreme Court held:

> (1) Federal courts have *power* under the federal habeas statute to grant relief despite the applicant's failure to have pursued a state remedy not available to him at the time he applies; the doctrine under which state procedural defaults are held to constitute an adequate and independent state ground barring direct Supreme Court review is not to be extended to limit the power granted the federal courts under the federal habeas statute. (2) Noia's failure to appeal was not a failure to exhaust "the remedies available in the courts of the State" as required by § 2254; that requirement re-

---

[16] Ann Woolhandler, *Demodeling Habeas*, 45 STAN. L. REV. 575, 580 (1993).

[17] *Brown* also made clear a petitioner does not have to present his federal claims to the state courts more than once, even if state law allowed the claims to be raised on direct appeal and then repeated in state collateral proceedings.

fers only to a failure to exhaust state remedies still open to the applicant at the time he files his application for habeas corpus in the federal court. (3) Noia's failure to appeal cannot under the circumstances be deemed an intelligent and understanding waiver of his right to appeal such as to justify the withholding of federal habeas relief.

Elaborating on the third holding, the Court stated that although state procedural defaults did not affect federal jurisdiction over habeas corpus petitions, the district courts did have a limited discretion to deny relief to applicants who have "deliberately by-passed the orderly procedures of the state courts and in so doing [have] forfeited [their] state court remedies." Noia had received a life sentence. The Court noted that had Noia successfully appealed and received a new trial, he might have lost again and received the death penalty. Under the circumstances, the Court held Noia's failure to appeal was not a deliberate circumvention of state procedures. Finally, the Court held that an applicant who has exhausted state remedies need not first seek certiorari in the United States Supreme Court before filing a habeas petition in federal district court. Why do you think the Court included this dictum?

Townsend v. Sain clarified (and appeared to liberalize) the standards for granting evidentiary hearings in habeas proceedings. The Court announced the following general standard:

> Where the facts are in dispute, the federal court in habeas corpus must hold an evidentiary hearing if the habeas applicant did not receive a full and fair evidentiary hearing in a state court, either at the time of trial or in a collateral proceeding. In other words a federal evidentiary hearing is required unless the state-court trier of fact has after a full hearing reliably found the relevant facts.

After stating that "[i]t would be unwise to overly particularize this test," the Court proceeded to particularize it, listing six circumstances in which a federal court must grant an evidentiary hearing to a habeas applicant:

> If (1) the merits of the factual dispute were not resolved in the state hearing; (2) the state factual determination is not fairly supported by the record as a whole; (3) the fact-finding procedure employed by the state court was not adequate to afford a full and fair hearing; (4) there is a substantial allegation of newly discovered evidence; (5) the material facts were not adequately developed at the state-court hearing; or (6) for any reason it appears that the state trier of fact did not afford the habeas applicant a full and fair fact hearing.

In discussing the fifth circumstance, the Court held that *Noia*'s deliberate-bypass standard should govern; that is, the petitioner could be held responsible for not adequately developing the facts only if the petitioner was guilty of "inexcusable neglect." Finally, the Court noted that even if a case satisfied none of the six criteria, a district court still retained discretion to hold a hearing. It is important to note that the dissenters did not disagree with the majority's general statement of the rule, balking only at the majority's six-part gloss on it and taking issue with the majority on application of the rule to the facts of the case.

In 1966, Congress codified habeas petitioners' entitlement to federal evidentiary hearings in what was then 28 U.S.C. § 2254(d). In doing so, it borrowed heavily from *Townsend*, although it created eight criteria instead of six. The statute also spoke not in terms of a mandatory evidentiary hearing, as had *Townsend*, but instead of the circumstances that would dispel the presumption of correctness of state fact-finding. Nonetheless, the statute was widely understood to have codified *Townsend*. As is explained more fully below, the Supreme Court rejected this understanding in *Keeney v. Tamayo-Reyes*, 504 U.S. 1, 112 S.Ct. 1715, 118 L.Ed.2d 318 (1992).

The final case in the 1963 trilogy, *Sanders v. United States*, clarified when federal courts could entertain second and subsequent habeas corpus petitions.[18] The Court held that the denial of a prior application should be given "[c]ontrolling weight" only if:

> (1) the same ground presented in the subsequent application was determined adversely to the applicant on the prior application, (2) the prior determination was on the merits, and (3) the ends of justice would not be served by reaching the merits of the subsequent application.

Brown v. Allen, augmented by the 1963 trilogy, opened wide the federal courthouse doors and invited state prisoners to enter. *Noia*, by forgiving petitioners' state procedural defaults unless state remedies had been deliberately by-passed and by requiring exhaustion only of presently available state remedies, opened to federal review thousands of constitutional questions lurking in the records of old state convictions that would not previously have been subject to review. By requiring federal evidentiary hearings unless the state court held a full and fair hearing and by relieving petitioners of responsibility for inadequate factual development unless they deliberately by-passed the opportunity to develop the facts, *Townsend* ordained many more hearings. Finally, by attaching no penalty to piecemeal applications, *Sanders* encouraged petitioners to split their claims and bring case after case.

Thousands of state prisoners accepted the invitation. In the 1940s and early 1950s, annual filings of habeas petitions in the federal district courts averaged in the mid-500s. The number of petitions increased

---

[18] *Sanders* was a post-conviction application by a federal prisoner under 28 U.S.C. § 2255, but the Court held that the same standards apply in state prisoners' habeas cases.

slowly after *Brown v. Allen*, reaching 822 in 1959.[19] After the 1963 trilogy, applications skyrocketed. In 1968, 6,488 petitions were filed, and by 1971, the number reached 8,372.[20]

The Warren Court's habeas corpus revolution did not occur in a vacuum; instead, it can be seen as one part—and perhaps a necessary part—of the Court's broader mission to reform American criminal justice at both the state and federal levels. During the 1950s and 1960s, the Court expanded criminal defendants' Fourth, Fifth, Sixth, and Fourteenth Amendment rights. While the Court could announce the new rights in cases directly reviewing judgments of the highest state courts, it could not actually implement the new rights because it can hear only a limited number of cases. The lower federal courts, however, could scrutinize large numbers of individual state criminal cases. As Justice Harlan candidly admitted, "the threat of habeas serves as a necessary additional incentive for trial and appellate courts throughout the land to conduct their proceedings in a manner consistent with established constitutional standards." In addition, the Court's 1963 habeas trilogy allowed federal courts to go back in time to enforce rights deemed sufficiently fundamental to be applied retroactively.

Perhaps inevitably, the Warren Court's bold habeas jurisprudence invited a backlash. The passing of the Warren Court and the advent of the Burger and Rehnquist Courts led to increasing criticism of the broad scope of habeas corpus. Slowly at first, and then more rapidly in recent years, Congress and the Court have systematically restricted the scope of habeas. The Supreme Court has interpreted the habeas corpus statutes much more restrictively and has created a plethora of new procedural obstacles to using the writ. Statistics reflect these changes. The number of applications leveled off during the 1970s. Because state prison populations were increasing, the rate of filings per hundred prisoners decreased from 5.74 in 1971 to 2.68 in 1983.[21]

The number of applications grew slowly in the 1980s and early 1990s, reaching 14,726 in 1996.[22] The state prison population, however, rose even faster during these years, so the rate of habeas filings continued to decline. In 1996, after years of debate, Congress confirmed and expanded the Court's writ-curtailment project in the AEDPA.

---

[19] George P. Smith, II, *Title 28, Section 2255 of the United States Code—Motion to Vacate, Set Aside, or Correct Sentence: Effective or Ineffective Aid to a Federal Prisoner*, 40 NOTRE DAME L. 171, 175 (1964-65).

[20] DIRECTOR OF THE ADMINISTRATIVE OFFICE OF THE UNITED STATES COURTS, 1968 ANNUAL REPORT, at 194-95 table C-2; 1971 Annual Report at 263 table C-2.

[21] Judith Resnik, *Tiers*, 57 S. CAL. L. REV. 840, 945 (1984).

[22] JOHN SCALIA, BUREAU OF JUSTICE STATISTICS SPECIAL REPORT: PRISONER PETITIONS FILED IN U.S. DISTRICT COURTS, 2000, WITH TRENDS 1980-2000, at 2 (2002).

In short, there has been a counter-revolution. The cases that follow in this Chapter present the most significant victories of the counter-revolutionaries. In addition to digesting the doctrinal changes, be sure to focus on the issues of federalism, parity, and separation-of-powers that underlie the cases. Did the Warren Court act appropriately in providing a possible remedy to the thousands of state prisoners claiming violation of their federal constitutional rights, or did expanded habeas corpus cause offensive, unnecessary intrusion into state criminal justice systems? Have the Burger and Rehnquist Courts achieved a better balance between enforcement of constitutional rights and federalism concerns, or, in reversing course, have they gone too far in the opposite direction? Do the widespread constitutional deficiencies in state criminal justice systems that arguably existed in the 1950s still exist today? Does the fact that many state high courts have interpreted their own state constitutions to grant more protection to criminal defendants than the Supreme Court grants defendants under the federal Constitution suggest that an expansive federal habeas remedy is an unnecessary anachronism? Have the decisions of the Burger and Rehnquist Courts limiting habeas been principled or have they stretched the canons of statutory construction to the breaking point? Have these Courts violated separation-of-powers principles by interpreting the habeas statutes in unreasonable ways or by creating federal common law that flies in the face of Congressional intent? Finally, does their disregard for *stare decisis* amount to inappropriate judicial activism, or is it simply a necessary antidote to the inappropriate activism of the Warren Court? These underlying issues and the fact that since 1982 the Supreme Court has given plenary review to more than fifty habeas corpus cases testify to the importance of this topic in modern federal courts jurisprudence.

B.   THE STATUTORY STRUCTURE

The statutes governing federal habeas corpus appear at 28 U.S.C.A. §§ 2241-2266.[23] They may generate more questions than they answer, and that is particularly so today, because of the amendments contained in the Antiterrorism and Effective Death Penalty Act of 1996. The courts are struggling to interpret and clarify the Act's sometimes murky

---

[23] A brief word about vocabulary is appropriate. The statutes, particularly § 2243, reflect the common law heritage of habeas corpus. The writ originally required the custodian of a prisoner to present the prisoner to the court so the court could evaluate the legality of the detention. The writ itself was not a release from the custody; it was merely the instrument by which the inquiry was launched. Accordingly, § 2243 notes that the judge "shall forthwith award the writ * * * ," but follows that command by noting that the custodian shall make a return on the writ specifying the reasons that the detention is lawful. Nonetheless, today the writ is frequently equated with the relief sought: (most often) release from custody. Even the Supreme Court has lapsed into this misusage, as in *Coleman v. Thompson, infra* page 1164, in which the Court notes that the district court, after considering the petitioner's claims on the merits, "denied the petition." In more traditional parlance, the writ was granted but relief was denied.

language and confusing structure. As Professor Yackle observed:

> The new law is not well drafted. It bears the influence of various bills that were fiercely debated for nearly forty years. Along the way, proponents of habeas legislation adjusted their initiatives in light of contemporaneous events and circumstances: the Powell Committee Report in 1989, for example, as well as shifting levels of political support for particular measures and new Supreme Court decisions on point. Proponents often kept abreast of the times by adding new elements to their bills without, at the same time, reexamining old formulations in order to maintain an intellectually coherent whole. The result, I am afraid, is extraordinarily arcane verbiage that will require considerable time and resources to sort out.[24]

Section 2241 contains the basic authorization for federal judges to grant writs of habeas corpus. All three levels of the federal judiciary are authorized to grant a writ, but, for obvious reasons, Supreme Court justices and circuit judges may transfer an application to the district court having jurisdiction to entertain it. The Military Commissions Act of 2006[25] amended § 2241(e) to deny the federal courts jurisdiction to hear habeas petitions by aliens determined by the United States to have been properly detained as enemy combatants or to be awaiting such determination. Sections 2242 and 2243 contain relatively straightforward provisions for the application, return, and hearing of a habeas petition. Section 2244, entitled "Finality of determination," is the first section AEDPA substantially revised. It is lengthy and confusing; nonetheless, the language evinces a clear intent drastically to limit second or successive habeas corpus petitions by state prisoners. Prior to AEDPA, the Supreme Court announced rules greatly limiting second or successive petitions. Section D-5 explores whether amended § 2244 limits even further the circumstances when second or successive petitions can be filed. Two new procedural hurdles are apparent on the face of § 2244. First, a prisoner seeking to file a second or successive petition must get permission from a three-judge panel of the court of appeals. Second, § 2244(d) imposes a one-year limitation on state prisoners' habeas petitions, running generally from the time the state judgment became final "by the conclusion of direct review or the expiration of the time for seeking such review." More time is available in certain extraordinary circumstances. The one year period is tolled during the pendency of state post-conviction proceedings; however, the Court held in *Lawrence v. Florida*, __ U.S. __, 127 S.Ct. 1079, 166 L.Ed.2d 924 (2007), that the period is not tolled during the pendency of a petition for certiorari to the Supreme Court from the state court judgment rendered on direct review.

---

[24] Larry W. Yackle, *A Primer on the New Habeas Corpus Statute*, 44 BUFF.L.REV. 381, 281 (1996).

[25] Pub.L. 109-366, 120 Stat. 2600 (2006).

Sections 2245-2252 are short sections containing specific procedural directions for habeas proceedings. Section 2253, as amended in 1996, sharply limits appeals in habeas cases, proscribing appeals unless a circuit judge issues a certificate of appealability and defining appealability in terms of a petitioner's "substantial showing" of constitutional violation. What is a substantial showing? Given the denial of relief, the petitioner's showing clearly did not persuade the district court. We are familiar with standards of appellate review involving abuse of discretion or "clear error." Where does "substantial showing" fit on that spectrum? Prior to AEDPA, Section 2253 allowed an appeal if either a district or circuit judge issued a "certificate of probable cause." A certificate issued if a judge felt there was "probable cause to believe that the petitioner ha[d] raised a 'substantial question' that [was] at least not totally 'devoid of merit.' "[26] Although the courts never clearly articulated the distinction between frivolous and non-frivolous unsuccessful claims, it was plainly easier to appeal before AEDPA.

Section 2254 contains most of the major restrictions on habeas corpus applications by state prisoners. Section 2254(a) appears to permit broad review by authorizing a federal court to hear any application by a state prisoner claiming "that he is in custody in violation of the Constitution or laws or treaties of the United States." Subsequent subsections, however, impose substantial limitations. Section 2254(b) requires a petitioner to have exhausted any available state procedures for raising the question presented. What if a petition contains both exhausted and unexhausted claims? May a federal court hear the exhausted claims and dismiss the rest to allow the petitioner to comply with the statute as to the unexhausted claims, or, if the prisoner chooses to press the exhausted claims, does he waive his opportunity to re-present the unexhausted claims after presenting them to the state courts? Section D-3 addresses these questions. Section D-4 considers the related rule that a state procedural default by the petitioner (*e.g.*, letting the time to file a notice of appeal pass) will normally constitute an adequate and independent state ground barring federal habeas review.

Section 2254(d)(1) says a habeas petition "shall not be granted with respect to any claim that was adjudicated on the merits in State court proceedings" unless the state ruling "resulted in a decision that was contrary to, or involved an unreasonable application of, clearly established Federal law, as determined by the Supreme Court of the United States." Congress may have intended this provision to codify the Supreme Court's decision in *Teague v. Lane*, 489 U.S. 288, 109 S.Ct. 1060, 103 L.Ed.2d 334 (1989). *Teague* and § 2254(d)(1) raise many thorny issues. For example, how is a court to decide whether Supreme Court cases "clearly establish" a federal constitutional rule? And what does "resulted

---

[26] Donald H. Zeigler & Michele G. Hermann, *The Invisible Litigant: An Inside View of Pro Se Actions in the Federal Courts*, 47 N.Y.U.L.REV. 157, 220-21 (1972).

in a decision that was contrary to, or involved an unreasonable application of" mean? Does it simply mean incorrect, or does it require a higher degree of error? Section D-2 of this Chapter addresses these and related issues

Section 2254(e) addresses the weight to be given to state court factual findings and the circumstances permitting a federal evidentiary hearing. Prior to enactment of the current § 2254(e) of AEDPA, the Supreme Court substantially narrowed the standards *Townsend v. Sain* (1963) set forth and Congress incorporated in 1966 into what was then § 2254(d). Section 2254(e) appears further to limit petitioners' opportunities for federal evidentiary hearings, although by how much is still unclear. Section D-1 addresses these matters.

One special feature of AEDPA deserves separate comment. Sections 2261-2266 provide expedited procedures applicable only to capital cases and limit the grounds for relief that the federal courts may consider. Section 2261(e) specifically excludes ineffective assistance of counsel in post-conviction proceedings (state or federal) as a ground for federal habeas corpus relief, a point on which Congress must have been especially intent given that § 2254(i) already contained an identical provision. Section 2261(e) does, however, note that the court may appoint effective counsel to *replace* ineffective counsel *during* post-conviction proceedings. Section 2263 limits a prisoner's time to seek federal habeas relief in a capital case to 180 days from the time the conviction becomes final (subject to certain tolling provisions), half that permitted in non-capital cases under § 2244(d) (subject to quite similar tolling provisions), and § 2266 directs the inferior federal courts to give priority to capital cases and to complete their consideration within specified time limits. AEDPA also sharply limits stays of execution, including prohibiting them with respect to second or successive petitions "unless the court of appeals approves the filing * * * ." The statute also limits the scope of review, directing the district courts only to consider claims upon which the state courts have ruled, excepting only claims not presented to the state courts because of some violation of federal law by the state, claims based on a new federal right that is retroactive, or claims based on previously undiscoverable facts.

These features are not automatically available, however. Section 2261(b, c, d) establishes prerequisites that the state must satisfy to reap the benefit of these sections. It must establish a formal, regular procedure to appoint competent counsel for post-conviction procedures in the state courts. The state must formally and affirmatively offer post-conviction counsel to all capital prisoners; merely giving prisoners the right to counsel does not suffice. Such counsel cannot, without the consent of both the prisoner and counsel, have previously been involved in the trial or appeal of the case. Finally, the state's rules must explicitly "provide standards of competency for the appointment of such counsel." Early experience suggests that the lower federal courts will interpret these requirements quite strictly. Thus, district courts have required an "affirmative, institutionalized, formal commitment" to a post-conviction review system, something more "than the general supervision of a state high court." One court found that merely setting aside funds for a "general category of state court expenditures" did not establish a " 'mechanism for the compensation and payment of reasonable expenses' as required by § 2261(b)." On the other hand, the Fifth Circuit upheld Texas rules providing funds for post-conviction review but limiting attorney compensation to $7,500 and expenses to $2,500. With respect to the competence of post-conviction counsel, however, the same court found that a "flexible mechanism" for ensuring competent counsel, such as evaluation of attorney questionnaires on a case-by-case basis, failed to meet the statutory requirement of "explicit standards of competency." A court found that one state's standard of five years of membership in the state bar and two years' experience in criminal law failed to guarantee competency. A district court approved Virginia's approach because Virginia has a statute that establishes seven criteria by which to judge counsel's competency.[27] On balance, although Congress sought through these provisions to make good on AEDPA's title, lower court experience to date suggests that it will not be easy for states to qualify under this particular "fast-track" legislation.

A final ironic note: In 1997, the year after the AEDPA was enacted, the number of state prisoner petitions jumped by over 5,000, reaching 19,956. By 2000, 21,345 application were filed.[28] John Scalia, a researcher with the Department of Justice's Bureau of Justice Statistics, concluded after a mathematical analysis that "[b]etween April 1996 and September 2000 an estimated 18,000 additional habeas corpus petitions were filed in U.S. district courts by State prison inmates directly as a result of the enactment of the AEDPA."[29] Why legislation designed to curtail habeas petitions resulted instead in a dramatic increase is a mystery.

C.   HABEAS CORPUS AND THE WAR ON TERROR

The Bush Administration's "War on Terror" raises many controversial military, political, and legal issues. Intense controversy has centered on detained individuals. What are their rights, if any? Are they prisoners of war, entitled to the full protections of the Geneva Conven-

---

[27] VA. CODE. § 19.2-163.8(A):

> (i) license or permission to practice law in Virginia; (ii) general background in criminal litigation; (iii) demonstrated experience in felony practice at trial and appeal; (iv) experience in death penalty litigation; (v) familiarity with the requisite court system; (vi) current training in death penalty litigation; and (vii) demonstrated proficiency and commitment to quality representation.

[28] JOHN SCALIA, BUREAU OF JUSTICE STATISTICS SPECIAL REPORT: PRISONER PETITIONS FILED IN U.S. DISTRICT COURTS, 2000, WITH TRENDS 1980-2000, at 2 (2002).

[29] *Id.* at 7.

tions, or illegal "enemy combatants," with few or no rights? Should the military alone determine their status and punishments, or should some or all of their cases go to the federal criminal justice system? Should it matter whether they are aliens or American citizens, or whether the government is holding them inside or outside of United States territory? These are complex and profound issues that have engaged the attention of all three branches of government and the citizenry.

The materials in this section focus on one important aspect of the legal controversy, namely, what role the federal courts should play in determining the rights and status of individuals captured or arrested and labeled terrorists. By and large, the Bush Administration has sought to keep such individuals under military control and has argued for very limited federal court involvement. Congress has cooperated, at least as to aliens designated "enemy combatants." The federal courts have struggled with precedent and statutory language. The Supreme Court has been split, sometimes fractured. The larger issues sometimes seem submerged in a maze of technical distinctions as the Justices seek to cobble together a majority in each case.[30] The Court has managed to sidestep the looming constitutional question of whether Congress's withdrawal of habeas jurisdiction over the Guantanamo detainees and other aliens designated enemy combatants violates the Suspension Clause of the Constitution. *Boumediene v. Bush*, 476 F.3d 981 (D.C. Cir.), *cert. granted*, ___ U.S.___, 127 S.Ct. 3078, 168 L.Ed.2d 755 (2007), presents that issue squarely.

On June 28, 2004, the Supreme Court issued three decisions concerning detention of enemy combatants. *Hamdi v. Rumsfeld*, 542 U.S. 507, 124 S.Ct. 2633, 159 L.Ed.2d 578 (2004), involved an American citizen who resided in Afghanistan. Local authorities seized Hamdi, who turned him over to the U.S. military, which transferred him to Guantanamo Bay. When the government discovered Hamdi was an American citizen, it moved him to the naval brig in Virginia. The government designated Hamdi an enemy combatant and argued that it could hold him indefinitely, without any formal charges, proceedings or assignment of counsel. Hamdi's father filed a petition for a writ of habeas corpus in Virginia seeking release from detention and the full panoply of criminal constitutional protections.

Hamdi upheld habeas jurisdiction for an American citizen detained in the United States. But what about an alien detained at Guantanamo Bay, Cuba? The following case presents that issue.

---

[30] It is sometimes difficult to draw a line between the separation-of-powers issues recent cases and legislation present and the broader issues involved in the treatment of detainees. We attempt to draw that line but also encourage students to use the materials as a spring-board for discussion of the broader issues.

RASUL v. BUSH

Supreme Court of the United States, 2004.
542 U.S. 466, 124 S.Ct. 2686, 159 L.Ed.2d 548.

JUSTICE STEVENS delivered the opinion of the Court.

These two cases present the narrow but important question whether United States courts lack jurisdiction to consider challenges to the legality of the detention of foreign nationals captured abroad in connection with hostilities and incarcerated at the Guantanamo Bay Naval Base, Cuba.

I

On September 11, 2001, agents of the al Qaeda terrorist network hijacked four commercial airliners and used them as missiles to attack American targets. * * * In response to the attacks, Congress passed a joint resolution authorizing the President to use "all necessary and appropriate force against those nations, organizations, or persons he determines planned, authorized, committed, or aided the terrorist attacks * * * or harbored such organizations or persons." Authorization for Use of Military Force. Acting pursuant to that authorization, the President sent U.S. Armed Forces into Afghanistan to wage a military campaign against al Qaeda and the Taliban regime that had supported it.

Petitioners in these cases are 2 Australian citizens and 12 Kuwaiti citizens who were captured abroad during hostilities between the United States and the Taliban. Since early 2002, the U.S. military has held them—along with, according to the Government's estimate, approximately 640 other non-Americans captured abroad—at the Naval Base at Guantanamo Bay. The United States occupies the Base, which comprises 45 square miles of land and water along the southeast coast of Cuba, pursuant to a 1903 Lease Agreement executed with the newly independent Republic of Cuba in the aftermath of the Spanish-American War. Under the Agreement, "the United States recognizes the continuance of the ultimate sovereignty of the Republic of Cuba over the [leased areas]," while "the Republic of Cuba consents that during the period of the occupation by the United States * * * the United States shall exercise complete jurisdiction and control over and within said areas." In 1934, the parties entered into a treaty providing that, absent an agreement to modify or abrogate the lease, the lease would remain in effect "[s]o long as the United States of America shall not abandon the * * * naval station of Guantanamo."

In 2002, petitioners, through relatives acting as their next friends, filed various actions in the U.S. District Court for the District of Columbia challenging the legality of their detention at the Base. All alleged that none of the petitioners has ever been a combatant against the United States or has ever engaged in any terrorist acts.[4] They also al-

---

[4] Relatives of the Kuwaiti detainees allege that the detainees were taken captive "by local villagers seeking promised bounties or other financial rewards" while they were pro-

leged that none has been charged with any wrongdoing, permitted to consult with counsel, or provided access to the courts or any other tribunal.

The two Australians, Mamdouh Habib and David Hicks, each filed a petition for writ of habeas corpus, seeking release from custody, access to counsel, freedom from interrogations, and other relief. Fawzi Khalid Abdullah Fahad Al Odah and the 11 other Kuwaiti detainees filed a complaint seeking to be informed of the charges against them, to be allowed to meet with their families and with counsel, and to have access to the courts or some other impartial tribunal. They claimed that denial of these rights violates the Constitution, international law, and treaties of the United States. Invoking the court's jurisdiction under 28 U.S.C. §§ 1331 and 1350, among other statutory bases, they asserted causes of action under the Administrative Procedure Act, the Alien Tort Statute and the general federal habeas corpus statute.

Construing all three actions as petitions for writs of habeas corpus, the District Court dismissed them for want of jurisdiction. The court held, in reliance on our opinion in *Johnson v. Eisentrager* (1950) that "aliens detained outside the sovereign territory of the United States [may not] invok[e] a petition for a writ of habeas corpus." The Court of Appeals affirmed. Reading *Eisentrager* to hold that " 'the privilege of litigation' does not extend to aliens in military custody who have no presence in 'any territory over which the United States is sovereign,' " it held that the District Court lacked jurisdiction over petitioners' habeas actions, as well as their remaining federal statutory claims that do not sound in habeas. We granted certiorari and now reverse.

II

Congress has granted federal district courts, "within their respective jurisdictions," the authority to hear applications for habeas corpus by any person who claims to be held "in custody in violation of the Constitution or laws or treaties of the United States." 28 U.S.C. §§ 2241(a), (c)(3). The statute traces its ancestry to the first grant of federal court jurisdiction: Section 14 of the Judiciary Act of 1789 authorized federal courts to issue the writ of habeas corpus to prisoners "in custody, under or by colour of the authority of the United States, or committed for trial before some court of the same." In 1867, Congress extended the protections of the writ to "all cases where any person may be restrained of his or her liberty in violation of the constitution, or of any treaty or law of the United States."

Habeas corpus is, however, "a writ antecedent to statute, * * * throw-

---

viding humanitarian aid in Afghanistan and Pakistan, and were subsequently turned over to U.S. custody. The Australian David Hicks was allegedly captured in Afghanistan by the Northern Alliance, a coalition of Afghan groups opposed to the Taliban, before he was turned over to the United States. The Australian Mamdouh Habib was allegedly arrested in Pakistan by Pakistani authorities and turned over to Egyptian authorities, who in turn transferred him to U.S. custody.

ing its root deep into the genius of our common law." The writ appeared in English law several centuries ago, became "an integral part of our common-law heritage" by the time the Colonies achieved independence, and received explicit recognition in the Constitution, which forbids suspension of "[t]he Privilege of the Writ of Habeas Corpus * * * unless when in Cases of Rebellion or Invasion the public Safety may require it."

As it has evolved over the past two centuries, the habeas statute clearly has expanded habeas corpus "beyond the limits that obtained during the 17th and 18th centuries." But "[a]t its historical core, the writ of habeas corpus has served as a means of reviewing the legality of Executive detention, and it is in that context that its protections have been strongest." As Justice Jackson [dissenting] wrote in an opinion respecting the availability of habeas corpus to aliens held in U.S. custody:

> Executive imprisonment has been considered oppressive and lawless since John, at Runnymede, pledged that no free man should be imprisoned, dispossessed, outlawed, or exiled save by the judgment of his peers or by the law of the land. The judges of England developed the writ of habeas corpus largely to preserve these immunities from executive restraint.

Consistent with the historic purpose of the writ, this Court has recognized the federal courts' power to review applications for habeas relief in a wide variety of cases involving Executive detention, in wartime as well as in times of peace. The Court has, for example, entertained the habeas petitions of an American citizen who plotted an attack on military installations during the Civil War, *Ex parte Milligan* (1866), and of admitted enemy aliens convicted of war crimes during a declared war and held in the United States, *Ex parte Quirin* (1942), and its insular possessions, *In re Yamashita* (1946).

The question now before us is whether the habeas statute confers a right to judicial review of the legality of Executive detention of aliens in a territory over which the United States exercises plenary and exclusive jurisdiction, but not "ultimate sovereignty."

III

Respondents' primary submission is that the answer to the jurisdictional question is controlled by our decision in *Eisentrager*. In that case, we held that a Federal District Court lacked authority to issue a writ of habeas corpus to 21 German citizens who had been captured by U.S. forces in China, tried and convicted of war crimes by an American military commission headquartered in Nanking, and incarcerated in the Landsberg Prison in occupied Germany. The Court of Appeals in *Eisentrager* had found jurisdiction, reasoning that "any person who is deprived of his liberty by officials of the United States, acting under purported authority of that Government, and who can show that his confinement is in violation of a prohibition of the Constitution, has a right to the writ." In reversing that determination, this Court summarized the six critical facts in the case:

We are here confronted with a decision whose basic premise is that these prisoners are entitled, as a constitutional right, to sue in some court of the United States for a writ of *habeas corpus*. To support that assumption we must hold that a prisoner of our military authorities is constitutionally entitled to the writ, even though he (a) is an enemy alien; (b) has never been or resided in the United States; (c) was captured outside of our territory and there held in military custody as a prisoner of war; (d) was tried and convicted by a Military Commission sitting outside the United States; (e) for offenses against laws of war committed outside the United States; (f) and is at all times imprisoned outside the United States.

On this set of facts, the Court concluded, "no right to the writ of *habeas corpus* appears."

Petitioners in these cases differ from the *Eisentrager* detainees in important respects: They are not nationals of countries at war with the United States, and they deny that they have engaged in or plotted acts of aggression against the United States; they have never been afforded access to any tribunal, much less charged with and convicted of wrongdoing; and for more than two years they have been imprisoned in territory over which the United States exercises exclusive jurisdiction and control.

Not only are petitioners differently situated from the *Eisentrager* detainees, but the Court in *Eisentrager* made quite clear that all six of the facts critical to its disposition were relevant only to the question of the prisoners' *constitutional* entitlement to habeas corpus. The Court had far less to say on the question of the petitioners' *statutory* entitlement to habeas review. Its only statement on the subject was a passing reference to the absence of statutory authorization: "Nothing in the text of the Constitution extends such a right, nor does anything in our statutes."

Reference to the historical context in which *Eisentrager* was decided explains why the opinion devoted so little attention to question of statutory jurisdiction. In 1948, just two months after the *Eisentrager* petitioners filed their petition for habeas corpus in the U.S. District Court for the District of Columbia, this Court issued its decision in *Ahrens v. Clark*, a case concerning the application of the habeas statute to the petitions of 120 Germans who were then being detained at Ellis Island, New York, for deportation to Germany. The *Ahrens* detainees had also filed their petitions in the U.S. District Court for the District of Columbia, naming the Attorney General as the respondent. Reading the phrase "within their respective jurisdictions" as used in the habeas statute to require the petitioners' presence within the district court's territorial jurisdiction, the Court held that the District of Columbia court lacked jurisdiction to entertain the detainees' claims. *Ahrens* expressly reserved the question "of what process, if any, a person confined in an area not subject to the jurisdiction of any district court may employ to assert federal rights." But as the dissent noted, if the presence of the petitioner in the territorial jurisdiction of a federal district court were truly a jurisdictional requirement, there could be only one response to that question. ([O]pinion of Rutledge, J.).[7]

When the District Court for the District of Columbia reviewed the German prisoners' habeas application in *Eisentrager,* it thus dismissed their action on the authority of *Ahrens.* Although the Court of Appeals reversed the District Court, it implicitly conceded that the District Court lacked jurisdiction under the habeas statute as it had been interpreted in *Ahrens.* The Court of Appeals instead held that petitioners had a constitutional right to habeas corpus secured by the Suspension Clause, reasoning that "if a person has a right to a writ of habeas corpus, he cannot be deprived of the privilege by an omission in a federal jurisdictional statute." In essence, the Court of Appeals concluded that the habeas statute, as construed in *Ahrens,* had created an unconstitutional gap that had to be filled by reference to "fundamentals." In its review of that decision, this Court, like the Court of Appeals, proceeded from the premise that "nothing in our statutes" conferred federal-court jurisdiction, and accordingly evaluated the Court of Appeals' resort to "fundamentals" on its own terms.[8]

Because subsequent decisions of this Court have filled the statutory gap that had occasioned *Eisentrager's* resort to "fundamentals," persons detained outside the territorial jurisdiction of any federal district court no longer need rely on the Constitution as the source of their right to federal habeas review. In *Braden v. 30th Judicial Circuit Court of Ky.* (1973), this Court held, contrary to *Ahrens,* that the prisoner's presence within the territorial jurisdiction of the district court is not "an invariable prerequisite" to the exercise of district court jurisdiction under the federal habeas statute. Rather, because "the writ of habeas corpus does not act upon the prisoner who seeks relief, but upon the person who holds him in what is alleged to be unlawful custody," a district court acts "within [its] respective jurisdiction" within the meaning of § 2241 as long as "the custodian can be reached by service of process." *Braden* reasoned that its departure from the rule of *Ahrens* was warranted in light of developments that "had a profound impact on the continuing vitality of that decision." These developments included, notably, decisions of this

---

[7] Justice Rutledge wrote:

> [I]f absence of the body detained from the territorial jurisdiction of the court having jurisdiction of the jailer creates a total and irremediable void in the court's capacity to act, * * * then it is hard to see how that gap can be filled by such extraneous considerations as whether there is no other court in the place of detention from which remedy might be had * * * .

[8] Although Justice Scalia disputes the basis for the Court of Appeals' holding, what is most pertinent for present purposes is that this Court clearly understood the Court of Appeals' decision to rest on constitutional and not statutory grounds. ("[The Court of Appeals] concluded that any person, including an enemy alien, deprived of his liberty anywhere under any purported authority of the United States is entitled to the writ if he can show that extension to his case of any constitutional rights or limitations would show his imprisonment illegal; [and] that, *although no statutory jurisdiction of such cases is given,* courts must be held to possess it as part of the judicial power of the United States * * * " (emphasis added)).

Court in cases involving habeas petitioners "confined overseas (and thus outside the territory of any district court)," in which the Court "held, if only implicitly, that the petitioners' absence from the district does not present a jurisdictional obstacle to the consideration of the claim." *Braden* thus established that *Ahrens* can no longer be viewed as establishing "an inflexible jurisdictional rule," and is strictly relevant only to the question of the appropriate forum, not to whether the claim can be heard at all.

Because *Braden* overruled the statutory predicate to *Eisentrager*'s holding, *Eisentrager* plainly does not preclude the exercise of § 2241 jurisdiction over petitioners' claims.[9]

IV

Putting *Eisentrager* and *Ahrens* to one side, respondents contend that we can discern a limit on § 2241 through application of the "longstanding principle of American law" that congressional legislation is presumed not to have extraterritorial application unless such intent is clearly manifested. Whatever traction the presumption against extraterritoriality might have in other contexts, it certainly has no application to the operation of the habeas statute with respect to persons detained within "the territorial jurisdiction" of the United States. By the express terms of its agreements with Cuba, the United States exercises "complete jurisdiction and control" over the Guantanamo Bay Naval Base, and may continue to exercise such control permanently if it so chooses. Respondents themselves concede that the habeas statute would create federal-court jurisdiction over the claims of an American citizen held at the base. Considering that the statute draws no distinction between Americans and aliens held in federal custody, there is little reason to think that Congress intended the geographical coverage of the statute to vary depending on the detainee's citizenship. Aliens held at the base, no less than American citizens, are entitled to invoke the federal courts' authority under § 2241.

---

[9] The dissent argues that *Braden* did not overrule *Ahrens*' jurisdictional holding, but simply distinguished it. Of course, *Braden* itself indicated otherwise, and a long line of judicial and scholarly interpretations, beginning with then-Justice Rehnquist's dissenting opinion, have so understood the decision.

The dissent also disingenuously contends that the continuing vitality of *Ahrens*' jurisdictional holding is irrelevant to the question presented in these cases, "inasmuch as *Ahrens* did not pass upon any of the statutory issues decided by *Eisentrager*." But what Justice Scalia describes as *Eisentrager*'s statutory holding—"that, unaided by the canon of constitutional avoidance, the statute did not confer jurisdiction over an alien detained outside the territorial jurisdiction of the courts of the United States,"—is little more than the rule of *Ahrens* cloaked in the garb of *Eisentrager*'s facts. To contend plausibly that this holding survived *Braden*, Justice Scalia at a minimum must find a textual basis for the rule other than the phrase "within their respective jurisdictions"—a phrase which, after *Braden*, can no longer be read to require the habeas petitioner's physical presence within the territorial jurisdiction of a federal district court. Two references to the district of confinement in provisions relating to recordkeeping and pleading requirements in proceedings before circuit judges hardly suffice in that regard.

Application of the habeas statute to persons detained at the base is consistent with the historical reach of the writ of habeas corpus. At common law, courts exercised habeas jurisdiction over the claims of aliens detained within sovereign territory of the realm, as well as the claims of persons detained in the so-called "exempt jurisdictions," where ordinary writs did not run, and all other dominions under the sovereign's control. As Lord Mansfield wrote in 1759, even if a territory was "no part of the realm," there was "no doubt" as to the court's power to issue writs of habeas corpus if the territory was "under the subjection of the Crown." Later cases confirmed that the reach of the writ depended not on formal notions of territorial sovereignty, but rather on the practical question of "the exact extent and nature of the jurisdiction or dominion exercised in fact by the Crown."

In the end, the answer to the question presented is clear. Petitioners contend that they are being held in federal custody in violation of the laws of the United States. No party questions the District Court's jurisdiction over petitioners' custodians. Section 2241, by its terms, requires nothing more. We therefore hold that § 2241 confers on the District Court jurisdiction to hear petitioners' habeas corpus challenges to the legality of their detention at the Guantanamo Bay Naval Base.

V

In addition to invoking the District Court's jurisdiction under § 2241, the *Al Odah* petitioners' complaint invoked the court's jurisdiction under 28 U.S.C. § 1331, the federal question statute, as well as § 1350, the Alien Tort Statute. The Court of Appeals, again relying on *Eisentrager,* held that the District Court correctly dismissed the claims founded on § 1331 and § 1350 for lack of jurisdiction, even to the extent that these claims "deal only with conditions of confinement and do not sound in habeas," because petitioners lack the "privilege of litigation" in U.S. courts. Specifically, the court held that because petitioners' § 1331 and § 1350 claims "necessarily rest on alleged violations of the same category of laws listed in the habeas corpus statute," they, like claims founded on the habeas statute itself, must be "beyond the jurisdiction of the federal courts."

As explained above, *Eisentrager* itself erects no bar to the exercise of federal court jurisdiction over the petitioners' habeas corpus claims. It therefore certainly does not bar the exercise of federal-court jurisdiction over claims that merely implicate the "same category of laws listed in the habeas corpus statute." But in any event, nothing in *Eisentrager* or in any of our other cases categorically excludes aliens detained in military custody outside the United States from the " 'privilege of litigation' " in U.S. courts. The courts of the United States have traditionally been open to nonresident aliens. And indeed, § 1350 explicitly confers the privilege of suing for an actionable "tort * * * committed in violation of the law of nations or a treaty of the United States" on aliens alone. The fact that petitioners in these cases are being held in military custody is immaterial to the question of the District Court's jurisdiction over their nonhabeas statutory claims.

VI

Whether and what further proceedings may become necessary after respondents make their response to the merits of petitioners' claims are matters that we need not address now. What is presently at stake is only whether the federal courts have jurisdiction to determine the legality of the Executive's potentially indefinite detention of individuals who claim to be wholly innocent of wrongdoing. Answering that question in the affirmative, we reverse the judgment of the Court of Appeals and remand for the District Court to consider in the first instance the merits of petitioners' claims.

It is so ordered.

JUSTICE KENNEDY, concurring in the judgment.

The Court is correct, in my view, to conclude that federal courts have jurisdiction to consider challenges to the legality of the detention of foreign nationals held at the Guantanamo Bay Naval Base in Cuba. While I reach the same conclusion, my analysis follows a different course. Justice Scalia exposes the weakness in the Court's conclusion that *Braden v. 30th Judicial Circuit Court of Ky.* "overruled the statutory predicate to *Eisentrager's* holding." As he explains, the Court's approach is not a plausible reading of *Braden* or *Johnson v. Eisentrager.* In my view, the correct course is to follow the framework of *Eisentrager.*

Eisentrager considered the scope of the right to petition for a writ of habeas corpus against the backdrop of the constitutional command of the separation of powers. The issue before the Court was whether the Judiciary could exercise jurisdiction over the claims of German prisoners held in the Landsberg prison in Germany following the cessation of hostilities in Europe. The Court concluded the petition could not be entertained. The petition was not within the proper realm of the judicial power. It concerned matters within the exclusive province of the Executive, or the Executive and Congress, to determine.

* * *

The decision in *Eisentrager* indicates that there is a realm of political authority over military affairs where the judicial power may not enter. The existence of this realm acknowledges the power of the President as Commander in Chief, and the joint role of the President and the Congress, in the conduct of military affairs. A faithful application of *Eisentrager,* then, requires an initial inquiry into the general circumstances of the detention to determine whether the Court has the authority to entertain the petition and to grant relief after considering all of the facts presented. A necessary corollary of *Eisentrager* is that there are circumstances in which the courts maintain the power and the responsibility to protect persons from unlawful detention even where military affairs are implicated.

The facts here are distinguishable from those in *Eisentrager* in two critical ways, leading to the conclusion that a federal court may entertain the petitions. First, Guantanamo Bay is in every practical respect a United States territory, and it is one far removed from any hostilities. The opinion of the Court well explains the history of its possession by the United States. In a formal sense, the United States leases the Bay; the 1903 lease agreement states that Cuba retains "ultimate sovereignty" over it. At the same time, this lease is no ordinary lease. Its term is indefinite and at the discretion of the United States. What matters is the unchallenged and indefinite control that the United States has long exercised over Guantanamo Bay. From a practical perspective, the indefinite lease of Guantanamo Bay has produced a place that belongs to the United States, extending the "implied protection" of the United States to it.

The second critical set of facts is that the detainees at Guantanamo Bay are being held indefinitely, and without benefit of any legal proceeding to determine their status. In *Eisentrager,* the prisoners were tried and convicted by a military commission of violating the laws of war and were sentenced to prison terms. Having already been subject to procedures establishing their status, they could not justify "a limited opening of our courts" to show that they were "of friendly personal disposition" and not enemy aliens. Indefinite detention without trial or other proceeding presents altogether different considerations. It allows friends and foes alike to remain in detention. It suggests a weaker case of military necessity and much greater alignment with the traditional function of habeas corpus. Perhaps, where detainees are taken from a zone of hostilities, detention without proceedings or trial would be justified by military necessity for a matter of weeks; but as the period of detention stretches from months to years, the case for continued detention to meet military exigencies becomes weaker.

In light of the status of Guantanamo Bay and the indefinite pretrial detention of the detainees, I would hold that federal-court jurisdiction is permitted in these cases. This approach would avoid creating automatic statutory authority to adjudicate the claims of persons located outside the United States, and remains true to the reasoning of *Eisentrager*. For these reasons, I concur in the judgment of the Court.

JUSTICE SCALIA, with whom THE CHIEF JUSTICE and JUSTICE THOMAS join, dissenting.

The Court today holds that the habeas statute, 28 U.S.C. § 2241, extends to aliens detained by the United States military overseas, outside the sovereign borders of the United States and beyond the territorial jurisdictions of all its courts. This is not only a novel holding; it contradicts a half-century-old precedent on which the military undoubtedly relied, *Johnson v. Eisentrager*. The Court's contention that *Eisentrager* was somehow negated by *Braden v. 30th Judicial Circuit Court of Ky.* (1973)—a decision that dealt with a different issue and did not so much as mention *Eisentrager*—is implausible in the extreme. This is an irresponsible overturning of settled law in a matter of extreme importance to our forces currently in the field. I would leave it to Congress to change § 2241, and dissent from the Court's unprecedented holding.

I

As we have repeatedly said: "Federal courts are courts of limited jurisdiction. They possess only that power authorized by Constitution and statute, which is not to be expanded by judicial decree. It is to be presumed that a cause lies outside this limited jurisdiction * * * ." The petitioners do not argue that the Constitution independently requires jurisdiction here. Accordingly, this case turns on the words of § 2241, a text the Court today largely ignores. Even a cursory reading of the habeas statute shows that it presupposes a federal district court with territorial jurisdiction over the detainee. Section 2241(a) states: "Writs of habeas corpus may be granted by the Supreme Court, any justice thereof, the district courts and any circuit judge *within their respective jurisdictions.*" (Emphasis added).

It further requires that "[t]he order of a circuit judge shall be entered in the records of *the* district court of *the district wherein the restraint complained of is had.*" 28 U.S.C. § 2241(a) (emphases added). And § 2242 provides that a petition "addressed to the Supreme Court, a justice thereof or a circuit judge * * * shall state the reasons for not making application to *the* district court of *the district in which the applicant is held.*" (Emphases added). No matter to whom the writ is directed, custodian or detainee, the statute could not be clearer that a necessary requirement for issuing the writ is that *some* federal district court have territorial jurisdiction over the detainee. Here, as the Court allows, the Guantanamo Bay detainees are not located within the territorial jurisdiction of any federal district court. One would think that is the end of this case.

The Court asserts, however, that the decisions of this Court have placed a gloss on the phrase "within their respective jurisdictions" in § 2241 which allows jurisdiction in this case. That is not so. In fact, the only case in point holds just the opposite (and just what the statute plainly says). That case is *Eisentrager,* but to fully understand its implications for the present dispute, I must also discuss our decisions in the earlier case of *Ahrens v. Clark* and the later case of *Braden.*

In *Ahrens,* the Court considered "whether the presence within the territorial jurisdiction of the District Court of the person detained is prerequisite to filing a petition for a writ of habeas corpus." The *Ahrens* detainees were held at Ellis Island, New York, but brought their petitions in the District Court for the District of Columbia. Interpreting "within their respective jurisdictions," the Court held that a district court has jurisdiction to issue the writ only on behalf of petitioners detained within its territorial jurisdiction. It was "not sufficient * * * that the jailer or custodian alone be found in the jurisdiction."

Ahrens explicitly reserved "the question of what process, if any, a person confined in an area not subject to the jurisdiction of any district court may employ to assert federal rights." That question, the same question presented to this Court today, was shortly thereafter resolved in *Eisentrager* insofar as noncitizens are concerned. * * * The District Court, relying on *Ahrens,* dismissed the petitions because the petitioners were not located within its territorial jurisdiction. The Court of Appeals reversed. According to the Court today, the Court of Appeals "implicitly conceded that the District Court lacked jurisdiction under the habeas statute as it had been interpreted in *Ahrens,*" and "[i]n essence * * * concluded that the habeas statute, as construed in *Ahrens,* had created an unconstitutional gap that had to be filled by reference to 'fundamentals.'" That is not so. The Court of Appeals concluded that there *was* statutory jurisdiction. It arrived at that conclusion by applying the canon of constitutional avoidance: "[I]f the existing jurisdictional act be construed to deny the writ to a person entitled to it as a substantive right, the act would be unconstitutional. It should be construed, if possible, to avoid that result." In cases where there was no territorial jurisdiction over the detainee, the Court of Appeals held, the writ would lie at the place of a respondent with directive power over the detainee. "It is not too violent an interpretation of 'custody' to construe it as including those who have directive custody, as well as those who have immediate custody, where such interpretation is necessary to comply with constitutional requirements * * * . *The statute must be so construed,* lest it be invalid as constituting a suspension of the writ in violation of the constitutional provision." ([E]mphasis added).

This Court's judgment in *Eisentrager* reversed the Court of Appeals. The opinion was largely devoted to rejecting the lower court's constitutional analysis, since the doctrine of constitutional avoidance underlay its statutory conclusion. But the opinion *had* to pass judgment on whether the statute granted jurisdiction, since that was the basis for the judgments of both lower courts. A conclusion of no constitutionally conferred right would obviously not support reversal of a judgment that rested upon a statutorily conferred right. And absence of a right to the writ under the clear wording of the habeas statute is what the *Eisentrager* opinion held: "Nothing in the text of the Constitution extends such a right, *nor does anything in our statutes.*" ([E]mphasis added). "[T]hese prisoners at no relevant time were within any territory over which the United States is sovereign, and the scenes of their offense, their capture, their trial and their punishment *were all beyond the territorial jurisdiction of any court of the United States.*" The brevity of the Court's statutory analysis signifies nothing more than that the Court considered it obvious (as indeed it is) that, unaided by the canon of constitutional avoidance, the statute did not confer jurisdiction over an alien detained outside the territorial jurisdiction of the courts of the United States.

Eisentrager's directly-on-point statutory holding makes it exceedingly difficult for the Court to reach the result it desires today. To do so neatly and cleanly, it must either argue that our decision in *Braden* overruled *Eisentrager,* or admit that *it* is overruling *Eisentrager.* The former course would not pass the laugh test, inasmuch as *Braden* dealt with a detainee held within the territorial jurisdiction of a district court, and never *mentioned Eisentrager.* And the latter course would require the Court to explain why our almost categorical rule of *stare decisis* in statutory cases should be set aside in order to complicate the present war, *and,* having set it aside, to explain why the habeas statute does not mean what it plainly says. So instead the Court tries an oblique course: "*Braden,*" it claims, "overruled *the statutory predicate* to *Eisentrager's* holding," (emphasis added), by which it means the statutory analysis of *Ahrens.* Even assuming, for the moment, that *Braden* overruled some aspect of *Ahrens,* inasmuch as *Ahrens* did not pass upon any of the statutory issues decided by *Eisentrager,* it is hard to see how any of that case's "statutory predicate" could have been impaired.

But in fact *Braden* did not overrule *Ahrens;* it distinguished *Ahrens. Braden* dealt with a habeas petitioner incarcerated in Alabama. The petitioner filed an application for a writ of habeas corpus in Kentucky, challenging an indictment that had been filed against him in that Commonwealth and naming as respondent the Kentucky court in which the proceedings were pending. This Court held that Braden was in custody because a detainer had been issued against him by Kentucky, and was being executed by Alabama, serving as an agent for Kentucky. We found that jurisdiction existed in Kentucky for Braden's petition challenging the Kentucky detainer, notwithstanding his physical confinement in Alabama. *Braden* was careful to *distinguish* that situation from the general rule established in *Ahrens.*

> A further, *critical* development since our decision in *Ahrens* is the emergence of *new classes of prisoners* who are able to petition for habeas corpus because of the adoption of a more expansive definition of the 'custody' requirement of the habeas statute. The overruling of *McNally v. Hill* (1934), made it possible for prisoners in custody under one sentence to attack a sentence which they had not yet begun to serve. And it also enabled a petitioner held in one State to attack a detainer lodged against him by another State. In such a case, the State holding the prisoner in immediate confinement acts as agent for the demanding State, and the custodian State is presumably indifferent to the resolution of the prisoner's attack on the detainer. Here, for example, the petitioner is confined in Alabama, but his dispute is with the Commonwealth of Kentucky, not the State of Alabama. *Under these circumstances,* it would serve no useful purpose to apply the *Ahrens* rule and require that the action be brought in Alabama." ([E]mphases added).

This cannot conceivably be construed as an overturning of the *Ahrens* rule *in other circumstances.* Thus, *Braden* stands for the proposition, and only the proposition, that where a petitioner is in custody in multiple jurisdictions within the United States, he may seek a writ of habeas corpus in a jurisdiction in which he suffers legal confinement, though not physical confinement, if his challenge is to that legal confinement. Outside that class of cases, *Braden* did not question the general rule of *Ahrens* (much less that of *Eisentrager*). Where, as here, present physical custody is at issue, *Braden* is inapposite, and *Eisentrager* unquestionably controls.[4]

* * *

The reality is this: Today's opinion, and today's opinion alone, overrules *Eisentrager;* today's opinion, and today's opinion alone, extends the habeas statute, for the first time, to aliens held beyond the sovereign territory of the United States and beyond the territorial jurisdiction of its courts. No reasons are given for this result; no acknowledgment of its consequences made. By spurious reliance on *Braden* the Court evades explaining why *stare decisis* can be disregarded, *and why Eisentrager was wrong.* Normally, we consider the interests of those who have relied on our decisions. Today, the Court springs a trap on the Executive, subjecting Guantanamo Bay to the oversight of the federal courts even though it has never before been thought to be within their jurisdiction—and thus making it a foolish place to have housed alien wartime detainees.

II

In abandoning the venerable statutory line drawn in *Eisentrager,* the Court boldly extends the scope of the habeas statute to the four corners of the earth. Part III of its opinion asserts that *Braden* stands for the proposition that "a district court acts 'within [its] respective jurisdiction' within the meaning of § 2241 as long as 'the custodian can be reached by service of process.' " Endorsement of that proposition is repeated in Part IV. ("Section 2241, by its terms, requires nothing more [than the District Court's jurisdiction over petitioners' custodians]").

The consequence of this holding, as applied to aliens outside the country, is breathtaking. It permits an alien captured in a foreign theater of active combat to bring a § 2241 petition against the Secretary of Defense. Over the course of the last century, the United States has held millions of alien prisoners abroad. A great many of these prisoners

---

[4] * * * Justice Kennedy recognizes that *Eisentrager* controls, but misconstrues that opinion. He thinks it makes jurisdiction under the habeas statute turn on the circumstances of the detainees' confinement—including, apparently, the availability of legal proceedings and the length of detention. The *Eisentrager* Court mentioned those circumstances, however, only in the course of its *constitutional* analysis, and not in its application of the statute. It is quite impossible to read § 2241 as conditioning its geographic scope upon them. Among the consequences of making jurisdiction turn upon circumstances of confinement are (1) that courts would *always* have authority to inquire into circumstances of confinement, and (2) that the Executive would be unable to know with certainty that any given prisoner-of-war camp is immune from writs of habeas corpus. And among the questions this approach raises: When does definite detention become indefinite? How much process will suffice to stave off jurisdiction? If there is a terrorist attack at Guantanamo Bay, will the area suddenly fall outside the habeas statute because it is no longer "far removed from any hostilities"? Justice Kennedy's approach provides enticing law-school-exam imponderables in an area where certainty is called for.

would no doubt have complained about the circumstances of their capture and the terms of their confinement. The military is currently detaining over 600 prisoners at Guantanamo Bay alone; each detainee undoubtedly has complaints—real or contrived—about those terms and circumstances. The Court's unheralded expansion of federal-court jurisdiction is not even mitigated by a comforting assurance that the legion of ensuing claims will be easily resolved on the merits. To the contrary, the Court says that the "[p]etitioners' allegations * * * unquestionably describe 'custody in violation of the Constitution or laws or treaties of the United States.'" From this point forward, federal courts will entertain petitions from these prisoners, and others like them around the world, challenging actions and events far away, and forcing the courts to oversee one aspect of the Executive's conduct of a foreign war.

Today's carefree Court disregards, without a word of acknowledgment, the dire warning of a more circumspect Court in *Eisentrager:*

> To grant the writ to these prisoners might mean that our army must transport them across the seas for hearing. This would require allocation for shipping space, guarding personnel, billeting and rations. It might also require transportation for whatever witnesses the prisoners desired to call as well as transportation for those necessary to defend legality of the sentence. The writ, since it is held to be a matter of right, would be equally available to enemies during active hostilities as in the present twilight between war and peace. Such trials would hamper the war effort and bring aid and comfort to the enemy. They would diminish the prestige of our commanders, not only with enemies but with wavering neutrals. It would be difficult to devise more effective fettering of a field commander than to allow the very enemies he is ordered to reduce to submission to call him to account in his own civil courts and divert his efforts and attention from the military offensive abroad to the legal defensive at home. Nor is it unlikely that the result of such enemy litigiousness would be conflict between judicial and military opinion highly comforting to enemies of the United States.

These results should not be brought about lightly, and certainly not without a textual basis in the statute and on the strength of nothing more than a decision dealing with an Alabama prisoner's ability to seek habeas in Kentucky.

III

Part IV of the Court's opinion, dealing with the status of Guantanamo Bay, is a puzzlement.

* * *

The Court gives only two reasons why the presumption against extraterritorial effect does not apply to Guantanamo Bay. First, the Court says (without any further elaboration) that "the United States exercises 'complete jurisdiction and control' over the Guantanamo Bay Naval Base [under the terms of a 1903 lease agreement], and may continue to exercise such control permanently if it so chooses [under the terms of a 1934 Treaty]." But that lease agreement explicitly recognized "the continuance of the ultimate sovereignty of the Republic of Cuba over the [leased areas]," and the Executive Branch—whose head is "exclusively responsible" for the "conduct of diplomatic and foreign affairs,"—affirms that the lease and treaty do not render Guantanamo Bay the sovereign territory of the United States.

The Court does not explain how "complete jurisdiction and control" without sovereignty causes an enclave to be part of the United States for purposes of its domestic laws. Since "jurisdiction and control" obtained through a lease is no different in effect from "jurisdiction and control" acquired by lawful force of arms, parts of Afghanistan and Iraq should logically be regarded as subject to our domestic laws. Indeed, if "jurisdiction and control" rather than sovereignty were the test, so should the Landsberg Prison in Germany, where the United States held the *Eisentrager* detainees.

* * *

The last part of the Court's Part IV analysis digresses from the point that the presumption against extraterritorial application does not apply to Guantanamo Bay. Rather, it is directed to the contention that the Court's approach to habeas jurisdiction—applying it to aliens abroad—is "consistent with the historical reach of the writ." None of the authorities it cites comes close to supporting that claim. Its first set of authorities involves claims by aliens detained in what is indisputably domestic territory. Those cases are irrelevant because they do not purport to address the territorial reach of the writ. The remaining cases involve issuance of the writ to " 'exempt jurisdictions' " and "other dominions under the sovereign's control." These cases are inapposite for two reasons: Guantanamo Bay is not a sovereign dominion, and even if it were, jurisdiction would be limited to subjects.

* * *

Departure from our rule of *stare decisis* in statutory cases is always extraordinary; it ought to be unthinkable when the departure has a potentially harmful effect upon the Nation's conduct of a war. The Commander in Chief and his subordinates had every reason to expect that the internment of combatants at Guantanamo Bay would not have the consequence of bringing the cumbersome machinery of our domestic courts into military affairs. Congress is in session. If it wished to change federal judges' habeas jurisdiction from what this Court had previously held that to be, it could have done so. And it could have done so by intelligent revision of the statute,[7] instead of by today's clumsy, coun-

---

[7] It could, for example, provide for jurisdiction by placing Guantanamo Bay within the territory of an existing district court; or by creating a district court for Guantanamo Bay,

tertextual reinterpretation that confers upon wartime prisoners greater habeas rights than domestic detainees. The latter must challenge their present physical confinement in the district of their confinement, *see Rumsfeld v. Padilla* (2004), whereas under today's strange holding Guantanamo Bay detainees can petition in any of the 94 federal judicial districts. The fact that extraterritorially located detainees lack the district of detention that the statute requires has been converted from a factor that precludes their ability to bring a petition at all into a factor that frees them to petition wherever they wish—and, as a result, to forum shop. For this Court to create such a monstrous scheme in time of war, and in frustration of our military commanders' reliance upon clearly stated prior law, is judicial adventurism of the worst sort. I dissent.

Notes and Questions

1. *Rasul's* holding is clear. The federal courts have jurisdiction over habeas corpus petitions filed by the foreign nationals captured abroad and incarcerated at the Guantanamo Bay Naval Base in Cuba. It is less clear whether aliens captured by the military and held in other places around the world may also petition the federal courts. At the outset of his opinion, Justice Stevens calls the issue facing the Court "narrow," while Justice Scalia accuses the majority of "boldly extend[ing] the scope of the habeas statute to the four corners of the earth" by "permit[ting] an alien captured in a foreign theater of active combat to bring a § 2241 petition against the Secretary of Defense." The majority opinion appears to extend habeas jurisdiction beyond the Guantanamo detainees, but how far is anyone's guess.

a) Much turns on precedent, particularly *Johnson v. Eisentrager*, 339 U.S. 763, 70 S.Ct. 936, 94 L.Ed. 1255 (1950). *Eisentrager* denied habeas jurisdiction to military prisoners exhibiting six specific characteristics. What are those characteristics? Perhaps Justice Kennedy suggested the easiest and cleanest way to resolve *Rasul* in his opinion concurring in the judgment. He read *Eisentrager* as a separation-of-powers case. For prisoners exhibiting the *Eisentrager* characteristics, a habeas petition was not "within the proper realm of judicial power." Instead, the petition concerned matters properly within executive and legislative control. Because the *Rasul* facts are distinguishable from *Eisentrager,* Justice Kennedy believes the habeas petitions can go forward while the Court "remains true to the reasoning of *Eisentrager.*" How does Justice Kennedy think the cases are distinguishable? Why do the factual differences he identifies justify a different outcome? Justice Scalia contends that Justice Kennedy's approach of distinguishing *Eisentrager* on its facts raises "imponderables in an area where certainty is called for." What are the imponderables? Will they raise serious problems for the Executive, or are Justice Scalia's fears exaggerated?

b) Justices Stevens and Scalia argue at length about the Court of Appeals for the District of Columbia's reasoning in *Eisentrager*, apparently seeking support for their different views of the Supreme Court's reasoning. For Justice Stevens, the key issue is not separation of powers but instead

as it did for the Panama Canal Zone.

whether *Eisentrager* at base was about *constitutional* entitlement to habeas corpus under the Suspension Clause or about *statutory* entitlement under § 2241. Writing for a bare majority on this point, Justice Stevens concludes that *Eisentrager* was about constitutional entitlement. Because subsequent cases interpreting the habeas corpus statute expanded the statutory entitlement, "persons detained outside the territorial jurisdiction of any federal district court no longer need rely on the Constitution as the source of their right to federal habeas review." Justice Scalia argues that *Eisentrager* interpreted both the constitutional and statutory habeas provisions and allowed jurisdiction under neither. Justice Scalia goes on to argue that the majority can avoid *Eisentrager* only by overruling it, a step the majority appears not to want to take, or at least not to take directly. Ultimately, as Justice Kennedy claims, Justice Scalia may win the battle over whether one can reasonably read *Braden* to "overrule[] the statutory predicate to *Eisentrager*'s holding," but he loses the war on the issue of whether *Eisentrager* controls *Rasul*.

c) Consider why the majority wants to cast *Eisentrager* as a constitutional decision rather than a decision restricting both constitutional and statutory habeas corpus. Think again of the six characteristics of the *Eisentrager* detainees. Could the military duplicate those characteristics for prisoners captured in Afghanistan, Iraq, or in other countries around the globe? On Justice Scalia's reasoning, can the federal courts exercise habeas jurisdiction over such people? On Justice Stevens'? *Must* the federal courts exercise jurisdiction over habeas petitions by such people after *Rasul*, or is the Court merely leaving the possibility open?

2. The answer to the last question may depend in part on how much control and dominion the United States must exercise over the place where aliens are detained. Justice Stevens cites old English cases stating that habeas writs could run to "exempt jurisdictions" or to places that were "no part of the realm" if the territory was "under the subjection of the Crown." He asserts that later cases confirmed that the reach of the writ depended on the practical question of "the exact extent and nature of the jurisdiction or dominion exercised in fact by the Crown." Consider Iraq. Does the United States exercise sufficient dominion over that country to support habeas jurisdiction over aliens detained there? If not, did it before the official transfer of power on June 28, 2004? Would it be sufficient if the United States exercised dominion over the specific place where the prisoner was detained? Must a federal district court make a factual inquiry into the extent of American military control over a particular city or province in deciding whether to hear a petition from someone detained there?

3. Is this actually a case about Abu Ghraib Prison, even though the abuses that occurred there did not come to light until after the Court heard argument in *Rasul* case and were not a part of the record? Or, by leaving the territorial scope of habeas corpus unclear, is the Court signaling the Executive not to try to circumvent the Court's decision by moving the Guantanamo detainees to Afghanistan or to some other location not under such clear American control?

NOTE ON *RUMSFELD V. PADILLA*, 542 U.S. 426,
124 S.Ct. 2711, 159 L.Ed.2d 513 (2004)

Decided the same day as *Rasul*, this case clarified the law dealing with custody and venue in habeas corpus cases for petitioners physically confined within the United States. Padilla, an American citizen, was arrested at Chicago's O'Hare Airport as he stepped off a plane arriving from Pakistan. He was brought to the Southern District of New York on a material witness warrant and held in federal criminal custody. His assigned counsel moved to vacate the material witness warrant. Two days before the hearing on the motion, President Bush ordered Secretary of Defense Rumsfeld to seize Padilla as an enemy combatant. The same day, the government informed the district judge of the order in an *ex parte* proceeding and asked the court to vacate the material witness warrant. Padilla was immediately taken by the military and moved to a Navy brig in South Carolina, where he was held incommunicado. Two days later, his attorney filed a habeas corpus petition in the Southern District claiming the military detention violated several federal constitutional provisions and naming President Bush, Secretary Rumsfeld, and Melanie A. Marr, the Commander of the Naval brig as respondents.

The district court held that Rumsfeld's "personal involvement" in Padilla's military custody made him a proper respondent and that it could exercise jurisdiction over the Secretary under New York's long-arm statute. On the merits, the court held the President had authority to detain citizens seized on American soil as enemy combatants, although the court held Padilla had a right to controvert the alleged facts against him and to consult with counsel. The Second Circuit reversed. The court agreed that Secretary Rumsfeld was a proper respondent, reasoning that the Supreme Court has not required the immediate physical custodian to be named in cases where the petitioner is detained for "other than federal criminal violations." Under the unique facts of this case, Secretary Rumsfeld exercised "the legal reality of control" over Padilla. The court of appeals also agreed the district court had jurisdiction over Rumsfeld under the state long-arm statute. On the merits, the court of appeals reversed the district court, holding the President had no authority to detain Padilla militarily. Accordingly, the court ordered the Secretary to release Padilla from military custody within 30 days.

The Supreme Court divided the issue of whether the Southern District had jurisdiction over Padilla's habeas petition into two related subquestions: "First, who is the proper respondent to that petition? And second, does the Southern District have jurisdiction over him or her?" As to the first subquestion, the Court began by looking at the language of §§ 2242-43, which refer to "the person" having custody of the petitioner. The majority stated the language supports the "default rule" in "core challenges" to present physical confinement: the proper respondent is the warden of the facility where the petitioner is held, not the Attorney General or some other "remote supervisory official." Padilla argued that the Court had expanded the concept of custody to include various restrictions on liberty short of physical detention, and therefore the immediate physical custodian rule need not apply. The Court agreed with the premise but not the conclusion, because Padilla was physically confined and was challenging that confinement. Thus, cases like *Braden v. Kentucky*, 410 U.S. 484, 93 S.Ct. 1123, 35 L.Ed.2d 443 (1973), which considered an Alabama prisoner to be "in custody" in Kentucky where a detainer was lodged against him and thus allowed him to name as respondent the Kentucky court where the detainer was lodged, were simply inapposite. The Court also distinguished *Ex parte Endo*, 323 U.S. 283, 65 S.Ct. 209, 89 L.Ed. 243 (1944), which allowed the petitioner to name as her custodian in California respondent, even though she was detained in Utah. Endo had filed her petition in California while detained there *before* being moved to Utah. Because the California court properly acquired jurisdiction, it could continue to exercise it. Padilla, by contrast, was transferred to South Carolina two days *before* the New York habeas proceeding began, and thus the New York federal court did not properly acquire jurisdiction over the proceeding.

Concluding that South Carolina brig Commander Marr was Padilla's custodian and thus the proper respondent in a habeas petition, the Court turned to the question whether the New York federal court had jurisdiction over her. The Court concluded it did not. Section 2241(a) limits district courts to granting habeas relief "within their respective jurisdictions." In core habeas petitions challenging present physical confinement, the only court having jurisdiction over the custodian is a court in the district where the petitioner is detained. The Court stated that an important purpose of the rule is to avoid "rampant forum shopping" by habeas petitioners, who would otherwise be able to name high-level supervisory officials as respondents and file a petition wherever the officials were amenable to long-arm jurisdiction. The Court again distinguished *Braden* because the petitioner was challenging future, not present, custody. The Court also stated that *Braden* did not authorize extraterritorial service of process on a respondent. Braden served his future Kentucky custodian in Kentucky, where the habeas petition was filed. Thus, one should not read *Braden* to authorize courts to use state long-arm statutes to obtain jurisdiction over respondents located outside the district where the petition is filed. The Court also distinguished *Strait v. Laird*, 406 U.S. 341, 92 S.Ct. 1693, 32 L.Ed.2d 141 (1972), which upheld the jurisdiction of a California federal court over a habeas petition filed by a California resident not in physical custody against his "nominal" custodian, the commanding officer of the Army's records center, who was located in Indiana. In Padilla's case, there was no need to designate a "nominal" custodian because Padilla had a real custodian located in the same district where he was detained. Finally, the Court refused to make a special exception based on the important issues involved in the case.

Justices O'Connor, Scalia, Kennedy, and Thomas joined Chief Justice Rehnquist's opinion for the Court. Justice Kennedy filed a concurring opinion, which Justice O'Connor joined. He wrote separately "to state my understanding of how the statute should be interpreted in light of the Court's holding." Justice Kennedy's "understanding" appears to be at odds in important ways with Chief Justice Rehnquist's opinion. Since Justices Kennedy and O'Connor were a part of the five-justice majority, Justice Kennedy's opinion is critical to determining what rules emerge from this case. Most importantly, Justice Kennedy did not believe that the rules requiring a habeas petition to be filed against the immediate custodian in the district where the custodian is located to be limitations on subject matter jurisdiction. Rather, he viewed them as rules of venue or personal jurisdiction. Thus, the government can waive the rules. In addition, Justice Kennedy would have acknowledged exceptions to the rules beyond those recognized for nonphysical custody (*Strait*), dual custody (*Braden*) or removal of the petitioner from the district after the petition is filed (*Endo*). Specifically, if the government removed a prisoner from a district and concealed his whereabouts, a petition could be filed in the original district. Similarly, if the government informed counsel where the petitioner had been moved but then kept moving him so that a filing could not catch up, habeas would lie in the district or district from which the petitioner had been removed. Since none of these circumstances occurred in Padilla's case, Justice Kennedy concurred in the judgment of the Court.

Justice Stevens dissented, joined by Justices Souter, Ginsburg, and Breyer. Justice Stevens thought this case very close to *Endo*. The government removed Padilla from New York without notice to his counsel. Justice Stevens hypothesized that counsel would have filed a habeas petition immediately if she had been informed of the President's order to seize Padilla. In that instance, Padilla's immediate custodian would have been physically present in New York, acting on orders of the Secretary of Defense. The dissenters thought allowing the government to obtain a tactical advantage by proceeding *ex parte* was unfair. Moreover, when Padilla's counsel filed the petition two days later, she still had not been officially informed by the government where her client was located. Instead, she understood from the media that her client was in South Carolina.

Even if the habeas petition was considered filed after Padilla was removed from the district, Justice Stevens thought there was sufficient precedent to make an exception to usual practice. He accused the majority of being

> disingenuous at best to classify respondent's petition with run-of-the-mill collateral attacks on federal criminal convictions. On the contrary, this case is singular not only because it calls into question decisions made by the Secretary himself, but also because those decisions have created a unique and unprecedented threat to the freedom of every American citizen.

The dissenters agreed with Justices Kennedy and O'Connor that the question of the proper forum was not jurisdictional, thus forming a majority of six on this issue. The dissenters thought it a matter of venue.

When analyzed under venue principles, they thought the New York district court was the more convenient forum. The government initially brought Padilla to New York on a material witness warrant, and the New York district judge and local counsel were familiar with the legal and factual issues underlying his case.

Notes and Questions

1. Are the rules requiring a person in physical custody to bring his petition against the immediate custodian and in the district of detention rules of subject matter jurisdiction, venue or, perhaps, personal jurisdiction? Is there any way to know other than by counting votes? Is the fact that the Court has announced several exceptions to these rules determinative, as Justice Kennedy suggests, or does that merely imply that the rules are not about subject matter jurisdiction?

2. Was the majority right to distinguish *Endo*, or should it have extended *Endo* to cover this case, as Justice Stevens suggested?

3. Ironically, in habeas cases an American citizen detained in the United States may have less choice of forum than an alien detained abroad. Padilla must file his petition in South Carolina, while the Guantanamo detainees may be able to choose from several districts. In a footnote in *Padilla*, Chief Justice Rehnquist noted that in cases involving American citizens detained overseas, and thus not within the territory of any district court, the Court has permitted petitioners to name supervisory officials as respondents and to file their petitions in the districts where the respondents resided. Presumably, the same rule would apply to the aliens detained at Guantanamo. If a supervisory official, *e.g.* the Secretary of Defense, works in Washington, D.C., but resides in Virginia, a detainee might be able to file in either. If military officers in the chain of command lived or served in other districts, the petitioner might also proceed there.

4. Jose Padilla subsequently filed a habeas petition in the proper venue, and the case made its way to the Fourth Circuit , which upheld his detention as an enemy combatant. Perhaps sensing trouble in the Supreme Court in light of the 2004 *Hamdi* and *Padilla* decisions,[31] the government brought criminal charges against Mr. Padilla and transferred him to the civilian courts. He was convicted and on January 22, 2008, he was sentenced to seventeen years and four months in prison.

NOTE ON RECENT DEVELOPMENTS IN HABEAS CORPUS AND THE WAR ON TERROR

Congress responded to *Rasul* by passing the Detainee Treatment Act of 2005, Pub. L. 109-148, 119 Stat. 2739 (2005). The Act addressed a wide range of subject relating to persons detained in the War on Terror. Section 1005 restricted federal court habeas jurisdiction over aliens detained at Guantanamo Bay. Section 1005(e) of the Act amended 28

---

[31] The four dissenting Justices in *Padilla* made clear their belief that extended, incommunicado detention for the purpose of interrogation is unconstitutional, calling such detention "the hallmark of the Star Chamber."

U.S.C. § 2241, which contains general provisions on the power of federal courts to issue a writ of habeas corpus.: : "(e) Except as provided in section 1005 of the Detainee Treatment Act of 2005, no court, justice, or judge shall have jurisdiction to hear or consider—(1) an application for a writ of habeas corpus filed by or on behalf of an alien detained by the Department of Defense at Guantanamo Bay, Cuba." Subsection (2) similarly removes jurisdiction over any other actions by Guantanamo detainees relating to any aspect of their confinement if they are in military custody or are designated enemy combatants. Subsection (2) also provides limited review by the District of Columbia Circuit of an enemy combatant determination. Subsection (3) mirrors subsection (2) in restricting judicial review of final decisions of military commissions. The effective-date provision reads :

> (1) IN GENERAL—This section shall take effect on the date of the enactment of the Act.

> (2) REVIEW OF COMBAT STATUS TRIBUNAL AND MILITARY COMMISSION DECISIONS.—Paragraphs (2) and (3) of subsection (e) shall apply with respect to any claim whose review is governed by one of such paragraphs and that is pending on or after the date of the enactment of this Act.

Section 1005 was silent about whether subsection (1) applied to habeas petitions pending on the Act's enactment date.

Prior to the statute, the United States Supreme Court granted certiorari in *Hamdan v. Rumsfeld*, 546 U.S. 1002, 126 S.Ct. 622, 163 L.Ed.2d 504 (2005), a habeas case brought by an alien detained at Guantanamo Bay. The government argued that Congress' failure to explicitly reserve jurisdiction over pending habeas cases should erect a presumption against jurisdiction under existing precedent. The Court rejected this argument, applying the principle of statutory construction that a negative inference is appropriate when Congress excludes language from one section of a statute that it includes in other sections of the same statute. The Court found that Congress considered the "respective temporal reach" of all three subsections together and omitted subsection (1) from the directive that subsections (2) and (3) apply to pending cases "only after having rejected earlier proposed versions of the statute that would have included what is now paragraph (1) within the scope of that directive." This history weighed heavily against the Government's argument that subsection (1) applies to pending habeas cases. Justice Scalia filed a spirited dissent on this issue, arguing that the plain meaning of section 1005(e) required applying it to all pending cases. On the merits, the Court held that the military commission convened to try Hamdan could not proceed because its structure and procedures violated the Uniform Code of Military Justice and the Geneva Conventions.

Congress responded by passing the Military Commissions Act of 2006, Pub. L. No. 109-366, 120 Stat. 2600 (2006). Section 7 declared that "[n]o court, justice, or judge shall have jurisdiction" to entertain a habeas corpus petition or any other action against the federal government or its agents concerning "any aspect of the detention, transfer, treatment, trial or conditions of confinement" of an alien who has either been determined to be an enemy combatant or is awaiting such a determination. Section 7(b) declared that this prohibition "shall apply to all cases, without exception, pending on or after the date of enactment of this Act." On its face, the Act plainly appears to require dismissal of pending habeas petitions from Guantanamo detainees.

On February 20, 2007, the United States Court of Appeals for the District of Columbia Circuit decided *Boumediene v. Bush*, 476 F.3d 981 (D.C. Cir.), *cert. granted,* ___ U.S.___, 127 S.Ct. 3078, 168 L.Ed.2d 755 (2007), which involved consolidated appeals in cases brought by Guantanamo detainees. The majority and dissent agreed that the Act withdrew jurisdiction over pending cases, thus raising the issue of whether the Act violates the Suspension Clause[32] of the Constitution. The majority held that the Act did not violate the Suspension Clause because the writ simply did not extend to aliens without presence or property within the United States. The dissenting judge reached a contrary conclusion:

> The Suspension Clause limits the removal of habeas corpus, at least as the writ was understood at common law, to times of rebellion or invasion unless Congress provides as adequate alternative remedy. The writ would have reached the detainees at common law, and Congress has neither provided an adequate alternative remedy * * * nor invoked the exception to the Clause by making the required findings to suspend the writ.

Initially the Supreme court denied certiorari, but on June 29, 2007, it reversed itself. It will decide the case in the spring of 2008.

D.   FEDERAL COURT REVIEW OF STATE CONVICTIONS

1. *State Factual Findings and Federal Evidentiary Hearings*

When a federal habeas court holds an evidentiary hearing, it treads in an area of great sensitivity. Consider, after all, that the state has already held a full trial and has expended appellate time on the case as well. There is a state court record that contains "the facts." For the federal court to proceed in such circumstances clearly implies that the state court record is somehow defective and that the state court proceeding was not adequate to develop the relevant facts fully. That the states should take offense at the implication is not surprising.

---

[32] U.S. CONST. art. 1, § 9, cl. 2: "The Privilege of the Writ of Habeas Corpus shall not be suspended, unless when in Cases of Rebellion or Invasion the public Safety may require it."

As explained in Section A, *Townsend v. Sain* (1963) and the 1966 amendments to 28 U.S.C. § 2254(d) liberalized the standards for granting evidentiary hearings. Although § 2254(d) said that state factual findings "shall be presumed to be correct," the presumption was rebuttable in the circumstances the statute listed. When the state court hearing did not develop the material facts adequately (circumstance 5 in the *Townsend* list, circumstance 3 in the statute), *Townsend* held that the deliberate-bypass standard applied; that is, a hearing could be denied only if the petitioner was guilty of "inexcusable neglect."

Keeney v. Tamayo-Reyes (1992), shifted from the deliberate-bypass standard to a cause-and-prejudice standard that had developed in the context of prisoners' failure to raise legal arguments in state proceedings. The old standard placed the burden on the state to demonstrate that a petitioner had deliberately bypassed an opportunity to develop the material facts during state proceedings. Under the new standard, a prisoner was not entitled to an evidentiary hearing unless he could demonstrate good cause (some objective reason) for having failed to develop the facts in state court *and* prejudice—a substantial probability that the result in the state proceeding would have been different in a trial without the alleged constitutional violation. The shift to the cause-and-prejudice standard made it much more difficult for petitioners to obtain an evidentiary hearing.

AEDPA replaced § 2254(d) of the 1966 statute with a new provision, § 2254(e). Section 2254(e)(1) continues the presumption that state fact findings were correct. Section 2254(e)(2) contains a new provision governing cases where the material facts were not adequately developed at the state court hearing. The Supreme Court considered the new provision in the following case.

WILLIAMS (MICHAEL) v. TAYLOR
Supreme Court of the United States, 2000.
529 U.S. 420, 120 S.Ct. 1479, 146 L.Ed.2d 435.

JUSTICE KENNEDY delivered the opinion of the Court.

Petitioner Michael Wayne Williams received a capital sentence for the murders of Morris Keller, Jr., and Keller's wife, Mary Elizabeth. Petitioner later sought a writ of habeas corpus in federal court. Accompanying his petition was a request for an evidentiary hearing on constitutional claims which, he alleged, he had been unable to develop in state-court proceedings. The question in this case is whether 28 U.S.C. § 2254(e)(2) as amended by the Antiterrorism and Effective Death Penalty Act of 1996 (AEDPA), bars the evidentiary hearing petitioner seeks. If petitioner "has failed to develop the factual basis of [his] claim[s] in State court proceedings," his case is subject to § 2254(e)(2), and he may not receive a hearing because he concedes his inability to satisfy the statute's further stringent conditions for excusing the deficiency.

I

[Petitioner and Jeffrey Alan Cruse committed the murders in 1993. Cruse was the State's main witness. After the petitioner was convicted and sentenced to death, Cruse pleaded guilty in a separate proceeding. Upon the prosecutor's recommendation to spare Cruse' life because of his testimony against the petitioner, Cruse was sentenced to life imprisonment. Petitioner's conviction and sentence were upheld by the Virginia appellate courts, and the Supreme Court denied certiorari. Petitioner then filed a state collateral attack claiming the State failed to disclose a second plea agreement it had reached with Cruse. (An earlier agreement was revoked when prosecutors discovered Cruse had failed to admit some of his wrongdoing.) The state courts denied relief and the Supreme Court again denied certiorari.]

* * *

Petitioner filed a habeas petition in the United States District Court for the Eastern District of Virginia on November 20, 1996. In addition to his claim regarding the alleged undisclosed agreement between the Commonwealth and Cruse, the petition raised three claims relevant to questions now before us. First, petitioner claimed the prosecution had violated *Brady v. Maryland* (1963) in failing to disclose a report of a confidential pretrial psychiatric examination of Cruse. Second, petitioner alleged his trial was rendered unfair by the seating of a juror who at *voir dire* had not revealed possible sources of bias. Finally, petitioner alleged one of the prosecutors committed misconduct in failing to reveal his knowledge of the juror's possible bias.

The District Court granted an evidentiary hearing on the undisclosed agreement and the allegations of juror bias and prosecutorial misconduct but denied a hearing on the psychiatric report. Before the evidentiary hearing could be held, the Commonwealth filed an application for an emergency stay and a petition for a writ of mandamus and prohibition in the Court of Appeals. The Commonwealth argued that petitioner's evidentiary hearing was prohibited by 28 U.S.C. § 2254(e)(2). A divided panel of the Court of Appeals granted the emergency stay and remanded for the District Court to apply the statute to petitioner's request for an evidentiary hearing. On remand, the District Court vacated its order granting an evidentiary hearing and dismissed the petition, having determined petitioner could not satisfy § 2254(e)(2)'s requirements.

The Court of Appeals affirmed. It first considered petitioner's argument that § 2254(e)(2) did not apply to his case because he had been diligent in attempting to develop his claims in state court. Citing its decision in *Cardwell v. Greene,* the Court of Appeals agreed with petitioner that § 2254(e)(2) would not apply if he had exercised diligence in state court. The court held, however, that petitioner had not been diligent and so had "failed to develop" in state court the factual bases of his *Brady,* juror bias, and prosecutorial misconduct claims. The Court of Appeals concluded petitioner could not satisfy the statute's conditions for excusing his failure to develop the facts and held him barred from receiving an evidentiary hearing. The Court of Appeals ruled in the alternative that, even if § 2254(e)(2) did not apply, petitioner would be ineligible for an evidentiary hearing under the cause and prejudice standard of pre-AEDPA law.

Addressing petitioner's claim of an undisclosed informal agreement between the Commonwealth and Cruse, the Court of Appeals rejected it on the merits under 28 U.S.C. § 2254(d)(1) and, as a result, did not consider whether § 2254(e)(2) applied.

On October 18, 1999, petitioner filed an application for stay of execution and a petition for a writ of certiorari. On October 28, we stayed petitioner's execution and granted certiorari to decide whether § 2254(e)(2) precludes him from receiving an evidentiary hearing on his claims. We now affirm in part and reverse in part.

II

A

Petitioner filed his federal habeas petition after AEDPA's effective date, so the statute applies to his case. The Commonwealth argues AEDPA bars petitioner from receiving an evidentiary hearing on any claim whose factual basis was not developed in state court, absent narrow circumstances not applicable here. Petitioner did not develop, or raise, his claims of juror bias, prosecutorial misconduct, or the prosecution's alleged *Brady* violation regarding Cruse's psychiatric report until he filed his federal habeas petition. Petitioner explains he could not have developed the claims earlier because he was unaware, through no fault of his own, of the underlying facts. As a consequence, petitioner contends, AEDPA erects no barrier to an evidentiary hearing in federal court.

Section 2254(e)(2), the provision which controls whether petitioner may receive an evidentiary hearing in federal district court on the claims that were not developed in the Virginia courts, becomes the central point of our analysis. It provides as follows:

> If the applicant has failed to develop the factual basis of a claim in State court proceedings, the court shall not hold an evidentiary hearing on the claim unless the applicant shows that—
>
> (A) the claim relies on—
>
> (i) a new rule of constitutional law, made retroactive to cases on collateral review by the Supreme Court, that was previously unavailable; or
>
> (ii) a factual predicate that could not have been previously discov-

ered through the exercise of due diligence; and

(B) the facts underlying the claim would be sufficient to establish by clear and convincing evidence that but for constitutional error, no reasonable factfinder would have found the applicant guilty of the underlying offense.

By the terms of its opening clause the statute applies only to prisoners who have "failed to develop the factual basis of a claim in State court proceedings." If the prisoner has failed to develop the facts, an evidentiary hearing cannot be granted unless the prisoner's case meets the other conditions of § 2254(e)(2). Here, petitioner concedes his case does not comply with § 2254(e)(2)(B), so he may receive an evidentiary hearing only if his claims fall outside the opening clause.

* * *

B

We start, as always, with the language of the statute. Section 2254(e)(2) begins with a conditional clause, "[i]f the applicant has failed to develop the factual basis of a claim in State court proceedings," which directs attention to the prisoner's efforts in state court. We ask first whether the factual basis was indeed developed in state court, a question susceptible, in the normal course, of a simple yes or no answer. Here the answer is no.

The Commonwealth would have the analysis begin and end there. Under its no-fault reading of the statute, if there is no factual development in the state court, the federal habeas court may not inquire into the reasons for the default when determining whether the opening clause of § 2254(e)(2) applies. We do not agree with the Commonwealth's interpretation of the word "failed."

We do not deny "fail" is sometimes used in a neutral way, not importing fault or want of diligence. So the phrase "We fail to understand his argument" can mean simply "We cannot understand his argument." This is not the sense in which the word "failed" is used here, however.

We give the words of a statute their " 'ordinary, contemporary, common meaning,' " absent an indication Congress intended them to bear some different import. In its customary and preferred sense, "fail" connotes some omission, fault, or negligence on the part of the person who has failed to do something. To say a person has failed in a duty implies he did not take the necessary steps to fulfill it. He is, as a consequence, at fault and bears responsibility for the failure. In this sense, a person is not at fault when his diligent efforts to perform an act are thwarted, for example, by the conduct of another or by happenstance. Fault lies, in those circumstances, either with the person who interfered with the accomplishment of the act or with no one at all. We conclude Congress used the word "failed" in the sense just described. Had Congress intended a no-fault standard, it would have had no difficulty in making its intent plain. It would have had to do no more than use, in lieu of the phrase "has failed to," the phrase "did not."

* * *

Our interpretation of § 2254(e)(2)'s opening clause has support in *Keeney v. Tamayo-Reyes* (1992), a case decided four years before AEDPA's enactment. In *Keeney,* a prisoner with little knowledge of English sought an evidentiary hearing in federal court, alleging his *nolo contendere* plea to a manslaughter charge was not knowing and voluntary because of inaccuracies in the translation of the plea proceedings. The prisoner had not developed the facts of his claim in state collateral proceedings, an omission caused by the negligence of his state postconviction counsel. The Court characterized this as the "prisoner's failure to develop material facts in state court." We required the prisoner to demonstrate cause and prejudice excusing the default before he could receive a hearing on his claim, unless the prisoner could "show that a fundamental miscarriage of justice would result from failure to hold a federal evidentiary hearing."

Section 2254(e)(2)'s initial inquiry into whether "the applicant has failed to develop the factual basis of a claim in State court proceedings" echoes *Keeney*'s language regarding "the state prisoner's failure to develop material facts in state court." In *Keeney,* the Court borrowed the cause and prejudice standard applied to procedurally defaulted claims, *see Wainwright v. Sykes* (1977), deciding there was no reason "to distinguish between failing to properly assert a federal claim in state court and failing in state court to properly develop such a claim." As is evident from the similarity between the Court's phrasing in *Keeney* and the opening clause of § 2254(e)(2), Congress intended to preserve at least one aspect of *Keeney*'s holding: prisoners who are at fault for the deficiency in the state-court record must satisfy a heightened standard to obtain an evidentiary hearing. To be sure, in requiring that prisoners who have not been diligent satisfy § 2254(e)(2)'s provisions rather than show cause and prejudice, and in eliminating a freestanding "miscarriage of justice" exception, Congress raised the bar *Keeney* imposed on prisoners who were not diligent in state-court proceedings. Contrary to the Commonwealth's position, however, there is no basis in the text of § 2254(e)(2) to believe Congress used "fail" in a different sense than the Court did in *Keeney* or otherwise intended the statute's further, more stringent requirements to control the availability of an evidentiary hearing in a broader class of cases than were covered by *Keeney*'s cause and prejudice standard.

* * *

Interpreting § 2254(e)(2) so that "failed" requires lack of diligence or some other fault avoids putting it in needless tension with § 2254(d). A prisoner who developed his claim in state court and can prove the state court's decision was "contrary to, or involved an unreasonable application of, clearly established Federal law, as determined by the Supreme Court of the United States," is not barred from obtaining relief by § 2254(d)(1). If the opening clause of § 2254(e)(2) covers a request for an evidentiary hearing on a claim which was pursued with diligence but remained undeveloped in state court because, for instance, the prosecution concealed the facts, a prisoner lacking clear and convincing evidence of innocence could be barred from a hearing on the claim even if he could satisfy § 2254(d). See 28 U.S.C. § 2254(e)(2)(B). The "failed to develop" clause does not bear this harsh reading, which would attribute to Congress a purpose or design to bar evidentiary hearings for diligent prisoners with meritorious claims just because the prosecution's conduct went undetected in state court. We see no indication that Congress by this language intended to remove the distinction between a prisoner who is at fault and one who is not.

The Commonwealth argues a reading of "failed to develop" premised on fault empties § 2254(e)(2)(A)(ii) of its meaning. To treat the prisoner's lack of diligence in state court as a prerequisite for application of § 2254(e)(2), the Commonwealth contends, renders a nullity of the statute's own diligence provision requiring the prisoner to show "a factual predicate [of his claim] could not have been previously discovered through the exercise of due diligence." § 2254(e)(2)(A)(ii). We disagree.

The Commonwealth misconceives the inquiry mandated by the opening clause of § 2254(e)(2). The question is not whether the facts could have been discovered but instead whether the prisoner was diligent in his efforts. The purpose of the fault component of "failed" is to ensure the prisoner undertakes his own diligent search for evidence. Diligence for purposes of the opening clause depends upon whether the prisoner made a reasonable attempt, in light of the information available at the time, to investigate and pursue claims in state court; it does not depend, as the Commonwealth would have it, upon whether those efforts could have been successful. Though lack of diligence will not bar an evidentiary hearing if efforts to discover the facts would have been in vain, see § 2254(e)(2)(A)(ii), and there is a convincing claim of innocence, see § 2254(e)(2)(B), only a prisoner who has neglected his rights in state court need satisfy these conditions. The statute's later reference to diligence pertains to cases in which the facts could not have been discovered, whether there was diligence or not. In this important respect § 2254(e)(2)(A)(ii) bears a close resemblance to (e)(2)(A)(i), which applies to a new rule that was not available at the time of the earlier proceedings. ("[W]ords and people are known by their companions"). In these two parallel provisions Congress has given prisoners who fall within § 2254(e)(2)'s opening clause an opportunity to obtain an evidentiary hearing where the legal or factual basis of the claims did not exist at the time of state-court proceedings.

We are not persuaded by the Commonwealth's further argument

that anything less than a no-fault understanding of the opening clause is contrary to AEDPA's purpose to further the principles of comity, finality, and federalism. There is no doubt Congress intended AEDPA to advance these doctrines. Federal habeas corpus principles must inform and shape the historic and still vital relation of mutual respect and common purpose existing between the States and the federal courts. In keeping this delicate balance we have been careful to limit the scope of federal intrusion into state criminal adjudications and to safeguard the States' interest in the integrity of their criminal and collateral proceedings. * * *

It is consistent with these principles to give effect to Congress' intent to avoid unneeded evidentiary hearings in federal habeas corpus, while recognizing the statute does not equate prisoners who exercise diligence in pursuing their claims with those who do not. Principles of exhaustion are premised upon recognition by Congress and the Court that state judiciaries have the duty and competence to vindicate rights secured by the Constitution in state criminal proceedings. Diligence will require in the usual case that the prisoner, at a minimum, seek an evidentiary hearing in state court in the manner prescribed by state law. "Comity * * * dictates that when a prisoner alleges that his continued confinement for a state court conviction violates federal law, the state courts should have the first opportunity to review this claim and provide any necessary relief." For state courts to have their rightful opportunity to adjudicate federal rights, the prisoner must be diligent in developing the record and presenting, if possible, all claims of constitutional error. If the prisoner fails to do so, himself or herself contributing to the absence of a full and fair adjudication in state court, § 2254(e)(2) prohibits an evidentiary hearing to develop the relevant claims in federal court, unless the statute's other stringent requirements are met. Federal courts sitting in habeas are not an alternative forum for trying facts and issues which a prisoner made insufficient effort to pursue in state proceedings. Yet comity is not served by saying a prisoner "has failed to develop the factual basis of a claim" where he was unable to develop his claim in state court despite diligent effort. In that circumstance, an evidentiary hearing is not barred by § 2254(e)(2).

III

Now we apply the statutory test. If there has been no lack of diligence at the relevant stages in the state proceedings, the prisoner has not "failed to develop" the facts under § 2254(e)(2)'s opening clause, and he will be excused from showing compliance with the balance of the subsection's requirements. We find lack of diligence as to one of the three claims but not as to the other two.

A

Petitioner did not exercise the diligence required to preserve the claim that nondisclosure of Cruse's psychiatric report was in contravention of *Brady v. Maryland* (1963). The report concluded Cruse "ha[d] little recollection of the [murders of the Kellers], other than vague memories, as he was intoxicated with alcohol and marijuana at the time." The report had been prepared in September 1993, before petitioner was tried; yet it was not mentioned by petitioner until he filed his federal habeas petition and attached a copy of the report. Petitioner explained that an investigator for his federal habeas counsel discovered the report in Cruse's court file but state habeas counsel had not seen it when he had reviewed the same file. State habeas counsel averred as follows:

"Prior to filing [petitioner's] habeas corpus petition with the Virginia Supreme Court, I reviewed the Cumberland County court files of [petitioner] and of his co-defendant, Jeffrey Cruse* * *. I have reviewed the attached psychiatric evaluation of Jeffrey Cruse * * *. I have no recollection of seeing this report in Mr. Cruse's court file when I examined the file. Given the contents of the report, I am confident that I would remember it."

The trial court was not satisfied with this explanation for the late discovery. Nor are we.

There are repeated references to a "psychiatric" or "mental health" report in a transcript of Cruse's sentencing proceeding, a copy of which petitioner's own state habeas counsel attached to the state habeas petition he filed with the Virginia Supreme Court. The transcript reveals that Cruse's attorney described the report with details that should have alerted counsel to a possible *Brady* claim.

* * *

The transcript put petitioner's state habeas counsel on notice of the report's existence and possible materiality. The sole indication that counsel made some effort to investigate the report is an October 30, 1995, letter to the prosecutor in which counsel requested "[a]ll reports of physical and mental examinations, scientific tests, or experiments conducted in connection with the investigation of the offense, including but not limited to: * * * [a]ll psychological test or polygraph examinations performed upon any prosecution witness and all documents referring or relating to such tests * * *." After the prosecution declined the requests absent a court order, it appears counsel made no further efforts to find the specific report mentioned by Cruse's attorney. Given knowledge of the report's existence and potential importance, a diligent attorney would have done more. Counsel's failure to investigate these references in anything but a cursory manner triggers the opening clause of § 2254(e)(2).

As we hold there was a failure to develop the factual basis of this *Brady* claim in state court, we must determine if the requirements in the balance of § 2254(e)(2) are satisfied so that petitioner's failure is excused. Subparagraph (B) of § 2254(e)(2) conditions a hearing upon a showing, by clear and convincing evidence, that no reasonable factfinder would have found petitioner guilty of capital murder but for the alleged constitutional error. Petitioner concedes he cannot make this showing, and the case has been presented to us on that premise. For these reasons, we affirm the Court of Appeals' judgment barring an evidentiary hearing on this claim.

B

We conclude petitioner has met the burden of showing he was diligent in efforts to develop the facts supporting his juror bias and prosecutorial misconduct claims in collateral proceedings before the Virginia Supreme Court.

Petitioner's claims are based on two of the questions posed to the jurors by the trial judge at *voir dire*. First, the judge asked prospective jurors, "Are any of you related to the following people who may be called as witnesses?" Then he read the jurors a list of names, one of which was "Deputy Sheriff Claude Meinhard." Bonnie Stinnett, who would later become the jury foreperson, had divorced Meinhard in 1979, after a 17-year marriage with four children. Stinnett remained silent, indicating the answer was "no." Meinhard, as the officer who investigated the crime scene and interrogated Cruse, would later become the prosecution's lead-off witness at trial.

After reading the names of the attorneys involved in the case, including one of the prosecutors, Robert Woodson, Jr., the judge asked, "Have you or any member of your immediate family ever been represented by any of the aforementioned attorneys?" Stinnett again said nothing, despite the fact Woodson had represented her during her divorce from Meinhard.

In an affidavit she provided in the federal habeas proceedings, Stinnett claimed "[she] did not respond to the judge's [first] question because [she] did not consider [herself] 'related' to Claude Meinhard in 1994 [at *voir dire*] * * *. Once our marriage ended in 1979, I was no longer related to him." As for Woodson's earlier representation of her, Stinnett explained as follows: "When Claude and I divorced in 1979, the divorce was uncontested and Mr. Woodson drew up the papers so that the divorce could be completed. Since neither Claude nor I was contesting anything, I didn't think Mr. Woodson 'represented' either one of us."

Woodson provided an affidavit in which he admitted "[he] was aware that Juror Bonnie Stinnett was the ex-wife of then Deputy Sheriff Claude Meinhard and [he] was aware that they had been divorced for some time." Woodson stated, however, "[t]o [his] mind, people who are related only by marriage are no longer 'related' once the marriage ends in divorce." Woodson also "had no recollection of having been involved as a private attorney in the divorce proceedings between Claude Meinhard and Bonnie Stinnett." He explained that "[w]hatever [his] involvement was in the 1979 divorce, by the time of trial in 1994[he] had completely forgotten about it."

Even if Stinnett had been correct in her technical or literal interpretation of the question relating to Meinhard, her silence after the first question was asked could suggest to the finder of fact an unwillingness to be forthcoming; this in turn could bear on the veracity of her explanation for not disclosing that Woodson had been her attorney. Stinnett's failure to divulge material information in response to the second question was misleading as a matter of fact because, under any interpretation, Woodson had acted as counsel to her and Meinhard in their divorce. Coupled with Woodson's own reticence, these omissions as a whole disclose the need for an evidentiary hearing. It may be that petitioner could establish that Stinnett was not impartial, or that Woodson's silence so infected the trial as to deny due process.

In ordering an evidentiary hearing on the juror bias and prosecutorial misconduct claims, the District Court concluded the factual basis of the claims was not reasonably available to petitioner's counsel during state habeas proceedings. After the Court of Appeals vacated this judgment, the District Court dismissed the petition and the Court of Appeals affirmed under the theory that state habeas counsel should have discovered Stinnett's relationship to Meinhard and Woodson.

We disagree with the Court of Appeals on this point. The trial record contains no evidence which would have put a reasonable attorney on notice that Stinnett's nonresponse was a deliberate omission of material information. State habeas counsel did attempt to investigate petitioner's jury, though prompted by concerns about a different juror. Counsel filed a motion for expert services with the Virginia Supreme Court, alleging "irregularities, improprieties and omissions exist[ed] with respect to the empaneling [sic] of the jury." Based on these suspicions, counsel requested funding for an investigator "to examine all circumstances relating to the empanelment of the jury and the jury's consideration of the case." The Commonwealth opposed the motion, and the Virginia Supreme Court denied it and dismissed the habeas petition, depriving petitioner of a further opportunity to investigate. The Virginia Supreme Court's denial of the motion is understandable in light of petitioner's vague allegations, but the vagueness was not the fault of petitioner. Counsel had no reason to believe Stinnett had been married to Meinhard or been represented by Woodson. The underdevelopment of these matters was attributable to Stinnett and Woodson, if anyone. We do not suggest the State has an obligation to pay for investigation of as yet undeveloped claims; but if the prisoner has made a reasonable effort to discover the claims to commence or continue state proceedings, § 2254(e)(2) will not bar him from developing them in federal court.

The Court of Appeals held state habeas counsel was not diligent because petitioner's investigator on federal habeas discovered the relationships upon interviewing two jurors who referred in passing to Stinnett as "Bonnie Meinhard." The investigator later confirmed Stinnett's prior marriage to Meinhard by checking Cumberland County's public records. We should be surprised, to say the least, if a district court familiar with the standards of trial practice were to hold that in all cases diligent counsel must check public records containing personal information pertaining to each and every juror. Because of Stinnett and Woodson's silence, there was no basis for an investigation into Stinnett's marriage history. Section 2254(e)(2) does not apply to petitioner's related claims of juror bias and prosecutorial misconduct.

We further note the Commonwealth has not argued that petitioner could have sought relief in state court once he discovered the factual bases of these claims some time between appointment of federal habeas counsel on July 2, 1996, and the filing of his federal habeas petition on November 20, 1996. * * * As state postconviction relief was no longer available at the time the facts came to light, it would have been futile for petitioner to return to the Virginia courts. In these circumstances, though the state courts did not have an opportunity to consider the new claims, petitioner cannot be said to have failed to develop them in state court by reason of having neglected to pursue remedies available under Virginia law.

Our analysis should suffice to establish cause for any procedural default petitioner may have committed in not presenting these claims to the Virginia courts in the first instance. Questions regarding the standard for determining the prejudice that petitioner must establish to obtain relief on these claims can be addressed by the Court of Appeals or the District Court in the course of further proceedings. These courts, in light of cases such as *Smith* ("[T]he remedy for allegations of juror partiality is a hearing in which the defendant has the opportunity to prove actual bias"), will take due account of the District Court's earlier decision to grant an evidentiary hearing based in part on its belief that "Juror Stinnett deliberately failed to tell the truth on voir dire."

                                   IV

Petitioner alleges the Commonwealth failed to disclose an informal plea agreement with Cruse. The Court of Appeals rejected this claim on the merits under § 2254(d)(1), so it is unnecessary to reach the question whether § 2254(e)(2) would permit a hearing on the claim.

The judgment of the Court of Appeals is affirmed in part and reversed in part, and the case is remanded for further proceedings consistent with this opinion.

It is so ordered.

Notes and Questions

1.   As *Williams* reflects, AEDPA supersedes *Townsend*, the 1966 amendment to § 2254(d), and *Tamayo-Reyes* for some purposes. *Tamayo-*

Reyes substituted the cause-prejudice standard for *Townsend*'s deliberate-bypass standard when a petitioner sought a federal evidentiary hearing on the ground that state proceedings did not develop the material facts adequately. What is left of the cause-prejudice standard in such cases after *Williams*? When does it apply? When does § 2254(e)(2) supersede it?

2. Look at the language of § 2254(e)(2). *Williams* tells us only that by replacing the cause-prejudice standard with this provision, Congress "raised the bar *Keeney* [*v. Tamayo-Reyes*] imposed on prisoners who were not diligent in state-court proceedings." How much did Congress raise the bar? To satisfy the "prejudice" element, a petitioner needs to show a substantial probability that the result of the state proceeding would have been different in a trial without the constitutional violation. What exactly must a petitioner show under § 2254(e)(2)(B)? How does that compare to "prejudice?"

3. Remember that *Townsend* and the 1966 amendments to then § 2254(d) laid out many circumstances requiring an evidentiary hearing. *Tamayo-Reyes*, § 2254(e)(2), and *Williams* all appear to apply only to the single circumstance when the state court hearing did not develop the material facts adequately. The only other provision of current law dealing with a review of state factual findings is in § 2254(d)(2), which states that a court shall *not* grant a state prisoner's application for a writ of habeas corpus that the state court adjudicated on the merits unless the state adjudication "resulted in a decision that was based on an unreasonable determination of the facts in light of the evidence presented in the State court proceeding." What happened to all of the other particular circumstances for granting a federal evidentiary hearing listed in *Townsend* and the former § 2254(d)? Has AEDPA eliminated them by omission? Should the general language of current § 2254(d)(2) be interpreted to encompass the other circumstances or should the other *Townsend* circumstances have a continuing life of their own? If your answer to the last question is "yes," consider whether a Supreme Court decision survives when Congress codifies it and subsequently deletes the codification. If your answer is "no," what do you make of *Tamayo-Reyes*'s statement that "it is evident that [the 1966 version of] § 2254(d) does not codify *Townsend*'s specifications of when a hearing is required?" At least one district judge has concluded that the answer should by "yes." *See Lawrie v. Snyder*, 9 F.Supp.2d 428 (D.Del. 1998) ("The remainder of *Townsend*, however, appears to have been left intact, including the other five factors under which an evidentiary hearing is mandatory, as well as the court's overriding ability to hold a hearing in its discretion.").

Professor Yackle attempts to resolve this interpretive problem by a liberal reading of the current sections (d)(2) and (e)(1):

> Under [(d)(2)], a federal court can scarcely be indifferent to the process by which a state court reached a factual finding or the evidentiary support that finding enjoys.

> I read § 2254(e)(1) to drop the specific procedural and substantive standards contained in the former § 2254(d). But I do not read it to dispense with a federal court's rudimentary responsibility to ensure that it is deciding a constitutional claim based on factual findings that

were forged in a procedurally adequate way and were anchored in a sufficient evidentiary record. In this sense, § 2254(e)(1) departs from prior law, but only to substitute general notions of procedural regularity and substantive accuracy for detailed statutory standards.

Larry W. Yackle, *Federal Evidentiary Hearings Under the New Habeas Corpus Statute*, 6 B.U.PUB.INT.L.J. 135, 141 (1996) (footnotes omitted).

4. The Supreme Court applied § 2254(d)(2) in *Rice v. Collins*, 546 U.S. 333, 126 S.Ct. 969, 163 L.Ed.2d 824 (2006), reversing a Ninth Circuit determination that the state court made an unreasonable determination of the facts in the light of the evidence presented. The petitioner claimed the prosecutor improperly used a peremptory challenge to excuse a juror because of her race. The Court characterized the prosecutor's explanation of the challenge to the trial judge as "unorganized," but noted that the prosecutor provided a number of permissible and plausible race-neutral reasons. The Court stated that reasonable minds reviewing the trial record might differ about the prosecutor's credibility, "but on habeas review[,] that does not suffice to supersede the trial court's credibility determination." *Rice* suggests federal judges should be reluctant to second guess fact determinations by state trial judges when those determinations rest on assessment of subjective factors such as demeanor and credibility. Does this seem unreasonable?

In *Schriro v. Landrigan*, __ U.S. __, 127 S.Ct. 1933, 167 L.Ed.2d 836 (2007), the Court again reversed a Ninth Circuit decision that a state court made an unreasonable determination of the facts in light of the evidence presented. Landrigan sought state and federal post-conviction relief from his Arizona murder conviction and death sentence.[33] In those applications, he claimed ineffective assistance of counsel because his trial attorney failed fully to explore mitigating evidence during the sentencing phase of the proceedings. The en banc Ninth Circuit held the district court erred in failing to hold an evidentiary hearing. The Supreme Court reversed, relying on the high threshold for relief specified in § 2254(d)(2). Under that provision, the federal court may not grant habeas relief simply because a federal court believes a state court's factual findings are incorrect. Instead, the state court's determination must be "unreasonable." The majority stressed that Landrigan was a violent, multiple murderer. Moreover, he explicitly prohibited defense counsel from presenting mitigating testimony from his mother and ex-wife during the sentencing proceedings. From this the state courts could reasonably determine that counsel was not ineffective. The dissenters argued that Landrigan's waiver of his rights was not knowing and intelligent, and in any event did not cover other mitigating evidence that would have been discovered if counsel had done a thorough investigation. The dissenters concluded an evidentiary hearing was warranted.

---

[33] He had previously been in an Oklahoma prison serving time for second degree murder. While there, he assaulted an inmate, which led to a conviction for assault and battery with a deadly weapon. Three years after that conviction, he had escaped from prison.

2. *Constitutional Claims Cognizable on Habeas Corpus*

Brown v. Allen (1953) greatly expanded habeas corpus by holding that federal courts generally must review federal constitutional claims raised by state prisoners if the petitioner exhausted available state court remedies. Notwithstanding *Brown*'s blanket nature, *Stone v. Powell*, 428 U.S. 465, 96 S.Ct. 3037, 49 L.Ed.2d 1067 (1976), held that federal habeas corpus does not extend to relitigation of Fourth Amendment claims when the state provides a full and fair opportunity to litigate them. The majority based its ruling on two themes: 1) the exclusionary rule being not a personal right but rather a judicially-created remedy for the benefit of society as a deterrent measure, and 2) that the interests the rule protects do not affect the integrity of the trial itself. Justice Brennan dissented vigorously, decrying the majority's "arrogation of power committed solely to Congress."

Many speculated that *Stone* presaged a general restricting of federal habeas jurisdiction because state courts generally provide opportunities to litigate federal claims. The defense community's alarm, at least on that ground, appears to have been premature. *Rose v. Mitchell*, 443 U.S. 545, 99 S.Ct. 2993, 61 L.Ed.2d 739 (1979), declined to extend *Stone* to a challenge to an allegedly racially discriminatory grand jury system, and *Jackson v. Virginia*, 443 U.S. 307, 99 S.Ct. 2781, 61 L.Ed.2d 560 (1979) ruled that *Stone* does not apply to a challenge based on the constitutionality of the reasonable doubt standard of criminal guilt. The latter issue goes directly to the integrity of the trial process as a manner of determining guilt, but the former is not so easily related to it. *Kimmelman v. Morrison* (1986) refused to extend *Stone* to Sixth Amendment claims of ineffective assistance of counsel where the claim of inadequate representation rested on failure to make a timely motion to suppress evidence allegedly seized in violation of the Fourth Amendment. The state argued that every Fourth Amendment claim where the defendant loses or defaults in raising it will thus be litigated in federal court in Sixth Amendment guise. The Court responded that the rigorous standard for ineffective assistance claims that *Strickland v. Washington*, 466 U.S. 668, 104 S.Ct. 2052, 80 L.Ed.2d 674 (1984), set forth would prevent this easy circumvention of *Stone v. Powell*. Finally, *Withrow v. Williams*, 507 U.S. 680, 113, S.Ct. 1745, 123 L.Ed.2d 407 (1993), declined to extend *Stone* to claims involving confessions obtained in violation of *Miranda v. Arizona*, 384 U.S. 436, 86 S.Ct. 1602, 16 L.Ed.2d 694 (1966). Has the Court implicitly limited *Stone* to Fourth Amendment claims?

TEAGUE v. LANE

Supreme Court of the United States, 1989.

489 U.S. 288, 109 S.Ct. 1060, 103 L.Ed.2d 334.

JUSTICE O'CONNOR announced the judgment of the Court and delivered the opinion of the Court with respect to Parts I, II, and III, and an opinion with respect to Parts IV and V, in which THE CHIEF JUSTICE, JUSTICE SCALIA, and JUSTICE KENNEDY join.

In *Taylor v. Louisiana*, this Court held that the Sixth Amendment required that the jury venire be drawn from a fair cross section of the community. The Court stated, however, that "in holding that petit juries must be drawn from a source fairly representative of the community we impose no requirement that petit juries actually chosen must mirror the community and reflect the various distinctive groups in the population. Defendants are not entitled to a jury of any particular composition." The principal question presented in this case is whether the Sixth Amendment's fair cross section requirement should now be extended to the petit jury. Because we adopt Justice Harlan's approach to retroactivity for cases on collateral review, we leave the resolution of that question for another day.

I

Petitioner, a black man, was convicted by an all-white Illinois jury of three counts of attempted murder, two counts of armed robbery, and one count of aggravated battery. During jury selection for petitioner's trial, the prosecutor used all 10 of his peremptory challenges to exclude blacks. Petitioner's counsel used one of his 10 peremptory challenges to exclude a black woman who was married to a police officer. After the prosecutor had struck six blacks, petitioner's counsel moved for a mistrial. The trial court denied the motion. When the prosecutor struck four more blacks, petitioner's counsel again moved for a mistrial, arguing that petitioner was "entitled to a jury of his peers." The prosecutor defended the challenges by stating that he was trying to achieve a balance of men and women on the jury. The trial court denied the motion, reasoning that the jury "appear[ed] to be a fair [one]."

[Teague pursued his direct appeals in Illinois. The Illinois and United States Supreme Courts denied review. Teague then sought federal habeas relief, arguing that, even before *Batson v. Kentucky*, under *Swain v. Alabama* a prosecutor who offered an explanation on his use of peremptory challenges could be questioned further. The lower federal courts rejected that argument and ruled that the fair cross section rule only applied to jury venires, not to juries selected from such venires. Since Teague's conviction became final before *Batson* was decided, the courts declined to afford him relief based on that case.]

* * *

II

Petitioner's first contention is that he should receive the benefit of our decision in *Batson* even though his conviction became final before *Batson* was decided. Before addressing petitioner's argument, we think it helpful to explain how *Batson* modified *Swain*. *Swain* held that a "State's purposeful or deliberate denial" to blacks of an opportunity to serve as jurors solely on account of race violates the Equal Protection Clause of the Fourteenth Amendment. * * *

In *Batson*, the Court overruled that portion of *Swain* setting forth the evidentiary showing necessary to make out a *prima facie* case of racial discrimination under the Equal Protection Clause. The Court held that a defendant can establish a *prima facie* case by showing that he is a "member of a cognizable racial group," that the prosecutor exercised "peremptory challenges to remove from the venire members of the defendant's race," and that those "facts and any other relevant circumstances raise an inference that the prosecutor used that practice to exclude the veniremen from the petit jury on account of their race." Once the defendant makes out a *prima facie* case of discrimination, the burden shifts to the prosecutor "to come forward with a neutral explanation for challenging black jurors."

In *Allen v. Hardy*, the Court held that *Batson* constituted an "explicit and substantial break with prior precedent" because it overruled a portion of *Swain*. Employing the retroactivity standard of *Linkletter v. Walker*, the Court concluded that the rule announced in *Batson* should not be applied retroactively on collateral review of convictions that became final before *Batson* was announced. The Court defined final to mean a case " 'where the judgment of conviction was rendered, the availability of appeal exhausted, and the time for petition for certiorari had elapsed before our decision in' *Batson* * * * ."

Petitioner's conviction became final 2 years prior to *Batson*, thus depriving petitioner of any benefit from the rule announced in that case.

* * *

We find that *Allen v. Hardy* is dispositive, and that petitioner cannot benefit from the rule announced in *Batson*.

IV

Petitioner's third and final contention is that the Sixth Amendment's fair cross section requirement applies to the petit jury. As we noted at the outset, *Taylor* expressly stated that the fair cross section requirement does not apply to the petit jury. Petitioner nevertheless contends that the *ratio decidendi* of *Taylor* cannot be limited to the jury venire, and he urges adoption of a new rule. Because we hold that the rule urged by petitioner should not be applied retroactively to cases on collateral review, we decline to address petitioner's contention.

A

In the past, the Court has, without discussion, often applied a new constitutional rule of criminal procedure to the defendant in the case announcing the new rule, and has confronted the question of retroactivity later when a different defendant sought the benefit of that rule. In several cases, however, the Court has addressed the retroactivity question in the very case announcing the new rule. These two lines of cases do not have a unifying theme, and we think it is time to clarify how the question of retroactivity should be resolved for cases on collateral review.

* * *

In our view, the question "whether a decision [announcing a new rule should] be given prospective or retroactive effect should be faced at the time of [that] decision." Retroactivity is properly treated as a threshold question, for, once a new rule is applied to the defendant in the case announcing the rule, evenhanded justice requires that it be applied retroactively to all who are similarly situated. Thus, before deciding whether the fair cross section requirement should be extended to the petit jury, we should ask whether such a rule would be applied retroactively to the case at issue. This retroactivity determination would normally entail application of the *Linkletter* standard, but we believe that our approach to retroactivity for cases on collateral review requires modification.

It is admittedly often difficult to determine when a case announces a new rule, and we do not attempt to define the spectrum of what may or may not constitute a new rule for retroactivity purposes. In general, however, a case announces a new rule when it breaks new ground or imposes a new obligation on the States or the Federal Government. To put it differently, a case announces a new rule if the result was not dictated by precedent existing at the time the defendant's conviction became final. Given the strong language in *Taylor* and our statement that "[f]airness in [jury] selection has never been held to require proportional representation of races upon a jury," application of the fair cross section requirement to the petit jury would be a new rule.

Not all new rules have been uniformly treated for retroactivity purposes. Nearly a quarter of a century ago, in *Linkletter*, the Court attempted to set some standards by which to determine the retroactivity of new rules. The question in *Linkletter* was whether *Mapp v. Ohio*, which made the exclusionary rule applicable to the States, should be applied retroactively to cases on collateral review. The Court determined that the retroactivity of *Mapp* should be determined by examining the purpose of the exclusionary rule, the reliance of the States on prior law, and the effect on the administration of justice of a retroactive application of the exclusionary rule. Using that standard, the Court held that *Mapp* would only apply to trials commencing after that case was decided.

The *Linkletter* retroactivity standard has not led to consistent results. Instead, it has been used to limit application of certain new rules to cases on direct review, other new rules only to the defendants in the cases announcing such rules, and still other new rules to cases in which trials have not yet commenced. Not surprisingly, commentators have "had a veritable field day" with the *Linkletter* standard, with much of the discussion being "more than mildly negative."

Application of the *Linkletter* standard led to the disparate treatment of similarly situated defendants on direct review. * * * This inequity also generated vehement criticism.

Dissatisfied with the *Linkletter* standard, Justice Harlan advocated a different approach to retroactivity. He argued that new rules should always be applied retroactively to cases on direct review, but that generally they should not be applied retroactively to criminal cases on collateral review.

In [1987], we rejected as unprincipled and inequitable the *Linkletter* standard for cases pending on direct review at the time a new rule is announced, and adopted the first part of the retroactivity approach advocated by Justice Harlan. We agreed with Justice Harlan that "failure to apply a newly declared constitutional rule to criminal cases pending on direct review violates basic norms of constitutional adjudication." We gave two reasons for our decision. First, because we can only promulgate new rules in specific cases and cannot possibly decide all cases in which review is sought, "the integrity of judicial review" requires the application of the new rule to "all similar cases pending on direct review." * * * Second, because "selective application of new rules violates the principle of treating similarly situated defendants the same," we refused to continue to tolerate the inequity that resulted from not applying new rules retroactively to defendants whose cases had not yet become final. Although new rules that constituted clear breaks with the past generally were not given retroactive effect under the *Linkletter* standard, we held that "a new rule for the conduct of criminal prosecutions is to be applied retroactively to all cases, state or federal, pending on direct review or not yet final, with no exception for cases in which the new rule constitutes a 'clear break' with the past."

The *Linkletter* standard also led to unfortunate disparity in the treatment of similarly situated defendants on collateral review. * * * This disparity in treatment was a product of two factors: our failure to treat retroactivity as a threshold question and the *Linkletter* standard's inability to account for the nature and function of collateral review. Having decided to rectify the first of those inadequacies, we now turn to the second.

B

Justice Harlan believed that new rules generally should not be applied retroactively to cases on collateral review. He argued that retroactivity for cases on collateral review could "be responsibly [determined] only by focusing, in the first instance, on the nature, function, and scope of the adjudicatory process in which such cases arise. The relevant frame of reference, in other words, is not the purpose of the new rule whose benefit the [defendant] seeks, but instead the purposes for which the writ of habeas corpus is made available." With regard to the nature of habeas corpus, Justice Harlan wrote:

Habeas corpus always has been a collateral remedy, providing an avenue for upsetting judgments that have become otherwise final. It is not designed as a substitute for direct review. The interest in leaving concluded litigation in a state of repose, that is, reducing the controversy to a final judgment not subject to further judicial revision, may quite legitimately be found by those responsible for defining the scope of the writ to outweigh in some, many, or most instances the competing interest in readjudicating convictions according to all legal standards in effect when a habeas petition is filed.

Given the "broad scope of constitutional issues cognizable on habeas," Justice Harlan argued that it is "sounder, in adjudicating habeas petitions, generally to apply the law prevailing at the time a conviction became final than it is to seek to dispose of [habeas] cases on the basis of intervening changes in constitutional interpretation." As he had explained,

> the threat of habeas serves as a necessary additional incentive for trial and appellate courts throughout the land to conduct their proceedings in a manner consistent with established constitutional standards. In order to perform this deterrence function, * * * the habeas court need only apply the constitutional standards that prevailed at the time the original proceedings took place.

Justice Harlan identified only two exceptions to his general rule of nonretroactivity for cases on collateral review. First, a new rule should be applied retroactively if it places "certain kinds of primary, private individual conduct beyond the power of the criminal law-making authority to proscribe." Second, a new rule should be applied retroactively if it requires the observance of "those procedures that * * * are 'implicit in the concept of ordered liberty.'" [Citing *Palko v. Connecticut*.]

* * *

We agree with Justice Harlan's description of the function of habeas corpus. * * * Rather, we have recognized that interests of comity and finality must also be considered in determining the proper scope of habeas review. Thus, if a defendant fails to comply with state procedural rules and is barred from litigating a particular constitutional claim in state court, the claim can be considered on federal habeas only if the defendant shows cause for the default and actual prejudice resulting therefrom. We have declined to make the application of the procedural default rule dependent on the magnitude of the constitutional claim at issue, or on the State's interest in the enforcement of its procedural rule.

* * *

Application of constitutional rules not in existence at the time a conviction became final seriously undermines the principle of finality which is essential to the operation of our criminal justice system. Without finality, the criminal law is deprived of much of its deterrent effect.

* * *

The "costs imposed upon the State[s] by retroactive application of new rules of constitutional law on habeas corpus * * * generally far outweigh the benefits of this application." In many ways the application of new rules to cases on collateral review may be more intrusive than the enjoining of criminal prosecutions, for it continually forces the States to marshal resources in order to keep in prison defendants whose trials and appeals conformed to then-existing constitutional standards. Furthermore, as we recognized, "[s]tate courts are understandably frustrated when they faithfully apply existing constitutional law only to have a federal court discover, during a [habeas] proceeding, new constitutional commands."

We find these criticisms to be persuasive, and we now adopt Justice Harlan's view of retroactivity for cases on collateral review. Unless they fall within an exception to the general rule, new constitutional rules of criminal procedure will not be applicable to those cases which have become final before the new rules are announced.

V

Petitioner's conviction became final in 1983. As a result, the rule petitioner urges would not be applicable to this case, which is on collateral review, unless it would fall within an exception.

The first exception suggested by Justice Harlan—that a new rule should be applied retroactively if it places "certain kinds of primary, private individual conduct beyond the power of the criminal law-making authority to proscribe,"—is not relevant here. * * *

The second exception suggested by Justice Harlan—that a new rule should be applied retroactively if it requires the observance of "those procedures that * * * are 'implicit in the concept of ordered liberty,' "—we apply with a modification. The language used by Justice Harlan * * * leaves no doubt that he meant the second exception to be reserved for watershed rules of criminal procedure * * * .

Justice Harlan had reasoned that one of the two principal functions of habeas corpus was "to assure that no man has been incarcerated under a procedure which creates an impermissibly large risk that the innocent will be convicted," and concluded "from this that all 'new' constitutional rules which significantly improve the pre-existing fact-finding procedures are to be retroactively applied on habeas." Justice Harlan gave three reasons for [later] shifting to the less defined *Palko* approach. First, he observed that recent precedent led "ineluctably * * * to the conclusion that it is not a principal purpose of the writ to inquire whether a criminal convict did in fact commit the deed alleged." Second, he noted that cases gave him reason to doubt the marginal effectiveness of claimed improvements in factfinding. Third, he found "inherently intractable the purported distinction between those new rules that are designed to improve the factfinding process and those designed principally to further other values."

We believe it desirable to combine the accuracy element of the * * * second exception with the * * * requirement that the procedure at issue must implicate the fundamental fairness of the trial. * * * [O]ur cases have moved in the direction of reaffirming the relevance of the likely accuracy of convictions in determining the available scope of habeas review. * * * [W]e believe that Justice Harlan's concerns about the difficulty in identifying both the existence and the value of accuracy-enhancing procedural rules can be addressed by limiting the scope of the second exception to those new procedures without which the likelihood of an accurate conviction is seriously diminished.

Because we operate from the premise that such procedures would be so central to an accurate determination of innocence or guilt, we believe it unlikely that many such components of basic due process have yet to emerge. We are also of the view that such rules are "best illustrated by recalling the classic grounds for the issuance of a writ of habeas corpus—that the proceeding was dominated by mob violence; that the prosecutor knowingly made use of perjured testimony; or that the conviction was based on a confession extorted from the defendant by brutal methods."

An examination of our decision in *Taylor* applying the fair cross section requirement to the jury venire leads inexorably to the conclusion that adoption of the rule petitioner urges would be a far cry from the kind of absolute prerequisite to fundamental fairness that is "implicit in the concept of ordered liberty." * * * Because the absence of a fair cross section on the jury venire does not undermine the fundamental fairness that must underlie a conviction or seriously diminish the likelihood of obtaining an accurate conviction, we conclude that a rule requiring that petit juries be composed of a fair cross section of the community would not be a "bedrock procedural element" that would be retroactively applied under the second exception we have articulated.

Were we to recognize the new rule urged by petitioner in this case, we would have to give petitioner the benefit of that new rule even though it would not be applied retroactively to others similarly situated. In the words of Justice Brennan, such an inequitable result would be "an unavoidable consequence of the necessity that constitutional adjudications not stand as mere dictum." But the harm caused by the failure to treat similarly situated defendants alike cannot be exaggerated: such inequitable treatment "hardly comports with the ideal of 'administration of justice with an even hand.'" Our refusal to allow such disparate treatment in the direct review context led us to adopt the first part of Justice Harlan's retroactivity approach in *Griffith*. "The fact that the new rule may constitute a clear break with the past has no bearing on the 'actual inequity that results' when only one of many similarly situated defendants receives the benefit of the new rule."

If there were no other way to avoid rendering advisory opinions, we might well agree that the inequitable treatment described above is "an insignificant cost for adherence to sound principles of decision-making." But there is a more principled way of dealing with the problem. We can simply refuse to announce a new rule in a given case unless the rule would be applied retroactively to the defendant in the case and to all others similarly situated. We think this approach is a sound one. Not only does it eliminate any problems of rendering advisory opinions, it also avoids the inequity resulting from the uneven application of new rules to similarly situated defendants. We therefore hold that, implicit in the retroactivity approach we adopt today, is the principle that habeas corpus cannot be used as a vehicle to create new constitutional rules of criminal procedure unless those rules would be applied retroactively to all defendants on collateral review through one of the two exceptions we have articulated. Because a decision extending the fair cross section requirement to the petit jury would not be applied retroactively to cases on collateral review under the approach we adopt today, we do not address petitioner's claim.

For the reasons set forth above, the judgment of the Court of Appeals is affirmed.

It is so ordered.

JUSTICE STEVENS, with whom JUSTICE BLACKMUN joins as to Part I, concurring in part and concurring in the judgment.

I

* * *

I do not agree * * * with the plurality's dicta proposing a "modification" of Justice Harlan's fundamental fairness exception. "[I]t has been the law, presumably for at least as long as anyone currently in jail has been incarcerated," Justice Harlan wrote, "that procedures utilized to convict them must have been fundamentally fair, that is, in accordance with the command of the Fourteenth Amendment that '[n]o State shall * * * deprive any person of life, liberty, or property, without due process of law.'" He continued: "[T]he writ ought always to lie for claims of nonobservance of those procedures that, as so aptly described by Mr. Justice Cardozo, are 'implicit in the concept of ordered liberty.' * * *" In embracing Justice Cardozo's notion that errors "violat[ing] those 'fundamental principles of liberty and justice which lie at the base of all our civil and political institutions,'" must be rectified, Justice Harlan expressly rejected a previous statement linking the fundamental fairness exception to factual innocence.

The plurality wrongly resuscitates Justice Harlan's early view, indicating that the only procedural errors deserving correction on collateral review are those that undermine "an accurate determination of innocence or guilt * * * ." I cannot agree that it is "unnecessarily anachronistic," to issue a writ of habeas corpus to a petitioner convicted in a manner that violates fundamental principles of liberty. * * * Even when assessing errors at the guilt phase of a trial, factual innocence is too capricious a factor by which to determine if a procedural change is sufficiently "bedrock" or "watershed" to justify application of the fundamental fairness exception.

* * *

JUSTICE BRENNAN, with whom JUSTICE MARSHALL joins, dissenting.

Today a plurality of this Court, without benefit of briefing and oral argument, adopts a novel threshold test for federal review of state criminal convictions on habeas corpus. It does so without regard for—indeed, without even mentioning—our contrary decisions over the past 35 years delineating the broad scope of habeas relief. The plurality further appears oblivious to the importance we have consistently accorded the principle of *stare decisis* in nonconstitutional cases. Out of an exaggerated concern for treating similarly situated habeas petitioners the same, the plurality would for the first time preclude the federal courts from considering on collateral review a vast range of important constitutional challenges; where those challenges have merit, it would bar the vindication of personal constitutional rights and deny society a check against further violations until the same claim is presented on direct review. In my view, the plurality's "blind adherence to the principle of treating like cases alike" amounts to "letting the tail wag the dog" when it stymies the resolution of substantial and unheralded constitutional questions. Because I cannot acquiesce in this unprecedented curtailment of the reach of the Great Writ, particularly in the absence of any discussion of these momentous changes by the parties or the lower courts, I dissent.

I

The federal habeas corpus statute provides that a federal court "shall entertain an application for a writ of habeas corpus in behalf of a person in custody pursuant to the judgment of a State court only on the ground that he is in custody in violation of the Constitution or laws or treaties of the United States." For well over a century, we have read this statute and its forbears to authorize federal courts to grant writs of habeas corpus whenever a person's liberty is unconstitutionally restrained. Shortly after the Habeas Corpus Act of 1867 empowered federal courts to issue writs of habeas corpus to state authorities, we noted: "This legislation is of the most comprehensive character. It brings within the habeas corpus jurisdiction of every court and of every judge every possible case of privation of liberty contrary to the National Constitution, treaties, or laws. It is impossible to widen this jurisdiction." Nothing has happened since to persuade us to alter that judgment. * * * Our subsequent rulings have not departed from that teaching in cases where the presentation of a petitioner's claim on collateral review is not barred by a procedural default.

In particular, our decisions have made plain that the federal courts may collaterally review claims such as Teague's once state remedies have been exhausted.

* * *

II

* * *

D

These are massive changes, unsupported by precedent.[6] They also lack a reasonable foundation. By exaggerating the importance of treating like cases alike and granting relief to all identically positioned habeas petitioners or none, "the Court acts as if it has no choice but to follow a mechanical notion of fairness without pausing to consider 'sound principles of decisionmaking.'" Certainly it is desirable, in the interest of fairness, to accord the same treatment to all habeas petitioners with the same claims. Given a choice between deciding an issue on direct or collateral review that might result in a new rule of law that would not warrant retroactive application to persons on collateral review other than the petitioner who brought the claim, we should ordinarily grant certiorari and decide the question on direct review. Following our decision in *Griffith v. Kentucky*, a new rule would apply equally to all persons whose convictions had not become final before the rule was announced, whereas habeas petitioners other than the one whose case we decided might not benefit from such a rule if we adopted it on collateral review. Taking cases on direct review ahead of those on habeas is especially attractive because the retrial of habeas petitioners usually places a heavier burden on the States than the retrial of persons on direct review. Other things being equal, our concern for fairness and finality ought to therefore lead us to render our decision in a case that comes to us on direct review.

Other things are not always equal, however. Sometimes a claim which, if successful, would create a new rule not appropriate for retroactive application on collateral review is better presented by a habeas case than by one on direct review. In fact, sometimes the claim is only presented on collateral review. In that case, while we could forgo deciding

---

[6] The plurality's claim that "our cases have moved in the direction of reaffirming the relevance of the likely accuracy of convictions in determining the available scope of habeas review," has little force. Two of the cases it cites discuss the conditions under which a habeas petitioner may obtain review even though his claim would otherwise be procedurally barred. They do not hold that a petitioner's likely guilt or innocence bears on the cognizability of habeas claims in the absence of procedural default. And the Court has limited *Stone v. Powell* to Fourth Amendment exclusionary rule claims, passing up several opportunities to extend it.

the issue in the hope that it would eventually be presented squarely on direct review, that hope might be misplaced, and even if it were in time fulfilled, the opportunity to check constitutional violations and to further the evolution of our thinking in some area of the law would in the meanwhile have been lost. In addition, by preserving our right and that of the lower federal courts to hear such claims on collateral review, we would not discourage their litigation on federal habeas corpus and thus not deprive ourselves and society of the benefit of decisions by the lower federal courts when we must resolve these issues ourselves.

The plurality appears oblivious to these advantages of our settled approach to collateral review. Instead, it would deny itself these benefits because adherence to precedent would occasionally result in one habeas petitioner's obtaining redress while another petitioner with an identical claim could not qualify for relief.[7] In my view, the uniform treatment of habeas petitioners is not worth the price the plurality is willing to pay. Permitting the federal courts to decide novel habeas claims not substantially related to guilt or innocence has profited our society immensely. Congress has not seen fit to withdraw those benefits by amending the statute that provides for them. And although a favorable decision for a petitioner might not extend to another prisoner whose identical claim has become final, it is at least arguably better that the wrong done to one person be righted than that none of the injuries inflicted on those whose convictions have become final be redressed, despite the resulting inequality in treatment.

* * *

Notes and Questions

1. a) When does existing precedent clearly dictate a decision? In *Wood v. Strickland*, 420 U.S. 308, 95 S.Ct. 992, 43 L.Ed.2d 214 (1975), a case involving official immunity to § 1983 claims, Justice Powell argued strongly that "settled, indisputable law" and "unquestioned constitutional rights" were chimeras and unworkable as a standard of liability, but in *Harlow v. Fitzgerald*, 457 U.S. 800, 102 S.Ct. 2727, 73 L.Ed.2d 396 (1982), he ruled that officials have immunity from § 1983 actions only "insofar as their conduct does not violate clearly established statutory or constitutional rights of which a reasonable person would have known." How many cases that recognize constitutional rights are "dictated by existing precedent"? If precedent

---

[7] The plurality's complaint that prior retroactivity decisions have sometimes led to more than one habeas petitioner's reaping the benefit of a new rule while most habeas petitioners obtained no relief because of "our failure to treat retroactivity as a threshold question" is misguided. The disparity resulting from our deciding three years later not to apply retroactively the rule of *Edwards v. Arizona* should not be ascribed to our failure to make retroactivity a threshold question, but rather to our failure to decide the retroactivity question at the same time that we decided the merits issue. If both decisions are made contemporaneously, then only one exception need be made to the rule of equal treatment. The plurality may find even this slight inequality unacceptable, but the magnitude of the disparity is not and need not be as large as its example suggests.

so clearly dictates a particular result, how does the case survive for Supreme Court review? Conversely, should one conclude that whenever the Supreme Court grants plenary review, either the precedent was not clearly established or the lower courts ignored their constitutional responsibility?

b) The Court has made clear that a case need not be on all fours to establish precedent sufficiently clear to avoid *Teague*. *Stringer v. Black*, 503 U.S. 222, 112 S.Ct. 1130, 117 L.Ed.2d 367 (1992), found that although no single case established the rule upon which the petitioner relied, a "long line of authority" strongly suggested it; *Teague* did not bar review. Still, it remains unclear just how much not-directly-on-point precedent is enough.

c) Thus far, neither the Supreme Court nor the inferior federal courts have had an easy time defining what a new rule is. In *Butler v. McKellar*, 494 U.S. 407, 110 S.Ct. 1212, 108 L.Ed.2d 347 (1990), the majority held that reasonable disagreement among courts or counsel about the outcome of a case meant that the result was not dictated by existing precedent and therefore was "new." Does that mean that whenever there is a dissenting opinion or a split among the circuits on an issue that it is by definition "new" and cannot be considered on collateral review? *See also Saffle v. Parks*, 494 U.S. 484, 110 S.Ct. 1257, 108 L.Ed.2d 415 (1990) (disagreement among lower courts establishes a rule as "new" as long as it is "logically distinct" from precedent); *Beard v. Banks*, 546 U.S. 406, 124 S.Ct. 2504, 159 L.Ed.2d 494 (2004) (dissent by four Justices reasoning that existing Supreme Court precedent did not compel result adopted by majority precludes finding that the result was dictated by precedent because the unlawfulness of conviction was not apparent to all reasonable jurists).

Sawyer v. Smith, 497 U.S. 227, 110 S.Ct. 2822, 111 L.Ed.2d 193 (1990), decided a few months after *Butler* and *Saffle*, demonstrates both the rigor of the new retroactivity test and the difficulty of applying it. Sawyer was convicted of murder and sentenced to death. He argued that the prosecutor intentionally sought to diminish the jury's sense of responsibility for the death sentence in violation of *Caldwell v. Mississippi*, 472 U.S. 320, 105 S.Ct. 2633, 86 L.Ed.2d 231 (1985), decided a year after final entry of Sawyer's conviction. The Supreme Court declined to reach the question of *Caldwell*'s scope, finding *Teague* dispositive.

> Our review of the relevant precedents that preceded *Caldwell* convinces us that it is a new rule for purposes of *Teague*. * * * The rule of *Teague* serves to "validat[e] reasonable, good-faith interpretations of existing precedents made by state courts even though they are shown to be contrary to later decisions." * * * The principle announced in *Teague* serves to ensure that gradual developments in the law over which reasonable jurists may disagree are not later used to upset the finality of state convictions valid when entered. This is but a recognition that the purpose of federal habeas corpus is to ensure that state convictions comply with the federal law in existence at the time the conviction became final, and not to provide a mechanism for the continuing reexamination of final judgments based upon later emerging legal doctrine.

* * *

Petitioner contends that the second *Teague* exception should be read to include new rules of capital sentencing that "preserve the accuracy and fairness of capital sentencing judgments." But this test looks only to half of our definition of the second exception. Acceptance of petitioner's argument would return the second exception to the broad definition that Justice Harlan first proposed in *Desist*, but later abandoned in *Mackey*, under which new rules that "significantly improve the pre-existing fact-finding procedures are to be retroactively applied on habeas." In *Teague*, we modified Justice Harlan's test to combine the accuracy element of the *Desist* test with the *Mackey* limitation of the exception to watershed rules of fundamental fairness. It is thus not enough under *Teague* to say that a new rule is aimed at improving the accuracy of trial. More is required. A rule that qualifies under this exception must not only improve accuracy, but also "alter our understanding of the *bedrock procedural elements*" essential to the fairness of a proceeding.

In a similar case, the Tenth Circuit concluded that although *Caldwell* announced a new rule for *Teague* purposes, it fell within the second *Teague* exception. *Hopkinson v. Shillinger*, 888 F.2d 1286 (10th Cir.1989) (en banc).

But *Caldwell* did not spring full grown from the Supreme Court's brow in 1985. *Donnelly v. DeChristoforo*, 416 U.S. 637, 94 S.Ct. 1868, 40 L.Ed.2d 431 (1974), substantially foreshadowed it. Professor Arkin notes the difficulty inherent in the Court's reasoning linking *Donnelly* and *Caldwell*.

> Having concluded that *Caldwell* was novel within the meaning of *Teague*, Justice Kennedy next considered whether it fell within either of the *Teague* exceptions. * * * [B]oth the Tenth Circuit and a significant minority of the Fifth Circuit believed that *Caldwell* fell within the second exception because it enhanced the reliability of capital sentencing. Indeed, Justice Kennedy himself strongly—and inexplicably, given the Court's ultimate position—emphasized that the *Caldwell* rule grew out of the Court's concern for the reliability in the capital sentencing process. Justice Kennedy, however, announced that enhancement of accuracy was not enough. * * * As Justice Kennedy explained, the bedrock procedural element of fairness in prosecutorial comment was already established by the due process based protections of *Donnelly v. DeChristoforo*. Thus, *Caldwell* did not effect a fundamental change in the legal community's understanding of the bedrock procedural elements necessary to a fair and accurate determination, but merely added to existing procedural guarantees, thereby falling outside *Teague*'s second exception. Justice Kennedy's opinion is a curious one. Having found *Caldwell* to be novel in the first place, Justice Kennedy was forced by his own reasoning to argue that, in the final analysis, it was not novel enough to be applied retroactively [under the second *Teague* exception].

Marc M. Arkin, *The Prisoner's Dilemma: Life in the Lower Federal Courts After* Teague v. Lane, 69 N.C. L. REV. 371, 388-89 (1991). Professor Arkin concludes "that *Sawyer* bears all the earmarks of an end-of-term opinion and fails to confront many of the questions raised by the Fifth Circuit * * * ." Nonetheless, "almost uniformly, the lower courts—even if expressing bewilderment at the Supreme Court's own disagreements—have * * * followed the 'hard core' *Teague* justices, holding most claims to be novel and to fall outside the *Teague* exceptions."

Gray v. Netherland, 518 U.S. 152, 116 S.Ct. 2074, 135 L.Ed.2d 457 (1996), offers a new glimpse of how broad *Teague* can be and how difficult it may be for habeas petitioners to establish that the rule that they wish the courts to apply is not new for *Teague* purposes. Gray was convicted of capital murder. Early in the trial, Gray's counsel moved the court to require "the prosecution to disclose the evidence it planned to introduce in the penalty phase" of the trial. The prosecutor responded that he would introduce only statements petitioner had made with respect to two other killings (the Sorrell murders). On the evening after the jury brought in a verdict of guilty, the prosecutor advised defense counsel that he intended to introduce extensive evidence linking Gray with the other murders at the penalty phase of the trial, scheduled to begin the following morning. The trial court and state appellate courts rejected counsel's objections to the surprise evidence. The federal district court granted Gray's petition for a writ, finding that "[p]etitioner was confronted and surprised by the testimony of officer Slezak and Dr. Presswalla," and further noted that the surprise "violated [petitioner's] right to fair notice and rendered the hearing clearly unreliable." The Fourth Circuit reversed.

A 5-4 majority of the Court affirmed the Court of Appeals's decision. Chief Justice Rehnquist divided Gray's claim into two parts: the prosecutor's failure to give notice of the evidence that the Commonwealth would present at the penalty phase of the trial and the prosecutor's affirmative misrepresentation to defense counsel of the evidence that he would seek to introduce. The Court refused to review the misrepresentation claim, remanding for consideration of whether Gray had timely raised and preserved it in the state proceedings and whether, if he had not, the Commonwealth timely raised and preserved the state procedural default as a bar to federal habeas consideration of the claim.

With respect to the notice-of-evidence claim, the Chief Justice began by noting *Teague*'s focus: "We have concluded that the writ's purpose may be fulfilled with the least intrusion necessary on States' interest of the finality of criminal proceedings by applying constitutional standards contemporaneous with the habeas petitioner's conviction to review his petition." The Court noted that Gray's counsel did not request additional time to respond to the state's evidence, but instead moved to exclude it.

> On these facts, for petitioner to prevail on his notice-of-evidence claim, he must establish that due process requires that he receive more than a day's notice of the Commonwealth's evidence. He must also establish that due process required a continuance whether or not he sought one, or that, if he chose not to seek a continuance, exclusion was the only appropriate remedy for the inadequate notice. We conclude that only

the adoption of a new constitutional rule could establish these propositions.

Thus, the majority refused relief on the notice-of-evidence claim.

Justice Ginsburg filed a strong dissent, joined by Justices Stevens, Souter and Breyer. She found no new rule implicated in Gray's claim and focused on the prosecutor's conduct as seen by the district court:

> "The consequences of this surprise," the District Court found, "could not have been more devastating." Most critically, the prosecutor's "statements only" assurance led defense counsel to forgo investigation of the details of the Sorrell murders, including a review of the evidence collected by the Chesapeake police department during its investigation of the crimes. Had Gray's lawyers conducted such a review, they could have shown that none of the forensic evidence collected by the Chesapeake police directly linked Gray to the Sorrell murders. Moreover, the evidence the Chesapeake police did obtain "strongly suggested that Timothy Sorrell"—[the victims' husband and father]—actually committed the murders."

Justice Ginsburg took strong issue with the majority's characterization of the rule whose benefit Gray sought as new.

> There is nothing "new" in a rule that capital defendants must be afforded a meaningful opportunity to defend against the State's penalty phase evidence. As this Court affirmed more than a century ago: "Common justice requires that no man shall be condemned in his person or property without * * * an opportunity to make his defence." * * *

> In *Gardner v. Florida*, the principal decision relied upon by the District Court, we confirmed that the sentencing phase of a capital trial "must satisfy the requirements of the Due Process Clause." *Gardner* presented the question whether a defendant was denied due process when the trial judge sentenced him to death relying in part on a presentence report, including a confidential portion not disclosed to defense counsel. Counsel's deprivation of an "opportunity * * * to challenge the accuracy or materiality" of the undisclosed information, the *Gardner* plurality reasoned, left a manifest risk that "some of the information accepted in confidence may [have been] erroneous, or * * * misinterpreted." As a basis for a death sentence, *Gardner* teaches, information unexposed to adversary testing does not qualify as reliable. * * *

> Urging that *Gardner* fails to "dictate" a decision for Gray here, the Commonwealth relies on the Fourth Circuit's reasoning to this effect: *Gardner* was a case about "secrecy"; Gray's case is about "surprise." Therefore, Gray seeks an extension, not an application, of *Gardner*, in *Teague* parlance, a "new rule." * * *

> *Teague* is not the straightjacket the Commonwealth misunderstands it to be. *Teague* requires federal courts to decide a habeas petitioner's constitutional claims according to the "law prevailing at the time [his]

conviction became final." But *Teague* does not bar federal habeas courts from applying, in "a myriad of factual contexts," law that is settled—here, the right to a meaningful chance to defend against or explain charges pressed by the State.

Note that one's position on whether or not a rule is new for *Teague* purposes may depend on how specifically one characterizes the principle whose application the prisoner seeks. The *Gray* majority characterizes the rule as saying that a defendant is constitutionally entitled to a certain length of notice or a certain remedy if adequate notice is not forthcoming. The dissent views the rule as a requirement that the defendant in a capital case have a reasonable opportunity to confront and contest charges against him. A life turns on the difference. Is federalism materially more or less offended according to whether one accepts the majority's or dissent's characterization?

O'Dell v. Netherland, 521 U.S. 151, 117 S.Ct. 1969, 138 L.Ed.2d 351 (1997), also a capital case, may be an even more rigorous application of *Teague*. The prosecutor argued that the jury should impose the death penalty because O'Dell would otherwise constitute a serious, continuing threat to society. State law, however, allowed only the death penalty or life imprisonment without possibility of parole. The trial court refused a defense request to charge the jury that the defendant was ineligible for parole if the jury recommended a life sentence, and the jury recommended death.

When O'Dell sought federal habeas relief, the district court ruled that he was entitled to be resentenced if he could show that he was in fact ineligible for parole. The court based its ruling on *Simmons v. United States* (1994), in which the prosecution had also sought the death penalty on the basis of the defendant's future dangerousness. In the Supreme Court, Justice Thomas, writing for the majority, observed:

> A plurality of the Court noted that a prosecutor's future dangerousness argument will "necessarily [be] undercut" by "the fact that the alternative sentence to death is life without parole." The plurality, relying on *Gardner v. Florida* (1977) and *Skipper v. South Carolina* (1986), concluded that "because truthful information of parole ineligibility allows the defendant to 'deny or explain' the showing of future dangerousness, due process plainly requires that he be allowed to bring it to the jury's attention."

Justice Thomas characterized three other votes as follows:

> Justice O'Connor, joined by the Chief Justice and Justice Kennedy, concurred in the judgment, providing the dispositive votes necessary to sustain it. The concurrence recognized:

> [The Court has] previously noted with approval * * * that "[m]any state courts have held it improper for the jury to consider or to be informed—through argument or instruction—of the possibility of commutation, pardon, or parole." The decision whether or not to inform the jury of the possibility of early release is generally left to the States.

All of this caused two problems for O'Dell. First, the Court announced *Sim-*

mons in 1994. O'Dell's conviction became final for *Teague* purposes in 1988, so one issue was whether *Simmons* was a *Teague* "new" rule. Second, the *O'Dell* Court could not agree on *Simmons*'s import.

Simmons rested, to some disputed degree, on the Court's decisions in *Gardner v. Florida* and *Skipper v. South Carolina*, both of which antedated O'Dell's conviction. In *Gardner*, the trial court sentenced the defendant to death on the basis of a presentence report that the defense never saw. A plurality held that due process required resentencing of a prisoner whose "death sentence was imposed, at least in part, on the basis of information which he had no opportunity to deny or explain." Justice White concurred in the judgment on the ground that the Eighth Amendment prohibited "selecting people for the death penalty * * * [on the basis of] secret information relevant to the character and record of the individual offender."

In *Skipper*, the prosecution argued for the death penalty on the ground that the defendant would be an unacceptable danger even in prison. The trial court refused to permit the defense to introduce evidence of Skipper's good behavior in prison previously. The Court ruled that *Eddings v. Oklahoma*, an Eighth Amendment case, and due process required that the defendant be permitted to present potentially mitigating evidence and that the court could not sentence him to die without having permitted him to contest the prosecution's argument.

The *O'Dell* majority distinguished *Skipper* on the ground that it concerned personal characteristics of the defendant, not the state of the law. It distinguished *Gardner* by viewing the narrow ground of Justice White's concurrence as the true holding of the case, since there were not five votes for the plurality's rationale. The majority also noted that the seven opinions in *Gardner* demonstrated that the Court in *Simmons* had not felt compelled to find as it did on the basis of that case, and concluded:

> In *Skipper*, too, the evidence that the defendant was unconstitutionally prevented from adducing was evidence of his past behavior. It is a step from a ruling that a defendant must be permitted to present evidence of that sort to a requirement that he be afforded an opportunity to describe the extant legal regime.

So saying, the Court found *Simmons* to be new for *Teague* purposes and therefore unavailable to O'Dell in the federal habeas proceeding. The majority also rejected O'Dell's argument that *Simmons* fell within the second *Teague* exception:

> Unlike the sweeping rule of *Gideon* [*v. Wainwright*], which established the affirmative right to counsel in all felony cases, the narrow right of rebuttal that *Simmons* affords to defendants in a limited class of capital cases has hardly " ' "alter[ed] our understanding of the *bedrock procedural elements*" ' essential to the fairness of a proceeding." ([E]mphasis in *Teague*). *Simmons* possesses little of the "watershed" character envisioned by *Teague*'s second exception.

The dissenters, of course, saw it differently. As Justice Stevens observed for four Members of the Court:

In my view, the right in *Simmons*—the right to respond to an inaccurate or misleading argument—is surely a bedrock procedural element of a full and fair hearing. As Justice O'Connor recognized in her opinion in *Simmons*, this right to rebut the prosecutor's arguments is a "hallmar[k] of due process." When a defendant is denied the ability to respond to the state's case against him, he is deprived of "his fundamental constitutional right to a fair opportunity to present a defense."

Nonetheless, four is not a majority of nine, and Maryland executed O'Dell.

Is the Court's characterization of the Justices' lineup in *Simmons* accurate? Justice Thomas describes Justice O'Connor's concurrence as "providing the dispositive votes necessary to sustain" the judgment. That opinion, as he notes, did take the position that the defendant was entitled to rebut the state's argument of future dangerousness with a showing of parole ineligibility. Arguably, though, Justice Thomas does not give Justice O'Connor full credit, for as part of the same discussion, she noted:

> [D]espite our general deference to state decisions regarding what the jury should be told about sentencing, I agree that due process requires that the defendant be allowed to do so in cases in which the only available alternative sentence to death is life imprisonment without possibility of parole and the prosecution argues that the defendant will pose a threat to society in the future.

512 U.S. at 177, 114 S.Ct. at 2201, 129 L.Ed.2d at 151. Thus, seven Members of the Court subscribed the principle that due process entitles a defendant to argue his ineligibility for parole to rebut the prosecution's argument of future dangerousness. Given that agreement, is it significant that the principle was explained in two opinions instead of one?

Are *Skipper* and *Gardner* properly distinguishable in the way that the majority attempts? Would the majority's argument with respect to those two cases be just as strong if the prosecutor had stated to the jury, "This man may be released into society if you do not impose the death penalty now," or would that have been, in the words of *Skipper*, " 'information which [the defendant] had no opportunity to deny or explain' "?

Due process prohibits a prosecutor from knowingly presenting perjured testimony. *See, e.g., Napue v. Illinois*, 360 U.S. 264, 79 S.Ct. 1173, 3 L.Ed.2d 1217 (1959); *Mooney v. Holohan*, 294 U.S. 103, 55 S.Ct. 340, 79 L.Ed. 791 (1935). Are the prosecutor's actions in *O'Dell* or as hypothesized in the paragraph above sufficiently different for due process purposes that the rule of *Simmons* should be viewed as a new rule for *Teague* purposes? If the rule is "new," should cases like *Napue* and *Mooney* affect the Court's view of whether it is "implicit in the concept of ordered liberty"?

Suppose instead of arguing as he did to the jury, the prosecutor called a law professor as an expert witness on state law. If the witness testified falsely that O'Dell could be paroled if given a life sentence, would that present a due process problem? If so, is it a new or an old problem for *Teague* purposes? Does the option of cross-examination in this hypothetical make it distinguishable from *O'Dell*? Should it?

Whorton v. Bockting, __ U.S. __, 127 S.Ct. 1173, 167 L.Ed.2d 1
(2007), continued the Court's practice of defining "new rule" very broadly
for *Teague* purposes but defining the exceptions that would allow a new rule
to apply in a collateral proceeding very narrowly. *Crawford v. Washington*,
541 U.S. 36, 124 S.Ct. 1354, 158 L.Ed.2d 177 (2004), redefined the Sixth
Amendment's Confrontation Clause. Prior to *Crawford*, *Ohio v. Roberts*, 448
U.S. 56, 100 S.Ct. 2531, 65 L.Ed.2d 597 (1980), allowed admission of a hearsay statement by a declarant unavailable to testify if the statement "bore
sufficient indicia of reliability," either because the statement fell within a
firmly rooted exception to the hearsay rule or bore "particularized guarantees of trustworthiness." *Crawford* overruled *Roberts*, holding that
"[t]estimonial statements of witnesses absent from trial" are admissible
"only where the declarant is unavailable *and* only where the defendant had
a prior opportunity to cross-examine [the witness]." (Emphasis added.)
Quoting *Saffle* and *Teague*, the Court said a rule is "new" if it is not "dictated
by precedent existing at the time the defendant's conviction became final."
Finding *Crawford* "flatly inconsistent" with *Roberts*, the Court held that
Crawford established a new rule of criminal procedure.

The *Whorton* Court noted that a new rule of procedure applies retroactively in a collateral proceeding only if it is a " 'watershed rul[e] of criminal
procedure' implicating the fundamental fairness and accuracy of the criminal proceeding" (again quoting *Saffle* and *Teague*). A new rule is a watershed only if it is necessary to prevent an impermissibly large risk of an inaccurate conviction and "alter[s] our understanding of the bedrock procedural
elements essential to the fairness of a proceeding." The Court noted that
while excluding uncross-examined hearsay statements might improve the
accuracy of trial, absence of this safeguard nonetheless did not pose an
"impermissibly large risk" of an inaccurate conviction. Nor did *Crawford*
find a new, previously *undiscovered* part of the bedrock because live testimony and cross-examination have long been considered important procedural guarantees.

If the *Crawford* rule is not a watershed, it is difficult to imagine
what new rule might be. The Court stated it to be "unlikely" that any such
rules will emerge, and noted that in the years since *Teague*, it has rejected
every claim that a new rule satisfied the requirements for watershed status.

Fiore v. White, 531 U.S. 225, 121 S.Ct. 712, 148 L.Ed.2d 629 (2001),
demonstrates that the federal courts still encounter difficulty in figuring out
when the state courts have announced a "new" rule. The Pennsylvania
courts convicted Fiore of operating a hazardous waste facility without a
permit. The trial court accepted the state's argument that Fiore had so
grossly overstepped the limitations of the permit he held that he effectively
was operating without a permit. The intermediate appellate court affirmed,
and the Pennsylvania Supreme Court declined to review the case. That
court later did review and reverse the conviction of Fiore's co-defendant, ruling that the statute's specification of operating *without* a permit precluded
conviction for violating a permit's terms, no matter how egregiously. Fiore
thereupon sought state collateral relief and, when unsuccessful, brought a
habeas petition to the federal courts. The United States Court of Appeals for

the Third Circuit reversed the district court's grant of the writ in the belief that Pennsylvania's Supreme Court had announced a new rule of law not applicable to Fiore. The United States Supreme Court reversed in a *per curiam* decision. It did so because it had certified to the Pennsylvania Supreme Court the question of whether that court's interpretation of the statute in the later case "state[d] the correct interpretation of the law of Pennsylvania at the date Fiore's conviction became final * * * ." The Pennsylvania Supreme Court replied that it did and that the case "did not announce a new rule of law. Our ruling merely clarified the plain language of the statute * * * ." Note the confusion on all three levels of federal courts. The District Court, granting habeas relief, felt that the rule was clearly not new within the meaning of *Teague*. The Court of Appeals felt that it clearly was. The United States Supreme Court declined to guess.

(d) The *Teague* plurality believes that retroactivity is a threshold issue; that is, a court must decide whether a new rule will be applied retroactively before deciding whether to announce the rule. The plurality then adopts Justice Harlan's suggestion that new rules not be applied retroactively if announced in cases on collateral review, except in two very limited circumstances. From these premises, the plurality concludes that new rules cannot be announced at all in a collateral proceeding. The plurality reaches this conclusion because of problems the justices perceive with announcing a new rule but not applying the rule retroactively. A court might decide not to apply the rule to the petitioner or to others similarly situated. What does the plurality suggest would be wrong with that? A court might apply the new rule just to the petitioner and not to others similarly situated. What does the plurality say would be wrong with that? Having found these alternatives unacceptable, the plurality is left with the conclusion that new rules simply cannot be announced in habeas corpus cases.

e) To make the threshold retroactivity decision, is a court forced to hypothesize a substantive rule in order to test its novelty? Where the hypothesized rule would not be retroactive, has not the court rendered an advisory opinion? Professor Arkin describes how the lower courts have apparently finessed the issue.

> When a petitioner is claiming relief under an after-decided rule, courts treat the requirement that retroactivity is to be given threshold consideration as one of priority; they simply decide the retroactivity of petitioner's claims—with whatever weighing of the merits is practically necessary—before proceeding to any other issue. Indeed, the fact that the issue of threshold consideration was passed over entirely by the Supreme Court in its affirmance of *Sawyer* [*v. Butler*] may well signal a recognition that the extreme position of *Teague* was unworkable from the start. Certainly, no court has expended much effort sorting out novelty from the constitutional merits.

Marc M. Arkin, *The Prisoner's Dilemma: Life in the Lower Federal Courts After* Teague v. Lane, 69 N.C. L. REV. 371, 397-98 (1991).

Tyler v. Cain, 533 U.S. 656, 121 S.Ct. 2478, 150 L.Ed.2d 632 (2001), may have made it even more difficult for a state prisoner to take advantage of a new constitutional rule that the Supreme Court has recognized. A jury convicted Tyler of second-degree murder upon an instruction relating to the meaning of "proof beyond a reasonable doubt" that the Court later found unconstitutional in its *per curiam* decision in *Cage v. Louisiana*, 498 U.S. 39, 111 S.Ct. 328, 112 L.Ed.2d 339 (1990). That decision alone did not make the new rule retroactive, but in *Sullivan v. Louisiana*, 508 U.S. 275, 113 S.Ct. 2078, 124 L.Ed.2d 182 (1993), the Court held that the *Cage* rule was structural, not subject to harmless-error analysis and would "always invalidate the conviction." Tyler argued that the *Cage-Sullivan* combination "made" the *Cage* rule retroactive within the meaning of AEDPA, § 2244(b)(1)(A). The Court's five-member majority disagreed: "Based on the plain meaning of the text read as a whole, we conclude that 'made' means 'held' and, thus, the requirement is satisfied only if this Court has held that the new rule is retroactively applicable to cases on collateral review." Justice Thomas's opinion then noted that neither *Cage* nor *Sullivan* so held, and that "[m]ultiple cases can render a new rule retroactive only if the holdings in those cases necessarily dictate retroactivity of the new rule." Dissenting, Justice Breyer, joined by Justices Stevens, Souter and Ginsburg, argued that the majority misread the statute to require a formal holding by the Court and that in any event, the *Cage-Sullivan* duo made clear that the *Cage* rule was retroactive under the Court's long-existing standards.

The majority also noted that

> [b]ecause Tyler's habeas application was his second, the District Court was required to dismiss it unless Tyler showed that this Court already had made Cage retroactive. * * * We cannot decide today whether *Cage* is retroactive to cases on collateral review, because that distinction would not help Tyler in this case. Any statement on *Cage*'s retroactivity would be *dictum*, so we decline to comment further on the issue.

Query how, after *Tyler*, a rule can become retroactive. The Court that announces the rule cannot also make it retroactive; that would be *dictum* under Justice Thomas's analysis. If the Court in *Tyler* cannot do so either, has the Court foreclosed all possibility of the rule being declared retroactive? Not necessarily; a prisoner presenting his first federal habeas application and therefore not facing the additional hurdles that confront a second or subsequent petition may seek such a holding. Note, however, that this presents again the possible anomaly of prisoners convicted of the same offense at the same trial on the same jury instruction having their fate determined by the speed with which their appeals and state post-conviction remedies run. If one prisoner's first federal habeas application antedates the announcement of the new rule's retroactivity and the other postdates it, only the latter's second federal habeas petition will result in relief.

f) How will the courts interpret the *Teague* exceptions? The first, concerning primary conduct exempted from punishment, will arise much less frequently than the second, referring to procedures "implicit in the concept of ordered liberty." In *Butler v. McKellar* (1990), the majority took a narrow view of the second, focusing not upon procedural fairness itself but instead only upon rules that enhance the accuracy of trial results and what Justice Kennedy termed "bedrock procedural elements."

g) It is not yet clear whether a state litigant can waive *Teague* problems, but the Supreme Court has effectively held that the state courts cannot. In *Horn v. Banks*, 536 U.S. 266, 122 S.Ct. 2147, 153 L.Ed.2d 301 (2002), petitioner sought habeas relief after the state courts affirmed his murder conviction and denied post-conviction relief. He argued in his state and federal petitions that *Mills v. Maryland*, 486 U.S. 367, 108 S.Ct. 1860, 100 L.Ed.2d 384 (1988), which postdated petitioner's conviction by six years, compelled the state to afford him a new sentencing proceeding because the sentencing court's charge implied that the jury had to be unanimous with respect to the existence of mitigating factors. The state courts denied relief on the ground that the procedure at Banks's sentencing did not violate *Mills*, but they did not consider *Teague*. The Third Circuit granted relief, foregoing a *Teague* analysis because "we do not need to focus on anything other than the reasoning and determination of the Pennsylvania Supreme Court." A *per curiam* Supreme Court reversed, holding that "the Court of Appeals committed a clear error by failing to perform a *Teague* analysis," and describing *Teague* analysis as a threshold question.

2. *Teague* divides constitutional rights into two categories: those that are retroactive and those that are not. After *Teague*, how will previously-unrecognized constitutional rights receive the federal courts' *imprimatur*?

3. Should the Court's willingness to recognize new constitutional rights in a *Teague* situation vary according to whether the prisoner argued them in state proceedings on direct appeal?

4. The Court disapproves disparity of treatment among similarly-situated individuals, arguing that recognition of a new but non-retroactive constitutional entitlement on habeas would allow only the petitioner to benefit, not others convicted at the same time.

a) Suppose all individuals convicted on a given day whose cases present a new constitutional question were to persevere through the state appellate and federal habeas corpus processes. What becomes of the anomaly the Court perceives? To the extent that it disappears, does a petitioner in Teague's position suffer because other prisoners had less astute counsel?

b) Suppose Teague and another person involved in the same incident were convicted on the same day but in separate trials. If Teague's state appellate process ran particularly quickly and his confederate's did not, is it not possible that the confederate would receive the benefit of a newly-recognized constitutional right during his direct appeal while Teague would not because his trip through the appellate process was more expeditious?

5. Should *Teague* apply to petitions by federal prisoners? Symmetry may suggest that it should, but if federalism concerns motivated the *Teague* Court, *Teague*'s rationale cannot apply to federal prisoners. (Of course, federalism was not the only rationale underlying *Teague*; concerns about finality and equality among similarly-situated prisoners implicate federal-prisoner habeas as well.)

6. Justice Brennan's dissent argued that the federal courts recognized many constitutional rights in habeas corpus cases. *Teague* halts that phenomenon. Although only a plurality supported the *Teague* rule, the Court has since made clear its intention to apply it rigorously. In *Penry v. Lynaugh*, 492 U.S. 302, 109 S.Ct. 2934, 106 L.Ed.2d 256 (1989), a majority ruled that *Teague* applies to whether the Constitution permits execution of a retarded prisoner. The Court reached the merits because existing precedent dictated the claimed right, but in three subsequent decisions, the Court applied *Teague* in capital cases and refused review. Justice Brennan dissented vigorously:

> [Applying *Teague* to capital cases] means that a person may be killed although he or she has a sound constitutional claim that would have barred his or her execution had this Court only announced the constitutional rule before his or her conviction and sentence became final. It is intolerable that the difference between life and death should turn on such a fortuity of timing and beyond my comprehension that a majority of this Court will so blithely allow a State to take a human life though the method by which the sentence was determined violates our Constitution.

7. Under *Teague*, a new rule of criminal procedure announced after a state prisoner's conviction becomes final may not be applied in federal habeas proceedings unless it is a "watershed" rule of procedure that implicates the fundamental fairness and accuracy of the criminal process. Whether this retroactivity standard is met in a federal habeas case plainly is a matter of federal law. May a state court, however, in state collateral proceedings allow retroactive application of a new federal rule when federal law would not allow retroactive application? The Supreme Court answered in the affirmative in *Danforth v. Minnesota*, __ U.S. __, 128 S.Ct. 1029, __ L.Ed.2d__ (2008).

Petitioner was convicted in 1996 in Minnesota of criminal sexual conduct. The state presented the six year-old victim's testimony by videotaped interview. After petitioner's conviction became final, the United States Supreme Court decided *Crawford v. Washington*, 541 U.S. 36, 124 S.Ct. 1354, 158 L.Ed.2d 177 (2004), which changed the contours of the Sixth Amendment Confrontation Clause. Danforth promptly filed a state post-conviction petition claiming admission of the videotape violated *Crawford* standards. Anticipating the Supreme Court decision in *Whorton v. Bockting*, ___ U.S. __, 127 S.Ct. 1173, 167 L.Ed.2d 1 (2007) (*supra* at 1120), the state courts determined that the new rule of criminal procedure *Crawford* announced was not a "watershed" rule, and thus, under *Teague,* could not apply retroactively. The Minnesota Supreme Court explicitly held that state courts are not free to give United States Supreme Court decisions announcing new rules broader retroactive application than the United States Supreme Court would give them.

The Supreme Court disagreed, holding that *Whorton*, *Teague*, and other precedents neither required state courts to follow federal retroactivity rules in state post-conviction proceedings nor prohibited them from following the federal rules. After a somewhat confusing review of "our somewhat confused and confusing 'retroactivity' cases," Justice Stevens's majority opinion carefully examined Justice O'Connor's opinion in *Teague*, and found no indication that it was meant to apply beyond "the unique context of federal habeas." Nor did other Supreme Court precedent require state courts to follow the *Teague* retroactivity rules. Minnesota argued that while a state may grant their citizens broader protection than federal law requires, a state may not do so "by judicial misconstruction of federal law." The Court concluded, however, that giving broader retroactive effect to a new Supreme Court criminal procedure rule was not "misconstruing the federal *Teague* standard," but rather "develop[ing] state law to govern retroactivity in state postconviction proceedings." Finding nothing in federal law to prohibit the states from following such a course, the Court reversed.

Chief Justice Roberts, joined by Justice Kennedy, dissented. The Chief Justice viewed the precedent differently, presenting quotations from earlier cases suggesting the states are required to follow federal retroactivity law. In addition, he argued that retroactivity is not a separate remedial issue that can be split from the underlying right because "when we ask whether and to what extent a rule will be retroactively applied, we are asking what law—new or old—will apply." More broadly, he argued that a uniform federal rule was essential to avoid haphazard and unequal application of federal law from state to state.

8. *Teague* has provoked considerable critical scholarly commentary. One commentator suggested strongly that the decision damages the Court's institutional integrity.

> The decisions in *Teague* and its progeny are subject to criticism on several fronts. The judicial crafting of the *Teague* decision was uneven at best, all too disingenuous at worst. The Court adopted an extremely restrictive view of habeas corpus jurisdiction and did so virtually as a passing aside. For anyone familiar with the climate surrounding the decision it is difficult to conclude that the Court's determination was the product of much more than unseemly impatience with a Congress that was considering related issues, but evidently too slowly for the Court. Moreover, the result in the *Teague* cases plainly was the work of a Court anxious to speed the pace of executions.

* * *

> None of the *Teague* decisions seriously discussed [the] radical redefinition of habeas corpus. Rather, the Court disingenuously characterized *Teague* as nothing more than one further decision in a long line of cases attempting to resolve perplexing problems regarding the retroactivity of criminal constitutional rules. The entire premise of *Teague* was that existing retroactivity rules denied "even-handed justice" to "similarly situated" individuals seeking application of constitutional rules in their cases. Thus, *Teague* masqueraded as an exercise in achieving fairness. Moreover, in doing so the *Teague* Court purported to adopt a theory of retroactivity advanced by Justice Harlan twenty years ago. *Teague*, however, did neither of these things, or at least it

did not do them very well.

Barry Friedman, *Habeas and Hubris*, 45 VAND.L.REV.. 797, 800, 803 (1992). *See also, e.g.*, Vivian Berger, *Justice Delayed or Justice Denied—A Comment on Recent Proposals to Reform Death Penalty Habeas Corpus*, 90 COLUM. L. REV. 1665 (1990); Richard H. Fallon, Jr. & Daniel J. Meltzer, *New Law, Nonretroactivity and Constitutional Remedies*, 104 HARV.L.REV. 1731 (1991).

9. In June, 1988, Chief Justice Rehnquist formed the *Ad Hoc* Committee on Federal Habeas Corpus in Capital Cases to examine the "necessity and desirability of legislation directed toward avoiding delay and the lack of finality" in capital cases. Former Justice Powell chaired the Committee, which reported suggested additions to Title 28. Senator Thurmond introduced the Committee's proposals in Congress. Neither that bill nor two similar bills became law, but the Court later decided cases that embodied many of the suggested changes. Did the formation of the Committee and the introduction of legislation embodying its proposals suggest that they are not a part of the then-existing statutory structure? If so, was it proper for the Court to create rules in the face of statutory incompleteness and congressional inaction? If the decisions did not rest on constitutional grounds, what justified creating federal common law? If they did rest on constitutional grounds, why did Chief Justice Rehnquist and the Committee feel that legislation was necessary?

9. For those who thought that the cause-and-prejudice rule of *Wainwright v. Sykes* (reaffirmed in *Coleman v. Thompson* and discussed in Section G below) could not be narrowed, *Teague* must have come as an unpleasant surprise. After those cases, a petitioner could have a state procedural default excused by showing that the rule upon which he relied "is so novel that its legal basis is not reasonably available to counsel." Suppose a prisoner today makes that showing. What does his success earn him? Similarly, a petitioner who wishes to file a second habeas petition will, under the federal rules, suffer dismissal if he "fails to allege new or different grounds for relief and the prior determination was on the merits." But if he does allege new grounds, how will he avoid the retroactivity trap of *Teague*?

> In any event, the relationship between the various definitions of novelty is a troubling question. Courts apparently believe that novelty for purposes of excusing procedural default or a successive petition is the same as novelty for purposes of barring retroactive application of a rule unless it falls within a *Teague* exception. Under current practice, this raises a cruel dilemma for petitioners. Under whatever practice develops as a result of the *Teague* regime, this dynamic is likely to lead to a further increase in the number, variety, and ingenuity of claims raised on direct appeal; indeed, it is likely to lead to the placing of even greater importance on the prisoner's direct appeal.

Marc M. Arkin, *The Prisoner's Dilemma: Life in the Lower Federal Courts After* Teague v. Lane, 69 N.C. L. REV. 371, 413 (1991).

WILLIAMS (TERRY) v. TAYLOR

Supreme Court of the United States, 2000.
529 U.S. 362, 120 S.Ct. 1495, 146 L.Ed.2d 389.

JUSTICE STEVENS announced the judgment of the Court and delivered the opinion of the Court with respect to Parts, I, III, and IV, and an opinion with respect to Parts II and V.[*]

The questions presented are whether Terry Williams' constitutional right to the effective assistance of counsel as defined in *Strickland v. Washington*, was violated, and whether the judgment of the Virginia Supreme Court refusing to set aside his death sentence "was contrary to, or involved an unreasonable application of, clearly established Federal law, as determined by the Supreme Court of the United States," within the meaning of 28 U.S.C. § 2254(d)(1). We answer both questions affirmatively.

I

On November 3, 1985, Harris Stone was found dead in his residence on Henry Street in Danville, Virginia. Finding no indication of a struggle, local officials determined that the cause of death was blood alcohol poisoning, and the case was considered closed. Six months after Stone's death, Terry Williams, who was then incarcerated in the "I" unit of the city jail for an unrelated offense, wrote a letter to the police stating that he had killed " 'that man down on Henry Street' " and also stating that he " 'did it' " to that " 'lady down on West Green Street' " and was " 'very sorry.' " The letter was unsigned, but it closed with a reference to "I cell." The police readily identified Williams as its author, and, on April 25, 1986, they obtained several statements from him. In one Williams admitted that, after Stone refused to lend him " 'a couple of dollars,' " he had killed Stone with a mattock and took the money from his wallet. In September 1986, Williams was convicted of robbery and capital murder.

At Williams' sentencing hearing, the prosecution proved that Williams had been convicted of armed robbery in 1976 and burglary and grand larceny in 1982. The prosecution also introduced the written confessions that Williams had made in April. The prosecution described two auto thefts and two separate violent assaults on elderly victims perpetrated after the Stone murder. On December 4, 1985, Williams had started a fire outside one victim's residence before attacking and robbing him. On March 5, 1986, Williams had brutally assaulted an elderly woman on West Green Street—an incident he had mentioned in his letter to the police. That confession was particularly damaging because other evidence established that the woman was in a "vegetative state" and not expected to recover. Williams had also been convicted of arson for setting a fire in the jail while awaiting trial in this case. Two expert

---

[*] Justice Souter, Justice Ginsburg, and Justice Breyer join this opinion in its entirety. Justice O'Connor and Justice Kennedy join Parts I, III, and IV of this opinion.

witnesses employed by the State testified that there was a "high probability" that Williams would pose a serious continuing threat to society.

The evidence offered by Williams' trial counsel at the sentencing hearing consisted of the testimony of Williams' mother, two neighbors, and a taped excerpt from a statement by a psychiatrist. One of the neighbors had not been previously interviewed by defense counsel, but was noticed by counsel in the audience during the proceedings and asked to testify on the spot. The three witnesses briefly described Williams as a "nice boy" and not a violent person. The recorded psychiatrist's testimony did little more than relate Williams' statement during an examination that in the course of one of his earlier robberies, he had removed the bullets from a gun so as not to injure anyone.

In his cross-examination of the prosecution witnesses, Williams' counsel repeatedly emphasized the fact that Williams had initiated the contact with the police that enabled them to solve the murder and to identify him as the perpetrator of the recent assaults, as well as the car thefts. In closing argument, Williams' counsel characterized Williams' confessional statements as "dumb," but asked the jury to give weight to the fact that he had "turned himself in, not on one crime but on four * * * that the [police otherwise] would not have solved." The weight of defense counsel's closing, however, was devoted to explaining that it was difficult to find a reason why the jury should spare Williams' life.[2]

The jury found a probability of future dangerousness and unanimously fixed Williams' punishment at death. The trial judge concluded that such punishment was "proper" and "just" and imposed the death sentence. The Virginia Supreme Court affirmed the conviction and sentence. It rejected Williams' argument that when the trial judge imposed sentence, he failed to give mitigating weight to the fact that Williams had turned himself in.

State Habeas Corpus Proceedings

In 1988 Williams filed for state collateral relief in the Danville Circuit Court. The petition was subsequently amended, and the Circuit Court (the same judge who had presided over Williams' trial and sentencing) held an evidentiary hearing on Williams' claim that trial counsel had been ineffective.[3] Based on the evidence adduced after two days

---

[2] In defense counsel's words: "I will admit too that it is very difficult to ask you to show mercy to a man who maybe has not shown much mercy himself. I doubt very seriously that he thought much about mercy when he was in Mr. Stone's bedroom that night with him. I doubt very seriously that he had mercy very highly on his mind when he was walking along West Green and the incident with Alberta Stroud. I doubt very seriously that he had mercy on his mind when he took two cars that didn't belong to him. Admittedly it is very difficult to get us [sic, probably intending "up"] and ask that you give this man mercy when he has shown so little of it himself. But I would ask that you would."

[3] While Williams' petition was pending before the Circuit Court, Virginia amended its state habeas statute to vest in the State Supreme Court exclusive jurisdiction to award

of hearings, Judge Ingram found that Williams' conviction was valid, but that his trial attorneys had been ineffective during sentencing. Among the evidence reviewed that had not been presented at trial were documents prepared in connection with Williams' commitment when he was 11 years old that dramatically described mistreatment, abuse, and neglect during his early childhood, as well as testimony that he was "borderline mentally retarded," had suffered repeated head injuries, and might have mental impairments organic in origin. The habeas hearing also revealed that the same experts who had testified on the State's behalf at trial believed that Williams, if kept in a "structured environment," would not pose a future danger to society.

Counsel's failure to discover and present this and other significant mitigating evidence was "below the range expected of reasonable, professional competent assistance of counsel." Counsel's performance thus "did not measure up to the standard required under the holding of *Strickland*, and [if it had,] there is a reasonable probability that the result of the sentencing phase would have been different." Judge Ingram therefore recommended that Williams be granted a rehearing on the sentencing phase of his trial.

The Virginia Supreme Court did not accept that recommendation. Although it assumed, without deciding, that trial counsel had been ineffective, it disagreed with the trial judge's conclusion that Williams had suffered sufficient prejudice to warrant relief. Treating the prejudice inquiry as a mixed question of law and fact, the Virginia Supreme Court accepted the factual determination that available evidence in mitigation had not been presented at the trial, but held that the trial judge had misapplied the law in two respects. First, relying on our decision in *Lockhart v. Fretwell*, the court held that it was wrong for the trial judge to rely " 'on mere outcome determination' " when assessing prejudice. Second, it construed the trial judge's opinion as having "adopted a *per se* approach" that would establish prejudice whenever any mitigating evidence was omitted.

The court then reviewed the prosecution evidence supporting the "future dangerousness" aggravating circumstance, reciting Williams' criminal history, including the several most recent offenses to which he had confessed. In comparison, it found that the excluded mitigating evidence—which it characterized as merely indicating "that numerous people, mostly relatives, thought that defendant was nonviolent and could cope very well in a structured environment"—"barely would have altered the profile of this defendant that was presented to the jury." On this basis, the court concluded that there was no reasonable possibility that the

---

writs of habeas corpus in capital cases. Shortly after the Circuit Court held its evidentiary hearing, the Supreme Court assumed jurisdiction over Williams' petition and instructed the Circuit Court to issue findings of fact and legal recommendation[s] regarding Williams' ineffective-assistance claims.

omitted evidence would have affected the jury's sentencing recommendation, and that Williams had failed to demonstrate that his sentencing proceeding was fundamentally unfair.

Federal Habeas Corpus Proceedings

Having exhausted his state remedies, Williams sought a federal writ of habeas corpus. After reviewing the state habeas hearing transcript and the state courts' findings of fact and conclusions of law, the federal trial judge agreed with the Virginia trial judge: The death sentence was constitutionally infirm.

After noting that the Virginia Supreme Court had not addressed the question whether trial counsel's performance at the sentencing hearing fell below the range of competence demanded of lawyers in criminal cases, the judge began by addressing that issue in detail. He identified five categories of mitigating evidence that counsel had failed to introduce,[4] and he rejected the argument that counsel's failure to conduct an adequate investigation had been a strategic decision to rely almost entirely on the fact that Williams had voluntarily confessed.

According to Williams' trial counsel's testimony before the state habeas court, counsel did not fail to seek Williams' juvenile and social services records because he thought they would be counterproductive, but because counsel erroneously believed that " 'state law didn't permit it.' " Counsel also acknowledged in the course of the hearings that information about Williams' childhood would have been important in mitigation. And counsel's failure to contact a potentially persuasive character witness was likewise not a conscious strategic choice, but simply a failure to return that witness' phone call offering his service. Finally, even if counsel neglected to conduct such an investigation at the time as part of a tactical decision, the District Judge found, tactics as a matter of reasonable performance could not justify the omissions.

Turning to the prejudice issue, the judge determined that there was " 'a reasonable probability that, but for counsel's unprofessional errors, the result of the proceeding would have been different.' *Strickland*." He found that the Virginia Supreme Court had erroneously assumed that *Lockhart* had modified the *Strickland* standard for determining prejudice, and that it had made an important error of fact in discussing its

---

4   (i) Counsel did not introduce evidence of the Petitioner's background * * * . (ii) Counsel did not introduce evidence that Petitioner was abused by his father. (iii) Counsel did not introduce testimony from correctional officers who were willing to testify that defendant would not pose a danger while incarcerated. Nor did counsel offer prison commendations awarded to Williams for his help in breaking up a prison drug ring and for returning a guard's wallet. (iv) Several character witnesses were not called to testify * * * . [T]he testimony of Elliott, a respected CPA in the community, could have been quite important to the jury * * * . (v) Finally, counsel did not introduce evidence that Petitioner was borderline mentally retarded, though he was found competent to stand trial.

finding of no prejudice.[5]   Having introduced his analysis of Williams' claim with the standard of review applicable on habeas appeals provided by 28 U.S.C. § 2254(d), the judge concluded that those errors established that the Virginia Supreme Court's decision "was contrary to, or involved an unreasonable application of, clearly established Federal law" within the meaning of § 2254(d)(1).

The Federal Court of Appeals reversed.   It construed § 2254(d)(1) as prohibiting the grant of habeas corpus relief unless the state court "decided the question by interpreting or applying the relevant precedent in a manner that reasonable jurists would all agree is unreasonable."   Applying that standard, it could not say that the Virginia Supreme Court's decision on the prejudice issue was an unreasonable application of the tests developed in either *Strickland* or *Lockhart*.   It explained that the evidence that Williams presented a future danger to society was "simply overwhelming"; it endorsed the Virginia Supreme Court's interpretation of *Lockhart*, and it characterized the state court's understanding of the facts in this case as "reasonable."

We granted certiorari and now reverse.

II

In 1867, Congress enacted a statute providing that federal courts "shall have power to grant writs of habeas corpus in all cases where any person may be restrained of his or her liberty in violation of the constitution, or of any treaty or law of the United States * * * ."   Over the years, the federal habeas corpus statute has been repeatedly amended, but the scope of that jurisdictional grant remains the same.   It is, of course, well settled that the fact that constitutional error occurred in the proceedings that led to a state-court conviction may not alone be sufficient reason for concluding that a prisoner is entitled to the remedy of habeas.   On the other hand, errors that undermine confidence in the fundamental fairness of the state adjudication certainly justify the issuance of the federal writ.   The deprivation of the right to the effective assistance of counsel recognized in *Strickland* is such an error.

The warden here contends that federal habeas corpus relief is prohibited by the amendment to 28 U.S.C. § 2254, enacted as a part of the Antiterrorism and Effective Death Penalty Act of 1996 (AEDPA).   The

---

[5]   Specifically, the Virginia Supreme Court found no prejudice, reasoning: "The mitigation evidence that the prisoner says, in retrospect, his trial counsel should have discovered and offered barely would have altered the profile of this defendant that was presented to the jury.   At most, this evidence would have shown that numerous people, mostly relatives, thought that defendant was nonviolent and could cope very well in a structured environment."   The Virginia Supreme Court ignored or overlooked the evidence of Williams' difficult childhood and abuse and his limited mental capacity.   It is also unreasonable to characterize the additional evidence as coming from "mostly relatives."   As stated, Bruce Elliott, a respected professional in the community, and several correctional officers offered to testify on Williams behalf.

relevant portion of that amendment provides:

> (d) An application for a writ of habeas corpus on behalf of a person in custody pursuant to the judgment of a State court shall not be granted with respect to any claim that was adjudicated on the merits in State court proceedings unless the adjudication of the claim—
>
> > (1) resulted in a decision that was contrary to, or involved an unreasonable application of, clearly established Federal law, as determined by the Supreme Court of the United States * * * .

In this case, the Court of Appeals applied the construction of the amendment that it had adopted in its earlier opinion in *Green v. French.* It read the amendment as prohibiting federal courts from issuing the writ unless:

> (a) the state court decision is in "square conflict" with Supreme Court precedent that is controlling as to law and fact or (b) if no such controlling decision exists, the state court's resolution of a question of pure law rests upon an objectively unreasonable derivation of legal principles from the relevant [S]upreme [C]ourt precedents, or if its decision rests upon an objectively unreasonable application of established principles to new facts.

Accordingly, it held that a federal court may issue habeas relief only if "the state courts have decided the question by interpreting or applying the relevant precedent in a manner that reasonable jurists would all agree is unreasonable."

We are convinced that that interpretation of the amendment is incorrect. It would impose a test for determining when a legal rule is clearly established that simply cannot be squared with the real practice of decisional law.[9] It would apply a standard for determining the "reasonableness" of state-court decisions that is not contained in the statute itself, and that Congress surely did not intend. And it would wrongly require the federal courts, including this Court, to defer to state judges' interpretations of federal law.

As the Fourth Circuit would have it, a state-court judgment is "unreasonable" in the face of federal law only if all reasonable jurists would

---

[9] Although we explain our understanding of "clearly established law," we note that the Fourth Circuit's construction of the amendment's inquiry in this respect is especially problematic. It separates cases into those for which a "controlling decision" exists and those for which no such decision exists. The former category includes very few cases, since a rule is "controlling" only if it matches the case before the court both "as to law and fact," and most cases are factually distinguishable in some respect. A literal application of the Fourth Circuit test would yield a particularly perverse outcome in cases involving the *Strickland* rule for establishing ineffective assistance of counsel, since that case, which established the "controlling" rule of law on the issue, contained facts insufficient to show ineffectiveness.

agree that the state court was unreasonable. Thus, in this case, for example, even if the Virginia Supreme Court misread our opinion in *Lockhart*, we could not grant relief unless we believed that none of the judges who agreed with the state court's interpretation of that case was a "reasonable jurist." But the statute says nothing about "reasonable judges," presumably because all, or virtually all, such judges occasionally commit error; they make decisions that in retrospect may be characterized as "unreasonable." Indeed, it is most unlikely that Congress would deliberately impose such a requirement of unanimity on federal judges. As Congress is acutely aware, reasonable lawyers and lawgivers regularly disagree with one another. Congress surely did not intend that the views of one such judge who might think that relief is not warranted in a particular case should always have greater weight than the contrary, considered judgment of several other reasonable judges.

The inquiry mandated by the amendment relates to the way in which a federal habeas court exercises its duty to decide constitutional questions; the amendment does not alter the underlying grant of jurisdiction in § 2254(a).[10]   When federal judges exercise their federal-question jurisdiction under the "judicial Power" of Article III of the Constitution, it is "emphatically the province and duty" of those judges to "say what the law is." At the core of this power is the federal courts' independent responsibility— independent from its coequal branches in the Federal Government, and independent from the separate authority of the several States—to interpret federal law. A construction of AEDPA that would require the federal courts to cede this authority to the courts of the States would be inconsistent with the practice that federal judges have traditionally followed in discharging their duties under Article III of the Constitution. If Congress had intended to require such an important change in the exercise of our jurisdiction, we believe it would have spoken with much greater clarity than is found in the text of AEDPA.

This basic premise informs our interpretation of both parts of § 2254(d)(1): first, the requirement that the determinations of state courts be tested only against "clearly established Federal law, as determined by the Supreme Court of the United States," and second, the prohibition on the issuance of the writ unless the state court's decision is

---

[10] Indeed, Congress roundly rejected an amendment to the bill eventually adopted that directly invoked the text of the jurisdictional grant, 28 U.S.C. § 2254(a) (providing that the federal courts "shall entertain an application for a writ of habeas corpus" (emphasis added)). The amendment read: "Notwithstanding any other provision of law, an application for a writ of habeas corpus in behalf of a person in custody pursuant to a judgment or order of a State court shall not be entertained by a court of the United States unless the remedies in the courts of the State are inadequate or ineffective to test the legality of the person's detention." ([A]mendment of Sen. Kyl) (emphasis added). In speaking against the Kyl amendment, Senator Specter (a key proponent of the eventual habeas reform) explained that when "dealing with the question of jurisdiction of the Federal courts to entertain questions on Federal issues, on constitutional issues, I believe it is necessary that the Federal courts retain that jurisdiction as a constitutional matter."

"contrary to, or involved an unreasonable application of," that clearly established law. We address each part in turn.

The "clearly established law" requirement

In *Teague v. Lane*, we held that the petitioner was not entitled to federal habeas relief because he was relying on a rule of federal law that had not been announced until after his state conviction became final. The antiretroactivity rule recognized in Teague, which prohibits reliance on "new rules," is the functional equivalent of a statutory provision commanding exclusive reliance on "clearly established law." Because there is no reason to believe that Congress intended to require federal courts to ask both whether a rule sought on habeas is "new" under Teague—which remains the law—and also whether it is "clearly established" under AEDPA, it seems safe to assume that Congress had congruent concepts in mind. It is perfectly clear that AEDPA codifies Teague to the extent that Teague requires federal habeas courts to deny relief that is contingent upon a rule of law not clearly established at the time the state conviction became final.[12]

Teague's core principles are therefore relevant to our construction of this requirement. Justice Harlan recognized the "inevitable difficulties" that come with "attempting 'to determine whether a particular decision has really announced a "new" rule at all or whether it has simply applied a well-established constitutional principle to govern a case which is closely analogous to those which have been previously considered in the prior case law.'" But *Teague* established some guidance for making this determination, explaining that a federal habeas court operates within the bounds of comity and finality if it applies a rule "dictated by precedent existing at the time the defendant's conviction became final." ([E]mphasis deleted). A rule that "breaks new ground or imposes a new obligation on the States or the Federal Government," falls outside this universe of federal law.

To this, AEDPA has added, immediately following the "clearly estab-

---

[12] We are not persuaded by the argument that because Congress used the words "clearly established law" and not "new rule," it meant in this section to codify an aspect of the doctrine of executive qualified immunity rather than *Teague*'s antiretroactivity bar. The warden refers us specifically to § 2244(b)(2)(A) and 28 U.S.C. § 2254(e)(2), in which the statute does in so many words employ the "new rule" language familiar to *Teague* and its progeny. Congress thus knew precisely the words to use if it had wished to codify *Teague per se*. That it did not use those words in § 2254(d) is evidence, the argument goes, that it had something else in mind entirely in amending that section. We think, quite the contrary, that the verbatim adoption of the *Teague* language in these other sections bolsters our impression that Congress had *Teague*—and not any unrelated area of our jurisprudence—specifically in mind in amending the habeas statute. These provisions, seen together, make it impossible to conclude that Congress was not fully aware of, and interested in codifying into law, that aspect of this Court's habeas doctrine. We will not assume that in a single subsection of an amendment entirely devoted to the law of habeas corpus, Congress made the anomalous choice of reaching into the doctrinally distinct law of qualified immunity, for a single phrase that just so happens to be the conceptual twin of a dominant principle in habeas law of which Congress was fully aware.

lished law" requirement, a clause limiting the area of relevant law to that "determined by the Supreme Court of the United States." If this Court has not broken sufficient legal ground to establish an asked-for constitutional principle, the lower federal courts cannot themselves establish such a principle with clarity sufficient to satisfy the AEDPA bar. In this respect, we agree with the Seventh Circuit that this clause "extends the principle of *Teague* by limiting the source of doctrine on which a federal court may rely in addressing the application for a writ."

* * *

A rule that fails to satisfy the foregoing criteria is barred by *Teague* from application on collateral review, and, similarly, is not available as a basis for relief in a habeas case to which AEDPA applies.

In the context of this case, we also note that, as our precedent interpreting *Teague* has demonstrated, rules of law may be sufficiently clear for habeas purposes even when they are expressed in terms of a generalized standard rather than as a bright-line rule. As Justice Kennedy has explained:

> If the rule in question is one which of necessity requires a case-by-case examination of the evidence, then we can tolerate a number of specific applications without saying that those applications themselves create a new rule * * *. Where the beginning point is a rule of this general application, a rule designed for the specific purpose of evaluating a myriad of factual contexts, it will be the infrequent case that yields a result so novel that it forges a new rule, one not dictated by precedent.

Moreover, the determination whether or not a rule is clearly established at the time a state court renders its final judgment of conviction is a question as to which the "federal courts must make an independent evaluation."

It has been urged, in contrast, that we should read *Teague* and its progeny to encompass a broader principle of deference requiring federal courts to "validat[e] 'reasonable, good-faith interpretations' of the law" by state courts. The position has been bolstered with references to our statements elucidating the "new rule" inquiry as one turning on whether "reasonable jurists" would agree the rule was not clearly established. This presumption of deference was in essence the position taken by three Members of this Court in *Wright* (opinion of Thomas, J.) ("[A] federal habeas court must defer to the state court's decision rejecting the claim unless that decision is patently unreasonable.").

Teague, however, does not extend this far. The often repeated language that *Teague* endorses "reasonable, good-faith interpretations" by state courts is an explanation of policy, not a statement of law. The *Teague* cases reflect this Court's view that habeas corpus is not to be used as a second criminal trial, and federal courts are not to run rough-

shod over the considered findings and judgments of the state courts that
conducted the original trial and heard the initial appeals. On the contrary, we have long insisted that federal habeas courts attend closely to
those considered decisions, and give them full effect when their findings
and judgments are consistent with federal law. But as Justice O'Connor
explained in *Wright*:

> [T]he duty of the federal court in evaluating whether a rule is
> "new" is not the same as deference; * * * *Teague* does not direct
> federal courts to spend less time or effort scrutinizing the existing
> federal law, on the ground that they can assume the state courts
> interpreted it properly.

> [T]he maxim that federal courts should "give great weight to the
> considered conclusions of a coequal state judiciary" * * * does not
> mean that we have held in the past that federal courts must pre-
> sume the correctness of a state court's legal conclusions on habeas,
> or that a state court's incorrect legal determination has ever been
> allowed to stand because it was reasonable. We have always held
> that federal courts, even on habeas, have an independent obligation
> to say what the law is.

We are convinced that in the phrase, "clearly established law," Congress did not intend to modify that independent obligation.

The "contrary to, or an unreasonable application of," requirement

The message that Congress intended to convey by using the phrases,
"contrary to" and "unreasonable application of" is not entirely clear. The
prevailing view in the Circuits is that the former phrase requires *de novo*
review of "pure" questions of law and the latter requires some sort of
"reasonability" review of so-called mixed questions of law and fact.

We are not persuaded that the phrases define two mutually exclusive categories of questions. Most constitutional questions that arise in
habeas corpus proceedings—and therefore most "decisions" to be made—
require the federal judge to apply a rule of law to a set of facts, some of
which may be disputed and some undisputed. For example, an erroneous conclusion that particular circumstances established the voluntariness of a confession, or that there exists a conflict of interest when one
attorney represents multiple defendants, may well be described either as
"contrary to" or as an "unreasonable application of" the governing rule of
law. In constitutional adjudication, as in the common law, rules of law
often develop incrementally as earlier decisions are applied to new factual situations. But rules that depend upon such elaboration are hardly
less lawlike than those that establish a bright-line test.

Indeed, our pre-AEDPA efforts to distinguish questions of fact, questions of law, and "mixed questions," and to create an appropriate standard of habeas review for each, generated some not insubstantial differences of opinion as to which issues of law fell into which category of

question, and as to which standard of review applied to each. We thus think the Fourth Circuit was correct when it attributed the lack of clarity in the statute, in part, to the overlapping meanings of the phrases "contrary to" and "unreasonable application of."

The statutory text likewise does not obviously prescribe a specific, recognizable standard of review for dealing with either phrase. Significantly, it does not use any term, such as "de novo" or "plain error," that would easily identify a familiar standard of review. Rather, the text is fairly read simply as a command that a federal court not issue the habeas writ unless the state court was wrong as a matter of law or unreasonable in its application of law in a given case. The suggestion that a wrong state-court "decision"—a legal judgment rendered "after consideration of *facts, and * * * law*," BLACK'S LAW DICTIONARY 414 (7th ed.1999) (emphasis added)—may no longer be redressed through habeas (because it is unreachable under the "unreasonable application" phrase) is based on a mistaken insistence that the § 2254(d)(1) phrases have not only independent, but mutually exclusive, meanings. Whether or not a federal court can issue the writ "under [the] 'unreasonable application' clause," the statute is clear that habeas may issue under § 2254(d)(1) if a state court "decision" is "contrary to * * * clearly established Federal law." We thus anticipate that there will be a variety of cases, like this one, in which both phrases may be implicated.

Even though we cannot conclude that the phrases establish "a body of rigid rules," they do express a "mood" that the federal judiciary must respect. In this respect, it seems clear that Congress intended federal judges to attend with the utmost care to state-court decisions, including all of the reasons supporting their decisions, before concluding that those proceedings were infected by constitutional error sufficiently serious to warrant the issuance of the writ. Likewise, the statute in a separate provision provides for the habeas remedy when a state-court decision "was based on an unreasonable determination of the facts *in light of the evidence presented in the State court proceeding.*" ([E]mphasis added). While this provision is not before us in this case, it provides relevant context for our interpretation of § 2254(d)(1); in this respect, it bolsters our conviction that federal habeas courts must make as the starting point of their analysis the state courts' determinations of fact, including that aspect of a "mixed question" that rests on a finding of fact. AEDPA plainly sought to ensure a level of "deference to the determinations of state courts," provided those determinations did not conflict with federal law or apply federal law in an unreasonable way. Congress wished to curb delays, to prevent "retrials" on federal habeas, and to give effect to state convictions to the extent possible under law. When federal courts are able to fulfill these goals within the bounds of the law, AEDPA instructs them to do so.

On the other hand, it is significant that the word "deference" does not appear in the text of the statute itself. Neither the legislative history, nor the statutory text, suggests any difference in the so-called "deference" depending on which of the two phrases is implicated.[13] Whatever "deference" Congress had in mind with respect to both phrases, it surely is not a requirement that federal courts actually defer to a state-court application of the federal law that is, in the independent judgment of the federal court, in error. As Judge Easterbrook noted with respect to the phrase "contrary to": "Section 2254(d) requires us to give state courts' opinions a respectful reading, and to listen carefully to their conclusions, but when the state court addresses a legal question, it is the law 'as determined by the Supreme Court of the United States' that prevails."[14]

Our disagreement with Justice O'Connor about the precise meaning of the phrase "contrary to," and the word "unreasonable," is, of course, important, but should affect only a narrow category of cases. The sim-

---

[13] As Judge Easterbrook has noted, the statute surely does not require the kind of "deference" appropriate in other contexts: "It does not tell us to 'defer' to state decisions, as if the Constitution means one thing in Wisconsin and another in Indiana. Nor does it tell us to treat state courts the way we treat federal administrative agencies. Deference * * * depends on delegation. Congress did not delegate interpretive or executive power to the state courts. They exercise powers under their domestic law, constrained by the Constitution of the United States. 'Deference' to the jurisdictions bound by those constraints is not sensible."

[14] The Court advances three reasons for adopting its alternative construction of the phrase "unreasonable application of." First, the use of the word "unreasonable" in the statute suggests that Congress was directly influenced by the "patently unreasonable" standard advocated by Justice Thomas in his opinion in *Wright v. West*; second, the legislative history supports this view; and third, Congress must have intended to change the law more substantially than our reading 28 U.S.C. § 2254(d)(1) permits.

None of these reasons is persuasive. First, even though, as the Court recognizes, the term "unreasonable" is "difficult to define," neither the statute itself nor the Court's explanation of it, suggests that AEDPA's "unreasonable application of" has the same meaning as Justice Thomas' " 'patently unreasonable' " standard mentioned in his dictum in *Wright*. To the extent the "broader debate" in *Wright* touched upon the Court's novel distinction today between what is "wrong" and what is "unreasonable," it was in the context of a discussion not about the *standard of review* habeas courts should use for law-application questions, but about whether a rule is "new" or "old" such that *Teague*'s retroactivity rule would bar habeas relief; Justice Thomas contended that *Teague* barred habeas "whenever the state courts have interpreted old precedents *reasonably*, not [as Justice O'Connor suggested] only when they have done so 'properly.' " *Teague*, of course, as Justice O'Connor correctly pointed out, "did not establish a standard of review at all"; rather than instructing a court how to review a claim, it simply asks, in absolute terms, *whether* a rule was clear at the time of a state-court decision. We thus do not think *Wright* "confirms" anything about the meaning of § 2254(d)(1), which is, as our division reflects, anything but "clear."

As for the other bases for Justice O'Connor's view, the only two specific citations to the legislative history upon which she relies do no more than beg the question. One merely quotes the language of the statute without elaboration, and the other goes to slightly greater length in stating that state-court judgments must be upheld unless "unreasonable." Neither sheds any light on what the content of the hypothetical category of "decisions" that are wrong but nevertheless not "unreasonable." Finally, while we certainly agree with the Court that AEDPA wrought substantial changes in habeas law, there is an obvious fallacy in the assumption that because the statute changed pre-existing law in some respects, it must have rendered this specific change here.

plest and first definition of "contrary to" as a phrase is "in conflict with." In this sense, we think the phrase surely capacious enough to include a finding that the state-court "decision" is simply "erroneous" or wrong. (We hasten to add that even "diametrically different" from, or "opposite" to, an established federal law would seem to include "decisions" that are wrong in light of that law.) And there is nothing in the phrase "contrary to"—as Justice O'Connor appears to agree—that implies anything less than independent review by the federal courts. Moreover, state-court decisions that do not "conflict" with federal law will rarely be "unreasonable" under either her reading of the statute or ours. We all agree that state-court judgments must be upheld unless, after the closest examination of the state-court judgment, a federal court is firmly convinced that a federal constitutional right has been violated. Our difference is as to the cases in which, at first-blush, a state-court judgment seems entirely reasonable, but thorough analysis by a federal court produces a firm conviction that that judgment is infected by constitutional error. In our view, such an erroneous judgment is "unreasonable" within the meaning of the act even though that conclusion was not immediately apparent.

In sum, the statute directs federal courts to attend to every state-court judgment with utmost care, but it does not require them to defer to the opinion of every reasonable state-court judge on * * * federal law. If, after carefully weighing all the reasons for accepting a state court's judgment, a federal court is convinced that a prisoner's custody—or, as in this case, his sentence of death—violates the Constitution, that independent judgment should prevail. Otherwise the federal "law as determined by the Supreme Court of the United States" might be applied by the federal courts one way in Virginia and another way in California. In light of the well-recognized interest in ensuring that federal courts interpret federal law in a uniform way,[15] we are convinced that Congress did not intend the statute to produce such a result.

III

In this case, Williams contends that he was denied his constitutionally guaranteed right to the effective assistance of counsel when his trial lawyers failed to investigate and to present substantial mitigating evidence to the sentencing jury. The threshold question under AEDPA is whether Williams seeks to apply a rule of law that was clearly established at the time his state-court conviction became final. That question is easily answered because the merits of his claim are squarely governed by our holding in *Strickland*.

---

[15] Indeed, a contrary rule would be in substantial tension with the interest in uniformity served by Congress' modification in AEDPA of our previous *Teague* jurisprudence—now the law on habeas review must be "clearly established" by this Court alone. It would thus seem somewhat perverse to ascribe to Congress the entirely inconsistent policy of perpetuating disparate readings of our decisions under the guise of deference to anything within a conceivable spectrum of reasonableness.

We explained in *Strickland* that a violation of the right on which Williams relies has two components:

> First, the defendant must show that counsel's performance was deficient. This requires showing that counsel made errors so serious that counsel was not functioning as the "counsel" guaranteed the defendant by the Sixth Amendment. Second, the defendant must show that the deficient performance prejudiced the defense. This requires showing that counsel's errors were so serious as to deprive the defendant of a fair trial, a trial whose result is reliable.

To establish ineffectiveness, a "defendant must show that counsel's representation fell below an objective standard of reasonableness." To establish prejudice he "must show that there is a reasonable probability that, but for counsel's unprofessional errors, the result of the proceeding would have been different. A reasonable probability is a probability sufficient to undermine confidence in the outcome."

It is past question that the rule set forth in *Strickland* qualifies as "clearly established Federal law, as determined by the Supreme Court of the United States." That the *Strickland* test "of necessity requires a case-by-case examination of the evidence," obviates neither the clarity of the rule nor the extent to which the rule must be seen as "established" by this Court. This Court's precedent "dictated" that the Virginia Supreme Court apply the *Strickland* test at the time that court entertained Williams' ineffective-assistance claim. And it can hardly be said that recognizing the right to effective counsel "breaks new ground or imposes a new obligation on the States." Williams is therefore entitled to relief if the Virginia Supreme Court's decision rejecting his ineffective-assistance claim was either "contrary to, or involved an unreasonable application of," that established law. It was both.

IV

The Virginia Supreme Court erred in holding that our decision in *Lockhart v. Fretwell* modified or in some way supplanted the rule set down in *Strickland*. It is true that while the *Strickland* test provides sufficient guidance for resolving virtually all ineffective-assistance-of-counsel claims, there are situations in which the overriding focus on fundamental fairness may affect the analysis. Thus, on the one hand, as *Strickland* itself explained, there are a few situations in which prejudice may be presumed. And, on the other hand, there are also situations in which it would be unjust to characterize the likelihood of a different outcome as legitimate "prejudice." Even if a defendant's false testimony might have persuaded the jury to acquit him, it is not fundamentally unfair to conclude that he was not prejudiced by counsel's interference with his intended perjury.

Similarly, in *Lockhart*, we concluded that, given the overriding interest in fundamental fairness, the likelihood of a different outcome attributable to an incorrect interpretation of the law should be regarded as a potential "windfall" to the defendant rather than the legitimate "prejudice" contemplated by our opinion in *Strickland*. The death sentence that Arkansas had imposed on Bobby Ray Fretwell was based on an aggravating circumstance (murder committed for pecuniary gain) that duplicated an element of the underlying felony (murder in the course of a robbery). Shortly before the trial, the United States Court of Appeals for the Eighth Circuit had held that such "double counting" was impermissible, but Fretwell's lawyer (presumably because he was unaware of the * * * decision) failed to object to the use of the pecuniary gain aggravator. Before Fretwell's claim for federal habeas corpus relief reached this Court, the case was overruled. Accordingly, even though the Arkansas trial judge probably would have sustained a timely objection to the double counting, it had become clear that the State had a right to rely on the disputed aggravating circumstance. Because the ineffectiveness of Fretwell's counsel had not deprived him of any substantive or procedural right to which the law entitled him, we held that his claim did not satisfy the "prejudice" component of the Strickland test.

Cases such as *Nix v. Whiteside* and *Lockhart v. Fretwell* do not justify a departure from a straightforward application of *Strickland* when the ineffectiveness of counsel does deprive the defendant of a substantive or procedural right to which the law entitles him.[18] In the instant case, it is undisputed that Williams had a right—indeed, a constitutionally protected right—to provide the jury with the mitigating evidence that his trial counsel either failed to discover or failed to offer.

Nevertheless, the Virginia Supreme Court read our decision in *Lockhart* to require a separate inquiry into fundamental fairness even when Williams is able to show that his lawyer was ineffective and that his ineffectiveness probably affected the outcome of the proceeding. It wrote:

> The prisoner argues there "is a 'reasonable probability' that at least one juror would have been moved to spare Petitioner's life had he heard" the mitigation evidence developed at the habeas hearing that was not presented at the trial. Summarizing, he contends there "is a 'reasonable probability' that had at least one juror heard any of this evidence—let alone all of this evidence—the outcome of this case would have been different."

We reject these contentions. The prisoner's discussion flies in

---

[18] In her concurring opinion in *Lockhart*, Justice O'Connor stressed this precise point.

I write separately only to point out that today's decision will, in the vast majority of cases, have no effect on the prejudice inquiry under *Strickland*. The determinative question—whether there is "a reasonable probability that, but for counsel's unprofessional errors, the result of the proceeding would have been different,"—remains unchanged. This case, however, concerns the unusual circumstance where the defendant attempts to demonstrate prejudice based on considerations that, as a matter of law, ought not inform the inquiry.

the face of the Supreme Court's admonition in *Lockhart* that "an analysis focusing solely on mere outcome determination, without attention to whether the result of the proceeding was fundamentally unfair or unreliable, is defective."

Unlike the Virginia Supreme Court, the state trial judge omitted any reference to *Lockhart* and simply relied on our opinion in *Strickland* as stating the correct standard for judging ineffective-assistance claims. With respect to the prejudice component, he wrote:

> Even if a Petitioner shows that counsel's performance was deficient, however, he must also show prejudice. Petitioner must show "that there is a reasonable probability that but for counsel's unprofessional errors, the result * * * would have been different." "A reasonable probability is a probability sufficient to undermine confidence in the outcome." Indeed, it is insufficient to show only that the errors had some conceivable effect on the outcome of the proceeding, because virtually every act or omission of counsel would meet that test. The petitioner bears the "highly demanding" and "heavy burden" in establishing actual prejudice.

The trial judge analyzed the ineffective-assistance claim under the correct standard; the Virginia Supreme Court did not.

We are likewise persuaded that the Virginia trial judge correctly applied both components of that standard to Williams' ineffectiveness claim. Although he concluded that counsel competently handled the guilt phase of the trial, he found that their representation during the sentencing phase fell short of professional standards—a judgment barely disputed by the State in its brief to this Court. The record establishes that counsel did not begin to prepare for that phase of the proceeding until a week before the trial. They failed to conduct an investigation that would have uncovered extensive records graphically describing Williams' nightmarish childhood, not because of any strategic calculation but because they incorrectly thought that state law barred access to such records. Had they done so, the jury would have learned that Williams' parents had been imprisoned for the criminal neglect of Williams and his siblings, that Williams had been severely and repeatedly beaten by his father, that he had been committed to the custody of the social services bureau for two years during his parents' incarceration (including one stint in an abusive foster home), and then, after his parents were released from prison, had been returned to his parents' custody.

Counsel failed to introduce available evidence that Williams was "borderline mentally retarded" and did not advance beyond sixth grade in school. They failed to seek prison records recording Williams' commendations for helping to crack a prison drug ring and for returning a guard's missing wallet, or the testimony of prison officials who described Williams as among the inmates "least likely to act in a violent, dangerous or provocative way." Counsel failed even to return the phone call of a certified public accountant who had offered to testify that he had visited Williams frequently when Williams was incarcerated as part of a prison ministry program, that Williams "seemed to thrive in a more regimented and structured environment," and that Williams was proud of the carpentry degree he earned while in prison.

Of course, not all of the additional evidence was favorable to Williams. The juvenile records revealed that he had been thrice committed to the juvenile system—for aiding and abetting larceny when he was 11 years old, for pulling a false fire alarm when he was 12, and for breaking and entering when he was 15. But as the Federal District Court correctly observed, the failure to introduce the comparatively voluminous amount of evidence that did speak in Williams' favor was not justified by a tactical decision to focus on Williams' voluntary confession. Whether or not those omissions were sufficiently prejudicial to have affected the outcome of sentencing, they clearly demonstrate that trial counsel did not fulfill their obligation to conduct a thorough investigation of the defendant's background.

We are also persuaded, unlike the Virginia Supreme Court, that counsel's unprofessional service prejudiced Williams within the meaning of *Strickland*. After hearing the additional evidence developed in the postconviction proceedings, the very judge who presided at Williams' trial and who once determined that the death penalty was "just" and "appropriate," concluded that there existed "a reasonable probability that the result of the sentencing phase would have been different" if the jury had heard that evidence. We do not agree with the Virginia Supreme Court that Judge Ingram's conclusion should be discounted because he apparently adopted "a *per se* approach to the prejudice element" that placed undue "emphasis on mere outcome determination." Judge Ingram did stress the importance of mitigation evidence in making his "outcome determination," but it is clear that his predictive judgment rested on his assessment of the totality of the omitted evidence rather than on the notion that a single item of omitted evidence, no matter how trivial, would require a new hearing.

The Virginia Supreme Court's own analysis of prejudice reaching the contrary conclusion was thus unreasonable in at least two respects. First, as we have already explained, the State Supreme Court mischaracterized at best the appropriate rule, made clear by this Court in *Strickland*, for determining whether counsel's assistance was effective within the meaning of the Constitution. While it may also have conducted an "outcome determinative" analysis of its own, it is evident to us that the court's decision turned on its erroneous view that a "mere" difference in outcome is not sufficient to establish constitutionally ineffective assistance of counsel. Its analysis in this respect was thus not only "contrary to," but also, inasmuch as the Virginia Supreme Court relied on the inapplicable exception recognized in *Lockhart*, an "unreasonable application of" the clear law as established by this Court.

Second, the State Supreme Court's prejudice determination was unreasonable insofar as it failed to evaluate the totality of the available mitigation evidence—both that adduced at trial, and the evidence adduced in the habeas proceeding—in reweighing it against the evidence in aggravation. This error is apparent in its consideration of the additional mitigation evidence developed in the postconviction proceedings. The court correctly found that as to "the factual part of the mixed question," there was "really * * * n[o] * * * dispute" that available mitigation evidence was not presented at trial. As to the prejudice determination comprising the "legal part" of its analysis, it correctly emphasized the strength of the prosecution evidence supporting the future dangerousness aggravating circumstance.

But the state court failed even to mention the sole argument in mitigation that trial counsel did advance—Williams turned himself in, alerting police to a crime they otherwise would never have discovered, expressing remorse for his actions, and cooperating with the police after that. While this, coupled with the prison records and guard testimony, may not have overcome a finding of future dangerousness, the graphic description of Williams' childhood, filled with abuse and privation, or the reality that he was "borderline mentally retarded," might well have influenced the jury's appraisal of his moral culpability. The circumstances recited in his several confessions are consistent with the view that in each case his violent behavior was a compulsive reaction rather than the product of cold-blooded premeditation. Mitigating evidence unrelated to dangerousness may alter the jury's selection of penalty, even if it does not undermine or rebut the prosecution's death-eligibility case. The Virginia Supreme Court did not entertain that possibility. It thus failed to accord appropriate weight to the body of mitigation evidence available to trial counsel.

V

In our judgment, the state trial judge was correct both in his recognition of the established legal standard for determining counsel's effectiveness, and in his conclusion that the entire postconviction record, viewed as a whole and cumulative of mitigation evidence presented originally, raised "a reasonable probability that the result of the sentencing proceeding would have been different" if competent counsel had presented and explained the significance of all the available evidence. It follows that the Virginia Supreme Court rendered a "decision that was contrary to, or involved an unreasonable application of, clearly established Federal law." Williams' constitutional right to the effective assistance of counsel as defined in *Strickland* was violated.

Accordingly, the judgment of the Court of Appeals is reversed, and the case is remanded for further proceedings consistent with this opinion.

It is so ordered.

JUSTICE O'CONNOR delivered the opinion of the Court with respect to Part II (except as to the footnote), concurred in part, and concurred in the judgment.*

* * * The relevant provision prohibits a federal court from granting an application for a writ of habeas corpus with respect to a claim adjudicated on the merits in state court unless that adjudication "resulted in a decision that was contrary to, or involved an unreasonable application of, clearly established Federal law, as determined by the Supreme Court of the United States." The Court holds today that the Virginia Supreme Court's adjudication of Terry Williams' application for state habeas corpus relief resulted in just such a decision. I agree with that determination and join Parts I, III, and IV of the Court's opinion. Because I disagree, however, with the interpretation of § 2254(d)(1) set forth in Part II of Justice Stevens' opinion, I write separately to explain my views.

I

Before 1996, this Court held that a federal court entertaining a state prisoner's application for habeas relief must exercise its independent judgment when deciding both questions of constitutional law and mixed constitutional questions (*i.e.*, application of constitutional law to fact). In other words, a federal habeas court owed no deference to a state court's resolution of such questions of law or mixed questions. In * * * *Wright v. West*, we revisited our prior holdings by asking the parties to address the following question in their briefs:

> In determining whether to grant a petition for writ of habeas corpus by a person in custody pursuant to the judgment of a state court, should a federal court give deference to the state court's application of law to the specific facts of the petitioner's case or should it review the state court's determination *de novo*?" Although our ultimate decision did not turn on the answer to that question, our several opinions did join issue on it.

Justice Thomas, announcing the judgment of the Court, acknowledged that our precedents had "treat[ed] as settled the rule that mixed constitutional questions are 'subject to plenary federal review' on habeas." He contended, nevertheless, that those decisions did not foreclose the Court from applying a rule of deferential review for reasonableness in future cases. According to Justice Thomas, the reliance of our precedents on *Brown v. Allen* was erroneous because the Court in *Brown* never explored in detail whether a federal habeas court, to deny a state prisoner's application, must conclude that the relevant state-court adjudication was "correct" or merely that it was "reasonable." Justice Thomas suggested that the time to revisit our decisions may have been at

---

* Justice Kennedy joins this opinion in its entirety. The Chief Justice and Justice Thomas join this opinion with respect to Part II. Justice Scalia joins this opinion with respect to Part II, except as to the footnote.

hand, given that our more recent habeas jurisprudence in the nonretro-activity context, *see, e.g., Teague v. Lane,* had called into question the then-settled rule of independent review of mixed constitutional questions.

I wrote separately in *Wright* because I believed Justice Thomas had "understate[d] the certainty with which *Brown v. Allen* rejected a deferential standard of review of issues of law." I also explained that we had considered the standard of review applicable to mixed constitutional questions on numerous occasions and each time we concluded that federal habeas courts had a duty to evaluate such questions independently.
* * *

* * * Under the federal habeas statute as it stood in 1992, then, our precedents dictated that a federal court should grant a state prisoner's petition for habeas relief if that court were to conclude in its independent judgment that the relevant state court had erred on a question of constitutional law or on a mixed constitutional question.

If today's case were governed by the federal habeas statute prior to Congress' enactment of AEDPA in 1996, I would agree with Justice Stevens that Williams' petition for habeas relief must be granted if we, in our independent judgment, were to conclude that his Sixth Amendment right to effective assistance of counsel was violated.

II

A

Williams' case is *not* governed by the pre-1996 version of the habeas statute. Because he filed his petition in December 1997, Williams' case is governed by the statute as amended by AEDPA. * * *

Accordingly, for Williams to obtain federal habeas relief, he must first demonstrate that his case satisfies the condition set by § 2254(d)(1). That provision modifies the role of federal habeas courts in reviewing petitions filed by state prisoners.

Justice Stevens' opinion in Part II essentially contends that § 2254(d)(1) does not alter the previously settled rule of independent review. Indeed, the opinion concludes its statutory inquiry with the somewhat empty finding that § 2254(d)(1) does no more than express a " 'mood' that the federal judiciary must respect." For Justice Stevens, the congressionally enacted "mood" has two important qualities. First, "federal courts [must] attend to every state-court judgment with utmost care" by "carefully weighing all the reasons for accepting a state court's judgment." Second, if a federal court undertakes that careful review and yet remains convinced that a prisoner's custody violates the Constitution, "that independent judgment should prevail."

* * * Justice Stevens' interpretation of § 2254(d)(1) gives the 1996 amendment no effect whatsoever. The command that federal courts

should now use the "utmost care" by "carefully weighing" the reasons supporting a state court's judgment echoes our pre-AEDPA statement * * * that federal habeas courts "should, of course, give great weight to the considered conclusions of a coequal state judiciary." Similarly, the requirement that the independent judgment of a federal court must in the end prevail essentially repeats the conclusion we reached in the very next sentence * * * with respect to the specific issue presented there: "But, as we now reaffirm, the ultimate question whether, under the totality of the circumstances, the challenged confession was obtained in a manner compatible with the requirements of the Constitution *is a matter for independent federal determination.*" ([E]mphasis added).

That Justice Stevens would find the new § 2254(d)(1) to have no effect on the prior law of habeas corpus is remarkable given his apparent acknowledgment that Congress wished to bring change to the field. That acknowledgment is correct and significant to this case. It cannot be disputed that Congress viewed § 2254(d)(1) as an important means by which its goals for habeas reform would be achieved.

Justice Stevens arrives at his erroneous interpretation by means of one critical misstep. He fails to give independent meaning to both the "contrary to" and "unreasonable application" clauses of the statute. By reading § 2254(d)(1) as one general restriction on the power of the federal habeas court, Justice Stevens manages to avoid confronting the specific meaning of the statute's "unreasonable application" clause and its ramifications for the independent-review rule. It is, however, a cardinal principle of statutory construction that we must " 'give effect, if possible, to every clause and word of a statute.' " Section 2254(d)(1) defines two categories of cases in which a state prisoner may obtain federal habeas relief with respect to a claim adjudicated on the merits in state court[:] * * * if the relevant state-court decision was either (1) *"contrary to * * ** clearly established Federal law, as determined by the Supreme Court of the United States," or (2) *"involved an unreasonable application of * * ** clearly established Federal law, as determined by the Supreme Court of the United States." (Emphases added.)

The Court of Appeals for the Fourth Circuit properly accorded both the "contrary to" and "unreasonable application" clauses independent meaning. * * * With respect to the first of the two statutory clauses, the Fourth Circuit held in *Green* that a state-court decision can be "contrary to" this Court's clearly established precedent in two ways. First, a state-court decision is contrary to this Court's precedent if the state court arrives at a conclusion opposite to that reached by this Court on a question of law. Second, a state-court decision is also contrary to this Court's precedent if the state court confronts facts that are materially indistinguishable from a relevant Supreme Court precedent and arrives at a result opposite to ours.

The word "contrary" is commonly understood to mean "diametrically different," "opposite in character or nature," or "mutually opposed." The text of § 2254(d)(1) therefore suggests that the state court's decision must be substantially different from the relevant precedent of this Court. The Fourth Circuit's interpretation of the "contrary to" clause accurately reflects this textual meaning. A state-court decision will certainly be contrary to our clearly established precedent if the state court applies a rule that contradicts the governing law set forth in our cases. * * * A state-court decision will also be contrary to this Court's clearly established precedent if the state court confronts a set of facts that are materially indistinguishable from a decision of this Court and nevertheless arrives at a result different from our precedent. Accordingly, in either of these two scenarios, a federal court will be unconstrained by § 2254(d)(1) because the state-court decision falls within that provision's "contrary to" clause.

On the other hand, a run-of-the-mill state-court decision applying the correct legal rule from our cases to the facts of a prisoner's case would not fit comfortably within § 2254(d)(1)'s "contrary to" clause. Assume, for example, that a state-court decision on a prisoner's ineffective-assistance claim correctly identifies *Strickland* as the controlling legal authority and, applying that framework, rejects the prisoner's claim. Quite clearly, the state-court decision would be in accord with our decision in *Strickland* as to the legal prerequisites for establishing an ineffective-assistance claim, even assuming the federal court considering the prisoner's habeas application might reach a different result applying the *Strickland* framework itself. It is difficult, however, to describe such a run-of-the-mill state-court decision as "diametrically different" from, "opposite in character or nature" from, or "mutually opposed" to *Strickland*, our clearly established precedent. Although the state-court decision may be contrary to the federal court's conception of how *Strickland* ought to be applied in that particular case, the decision is not "mutually opposed" to *Strickland* itself.

Justice Stevens would instead construe § 2254(d)(1)'s "contrary to" clause to encompass such a routine state-court decision. That construction, however, saps the "unreasonable application" clause of any meaning. If a federal habeas court can, under the "contrary to" clause, issue the writ whenever it concludes that the state court's *application* of clearly established federal law was incorrect, the "unreasonable application" clause becomes a nullity. We must, however, if possible, give meaning to every clause of the statute. Justice Stevens not only makes no attempt to do so, but also construes the "contrary to" clause in a manner that ensures that the "unreasonable application" clause will have no independent meaning. We reject that expansive interpretation of the statute. Reading § 2254(d)(1)'s "contrary to" clause to permit a federal court to grant relief in cases where a state court's error is limited to the manner in which it *applies* Supreme Court precedent is suspect given the logical and natural fit of the neighboring "unreasonable application" clause to such cases.

The Fourth Circuit's interpretation of the "unreasonable application" clause of § 2254(d)(1) is generally correct. That court held in *Green* that a state-court decision can involve an "unreasonable application" of this Court's clearly established precedent in two ways. First, a state-court decision involves an unreasonable application of this Court's precedent if the state court identifies the correct governing legal rule from this Court's cases but unreasonably applies it to the facts of the particular state prisoner's case. Second, a state-court decision also involves an unreasonable application of this Court's precedent if the state court either unreasonably extends a legal principle from our precedent to a new context where it should not apply or unreasonably refuses to extend that principle to a new context where it should apply.

A state-court decision that correctly identifies the governing legal rule but applies it unreasonably to the facts of a particular prisoner's case certainly would qualify as a decision "involv[ing] an unreasonable application of * * * clearly established Federal law." Indeed, we used the almost identical phrase "application of law" to describe a state court's application of law to fact in the certiorari question we posed to the parties in *Wright*.*

The Fourth Circuit also held in *Green* that state-court decisions that unreasonably extend a legal principle from our precedent to a new context where it should not apply (or unreasonably refuse to extend a legal principle to a new context where it should apply) should be analyzed under § 2254(d)(1)'s "unreasonable application" clause. Although that holding may perhaps be correct, the classification does have some problems of precision. Just as it is sometimes difficult to distinguish a mixed question of law and fact from a question of fact, it will often be difficult to identify separately those state-court decisions that involve an unreasonable application of a legal principle (or an unreasonable failure to apply a legal principle) to a new context. Indeed, on the one hand, in some cases it will be hard to distinguish a decision involving an unreasonable extension of a legal principle from a decision involving an unreasonable application of law to facts. On the other hand, in many of the same cases it will also be difficult to distinguish a decision involving an unreasonable extension of a legal principle from a decision that "arrives at a conclusion opposite to that reached by this Court on a question of law." Today's case does not require us to decide how such "extension of legal principle" cases should be treated under § 2254(d)(1). For now it is

---

* The legislative history of § 2254(d)(1) also supports this interpretation. ("[U]nder the bill deference will be owed to State courts' decisions on the application of Federal law to the facts. Unless it is unreasonable, a State court's decision applying the law to the facts will be upheld"); ("[W]e allow a Federal court to overturn a State court decision only if it is contrary to clearly established Federal law or if it involves an 'unreasonable application' of clearly established Federal law to the facts").

sufficient to hold that when a state-court decision unreasonably applies the law of this Court to the facts of a prisoner's case, a federal court applying § 2254(d)(1) may conclude that the state-court decision falls within that provision's "unreasonable application" clause.

B

There remains the task of defining what exactly qualifies as an "unreasonable application" of law under § 2254(d)(1). The Fourth Circuit held in *Green* that a state-court decision involves an "unreasonable application of * * * clearly established Federal law" only if the state court has applied federal law "in a manner that reasonable jurists would all agree is unreasonable." The placement of this additional overlay on the "unreasonable application" clause was erroneous. It is difficult to fault the Fourth Circuit for using this language given the fact that we have employed nearly identical terminology to describe the related inquiry undertaken by federal courts in applying the nonretroactivity rule of *Teague*. * * *

Defining an "unreasonable application" by reference to a "reasonable jurist," however, is of little assistance to the courts that must apply § 2254(d)(1) and, in fact, may be misleading. Stated simply, a federal habeas court making the "unreasonable application" inquiry should ask whether the state court's application of clearly established federal law was objectively unreasonable. The federal habeas court should not transform the inquiry into a subjective one by resting its determination instead on the simple fact that at least one of the Nation's jurists has applied the relevant federal law in the same manner the state court did in the habeas petitioner's case. The "all reasonable jurists" standard would tend to mislead federal habeas courts by focusing their attention on a subjective inquiry rather than on an objective one. * * * As I explained in *Wright* with respect to the "reasonable jurist" standard in the *Teague* context, "[e]ven though we have characterized the new rule inquiry as whether 'reasonable jurists' could disagree as to whether a result is dictated by precedent, the standard for determining when a case establishes a new rule is 'objective,' and the mere existence of conflicting authority does not necessarily mean a rule is new."

The term "unreasonable" is no doubt difficult to define. That said, it is a common term in the legal world and, accordingly, federal judges are familiar with its meaning. For purposes of today's opinion, the most important point is that an *unreasonable* application of federal law is different from an *incorrect* application of federal law. Our opinions in *Wright*, for example, make that difference clear. Justice Thomas' criticism of this Court's subsequent reliance on *Brown* turned on that distinction. The Court in *Brown*, Justice Thomas contended, held only that a federal habeas court must determine whether the relevant state-court adjudication resulted in a " 'satisfactory conclusion.' " In Justice Thomas' view, *Brown* did not answer "the question whether a 'satisfactory' conclusion was one that the habeas court considered correct, as opposed to merely *reasonable*." ([E]mphases in original). In my separate opinion in *Wright*, I made the same distinction, maintaining that "a state court's *incorrect* legal determination has [never] been allowed to stand because it was *reasonable*. We have always held that federal courts, even on habeas, have an independent obligation to say what the law is." ([E]mphases added). In § 2254(d)(1), Congress specifically used the word "unreasonable," and not a term like "erroneous" or "incorrect." Under § 2254(d)(1)'s "unreasonable application" clause, then, a federal habeas court may not issue the writ simply because that court concludes in its independent judgment that the relevant state-court decision applied clearly established federal law erroneously or incorrectly. Rather, that application must also be unreasonable.

Justice Stevens turns a blind eye to the debate in *Wright* because he finds no indication in § 2254(d)(1) itself that Congress was "directly influenced" by Justice Thomas' opinion in *Wright*. As Justice Stevens himself apparently recognizes, however, Congress need not mention a prior decision of this Court by name in a statute's text in order to adopt either a rule or a meaning given a certain term in that decision. In any event, whether Congress intended to codify the standard of review suggested by Justice Thomas in *Wright* is beside the point. *Wright* is important for the light it sheds on § 2254(d)(1)'s requirement that a federal habeas court inquire into the reasonableness of a state court's application of clearly established federal law. The separate opinions in *Wright* concerned the very issue addressed by § 2254(d)(1)'s "unreasonable application" clause—whether, in reviewing a state-court decision on a state prisoner's claims under federal law, a federal habeas court should ask whether the state-court decision was correct or simply whether it was reasonable. Justice Stevens' claim that the debate in *Wright* concerned only the meaning of the *Teague* nonretroactivity rule is simply incorrect. As even a cursory review of Justice Thomas' opinion and my own opinion reveals, both the broader debate and the specific statements to which we refer concerned precisely the issue of the standard of review to be employed by federal habeas courts. The *Wright* opinions confirm what § 2254(d)(1)'s language already makes clear—that an *unreasonable* application of federal law is different from an *incorrect* or *erroneous* application of federal law.

Throughout this discussion the meaning of the phrase "clearly established Federal law, as determined by the Supreme Court of the United States" has been put to the side. That statutory phrase refers to the holdings, as opposed to the *dicta*, of this Court's decisions as of the time of the relevant state-court decision. In this respect, the "clearly established Federal law" phrase bears only a slight connection to our *Teague* jurisprudence. With one caveat, whatever would qualify as an old rule under our *Teague* jurisprudence will constitute "clearly established Federal law, as determined by the Supreme Court of the United States" under § 2254(d)(1). The one caveat, as the statutory language makes clear, is that § 2254(d)(1) restricts the source of clearly established law to this Court's jurisprudence.

In sum, § 2254(d)(1) places a new constraint on the power of a federal habeas court to grant a state prisoner's application for a writ of habeas corpus with respect to claims adjudicated on the merits in state court. Under § 2254(d)(1), the writ may issue only if one of the following two conditions is satisfied—the state-court adjudication resulted in a decision that (1) "was contrary to * * * clearly established Federal law, as determined by the Supreme Court of the United States," or (2) "involved an unreasonable application of * * * clearly established Federal law, as determined by the Supreme Court of the United States." Under the "contrary to" clause, a federal habeas court may grant the writ if the state court arrives at a conclusion opposite to that reached by this Court on a question of law or if the state court decides a case differently than this Court has on a set of materially indistinguishable facts. Under the "unreasonable application" clause, a federal habeas court may grant the writ if the state court identifies the correct governing legal principle from this Court's decisions but unreasonably applies that principle to the facts of the prisoner's case.

III

Although I disagree with Justice Stevens concerning the standard we must apply under § 2254(d)(1) in evaluating Terry Williams' claims on habeas, I agree with the Court that the Virginia Supreme Court's adjudication of Williams' claim of ineffective assistance of counsel resulted in a decision that was both contrary to and involved an unreasonable application of this Court's clearly established precedent. Specifically, I believe that the Court's discussion in Parts III and IV is correct and that it demonstrates the reasons that the Virginia Supreme Court's decision in Williams' case, even under the interpretation of § 2254(d)(1) I have set forth above, was both contrary to and involved an unreasonable application of our precedent.

* * *

To be sure, as The Chief Justice notes, the Virginia Supreme Court did also inquire whether Williams had demonstrated a reasonable probability that, but for his trial counsel's unprofessional errors, the result of his sentencing would have been different. It is impossible to determine, however, the extent to which the Virginia Supreme Court's error with respect to its reading of *Lockhart* affected its ultimate finding that Williams suffered no prejudice. For example, at the conclusion of its discussion of whether Williams had demonstrated a reasonable probability of a different outcome at sentencing, the Virginia Supreme Court faulted the Virginia Circuit Court for its "emphasis on mere outcome determination, without proper attention to whether the result of the criminal proceeding was fundamentally unfair or unreliable." As the Court explains, however, Williams' case did not implicate the unusual circumstances present in cases like *Lockhart* or *Nix v. Whiteside*. Accordingly, for the very reasons I set forth in my *Lockhart* concurrence, the emphasis on outcome was entirely appropriate in Williams' case.

Third, I also agree with the Court that, to the extent the Virginia Supreme Court did apply *Strickland*, its application was unreasonable. * * * The Virginia Supreme Court's decision reveals an obvious failure to consider the totality of the omitted mitigation evidence. For that reason, and the remaining factors discussed in the Court's opinion, I believe that the Virginia Supreme Court's decision "involved an unreasonable application of * * * clearly established Federal law, as determined by the Supreme Court of the United States."

Accordingly, although I disagree with the interpretation of § 2254(d)(1) set forth in Part II of Justice Stevens' opinion, I join Parts I, III, and IV of the Court's opinion and concur in the judgment of reversal.

[Chief Justice Rehnquist, joined by Justices Scalia and Thomas, agreed with the Court's analytical framework as set out in Justice Stevens's and O'Connor's opinions. He diverged, however, from the Court's conclusion that the omitted evidence might have changed the result, finding as a practical matter that the omission was similar to harmless error.]

Notes and Questions

1. Both Justice Stevens and Justice O'Connor address, at least to some extent, the relationship between *Teague v. Lane* (1989), *supra* at 1101, and the current version of § 2254(d)(1), enacted as part of the AEDPA in 1996. The exact relationship, however, is unclear. *Teague* held that new constitutional rules of criminal procedure cannot be announced in habeas corpus cases unless such rules apply retroactively to all defendants on collateral review under one of the *Teague* two exceptions. Thus, habeas petitioners basically are limited to asserting claims based on "old rules," that is, rules that existed when their convictions became final. Section 2254(d)(1) prohibits the grant of a state prisoner's habeas petition unless the state adjudication of the claim "resulted in a decision that was contrary to, or involved an unreasonable application of, clearly established Federal law, as determined by the Supreme Court of the United States." The use of the phrase "clearly established Federal law" raised the question whether Congress meant to codify the holding of *Teague*. The circuit courts disagreed.

Justice Stevens, speaking only for himself and three other Justices on this point in *Williams*, states that *Teague*'s prohibition of reliance on new rules "is the functional equivalent of [the] statutory provision commanding exclusive reliance on 'clearly established law.'" Consequently, he concludes that "AEDPA codifies *Teague* to the extent that *Teague* requires federal habeas courts to deny relief that is contingent upon a rule of law not clearly established at the time the state conviction became final." Justice O'Connor, speaking for a majority on this point, appears to agree, although she points out (and Justice Stevens agrees) that the statute limits "clearly established law" to that "determined by the Supreme Court." The additional language of the § 2254(d)(1) ("a decision that was contrary to, or involved an unreasonable application of" clearly established law) is not taken from *Teague*, and this muddies the waters considerably.

The Court revisited the question of the relationship between *Teague* and § 2254(d)(1) in *Horn v. Banks*, 536 U.S. 266, 122 S.Ct. 2147, 153 L.Ed.2d 301 (2002). *Banks*, a *per curiam* opinion, stated that *Teague* has a continued authority independent of AEDPA:

> While it is of course a necessary prerequisite to federal habeas relief that a prisoner satisfy the AEDPA standard of review set forth in 28 U.S.C. § 2254(d) ("[a]n application * * * shall not be granted * * * *unless*" the AEDPA standard of review is satisfied (emphasis added)), none of our post-AEDPA cases have suggested that a writ of habeas corpus should automatically issue if a prisoner satisfies the AEDPA standard, or that AEDPA relieves courts from the responsibility of addressing properly raised *Teague* arguments. To the contrary, if our post-AEDPA cases suggest anything about AEDPA's relationship to *Teague*, it is that the AEDPA and *Teague* inquires are distinct. Thus, in addition to performing any analysis required by AEDPA, a federal court considering a habeas petition must conduct a threshold *Teague* analysis when the issue is properly raised by the state.

It would have been helpful if the Court had explained each inquiry and specified exactly *how* the AEDPA and *Teague* inquiries are different rather than simply asserting it. Because the Court spoke so generally, the relationship between *Teague* and § 2254(d)(1) remains unclear. Consider Larry Yackle's recent summary of the relationship: "The statute neither displaces nor codifies the *Teague* doctrine wholesale. It is accurate to say only that § 2254(d) absorbs the central ideas in *Teague* into a statutory framework for handling habeas petitions, seeking, in effect, to upset prior state court decisions on the merits of prisoners' claims." LARRY W. YACKLE, FEDERAL COURTS 567 (2d ed. 2003).

2. a) Justice Stevens says that whether a particular rule is "clearly established" is itself a federal question. If the federal courts find that a rule is not clearly established, how will it ever become so? Pursuant to § 2254(d)(1), even the Supreme Court cannot order habeas relief if the federal rule was not clearly established. Has Congress effectively put a cap on the scope of federal rights to which a state prisoner is entitled?

b) Section 2254(d)(1) now clearly limits the source of federal constitutional law binding on the states to Supreme Court decisions. Does that effectively put pressure on the Court to accept for review cases in which the Circuits are unanimous (and correct in the Court's view) about the existence of a constitutional rule? If so, is that a wise use of Supreme Court resources? Should Congress or the Court make that decision,?

3. a) Justice Stevens thinks the phrases "contrary to" and "unreasonable application of" are not mutually exclusive, and that Congress did not

mean to alter the settled rule that federal habeas courts may conduct essentially *de novo* review of state court decisions of issues of law and the application of law to fact. Justice O'Connor thinks the phrases impose different standards (and has the majority to prove it). Justice Stevens' attempt to merge them, she contends, "saps the 'unreasonable application' clause of any meaning." If you were on the Court, how would you vote? Why?

b) Note that Justice O'Connor endorses the Fourth Circuit's categorization of the kinds of cases that will fall under the two phrases. It is interesting to juxtapose her characterization of the cases in each category:

> First, a state-court decision is contrary to this Court's precedent if the state court arrives at a conclusion opposite to that reached by this Court on a question of law. Second, a state-court decision is also contrary to this Court's precedent if the state court confronts facts that are materially indistinguishable from a relevant Supreme Court precedent and arrives at a result opposite to ours.

> * * *

> [Third,] a state-court decision involves an unreasonable application of this Court's precedent if the state court identifies the correct governing legal rule from this Court's cases but unreasonably applies it to the facts of the particular state prisoner's case. [Fourth,] a state-court decision also involves an unreasonable application of this Court's precedent if that state court either unreasonably extends a legal principle from our precedent to a new context where it should not apply or unreasonably refuses to extend that principle to a new context where it should apply.

How different are the second and third categories? If the state court confronts materially indistinguishable facts and reaches an opposite result, is that different from a state court using the correct rule but unreasonably applying it to the facts? How can we know that the state court application is unreasonable save by comparing the state case with the facts of the Supreme Court case that announced the rule (and perhaps other Supreme Court cases that elaborated it)? If you think the second and third categories are different, can you construct cases that would satisfy one but not the other? Is it also possible that there are cases that satisfy both?

To the extent that the two categories do overlap, does that give some support, however unintended, to Justice Stevens' view that the two statutory phrases overlap? Assuming that they do, does the fourth category nonetheless give "unreasonable application of" something to do, thus supporting Justice O'Connor's criticism of Justice Stevens' approach?

4. Having concluded that the phrases "contrary to" and "unreasonable application of" have different meanings, Justice O'Connor interprets the latter in a way that imposes a substantial new restriction on federal habeas corpus review of state convictions. Admitting that the term "unreasonable" is difficult to define, Justice O'Connor defines it in the negative. According to her, what is an unreasonable application of federal law *not*? In assessing whether a state court decision involved an unreasonable application of fed-

eral law, should the federal court apply an objective or subjective standard?

5. a) Justice O'Connor's reading of "unreasonable application of" suggested that federal courts should give some degree of deference to state court determinations of issues of federal law and mixed questions of law and fact. Because Justice O'Connor agrees with Justice Stevens that even by her definitions the Virginia Supreme Court's denial of relief to Terry Williams was both contrary to and involved an unreasonable application of the *Strickland v. Washington* standards, *Williams* does not make clear how much deference state rulings should get.

b) Should federal courts defer to state interpretations of federal law? Assume that Congress indeed intended to codify a rule of deference by federal courts to opinions of state courts on federal law. Is that permissible, or does it violate separation of powers by intruding on the judicial function? Could Congress simply withdraw Supreme Court power to review such adjudications under § 1257 (*cf. Martin v. Hunter's Lessee*), making them unreviewable, thus making impossible Supreme Court review of state court decisions on federal constitutional matters?

c) Still with respect to the authoritativeness of federal courts in the area of federal law, does or should their authoritativeness differ according to whether they are reviewing a pure statement of federal law by the state courts or an application of federal law to the facts? If so, why are federal court decisions less authoritative in one area than the other? If not, then what are we to make of the two phrases that lie at the heart of this case: "contrary to" and "unreasonable application of?"

6. Perhaps hoping to lessen the impact of Justice O'Connor's differentiation of "contrary to" and "unreasonable application of," Justice Stevens predicted that the difference in meaning "should affect only a narrow category of cases," because "state-court decisions that do not 'conflict' with federal law will rarely be 'unreasonable' under either her reading of the statute or ours." This proved to be a very poor prediction. Since *Williams* was decided, the Court has made clear that state court determinations of federal law should receive great deference. Indeed, the Court has been watchful of the circuit courts and has reversed any decision in which circuit judges stray into applying a standard of review that looks anything like *de novo*.

a) In *Bell v. Cone*, 535 U.S. 685, 122 S.Ct. 1842, 152 L.Ed. 2d 914 (2002), the petitioner contended, as had Terry Williams, that his counsel rendered ineffective assistance under the *Strickland* standard during his sentencing hearing. The Sixth Circuit granted the writ because Cone's attorney did not ask for mercy following the prosecutor's final argument and thus did not subject the State's call for the death penalty to "meaningful adversarial testing." The Court of Appeals found the state courts' denial of relief to be an unreasonable application of the clearly established law announced in *Strickland*. The Supreme Court reversed. Chief Justice Rehnquist began by firmly reiterating that the phrases "contrary to" and "unreasonable application of" have different meanings. "The focus of the latter inquiry is on whether the state court's application of clearly established federal law is objectively unreasonable, and we stressed in *Williams* that an unreasonable application is different from an incorrect one." Chief Justice Rehnquist noted the petitioner had to overcome two levels of deference. First, under *Strickland*, judicial scrutiny of counsel's performance must be highly deferential. Second, under § 2254(d)(1), "it is not enough to convince a federal habeas court that, in its independent judgment, the state court decision applied *Strickland* incorrectly. Rather, he must show that the Tennessee Court of Appeals applied *Strickland* to the facts of his case in an objectively unreasonable manner." After reviewing the facts, the Court concluded petitioner could not satisfy the § 2254(d)(1) standard.

b) *Woodford v. Visciotti*, 537 U.S. 19, 123 S.Ct. 357, 154 L.Ed.2d 279 (2002), also involved a claim of ineffective assistance of counsel during the sentencing phase that resulted in imposition of the death penalty. In a *per curiam* opinion, the Court reversed a grant of habeas relief by the Ninth Circuit and chided the lower court for substituting its judgment for that of the California Supreme Court. The state court presumed that counsel's performance was constitutionally inadequate because of a failure to present evidence of mitigating circumstances. Nonetheless, the California high court denied relief because it did not believe there was a reasonable probability that but for counsel's errors and omissions, the sentencing authority would have found that the balance of aggravating and mitigating circumstances did not warrant the death penalty. The evidence of mitigating circumstances that counsel failed to present was extensive. Petitioner had some brain damage and had grown up in a dysfunctional family where he suffered continual psychological abuse. He also had club feet and a possible seizure disorder. The Ninth Circuit concluded it was reasonably probable the jury would have struck the balance differently with full information, and thus the California Supreme Court decision was both contrary to and an unreasonable application of federal law. In addition, the circuit court concluded that the determination that Visciotti suffered no prejudice from his counsel's deficiencies was "objectively unreasonable." The Supreme Court reiterated that a habeas court may not issue a writ simply because it concludes a state court applied federal law incorrectly. Even though the Ninth Circuit may have been correct in concluding the aggravating factors were not overwhelming, the California Supreme Court had written a detailed opinion carefully weighing the aggravating and mitigating evidence and reaching the opposite conclusion. The federal court was not free to substitute its independent judgment for that of the state court.

c) The Supreme Court again reversed the grant of a habeas petition in *Lockyer v. Andrade*, 538 U.S. 63, 123 S.Ct. 1166, 155 L.Ed.2d 144 (2003). Petitioner received two consecutive 25-years-to-life sentences under California's "three strikes" law for stealing nine videotapes from Kmart. On appeal, he argued the sentences violated the Eighth Amendment prohibition against cruel and unusual punishment because they were grossly disproportionate to the offenses he committed. Following its own precedent, the Ninth Circuit held that an unreasonable application of federal law occurs "when our independent review of the legal question 'leaves us with a "firm conviction" that one answer, the one rejected by the [state] court, was correct and the other, the application of the federal law that the [state] court adopted was erroneous—in other words, that clear error occurred.' " The Supreme

Court rejected this definition, holding that a clearly wrong state court decision is not necessarily objectively unreasonable. "The gloss of clear error fails to give proper deference to state courts by conflating error (even clear error) with unreasonableness," the Court stated, citing *Williams, Cone* and *Viscotti*. The Court concluded that because under its own case law the precise contours of the proportionality principle are unclear, the California court's denial of relief was not objectively unreasonable.

d) In *Price v. Vincent*, 538 U.S. 634, 123 S.Ct. 1848, 155 L.Ed.2d 877 (2003), the Supreme Court again criticized the Sixth Circuit for misapplying § 2254(d)(1). At the close of the prosecution's case, the trial judge appeared to grant a defense motion for a directed verdict of acquittal on the first degree murder charge because of insufficient evidence of premeditation. The trial judge subsequently changed his mind, and the issue went to the jury, which convicted the petitioner of first degree murder. The Michigan Court of Appeals reversed on double jeopardy grounds, but the Michigan Supreme Court reinstated the conviction, concluding the trial judge's comments were not sufficiently final to constitute a judgment of acquittal terminating jeopardy. The U.S. Supreme Court reversed the Sixth Circuit's grant of the writ. Chief Justice Rehnquist stated, "Although the Court of Appeals recited [the] standard [of § 2254(d)(1)], it proceeded to evaluate respondent's claim *de novo* rather than through the lens of § 2254(d), apparently because it 'agreed with the district court that whether the state trial judge acquitted [respondent] of first-degree murder is a question of law and not one of fact.'" The Court concluded that the Michigan Supreme Court decision was not contrary to and did not involve an objectively unreasonable application of established federal law.

Has the Supreme Court in effect adopted an abuse-of-discretion standard in habeas corpus cases for review of questions of law and mixed question of law and fact? If an objectively unreasonable application of federal law is different from an abuse of discretion, what is the difference?

What do you think of a good-faith standard of review of state court federal law decisions? Would that standard convert the constitutional principles that might be involved in a particular case from rights of the defendant to a simple restraint on malicious courts? Would it have a tendency to make constitutional law whatever state judges think it is, so long as they think it in good faith? If so, what would happen to the authoritativeness of the law, particularly law "clearly established by the Supreme Court"?

e) *Wiggins v. Smith*, 539 U.S. 510, 123 S.Ct. 2527, 156 L.Ed.2d 471 (2003), involved an unusual twist. In a case very similar to *Williams v. Taylor* on the facts, the petitioner managed to convince the Court he had overcome the twin hurdles of *Strickland* and § 2254(d)(1). The Court therefore reversed the judgment of the Fourth Circuit denying habeas relief. Justice Scalia, joined by Justice Thomas, in dissent, argued that the Court violated its own precedent limiting relief to claims based on federal law that was clearly established at the time of the state court decision. The majority relied heavily on *Williams* in granting relief, and *Williams* postdated the Maryland court's decision denying Wiggins's Sixth Amendment claim. Thus,

Justice Scalia concluded, the law underlying the grant of relief was not clearly established when the state court acted. The majority disagreed, contending it was simply applying the established *Strickland* standards.

f) In *Brown v. Payton*, 544 U.S. 13, 125 S.Ct. 1432, 161 L.Ed.2d 334 (2005), the Court held that a state court ruling, even if wrong, was not unreasonable, and it reversed a Ninth Circuit decision that had granted habeas relief. *Boyde v. California*, 494 U.S. 370, 110 S.Ct. 1190, 108 L.Ed.2d 316 (1990), held that a California jury instruction permitting a sentencing jury in a capital case to consider "[a]ny other circumstance which extenuates the gravity of the crime even though it is not a legal excuse for the crime * * *" was constitutional and did not improperly suggest to a jury that it could not consider post-crime conduct by the defendant in mitigation. In *Payton*, the prosecutor's closing argument incorrectly urged that the jury could not consider post-crime conduct. The trial court admonished the jury that the prosecutor's comments were only argument, but it did not specifically instruct the jury that the prosecutor's interpretation of the law was wrong. The jury recommended a death sentence, which the judge imposed. The California Supreme Court affirmed Payton's conviction and sentence. Applying *Boyde* to this case, the court held there was no reasonable likelihood the jury thought it was required to disregard Payton's post-crime mitigating evidence.

In granting habeas relief, the Ninth Circuit assumed that a jury would consider post-crime evidence of a defendant's religious conversion and good behavior in prison. Given the prosecutor's argument that the jury could not legally consider such evidence, and the trial court's failure to correct this error, it was likely the jury was misled, and it was an unreasonable application of U.S. Supreme Court precedent to hold to the contrary.

The Supreme Court disagreed:

> [T]he California Supreme Court's conclusion that the jury was not reasonably likely to have accepted the prosecutor's narrow view of [the state law allowing the jury to consider extenuating circumstances] was an application of *Boyde* to similar but not identical facts. Even on the assumption that its conclusion was incorrect, it was not unreasonable, and is therefore just the type of decision that AEDPA shields on habeas review.

Justice Souter, dissenting for himself and Justices Stevens and Ginsburg, agreed with the Ninth Circuit's reasoning, stating "[i]t was reasonably likely in these circumstances that the jury failed to consider Payton's mitigating evidence, and in concluding otherwise, the Supreme Court of California unreasonably applied settled law, with substantially injurious effects."

3. *Exhaustion of Remedies*

The federal courts have long required state prisoners to exhaust available state remedies before filing a habeas petition in federal court. Congress codified this requirement in 1948, but the statute did not address how the courts should deal with so-called "mixed" petitions— petitions containing both exhausted and unexhausted claims. In *Rose v.*

Lundy, 455 U.S. 509, 102 S.Ct. 1198, 71 L.Ed.2d 379 (1982), the Supreme Court held a district court must dismiss mixed petitions, thus leaving the petitioner with the choice of returning to state court to adjudicate unexhausted claims or amending the petition to present only exhausted claims.

Congress addressed exhaustion requirements in AEDPA (1996):

§ 2254

* * *

    (b)(1) An application for a writ of habeas corpus on behalf of a person in custody pursuant to the judgment of a State court shall not be granted unless it appears that

        (A) the applicant has exhausted the remedies available in the courts of the State; or

        (B)   (i)   there is an absence of available state corrective process; or

            (ii) circumstances exist that render such process ineffective to protect the rights of the applicant.

    (2) An application for a writ of habeas corpus may be denied on the merits, notwithstanding the failure of the applicant to exhaust the remedies available in the courts of the State.

    (3) A State shall not be deemed to have waived the exhaustion requirement or be estopped from reliance upon the requirement unless the State, through counsel, expressly waives the requirement.

    (c) An applicant shall not be deemed to have exhausted the remedies available in the courts of the State, within the meaning of this section, it he has the right under the law of the State to raise, by any available procedure, the question presented.

AEDPA left the basic exhaustion requirements of § 2254 unchanged. Note that the statute does specifically permit the habeas court to rule on an unexhausted claim provided that the court rules *against* the prisoner. The statute also prohibits the federal courts from inferring state waiver of the requirement or from finding that the state is estopped to raise the issue, requiring instead an explicit waiver through counsel. What do these two provisions tell us about the nature of even Congress's exhaustion rule?

The amended exhaustion provisions do not say what should happened to mixed petitions of the type presented in *Lundy*. Should the courts continue to dismiss such petitions in their entirety, or should they hear the exhausted claims and dismiss only the unexhausted ones? If the former, then has Congress implicitly taken the position that a prisoner who has some claims that are ripe for federal adjudication and some that are not should remain imprisoned until all are ripe, despite the fact that the earlier-ripened claims may be sufficient to secure his release? Is the prisoner thus faced with the dilemma of abandoning some (perhaps winning) claims or suffering longer-than-necessary imprisonment?

What does AEDPA mean when it refers in § 2254(c) to "any available procedure" for raising a claim in the state courts? Does that include having sought certiorari from the state's highest court even in the face of indications that the court only wishes to receive petitions for review if the case presents unsettled issues of law with broad application rather than fact-specific claims relating to the application of established law? *O'Sullivan v. Boerckel*, 526 U.S. 838, 119 S.Ct. 1728, 144 L.Ed.2d 1 (1999), answered affirmatively. Boerckel sought federal habeas relief on six grounds, only three of which he had sought (unsuccessfully) to present to the Illinois Supreme Court through certiorari. Illinois had a rule discussing the scope of its Supreme Court's discretion; it referred *inter alia* to "the general importance of the question presented; the existence of a conflict between the decision sought to be reviewed and a decision of the Supreme Court, or of another division of the Appellate Court; [and] the need for the exercise of the Supreme Court's supervisory authority * * * ." Boerckel argued that the three excluded claims related to "routine allegations of error" and were highly fact-specific, involving only particularized application of well established legal principles. A six-to-three Court ruled that he should have given Illinois's Supreme Court the opportunity to exercise its discretion and that his failure to do so constituted a procedural default barring federal consideration of the omitted claims. The majority did appear to leave room for states to pass rules of discretionary review that make it clear that such review is "unavailable" to certain types of cases.

Justice Stevens's dissent accused the majority of confusing the exhaustion and procedural default doctrines. He argued that the Court actually showed less, not more, respect for the states, by threatening to flood their discretionary review processes with futile petitions, wasting state judicial time and delaying inevitable federal habeas review. Assuming that Justice Stevens is correct about the Illinois Supreme Court's not wanting to be troubled with appeals on fact-intensive claims with no systemic importance, how would you craft a certiorari policy the embodies that goal without excluding cases that the court might want to hear?

Generally, a petitioner who uses one of several available means to present a claim to the state court satisfies the exhaustion requirement. Once the state's highest court has either rejected the claim or denied discretionary review, exhaustion is complete. Is this a reasonable interpretation of § 2254(c) (unchanged by AEDPA), which apparently precludes review if there is "any" available procedure? Why should one not understand that word to include, in addition to applications to the state's

highest court for discretionary review, requests for rehearing, resort to
the extraordinary writs, and invocation of state habeas corpus procedures? Is it of any significance that AEDPA reenacted this section without change?

Does the majority's view place state prisoners in an impossible position with respect to characterizing their claims? Professor Carlos
Vasquez has suggested that this creates an irreconcilable conflict for
state prisoners. Given the ordinary workings of a discretionary review
procedure, persons seeking discretionary review will have no realistic
possibility of obtaining it unless they can demonstrate that the issues
they raise are novel and, as Justice Stevens says, "of broad significance."
Yet to make such a showing in the state's certiorari proceeding may undermine the chance to secure federal habeas corpus relief, since the doctrine of *Teague v. Lane*, supplemented now by 28 U.S.C. § 2254(d), requires a decision to have been "contrary to * * * clearly established Federal law, as determined by the Supreme Court of the United States" to
be reviewable by federal habeas corpus. How likely is it that an issue
will satisfy both of those criteria?

What policies does the Court serve by dismissing exhausted claims
joined with unexhausted ones? How does deferring federal adjudication
serve those policies? In this connection, consider one of the perhaps unanticipated effects that AEDPA may have. The statute establishes a
one-year filing deadline, typically running from the end of the direct review process. *Lundy* directs the federal courts to dismiss petitions containing exhausted and unexhausted claims, and threatens prisoners
with the loss of the unexhausted claims if the prisoners press on with
only the exhausted claims. "The idea in Lundy is to encourage prisoners
to slow down litigation of some claims until all are ready for federal adjudication." Larry W. Yackle, *A Primer on the New Habeas Corpus Statute*, 44 BUFF.L.REV. 381, 387 (1996). Suppose a prisoner faces the one-
year filing deadline with respect to some (exhausted) claims but has not
completed state proceedings with respect to other (obviously unexhausted) claims. What is he to do?

AEDPA directs that "[a] claim presented in a second or successive
habeas corpus application under section 2254 that was presented in a
prior application shall be dismissed." If a district court follows *Lundy*
and dismisses a mixed petition at the outset without any consideration
of the merits, were the claims in such a petition "presented"? *Stewart v.
Martinez-Villareal*, 523 U.S. 637, 118 S.Ct. 1618, 140 L.Ed.2d 849
(1998), says no.

Slack v. McDaniel, 529 U.S. 473, 120 S.Ct. 1595, 146 L.Ed.2d 542
(2000), elaborated a bit on the treatment of mixed petitions under
AEDPA. Slack had filed an original federal habeas petition that contained exhausted and unexhausted claims. He asked the district court
to hold his action in abeyance while he exhausted his remaining claims

in the state courts. The court instead dismissed the petition without prejudice, noting specifically that Slack was entitled to renew the petition after exhausting his state remedies. When Slack refiled a petition containing all of the original claims and some new ones, the state objected, arguing that the inclusion of new claims made the petition a "second or successive petition" that constituted abuse of the writ. The district court dismissed the new claims. The Ninth Circuit affirmed that action, but also dismissed the remainder of the petition on *Rose v. Lundy* grounds. The Supreme Court reversed, holding that "[a] habeas petition filed in the district court after an initial habeas petition was unadjudicated on its merits and dismissed for failure to exhaust state remedies is not a second or successive petition." *Lundy*, said the Court, intended only to avoid piecemeal adjudication; here the prisoner had done exactly what *Lundy* contemplated. Justices Scalia and Thomas dissented from the part of the Court's holding that allowed the inclusion of the new claims. Note the bind in which their interpretation of *Lundy* puts the prisoner. What is the dilemma that he faces?

The court dismissed the mixed petition in *Slack* without prejudice before adjudication of any claims on the merits. By contrast, in *Burton v. Stewart*, __ U.S. __, 127 S.Ct. 793, 166 L.Ed.2d 628 (2007), the petitioner chose to proceed on the exhausted claims disputing the constitutionality of his convictions while not pressing his sentencing claims that were pending in state court when he filed his federal habeas petition. Three years after the federal courts denied his exhausted claims on the merits, petitioner filed another federal petition raising his sentencing claims. The Ninth Circuit held that the second petition was not "second or successive" within the meaning of § 2244(b)(2) because the petitioner had a good excuse for not presenting his sentencing claims; namely that they were pending in state court when the first habeas petition was filed and thus were not ripe for federal review. The Supreme Court reversed, stating:

> There is no basis in our cases for supposing, as the Ninth Circuit did, that a petitioner with unexhausted claims who chooses * * * to proceed to adjudication of his exhausted claims * * * may later assert that a subsequent petition is not "second or successive" precisely because his new claims were unexhausted at the time he filed his first petition. This reasoning conflicts with both *Lundy* and § 2244(b) and would allow prisoners to file separate habeas petitions in the not uncommon situation where a conviction is upheld but a sentence is reversed.

Such a result, said the Court, would be inconsistent with the goals of reducing piecemeal litigation and streamlining federal habeas proceedings. The Court distinguished *Slack* because there the first petition was dismissed before any claims were adjudicated on the merits. In that circumstance, the second petition is treated as another first petition. Burton's case was different because the lower court had adjudicated the exhausted claims in the first petition on the merits.

4. *The Effect of State Procedural Defaults*

COLEMAN v. THOMPSON
Supreme Court of the United States, 1991.
501 U.S. 722, 111 S.Ct. 2546, 115 L.Ed.2d 640.

JUSTICE O'CONNOR delivered the opinion of the Court.

This is a case about federalism. It concerns the respect that federal courts owe the States and the States' procedural rules when reviewing the claims of state prisoners in federal habeas corpus.

I

A Buchanan County, Virginia, jury convicted Roger Keith Coleman of rape and capital murder and fixed the sentence at death for the murder. The trial court imposed the death sentence, and the Virginia Supreme Court affirmed both the convictions and the sentence. This Court denied certiorari.

Coleman then filed a petition for a writ of habeas corpus in the Circuit Court for Buchanan County, raising numerous federal constitutional claims that he had not raised on direct appeal. After a two-day evidentiary hearing, the Circuit Court ruled against Coleman on all claims.

Coleman filed his notice of appeal with the Circuit Court * * * 33 days after the entry of final judgment. Coleman subsequently filed a petition for appeal in the Virginia Supreme Court. The Commonwealth of Virginia, as appellant, filed a motion to dismiss the appeal. The sole ground for dismissal urged in the motion was that Coleman's notice of appeal had been filed late. Virginia Supreme Court Rule 5:9(a) provides that no appeal shall be allowed unless a notice of appeal is filed with the trial court within 30 days of final judgment.

The Virginia Supreme Court did not act immediately on the Commonwealth's motion, and both parties filed several briefs on the subject of the motion to dismiss and on the merits of the claims in Coleman's petition. On May 19, 1987, the Virginia Supreme Court issued the following order, dismissing Coleman's appeal:

> On December 4, 1986 came the appellant, by counsel, and filed a petition for appeal in the above-styled case.

> Thereupon came the appellee, by the Attorney General of Virginia, and filed a motion to dismiss the petition for appeal; on December 19, 1986 the appellant filed a memorandum in opposition to the motion to dismiss; on December 19, 1986 the appellee filed a reply to the appellant's memorandum; on December 23, 1986 the appellee filed a brief in opposition to the petition for appeal; on December 23, 1986 the appellant filed a surreply in opposition to the appellee's motion to dismiss; and on January 6, 1987 the appellant filed a reply brief.

Upon consideration whereof, the motion to dismiss is granted and the petition for appeal is dismissed.

This Court again denied certiorari.

Coleman next filed a petition for writ of habeas corpus in the United States District Court for the Western District of Virginia. In his petition, Coleman presented four federal constitutional claims he had raised on direct appeal in the Virginia Supreme Court and seven claims he had raised for the first time in state habeas. The District Court concluded that, by virtue of the dismissal of his appeal by the Virginia Supreme Court in state habeas, Coleman had procedurally defaulted the seven claims. The District Court nonetheless went on to address the merits of all 11 of Coleman's claims. The court ruled against Coleman on all of the claims and denied the petition.

The United States Court of Appeals for the Fourth Circuit * * * held that Coleman had defaulted all of the claims that he had presented for the first time in state habeas. Coleman argued that the Virginia Supreme Court had not "clearly and expressly" stated that its decision in state habeas was based on a procedural default, and therefore the federal courts could not treat it as such under the rule of *Harris v. Reed* (1989). The Fourth Circuit disagreed. It concluded that the Virginia Supreme Court had met the "plain statement" requirement of *Harris* by granting a motion to dismiss that was based solely on procedural grounds. The Fourth Circuit held that the Virginia Supreme Court's decision rested on independent and adequate state grounds and that Coleman had not shown cause to excuse the default. As a consequence, federal review of the claims Coleman presented only in the state habeas proceeding was barred. We granted certiorari to resolve several issues concerning the relationship between state procedural defaults and federal habeas review, and now affirm.

II

A

This Court will not review a question of federal law decided by a state court if the decision of that court rests on a state law ground that is independent of the federal question and adequate to support the judgment. This rule applies whether the state law ground is substantive or procedural. In the context of direct review of a state court judgment, the independent and adequate state ground doctrine is jurisdictional. Because this Court has no power to review a state law determination that is sufficient to support the judgment, resolution of any independent federal ground for the decision could not affect the judgment and would therefore be advisory.

We have applied the independent and adequate state ground doctrine not only in our own review of state court judgments, but in deciding whether federal district courts should address the claims of state prisoners in habeas corpus actions. The doctrine applies also to bar federal habeas when a state court declined to address a prisoner's federal claims because the prisoner had failed to meet a state procedural requirement. * * *

The basis for application of the independent and adequate state ground doctrine in federal habeas is somewhat different than on direct review by this Court. When this Court reviews a state court decision on direct review pursuant to 28 U.S.C. § 1257 it is reviewing the judgment; if resolution of a federal question cannot affect the judgment, there is nothing for the Court to do. This is not the case in habeas. When a federal district court reviews a state prisoner's habeas corpus petition pursuant to 28 U.S.C. § 2254 it must decide whether the petitioner is "in custody in violation of the Constitution or laws or treaties of the United States." The court does not review a judgment, but the lawfulness of the petitioner's custody *simpliciter*.

Nonetheless, a state prisoner is in custody pursuant to a judgment. When a federal habeas court releases a prisoner held pursuant to a state court judgment that rests on an independent and adequate state ground, it renders ineffective the state rule just as completely as if this Court had reversed the state judgment on direct review. In such a case, the habeas court ignores the State's legitimate reasons for holding the prisoner.

In the habeas context, the application of the independent and adequate state ground doctrine is grounded in concerns of comity and federalism. Without the rule, a federal district court would be able to do in habeas what this Court could not do on direct review; habeas would offer state prisoners whose custody was supported by independent and adequate state grounds an end run around the limits of this Court's jurisdiction and a means to undermine the State's interest in enforcing its laws.

When the independent and adequate state ground supporting a habeas petitioner's custody is a state procedural default, an additional concern comes into play. This Court has long held that a state prisoner's federal habeas petition should be dismissed if the prisoner has not exhausted available state remedies as to any of his federal claims. This exhaustion requirement is also grounded in principles of comity; in a federal system, the States should have the first opportunity to address and correct alleged violations of state prisoner's federal rights. * * *

These same concerns apply to federal claims that have been procedurally defaulted in state court. Just as in those cases in which a state prisoner fails to exhaust state remedies, a habeas petitioner who has failed to meet the State's procedural requirements for presenting his federal claims has deprived the state courts of an opportunity to address those claims in the first instance. A habeas petitioner who has defaulted his federal claims in state court meets the technical requirements for exhaustion; there are no state remedies any longer "available" to him. In the absence of the independent and adequate state ground doctrine in federal habeas, habeas petitioners would be able to avoid the exhaustion requirement by defaulting their federal claims in state court. The independent and adequate state ground doctrine ensures that the State's interest in correcting their own mistakes is respected in all federal habeas cases.

B

* * *

In *Michigan v. Long* (1983), * * * in order to minimize the costs associated with resolving ambiguities in state court decisions while still fulfilling our obligation to determine if there was an independent and adequate state ground for the decision, we established a conclusive presumption of jurisdiction in these cases:

> [W]hen, as in this case, a state court decision fairly appears to rest primarily on federal law, or to be interwoven with the federal law, and when the adequacy and independence of any possible state law ground is not clear from the face of the opinion, we will accept as the most reasonable explanation that the state court decided the case the way it did because it believed that federal law required it to do so.

After *Long*, a state court that wishes to look to federal law for guidance or as an alternative holding while still relying on an independent and adequate state ground can avoid the presumption by stating "clearly and expressly that [its decision] is * * * based on bona fide separate, adequate, and independent grounds."

In *Caldwell v. Mississippi* (1985) we applied the *Long* presumption in the context of an alleged independent and adequate state procedural ground.

Long and *Caldwell* were direct review cases. We first considered the problem of ambiguous state court decisions in the application of the independent and adequate state ground doctrine in a federal habeas case in *Harris v. Reed*. * * *

The situation presented to this Court was nearly identical to that in *Long* and *Caldwell*: a state court decision that fairly appeared to rest primarily on federal law in a context in which a federal court has an obligation to determine if the state court decision rested on an independent and adequate state ground. "Faced with a common problem, we adopt[ed] a common solution." *Harris* applied in federal habeas the presumption this Court adopted in *Long* for direct review cases. Because the Illinois Appellate Court did not "clearly and expressly" rely on waiver as a ground for rejecting Harris' ineffective assistance of counsel claims, the *Long* presumption applied and Harris was not barred from federal habeas.

After *Harris*, federal courts on habeas corpus review of state prisoner claims, like this Court on direct review of state court judgments, will presume that there is no independent and adequate state ground for a state court decision when the decision "fairly appears to rest primarily on federal law, or to be interwoven with the federal law, and when the adequacy and independence of any possible state law ground is not clear from the face of the opinion." In habeas, if the decision of the last state court to which the petitioner presented his federal claims fairly appeared to rest primarily on resolution of those claims, or to be interwoven with those claims, and did not clearly and expressly rely on an independent and adequate state ground, a federal court may address the petition.[1]

III

A

Coleman contends that the presumption of *Long* and *Harris* applies in this case, and precludes a bar to habeas, because the Virginia Supreme Court's order dismissing Coleman's appeal did not "clearly and expressly" state that it was based on state procedural grounds. Coleman reads *Harris* too broadly. A predicate to the application of the *Harris* presumption is that the decision of the last state court to which the petitioner presented his federal claims must fairly appear to rest primarily on federal law or to be interwoven with federal law.

* * *

Coleman urges a broader rule: that the presumption applies in all cases in which a habeas petitioner presented his federal claims to the state court. This rule makes little sense. * * * The presumption, like all conclusive presumptions, is designed to avoid the costs of excessive inquiry where a *per se* rule will achieve the correct result in almost all cases. * * *

Per se rules should not be applied, however, in situations where the generalization is incorrect as an empirical matter; the justification for a conclusive presumption disappears when application of the presumption will not reach the correct result most of the time. The *Long* and *Harris* presumption works because in the majority of cases in which a state court decision fairly appears to rest primarily on federal law or to be interwoven with such law, and the state court does not plainly state that it is relying on an independent and adequate state ground, the state court decision did not in fact rest on an independent and adequate state ground. We accept errors in those small number of cases where there was nonetheless an independent and adequate state ground in exchange

---

[1] This rule does not apply if the petitioner failed to exhaust state remedies and the court to which petitioner would be required to present his claims in order to meet the exhaustion requirement would now find the claims procedurally barred. In such a case there is a procedural default for purposes of federal habeas regardless of the decision of the last state court to which the petitioner actually presented his claims.

for a significant reduction in the costs of inquiry.

The tradeoff is very different when the factual predicate does not exist. In those cases in which it does not fairly appear that the state court rested its decision primarily on federal grounds, it is simply not true that the "most reasonable explanation" is that the state judgment rested on federal grounds. * * * Any efficiency gained by applying a conclusive presumption, and thereby avoiding inquiry into state law, is simply not worth the cost in the loss of respect for the State that such a rule would entail.

* * *

In any event, we decline to establish such a rule here, for it would place burdens on the States and state courts in exchange for very little benefit to the federal courts. We are, as an initial matter, far from confident that the empirical assumption of the argument for such a rule is correct. It is not necessarily the case that state courts will take pains to provide a clear and express statement of procedural default in all cases, even after announcement of the rule. State courts presumably have a dignitary interest in seeing that their state law decisions are not ignored by a federal habeas court, but most of the price paid for federal review of state prisoner claims is paid by the State. When a federal habeas court considers the federal claims of a prisoner in state custody for independent and adequate state law reasons, it is the State that must respond. It is the State that pays the price in terms of the uncertainty and delay added to the enforcement of its criminal laws. It is the State that must retry the petitioner if the federal courts reverse his conviction. If a state court, in the course of disposing of cases on its overcrowded docket, neglects to provide a clear and express statement of procedural default, or is insufficiently motivated to do so, there is little the State can do about it. Yet it is primarily respect for the State's interests that underlies the application of the independent and adequate state ground doctrine in federal habeas.

A broad presumption would also put too great a burden on the state courts. It remains the duty of the federal courts, whether this Court on direct review, or lower federal courts in habeas, to determine the scope of the relevant state court judgment. We can establish a *per se* rule that eases the burden of inquiry on the federal courts in those cases where there are few costs to doing so, but we have no power to tell state courts how they must write their opinions. We encourage state courts to express plainly, in every decision potentially subject to federal review, the grounds upon which its judgment rests, but we will not impose on state courts the responsibility for using particular language in every case in which a state prisoner presents a federal claim—every state appeal, every denial of state collateral review—in order that federal courts might not be bothered with reviewing state law and the record in the case.

Nor do we believe that the federal courts will save much work by applying the *Harris* presumption in all cases. * * * In the absence of a clear indication that a state court rested its decision on federal law, a federal court's task will not be difficult.

* * *

B

The *Harris* presumption does not apply here. Coleman does not argue, nor could he, that it "fairly appears" that the Virginia Supreme Court's decision rested primarily on federal law or was interwoven with such law. The Virginia Supreme Court stated plainly that it was granting the Commonwealth's motion to dismiss the petition for appeal. That motion was based solely on Coleman's failure to meet the Supreme Court's time requirements. There is no mention of federal law in the Virginia Supreme Court's three-sentence dismissal order. It "fairly appears" to rest primarily on state law.

* * *

IV

In *Daniels v. Allen* (1953), the companion case to *Brown v. Allen*, we confronted a situation nearly identical to that here. Petitioners were convicted in a North Carolina trial court, and then were one day late in filing their appeal as of right in the North Carolina Supreme Court. That court rejected the appeals as procedurally barred. We held that federal habeas was also barred unless petitioners could prove that they were "detained without opportunity to appeal because of lack of counsel, incapacity, or some interference by officials."

Fay v. Noia (1963) overruled this holding. Noia failed to appeal at all in state court his state conviction, and then sought federal habeas review of his claim that his confession had been coerced. This Court held that such a procedural default in state court does not bar federal habeas review unless the petitioner has deliberately bypassed state procedures by intentionally forgoing an opportunity for state review. *Fay* thus created a presumption in favor of federal habeas review of claims procedurally defaulted in state court. The Court based this holding on its conclusion that a State's interest in orderly procedure are sufficiently vindicated by the prisoner's forfeiture of his state remedies. "Whatever residuum of state interest there may be under such circumstances is manifestly insufficient in the face of the federal policy * * * of affording an effective remedy for restraints contrary to the Constitution."

Our cases after *Fay* that have considered the effect of state procedural default on federal habeas review have taken a markedly different view of the important interests served by state procedural rules.

* * *

We concluded in *Francis* [*v. Henderson* (1976), a case challenging grand jury composition where defendant failed to raise the issue as required by state law] that a proper respect for the States required that federal courts give to the state procedural rule the same effect they give to the federal rule * * *. We held that Francis' claim was barred in federal habeas unless he could establish cause and prejudice.

Wainwright v. Sykes (1977) applied the cause and prejudice standard more broadly. Sykes did not object at trial to the introduction of certain inculpatory statements he had earlier made to the police. Under Florida law, this failure barred state courts from hearing the claim on either direct appeal or state collateral review. We recognized that this contemporaneous objection rule served strong state interests in the finality of its criminal litigation. To protect these interests, we adopted the same presumption against federal habeas review of claims defaulted in state court for failure to object at trial that *Francis* had adopted in the grand jury context: the cause and prejudice standard. "We believe the adoption of the *Francis* rule in this situation will have the salutary effect of making the state trial on the merits the 'main event,' so to speak, rather than a 'tryout on the road' for what will later be the determinative federal habeas hearing."

In so holding, *Wainwright* limited *Fay* to its facts. The cause and prejudice standard in federal habeas evinces far greater respect for state procedural rules than does the deliberate bypass standard of *Fay*. These incompatible rules are based on very different conceptions of comity and of the importance of finality in state criminal litigation. In *Wainwright*, we left open the question whether the deliberate bypass standard still applied to a situation like that in *Fay*, where a petitioner has surrendered entirely his right to appeal his state conviction. We rejected explicitly, however, "the sweeping language of *Fay v. Noia*, going far beyond the facts of the case eliciting it."

Our cases since *Sykes* have been unanimous in applying the cause and prejudice standard. *Engle v. Isaac* (1982) held that the standard applies even in cases in which the alleged constitutional error impaired the truthfinding function of the trial. Respondents had failed to object at trial to jury instructions that placed on them the burden of proving self defense. Ohio's contemporaneous objection rule barred respondents' claim on appeal that the burden should have been on the State. We held that this independent and adequate state ground barred federal habeas as well, absent a showing of cause and prejudice.

Recognizing that the writ of habeas corpus "is a bulwark against convictions that violate fundamental fairness," we also acknowledged that "the Great Writ entails significant costs." The most significant of these is the cost to finality in criminal litigation that federal collateral review of state convictions entails * * *. Moreover, "[f]ederal intrusions into state criminal trials frustrate both the States' sovereign power to punish offenders and their good-faith attempts to honor constitutional rights." These costs are particularly high, we explained, when a state prisoner, through a procedural default, prevents adjudication of his constitutional claims in state court. Because these costs do not depend on the type of claim the prisoner raised, we reaffirmed that a state procedural default of any federal claim will bar federal habeas unless the petitioner demonstrates cause and actual prejudice. We also explained in *Engle* that the cause and prejudice standard will be met in those cases where review of a state prisoner's claim is necessary to correct "a fundamental miscarriage of justice." ("[W]here a constitutional violation has probably resulted in the conviction of one who is actually innocent, a federal habeas court may grant the writ even in the absence of a showing of cause for the procedural default").

* * *

We now make it explicit: In all cases in which a state prisoner has defaulted his federal claims in state court pursuant to an independent and adequate state procedural rule, federal habeas review of the claims is barred unless the prisoner can demonstrate cause for the default and actual prejudice as a result of the alleged violation of federal law, or demonstrate that failure to consider the claims will result in a fundamental miscarriage of justice. *Fay* was based on a conception of federal/state relations that undervalued the importance of state procedural rules. The several cases after *Fay* that applied the cause and prejudice standard to a variety of state procedural defaults represent a different view. We now recognize the important interest in finality served by state procedural rules, and the significant harm to the States that results from the failure of federal courts to respect them.

* * *

V

A

Coleman maintains that there was cause for his default. The late filing was, he contends, the result of attorney error of sufficient magnitude to excuse the default in federal habeas.

Murray v. Carrier (1986) considered the circumstances under which attorney error constitutes cause. Carrier argued that his attorney's inadvertence in failing to raise certain claims in his state appeal constituted cause for the default sufficient to allow federal habeas review. We rejected this claim, explaining that the costs associated with an ignorant or inadvertent procedural default are no less than where the failure to raise a claim is a deliberate strategy: it deprives the state courts of the opportunity to review trial errors. When a federal habeas court hears such a claim, it undercuts the State's ability to enforce its procedural rules just as surely as when the default was deliberate. We concluded: "So long as a defendant is represented by counsel whose performance is not constitutionally ineffective under the standard established in *Strickland v. Washington*, we discern no inequity in requiring him to bear the risk of attorney error that results in a procedural default."

Applying the *Carrier* rule as stated, this case is at an end. There is no constitutional right to an attorney in state post-conviction proceedings. * * *

Coleman attempts to avoid this reasoning by arguing that *Carrier* does not stand for such a broad proposition. He contends that *Carrier* applies by its terms only in those situations where it is possible to state a claim for ineffective assistance of counsel. Where there is no constitutional right to counsel, Coleman argues, it is enough that a petitioner demonstrate that his attorney's conduct would meet the *Strickland* standard, even though no independent Sixth Amendment claim is possible.

* * *

Attorney ignorance or inadvertence is not "cause" because the attorney is the petitioner's agent when acting, or failing to act, in furtherance of the litigation, and the petitioner must "bear the risk of attorney error." Attorney error that constitutes ineffective assistance of counsel is cause, however. This is not because, as Coleman contends, the error is so bad that "the lawyer ceases to be an agent of the petitioner." In a case such as this, where the alleged attorney error is inadvertence in failing to file a timely notice, such a rule would be contrary to well-settled principles of agency law. Rather, as *Carrier* explains, "if the procedural default is the result of ineffective assistance of counsel, the Sixth Amendment itself requires that responsibility for the default be imputed to the State." In other words, it is not the gravity of the attorney's error that matters, but that it constitutes a violation of petitioner's right to counsel, so that the error must be seen as an external factor, *i.e.*, "imputed to the State."

Where a petitioner defaults a claim as a result of the denial of the right to effective assistance of counsel, the State, which is responsible for the denial as a constitutional matter, must bear the cost of any resulting default and the harm to state interests that federal habeas review entails. A different allocation of costs is appropriate in those circumstances where the State has no responsibility to ensure that the petitioner was represented by competent counsel. As between the State and the petitioner, it is the petitioner who must bear the burden of a failure to follow state procedural rules. In the absence of a constitutional violation, the petitioner bears the risk in federal habeas for all attorney errors made in the course of the representation, as *Carrier* says explicitly.

B

Among the claims Coleman brought in state habeas, and then again in federal habeas, is ineffective assistance of counsel during trial, sentencing, and appeal. Coleman contends that, at least as to these claims, attorney error in state habeas must constitute cause. This is because, under Virginia law at the time of Coleman's trial and direct appeal, ineffective assistance of counsel claims related to counsel's conduct during trial or appeal could be brought only in state habeas. Coleman argues that attorney error in failing to file timely in the first forum in which a federal claim can be raised is cause.

We reiterate that counsel's ineffectiveness will constitute cause only if it is an independent constitutional violation. * * * [T]here is no right to counsel in state collateral proceedings. For Coleman to prevail, therefore, there must be an exception to the rule * * * in those cases where state collateral review is the first place a prisoner can present a challenge to his conviction. We need not answer this question broadly, however, for one state court has addressed Coleman's claims: the state habeas trial court. The effectiveness of Coleman's counsel before that court is not at issue here. Coleman contends that it was the ineffectiveness of his counsel during the appeal from that determination that constitutes cause to excuse his default. We thus need to decide only whether Coleman had a constitutional right to counsel on appeal from the state habeas trial court judgment. We conclude that he did not.

* * *

Coleman has had his "one and only appeal," if that is what a state collateral proceeding may be considered; the Buchanan County Circuit Court, after a two-day evidentiary hearing, addressed Coleman's claims of trial error, including his ineffective assistance of counsel claims. What Coleman requires here is a right to counsel on appeal from that determination. Our case law will not support it.

* * *

Because Coleman had no right to counsel to pursue his appeal in state habeas, any attorney error that led to the default of Coleman's claims in state court cannot constitute cause to excuse the default in federal habeas. As Coleman does not argue in this Court that federal review of his claims is necessary to prevent a fundamental miscarriage of justice, he is barred from bringing these claims in federal habeas. Accordingly, the judgment of the Court of Appeals is

Affirmed.

JUSTICE BLACKMUN, with whom JUSTICE MARSHALL and JUSTICE STEVENS join, dissenting.

Federalism; comity; state sovereignty; preservation of state resources; certainty: the majority methodically inventories these multifarious state interests before concluding that the plain-statement rule of *Michigan v. Long* does not apply to a summary order. One searches the majority's opinion in vain, however, for any mention of petitioner Coleman's right to a criminal proceeding free from constitutional defect or his interest in finding a forum for his constitutional challenge to his conviction and sentence of death. Nor does the majority even allude to the "important need for uniformity in federal law," which justified this Court's adoption of the plain-statement rule in the first place. Rather, displaying obvious exasperation with the breadth of substantive federal habeas doctrine and the expansive protection afforded by the Fourteenth Amendment's guarantee of fundamental fairness in state criminal proceedings, the Court today continues its crusade to erect petty procedural barriers in the path of any state prisoner seeking review of his federal constitutional claims. Because I believe that the Court is creating a Byzantine morass of arbitrary, unnecessary, and unjustifiable impediments to the vindication of federal rights, I dissent.

I

The Court cavalierly claims that "[t]his is a case about federalism," and proceeds without explanation to assume that the purposes of federalism are advanced whenever a federal court refrains from reviewing an ambiguous state court judgment. Federalism, however, has no inherent normative value: it does not, as the majority appears to assume, blindly protect the interests of States from any incursion by the federal courts. Rather, federalism secures to citizens the liberties that derive from the diffusion of sovereign power. * * * In this context, it cannot lightly be assumed that the interests of federalism are fostered by a rule that impedes federal review of federal constitutional claims.

Moreover, the form of federalism embraced by today's majority bears little resemblance to that adopted by the Framers of the Constitution and ratified by the original States. The majority proceeds as if the sovereign interests of the States and the Federal Government were co-equal. Ours, however, is a federal republic, conceived on the principle of a supreme federal power and constituted first and foremost of citizens, not of sovereign States. The citizens expressly declared: "This Constitution, and the Laws of the United States which shall be made in Pursuance thereof * * * shall be the supreme Law of the Land." * * * The ratification of the Fourteenth Amendment by the citizens of the several States expanded federal powers even further, with a corresponding diminution of state sovereignty. Thus, "the sovereignty of the States is limited by the Constitution itself."

Federal habeas review of state court judgments, respectfully employed to safeguard federal rights, is no invasion of State sovereignty. Since 1867, Congress has acted within its constitutional authority to " 'interpose the federal courts between the States and the people, as guardians of the people's federal rights—to protect the people from unconstitutional action.' " Justice Frankfurter, in his separate opinion in *Brown v. Allen*, recognized this: "Insofar as [federal habeas] jurisdiction enables federal district courts to entertain claims that State Supreme Courts have denied rights guaranteed by the United States Constitution, it is not a case of a lower court sitting in judgment on a higher court. It is merely one aspect of respecting the Supremacy Clause of the Constitution whereby federal law is higher than State law." Thus, the considered exercise by federal courts—in vindication of fundamental constitutional rights—of the habeas jurisdiction conferred on them by Congress exemplifies the full expression of this Nation's federalism.

* * *

II

* * *

B

* * * In its attempt to justify a blind abdication of responsibility by the federal courts, the majority's opinion marks the nadir of the Court's recent habeas jurisprudence, where the discourse of rights is routinely replaced with the functional dialect of interests. The Court's habeas jurisprudence now routinely, and without evident reflection, subordinates fundamental constitutional rights to mere utilitarian interests. Such unreflective cost-benefit analysis is inconsistent with the very idea of rights. The Bill of Rights is not, after all, a collection of technical interests, and "surely it is an abuse to deal too casually and too lightly with rights guaranteed" therein. *Brown v. Allen* (opinion of Frankfurter, J.).

It is well settled that the existence of a state procedural default does not divest a federal court of jurisdiction on collateral review. Rather, the important office of the federal courts in vindicating federal rights gives way to the States' enforcement of their procedural rules to protect the States' interest in being an equal partner in safeguarding federal rights. This accommodation furthers the values underlying federalism in two ways. First, encouraging a defendant to assert his federal rights in the appropriate state forum makes it possible for transgressions to be arrested sooner and before they influence an erroneous deprivation of liberty. Second, thorough examination of a prisoner's federal claims in state court permits more effective review of those claims in federal court, honing the accuracy of the writ as an implement to eradicate unlawful detention. The majority ignores these purposes in concluding that a State need not bear the burden of making clear its intent to rely on such a rule. When it is uncertain whether a state court judgment denying relief from federal claims rests on a procedural bar, it is inconsistent with federalism principles for a federal court to exercise discretion to decline to review those federal claims.

* * *

The majority's attempt to distinguish between the interests of state courts and the interests of the States in this context is inexplicable. States do not exist independent of their officers, agents, and citizens. Rather, "[t]hrough the structure of its government, and the character of those who exercise government authority, a State defines itself as a sovereign." *See also Ex parte Virginia* ("A State acts by its legislative, its executive, or its judicial authorities. It can act in no other way"). The majority's novel conception of dichotomous interests is entirely unprecedented.

* * *

III

* * * Whether unprofessional attorney conduct in a state postconviction proceeding should bar federal habeas review of a state prisoner's conviction and sentence of death is not a question of costs to be allocated most efficiently. It is, rather, another circumstance where this Court must determine whether federal rights should yield to state interests. * * *

The majority first contends that this Court's decision in *Murray v. Carrier* expressly resolves this issue. Of course, that cannot be so, as the procedural default at issue in *Murray* occurred on direct review, not collateral attack, and this Court has no authority to resolve issues not before it. Moreover, notwithstanding the majority's protestations to the contrary, the language of *Murray* strongly suggests that the Court's resolution of the issue would have been the same regardless of when the procedural default occurred. The Court in *Murray* explained: "A State's procedural rules serve vital purposes at trial, on appeal, and *on state collateral attack* " (emphasis added). Rejecting Carrier's argument that, with respect to the standard for cause, procedural defaults on appeal should be treated differently from those that occur during the trial, the Court stated that "the standard for cause should not vary depending on the timing of a procedural default or on the strength of an uncertain and difficult assessment of the relative magnitude of the benefits attributable to the state procedural rules that attach at *each successive stage of the judicial process*" (emphasis added).

The rule foreshadowed by this language, which the majority today evades, most faithfully adheres to a principled view of the role of federal habeas jurisdiction. As noted above, federal courts forgo the exercise of their habeas jurisprudence over claims that are procedurally barred out of respect for the state interests served by those rules. Recognition of state procedural forfeitures discourages petitioners from attempting to avoid state proceedings, and accommodates the State's interest in finality. No rule, however, can deter gross incompetence. To permit a procedural default caused by attorney error egregious enough to constitute ineffective assistance of counsel to preclude federal habeas review of a state prisoner's federal claims in no way serves the State's interest in preserving the integrity of its rules and proceedings. The interest in finality, standing alone, cannot provide a sufficient reason for a federal habeas court to compromise its protection of constitutional rights.

The majority's conclusion that Coleman's allegations of ineffective assistance of counsel, if true, would not excuse a procedural default that occurred in the state post-conviction proceeding is particularly disturbing because, at the time of Coleman's appeal, state law precluded defendants from raising certain claims on direct appeal. As the majority acknowledges, under state law as it existed at the time of Coleman's trial and appeal, Coleman could raise his ineffective assistance of counsel claim with respect to counsel's conduct during trial and appeal only in state habeas.

* * *

* * * "[F]undamental fairness is the central concern of the writ of habeas corpus." It is the quintessence of inequity that the Court today abandons that safeguard while continuing to embrace the cause and prejudice standard.

I dissent.

Notes and Questions

1. a) The majority notes that the adequate-and-independent-state-ground rule is a jurisdictional limitation of direct review and links that assertion to the inhibition against advisory opinions. Although the Court's disinclination to render advisory opinions is two centuries old, why is it a jurisdictional bar? From what constitutional provision does it derive?

b) The Court clearly feels that the rule is not jurisdictional in cases of collateral review. Why not? Why should the presence of a state ground for decision either always or never preclude review? If there is a distinction, does it shed any light on whether the rule is *always* jurisdictional in the context of direct review?

c) The Court reaffirmed the non-jurisdictional nature of the state-procedural-default rule in the habeas context in *Trest v. Cain*, 522 U.S. 87, 118 S.Ct. 478, 139 L.Ed.2d 444 (1997), holding that "a procedural default, that is, a critical failure to comply with state procedural law, is not a jurisdictional matter." Justice Breyer's opinion for a unanimous Court viewed state procedural default as a defense that the state must preserve. The Court also recognized that there is uncertainty about whether a habeas court may raise the issue *sua sponte*, but declined to reach that question because the Fifth Circuit had thought itself compelled to raise the issue, the petition for certiorari had not embraced that question, and the factual record was inadequate to permit the court to adjudicate that issue.

2. a) *Coleman* reaffirms the decision in *Harris v. Reed* to apply the standards for interpreting ambiguous state court decisions developed in the context of direct Supreme Court review in *Michigan v. Long* and *Caldwell v. Mississippi* to habeas corpus cases. Thus, both the Supreme Court and district courts faced with an ambiguous state court decision will presume there is no independent and adequate state ground barring federal review if the state court decision "fairly appears to rest primarily on federal law, or to be interwoven with the federal law" unless the adequacy and independence of

any possible state law ground is clear from the face of the state court opinion. While there clearly is logic in the Court's determination when "[f]aced with a common problem [to] adopt a common solution," there also is irony. The *Michigan v. Long* standard expanded the Supreme Court's jurisdiction. Presuming the state court decision did not rest upon an adequate and independent state ground enabled the Court in *Long* to review and reverse a state court ruling that granted the defendant relief on the grounds his Fourth Amendment rights were violated. The *Michigan v. Long* standard, however, also expands the scope of habeas corpus, making it easier for district courts to review state court decisions denying petitioners' federal constitutional claims. This expansion runs counter to the Court's apparent desire to limit the scope of habeas corpus.

b) The Court of Appeals and the Supreme Court both concluded the Virginia Supreme Court decision rested on an adequate and independent state ground, so Coleman could not rely on *Long*. Do you agree?

c) Justice Blackmun, dissenting, accuses the majority of embracing a federalism that "blindly protect[s] the interests of the States from any incursion by the federal courts." He contends federal habeas review, "respectfully employed to safeguard federal rights, is no invasion of State sovereignty." Who is right?

3. *Wainwright v. Sykes*, 433 U.S. 72, 97 S.Ct. 2497, 53 L.Ed.2d 594 (1977), upon which *Coleman* so heavily relies, deserves extended consideration. Sykes challenged a conviction based in part upon his own statement. Counsel had not objected to the introduction of the statement, violating the state's contemporaneous objection rule. Sykes argued in the federal proceeding that he had not understood his *Miranda* rights and persuaded the district court to order a hearing on the question of the voluntariness of his statement. The Supreme Court denied habeas relief, adopting the cause-and-prejudice standard echoed in *Coleman*.

a) In rejecting the "deliberate bypass" standard in favor of the "cause and prejudice" standard, *Sykes* noted (and *Coleman* echoes) that "proper respect" for the states and their adjudicative processes compels the latter standard. From whence do either the cause-and-prejudice standard or the deliberate-bypass standard derive? Are they constitutionally compelled or are they prudential limitations on federal judicial power?

b) The *Sykes* Court adopted the cause-and-prejudice standard because it worried that a more lenient rule encouraged "sandbagging."

> We think that the [deliberate bypass] rule of *Fay v. Noia*, broadly stated, may encourage "sandbagging" on the part of defense lawyers, who may take their chances on a verdict of not guilty in a state trial court with the intent to raise their constitutional claims in a federal habeas court if their initial gamble does not pay off. The refusal of federal habeas courts to honor contemporaneous-objection rules may also make state courts themselves less stringent in their enforcement. Under the rule of *Fay v. Noia*, state appellate courts know that a federal constitutional issue raised for the first time in the proceeding be-

fore them may well be decided in any event by a federal habeas tribunal. Thus, their choice is between addressing the issue notwithstanding the petitioner's failure to timely object, or else face the prospect that the federal habeas court will decide the question without the benefit of their views.

Justice Brennan's dissent insisted that sandbagging was unlikely because it would violate even the deliberate-bypass standard. He argued that the majority's new rule was inconsistent with proper respect for constitutional rights and established law regarding their abandonment.

> [T]here are times when the failure to heed a state procedural requirement stems from an intentional decision to avoid the presentation of constitutional claims to the state forum. *Fay* was not insensitive to this possibility. Indeed, the very purpose of its bypass test is to detect and enforce such intentional procedural forfeitures of outstanding constitutionally based claims. *Fay* does so through application of the longstanding rule used to test whether action or inaction on the part of a criminal defendant should be construed as a decision to surrender the assertion of rights secured by the Constitution: To be an effective waiver, there must be "an intentional relinquishment or abandonment of a known right or privilege." Incorporating this standard, *Fay* recognized that if one "understandingly and knowingly forewent the privilege of seeking to vindicate his federal claims in the state courts, whether for strategic, tactical or any other reasons that can fairly be described as the deliberate by-passing of state procedures, then it is open to the federal court on habeas to deny him all relief * * * ." For this reason, the Court's assertion that it "think[s]" that the *Fay* rule encourages intentional "sandbagging" on the part of the defense lawyers is without basis; certainly the Court points to no cases or commentary arising during the past 15 years of actual use of the *Fay* test to support this criticism. Rather, a consistent reading of case law demonstrates that the bypass formula has provided a workable vehicle for protecting the integrity of state rules in those instances when such protection would be both meaningful and just.

Apart from questions of the proper standard for surrender of important constitutional rights, discussed below, consider whether sandbagging is practical. Assuming defense counsel could conceal deliberate failure to raise an issue, what does it profit the defense in a criminal case to hold it back? Raising the objection at trial in *Sykes* presumably would have made conviction less likely. What advantage did the defense reap by foregoing that possibility? If Sykes's conviction were vacated on federal review, that would not necessarily end the proceedings; the state could retry him without the tainted evidence. The additional expense to the state is clear, but that is hardly a benefit to the defendant. What can sandbagging accomplish?

c) *Sykes* and *Coleman* also raise questions about the ease or difficulty of losing constitutional rights. In *Sykes*, the petitioner sought to assert a Fifth Amendment right. In *Coleman*, petitioner urged several constitutional defects in the state proceedings[34] that the Court barred because Coleman's counsel had filed a state notice of appeal three days late. In both cases, the Court found that the asserted constitutional rights had been waived. In *Sykes*, Justice Brennan took sharp issue with the majority, arguing that *Johnson v. Zerbst*, 304 U.S. 458, 58 S.Ct. 1019, 82 L.Ed. 1461 (1938), which required a knowing and deliberate waiver by the defendant, should continue to govern waiver of constitutional rights. The majority, shifting away from that standard, noted:

> We leave open for resolution in future decisions the precise definition of the "cause"-and-"prejudice" standard, and note here only that it is narrower than the standard set forth in dicta in *Fay v. Noia*, which would make federal habeas review generally available to state convicts absent a knowing and deliberate waiver of the federal constitutional contention.

Thus, the majority clearly repudiated *Johnson v. Zerbst* in this context.

In *Sykes*, the defendant's failure contemporaneously to object to introduction of his statement waived his right to do so. In *Edelman v. Jordan*, 415 U.S. 651, 94 S.Ct. 1347, 39 L.Ed.2d 662 (1974), the Court ruled on whether Illinois's participation in a federal program waived the state's Eleventh Amendment immunity. Refusing to find waiver, the majority said:

> Constructive consent is not a doctrine commonly associated with the surrender of constitutional rights, and we see no place for it here. In deciding whether a State has waived its constitutional protection under the Eleventh Amendment, we will find waiver only where stated "by the most express language or by such overwhelming implications from the text as [will] leave no room for any other reasonable construction."[a]

Plainly, *Sykes/Coleman* and *Edelman* are flatly inconsistent as to the conduct necessary to waive a constitutional right. Are the different standards for state and individual waiver justifiable?

4. The cause-and-prejudice standard has been used to judge petitioners' performance as litigators in at least three contexts in habeas corpus cases. In *Tamayo-Reyes*, discussed at page 1088, the Court substituted the cause-and-prejudice standard for *Townsend*'s deliberate-bypass standard when a petitioner sought a federal evidentiary hearing on the ground that the material facts were not adequately developed in state proceedings. *Sykes/Coleman* applied the standard to decide whether to excuse a petitioner's procedural default in state court. *McCleskey v. Zant*, 499 U.S. 467,

---

[34] Coleman argued, *inter alia*, the following: pre-judgment of his case one juror, ineffective assistance of counsel, exclusion, in violation of Witherspoon v. Illinois, 391 U.S. 510, 88 S.Ct. 1770, 20 L.Ed.2d 776 (1968), of jurors opposed to the death penalty, and the prosecution's failure to disclose exculpatory evidence.

[a] [AUTHORS' NOTE] The Court did note that the Eleventh Amendment concerns an area in which sovereignties collide, paying homage to the special position of the Eleventh Amendment. Nonetheless, the Court's thoughts on waiver were expressed in terms far broader than necessary merely to defer to the Eleventh Amendment.

111 S.Ct. 1454, 113 L.Ed.2d 517 (1991), applies the standard to determine whether a petitioner should be allowed to file a successive habeas petition presenting claims not presented in an earlier petition. Given the wide application of the cause-and-prejudice standard in habeas cases, it is surprising that it is not better defined. As the Court has candidly admitted, it has never "attempted to establish conclusively the contours of the standard." The Court has provided no "precise content" defining "cause," and the meaning of "prejudice remains an "open question" in most contexts. Nonetheless, some guidelines have emerged for both.

a) *Reed v. Ross*, 468 U.S. 1, 104 S.Ct. 2901, 82 L.Ed.2d 1 (1984), held that a petitioner may have good cause for not raising a constitutional claim when the claim was not recognized at the time of his state proceedings. *Teague v. Lane* obviously limited the utility of this holding to petitioners because it prohibited consideration of constitutional claims not recognized before the petitioner's state proceedings became final, except in extremely limited circumstances. *Murray v. Carrier*, discussed in *Coleman*, makes clear that a petitioner can establish good cause for error in state proceedings if counsel is constitutionally ineffective under *Strickland v. Washington*. *Murray* also stated that establishing cause would "ordinarily turn on whether the prisoner can show that some objective factor external to the defense impeded counsel's efforts to comply with the State's procedural rule," and suggested that "some interference by officials" would qualify. Subsequently, *Strickler v. Greene*, 527 U.S. 263, 119 S.Ct. 1936, 144 L.Ed.2d 286 (1999), found that the prosecutor's failure to provide defense counsel with exculpatory material (in violation of *Brady v. Maryland* (1963)) established cause for counsel's failure to use the material during the guilt and sentencing phases of the state proceedings.

Edwards v. Carpenter, 529 U.S. 446, 120 S.Ct. 1587, 146 L.Ed.2d 518 (2000), caused (so to speak) the Court again to confront the relationship between ineffective-assistance claims and state procedural default. Perhaps not surprisingly, the Court reaffirmed that ineffective assistance may satisfy the cause requirement for a procedurally defaulted claim, but the Court also added another layer to the analysis by holding that the prisoner may default the ineffective-assistance claim itself. In this event, the prisoner would have to seek state habeas relief based on the second default, showing cause and prejudice for defaulting the ineffective-assistance claim. If successful in that endeavor, the prisoner would still have the challenge of demonstrating cause and prejudice for the underlying constitutional claim. Thus, he would have to prove two levels of cause and prejudice. Justice Breyer and Stevens, although they concurred in the result, thought that the federal court should evaluate the defaulted ineffective-assistance claim in the first instance. The majority, on the other hand, viewed that possibility as an end run around *Murray v. Carrier*'s exhaustion requirement.

b) The meaning of "prejudice" may be even less certain. *United States v. Frady*, 456 U.S. 152, 102 S.Ct. 1584, 71 L.Ed.2d 816 (1982), explained that to find prejudice, a court must determine "not merely [that] the instruction is undesirable, erroneous, or even universally condemned," but instead "whether the ailing instruction by itself so infected the entire trial that the resulting convictions violated due process." *Strickler v. Greene* stated that prejudice exists only if "there is a reasonable probability that the result of the trial would have been different if the suppressed documents had been disclosed to the defense." Moreover, said the Court, "the adjective is important. The question is not whether the defendant would more likely than not have received a different verdict with the evidence, but whether in its absence he received a fair trial, understood as a trial resulting in a verdict worthy of confidence." In *Schlup v. Delo*, 513 U.S. 298, 115 S.Ct. 851, 130 L.Ed.2d 808 (1995), by contrast, Justice O'Connor stated in a concurrence that prejudice "requires only a reasonable probability that, absent the errors, the factfinder would have had a reasonable doubt respecting guilt."

c) Despite vagueness and possible inconsistencies in the Court's definitions of cause and prejudice, it seems clear that petitioners will be hard pressed to show both. Coleman could not even show cause, and while Strickler showed cause by the prosecutor's withholding of *Brady* material, the Court found there was only a reasonable *possibility* (not *probability*) that availability of the material would have produced a different result, either at the guilt or sentencing phase. Returning to *Coleman*, petitioner claimed that his attorney's failure to file a timely appeal from the state trial court's denial of the habeas petition was ineffective assistance under *Strickland v. Washington*, which is one of the ways a petitioner can establish cause. The majority thought it unnecessary to decide this claim. Why?

5. The Court notes that a petitioner must exhaust available state remedies as a prerequisite to federal habeas review. How does this relate to the rule that a state procedural default constitutes an adequate and independent state ground barring habeas review? Do the two limitations merely complement each other, or is the procedural-default rule necessary to enforce the exhaustion requirement? If the latter, which of the procedural default standards—deliberate bypass or cause-and-prejudice—will result in a more rigorous enforcement of the exhaustion requirement?

6. *Coleman* raises questions on many levels, some concerning the "federalism" on which Justice O'Connor focuses. Lurking in the background, however, is a more general issue about federal habeas corpus. Perhaps only by considering what the institution of federal habeas is supposed to do can one sensibly approach federalism and other problems. Justice Blackmun's dissent suggests as much. Is he correct? Is there a "chicken and egg" problem with respect to which issue drives the inquiry?

5. *The Problem of Successive Petitions*

Sanders v. United States (1963) set permissive standards for second or successive habeas petitions. The court could dismiss such petitions without reaching the merits only if an earlier petition presenting the same claim had been denied on the merits *and* the ends of justice would not be served by reaching the merits of the subsequent petition. The court could deny subsequent applications based on new grounds or on grounds not previously determined on the merits only if the petitioner was guilty of abuse of the writ. If the court found that the failure to raise the present claim in a previous application was a deliberate bypass within the meaning of *Fay v. Noia* (1963), that was an abuse. Thus, res judicata, which precludes not only claims that were litigated but also claims that might have been litigated in an earlier lawsuit, had only limited application in habeas cases. In 1966, Congress essentially codified this standard in an amendment to § 2244(b).

Coleman v. Thompson (1991), presented at page 1164, formally interred *Fay v. Noia*. *McCleskey v. Zant*, 499 U.S. 467, 111 S.Ct. 1454, 113 L.Ed.2d 517 (1991) did the same to *Sanders* by applying the cause-and-prejudice standard to successive petitions:

> We conclude from the unity of structure and purpose in the jurisprudence of state procedural defaults and abuse of the writ that the standard for excusing a failure to raise a claim at the appropriate time should be the same in both contexts. We have held that a procedural default will be excused upon a showing of cause and prejudice. We now hold that the same standard applies to determine if there has been an abuse of the writ through inexcusable neglect.

> In procedural default cases, the cause standard requires the petitioner to show that "some objective factor external to the defense impeded counsel's efforts" to raise the claim in state court. Objective factors that constitute cause include " 'interference by officials' " that makes compliance with the state's procedural rule impracticable, and "a showing that the factual or legal basis for a claim was not reasonably available to counsel." In addition, constitutionally "ineffective assistance of counsel * * * is cause." Attorney error short of ineffective assistance of counsel, however, does not constitute cause and will not excuse a procedural default. Once the petitioner has established cause, he must show " 'actual prejudice' resulting from the errors of which he complains."

> Federal courts retain the authority to issue the writ of habeas corpus in a further, narrow class of cases despite a petitioner's failure to show cause for a procedural default. These are extraordinary instances when a constitutional violation probably has caused the conviction of one innocent of the crime. We have described this class of cases as implicating a fundamental miscarriage of justice.

> The cause and prejudice analysis we have adopted for cases of procedural default applies to an abuse of the writ inquiry in the following manner. When a prisoner files a second or subsequent application, the government bears the burden of pleading abuse of the writ. The government satisfies this burden if, with clarity and particularity, it notes petitioner's prior writ history, identifies the claims that appear for the first time, and alleges that petitioner has abused the writ. The burden to disprove abuse then becomes petitioner's. To excuse his failure to raise the claim earlier, he must show cause for failing to raise it and prejudice therefrom as those

concepts have been defined in our procedural default decisions. The petitioner's opportunity to meet the burden of cause and prejudice will not include an evidentiary hearing if the district court determines as a matter of law that petitioner cannot satisfy the standard. If petitioner cannot show cause, the failure to raise the claim in an earlier petition may nonetheless be excused if he or she can show that a fundamental miscarriage of justice would result from a failure to entertain the claim. Application of the cause and prejudice standard in the abuse of the writ context does not mitigate the force of *Teague v. Lane*, which prohibits, with certain exceptions, the retroactive application of new law to claims raised in federal habeas. Nor does it imply that there is a constitutional right to counsel in federal habeas corpus.

In 1996, AEDPA amended the language of § 2244 that governed successive petitions and abuse of the writ. Whether one considers *McClesky* still to be good law depends on whether one reads the new language to codify *McClesky* or to impose even greater restrictions on successive petitions. The applicable provisions of § 2244 read as follows:

(b) (1) A claim presented in a second or successive habeas corpus application under section 2254 that was presented in a prior application shall be dismissed.

(2) A claim presented in a second or successive habeas corpus application under section 2254 that was not presented in a prior application shall be dismissed unless—

(A) the applicant shows that the claim relies on a new rule of constitutional law, made retroactive to cases on collateral review by the Supreme Court, that was previously unavailable; or

(B) (i) the factual predicate for the claim could not have been discovered previously through the exercise of due diligence; and

(ii) the facts underlying the claim, if proven and viewed in light of the evidence as a whole, would be sufficient to establish by clear and convincing evidence that, but for constitutional error, no reasonable factfinder would have found the applicant guilt of the underlying offense.

Notice that the statute does not use the language "cause and prejudice." Review the guidelines for cause and prejudice described in note 4 following *Coleman*. What similarities do you see between the guidelines and the language of the statute? What differences? Do you think the statute imposes any new restrictions on successive petitions? In an extended discussion, *Daniels v. United States*, 254 F.3d 1180, 1195-98 (10th Cir. 2001), concluded that AEDPA replaces the old cause-and-prejudice and *Teague* standards but then interprets the new language to mean almost the same thing as the old standards. Section 2244(b)(3) contains one requirement that is indisputably new. Before filing a second or successive petition permitted under (b)(2), the applicant must receive permission from the appropriate court of appeals.

As difficult as the questions in the preceding paragraph are to answer, § 2244(b) poses even more difficult questions when petitioners claim they are actually innocent. In a series of cases decided before AEDPA where petitioners claimed they could make compelling showings of innocence, the Court relied upon its general equitable powers to establish standards for entertaining a first, second or successive habeas petition despite a state procedural default or other defect that would normally preclude federal review. Moreover, if the petitioner was able to present strong evidence of innocence in a second or successive federal petition, the Court did not pay much attention to whether the petition repeated a claim raised in an earlier federal petition or presented a claim that might have been but was not raised in the earlier petition. The cases were not consistent, however, in specifying the burden of proof a petitioner must satisfy to obtain relief.

The Court addressed this inconsistency in *Schlup v. Delo*, 513 U.S. 298, 115 S.Ct. 851, 130 L.Ed.2d 808 (1995). *Schlup* held that a person whose petition would otherwise be barred as a successive petition or for some procedural default could have the petition heard because of "actual innocence" by showing that "a constitutional violation has probably resulted in the conviction of one who is actually innocent." The Court made clear it was adopting a "more likely than not" or preponderance standard rather than the "clear and convincing evidence" standard the dissenters proposed.

Consider again the language of § 2244 (b). Note that (b)(1) and (b)(2) distinguish between claims presented in a second or successive petition that were presented in a prior application and claims that were not. Under (b)(1), claims that were previously presented "shall be dismissed," period. Under (b)(2), claims that were not presented can be heard if the conditions of (b)(2)(A) or (B) can be satisfied.

By adopting a preponderance standard, *Schlup v. Delo* could be seen to overrule *Sawyer v. Whitley*, 505 U.S. 333, 112 S.Ct. 2514, 120 L.Ed.2d 269 (1992), a case involving a challenge to the death penalty on the basis of actual innocence. *Sawyer* held the petitioner must "show with clear and convincing evidence that but for the constitutional error at his sentencing hearing, no reasonable juror could have found him eligible for the death penalty." Section 2244(b)(2)(B)(ii) could be read to overrule *Schlup* and reinstate the clear-and-convincing evidence standard for a successive petition claiming actual innocence. Both *Sawyer* and *Schlup* may be alive and well however, depending on how one reads *Calderon v. Thompson*, 523 U.S. 538, 118 S.Ct. 1489, 140 L.Ed.2d 728 (1998). Thompson was convicted of rape and murder and sentenced to death. After exhausting state remedies, he filed a federal habeas petition. The district court granted relief as to the rape conviction and the rape special circumstances on grounds of ineffective assistance of counsel and ruled the death sentence invalid. The court did not disturb the murder conviction. The court of appeals reversed the rape conviction, affirmed the murder conviction, and reinstated the death sentence. After a flurry of additional applications to the court of appeals, the Supreme Court, the district court, and the Governor of California, all of which were denied, two days before his execution date a divided en banc panel of the court of appeals recalled the Court's mandate of June 11, 1997, that had denied all relief. The Court of Appeals took this action because of "procedural misunderstandings within [the] court," and to avoid "a miscarriage of justice." The court then proceeded to rule much as the district court had ruled, although it "remanded the question of the murder conviction for [the District Court's] initial consideration in light of our vacatur of the rape conviction."

The Supreme Court reversed, holding that in the circumstances of the case, recalling the mandate was an abuse of discretion. California argued that the court of appeals acted on the basis of a second or successive petition, thus calling § 2244(b) directly into operation. The Court accepted the court of appeals' word that it acted *sua sponte* on the basis of Thompson's first federal habeas petition, not on the basis of later filings. Thus, § 2244(b) was not technically applicable. Nonetheless, the Court looked to the statute to "inform our consideration." After reviewing § 2244(b)(2)'s language, the Court said the following:

> It is true that the miscarriage of justice standard we adopt today is somewhat more lenient than the standard in § 2244(b)(2)(B). See, *e.g.*, § 2244(b)(2)(B)(i)(factual predicate for claim must "not have been discoverable previously through the exercise of due diligence"). The miscarriage of justice standard is altogether consistent, however, with AEDPA's central concern that the merits of concluded criminal proceedings not be revisited in the absence of a strong showing of factual innocence. And, of course, the rules applicable in all cases where the court recalls its mandate further ensure the practice is limited to the most rare and extraordinary case.

Equating "miscarriage of justice" and "actual innocence," the Court then analyzed Thompson's case under the actual innocence standards articulated in the line of cases culminating in *Schlup*. The Court made clear that *Schlup* did not overrule *Sawyer* on the burden of proof issue. *Sawyer*'s clear-and-convincing standard applies when a capital petitioner challenges the circumstances making him eligible for the death penalty, while *Schlup*'s more likely than not standard applies when the petitioner claims he did not commit the underlying crime.

One can read *Thompson* in different ways. Because § 2244(b) was not technically applicable, the standards of the *Schlup* line of cases may apply only when the petitioner claims actual innocence in his first habeas petition, and some stricter set of standards may apply if the actual innocence claim is asserted in a second or successive petition. On the other hand, the Court relies heavily on the statute in construing the Court-created miscarriage of justice standard. In addition, although the Court states that the *Schlup* actual innocence standards are "somewhat more lenient" than the § 2244(b)(2)(B) standards, it does not explain what the differences might be, other than the cryptic reference to § 2244(b)(2)(B)(i). Does the Court mean to suggest that a miscarriage of justice claim could be raised in an initial petition even though the evidence submitted in support of the claim *was* "discoverable previously through the exercise of due diligence?" In addition, the Court makes no reference to the apparent difference between *Schlup*'s more likely than not standard and the statute's clear and convincing standard when stating that the caselaw standard is somewhat more lenient, despite the fact the Court contrasts these standards a few paragraphs later in distinguishing *Schlup* and *Sawyer*. What do you think? Is there one set of actual innocence standards for initial habeas applications and a different set for second or successive applications, or are the standards actually very similar? One thing is clear—it is a rare petitioner who will be able to satisfy either.

The Court revisited the standards for adjudicating actual-innocence and miscarriage-of-justice claims in *House v. Bell*, 547 U.S. 518, 126 S.Ct. 2064, 165 L.Ed.2d 1 (2006). As often happens in this highly technical, complex area of the law, the opinion raised many questions. Whether it answered any is questionable.

Paul House was convicted of murder and sentenced to death in Tennessee. The state supreme court affirmed. House sought collateral relief in state court claiming, *inter alia*, ineffective assistance of counsel and improper jury instructions. The trial court denied the petition; the Tennessee intermediate appellate court affirmed, and both the Tennessee and United States Supreme Courts denied review. House then filed a second petition in state court, reasserting his ineffective-assistance claim and requesting investigative or expert assistance. The Tennessee Supreme Court affirmed denial of this petition because, under Tennessee law, the claims were either waived or previously determined. House next filed a federal habeas corpus petition raising several claims of ineffective assistance of counsel and prosecutorial misconduct. The district court concluded that the state procedural defaults precluded review but held a hearing to determine whether House might satisfy the actual-innocence exception to the procedural default rules. Ultimately, the court held that House had "neither demonstrated actual innocence of the murder under *Schlup* nor established that he was ineligible for the death penalty under *Sawyer*." The *en banc* Sixth Circuit affirmed the district court decision by an 8-7 vote, and the Supreme Court granted certiorari.

After a lengthy review of the factual record, the Court discussed the proper rules for cases raising actual innocence claims. To satisfy the

Schlup standard for forgiving a procedural default, a petitioner must show that "it is more likely than not that no reasonable juror would have found petitioner guilty beyond a reasonable doubt." The Court also reiterated *Schlup*'s rule that making such a showing does not by itself entitle the petitioner to relief; rather, it earns him only a review of the merits of the constitutional claims he raises. Later in the opinion, the Court explained, citing *Herrera v. Collins*, 506 U.S. 390, 113 S.Ct. 853, 122 L.Ed.2d 203 (1993), that while there may be some cases where evidence of innocence is so overwhelming that it would be unconstitutional to execute the defendant for that reason alone, *House* was not such a case.

Is this a reasonable rule? If it is more likely than not that no reasonable juror would have convicted the petitioner, why isn't that enough to merit relief? In addition, once a court has decided that no reasonable juror would have convicted the petitioner, won't that as a practical matter affect the court's consideration of the constitutional issues?

One cannot do justice to the Court's further guidance on how to evaluate evidence in such cases by mere summary or paraphrase; one must experience it *verbatim*:

> For purposes of this case several features of the *Schlup* standard bear emphasis. First, although "[t]o be credible" a gateway claim requires "new reliable evidence—whether it be exculpatory scientific evidence, trustworthy eyewitness accounts, or critical physical evidence—that was not presented at trial," the habeas court's analysis is not limited to such evidence. There is no dispute in this case that House has presented some new reliable evidence; the State has conceded as much. In addition, because the District court held an evidentiary hearing in this case, and because the State does not challenge the court's decision to do so, we have no occasion to elaborate on *Schlup*'s observation that when considering an actual-innocence claim in the context of a request for an evidentiary hearing, the District Court need not "test the new evidence by a standard appropriate for deciding a motion for summary judgment," but rather may "consider how the timing of the submission and the likely credibility of the affiants bear on the probable reliability of that evidence." Our review in this case addresses the merits of the *Schlup* inquiry, based on a fully developed record, and with respect to that inquiry *Schlup* makes plain that the habeas court must consider " 'all the evidence,' " old and new, incriminating and exculpatory, without regard to whether it would necessarily be admitted under "rules of admissibility that would govern at trial." Based on this total record, the court must make "a probabilistic determination about what reasonable, properly instructed jurors would do." The court's function is not to make an independent factual determination about what likely occurred, but rather to assess the likely impact of the evidence on reasonable jurors.

This language appears to give district judges broad leeway to consider all available evidence. How can a district judge consider the "likely impact of [inadmissible] evidence on reasonable jurors"? Surely the Court cannot be implying that if House receives another trial the court should allow inadmissible evidence into the record. What is the point of having the court on collateral review consider evidence that a juror, reasonable or not, should never see or hear? In addition, is there any practical difference between making "an independent factual determination about what likely occurred" and assessing "the likely impact of the evidence on reasonable jurors?" In other words, won't the likely impact of the evidence on jurors depend upon their making a factual determination of what likely occurred?

Finally, the Court rejected the state's argument that the Court was bound by the district court's factual findings absent a showing a clear error. This portion of the Court's opinion is also less than clear.

> The State also argues that the District Court's findings in this case tie our hands, precluding a ruling in House's favor absent a showing of clear error as to the District Court's specific determinations. This view overstates the effect of the District Court's ruling. Deference is given to a trial court's assessment of evidence presented to it in the first instance. Yet the *Schlup* inquiry, we repeat, requires a holistic judgment about " 'all the evidence,' " and its likely effect on reasonable jurors applying the reasonable-doubt standard. As a general rule, the inquiry does not turn on discrete findings regarding disputed points of fact, and "[i]t is not the district court's independent judgment as to whether reasonable doubt exists that the standard addresses." Here, although the District Court attentively managed complex proceedings, carefully reviewed the extensive record, and drew certain conclusions about the evidence, the court did not clearly apply *Schlup*'s predictive standard regarding whether reasonable jurors would have reasonable doubt.

The Court does not appear to adopt either the usual abuse-of-discretion or *de-novo* standards, but something in between. Having concluded that House made the required gateway showing to excuse his state procedural default, the Court reversed and remanded for consideration of House's constitutional claims.

Gonzalez v. Crosby, 545 U.S. 524, 125 S.Ct. 2641, 162 L.Ed.2d 480 (2005), considered whether a motion for relief from judgment under FED. R. CIV. P. 60(b) should be subject to the additional restrictions that apply to second or successive habeas petitions. The Court held that if a Rule 60(b) motion presented an old or new claim, it should be considered a second or successive petition, while if no claim was presented, it should not: "If neither the motion itself nor the federal judgment from which it seeks relief substantively addresses federal grounds for setting aside the movant's state conviction, allowing the motion to proceed as denominated creates no inconsistency with the habeas statutes or rules." The Court concluded that Crosby's motion, which alleged merely that the federal court misapplied the federal statute of limitations, was not a second or successive petition. (The Court subsequently held, however, that petitioner's motion should be denied because it failed to set forth sufficiently "extraordinary circumstances" justifying relief.) The Court also identified other instances in which a 60(b) motion may play a valid role in habeas proceedings, such as relieving a party from the effect of a default judgment mistakenly entered against them or allowing *vacatur* of a judgment void for lack of subject matter jurisdiction.

A petitioner may avoid the prohibition of a second or successive petition if the claim raised in the subsequent petition is based on facts that did not exist at the time the first petition was filed. In *Panetti v. Quarterman,* __ U.S. __, 127 S.Ct. 2842, 168 L.Ed.2d 662 (2007), a Texas state court convicted petitioner of capital murder and sentenced him to death. At trial, he had claimed he was not guilty by reason of insanity, and he pressed this claim on appeal and in a federal habeas petition without success. Petitioner then filed a second federal habeas petition, claiming that his mental illness made him incompetent to be executed. The federal court stayed the application to allow the state trial judge to consider the matter. When the trial judge denied relief, the petitioner returned to federal court. The Supreme Court held that § 2244(b) did not bar the second habeas petition. *Ford v. Wainwright,* 477 U.S. 399, 106 S.Ct. 2595, 91 L.Ed.2d 335 (1986), held that the Eighth Amendment prohibits execution of a prisoner who is presently insane, even if he was earlier found competent to stand trial. Thus, a person facing death must be allowed to present evidence about his current mental state, and a federal court may hear such a claim, even if it comes in a second habeas petition. The Court reasoned that disallowing the second petition would work "seemingly perverse" results:

> A prisoner would be faced with two options: forgo the opportunity to raise a *Ford* claim in federal court; or raise the claim in a first federal habeas application (which generally must be filed within one year of the relevant state-court ruling), even though it is premature. The dilemma would apply not only to prisoners with mental conditions indicative of incompetency but also those with no early sign of mental illness. All prisoners are at risk of deteriorations in their mental state. As a result, conscientious defense attorneys would be obliged to file unripe (and in many cases, meritless) *Ford* claims in each and every § 2254 application. This counterintuitive approach would add to the burden imposed on courts, applicants, and the States, with no clear advantage to any.

State prisoners sometimes seek to avoid the severe restrictions on successive habeas petitions by raising their claims in a plenary civil action under 42 U.S.C. § 1983. Although the federal courts generally disallow this gambit, it has been successful in a few instances. *Hill v.*

McDonough, 547 U.S. 573, 126 S.Ct. 2096, 165L.Ed 2d 44 (2006), allowed a Florida death row inmate to bring a § 1983 action challenging the lethal injection procedure the state was likely to use on him. Hill claimed the procedure would cause him severe pain, thus violating the Eighth Amendment's prohibition of cruel and unusual punishments. Because Hill did not challenge the lethal injection sentence as a general matter and appeared to leave the state free to use an alternative lethal injection procedure, the lawsuit would not actually bar implementation of the sentence and thus could proceed.

The proper line of demarcation between habeas corpus and § 1983 claims has concerned the Court for some time. Many of the procedural restrictions on habeas corpus do not exist in § 1983 cases, thus giving state prisoners an incentive to raise their claims under that statute. The Supreme Court first considered the issue in *Preiser v. Rodriguez*, 411 U.S. 475, 93 S.Ct. 1827, 36 L.Ed.2d 439 (1973). In 1973, the main impediment to access to a federal forum in habeas cases was the requirement that a prisoner exhaust available state remedies before proceeding to federal court. Because there is no exhaustion requirement in § 1983 actions,[35] they provided an attractive alternative to habeas corpus. *Preiser* set the dividing line as follows: "[W]hen a state prisoner is challenging the very fact or duration of his physical imprisonment, and the relief he seeks is a determination that he is entitled to immediate release or a speedier release * * * his sole federal remedy is a writ of habeas corpus." Challenges to the *conditions* of confinement, by contrast, could be brought in section 1983 actions.

The *Preiser* standard worked reasonably well in the main, but applying it was sometimes uncertain. The lethal injection cases provide a dramatic example. *Nelson v. Campbell*, 541 U.S. 637, 124 S.Ct. 2117, 158 L.Ed.2d 924 (1994), presaged *Hill v. McDonough*. Three days before he was to die by lethal injection, Nelson filed a § 1983 action in federal court. Nelson had severely compromised peripheral veins from drug abuse, and he challenged the so-called "cut-down" procedure the warden planned to use to gain access to a vein as cruel and unusual punishment and deliberate indifference to his serious medical needs in violation of the Eighth Amendment. The district court and court of appeals held Nelson's action the "functional equivalent" of a habeas corpus proceeding and denied relief because Nelson had filed a previous federal habeas petition and could not surmount the restrictions on successive petitions.

In her opinion for a unanimous Court, Justice O'Connor explained the difficulty in applying the *Preiser* standard to Nelson's claims. She noted that the labels "conditions of confinement" and "fact or duration" of confinement were not "particularly apt." Nor did a suit seeking to enjoin

---

[35] *See* Patsy v. Board of Regents, 457 U.S. 496, 102 S.Ct. 2557, 73 L.Ed.2d 172 (1982), text at 715; Monroe v. Pape, 365 U.S. 167, 81 S.Ct. 473, 5 L.Ed.2d 492 (1961), *supra* at 510.

a particular means of execution directly call into question the "fact" or "validity" of the sentence. On the other hand, when a state has directed that executions be by lethal injection, the Court may rule that a suit seeking to enjoin lethal injections permanently is a challenge to the fact of the sentence itself. In addition, while it "makes little sense" to talk about the "duration" of a death sentence, allowing a § 1983 action clearly delays imposition of the sentence. Ultimately, the Court held Nelson's lawsuit could proceed, reasoning that Nelson was not actually challenging the sentence itself. Because the "cut-down" procedure was not necessary to the lethal injection, the sentence could be implemented by other means.

The analysis in *Hill v. McDonough* proceeded along similar lines. Although Hill challenged the chemical injection sequence rather than a surgical procedure prior to the injections, he did not actually ask to stop his execution or to change the sentence. Hill, like Nelson, sought only to enjoin state officials from executing him in the manner they presently intended.

6. *Time Limits*

AEDPA imposes a one-year limitation period for filing a federal habeas petition, measured generally (with certain limited exceptions) from the time direct state review is final. The statute tolls the limitation for the time during which a properly filed application for state collateral review is pending. The statutory provisions read as follows:

§ 2244. Finality of Determination

* * * *

(d)(1) A 1-year period of limitation shall apply to an application for a writ of habeas corpus by a person in custody pursuant to the judgment of a State court. The limitation period shall run from the latest of—

> (A) the date on which the judgment became final by the conclusion of direct review or the expiration of the time for seeking such review;

> (B) the date on which the impediment to filing an application created by State action in violation of the Constitution or laws of the United States if removed, if the applicant was prevented from filing by such State action;

> (C) the date on which the constitutional right asserted was initially recognized by the Supreme Court, if the right has been newly recognized by the Supreme Court and made retroactively applicable to cases on collateral review; or

> (D) the date on which the factual predicate of the claim or claims presented could have been discovered through the ex-

ercise of due diligence.

(2) The time during which a properly filed application for State post-conviction or other collateral review with respect to the pertinent judgment or claim is pending shall not be counted toward any period of limitation under this subsection.

Several issues as to the proper interpretation of these provisions reached the Supreme Court in recent terms. *Day v. McDonough*, 547 U.S. 198, 126 S.Ct. 1675, 164 L.Ed.2d 376 (2006), held that district courts are permitted, but not obliged, to consider the timeliness of a state prisoner's habeas petition *sua sponte*. In answering Day's petition, the state failed to raise § 2244(d)'s one-year limitation as a defense. The state mistakenly overlooked controlling Eleventh Circuit precedent, which, if applied, would require dismissal of the petition as untimely. A federal Magistrate Judge noticed the state's computation error and recommended the petition be dismissed. The district court adopted the recommendation, and the Eleventh Circuit affirmed.

Day argued that under the applicable habeas corpus rules, the Federal Rules of Civil Procedure should govern. Under Federal Rules 8(c) and 12(b), a defendant waives a statute of limitations defense that is not raised in its answer. The Court declined to apply these rules in this situation, applying a more flexible, discretionary approach. Where the state had not affirmatively decided to waive the defense and failure to raise it resulted from a mathematical error, the Court thought dismissal was appropriate. The Court noted that instead of acting on its own motion, the Magistrate Judge might have invited the state to amend it's answer when the Judge noticed the computation error. Because this procedure would have resulted in dismissal of the petition, it seemed unreasonable to require a different result simply because the Magistrate Judge acted *sua sponte*.

Mayle v. Felix, 545 U.S. 644, 125 S.Ct. 2562, 162 L.Ed.2d 582 (2005), considered the relation between § 2244(d)(1) and FED. R. CIV. P. 15(c)(2). Title 28 U.S.C. § 2242 states that a habeas petition "may be amended or supplemented as provided in the rules of procedure applicable to civil actions." Rule 15(c)(2) states that an amendment of a pleading relates back to the date of the original pleading when "the claim or defense asserted in the amended pleading arose out of the conduct, transaction, or occurrence set forth or attempted to be set forth in the original pleading." Felix was convicted in California state court of murder and robbery. He filed a timely federal habeas petition alleging that introduction of videotaped statements of a prosecution witness violated his Sixth Amendment right to confront witnesses against him. After the one-year limitation period had run, Felix attempted to amend his petition to include a claim that introduction of his own statements violated the Fifth Amendment because the convictions were coerced. The issue, then, was whether the claim in the amended petition arose out the "conduct, transaction, or occurrence" set forth in Felix's original petition.

The Ninth Circuit held the two claims were sufficiently related to allow relation back. The majority concluded that the relevant "transaction" for Rule 15(c)(2) purposes was the "trial and conviction in state court." The majority feared a more stringent standard would "unduly strai[n] the usual meaning of 'conduct, transaction, or occurrence'" by dividing the trial and conviction into "a series of perhaps hundreds of individual occurrences." The Supreme Court reversed, siding with those courts of appeals that allow relation back only when the original and new claims arise from the same core facts, and not when the claims are separate in "both time and type." The Court held Felix's claims were based on different facts and arose at different points in the criminal proceeding. The Court thought the more restrictive approach to be consistent with precedent applying Rule 15(c)(2) in regular, non-habeas civil cases and labeled the Ninth Circuit approach "boundless" because "[a] miscellany of claims for relief could be raised later rather than sooner and relate back, for 'conduct, transaction, or occurrence' would be defined to encompass any pretrial, trial, or post-trial error that could provide a basis for challenging the conviction." Congress enacted the one-year time limitation to promote the finality of criminal convictions. In the Court's view, the limitation would have "slim significance" if claims asserted after one year could be revived simply because they arise from the same trial, conviction, or sentence as the timely claims.

Justice Souter, joined by Justice Stevens, dissented. He noted that under Rule 15(a), amendment as of right can occur only before service of a responsive pleading, and that leave of court is required thereafter. District judges thus may refuse permission if there is unjustifiable delay or prejudice to the state. The dissenters also accepted Felix's argument that the relevant transaction was the trial because the claims concerning the videotape of a prosecution witness and the pretrial statements taken from Felix ripened only when the prosecutor sought to introduce them at trial. Justice Souter also argued that the majority's definition of "transaction or occurrence" was inconsistent with the broad definition of those words in the claim preclusion context. Modern claim preclusion prohibits a party from asserting any claims that were or might have been raised in a prior proceeding "with respect to all or any part of the transaction, or series of connected transactions, out of which the action arose." Justice Souter contended this definition of "transaction or occurrence" is the one used in another section of the same habeas statute, § 2244. Section 2244(b)(1) requires dismissal of a claim presented in a second or successive habeas petition that was not presented prior application, with very limited exceptions. Finally, the dissent argued that the consequences of the majority's rule would fall most heavily on the shoulders of indigent litigants. A lawyer hired at the outset to file a habeas petition will generally include all potentially meritorious claims. Almost all prisoners file habeas petitions *pro se*, however, and it is generally only later, if the petition appears to have some merit, that the petitioner gets appointed counsel. "Hobbling" appointed counsel by refusing to allow additional claims to relate back to the time of original filing "limits the capacity of appointed counsel to provide the service that a paid lawyer, hired at the outset, can give a client."

Title 28 U.S.C. § 2255 imposes a one-year limitation on federal prisoners to move to vacate, set aside, or correct a sentence. In language that is identical to § 2244(d)(1)(C), the one-year period may be measured from "the date on which the right asserted was initially recognized by the Supreme Court, if that right has been newly recognized by the Supreme Court and made retroactively applicable to cases on collateral review." *Dodd v. United States,* 545 U.S. 353, 125 S.Ct. 2478, 162 L.Ed.2d 343 (2005), held that the one-year period runs from the date the Supreme Court recognized the new right, and not from the date the Court made the right retroactive.[36] Justice O'Connor, who wrote the majority opinion, believed the text of the statute was dispositive: The statute "unequivocally identifies one, and only one, date from which a 1-year limitation is measured: 'the date on which the right asserted was initially recognized by the Supreme Court.'" She read the second clause— "if that right has been newly recognized by the Supreme Court and made retroactively applicable to cases on collateral review"—to impose conditions on the applicability of the subsection. This means the date on which the Supreme Court initially recognized the new right does not apply at all if the conditions in the second clause are not satisfied. Conversely, if the conditions are satisfied, the time runs from the specified date; namely, the date on which the right was initially recognized.

Justice Stevens dissented, joined by Justices Souter, Ginsberg, and Breyer. Justice Stevens did not think the statute to be as clear as the majority claimed. It could easily be interpreted to make the one-year period run only when the Supreme Court recognized the new right *and* when the new right was made retroactive. Justice Stevens thought the majority's interpretation often would lead to absurd results that Congress could not have intended. Noting that a decision about the retroactivity of a new right often is not made within one year of the decision recognizing the right, Justice Stevens reasoned that "[i]t would make no sense for Congress, in the same provision, both to recognize a potential basis for habeas relief and also make it highly probable that the statute of limitation would bar relief before the claim can [sic] be brought." He also pointed out that the majority's interpretation would effectively nullify 28 U.S.C. § 2244(b)(2)(A), which allows a new claim presented in a second or successive habeas petition to go forward if "the applicant shows that the claim relies on a new rule of constitutional law, made retroactive to cases on collateral review by the Supreme Court, that was

---

[36] Since § 2244(d)(1)(C) and § 2255 have identical language, it seems reasonable to presume the holding of *Dodd* will apply to § 2254 cases.

previously unavailable."

Pace v. DiGuglielmo, 544 U.S. 408, 125 S.Ct. 1807, 161 L.Ed.2d 669 (2005), addressed a relatively narrow question about the tolling provision of § 2244(d)(2). In order to toll the one-year limitation period, a state post-conviction application must be "properly filed." *Artuz v. Bennett*, 531 U.S. 4, 121 S.Ct. 361, 148 L.Ed.2d 213 (2000), held that an application is properly filed when it is delivered and accepted by an appropriate court officer and satisfies applicable state laws and rules governing filings, such as rules prescribing the form of the application, a filing fee, and time limits. Because applications are different from claims, an application is properly filed even though the legal claims might lack merit or be procedurally barred under state law. *Pace* addressed an issue left open in *Artuz*; namely, whether certain exceptions to a timely filing requirement can prevent a late application from being considered improperly filed. The district court reasoned that because a state judge must decide whether an otherwise late petition fits within the statutory exceptions to a time limit, the time limit is not a "condition to filing" but rather a "condition to obtaining relief," and thus a petition can be "properly filed" as defined in *Artuz* even though it is filed late. The Third Circuit reversed and the Supreme Court affirmed. The Court saw no reason to treat a basic time limit and exceptions to that limit differently for § 2244(d)(2) purposes. The dissent argued, *inter alia*, that the majority rule would result in a flood of new federal filings. State prisoners trying in good faith to exhaust state remedies may ultimately find their state petition was not "properly filed" and thus that the one-year federal statute of limitations has run. To protect themselves, they are likely to file a "protective" petition in federal court and ask the federal court to stay the federal proceeding until state remedies are exhausted.

28 U.S.C. § 2244(d)(2) tolls the one-year limitation period during the time when state collateral challenges are pending. In *Carey v. Saffold*, 536 U.S. 214, 122 S.Ct. 2134, 153 L.Ed.2d 260 (2002), the Supreme Court held that the proceeding is "pending" for § 2244(d)(2) purposes during the period from a lower state court's final judgment in a collateral proceeding to the filing of a notice of appeal to a higher court. Most states require an appellant to file a notice of appeal within a few days of final judgment, so tolling the limitation period does not undermine with the reasons for having one. California follows a different procedure. It permits the petitioner to file new original petitions in successively higher state courts as long as they come within a "reasonable time." In *Carey*, petitioner promptly filed after an adverse decision in the California Superior Court, but when the California Court of Appeal ruled against him, he allowed 4½ months to elapse before seeking relief from the California Supreme Court, which denied Saffold's petition "on the merits and for lack of diligence." One week after that decision, Saffold sought federal habeas relief.

When the case reached Washington, the Court vacated the judgment for the petitioner and directed the Ninth Circuit to determine whether the California Supreme Court thought the appeal was timely and denied it on the merits or thought the appeal was untimely and denied it for that reason. The United States Supreme Court stated that the words "lack of diligence" did not necessarily mean Saffold was untimely seeking relief from the California Supreme Court, because the lack of diligence might have referred to some earlier delay not relevant to whether Saffold timely sought relief from the California Supreme Court. The five-member majority also observed that the words "on the merits" might not have necessarily meant the application was timely, because courts sometimes deny a case on the merits even though it is untimely. Unfortunately, the Court left it unclear how the Ninth Circuit should proceed if it could not rely on any of the words the California Supreme Court used, although they certifying the question of timeliness to the California Supreme Court for clarification. This rather bizarre approach caused Justice Kennedy's dissent to heap some perhaps well deserved scorn on the majority's method of analysis.

The issue arose again in *Evans v. Chavis*, 546 U.S. 189, 126 S.Ct. 846, 163 L.Ed.2d 684 (2006). Chavis waited more than three years from the lower court decision to file a further petition. The California Supreme Court stated only that the "Petition for writ of habeas corpus is DENIED." The Ninth Circuit held the federal limitation period was tolled during the time between the lower court decision and the filing of the notice of appeal. The court concluded that the California Supreme Court decision was on the merits because of a long-standing presumption that denial of a habeas petition by the California Supreme Court without comment or citation is a decision on the merits. The United States Supreme Court reversed, holding the Ninth Circuit approach at odds with its decision in *Carey*. If use of the words "on the merits" in *Carey* did not necessarily mean the denial was on the merits, the Court did not see how the *absence* of those words could automatically warrant a holding that the filing was on the merits. In the absence of clear direction from the California Supreme Court, the federal courts are to "examine the delay in each case and determine what the state courts would have held in respect to timeliness." How one determines what a collegial body would have thought was apparently left as an exercise for the lower courts. The Court recognized the practical problem the federal courts faced when interpreting a "reasonable time" standard with no guidance from the state courts on whether the petitioner had met that standard. The Court said it understood the Ninth Circuit's desire to create a workable rule, but that the rule the Circuit chose conflicted with the approach *Carey* mandated. The Court went on essentially to beg the California courts and legislature to resolve this problem and made several suggestions as to how they might do so. Finally, the Court held Chavis' application to the California Supreme Court to be untimely.

Rhines v. Weber, 544 U.S. 269, 125 S.Ct. 1528, 161 L.Ed.2d 440

(2005), addressed the interplay between the rules governing mixed petitions and the one-year statute of limitations in 28 U.S.C. § 2244(d). If a state prisoner files a petition within the limitation period, and the district court determines it to be a mixed petition after the one-year period has run, may the petitioner exercise the *Rose v. Lundy* option of returning to state court to present the unexhausted claims, later to present all of his claims to the federal court, or does § 2244(d) bar a return to federal court? In *Rhines*, the district court granted the petitioner's motion to hold his habeas petition in abeyance (rather than dismiss it) while he returned to state court to present his unexhausted claims, but the Court of Appeals held the district had no authority to do this except in "truly exceptional" cases.

The Supreme Court held that a stay in these circumstances may be appropriate, although it imposed several conditions. The Court thought a stay may be appropriate because a contrary rule would put petitioners in an unfair position. If a petitioner files a timely mixed petition, and the court dismisses it under *Rose*, the petitioner is likely to forfeit federal review of any of his claims because of the one-year limitation period. Thus, the petitioner's only course would be to drop his unexhausted claims, forfeiting any chance for federal court review of those claims. The Court cautioned against too frequent use of stay and abeyance, which it thought would undermine AEDPA's twin goals of reducing delays in the execution of sentences and streamlining habeas proceedings. Thus, a stay should be granted only if 1) there was "good cause" for the failure to exhaust all claims; 2) the unexhausted claims are not plainly meritless; 3) the petitioner complies with any time limits set by the district court for pursuing state review; and 4) the petitioner does not engage in "abusive litigation tactics or intentional delay."

Index

References are to pages

ABSTENTION
See *Burford* Abstention; *Colorado River* Abstention; *Thibodaux* Abstention; *Younger* Abstention

ADEQUATE AND INDEPENDENT STATE GROUND
See Habeas Corpus; Supreme Court Review of State Court Decisions

ADVISORY OPINIONS
See also, Adequate and Independent State Ground
Generally, 25-34
Adequate and independent state ground, 913, 914, 1166
Congressional authorization, 27-34
Declaratory Judgments, 33-34
Habeas corpus, 1166
Jay-Jefferson correspondence, 25-26

ANTI-INJUNCTION ACT
Generally, 746-761
Exceptions
Express authorization, 749, 758-760
Necessary in aid of jurisdiction, 749-752, 760
Protecting judgments or orders, 749-752, 754-757, 760, 1048
Federal-state Friction, 747-749
Injunctions against parties, 749
Pending litigation, 996
Younger abstention, 787-788, 792-793, 827-828

ANTI-TERRORISM AND EFFECTIVE DEATH PENALTY ACT OF 1996
Generally, 1053, 1058, 1059, 1063
Actual innocence, 11861186
Death penalty provisions, 1062, 1063
Deference to state legal rulings, 1088, 1156, 1158
Evidentiary hearings, 11561087-1088, 1091-1094
Exhaustion of state remedies, 1055, 1099
New rules of decision, 1112
Successive Petitions, 1060, 1062, 1183-1193
Teague, relation to, 1134-1136, 1146-1150, 1153-1154

ARTICLE I COURTS
See Legislative Courts

BURFORD ABSTENTION
Generally, 841-865
Complex administrative process, 843-844, 853, 858
Complex issues of state law, 844-847, 852, 859, 868-869

Conflicts between federal and state rulings, 846-847, 859
Damage actions, 855-865
Stay only, 857-858, 861, 863-864
Deference to state sovereign, 858
Desirability of single, authoritative court, 845-846, 870-871
Discretionary relief generally, 851, 860, 861
Equitable discretion, 859-860
Exceptional circumstances, 853, 855, 856, 864, 868
Federalism, 862-863
Federal questions jurisdiction, 851
Forecast of state law distinguished, 849
Interference with state regulatory schemes, 845-846,
Local issues, 852
Narrow exception, 862
Parity, 850
Separation of powers, 848, 850, 856, 862, 865, 878
Trial *de novo* in state court, 845
Unified determination of policy, 847

CHOICE OF LAW
Admiralty, 439-440
Antitrust, 439-440
Determining state law, 431-432
Federal government as a party, 391, 413-415
Foreign relations, 392-393
Preemption, 393-395
Statute of limitations, 395, 499-506

CIVIL RIGHTS ACT OF 1871
See also, Fourteenth Amendment
Generally, 509-531
Color of state law, 513-514, 519-526
Common-law immunities, 576-580
Custom or usage, 545-546, 552-554
Due process
Pre-deprivation hearing, 598-600, 603-605
Municipal liability
Generally, 514-515, 526, 531-576
Deliberate action, 555
Deliberate indifference, 553-554, 556-571, 601-603
Failure to act as policy, 553-556
Respondeat superior, 544-546, 547-548, 550-552, 556-557, 560, 563, 568-571, 574
Single decision as policy, 552-553, 557-562
Negligence, 600-601
Sherman Amendment, 514-515, 532-541, 547, 550

State remedies
    Authorized/unauthorized activity, 516-
       518, 520-524, 527-528, 598-600,
       605, 642
    Irrelevant to scope of § 1983, 512-513,
       600-605
    Private individuals, 528
    State-employed professionals, 528
    Ultra vires actions, 527-528

COLORADO RIVER ABSTENTION
    Generally, 865-878
Concurrent state proceedings, 869-870
Conflicting claims to a res, 870
Declaratory judgments, 876-878
Parallel state litigation, 869-870

CONGRESSIONAL CONTROL OF FEDERAL JURISDICTION
    Generally, 163-221
Case-or-Controversy Clause, 217
Circumventing Supreme Court decisions, 163
    Separation of powers, 163, 175, 187-189, 199-221
Essential functions thesis, 176
    And uniformity, 177
    Limits on congressional power, 177-180
Exceptions Clause, 163-180
Extradition, 219-220
Final decision, 218-219
Inferior federal courts
    And discretionary Supreme Court review, 195
    Implied congressional control of jurisdiction, 193-194
    Lack of congressional power to abolish, 193-195
    Organization and existence, 187
Interbranch cooperation, 216
Legislative review of judicial decisions, 216
Necessity of some jurisdiction, 196-198
Prison Litigation Reform Act, 220
Reinstating dismissed cases, 201
Repealer Act, 165-167, 168-170
Retroactive legislation, 204-205, 211-211
    Classes of cases, 205-206
    Relief from judgments distinguished, 208, 218
Rules of decision not within Exceptions Clause, 187
Separation of powers generally, 201-206, 213
Supremacy, 175-176
Supreme Court appellate jurisdiction
    Alternative bases for, 172
    Constitutionally subject to limits, 170
    Necessity of affirmative grant by Congress, 166-166
    Pending cases, congressional power to oust jurisdiction, 171, 191, 205

DECLARATORY JUDGMENTS
    See also, Advisory Opinions; Federal Question Jurisdiction
And well-pleaded complaints, see Federal Question Jurisdiction, Well-Pleaded Complaint
Procedural purpose of Declaratory Judgment Act, 304, 310-311, 319
Ripeness, 105

ELEVENTH AMENDMENT
    Generally, 607-743
Amenability of states to suit generally, 610, 613-615
Appeals from state court, 613-614
Article I abrogation, 695, 697, 700-703
Availability of state forum, 662
Chisholm v. Georgia, 607, 609-610, 611, 613, 615, 617-618, 631, 642, 648, 692, 704-704, 706-708, 711, 712-712, 714, 717, 725, 731
Citizens of state sued, 609, 612, 648, 709
Commerce power, 695-696
Common law immunity, 618, 695
Congressional abrogation of immunity, 658, 669, 672-688, 695, 699, 703-704, 709, 710
Consent to suit, 4, 613, 618, 645, 657, 658
Detailed remedial scheme, 705-706, 729-730, 732-733
Dignity of states, 643-644, 700, 723, 733
Diversity jurisdiction, 616, 618, 695, 712, 713-715, 717, 721, 724
Divided sovereignty, 713, 722-724
Federal question cases, 609, 612-615, 709
Fourteenth Amendment as not modifying, 638
Fourteenth Amendment enforcement powers, scope of, 675-694
Functional equivalence, 664-665
Hans immunity non-constitutional, 716-717, 719
Illegal act not state's act, 634, 738
Irrelevance of relief sought, 700
Jurisdiction, limit on, 653, 662, 702, 704, 708, 709, 729-730, 768
Jurisprudence in all civilized nations, 704
Literal reading disfavored, 704
Money awards, 7, 649-651
Need to interpret federal law, 663, 743
Officials as the state, 629, 631-634, 649, 665
Partakes of jurisdictional bar, 653, 710
Pendent jurisdiction, See Supplemental claims, this topic
Property claims, 661-665
Prospective relief, 629-635, 648-649, 661, 663, 713, 726
Reception of common law, 719-720
Relief sought irrelevant, 700
Retrospective relief, 647-650, 661, 663, 726
Sedgwick amendment, 714-715

Sovereign immunity exceeds, 741-743

Sovereigns versus sovereigns, suits by, 641-642, 733

States as "persons"
    § 1983, 670-671
    False Claims Act, 671

Stripping state officials of state identity, 634, 639, 661, 738

Subject matter jurisdiction, limiting, 617-618

Supplemental claim, 736-740

Supremacy, 663, 718, 738

Surrender in the plan of the Conventions, 611, 655, 662, 695, 703, 713-714, 721, 733

Waiver by states, 651-652, 657. 660-661

***ERIE* CHOICE OF LAW**
    See Choice of Law

EXHAUSTION OF ADMINISTRATIVE REMEDIES
    Generally, 761-773

And Civil Rights Act of 1871, 763-768

Federal docket pressures, 770

Jurisdiction, 770

Separation of powers, 769, 772-773

Stare decisis generally, 763

State judicial proceedings, 772

FEDERAL COMMON LAW
    See also, Choice of Law; Implied Rights of Action; Separation of Powers
    Generally, 373-508

By congressional direction, 236, 433-438

Displacing state law, 407-408, 422-423

Exercise of constitutional function, 388

Federal charter, 422

Filling in statutory interstices, 499-506

New *Erie* doctrine, 421-422, 469, 506

Rules of Decision Act, 381-382
    Not addressed to diversity, 383-384

Significant conflict with state law, 407-408, 422-423

State law as, 388, 392, 395-406, 422-423, 427-429

Technique for creating, 375

Uniformity, 384-386, 388, 389-391, 422

FEDERAL QUESTION JURISDICTION
    Generally, 223-320

Actual contested issue
    Not required, 250,
    Required, 233-234, 270-272

All Writs Act, relation to, 288

Anticipated defense, 250-251, 304, 309

Capacity to sue as granting, 226-227, 230, 234-236

Co-extensive with Supreme Court appellate jurisdiction, 228

Constitutional limitations, 225-246, 255-262

Declaratory judgments, 302-320

Federal element of state claim, 266, 275, 281-283

Genuine controversy, see issue, this topic

In state courts, 639-641

Ingredient of cause, 229

Judicial case defined, 227

Jurisdictional statutes alone not creating, 260-260

Law creating the cause of action, 264, 267-268, 274, 284-285, 309

Mixed federal and state issues, 228, 232

Multiple grounds for relief, 285-286

Not self-executing, 223-224

Original jurisdiction of Supreme Court, 228

Outcome-determinative test, 229, 258, 266, 270, 274, 274, 258

Patent cases, 252

Preemption of state claim, 253-255, 276, 313-315

Private federal cause of action, absence of, 274-275, 280, 282-282

Protective jurisdiction
    Generally, 236-246
    And parity, 240
    Congressional commands to fashion common law, 236
    Remoteness of issue, 230-230, 233, 271-272, 259-259

Separation of powers, 244-245

Sovereign immunity as, 256

State declaratory judgment actions, 310-311

State law claims, 262-272, 284-285

Statutory development, 224-225, 246-249

Sua sponte consideration of jurisdiction, 250, 266

Substantial question, 309

Substantiality of federal issue, 272-286

Time to determine, 236

Well-pleaded complaint, 249-255, 268-270, 308
    As federal common law, not interpretive limit, 260-260
    Not applicable to Article III, 260-261
    Patent cases, 305
    Procedural change only, 304
    State declaratory judgment cases, 306-316

FOURTEENTH AMENDMENT
    See also, Civil Rights Act of 1871

Authorized/unauthorized activities, 516-526,,546-547, 551, 604-605

Mental element, 600-603

HABEAS CORPUS
    Generally, 1051-1199

Actual innocence, 1186-1199

Adequate and independent state ground, 1165-1169, 1178

Cause-and-prejudice standard, 1088, 1090, 1152-1153, 1170-1172, 1177, 1179-1183, 1185

Custody, 1051, 1061, 1066-1071, 1074-

1077, 1082-1085
Deliberate bypass, 1170, 1179, 1183
Dictated by precedent, 1104, 1112-1117, 1135-1136
Enemy combatants, 1063-1085
Evidentiary hearing, standards, 1056-1057, 1062, 1087-1100
Exhaustion, 1094, 1159-1163, 1166, 1183
    Abuse of writ, 1163, 1183-1193
    Forfeiture of unexhausted claims, 1061
    Mixed petitions, 1159-1163
    Procedural default, 1091-1094, 1106, 1115, 1126, 1161-1162, 1164-1183
    Successive petitions, 1183-1199
    Total exhaustion rule, 1159-1163
Federalism, 1051-1052, 1166-1167
Fourth Amendment claims, 6, 14-15, 1101
Full and fair state hearing, 1055-1057, 1101
Harmless error, 1122, 1153
History, 1054-1059
Ineffective assistance of counsel, 1062-1063, 1101, 1128-1130, 1140-1144, 1148, 1152-1153, 1156-1157, 1167-1167, 1172- 1174, 1177-1178, 11821184
New rules, 1103-1126
Plain statement rule, 1167-1168
Procedural default, 1056-1057, 1061, 1091-1106, 1111, 1115, 1126, 1161, 1164-1183
Relitigating facts, 1056-1057, 1087-1100
Res judicata, 1055, 1184
Retroactivity, 1103-1107, 1104
    And similarly situated parties, 1108, 1123
    Threshold question, 1104, 1121
Separation of powers, 1126
Sixth Amendment claims, see Ineffective assistance of counsel, this topic
Statutory structure, 1059-1063
    Codification of case law, 1185-1199
Successive petitions, 1183-1199
    Abuse of writ, 1183-1185, 1187
    Cause-and-prejudice standard, 1183-1186
Territorial reach, 1063-1085

IMMUNITIES
Clearly established rights, 584, 585-591
Deliberate indifference, 494, 553-554, 556, 558-560, 568, 601-602
Federal Tort Claims Act, 410, 416-417
Government contractors, 406-423
Implied, 406-423
Officials
    Generally, 576-598
    Judges, 576-577, 578-579
    Legislators, 577-578
    Prosecutors, 577
    Witnesses, 577
Separation of powers, 412, 417-418
Sequence of inquiry, 586

Summary judgment and discovery, 583-585, 591-592, 593-594

IMPLIED RIGHTS Of ACTION
    See also, Federal Common Law; Separation of Powers
    Generally, 440-499
All Writs Act, 454
Civil Service Reform Act, 478-479
Constitutional provisions, 440-455, 480-499
Expanding federal jurisdiction, 468, 470-471
Federal regulations, to enforce, 498-499
Four-factor test, 456
Fourth Amendment, 440-455
Government employees, 484
History, 455-457
Military personnel, 483, 490
Parental Kidnaping Prevention Act, 476-478
Private entities acting under color of federal law, 496-498
Rivers and Harbors Act, 471-476
Securities Exchange Commission Act, 199-200, 456
Separation of powers, 10-12, 450-453, 464, 478-479, 487
Social Security Act, 480-493
Special factors counseling hesitation, 443, 453, 484-486

JOHNSON ACT, 761, 848-849

JUSTICIABILITY
    See Advisory Opinions; Mootness; Political Questions; Ripeness; Standing
Case or controversy, 23, 29-33

KU KLUX ACT
    See Civil Rights Act of 1871

LEGISLATIVE COURTS
    Generally, 321-371
Adjunct courts, 332, 349
Administrative agencies, 322, 328-330, 345
Appeals from, 323-324
Article III functions in non-Article III courts, 333-335, 341-343
Article III judges, 321, 325-326
Bankruptcy courts, 322-351
Creation of new substantive rights, 335
Essential attributes of judicial power, 335-336
Factfinding, 333-334
Federalism, 359-360
Intrusion on Article III courts, 362-364
Judicial matters, 328-330
Magistrates, 367-371
Military courts, 328, 345
Not exceptional circumstance, 330
Powers of judges, 323
Public rights, 328-330, 345, 351, 358, 361, 366

Referee system, 323
Review of judgments, 322, 344
Scope of operation, 345
Separation of powers, 324-335, 341-343,
    346-347, 354-359, 361-363
Specialized courts, 331
State law claims, 323
Tax Court, 321-322
Territorial courts, 321, 327-328, 345
Territories and districts
    Article I power to govern, 327-328
Waiver by parties of Article III rights, 355-
    356

MOOTNESS
    Generally, 23-24, 111-144
Amendment of statute, 118-119
Capable of repetition, 114, 117-118
Case or controversy, 112-115, 121-122
Change in complainant's status, 118-119
Change in practice, 118-119
Class actions, 119-121
Effective judgment, 113-114
Prudential doctrine, 121-122
Relation to standing, 132-133, 144
Voluntary cessation of conduct, 113-114,
    115, 118-119, 143

**PARITY OF STATE AND FEDERAL
COURTS,**
    See also, *Younger* Abstention,
    Generally, 13-21

POLITICAL QUESTIONS
    Generally, 24, 144-162
As prudential question, 156-157
Checks and balances, 149, 152
Constitutionality of legislative acts, 151-
    153
Finality, 149-150
Guaranty Clause, 159-160
Lack of judicial standards, 146, 158
Legislative apportionment, 159
Merits as determinant, 158-159
Qualifications for office, 150, 153
Textual commitment to coordinate political
    department, 146, 148-149, 151-153,
    160-161

PRISON LITIGATION REFORM ACT,
220-221

PULLMAN ABSTENTION
    Generally, 774-785
Avoiding unnecessary rulings of federal
    law, 775, 778-780
Certifying questions to state courts, 778-
    780
Discretion, 776
Diversity cases, 777-778
Friction with state laws, 776
Modifying constitutional issue, 778-780
Procedure, 781-785
State constitutional provisions, 778

Unclear state law, 775-776, 777-778, 779

RIPENESS
    Generally, 23, 100-111
And standing, 104-105
Case or controversy, 105, 111
Declaratory judgments, 105-106
Discretionary enforcement, 102, 109-110
Factual specificity, 101, 107-110
Fitness for judicial decision, 101, 107-110
Hardship of withholding consideration,
    101-104
Separation of powers, 101-102

ROOKER-FELDMAN DOCTRINE
    Generally, 993-1050
Abuse of process, 1048
Administrative proceedings, 1001-1002,
    1003
And jurisdiction, 1002, 1005, 1007, 1040
Anti-Injunction Act, 996
Appeal vs. collateral attack, 996
Appellate jurisdiction of inferior federal
    courts, 995, 1002, 1012-1014, 1011,
    1015, 1016-1017, 1022, 1033-1034,
    1038
Artful pleading, 1027-1028, 1030
Bar admission and reinstatement
    Disbarment, 1021
    Generally, 997-1009, 1019-1029
Character of the proceeding, 1003-1004
Characterization of state proceedings as
    judicial, 1006
    Federal characterization determinative,
        1003
Civil rights claims generally, 1045-1047
Claims not adjudicated in state courts,
    1041
Claims of right, 1001
Class actions generally, 1031-1042
Class of beneficiaries, 1023
Constitutionally compelled, 1009
Continued government practices, 1046-
    1047
1034, 1038-1039, 1042
Detail in pleadings, 1024
Dignity of state courts, 1010
Distinct injury, 1016, 1017-1017, 1019,
    1033
Federal habeas corpus, 996-997
Federal plaintiff as state defendant, 1034
Federal plaintiff as state plaintiff, 1034
Full Faith and Credit Act, 1016-1017, 1049
General challenges to rules, 1005-1006,
    1022-1026
Inextricably intertwined issues, 1006, 1013,
    1017-1019, 1023, 1026-1027, 1032-
    1033, 1034, 1035, 1045-1046
Injury from independent act or state court
    judgment, 1016, 1017, 1033-1035
"Judicial" decisions or proceedings, 1001-
    1004, 1009-1010, 1022-1024
Jurisdiction of inferior federal courts, 995,

1002, 1005-1007, 1011, 1012-1014, 1016-1017, 1015, 1022-1024, 1033-1034, 1038-1039
Lack of state jurisdiction, 1032-1033, 1034-1038, 1038-1039, 1042-1043
Legislative proceedings, 1003
Malpractice litigation, 1037-1041
Ministerial actions, 1004
Personal jurisdiction, 1032, 1033, 1041
Precedence over res judicata, 1011, 1016
Questionable state court judgments, 1035
Rationales, 1040
Related claims, 1040
Relief requested, 1024
Res judicata, 996, 1007, 1013, 1017, 1018, 1028, 1029, 1034, 1042, 1049
Setting aside state judgment, 975
Simultaneous federal and state proceedings, 1011
Standing, 1049
Three-Judge Court Act, 993-994

RULES OF DECISION ACT
See Federal Common Law

SEPARATION OF POWERS
See also, Exhaustion of Administrative Remedies; Federal Common Law; Federal Question Jurisdiction; Habeas Corpus; Immunities; Implied Rights of Action; Legislative Courts; Political Questions; Ripeness; Standing; *Younger* Abstention
Generally, 8-13
Common law powers of federal courts
Generally, 10-12
Command of legislature to create common law, 11
Executive, 9-10
Implied rights of action, 10-12
Interlocking control, 8-9
Judiciary, 10-12
Non-judicial review of judicial decisions, 27
Not discussed in Constitution, 12-13
Standing, 43, 51-52
Structural safeguard, 210

STANDING
Generally, 23, 34-99
Aggrieved party, 99
Associational standing, 98
Case or controversy, 37-39
Causation, See Traceability and Redressability
Citizens, 40-41, 88-92
Congressionally-created, 88-92
Constitutional components generally, 38-39, 80-92
Continuing governmental practices, 54-55, 1046-1047
Criminal statutes, 55-56
Generalized grievances, 42-43, 80-84

Injunctive relief, 56
Injury in fact, 38-43, 67-68, 70-73, 83-84
Government illegal action, 40-41
Personalized injury, 40-41, 44-45, 128-129, 136-138, 141-142
Stigmatizing injury, 40-41
Legislators, 55
Nexus, 84, 85-86
Organizations, interests of members, 98
Protected legal interest, 92-96
Prudential components generally, 38, 81-84, 88, 92-98
Redressability, 41-42, 55-59, 64, 65, 72, 73, 74-76, 77, 79, 87, 130-131, 138-140, 141-142, 143
Relation to mootness, 132-133, 144
Separation of powers, 42-43, 51, 52, 53-79,
Tax liability, 37
Taxpayers, 85-88, 96-98
Third-party standing, 96-98, 99
Time of determination, 59-60
Traceability of injury to defendant's conduct, 41-42, 46-48, 55-59, 65, 70-71, 74-75, 65, 76
Voters, 83-84
Widely-shared harm
See Generalized Grievances, this topic
Zones of protected interests, 83, 92-96
Third-party beneficiaries, 95

STATE ACTION
See Fourteenth Amendment

STATE LAW SOVEREIGN IMMUNITY
Against federal claims in state court, 639-640, 732-732

SUPREME COURT REVIEW OF STATE COURTS
Generally, 879-991
Adequacy of state ground, 901-903
As constitutional imperative, 900, 902-903, 914
As prudential rule, 900
As statutory command, 900
Clear statement rule, 913, 1167, 1168
Due process and state procedures, 959, 962-963, 969
Legitimate state interest, 959, 964-968, 971-971
Necessity of state reliance on procedural default, 955, 957
Procedural state law, 946-991
Contemporaneous objection rule, 959969
Excusing procedural default, 967-968, 972
Legitimate state interests, 971
Adequate and independent state ground, 884-972
Substantive state law, 901-946
Unclear basis for state decision, 906-926
Waiver of constitutional rights, 958-961

Advisory opinions, 914, 958
Facts, review of, 930-946
    Evidentiary insufficiency, 933-934, 937
    Intermingled state and federal issues, 937, 938-946
    Sham, state findings as, 934
Final judgments
    Generally, 972-991
    Exceptions, 974-979
    Federalism, 981-982
Incorporation
    Federal, of state law, 929-930
    State, of federal law, 926-929
Independence of state ground, 903-926
Presumption of jurisdiction, 913, 1167-1170
Scope of review, 881, 884-901
Seeking clarification, 908-909, 920-921
Statutory development, 882-883
Substantiality of federal issue, 883

TAX INJUNCTION ACT, 761

THIBODAUX **ABSTENTION**
    Generally, 854-855, 868-869
Dismissal *versus* stay, 857-858
Eminent domain, 854-855, 857-858, 871-872
Sovereign prerogative, 854, 871

YOUNGER **ABSTENTION**
    Generally, 785-841
Administrative proceedings, 834-835
And Civil Rights Act of 1871, 828-829
And injunctive relief, 812-813
Anti-Injunction Act, 787, 791, 792-793, 798, 827-828
As constitutional imperative, 798-799
As policy, 786, 798-799
Attorney discipline, 835
Bad-faith prosecutions, 788-789, 810
Chilling effect, 789-790
Civil enforcement proceedings, 831-834, 836-838
Contempt proceedings, 832
Declaratory Judgment Act, 805-806, 807-810
Declaratory judgments, 799-812
    As predicates for further relief, 808, 809, 812
    Equity, 787-789
    Res judicata effect, 808, 809, 812
Executive actions, 836
Federal-state friction, 808-809
Flagrant unconstitutionality, 791, 796-798

Later-commenced state action, 808, 813-822
Legislative actions, 838-840
Neglect proceedings, 832-834
No adequate remedy at law, 788-789, 795-796
Parity of federal and state courts, 14-21, 798
Pending actions, 6, 789, 792, 803
Proceedings of substance on the merits, 816, 818, 820
Quasi-criminal proceedings, 822-829
Role of federal courts, 804-806, 819
Separation of powers, 793
Subject matter jurisdiction, 830-831
Subsequent state actions, 808
Suppression motions, 800
Threatened prosecutions, 785-786, 801-802
Waiver, 799, 831